Great Britain & Ireland 2011

Contents

INTRODUCTION

Our Centennial Edition! 5

1911-2011...
What a difference a century makes! 6

Commitments 4
How to use this guide 8
Classification & awards 10
Facilities & services 12
Prices 13
Towns 14
Town plans 15

AWARDS 2011

Starred establishments 1
Bib Gourmand 2
Bib Hotel 2
Particularly pleasant hotels & guesthouses 30
Particularly pleasant restaurants & pubs 3

100

Commitments

"This volume was created at the turn of the century and will last at least as long".

This foreword to the very first edition of the MICHELIN Guide, written in 1900, has become famous over the years and the guide has lived up to the prediction. It is read across the world and the key to its popularity is the consistency of its commitment to its readers, which is based on the following promises.

The MICHELIN guide's commitments:

Anonymous inspections: our inspectors make regular and anonymous visits to hotels and restaurants to gauge the quality of products and services offered to an ordinary customer. They settle their own bill and may then introduce themselves and ask for more information about the establishment. Our readers' comments are also a valuable source of information, which we can then follow up with another visit of our own.

Independence: Our choice of establishments is a completely independent one, made for the benefit of our readers alone. The decisions to be taken are discussed around the table by the inspectors and the editor. The most important awards are decided at a European level. Inclusion in the guide is completely free of charge.

Selection and choice: The guide offers a selection of the best hotels and restaurants in every category of comfort and price. This is only possible because all the inspectors rigorously apply the same methods.

Annual updates: All the practical information, the classifications and awards are revised and updated every single year to give the most reliable information possible.

Consistency: The criteria for the classifications are the same in every country covered by the MICHELIN guide.

... and our aim: to do everything possible to make travel, holidays and eating out a pleasure, as part of Michelin's ongoing commitment to improving travel and mobility.

Our Centennial Edition!

Dear Readers

The 2011 edition of the Michelin Guide Great Britain and Ireland is a very special one, because this year marks its 100th anniversary.

The first Guide to the British Isles was published in 1911, with the aim of helping the earliest intrepid motorists on their travels. Instructional in nature, it contained a wealth of practical information including advice on changing tyres and information about road quality, as well as details about hotels, Michelin tyre stockists and repair shops for the inevitable breakdowns.

Dark blue in colour rather than red, this Guide ran for five editions, with a break in production due to the First World War. The Guide resumed in 1922 when its title was changed to Great Britain (with Ireland not included) and this ran until 1930. The current Great Britain and Ireland Guide was re-launched in 1974 and has been published every year since.

Over the years the Guide has responded to changes in society, adapting to the needs of its readers and their dining and travel habits, improving content and adding descriptive text for the first time in 2003. While back in 1911, amenities such as central heating and electric lights were deemed worthy of note; in 2011, these have been replaced by air conditioning, wi-fi internet access and saunas...

Michelin stands for reliability, independence, confidentiality, anonymity...and a whole set of values with which our readers identify; not forgetting of course the famous stars which denote excellence in cuisine.

For these reasons and as a tribute to our beginnings, this year's guide points out establishments recommended in both the 1911 and 2011 Guides with a new symbol (100) – the special Hundred Years award.

Readers and their valuable letters and comments have played a significant role in the Guide's success up to the present day. Thanks to your support, we have been able to publish a Guide that has reached its landmark centenary, and we hope that you will continue to support us as we travel on through the 21st century.

1911-2011... What a difference a century makes!

The first edition of the Michelin Guide to the British Isles appeared in 1911 and, like the other European Guides which came before, it complemented the company's flourishing tyre business. Offered free of charge, it was available from all Michelin tyre dealers, as well as from every hotel listed within it.

1911-1920 ➜ In the beginning

From the very beginning, the guide placed its emphasis on practical information and was packed with notes on tyres, car engines, routes and distances in order to alleviate travellers' fears about breaking down. Thanks to its straightforward advice, the guide became known as the motorist's vade-mecum.

In 1920 Michelin began to market it commercially. This provided the opportunity to delete all advertising from the guide's pages and, by so doing, to assert the independence which is still such an important feature of the guide today.

1922-1930 ➜ Roaring through the Twenties

When the guide resumed in 1922, its title had changed to The Michelin Guide to Great Britain. Ireland was not included – a consequence of the partitioning of Ireland in 1921.

In the 1920s, car ownership began to expand to include the middle classes and, by the time of the next Guide to Great Britain in 1923, there were more than 1,000,000 cars travelling on British roads.

With each subsequent edition of The Michelin Guide came a desire for improvement and this led to the inclusion of restaurants for the first time in 1925.

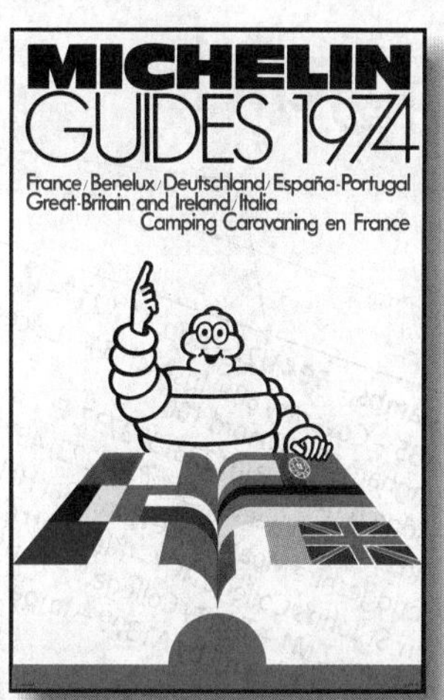

Restaurants were classified using stars, but these referred only to comfort levels and had no gastronomic relevance. After 1927, this classification changed to a one to five diamond system.

1974-1999 ➜ Reach for the Stars

After a 43 year absence, The Red Guide to Great Britain & Ireland was re-launched in 1974; no longer a handbook for drivers, but a hotel and restaurant guide.

Four years work went into producing the 1974 edition with over 15,000 establishments being assessed and evaluated by our own professional, anonymous inspectors. The result was a guide to 2,330 hotels, 331 motels and 981 restaurants located in over 1,400 towns and villages throughout the UK and Ireland.

The 1974 edition of the Guide to Great Britain and Ireland, with its distinctive new red cover, also saw the appearance of the first stars as we know them today. Awarded for the quality of the food, they have been a permanent feature of the guide since. They have also proved to be a great talking point!

In the 1974 edition, only 25 restaurants were considered to be worthy of a star. Today we have a galaxy of stars in a multitude of establishments; from country pubs, to Indian restaurants...and simple bistros to city hotspots.

2000-2011 ➜ Into the 21st Century

Growing prosperity, increased mobility, immigration and mass tourism have changed the culinary and travel habits of the British people over the last century, and the Michelin Guide has continually evolved in order to reflect this.

Good food doesn't have to be expensive, and one historic moment was the appearance of the Bib Gourmand in 1997. This award is given to restaurants offering good quality cuisine at modest prices. Its counterpart, the Bib Hotel, followed in 2004.

A new Guide to Eating out in Pubs was launched a year later, featuring 500 of the best dining pubs throughout Britain and Ireland. This was followed by a guide to London Restaurants and Hotels, containing in-depth descriptions of over 450 London restaurants.

The Michelin Man, Bibendum, has also changed a little over the years: he's stopped smoking, has lost weight and is fitter than ever – not bad for a centenarian!

How to use this guide

TOURIST INFORMATION

Distances from the main towns, tourist offices, local tourist attractions, means of transport, golf courses and leisure activities...

HOTELS

From 🏨🏨🏨🏨🏨 to 🏠, ⌂: categories of comfort.
In red 🏨🏨🏨🏨🏨... 🏠, ⌂: the most pleasant.

100 YEARS OLD!

Establishment included in the guide in 1911.

RESTAURANTS AND PUBS

From XXXXX to X, 🍺: categories of comfort.
In red XXXXX... X, 🍺: the most pleasant.

STARS

✿✿✿ Worth a special journey.
✿✿ Worth a detour.
✿ A very good restaurant.

GOOD FOOD AND ACCOMMODATION AT MODERATE PRICES

Bib Gourmand

Bib Hotel

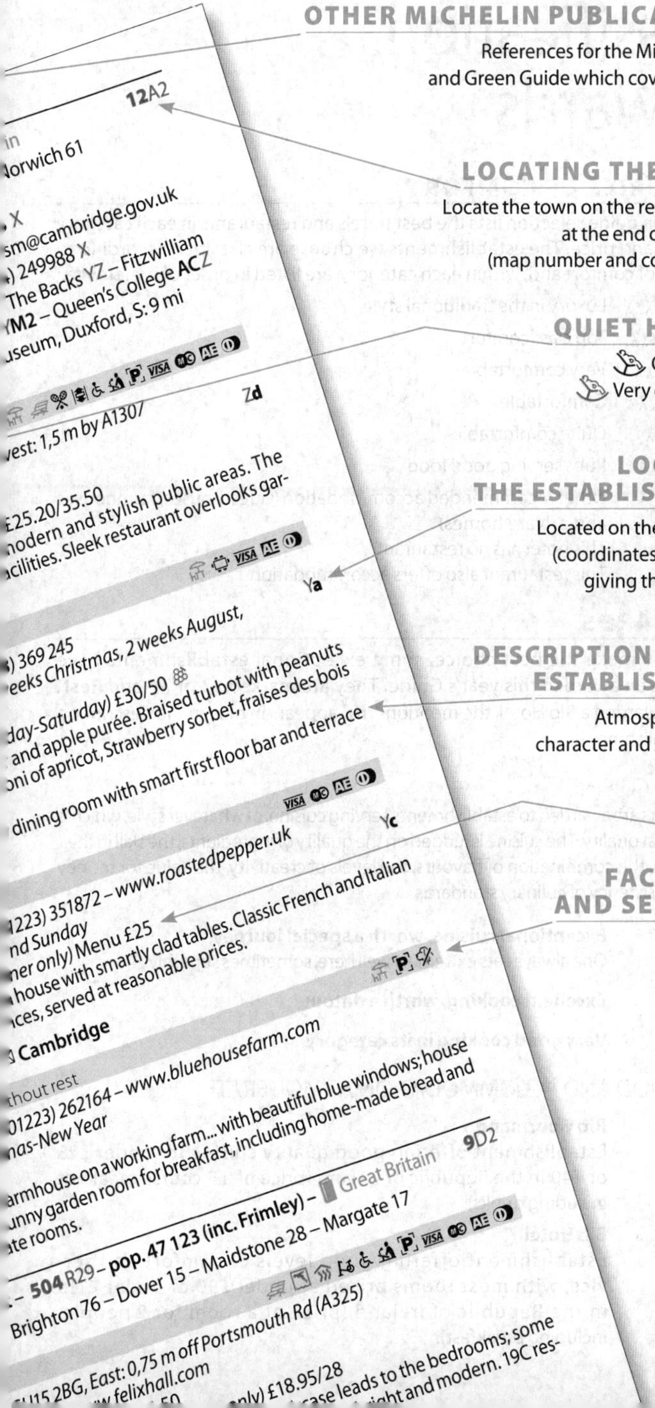

OTHER MICHELIN PUBLICATIONS

References for the Michelin map and Green Guide which cover the area.

LOCATING THE TOWN

Locate the town on the regional map at the end of the guide (map number and coordinates).

QUIET HOTELS

Quiet hotel.
Very quiet hotel.

LOCATING THE ESTABLISHMENT

Located on the town plan (coordinates and letters giving the location).

DESCRIPTION OF THE ESTABLISHMENT

Atmosphere, style, character and specialities.

PRICES

FACILITIES AND SERVICES

Classification & awards

CATEGORIES OF COMFORT

The Michelin guide selection lists the best hotels and restaurants in each category of comfort and price. The establishments we choose are classified according to their levels of comfort and, within each category, are listed in order of preference.

🏨🏨🏨🏨🏨	XXXXX	Luxury in the traditional style
🏨🏨🏨🏨	XXXX	Top class comfort
🏨🏨🏨	XXX	Very comfortable
🏨🏨	XX	Comfortable
🏨	X	Quite comfortable
	🍺	Pubs serving good food
🏠		Other recommended accommodation (Guesthouses, farmhouses and private homes)
without rest.		This hotel has no restaurant
with rm		This restaurant also offers accommodation

THE AWARDS

To help you make the best choice, some exceptional establishments have been given an award in this year's Guide. They are marked ✿ or ☺ and **Rest**. For those awarded a Bib Hotel, the mention "**rm**" appears in blue in the description of the establishment.

THE BEST CUISINE

Michelin stars are awarded to establishments serving cuisine, of whatever style, which is of the highest quality. The cuisine is judged on the quality of ingredients, the skill in their preparation, the combination of flavours, the levels of creativity, the value for money and the consistency of culinary standards.

✿✿✿ **Exceptional cuisine, worth a special journey**
One always eats extremely well here, sometimes superbly.

✿✿ **Excellent cooking, worth a detour**

✿ **Very good cooking in its category**

GOOD FOOD AND ACCOMMODATION AT MODERATE PRICES

☺ **Bib Gourmand**
Establishment offering good quality cuisine for under £28 or €40 in the Republic of Ireland (price of a 3 course meal not including drinks).

☺ **Bib Hotel**
Establishment offering good levels of comfort and service, with most rooms priced at under £90 or under €115 in the Republic of Ireland (price of a room for 2 people, including breakfast).

PLEASANT HOTELS AND RESTAURANTS

Symbols shown in red indicate particularly pleasant or restful establishments: the character of the building, its décor, the setting, the welcome and services offered may all contribute to this special appeal.

⌂, ⌂ to ⌂⌂⌂⌂⌂ **Pleasant hotels & guesthouses**

🍺, X to XXXXX **Pleasant restaurants & pubs**

OTHER SPECIAL FEATURES

As well as the categories and awards given to the establishment, Michelin inspectors also make special note of other criteria which can be important when choosing an establishment.

LOCATION

If you are looking for a particularly restful establishment, or one with a special view, look out for the following symbols:

Quiet hotel

Very quiet hotel

Interesting view

Exceptional view

WINE LIST

If you are looking for an establishment with a particularly interesting wine list, look out for the following symbol:

Particularly interesting wine list

This symbol might cover the list presented by a sommelier in a luxury restaurant or that of a simple pub or restaurant where the owner has a passion for wine. The two lists will offer something exceptional but very different, so beware of comparing them by each other's standards.

SMOKING

In Great Britain and the Republic of Ireland the law prohibits smoking in all pubs, restaurants and hotel public areas.

Facilities & services

30 rm	Number of rooms
	Lift (elevator)
A/C	Air conditioning (in all or part of the establishment)
	Fast Internet access in bedrooms
	Wi-fi Internet access in bedrooms
	Establishment at least partly accessible to those of restricted mobility
	Special facilities for children
	Meals served in garden or on terrace
Spa	An extensive facility for relaxation and well-being
	Sauna – Exercise room
	Swimming pool: outdoor or indoor
	Garden – Park
18	Tennis court – Golf course and number of holes
	Fishing available to hotel guests. A charge may be made
	Equipped conference room
	Private dining rooms
	Hotel garage (additional charge in most cases)
	Car park for customers only
	No dogs allowed (in all or part of the establishment)
	Nearest Underground station (in London)
May-October	Dates when open, as indicated by the hotelier

Prices

Prices quoted in this guide were supplied in autumn 2010 and apply to low and high seasons. They are subject to alteration if goods and service costs are revised. By supplying the information, hotels and restaurants have undertaken to maintain these rates for our readers.
In some towns, when commercial, cultural or sporting events are taking place the hotel rates are likely to be considerably higher.
Prices are given in £ sterling, except for the Republic of Ireland where euros are quoted.
All accommodation prices include both service and V.A.T. All restaurant prices include V.A.T. Service is also included when an **s** appears after the prices.
Where no **s** is shown, prices may be subject to the addition of a variable service charge which is usually between 10 % - 15 %.
(V.A.T. does not apply in the Channel Islands).
Out of season, certain establishments offer special rates. Ask when booking.

RESERVATION AND DEPOSITS

Some hotels will require a deposit which confirms the commitment of both the customer and the hotelier. Ask the hotelier to provide you with all the terms and conditions applicable to your reservation in their written confirmation.

CREDIT CARDS

	Credit cards accepted by the establishment:
AE Ⓓ MC VISA	American Express – Diners Club – MasterCard – Visa

ROOMS

rm 🚹 50.00/90.00	Lowest price 50.00 and highest price 90.00 for a comfortable single room
rm 🚹🚹 70.00/120.00	Lowest price 70.00 and highest price 120.00 for a double or twin room for 2 people
rm ☕ 55.00/85.00	Full cooked breakfast (whether taken or not) is included in the price of the room
☕ 6.00	Price of breakfast

SHORT BREAKS

Many hotels offer a special rate for a stay of two or more nights which comprises dinner, room and breakfast usually for a minimum of two people. Please enquire at hotel for rates.

RESTAURANT

Set meals: lowest price £13.00, highest price £28.00, usually for a 3 course meal. The lowest priced set menu is often only available at lunchtimes.
A la carte meals: the prices represent the range of charges from a simple to an elaborate 3 course meal.

s	Service included
🎭	Restaurants offering lower priced pre and/or post theatre menus

🏠: Dinner in this category of establishment is sometimes communal and meals are not always available every evening. It will generally be a limited menu, served at a set time, to residents only. Lunch is rarely offered. Many will not be licensed to sell alcohol.

Towns

GENERAL INFORMATION

✉ **York**	Postal address
501 M27, ⑩	Michelin map and co-ordinates or fold
Great Britain	See the Michelin Green Guide Great Britain
pop. 1057	Population Source: 2001 Census (Key Statistics for Urban Areas) Crown copyright 2004
BX **a**	Letters giving the location of a place on a town plan
18	Golf course and number of holes (handicap sometimes required, telephone reservation strongly advised)
✳ ⋞	Panoramic view, viewpoint
✈	Airport
⛴	Shipping line (passengers & cars)
⛴	Passenger transport only
i	Tourist Information Centre

STANDARD TIME

In winter, standard time throughout the British Isles is Greenwich Mean Time (GMT). In summer, British clocks are advanced by one hour to give British Summer Time (BST). The actual dates are announced annually but always occur over weekends in March and October.

TOURIST INFORMATION

STAR-RATING

★★★	Highly recommended
★★	Recommended
★	Interesting
AC	Admission charge

LOCATION

◉	Sights in town
◎	On the outskirts
N, S, E, W	The sight lies North, South, East or West of the town
A 22	Take road A 22, indicated by the same symbol on the Guide map
2 mi.	Distance in miles (In the Republic of Ireland kilometres are quoted).

Town plans

@ ● a Hotels – restaurants

SIGHTS

Place of interest
Interesting place of worship

ROADS

M 1 Motorway
Numbered junctions: complete, limited
Dual carriageway with motorway characteristics
Main traffic artery
A 2 Primary route (GB) and National route (IRL)
One-way street – Unsuitable for traffic or street subject to restrictions
Pedestrian street – Tramway
Piccadilly P Shopping street – Car park – Park and Ride
Gateway – Street passing under arch – Tunnel
15'5 Low headroom (16'6" max.) on major through routes
Station and railway
Funicular – Cable-car
B Lever bridge – Car ferry

VARIOUS SIGNS

Tourist Information Centre
Church/Place of worship - Mosque – Synagogue
Communications tower or mast – Ruins
Garden, park, wood – Cemetery
Stadium - Racecourse - Golf course
Golf course (with restrictions for visitors) – Skating rink
Outdoor or indoor swimming pool
View – Panorama
Monument – Fountain – Hospital – Covered market
Pleasure boat harbour – Lighthouse
Airport – Underground station – Coach station
Ferry services: passengers and cars
Main post office
Public buildings located by letter:
C H J County Council Offices – Town Hall – Law Courts
M T U Museum – Theatre – University, College
POL. Police (in large towns police headquarters)

LONDON

BRENT WEMBLEY Borough – Area
Borough boundary
Congestion Zone – Charge applies Monday-Friday 07.00-18.00
Nearest Underground station to the hotel or restaurant

Awards 2011

Starred establishments 2011

The colour corresponds to the establishment with the most stars in this location.

London	This location has at least one 3 star restaurant	✻✻✻
Dublin	This location has at least one 2 star restaurant	✻✻
Edinburgh	This location has at least one 1 star restaurant	✻

Lochinver

Sleat

Fort William

Dalry

Malahide

Dublin

REPUBLIC OF IRELAND

Ardmore

Rock

ISLES OF SCILLY

GUERNSEY

JERSEY

La Pulente

St Helier

SHETLAND
ISLANDS
ORKNEY
ISLANDS
Nairn
SCOTLAND
Auchterarder
Peat Inn
Elie
Edinburgh
Linlithgow
Leith
Pooley Bridge
Ambleside
Windermere
Ramsgill-
in-Nidderdale
Cartmel
Bolton Abbey
Ilkley
South Dalton
Langho
ENGLAND
Birkenhead
Sheffield
Chester
Baslow
Llandrillo
Nottingham
Morston
Machynlleth
Clipsham
Hunstanton
Hambleton
Birmingham
Royal Leamington Spa
Titley
Ludlow
Winchcombe
Upper Slaughter
Cambridge
WALES
Cheltenham
Murcott
Woburn
Llanddewi
Skirrid
Welwyn Garden City
Whitebrook
Malmesbury
Great Milton
Bristol
Marlow
London
Colerne
Little Bedwyn
Chew Magna
Shinfield
Ripley
Seasalter
Castle Combe
Faversham
Bray
Biddenden
Knowstone
Bagshot
Winchester
Cranbrook
Petersfield
Cuckfield
Chagford
Dorchester
Bodiam
Beaulieu
Emsworth
Torquay
Ventnor

Starred establishments

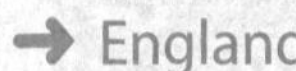

→ England

Bray	Fat Duck
Bray	Waterside Inn
London / City of Westminster	Alain Ducasse at The Dorchester
London / Kensington and Chelsea	Gordon Ramsay

✿✿

→ *In red the 2011 Rising Stars for* ✿✿✿

→ England

Cambridge	Midsummer House	
Chagford	Gidleigh Park	
Cheltenham	Le Champignon Sauvage	
London / Camden	Pied à Terre	
London / City of Westminster	L'Atelier de Joël Robuchon	
London / City of Westminster	Le Gavroche	
London / City of Westminster	Hélène Darroze at The Connaught	**N**
London / City of Westminster	Hibiscus	
London / City of Westminster	Marcus Wareing at The Berkeley	
London / City of Westminster	Square	
London / Kensington and Chelsea	The Ledbury	
Malmesbury	Whatley Manor	
Oxford / Great Milton	Le Manoir aux Quat' Saisons	
Rock	Restaurant Nathan Outlaw	**N**

→ Scotland

Auchterarder	Andrew Fairlie at Gleneagles

→ Republic of Ireland

Dublin	Patrick Guilbaud

→ **N** *New*

→ *In red the 2011 Rising Stars for* ✿✿

→ England

Ambleside	The Samling
Bagshot	Michael Wignall at The Latymer (at Pennyhill Park Hotel)
Baslow	Fischer's at Baslow Hall
Bath / Colerne	The Park (at Lucknam Park Hotel)
Beaulieu	The Terrace (at Montagu Arms Hotel)
Beverley / South Dalton	The Pipe and Glass Inn
Biddenden	West House
Birkenhead	Fraiche
Birmingham	Purnell's
Birmingham	Simpsons
Birmingham	Turners
Blackburn / Langho	Northcote
Blakeney / Morston	Morston Hall
Bodiam	Curlew **N**
Bolton Abbey	Burlington (at Devonshire Arms Country House Hotel)
Bourton-on-the-Water / Upper Slaughter	Lords of the Manor
Bray	Royal Oak
Bristol	Casamia
Castle Combe	Manor House H. and Golf Club
Chester	Simon Radley at The Chester Grosvenor
Chew Magna	Pony and Trap **N**
Cranbrook	Apicius
Cuckfield	Ockenden Manor
Dorchester	Sienna
Emsworth	36 on the Quay
Faversham	Read's
Grange-over-Sands / Cartmel	L'Enclume
Hunstanton	The Neptune
Ilkley	Box Tree
Jersey / La Pulente	Atlantic
Jersey / St Helier	Bohemia (at The Club Hotel and Spa)
Kington / Titley	The Stagg Inn
London / Bromley	Chapter One
London / Camden	Hakkasan
London / City of London	Club Gascon
London / City of London	Rhodes Twenty Four
London / City of Westminster	Amaya
London / City of Westminster	Apsleys (at Lanesborough Hotel)
London / City of Westminster	Arbutus
London / City of Westminster	L'Autre Pied
London / City of Westminster	Benares
London / City of Westminster	Galvin at Windows (at London Hilton Hotel)

London / City of Westminster	Gauthier - Soho	**N**
London / City of Westminster	Greenhouse	
London / City of Westminster	Kai	
London / City of Westminster	Locanda Locatelli	
London / City of Westminster	Maze	
London / City of Westminster	Murano	
London / City of Westminster	Nobu (at The Metropolitan Hotel)	
London / City of Westminster	Nobu Berkeley St	
London / City of Westminster	Pétrus	**N**
London / City of Westminster	Quilon	
London / City of Westminster	Rhodes W1 (Restaurant)	
London / City of Westminster	Semplice	
London / City of Westminster	Seven Park Place (at St James's Hotel and Club)	**N**
London / City of Westminster	Sketch (The Lecture Room and Library)	
London / City of Westminster	Tamarind	
London / City of Westminster	Texture	
London / City of Westminster	Umu	
London / City of Westminster	Wild Honey	
London / City of Westminster	Yauatcha	
London / City of Westminster	Zafferano	
London / Hammersmith and Fulham	Harwood Arms	
London / Hammersmith and Fulham	River Café	
London / Hounslow	La Trompette	
London / Islington	St John	
London / Kensington and Chelsea	Kitchen W8	**N**
London / Kensington and Chelsea	Rasoi	
London / Kensington and Chelsea	Tom Aikens	
London / Richmond-upon-Thames	Bingham Restaurant (at Bingham Hotel)	
London / Richmond-upon-Thames	The Glasshouse	
London / Richmond-upon-Thames	Petersham Nurseries Café	**N**
London / Tower Hamlets	Galvin La Chapelle	**N**
London / Tower Hamlets	Viajante	**N**
London / Wandsworth	Chez Bruce	
Ludlow	La Bécasse	
Ludlow	Mr Underhill's at Dinham Weir	
Marlborough / Little Bedwyn	Harrow at Little Bedwyn	
Marlow	Adam Simmonds at Danesfield House	**N**
Marlow	The Hand and Flowers	
Murcott	The Nut Tree	
Nottingham	Restaurant Sat Bains	
Oakham / Hambleton	Hambleton Hall	
Pateley Bridge / Ramsgill-in-Nidderdale	Yorke Arms	
Petersfield	JSW	
Reading / Shinfield	L'Ortolan	
Ripley (Surrey)	Drake's	
Royal Leamington Spa	Mallory Court	
Sheffield	Old Vicarage	

South Molton / Knowstone	The Masons Arms	
Stamford / Clipsham	The Olive Branch and Beech House	
Torquay	Room in the Elephant	
Ullswater / Pooley Bridge	Sharrow Bay Country House	
Welwyn Garden City	Auberge du Lac	
Whitstable / Seasalter	The Sportsman	
Wight (Isle of) / Ventnor	Hambrough	
Winchcombe	5 North St	
Winchester	The Black Rat	**N**
Windermere	Holbeck Ghyll	
Woburn	Paris House	**N**

→ Scotland

Dalry	Braidwoods
Edinburgh	Number One (at Balmoral Hotel)
Edinburgh	21212
Edinburgh / Leith	Kitchin
Edinburgh / Leith	Martin Wishart
Edinburgh / Leith	Plumed Horse
Elie	Sangster's
Fort William	Inverlochy Castle
Linlithgow	Champany Inn
Lochinver	Albannach
Nairn	Boath House
Peat Inn	Peat Inn
Portpatrick	Knockinaam Lodge
Skye (Isle of) / Sleat	Kinloch Lodge

→ Wales

Abergavenny / Llanddewi Skirrid	The Walnut Tree
Llandrillo	Tyddyn Llan
Machynlleth	Ynyshir Hall
Monmouth / Whitebrook	Crown at Whitebrook

→ Republic of Ireland

Ardmore	House (at Cliff House Hotel)
Dublin	Chapter One
Dublin	L'Ecrivain
Dublin	Thornton's (at The Fitzwilliam Hotel)
Malahide	Bon Appétit

→ *The 2011 Rising Stars for* ✿

Alkham	The Marquis
Amersham	Artichoke
Edinburgh	Castle Terrace
Helmsley / Oldstead	Black Swan

The 2011 Bib Gourmand

• Places with at least one Bib Gourmand establishment.

SHETLAND ISLANDS
ORKNEY ISLANDS
SCOTLAND
Edinburgh
Sorn
Peebles
Durham
Hutton Magna
Hurworth-on-Tees
Masham
Sutton-on-the-Forest
Thornton
Gisburn
Ferrensby
Wiswell
Beverley
Leeds
Bury
Oldham
Sheffield
Alderley Edge
Birchover
Burnham Market
ENGLAND
Stathern
Itteringham
WALES
Stamford
Stanton
Stoke Holy Cross
Stratford-upon-Avon
Bury St. Edmunds
Stow-on-the-Wold
Little Wilbraham
Woolhope
Kingham
Aldeburgh
Chipping Norton
Abergavenny
Burford
Oxford
Burchett's Green
Kelvedon
Tetbury
Seer Green
Bristol
Toot Baldon
London
Backwell
East Chisenbury
Preston Candover
Windlesham
Wells
Ramsgate
Bray-on-Thames
Bruton
Longstock
West Hoathly
Henfield
Rockbeare
Droxford
Wimborne St. Giles
Hove
Brighton
Hastings and St Leonards

Bib Gourmand

Good food at moderate prices

→ England

Aldeburgh	Lighthouse	
Alderley Edge	The Wizard	
Backwell	The New Inn	**N**
Barnard Castle / Hutton Magna	The Oak Tree Inn	
Beaconsfield / Seer Green	The Jolly Cricketers	**N**
Beverley	Whites	
Blackpool / Thornton	Twelve	
Bray	The Hinds Head	
Brighton	Chilli Pickle	**N**
Brighton / Hove	The Ginger Pig	
Brighton / Hove	The Meadow	
Bristol	Greens' Dining Room	
Bruton	At The Chapel	
Burford	The Carpenter's Arms	**N**
Burnham Market	Hoste Arms	
Bury	The Waggon	
Bury St Edmunds	Pea Porridge	**N**
Cambridge / Little Wilbraham	The Hole in the Wall	
Chipping Norton	Masons Arms	
Clitheroe / Wiswell	Freemasons Country Inn	**N**
Darlington / Hurworth-on-Tees	The Bay Horse	
Droxford	The Bakers Arms	
Durham	Bistro 21	
East Chisenbury	Red Lion Freehouse	
Exeter / Rockbeare	Jack in the Green Inn	
Gisburn	La Locanda	**N**
Guernsey / St Saviour (Guernsey)	Pavilion	
Hastings and St. Leonards	St Clements	
Henfield	The Ginger Fox	
Itteringham	Walpole Arms	
Kelvedon	George and Dragon	
Kingham	The Kingham Plough	
Knaresborough / Ferrensby	General Tarleton Inn	
Leeds	Piazza by Anthony	
London / Camden	Bradley's	
London / Camden	Giaconda Dining Room	
London / Camden	Great Queen Street	
London / Camden	Market	
London / Camden	Salt Yard	
London / City of London	Goldfish City	**N**
London / City of London	28°-50°	**N**
London / City of Westminster	Al Duca	
London / City of Westminster	Bar Trattoria Semplice	
London / City of Westminster	Benja	
London / City of Westminster	Bocca di Lupo	
London / City of Westminster	Dehesa	
London / City of Westminster	Hereford Road	
London / City of Westminster	Iberica	**N**
London / City of Westminster	Polpo	**N**
London / City of Westminster	Terroirs	
London / Hounslow	Charlotte's Bistro	**N**
London / Islington	Comptoir Gascon	
London / Islington	The Drapers Arms	
London / Islington	500	

→ **N** *New*

London / Islington	Medcalf	
London / Islington	Metrogusto	
London / Islington	Morito	**N**
London / Islington	Trullo	**N**
London / Kensington and Chelsea	Malabar	
London / Lambeth	Canton Arms	**N**
London / Lewisham	Chapters	
London / Richmond-upon-Thames	Brown Dog	
London / Richmond-upon-Thames	Mango and Silk	
London / Richmond-upon-Thames	Simply Thai	**N**
London / Southwark	Anchor and Hope	
London / Southwark	Zucca	**N**
London / Tower Hamlets	Cafe Spice Namaste	
London / Tower Hamlets	Galvin Café a Vin	**N**
Maidenhead / Burchett''s Green	Crown	**N**
Masham	Vennell's	
Matlock / Birchover	The Druid Inn	
Melton Mowbray / Stathern	Red Lion Inn	
Millbrook / Freathy	The View	
Norwich / Stoke Holy Cross	Wildebeest Arms	
Oldham	The White Hart Inn	
Oxford	The Magdalen Arms	**N**
Oxford / Toot Baldon	The Mole Inn	
Padstow	Rick Stein's Café	
Preston Candover	Purefoy Arms	**N**
Ramsgate	Age and Sons	
St Ives	Black Rock	**N**
Sheffield	Artisan	
Stamford	Jim's Yard	
Stanton	Leaping Hare	
Stockbridge / Longstock	The Peat Spade Inn	
Stow-on-the-Wold	The Old Butchers	
Stratford-upon-Avon	Malbec Petit Bistro	
Sutton-on-the-Forest	Rose and Crown	
Tetbury	The Gumstool Inn	
Wadebridge / St Kew	St Kew Inn	
Wells	Old Spot	
West Hoathly	The Cat Inn	**N**
Wimborne St Giles	The Bull Inn	**N**
Windlesham	The Bee	
Woolhope	The Butchers Arms	

→ Scotland

Edinburgh	Dogs	
Kintyre (Peninsula) / Kilberry	Kilberry Inn	
Peebles	Osso	**N**
Sorn	The Sorn Inn	

→ Wales

Abergavenny	The Hardwick	

→ Northern Ireland

Ballyclare	Oregano	
Belfast	Cayenne	
Warrenpoint	Restaurant 23	

→ Republic of Ireland

Adare	White Sage	
Cashel (Tipperary)	Cafe Hans	
Clonegall	Sha Roe Bistro	
Dingle	The Chart House	
Dublin	La Maison	
Dublin	Pichet	
Dublin	The Pig's Ear	
Duncannon	Aldridge Lodge	
Dundalk	Rosso	
Durrus	Good Things Cafe	
Kinsale	Fishy Fishy Cafe	
Lisdoonvarna	Wild Honey Inn	
Lismore	O'Brien Chop House	
Roundstone	O'Dowd's	**N**

Bib Hotel

Good accommodation at moderate prices

➜ England

Aldeburgh / Friston	Old School	
Armscote	Willow Corner	
Barnard Castle	Greta House	
Barnard Castle	Homelands	
Bishop's Stortford / Stansted Mountfitchet	Chimneys	
Bodmin	Bokiddick Farm	
Bourton-on-the-Water	Coombe House	
Bovey Tracey	Brookfield House	
Bungay / Earsham	Earsham Park Farm	N
Bury St Edmunds / Beyton	Manorhouse	
Cheddleton	Choir Cottage	
Deddington	The Old Post House	
Devizes / Potterne	Blounts Court Farm	
Doddington	Old Vicarage	N
Earl Stonham	Bays Farm	N
Eastbourne	Brayscroft	
Ely / Little Thetford	Springfields	
Harrogate / Kettlesing	Knabbs Ash	
Hartland	Golden Park	
Henfield / Wineham	Frylands	
Hexham	West Close House	
Holbeach	Pipwell Manor	
Kenilworth	Victoria Lodge	
Kirkwhelpington	Shieldhall	
Leyburn	Clyde House	
Longtown	Bessiestown Farm	
Morpeth / Longhorsley	Thistleyhaugh Farm	
Oxhill	Oxbourne House	
Penrith	Brooklands	N
Pickering	Bramwood	
Ripon	Sharow Cross House	
Ross-on-Wye / Kerne Bridge	Lumleys	
Salisbury / Little Langford	Little Langford Farmhouse	
Scarborough	Alexander	
Southend-on-Sea	Beaches	
Stow-on-the-Wold	Number Nine	
Torquay	Colindale	
Tynemouth	Martineau Guest House	
Wallingford	North Moreton House	
Wareham	Gold Court House	
Wells / Easton (Somerset)	Beaconsfield Farm	
Whitby / Briggswath	Lawns	
York	Alexander House	N

➜ Scotland

Anstruther	The Spindrift
Auchencairn	Balcary Mews
Aultbea	Mellondale
Ayr	Coila
Ayr	No.26 The Crescent
Ballater	Moorside House
Blairgowrie	Gilmore House
Carnoustie	The Old Manor

➜ **N** *New*

Crieff	Merlindale	
Dunkeld	Letter Farm	
Edinburgh	Beverley	
Forres / Dyke	Old Kirk	
Glendevon	Tormaukin Inn	
Jedburgh	Willow Court	**N**
Kingussie	Hermitage	
Montrose	36 The Mall	
Nairn	Bracadale House	
Peebles	Rowanbrae	**N**
Perth	Taythorpe	
Pitlochry	Dunmurray Lodge	
Skye (Isle of) / Broadford	Tigh an Dochais	
Skye (Isle of) / Dunvegan	Roskhill House	
Stevenston	Ardeer Farm Steading	
Strathpeffer	Craigvar	
Thornhill	Gillbank House	
Ullapool	Point Cottage	
Wick	The Clachan	**N**

→ Wales

Aberaeron	Llys Aeron	
Betws Garmon	Betws Inn	
Colwyn Bay	Rathlin Country House	
Dolgellau	Tyddyn Mawr	
Llandudno	Abbey Lodge	
Llandudno	Lympley Lodge	
Llanuwchllyn	Eifionydd	
Ruthin	Firgrove	

→ Northern Ireland

Bangor	Cairn Bay Lodge	
Belfast	Ravenhill House	
Crumlin	Caldhame Lodge	

→ Republic of Ireland

Ballyvaughan	Drumcreehy House	
Bansha	Rathellen House	**N**
Cashel (Tipperary)	Aulber House	
Castlegregory	Shores Country House	
Donegal	Ardeevin	
Dundalk	Rosemount	
Kinsale / Barrells Cross	Rivermount House	
Oughterard	Railway Lodge	
Oughterard	Waterfall Lodge	
Toormore	Fortview House	
Tramore	Glenorney	

Particularly pleasant hotels & guesthouses

England

Dogmersfield Four Seasons
London / City of Westminster Berkeley
London / City of Westminster Claridge's
London / City of Westminster Connaught
London / City of Westminster Dorchester
London / City of Westminster Mandarin Oriental Hyde Park
London / City of Westminster The Ritz
London / City of Westminster Savoy
New Milton Chewton Glen
Oxford / Great Milton Le Manoir aux Quat' Saisons
Taplow Cliveden

England

Aylesbury Hartwell House
Bath Royal Crescent
Bath / Colerne Lucknam Park
Chagford Gidleigh Park
Jersey / St Saviour (Jersey) Longueville Manor
London / City of Westminster The Goring
London / City of Westminster One Aldwych
London / City of Westminster Soho
Lyndhurst Lime Wood
Malmesbury Whatley Manor
Newbury The Vineyard at Stockcross
North Bovey Bovey Castle
Ston Easton Ston Easton Park

Scotland

Ballantrae Glenapp Castle
Bishopton Mar Hall
Eriska (Isle of) Isle of Eriska
Fort William Inverlochy Castle

Republic of Ireland

Dublin Merrion
Kenmare Park
Killarney Killarney Park

England

Abberley Elms
Amberley Amberley Castle
Bath Bath Priory
Beaulieu Montagu Arms
Bolton Abbey Devonshire Arms Country House
Bourton-on-the-Water / Lower Slaughter Lower Slaughter Manor
Bourton-on-the-Water / Upper Slaughter Lords of the Manor
Broadway Buckland Manor
Castle Combe Manor House H. and Golf Club
Dedham Maison Talbooth
Evershot Summer Lodge
Gillingham Stock Hill Country House
Guernsey / St Peter Port Old Government House H. and Spa

Jersey / La Pulente	Atlantic
London / Camden	Charlotte Street
London / Camden	Covent Garden
London / City of Westminster	Dukes
London / City of Westminster	Halkin
London / City of Westminster	Stafford
London / Kensington and Chelsea	Blakes
London / Kensington and Chelsea	The Capital
London / Kensington and Chelsea	Draycott
London / Kensington and Chelsea	The Milestone
London / Kensington and Chelsea	The Pelham
Newcastle upon Tyne	Jesmond Dene House
Oakham / Hambleton	Hambleton Hall
Royal Leamington Spa	Mallory Court
Scilly (Isles of)	St Martin's on the Isle
Tetbury	Calcot Manor
Ullswater / Pooley Bridge	Sharrow Bay Country House
Winchester / Sparsholt	Lainston House
Windermere / Bowness-on-Windermere	Gilpin Lodge
Yarm	Judges Country House
York	Middlethorpe Hall

→ Scotland

Blairgowrie	Kinloch House
Edinburgh	Prestonfield
Torridon	The Torridon

→ Wales

Llandudno	Bodysgallen Hall
Llangammarch Wells	Lake Country House and Spa

→ Republic of Ireland

Ardmore	Cliff House
Ballyvaughan	Gregans Castle
Dublin	Dylan
Mallow	Longueville House

→ England

Ambleside	The Samling
Bath	Queensberry
Bigbury-on-Sea	Burgh Island
Blakeney / Morston	Morston Hall
Brampton	Farlam Hall
Burnham Market	Hoste Arms
Cheltenham	The Hotel
Chester	Green Bough
Cirencester / Barnsley	Barnsley House
Cuckfield	Ockenden Manor
Frome	Babington House
Helmsley	Feversham Arms
Horley	Langshott Manor
King's Lynn / Grimston	Congham Hall
Lewdown	Lewtrenchard Manor
London / City of Westminster	Dorset Square
London / Kensington and Chelsea	Egerton House
London / Kensington and Chelsea	Knightsbridge
London / Kensington and Chelsea	The Levin
London / Kensington and Chelsea	Number Sixteen
Newquay / Mawgan Porth	Scarlet
North Walsham	Beechwood
Orford	Crown and Castle
Rushlake Green	Stone House
St Mawes	Tresanton
Scilly (Isles of)	Hell Bay
Southampton / Netley Marsh	Hotel TerraVina
Tavistock / Milton Abbot	Hotel Endsleigh
Torquay / Maidencombe	Orestone Manor
Wareham	Priory
Windermere	Holbeck Ghyll

Scotland

Abriachan	Loch Ness Lodge
Achiltibuie	Summer Isles
Arran (Isle of)	Kilmichael Country House
Killin / Ardeonaig	Ardeonaig
Lochearnhead / Balquhidder	Monachyle Mhor
Nairn	Boath House
Port Appin	Airds
Portpatrick	Knockinaam Lodge
Skye (Isle of) / Sleat	Kinloch Lodge

Wales

Llandudno	Osborne House
Machynlleth	Ynyshir Hall
Swansea / Llanrhidian	Fairyhill
Talsarnau	Maes-y-Neuadd

Republic of Ireland

Arthurstown	Dunbrody Country House
Ballingarry	Mustard Seed at Echo Lodge
Kinsale	Perryville House

England

Ashwater	Blagdon Manor
Bourton-on-the-Water	Dial House
Burnham Market	Vine House
Chillington	whitehouse
Coln St Aldwyns	New Inn At Coln
Dartmouth / Kingswear	Nonsuch House
Helmsley / Harome	Cross House Lodge at The Star Inn
Keswick / Portinscale	Swinside Lodge
Ludlow	De Grey's Town House
Lynton / Martinhoe	Old Rectory
Moccas	Moccas Court
Porlock	Oaks
Portscatho	Driftwood
Salisbury / Teffont Magna	Howard's House
Windermere / Bowness-on-Windermere	Gilpin Lake House

Scotland

Kelso / Ednam	Edenwater House
Kirkbean	Cavens
Mull (Isle of) / Tiroran	Tiroran House
Skye (Isle of)	Toravaig House
Tain / Cadboll	Glenmorangie House

Wales

Betws-y-Coed	Tan-y-Foel Country House
Conwy / Llansanffraid Glan Conwy	Old Rectory Country House
Dolgellau	Ffynnon

Republic of Ireland

Bagenalstown	Kilgraney Country House
Castlelyons	Ballyvolane House
Dingle	Emlagh Country House
Lahinch	Moy House

England

Arnside	Number 43
Ash	Great Weddington
Austwick	Austwick Hall
Beverley	Burton Mount
Blackpool	Number One St Lukes
Bridport / Burton Bradstock	Norburton Hall
Brighton	Kemp Townhouse
Broad Oak	Fairacres
Cheltenham	Thirty Two
Chipping Campden / Broad Campden	Malt House

Clun	Birches Mill
Crackington Haven	Manor Farm
Cranbrook	Cloth Hall Oast
East Hoathly	Old Whyly
Hawkshead / Far Sawrey	West Vale
Haworth	Ashmount Country House
Ivychurch	Olde Moat House
Kendal	Beech House
Lavenham	Lavenham Priory
Ledbury / Kynaston	Hall End
Lizard	Landewednack House
Man (Isle of) / Douglas	Birchfield House
Marazion / Perranuthnoe	Ednovean Farm
Marazion / St Hilary	Ennys
Moreton-in-Marsh	The Old School
North Bovey	Gate House
Padstow	Treverbyn House
Padstow	Woodlands Country House
Pershore / Eckington	Eckington Manor
Pickering	17 Burgate
Pickering / Levisham	Moorlands Country House
Ripon	Sharow Cross House
St Austell / Tregrehan	Anchorage House
Shrewsbury	Pinewood House
Stow-on-the-Wold / Lower Swell	Rectory Farmhouse
Stratford-upon-Avon	Cherry Trees
Stratford-upon-Avon / Pillerton Priors	Fulready Manor
Tavistock / Chillaton	Tor Cottage
Teignmouth	Thomas Luny House
Thursford Green	Holly Lodge
Warkworth	Roxbro House
Wold Newton	Wold Cottage

→ Scotland

Ballantrae	Cosses Country House
Bute (Isle of) / Ascog	Balmory Hall
Connel	Ards House
Drumbeg	Blar na Leisg at Drumbeg House
Edinburgh	Davenport House
Fortrose	Water's Edge
Fort William	Grange
Grantown-on-Spey	Dulaig
Islay (Isle of) / Ballygrant	Kilmeny
Linlithgow	Arden House
Lochinver	Ruddyglow Park Country House
Mainland (Orkney Islands) / Harray	Holland House
Mull (Isle of) / Gruline	Gruline Home Farm
Skirling	Skirling House
Skye (Isle of) / Bernisdale	Spoons
Strathpeffer	Craigvar
Tain / Nigg	Wemyss House

→ Wales

Anglesey (Isle of) / Beaumaris	Cleifiog
Anglesey (Isle of) / Menai Bridge	Neuadd Lwyd
Betws-y-Coed / Penmachno	Penmachno Hall
Dolfor	Old Vicarage
Dolgellau	Tyddyn Mawr
Pwllheli / Boduan	The Old Rectory
St Clears	Coedllys Country House

→ Northern Ireland

Ballintoy	Whitepark House
Dungannon	Grange Lodge
Holywood	Beech Hill

→ Republic of Ireland

Castlegregory	Shores Country House
Cong	Ballywarren House
Fethard	Mobarnane House
Kanturk	Glenlohane
Kenmare	Sallyport House
Kilkenny	Blanchville House
Portlaoise	Ivyleigh House
Toormore	Fortview House

Particularly pleasant restaurants & pubs

England

London / City of Westminster The Ritz Restaurant

England

Bath / Colerne The Park (at Lucknam Park Hotel)
Bolton Abbey Burlington (at Devonshire Arms Country House Hotel)
Bray Waterside Inn
London / City of Westminster Hélène Darroze at The Connaught
London / City of Westminster Marcus Wareing at The Berkeley
Winteringham Winteringham Fields

Republic of Ireland

Dublin Patrick Guilbaud

England

Baslow Fischer's at Baslow Hall
Birmingham Simpsons
Blackburn / Langho Northcote
Cambridge Midsummer House
Dedham Le Talbooth
Faversham Read's
Grange-over-Sands / Cartmel L'Enclume
Ilkley Box Tree
Lavenham The Great House
London / City of London Coq d'Argent
London / City of Westminster Cecconi's
London / City of Westminster Pétrus
London / City of Westminster Quo Vadis
London / City of Westminster Scott's
London / City of Westminster The Wolseley
London / Hackney Boundary
London / Kensington and Chelsea Bibendum
London / Tower Hamlets Galvin La Chapelle
Newcastle upon Tyne Fisherman's Lodge
Pateley Bridge / Ramsgill-in-Nidderdale Yorke Arms
Petersfield JSW
Reading / Shinfield L'Ortolan
Skipton / Hetton Angel Inn and Barn Lodgings
Tavistock / Gulworthy The Horn of Plenty
Welwyn Garden City Auberge du Lac
Woburn Paris House

Scotland

Edinburgh 21212
Peat Inn Peat Inn

Wales

Llandrillo Tyddyn Llan

England

Alkham The Marquis
Arlingham The Old Passage Inn
Bath / Colerne The Brasserie (at Lucknam Park Hotel)
Bildeston The Bildeston Crown
Brockenhurst Simply at Whitley Ridge
Burnham Market Hoste Arms
Bury St Edmunds Maison Bleue
Cheltenham Daffodil
Grantham / Great Gonerby Harry's Place
Grantham / Hough-on-the-Hill The Brownlow Arms
Kirkby Lonsdale Hipping Hall
London / Camden Hakkasan
London / Camden Mon Plaisir
London / City of Westminster Le Café Anglais
London / City of Westminster Clos Maggiore
London / City of Westminster J. Sheekey
London / City of Westminster Rules
London / City of Westminster Wild Honey
London / Hammersmith and Fulham River Café
Ludlow Mr Underhill's at Dinham Weir
Malmesbury Le Mazot (at Whatley Manor Hotel)
Newquay / Watergate Bay Fifteen Cornwall
Padstow Paul Ainsworth at No.6
Padstow The Seafood
Sark La Sablonnerie
Stanton Leaping Hare
Yeovil / Barwick Little Barwick House

Scotland

Kingussie Cross at Kingussie
Lochinver Albannach
Skye (Isle of) / Dunvegan The Three Chimneys and The House Over-By

Wales

Pwllheli Plas Bodegroes

Republic of Ireland

Aran Islands / Inishmaan Inis Meáin Restaurant and Suites
Celbridge La Serre
Clogheen Old Convent
Dublin Locks Brasserie
Dunfanaghy The Mill
Dunkineely Castle Murray House
Kenmare Lime Tree
Kilbrittain Casino House

England

Ashburton Agaric
Bournemouth West Beach
Bray / Bray Marina Riverside Brasserie
Jersey / Gorey Suma's
Jersey / Green Island Green Island
Jersey / St Brelades Bay Oyster Box
London / City of Westminster L'Atelier de Joël Robuchon
London / City of Westminster Bocca di Lupo
London / City of Westminster Dehesa
London / City of Westminster J. Sheekey Oyster Bar
London / Islington Comptoir Gascon
London / Islington Trullo
London / Kensington and Chelsea Bibendum Oyster Bar
London / Richmond-upon-Thames Petersham Nurseries Café
London / Southwark Oxo Tower Brasserie
London / Southwark Zucca
Mousehole Cornish Range
St Ives Porthminster Beach Cafe
Shaldon ODE
Stow-on-the-Wold / Daylesford Cafe at Daylesford Organic
Studland Shell Bay
Summercourt Viners
West Malling Swan

Scotland

Kingairloch Boathouse and Steadings
Thurso / Scrabster The Captain's Galley

Republic of Ireland

Barna O'Grady's on the Pier
Dingle The Chart House

England

Alton / Lower Froyle The Anchor Inn
Ambleside Drunken Duck Inn
Barnard Castle / Romaldkirk Rose and Crown
Bath / Combe Hay The Wheatsheaf
Baughurst The Wellington Arms
Beverley / South Dalton The Pipe and Glass Inn
Biggleswade / Old Warden Hare and Hounds
Bolnhurst The Plough at Bolnhurst
Bray The Hinds Head
Burford / Swinbrook The Swan Inn
Chichester / Chilgrove Fish House
Chichester / East Lavant The Royal Oak Inn
Cirencester / Barnsley Village Pub
Cirencester / Sapperton The Bell
Clitheroe / Wiswell Freemasons Country Inn
Helmsley / Harome The Star Inn
Helmsley / Oldstead Black Swan
Kendal / Crosthwaite The Punch Bowl Inn
Keyston The Pheasant
Lydford The Dartmoor Inn
Marlow The Hand and Flowers
Milton Keynes / Newton Longville The Crooked Billet
Mistley The Mistley Thorn
Shefford The Black Horse
Skipton / Hetton Angel Inn
South Molton / Knowstone The Masons Arms
Stamford / Clipsham The Olive Branch and Beech House
Stockbridge / Longstock The Peat Spade Inn
Stoke-by-Nayland The Crown
Stokenchurch / Radnage The Three Horseshoes Inn
Sutton-on-the-Forest Rose and Crown
Tarr Steps Tarr Farm Inn
Taunton / Triscombe Blue Ball Inn
Woburn The Birch
Woolhope The Butchers Arms

Wales

Aberaeron Harbourmaster
Brecon The Felin Fach Griffin
Caersws / Pontdolgoch The Talkhouse
Skenfrith The Bell at Skenfrith

Further information

Beer...

It's no exaggeration to say that beer and its consumption has pretty much defined popular conception of the British character for hundreds of years. From humble alehouse, via ubiquitous urban tavern, to agreeable coaching inn – all manner of drinking establishments have lined the British highway and byway since medieval times. As an example of the popularity of the properties of ale, by the fourteenth century there were over 350 taverns in London alone, while exactly 400 years ago you could have wandered round the capital's Square Mile and found over a thousand alehouses.

The quality of the beverage proffered to thirsty customers has varied as much as the fixtures and fittings but, generally speaking, the production of beer has followed a time-honoured recipe of four ingredients: barley, hops, yeast and water. The perfect pint begins with barley - the classic beer-making grain - and a clean, plentiful water supply coming together in a maltings, creating sugar for fermentation. The result looks like thin porridge; this boiling sludge is then filtered to a brown, hazy liquid called sweet wort.

Malt imparts sweetness to a beer and so, to give it balance, the addition of hops provides a bitter element to the mix. The hops need to be boiled to release their bitterness; it's at this point the true process of brewing is enacted. Eventually, the 'hopped wort' is cooled and filtered, in preparation for the key operation: fermentation. To ferment the beer, the brewers' little miracle-worker – yeast – is added to the fermentation vessels. Yeast is a living micro-organism, and its great claim to fame (apart from filling jars of Marmite!) is being able to convert the sugars into alcohol, carbon dioxide gas and a host of subtle flavours. With real ale, a secondary fermentation takes place when the finished product is safely ensconced in its barrel or cask, a process known as conditioning which happens before it leaves the brewery, and later, as it lies in the pub cellar. The final link in the chain is the publican, who (hopefully) oversees that decent pint gushing enticingly from the hand pump!

... and Whisky

Translated from the Gaelic term 'water of life', whisky depends for its very existence on the classic qualities of H2O. The local water supply dictates the nature of your glass of whisky; above and beyond that, the characteristics of the drink itself can range from spicy and aromatic to stylish and fruity, from light and fragrant to seaweedy and peaty. The classic Scotch whisky - only produced in the ideal natural environment of Scotland - makes full use of plentiful water supplies: barley is steeped in water for two to three days to turn it into malt, and then dried in a kiln traditionally fuelled by peat, before being ground in a mill.

The milled malt is called grist, and when hot water is added, the mixture is fed into a mash tun. This is where the sugars from malting dissolve, and the resulting solution – wort – oozes through the floor of the tun, to be passed into large wooden or stainless steel vessels. Add yeast, and fermentation occurs, with the sugars turning to alcohol. By now, this looks something like beer, but when it's distilled – a two-pronged process in which condensing vapours are captured - any resemblance to ale is long gone! By the time the different parts of the distillation are gathered together and redistilled, the resultant liquid – the new-make whisky – is ready to spend the next three years (by law) in oak casks maturing: the wood enhances the final aroma and flavour. Whisky makers enjoy a certain pact with the heavens: as the liquid matures, some of it evaporates into the ether, and this is known as the 'Angels' Share'...

Irish whiskey (note the extra 'e') differs slightly from the Scottish version, and not just in the spelling. It's traditionally made from cereals, and peat is hardly ever used in the malting process, so there's a lack of the smoky, earthy characteristics found over the Irish Sea. It's also encouraged to sit around for a much longer time: the maturation period is seven years, more than twice that of Scotch.

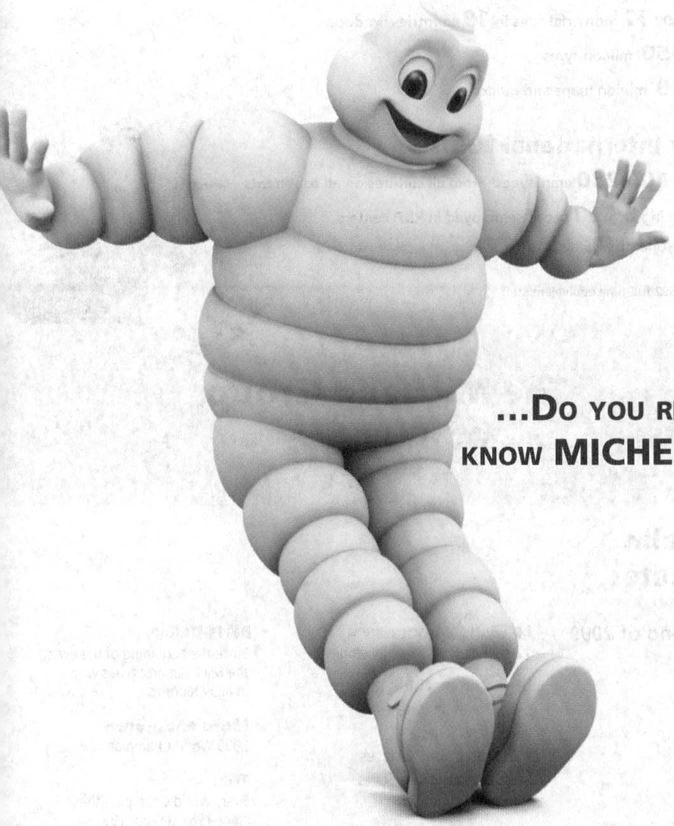

The world No.1 in tyres with 16.3% of the market

A business presence in over 170 countries

A manufacturing footprint at the heart of markets

In 2009 **72** industrial sites in **19** countries produced:

- **150** million tyres
- **10** million maps and guides

Highly international teams

Over **109 200** employees* from all cultures on all continents including **6 000** people employed in R&D centers in Europe, the US and Asia.

*102 692 full-time equivalent staff

The Michelin Group at a glance

Michelin competes

At the end of 2009

- **Le Mans 24-hour race**
  12 consecutive years of victories
- **Endurance 2009**
  • 6 victories on 6 stages in Le Mans Series
  • 12 victories on 12 stages in American Le Mans Series
- **Paris-Dakar**
  Since the beginning of the event, the Michelin group has won in all categories
- **Moto endurance**
  2009 World Champion
- **Trial**
  Every World Champion title since 1981 (except 1992)

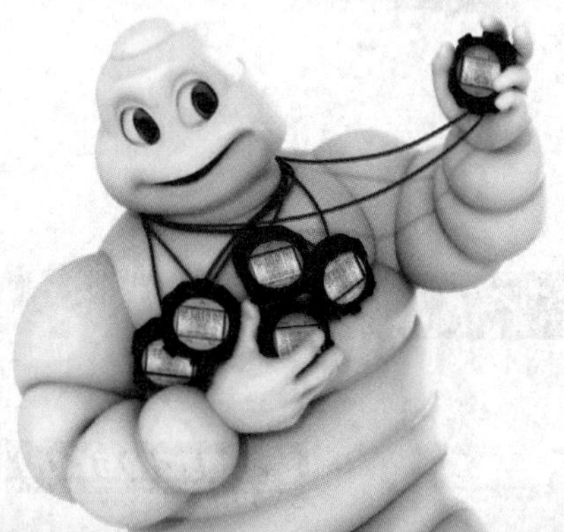

Michelin, established close to its customers

○ 72 plants in 19 countries

- Algeria
- Brazil
- Canada
- China
- Colombia
- France
- Germany
- Hungary
- Italy
- Japan
- Mexico
- Poland
- Romania
- Russia
- Serbia
- Spain
- Thailand
- UK
- USA

A Technology Center spread over 3 continents

- Asia
- Europe
- North America

Natural rubber plantations

- Brazil

Our mission

To make a sustainable contribution to progress in the mobility of goods and people by enhancing freedom of movement, safety, efficiency and the pleasure of travelling.

Michelin: committed to environmental-friendliness

Michelin, world leader in low rolling resistance tyres, actively reduces fuel consumption and vehicle gas emission.

For its products, Michelin develops state-of-the-art technologies in order to:
- Reduce fuel consumption, while improving overall tire performance.
- Increase life cycle to reduce the number of tyres to be processed at the end of their useful lives;
- Use raw materials which have a low impact on the environment.

Furthermore, at the end of 2008, 99.5% of tyre production in volume was carried out in ISO 14001* certified plants.

Michelin is committed to implementing recycling channels for end-of-life tyres.

*environmental certification

Passenger Car
Light Truck

Truck

Michelin
a key mobility enabler

Earthmover

Aircraft

Agricultural

Two-wheel

Distribution

Partnered with vehicle manufacturers, in tune with users, active in competition and in all the distribution channels, Michelin is continually innovating to promote mobility today and to invent that of tomorrow.

Maps and Guides

ViaMichelin, travel assistance services

Michelin Lifestyle, for your travel accessories

MICHELIN plays on balanced performance

- **Long tyre life**
- **Fuel savings**
- **Safety on the road**

... MICHELIN tyres provide you with the best performance, without making a single sacrifice.

The MICHELIN tyre pure technology

1 Tread
A thick layer of rubber provides contact with the ground. It has to channel water away and last as long as possible.

2 Crown plies
This double or triple reinforced belt has both vertical flexibility and high lateral rigidity. It provides the steering capacity.

3 Sidewalls
These cover and protect the textile casing whose role is to attach the tyre tread to the wheel rim.

4 Bead area for attachment to the rim
Its internal bead wire clamps the tyre firmly against the wheel rim.

5 Inner liner
This makes the tyre almost totally impermeable and maintains the correct inflation pressure.

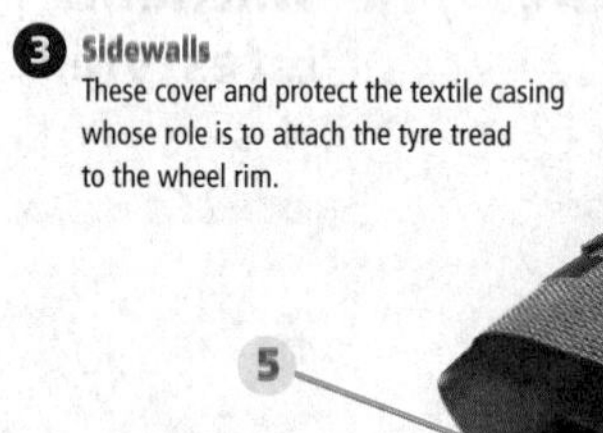

Heed the MICHELIN Man's advice

To improve safety:

- I drive with the correct tyre pressure
- I check the tyre pressure every month
- I have my car regularly serviced
- I regularly check the appearance of my tyres (wear, deformation)
- I am responsive behind the wheel
- I change my tyres according to the season

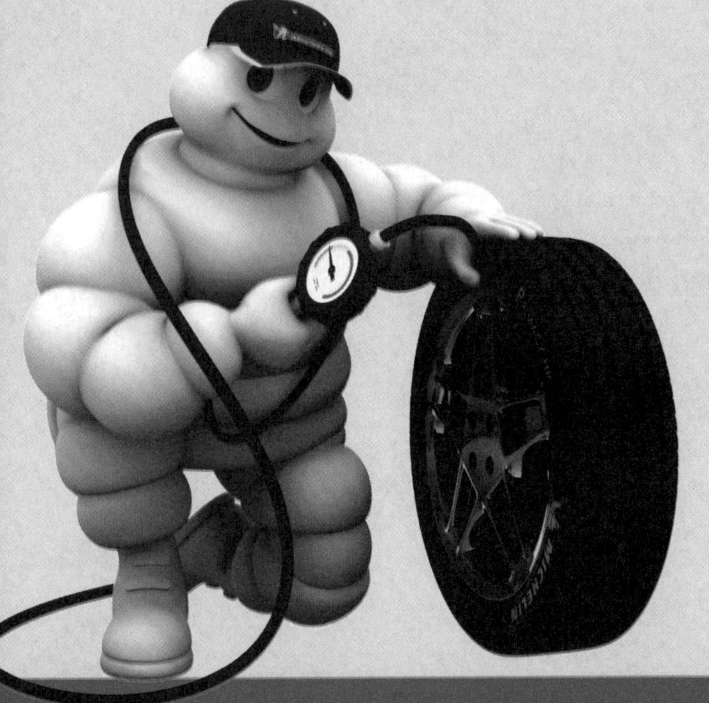

Great Britain

C. Labonne/MICHELIN

England
Channel Islands • Isle of Man

ABBERLEY – Worcestershire – 503 M27 – pop. 654 – ✉ Worcester 18 B2

London 137 mi – Birmingham 27 mi – Worcester 13 mi

Elms

West : 2 mi on A 443 ✉ WR6 6AT – ☎ (01299) 896 666 – www.theelmshotel.co.uk

23 rm (dinner included) – †£ 200/315 ††£ 330/510

Rest ***Brooke Room*** – Menu £ 21/50 – Carte £ 19/31

Rest ***Pear Terrace*** – Carte £ 24/27

◆ Impressive Queen Anne house built in 1710. Inside, modern colours and fabrics blend with traditional furnishings. Bedrooms are split between the house and stables; most boast country views. Child friendly. Impressive spa. Fine dining room offers modern menu. Informal restaurant in spa serves snacks and traditional fare.

ABBOTSBURY – Dorset – 503 M32 – pop. 422 3 B3

London 146 mi – Bournemouth 44 mi – Exeter 50 mi – Weymouth 10 mi

Town★★ - Chesil Beach★★ - Swannery★ **AC** – Sub-Tropical Gardens★ **AC**

St Catherine's Chapel★, 0.5 mi uphill (30 mn rtn on foot). Maiden Castle★★ (≤★) NE : 7.5 m

Abbey House without rest

Church St ✉ DT3 4JJ – ☎ (01305) 871 330 – www.theabbeyhouse.co.uk – March-October

5 rm – ††£ 95/100

◆ Historic stone house; part-15C abbey infirmary. Garden holds a unique Benedictine water mill. Breakfast room with low beamed ceiling and fireplace. Cosy bedrooms.

ENGLAND

ABINGDON – Oxfordshire – 503 Q28 – pop. 36 010 Great Britain 10 B2

London 64 mi – Oxford 6 mi – Reading 25 mi

from Abingdon Bridge to Oxford (Salter Bros. Ltd) 2 daily (summer only)

Visitor Information Point , Town Council , Abbey Close ☎ (01235) 522711

Drayton Park Drayton Steventon Rd, ☎ (01235) 550 607

Town★ – County Hall★

at Marcham West : 3 mi on A 415

Rafters without rest

Abingdon Rd, on A 415 ✉ OX13 6NU – ☎ (01865) 391 298 – www.bnb-rafters.co.uk

4 rm – †£ 59/85 ††£ 120

◆ Modern, well-equipped bedrooms; the superior room, with luxury bathroom and balcony, is best. Friendly owner offers substantial, locally sourced breakfast. Massage chair for relaxation.

ABINGER HAMMER – Surrey – 504 S30 7 C2

London 35 mi – Brighton 40 mi – Dover 91 mi – Portsmouth 50 mi

Drakes on the Pond

Dorking Rd, on A 25 ✉ RH5 6SA – ☎ (01306) 731 174 – www.drakesonthepond.com – Closed 2 weeks August, Christmas, Sunday and Monday

Rest – Menu £ 25 (lunch) – Carte dinner £ 43/54

◆ Long-standing neighbourhood restaurant – formerly a cowshed – run by husband and wife: he cooks, she leads front of house. Long, narrow room with bright walls. Simply presented, classic dishes.

ALDEBURGH – Suffolk – 504 Y27 – pop. 2 654 15 D3

London 97 mi – Ipswich 24 mi – Norwich 41 mi

152 High St ☎ (01728) 453637, atic@suffolkcoastal.gov.uk

ThorpenessHotel and Golf Course Thorpeness, ☎ (01728) 452 176

Wentworth
Wentworth Rd. ✉ *IP15 5BD* – ✆ *(01728) 452 312*
– *www.wentworth-aldeburgh.com*
35 rm – †£ 103/133 ††£ 195/219
Rest – Menu £ 23 (dinner) – Carte lunch £ 16/24
♦ Carefully furnished, traditional seaside hotel; coast view bedrooms are equipped with binoculars and all have a copy of 'Orlando the Marmalade Cat'; a story set in the area. Formal dining room offers mix of brasserie and classic dishes.

Brudenell
The Parade ✉ *IP15 5BU* – ✆ *(01728) 452 071* – *www.brudenellhotel.co.uk*
44 rm – †£ 100/159 ††£ 245/295 **Rest** – Carte £ 25/35
♦ Contemporary hotel situated right on the beach, with a relaxed ambience and superb sea views. Bedrooms feature modern bathrooms and up-to-date facilities. Informal, split-level bar/restaurant offers an accessible menu of modern classics to suit every taste.

Lighthouse
77 High St ✉ *IP15 5AU* – ✆ *(01728) 453 377*
– *www.thelighthouserestaurant.co.uk*
Rest – *(booking essential)* Carte £ 21/32
♦ Busy, unpretentious bistro boasts a wealth of Suffolk produce from local meats to Aldeburgh cod and potted shrimps. Rustic, flavourful dishes with strong Mediterranean influences. Good choice of wines, amiable service and a warm, relaxing ambience.

at Friston Northwest : 4 mi by A 1094 on B 1121 – ✉ Aldeburgh

Old School without rest
✉ *IP17 1NP* – ✆ *(01728) 688 173* – *www.fristonoldschool.co.uk*
3 rm – †£ 50/60 ††£ 70/80
♦ Red-brick former school house with pleasant gardens. Good-sized bedrooms boast attractive furnishings, modern bathrooms and nice views. Communal breakfasts include a 'Full Suffolk', locally smoked kippers and milk from the nearby dairy. Run by lovely owners.

ALDERLEY EDGE – Cheshire – 502 N24 – pop. 5 280 — 20 B3

London 187 mi – Chester 34 mi – Manchester 14 mi – Stoke-on-Trent 25 mi
Wilmslow Mobberley Great Warford, ✆ (01565) 872 148

Alderley Edge
Macclesfield Rd ✉ *SK9 7BJ* – ✆ *(01625) 583 033* – *www.alderleyedgehotel.com*
– *Closed Christmas*
49 rm – †£ 85/150 ††£ 120/145, £ 15 – 1 suite
Rest ***The Alderley*** – see restaurant listing
♦ Well-run, early Victorian country house in affluent village. Smart landscaped gardens; compact, fairly formal interior. Modern, leather-furnished guest areas. More classically styled bedrooms.

The Alderley – at Alderley Edge Hotel
✉ *SK9 7BJ* – ✆ *(01625) 583 033* – *www.alderleyedgehotel.com* – *Closed Christmas and Sunday*
Rest – Menu £ 22/30 – Carte £ 43/46
♦ Formal restaurant with full-length windows and long-standing reputation. Modern British menus display some interesting combinations and unusual twists. Good value lunch and daily evening menus.

London Road Restaurant and Wine Bar
46 London Rd ✉ *SK9 7DZ* – ✆ *(01625) 584 163* – *www.heathcotes.co.uk*
Rest – Menu £ 15/20 – Carte £ 19/40
♦ Sleek, modern brasserie with bar, basement, private dining room and terrace. Large menus offer modern European dishes with Northern influences; cooking is clean and unfussy.

ENGLAND

The Wizard
Macclesfield Rd, Southeast : 1.25 mi on B 5087 ✉ SK10 4UB – ✆ (01625) 584 000 – www.ainscoughs.co.uk – Closed 25 December
Rest – Carte £ 20/40
◆ Characterful, dog-friendly, 200 year old pub with flag floors, wood beams and open fires. Seasonal menu of traditional dishes, including pub favourites and the occasional Mediterranean influence. Small tapas-style plates provide nibbles for drinkers.

ALDERNEY – **C.I.** – **503** Q33 – **see Channel Islands**

ALDFIELD – **N. Yorks.** – **502** P21 – **see Ripon**

ALFRISTON – **East Sussex** – **504** U31 – **pop. 1 721** – ✉ **Polegate** **8** A3
London 66 mi – Eastbourne 9 mi – Lewes 10 mi – Newhaven 8 mi

Moonrakers with rm
High St ✉ BN2 5TD – ✆ (01323) 871 199 – www.moonrakersrestaurant.co.uk – Closed 2-16 January, Sunday dinner, Monday and Tuesday
1 rm – £ 175/205
Rest – *(booking essential)* Menu £ 19 (weekday lunch) – Carte £ 32/47
◆ Charming 16C cottage with heavy beams, inglenook fireplace and lovely terrace. Interesting dishes display classic flavour combinations with modern twists. Ingredients are handled with care. A stylish, beamed bedroom with sitting room occupies the first floor.

Wingrove House with rm
High St ✉ BN26 5TD – ✆ (01323) 870 276 – www.wingrovehousealfriston.com – Closed 25 December
5 rm – £ 125/155 £ 125/155 **Rest** – Carte £ 21/38
◆ Imposing colonial-style house; personally run, with relaxed, informal feel. Spacious, contemporary brasserie, wood-floored lounge and pleasant terrace. Modern menu of brasserie dishes served by a bright team. Understated, stylish bedrooms; some with balconies.

The George Inn with rm
rm,
High St ✉ BN26 5SY – ✆ (01323) 870 319 – www.thegeorge-alfriston.com – Closed 25-26 December
6 rm – £ 60 £ 90/130 **Rest** – Carte £ 20/30
◆ Characterful 14C stone and timber pub in a delightful village on the Southdown Way. Menu offers sharing boards and restaurant-style dishes, with pub classics appearing as specials. Comfy, simply furnished bedrooms; Bob Hall, with its 13C murals, is the best.

ALKHAM – **Kent** – **504** X30 – **pop. 607** **9** D2
London 72 mi – Bexley 61 mi

The Marquis with rm
Alkham Valley Rd ✉ CT15 7DF – ✆ (01304) 873 410 – www.themarquisatalkham.co.uk
5 rm – £ 65/85 £ 145/165
Rest – *(closed Sunday dinner and Monday lunch)* Menu £ 20/25 – Carte £ 40/51
◆ Fashionable former pub with smart bar, stylish dining room and relaxed atmosphere. Accomplished cooking features classical combinations with original touches. Portions are generous and presentation, modern. A six course tasting menu is available. Chic, spacious bedrooms boast luxury bathrooms; some are in an annexe.

ALNWICK – **Northumberland** – **501** O17 – **pop. 7 767** Great Britain **24** B2
London 320 mi – Edinburgh 86 mi – Newcastle upon Tyne 34 mi
2 The Shambles ✆ (01665) 510 665, alnwicktic@alnwick.gov.uk
Swansfield Park, ✆ (01665) 602 632
Town ★ - Castle★★ **AC**
Dunstanburgh Castle★ **AC**, NE : 8 mi by B 1340 and Dunstan rd (last 2.5 mi on foot)

Greycroft without rest

Croft Pl, via Prudhoe St ✉ NE66 1XU – ☎ (01665) 602 127 – www.greycroft.co.uk – Closed January

6 rm – ♦£ 55/85 ♦♦£ 110/120

♦ Quiet 19C house, 5min walk from Alnwick castle. Bedrooms individually decorated to a high standard; breakfast in airy conservatory overlooking walled garden. Hospitable owners.

Aln House without rest

South Rd, Southeast : 0.75 mi by B 6346 on Newcastle rd ✉ NE66 2NZ – ☎ (01665) 602 265 – www.alnhouse.co.uk – Closed 24-26 December

6 rm – ♦£ 55/85 ♦♦£ 80/90

♦ Semi detached Edwardian house with mature front and rear gardens, an easy walk from castle. Homely lounge enhanced by personal touches. Individually appointed rooms.

Blackmore's with rm

24 Bondgate Without ✉ NE66 1PN – ☎ (01665) 602 395 – www.blackmoresofalnwick.com – Closed 24-25 December

14 rm – ♦£ 70/100 ♦♦£ 95/120

Rest – *(dinner only)* Menu £ 20 – Carte £ 18/30

♦ 18C stone building with modern, open-plan interior and central bar. Bistro serves menu of mainly pub classics; first floor restaurant, with interesting display of clocks, offers more ambitious fare. Well-kept, contemporary bedrooms in chocolate tones.

at North Charlton North : 6.75 mi by A 1 – ✉ Alnwick

North Charlton Farm without rest

✉ NE67 5HP – ☎ (01665) 579 443 – www.northcharltonfarm.co.uk

3 rm – ♦£ 50 ♦♦£ 80

♦ Attractive house on working farm with agricultural museum. Offers traditional accommodation. Each bedroom is individually decorated and has countryside views.

at Chathill North : 8.75 mi by A 1 off B 6347

Doxford Hall H. and Spa

✉ NE67 5DN – ☎ (01665) 589 700 – *www.doxfordhall.com*

23 rm – ♦£ 96/161 ♦♦£ 132/280 – 2 suites

Rest ***George Runciman*** – Menu £ 19 (lunch) – Carte dinner £ 34/47

♦ 18C house with recent extensions and well-appointed spa. Spacious bedrooms, styled to complement original house; all have mod cons including flat screens, while impressive feature beds add a sense of luxury. Interesting modern cuisine served in formal dining room.

ALSTONEFIELD – Staffordshire – 504 O24 — 19 C1

London 157 mi – Birmingham 66 mi – Liverpool 77 mi – Leeds 88 mi

The George

✉ DE6 2FX – ☎ (01335) 310 205 – www.thegeorgeatalstonefield.com – Closed 25 December

Rest – Carte £ 19/39

♦ Simply furnished, family-run pub with roaring fire and relaxed, cosy atmosphere. Daily changing menus offer well-priced, down-to-earth dishes; good 'on toast' section at lunch.

ALTON – Hampshire – 504 R30 – pop. 16 051 — 6 B2

London 53 mi – Reading 24 mi – Southampton 29 mi – Winchester 18 mi

7 Cross and Pillory Lane ☎ (01420) 88448, petersfieldinfo@btconnect.com

Old Odiham Rd, ☎ (01420) 82 042

at Lower Froyle Northeast : 4.5 mi by A 31

The Anchor Inn with rm

✉ *GU34 4NA* – ✆ *(01420) 23 261* – *www.anchorinnatlowerfroyle.co.uk* – *Closed 25 December*

5 rm – †£ 90/120 ††£ 90/120 **Rest** – Carte £ 25/35

◆ Part-whitewashed, part-tile hung 14C building in pretty countryside, boasting low-beams, open fires and bric-a-brac aplenty. Good-sized menus offer classic pub dishes with a refined edge; cooking is hearty and flavoursome. Bedrooms are fittingly characterful.

ALTRINCHAM – Greater Manchester – 502 N23 – pop. 40 695 20 B3

London 191 mi – Chester 30 mi – Liverpool 30 mi – Manchester 8 mi

20 Stamford New Rd ✆ (0161) 912 5931, tourist.information@ trafford.gov.uk

Altrincham Municipal Timperley Stockport Rd, ✆ (0161) 928 0761

Dunham Forest Oldfield Lane, ✆ (0161) 928 2605

Ringway Hale Barns Hale Mount, ✆ (0161) 980 2630

The Victoria

29 Stamford St ✉ *WA14 1EX* – ✆ *(0161) 613 1855* – *Closed 26 December, 1 January and Sunday dinner*

Rest – Menu £ 16 (dinner) – Carte £ 23/32

◆ Traditional looking pub in town centre. Sandwiches and light bites on bar menu. À la carte offers classic dishes with a modern twist; locally sourced ingredients to the fore.

at Little Bollington Southwest : 3.25 mi on A 56 – ✉ Altrincham

Ash Farm without rest

Park Lane ✉ *WA14 4TJ* – ✆ *(0161) 929 9290* – *www.ashfarm.co.uk*

3 rm – †£ 49/59 ††£ 75/82

◆ 18C former farmhouse with large garden, modern pine-furnished breakfast room and comfy, boho lounge. Traditional, antique-furnished bedrooms have a pleasant country house style. Friendly owners.

ALVESTON – Warks. – 504 OP27 – see Stratford-upon-Avon

AMBERLEY – West Sussex – 504 S31 – pop. 525 – ✉ Arundel 7 C2

Great Britain

London 56 mi – Brighton 24 mi – Portsmouth 31 mi

Bignor Roman Villa (mosaics★) **AC**, NW : 3.5 mi by B 2139 via Bury

Amberley Castle

Southwest : 0.5 mi on B 2139 ✉ *BN18 9LT* – ✆ *(01798) 831 992* – *www.amberleycastle.co.uk*

13 rm – †£ 230/285 ††£ 425/520 – 6 suites

Rest ***Queen's Room*** – *(booking essential)* Menu £ 30/65

◆ Stunning 12C castle with original stonework, old battlements and evidence of a moat. Charming grounds with gardens, lakes and a croquet lawn; matched inside by a characterful array of rooms packed with armour and heraldic antiques. Sumptuous bedrooms boast spa baths. Large, elegant dining room serves complex dishes.

AMBLESIDE – Cumbria – 502 L20 – pop. 3 064 Great Britain 21 A2

London 278 mi – Carlisle 47 mi – Kendal 14 mi

Central Buildings, Market Cross ✆ (015394) 32582 AZ, amblesidetic@ southlakeland.gov.ukMain Car Park BY

Lake Windermere★★ – Dove Cottage, Grasmere★ **AC** AY **A** – Brockhole National Park Centre★ **AC**, SE : 3 mi by A 591 AZ. Wrynose Pass★★, W : 7.5 mi by A 593 AY – Hard Knott Pass★★, W : 10 mi by A 593 AY

AMBLESIDE

Street	Grid	No.
Borrans Rd	BY	2
Cheapside	AZ	4
Church St	AZ	6
Compston St	AZ	8
Kelsick Rd	AZ	12
King St	AZ	13
Lake Rd	AZ	
Market Pl.	AZ	14
North Rd	AZ	17
Old Lake Rd	AZ	20
St Mary's Lane	AZ	22
Smithy Brow	AZ	23

GRASMERE

Street	Grid	No.
Broadgate	BZ	3
Easedale Rd	BZ	10
Swan Lane	AY	24

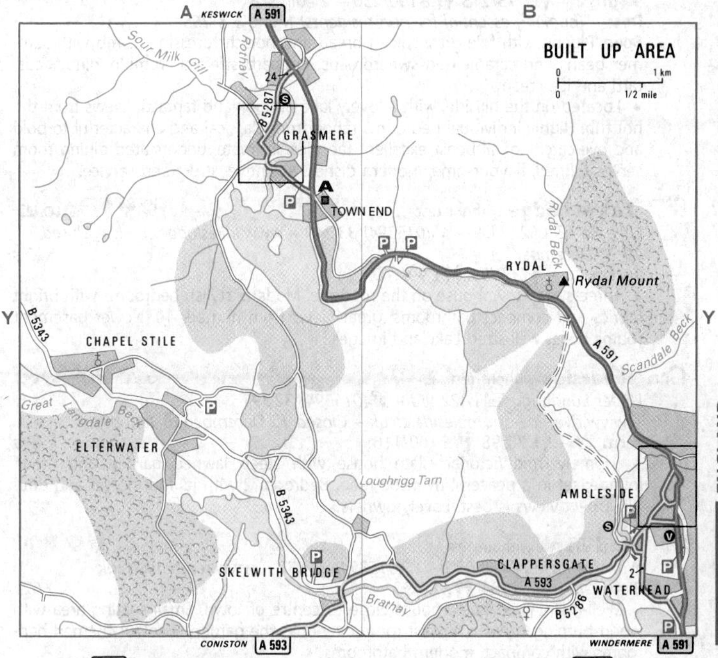

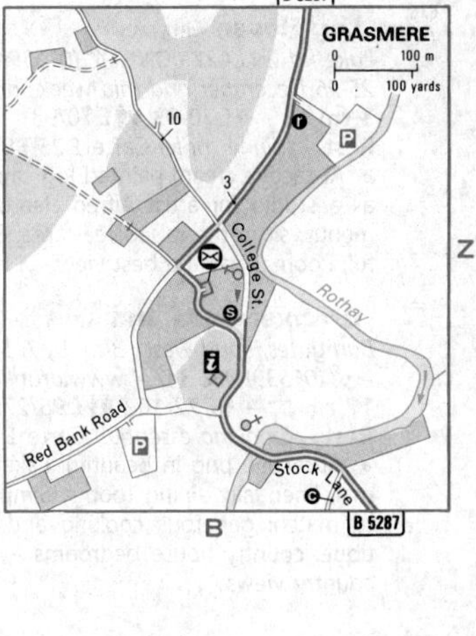

BUILT UP AREA

0 1 km
0 1/2 mile

KESWICK A 591
Sour Milk Gill
Rothay
B 5287
GRASMERE
TOWN END
Rydal Beck
RYDAL
Rydal Mount
B 5343
CHAPEL STILE
A 591
Scandale Beck
Great Langdale Beck
ELTERWATER
Loughrigg Tarn
B 5343
AMBLESIDE
SKELWITH BRIDGE
CLAPPERSGATE
A 593
WATERHEAD
Brathay
B 5286
CONISTON A 593
WINDERMERE A 591

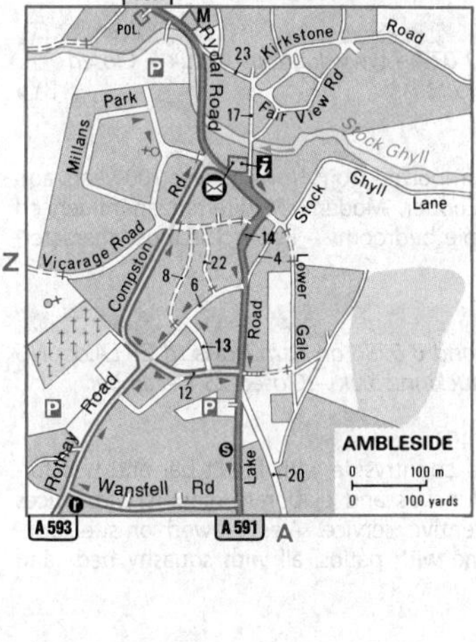

AMBLESIDE

0 100 m
0 100 yards

A 591
POL.
Rydal Road
Kirkstone Road
Fair View Rd
Park
Millans Park
Stock Ghyll
Stock Ghyll Lane
Rd
Vicarage Road
Compston Rd
Lower Gale
Road
Rothay Road
Wansfell Rd
Lake Road
A 593
A 591

GRASMERE

0 100 m
0 100 yards

B 5287
College St.
Rothay
Red Bank Road
Stock Lane
B 5287

ENGLAND

The Samling

Ambleside Rd, South : 1.5 mi on A 591 ✉ LA23 1LR – ✆ (015394) 31 922 – www.thesamlinghotel.co.uk
9 rm – £ 175/215 £ 190/230 – 2 suites
Rest – *(booking essential for non-residents)* Menu £ 33/55
Spec. Pigeon with foie gras, spiced bread and borscht dressing. Lamb with summer beans and caramelised sweetbreads. Rhubarb streusel crumble, ginger custard and ice cream.
◆ Located on the hillside, with a lovely lake outlook and fantastic views from the hot tub. Highly individual bedrooms range from classical and characterful to bold and eye-catching; all boast excellent facilities. Intimate, understated dining room serves refined, flavoursome, modern dishes. Attentive, structured service.

Lakes Lodge without rest

Lake Rd ✉ LA22 0DB – ✆ (015394) 33 240 – www.lakeslodge.co.uk – Closed 19-27 December AZ**s**
16 rm – £ 69/99 £ 99/149
◆ Three-storey townhouse on the roadside. Modern, stylish bedrooms with bright fabrics and compact bathrooms; great views from number 10. Newer basement rooms boast wall-sized Lakeland images.

Riverside without rest

Under Loughrigg ✉ LA22 9LJ – ✆ (015394) 32 395 – www.riverside-at-ambleside.co.uk – Closed 15 December-28 January
6 rm – £ 75/98 £ 100/116 BY**s**
◆ Homely, mid-Victorian slate house with steep lawned garden and fire-lit lounge; set in a peaceful riverside road. Bedroom 2 with its four-poster and double-aspect views is best. Lovely owners.

Red Bank without rest

Wansfell Rd ✉ LA22 0EG – ✆ (015394) 34 637 – www.red-bank.co.uk
3 rm – £ 70/84 £ 80/90 AZ**r**
◆ Well-maintained guest house close to centre of town. Small seating area with wood burning stove; breakfast room overlooks the garden. 3 colour-themed bedrooms with compact, modern bathrooms.

Log House with rm

Lake Rd ✉ LA22 0DN – ✆ (015394) 31 077 – www.loghouse.co.uk – Closed 25-26 December and mid week January BY**v**
3 rm – £ 70/93 £ 70/93
Rest – *(dinner only)* Carte £ 25/38 **s**
◆ Attractive cream-painted log cabin, imported from Norway over 100 years ago as a studio for artist Alfred Heaton Cooper. Modern, Mediterranean-influenced menus; sit in the raised rear area. Simple bedrooms – Room 1 is most characterful; Room 3 has the best view.

Drunken Duck Inn with rm

Barngates, Southwest : 3 mi by A 593 and B 5286 on Tarn Hows rd ✉ LA22 0NG – ✆ (01539) 436 347 – www.drunkenduckinn.co.uk – Closed 25 December
17 rm – £ 72/102 £ 95/275
Rest – *(booking essential)* Carte £ 20/40
◆ Attractive pub in beautiful Lakeland countryside with fire-lit bar and two formal, linen-laid dining rooms. Simple lunches and elaborate dinners with prices to match; generous cooking and attentive service. Ales brewed on-site. Boutique, country house bedrooms – some with patios, all with squashy beds and country views.

AMERSHAM (Old Town) – Buckinghamshire – 504 S29 – pop. 21 470 — 11 D2

London 29 mi – Aylesbury 16 mi – Oxford 33 mi
Little Chalfont Lodge Lane, ✆ (01494) 764 877

ENGLAND

XX **Artichoke**

9 Market Sq. ✉ HP7 0DF – ✆ (01494) 726 611 – www.artichokerestaurant.co.uk – Closed 1 week Easter, last week August, first week September, 1 week Christmas, Sunday and Monday.

Rest – *(booking essential at dinner)* Menu £ 23/40 – Carte lunch £ 32/45

◆ 16C brick house with smart façade; an artichoke etched on its window. Narrow room with stylish, modern look but retaining period detail. Accomplished, well-presented cooking.

X **Gilbey's**

1 Market Sq. ✉ HP7 0DF – ✆ (01494) 727 242 – www.gilbeygroup.com – Closed 24-29 December and 1 January

Rest – *(booking essential)* Menu £ 22 (weekday lunch) – Carte £ 30/35

◆ Part of a former 17C school, this busy neighbourhood restaurant is cosy and informal with modern artwork on walls. Eclectic range of British cooking with global influences.

AMPLEFORTH – N. Yorks. – 502 Q21 – see Helmsley

ANSTEY – Hertfordshire 12 B2

London 38 mi – Croydon 71 mi – Barnet 35 mi – Ealing 47 mi

Anstey Grove Barn without rest

on Meesden rd ✉ SG9 0BJ – ✆ (01763) 848 828 – www.ansteygrovebarn.co.uk

6 rm – £ 65 £ 100

◆ Converted barn on what was once a working pig farm. Simply furnished, homely bedrooms named after breeds of pig; the best is Old Yorkshire with its four-poster and roll-top bath.

APPLEBY-IN-WESTMORLAND – Cumbria – 502 M20 – pop. 2 862 21 B2

London 285 mi – Carlisle 33 mi – Kendal 24 mi – Middlesbrough 58 mi

Moot Hall, Boroughgate ✆ (017683) 51177, tic@applebytown.org.uk

Appleby Brackenber Moor, ✆ (017683) 51 432

Appleby Manor Country House

Roman Rd, East : 1 mi by B 6542 and Station Rd ✉ CA16 6JB – ✆ (017683) 51 571 – www.applebymanor.co.uk – Closed 24-26 December

31 rm – £ 140/160 £ 140/260 **Rest** – Carte £ 27/36 **s**

◆ Family-run, Victorian gentleman's residence with mature gardens and more recent extensions. Spacious, traditionally styled guest areas; small leisure suite. Bedrooms in original house are the most characterful. Two-roomed, formal restaurant offers classical menus.

Tufton Arms

Market Sq ✉ CA16 6XA – ✆ (017683) 51 593 – www.tuftonarmshotel.co.uk – Closed 25-26 December

20 rm – £ 77/92 £ 130 **Rest** – Menu £ 30 (dinner) – Carte £ 17/29

◆ 16C former coaching inn in traditional market town boasts contemporary interior; chic, comfortable bedrooms in bold colours. Fishing, shooting and stalking can be arranged. Easy-going menu served in modern dining room.

APPLEDORE – Devon – 503 H30 – pop. 2 187 2 C1

London 228 mi – Barnstaple 12 mi – Exeter 46 mi – Plymouth 61 mi

Town★

West Farm without rest

Irsha St, West : 0.25 mi ✉ EX39 1RY – ✆ (01237) 425 269

3 rm – £ 65 £ 100

◆ 17C house, boasting particularly pleasant garden at the back, in a charming little coastal village. Delightfully appointed sitting room. Bedrooms feel comfortable and homely.

APPLETREEWICK – North Yorkshire – 502 O21 — 22 B2

London 236 mi – Harrogate 25 mi – Skipton 11 mi

Knowles Lodge without rest

South : 1 mi on Bolton Abbey rd ✉ BD23 6DQ – ✆ (01756) 720 228 – www.knowleslodge.com

4 rm – £ 60/65 £ 100

♦ Unusual Canadian ranch-house style guesthouse, clad in timber and sited in quiet dales location. Large sitting room with fine outlook. Cosy bedrooms have garden views.

ARLINGHAM – Gloucestershire – 503 M28 – pop. 377 – ✉ Gloucester — 4 C1

London 120 mi – Birmingham 69 mi – Bristol 34 mi – Gloucester 16 mi

The Old Passage Inn with rm

Passage Rd, West : 0.75 mi ✉ GL2 7JR – ✆ (01452) 740 547 – www.theoldpassageinn.com – Closed Sunday dinner and Monday, restricted opening in winter

3 rm – £ 60/130 £ 80/150, £ 8.95

Rest – Seafood – Menu £ 20 (lunch) – Carte £ 34/45

♦ Eye-catching, former inn with bright yellow interior and colourful local artwork. Appealing seafood menus; unfussy cooking relies on the quality of the produce. Smart rooms with river views.

ENGLAND

ARMSCOTE – Warwickshire – 504 P27 — 19 C3

London 91 mi – Birmingham 36 mi – Oxford 38 mi

Willow Corner without rest

✉ CV37 8DE – ✆ (01608) 682 391 – www.willowcorner.co.uk – Restricted opening in winter

3 rm – £ 55 £ 75

♦ Lovely thatched property in quaint village with stable door, mullioned windows and low ceilings. Pretty bedrooms with thoughtful extras; homemade biscuits and tea on arrival.

ARNSIDE – Cumbria – 502 L21 – pop. 2 301 — 21 3A

London 257 mi – Liverpool 74 mi – Manchester 69 mi – Bradford 97 mi

Number 43

43 The Promenade ✉ LA5 0AA – ✆ (01524) 762 761 – www.no43.org.uk

6 rm – £ 120 £ 190 **Rest** – Menu £ 23

♦ Stylishly converted Victorian townhouse boasting superb estuary and fell views. Contemporary bedrooms with smart bathrooms, quality furnishings and good facilities. Comfy, open-plan lounge and dining room. Home-cooked meals by arrangement; lighter sharing platters every evening. Have breakfast on glass-enclosed terrace.

ARUNDEL – West Sussex – 504 S31 – pop. 3 297 Great Britain — 7 C2

London 58 mi – Brighton 21 mi – Southampton 41 mi – Worthing 9 mi

61 High St ✆ (01903) 882268, arundel.vic@arun.gov.uk

Castle★★ AC

The Town House with rm

65 High St ✉ BN18 9AJ – ✆ (01903) 883 847 – www.thetownhouse.co.uk – Closed last 2 weeks February, last 2 weeks October, 25 December, Sunday and Monday

4 rm – £ 75 £ 130 **Rest** – Menu £ 20/30

♦ Early 17C house displaying original sugar glass windows and impressive Renaissance ceiling with gilded walnut panelling. Smartly laid, intimate dining room. Confidently executed, tried-and-tested dishes with a classical base. Modern, well-equipped bedrooms.

XX **Arundel House** with rm

11 High St ✉ BN18 9AD – ✆ (01903) 882 136 – www.arundelhouseonline.com – Closed 24-31 December, Sunday and Monday

5 rm – †£ 75/140 ††£ 75/140

Rest – Menu £ 22/32 – Carte £ 28/38

◆ Proudly run, bow-fronted high street restaurant, its smart, neutrally hued walls hung with black and white pictures. Monthly changing menus of simple, understated dishes with an emphasis on fish and game. Simple yet stylish modern bedrooms complete the picture.

at Burpham **Northeast : 3 mi by A 27 – ✉ Arundel**

Burpham Country House

The Street ✉ BN18 9RJ – ✆ (01903) 882 160 – www.burphamcountryhouse.com – Closed January and Christmas.

10 rm – †£ 50/90 ††£ 110/140

Rest – *(closed Tuesday-Wednesday November-February, Sunday and Monday) (dinner only)* Menu £ 26

◆ Reputedly a hunting lodge for the Duke of Norfolk, this tranquil hotel constitutes the ideal 'stress remedy break'. Calm, pastel-coloured bedrooms overlook exquisite gardens. Seasonal menu of classic dishes served in dining room and conservatory.

George and Dragon

Main St ✉ BN18 9RR – ✆ (01903) 883 131 – www.georgeanddragoninnburpham.com

Rest – Carte £ 21/32

◆ It's all in the name: a good old-fashioned English pub with a rustic bar, linen-clad dining room and relaxed feel. Cooking features British classics, old pub favourites and daily specials.

ASCOT – Windsor and Maidenhead – 504 R29 – pop. 15 761 — 11 D3

London 36 mi – Reading 15 mi

Mill Ride Ascot, ✆ (01344) 886 777

Coworth Park

London Rd., East : 2.75 mi on A 329 ✉ SL5 7SE – ✆ (01344) 876 600 – www.coworthpark.com

55 rm – †£ 258/498 ††£ 372/612 – 15 suites

Rest *John Campbell at Coworth Park* – Menu £ 25/60

Rest *Barn* – Carte £ 23/30

◆ 17C property set in 246 acres and boasting its own championship polo pitches. Comfortable, stylish guest areas; superb spa. Beautiful bedrooms feature bespoke furniture, marble bathrooms and a high level of facilities. Fine dining restaurant serves inventive, original cooking. Rustic bistro offers hearty classics.

Berystede

Bagshot Rd, Sunninghill, South : 1.5 mi on A 330 ✉ SL5 9JH – ✆ (0844) 879 91 04 – www.macdonaldhotels.co.uk/berystede

121 rm – †£ 99/239 ††£ 99/239 – 5 suites

Rest *Hyperion* – *(dinner only and Sunday lunch)* Carte £ 24/36

◆ Turreted red brick Victorian house in mature gardens, boasts classically-styled lounge, panelled bar with terrace and variously-sized bedrooms, with warm, contemporary feel. Formal dining at Hyperion, with classic menus and countryside outlook.

XX **Ascot Oriental**

East : 2.25 mi on A 329 ✉ SL5 0PU – ✆ (01344) 621 877 – www.ascotoriental.com – Closed 25-26 December

Rest – Chinese – Menu £ 28/29 – Carte £ 32/46

◆ Stylish modern restaurant with a vibrantly hued interior. Private dining in attractive conservatory. An interesting menu of Chinese dishes prepared with originality and verve.

ENGLAND

ASCOTT-UNDER-WYCHWOOD – Oxfordshire – 504 P28 – pop. 524 10 A2

London 83 mi – Birmingham 66 mi – Bristol 69 mi – Leicester 73 mi

The Swan Inn with rm

4 Shipton Rd ✉ OX7 6AY – ✆ (01993) 832 332 – www.swanatascott.com – Closed Sunday dinner and Monday

5 rm – †£ 75 ††£ 75/125

Rest – *(booking advisable at dinner)* Carte £ 21/30

♦ Traditional community pub with great atmosphere. Classic, quality cooking with dishes like pork belly or sausage and mash – and everything from the bread to the chips homemade. Contemporary bedrooms.

ASENBY – N. Yorks. – see Thirsk

ASH – Kent – 504 X30 9 D2

London 70 mi – Canterbury 9 mi – Dover 15 mi

Great Weddington

Northeast : 0.5 mi by A 257 on Weddington rd ✉ CT3 2AR – ✆ (01304) 813 407 – www.greatweddington.co.uk – Closed 25 December-1 January

4 rm – †£ 100/120 ††£ 100/120 **Rest** – Menu £ 38

♦ Charming Regency country house, ideally located for Canterbury and Dover. Well appointed drawing room and terrace. Thoughtfully furnished, carefully co-ordinated rooms. Communal dining room; owner an avid cook.

ASHBOURNE – Derbyshire – 502 O24 – pop. 5 020 Great Britain 16 A2

London 146 mi – Birmingham 47 mi – Manchester 48 mi – Nottingham 33 mi

13 Market Pl ✆ (01335) 343666, ashbourneinfo@derbyshiredales.gov.uk

Dovedale★★ (Ilam Rock★) NW : 6 mi by A 515

Callow Hall

Mappleton Rd, West : 0.75 mi by Union St (off Market Pl) ✉ DE6 2AA – ✆ (01335) 300 900 – www.callowhall.co.uk

15 rm – †£ 105/140 ††£ 150/195 – 1 suite

Rest – Menu £ 25/42 – Carte £ 34/43

♦ Victorian country house in 44 acres of gardens, fields and woodland. Individually styled bedrooms boast original features, well-appointed bathrooms, and quality fabrics and furnishings. Daily changing menus feature local produce and tasty home-smoked salmon.

the dining room

33 St Johns St ✉ DE6 1GP – ✆ (01335) 300 666 – www.thediningroomashbourne.co.uk – Closed 2 weeks Christmas, 1 week Easter, 1 week September, Sunday and Monday

Rest – *(dinner only) (booking essential)* Menu £ 37/45

♦ Modern, stylish décor blends agreeably with period features including a cast iron range. Well-sourced, seasonal ingredients inform intricate modern dishes on 7 or 16 course tasting menus.

ASHBURTON – Devon – 503 I32 – pop. 3 309 2 C2

London 220 mi – Exeter 20 mi – Plymouth 25 mi

Dartmoor National Park★★

Agaric with rm

30 and 36 North St ✉ TQ13 7QD – ✆ (01364) 654 478 – www.agaricrestaurant.co.uk – Closed 2 weeks Christmas, 1 week August, Sunday-Tuesday and Saturday lunch

4 rm – †£ 50/85 ††£ 130 **Rest** – *(booking essential)* Carte £ 30/41

♦ 200 year-old house, selling home-made jams, fudge and olives. Relaxed neighbourhood restaurant using a blend of cooking styles. Very stylish, individually themed bedrooms.

ASHFORD-IN-THE-WATER – Derbs. – 502 O24 – see Bakewell

ASHFORD – Kent – 504 W30 – pop. 58 936 9 C2

London 56 mi – Canterbury 14 mi – Dover 24 mi – Hastings 30 mi

Access Channel Tunnel : Eurostar information and reservations ✆ (08705) 186186

18 The Churchyard ✆ (01233) 629165, tourism@ashford.gov.uk

Eastwell Manor

Eastwell Park, Boughton Lees, North : 3 mi by A 28 on A 251 ✉ TN25 4HR – ✆ (01233) 213 000 – www.eastwellmanor.co.uk

20 rm – £ 110/265 £ 295 – 22 suites – £ 270/445

Rest *Manor* – Menu £ 18/38 – Carte £ 40/61

Rest *Brasserie* – ✆ (01233) 213 100 *(Closed Sunday dinner)* Menu £ 20 (dinner) – Carte £ 14/32

♦ Mansion house in formal gardens, replete with interesting detail including carved panelled rooms and stone fireplaces. Smart individual bedrooms. Manor offers seasonal menus. Swish brasserie in luxury spa with marbled entrance hall.

ASHWATER – Devon – 503 H31 2 C2

London 218 mi – Bude 16 mi – Virginstow 3 mi

Blagdon Manor

Northwest : 2 mi by Holsworthy rd on Blagdon rd ✉ EX21 5DF – ✆ (01409) 211 224 – www.blagdon.com – Closed January, Monday and Tuesday

7 rm – £ 85 £ 200 **Rest** – *(booking essential)* Menu £ 20/38

♦ Proudly run former farmhouse in peaceful, rural location. Modern country house bedrooms, spotlessly kept, named after surrounding villages. Library, lounges and flag-floored bar. Classically-based cooking with a modern touch, served in dining room with conservatory extension.

ASKRIGG – North Yorkshire – 502 N21 – pop. 1 002 – ✉ Leyburn 22 A1

London 251 mi – Kendal 32 mi – Leeds 70 mi – Newcastle upon Tyne 70 mi

Yorebridge House

Bainbridge, West : 1 mi ✉ DL8 3EE – ✆ (01969) 652 060 – www.yorebridgehouse.com

11 rm – £ 135/215 £ 160/240

Rest – *(booking essential for non residents)* Menu £ 43 – Carte £ 23/43

♦ Lovingly restored former school with warm, hospitable owners. Modern, stylish and comfortable interior. Individually designed bedrooms, some with hot tubs. Locally sourced produce in relaxing dining room.

ASTON CANTLOW – Warwickshire – 503 O27 – pop. 1 843 19 C3

Great Britain

London 106 mi – Birmingham 20 mi – Stratford-upon-Avon 5 mi

Mary Arden's House★ **AC**, SE : 2 mi by Wilmcote Lane and Aston Cantlow Rd

The King's Head

21 Bearley Rd ✉ B95 6HY – ✆ (01789) 488 242 – www.thekh.co.uk – Closed 25 December

Rest – Menu £ 15 – Carte £ 22/30

♦ Characterful black and white timbered, part 15C inn, set in a picturesque village. Seasonal menus feature traditional pub dishes, with local meats and fish to the fore. Regular duck suppers.

ASTON CLINTON – Buckinghamshire – 504 R28 – pop. 4 038 – ✉ Aylesbury 11 C2

London 42 mi – Aylesbury 4 mi – Oxford 26 mi

West Lodge

45 London Rd ✉ HP22 5HL – ✆ (01296) 630 362 – www.westlodge.co.uk

9 rm – £ 55/72 £ 82/87

Rest – *(closed Sunday) (dinner only)* Menu £ 24 – Carte £ 24/29

♦ 19C former hunting lodge for Rothschild estate with walled Victorian garden. Bedrooms in converted outbuilding are largest/quietest. Balloon theme throughout adds interest. Conservatory dining room serving residents only.

ENGLAND

ASTON ROWANT – Oxfordshire – pop. 2 512 **11** C2

London 45 mi – Coventry 69 mi

The Lambert Arms

London Rd, on A 40 ✉ OX49 5SB – ✆ (01844) 351 496 – www.lambertarms.com

42 rm – †£ 79/85 ††£ 89/95, ☕ £ 5.95

Rest – *(Closed Sunday dinner)* Carte £ 20/37 **s**

♦ Traditional timbered inn boasts comfortable, modernised interior, with spacious, well-equipped bedrooms in purpose-built extension. Good French breakfasts. Contemporary dishes served in restaurant or spacious bar.

ASTON TIRROLD – Oxfordshire **10** B3

London 58 mi – Reading 16 mi – Streatley 4 mi

The Sweet Olive at The Chequers Inn

Baker St ✉ OX11 9DD – ✆ (01235) 851 272 – www.sweet-olive.com – Closed 2 weeks February, 1 week July, 25 December, Sunday dinner and Wednesday

Rest – *(booking essential)* Carte £ 24/30

♦ Red-brick Victorian pub at heart of the village; cosy, welcoming and popular with the locals. Gallic owners offer French-influenced menu and interesting selection of fine wines.

ATCHAM – Shrops. – **503** L25 – see Shrewsbury

AYTHORPE RODING – Essex – see Great Dunmow

ATTLEBOROUGH – Norfolk – **504** X26 – pop. 6 530 **15** C2

London 101 mi – Norwich 19 mi – Ipswich 42 mi – Peterborough 87 mi

Mulberry Tree with rm

Station Rd ✉ NR17 2AS – ✆ (01953) 452 124 – www.the-mulberry-tree.co.uk – Closed 25 December, 1 January and Sunday

5 rm ☕ – †£ 73 ††£ 95 **Rest** – Carte £ 22/34

♦ Contemporary bar/restaurant set in imposing brick-built property with pleasant terrace and bowling green. Bar menu popular at lunch. À la carte offers attractively presented, globally influenced, modern dishes. Stylish, very comfortable bedrooms.

AUGHTON – Lancashire – **502** L23 – pop. 8 342

London 217 mi – Liverpool 13 mi – Manchester 40 mi – Bradford 68 mi

The Swan Inn with rm

2 Springfield Rd. ✉ L39 6ST – ✆ (01695) 421 450 – www.mpwrestaurants.co.uk

12 rm ☕ – †£ 50/70 ††£ 60/140 **Rest** – Menu £ 20 – Carte £ 27/52

♦ Sizeable, smartly refurbished restaurant with linen-laid tables; its walls decorated with cartoons from Marco Pierre White's private collection. Accessible menu of modern British cooking with some locally influenced dishes. Stylish, contemporary bedrooms.

AUSTWICK – North Yorkshire – **502** M21 – pop. 467 – ✉ Lancaster (lancs.) **22** A2

London 259 mi – Kendal 28 mi – Lancaster 20 mi – Leeds 46 mi

Traddock

✉ LA2 8BY – ✆ (015242) 51 224 – www.thetraddock.co.uk

12 rm ☕ – †£ 80/105 ††£ 135/190

Rest – *(booking essential for non-residents)* Carte £ 28/32

♦ Georgian country house – formerly a private residence – named after an old horse trading paddock. Modern interior with bright, airy lounges. Bedrooms boast feature beds, rural views and roll-top baths. Formal dining room serves modern versions of old classics.

Austwick Hall

Southeast : 0.5 mi on Townend Ln. ✉ LA2 8BS – ✆ (015242) 51 794 – www.austwickhall.co.uk

5 rm ☕ – †£ 160 ††£ 175 **Rest** – Carte £ 25/35

♦ Spacious and comfortable house with open fires and welcoming atmosphere. Located in a delightful village on the edge of the dales. Very much a family concern. A strong organic base to the cooking.

Wood View without rest
The Green ✉ LA2 8BB – ✆ (015242) 51 190 – www.woodviewbandb.com
– Closed January and November
5 rm – **††**£ 55/76
◆ In a charming spot on the village green, the cottage dates back to 17C with many of the original features still in place including exposed rafters in several bedrooms.

AYLESBURY – Buckinghamshire – 504 R28 – pop. 69 021 — 11 C2

Great Britain

London 46 mi – Birmingham 72 mi – Northampton 37 mi – Oxford 22 mi

The Kings Head, Kings Head Passage off Market Square ✆ (01296) 330559, tic@aylesburyvaledc.gov.uk

Weston Turville New Rd, ✆ (01296) 424 084

Aylesbury Golf Centre Bierton Hulcott Lane, ✆ (01296) 393 644

Waddesdon Manor★★, NW : 5.5 mi by A 41 – Chiltern Hills★

Hartwell House
Oxford Rd, Southwest : 2 mi on A 418 ✉ HP17 8NR – ✆ (01296) 747 444
– www.hartwell-house.com
36 rm – **†**£ 170/200 **††**£ 280 – 10 suites
Rest *The Soane* – Menu £ 22/38 (weekdays) – Carte dinner £ 37/49
◆ Where Louis XVIII exiled King of France was once resident. Impressive palatial house in 90 acres of parkland, boasting luxurious lounges, ornate furnishings and magnificent antique-filled bedrooms. Restaurant offers good value lunches and traditional country house cooking.

AYLESFORD – Kent – 504 V30 — 8 B1

London 37 mi – Maidstone 3 mi – Rochester 8 mi

Hengist
7-9 High St ✉ ME20 7AX – ✆ (01622) 719 273 – www.hengistrestaurant.co.uk
– Closed Monday
Rest – Menu £ 15 (lunch) **s** – Carte £ 35/48 **s**
◆ Converted 16C town house, elegantly appointed throughout, with bonus of exposed rafters and smart private dining room upstairs. Accomplished modern cooking with seasonal base.

AYLMERTON – Norfolk – 504 X25 — 15 D1

London 138 mi – Norwich 25 mi – East Dereham 26 mi – Taverham 23 mi

Eiders without rest
Holt Rd ✉ NR11 8QA – ✆ (01263) 837 280 – www.eiders.co.uk
– Closed 24 December -7 January
6 rm – **†**£ 70/80 **††**£ 100/125
◆ Whitewashed house with large lawned gardens, ornamental pond and swimming pool. Modern, spacious, ground floor bedrooms, 3 with balconies and pond views; excellent bathrooms.

AYNHO – Northamptonshire – 504 Q28 – pop. 632 — 16 B3

London 73 mi – Birmingham 66 mi – Leicester 62 mi – Coventry 48 mi

Cartwright
1-5 Croughton Rd ✉ OX17 3BE – ✆ (01869) 811 885
– www.oxfordshire-hotels.co.uk
21 rm – **†**£ 99 **††**£ 110/130
Rest – *(Closed 25 December)* Menu £ 16/20 – Carte £ 27/37
◆ Modernised 16C inn, ideally placed for Silverstone and Bicester Village. Spacious bedrooms come with complimentary wi-fi and are split between main house and rear conversion. Dining is an informal affair, with a seasonal menu of robust dishes.

ENGLAND

AYSGARTH – North Yorkshire – 502 O21 22 A1

London 249 mi – Ripon 28 mi – York 56 mi

George and Dragon Inn with rm

DL8 3AD – (01969) 663 358 – www.georgeanddragonaysgarth.co.uk
– *Closed 2 weeks January*

7 rm – †£ 40/65 ††£ 80/100 **Rest** – Menu £ 13/16 – Carte £ 15/30

◆ Laid-back coaching inn set in the National Park, close to the breathtaking River Ure waterfalls. Unfussy pub classics include plenty of local meats, game and proper old-fashioned puddings. Comfy, individually styled bedrooms; some with whirlpool baths.

BABBACOMBE – Torbay – 503 J32 – see Torquay

BACKWELL – North Somerset – 503 L29 – pop. 5 455 3 B2

London 127 mi – Bristol 9 mi – Cardiff 48 mi – Swansea 83 mi

The New Inn

86 West Town Rd BS48 3BE – (01275) 462 199
– *www.newinn-backwell.co.uk*

Rest – Carte £ 20/28

◆ Pretty 18C stone pub with welcoming, open-fired bar and more formal dining area. Stylish, modern cooking; appealing menus of precisely prepared, elegant dishes and interesting side plates.

ENGLAND

BAGSHOT – Surrey – 504 R29 – pop. 5 247 7 C1

London 37 mi – Reading 17 mi – Southampton 49 mi

Windlesham Grove End, (01276) 452 220

Pennyhill Park

London Rd , Southwest : 1 mi on A 30 GU19 5EU
– (01276) 471 774 – *www.exclusivehotels.co.uk*

112 rm – †£ 195/295 ††£ 295, £ 20 – 11 suites

Rest *Michael Wignall at The Latymer* – see restaurant listing

Rest *Brasserie* – *(closed Saturday lunch) (buffet lunch)* Carte dinner £ 33/54

◆ Impressive 19C manor house in 123 acres. Classical guest areas with modern touches; spacious bedrooms with period furnishings and great views. Has one of the best spas in Europe. Afternoon tea in comfy lounge. Carvery lunch in brasserie, which opens onto garden.

Michael Wignall at The Latymer – at Pennyhill Park Hotel

London Rd , Southwest : 1 mi on A30 GU19 5EU
– (01276) 486 156 – *www.exclusivehotels.co.uk*
– *Closed 1-16 January, Saturday lunch, Sunday and Monday*

Rest – *(booking essential)* Menu £ 32/58

Spec. Crab and verbena ravioli with sea trout and scallops. Suckling pig with butter bean purée and pork popcorn. Parfait of strawberries with mint ice cream and Pimm's espuma.

◆ Elegant hotel dining room with oak-clad walls, glass-enclosed chef's table and quality place settings. Cooking is careful, precise and uses only quality ingredients; a concise à la carte offers ambitious, original dishes that are full of flavour. Formal service.

BAKEWELL – Derbyshire – 502 O24 – pop. 3 676 Great Britain 16 A1

London 160 mi – Derby 26 mi – Manchester 37 mi – Nottingham 33 mi

Old Market Hall, Bridge St (01629) 816558, bakewell@peakdistrict.gov.uk

Chatsworth★★★ (Park and Garden★★★) **AC**, NE : 2.5 mi by A 619
– Haddon Hall★★ **AC**, SE : 2 mi by A 6

at Ashford-in-the-Water **Northwest : 1.75 mi by A 6 and A 6020 – ✉ Bakewell**

Riverside House

Fennel St ✉ DE45 1QF – ✆ (01629) 814 275 – www.riversidehousehotel.co.uk
14 rm (dinner included) – †£ 155 ††£ 195
Rest ***Riverside Room*** – Menu £ 15/45

◆ Homely former shooting lodge with gardens running down to the river. Cosy open-fired bar and elegant drawing room. Well-furnished bedrooms with good extras – some have views, some in the wing open onto a terrace. Classical dining takes place over several rooms.

River Cottage without rest

Buxton Rd, Ashford-in-the-Water ✉ DE45 1QP – ✆ (01629) 813 327 – www.rivercottageashford.co.uk – Closed January and December
4 rm – †£ 95/110 ††£ 100/135

◆ Traditional stone cottage by the River Wye, with delightful gardens and terrace. Bedrooms blend modern furnishings and antique furniture. Complimentary wines and afternoon tea.

BALSALL COMMON – **W. Mids.** – **see Coventry**

BAMBURGH – **Northumberland** – **501** O17 – **pop. 582** Great Britain **24** B1

London 337 mi – Edinburgh 77 mi – Newcastle upon Tyne 51 mi

Castle★ **AC**

Lord Crewe Arms

rest,

Front St ✉ NE69 7BL – ✆ (01668) 214 243 – www.lordcrewe.co.uk – Closed January and December
17 rm – †£ 60/98 ††£ 78/150
Rest ***Olive Tree*** – *(bar lunch)* Carte £ 20/32

◆ Privately owned, 17C former coaching inn, in the shadow of the Norman castle. Spacious, comfy lounge and contemporary bedrooms. Characterful, beamed bar is more rustic in style. Italian classics in The Olive Tree.

at Waren Mill **West : 2.75 mi on B 1342 – ✉ Belford**

Waren House

✉ NE70 7EE – ✆ (01668) 214 581 – www.warenhousehotel.co.uk
12 rm (dinner included) – †£ 123/155 ††£ 197/240 – 3 suites
Rest – *(dinner only)* Menu £ 35

◆ Personally run country house set in mature, tranquil grounds. Bedrooms, named after the owners' family members, mix classic and modern styles: some have four-posters and coastal views. Formal dining room boasts ornate ceiling; menus showcase local ingredients.

BAMPTON – **Devon** – **503** J31 – **pop. 1 617** **2** D1

London 189 mi – Exeter 18 mi – Minehead 21 mi – Taunton 15 mi

Bark House

Oakfordbridge, West : 3 mi by B 3227 on A 396 ✉ EX16 9HZ – ✆ (01398) 351 236 – www.thebarkhouse.co.uk
6 rm – †£ 54/64 ††£ 100
Rest – *(closed Sunday dinner and Monday) (dinner only and Sunday lunch) (booking essential for non-residents)* Menu £ 20/22

◆ Simple, homely hotel; formerly used as a wood store for the local tannery. Bedrooms boast contemporary fabrics and modern bathrooms. One leads to a small garden; another has a balcony. Honest home cooking, coupled with good bin ends from the owner's wine business.

The Quarrymans Rest with rm

Briton St ✉ EX16 9LN – ✆ (01398) 331 480 – www.thequarrymansrest.co.uk – Closed Sunday dinner
3 rm – †£ 45 ††£ 85 **Rest** – Carte £ 20/28

◆ 17C inn with relaxed, open-fired bar/lounge and more formal, intimate restaurant. Locally sourced produce to the fore on seasonal menu of tried-and-tested classics, with the occasional Asian influence. Clean, fresh, uncluttered bedrooms.

BANBURY – Oxfordshire – 503 P27 – pop. 43 867 Great Britain 10 B1

London 76 mi – Birmingham 40 mi – Coventry 25 mi – Oxford 23 mi
Spiceball Park Rd ✆ (01295) 259855, banbury.tic@cherwell-dc.gov.uk
Cherwell Edge Chacombe, ✆ (01295) 711 591
Upton House★ **AC**, NW : 7 mi by A 422

Banbury House
Oxford Rd ✉ OX16 9AH – ✆ (01295) 259 361 – www.banburyhouse.co.uk – Closed 24 December-2 January
64 rm – 🚹£ 52/190 🚹🚹£ 62/190, ☕ £ 15
Rest – *(closed Sunday dinner) (bar lunch)* Menu £ 25
◆ Georgian property combining the traditional with the more modern. Well-maintained bedrooms in contemporary styles. Bar popular for lunchtime snacks. Restaurant offers contemporary British menu.

at Milton South : 5.5 mi by A 4260 – ✉ Banbury

The Black Boy Inn
✉ OX15 4HH – ✆ (01295) 722 111 – www.blackboyinn.com – Closed Sunday dinner
Rest – Menu £ 15 (Monday-Thursday) – Carte £ 27/38
◆ 16C sand-coloured stone pub with traditional bar and spacious garden; popular with the locals. Wide-ranging à la carte displays largely British dishes and the odd international flavour.

at Sibford Gower West : 8 mi by B 4035 – ✉ Banbury

The Wykham Arms
Temple Mill Rd ✉ OX15 5RX – ✆ (01295) 788 808 – www.wykhamarms.co.uk – Closed Sunday dinner and Monday
Rest – Carte £ 26/31
◆ Thatched stone pub set down country lanes in a small village. Featuring local produce, menus range from bar snacks and lights bites to the full 3 courses. Good range of wines by the glass.

ENGLAND

BARNARD CASTLE – Durham – 502 O20 – pop. 6 714 Great Britain 24 A3

London 258 mi – Carlisle 63 mi – Leeds 68 mi – Middlesbrough 31 mi
Woodleigh, Flatts Rd ✆ (01833) 690909, tourism@teesdale.gov.uk
Harmire Rd, ✆ (01833) 638 355
Bowes Museum★ **AC**
Raby Castle★ **AC**, NE : 6.5 mi by A 688

Greta House without rest
89 Galgate ✉ DL12 8ES – ✆ (01833) 631 193 – www.gretahouse.co.uk
3 rm ☕ – 🚹£ 50 🚹🚹£ 72
◆ Neat terraced Victorian house with traditional lounge and stylish, contemporary, individually decorated bedrooms; Room 3 is the best, with its feature bath and shower. Excellent hospitality. Complimentary sherry and homemade biscuits on arrival.

Homelands
85 Galgate ✉ DL12 8ES – ✆ (01833) 638 757 – www.homelandsguesthouse.co.uk
5 rm ☕ – 🚹£ 50/63 🚹🚹£ 70/73 **Rest** – Menu £ 20
◆ Immaculately maintained Victorian terraced house set on main road. Cosy lounge and compact but individually furnished, well-priced bedrooms; four are in the house and one is at the bottom of the long, mature rear garden. Charming owners. Simple, home-cooked dinners by arrangement.

at Whorlton East : 4.75 mi by A 67

The Bridge Inn
✉ DL12 8XD – ✆ (01833) 627 341 – www.thebridgeinnrestaurant.co.uk – Closed first 2 weeks January, Sunday and Monday lunch
Rest – Menu £ 17 – Carte £ 22/37
◆ Sit in traditional bar or spacious, contemporary restaurant to enjoy precise, accomplished cooking with well-matched flavours. Big city dining in a beautiful countryside location.

at Greta Bridge Southeast : 4.5 mi off A 66 – ✉ Barnard Castle

The Morritt
✉ *DL12 9SE* – ✆ *(01833) 627 232* – *www.themorritt.co.uk*
27 rm – ♦£ 100/175 ♦♦£ 175/200
Rest ***The Morritt*** – Carte £ 25/37
Rest ***Bistro/Bar*** – Menu £ 10 (weekday lunch) – Carte £ 19/27
♦ Personally run, 19C former coaching inn displaying a pleasant mix of old and new. Individually designed bedrooms blend contemporary décor with antiques, four-posters and interesting bedsteads. Oak panelled restaurant and cosy bistro offer modern menu. All day snacks available in the bar.

at Hutton Magna Southeast : 7.25 mi by A 66

The Oak Tree Inn
✉ *DL11 7HH* – ✆ *(01833) 627 371* – *Closed 25-27 December and 1-2 January*
Rest – *(dinner only) (booking essential)* Carte £ 26/33
♦ Small but charming whitewashed pub consisting of a single room. Run by a husband and wife team, he cooks, while she serves. Cooking is hearty and flavoursome with a rustic French feel.

at Romaldkirk Northwest : 6 mi by A 67 on B 6277 – ✉ Barnard Castle

Rose and Crown with rm
✉ *DL12 9EB* – ✆ *(01833) 650 213* – *www.rose-and-crown.co.uk*
– *Closed 24-26 December*
12 rm – ♦£ 92 ♦♦£ 165
Rest – Carte £ 17/29
Rest ***The Restaurant*** – *(dinner only)* Menu £ 18/33
♦ Quintessential 18C English inn, set by Saxon church and surrounded by village greens. Choice of atmospheric bar adorned with horse brasses or rear brasserie serving classical fare. More formal restaurant offers seasonally changing four course dinner. Cosy, classical bedrooms boast flat screen TVs and Bose radios.

ENGLAND

BARNSLEY – Gloucestershire – **503** O28 – see Cirencester

BARNSTAPLE – Devon – **503** H30 – pop. 30 765 — 2 C1

London 222 mi – Exeter 40 mi – Taunton 51 mi
36 Boutport St ✆ (01271) 375000
Chulmleigh - Leigh Rd, ✆ (01769) 580 519
Town★ - Long Bridge★
Arlington Court★★ (Carriage Collection★) **AC**, NE : 6 mi by A 39

Old Custom House
The Strand ✉ *EX31 1EU* – ✆ *(01271) 370 123* – *www.jamesduckett.co.uk*
– *Closed 1-13 January, Sunday and Monday except Mothering Sunday*
Rest – Menu £ 17 (lunch) – Carte dinner £ 27/37
♦ Brightly painted restaurant by the river. Rustic interior with chunky tables and wood-panelled private room. Flavoursome, classical dishes with modern presentation. Tasting menu available.

BARRASFORD – Northumberland — 24 A2

London 309 mi – Newcastle upon Tyne 29 mi – Sunderland 42 mi – Middlesbrough 66 mi

Barrasford Arms with rm
✉ *NE48 4AA* – ✆ *(01434) 681 237* – *www.barrasfordarms.co.uk*
– *Closed 25 December, 1 January, Sunday dinner and Monday lunch*
7 rm – ♦£ 45/65 ♦♦£ 65/85 **Rest** – Menu £ 13 (lunch) – Carte £ 22/30
♦ Close to Kielder Water and Hadrian's Wall, this personally run 19C stone inn has a traditional, homely atmosphere. Pub classics served at lunch; more substantial dishes at dinner. Modern, comfortable bedrooms.

BARROWDEN – Rutland 17 C2

London 94 mi – Peterborough 17 mi – Stamford 8 mi

Exeter Arms with rm

28 Main St ✉ LE15 8EQ – ✆ (01572) 747 247 – www.exeterarmsrutland.co.uk – Closed Sunday dinner and Monday lunch

3 rm – £ 45 £ 79 **Rest** – Carte £ 19/25

◆ Traditional village inn with pleasant views over the green and duck pond. Menus offer well-priced, classical combinations. To the rear is the pub's very own micro-brewery. Simple, cottage-style bedrooms overlook the water.

BARTON-ON-SEA – Hampshire – 503 P31 6 A3

London 108 mi – Bournemouth 11 mi – Southampton 24 mi – Winchester 35 mi

Pebble Beach with rm

Marine Dr ✉ BH25 7DZ – ✆ (01425) 627 777 – www.pebblebeach-uk.com

3 rm – £ 70 £ 100, £ 6.50 **Rest** – Seafood – Carte £ 30/51

◆ Large, split-level restaurant with open-plan kitchen, fish tank and white baby grand piano. Metal-furnished terrace boasts impressive Solent and Isle of Wight views. Extensive, seasonally changing menus centred around local seafood. Good-sized, homely bedrooms.

ENGLAND

BARWICK – Somerset – 503 M31 – see Yeovil

BASHALL EAVES – Lancashire – 502 M23 – see Clitheroe

BASILDON – Essex – 504 V29 – pop. 99 876 13 C3

London 30 mi – Chelmsford 17 mi – Southend-on-Sea 13 mi

18 Clayhill Lane, Kingswood, ✆ (01268) 533 297

9 Langdon Hills, Lower Dunton Rd, Bulphan ✆ (01268) 548 444

at Wickford North : 5.25 mi by A 132 – ✉ Basildon

Chichester rm, rest,

Old London Rd, Rawreth, East : 2.75 mi by A 129 ✉ SS11 8UE – ✆ (01268) 560 555 – www.thechichesterhotel.com

35 rm – £ 45/69 £ 45/69, £ 10

Rest *Chichester* – *(dinner only and Sunday lunch)* Menu £ 17/20 – Carte £ 18/27

◆ Surrounded by rolling farmland, a smart, red-brick hotel with a comfy lounge, pleasant courtyard garden and clean, modern bedrooms. Popular with business-people midweek and leisure guests at weekends. Restaurant offers a good range of traditionally based dishes.

BASLOW – Derbyshire – 502 P24 – pop. 1 184 – ✉ Bakewell 16 A1

Great Britain

London 161 mi – Derby 27 mi – Manchester 35 mi – Sheffield 13 mi

Chatsworth★★★ (Park and Garden★★★) **AC**

Cavendish

Church Ln, on A 619 ✉ DE45 1SP – ✆ (01246) 582 311 – www.cavendish-hotel.net

23 rm – £ 133/147 £ 169/219, £ 18.95 – 1 suite

Rest *The Gallery* – Menu £ 41

Rest *Garden Room* – Carte £ 23/36

◆ Elegant hotel on the Chatsworth Estate, boasting lovely parkland views. Bedrooms have a cosy, country house feel and a slightly contemporary edge. Some of the furniture and paintings come from Chatsworth House. Formal Gallery restaurant serves traditional menus. Garden Room offers all day dining and afternoon teas.

XXX Fischer's at Baslow Hall with rm

Calver Rd, on A 623 ✉ DE45 1RR – ☎ (01246) 583 259 – www.fischers-baslowhall.co.uk – Closed 25-26 December

10 rm – †£ 100/140 ††£ 150/220 – 1 suite

Rest – *(closed Sunday dinner to non-residents and Monday lunch) (booking essential)* Menu £ 33/72

Spec. Foie gras with peach meringue and Martini. Sirloin and Jacob's Ladder of beef with pickled baby beets. Raspberry soufflé with raspberry sorbet.

◆ Edwardian manor house with impressive formal grounds and walled vegetable garden. Classically based and accomplished cooking, with the occasional modern twist, uses much local produce. Comfortable bedrooms in main house; garden rooms larger.

X Rowley's

Church St ✉ DE45 1RY – ☎ (01246) 583 880 – www.rowleysrestaurant.co.uk – Closed Sunday dinner

Rest – *(booking advisable)* Menu £ 24 (lunch) – Carte £ 26/32

◆ Contemporary restaurant and bar set over two floors; downstairs with view of open plan kitchen. Modern menu, with produce sourced from in and around Peak District.

BASSENTHWAITE – Cumbria – 501 K19 – pop. 433 — 21 A2

London 300 mi – Carlisle 24 mi – Keswick 7 mi

Pheasant

rest,

Southwest : 3.25 mi by B 5291 on Wythop Mill Rd, ✉ CA13 9YE – ☎ (017687) 76 234 – www.the-pheasant.co.uk – Closed 25 December

15 rm – †£ 85/115 ††£ 194/210

Rest *Bistro at The Pheasant* – Carte £ 26/34

Rest *Dining Room* – Menu £ 28/38

◆ 16C whitewashed coaching inn with hugely characterful bars, comfy lounge and traditional styled bedrooms - some with lovely country views. Home-cooked dishes in laid-back, oak-furnished Bistro. Daily changing menu and garden outlook in more formal Dining Room.

Overwater Hall

Northeast : 2.5 mi by Uldale rd on Overwater rd ✉ CA7 1HH – ☎ (017687) 76 566 – www.overwaterhall.co.uk – Closed 2-13 January and mid-week early December

11 rm (dinner included) – †£ 100/180 ††£ 170/260

Rest – *(closed Monday lunch)* Menu £ 45 (dinner) – Carte lunch £ 20/28

◆ Castellated Georgian manor house built in 1811, set in 18 acres of mature gardens. Three good-sized lounges, one with a bar. Large, boldly patterned bedrooms with rich fabrics and good quality bathrooms. Formal dining room offers a traditional country house menu.

Y. Duhamel/MICHELIN

BATH

County: Bath and North East Somerset
Michelin regional map: **503** M29
London 119 mi – Bristol 13 mi
– Southampton 63 mi
– Taunton 49 mi

Population: 90 144
Great Britain
Map reference: **4** C2

PRACTICAL INFORMATION

Tourist Information

Abbey Chambers, Abbey Church Yard ✆ (0906) 711 2000, tourism@bathnes.gov.uk

Golf Courses

27 Tracy Park Wick Bath Rd, ✆(0117) 937 18 00

18 Lansdown, ✆(01225) 422 138

9 Entry Hill, ✆(01225) 834 248

SIGHTS

In town

City★★★ - Royal Crescent★★★ AV (No.1 Royal Crescent★★**AC** AV **A**) – The Circus★★★ AV – Museum of Costume★★★ **AC** AV **M7** – Roman Baths★★ **AC** BX **D** – Holburne Museum and Crafts Study Centre★★ **AC** Y **M5** – Pump Room★ BX **B** - Assembly Rooms★ AV – Bath Abbey★ BX – Pulteney Bridge★ BV – Bath Industrial Heritage Centre★ **AC** AV **M1** – Lansdown Crescent★★ (Somerset Place★) Y – Camden Crescent★ Y – Beckford Tower and Museum **AC** (prospect★) Y **M6** – Museum of East Asian Art★ AV **M9** – Orange Grove★ BX

On the outskirts

Claverton (American Museum★★ **AC**, Claverton Pumping Station★ **AC**) E : 3 mi by A 36 Y

In the surrounding area

Corsham Court★★ **AC**, NE : 8.5 mi by A 4 – Dyrham Park★ **AC**, N : 6.5 mi by A 4 and A 46

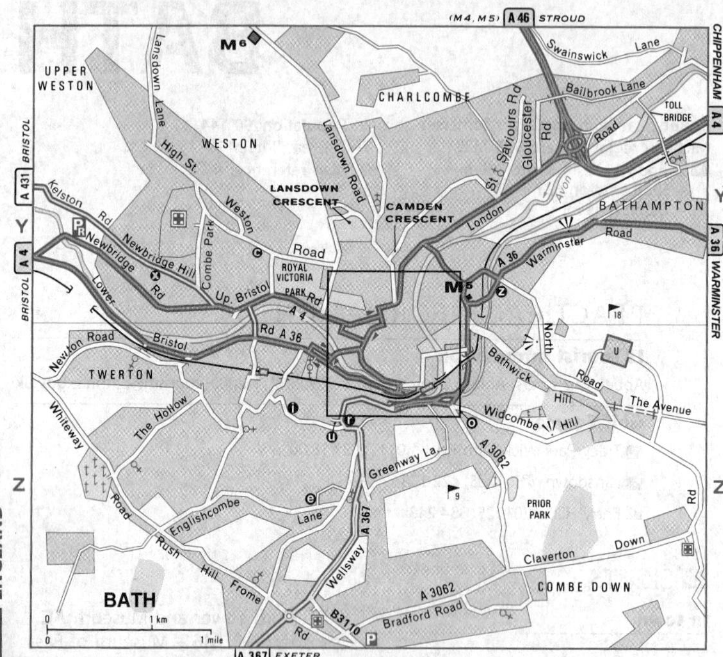

Royal Crescent

16 Royal Cres ✉ BA1 2LS – ✆ (01225) 823 333
– www.royalcrescent.co.uk AV**a**

35 rm ☕ – 👤£ 325 👥£ 345 – 10 suites

Rest *The Dower House* – see restaurant listing

♦ Professionally run townhouse in sweeping Georgian crescent, boasting smart fire-lit entrance, period drawing room/library and stylish spa. Elegant Georgian bedrooms display antiques.

Bath Spa

rm, rest,

Sydney Rd ✉ BA2 6JF – ✆ (0844) 879 91 06
– www.macdonaldhotels.co.uk Y**z**

118 rm – 👤£ 135/295 👥£ 135/295, ☕ £ 16 – 11 suites

Rest *Vellore* – *(dinner only) (booking essential)* Menu £ 35/40

Rest *Alfresco* – Carte £ 24/31

♦ Impressive 19C mansion in mature gardens, with newer wing. Period lounges and contemporary bedrooms; full butler service in Imperial Suites. Superb spa. Impressive, formal Georgian dining room with Corinthian columns. Informal Alfresco offers classic grill menu.

Bath Priory

Weston Rd ✉ BA1 2XT – ✆ (01225) 331 922
– www.thebathpriory.co.uk Y**c**

27 rm ☕ – 👤£ 180/220 👥£ 195/390

Rest – Menu £ 25/69

♦ Impressive Georgian house with mature gardens, classical guest areas, sumptuous sitting room and smart spa. Luxurious bedrooms blend the traditional and the modern. Designer bathrooms. Two dining rooms; the smaller more romantic, the larger more modern. Ambitious cooking uses some unexpected combinations.

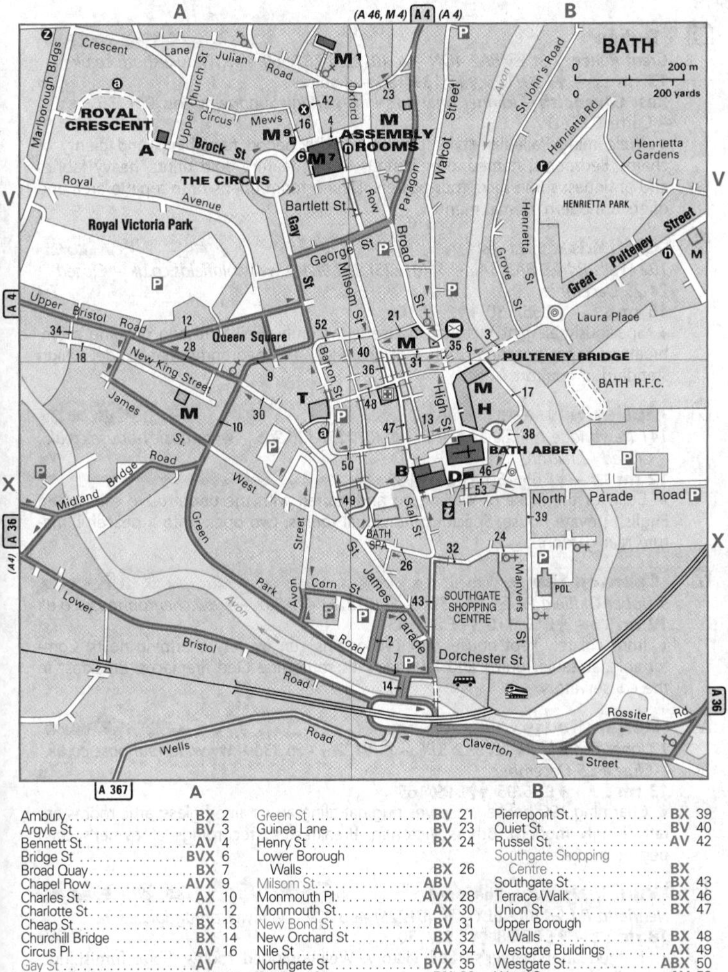

BATH

Street	Grid	No.
Ambury	BX	2
Argyle St	BV	3
Bennett St	AV	4
Bridge St	BVX	6
Broad Quay	BX	7
Chapel Row	AVX	9
Charles St	AX	10
Charlotte St	AV	12
Cheap St	BX	13
Churchill Bridge	BX	14
Circus Pl.	AV	16
Gay St	AV	
Grand Parade	BX	17
Great Stanhope St	AV	18
Green St	BV	21
Guinea Lane	BV	23
Henry St	BX	24
Lower Borough Walls	BX	26
Milsom St	ABV	
Monmouth Pl.	AVX	28
Monmouth St	AX	30
New Bond St	BV	31
New Orchard St	BX	32
Nile St	AV	34
Northgate St	BVX	35
Old Bond St	BX	36
Orange Grove	BX	38
Pierrepont St	BX	39
Quiet St	BV	40
Russel St	AV	42
Southgate Shopping Centre	BX	
Southgate St	BX	43
Terrace Walk	BX	46
Union St	BX	47
Upper Borough Walls	BX	48
Westgate Buildings	AX	49
Westgate St	ABX	50
Wood St	AV	52
York St	BX	53

Homewood Park

Abbey Ln, Hinton Charterhouse, Southeast : 6.5 mi on A 36 ⊠ BA2 7TB – ✆ (01225) 723 731 – www.homewoodpark.co.uk

19 rm ☕ – 🚹£ 185/245 🚹🚹£ 495 – 2 suites **Rest** – Menu £ 19/45

◆ Remotely set country house with fashionable interior. Charming guest areas – many boasting open fires – and contemporary bedrooms with bold colour schemes. Superb spa and treatment facilities. Dining split between 3 rooms. Modern dishes are stylishly presented.

Queensberry

Russel St ⊠ BA1 2QF – ✆ (01225) 447 928 – www.thequeensberry.co.uk

29 rm – 🚹£ 130/185 🚹🚹£ 130/500, ☕ £ 15 AV**x**

Rest *Olive Tree* – see restaurant listing

◆ Classy boutique merger of Georgian town house décor with contemporary furnishing, understated style and well-chosen detail. Ample, unfussy rooms; pretty courtyard garden.

ENGLAND

Dukes
Great Pulteney St ✉ *BA2 4DN* – *(01225) 787 960* – *www.dukesbath.co.uk*
13 rm – £ 99/125 £ 139/199 – 4 suites BV**n**
Rest *Cavendish* – *(dinner only and lunch Friday-Sunday)* Menu £ 16/35 – Carte £ 25/41
◆ Welcoming Palladian-style townhouse with period furnishings and plenty of charm. Bedrooms, named after famous Dukes, feature bold prints, heavy fabrics and antiques; some have four-posters. Dining room opens onto a patio area and offers a modern, formal menu.

Oldfields without rest
102 Wells Rd ✉ *BA2 3AL* – *(01225) 317 984* – *www.oldfields.co.uk* – *Closed 24-25 December* Z**u**
16 rm – £ 55/150 £ 89/160
◆ Spaciously elegant Victorian house with comfy, well-furnished drawing room, breakfast room boasting 'Bath rooftops' view and bedrooms that exude a high standard of comfort.

Apsley House without rest
141 Newbridge Hill ✉ *BA1 3PT* – *(01225) 336 966* – *www.apsley-house.co.uk* – *Closed Christmas* Y**x**
12 rm – £ 65/150 £ 70/165
◆ Built for the Duke of Wellington and staffed with the unobtrusive calm of an English private house. Spacious individual rooms; two open onto a peaceful, mature rear garden.

Cheriton House without rest
9 Upper Oldfield Pk ✉ *BA2 3JX* – *(01225) 429 862* – *www.cheritonhouse.co.uk*
12 rm – £ 60/110 £ 85/145 Z**u**
◆ Immaculately kept house with 19C origins, run by very charming hosts. Comfortable, sizeable rooms and lounge, with some fine tiled fireplaces. Breakfast in the conservatory.

Dorian House without rest
1 Upper Oldfield Pk ✉ *BA2 3JX* – *(01225) 426 336* – *www.dorianhouse.co.uk* – *Closed 25 December* Z**u**
13 rm – £ 65/95 £ 99/165
◆ Charming 19C house preserves original tiling and stained glass; attic rooms are refreshingly modern, others Victorian. Breakfast to recordings of owner's cello performances.

Villa Magdala without rest
Henrietta Rd ✉ *BA2 6LX* – *(01225) 466 329* – *www.villamagdala.co.uk*
18 rm – £ 85/98 £ 98/150 BV**r**
◆ Named after Napier's 1868 victory. Well-equipped rooms, floral furnishings; carefully preserved ornate balustrade and showpiece bedroom with four-poster and chaise longue.

One Three Nine without rest
139 Wells Rd ✉ *BA2 3AL* – *(01225) 314 769* – *www.139bath.co.uk* – *Closed 24-25 December* Z**r**
10 rm – £ 65/165 £ 99/175
◆ Unassuming Victorian building conceals the chic, bold décor of a stylish boutique hotel. Individually styled bedrooms may include four-posters or spa baths. Excellent terrace breakfast.

Town House without rest
7 Bennett St ✉ *BA1 2QJ* – *(01225) 422 505* – *www.thetownhousebath.co.uk* – *Closed January* AV**c**
3 rm – £ 130 £ 130
◆ Welcoming 18C house in excellent location, designed by John Wood and rebuilt after war damage. Spacious bedrooms with South African wildlife décor. Communal breakfast.

ENGLAND

Lavender House without rest
17 Bloomfield Pk, (off Bloomfield Rd) ✉ BA2 2BY – ☎ (01225) 314 500 – www.lavenderhouse-bath.com Z**s**
4 rm – £ 65 £ 90/120
◆ New owners have made a major investment in this Edwardian house. Rooms have plenty of antiques but also boast a modern, clean feel. Breakfast is served family-style.

Athole House without rest
33 Upper Oldfield Pk ✉ BA2 3JX – ☎ (01225) 320 000 – www.atholehouse.co.uk Z**i**
4 rm – £ 55/75 £ 85/105
◆ Spacious, bay windowed Victorian guesthouse with large garden, away from city centre. Bright breakfast room; conservatory lounge. Light, airy, contemporary bedrooms.

Dower House – at The Royal Crescent Hotel
16 Royal Cres ✉ BA1 2LS – ☎ (01225) 823 333 – www.royalcrescent.co.uk AV**a**
Rest – Menu £ 25/60
◆ Plush, contemporary dining room with swish bar, spacious lounge and lovely garden. Creative, seasonal cooking is underpinned by a French base. Attentive, understated service.

Olive Tree – at Queensberry Hotel
Russel St ✉ BA1 2QF – ☎ (01225) 447 928 – www.thequeensberry.co.uk – Closed Monday lunch AV**x**
Rest – Menu £ 20 (lunch) – Carte £ 45/57
◆ Up-to-date restaurant with a classy, stylish and contemporary ambience. Modern artworks adorn the split-level basement. Modern British cooking. Helpful staff.

Bistro La Barrique
31 Barton St ✉ BA1 1HG – ☎ (01225) 463 861 – www.bistrolabarrique.co.uk – Closed 25-26 December and 1 January AX**a**
Rest – French – Menu £ 14 (early dinner) – Carte £ 18/26
◆ Unpretentious bistro-style restaurant, with sheltered courtyard for terrace dining. Small, good value menu of 'petits plats'; classic French dishes with some Mediterranean twists.

Casanis
4 Saville Row ✉ BA1 2QP – ☎ (01225) 780 055 – www.casanis.co.uk – Closed 25-26 December, 1 January, 1 week spring, 1 week summer, Sunday and Monday AV**n**
Rest – French – *(booking essential)* Menu £ 22 (lunch and early dinner) – Carte £ 28/36
◆ Sweet French bistro set in an elegant Georgian building near the Assembly Rooms. Exposed wooden floors, clothed tables and a tiny rear courtyard. Skilful cooking of classic French dishes.

The Marlborough Tavern
35 Marlborough Buildings ✉ BA1 2LY – ☎ (01225) 423 731 – www.marlborough-tavern.com – Closed 25 December AV**z**
Rest – *(booking advisable)* Carte £ 25/35
◆ Spacious, modern pub next to the park and Royal Crescent, boasting funky flock wallpaper, scrubbed wooden floors and local artwork. Unfussy, hearty, classical dishes use very local produce.

White Hart
Widcombe Hill ✉ BA2 6AA – ☎ (01225) 338 053 – www.whitehartbath.co.uk – Closed Sunday dinner and bank holidays Z**o**
Rest – *(booking essential at dinner)* Carte £ 22/28
◆ Appealing pub on south east edge of the city centre, with a local following and a neighbourhood feel. Generous portions of hearty cooking; smaller tapas plates also popular.

at Box **Northeast : 4.75 mi on A 4 - Y - ✉ Bath**

The Northey

Bath Rd ✉ SN13 8AE – ✆ (01225) 742 333 – www.ohhcompany.co.uk
Rest – Menu £ 16 (lunch) – Carte £ 24/32
◆ Traditional-looking, family-run stone coaching inn with open-plan interior, large dining room and vast bar. Appealing monthly menus feature unfussy, seasonal British dishes; fish is a strength.

at Colerne **Northeast : 6.5 mi by A 4 - Y - Batheaston rd and Bannerdown Rd – ✉ Chippenham**

Lucknam Park

North : 0.5 mi on Marshfield rd ✉ SN14 8AZ – ✆ (01225) 742 777 – www.lucknampark.co.uk
36 rm – †£ 295 ††£ 475, ☕ £ 20 – 5 suites
Rest ***The Park and The Brasserie*** – see restaurant listing
◆ Grand Palladian mansion with tree-lined drive, rich décor, luxurious furnishings and sumptuous fabrics. Top class facilities include impressive spa complex and renowned equestrian centre. Extremely comfortable bedrooms.

The Park – at Lucknam Park Hotel

North : 0.5 mi on Marshfield rd ✉ SN14 8AZ – ✆ (01225) 742 777 – www.lucknampark.co.uk – Closed Sunday dinner and Monday
Rest – *(dinner only and Sunday lunch) (booking essential)* Menu £ 68 **s**
Spec. Scallops with smoked haddock brandade, baby carrots and cumin. Loin of venison with pumpkin and sage risotto fritters. Chocolate tart with cherries and pistachio.
◆ Located within an impressive mansion, an opulent dining room with skilled, amiable service and a knowledgeable kitchen team. Classical menus display modern European influences, with dishes expertly crafted from locally sourced farm produce.

The Brasserie – at Lucknam Park Hotel

North : 0.5 mi on Marshfield rd ✉ SN14 8AZ – ✆ (01225) 742 777 – www.lucknampark.co.uk
Rest – Menu £ 21/28 **s** – Carte £ 33/45 **s**
◆ Linen-laid brasserie in state-of-the-art spa complex, boasting spacious bar-lounge and airy dining room with full-length windows. Precise, modern cooking in well-judged combinations; healthy options available. BBQs on the terrace in summer.

at Monkton Combe **Southeast : 4.5 mi by A 36 - Y – ✉ Bath**

Wheelwrights Arms with rm

Church Ln ✉ BA2 7HB – ✆ (01225) 722 287 – www.wheelwrightsarms.co.uk
7 rm ☕ – †£ 85 ††£ 145
Rest – Menu £ 14 (weekday lunch) – Carte £ 20/30
◆ Charming 18C former carpenter's workshop in a sleepy little village, displaying exposed stone walls, parquet floors and open fires. Wide-ranging, traditional menus; mainly fish specials. Individually designed bedrooms are modern with rustic overtones.

at Combe Hay **Southwest : 5 mi by A 367 – ✉ Bath**

The Wheatsheaf with rm

✉ BA2 7EG – ✆ (01225) 833 504 – www.wheatsheafcombehay.com – Closed Sunday dinner and Monday except bank holidays when open for lunch
3 rm ☕ – †£ 140 ††£ 140 **Rest** – Carte £ 15/35
◆ A modern take on the classical country pub; remotely set in a pretty village, with chic styling, open fires, comfy sofas and a relaxed atmosphere. Contemporary presentation of flavourful, seasonal dishes. Spacious, modern bedrooms boast a quality feel.

ENGLAND

BATTLE – East Sussex – **504** V31 – **pop. 5 190** Great Britain **8** B3

London 55 mi – Brighton 34 mi – Folkestone 43 mi – Maidstone 30 mi

Battle and Bexhill TIC, Battle Abbey, High St (01424) 773721, battletic@rother.gov.uk

Town★ – Abbey and Site of the Battle of Hastings★ **AC**

XX **Nobles**

17 High St TN33 OAE – (01424) 774 422 – www.noblesrestaurant.co.uk – Closed Christmas-New Year, Sunday dinner and bank holiday Mondays

Rest – Menu £ 14 (lunch)/18 (weekday dinner) – Carte £ 27/38

◆ Simple, tasteful eatery with terrace, in heart of historical high street. Regularly changing menus offer unfussy classical dishes of local seasonal produce, with the occasional twist.

Don't confuse the couvert rating X with the stars ✿! Couverts defines comfort and service, while stars are awarded for the best cuisine across all categories of comfort.

BAUGHURST – Hampshire **6** B1

London 61 mi – Camberley 28 mi – Farnborough 27 mi

The Wellington Arms

Baughurst Rd, Southwest : 0.5 mi RG26 5LP – (0118) 982 0110 – www.thewellingtonarms.com – Closed Sunday dinner

Rest – *(booking essential)* Menu £ 18 (weekday lunch) – Carte £ 18/34

◆ Smart, cream pub boasting its own pigs, chickens, bees, herb beds and vegetable gardens. Produce is strictly local and home-grown/reared/made. Blackboard menus feature 6 dishes per course, which are replaced as produce runs out. Cooking is generous and satisfying.

BEACONSFIELD – Buckinghamshire – **504** S29 – **pop. 12 292** **11** D3

London 26 mi – Aylesbury 19 mi – Oxford 32 mi

Beaconsfield Seer Green, (01494) 676 545

Crazy Bear

73 Wycombe End HP9 1LX – (01494) 673 086 – www.crazybeargroup.co.uk

10 rm – ††£ 345/430, £ 15

Rest ***The Thai*** – see restaurant listing

Rest ***English*** – *(booking advisable)* Menu £ 20 (lunch) – Carte £ 26/38

◆ Theatrical bedrooms each with their own unique features including leather padded walls and baths which fill from the ceiling. Bars are the ultimate in boutique style, with rich, flamboyant décor. Voluptuous style and European menu in the English restaurant.

XX **The Thai** – at Crazy Bear Hotel

73 Wycombe End HP9 1LX – (01494) 673 086 – www.crazybeargroup.co.uk – Closed Sunday and Monday

Rest – Thai – *(dinner only) (booking essential)* Menu £ 47 – Carte £ 33/57

◆ Dine on authentic, well presented Thai dishes in sumptuous surroundings, with a theatrical design that includes chandeliers, flock wallpaper and studded leather chairs. Personable service.

ENGLAND

at Seer Green Northeast : 2.5 mi by A 355 – ✉ Buckinghamshire

The Jolly Cricketers

24 Chalfont Rd ✉ HP9 2YG – ✆ (01494) 676 308 – Closed Sunday dinner and Monday

Rest – Carte £ 22/32

◆ A charming Victorian pub filled with a host of cricketing memorabilia. Friendly staff and an appealing menu that mixes classics with more modern influences. Excellent condition beers.

at Wooburn Common Southwest : 3.5 mi by A 40 – ✉ Beaconsfield

Chequers Inn

Kiln Ln, Southwest : 1 mi on Bourne End rd ✉ HP10 0JQ – ✆ (01628) 529 575 – www.chequers-inn.com

17 rm – †£ 83/100 ††£ 88/108, ☐ £ 9.95

Rest – Menu £ 18/23 – Carte £ 28/41

◆ Attractive 17C red-brick former inn: family-owned and run since 1975. Cosy beamed bar and spacious leather-furnished lounge. Good-sized bedrooms boast flat screen TVs and wi-fi. Choice of bar snacks, or more ambitious dishes in the clothed rear restaurant.

BEADNELL – Northumberland – 501 P17 — 24 B1

London 341 mi – Edinburgh 81 mi – Newcastle upon Tyne 47 mi

Beach Court without rest

Harbour Rd ✉ NE67 5BJ – ✆ (01665) 720 225 – www.beachcourt.com – Restricted opening in winter

3 rm ☐ – †£ 75 ††£ 99/159

◆ Mock-baronial house, superbly set right on the beachfront: ask for the turret room. Traditionally furnished, with bric-a-brac aplenty and doves in the garden. Excellent hospitality.

BEAMHURST – Staffs. – see Uttoxeter

BEAMINSTER – Dorset – 503 L31 – pop. 2 791 — 3 B3

London 154 mi – Exeter 45 mi – Taunton 30 mi – Weymouth 29 mi

Chedington Court South Perrott, ✆ (01935) 891 413

Bridge House

3 Prout Bridge ✉ DT8 3AY – ✆ (01308) 862 200 – www.bridge-house.co.uk

13 rm ☐ – †£ 126/160 ††£ 220/255

Rest – Menu £ 25 – Carte dinner £ 28/57

◆ Hugely characterful 13C former priest's house, with newer extensions. Traditionally furnished, flag-floored lounges boast inglenook fireplaces. Mix of classical and modern bedrooms. Linen-laid restaurant with conservatory and terrace offers brasserie-style menu.

The Wild Garlic

4 The Square ✉ DT8 3AS – ✆ (01308) 861 446 – www.thewildgarlic.co.uk – Closed Sunday-Tuesday and bank holidays

Rest – *(booking essential)* Carte £ 28/38

◆ Pretty, rustic restaurant in charming town; ask for a window table overlooking the square. Run by 2009 Masterchef winner, who is a keen forager. Appealing menu supplemented by blackboard specials.

BEARSTED – Kent – 504 V30 – see Maidstone

Good food at moderate prices? Look for the Bib Gourmand.

ENGLAND

BEAULIEU – Hampshire – **503** P31 – **pop. 726** – ✉ **Brockenhurst** **6** B2

Great Britain

London 102 mi – Bournemouth 24 mi – Southampton 13 mi – Winchester 23 mi

Town★★ - National Motor Museum★★ **AC**

Buckler's Hard★ (Maritime Museum★ **AC**) SE : 2 m

Montagu Arms

Palace Ln ✉ *SO42 7ZL* – ✆ *(01590) 612 324 – www.montaguarmshotel.co.uk*

18 rm – £ 140 £ 220 – 4 suites

Rest *The Terrace* – see restaurant listing

Rest *Monty's Brasserie* – Carte £ 22/33

◆ Well-run 18C inn with characterful parquet floors and wood-panelled walls. Country house style bedrooms boast antiques and modern facilities. Airy wicker-furnished conservatory, pleasant terrace and lovely gardens. Informal Monty's serves home-cooked classics.

The Terrace – at Montagu Arms Hotel

Palace Ln. ✉ *SO42 7ZL* – ✆ *(01590) 612 324 – www.montaguarmshotel.co.uk*

Rest – *(closed Monday and lunch Tuesday)* Menu £ 23 (lunch) – Carte dinner £ 53/63

Spec. Tarte fine of beetroot with caramelised onions and mackerel. Wild sea bass with Jersey Royal potatoes, crab and samphire. Dark chocolate delice with lavender ice cream.

◆ Traditional country house dining room with wood-panelled lounge. Good-sized, linen-laid tables; polite, efficient service. Lovely garden outlook from terrace. Precisely prepared, top quality produce used in refined, classically based dishes with modern touches.

The sun's out? Then enjoy eating outside on the terrace:

BEDFORD – Bedfordshire – **504** S27 – **pop. 82 488** **12** A1

London 59 mi – Cambridge 31 mi – Colchester 70 mi – Leicester 51 mi

Town Hall, St Paul's Sq ✆ (01234) 221 712, touristinfo@bedford.gov.uk

Bedfordshire Biddenham Bromham Rd, ✆ (01234) 261 669

Mowsbury Kimbolton Rd, ✆ (01234) 772 700

Plan on next page

at Elstow South : 2 mi by A 6 – ✉ **Bedford**

St Helena

High St ✉ *MK42 9XP* – ✆ *(01234) 344 848 – www.sthelenarestaurant.com – Closed 24 December-5 January, Sunday, Monday, and lunch Saturday and Tuesday* **Yr**

Rest – Menu £ 31/38

◆ Delightful, antique-filled house with mature gardens and popular conservatory. Small rooms and low ceilings add warmth and atmosphere. Classical menus display some Italian influences.

at Bourne End Northwest : 8 mi by A 6

Bourne End Farm without rest

East : 0.5 mi by Bourne End rd ✉ *MK44 1QS* – ✆ *(01234) 783 184 – www.bourneendfarm.co.uk*

3 rm – £ 60/80 £ 80/90

◆ Spotless house in over 100 acres of arable farmland; comfortable, simply furnished bedrooms with showers; cosy lounge and charming hosts. Communal farm breakfast in dining room.

ENGLAND

BEDFORD

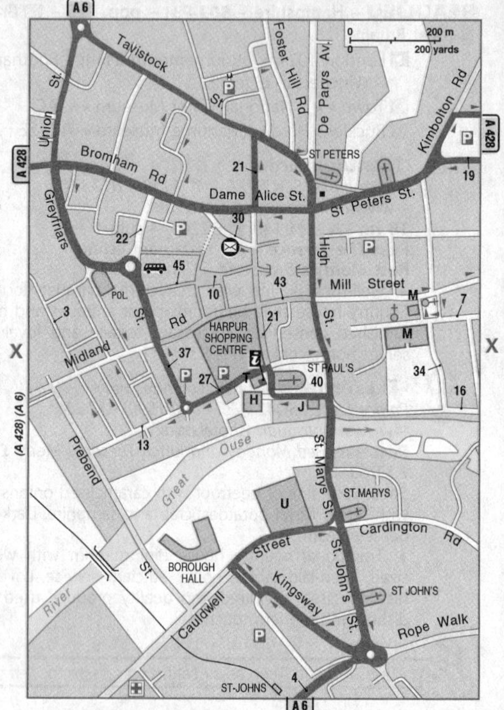

ENGLAND

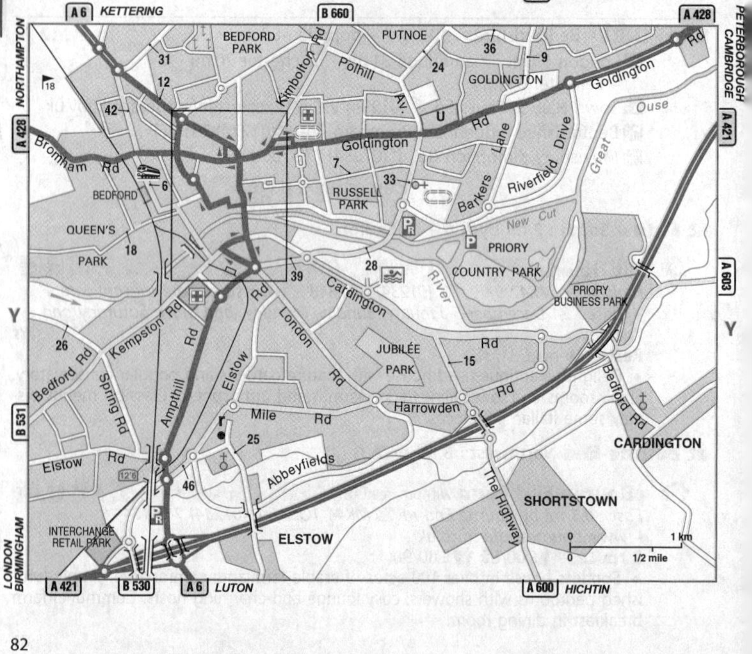

BEELEY – Derbyshire – pop. 165 **16** B1

London 160 mi – Derby 26 mi – Matlock 5 mi

The Devonshire Arms with rm

Devonshire Sq ✉ DE4 2NR – ✆ (01629) 733 259 – www.devonshirebeeley.co.uk

8 rm – †£ 99 ††£ 175

Rest – Carte £ 20/36

◆ Stone inn close to Chatsworth House and owned by the Estate. Rustic bar; modern extension with lovely views. Unusual starters followed by classics and daily 'market' dishes. Tasty afternoon teas. Beamed bedrooms in main house; larger, brighter rooms next door.

BELCHFORD – Lincolnshire – **502** T24 – ✉ Horncastle **17** C1

London 169 mi – Horncastle 5 mi – Lincoln 28 mi

The Blue Bell Inn

1 Main Rd ✉ LN9 6LQ – ✆ (01507) 533 602 – Closed 2 weeks mid January, Sunday dinner and Monday

Rest – Carte £ 17/28

◆ A traditionally styled whitewashed pub, popular with walkers on the Viking Way. Numerous blackboard menus list sandwiches, pub favourites and more ambitious choices.

BELFORD – Northumberland – **501** O17 – pop. 1 177 **24** A1

London 335 mi – Edinburgh 71 mi – Newcastle upon Tyne 49 mi

Belford South Rd, ✆ (01668) 213 323

Market Cross without rest

1 Church St ✉ NE70 7LS – ✆ (01668) 213 013 – www.marketcross.net

4 rm – †£ 50/80 ††£ 80/110

◆ 200 year-old stone house in rural town centre. Warmly decorated lounge, homely touches in tasteful bedrooms. Wide, locally inspired breakfast choice in cosy pine surroundings.

BELPER – Derbyshire – **502** P24 – pop. 21 938 **16** B2

London 141 mi – Birmingham 59 mi – Leicester 40 mi – Manchester 55 mi

at Shottle Northwest : 4 mi by A 517 – ✉ Belper

Dannah Farm Country House without rest

Bowmans Lane, North : 0.25 mi by Alport rd ✉ DE56 2DR – ✆ (01773) 550 273 – www.dannah.co.uk – Closed 24-26 December

4 rm – †£ 75/95 ††£ 150/250 – 4 suites

◆ Family-run converted farmhouse - part of a working farm. Spacious, contemporary bedrooms are diverse in style; the two level Studio suite includes hot tub and spiral staircase.

BELTON – Leics. – see Loughborough

BENENDEN – Kent – **504** V30 **8** B2

London 55 mi – Croydon 49 mi – Barnet 81 mi – Ealing 85 mi

Ramsden Farm without rest

Dingleden Ln, Southeast : 1 mi by B 2086 ✉ TN17 4JT – ✆ (01580) 240 203 – www.ramsdenfarmcottage.co.uk

3 rm – †£ 65/110 ††£ 80/110

◆ Attractive clapperboard house with modern styling, a refreshingly relaxed air and fine countryside views. Spacious, up-to-date bedrooms; luxurious, modern bathrooms with underfloor heating.

BEPTON – W. Sussex – see Midhurst

ENGLAND

BERKHAMSTED – Hertfordshire – 504 S28 – pop. 18 800 12 A2

Great Britain

London 34 mi – Aylesbury 14 mi – St Albans 11 mi

Whipsnade Wild Animal Park★ **AC**, N : 9.5 mi on A 4251, B 4506 and B 4540

Eatfish

163-165 High St ✉ HP4 3HB – ✆ (01442) 879 988 – www.eatfish.co.uk – Closed 25-26 December

Rest – Seafood – Menu £ 15 (lunch) – Carte £ 24/35

◆ Well-run neighbourhood seafood restaurant with linen-laid tables and a characterful, rustic feel. Flexible menu, with large/smaller portions. Summer terrace and a young, friendly team.

BERWICK-UPON-TWEED – Northumberland – 501 O16 24 A1 – pop. 12 870 Great Britain

London 349 mi – Edinburgh 57 mi – Newcastle upon Tyne 63 mi

106 Marygate ✆ (01289) 330733, tourism@berwick-upon-tweed.gov.uk

Goswick, ✆ (01289) 387 256

Magdalene Fields, ✆ (01289) 306 130

Town★★ - Walls★

Foulden★, NW : 5 mi – Paxton House (Chippendale furniture★) **AC**, W : 5 mi by A 6105, A 1 and B 6461. St Abb's Head★★ (≤★), NW : 12 mi by A 1, A 1107 and B 6438 - SW : Tweed Valley★★ – Eyemouth Museum★ **AC**, N : 7.5 mi by A 1 and A 1107 – Holy Island★ (Priory ruins★ **AC**, Lindisfarne Castle★ **AC**), SE : 9 mi by A 1167 and A 1 – Manderston★ (stables★), W : 13 mi by A 6105 - Ladykirk (Kirk o'Steil★), SW : 8.5 mi by A 698 and B 6470

1 Sallyport

1 Sallyport, off Bridge St ✉ TD15 1EZ – ✆ (01289) 308 827 – www.sallyport.co.uk

6 rm – †£ 85/120 ††£ 140/150 **Rest** – Carte £ 19/35 **s**

◆ 17C Grade II listed house on cobbled alley. The bedrooms are a strong point: they boast a boutique style, with a high standard of facilities, and lots of homely extra touches. Characterful farmhouse kitchen style dining room.

BEVERLEY – East Riding of Yorkshire – 502 S22 – pop. 29 110 23 D2 – ✉ Kingston-Upon-Hull Great Britain

London 188 mi – Kingston-upon-Hull 8 mi – Leeds 52 mi – York 29 mi

34 Butcher Row ✆ (01482) 867430, beverley.tic@vhey.co.uk

The Westwood, ✆ (01482) 868 757

Town★ - Minster★★ – St Mary's Church★

Burton Mount

Malton Rd, Cherry Burton , Northwest : 2.75 mi by A 164, B 1248 on Leconfield rd ✉ HU17 7RA – ✆ (01964) 550 541 – www.burtonmount.co.uk

3 rm – †£ 64 ††£ 91 **Rest** – Menu £ 32

◆ Homely red brick house overlooking large, mature gardens. Dining room boasts French windows opening onto the terrace. Comfy bedrooms display heavy fabrics and dark wood furniture. Good breakfasts; dinners of well sourced local produce cooked on the Aga.

Whites

12a North Bar Without ✉ HU17 7AB – ✆ (01482) 866 121 – www.whitesrestaurant.co.uk – Closed Christmas and New Year, 1 week August, Sunday and Monday

Rest – *(booking advisable)* Menu £ 16/20 (midweek) – Carte dinner £ 28/37

◆ Friendly restaurant and patisserie; its intimate inner hung with vivid ceramics. Good value, classical dishes are cooked with skill and care. Freshly baked cakes and a wide selection of homemade petits fours. Relaxed, informal atmosphere.

at Tickton Northeast : 3.5 mi by A 1035 – ✉ Kingston-Upon-Hull

Tickton Grange

on A 1035 ✉ HU17 9SH – ☎ (01964) 543 666 – www.beverleyticktongrange.co.uk – Restricted opening at Christmas

21 rm – †£ 93 ††£ 125/145

Rest *Champagne* – Menu £ 23/30

♦ Warm, welcoming, family-run hotel. Bedrooms blend Georgian and contemporary architecture, and display antique and period-inspired furniture. Richly swagged fabrics and open fires in an inviting lounge. Dine in Georgian style; large bay windows look onto the lawn.

at South Dalton Northwest : 5 mi by A 164 and B 1248 – ✉ Beverley

The Pipe and Glass Inn (James Mackenzie) with rm

West End ✉ HU17 7PN – ☎ (01430) 810 246 – www.pipeandglass.co.uk – Closed 2 weeks January, Sunday dinner and Monday except bank holidays

2 rm – †£ 150 ††£ 150 **Rest** – Carte £ 21/40

Spec. Potted Gloucester Old Spot pork with crackling salad. Yorkshire Wolds mutton hotpot with wild garlic dumplings. Blood orange burnt cream with East Yorkshire sugar cakes.

♦ Warm, bustling and inviting pub, personally run by experienced owners. Generous portions of carefully executed, flavourful cooking, with judicious use of local, seasonal and traceable produce. Luxury, designer bedrooms boast all mod cons and have their own patios overlooking estate woodland. Breakfast served in bedrooms.

BEYTON – Suffolk – **504** W27 – see Bury St Edmunds

BIBURY – Gloucestershire – **503** O28 – **pop. 570** – ✉ Cirencester **4** D1

Great Britain

London 86 mi – Gloucester 26 mi – Oxford 30 mi

Village★

Swan

✉ *GL7 5NW – ☎ (01285) 740 695 – www.cotswold-inns-hotels.co.uk/swan*

19 rm – †£ 160/200 ††£ 160/283 – 3 suites

Rest *Gallery* – *(dinner only)* Menu £ 35

Rest *Café Swan* – Menu £ 33 (dinner) – Carte £ 25/27

♦ Ivy-clad 17C coaching inn with private gardens; idyllic village location by a trout stream. Comfortable rooms with a contemporary edge. Gallery is formally stylish and spacious. Café Swan is a brasserie with stone-flagged courtyard.

Cotteswold House without rest

Arlington, on B 4425 ✉ GL7 5ND – ☎ (01285) 740 609 – www.cotteswoldhouse.net

3 rm – †£ 55 ††£ 75

♦ Set in a manicured garden outside the picturesque village. Homely, spotless and modestly priced bedrooms, comprehensively remodelled behind a Victorian façade.

BICESTER – Oxfordshire – **504** Q28 – **pop. 31 113** **10** B2

London 66 mi – Birmingham 70 mi – Leicester 66 mi – Coventry 51 mi

Villandry

26 B&C, 50 Pingle Drive, Bicester Village Outlet Shopping, on A 421 at junction of A 41 ✉ OX26 6WD – ☎ (01869) 355 070 – www.villandry.com

Rest – *(Bookings not accepted at lunch)* Carte £ 21/32

♦ Rest tired shoppers' feet at this bustling bistrot; an outpost of the popular London foodstore. Fresh, tasty modern cooking, from classic French dishes to rotisserie steaks.

ENGLAND

BIDDENDEN – Kent – 504 V30 – pop. 2 205 Great Britain 9 C2

London 52 mi – Ashford 13 mi – Maidstone 16 mi

Bodiam Castle★★, S : 10 mi by A 262, A 229 and B 2244 – Sissinghurst Garden★, W : 3 mi by A 262 – Battle Abbey★, S : 20 mi by A 262, A 229, A 21 and A 2100

Barclay Farmhouse without rest

Woolpack Corner, South : 0.5 mi by A 262 on Benenden rd ✉ TN27 8BQ – ✆ (01580) 292 626 – www.barclayfarmhouse.co.uk

3 rm – £ 65 £ 95

◆ Set in an acre of pleasant garden: well-priced, very comfortable accommodation with fine French oak flooring and furniture. Inventive breakfasts in the barn conversion.

West House (Graham Garrett)

28 High St ✉ TN27 8AH – ✆ (01580) 291 341 – www.thewesthouserestaurant.co.uk – Closed Christmas-New Year, 2 weeks late July, Saturday lunch, Sunday dinner and Monday

Rest – Menu £ 25/35

Spec. Smoked haddock carpaccio with bacon dressing and pea shoots. Marsh lamb cutlet and sweetbreads with broad beans. White chocolate honeycomb parfait with dark chocolate sorbet.

◆ Pretty part 16C former weavers' cottages in picturesque village. Charming beamed interior with inglenook and modern artwork. Concise seasonal menu; confident and technically skilled cooking allows the ingredients to shine.

The Three Chimneys

Hareplain Rd, West : 1.5 mi by A 262 ✉ TN27 8LW – ✆ (01580) 291 472 – www.thethreechimneys.co.uk – Closed 25 and 31 December

Rest – *(booking essential)* Carte £ 25/32

◆ Delightful pub with charming terrace and garden, dating back to 1420 and boasting a roaring fire, dimly lit low-beamed rooms and an old world feel. Largely British dishes and nursery puddings.

Don't confuse the couvert rating with the stars!
Couverts defines comfort and service, while stars are awarded for the best cuisine across all categories of comfort.

BIGBURY – Devon – 503 I33 2 C3

London 195 mi – Exeter 41 mi – Plymouth 22 mi

Kingsbridge★, E : 13 mi by B 3392 and A 379

The Oyster Shack

Milburn Orchard Farm, Stakes Hill, East : 1 mi on Easton rd ✉ TQ7 4BE – ✆ (01548) 810 876 – www.oystershack.co.uk – Closed 4 January-1 February

Rest – Seafood – *(booking essential)* Carte £ 23/36

◆ Eccentric venue; half a lovely covered terrace, decorated with fishing nets. Seafood, particularly local oyster dishes; classic and modern dishes using the freshest produce.

BIGBURY-ON-SEA – Devon – 503 I33 – pop. 600 – ✉ Kingsbridge 2 C3

London 196 mi – Exeter 42 mi – Plymouth 23 mi

Burgh Island

South : 0.5 mi by sea tractor ✉ TQ7 4BG – ✆ (01548) 810 514 – www.burghisland.com

14 rm – £ 300/410 £ 420 – 10 suites – £ 410/620

Rest – *(dinner only and Sunday lunch) (booking essential for non-residents)* Menu £ 45/57

◆ Unique Grade II listed 1930s country house in private island setting: stylishly romantic Art Deco interior. Charmingly individual rooms with views: some have fantastic style. Ballroom dining: dress in black tie. Owners pride themselves on accomplished cooking.

Henley

Folly Hill ✉ TQ7 4AR – ☎ (01548) 810 240 – www.thehenleyhotel.co.uk – April-October
5 rm – †£ 75 ††£ 136
Rest – *(dinner only) (booking essential for non-residents)* Menu £ 34
♦ Charming hotel with superb views over Burgh Island and Bolt Tail. Homely lounge, wicker-furnished conservatory and comfy bedrooms that cross New England and English Country styles; room 2 boasts double-aspect views. Concise, unfussy dinners use local ingredients.

BIGGLESWADE – Bedfordshire – 504 T27 – pop. 15 383 — 12 B1

London 46 mi – Bedford 12 mi – Luton 24 mi

at Old Warden West : 3.5 mi by A 6001 off B 658 – ✉ Biggleswade

Hare & Hounds

The Village ✉ SG18 9HQ – ☎ (01767) 627 225 – www.hareandhoundsoldwarden.co.uk – Closed Sunday dinner and Monday except bank holidays
Rest – Carte £ 22/28
♦ Charming picture postcard pub set in an idyllic village. Monthly changing à la carte offers hearty, flavoursome dishes; blackboard menu presents classic pub fare. Homemade bread and pasta.

BILDESTON – Suffolk – 504 W27 — 15 C3

London 85 mi – Bury St Edmunds 18 mi – Ipswich 15 mi

The Bildeston Crown with rm

104 High St ✉ IP7 7EB – ☎ (01449) 740 510 – www.thebildestoncrown.co.uk
12 rm – †£ 90 ††£ 250 **Rest** – Menu £ 22 – Carte £ 26/40
♦ Old beamed inn with lovely courtyard. Stylish, modern interior with 2 bars, a smart lounge and formal restaurant; warm colours and open fires feature. Choose from classics, an ambitious à la carte or tasting menu. Elaborate, artistic cooking. Luxurious bedrooms boast bold colours, designer furniture and chic bathrooms.

ENGLAND

BIRCHOVER – Derbs. – see Matlock

BIRKENHEAD – Merseyside – 502 K23 – pop. 83 729 — 20 A3

London 222 mi – Liverpool 2 mi
Access Mersey Tunnels (toll)
to Liverpool and Wallasey (Mersey Ferries) frequent services daily
Arrowe Park Woodchurch, ☎ (0151) 677 1527
Prenton Golf Links Rd, ☎ (0151) 609 3426

Plan : see Liverpool p. 3

Fraiche (Marc Wilkinson)

11 Rose Mount, Oxton, Southwest : 2.25 mi by A 552 and B 5151 ✉ CH43 5SG – ☎ (0151) 652 2914 – www.restaurantfraiche.com – Closed first 2 weeks January, Monday and Tuesday
Rest – *(dinner only and lunch Friday-Saturday) (booking essential)*
Menu £ 26/60
Spec. Scallops with kohlrabi cream and Iberico ham consommé. Duck with vanilla poached turnip and verjus dressing. Apple soup with yoghurt ice and pistachio cake.
♦ Stylish, sophisticated restaurant displaying interesting glass friezes. Choice of 3 set menus. Creative, modern dishes use excellent quality ingredients from around the globe. Unusual combinations; impressive presentation. Knowledgeable, personable service.

K. Blackwell/MICHELIN

BIRMINGHAM

County: West Midlands
Michelin regional map: **503** O26
London 122 mi – Bristol 91 mi
– Liverpool 103 mi
– Manchester 86 mi

Population: 970 892
Great Britain
Map reference: **19** C2

PRACTICAL INFORMATION

Tourist Information

The Rotunda, 150 New St ✆ (0121) 202 5000

Airport

Birmingham International Airport : ✆ (0844) 576 6000, E : 6.5 mi by A 45 DU

Golf Courses

Edgbaston Church Rd, ✆ (0121) 454 1736

Hilltop Handsworth Park Lane, ✆ (0121) 554 4463

Hatchford Brook Sheldon Coventry Rd, ✆ (0121) 743 9821

Brandhall Warley Heron Rd, Oldbury, ✆ (0121) 552 2195

Harborne Church Farm Harborne Vicarage Rd, ✆ (0121) 427 1204

SIGHTS

IN TOWN

City★ – Museum and Art Gallery★★ LY **M2** – Barber Institute of Fine Arts★★ (at Birmingham University) EX **U** – Cathedral of St Philip (stained glass portrayals★) LMY – Millennium Point FV

ON THE OUTSKIRTS

Aston Hall★★ FV **M**

IN THE SURROUNDING AREA

Black Country Museum★, Dudley, NW : 10 mi by A 456 and A 4123 AU – Bournville★, SW : 4 mi on A 38 and A 441

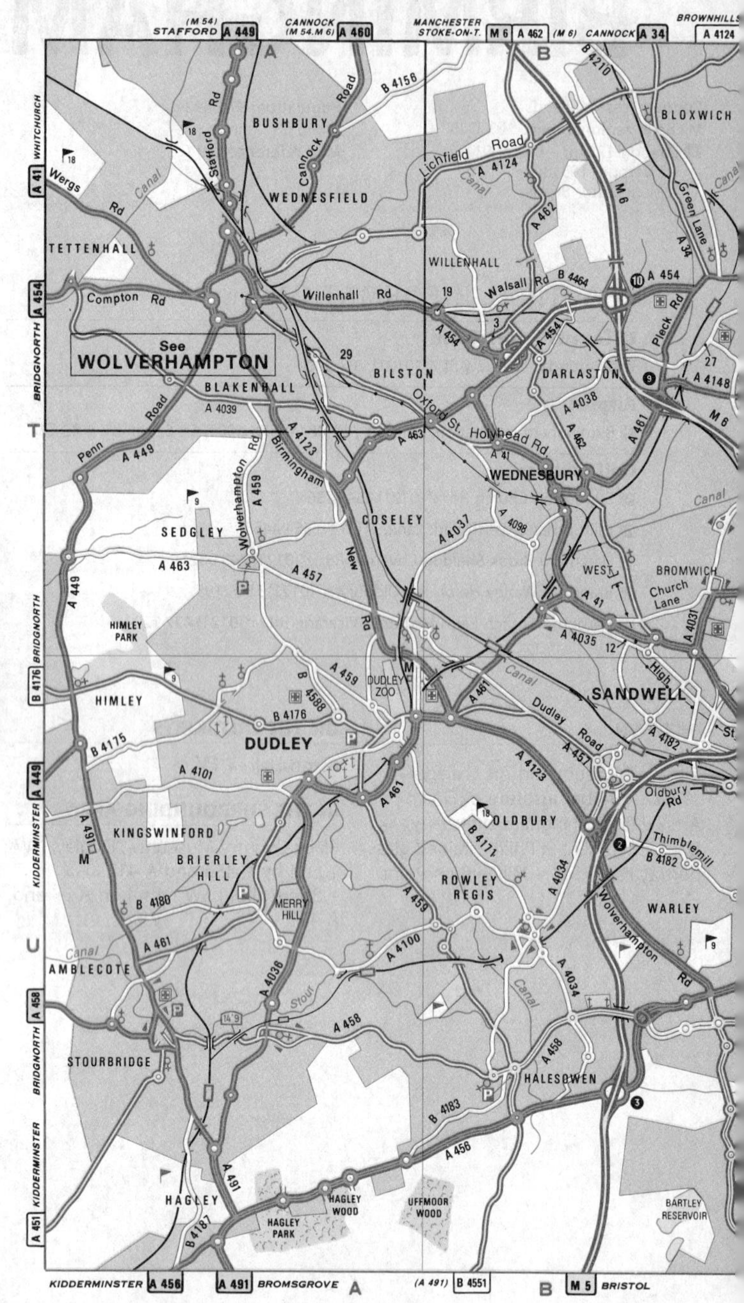

(M 54) STAFFORD A 449
CANNOCK (M 54.M 6) A 460
MANCHESTER STOKE-ON-T. M 6 A 462
(M 6) CANNOCK A 34
BROWNHILLS A 4124
WHITCHURCH A 41
BRIDGNORTH A 454
BRIDGNORTH B 4176
KIDDERMINSTER A 449
BRIDGNORTH A 458
KIDDERMINSTER A 451
KIDDERMINSTER A 456
A 491 BROMSGROVE
(A 491) B 4551
M 5 BRISTOL
ENGLAND
BUSHBURY
WEDNESFIELD
TETTENHALL
BLOXWICH
WILLENHALL
See WOLVERHAMPTON
BLAKENHALL
BILSTON
DARLASTON
WEDNESBURY
COSELEY
SEDGLEY
WEST BROMWICH
HIMLEY PARK
HIMLEY
DUDLEY
DUDLEY ZOO
SANDWELL
OLDBURY
KINGSWINFORD
BRIERLEY HILL
MERRY HILL
ROWLEY REGIS
WARLEY
AMBLECOTE
STOURBRIDGE
HALESOWEN
HAGLEY
HAGLEY WOOD
HAGLEY PARK
UFFMOOR WOOD
BARTLEY RESERVOIR
Wergs Rd
Compton Rd
Stafford Rd
Cannock Road
Lichfield Road
Willenhall Rd
Walsall Rd
Green Lane
Pleck Rd
Penn Road
Wolverhampton Rd
Birmingham New Rd
Oxford St.
Holyhead Rd
Church Lane
High St
Dudley Road
Oldbury Rd
Thimblemill
Wolverhampton Rd
Canal
Stour

BIRMINGHAM AND WOLVERHAMPTON

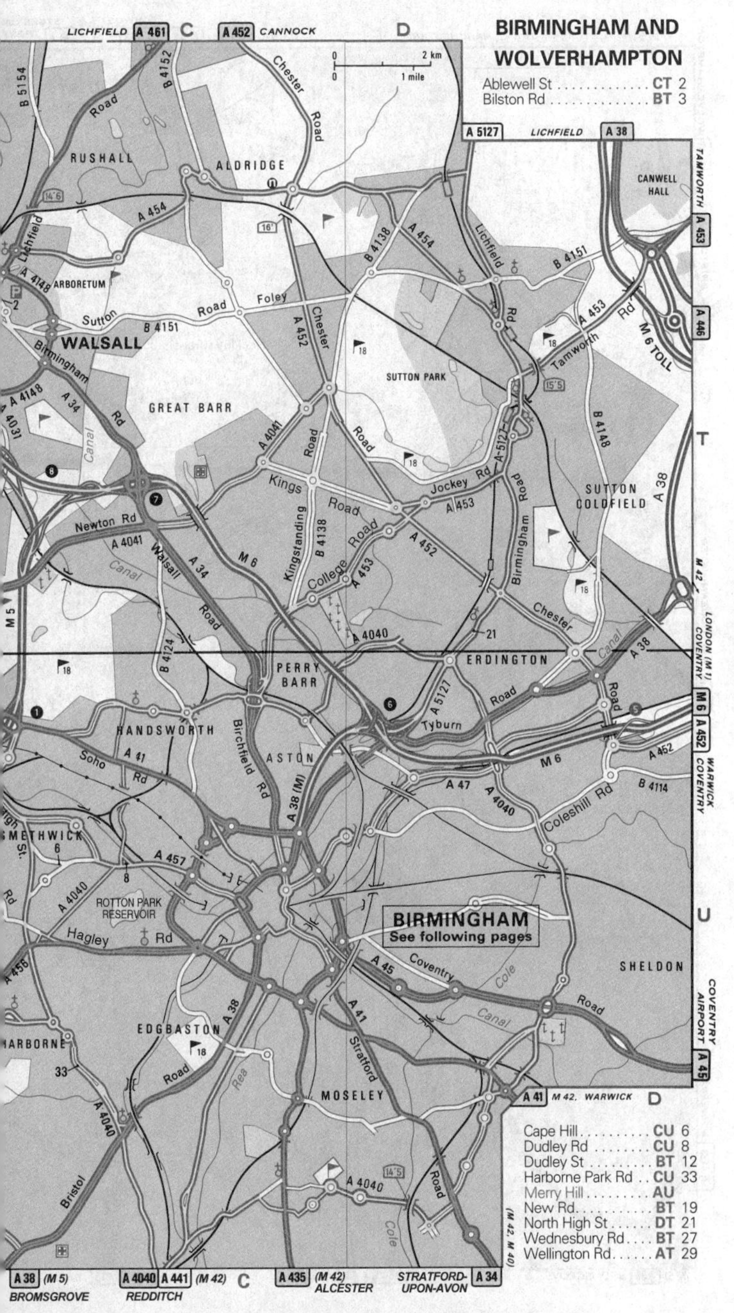

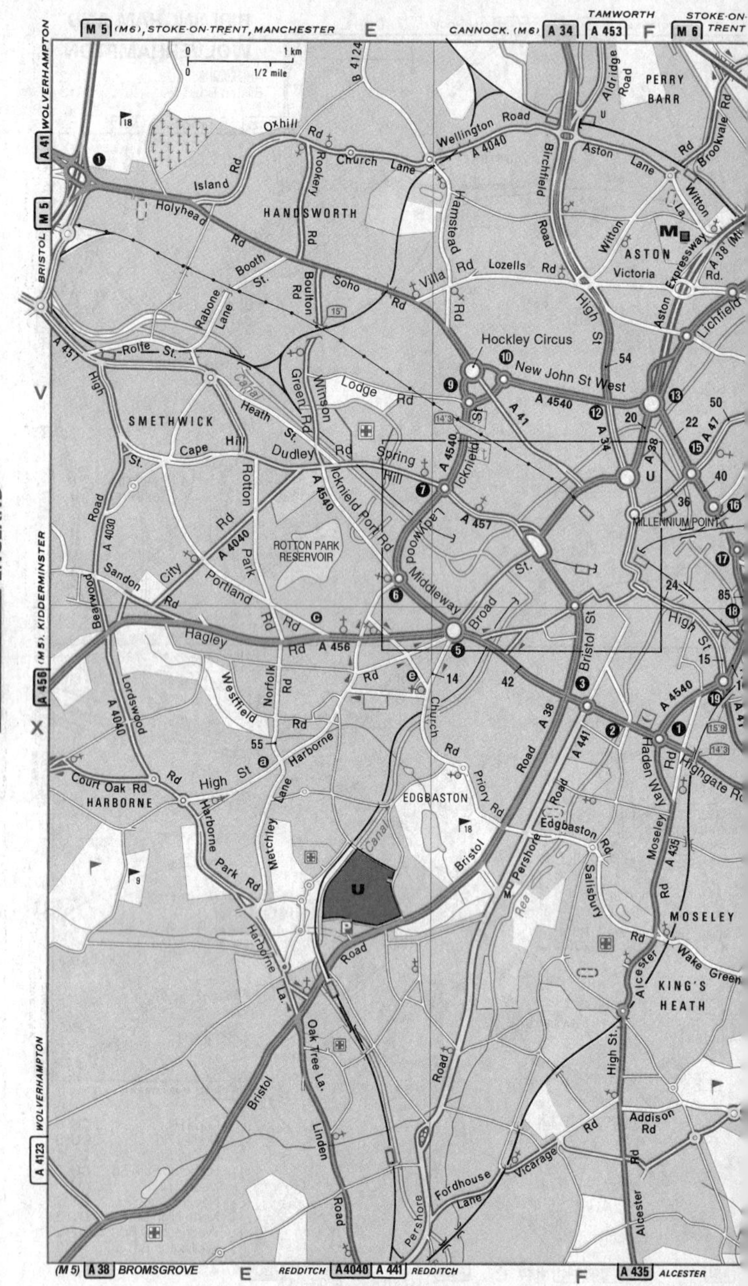
M 5 (M6), STOKE-ON-TRENT, MANCHESTER
CANNOCK, (M6) A 34
TAMWORTH A 453
STOKE-ON-TRENT M 6
A 41 WOLVERHAMPTON
M 5 BRISTOL
A 456 (M 5), KIDDERMINSTER
A 4123 WOLVERHAMPTON
(M 5) A 38 BROMSGROVE
REDDITCH A4040
A 441 REDDITCH
A 435 ALCESTER
1 km
1/2 mile
PERRY BARR
HANDSWORTH
ASTON
SMETHWICK
ROTTON PARK RESERVOIR
HARBORNE
EDGBASTON
MOSELEY
KING'S HEATH
Hockley Circus
MILLENNIUM POINT
Holyhead Rd
Oxhill Rd
Church Lane
Wellington Road
Aston Lane
Birchfield Road
Aldridge Road
Brookvale Rd
Witton La.
Witton Rd
Aston Expressway
Victoria Rd.
Lichfield
Island Rd
Rookery Rd
Hamstead Rd
Lozells Rd
Villa Rd
Booth St.
Soho Rd
Boulton Rd
Rabone Lane
Rolfe St.
High St
New John St West
Lodge Rd
Winson Green Rd
Heath St.
Cape Hill
Dudley Rd
Spring Hill
Icknield St
Icknield Port Rd
Ladywood Middleway
Rotton Park
City Rd
Portland Rd
Sandon Rd
Bearwood Road
Hagley Rd
Broad St.
Bristol St
Westfield Rd
Norfolk Rd
Lordswood Rd
Court Oak Rd
Harborne Rd
High St
Harborne Park Rd
Harborne Lane
Matchley Lane
Church Rd
Priory Rd
Bristol Road
Pershore Road
Edgbaston Rd
Salisbury Rd
Haden Way
Highgate Rd
Moseley Rd
Wake Green
Alcester Rd
High St.
Addison Rd
Vicarage Rd
Fordhouse Lane
Oak Tree La.
Linden Road
Bristol Road
Canal
Rea
A 4040
A 457
A 4030
A 4540
A 41
A 34
A 38
A 47
A 456
A 441
A 435
B 4124
54
50
20
22
40
36
24
85
15
14
42
55
U
M
P
E
F
V
X

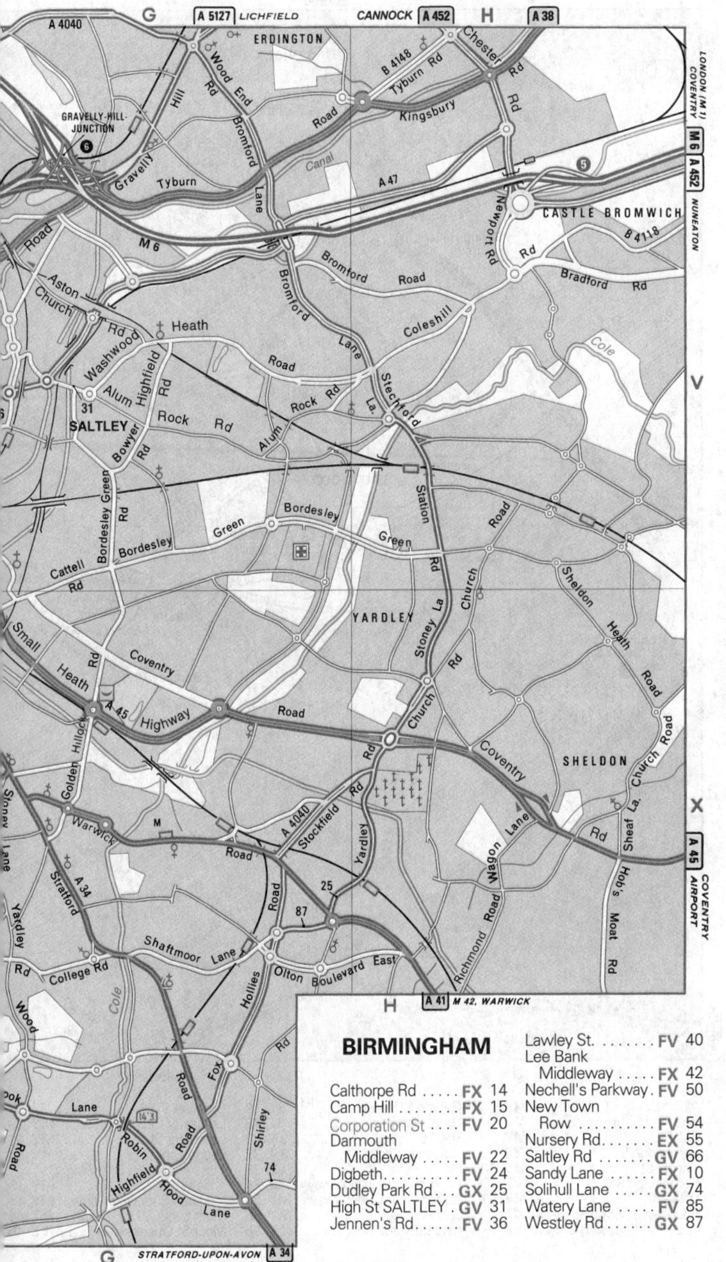

BIRMINGHAM

Calthorpe Rd . . . . . FX 14
Camp Hill . . . . FX 15
Corporation St . . . . FV 20
Darmouth
Middleway . . . . . FV 22
Digbeth. . . . . FV 24
Dudley Park Rd . . . GX 25
High St SALTLEY . GV 31
Jennen's Rd. . . . . . FV 36
Lawley St. . . . . FV 40
Lee Bank
Middleway . . . . . FX 42
Nechell's Parkway . FV 50
New Town
Row . . . . FV 54
Nursery Rd. . . . . . . EX 55
Saltley Rd . . . . GV 66
Sandy Lane . . . . . . FX 10
Solihull Lane . . . . . GX 74
Watery Lane . . . . . FV 85
Westley Rd . . . . . . GX 87

ENGLAND

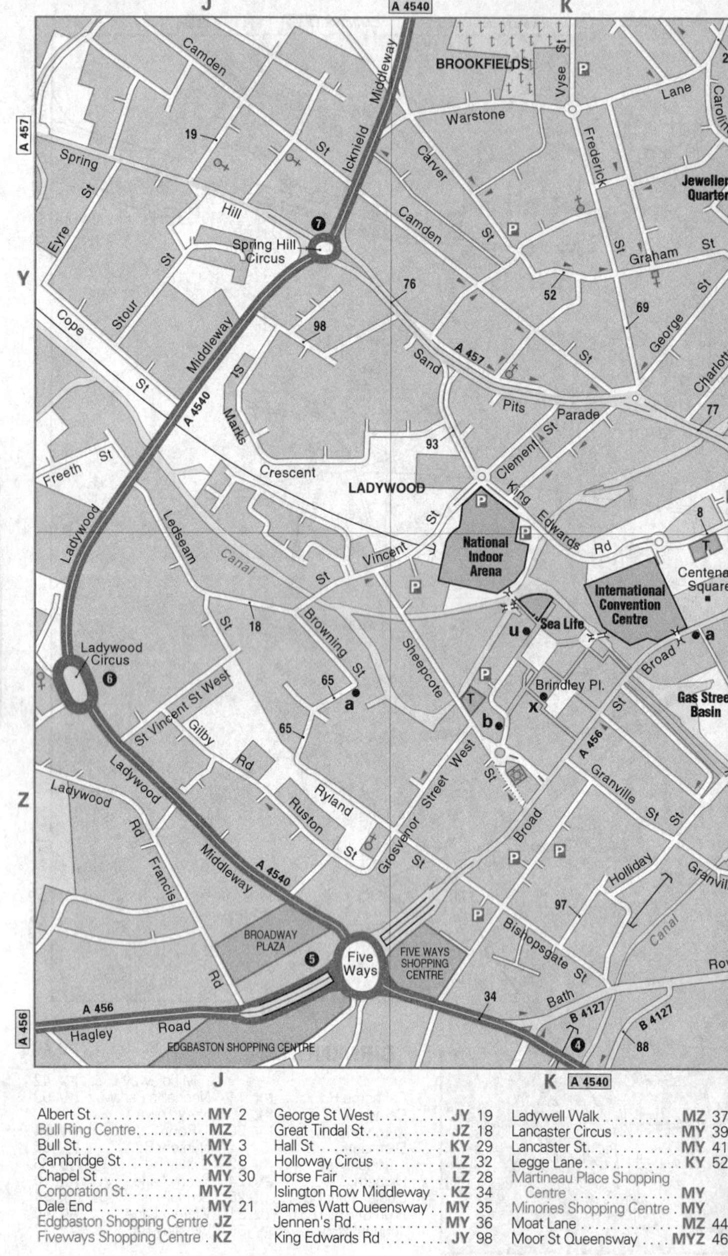

Albert St . . . . **MY** 2
Bull Ring Centre . . . . **MZ**
Bull St . . . . **MY** 3
Cambridge St . . . . **KYZ** 8
Chapel St . . . . **MY** 30
Corporation St . . . . **MYZ**
Dale End . . . . **MY** 21
Edgbaston Shopping Centre **JZ**
Fiveways Shopping Centre . **KZ**

George St West . . . . **JY** 19
Great Tindal St . . . . **JZ** 18
Hall St . . . . **KY** 29
Holloway Circus . . . . **LZ** 32
Horse Fair . . . . **LZ** 28
Islington Row Middleway . . **KZ** 34
James Watt Queensway . . **MY** 35
Jennen's Rd . . . . **MY** 36
King Edwards Rd . . . . **JY** 98

Ladywell Walk . . . . **MZ** 37
Lancaster Circus . . . . **MY** 39
Lancaster St . . . . **MY** 41
Legge Lane . . . . **KY** 52
Martineau Place Shopping Centre . . . . **MY**
Minories Shopping Centre . **MY**
Moat Lane . . . . **MZ** 44
Moor St Queensway . . . . **MYZ** 46

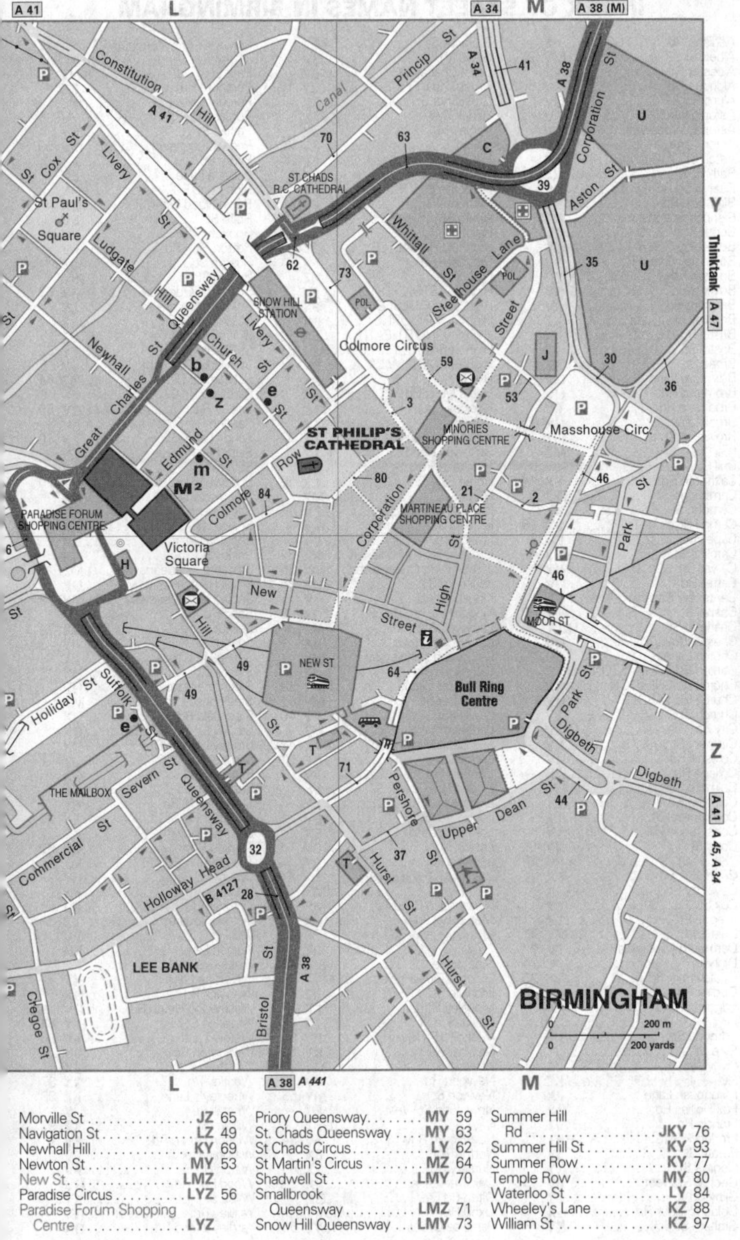
A 41
L
A 34
M
A 38 (M)
Constitution
Hill
A 41
Canal
Princip
St
A 34
41
A 38
Corporation
St
U
C
70
63
39
Aston
St
St Paul's
Square
Cox
St
Livery
St
ST CHADS
R.C. CATHEDRAL
Whittall
St
Ludgate
Hill
Queensway
62
73
Steelhouse
Lane
POL
35
U
SNOW HILL
STATION
POL
Street
Y
Thinktank
A 47
Newhall
St
Church
Livery
St
Colmore Circus
J
30
36
59
b
z
e
St
3
53
Great
Charles
St
ST PHILIP'S
CATHEDRAL
MINORIES
SHOPPING CENTRE
Masshouse Circ.
Edmund
St
m
Row
80
46
M²
Colmore
84
Corporation
21
2
St
PARADISE FORUM
SHOPPING CENTRE
MARTINEAU PLACE
SHOPPING CENTRE
Park
ENGLAND
6
Victoria
Square
St
H
46
New
High
St
MOOR ST
Street
Hill
49
NEW ST
64
Bull Ring
Centre
Park
St
Holliday
St
Suffolk
49
e
St
Digbeth
Z
T
71
Digbeth
THE MAILBOX
Severn
St
Queensway
Pershore
St
44
A 41
A 45, A 34
Commercial
St
32
Upper
Dean
37
T
Hurst
St
Holloway
Head
B 4127
28
LEE BANK
St
A 38
Hurst
St
Bristol
Cregoe
St
BIRMINGHAM
0
200 m
0
200 yards
L
A 38
A 441
M

INDEX OF STREET NAMES IN BIRMINGHAM

Hyatt Regency
2 Bridge St ✉ B1 2JZ – ✆ (0121) 643 1234 – www.birmingham.regency.hyatt.com
315 rm – †£ 209 ††£ 209, ☕ £ 15.75 – 4 suites KZ**a**
Rest *Aria* – Menu £ 15 – Carte £ 27/42
◆ Striking mirrored exterior. Glass enclosed lifts offer panoramic views. Sizeable rooms with floor to ceiling windows. Covered link with International Convention Centre. Contemporary style restaurant in central atrium; modish cooking.

Malmaison
Mailbox, 1 Wharfside St ✉ B1 1RD – ✆ (0121) 246 5000 – www.malmaison.com
184 rm – †£ 170 ††£ 170/350, ☕ £ 13.95 – 1 suite LZ**e**
Rest *Brasserie* – Menu £ 16 (dinner) – Carte £ 26/33
◆ Stylish, modern boutique hotel, forms centrepiece of Mailbox development. Chic bar. Spacious, contemporary bedrooms with every modern facility; superb petit spa. Brasserie serving contemporary French-influenced cooking at reasonable prices.

Hotel Du Vin
25 Church St ✉ B3 2NR – ✆ (0121) 200 0600 – www.hotelduvin.com
66 rm – †£ 160 ††£ 175/205, ☕ £ 14.50 LY**e**
Rest *Bistro* – Carte £ 35/45
◆ Former 19C eye hospital in heart of shopping centre; has relaxed, individual, boutique style. Low lighting in rooms of muted tones: Egyptian cotton and superb bathrooms. Champagne in "bubble lounge"; Parisian style brasserie.

City Inn
1 Brunswick Sq, Brindley Pl ✉ B1 2HW – ✆ (0121) 643 1003 – www.cityinn.com
238 rm ☕ – †£ 79/225 ††£ 89/235 KZ**b**
Rest *City Café* – ✆ (0121) 633 6300 – Menu £ 15/17 **s** – Carte £ 24/31 **s**
◆ In heart of vibrant Brindley Place; the spacious atrium with bright rugs and blond wood sets the tone for equally stylish bedrooms. Corporate friendly with many meeting rooms. Eat in restaurant, terrace or bar.

Simpsons (Andreas Antona) with rm
20 Highfield Rd, Edgbaston ✉ B15 3DU – ✆ (0121) 454 3434
– www.simpsonsrestaurant.co.uk – Closed bank holidays EX**e**
4 rm – †£ 225 ††£ 225
Rest – Contemporary – *(closed Sunday dinner)* Menu £ 30/33 – Carte £ 40/53
Spec. Scallops with chorizo, tomato and squid. Aberdeenshire beef with braised cheek ravioli and toasted peanuts. Turrón parfait with raspberries.
◆ Smart Georgian mansion with stylish lounges, pleasant garden terrace and summer house. Tables are well-spaced; service is formal and efficient. Classical menu displays Mediterranean influences, contemporary twists and excellent produce. Spacious bedrooms boast French country styling.

Purnell's (Glynn Purnell)
55 Cornwall St ✉ B3 2DH – ✆ (0121) 212 9799 – www.purnellsrestaurant.com
– Closed Christmas-New Year, 1 week Easter, 2 weeks summer, Saturday lunch, Sunday and Monday LY**b**
Rest – Modern – Menu £ 25/45
Spec. Salad of crab with apple and smoked paprika honeycomb. Lamb with butterbeans, pigs trotter and cauliflower. Pavlova with raspberry and mint sorbet.
◆ Passionately run, stylish restaurant in sizeable red-brick property with large lounge. Refined and modern cooking displays plenty of original and individual touches. The tasting menus are particularly innovative in style.

Opus
54 Cornwall St ✉ B3 2DE – ✆ (0121) 200 2323 – www.opusrestaurant.co.uk
– Closed 24 December-6 January, Saturday lunch, Sunday and bank holidays LY**z**
Rest – Modern – Menu £ 19 (lunch/early dinner)/28 – Carte £ 33/46
◆ Set in the heart of the financial district; its name means 'hard work'. Floor-to-ceiling windows, cocktail bar and chef's table. Modern menus of precisely prepared, wholesome dishes.

ENGLAND

XXX **Asha's**

12-22 Newhall St ✉ B3 3LX – ✆ (0121) 200 27 67 – www.ashasuk.co.uk – Closed Saturday and Sunday lunch LY**m**

Rest – Indian – Menu £ 13/25 – Carte £ 26/39

◆ Smart restaurant with delightful décor and vivid artwork. Owned by renowned artiste/gourmet Asha Bhosle. Authentic North West Indian cuisine cooked by chefs originally from that region.

XXX **Edmunds**

6 Central Sq, Brindley Pl ✉ B1 2JB – ✆ (0121) 633 4944 – www.edmundsbirmingham.com – Closed 1 week spring, 1 week summer, 1 week autumn, 1 week winter, Saturday lunch, Sunday and bank holidays

Rest – Modern European – Menu £ 19/40 KZ**x**

◆ Formal restaurant in heart of city. Smart interior with neutral décor and modern lighting. Immaculately laid tables boast fine china and glassware. Smart, attentive staff.

XX **Asquiths**

1 Montague Rd ✉ B16 9HN – ✆ (0121) 455 0999 – www.theasquith.com – Closed Christmas-New Year, Easter, 2 weeks summer, Sunday dinner and lunch Monday-Wednesday EX**c**

Rest – French – *(booking essential)* Menu £ 20/35

◆ Two-roomed neighbourhood restaurant in extended red-brick coach house; conservatory overlooks a small garden. Daily changing menu of skilful French cooking; smooth, assured flavours.

XX **Turners** (Richard Turner)

69 High St, Harborne ✉ B17 9NS ✆ (0121) 426 4440 – www.turnersofharborne.com – Closed last week August, Sunday and Monday EX**a**

Rest – Modern *(booking essential) (Saturday dinner tasting menu only)* Menu £ 25/49

Spec. Scallops with peas, broad beans, quails egg and belly pork. Loin of veal with caramelised sweetbreads, white asparagus and truffle sauce. Chocolate tart with salted caramel ice cream and popcorn panna cotta.

◆ Neat neighbourhood restaurant in suburban parade, with wood panels, etched mirrors and velvet chairs. Concise à la carte and tasting menus offer refined, flavoursome dishes of accomplished, classical cooking with modern touches. Formal, structured service.

XX **Loves**

The Glasshouse, Canal Sq ✉ B16 8FL – ✆ (0121) 454 5151 – www.loves-restaurant.co.uk – Closed 2 weeks August, 2 weeks Christmas, Sunday and Monday JZ**a**

Rest – Inventive – Menu £ 25/40

◆ Situated on the ground floor of an apartment block on the canal basin, with spacious, contemporary interior and smartly laid tables. Cooking uses modern techniques and presentation.

XX **Lasan**

3-4 Dakota Buildings, James St, St Pauls Sq ✉ B3 1SD – ✆ (0121) 212 3664 – www.lasangroup.com – Closed 25 December and Saturday lunch

Rest – Indian – Carte £ 30/51 KY**a**

◆ Jewellery quarter restaurant of sophistication and style; good quality ingredients allow the clarity of the spices to shine through in this well-run Indian establishment.

XX **Bank**

4 Brindley Pl ✉ B1 2JB – ✆ (0121) 633 4466 – www.bankrestaurants.com – Closed 1 January and 26 December KZ**u**

Rest – Modern – Menu £ 15 (lunch and early dinner) – Carte £ 20/38

◆ Capacious, modern and busy bar-restaurant where chefs can be watched through a glass wall preparing the tasty modern dishes. Pleasant terrace area.

BISHOP'S STORTFORD – Hertfordshire – 504 U28 – pop. 35 325 **12** B2

London 34 mi – Cambridge 27 mi – Chelmsford 19 mi – Colchester 33 mi

Stansted Airport : ✆ (0844) 3351803, NE : 3.5 m

2 Market Square ✆ (01279) 655831, tic@bishopsstortford.org

Audley End★★ **AC**, N : 11 mi by B 1383

ENGLAND

Cottage without rest

71 Birchanger Ln, Northeast : 2.25 mi by B 1383 on Birchanger rd ✉ CM23 5QA – ☎ (01279) 812 349 – www.thecottagebirchanger.co.uk – Closed Christmas-New Year

14 rm – †£ 45/65 ††£ 70/85

◆ Rurally-set part 17/18C cottages - yet close to airport. Cosy reception rooms with oak panelling and exposed beams. Conservatory style breakfast room and homely bedrooms.

Lemon Tree

14-16 Water Ln ✉ CM23 2LB – ☎ (01279) 757 788 – www.lemontree.co.uk – Closed 25-26 December, Sunday dinner and bank holidays

Rest – Carte £ 28/38

◆ Cosy, vibrant restaurant in centre of town. Light and airy dining rooms, open bar; spacious private dining room on first floor. Wide-ranging menu, locally sourced ingredients.

Host

4 The Corn Exchange, Market Sq ✉ CM23 3UU – ☎ (01279) 657 000 – www.hostrestaurant.co.uk – Closed 26 December, Sunday dinner and bank holiday Mondays

Rest – Menu £ 15 (midweek) – Carte dinner £ 18/39

◆ Grade I listed building with unique roof terrace. Main restaurant has industrial feel, with modern bar and open kitchen. Oft-changing menu incorporates global influences.

at Stansted Mountfitchet **Northeast : 3.5 mi by B 1383 on B 1051 – ✉ Bishop'S Stortford**

Chimneys without rest

44 Lower St, on B 1351 ✉ CM24 8LR – ☎ (01279) 813 388 – www.chimneysguesthouse.co.uk

4 rm – †£ 55/60 ††£ 78

◆ Charming 17C house with friendly hosts, beamed ceilings, snug breakfast room and homely lounge. Comfy bedrooms - single has largest bathroom. Usefully located for airport.

at Great Hallingbury **East : 3 mi by A 1060 and Great Hallingbury rd.**

Great Hallingbury Manor

✉ CM22 7TJ – ☎ (01279) 506 475 – www.greathallingburymanor.com

31 rm – †£ 90/160 ††£ 120/250, £ 14.50

Rest *Anton's* – see restaurant listing

◆ Tudor-style hotel, 5min from Stansted airport. Good-sized, stylish bedrooms with excellent beds and flat screen TVs; most have wet room showers; two have roll-top baths.

Anton's – at Great Hallingbury Manor Hotel

✉ CM22 7TJ – ☎ (01279) 506 475 – www.antonsrestaurant.co.uk

Rest – *(booking advisable)* Menu £ 25 – Carte £ 28/45

◆ Formally laid, modern restaurant behind hotel, with piano, bar and terrace. Classic dishes presented in a modern style, some with a slight Oriental twist. Good breads; hearty puddings.

at Hatfield Heath **Southeast : 6 mi on A 1060 – ✉ Bishop's Stortford**

Down Hall Country House rest,

South : 1.5 mi by Matching Ln ✉ CM22 7AS – ☎ (01279) 731 441 – www.downhall.co.uk

99 rm – †£ 84/165 ††£ 89/235

Rest *Grill Room* – *(closed Saturday lunch)* Menu £ 24 (dinner) – Carte £ 28/38

◆ Stunning 19C mansion with formal gardens, fountain and helipad. Classical guest areas boast ornate plasterwork. Lovely lounge for afternoon tea. Dark wood furnished bedrooms in wing; characterful feature rooms in main house. Modern restaurant with accessible menu.

BISHOPSTONE – Swindon – **503** P29 – see Swindon

ENGLAND

London 228 mi – Leeds 47 mi – Liverpool 39 mi – Manchester 24 mi

50-54 Church St ✆ (01254) 688040, visit@blackburn.gov.uk

Pleasington, ✆ (01254) 202 177

Wilpshire 72 Whalley Rd, ✆ (01254) 248 260

Great Harwood Harwood Bar, Whalley Rd, ✆ (01254) 884 391

The Clog & Billycock

Billinge End Rd, Pleasington , West : 2 mi by A 677 ✉ BB2 6QB – ✆ (01254) 201 163 – www.theclogandbillycock.com – Closed 25 December
Rest – Carte £ 17/26

♦ Spacious, modern, open-plan pub. Extensive menus offer plenty of choice and display a strong Lancastrian slant; cooking is rustic and generous. Most produce is sourced from within 20 miles.

at Langho North : 4.5 mi on A 666 – ✉ Whalley

Northcote (Nigel Haworth) with rm

Northcote Rd, North : 0.5 mi on A 59 at junction with A 666 ✉ BB6 8BE – ✆ (01254) 240 555 – www.northcote.com – Closed 25 December
14 rm – ♦£ 200/215 ♦♦£ 235/260
Rest – Menu £ 25 (lunch) – Carte £ 40/56
Spec. Lobster with new potato salad and lemon caviar. Grouse with leeks, heather jelly and roast potatoes. Valrhona chocolate with smoked nuts and salted sheep's milk ice cream.

♦ Smartly refurbished restaurant in red-brick Victorian house. Traceability and food miles are all-important to this team, with regional ingredients and local suppliers the stars of the show; some produce travelling only a few metres from their own organic gardens. Elegant, contemporary bedrooms boast designer touches.

at Mellor Northwest : 3.25 mi by A 677 – ✉ Blackburn

Stanley House

Southwest : 0.75 mi by A 677 and Further Lane ✉ BB2 7NP – ✆ (01254) 769 200 – www.stanleyhouse.co.uk – Closed 1 week January
12 rm – ♦£ 99/178 ♦♦£ 119/235
Rest *Cassis* – see restaurant listing

♦ 17C manor with superb rural views houses elegantly proportioned rooms defined by wonderfully rich colours. Bar and conference facilities in converted farmhouse.

Millstone

Church Ln. ✉ BB2 7JR – ✆ (01254) 813 333 – www.shirehotels.com
22 rm – ♦£ 74 ♦♦£ 99/125 – 1 suite
Rest – *(bar lunch)* Menu £ 32 – Carte approx. £ 31

♦ Attractive sandstone former coaching inn set in a quiet village. Pub-style bar with log fire and comfy sofas. Cosy, well-kept bedrooms have matching floral patterns and good modern facilities. Traditional wood-panelled dining room offers accessible menu.

Cassis – at Stanley House Hotel

Southwest : 0.75 mi by A 677 and Further Lane ✉ BB2 7NP – ✆ (01254) 769 200 – www.stanleyhouse.co.uk
Rest – *(Closed 1-14 January, Sunday dinner, Monday and Tuesday)*
Menu £ 24/33 – Carte dinner £ 33/47

♦ Independent from main hotel. Name derives from rich blackcurrant theme throughout! Vast raised mezzanine for apéritifs. Weekly evolving menus with vibrant Lancashire accent.

ENGLAND

BLACKPOOL

Street	Grid	No.
Abingdon St	AY	2
Adelaide St	AY	3
Ansdell Rd	BZ	4
Blackpool Old Rd	BY	5
Burlington Rd West	AZ	6
Caunce St	AY	7
Central Drive	BZ	8
Cherry Tree Rd	BZ	9
Church St	AY	
Clifton St	AY	12
Condor Grove	BZ	13
Cookson St	AY	14
Deansgate	AY	15
Garstang Rd West	BY	16
George St	AY	17
Grange Rd	BY	19
Grasmere Rd	BZ	20
Grosvenor St	AY	21
High St	AY	22
Hornby Rd	BY	
Hounds Hill Centre	AY	
King St	AY	23
Lark Hill St	AY	24
New Bonny St	AY	25
North Park Drive	BY	26
Pleasant St	AY	27
Plymouth Rd	BY	28
Poulton Rd	BY	29
Queen's Promenade	BY	
Reads Ave	BZ	32
Rigby Rd	BZ	33
Seaside Way	BZ	34
South King St	AY	35
South Park Drive	BZ	36
Talbot Square	AY	39
Topping St	AY	40
Westcliffe Drive	BY	41

ENGLAND

BLACKPOOL – Blackpool – **502** K22 – pop. 142 283 Great Britain **20** A2

London 246 mi – Leeds 88 mi – Liverpool 56 mi – Manchester 51 mi
Blackpool Airport : ✆ (0844) 4827171, S : 3 mi by A 584
1 Clifton St ✆ (01253) 478222, tic@blackpool.gov.uk
Blackpool Park North Park Drive, ✆ (01253) 397 916
Poulton-le-Fylde Breck Rd, Myrtle Farm, ✆ (01253) 892 444
Tower★ **AC** AY **A**

Plan on preceding page

Number One South Beach
rm,
4 Harrowside West ✉ FY4 1NW – ✆ (01253) 343 900 – www.numberonehotels.com
13 rm – †£ 75/140 ††£ 120/150 – 1 suite BZ**v**
Rest – *(dinner only and Sunday lunch)* Carte £ 23/32
♦ Modernised hotel set back off promenade. Contemporary interior with stylish, boldly coloured bedrooms; two with four-posters. Superb bathrooms boast whirlpool baths and TVs. Interesting menus are largely made up of free range, organic and fair trade produce.

Number One St Lukes without rest
1 St Lukes Rd ✉ FY4 2EL – ✆ (01253) 343 901 – www.numberoneblackpool.com
3 rm – †£ 75/100 ††£ 120/130 AZ**a**
♦ Engagingly run, enticingly stylish guesthouse. The good value nature of the establishment is further enhanced by an elegant breakfast room and luxuriously appointed bedrooms.

ENGLAND

at Thornton Northeast : 5.5 mi by A 584 - BY - on B 5412 – ✉ Blackpool

Twelve
Marsh Mill, Fleetwood Rd North, North : 0.5 mi on A 585 ✉ FY5 4JZ – ✆ (01253) 821 212 – www.twelve-restaurant.co.uk – Closed first 2 weeks January and Monday
Rest – *(dinner only and Sunday lunch)* Menu £ 19/26 – Carte £ 32/42
♦ Spacious restaurant where brick walls, exposed pipework and grey beams contribute to a slightly industrial feel. Passionately run by dynamic owner and friendly team. Good value menus offer interesting, well-executed modern dishes with the odd innovative touch.

BLAKENEY – Norfolk – **504** X25 – pop. 1 628 – ✉ Holt **15** C1

London 127 mi – King's Lynn 37 mi – Norwich 28 mi

Blakeney
The Quay ✉ NR25 7NE – ✆ (01263) 740 797 – www.blakeneyhotel.co.uk
63 rm (dinner included) – †£ 132/217 ††£ 288/314
Rest – Menu £ 28 (dinner) – Carte lunch £ 28/43
♦ Traditional hotel on the quayside with views of estuary and a big sky! Sun lounge a delightful spot for the vista. Bedrooms vary in size and décor, some with private patio. Armchair dining with estuary views.

Blakeney House without rest
High St ✉ NR25 7NX – ✆ (01263) 740 561 – www.blakeneyhouse.com – Closed 4 days at Christmas and 1 week early January
8 rm – †£ 80/95 ††£ 120/150
♦ Substantial Victorian house tucked away in a tranquil spot on the High Street. Spacious, individually decorated, up-to-date bedrooms. Pleasant breakfast room with garden views.

Moorings
High St ✉ NR25 7NA – ✆ (01263) 740 054 – www.blakeney-moorings.co.uk – Closed 2 weeks January, Sunday, Monday dinner except August and bank holidays and midweek November-March
Rest – *(booking essential) (light lunch)* Carte £ 26/34
♦ Bright village bistro near the quayside, offering popular light lunches. Classical dinner menu boasts unfussy, seasonal dishes, including game and local seafood. Tasty puddings.

The White Horse with rm
4 High St ✉ NR25 7AL – ✆ (01263) 740 574 – www.blakeneywhitehorse.co.uk – Closed 25 December
9 rm – †£ 60/90 ††£ 60/140 **Rest** – *(booking advisable)* Carte £ 20/35
◆ Brick and flint former coaching inn set by the harbour. Traditional, hearty pub favourites on lunch menu. Evening à la carte features seasonal dishes and some interesting combinations. Modern bedrooms come in various shapes and sizes.

at Cley next the Sea East : 1.5 mi on A 149 – ✉ Holt

Cley Windmill
The Quay ✉ NR25 7RP – ✆ (01263) 740 209 – www.cleywindmill.co.uk
8 rm – †£ 122/165 ††£ 122/165
Rest – *(dinner only) (booking essential to non residents)* Menu £ 33
◆ Restored 18C redbrick windmill in salt marshes with a viewing gallery: a bird-watcher's paradise. Neatly kept rooms, full of character, in the mill, stable and boatshed. Flagstoned dining room; communal table.

at Wiveton South : 1 mi by A149 on Wiveton Rd

The Wiveton Bell with rm
Blakeney Rd ✉ NR25 7TL – ✆ (01263) 740 101 – www.wivetonbell.com – Closed 25 December
4 rm – †£ 90/120 ††£ 90/120 **Rest** – *(booking essential)* Carte £ 18/30
◆ Characterful pub with colourful garden; surrounded by salt marshes and nature reserves. Comfy, modern bar and airy conservatory. Menus offer traditional British dishes with some international influences. Charming bedrooms come with a tuck-box for breakfast in bed.

at Morston West : 1.5 mi on A 149 – ✉ Holt

Morston Hall (Galton Blackiston)
The Street ✉ NR25 7AA – ✆ (01263) 741 041 – www.morstonhall.com – Closed 1-28 January and 24-26 December
13 rm (dinner included) – †£ 200/250 ††£ 330/340
Rest – *(dinner only and Sunday lunch) (booking essential) (set menu only)* Menu £ 34/56
Spec. Ox tongue on broad bean purée with petit pois and shallot jus. Lobster with cabbage and champagne bisque sauce. Blackcurrant soufflé with clotted cream ice cream.
◆ Attractive country house with manicured gardens and antique-filled guest areas. Annexed bedrooms are largest, most luxurious and display subtle contemporary touches. Formal 4 course daily menu offers well-balanced, local, seasonal dishes. Cooking is classical, sophisticated and exhibits a delicate, modern touch.

BLANDFORD FORUM – Dorset – 503 N31 – pop. 9 854 — 4 C3

London 124 mi – Bournemouth 17 mi – Dorchester 17 mi – Salisbury 24 mi
1 Greyhound Yard ✆ (01258) 454770, blandfordtic@north-dorset.gov.uk
Ashley Wood Wimbourne Rd, ✆ (01258) 452 253
Town★
Kingston Lacy★★ **AC**, SE : 5.5 mi by B 3082 – Royal Signals Museum★, NE : 2 mi by B 3082. Milton Abbas★, SW : 8 mi by A 354 – Sturminster Newton★, NW : 8 mi by A 357

Portman Lodge without rest
Whitecliff Mill St ✉ DT11 7BP – ✆ (01258) 453 727 – www.portmanlodge.co.uk – Closed 24 December-5 January
3 rm – †£ 50 ††£ 70
◆ Red-brick guesthouse boasting many original Victorian features. Guest areas display artefacts from the owners' travels. Plush breakfast room or terrace dining in summer. Classical bedrooms.

at Iwerne Minster North : 6 mi on A 350

The Talbot with rm

Blanford Rd ✉ DT11 8QN – ✆ (01747) 811 269 – www.the-talbot.com

5 rm – †£ 60/75 ††£ 75/105 **Rest** – Carte £ 18/28

◆ Pleasant and unfussy mock-Elizabethan inn. Hearty and generous cooking features British classics at lunch and substantial, regularly-changing dishes in the evening. Rooms are comfortable, well-appointed and up-to-date.

at Farnham Northeast : 7.5 mi by A 354 – ✉ Blandford Forum

Farnham Farm House without rest

North : 1 mi by Shaftesbury rd ✉ DT11 8DG – ✆ (01725) 516 254 – www.farnhamfarmhouse.co.uk – Closed 25-26 December

3 rm – †£ 70 ††£ 90

◆ Attractive farmhouse in peaceful location. Homely, individually furnished bedrooms with country views. Swimming pool and therapy centre on site. Breakfast features local produce; picnics available.

The Museum Inn with rm

✉ DT11 8DE – ✆ (01725) 516 261 – www.museuminn.co.uk – Closed 25 December

8 rm – †£ 110 ††£ 165 **Rest** – *(bookings not accepted)* Carte £ 30/44

◆ Part-thatched 17C country pub, in a picture postcard village. Menu offers British classics with a Mediterranean edge; cooking is seasonal, unfussy and local. Bedrooms range from small and cottagey, to spacious with a four-poster.

at Shapwick Southeast : 7.5 mi by B 3082

The Anchor

West St ✉ DT11 9LB – ✆ (01258) 857 269 – www.anchorshapwick.co.uk – Closed Sunday dinner

Rest – Carte £ 16/35

◆ Traditionally furnished village pub, with flag floors, open fires and friendly staff. Unfussy, modern cooking. Daily changing menus feature game from local estates and plenty of offal.

BLEDINGTON – Oxon. – 503 P28 – see Stow-on-the-Wold

BLOCKLEY – Gloucestershire – 503 O27 – pop. 1 668 – ✉ Moreton-In-Marsh 4 D1

London 91 mi – Birmingham 39 mi – Oxford 34 mi

Lower Brook House

Lower St ✉ GL56 9DS – ✆ (01386) 700 286 – www.lowerbrookhouse.com – Closed Christmas and early January

6 rm – †£ 80/185 ††£ 80/185

Rest – *(closed Sunday) (dinner only)* Carte £ 25/33

◆ Personally run, adjoining 17C Cotswold stone cottages with huge inglenooks, beams and flagged floors. Characterful and stylish from every aspect. Individually appointed rooms. Imaginative evening menus of local Cotswold produce.

BODIAM CASTLE – East Sussex – 504 V30 Great Britain 8 B2

London 58 mi – Cranbrook 7 mi – Hastings 13 mi

Castle★★

Battle Abbey★, S : 10 mi by B 2244, B 2089, A 21 and minor rd – Rye★★, SW : 13 mi by A 268

Curlew

Junction Rd, Northwest : 1.5 mi at junction with B 2244 ✉ TN32 5UY – ✆ (01580) 861 394 – www.thecurlewrestaurant.co.uk – Closed 2 weeks spring, 2 weeks autumn, 25-26 December, Monday and Tuesday

Rest – British – Menu £ 22 (lunch) – Carte £ 28/32

Spec. Duck egg with watercress, bacon and black pudding. Slow-cooked lamb shoulder with artichoke and mint dripping. Cherry batter with cherry blossom and honey ice-cream.

◆ Stylish restaurant with laid-back lounge, cow motif wallpaper and bespoke leather banquettes. Concise British menu offers accomplished, classically based dishes, interpreted in modern ways. Preparation is careful, execution is precise and presentation is appealing.

BODMIN – Cornwall – 503 F32 – pop. 12 778 1 B2

London 270 mi – Newquay 18 mi – Plymouth 32 mi – Truro 23 mi

Shire Hall, Mount Folly ✆ (01208) 76616, bodmintic@visit.org.uk

St Petroc Church★

Bodmin Moor★★ - Lanhydrock★★, S : 3 mi by B 3269 – Blisland★ (Church★), N : 5.5 mi by A 30 and minor roads – Pencarrow★, NW : 4 mi by A 389 and minor roads – Cardinham (Church★), NE : 4 mi by A 30 and minor rd – St Mabyn (Church★), N : 5.5 mi by A 389, B 3266 and minor rd. St Tudy★, N : 7 mi by A 389, B 3266 and minor rd

Trehellas House

Washaway, Northwest: 3 mi on A 389 ✉ PL30 3AD – ✆ (01208) 72 700 – www.trehellashouse.co.uk

12 rm – ♦£ 50/68 ♦♦£ 65/160

Rest – *(closed Monday lunch)* Menu £ 15 (lunch) – Carte £ 28/40

♦ Relaxed, personally run country house with keen owners. Bedrooms divided between main house and converted stable. Cosy and cottagey feel without being chintzy. Traditional cooking; venison a speciality.

Bokiddick Farm without rest

Lanivet, South : 5 mi by A 30 following signs for Lanhydrock and Bokiddick ✉ PL30 5HP – ✆ (01208) 831 481 – www.bokiddickfarm.co.uk – Closed Christmas and New Year

5 rm – ♦£ 45/50 ♦♦£ 72/76

♦ Sizeable house on dairy farm: do take a quick tour. Warm welcome assured. Neat, well priced rooms with added amenities in old house; smart stable conversion for more rooms.

BOLNHURST – Bedfordshire 12 A1

London 64 mi – Bedford 8 mi – St Neots 7 mi

The Plough at Bolnhurst

Kimbolton Rd, South : 0.5 mi on B 660 ✉ MK44 2EX – ✆ (01234) 376 274 – www.bolnhurst.com – Closed 2 weeks January, Sunday dinner and Monday

Rest – Menu £ 18 (weekday lunch) – Carte £ 24/38

♦ Smart, cosy whitewashed pub with rustic bar, modern restaurant, lovely garden and bustling atmosphere. Menus change with the seasons but always feature a 28-day aged Aberdeenshire steak selection, strong Mediterranean influences and good old fashioned puddings.

BOLTON ABBEY – North Yorkshire – 502 O22 – pop. 117 22 B2

– ✉ **Skipton** Great Britain

London 216 mi – Harrogate 18 mi – Leeds 23 mi – Skipton 6 mi

Bolton Priory★ **AC**

Devonshire Arms Country House

✉ BD23 6AJ – ✆ (01756) 710 441 – www.devonshirehotels.co.uk

38 rm – ♦£ 159 ♦♦£ 238 – 2 suites

Rest *Burlington and Brasserie* – see restaurant listing

♦ Fine period coaching inn, with antique-furnished guest areas and vast art collection. Compact bedrooms in extension, recently refurbished in bright, contemporary country house style. Refurbishment to continue in main house. Good spa and leisure. Smooth service.

Burlington – at Devonshire Arms Country House Hotel

✉ BD23 6AJ – ✆ (01756) 710 441 – www.devonshirehotels.co.uk

Rest – *(closed 3-11 January, Tuesday October-March and Monday) (dinner only and Sunday lunch) (booking essential)* Menu £ 65

Spec. Scallops with celeriac and smoked eel. Lamb with broccoli purée, olive gnocchi and goat's cheese. Caramelised apple pie mousse with apple sorbet and filo.

♦ Elegant, antique-filled dining room with polished tables and oil paintings. Structured, formal service. Ambitious, creative cooking captures modern trends; elaborate dishes are artistically presented, displaying the chef's obvious passion.

ENGLAND

XX **Brasserie** – at Devonshire Arms Country House Hotel

✉ *BD23 6AJ* – *✆ (01756) 710 710*
– *www.devonshirehotels.co.uk*
Rest – Carte £ 22/29

♦ A contrast to the restaurant in atmosphere and design. This is a modern, vividly decorated brasserie; the kitchen produces carefully prepared, satisfying brasserie favourites.

BOLTON-BY-BOWLAND – Lancashire – 502 M/N22 Great Britain 20 B2

London 246 mi – Blackburn 17 mi – Skipton 15 mi

Skipton - Castle★, E : 12 mi by A 59 – Bolton Priory★, E : 17 mi by A 59

Middle Flass Lodge

Settle Rd, North : 2.5 mi by Clitheroe rd on Settle rd ✉ *BB7 4NY* – *✆ (01200) 447 259* – *www.middleflasslodge.co.uk*
7 rm – †£ 45/50 ††£ 62/75
Rest – Menu £ 30

♦ Friendly, welcoming owners in a delightfully located barn conversion. Plenty of beams add to rustic effect. Pleasantly decorated, comfy rooms with countryside outlook. Blackboard's eclectic menu boasts local, seasonal backbone.

BONCHURCH – Isle of Wight – 504 P32 – see Wight (Isle of)

BORDON – Hampshire 504 R 30

London 54 mi – Croydon 57 mi – Barnet 67 mi – Ealing 49 mi

Groomes

Frith End, North : 2.75 mi by A 325 on Frith End Sand Pit rd ✉ *GU35 0QR* – *✆ (01420) 489 858* – *www.groomes.co.uk*
7 rm – †£ 90 ††£ 144
Rest – Carte £ 21/33

♦ Former farmhouse set in 185 acres, with lawned gardens and wood-furnished terrace. Good-sized bedrooms boast modern facilities; some have free-standing roll-top baths. Two tables of six for communal dining; set menus of home-cooked dishes make use of local produce.

BOREHAM – Essex – 504 V27 – see Chelmsford

BOROUGHBRIDGE – North Yorkshire – 502 P21 – pop. 3 311 22 B2

London 215 mi – Leeds 19 mi – Middlesbrough 36 mi – York 16 mi

2 Fishergate ✆ (01423) 323 373

XX **thediningroom**

20 St James's Sq ✉ *YO51 9AR* – *✆ (01423) 326 426* – *www.thediningroomonline.co.uk* – *Closed first week January, 26 December, Sunday dinner and Monday*
Rest – *(dinner only and Sunday lunch) (booking essential)* Menu £ 29 – Carte £ 30/34

♦ Characterful, bow-fronted cottage with courtyard terrace. Modern lounge-bar and intimate beamed restaurant. Set price menu offers hearty, boldly flavoured, Mediterranean-influenced dishes.

at Roecliffe West : 1 mi

The Crown Inn with rm

✉ *YO51 9LY* – *✆ (01423) 322 300* – *www.crowninnroecliffe.com* – *Closed Sunday dinner*
4 rm – †£ 100 ††£ 130
Rest – Menu £ 20 (dinner) – Carte £ 19/26

♦ Smart 16C inn with stylish country interior, set by a delightful village green. Good-sized menus offer a nice balance of meat and fish, and a dedicated 'meat free' selection. Well-chosen wine list. Smart bedrooms with antique-style furnishings and feature beds.

BOSCASTLE - Cornwall - 503 F31 1 B2

London 260 mi – Bude 14 mi – Exeter 59 mi – Plymouth 43 mi

Village★

Poundstock Church★ – Tintagel Old Post Office★

Boscastle House without rest

Tintagel Rd, South : 0.75 mi on B 3263 ✉ PL35 OAS – ✆ (01840) 250 654 – www.boscastlehouse.com

6 rm – ££ 120

• Modern styling in a detached Victorian house. Bedrooms are light and spacious, with roll-top baths and walk-in showers. Hearty breakfasts, cream teas and a calm, relaxing air.

Trerosewill Farm without rest

Paradise, South : 1 mi off B 3263 ✉ PL35 0BL – ✆ (01840) 250 545 – www.trerosewill.co.uk – March-November

9 rm – £ 40/60 £ 70/105

• Modern guesthouse on 50 acre working farm, affording fine views of the coast and close to good clifftop walks. Conservatory breakfast room. Bedrooms in matching patterns, some with jacuzzis.

Old Rectory without rest

St Juliot, Northeast : 2.5 mi by B 3263 ✉ PL35 0BT – ✆ (01840) 250 225 – www.stjuliot.com – Mid-February-mid-November

4 rm – £ 50/70 £ 92/99

• Communal breakfast room; much of the produce used comes from the Victorian walled garden. Characterful bedrooms; one in the converted stables. Thomas Hardy once stayed here.

Guesthouses don't provide the same level of service as hotels. They are often characterised by a warm welcome and a décor which reflects the owner's personality. Those shown in red are particularly pleasant.

BOSHAM - W. Sussex - 504 R31 - see Chichester

BOSTON SPA - West Yorkshire - 502 P22 - pop. 5 952 22 B2

London 127 mi – Harrogate 12 mi – Leeds 12 mi – York 16 mi

Four Gables without rest

Oaks Lane, West : 0.25 mi by A 659 ✉ LS23 6DS – ✆ (01937) 845 592 – www.fourgables.co.uk – Closed January and Christmas

4 rm – £ 60 £ 73/88

• Down a quiet private road, a Grade II listed Arts and Crafts house with period fireplaces, stripped oak and terracotta tile floors. Traditional, individually decorated rooms. Manicured garden.

BOUGHTON MONCHELSEA - Kent - pop. 2 863 8 B2

London 46 mi – Southend-on-Sea 60 mi – Basildon 48 mi – Maidstone 4 mi

The Mulberry Tree

Hermitage Lane, South : 1.5 mi by Park Lane and East Hall Hill ✉ ME17 4DA – ✆ (01622) 749 082 – www.themulberrytreekent.co.uk – Closed Sunday dinner and Monday

Rest – Menu £ 16 (lunch and weekday dinner) – Carte £ 26/33

• Remotely situated, stylishly decorated, family-owned restaurant with enclosed garden. Daily-changing menus offer modern, tasty dishes, homemade, using the best local produce.

BOURNE END - Hertfordshire - See Bedford

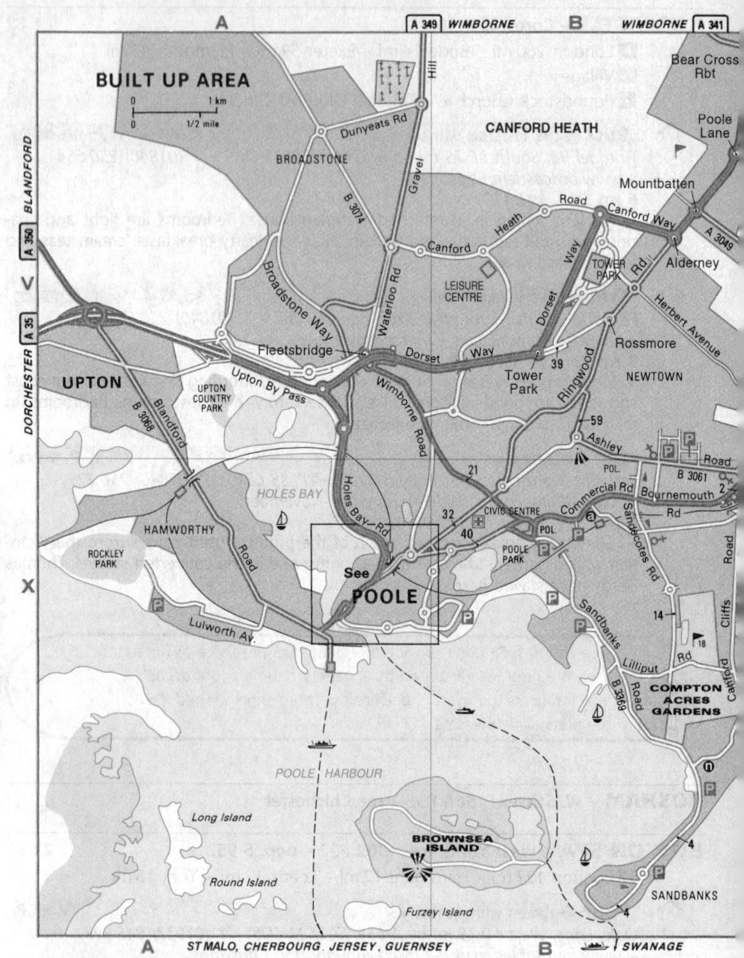

BOURNEMOUTH AND POOLE

Archway Rd . . . . **BX** 2
Banks Rd . . . . **BX** 4
Boscombe Overcliff Rd . . . . **EX** 6
Boscombe Spa Rd . . . . **DX** 7
Branksome Wood Rd . . . . . **CY** 9
Chessel Ave . . . . **EX** 10
Clarendon Rd . . . . **CX** 12
Commercial Rd . . . . **CY** 13
Compton Ave . . . . **BX** 14
Cranleigh Rd . . . . **EV** 16
Durley Rd . . . . **CZ** 17
Ensbury Park Rd . . . . **CV** 19
Exeter Rd . . . . **CDZ** 20
Fernside Rd . . . . **ABX** 21
Fir Vale Rd . . . . **DY** 23
Gervis Pl . . . . **DY** 24
Gloucester Rd . . . . **EV** 26
Hampshire Centre . . . . **DV**
Hinton Rd . . . . **DZ** 27
Lansdowne Rd . . . . **DY** 30
Lansdowne (The) . . . . **DY** 28
Leven Ave . . . . **CX** 31
Longfleet Rd . . . . **BX** 32
Madeira Rd . . . . **DY** 34
Manor Rd . . . . **EY** 35
Meyrick Rd . . . . **EYZ** 36
Old Christchurch Rd . . . . . . **DY**
Old Wareham Rd . . . . **BV** 39
Parkstone Rd . . . . **BX** 40
Pinecliff Rd . . . . **CX** 42
Post Office Rd . . . . **CY** 43
Priory Rd . . . . **CZ** 45
Queen's Rd . . . . **CX** 46
Richmond Hill . . . . **CY** 47
Richmond Park Rd . . . . **DV** 48
Russell Cotes Rd . . . . **DZ** 49
St Michael's Rd . . . . **CZ** 51
St Paul's Rd . . . . **EY** 52
St Peter's Rd . . . . **DY** 53
St Stephen's Rd . . . . **CY** 55
St Swithuns Rd South . . . . . **EY** 56
Seabourne Rd . . . . **EV** 57
Seamoor Rd . . . . **CX** 58
Sea View Rd . . . . **BV** 59
Southbourne Grove . . . . . . **EX** 61
Southbourne Overcliff Drive . . **EX** 62
Sovereign Shopping Centre . **EX**
Square (The) . . . . **CY** 63
Suffolk Rd . . . . **CY** 64
Surrey Rd . . . . **CX** 66
Triangle (The) . . . . **CY** 67
Upper Hinton Rd . . . . **DZ** 68
Wessex Way . . . . **CX** 70
Western Rd . . . . **CX** 73
Westover Rd . . . . **DZ** 75
West Cliff Promenade . . . . . **CZ** 71

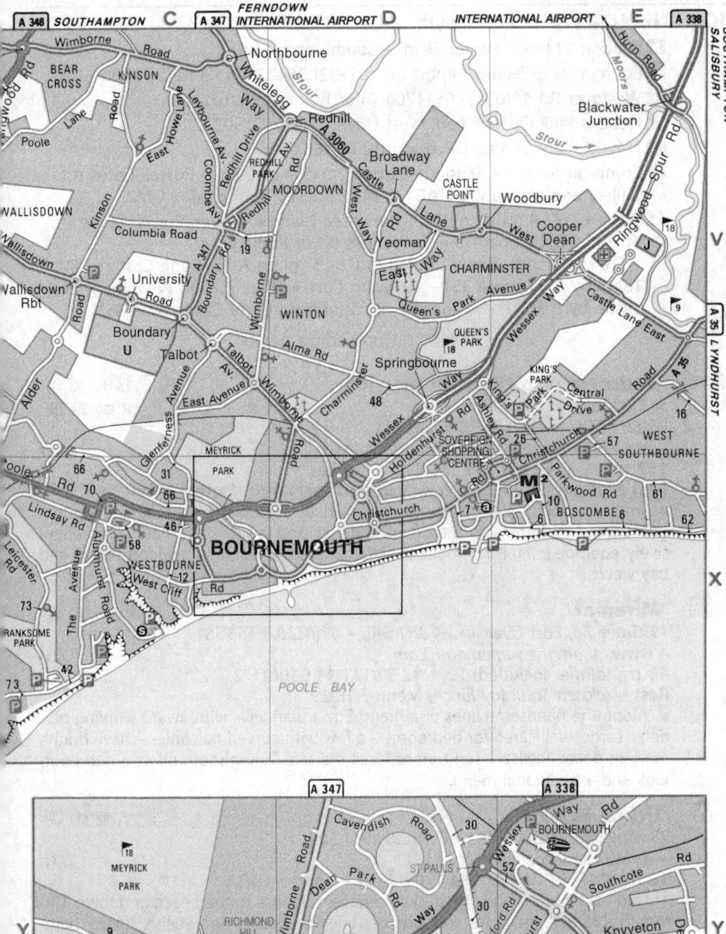

A 348 SOUTHAMPTON C A 347 FERNDOWN INTERNATIONAL AIRPORT D INTERNATIONAL AIRPORT E A 338

SOUTHAMPTON SALISBURY

Wimborne Road
BEAR CROSS
KINSON
Northbourne
Whitelegg Way
Stour
Redhill
A 3060
Blackwater Junction
Stour
Poole Lane
Road
East Howe Lane
Leybourne Av.
Redhill Drive
REDHILL PARK
Broadway Lane
Castle
Spur Rd
WALLISDOWN
Kinson
Coombe Av.
MOORDOWN
West Way
CASTLE POINT
Woodbury
Ringwood
Yeoman
Cooper Dean
Columbia Road
19
Lane
West
Wallisdown
A 347
Boundary Rd
Wimborne
East Way
CHARMINSTER
V
Wallisdown Rbt
University
Road
Avenue
Queen's Park
Wessex Way
Castle Lane East
Boundary
U
Talbot
WINTON
QUEEN'S PARK
18
A 35 LYNDHURST
Talbot Av.
Alma Rd
Springbourne
KING'S PARK
Alder
Glenferness Avenue
East Avenue
Wimborne Road
Charminster
48
Way
King's Park
Central Drive
Road
A 35
16
MEYRICK
Wessex
Holdenhurst Rd
Ashley Rd
SOVEREIGN SHOPPING CENTRE
26
Christchurch
57
WEST SOUTHBOURNE
Poole Rd
66
70
MEYRICK PARK
31
66
Rd
M²
Parkwood Rd
61
Lindsay Rd
58
46
Christchurch
7
10
BOSCOMBE
6
62
Leicester Rd
The Avenue
Alumhurst Road
WESTBOURNE
12
West Cliff
BOURNEMOUTH
Rd
X
73
BRANKSOME PARK
42
73
POOLE BAY

ENGLAND

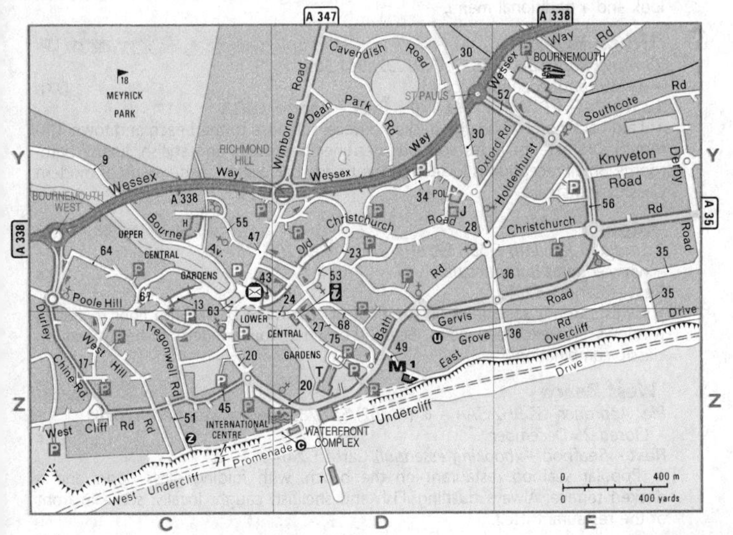

BOURNEMOUTH – Bournemouth – 503 O31 – pop. 167 527 4 D3

London 114 mi – Bristol 76 mi – Southampton 34 mi

Bournemouth (Hurn) Airport : (01202) 364000, N : 5 mi by Hurn - DV

Westover Rd (0845) 0511700, info@bournemouth.gov.uk

Queens Park Queens Park West Drive, (01202) 302 611

Meyrick Park Central Drive, (01202) 786 000

Compton Acres★★ (English Garden ≤★★★) **AC** AX – Russell-Cotes Art Gallery and Museum★★ **AC** DZ **M1** - Shelley Rooms **AC** EX **M2**

Poole★, W : 4 mi by A 338 – Brownsea Island★ (Baden-Powell Stone ≤★★) **AC**, by boat from Sandbanks BX or Poole Quay – Christchurch★ (Priory Church★) E : 4.5 mi on A 35. Corfe Castle★, SW : 18 mi by A 35 and A 351 – Lulworth Cove★ (Blue Pool★) W : 8 mi of Corfe Castle by B 3070 – Swanage★, E : 5 mi from Corfe Castle by A 351

Plans on preceding pages

Bournemouth Highcliff Marriott

St Michael's Rd, West Cliff rm,
BH2 5DU – (01202) 557 702
– www.bournenmouthhighcliffmarriott.co.uk CZ**z**

157 rm – £ 150 £ 150/170 – 3 suites

Rest *Highcliff Grill* – *(dinner only and Sunday lunch)* Carte £ 28/44

◆ Imposing white clifftop landmark, linked by funicular to the beach. Modern guest areas. Bedrooms, in the grand tradition, and leisure centre are comprehensively equipped. Informal, modern restaurant with steak and seafood menu, and bay views.

Miramar

19 Grove Rd, East Overcliff BH1 3AL – (01202) 556 581
– www.miramar-bournemouth.com DZ**u**

43 rm (dinner included) – £ 50/111 £ 100/172

Rest – *(closed Saturday lunch)* Menu £ 18/29

◆ Along the handsome lines of a grand Edwardian villa, with award winning gardens. Large, well-cared for bedrooms – a few with curved balconies – have bright, modern décor. Pleasant sun terrace faces the sea. Dining room offers a good outlook and a traditional menu.

Urban Beach

23 Argyll Rd BH5 1EB – (01202) 301 509
– www.urbanbeachhotel.co.uk DX**a**

12 rm – £ 70/170 £ 170 **Rest** – Carte £ 18/33

◆ Laid-back hotel with large decked terrace, set close to the beach and town. Unremarkable exterior hides spacious designer bedrooms and stylish, luxury bathrooms. Small reception is located in the trendy bar/bistro. Large menu of modern classics and steaks.

Edge

2 Studland Rd., (4th Floor) BH4 8JA – (01202) 757 007
– www.edgerestaurant.co.uk CX**s**

Rest – Carte £ 32/46

◆ Stylish, trendy restaurant on top floor of apartment block, with floor to ceiling windows and excellent views. Seafood-based menu; modern dishes styled on classic combinations.

West Beach

Pier Approach BH2 5AA – (01202) 587 785 – www.west-beach.co.uk
– Closed 25 December DZ**c**

Rest – Seafood – *(booking essential)* Carte £ 24/40

◆ Popular seafood restaurant on the beach, with folding glass doors and a decked terrace. Always bustling. Fish and shellfish caught locally; some in front of the restaurant itself.

BOURTON-ON-THE-HILL – Glos. – see Moreton-in-Marsh

BOURTON-ON-THE-WATER – Gloucestershire – 503 O28 – pop. 3 093 Great Britain 4 D1

London 91 mi – Birmingham 47 mi – Gloucester 24 mi – Oxford 36 mi

Town★

Northleach (Church of SS. Peter and Paul★, Wool Merchants' Brasses★), SW : 5 mi by A 429

Dial House

The Chestnuts, High St ✉ *GL54 2AN* – ✆ *(01451) 822 244 – www.dialhousehotel.com*

15 rm – †£ 120/150 ††£ 195/240

Rest – *(booking essential for non-residents)* Carte £ 33/39

♦ House of Cotswold stone - the oldest in the village - with lovely lawned gardens and drawing room. Bedrooms mix of the contemporary and the floral; those in extension are smaller. Refined cooking makes good use of local ingredients.

Coombe House without rest

Rissington Rd ✉ *GL54 2DT* – ✆ *(01451) 821 966 – www.coombehouse.net – restricted opening October-March*

5 rm – †£ 50/60 ††£ 70/90

♦ Creeper-clad 1920s house on the quiet outskirts of the village, near the local bird sanctuary. Homely lounge and spotless, comfortable, cottage style bedrooms in soft chintz.

at Lower Slaughter Northwest : 1.75 mi by A 429 – ✉ Cheltenham

Lower Slaughter Manor

✉ *GL54 2HP* – ✆ *(01451) 820 456 – www.lowerslaughter.co.uk*

19 rm – †£ 230/850 ††£ 310/850 **Rest** – Menu £ 26/55 – Carte £ 42/60

♦ Beautiful listed part 17C manor in warm Cotswold stone with lovely garden. Open fires and period detail throughout; furnishings and fabrics rich yet contemporary. Smart, boldly coloured bedrooms. Elegant dining room with French-influenced menu.

Washbourne Court

✉ *GL54 2HS* – ✆ *(01451) 822 143 – www.washbournecourt.co.uk*

26 rm – †£ 135/225 ††£ 135/235 – 4 suites

Rest – *(bar lunch Monday-Saturday)* Menu £ 45 (dinner)

♦ Stone-built former manor house with pleasant cottage annexes. Stylish interior boasts marble floored reception, contemporary bedrooms, comfy lounges and low-beamed bar with terrace. Local produce a feature in the dark wood-furnished dining room.

at Upper Slaughter Northwest : 2.5 mi by A 429 – ✉ Bourton-On-The-Water

Lords of the Manor

✉ *GL54 2JD* – ✆ *(01451) 820 243 – www.lordsofthemanor.com*

24 rm – †£ 195 ††£ 310/570 – 2 suites

Rest – *(dinner only and Sunday lunch)* Menu £ 59

Spec. Terrine of foie gras and smoked eel with pain d'épices. Rib of beef with smoked tongue, leeks and pommes Anna. Chocolate tart with passion fruit sorbet and chocolate ganache.

♦ Charming and attractive 17C former rectory set in pretty Cotswold village, with neat and mature gardens. Comfortable sitting rooms and subtly contemporary bedrooms. Formal dining room where the classically based cooking is given a modern twist.

BOVEY TRACEY – Devon – 503 I32 – pop. 4 514 – ✉ Newton Abbot 2 C2

London 214 mi – Exeter 14 mi – Plymouth 32 mi

18 Stover Bovey Rd, Newton Abbot, ✆ (01626) 352 460

St Peter, St Paul and St Thomas of Canterbury Church★

Dartmoor National Park★★

ENGLAND

Brookfield House without rest 

Challabrook Ln., Southwest : 0.75 mi by Brimley rd ✉ TQ13 9DF – ☎ (01626) 836 181 – www.brookfield-house.com – February-November

3 rm – †£ 51/55 ††£ 72/80

◆ Well-kept early Edwardian house in two acres of attractive gardens, and surrounded by Dartmoor. Simple, classic styling; the three large, immaculately appointed bedrooms are named after flowers and Iris, which gets all-day sunlight, is the most popular.

BOWNESS-ON-WINDERMERE – Cumbria – 502 L20 – see Windermere

BOX – Bath & North East Somerset – 503 N29 – see Bath

BRADFIELD – Essex – see Mistley

BRADFORD-ON-AVON – Wiltshire – 503 N29 – pop. 9 072 **4** C2

London 118 mi – Bristol 24 mi – Salisbury 35 mi – Swindon 33 mi

50 St Margarets St ☎ (01225) 865797, tic@bradfordonavon.co.uk

Town★★ - Saxon Church of St Lawrence★★ - Tithe Barn★ – Bridge★

Great Chalfield Manor★ (All Saints★) **AC**, NE : 3 mi by B 3109 – Westwood Manor★ **AC**, S : 1.5 mi by B 3109 – Top Rank Tory (≤★). Bath★★★, NW : 7.5 mi by A 363 and A 4 – Corsham Court★★ **AC**, NE : 6.5 mi by B 3109 and A 4

Woolley Grange

Woolley Green, Northeast : 0.75 mi by B 3107 on Woolley St ✉ BA15 1TX – ☎ (01225) 864 705 – www.woolleygrangehotel.co.uk

19 rm – †£ 90/195 ††£ 295/315 – 7 suites

Rest – Menu £ 20/40 – Carte £ 20/28

◆ Modern art, period furniture: innumerable charming details spread through the rooms of a beautiful Jacobean manor. This is a hotel very much geared to families. Classic British cooking in restaurant, conservatory or terrace.

Bradford Old Windmill

4 Masons Lane, on A 363 ✉ BA15 1QN – ☎ (01225) 866 842 – www.bradfordoldwindmill.co.uk – March-November

3 rm – †£ 79/99 ††£ 99/120 **Rest** – Menu £ 25

◆ 1807 windmill in redressed local stone; Gothic windows and restored bridge. Rooms and circular lounge, stacked with books and curios, share a homely, unaffected quirkiness. Flavourful vegetarian menus.

at Holt East : 2 mi on B 3107 – ✉ Bradford-On-Avon

The Tollgate Inn with rm

Ham Grn ✉ BA14 6PX – ☎ (01225) 782 326 – www.tollgateholt.co.uk – Closed 25 December, 1 January, Sunday dinner and Monday

4 rm – †£ 50/100 ††£ 80/100

Rest – *(booking essential)* Menu £ 15/20 – Carte £ 20/30

◆ 16C pub featuring a cosy, fire-lit bar, two traditional dining rooms and a delightful terrace and garden. Daily changing menu focuses on local produce, with light bites at lunch and more robust dishes at dinner. Comfortable, thoughtfully appointed bedrooms.

BRADWELL – 504 O24 – pop. 1 728 – ✉ Derbyshire **16** A1

London 170 mi – Birmingham 99 mi – Liverpool 66 mi – Leeds 48 mi

Samuel Fox with rm

Stretfield Rd ✉ S33 9JT – ☎ (01433) 621 562 – www.samuelfox.co.uk

4 rm – †£ 75 ††£ 115 **Rest** – Menu £ 15 – Carte £ 19/29

◆ Smart, stone-built inn with the fresh, light feel of a French bistro. Set price lunch menu and evening à la carte offer simple, flavourful dishes, with game in the winter and fish specials in the summer. Efficient, cheery service. Comfortable modern bedrooms.

ENGLAND

BRAITHWAITE – Cumbria – **502** K20 – see Keswick

BRAMFIELD – Suffolk – **504** Y27 – pop. 1 778 – ✉ Ipswich **15** D2

London 215 mi – Ipswich 27 mi – Norwich 28 mi

Queen's Head

The Street ✉ IP19 9HT – ✆ (01986) 784 214 – www.queensheadbramfield.co.uk

Rest – Carte £ 19/26

♦ Characterful, personally run, cream-washed pub set in the heart of a small village. Local, seasonal produce informs the classical daily menu; organic ingredients are used where possible.

BRAMPTON – Cumbria – **501** L19 – pop. 3 965 Great Britain **21** B1

London 317 mi – Carlisle 9 mi – Newcastle upon Tyne 49 mi

Moot Hall, Market Pl ✆ (016977) 3433

Talkin Tarn, ✆ (016977) 2255

Hadrian's Wall★★, NW : by A 6077

Farlam Hall

Southeast : 2.75 mi on A 689 ✉ CA8 2NG – ✆ (016977) 46 234 – www.farlamhall.co.uk – Closed 3-13 January and 24-30 December

12 rm (dinner included) – £ 185 £ 356

Rest – *(dinner only) (booking essential for non-residents)* Menu £ 45

♦ Long-standing, family-owned Victorian country house. Comfortable guest areas overlook ornamental gardens and lake. Traditionally decorated bedrooms boast Bose radios and flat screen TVs. Fine, formal dining in sumptuous restaurant. Attentive, pristine service.

BRANCASTER STAITHE – Norfolk **15** C1

London 131 mi – King's Lynn 25 mi – Boston 57 mi – East Dereham 27 mi

White Horse with rm

✉ PE31 8BY – ✆ (01485) 210 262 – www.whitehorsebrancaster.co.uk

15 rm – £ 75/95 £ 90/130

Rest – *(booking essential)* Carte £ 19/31

♦ Elevated position affords beautiful coastal views from rear conservatory and terrace, while landscaped front terrace boasts parasols, heaters and lights. Varied menu with local seafood. Up-to-date, comfortable bedrooms.

Jolly Sailors

✉ PE31 8BJ – ✆ (01485) 210 314 – www.jollysailorsbrancaster.co.uk

Rest – Carte £ 14/25

♦ Characterful, rustic pub with welcoming open fire. Simple menu ranges from light bites such as a ploughman's, to freshly made pizzas and pub classics; all followed by tasty nursery puddings.

BRANSCOMBE – Devon – **503** K31 – pop. 501 – ✉ Seaton **2** D2

London 167 mi – Exeter 20 mi – Lyme Regis 11 mi

Village★

Seaton (★★), NW : 3 m – Colyton★

Masons Arms with rm

✉ EX12 3DJ – ✆ (01297) 680 300 – www.masonsarms.co.uk

21 rm – £ 56/80 £ 122/175

Rest – Menu £ 30 (dinner) – Carte £ 21/31

♦ Immensely charming 14C inn set in a picturesque village. Much of the produce is locally sourced, with crab landed on the nearby beach and local meats roasted on the spit over the fire. Individually styled bedrooms boast beams and antiques.

BRAY – Windsor and Maidenhead – **504** R29 – pop. 8 121 – ✉ Maidenhead **11** C3

London 34 mi – Reading 13 mi

Plan : see Maidenhead

XXXX **Waterside Inn** (Alain Roux) with rm

✿✿✿ *Ferry Rd. ✉ SL6 2AT – ✆ (01628) 620 691 – www.waterside-inn.co.uk – Closed 26 December-3 February* Xs

8 rm ☕ – 🚹£ 190/290 🚹🚹£ 190/290 – 3 suites

Rest – French – *(closed Tuesday except dinner June-August and Monday) (booking essential)* Menu £ 57/140 – Carte £ 111/146

Spec. Tronçonnettes de homard poêlées minute au Porto blanc. Filets de lapereau grillés, sauce à l'armagnac et aux marrons glacés. Péché Gourmand selon "Alain" et "Michel".

◆ Few restaurants can match this glorious setting on the Thames, with the terrace an enchanting spot for an aperitif. Enjoy classic French cuisine, prepared with great care, in elegant surroundings. Service is charming and expertly organised. Luxurious bedrooms are spacious and chic.

XXX **Fat Duck** (Heston Blumenthal)

✿✿✿ *High St ✉ SL6 2AQ – ✆ (01628) 580 333 – www.fatduck.co.uk – Closed 17 December-10 January, Sunday dinner and Monday* Xe

Rest – *(booking essential 2 months in advance) (set menu only)* Menu £ 160

Spec. Jelly of quail with crayfish cream, chicken liver parfait, truffle toast. Salmon poached in liquorice, artichoke, vanilla mayonnaise and golden trout roe. Black Forest gâteau with kirsch ice cream.

◆ Low-beamed, converted pub where history and science combine in an exciting, innovative alchemy of contrasting flavours and textures. It's very stimulating and involving; the attentive team are on hand to guide you through the experience.

XX **Caldesi in Campagna**

Old Mill Ln ✉ SL6 2BG – ✆ (01628) 788 500 – www.caldesi.com – Closed 25 December, 1 January, Sunday dinner, Monday and bank holidays

Rest – Italian – Menu £ 23 (lunch) – Carte £ 31/53 Xx

◆ Welcoming former pub with smart interior, conservatory and decked garden with wood fired oven. Flavoursome Italian cooking displays Ligurian, Tuscan and Sicilian influences.

The Hinds Head

High St ✉ SL6 2AB – ✆ (01628) 626 151 – www.hindsheadhotel.co.uk – Closed 25-26 December and Sunday dinner Xe

Rest – *(booking essential)* Menu £ 28 – Carte £ 25/40

◆ Our Pub of the Year 2011 sits at the heart of a pretty village. Dark panelling and log fires provide a characterful, almost medieval feel. Food is down-to-earth, with classic, comforting dishes and traditional desserts. Dishes are fiercely British and big on flavour; rich, simple and satisfying.

Royal Oak

✿ *Paley Street, Southwest : 3.5 mi by A 308, A 330 on B 3024 ✉ SL6 3JN – ✆ (01628) 620 541 – www.theroyaloakpaleystreet.com – Closed Sunday dinner and bank holiday Mondays*

Rest – Menu £ 22 (lunch) – Carte £ 30/45

Spec. Lasagne of rabbit with wild mushrooms and chervil. Peppered haunch of venison with creamed spinach and sauce poivrade. Eton mess.

◆ A warm and welcoming beamed dining pub, with service that gets the tone just right. The menu champions British produce and is very appealing. This is skilled, confident cooking which sensibly avoids over-elaboration; game is handled deftly.

Crown

High St. ✉ SL6 2AH – ✆ (01628) 621 936 – www.thecrownatbray.co.uk – Closed 25-26 December

Rest – Carte £ 22/35

◆ Charmingly restored 16C inn with low-beamed, atmospheric fire-lit bar and lighter, more formal, cottage-style dining room. Wide-ranging British menu of robust, flavoursome dishes.

at Bray Marina Southeast : 2 mi by B 3208, A 308 - X - on Monkey Island Lane – ✉ Bray-On-Thames

Riverside Brasserie

(follow road through the marina) ✉ *SL6 2EB* – ✆ *(01628) 780 553 – www.riversidebrasserie.co.uk – April-September*

Rest – *(booking essential)* Carte £ 39/50

◆ Marina boathouse, idyllically set on the banks of the Thames. Very simply appointed interior and decked terrace. Inventive cooking in informal, busy and buzzy surroundings.

BRAYE – C.I. – **503** Q33 – see Channel Islands (Alderney)

BRAY MARINA – Windsor & Maidenhead – see Bray-on-Thames

BREARTON – North Yorkshire **22** B2

London 216 mi – Leeds 23 mi – Sheffield 67 mi – Manchester 77 mi

The Malt Shovel

Main St ✉ *HG3 3BX* – ✆ *(01423) 862 929 – www.themaltshovelbrearton.co.uk – Closed Monday, Tuesday and Sunday dinner*

Rest – Carte £ 27/42

◆ Quirky, shabby-chic pub run by the Bleikers, who also own the famous smokehouse. Classical dishes with continental flavours; lots of smoked seasonal produce. Tapas-style small plates at lunch.

BREEDON ON THE HILL – Leics. – see Castle Donington

BRENTWOOD – Essex – **504** V29 – **pop. 47 593** **13** C2

London 22 mi – Chelmsford 11 mi – Southend-on-Sea 21 mi

44 High St ✆ (01277) 200300, enquiries@brentwood.gov.uk

Bentley G. & C.C. Ongar Rd, ✆ (01277) 373 179

Warley Park Little Warley Magpie Lane, ✆ (01277) 224 891

Marygreen Manor

London Rd, Southwest : 1.25 mi on A 1023 ✉ *CM14 4NR* – ✆ *(01277) 225 252 – www.marygreenmanor.co.uk*

56 rm – †£ 75/150 ††£ 90/150, ☕ £ 14.50

Rest *Tudors* – see restaurant listing

◆ Charming Tudor building with wood panelled rooms and open fires. Bedrooms split between main house and courtyard - some named after Henry VIII's wives. Professionally run.

Tudors – at Marygreen Manor Hotel

London Rd, Southwest : 1.25 mi on A 1023 ✉ *CM14 4NR* – ✆ *(01277) 225 252 – www.marygreenmanor.co.uk – Closed dinner Sunday and bank holidays*

Rest – Menu £ 34/40

◆ Spacious Tudor-style dining room with stained glass, wood beams and tapestries. Well-spaced, dressed tables and formal service. Appealing, modern food with a seasonal base.

BRIDGNORTH – Shropshire – **502** M26 – **pop. 11 891** Great Britain **18** B2

London 146 mi – Birmingham 26 mi – Shrewsbury 20 mi – Worcester 29 mi

The Library, Listley St ✆ (01746) 763257, bridgnorth.tourism@shropshire.gov.uk

Stanley Lane, ✆ (01746) 763 315

Ironbridge Gorge Museum★★ **AC** (The Iron Bridge★★ - Coalport China Museum★★ - Blists Hill Open Air Museum★★ - Museum of the Gorge and Visitor Centre★) NW : 8 mi by B 4373

ENGLAND

at Worfield Northeast : 4 mi by A 454 – ✉ Bridgnorth

Old Vicarage
✉ *WV15 5JZ – ✆ (01746) 716 497 – www.oldvicarageworfield.com*
14 rm – †£ 73 ††£ 95 **Rest** – *(booking essential)* Menu £ 23/35
◆ Antiques, rare prints and rustic pottery: a personally run Edwardian parsonage in a rural setting with thoughtfully appointed bedrooms, some in the coach house. Delightful orangery dining room overlooking garden; modern British cooking.

BRIDPORT – Dorset – 503 L31 – pop. 12 977 — 3 B3

London 150 mi – Exeter 38 mi – Taunton 33 mi – Weymouth 19 mi
47 South St ✆ (01308) 424901, bridport.tic@westdorset-dc.gov.uk
Bridport and West Dorset West Bay East Cliff, ✆ (01308) 422 597
Mapperton Gardens★, N : 4 mi by A 3066 and minor rd. Lyme Regis★ - The Cobb★, W : 11 mi by A 35 and A 3052

Roundham House without rest
Roundham Gdns, West Bay Rd, South : 1 mi by B 3157 ✉ DT6 4BD – ✆ (01308) 422 753 – www.roundhamhouse.co.uk – June-October
8 rm – †£ 49/85 ††£ 95/125
◆ Sizeable Edwardian house displaying rich colours and period furnishings. Comfy lounge; modern bedrooms with bold feature walls and good comforts. Elevated position offers pleasant country views.

Riverside
West Bay, South : 1.75 mi by B 3157 ✉ DT6 4EZ – ✆ (01308) 422 011 – www.thefishrestaurant-westbay.co.uk – Closed 27 November-12 Februrary, Monday except Bank Holidays and Sunday dinner
Rest – Seafood – *(booking essential)* Menu £ 24 (weekday lunch) – Carte £ 26/39
◆ Long-standing seafood restaurant with harbour views; accessed via a bridge. Good value daily menu offers extremely fresh, straightforward dishes crafted from local produce. Plenty of choice.

The Bull with rm
34 East St ✉ DT6 3LF – ✆ (01308) 422 878 – www.thebullhotel.co.uk
19 rm – †£ 70/110 ††£ 150/190 **Rest** – Carte £ 18/38
◆ Boutique, regency style inn displaying an eclectic mix of period features and chic, contemporary décor. Local meats and Lyme Bay fish are showcased in classic brasserie dishes. Uniquely styled, modern bedrooms boast bold feature walls and stylish bathrooms.

at Burton Bradstock Southeast : 2 mi by B 3157

Norburton Hall without rest
Shipton Ln ✉ DT6 4NQ – ✆ (01308) 897 007 – www.norburtonhall.com
3 rm – †£ 90/120 ††£ 130/220
◆ Spacious Edwardian Arts and Crafts house with coastal views and 6 acres of mature grounds. Woodwork, ornate carvings and period furniture abound; classical bedrooms, modern shower rooms.

BRIGGSWATH – N. Yorks. – 502 S20 – see Whitby

BRIGHOUSE – West Yorkshire – 502 O22 – pop. 32 360 — 22 B2

London 213 mi – Bradford 12 mi – Burnley 28 mi – Leeds 15 mi
Crow Nest Park Hove Edge Coach Rd, ✆ (01484) 401 121

Brook's
6 Bradford Rd ✉ HD6 1RW – ✆ (01484) 715 284 – www.brooks-restaurant.co.uk – Closed 10 days January, 10 days summer, Sunday and some bank holidays
Rest – *(dinner only)* Menu £ 17 (weekday dinner) – Carte £ 29/32
◆ Long-standing, very personally run restaurant, where eclectic art fills the walls. Pleasant wine bar and upstairs lounge. Robust, tasty, interesting dishes; kangaroo and zebra sometimes feature.

ENGLAND

London 53 mi – Portsmouth 48 mi – Southampton 61 mi
Shoreham Airport : ✆ (01273) 467373, W : 8 mi by A 27 AV
Royal Pavilion Shops ✆ (01273) 292595, brighton-tourism@ brighton-hove.gov.uk
East Brighton Roedean Rd, ✆ (01273) 604 838
The Dyke Devil's Dyke Rd, Devil's Dyke, ✆ (01273) 857 296
Hollingbury Park Ditchling Rd, ✆ (01273) 552 010
Waterhall Waterhall Rd, ✆ (01273) 508 658
Town★★ - Royal Pavilion★★★ **AC** CZ – Seafront★★ – The Lanes★ BCZ – St Bartholomew's★ **AC** CX **B**
Devil's Dyke (<★) NW : 5 mi by Dyke Rd (B 2121) BY

Plans on following pages

Hotel du Vin
2-6 Ship St ✉ BN1 1AD – ✆ (01273) 718 588 – www.hotelduvin.com
49 rm – †£ 230 ††£ 230, ☕ £ 14.95 CZ**a**
Rest *Bistro* – *(booking essential)* Carte £ 35/45
♦ 19C part-Gothic building where style is the keyword. Lounge-bar full of wine books; mezzanine cigar gallery with billiard table; striking bedrooms, some boasting terraces. Relaxed brasserie offers British/European classics and predictably huge wine selection.

Drakes
43-44 Marine Par. ✉ BN2 1PE – ✆ (01273) 696 934 – www.drakesofbrighton.com CZ**u**
20 rm – †£ 105/150 ††£ 210/260, ☕ £ 12.50
Rest *Restaurant* – see restaurant listing
♦ Pair of 18C townhouses on the promenade. Stylish, modern interior with cocktail bar. Chic bedrooms boast bamboo flooring, wooden feature walls, good mod cons and wet rooms; city or sea views.

Myhotel Brighton
17 Jubilee St ✉ BN1 1GE – ✆ (01273) 900 300 – www.myhotels.com
80 rm – †£ 160/190 ††£ 190/270, ☕ £ 7.95 CY**z**
Rest *Myhotel Brighton* – Carte £ 21/34
♦ Contemporary glass cube, set in the heart of town. Whacky, designer interior with relaxed vibe and stylish bar. Quirky, minimalist bedrooms boast the latest technological extras. Modern European menu served in informal brasserie and courtyard.

Kemp Townhouse without rest
21 Atlingworth St. ✉ BN2 1PL – ✆ (01273) 681 400 – www.kemptownhousebrighton.com – Closed 2-15 January CZ**n**
9 rm ☕ – †£ 95/145 ††£ 215
♦ Stylish, very personally run 19C townhouse. Bedrooms have an uncluttered, classic style and compact wet rooms; those facing the front are larger and more comfortable. 2 four-posters.

Paskins without rest
18-19 Charlotte St ✉ BN2 1AG – ✆ (01273) 601 203 – www.paskins.co.uk
19 rm ☕ – †£ 50/75 ††£ 80/90 CV**e**
♦ Quirky, personally run guesthouse. Small, modern bedrooms are simply furnished and well-kept. Showers only – to save water – and eco-toiletries. Organic breakfast features homemade sausages.

brightonwave without rest
10 Madeira Pl. ✉ BN2 1TN – ✆ (01273) 676 794 – www.brightonwave.com
8 rm ☕ – †£ 60/100 ††£ 150/175 CZ**s**
♦ Personally run Victorian townhouse featuring ever-changing artwork. Contemporary bedrooms: the front facing and garden rooms are the largest and most comfortable. One modern four-poster.

BRIGHTON AND HOVE

See following page

BUILT UP AREA

0 — 1 km
0 — 1/2 mile

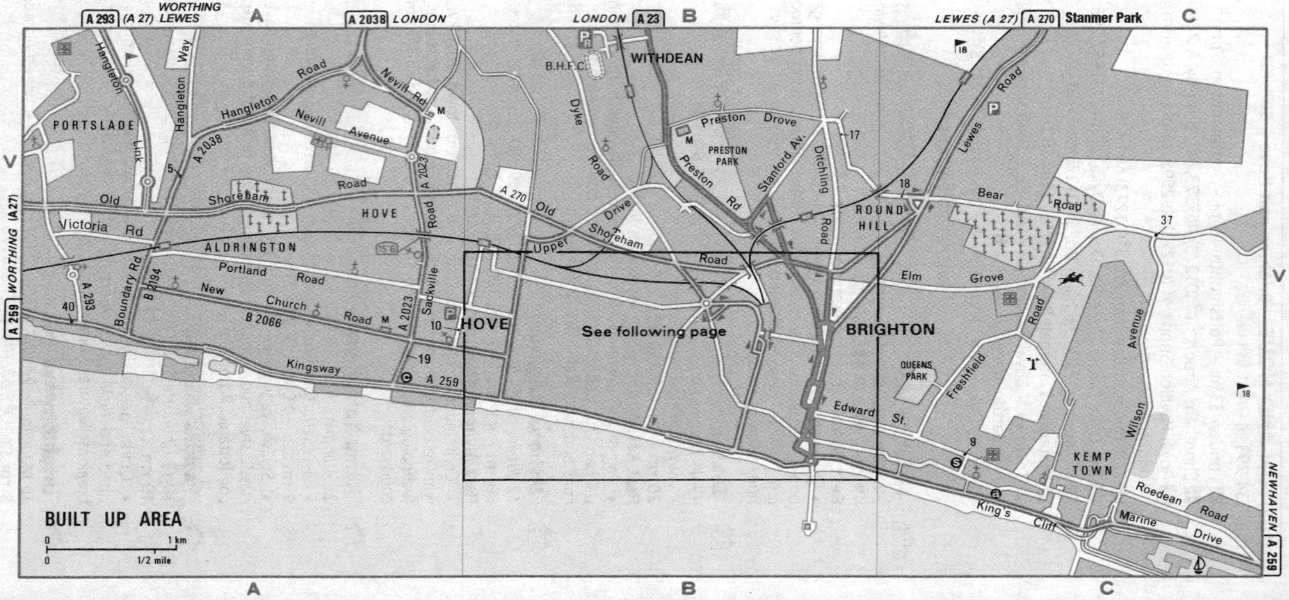

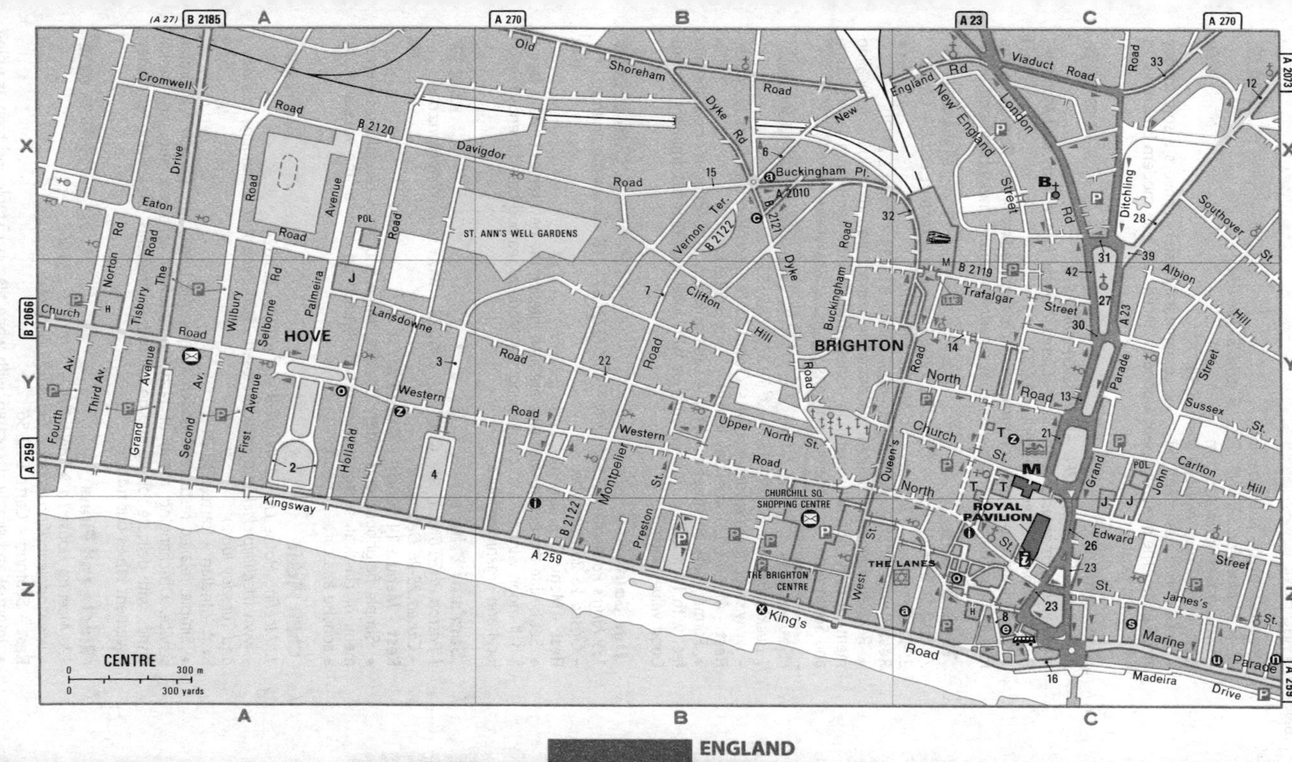
BRIGHTON
HOVE
ROYAL PAVILION
THE LANES
CHURCHILL SQ. SHOPPING CENTRE
THE BRIGHTON CENTRE
ST. ANN'S WELL GARDENS
Kingsway
King's Road
Western Road
North Road
Queen's Road
Church St.
Marine Parade
Madeira Drive
Dyke Rd
London Rd
Viaduct Road
Grand Parade
CENTRE
0
300 m
0
300 yards

ENGLAND

Restaurant – at Drakes Hotel
43-44 Marine Par. ✉ *BN2 1PE* – ✆ *(01273) 696 934*
– *www.drakesofbrighton.com* CZ**u**
Rest – *(booking advisable)* Menu £ 39
◆ Set in hotel basement, this cool, contemporary eatery conveys a soft, moody atmosphere. The menus present a good balanced choice of modern British dishes with Gallic twists.

Gingerman
21A Norfolk Sq ✉ *BN1 2PD* – ✆ *(01273) 326 688*
– *www.gingermanrestaurants.com – Closed 2 weeks late January and Monday*
Rest – *(booking essential)* Menu £ 18/32 BZ**i**
◆ Tucked away off the promenade; French and Mediterranean flavours to the fore in a confident, affordable, modern repertoire: genuine neighbourhood feel.

Terre à Terre
71 East St ✉ *BN1 1HQ* – ✆ *(01273) 729 051 – www.terreaterre.co.uk – Closed 25-26 December, 1 January and Monday in winter* CZ**e**
Rest – Vegetarian – *(booking essential)* Menu £ 15/33 – Carte £ 21/30
◆ Relaxed, friendly restaurant decorated in warm burgundy colours. Appealing menu of tasty, original vegetarian dishes which include items from Japan, China and South America. Generous portions.

Sevendials
1 Buckingham Pl. ✉ *BN1 3TD* – ✆ *(01273) 885 555*
– *www.sevendialsrestaurant.co.uk – Closed 25-26 December and Sunday dinner*
Rest – Menu £ 13 (weekday lunch) – Carte £ 22/31 BX**a**
◆ Former bank on street corner: the vault now acts as function room. Light, airy feel with high ceiling. Modern menus with local ingredients admirably to fore. Good value lunch.

Due South
139 King's Rd Arches ✉ *BN1 2FN* – ✆ *(01273) 821 218 – www.duesouth.co.uk*
– *Closed 25-26 December* BZ**x**
Rest – Menu £ 15 (lunch) – Carte £ 22/47
◆ Set beside the beach, with pleasant arch interior: the best tables upstairs facing a half-moon window and overlooking sea. Modern, seafood-based menus rely on local and organic produce.

Sam's of Brighton
1 Paston Pl ✉ *BN2 1HA* – ✆ *(01273) 676 222 – www.samsofbrighton.co.uk*
– *Closed 25-26 December* CV**a**
Rest – Menu £ 14 (lunch) – Carte £ 21/31
◆ Simple neighbourhood eatery boasting three enormous candelabras. Simple menu of classical, seasonal dishes. Early brunch on offer at the weekend and a concise à la carte at noon.

Chilli Pickle
42 Meeting House Ln. ✉ *BN1 1HB* – ✆ *(01273) 323 824*
– *www.thechillipicklebistro.co.uk – Closed 25-26 December, 1 January, Monday and Tuesday lunch* CZ**o**
Rest – Indian – Carte £ 18/31
◆ Simple, relaxed restaurant hidden away in the Lanes, with friendly welcoming service. Oft-changing menu of tasty, thoughtfully prepared, authentic Indian dishes, with delicate spicing and good quality ingredients. Great value for money; pavement tables out front.

Riddle and Finns
12b Meeting House Ln ✉ *BN1 1HB* – ✆ *(01273) 323 008*
– *www.riddleandfinns.co.uk – Closed 25 December* CZ**i**
Rest – Seafood – Carte £ 22/56
◆ Informal and simply decorated, with white tiles, bar stools and high, marble-topped tables for communal dining. Well-executed, classical seafood dishes; polite, attentive service.

ENGLAND

Blenio Bistro

87-93 Dyke Rd. ✉ BN1 3JE – ✆ (01273) 220 220 – www.bleniobistro.com – Closed Monday and Tuesday BX**c**

Rest – Carte £ 24/36

♦ Friendly, passionately run neighbourhood bistro. Simply furnished, with exposed brick, food-related art and pleasant terrace. Regularly changing menu ranges from snacks to the full 3 courses.

The Ginger Dog

12 College Pl. ✉ BN2 1HN – ✆ (01273) 620 990 – www.gingermanrestaurants.com CV**s**

Rest – Carte £ 30/40

♦ Warm and welcoming shabby-chic pub; part of the growing local 'Ginger' empire. Fresh produce is to the fore on the menu, which is mostly in a British vein but with the odd nod to Italy.

at Hove

The Meadow

64 Western Rd ✉ BN3 2JQ – ✆ (01273) 721 182 – www.themeadowrestaurant.co.uk – Closed 25 December, Sunday dinner and Monday AY**o**

Rest – Menu £ 15 (lunch and early dinner) – Carte £ 22/34

♦ Airy, split-level dining room with small shop. Its name symbolises the chef's vision to support local producers – the 'grass roots' of the restaurant. Beasts are bought in whole; some items are from his parents' garden or foraged for. Unfussy, classical cooking.

Graze

42 Western Rd. ✉ BN3 1JD – ✆ (01273) 823 707 – www.graze-restaurant.co.uk – Closed 25-26 and 31 December, Sunday dinner and Monday AY**z**

Rest – Menu £ 16 (weekday lunch) – Carte £ 27/37

♦ Lively neighbourhood eatery with quirky, informal feel. Cooking is elaborate and adventurous: good value midweek menu; 7 course tapas-style tasting menu must be ordered in advance for lunch.

The Ginger Pig

3 Hove St ✉ BN3 2TR – ✆ (01273) 736 123 – www.gingermanrestaurants.com

Rest – Carte £ 25/30 AV**c**

♦ Smart building by the seafront – formerly a hotel – boasting a mortar ship relief and beautifully restored revolving door. Menus offer precise, flavoursome British dishes and vegetarians are well-catered for. Great value set menus. Service copes well under pressure.

ENGLAND

BRIMSCOMBE – Glos. – **503** N28 – see Stroud

BALTIC
FERRY
NUMBER SEVEN
MULTI STOP

BRISTOL

County: City of Bristol
Michelin regional map: **503** M29
London 121 mi – Birmingham 91 mi
Population: 420 556

Great Britain
Map reference: **4** C2

PRACTICAL INFORMATION

Tourist Information

Explore-at-Bristol, Harbourside ✆ (0333) 321 0101, ticharbourside@destinationbristol.co.uk

Airport

Bristol Airport : ✆ (0871) 334 4444, SW : 7 mi by A 38 AX

Bridge

Severn Bridge (toll)

Golf Courses

Short Lodge GC Carsons Rd, ✆ (0117) 956 5501

Clifton Beggar Clifton Bush Lane, Failand, ✆ (01275) 393 474

Knowle, Fairway Brislington West Town Lane, ✆ (0117) 977 0660

Long Ashton Clarken Coombe, ✆ (01275) 392 229

Stockwood Vale Keynsham Stockwood Lane, ✆ (0117) 986 6505

SIGHTS

In town

City★★ – St Mary Redcliffe★★ DZ - At-Bristol★★ CZ - Brandon Hill★★ AX - Georgian House★★ AX **K** – Bristol Museum★★ CZ **M3** - Brunel's ss Great Britain and Maritime Heritage Centre★ **AC** AX **S2** – The Old City★ CYZ : Theatre Royal★★ CZ **T** - Merchant Seamen's Almshouses★ CZ **Q** – St Stephen's City★ CY **S1** - St John the Baptist★ CY – College Green★ CYZ (Bristol Cathedral★, Lord Mayor's Chapel★) – City Museum and Art Gallery★ AX **M1**

On the outskirts

Clifton★★ AX (Clifton Suspension Bridge★★ (toll), RC Cathedral of St Peter and St Paul★★ **F1**, Bristol Zoological Gardens★★ **AC**, Village★) – Blaise Hamlet★★ - Blaise Castle House Museum★, NW : 5 mi by A 4018 and B 4057 AV

In the surrounding area

Bath★★★, SE : 13 mi by A 4 BX – Chew Magna★ (Stanton Drew Stone Circles★ **AC**) S : 8 mi by A 37 - BX - and B 3130 – Clevedon★ (Clevedon Court★ **AC**, ⩽★) W : 11.5 mi by A 370, B 3128 - AX - and B 3130

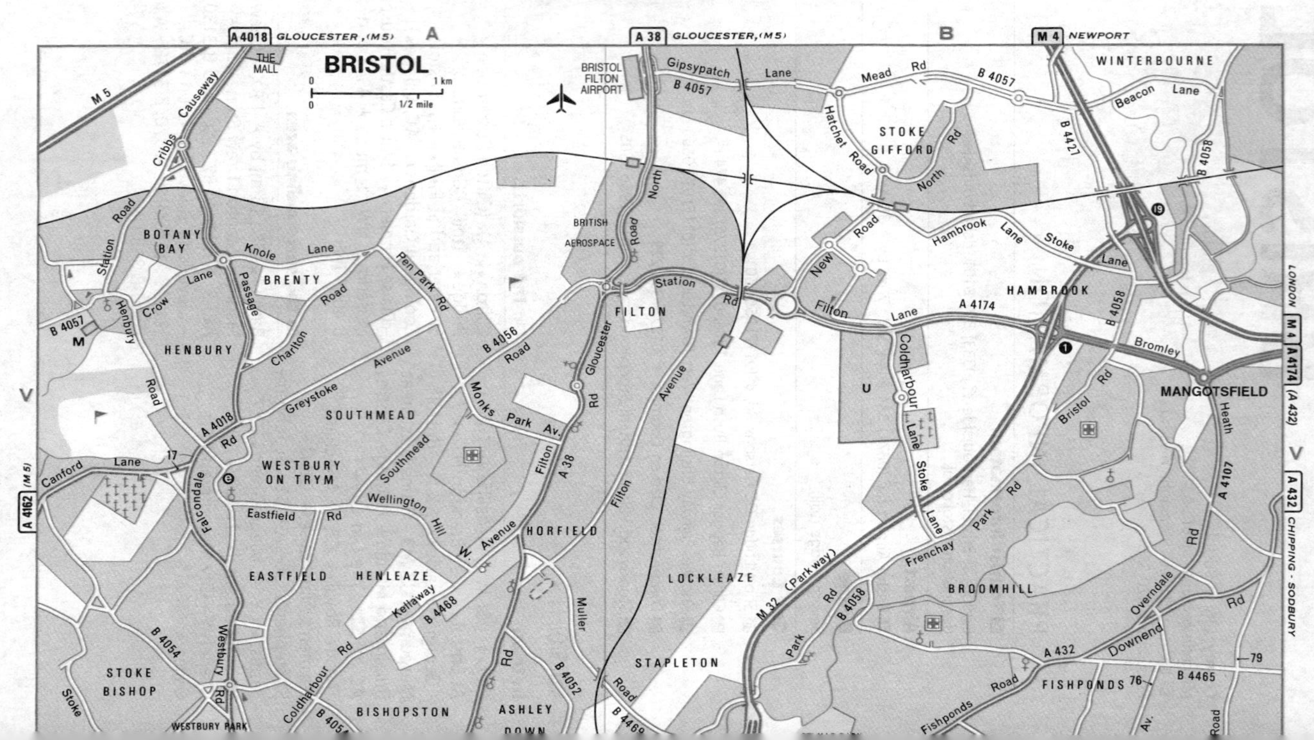
ENGLAND
A 4018 GLOUCESTER, (M5)
A 38 GLOUCESTER, (M5)
M 4 NEWPORT
LONDON M 4 A 4174 (A 432)
A 432 CHIPPING - SODBURY
A 4162 (M 5)
BRISTOL
0 1 km
0 1/2 mile
THE MALL
BRISTOL FILTON AIRPORT
BRITISH AEROSPACE
WINTERBOURNE
STOKE GIFFORD
HAMBROOK
MANGOTSFIELD
BOTANY BAY
BRENTY
HENBURY
FILTON
SOUTHMEAD
WESTBURY ON TRYM
HORFIELD
LOCKLEAZE
BROOMHILL
EASTFIELD
HENLEAZE
STAPLETON
FISHPONDS
STOKE BISHOP
BISHOPSTON
ASHLEY DOWN
WESTBURY PARK
M 5
Cribbs Causeway
Station Road
Knole Lane
Crow Lane
Henbury Road
Passage Road
Charlton Road
Pen Park Rd
B 4056 Road
Greystoke Avenue
A 4018 Rd
Canford Lane
Falcondale Rd
Southmead Rd
Monks Park Av.
Gloucester Rd
Filton A 38
Wellington Hill W.
Eastfield Rd
Kellaway Av B 4468
Coldharbour Rd
B 4054
Westbury Rd
Stoke
Gipsypatch Lane
B 4057
North Road
Station Rd
Filton Avenue
Muller Road
B 4052
B 4469
Mead Rd
Hatchet Road
North Rd
Beacon Lane
B 4427
B 4058
New Road
Hambrook Lane
Stoke Lane
Filton Lane
A 4174
Coldharbour Lane
Stoke Lane
Bromley Heath
Bristol Rd
A 4107
Frenchay Park Rd
M 32 (Park way)
Park Rd
Overndale Rd
Downend Rd
A 432
B 4465
Fishponds Road
Av.
Road
17
76
79
U
M

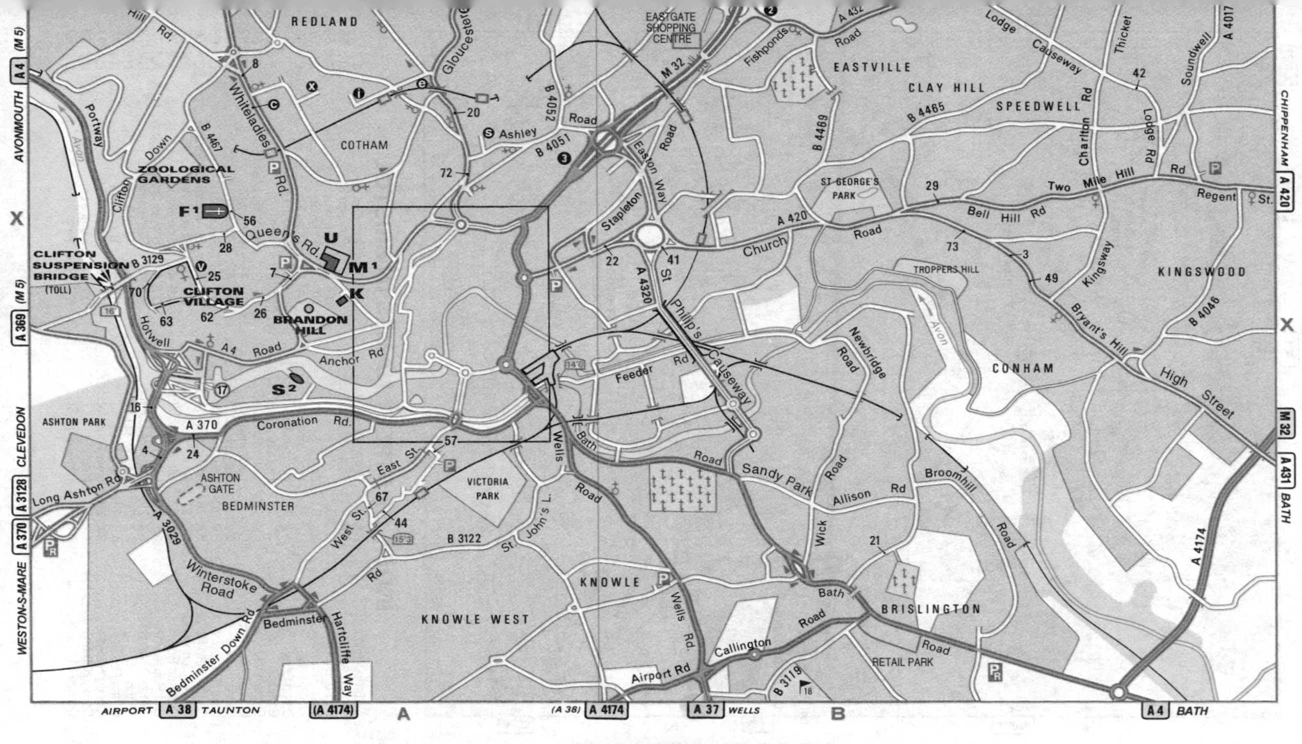
REDLAND
EASTGATE SHOPPING CENTRE
EASTVILLE
CLAY HILL
SPEEDWELL
COTHAM
ZOOLOGICAL GARDENS
ST GEORGE'S PARK
KINGSWOOD
TROPPERS HILL
CLIFTON SUSPENSION BRIDGE (TOLL)
CLIFTON VILLAGE
BRANDON HILL
CONHAM
ASHTON PARK
ASHTON GATE
BEDMINSTER
VICTORIA PARK
KNOWLE
KNOWLE WEST
BRISLINGTON
RETAIL PARK
Avon
Portway
Clifton Down
Hill Rd.
Whiteladies Rd.
Queen's Rd.
Gloucester
Ashley
Fishponds Road
Lodge Causeway
Thicket
Soundwell
Charlton Rd
Lodge Rd
Two Mile Hill Rd
Regent St.
Bell Hill Rd
Church Road
Kingsway
Bryant's Hill
High Street
Easton Way
Stapleton Road
Philip's Causeway
Feeder Rd
Anchor Rd
Hotwell Road
Coronation Rd.
Newbridge Road
Sandy Park Road
Wick Road
Allison Rd
Broomhill Road
Bath Road
Wells Road
Wells Rd.
East St.
West St.
St. John's L.
Long Ashton Rd
Winterstoke Road
Bedminster Down Rd
Hartcliffe Way
Airport Rd
Callington Road
AVONMOUTH A 4 (M 5)
A 369 (M 5)
CLEVEDON A 3128 A 370 WESTON-S-MARE
AIRPORT A 38 TAUNTON
(A 4174)
(A 38) A 4174
A 37 WELLS
A 4 BATH
M 32 A 431 BATH
CHIPPENHAM A 420
ENGLAND

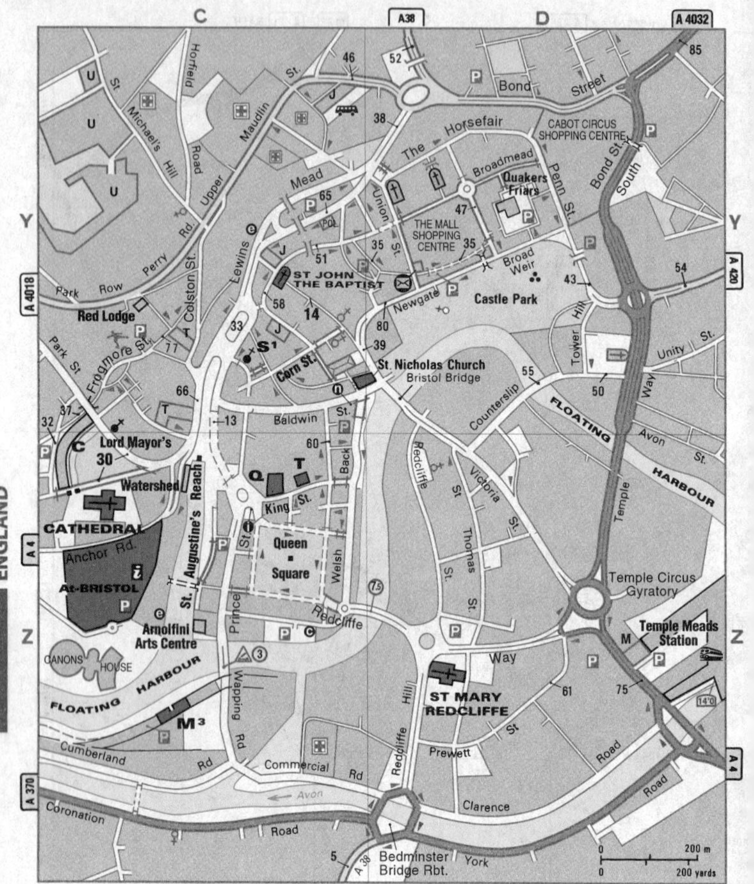

INDEX OF STREET NAMES IN BRISTOL

Hotel du Vin

The Sugar House ✉ *BS1 2NU – ✆ (0117) 925 5577 – www.hotelduvin.com*
40 rm – †£ 125/160 ††£ 125/260, ☕ £ 14.50 CY**e**
Rest ***Bistro*** – *(booking essential)* Carte £ 26/42
◆ A massive chimney towers over the 18C sugar refinery; stylish loft rooms in minimalist tones: dark leather and wood, low-slung beds, Egyptian linen and subtle wine curios. Noisy, bustling bar and bistro; plenty of classics. Good wine list.

Brigstow Bristol

5-7 Welsh Back ✉ *BS1 4SP – ✆ (0117) 929 1030 – www.mercure.com*
115 rm – †£ 159 ††£ 159, ☕ £ 13.95 – 1 suite CY**n**
Rest ***Ellipse*** – Carte £ 17/26 **s**
◆ Smart city centre hotel in charming riverside location. Stylish public areas typified by lounges and mezzanine. Modern, brightly coloured bedrooms are full of curves: both bedrooms and bathrooms feature plasma TVs. Modern brasserie and bar overlook river.

Casamia (Jonray and Peter Sanchez-Iglesias)

38 High St, Westbury-on-Trym, Northwest : 2 mi by A 4018 ✉ *BS9 3DZ – ✆ (0117) 959 2884 – www.casamiarestaurant.co.uk – Closed 25-26 December, 1 January, Sunday and Monday* AV**e**
Rest – Italian – *(dinner only and Saturday lunch) (booking advisable set menu only)* Menu £ 38/55
Spec. Beetroot risotto. Roast best end of lamb with kidney, parsley, swede and cucumber. Amadei chocolate.
◆ Proudly and professionally run former trattoria; simply decorated, with linen-covered tables and leather-furnished bar for aperitifs. Skilful, innovative, flavourful cooking from ambitious brothers. Classic Italian dishes are given modern, cutting edge twists.

Bordeaux Quay (The Restaurant)

V-Shed, Canons Way (1st Floor) ✉ *BS1 5UH – ✆ (0117) 943 1200 – www.bordeaux-quay.co.uk – Closed 24-28 December, Sunday dinner, Monday and lunch in August* CZ**e**
Rest – Menu £ 25/29 – Carte £ 25/44
◆ Huge harbourside emporium that's 100% organic. Ground floor houses deli, bakery, cookery school and relaxed bar. Linen-laid restaurant above offers seasonal, Mediterranean-influenced menu.

Bell's Diner

1-3 York Rd, Montpelier ✉ *BS6 5QB – ✆ (0117) 924 0357 – www.bellsdiner.co.uk – Closed Sunday, lunch Monday and Saturday, and bank holidays* AX**s**
Rest – *(booking essential at dinner)* Carte £ 30/40
◆ Shabby-chic neighbourhood restaurant, characterfully decorated with old bottles and flour sacks. Modern, French-inspired menus include a serious tasting selection – accompanied by wine flights.

Riverstation

The Grove, Harbourside ✉ *BS1 4RB – ✆ (0117) 914 4434 – www.riverstation.co.uk – Closed 24-26 December and Sunday dinner*
Rest – Menu £ 15/18 (weekdays) – Carte £ 25/35 CZ**c**
◆ Great riverside location: watch canal boats pass by from the terrace. Bar offers all day dining with breakfast, brunch and meze plates. Upstairs café offers more substantial modern European fare.

Rockfish Grill

128 Whiteladies Rd ✉ *BS8 2RS – ✆ (0117) 973 73 84 – www.rockfishgrill.co.uk – Closed 25-31 December, first week January, Sunday and Monday*
Rest – Seafood – *(booking essential)* Menu £ 15 – Carte £ 25/38 AX**c**
◆ Well-run and busy, with polite, friendly service. Daily changing menus focus on fresh, simply prepared fish and seafood, cooked in the charcoal josper oven. Owners' fishmongers is adjacent.

ENGLAND

Culinaria
1 Chandos Rd., Redland ✉ BS6 6PG – ☎ (0117) 973 7999 – www.culinariabristol.co.uk – Closed Christmas-New Year, 1 week spring, 2 weeks summer and Sunday-Wednesday AX**x**
Rest – Menu £ 20 (lunch) – Carte £ 26/33
◆ Combined deli and eatery; the personally run diner is informal with lots of light and space. Sound cooking behind a collection of Mediterranean, English and French dishes.

Greens' Dining Room
25 Zetland Rd ✉ BS6 7AH – ☎ (0117) 924 64 37 – www.greensdiningroom.com – Closed 1 week Christmas, last 2 weeks August, Sunday and Monday
Rest – *(booking essential)* Menu £ 28 (dinner) – Carte £ 20/30 AX**e**
◆ Family-run neighbourhood eatery set in residential area, with an intimate, homely interior and a convivial atmosphere. Good value, daily changing menu: unfussy, Italian-influenced dishes rely on natural flavours and carefully sourced produce. Chatty service.

The Albion Public House and Dining Rooms
Boyces Ave, Clifton Village ✉ BS8 4AA – ☎ (0117) 973 3522 – www.thealbionclifton.co.uk – Closed 25 December, 1 January, Sunday dinner and Monday AX**v**
Rest – *(booking essential)* Menu £ 30 (dinner) – Carte £ 24/39
◆ Trendy Grade II listed pub at the heart of the village. Unfussy, highly seasonal menu changes twice a day; everything is homemade. BBQs held on the pleasant terrace every Sunday evening.

The Kensington Arms
35-37 Stanley Rd ✉ BS6 6NP – ☎ (0117) 944 6444 – www.thekensingtonarms.co.uk – Closed 25 December and Sunday dinner
Rest – Carte £ 20/30 AX**i**
◆ Welcoming neighbourhood pub with traditional bar, impressive high-ceilinged dining room and charming Victorian style. Menus change every two months and have a strong British and seasonal base.

Robin Hood's Retreat
197 Gloucester Rd ✉ BS7 8BG – ☎ (0117) 924 8639 – www.robinhoodsretreat.co.uk – Closed 25 December AX**a**
Rest – *(booking advisable at dinner)* Menu £ 20 (lunch and early dinner) – Carte £ 25/32
◆ Red-brick, Victorian pub in busy part of city, with characterful bar and relaxed atmosphere. Daily changing menus offer hearty, flavourful interpretations of British classics.

BROAD CAMPDEN – Glos. – see Chipping Campden

BROAD OAK – East Sussex – **504** V31 **8** B3
London 62 mi – Hastings 8 mi – Rye 7 mi

Fairacres without rest
Udimore Rd, on B 2089 ✉ TN31 6DG – ☎ (01424) 883 236 – www.fairacresrye.co.uk – Closed Christmas - New Year
3 rm – †£ 60 ††£ 100
◆ Listed 17C cottage in picture-postcard pink. Big breakfasts under low beams. Individual rooms: one overlooks superb magnolia tree in garden. All have many thoughtful extras.

BROADSTAIRS – Kent – **504** Y29 – **pop. 22 712** **9** D1
London 77 mi – Canterbury 18 mi – Ramsgate 2 mi

Burrow House without rest
Granville Rd. ✉ CT10 1QD – ☎ (01843) 601 817 – www.burrowhouse.com – Closed 20 December-1 January
4 rm – †£ 80/115 ††£ 95/145
◆ Tastefully restored and subtly modernised Victorian house close to sea front. Bedrooms blend contemporary décor and fine antique furniture. Gourmet dinners by arrangement. Substantial breakfasts.

London 93 mi – Birmingham 36 mi – Cheltenham 15 mi – Oxford 38 mi

1 Cotswold Court (01386) 852937

Town★

Country Park (Broadway Tower ★★★), SE : 2 mi by A 44 – Snowshill Manor★ (Terrace Garden★) **AC**, S : 2.5 m

Buckland Manor

WR12 7LY – (01386) 852 626 – www.bucklandmanor.com
14 rm – £ 195/300 £ 225/320
Rest – *(booking essential for non-residents)* Menu £ 20 (lunch) – Carte £ 43/52
◆ Secluded part 13C country house with beautiful gardens. Individually furnished bedrooms boast high degree of luxury. Fine service throughout as old-world serenity prevails. Restaurant boasts elegant crystal, fine china and smooth service.

Lygon Arms

rest,

High St WR12 7DU – (01386) 852 255 – www.barcelo-hotels.co.uk/lygonarms
77 rm – £ 124/174 £ 225/289 – 6 suites
Rest *Goblets* – see restaurant listing
Rest *Great Hall* – *(dinner only and Sunday lunch)* Menu £ 25/43 – Carte approx. £ 63 **s**
◆ Superbly enticing, quintessentially English coaching inn with many 16C architectural details in its panelled, beamed interiors, and in rooms that Charles I and Cromwell once stayed in. Refined dining amongst baronial splendours, including a minstrels' gallery.

Broadway

The Green WR12 7AA – (01386) 852 401 – www.cotswold-inns-hotels.co.uk
19 rm – £ 155 £ 175
Rest *Courtyard* – Menu £ 15/28
◆ Characterful 16C inn set on the green in the heart of the village; originally an abbot's retreat. Classically styled guest areas. Crisp, light colour schemes in more modern bedrooms. Timbered, horse racing themed bar. Modern British cooking and good value lunches.

The Olive Branch without rest

78 High St WR12 7AJ – (01386) 853 440 – www.theolivebranch-broadway.com
8 rm – £ 58/78 £ 85/110
◆ A 1590s former staging post on the high street run by a friendly husband and wife team. Flagged floors, sandstone walls and compact bedrooms with a few charming touches.

Windrush House without rest

Station Rd WR12 7DE – (01386) 853 577 – www.windrushhouse.com
5 rm – £ 75 £ 90
◆ Fresh, modern guesthouse with landscaped garden, set in a picturesque village. Comfortable lounge. Light, airy bedrooms come with homemade biscuits; some boast wrought iron beds.

Russell's with rm

20 High St WR12 7DT – (01386) 853 555 – www.russellsofbroadway.co.uk – Closed Sunday dinner except bank holidays when closed Monday dinner
7 rm – £ 98/158 £ 98/300
Rest – Menu £ 16 (weekdays) – Carte £ 29/36
◆ Behind the splendid Cotswold stone façade lies a stylish modern restaurant with terrace front and rear. Seasonally influenced, regularly changing menus. Smart, comfy bedrooms.

Goblets – at The Lygon Arms Hotel

High St WR12 7DU – (01386) 854 418 – www.barcleo-hotels.co.uk/lygonarms.co.uk
Rest – *(booking essential)* Menu £ 25/38 – Carte approx. £ 63
◆ Characterfully firelit in rustic dark oak. Modern dining room at front more atmospheric than one to rear. Menus of light, tasty, seasonal dishes offered.

BROCKENHURST – Hampshire – 503 P31 – pop. 2 865 Great Britain 6 A2

London 99 mi – Bournemouth 17 mi – Southampton 14 mi – Winchester 27 mi

Brockenhurst Manor Sway Rd, ☎ (01590) 623 332

New Forest★★ (Rhinefield Ornamental Drive★★, Bolderwood Ornamental Drive★★)

Rhinefield House

Rhinefield Rd, Northwest : 3 mi ✉ *SO42 7QB – ☎ (01590) 625 600 – www.rhinefieldhousehotel.co.uk*

50 rm – †£ 179/245 ††£ 189/255 – 1 suite

Rest *Armada* – ☎ (01590) 622 922 *(dinner only and Sunday lunch)* Menu £ 45

Rest *The Brasserie* – ☎ (01590) 622 922 – Carte £ 27/33

◆ Impressive country house with ornamental pond, parterres and yew maze, in 40 acres of tranquil forest parkland. Period features include ornate wood carvings. Contemporary bedrooms boast the latest mod cons; rooms in the original house are more characterful. Fine dining in Armada. Relaxed Brasserie with terrace.

New Park Manor

Lyndhurst Rd, North : 1.5 mi on A 337 ✉ *SO42 7QH – ☎ (01590) 623 467 – www.newparkmanorhotel.co.uk*

24 rm – †£ 105/135 ††£ 105/135

Rest *The Stag* – Menu £ 20/43

◆ Extended, elegantly proportioned former hunting lodge built by Charles II on his return from France. Classic bedrooms in the main house; those in the Forest Wing are more contemporary. Candlelit fine dining.

The Cloud

Meerut Rd ✉ *SO42 7TD – ☎ (01590) 622 165 – www.cloudhotel.co.uk – Closed 28 December-14 January*

18 rm (dinner included) – †£ 80/89 ††£ 130/178

Rest *Encore* – Menu £ 17/31

◆ Well-kept hotel made up of four cottages, set on the edge of a pretty New Forest town; photos attest to the owner's past as a tiller girl. Neat, tidy bedrooms. Busy, linen-laid restaurant with conservatory extension and theatrical theme; traditional menus.

Cottage Lodge without rest

Sway Rd ✉ *SO42 7SH – ☎ (01590) 622 296 – www.cottagelodge.co.uk – Closed weekdays 1 January-14 February*

12 rm – †£ 50/110 ††£ 110/170

◆ 300-year old former forester's cottage in the heart of the village: proudly run by welcoming owner. Low oak beamed ceiling, cosy snug bar and large, neatly appointed rooms.

Simply at Whitley Ridge with rm

Beaulieu Rd, East : 1 mi on B 3055 ✉ *SO42 7QL – ☎ (01590) 622 354 – www.whitleyridge.co.uk – Closed January-February*

18 rm – †£ 115/135 ††£ 125/195, £ 7.95

Rest – Menu £ 20 (lunch) – Carte £ 31/39

◆ Georgian house in 14 acres of mature gardens, in charming New Forest setting. Formal brasserie offers good value, flavoursome, hearty dishes, with New Forest produce to the fore. Keen, attentive service. Stylish, modern lounges; attractive terraces. Spacious, contemporary bedrooms offer a good level of facilities.

Thatched Cottage with rm

16 Brookley Rd. ✉ *SO42 7RR – ☎ (01590) 623 090 – www.thatchedcottage.co.uk*

5 rm – †£ 70/90 ††£ 110/130, £ 8.50

Rest – *(closed Sunday dinner, Monday and Tuesday) (booking essential)* Menu £ 17/22

◆ Longstanding restaurant set in traditional, very individually styled 17C farmhouse, with wood-furnished terrace and open kitchen. Classic dishes on locally sourced menu. Cottage-style bedrooms.

at Sway Southwest : 3 mi by B 3055 – ✉ Lymington

XX **Nurse's Cottage** with rm — AC rest, P VISA MC AE

Station Rd ✉ SO41 6BA – ☎ (01590) 683 402 – www.nursescottage.co.uk – Closed 3 weeks March and 3 weeks November-December

5 rm (dinner included) – †£ 93/98 ††£ 200/215

Rest – *(dinner only) (booking essential)* Menu £ 28

♦ Personally run, welcoming conservatory restaurant with an intimate charm. Traditional menus make good use of Hampshire's larder and much thought goes into the wine list. Pristine, comfy bedrooms with pretty details.

BROCKTON – **Shrops.** – **see Much Wenlock**

BROMFIELD – **Shrops.** – **503** L26 – **see Ludlow**

BRUNDALL – **Norfolk** – **504** Y26 – **pop. 5 832** — **15** D2

London 118 mi – Great Yarmouth 15 mi – Norwich 8 mi

XX **Lavender House** — P VISA MC

39 The Street ✉ NR13 5AA – ☎ (01603) 712 215 – www.thelavenderhouse.co.uk – Closed 26 December-7 January, Sunday and Monday

Rest – *(dinner only and Sunday lunch) (booking advisable)* Menu £ 40

♦ Characterful low-ceilinged thatched cottage with comfy lounge and bar, cosy dining rooms and impressive 8-seater table in kitchen. Original monthly menus display interesting modern twists.

BRUNTINGTHORPE – **Leicestershire** Great Britain — **16** B3

London 96 mi – Leicester 10 mi – Market Harborough 15 mi

Leicester - Museum and Art Gallery★, Guildhall★ and St Mary de Castro Church★, N : 11 mi by minor rd and A 5199

The Joiners — P VISA MC

Church Walk ✉ LE17 5QH – ☎ (0116) 247 8258 – www.thejoinersarms.co.uk – Closed Sunday dinner and Monday

Rest – *(booking essential)* Menu £ 14 (lunch) – Carte £ 22/28

♦ Neat and tidy whitewashed pub with characterful interior. Good value menus offer a mix of refined pub classics and brasserie-style dishes, cooked and presented in a straightforward manner.

BRUSHFORD – **Somerset** – **503** J30 – **see Dulverton**

BRUTON – **Somerset** – **503** M30 – **pop. 2 982** — **4** C2

London 118 mi – Bristol 27 mi – Bournemouth 44 mi – Salisbury 35 mi

Stourhead★★★ **AC**, W : 8 mi by B 3081

X **At The Chapel** — VISA MC

High St ✉ BA10 0AE – ☎ (01749) 814 070 – www.atthechapel.co.uk – Closed Sunday dinner and Monday

Rest – Carte £ 19/33

♦ Informal, wood-floored restaurant in former chapel, with bakery to one side and wine shop to the other. Well-priced, daily changing menus offer rustic, Mediterranean-influenced dishes, with wood-fired pizzas a speciality in the evenings. Friendly service.

BRYHER – **Cornwall** – **503** A/B34 – **see Scilly (Isles of)**

BUCKDEN – **Cambridgeshire** – **504** T27 – **pop. 2 385** — **14** A2
– ✉ **Huntingdon**

London 65 mi – Bedford 15 mi – Cambridge 20 mi – Northampton 31 mi

ENGLAND

The George
High St ✉ PE19 5XA – ✆ (01480) 812 300 – www.thegeorgebuckden.com
12 rm – ♦£ 95/100 ♦♦£ 145
Rest ***Brasserie*** – see restaurant listing
◆ Delightfully restored former 19C coaching inn with stylish, contemporary look, typified by leather tub chairs and sofas. Smart bedrooms are all named after famous Georges.

Brasserie – at The George Hotel
High St ✉ PE19 5XA – ✆ (01480) 812 300 – www.thegeorgebuckden.com
Rest – Carte £ 24/37
◆ Spacious, modern brasserie serving a range from traditional English game to Mediterranean and Moroccan influenced dishes. French windows lead to courtyard, creating airy feel.

BUCKHORN WESTON – Dorset 4 C3

London 117 mi – Poole 36 mi – Bath 33 mi – Weymouth 37 mi

Stapleton Arms with rm
Church Hill ✉ SP8 5HS – ✆ (01963) 370 396 – www.thestapletonarms.com
4 rm – ♦£ 72/90 ♦♦£ 80/120 **Rest** – Carte £ 18/27
◆ Stylish, shabby-chic pub with elegant dining room; muddy boots, dogs and children are all welcome. Wide-ranging menu offers traditional choices with some Mediterranean touches. Spacious, contemporary bedrooms – some boast underfloor heating.

BUCKINGHAM – Buckinghamshire – 503 Q27 – pop. 12 512 11 C1

Great Britain

London 64 mi – Birmingham 61 mi – Northampton 20 mi – Oxford 25 mi
Silverstone Stowe Silverstone Rd, ✆ (01280) 850 005
Tingewick Rd, ✆ (01280) 815 566
Stowe Gardens★★, NW : 3 mi by minor rd. Claydon House★ **AC**, S : 8 mi by A 413

Villiers
rest,
3 Castle St ✉ MK18 1BS – ✆ (01280) 822 444 – www.oxfordshire-hotels.co.uk
43 rm – ♦£ 95/150 ♦♦£ 110/165 – 3 suites
Rest ***Villiers*** – Menu £ 16/20 – Carte £ 29/36
◆ Professionally run hotel on central street. Spacious, bedrooms vary in style: some boasting original beams and eaves; all equally comfy with large, well-kept bathrooms. Modern restaurant offers appealing British menu. Locals often pop in to the lounges for coffee.

BUCKLAND MARSH – Oxfordshire – pop. 2 243 10 A2

London 76 mi – Faringdon 4 mi – Oxford 15 mi

The Trout at Tadpole Bridge with rm
✉ SN7 8RF – ✆ (01367) 870 382 – www.troutinn.co.uk – Closed Sunday dinner November-April except bank holidays
6 rm – ♦£ 80 ♦♦£ 120 **Rest** – Carte £ 20/35
◆ Smart pub with attractive garden leading down to the Thames. Concise menu consists of classic Gallic dishes with contemporary touches; seafood and game often feature as specials. Comfy bedrooms exceed expectations. Private moorings available.

BUCKLAND NEWTON – Dorset – 503 M31 4 C3

London 214 mi

Gaggle of Geese
✉ DT2 7BS – ✆ (01300) 345 249 – www.thegaggle.co.uk
– Closed 25 December, dinner 26 December and 1 January
Rest – Carte £ 22/34
◆ Relaxed, shabby-chic pub run by experienced owners. Oft-changing menus use excellent quality produce including fruit, veg and herbs from garden. Hearty cooking; refined presentation.

BUDE – Cornwall – 503 G31 – pop. 3 681 — 1 B2

London 252 mi – Exeter 51 mi – Plymouth 50 mi – Truro 53 mi

Visitor Centre, The Crescent ✆ (01288) 354240, budetic@visitbude.info

Burn View, ✆ (01288) 352 006

The Breakwater★★ – Compass Point (≤★)

Poughill★ (church★★), N : 2.5 mi - E : Tamar River★★ – Kilkhampton (Church★), NE : 5.5 mi by A 39 – Stratton (Church★), E : 1.5 mi – Launcells (Church★), E : 3 mi by A 3072 – Marhamchurch (St Morwenne's Church★), SE : 2.5 mi by A 39 – Poundstock★ (≤★★, church★, guildhouse★), S : 4.5 mi by A 39. Morwenstow (cliffs★★, church★), N : 8.5 mi by A 39 and minor roads - Jacobstow (Church★), S : 7 mi by A 39

Falcon

Breakwater Rd ✉ EX23 8SD – ✆ (01288) 352 005 – www.falconhotel.com – Closed 25 December

29 rm – ♦£ 65/83 ♦♦£ 130/140 – 1 suite

Rest – *(bar lunch Monday-Saturday)* Carte £ 26/30 **s**

♦ An imposing, personally run hotel with the proudly traditional character of a bygone age. Contemporary and classic blend in bedrooms. Separate private garden. Formal dining.

BUDLEIGH SALTERTON – Devon – 503 K32 – pop. 4 801 — 2 D2

London 182 mi – Exeter 16 mi – Plymouth 55 mi

Fore St ✆ (01395) 445275, budleigh.tic@btconnect.com

East Devon Links Rd, Budleigh Salterton, ✆ (01395) 443 370

East Budleigh (Church★), N : 2.5 mi by A 376 – Bicton★ (Gardens★) **AC**, N : 3 mi by A 376

The Long Range

5 Vales Rd, by Raleigh Rd ✉ EX9 6HS – ✆ (01395) 443 321 – www.thelongrangehotel.co.uk – Closed 19 October-4 November and New Year

9 rm – ♦£ 49/78 ♦♦£ 100/120 **Rest** – Menu £ 27

♦ Homely and unassuming guesthouse, personally run in quiet residential street. Sun lounge with bright aspect, overlooking broad lawn and neat borders. Simple, unfussy rooms. Tasty, locally sourced dishes in a comfy dining room.

BUNBURY – 502 M24 – ✉ Tarporley — 20 A3

London 183 mi – Birmingham 68 mi – Liverpool 39 mi – Sheffield 87 mi

Yew Tree Inn

Long Ln, Spurstow ✉ CW6 9RD – ✆ (01829) 260 274 – www.theyewtreebunbury.com – Closed 25 December

Rest – Carte £ 19/29

♦ Characterful country dining pub featuring central bar surrounded by traditionally furnished rooms. Homemade dishes utilise local, seasonal produce; try the chips cooked in beef dripping.

BUNGAY – Suffolk – 504 Y26 – pop. 4 895 Great Britain — 15 D2

London 108 mi – Beccles 6 mi – Ipswich 38 mi

Norwich★★ - Cathedral★★, Castle Museum★, Market Place★, NW : 15 mi by B 1332 and A 146

Castle Inn with rm

35 Earsham St ✉ NR35 1AF – ✆ (01986) 892 283 – www.thecastleinn.net – Closed Sunday dinner

4 rm – ♦£ 65 ♦♦£ 85 **Rest** – Menu £ 17 (lunch) – Carte £ 17/30

♦ Sky-blue pub with open-plan dining area and intimate rear bar. Fresh, simple and seasonal country based cooking; the Innkeeper's platter of local produce is a perennial favourite. Tasty homemade cakes and cookies on display. Homely, comfortable bedrooms.

at Earsham Southwest : 3 mi by A 144 and A 143 – ✉ Bungay

Earsham Park Farm without rest
Old Railway Rd, on A 143 ✉ NR35 2AQ – ☎ (01986) 892 180
– www.earsham-parkfarm.co.uk
4 rm – †£ 50/70 ††£ 80/100
◆ Isolated red-brick Victorian farmhouse, surrounded by working farm which supplies the produce for breakfast. Well appointed rooms with rural names.

BURCHETT'S GREEN – Windsor and Maidenhead – **504** R29 – see Maidenhead

---

BURCOMBE – Wilts. – see Salisbury

BURFORD – Oxfordshire – **503** P28 – **pop. 1 171** **10** A2

London 76 mi – Birmingham 55 mi – Gloucester 32 mi – Oxford 20 mi
The Brewery, Sheep St ☎ (01993) 823558, burford.vic@westoxon.gov.uk
Burfotd Golf Club, ☎ (01993) 822 583

Bay Tree
Sheep St ✉ OX18 4LW – ☎ (01993) 822 791 – www.cotswold-inns-hotels.co.uk/bay-tree
21 rm – †£ 120/130 ††£ 170/210 **Rest** – Menu £ 20/32 – Carte £ 23/31
◆ Characterful, creeper-clad 16C house with coaching inn style, antique furnishings and original features. Two front lounges with vast stone fireplaces. Comfortable bedrooms. Light, airy restaurant overlooking beautiful landscaped garden.

Burford House
99 High St ✉ OX18 4QA – ☎ (01993) 823 151 – www.burfordhouse.co.uk
8 rm – †£ 124 ††£ 179/199
Rest – *(closed Sunday) (lunch only and dinner Thursday-Saturday)*
Menu £ 16/35 – Carte lunch £ 17/24
◆ Characterful 17C B&W timbered townhouse. Lounge and garden room have a subtle, contemporary edge, while comfy, individually decorated bedrooms are more traditional in style. Good breakfasts, homely lunches and gourmet dinners in informal restaurant.

Cotland House without rest
Fulbrook Hill, Fulbrook, Northeast : 0.5 mi on A 361 ✉ OX18 4BH – ☎ (01993) 822 382 – www.cotlandhouse.com
4 rm – †£ 45/70 ††£ 90/110
◆ Bright, modern house in Cotswold stone; its cool, light décor tinged with Gallic style. Neatly kept by friendly owner, with candles, magazines, fresh flowers and top-name toiletries.

The Lamb Inn with rm
✉ OX18 4LR – ☎ (01993) 823 155 – www.cotswold-inns-hotels.co.uk
17 rm – †£ 81/150 ††£ 141/265 **Rest** – Carte £ 35/45
◆ 15C weavers' cottage set in a charming town. Bar offers light bites and afternoon tea; the restaurant, a daily market and set menu. Ambitious cooking is robust and classically based. Bedrooms are cosy; Rosie has its own garden.

The Highway Inn with rm
117 High St ✉ OX18 4RG – ☎ (01993) 823 661 – www.thehighwayinn.co.uk
– Closed first 2 weeks January and 25-26 December
9 rm – †£ 79/99 ††£ 89/140 **Rest** – Carte £ 20/35
◆ Characterful beamed inn dating from 1480. Simple, honest cooking of pub classics and delicious desserts, with an emphasis on local produce. Classic, cosy bedrooms.

The Carpenter's Arms
Fulbrook Hill, Northeast : 0.5 mi on A 361 ✉ OX18 4BH – ☎ (01993) 823 275
– www.thecarpentersarmsfulbrook.com – Closed Sunday dinner and Monday
Rest – Carte £ 20/27
◆ Its unassuming outer appearance gives little clue as the warm, inviting style within. Expect robust and competitively prices dishes, from grilled chops to cod with chickpea stew. Personally run.

at Swinbrook East : 2.75 mi by A 40 – ✉ Burford

The Swan Inn with rm

✉ *OX18 4DY – ✆ (01993) 823 339 – www.theswannswinbrook.co.uk – Closed 25-26 December*
6 rm ☕ – 🚹£ 100/120 🚹🚹£ 140/180
Rest – Carte £ 20/34
♦ Wisteria-clad, honey-coloured pub on the riverbank boasting a lovely garden filled with fruit trees. Charming interior displays an open oak frame and exposed stone walls hung with old photos. Monthly menu features the latest local produce and a modern take on older recipes. Well-appointed bedrooms have a luxurious feel.

BURLTON – Shropshire – ✉ Shrewsbury 18 B1

London 235 mi – Shrewsbury 10 mi – Wrexham 20 mi

The Burlton Inn with rm

✉ *SY4 5TB – ✆ (01939) 270 284 – www.burltoninn.com – Closed 25 December and Sunday dinner*
6 rm ☕ – 🚹£ 85 🚹🚹£ 85
Rest – Carte £ 18/32
♦ Characterful 18C whitewashed inn with pleasant terrace and pretty fountain. Keenly priced menus feature unfussy classical cooking, with lighter snacks at lunch and more adventurous dishes in the evening. Neat, wood-furnished bedrooms boast large bathrooms.

BURNHAM MARKET – Norfolk – 504 W25 – pop. 898 Great Britain 15 C1

London 128 mi – Cambridge 71 mi – Norwich 36 mi
Lambourne Dropmore Rd, ✆ (01628) 666 755
Holkham Hall★★ **AC**, E : 3 mi by B 1155

Hoste Arms

The Green ✉ *PE31 8HD – ✆ (01328) 738 777 – www.hostearms.co.uk*
34 rm ☕ – 🚹£ 113/161 🚹🚹£ 172/244 – 1 suite
Rest ***The Hoste Arms*** – see restaurant listing
♦ Extended 17C inn in heart of pretty village. Stylish, comfortable bedrooms boast a high level of facilities and include the eye-catching Zulu wing with its South African themed décor.

Vine House without rest

The Green ✉ *PE31 8HD – ✆ (01328) 738 777 – www.vinehouseboutiquehotel.co.uk*
6 rm ☕ – 🚹£ 128/183 🚹🚹£ 155/230 – 1 suite
♦ Stylish, comfortable and elegant rooms with great bathrooms at this extended Georgian house. Evening butler service for drinks. Reception and meals at Hoste Arms opposite.

Railway Inn without rest

Creake Rd. ✉ *PE31 8HD – ✆ (01328) 738 777 – www.hostearms.co.uk*
8 rm ☕ – 🚹£ 78/85 🚹🚹£ 94/101
♦ Former station house with derelict platform and carriage to rear. Stylish, contemporary bedrooms boast bold feature walls, modern furniture, retro fittings and good facilities.

Hoste Arms

The Green ✉ *PE31 8HD – ✆ (01328) 738 777 – www.hostearms.co.uk*
Rest – *(booking advisable)* Carte £ 25/37
♦ Extensive dining areas include rustic bar, informal conservatory and Moroccan garden. Classically based menus feature global influences, with emphasis on local produce. Friendly, polite service.

ENGLAND

BURNSALL – North Yorkshire – 502 O21 – pop. 108 – ✉ Skipton 22 A2

London 223 mi – Bradford 26 mi – Leeds 29 mi

Devonshire Fell

✉ *BD23 6BT – ✆ (01756) 729 000 – www.devonshirefell.co.uk*
10 rm – †£ 79/145 ††£ 173/210 – 2 suites
Rest – *(light lunch Monday-Saturday)* Menu £ 32
◆ Stone-built hotel – once a club for 19C mill owners – decorated with bold colours and striking, contemporary artwork. Spacious bedrooms boast dale views. Formal, linen-clad conservatory and more funky, modern brasserie; wide-ranging, modern menu.

The Red Lion with rm

✉ *BD23 6BU – ✆ (01756) 720 204 – www.redlion.co.uk*
25 rm – †£ 65/100 ††£ 80/153 – 4 suites
Rest – Menu £ 31 (dinner) – Carte £ 23/34
◆ Appealing stone inn on the riverbank with cosy bar, laid-back lounge and formally dressed dining room. Extensive menus offer local meat/fish/game, pub favourites and daily specials. Classic bedrooms have modern overtones; the annexe rooms are more contemporary.

BURPHAM – W. Sussex – 504 S30 – see Arundel

BURRINGTON – Devon – 503 I31 – pop. 533 2 C1

London 260 mi – Barnstaple 14 mi – Exeter 28 mi – Taunton 50 mi

Northcote Manor

Northwest : 2 mi on A 377 ✉ EX37 9LZ – ✆ (01769) 560 501 – www.northcotemanor.co.uk
14 rm – †£ 99/145 ††£ 130/215 – 1 suite
Rest – *(booking essential)* Menu £ 20/42 **s**
◆ Creeper-clad hall in the Torr Valley, dating from 1716. Fine fabrics and antiques in elegant, individually styled rooms; attention to well-judged detail lends air of idyllic calm. Country house restaurant features eye-catching murals.

BURTON BRADSTOCK – Dorset – 503 L31 – See Bridport

BURTON-UPON-TRENT – Staffordshire – 502 O25 – pop. 43 784 19 C1

London 128 mi – Birmingham 29 mi – Leicester 27 mi – Nottingham 27 mi

Customer Service Centre, Market Place ✆ (01283) 508000, reception@eaststaffsbc.gov.uk

Branston G. & C.C. Burton Rd, ✆ (01283) 528 320

Craythorne Stretton Craythorne Rd, ✆ (01283) 564 329

at Stretton Northwest : 3.25 mi by A 5121 (A 38 Derby) – ✉ Burton-Upon-Trent

Dovecliff Hall

Dovecliff Rd ✉ DE13 0DJ – ✆ (01283) 531 818 – www.dovecliffhallhotel.co.uk
15 rm – †£ 95 ††£ 120/225
Rest – *(closed Sunday dinner)* Menu £ 18/20 – Carte £ 28/41
◆ Imposing, listed 1790s house with lovely gardens and spacious rooms, nestling in an elevated position above the Trent. Airy bedrooms, most boasting garden vistas. Formal dining rooms in restaurant and delightful orangery.

BURY – Greater Manchester – 502 N23 – pop. 60 718 20 B2

London 211 mi – Leeds 45 mi – Liverpool 35 mi – Manchester 9 mi

The Met Art Centre, Market St ✆ (0161) 253 5111, touristinformation@bury.gov.uk

Greenmount, ✆ (01204) 883 712

The Waggon

131 Bury and Rochdale Old Rd, Birtle, East : 2 mi on B 6222 ✉ BL9 6UE – ☎ (01706) 622 955 – www.thewaggonatbirtle.co.uk – Closed 26 December-5 January, 2 weeks end July-August, Monday and Tuesday

Rest – *(dinner only and lunch Thursday, Friday and Sunday)* Menu £ 17 (weekday dinner) – Carte £ 22/28

◆ Unprepossessing façade hides a pleasantly decorated eatery with good value, no-nonsense cooking featuring a decidedly strong Lancashire base and the famous Bury Black Pudding.

BURY ST EDMUNDS – Suffolk – 504 W27 – pop. 36 218 15 C2

Great Britain

London 79 mi – Cambridge 27 mi – Ipswich 26 mi – Norwich 41 mi

6 Angel Hill ☎ (01284) 764667, tic@stedsbc.gov.uk

The Suffolk Golf and Spa Hotel Fornham St Genevieve, ☎ (01284) 706 777

Town★ - Abbey and Cathedral★

Ickworth House★ **AC**, SW : 3 mi by A 143

The Angel

3 Angel Hill ✉ IP33 1LT – ☎ (01284) 714 000 – www.theangel.co.uk

73 rm – †£ 100/170 ††£ 115/200 – 1 suite

Rest *The Eaterie* – Menu £ 16 (lunch) – Carte £ 18/40

◆ 15C inn near the Abbey Gardens with a fine Georgian façade. Rooms offer a bright, modern take on classic style: a few, named after famous visitors, have four poster beds. The Eaterie is in atmospheric 12C cellars.

Ounce House without rest

Northgate St ✉ IP33 1HP – ☎ (01284) 761 779 – www.ouncehouse.co.uk

5 rm – †£ 85/95 ††£ 125/135

◆ Two 1870s houses knocked together; well furnished with Victorian elegance. Spacious, individually styled bedrooms; well-chosen antiques contribute to a characterful interior.

Maison Bleue

30-31 Churchgate St ✉ IP33 1RG – ☎ (01284) 760 623 – www.maisonbleue.co.uk – Closed 3 weeks January, 2 weeks summer, Sunday and Monday

Rest – Seafood – Menu £ 20/30 – Carte £ 29/46

◆ 17C glass-fronted house with blue canopies, set in the heart of town. Chic, pastel grey colour scheme with modern landscapes. Well-presented cooking displays classic French roots, with fish the main element of the monthly changing menu. Formal, efficient service.

Pea Porridge

28-29 Cannon St. ✉ IP33 1JR – ☎ (01284) 700 200 – www.peaporridge.co.uk – Closed 2 weeks January, 2 weeks September, Sunday and Monday

Rest – *(booking advisable)* Menu £ 15 (lunch and mid-week dinner) – Carte £ 23/32

◆ Charming restaurant in cosy 19C brick cottage – a former bakery – well run by husband and wife team. Tasty, seasonal, country-style cooking with a strong Mediterranean bias. Great value lunch menus. Biodynamic and organic old world wines. Efficient service.

at Ixworth Northeast : 7 mi by A 143 – ✉ Bury St Edmunds

Theobalds

68 High St. ✉ IP31 2HJ – ☎ (01359) 231 707 – www.theobaldsrestaurant.co.uk – Closed 1 week early summer, Monday and dinner Sunday

Rest – *(dinner only and lunch Sunday, Wednesday and Friday)* Menu £ 29 (weekdays) – Carte £ 31/35

◆ Beamed part 16C cottage with a cosy firelit lounge. Friendly service and well-judged seasonal menus combine heartwarming favourites and contemporary dishes.

at Beyton East : 6 mi by A 14 – ✉ Bury St Edmunds

Manorhouse without rest
The Green ✉ IP30 9AF – ✆ (01359) 270 960 – www.beyton.com
4 rm – †£ 50/60 ††£ 70/76
◆ Part 15C Suffolk longhouse with mature garden in idyllic spot overlooking village green. Two rooms are in converted barn; all have a rustic feel to them. Personally run.

at Whepstead South : 4.5 mi by A 143 on B 1066

The White Horse
Rede Rd ✉ IP29 4SS – ✆ (01284) 735 760 – www.whitehorsewhepstead.co.uk – Closed 25-26 December and Sunday dinner
Rest – Carte £ 20/25
◆ Cheerfully run 17C village pub; choose between a characterful beamed room and the brighter Gallery with local artists' work. The kitchen's strength lies in the more conventional dishes.

at Horringer Southwest : 3 mi on A 143 – ✉ Bury St Edmunds

Ickworth
✉ IP29 5QE – ✆ (01284) 735 350 – www.lckworthhotel.co.uk
26 rm – †£ 170/325 ††£ 170/335 – 12 suites
Rest *Fredericks* – *(dinner only)* Menu £ 38
Rest *Conservatory* – Carte £ 22/36
◆ Family-orientated hotel set in the east wing of a grand 200 year old mansion: formerly home to the Marquise of Bristol and now owned by the National Trust. Set in 1,800 acres it boasts three airy drawing rooms and comfy bedrooms with views. Smart Fredericks overlooks gardens. Casual dining in impressive former orangery.

ENGLAND

BUSHEY – Hertfordshire – 504 S29 – pop. 17 001 — 12 A2

London 18 mi – Luton 21 mi – Watford 3 mi
Bushey Hall Bushey Hall Drive, ✆ (01923) 222 253
Bushey G. & C.C. High St, ✆ (020) 8950 2283

Plan : see Greater London (North-West) 1

st James
30 High St ✉ WD23 3HL – ✆ (020) 8950 2480 – www.stjamesrestaurant.co.uk – Closed Sunday BTc
Rest – Carte £ 25/31
◆ Long-standing, likeable restaurant with wood floored front room and bar, plus rear room for large parties. Appealing British menu shows real understanding of what guests want.

BUTTERMERE – Cumbria – 502 K20 – pop. 139 – ✉ Cockermouth — 21 A2

London 306 mi – Carlisle 35 mi – Kendal 43 mi

Wood House
Northwest : 0.5 mi on B 5289 ✉ CA13 9XA – ✆ (017687) 70 208 – www.wdhse.co.uk – April-October
3 rm – †£ 70/110 ††£ 110 **Rest** – Menu £ 29
◆ 16C house in a wonderfully serene lakeside setting with stunning views. Well-appointed lounge; antique furnished bedrooms. Meals cooked on the Aga using fresh seasonal, local ingredients and served family-style around an antique table.

BUXHALL – Suffolk – see Stowmarket

BUXTON – Derbyshire – 502 O24 – pop. 20 836 — 16 A1

London 172 mi – Derby 38 mi – Manchester 25 mi – Stoke-on-Trent 24 mi
The Crescent ✆ (01298) 25106, tourism@highpeak.gov.uk
Buxton and High Peak Townend, ✆ (01298) 26 263

Buxton's Victorian without rest

3A Broad Walk ✉ SK17 6JE – ☎ (01298) 78 759 – www.buxtonvictorian.co.uk – Closed Christmas-New Year

7 rm – †£ 60/80 ††£ 86/90

◆ Charming Victorian house built in 1860 for the Duke of Devonshire. Cosy lounge and breakfast room with views over boating lake and bandstand. Bedrooms boast period furniture.

Grendon without rest

Bishops Ln. , Southeast : 0.75 mi by A 53 ✉ SK17 6UN – ☎ (01298) 78 831 – www.grendonguesthouse.co.uk – Closed January

5 rm – †£ 50/70 ††£ 94

◆ Cosy Edwardian house on edge of town, built for a wealthy mill owner in the 1900s, with period features and pleasant gardens. Comfortable, traditionally furnished bedrooms.

BYLAND ABBEY – N. Yorks. – 502 Q21 – see Helmsley

CALLINGTON – Cornwall – 503 H32 – pop. 4 048 2 C2

London 237 mi – Exeter 53 mi – Plymouth 15 mi – Truro 46 mi

Langmans

3 Church St ✉ PL17 7RE – ☎ (01579) 384 933 – www.langmansrestaurant.co.uk

Rest – *(dinner only) (booking essential) (set menu only)* Menu £ 35

◆ Quaint double-fronted shop conversion; run by husband and wife team. Pre-dinner drinks in lounge followed by 6 course tasting menu in rear dining room. Refined, precise cooking.

CALLOW HILL – Worcestershire 19 C3

London 120 mi – Birmingham 26 mi – Coventry 35 mi – Wolverhampton 27 mi

The Royal Forester

✉ DY14 9XW – ☎ (01299) 266 286 – www.royalforesterinn.co.uk

Rest – Menu £ 13 – Carte dinner £ 20/36

◆ Pub dating from 1411; rustic dining room, relaxed atmosphere and bright, contemporary bar with grand piano. Simple, flavourful cooking and informative, bi-monthly menu. Fresh, modern, food-themed bedrooms; Aubergine, Pear and Cherry are the largest.

CALNE – Wiltshire – 503 O29 – pop. 13 789 4 C2

London 91 mi – Bristol 33 mi – Southampton 63 mi – Swindon 17 mi

Bowood House★ AC, (Library ≤★) SW : 2 mi by A 4 – Avebury★★ (The Stones★, Church★) E : 6 mi by A 4

Bowood

Derry Hill, West : 3 mi by A 4 on Derry Hill rd . ✉ SN11 9PQ – ☎ (01249) 822 228 – www.bowood.org

43 rm – †£ 150/180 ††£ 210/360

Rest *Shelburne* – *(dinner only and Sunday lunch)* Carte £ 30/44

Rest *Clubhouse Brasserie* – Carte £ 19/30

◆ Smart, professionally run, purpose-built hotel in grounds of Lord and Lady Lansdowne's Estate. Contemporary country house styling. Spacious bedrooms; some with balconies. Modern British cooking in formal Shelburne, with attractive terrace. Brasserie menu in golf clubhouse.

ENGLAND

CAMBRIDGE – Cambridgeshire – **504** U27 – **pop. 117 717** Great Britain **14** B3

London 55 mi – Coventry 88 mi – Ipswich 54 mi – Kingston-upon-Hull 137 mi

Cambridge City Airport : ✆ (01223) 373765, E : 2 mi on A 1303 X

The Guildhall, Paes Hill ✆ (0871) 2268006, info@cambridge.org

Cambridge Menzies Hotel Bar Hill, ✆ (01954) 780 098

Town★★★ – St John's College★★★ **AC** Y – King's College★★ (King's College Chapel★★★) Z The Backs★★ YZ – Fitzwilliam Museum★★ Z **M1** – Trinity College★★ Y – Clare College★ Z **B** – Kettle's Yard★ Y **M2** – Queen's College★ **AC** Z

Audley End★★, S : 13 mi on Trumpington Rd, A 1309, A 1301 and B 1383 – Imperial War Museum★, Duxford, S : 9 mi on M 11

Hotel du Vin

15-19 Trumpington St ✉ CB2 1QA – ✆ (01223) 227 330 – www.hotelduvin.com

41 rm – 🛉£ 180/230 🛉🛉£ 200/250 Z**u**

Rest ***Bistro*** – see restaurant listing

◆ Row of ex-university owned 18C houses; now a smart, stylish hotel. Contemporary bedrooms feature wine theme; 'Brown Brothers' comes with its own cinema. Relaxing, clubby bar.

Hotel Felix

Whitehouse Ln, Huntingdon Rd, Northwest : 1.5 mi by A 1307 ✉ CB3 0LX – ✆ (01223) 277 977 – www.hotelfelix.co.uk

52 rm – 🛉£ 160 🛉🛉£ 198, £ 7.50

Rest ***Graffiti*** – Menu £ 18 (lunch) – Carte dinner £ 27/37

◆ Privately owned Victorian mansion set in 3 acres of gardens with contemporary interior. Majority of bedrooms in extension; spacious and luxurious. Modern artwork decorates. Graffiti restaurant overlooks terrace and gardens.

Midsummer House (Daniel Clifford)

Midsummer Common ✉ CB4 1HA – ✆ (01223) 369 299 – www.midsummerhouse.co.uk – Closed 2 weeks Christmas-New Year, Sunday, Monday and lunch Tuesday Y**a**

Rest – Menu £ 35/73

Spec. Seared scallops with parmesan, confit lemon and Iberico ham. Slow cooked duck, baby gem, salt baked beetroot and orange jus. Apple tarte tatin, vanilla, garlic and bay leaf.

◆ Charming and idyllic location beside the River Cam; conservatory dining with fresh, bright feel. Visually impressive dishes reveal cooking that is confidently crafted; flavours are clear and pronounced. Tasting menu only Fri/Sat. Service is formal and well-timed.

Alimentum

152-154 Hills Rd ✉ CB2 8PB – ✆ (01223) 413 000 – www.restaurantalimentum.co.uk – Closed 23-30 December, Sunday dinner and bank holidays X**a**

Rest – Menu £ 17 (weekdays) – Carte £ 33/40

◆ Sleek, stylish restaurant with striking red and black décor and spacious cocktail bar. Modern menu has French base; dishes are clean and unfussy with some innovative touches.

22 Chesterton Road

22 Chesterton Rd ✉ CB4 3AX – ✆ (01223) 351 880 – www.restaurant22.co.uk – Closed 25 December-4 January, Sunday and Monday Y**c**

Rest – *(booking essential) (lunch by arrangement)* Menu £ 29

◆ Converted Victorian house with distinctive dining room decorated in rich colours. Monthly changing classical menu; tasty, good value French-influenced dishes. Formal service.

Bistro – at Hotel du Vin

15-19 Trumpington St ✉ CB2 1QA – ✆ (01223) 227 330 – www.hotelduvin.com

Rest – Menu £ 20 (lunch) – Carte £ 32/45 Z**u**

◆ Spacious brasserie with black banquettes and walls filled with wine memorabilia. Classic dishes presented in a modern style, with French undertones. Relaxed, buzzy ambience.

ENGLAND

CAMBRIDGE

Street	Grid	No.
Bridge St	Y	2
Coldham's Lane	X	5
Corn Exchange St	Z	6
Downing St	Z	7
Free School Lane	Z	12
Grafton Centre	Y	
Hobson St	Y	14
King's Parade	Z	15
Lion Yard Centre	Z	
Madingley Rd	X	16
Magdalene St	Y	17
Market Hill	YZ	18
Market St	Y	19
Milton Rd	Y	20
Newmarket Rd	Y	21
Northampton St	Y	22
Parker St	Z	23
Peas Hill	Z	25
Pembroke St	Z	26
Petty Cury	Z	27
Rose Crescent	Y	28
St Andrew's St	Z	30
St John's St	Y	31
Short St	Y	32
Sidney St	Y	34
Trinity St	Y	36
Trumpington Rd	Z	37
Wheeler St	Z	39

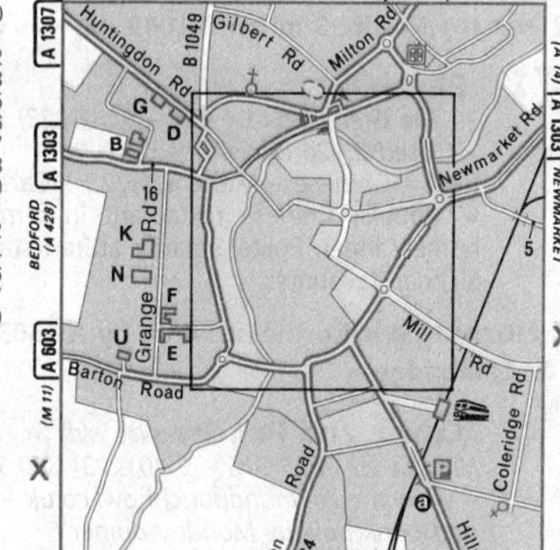

COLLEGES

College	Grid	Ref.
Christ's	Y	A
Churchill	X	B
Clare	Z	B
Clare Hall	X	N
Corpus Christi	Z	G[1]
Darwin	Z	D
Downing	Z	E[1]
Emmanuel	Z	F
Fitzwilliam	X	G
Gonville and Caius	Y	G[2]
Hugues Hall	Z	K
Jesus	Y	K
King's	Z	
Lucy Cavendish	Y	O[1]
Magdalene	Y	N
Newnham	X	E[2]
New Hall	X	D
Pembroke	Z	N
Peterhouse	Z	O[2]
Queen's	Z	
Robinson	X	K
St Catharine's	Z	R
St Edmund's House	Y	U
St John's	Y	
Selwyn	X	F
Sidney Sussex	Y	P
Trinity	Y	
Trinity Hall	Y	V
Wolfson	X	U

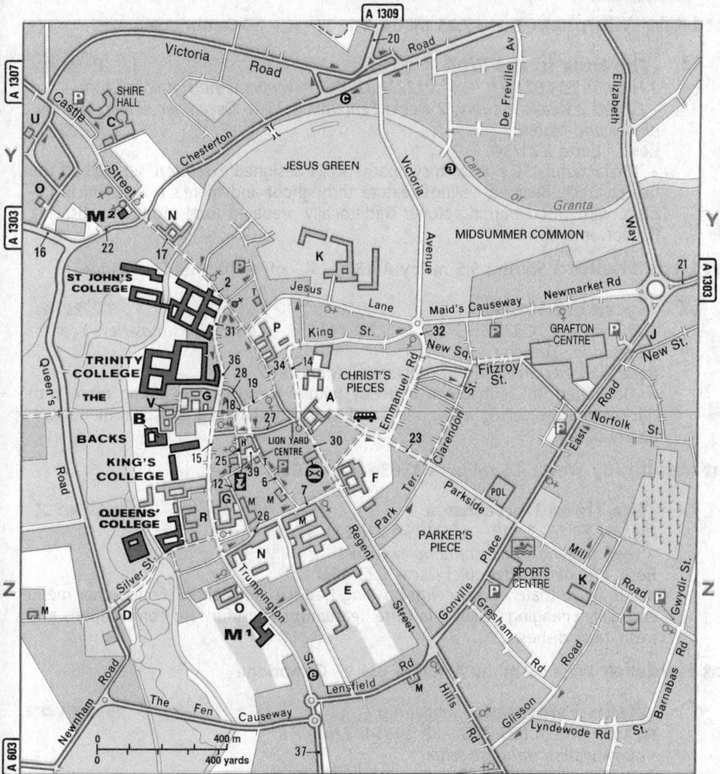

ENGLAND

at Histon North : 3 mi on B 1049 - X – ✉ Cambridge

XX **Phoenix**

20 The Green ✉ CB4 9JA – ✆ (01223) 233 766 – Closed 25-26 December

Rest – Chinese – Menu £ 19/25 – Carte £ 42/114

♦ Popular Chinese restaurant in former pub on village green. Comfortable, homely inner. Polite, smartly attired staff. Vast menu with plenty of Peking and Sichuan favourites.

at Horningsea Northeast : 4 mi by A 1303 - X - and B 1047 on Horningsea rd – ✉ Cambridge

Crown and Punchbowl with rm

High St ✉ CB25 9JG – ✆ (01223) 860 643 – www.thecrownandpunchbowl.co.uk – Closed 26-30 December, Sunday dinner and bank holiday Monday dinner

5 rm – †£ 74/95 ††£ 95

Rest – Menu £ 19/40

♦ Homely dining pub with formal service. Dishes display European influences and arrive in a mix of classic and more ambitious styles. Daily fish specials and a mix and match sausage board. Simple, tidy bedrooms are handy for the airport.

ENGLAND

at Little Wilbraham East : 7.25 mi by A 1303 - X – ✉ Cambridge

The Hole in the Wall

2 High St ✉ CB21 5JY – ✆ (01223) 812 282 – www.the-holeinthewall.com – Closed 2 weeks January, 2 weeks September, 25-26 December dinner, Sunday dinner and Monday

Rest – Carte £ 21/34

♦ Characterful 15C pub with sympathetically designed extension, set well off the beaten track. Beamed ceilings feature throughout and there's a large brick fire-place with wood burning stove. Traditionally prepared local produce; satisfying, flavoursome dishes.

at Little Shelford South : 5.5 mi by A 1309 - X - off A 10 – ✉ Cambridge

XX **Sycamore House**

1 Church St ✉ CB22 5HG – ✆ (01223) 843 396 – Closed Christmas-New Year and Sunday-Tuesday

Rest – *(dinner only) (booking essential)* Menu £ 27

♦ Converted 16C cottage in a sleepy hamlet. Long narrow dining room with thick walls, low ceiling and open fire. Frequently-changing, seasonal menu with hearty base.

at Madingley West : 4.5 mi by A 1303 - X – ✉ Cambridge

The Three Horseshoes

High St ✉ CB23 8AB – ✆ (01954) 210 221 – www.threehorseshoesmadingley.co.uk

Rest – *(booking advisable)* Carte £ 23/40

♦ Attractive thatched pub with bustling trattoria atmosphere. Concise bar menu and daily changing Italian à la carte, featuring straightforward combinations and fresh, tasty dishes.

at Hardwick West : 5 mi by A 1303 - X – ✉ Cambridge

Wallis Farmhouse without rest

98 Main St ✉ CB23 7QU – ✆ (01954) 210 347 – www.wallisfarmhouse.co.uk

4 rm – †£ 60 ††£ 90

♦ Remotely set Georgian house in picturesque village. Immaculately kept bed-rooms in a converted barn across courtyard. Breakfast served in main house. Spa-cious rear garden.

CAMPSEA ASH – Suffolk 15 D3

London 101 mi – Norwich 46 mi – Southend-on-Sea 76 mi – Ipswich 16 mi

Old Rectory

Station Rd ✉ IP13 0PU – ✆ (01728) 746 524 – www.theoldrectorysuffolk.com – Closed Christmas-New Year

7 rm – £ 75/95 £ 110/140

Rest – *(dinner only) (set menu only)* Menu £ 28

◆ Former Georgian rectory; now a stylish hotel with attractive gardens. Contemporary bedrooms; Oak is the most luxurious. Striking dining room with open fire. Dinner served on an ad hoc basis, so arrange when booking. Set 3 course menu; accomplished home cooking.

Fancy a last minute break?
Check hotel websites to take advantage of price promotions.

CANTERBURY – Kent – 504 X30 – pop. 43 552 Great Britain 9 D2

London 59 mi – Brighton 76 mi – Dover 15 mi – Maidstone 28 mi

12-13 Sun St, Buttermarket ✆ (01227) 378100, canterburyinformation@canterbury.gov.uk

City★★★ - Cathedral★★★ Y - St Augustine's Abbey★★ **AC** YZ **K** – King's School★ Y – Mercery Lane★ Y **12** - Christ Church Gate★ Y **D** – Museum of Canterbury★ **AC** Y **M1** – St Martin's Church★ Y **N** – West Gate Towers★ **AC** Y **R**

Plan on next page

Abode Canterbury

30-33 High St ✉ CT1 2RX – ✆ (01227) 766 266 – www.michaelcaines.com Y**a**

72 rm – £ 135/155 £ 135/155 – 1 suite

◆ Centrally located former coaching inn; heavily beamed, yet with a stylish, modern, boutique feel. Contemporary bedrooms, comfortable champagne bar and atmospheric first floor lounge.

Michael Caines – at Abode Canterbury Hotel

High St ✉ CT1 2RX – ✆ (01227) 826 684 – www.michaelcaines.com Y**a**

Rest – *(closed Sunday dinner)* Menu £ 13/25 – Carte £ 37/48

◆ Enjoy a glass of Champagne in smart bar before repairing to the upmarket restaurant to enjoy modern British cooking utilising a variety of styles and classical techniques.

Goods Shed

Station Rd West, St Dunstans ✉ CT2 8AN – ✆ (01227) 459 153 – www.thegoodsshed.net – Closed 25-26 December, 1 January, Sunday dinner and Monday Y**x**

Rest – Carte £ 28/35

◆ Once derelict railway shed, now a farmers' market that's open all day. Its eating area offers superbly fresh produce with no frills and real flavours very much to the fore.

at Lower Hardres South : 3 mi on B 2068 - Z – ✉ Canterbury

The Granville

Street End ✉ CT4 7AL – ✆ (01227) 700 402 – www.thegranvillecanterbury.com – Closed Sunday dinner and Monday

Rest – Carte £ 21/34

◆ Sizeable, family-run pub with Scandinavian-style, open-plan interior. Constantly evolving blackboard menu offers generous portions of unfussy, traditional dishes; veg is from the allotment.

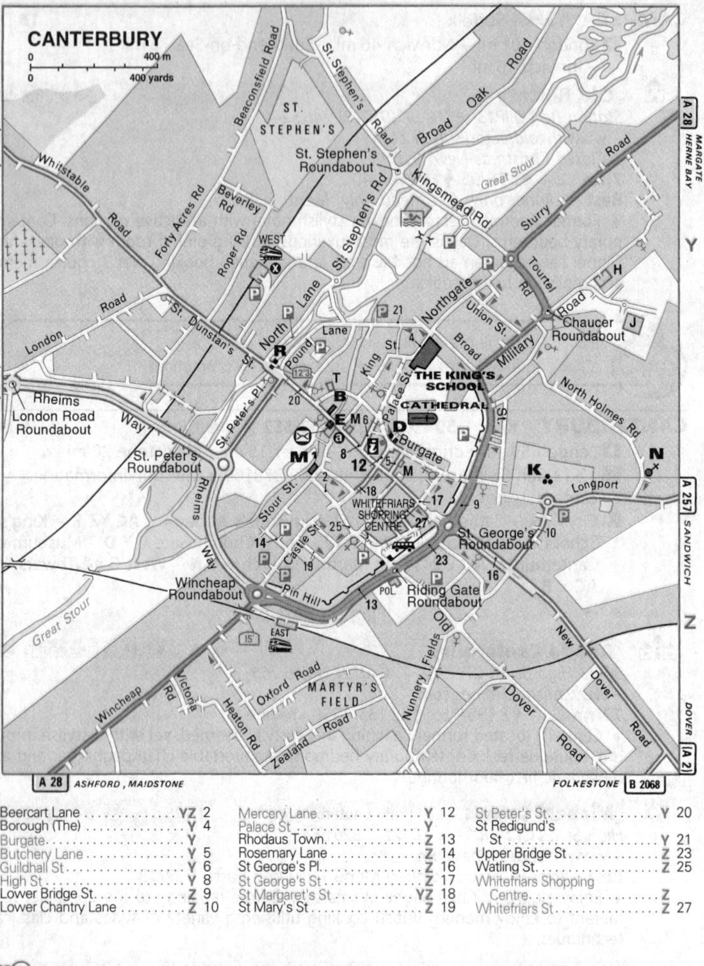

CANTERBURY

Beercart Lane	YZ	2
Borough (The)	Y	4
Burgate	Y	
Butchery Lane	Y	5
Guildhall St	Y	6
High St	Y	8
Lower Bridge St	Z	9
Lower Chantry Lane	Z	10
Mercery Lane	Y	12
Palace St	Y	
Rhodaus Town	Z	13
Rosemary Lane	Z	14
St George's Pl	Z	16
St George's St	Z	17
St Margaret's St	YZ	18
St Mary's St	Z	19
St Peter's St	Y	20
St Redigund's St	Y	21
Upper Bridge St	Z	23
Watling St	Z	25
Whitefriars Shopping Centre	Z	
Whitefriars St	Z	27

Good food at moderate prices? Look for the Bib Gourmand.

CARBIS BAY – Cornwall – 503 D33 – see St Ives

CARLISLE – Cumbria – 501 L19 – pop. 71 773 Great Britain 21 B1

- London 317 mi – Blackpool 95 mi – Edinburgh 101 mi – Glasgow 100 mi
- Carlisle Airport ✆ (01228) 573641, NW : 5.5 mi by A 7 - BY - and B 6264
- Old Town Hall, Green Market ✆ (01228) 625600, tourism@carlisle-city.gov.uk
- 18 Aglionby, ✆ (01228) 513 029
- 18 Stony Holme St Aidan's Rd, ✆ (01228) 625 511
- 9 Dalston Hall Dalston, ✆ (01228) 710 165
- Town★ - Cathedral★ (Painted Ceiling★) AY **E** – Tithe Barn★ BY **A**
- Hadrian's Wall★★, N : by A 7 AY

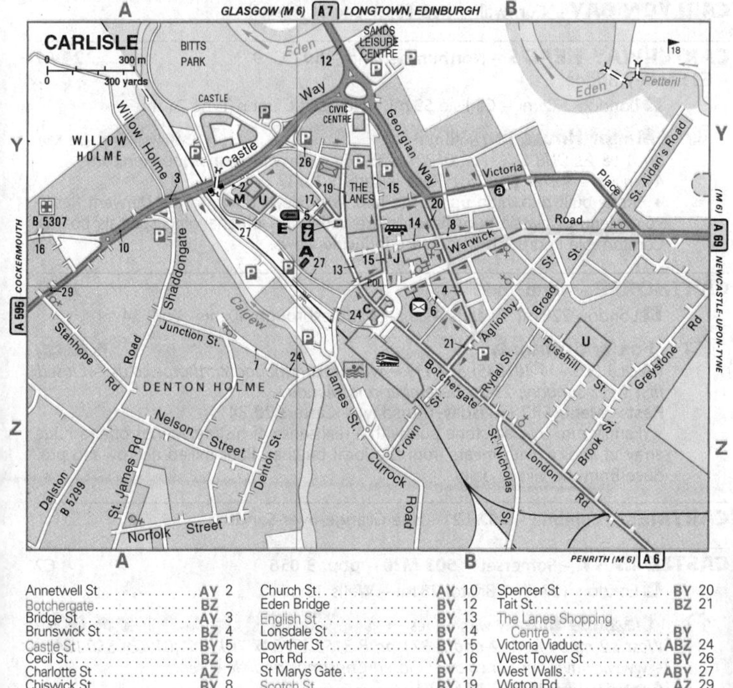

Annetwell St	AY	2	Church St	AY	10	Spencer St	BY	20
Botchergate	BZ		Eden Bridge	BY	12	Tait St	BZ	21
Bridge St	AY	3	English St	BY	13	The Lanes Shopping Centre	BY	
Brunswick St	BZ	4	Lonsdale St	BY	14	Victoria Viaduct	ABZ	24
Castle St	BY	5	Lowther St	BY	15	West Tower St	BY	26
Cecil St	BZ	6	Port Rd	AY	16	West Walls	ABY	27
Charlotte St	AZ	7	St Marys Gate	BY	17	Wigton Rd	AZ	29
Chiswick St	BY	8	Scotch St	BY	19			

Number Thirty One

31 Howard Pl. ✉ CA1 1HR – ✆ (01228) 597 080 – www.number31.co.uk – Closed 25 December BY**a**

4 rm – £ 60/65 £ 85/105 **Rest** – Menu £ 20

♦ Well-appointed, bay-windowed Victorian townhouse with sumptuous lounge and warm, immaculately-kept bedrooms. The large, comfortable Red Room on the top floor is the best. Richly decorated dining room with window onto plant-filled terrace.

at High Crosby **Northeast : 5 mi by A 7 - BY - and B 6264 off A 689 – ✉ Carlisle**

Crosby Lodge Country House

Crosby-on-Eden ✉ CA6 4QZ – ✆ (01228) 573 618 – www.crosbylodge.co.uk – Closed Christmas and New Year

11 rm – £ 90/105 £ 170/220

Rest – *(Sunday dinner residents only)* Carte £ 34/55

♦ Grade II listed, castellated house built in 1802. Warm ambience and welcoming hostess. Traditionally furnished lounge. Comfortable bedrooms with pleasant countryside outlook. Richly coloured dining room with polished brass around fireplace. Classic, homecooked food includes renowned sweet trolley.

CARLTON HUSTHWAITE – North Yorkshire – 502 Q21 — 22 B2

London 230 mi – Leeds 51 mi – Middlesbrough 32 mi – York 20 mi

Carlton Bore

✉ YO7 2BW – ✆ (01845) 501 265 – www.carltonbore.co.uk

Rest – Carte £ 19/23

♦ Characterful 17C stone inn offering appealing menu of well-priced, generously proportioned pub favourites. Three brightly decorated rooms and a warm, welcoming atmosphere.

CARLTON-IN-COVERDALE – N. Yorks. – 502 O21 – see Middleham

CARLYON BAY - Cornwall - 503 F33 - see St Austell

CARTERWAY HEADS - Northumberland - 501 O19 — 24 A2
- ✉ Shotley Bridge

London 272 mi - Carlisle 59 mi - Newcastle upon Tyne 21 mi

Manor House Inn with rm

on A 68 ✉ DH8 9LX - ☎ (01207) 255 268 - www.themanorhouseinn.com

4 rm - †£ 45 ††£ 75 **Rest** - Carte £ 13/37

◆ Stone-built pub, high up on the hills, with views down to the Derwent Reservoir. Menu of classic pub dishes; more variety on oft-changing specials boards. Comfortable bedrooms with peace-inducing views.

CARTHORPE - North Yorkshire — 22 B1

London 228 mi - Leeds 49 mi - Middlesbrough 40 mi - York 34 mi

Fox and Hounds

✉ DL8 2LG - ☎ (01845) 567 433 - www.foxandhoundscarthorpe.co.uk - Closed first week January, 25-26 December and Monday

Rest - Menu £ 17 (Tuesday-Thursday) - Carte £ 20/34

◆ Family run, ivy-clad stone pub with a real sense of history. Menus offer a huge array of choice, with meats from the local butcher, flour milled nearby and produce from the village dairy.

ENGLAND

CARTMEL - Cumbria - 502 L21 - see Grange-over-Sands

CASTLE CARY - Somerset - 503 M30 - pop. 3 056 — 4 C2

London 127 mi - Bristol 28 mi - Wells 13 mi

Clanville Manor without rest

West : 2 mi by B 3152 and A 371 on B 3153 ✉ BA7 7PJ - ☎ (01963) 350 124 - www.clanvillemanor.co.uk - Closed Christmas and New Year

4 rm - †£ 45/120 ††£ 90/120

◆ 18C house, charmingly cluttered. Heirlooms and antiques abound. Breakfasts served from the Aga. Walled garden boasts heated pool. Individual bedrooms, including four-poster.

at Lovington West : 4 mi by B 3152 and A 371 on B 3153 - ✉ Castle Cary

The Pilgrims at Lovington with rm

rm,

✉ BA7 7PT - ☎ (01963) 240 597 - www.thepilgrimsatlovington.co.uk - Closed Sunday dinner, Monday and lunch Tuesday

5 rm - †£ 80 ††£ 95/120 **Rest** - Carte £ 22/35

◆ Pristine and personally run; its unprepossessing outward appearance masking a charming interior. Appealing menu of British/Mediterranean dishes made with quality local produce. Comfortable, contemporary bedrooms, luxurious bathrooms and substantial breakfasts.

CASTLE COMBE - Wiltshire - 503 N29 - pop. 347 - ✉ Chippenham — 4 C2

London 110 mi - Bristol 23 mi - Chippenham 6 mi

Village★★

Manor House H. and Golf Club

✉ SN14 7HR - ☎ (01249) 782 206 - www.exclusivehotels.co.uk

44 rm - †£ 245 ††£ 245 - 4 suites

Rest ***The Bybrook*** - *(closed Monday lunch)* Menu £ 28/57

Spec. Seared scallops with butternut squash and chorizo. Slow cooked fillet of beef, cauliflower soubise, wild mushroom ravioli. Crème fraîche brûlée and chestnut financier.

◆ Fine period manor house in 365 acres of formal gardens and parkland. Interior exudes immense charm and style, with oak panelling and a host of open-fired lounges. Uniquely styled, luxurious bedrooms; many in the courtyard. Large dining room offers refined, carefully prepared dishes with a classical base. Slick service.

Castle Inn
✉ SN14 7HN – ✆ (01249) 783 030 – www.castle-inn.info – Closed 25 December
11 rm – 🛉£ 80/125 🛉🛉£ 175
Rest – Carte £ 20/34
◆ A hostelry dating back to the 12C in the middle of a delightful and historic village. Wooden beams and much character throughout. Breakfast in conservatory. Large and varied menu served in rustic bar.

CASTLE DONINGTON – Leicestershire – 502 P25 – pop. 5 977 — 16 B2
– ✉ Derby

London 123 mi – Birmingham 38 mi – Leicester 23 mi – Nottingham 13 mi
Nottingham East Midlands Airport : ✆ (0871) 919 9000, S : by B 6540 and A 453

at Breedon on the Hill Southwest : 4 mi by Breedon rd off A 453
– ✉ Castle Donington

The Three Horseshoes Inn
44-46 Main St ✉ DE73 8AN – ✆ (01332) 695 129 – www.thehorseshoes.com – Closed Sunday dinner
Rest – Carte £ 22/33
◆ Large, highly characterful, whitewashed pub with numerous interlinking rooms, cosy fires and pleasant terrace. Blackboard menus display robust, classical dishes of flavoursome, seasonal produce.

CATEL – C.I. – 503 P33 – see Channel Islands (Guernsey)

CAUNTON – Notts. – 502 R24 – see Newark-on-Trent

CERNE ABBAS – Dorset – 503 M31 — 4 C3

London 132 mi – Bristol - 60 mi – Cardiff 115 mi – Southampton 58 mi

The New Inn
14 Long St ✉ DT2 7JF – ✆ (01300) 341 274 – www.newinncerneabbas.com – Closed Sunday dinner November-March
Rest – Carte £ 18/30
◆ Sizeable pub set in picture postcard village, with exposed beams, decked terrace and vast garden. Freshly prepared, traditional dishes make good use of locally sourced produce.

CHADDESLEY CORBETT – Worcs. – 503 N26 – see Kidderminster

CHADWICK END – West Midlands – 503 O26 — 19 C2

London 106 mi – Birmingham 13 mi – Leicester 40 mi – Stratford-upon-Avon 16 mi

The Orange Tree 
Warwick Rd, on A 4141 ✉ B93 0BN – ✆ (01564) 785 364 – www.lovelypubs.co.uk – Closed 25 December and Sunday dinner
Rest – *(booking essential)* Menu £ 15 (weekdays) – Carte £ 15/28
◆ Large, contemporary pub with neat gardens, spacious terrace and buzzing atmosphere. Wide-ranging menu offers several dishes in two sizes, with tasty spit roast chicken a speciality.

CHAGFORD – Devon – 503 I31 – pop. 1 417 — 2 C2

London 218 mi – Exeter 17 mi – Plymouth 27 mi
Dartmoor National Park★★

Gidleigh Park (Michael Caines) rm,
Northwest : 2 mi by Gidleigh Rd ✉ TQ13 8HH – ☎ (01647) 432 367 – www.gidleigh.com
23 rm – 🛉£ 295 🛉🛉£ 500, 1 suite **Rest** – *(booking essential)* Menu £ 48/99
Spec. Salmon with Oscietra caviar, salmon jelly and Greek yoghurt vinaigrette. Duckling with star anise and orange braised chicory. Strawberry mousse with palmier biscuit, strawberry jelly and basil purée.
◆ Lovingly restored and extremely comfortable Arts and Crafts house set in 100 acres. Luxurious bedrooms boast impressive bathrooms; some have a balcony. Formal restaurant, where classical French menus showcase skilfully prepared, quality local produce. Tasting menu for Michael Caines' signature dishes.

22 Mill Street with rm
22 Mill St ✉ TQ13 8AW – ☎ (01647) 432 244 – www.22millst.com – Restricted opening January
2 rm – 🛉£ 109/129 🛉🛉£ 129/169, £ 12
Rest – *(closed Sunday and Monday) (booking essential)* Menu £ 42 **s**
◆ Smart, intimate restaurant on high street of scenic village, right in the heart of Dartmoor. Fresh and unfussy, with formally laid tables. An array of modern menus offer simply cooked, seasonal classics. Comfortable, rustic-style bedrooms.

at Sandypark Northeast : 2.25 mi on A 382 – ✉ Chagford

Mill End
on A 382 ✉ TQ13 8JN – ☎ (01647) 432 282 – www.millendhotel.com – Closed 3 weeks January
13 rm – 🛉£ 100 🛉🛉£ 150/170 – 1 suite **Rest** – *(dinner only)* Menu £ 42
◆ Well-maintained house with pleasant gardens; its comfy, antique-furnished lounge retaining a traditional charm. Classically styled bedrooms in original house; larger, more modern rooms in extension. A modern take on the classics in the bright, linen-laid restaurant.

Parford Well without rest
on Drewsteignton rd ✉ TQ13 8JW – ☎ (01647) 433 353 – www.parfordwell.co.uk – Closed Christmas and New Year
3 rm – 🛉£ 70/90 🛉🛉£ 90/100
◆ Tastefully maintained with superbly tended gardens. Elegant sitting room has plenty of books and French windows to garden. Two breakfast rooms. Homely, immaculate bedrooms.

at Easton Northeast : 1.5 mi on A 382 – ✉ Chagford

Easton Court without rest
Easton Cross ✉ TQ13 8JL – ☎ (01647) 433 469 – www.easton.co.uk
5 rm – 🛉£ 50/55 🛉🛉£ 75/80
◆ Well appointed accommodation and a high ceilinged lounge overlooking the immaculate gardens. Home made marmalade a speciality. Friendly atmosphere.

CHANNEL ISLANDS – 503 L/M33

ALDERNEY – Alderney – **503** M32 **5** B1
London 103 mi – Saint Helier 3 mi – Saint Anne 1 mi – Cherbourg 18 mi
Aurigny Air Services ☎ (01481) 822886
States Office, Island Hall, Royal Connaught Sq ☎ (01481) 822 811 marketing@visitalderney.com
Braye Bay★ – Mannez Garenne (≤★ from Quesnard Lighthouse) – Telegraph Bay★ – Vallee des Trois Vaux★ – Clonque Bay★

BRAYE – Alderney **5** B1

Braye Beach
✉ GY9 3XT – ☎ (01481) 824 300 – www.brayebeach.com
27 rm – 🛉£ 100/140 🛉🛉£ 140/200 **Rest** – Menu £ 19 – Carte approx. £ 33 **s**
◆ Smart, contemporary hotel set on edge of beach. Vaulted basement houses a series of lounges and a 19-seat cinema. Modern European cooking with a subtle seafood slant.

ENGLAND

GUERNSEY - Guernsey - **503** L32 - **pop. 58 867** 5 A2

London 139 mi - Saint Helier 2 mi - Saint Anne 2 mi - Cherbourg 18 mi

Guernsey Airport (01481) 237766, Aurigny Air (01481) 822 886

from St Peter Port to France (St Malo) and Jersey (St Helier) (Condor Ferries Ltd) 2 weekly - from St Peter Port to France (Dielette) (Manche Iles Express) (summer only) (60 mn) - from St Peter Port to Herm (Herm Seaway) (25 mn) - from St Peter Port to Sark (Isle of Sark Shipping Co. Ltd) (45 mn) - from St Peter Port to Jersey (St Helier) (HD Ferries) (1hr) - from St Peter Port to Jersey (St Helier) (Condor Ferries Ltd) daily

from St Peter Port to France (St Malo) and Jersey (St Helier) (Condor Ferries Ltd) - from St Peter Port to Jersey (St Helier) and Weymouth (Condor Ferries Ltd)

P.O. Box 23, North Esplanade (01481) 723552, enquiries@visitguernsey.com

Island★ - Pezeries Point★★ - Icart Point★★ - Côbo Bay★★ - St Martin's Point★★ - St Apolline's Chapel★ - Vale Castle★ - Fort Doyle★ - La Gran'mere du Chimquiere★ - Rocquaine Bay★ - Jerbourg Point★

CATEL/CASTEL - Guernsey 5 A2

Cobo Bay rest, VISA AE

Cobo Coast Rd GY5 7HB - (01481) 257 102 - www.cobobayhotel.com - Closed January-February

34 rm - £ 49/115 £ 79/185

Rest - *(dinner only)* Menu £ 28 **s** - Carte £ 22/31 **s**

♦ Modern hotel on sandy Cobo Bay; an ideal location for families. The rooms are pleasant with bright décor and some have the delightful addition of seaview balconies. Romantic dining with views of sunsets.

FERMAIN BAY - Guernsey 5 A2

Fermain Valley rm, rest, VISA AE

Fermain Ln GY1 1ZZ - (01481) 235 666 - www.fermainvalley.com

45 rm - £ 95/115 £ 215/245

Rest ***Valley Brasserie*** - Carte £ 25/34

♦ Fine sea views through the trees. Smart contemporary country house theme prevails: sleek lounges, decked terrace, library, and fresh, carefully appointed rooms with balconies. Informal restaurant offers fresh fish and simple grills. Beautiful terrace/view and marine photos by Beken.

KINGS MILLS - Guernsey 5 A2

Fleur du Jardin with rm VISA AE

Grand Moulins GY5 7JT - (01481) 257 996 - www.fleurdujardin.com

17 rm - £ 64/88 £ 88/136 - 1 suite **Rest** - Carte £ 24/33

♦ 15C stone inn with landscaped garden, heated terrace and rustic inner. Regularly changing menu offers mix of unfussy classics and more ambitious dishes. Specials feature island seafood. Well-equipped bedrooms; some in fresh New England style. Heated outdoor pool.

ST MARTIN - Guernsey - **pop. 6 267** 5 A2

St Peter Port 2 mi

Bella Luce VISA AE

La Fosse GY4 6EB - (01481) 238 764 - www.bellalucehotel.com - Closed January

23 rm - £ 104/160 £ 130/200

Rest ***Hemmingway*** - Menu £ 23 - Carte dinner £ 24/38

♦ Originally a Norman manor house; with a cosy beamed bar, cellar-like lounge and stylish, intimate interior featuring voluptuous velvets. Opulent bedrooms boast modern bathrooms. Pleasant gardens with pool. Hemmingway offers an eclectic array of modern dishes.

ENGLAND

La Barbarie

Saints Bay ✉ GY4 6ES – ✆ (01481) 235 217 – www.labarbariehotel.com – 11 March-30 October

26 rm – †£ 59/76 ††£ 77/136 – 1 suite **Rest** – *(bar lunch)* Carte £ 21/32

◆ Stone-built former priory with a welcoming, cottagey style. Characterful bar; well-kept pool and terrace. Bedrooms are traditional and comfortable. Seafood a speciality.

Auberge

Jerbourg Rd ✉ GY4 6BH – ✆ (01481) 238 485 – www.theauberge.gg – Closed January and Sunday dinner

Rest – *(booking essential)* Menu £ 19 (lunch) – Carte £ 26/31

◆ Superbly located informal modern restaurant, with attractive terrace boasting tranquil sea and island views. Artistic dishes display bold flavours. Quality island-caught fish is a favourite.

ST PETER PORT – Guernsey 5 A2

Rohais St Pierre Park, ✆ (01481) 727 039

Town★★ - St Peter's Church★ Z – Hauteville House★ **AC** Z – Castle Cornet★ (≤★) **AC** Z

Saumarez Park★ (Guernsey Folk Museum★), W : 2 mi by road to Catel Z – Little Chapel★, SW : 2.25 mi by Mount Durand road Z

Old Government House H. & Spa rm, rm,

St Ann's Pl ✉ GY1 2NU – ✆ (01481) 724 921 – www.theoghhotel.com Ya

61 rm – †£ 130/185 ††£ 140/185 – 1 suite

Rest *Governors* – *(booking essential)* Carte £ 34/53

Rest *Brasserie* – ✆ (01481) 738 604 – Menu £ 23 – Carte £ 30/40

◆ Fine 18C building; classically furnished, with many of its original features restored. Glorious ballroom, well-equipped spa and individually styled bedrooms with modern bathrooms. Intimate fine dining in Governors, where ambitious cooking has a French base. Smart yet informal Brasserie, with delightful outside terrace.

Nautique

Quay Steps ✉ GY1 2LE – ✆ (01481) 721 714 – www.lenautiquerestaurant.co.uk – Closed Saturday lunch and Sunday Zr

Rest – Menu £ 17 (lunch) **s** – Carte £ 24/34 **s**

◆ Quayside former warehouse with pleasant marina view and characterful, nautically themed interior; ask for a window seat. Large menu of generously sized, classic dishes, with fish a feature.

Pier 17

Albert Pier ✉ GY1 1AD – ✆ (01481) 720 823 – www.pier17restaurant.com – Closed Sunday Zx

Rest – Carte £ 26/32

◆ Set on a historic pier overlooking the harbour. Well-balanced menu displays traditional dishes with a modern edge, supplemented by tasty fish specials.

Swan Inn

St Julian's Ave ✉ GY1 1WA – ✆ (01481) 728 969 – Closed 25 December and Sunday

Rest – Carte £ 15/22 Yx

◆ Smart Victorian pub with bottle-green façade, traditional styling and good value early week menu. Choose hearty, satisfying dishes in the bar or more ambitious fare in the dining room.

ST SAVIOUR – Guernsey 5 A2

St Peter Port 4 mi

Farmhouse

Route des Bas Courtils ✉ GY7 9YF – ✆ (01481) 264 181 – www.thefarmhouse.gg

14 rm – †£ 100/155 ††£ 155/195 **Rest** – Carte £ 25/38

◆ Former farm restyled in boutique vein. Stylish, sumptuous bedrooms with high-tech amenities; bathrooms with heated floors. Pleasant garden and pool; terrace and kitchen garden. Contemporary cooking with international edge uses Island's finest produce in eclectic ways.

ENGLAND

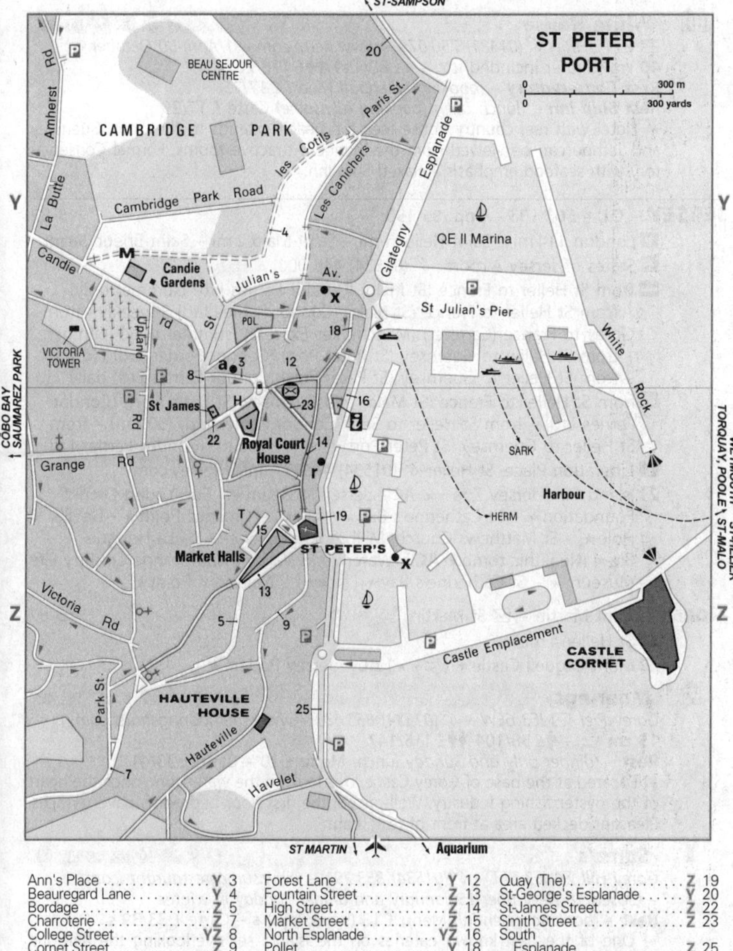

Ann's Place	Y 3	Forest Lane	Y 12	Quay (The)	Z 19
Beauregard Lane	Y 4	Fountain Street	Z 13	St-George's Esplanade	Y 20
Bordage	Z 5	High Street	Z 14	St-James Street	Z 22
Charroterie	Z 7	Market Street	Z 15	Smith Street	Z 23
College Street	YZ 8	North Esplanade	YZ 16	South Esplanade	Z 25
Cornet Street	Z 9	Pollet	Y 18		

Pavilion

Le Gron ✉ GY7 9RN – ✆ (01481) 264 165 – www.thepavilion.co.gg – Closed Christmas-mid January and Monday in winter

Rest – *(lunch only and dinner Friday-Saturday in summer)* Menu £ 20 (dinner) – Carte £ 21/28

◆ Farmhouse-style restaurant displaying exposed stone and beams. Menus offer something for everyone, from tea and cakes to full 3 courses. Fresh, simple, intelligent cooking. Desserts a must.

HERM – Herm – 503 M33 — 5 A2

London 142 mi – Saint Helier 5 mi – Saint Peter Port 5 mi – Saint-Malo 5 mi

to Guernsey (St Peter Port) (Herm Seaway) (20 mn)

Le Grand Monceau★

White House

✉ *GY1 3HR – ☎ (01481) 750 075 – www.herm.com – 1 April-30 October*
40 rm (dinner included) – †£ 88/119 ††£ 176/202
Rest *Conservatory* – *(booking essential)* Menu £ 17/25
Rest *Ship Inn* – *(lunch only) (booking advisable)* Carte £ 17/29
♦ Hotel with real country house feel: the beach extends to the door. Guernsey and Jethou can be viewed from the lounge. Attractive rooms. Formal Conservatory with seafood emphasis. Relaxed Ship Inn.

JERSEY – C.I. – 503 L33 – pop. 85 150 — 5 B2

London 114 mi – Saint Helier 1 mi – Saint-Malo 2 mi – Saint-Brieuc 58 mi

States of Jersey Airport : ☎ (01534) 446 000

from St Helier to France (St Malo) (Condor Ferries Ltd) (summer only) – from St Helier to France (St Malo) (Condor Ferries Ltd) 3 weekly - from Gorey to France (Carteret) (Manche Iles Express) (summer only) (60mn) – from St Helier to Guernsey (St Peter Port) (Condor Ferries Ltd) (50 mn) – from St Helier to Guernsey (St Peter Port) (Condor Ferries Ltd) daily

from St Helier to France (St Malo) and Guernsey (St Peter Port) (Condor Ferries Ltd) – from St Helier to Sark (Condor Ferries Ltd) (50 mn) – from St Helier to Guernsey (St Peter Port) and Weymouth (Condor Ferries Ltd)

Liberation Place, St Helier ☎ (01534) 448877, info@jersey.com

Island★★ - Jersey Zoo★★ **AC** – Jersey Museum★ - Eric Young Orchid Foundation★ – St Catherine's Bay★ (≤★★) – Grosnez Point★ - Devil's Hole★ – St Matthews Church, Millbrook (glasswork★) – La Hougue Bie★ (Neolithic tomb★ **AC**) - Waterworks Valley - Hamptonne Country Life Museum★ – St Catherine's Bay★ (≤★★) – Noirmont Point★

GOREY – Saint Martin – ✉ St Martin — 5 B2

St Helier 4 mi

Mont Orgueil Castle★ (≤★★) **AC** – Jersey Pottery★

Moorings

Gorey Pier ✉ *JE3 6EW – ☎ (01534) 853 633 – www.themooringshotel.com*
15 rm – †£ 58/104 ††£ 115/147
Rest – *(dinner only and Sunday lunch)* Menu £ 20 – Carte £ 33/41
♦ Located at the base of Gorey Castle, overlooking the waterfront, once the heart of the oyster fishing industry. Well-priced; the first floor bedrooms have terraces. Pleasant decked area at front of restaurant.

Suma's

Gorey Hill ✉ *JE3 6ET – ☎ (01534) 853 291 – www.sumasrestaurant .com – Closed 18 December-15 January and dinner Sunday in winter*
Rest – *(booking essential)* Menu £ 18 (weekdays) **s** – Carte £ 33/39 **s**
♦ One of the best known eateries on the island, set overlooking the harbour. Huge sliding glass doors and small heated terrace. Good value lunch and early evening menu. Local produce includes fresh island seafood; unfussy cooking displays Mediterranean influences.

Castle Green

La Route de la Cote ✉ *JE3 6DR – ☎ (01534) 840 218 – www.castlegreenjersey.co.uk – Closed Sunday dinner and Monday*
Rest – Carte £ 19/33
♦ Relaxed, friendly restaurant above Gorey Harbour, with decked terrace and southerly sea panorama. Accessible menu of modern classics, with plenty of Mediterranean dishes and fish specials.

Bass and Lobster

Gorey Coast Rd ✉ *JE3 6EU – ☎ (01534) 859 590 – www.bassandlobster.com – Closed Monday-Tuesday in winter, Monday lunch and Sunday in summer*
Rest – Menu £ 13/17 – Carte £ 24/37
♦ Bright, modern 'foodhouse' close to the beach. Seasonal island produce; fresh, tasty seafood and shellfish dominate the menu. Fantastic oysters; good value lunches. Smooth, effective service.

GREEN ISLAND – Saint Clement **5** B2

Green Island

St Clement ✉ JE2 6LS – ✆ (01534) 857 787 – www.greenisland.je – Closed 1 week Christmas-New Year, Sunday dinner and Monday

Rest – Mediterranean – *(booking essential)* Menu £ 18 (lunch) – Carte £ 30/42

♦ Charming, personally run restaurant with terrace and seaside kiosk. Internationally influenced dishes and seafood specials showcase island produce. Flavours are bold and perfectly judged.

GROUVILLE – Grouville **5** B2

St Helier 3 mi

Cafe Poste

La Rue de la ville ès Renauds ✉ JE3 9FY – ✆ (01534) 859 696 – www.cafeposte.co.uk – Closed 2 weeks November, 1 week spring, Monday and Tuesday

Rest – Menu £ 19 – Carte £ 29/40

♦ Popular neighbourhood restaurant – formerly a post office – with French country themed interior and cosy fire in winter. Eclectic menus include plenty of well-crafted seafood creations.

ROZEL BAY – Saint Martin – ✉ St Martin **5** B2

St Helier 6 mi

Chateau La Chaire

Rozel Valley ✉ JE3 6AJ – ✆ (01534) 863 354 – www.chateau-la-chaire.co.uk

12 rm – †£ 85/120 ††£ 95/295 – 2 suites

Rest – Menu £ 15/30 – Carte £ 40/47

♦ Impressive 19C country house and gardens; drawing room features original plaster ceiling. More contemporary bedrooms blend chic styling with period furniture; Room 2 has a delightful balcony. Conservatory dining room with popular terrace; good use of island ingredients.

ST AUBIN – Saint Brelade – ✉ St Brelade **5** B2

St Helier 4 mi

Somerville rest,

Mont du Boulevard, South : 0.75 mi via harbour ✉ JE3 8AD – ✆ (01534) 741 226 – www.dolanhotels.com

56 rm – †£ 105/170 ††£ 149/189

Rest *Tides* – Menu £ 16/30 **s** – Carte approx. £ 38

♦ Grand 19C hotel in stunning position above the town, with superb view over St Aubin Bay. Stylish public areas and bright bedrooms. The dining room features subtle, contemporary styling; most tables offer a view. Modern menus, with lobster specials in season.

Panorama without rest

La Rue du Crocquet ✉ JE3 8BZ – ✆ (01534) 742 429 – www.panoramajersey.com – Mid-April-mid-October

14 rm – †£ 40/109 ††£ 114/146

♦ Charming, personally run and immaculately kept hotel offering stunning bay and castle views and an extraordinary collection of teapots. Individually decorated bedrooms and comprehensive breakfasts.

ST BRELADE'S BAY – Saint Brelade – ✉ St Brelade **5** B2

St Helier 6 mi

Fishermen's Chapel (frescoes★)

Horizon rm, rest,

✉ JE3 8EF – ✆ (01534) 743 101 – www.handpicked.co.uk/lhorizon

99 rm – †£ 70/170 ††£ 140/280 – 7 suites

Rest *Grill* – *(dinner only)* Menu £ 43 **s**

Rest *Brasserie* – Menu £ 34 (dinner) – Carte £ 25/31

♦ Period hotel right on the beach and consequently popular for its stunning views from the terrace and some of its tastefully decorated front bedrooms. Serene indoor pool. Intimately styled grill room. Informal brasserie with lovely terrace overlooking the beach.

ENGLAND

St Brelade's Bay
La Route de la Baie ✉ JE3 8EF – ☎ (01534) 746 141 – www.stbreladesbayhotel.com – April-September
80 rm – †£ 93/212 ††£ 206/304 – 5 suites
Rest *Bay* – *(closed Monday and Tuesday lunch)* Menu £ 17/30 – Carte £ 32/38
◆ Traditional seafront hotel with mouth-watering views of bay and resplendent gardens with pool. Rattan furnished sitting room and spacious bedrooms. Friendly and family run. Front, sea-facing restaurant.

Oyster Box
La Route de la Baie ✉ JE3 8EF – ☎ (01534) 743 311 – www.oysterbox.co.uk – Closed 25-26 December, 1 January, Sunday dinner and Monday lunch
Rest – *(booking essential)* Carte £ 23/46
◆ Cool, modern restaurant on the beach with al fresco dining. Flexible menu featuring quality ingredients prepared in a fresh, simple manner.

ST HELIER – **Saint Helier** **5** B2

Jersey Museum★ **AC** Z - Elizabeth Castle (≤★) **AC** Z – Fort Regent (≤★ **AC**) Z

St Peter's Valley - German Underground Hospital★ **AC**, NW : 4 mi by A 1, A 11 St Peter's Valley rd and C 112

ENGLAND

Grand
The Esplanade ✉ JE2 3QA – ☎ (01534) 722 301 – www.grandjersey.com Y**u**
117 rm – †£ 109/195 ††£ 135/195 – 6 suites
Rest *Tassili* – *(dinner only Thursday-Saturday) (booking essential)* Menu £ 47
Rest *Victoria's* – *(dinner only and Sunday lunch)* Menu £ 25 – Carte £ 26/38
◆ Victorian hotel with pitched white façade overlooking St Aubin's Bay, given contemporary makeover. Strong leisure facilities and comfortable bedrooms. Tassili for formal dining. Brasserie style in Victoria's.

Club Hotel & Spa
Green St ✉ JE2 4UH – ☎ (01534) 876 500 – www.theclubjersey.com – Closed 25-30 December Z**e**
44 rm – †£ 130/215 ††£ 130/215, £ 7.50 – 2 suites
Rest *Bohemia* – see restaurant listing
◆ Well-run, fresh, modern hotel with pleasant poolside terrace. Bedrooms differ considerably but all are sleek and contemporary with good amenities and luxurious bathrooms.

Royal Yacht
Weighbridge ✉ JE2 3NF – ☎ (01534) 720 511 – www.theroyalyacht.com Z**b**
109 rm – †£ 135 ††£ 220 – 2 suites
Rest *Sirocco* – *(dinner only and Sunday lunch)* Menu £ 25 – Carte approx. £ 46
Rest *Grill* – Carte £ 16/32
◆ Set overlooking the harbour, with contemporary interior and splendid spa. The most spacious bedrooms look to the harbour; the quietest over the inner courtyard; suites feature hot tubs. Formal dining in first floor Sirocco, with its enviable view and Mediterranean menu. Nautical style in Grill, with steaks a speciality.

Eulah Country House without rest
Mont Cochon, Northwest : 2 mi by A 1 on B 27 ✉ JE2 3JA – ☎ (01534) 626 626 – www.eulah.co.uk
9 rm – †£ 105/125 ††£ 150/230
◆ Informally run Edwardian country house proves pleasantly unconventional. Stylish combined lounge and breakfast room, luxurious bedrooms and superb views of St Aubin's Bay.

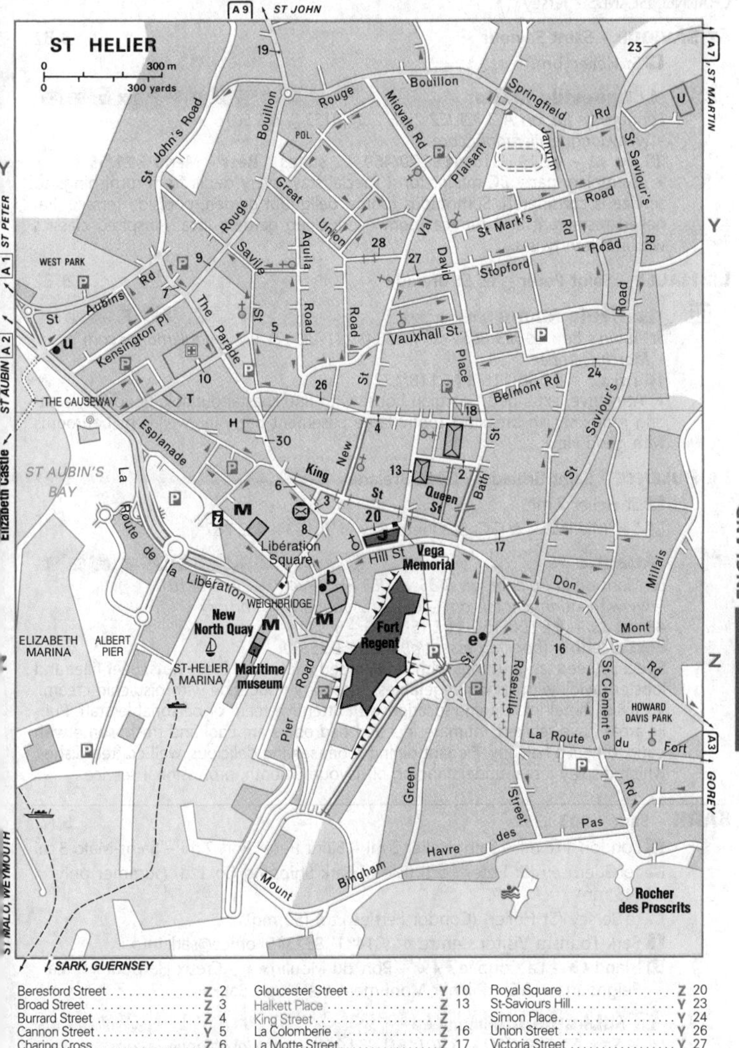

Beresford Street . . . . Z 2
Broad Street . . . . Z 3
Burrard Street . . . . Z 4
Cannon Street . . . . Y 5
Charing Cross . . . . Z 6
Cheapside . . . . Y 7
Conway Street . . . . Z 8
Elizabeth Place . . . . Y 9
Gloucester Street . . . . Y 10
Halkett Place . . . . Z 13
King Street . . . . Z
La Colomberie . . . . Z 16
La Motte Street . . . . Z 17
Minden Place . . . . Z 18
Queen Street . . . . Z
Queen's Road . . . . Y 19
Royal Square . . . . Z 20
St-Saviours Hill . . . . Y 23
Simon Place . . . . Y 24
Union Street . . . . Y 26
Victoria Street . . . . Y 27
Windsor Road . . . . Y 28
York Street . . . . Y 30

XXX **Bohemia** – at The Club Hotel & Spa

Green St ✉ JE2 4UH – ✆ (01534) 880 588 – www.bohemiajersey.com – Closed 25-30 December, Sunday and bank holiday Mondays **Ze**

Rest – Menu £ 22/50

Spec. Curry salted scallops with coconut dhal, onion bhaji and apple salad. Lamb with minted peas, goat's cheese and honeycomb. Rhubarb crumble soufflé with yoghurt, ginger and rhubarb fool.

◆ This stylish restaurant has been extended to include a chef's table. Comfy bar and very attentive serving team. Top quality produce is showcased in cooking that is well-judged and clever, without being gimmicky. Good choice of wines by the glass.

ST SAVIOUR – Saint Saviour 5 B2

St Helier 1 mi

Longueville Manor

Longueville Rd, on A 3 ✉ JE2 7WF – ✆ (01534) 725 501 – www.longuevillemanor.com

28 rm – †£ 195/315 ††£ 220/460 – 2 suites **Rest** – Menu £ 21/55 s

◆ Exemplary part 13C manor for a special stay; every detail from furnishings to service is considered. Sumptuous rooms, delightful garden, poolside terrace. Panelled restaurant and terrace room overlooking garden; locally-inspired classics with modern twists.

LA HAULE – Saint Peter – ✉ St Brelade 5 B2

La Haule Manor without rest

St Aubin's Bay ✉ JE3 8BS – ✆ (01534) 741 426 – www.lahaulemanor.com – March-October

16 rm – †£ 58/116 ††£ 118/172

◆ Attractive, extended Georgian house with fine coastal outlook. Period style sitting room; stylish breakfast room; large basement bar. Airy, well-kept bedrooms with good view.

LA PULENTE – Saint Brelade – ✉ St Brelade 5 B2

St Helier 7 mi

Les Mielles G. & C.C. St Ouens Bay, ✆ (01534) 482 787

ENGLAND

Atlantic

Le Mont de la Pulente, on B 35 ✉ JE3 8HE – ✆ (01534) 744 101 – www.theatlantichotel.com – Closed 2 January-4 February

49 rm – †£ 100/150 ††£ 150/250 – 1 suite

Rest *Ocean* – *(booking essential)* Menu £ 25/60

Spec. Sautéed langoustines with caramelised bacon and Brazil nuts. Beef fillet and lobster ravioli with spring vegetables. Raspberry nougatine with pistachio cream.

◆ Stylish hotel in stunning location with attentive team of personable staff. Public areas have relaxed, intimate feel and bedrooms are cool and fresh; some with patio, others a balcony. Elegant dining room serving delicious, well-crafted dishes, which display a real understanding of flavour. Smooth, professional service.

SARK – Sark – **503** L33 5 A2

London 116 mi – Saint Helier 3 mi – Saint Peter Port 2 mi – Saint-Malo 3 mi

to Guernsey (St Peter Port) (Isle of Sark Shipping Co. Ltd) (summer only) (45 mn)

to Jersey (St Helier) (Condor Ferries Ltd) (50 mn)

Sark Tourism Visitor Centre ✆ (01481) 832345, office@sark.info

Island★★ - La Coupáe★★★ – Port du Moulin★★ - Creux Harbour★ – La Seigneurie★ **AC** – Pilcher Monument★ – Hog's Back★

La Sablonnerie with rm

Little Sark ✉ GY9 OSD – ✆ (01481) 832 061 – www.lasablonnerie.com – mid-April-mid-October

20 rm (dinner included) – †£ 70/135 ††£ 139/270 – 2 suites

Rest – *(booking essential)* Menu £ 30 – Carte £ 25/37

◆ Charming, whitewashed 16C former farmhouse with beautiful gardens. Cosy, beamed interior with a comfortable lounge for aperitifs. Regularly changing, five course menu offers a classic style of cooking using produce from their own farm. Prompt service. Neat, tidy bedrooms; Room 14, in the former stables, is the best.

CHANNEL TUNNEL – Kent – **504** X30 – see Folkestone

CHAPEL-EN-LE-FRITH – Derbyshire – **504** O24 – pop. 6 581 **16** A1

London 175 mi – Sheffield 27 mi – Manchester 21 mi – Stoke-on-Trent 34 mi

High Croft without rest
Manchester Rd, West : 0.75 mi on B 5470 ✉ SK23 9UH – ✆ (01298) 814 843 – www.highcroft-guesthouse.co.uk
4 rm – ♦£ 65 ♦♦£ 105
◆ Edwardian house with period features and lovely mature garden. Comfortable bedrooms overlook surrounding hills and valleys; Atholl suite - a four poster with tub - is best.

CHARLTON – W. Sussex – 504 R31 – see Chichester

CHARMOUTH – Dorset – 503 L31 – pop. 1 497 – ✉ Bridport 3 B3

London 157 mi – Dorchester 22 mi – Exeter 31 mi – Taunton 27 mi

White House
2 Hillside, The Street ✉ DT6 6PJ – ✆ (01297) 560 411 – www.whitehousehotel.com – restricted opening in winter
6 rm – ♦£ 60/90 ♦♦£ 90/150
Rest – *(closed Sunday and Monday) (dinner only)* Menu £ 33
◆ Gleaming white Regency villa close to the Jurassic Coast, personally run by a friendly couple. Bedrooms feature cast iron/sleigh beds and flat screen TVs. Comfortable sitting room in period style. More modern, wood-furnished dining room; classic menus.

CHATHILL – Northumberland – see Alnwick

CHEDDLETON – Staffordshire – 502 N24 – pop. 2 719 – ✉ Leek 19 C1

London 125 mi – Birmingham 48 mi – Derby 33 mi – Manchester 42 mi

Choir Cottage without rest
Ostlers Lane, via Hollow Lane, (opposite Red Lion on A 520) ✉ ST13 7HS – ✆ (01538) 360 561 – www.choircottage.co.uk – Closed 25 December
3 rm – ♦£ 59/69 ♦♦£ 70/80
◆ Personally run 17C stone cottage, formerly owned by the church and let to the poor, with the rent used to buy choir gowns. Individually furnished bedrooms boast private outdoor seating areas; some have four-posters and one is split-level. Smart guest areas.

CHELMSFORD – Essex – 504 V28 – pop. 99 962 13 C2

London 33 mi – Cambridge 46 mi – Ipswich 40 mi – Southend-on-Sea 19 mi

Unit 3, Dukes Walk, Duke St ✆ (01245) 283400, chelmsfordvisitor.information@firstgroup.com

Barda
30-32 Broomfield Rd ✉ CM1 1SW – ✆ (01245) 357 799 – www.barda-restaurant.com – Closed Sunday dinner and Monday
Rest – Menu £ 17 – Carte £ 25/35
◆ Keenly run contemporary restaurant with large decked terrace. Simple, flavoursome dishes at lunch; more interesting, international cooking at dinner. Classical puddings display modern twists.

at Boreham Northeast : 3.5 mi on B 1137 (Springfield Rd)

Lion Inn
Main Rd ✉ CM3 3JA – ✆ (01245) 394 900 – www.lioninnhotel.co.uk – Closed 24-26 December
15 rm – ♦£ 105 ♦♦£ 150 **Rest** – Carte £ 20/39
◆ Keenly run, extended former pub with eco-friendly credentials and a French feel. Soundproofed bedrooms blend contemporary furnishings with antiques. Large open-plan lounge/brasserie with buzzy atmosphere; short menu of appealing, pub-style dishes.

ENGLAND

CHELTENHAM – Gloucestershire – 503 N28 – pop. 98 875 4 C1

London 99 mi – Birmingham 48 mi – Bristol 40 mi – Gloucester 9 mi

77 Promenade ✆ (01242) 522878, tic@cheltenham.gov.uk

Cleeve Hill, ✆ (01242) 672 025

Cotswold Hills Ullenwood, ✆ (01242) 515 264

Town★

Sudeley Castle★ (Paintings★) **AC**, NE : 7 mi by B 4632 A

Hotel du Vin

rm, VISA

Parabola Rd ✉ GL50 3AQ – ✆ (01242) 588 450 – www.hotelduvin.com

48 rm – †£ 155/300 ††£ 155/300, ☕ £ 10.95 – 1 suite BY**c**

Rest *Bistro* – Menu £ 16 (lunch) – Carte £ 24/35

◆ Stylish Regency house. Lounge features a chandelier made from wine glasses. Bedrooms are named after wines and boast contemporary furnishings and wine-themed artwork. Bistro-style restaurant with paved terrace offers classical menus with French influences.

The Hotel

VISA

38 Evesham Rd ✉ GL52 2AH – ✆ (01242) 518 898 – www.thehoteluk.co.uk

12 rm – †£ 155 ††£ 155, ☕ £ 19 CY**r**

Rest *Parkers* – see restaurant listing

◆ Stylish, modern hotel displaying bold, contemporary colours and striking furniture. Black marble floored reception, comfortable lounge and smart bar. Bedrooms – named after dukes and dignitaries – boast chic styling, good modern facilities and smart bathrooms.

Beaumont House without rest

VISA

56 Shurdington Rd ✉ GL53 0JE – ✆ (01242) 223 311 – www.bhhotel.co.uk

16 rm ☕ – †£ 69/80 ††£ 90/127 AX**u**

◆ Keenly run Georgian house with comfy drawing room and bar; breakfast room overlooks lawned garden. Refurbished bedrooms are stylish and contemporary with excellent bathrooms.

Lypiatt House without rest

VISA

Lypiatt Rd ✉ GL50 2QW – ✆ (01242) 224 994 – www.staylypiatt.co.uk

10 rm ☕ – †£ 75/90 ††£ 120 BZ**c**

◆ A privately owned, serene Victorian house with friendly service. Bedrooms on the top floor with dormer roof tend to be smaller than those on the other floors. Soft, pale colours.

Butlers without rest

VISA

Western Rd ✉ GL50 3RN – ✆ (01242) 570 771 – www.butlers-hotel.co.uk

9 rm ☕ – †£ 55/70 ††£ 85/120 BY**v**

◆ Personally managed hotel where bedrooms constitute a peaceful haven with stylish drapes and canopies. Rooms named after famous butlers; some overlook wooded garden to rear.

Thirty Two without rest

VISA

32 Imperial Sq ✉ GL50 1QZ – ✆ (01242) 771 110 – www.thirtytwoltd.com – closed 25-26 December BZ**e**

4 rm ☕ – †£ 160 ††£ 175

◆ Immaculate Regency house overlooking grassy city square. Stylish, beautifully appointed bedrooms with furniture designed by owner; superb bathrooms. Excellent facilities and extra touches.

Hanover House without rest

VISA

65 St George's Rd ✉ GL50 3DU – ✆ (01242) 541 297 – www.hanoverhouse.org – Closed 25 December BY**u**

3 rm ☕ – †£ 70 ††£ 100

◆ Early Victorian townhouse, perfectly located for seeing the city. Comfortable family lounge filled with books and portraits; spacious, tastefully furnished bedrooms. Organic breakfasts.

CHELTENHAM

Berkeley St . . . . CYZ 4
Clarence St . . . . CY 6
Crescent Terrace . . . . . BY 7
Deep St. . . . . AX 9
Dunalley St . . . . CY 10
Henrietta St. . . . . CY 13
High St . . . . BCY
High St PRESTBURY . AX 14
Keynsham Rd . . . . CZ 15
Knapp Rd. . . . . BY 16
Montpellier Ave. . . . . . BZ 17
Montpellier Walk . . . . . BZ 18
North St. . . . . CY 20
Norwood Rd . . . . BZ 21
Oriel Rd . . . . CZ 22
Pittville St . . . . CY 26
Portland St. . . . . CY 27
Promenade (The) . . . . . . BZCY 28
Regent Arcade Shopping Centre . . . . CY 29
Regent St . . . . CY 29
Rodney Rd. . . . . CY 30
Royal Well Rd . . . . . . BCY 32
St James St. . . . . CY 33
St Johns Ave . . . . CY 34
St Margaret's Rd . . . . . CY 35
Sandford Mill Rd . . . . . CZ 36
Sandford Terrace . . . . . CZ 37
Winchcombe St . . . . . . CY 38

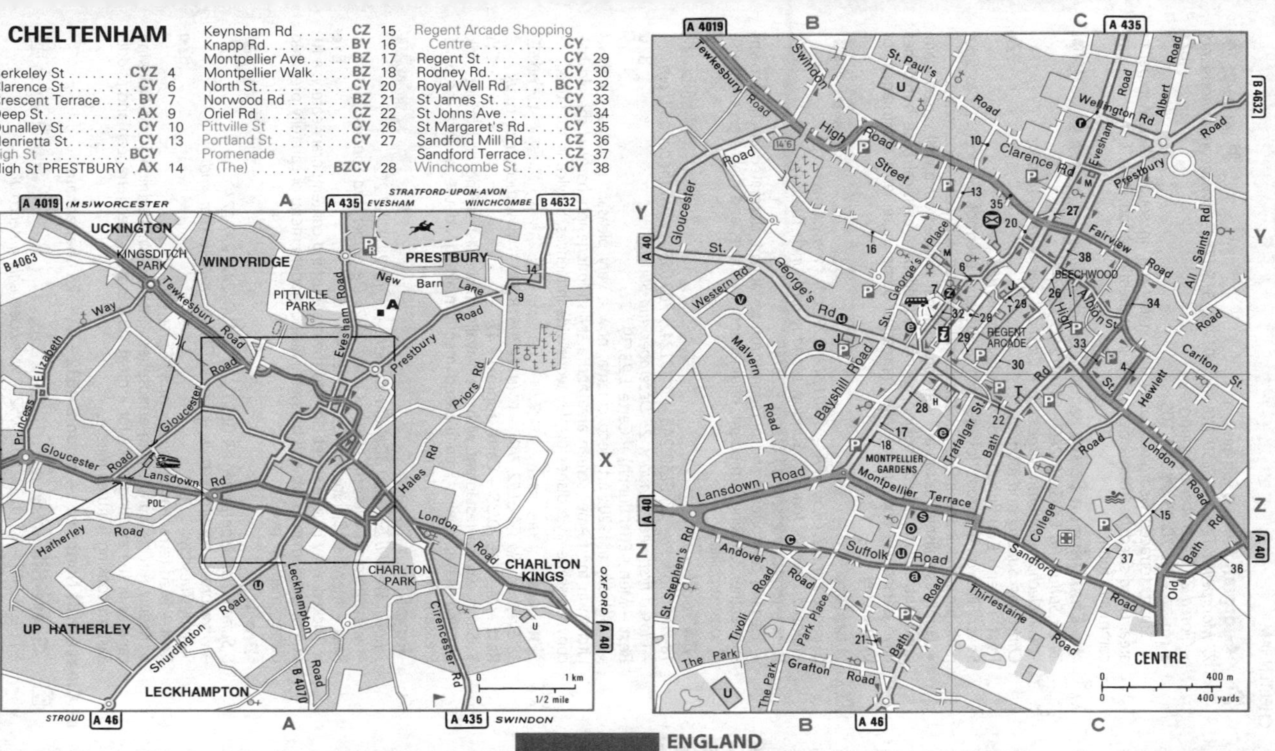

Georgian House without rest
77 Montpellier Terr. ✉ GL50 1XA – ☎ (01242) 515 577 – www.georgianhouse.net – Closed 22 December-5 January BZ**s**
3 rm – †£ 70/85 ††£ 85/105
◆ Smart, terraced Georgian house, hospitably run, in sought-after Montpellier area. Good-sized bedrooms decorated in authentic period style. Comfy, elegant communal rooms.

Le Champignon Sauvage (David Everitt-Matthias)
24-28 Suffolk Rd ✉ GL50 2AQ – ☎ (01242) 573 449 – www.lechampignonsauvage.com – Closed 3 weeks June, 10 days Christmas, Sunday and Monday BZ**a**
Rest – Menu £ 30 (lunch and weekday dinner)/55
Spec. Fillet of sea trout, lovage vichyssoise and beetroot. Gloucester Old Spot pork, pig's cheek and head. Chocolate and olive tart with fennel ice cream.
◆ Firmly established restaurant with professional service from a well-versed team. Confident, accomplished cooking is underscored by a classical base but dishes have personality and are visually impressive. Some ingredients are foraged for by the chef.

Lumière
Clarence Par. ✉ GL50 3PA – ☎ (01242) 222 200 – www.lumiere.cc – Closed 2 weeks January, Sunday, Monday and lunch Tuesday BCY**z**
Rest – *(booking essential)* Menu £ 25/45
◆ Elegant, comfortable and personally run restaurant, decorated in chic browns and leather. Cooking is modern, original and inventive, and makes excellent use of local suppliers.

ENGLAND

Daffodil
18-20 Suffolk Par. ✉ GL50 2AE – ☎ (01242) 700 055 – www.thedaffodil.com – Closed first week January, 25 December and Sunday BZ**u**
Rest – Menu £ 16 (lunch) – Carte £ 23/39
◆ Originally a 1920s art deco cinema, now a very pleasant restaurant with its kitchen in the former screen area and a stylish lounge in what was the old balcony. Brasserie-style dishes display worldwide influences. Service is attentive.

Parkers – at The Hotel
38 Evesham Rd ✉ GL52 2AH – ☎ (01242) 518 898 – www.thehoteluk.co.uk
Rest – Menu £ 20/35 – Carte approx. £ 47 CY**r**
◆ Smart, stylish restaurant with plain walls, minimalist styling and bright pink, brushed velvet chairs. French-based menus make good use of local produce. Pleasant enclosed rear terrace.

Royal Well Tavern
5 Royal Well Pl. ✉ GL50 3DN Cheltenham – ☎ (01242) 221 212 – www.theroyalwelltavern.com – Closed 25-26 December and Sunday
Rest – Menu £ 13 (lunch) – Carte £ 29/49 BY**e**
◆ Tucked away in side street close to theatre. Bustling contemporary eatery; a fusion of gentleman's club and brasserie. Rustic modern menu of carefully prepared dishes; many in two sizes.

Brosh
8 Suffolk Par. Montpellier ✉ GL50 2AB – ☎ (01242) 227 277 – www.broshrestaurant.co.uk – Closed Christmas-New Year and Sunday-Tuesday BZ**o**
Rest – Mediterranean – *(dinner only)* Carte £ 20/39
◆ Keenly run restaurant with atmospheric interior: dimmed lights and flickering candles in the evening make for a great vibe. Eastern Mediterranean and Middle Eastern cooking features mezze.

at Cleeve Hill Northeast : 4 mi on B 4632 - AX – ✉ Cheltenham

Cleeve Hill without rest
✉ GL52 3PR – ☎ (01242) 672 052 – www.cleevehill-hotel.co.uk
10 rm – †£ 45/65 ††£ 85/125
◆ Edwardian house in elevated spot; most bedrooms have views across Cleeve Common and the Malvern Hills. Breakfast room is in the conservatory; admire the landscape over coffee.

Malvern View with rm

✉ *GL52 3PR – ✆ (01242) 672 017 – www.malvernview.com – Closed 2 weeks January, Sunday and Monday*

6 rm – †£ 60/70 ††£ 85/100

Rest – Menu £ 17 (lunch) – Carte dinner £ 30/35

◆ Sandstone house with views of Malvern countryside and Cleeve Hill. Concise menu of classic dishes; hearty, flavoursome cooking. Good value lunch menu and friendly service. Boutique-style bedrooms boast bold feature walls and modern facilities; Room 1 is the largest.

at Shurdington Southwest : 3.75 mi on A 46 - AX – ✉ Cheltenham

Greenway

✉ *GL51 4UG – ✆ (01242) 862 352 – www.thegreenway.co.uk*

16 rm – †£ 160/290 ††£ 350/400 – 1 suite **Rest** – Menu £ 48

◆ Ivy-clad Elizabethan manor house set in large grounds and peaceful lawned gardens. Spacious, classically styled lounges and drawing rooms. Bedrooms have a typical country house feel. Smart spa facility. Garden and lily pond on view from formal restaurant.

CHERITON FITZPAINE – 503 J31 – ✉ Devon 2 C2

London 182 mi – Cardiff 108 mi – Plymouth 59 mi – Swansea 144 mi

Devon Wine School

Redyeates Farm, North : 0.75 mi by Way Rd turning left down unmarked road after Redyeates cross roads. ✉ EX17 4HG – ✆ (01363) 866 742 – www.devonwineschool.co.uk – Closed 1 week mid-May, 1 week early July and 25 December

5 rm – †£ 80/90 ††£ 100/130 **Rest** – Menu £ 33

◆ Delightful 17C farmhouse in idyllic rural spot; offering residential wine school run by a Master of Wine. Fresh, modern bedrooms; Saint Amour has its own private terrace and roll-top bath. Set dinner menu served at large table in vaulted barn.

ENGLAND

CHESTER – Cheshire – 502 L24 – pop. 80 121 Great Britain 20 A3

London 207 mi – Birkenhead 7 mi – Birmingham 91 mi – Liverpool 21 mi

Chester Visitor Centre, Vicars Lane ✆ (01244) 402111, tic@chester.gov.uk

Upton-by-Chester Upton Lane, ✆ (01244) 381 183

Curzon Park, ✆ (01244) 677 760

City★★ - The Rows★★ B – Cathedral★ B – City Walls★ B

Chester Zoo★ AC, N : 3 mi by A 5116

Plans on following pages

Chester Grosvenor H. and Spa

Eastgate ✉ CH1 1LT – ✆ (01244) 324 024 – www.chestergrosvenor.com – Closed 25-26 December **Ba**

76 rm – †£ 220 ††£ 350, £ 25 – 4 suites

Rest ***Simon Radley at The Chester Grosvenor and La Brasserie*** – see restaurant listing

◆ 19C hotel with grand black and white timbered façade; set close to the cathedral and historic city centre. Lavish interior displays rich décor, impressive antiques and luxurious bedrooms.

Doubletree by Hilton Chester

Warrington Rd., Northeast : 2 mi on A 56 ✉ CH2 3PD – ✆ (01244) 408 800 – www.doubletree-hilton.co.uk/chester – Closed 25-26 December **As**

140 rm – †£ 85/190 ††£ 85/190, £ 12.95

Rest – Menu £ 20 (dinner) **s** – Carte £ 16/30 **s**

Rest ***Marco Pierre White Steakhouse Bar*** – Beef specialities – ✆ (01244) 408 830 *(Closed Monday lunch and Sunday dinner)* Carte £ 27/49

◆ Smart, stylish hotel offering sleek, spacious bedrooms with super king-sized beds, bright white décor and modern facilities. State-of-the-art conference facilities. Superb spa with well-equipped leisure club. Modern steakhouse set in 18C manor house. Informal brasserie.

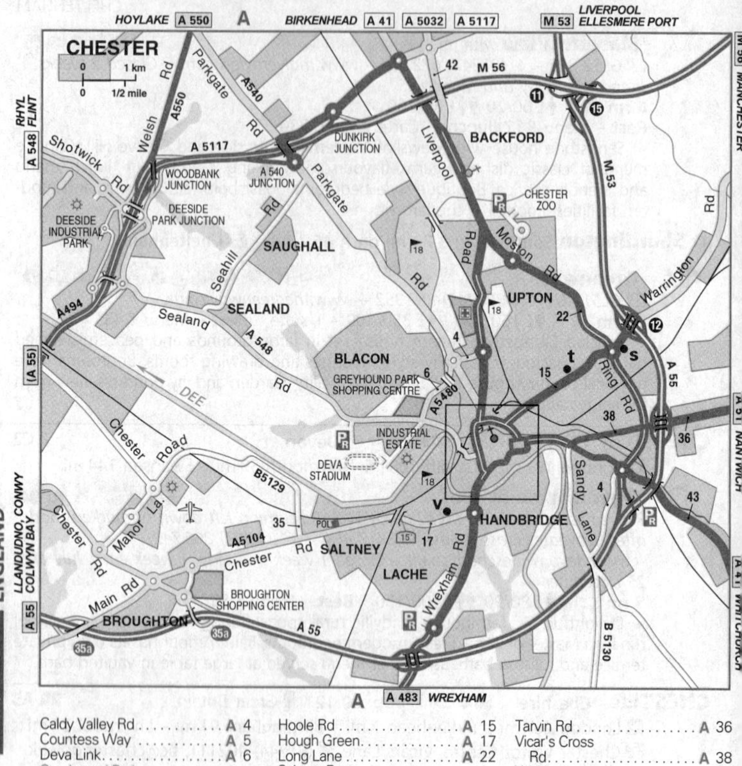

Abode Chester

rm,

Grosvenor Rd ✉ CH1 2DJ – ✆ (01244) 347 000 – www.abodehotels.co.uk

85 rm ☕ – 🚹£ 89/135 👥£ 89/135 Bz

Rest *Michael Caines* – see restaurant listing

Rest *MC Café Grill & Bar* – Menu £ 14 – Carte £ 23/34

◆ Imposing modern hotel opposite the castle and the racecourse; a short walk into the city. Four categories of bedroom; Enviable and Fabulous are the best. Ask for a room with a racecourse view. Ground floor MC Café Grill & Bar offers a modern brasserie menu.

Green Bough

60 Hoole Rd, on A 56 ✉ CH2 3NL – ✆ (01244) 326 241 – www.greenbough.co.uk – Closed 24 December-2 January At

13 rm ☕ – 🚹£ 85/125 👥£ 95/195 – 3 suites

Rest *Olive Tree* – *(dinner only)* Menu £ 25 – Carte £ 42/49

◆ Personally run and very comfortable hotel, boasting high quality decor; owner pays notable attention to detail. Individually styled, generously sized bedrooms: some in a country house style, others displaying bold, contemporary décor – many boast wrought iron feature beds. Dine formally in attractive surroundings.

Mitchell's of Chester without rest

28 Hough Grn, Southwest : 1 mi by A 483 on A 5104 ✉ CH4 8JQ – ✆ (01244) 679 004 – www.mitchellsofchester.com – Closed 21- 29 December Av

7 rm ☕ – 🚹£ 40/70 👥£ 70/95

◆ Large Victorian house, attractively restored and privately run. Homely breakfast room; lounge comes complete with parrot. Individually decorated bedrooms continue Victoriana feel.

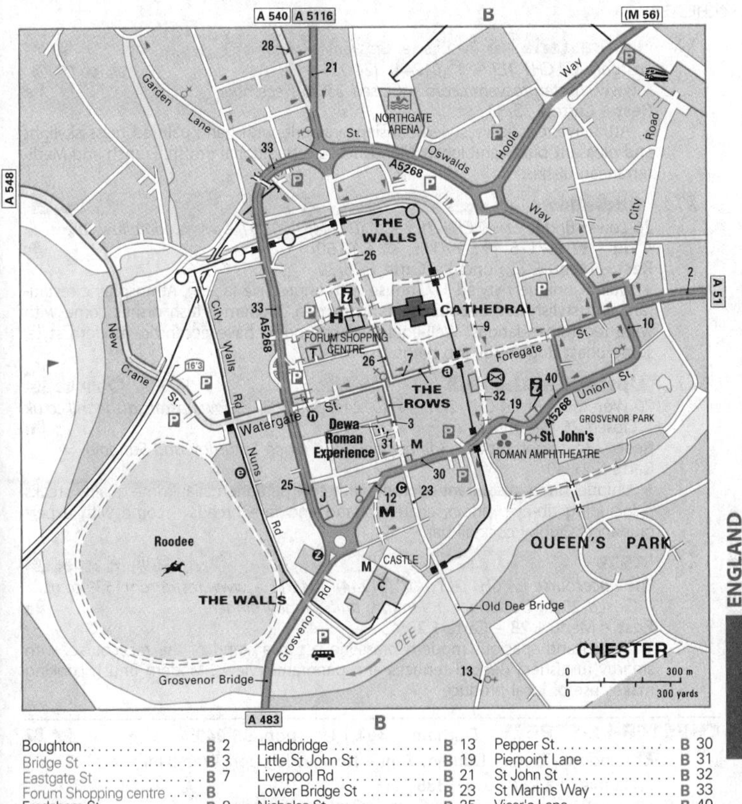

B

- Boughton . . . . . B 2
- Bridge St . . . . . B 3
- Eastgate St . . . . . B 7
- Forum Shopping centre . . . . . B
- Frodsham St . . . . . B 9
- Grosvenor Park Rd . . . . . B 10
- Grosvenor St . . . . . B 12
- Handbridge . . . . . B 13
- Little St John St . . . . . B 19
- Liverpool Rd . . . . . B 21
- Lower Bridge St . . . . . B 23
- Nicholas St . . . . . B 25
- Northgate St . . . . . B 26
- Parkgate Rd . . . . . B 28
- Pepper St . . . . . B 30
- Pierpoint Lane . . . . . B 31
- St John St . . . . . B 32
- St Martins Way . . . . . B 33
- Vicar's Lane . . . . . B 40
- Watergate St . . . . . B

XXXX **Simon Radley at The Chester Grosvenor**

Eastgate ✉ *CH1 1LT – ✆ (01244) 324 024*
– www.chestergrosvenor.com
– Closed 25-26 December, 1-10 January, Sunday and Monday **Ba**

Rest – *(dinner only)* Menu £ 69

Spec. Saddle of rabbit with smoked bacon macaroni, peas and poached langoustine. Roast grouse with saddle of hare, cocoa and cassis. Pistachio cantuccini and mandarin curd.

◆ Smart restaurant with fabric-covered walls, plush furnishings, stylish cocktail lounge and formal, detailed service. Quality ingredients come together in sophisticated dishes that boast creative, innovative touches. Attractive, modern presentation.

XX **Michael Caines** – at Abode Chester

Grosvenor Rd, (Fifth Floor) ✉ *CH1 2DJ*
– ✆ (01244) 405 820 – www.michaelcaines.com
– Closed Sunday **Bz**

Rest – Menu £ 13 (lunch and early dinner)/20
– Carte £ 35/54

◆ Fashionable spot for city dining, located on fifth floor of hotel. Menus combine a French base with a modern edge; try the tasting menu to fully appreciate the flavourful, artistic cooking.

XX **La Brasserie** – at The Chester Grosvenor H. Spa Hotel

Eastgate ✉ CH1 1LT – ☎ (01244) 324 024 – www.chestergrosvenor.com – Closed 25-26 December Ba

Rest – Carte £ 33/53

◆ Attractive, classically styled Parisian brasserie with hand-painted glass skylight and pleasant buzzy ambience. Menus feature traditional British, French and Mediterranean dishes.

XX **Oddfellows** with rm

20 Lower Bridge St ✉ CH1 1RS – ☎ (01244) 400 001 – www.oddfellows.biz

4 rm – †£ 99/175 ††£ 99/175, ☕ £ 12.50 Bc

Rest – Menu £ 13 (lunch) – Carte £ 26/39

◆ Quirky, uniquely styled 17C house with impressive façade. Atmospheric restaurant and stylish bar; Bedouin tents in garden. Modern British dishes come with wine recommendations. Well-equipped bedrooms have eccentric, modern style; some boast double roll-top baths.

XX **Upstairs at the Grill**

70 Watergate St ✉ CH1 2LA – ☎ (01244) 344 883 – www.upstairsatthegrill.co.uk – Closed 25 December Bn

Rest – Beef specialities – *(dinner only and lunch Saturday and Sunday)* Carte £ 21/40

◆ Unique, buzzy restaurant adorned with cow paraphernalia. Prime quality steaks – including rib-eye, sirloin, chateaubriand and rare breeds – come with expert guidance. Clubby cocktail bar.

XX **1539**

The Racecourse ✉ CH1 2LY – ☎ (01244) 304 611 – www.restaurant1539.co.uk – Closed 25-26 December, 1 January and Sunday dinner Be

Rest – Menu £ 28 – Carte £ 20/43

◆ Stylish and spacious modern brasserie set in a stand of the racecourse, with smartly furnished, decked terraces and panoramic views. Modern British cooking makes use of local produce.

ENGLAND

CHESTER-LE-STREET – Durham – 502 P19 – pop. 36 049 — 24 B2

London 275 mi – Durham 7 mi – Newcastle upon Tyne 8 mi

Lumley Park, ☎ (0191) 388 3218

Roseberry Grange Grange Villa, ☎ (0191) 370 0660

Lumley Castle

East : 1 mi on B 1284 ✉ DH3 4NX – ☎ (0191) 389 1111 – www.lumleycastle.com – Closed 25-26 December and 2 January

73 rm ☕ – †£ 69/145 ††£ 105/250 – 1 suite

Rest *Black Knight* – *(closed Saturday lunch)* Menu £ 22/34 **s** – Carte dinner £ 27/46 **s**

◆ Norman castle, without additions, underscoring its uniqueness. Rich, gothic interiors of carved wood, chandeliers, statues, tapestries, rugs. Rooms imbued with atmosphere. Restaurant offers classical dishes with an original twist.

CHEW MAGNA – Bath and North East Somerset – 503 M29 – pop. 1 187 — 4 C2

London 128 mi – Bristol 9 mi – Cardiff 52 mi – Bournemouth 89 mi

Pony & Trap (Josh Eggleton)

Knowle Hill, Newtown, South : 1.25 mi on Bishop Stuttard rd ✉ BS40 8TQ – ☎ (01275) 332 627 – www.theponyandtrap.co.uk – Closed Sunday dinner in winter and Monday

Rest – *(booking essential)* Carte £ 20/26

Spec. Scallops with Hodge Podge and cider reduction. Pork fillet and belly with celeriac purée and apple sauce. Rhubarb and ginger jelly with vanilla panna cotta.

◆ Cosy whitewashed pub in a tiny hamlet; its oversized dining room windows offering lovely country views. Twice-daily menu of extremely fresh, seasonal produce, including locally sourced, hung and smoked meats and fish. Classical cooking with clean, clear flavours.

Bear & Swan

13 South Par ✉ BS40 8SL – ✆ (01275) 331 100 – www.bearandswan.co.uk – Closed Sunday dinner
Rest – Carte £ 19/31
♦ Well-established village pub with delightful open-fired bar, candlelit dining room and loyal local following. Choice of fresh, homemade British pub classics or more European-influenced dishes.

CHICHESTER – West Sussex – 504 R31 – pop. 27 477 Great Britain 7 C2

London 69 mi – Brighton 31 mi – Portsmouth 18 mi – Southampton 30 mi
29a South St ✆ (01243) 775888, chitic@chichester.gov.uk
Goodwood Kennel Hill, ✆ (01243) 755 133
Chichester Golf Centre Hunston Village, ✆ (01243) 533 833
City★★ – Cathedral★★ BZ **A** – St Mary's Hospital★ BY **D** – Pallant House★ **AC** BZ **M**
Fishbourne Roman Palace★★ (mosaics★) **AC** AZ **R**. Weald and Downland Open Air Museum★★ **AC**, N : 6 mi by A 286 AY

Ship

57 North St. ✉ PO19 1NH – ✆ (01243) 778 000 – www.theshiphotel.net
36 rm – †£ 80/100 ††£ 99/175 **Rest** – Carte £ 20/33 BY**s**
♦ Grade II listed building, formerly home to one of Nelson's men. Some Georgian and Regency features remain, including a cantilevered wrought iron staircase. Stylish, contemporary bedrooms. Airy brasserie with modern menu; meat and game from nearby estate.

Comme ça

67 Broyle Rd, on A 286 ✉ PO19 6BD – ✆ (01243) 788 724 – www.commeca.co.uk – Closed 24 December-6 January AY**c**
Rest – French – Menu £ 25/35
♦ Stalwart of the local dining scene for many years. Classical French cooking ministered by Normand chef. Family lunches on Sundays; good value pre-theatre menu. Eat in the airy conservatory.

CHICHESTER

Street	Grid	No.
Birdham Rd	AZ	2
Bognor Rd	AZ	3
Chapel St	BY	6
Chartres (Av. de)	BZ	7
Chichester Arundel Rd	AY	8
East Pallant	BZ	9
East St	BZ	
Florence Rd	AZ	10
Hornet (The)	BZ	12
Kingsham Rd	BZ	13
Lavant Rd	AY	14
Little London	BY	15
Market Rd	BZ	16
Northgate	BY	17
North Pallant	BZ	19
North St	BYZ	
Oaklands Way	BY	18
St James's	AZ	21
St John's St	BZ	23
St Martin's Square	BY	24
St Pancras	BY	25
St Paul's Rd	BY	27
Sherborne Rd	AZ	28
Southgate	BZ	29
South Pallant	BZ	31
South St	BZ	
Spitalfield Lane	BY	32
Stockbridge Rd	AZ	33
Tower St	BY	35
Via Ravenna	AZ	37
Westhampnett Rd	AYZ	38
West Pallant	BZ	39

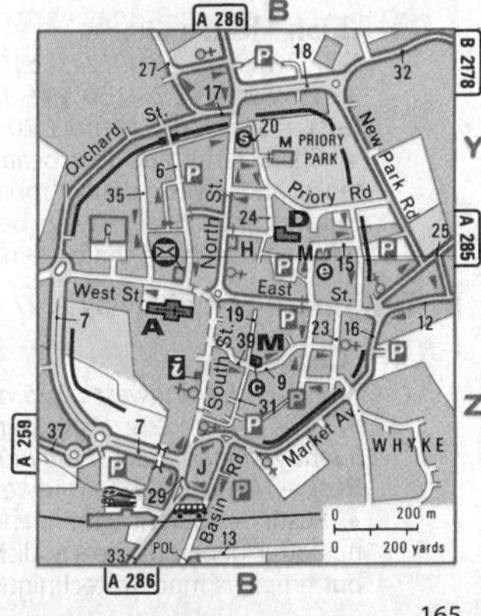

X **Field and Fork at Pallant House Gallery**
9 North Pallant ✉ PO19 1TJ – ✆ (01243) 770 827 – www.fieldandfork.co.uk – Closed 25-26 December, 1 January, Monday, dinner Sunday and Tuesday
Rest – Menu £ 27 (dinner) – Carte lunch £ 26/30 BZc
◆ Modern restaurant in striking Queen Anne building, with delightful courtyard and adjoining art gallery. Light dishes at lunch; more formal dinner menu. Fresh, seasonal produce used with care.

at Mid Lavant North 2 mi on A286

Rooks Hill without rest
Lavant Rd ✉ PO18 0BQ – ✆ (01243) 528 400 – www.rookshill.co.uk – Closed first 2 weeks January and 1 week Autumn
6 rm – †£ 75/105 ††£ 99/165
◆ Charming Grade II listed guesthouse with mix of contemporary styling and original features. Breakfast room opens into lovely terrace/garden. Well appointed bedrooms with attractive bathrooms. Large buffet breakfast.

The Earl of March
✉ PO18 0BQ – ✆ (01243) 533 993 – www.theearlofmarch.com – Closed Sunday dinner
Rest – Menu £ 22 (early dinner) – Carte £ 25/35
◆ 18C inn with perfect blend of country character and contemporary styling. Terrace with amazing views of the South Downs. Good quality, seasonal produce used in classic British dishes.

at East Lavant North : 2.5 mi off A 286 - AY – ✉ Chichester

The Royal Oak Inn with rm
Pook Ln ✉ PO18 0AX – ✆ (01243) 527 434 – www.royaloakeastlavant.co.uk
10 rm – †£ 60/135 ††£ 100/210 **Rest** – Carte £ 31/60
◆ 18C whitewashed inn with rustic, laid-back feel; arrive early for a spot by the fire. Cooking is fairly refined but steaks play an important role. There are interesting vegetarian options, a good cheese selection and plenty of wines by the glass. Spacious bedrooms are comfy and well-equipped; breakfast is a treat.

ENGLAND

at Charlton North : 6.25 mi by A 286 - AY – ✉ Chichester

The Fox Goes Free
✉ PO18 0HU – ✆ (01243) 811 461 – www.thefoxgoesfree.com – Closed 25 December
Rest – Carte £ 20/28
◆ Charming 17C flint pub with lovely South Downs outlook, pleasant garden and many original features. Dishes range from simple pub classics to more substantial local offerings; some to share.

at Chilgrove North : 6.5 mi by A 286 on B 2141

Fish House with rm
✉ PO18 9HX – ✆ (01243) 519 444 – www.thefishhouse.co.uk
15 rm – †£ 75/160 ††£ 95/210
Rest – Seafood – Menu £ 20 – Carte £ 28/47
◆ Characterful and low beamed, with marble topped bar, oyster counter, fish tanks and stylish dining room. Classical seafood à la carte with international touches. Individually styled bedrooms boast espresso machines, iPod docks and private hot tubs in the garden.

at Tangmere East : 2 mi by A 27 - AY – ✉ Chichester

XX **Cassons**
Arundel Rd, Northwest : 0.25 mi off A 27 (westbound) ✉ PO18 0DU – ✆ (01243) 773 294 – www.cassonsrestaurant.co.uk – Closed 26-30 December, Monday, Sunday dinner and Tuesday lunch
Rest – Menu £ 21/35 (midweek) – Carte £ 22/35
◆ Rustic restaurant with linen-laid tables and exposed brick walls. Set price menus offer generous, hearty dishes with bold flavours. Cooking is classically based but employs modern techniques.

at Sidlesham South : 5 mi on B 2145 - AZ

Landseer House without rest
Cow Ln. , South : 1.5 mi by B2145 and Keynor Lane. ✉ *PO20 7LN* – ☎ *(01243) 641 525* – *www.landseerhouse.co.uk*
6 rm – †£ 85/95 ††£ 95/200
◆ Delightful guesthouse with large conservatory and unusual furniture; set in 4½ acres of gardens by a nature reserve and harbour. Two bedrooms in the courtyard. Views to the Isle of Wight.

Crab and Lobster with rm
Mill Ln ✉ *PO20 7NB* – ☎ *(01243) 641 233* – *www.crab-lobster.co.uk*
4 rm – †£ 80 ††£ 150 **Rest** – *(booking advisable)* Carte £ 26/46
◆ Historic inn, superbly located on a nature reserve, with pretty gardens and a light, relaxed feel. Seasonal menu focuses on seafood. Very comfortable bedrooms have a modern, minimalist style; one has its own garden and an open fired stove.

at Bosham West : 4 mi by A 259 - AZ – ✉ Chichester

Millstream rm, rest,
Bosham Ln ✉ *PO18 8HL* – ☎ *(01243) 573 234* – *www.millstream-hotel.co.uk*
32 rm – †£ 85/129 ††£ 145/175 – 3 suites **Rest** – Menu £ 25/30
◆ Attractive hotel with a pretty garden that backs onto a stream bobbing with ducks. Cosy bedrooms display individually co-ordinated fabric furnishings, sand-wash fitted furniture and large windows. Seasonal, daily changing menus.

at Funtington Northwest : 4.75 mi by B 2178 - AY - on B 2146 – ✉ Chichester

Hallidays
Watery Ln. ✉ *PO18 9LF* – ☎ *(01243) 575 331* – *www.hallidays.info* – *Closed 2 weeks August, 1 week March, Saturday lunch, Sunday dinner, Monday and Tuesday*
Rest – Menu £ 20 (lunch)/35 – Carte £ 28/37
◆ A row of part-13C thatched cottages; confident and keen chef delivers a lively medley of frequently changing menus. Modern meals sit alongside classics; local produce plays a key role.

CHIEVELEY – West Berkshire – **503** Q29 **10** B3
London 60 mi – Newbury 5 mi – Swindon 25 mi

The Crab at Chieveley with rm
Wantage Rd, West : 2.5 mi by School Rd on B 4494 ✉ *RG20 8UE* – ☎ *(01635) 247 550* – *www.crabatchieveley.com*
13 rm – ††£ 195 **Rest** – Menu £ 20 (lunch) – Carte £ 31/62
◆ Thatched former inn, a lively venue, on a country road with wheat fields. Choice of bistro or restaurant for seafood menu. Highly original bedrooms themed as famous hotels.

CHILGROVE – West Sussex – **504** R31 – see Chichester

CHILLATON – Devon – **503** H32 – see Tavistock

CHILLINGTON – Devon – **503** I33 **2** C3
London 217 mi – Plymouth 26 mi – Torbay 20 mi – Torquay 22 mi

whitehouse
✉ *TQ7 2JX* – ☎ *(01548) 580 505* – *www.whitehousedevon.com*
6 rm – †£ 160/180 ††£ 230/250
Rest – *(booking advisable for non residents)* Carte £ 24/39
◆ Sizeable Georgian house with modern furnishings, relaxed atmosphere and beautiful gardens. Sumptuous, well appointed bedrooms, with large baths and handmade toiletries. Lovely dining room with casual, airy feel and appealing menu.

CHINNOR – Oxfordshire – **504** R28 – **pop. 5 407** Great Britain **11** C2
London 45 mi – Oxford 19 mi
Ridgeway Path★★

ENGLAND

at Sprigg's Alley Southeast : 2.5 mi by Bledlow Ridge rd – ✉ Chinnor

Sir Charles Napier

✉ *OX39 4BX – ✆ (01494) 483 011 – www.sircharlesnapier.co.uk – Closed 3 days Christmas, Sunday dinner and Monday except bank holidays*
Rest – Carte £ 30/40
◆ Attractive flint pub in a small hillside hamlet, with pleasant outside terrace and delightful gardens. Refined, French based dishes are skilfully prepared and full of flavour.

at Kingston Blount Southwest : 1.75 mi on B 4009 – ✉ Chinnor

Lakeside Town Farm without rest

Brook St, (off Sydenham rd) ✉ OX39 4RZ – ✆ (01844) 352 152 – www.townfarmcottage.co.uk
4 rm – 🛉£ 60 🛉🛉£ 100
◆ Set in lovely gardens on a working farm: flora and fauna abound. Cosy bedrooms with well-coordinated décor and thoughtful touches. Family-style breakfasts include homemade bread and jam.

CHIPPENHAM – Wiltshire – 503 N29 – pop. 33 189 — 4 C2

London 106 mi – Bristol 27 mi – Southampton 64 mi – Swindon 21 mi
Yelde Hall, Market Place ✆ (01249) 665970, tourism@chippenham.gov.uk
Monkton Park (Par Three), ✆ (01249) 653 928
Yelde Hall★
Corsham Court★★ **AC**, SW : 4 mi by A 4 – Sheldon Manor★ **AC**, W : 1.5 mi by A 420 – Biddestone★, W : 3.5 mi – Bowood House★ **AC** (Library ★) SE : 5 mi by A 4 and A 342. Castle Combe★★, NW : 6 mi by A 420 and B 4039

ENGLAND

at Stanton St Quintin North : 5 mi by A 429 – ✉ Chippenham

Stanton Manor

✉ *SN14 6DQ – ✆ (01666) 837 552 – www.stantonmanor.co.uk*
22 rm – 🛉£ 99/195 🛉🛉£ 195 **Rest** – Menu £ 15/35 – Carte £ 22/41
◆ Extended 19C manor in formal gardens; popular as a wedding venue. Appealing range of bedrooms, geared to corporate market; the deluxe rooms considerably better than the standards. Elegant restaurant uses produce from the garden.

CHIPPING CAMPDEN – Gloucestershire – 503 O27 – pop. 1 943 — 4 D1

London 93 mi – Cheltenham 21 mi – Oxford 37 mi – Stratford-upon-Avon 12 mi
Old Police Station ✆ (01386) 841206, visitchippingcampden@lineone.net
Town★
Hidcote Manor Garden★★ **AC**, NE : 2.5 m

Cotswold House

rest,

The Square ✉ GL55 6AN – ✆ (01386) 840 330 – www.cotswoldhouse.com
25 rm – 🛉£ 190/300 🛉🛉£ 210/325 – 3 suites
Rest *Hicks'* – see restaurant listing **Rest *Juliana's*** – *(closed Sunday and Monday except bank holidays) (dinner only)* Menu £ 50
◆ Enviably stylish Regency town house with graceful spiral staircase winding upwards to luxurious rooms, some very modern, boasting every mod con imaginable. Impressive service. Formal though stylish Juliana's for accomplished cooking with an original style.

Kings with rm

The Square ✉ GL55 6AW – ✆ (01386) 840 256 – www.kingscampden.co.uk
19 rm – 🛉£ 95/110 🛉🛉£ 149/189 **Rest** – Menu £ 16/28 – Carte £ 16/32
◆ Beautiful Cotswold stone house with champagne bar, beamed dining room and rear terrace. Large brasserie menu offers tasty, straightforward classics with modern Mediterranean influences. Stylish bedrooms display vivid colour schemes.

Hicks' – at Cotswold House Hotel

The Square ✉ GL55 6AN – ✆ (01386) 840 330 – www.cotswoldhouse.com
Rest – *(booking essential)* Carte £ 26/48
◆ Named after local benefactor. Booking advised; open all day serving locals and residents with modern varied menu. Morning coffees, afternoon teas, home-made cake available.

Eight Bells Inn with rm

Church St ✉ *GL55 6JG – ✆ (01386) 840 371 – www.eightbellsinn.co.uk – Closed 25 December*

7 rm – 🛉£ 65 🛉🛉£ 85/125 **Rest** – Menu £ 17 (weekdays) – Carte £ 25/32

◆ 14C pub close to the historic high street in an old wool merchant's town. Cooking is traditionally British – pies are the real thing, puddings are comforting and specials are just that, so arrive early. Bedrooms combine plenty of character with good mod cons.

at Mickleton North : 3.25 mi by B 4035, B 4081 on B 4632 – ✉ Chipping Campden

Three Ways House rest,

✉ *GL55 6SB – ✆ (01386) 438 429 – www.threewayshousehotel.com*

48 rm – 🛉£ 85/120 🛉🛉£ 140/235

Rest – *(bar lunch Monday-Saturday)* Menu £ 35 – Carte £ 24/33

◆ Built in 1870; renowned as home of the 'Pudding Club'. Two types of room, in original house or modern block, all very comfy and modern. Bar with antique tiled floor. Arcaded dining room; Pudding Club meets here to vote after tastings.

Nineveh Farm without rest

Southwest : 0.75 mi by B 4632 on B 4081 ✉ *GL55 6PS – ✆ (01386) 438 923 – www.stayinthecotswolds.co.uk*

5 rm – 🛉£ 75 🛉🛉£ 85

◆ Georgian farmhouse in pleasant garden. Warm welcome; local information in residents' lounge. Comfortable rooms with view in main house or with French windows in garden house.

at Ebrington East : 2 mi by B 4035

The Ebrington Arms with rm

✉ *GL55 6NH – ✆ (01386) 593 223 – www.theebringtonarms.co.uk*

3 rm – 🛉£ 90/100 🛉🛉£ 100/110 **Rest** – Carte £ 25/30

◆ Proper village local with beamed, flag-floored bar at its hub, set in charming chocolate box village. Robust, traditional dishes use local ingredients and up-to-date techniques. Bedrooms have countryside views; room three, with four-poster bed and luxury bathroom, is best.

at Paxford Southeast : 3 mi by B 4035 – ✉ Chipping Campden

Churchill Arms with rm

✉ *GL55 6XH – ✆ (01386) 594 000 – www.thechurchillarms.com*

4 rm – 🛉£ 55/75 🛉🛉£ 75/90 **Rest** – *(bookings not accepted)* Carte £ 20/35

◆ Traditional stone inn set in a lovely location, boasting homely, rustic interior and great views. Cooking displays a real mix of influences, from pub classics to more restaurant-style dishes. Cosy bedrooms with good outlooks – can be noisy before closing time.

at Broad Campden South : 1.25 mi by B 4081 – ✉ Chipping Campden

Malt House without rest

✉ *GL55 6UU – ✆ (01386) 840 295 – www.malt-house.co.uk – Closed Christmas and New Year*

7 rm – 🛉£ 85 🛉🛉£ 145/165

◆ For a rare experience of the countryside idyll, this 16C malting house is a must. Cut flowers from the gardens on view in bedrooms decked out in fabrics to delight the eye.

CHIPPING NORTON – Oxfordshire – 503 P28 – pop. 5 688 10 A1

London 77 mi – Oxford 22 mi – Stow-on-the-Wold 9 mi

Masons Arms

Banbury Rd, Swerford, Northeast : 5 mi on A 361 ✉ *OX7 4AP – ✆ (01608) 683 212 – www.masons-arms.com – Closed 24-26 December*

Rest – Menu £ 18/25 – Carte £ 21/35

◆ Stone-built inn with vast garden and pleasant countryside views. Good value menus display an eclectic mix of straightforward dishes, ranging from the traditional to the more exotic. All produce is traceable, meats are rare breed and breads/desserts are homemade.

ENGLAND

CHORLEY – Lancashire – 502 M23 – pop. 33 424 — 20 A2

London 222 – Blackpool 30 – Liverpool 33 – Manchester 26
Duxbury Park Duxbury Hall Rd, ☎ (01257) 265 380
Shaw Hill Hotel G. & C.C. Whittle-le-Woods Preston Rd, ☎ (01257) 269 221

XX **The Red Cat**
Blackburn Rd, Whittle-Le-Woods, Northeast : 2.5 m on A 674 ✉ PR6 8LL – ☎ (01257) 263 966 – www.theredcat.co.uk – Closed Monday and Tuesday
Rest – Carte £ 29/41
◆ Restored pub with original beams, stone walls and brick fireplaces. Unfussy, modern dishes display good ingredients and sound cooking in well presented, classic combinations.

CHORLTON-CUM-HARDY – Gtr Manchester – 502 N23 – see Manchester

CHRISTCHURCH – Dorset – 503 O31 – pop. 40 208 — 4 D3

London 111 mi – Bournemouth 6 mi – Salisbury 26 mi – Southampton 24 mi
49 High St ☎ (01202) 471780, enquiries@christchurchtourism.info
Highcliffe Castle Highcliffe-on-Sea 107 Lymington Rd, ☎ (01425) 272 953
Riverside Ave, ☎ (01202) 436 436
Town★ - Priory★
Hengistbury Head★ (≤★★) SW : 4.5 mi by A 35 and B 3059

Christchurch Harbour — rm, rm
95 Mudeford, East : 2 mi ✉ BH23 3NT – ☎ (01202) 483 434 – www.christchurch-harbour-hotel.co.uk
64 rm ☕ – †£ 220 ††£ 245
Rest *Jetty* – see restaurant listing
Rest – Menu £ 18/25 (weekday dinner) – Carte £ 28/37
◆ Busy hotel in a great spot, with pleasant drinks terrace and chic spa. Contemporary styling and plush bedrooms; choose between 'Inland' or 'Harbour'; the latter boasting either a balcony or terrace. Restaurant offers classically based cuisine.

Captain's Club
Wick Ferry, Wick Ln. ✉ BH23 1HU – ☎ (01202) 475 111 – www.captainsclubhotel.com
17 rm – †£ 149/199 ††£ 229/259, ☕ £ 15 – 12 suites
Rest *Tides* – see restaurant listing
◆ Eye-catching hotel displaying striking art deco and nautical influences. Floor to ceiling windows throughout; attractive river views. Sleek, unfussy bedrooms and suites. Stylish spa.

The Kings — rm, rest
18 Castle St. ✉ BH23 1DT – ☎ (01202) 588 933 – www.thekings-christchurch.co.uk
20 rm ☕ – ††£ 85/145
Rest *Brasserie* – Carte £ 19/38 **s**
◆ Lovingly restored late 17C former coaching inn, in the heart of the town, overlooking the priory, ruins and bowling green. Pretty, boutique style and well-appointed, contemporary bedrooms. Appealing ground floor bar and brasserie.

Druid House without rest
26 Sopers Ln ✉ BH23 1JE – ☎ (01202) 485 615 – www.druid-house.co.uk
9 rm ☕ – †£ 45/70 ††£ 70/100
◆ Bright, fresh inner in contrast to its exterior. Modern, slightly kitsch breakfast room; light, airy conservatory sitting room and smart bar. Spacious bedrooms, two with balconies.

XXX **Jetty** – at Christchurch Harbour Hotel
95 Mudeford, East : 2 mi ✉ BH23 3NT – ☎ (01202) 483 434 – www.christchurch-harbour-hotel.co.uk
Rest – Carte £ 30/40
◆ Contemporary, eco-friendly restaurant in a fantastic waterside setting. Local, seasonal produce includes crabs from just over the bay. Tasty specials are cooked on the josper charcoal grill.

XXX **Tides** – at Captain's Club Hotel
Wick Ferry, Wick Ln. ✉ *BH23 1HU – ☎ (01202) 475 111 – www.captainsclubhotel.com*
Rest – Menu £ 17/28 – Carte £ 31/49
◆ Stylish restaurant with water feature wall, oversized windows and river views. Modern, well judged cooking offers a wide choice, good combinations and some unusual formats.

XX **Splinters**
12 Church St ✉ *BH23 1BW – ☎ (01202) 483 454 – www.splinters.uk.com – Closed 1-10 January, Sunday and Monday*
Rest – Menu £ 15/26 (dinner Tuesday to Thursday) – Carte £ 26/39
◆ Family-run restaurant in cobbled street with bar, lounge and several cosy, characterful rooms; one with intimate booths. Unfussy, classical cooking uses good ingredients. Interesting wine list.

CHURCH ENSTONE – Oxfordshire – ✉ Chipping Norton 10 B1

London 72 mi – Banbury 13 mi – Oxford 38 mi

The Crown Inn
Mill Ln ✉ *OX7 4NN – ☎ (01608) 677 262 – Closed 26 December, 1 January and Sunday dinner*
Rest – Carte £ 19/28
◆ 17C inn set among pretty stone houses in a picturesque village. Meat, fruit and veg come from local farms and seafood is a speciality. Lunch offers pub favourites; puddings are homemade.

CHURCHILL – Oxfordshire – 503 P28 – pop. 502 – ✉ Chipping Norton 10 A1

London 79 mi – Birmingham 46 mi – Cheltenham 29 mi – Oxford 23 mi

The Chequers
Church Rd ✉ *OX7 6NJ – ☎ (01608) 659 393 – Closed 25 December*
Rest – Carte £ 18/23
◆ Traditional stone pub with unexpectedly stylish interior. Classical menus display the odd inventive touch but puddings are firmly rooted in the old school. Thursdays are roast duck nights.

CHURCH STRETTON – Shropshire – 502 L26 – pop. 3 841 18 B2

Great Britain

London 166 mi – Birmingham 46 mi – Hereford 39 mi – Shrewsbury 14 mi
Trevor Hill, ☎ (01694) 722 281
Wenlock Edge★, E : by B 4371

XX **The Studio**
✉ *SY6 6BY – ☎ (01694) 722 672 – www.thestudiorestaurant.net – Closed 3 weeks January, 1 week spring, 1 week autumn, Christmas-New Year and Sunday-Tuesday*
Rest – *(dinner only)* Menu £ 28
◆ Personally run former art studio; walls enhanced by local artwork. Pleasant rear terrace for sunny lunches. Tried-and-tested dishes: much care taken over local produce.

CIRENCESTER – Gloucestershire – 503 O28 – pop. 15 861 Great Britain 4 D1

London 97 mi – Bristol 37 mi – Gloucester 19 mi – Oxford 37 mi
Corinium Museum Park Street ☎ (01285) 654180, cirencestervic@cotswold.gov.uk
Bagendon Cheltenham Rd, ☎ (01285) 652 465
Town★ – Church of St John the Baptist★ – Corinium Museum★ (Mosaic pavements★) AC
Fairford : Church of St Mary★ (stained glass windows★★) E : 7 mi by A 417

No 12 without rest
12 Park St ✉ *GL7 2BW – ☎ (01285) 640 232 – www.no12cirencester.co.uk*
4 rm – †£ 70 ††£ 100
◆ 16C property with Georgian façade, hidden away in the old alleyways. Delightful rear walled garden. Excellent organic breakfast. Stylish rooms charmingly blend old and new.

ENGLAND

Old Brewhouse without rest

7 London Rd ✉ GL7 2PU – ✆ (01285) 656 099 – www.theoldbrewhouse.com – Closed Christmas

10 rm – †£ 56/65 ††£ 70/85

◆ Former 17C brewhouse with a cosy, cottagey ambience. Exposed stone in two breakfast rooms. Cast iron bedsteads adorn some of the rooms, all of which boast period character.

at Barnsley Northeast : 4 mi by A 429 on B 4425 – ✉ Cirencester

Barnsley House

✉ GL7 5EE – ✆ (01285) 740 000 – www.barnsleyhouse.com

11 rm – †£ 260 ††£ 455 – 7 suites

Rest – Menu £ 22 (lunch) **s** – Carte £ 33/43 **s**

◆ Impressive 17C Cotswold manor house. Contemporary interior, with hi tech bedrooms; largest and most modern in annexed courtyard. Well kept gardens, hydrotherapy pool, cinema. Dining room has pleasant outlook. Modern, interesting menus.

Village Pub with rm

✉ GL7 5EF – ✆ (01285) 740 421 – www.thevillagepub.co.uk

6 rm – †£ 90 ††£ 90/160 **Rest** – Carte £ 22/31

◆ Stylish pub with open fires and cosy feel. Appealing, daily changing menu of modern British dishes, with irresistible nibbles, locally sourced meats, charcuterie from Highgrove and comforting desserts. Individually decorated bedrooms; Six has a four-poster.

at Sapperton West : 5 mi by A 419 – ✉ Cirencester

The Bell

✉ GL7 6LE – ✆ (01285) 760 298 – www.foodatthebell.co.uk – Closed 25 December

Rest – Carte £ 26/33

◆ Charming pub in a pretty village. Wide-ranging, daily changing menu and seafood specials take on a refined yet rustic style, relying on local and regional produce. Interesting wine list.

CLACTON-ON-SEA – Essex – 504 X28 – pop. 51 284 13 D2

London 83 mi

at St Osyth West : 4.5 mi by A 133 and B 1027 – ✉

Park Hall without rest

Park Hall, East : 1.5 mi on B 1027 ✉ CO16 8HG – ✆ (01255) 820 922 – www.parkhall.info

3 rm – †£ 70 ††£ 120/130

◆ 14C antique-filled former monastery in 600 acres of arable farmland, with 5 acres of grounds, where peacocks roam free. Traditionally styled rooms come with many thoughtful extras.

CLANFIELD – Oxfordshire – 503 P28 – pop. 1 709 10 A2

London 75 mi – Oxford 24 mi – Swindon 16 mi

Cotswold Plough

Bourton Rd, on A 4095 ✉ OX18 2RB – ✆ (01367) 810 222 – www.cotswoldploughhotel.com – Closed 24-28 December

11 rm – †£ 85 ††£ 155

Rest ***Restaurant*** – see restaurant listing

◆ Charming hotel with delightful stone façade, located in the heart of a pretty village. Serene lounge with period fireplace. Comfortable, characterful bedrooms with a modern touch.

Restaurant – at Cotswold Plough Hotel

Bourton Rd, on A 4095 ✉ OX18 2RB – ✆ (01367) 810 222 – www.cotswoldploughhotel.com – Closed 24-28 December

Rest – Carte £ 20/29

◆ Accomplished modern cooking; strong on fish and game. Dining over several rooms at polished tables; pre and post-prandial drinks by the fire. Friendly, informal service.

ENGLAND

The Clanfield Tavern

Bampton Rd ✉ OX18 2RG – ✆ (01367) 810 223 – www.clanfieldtavern.com – Closed 25 December and Monday

Rest – Menu £ 16 – Carte £ 19/34

◆ Charming 17C mellow stone pub beside a babbling stream. Menus feature wholesome, seasonal pub dishes with beer suggestions, followed by old school puddings. Thursday steak nights feature a variety of breeds. 3 regularly changing ales with 1/3 pint glasses available.

CLAVERING – Essex – **504** U28 – **pop. 1 663** – ✉ **Saffron Walden** **12** B2

London 44 mi – Cambridge 25 mi – Colchester 44 mi – Luton 29 mi

The Cricketers with rm

✉ CB11 4QT ✆ (01799) 550 442 – www.thecricketers.co.uk – Closed 25-26 December

14 rm – †£ 65/75 ††£ 90/110 **Rest** – Menu £ 30 (dinner) – Carte £ 25/30

◆ Attractive whitewashed pub exuding old-world charm. Straightforward cooking is precise and flavoursome. Local produce is key – all veg comes from their son Jamie Oliver's garden. Simple modern bedrooms in courtyard, more traditional rooms in the pavilion.

CLEARWELL – Gloucestershire **4** C1

London 138 mi – Birmingham 85 mi – Bristol 31 mi – Cardiff 46 mi

Tudor Farmhouse

High St ✉ GL16 8JS – ✆ (01594) 833 046 – www.tudorfarmhousehotel.co.uk – Closed 24-27 December

20 rm – †£ 85 ††£ 190 **Rest** – Menu £ 33 (dinner) – Carte lunch £ 17/27

◆ Converted farm buildings in the heart of the Forest of Dean. Character bedrooms in original farmhouse feature beams, uneven floors and antique furniture. More modern bedrooms in two outbuildings. Restaurant offers classic, French-influenced dishes with a twist.

ENGLAND

CLEEVE HILL – Glos. – **503** N28 – see Cheltenham

CLENT – Worcestershire – **504** N26 Great Britain **19** C2

London 127 mi – Birmingham 12 mi – Hagley 2 mi

Black Country Museum★, N : 7 mi by A 491 and A 4036 – Birmingham★ - Museum and Art Gallery★★, Aston Hall★★, NE : 10 mi by A 491 and A 456

Bell & Cross

Holy Cross, West : 0.5 mi off A 491 (northbound carriageway) (Bromsgrove rd) ✉ DY9 9QL – ✆ (01562) 730 319 – www.bellandcrossclent.co.uk – Closed 25 December and dinner 26 and 31 December and 1 January

Rest – Menu £ 17 (weekdays) – Carte £ 18/27

◆ Charming pub down a maze of lanes, with colourful window boxes and country views. Light bites and pub classics at lunch; more ambitious dishes at dinner. Influences range from Asia to the Med.

CLEY NEXT THE SEA – Norfolk – **504** X25 – see Blakeney

CLIFTON – Cumbria – **502** L20 – see Penrith

CLIPSHAM – Rutland – see Stamford

CLITHEROE – Lancashire – **502** M22 – **pop. 14 697** **20** B2

London 64 mi – Blackpool 35 mi – Manchester 31 mi

Council Offices, Church Walk ✆ (01200) 425566,tourism@ribblevalley.gov.uk

Whalley Rd, ✆ (01200) 422 618

at Grindleton Northeast : 3 mi by A 671

Duke of York Inn

Brow Top ✉ BB7 4QR – ✆ (01200) 441 266 – www.dukeofyorkgrindleton.com – Closed 25 December and Monday except bank holidays

Rest – Menu £ 11 – Carte £ 18/28

◆ Ivy-clad pub in the heart of the Trough of Bowland, with views to Pendle Hill. Rustic bar and light, contemporary dining room. Good choice on seasonal menu, with plenty of regional dishes.

at Wiswell South : 3.75 mi by A 671 and Whalley rd

Freemasons Country Inn

8 Vicarage Fold ✉ BB7 9DF – ☎ (01254) 822 218 – www.freemasonswiswell.co.uk
Rest – Menu £ 15 – Carte £ 25/32
♦ Delightful pub, hidden away on a narrow lane. Flag floors, low beams and open fires downstairs; elegant, antique-furnished dining rooms upstairs. Interesting menu features modern versions of traditional pub dishes. Skilful cooking, with clear flavours. Charming service.

at Bashall Eaves Northwest : 3 mi by B6243

The Red Pump Inn with rm

Clitheroe Rd ✉ BB7 3DA – ☎ (01254) 826 227 – www.theredpumpinn.co.uk – Closed 2 weeks February, Tuesday in winter and Monday
3 rm – †£ 60/75 ††£ 75/115 **Rest** – Menu £ 15 – Carte £ 17/26
♦ One of the oldest pubs in the Ribble Valley, with traditional restaurant, rustic bar and charming fire-lit snug. Local produce features on seasonal menus, with game a speciality. Spacious bedrooms boast good facilities and views of Pendle Hill or Longridge Fell.

CLOVELLY – Devon – 503 G31 – pop. 439 – ✉ Bideford 1 B1

London 241 mi – Barnstaple 18 mi – Exeter 52 mi – Penzance 92 mi
Village★★
SW : Tamar River★★. Hartland : Hartland Church★ - Hartland Quay★ (viewpoint★★) - Hartland Point ≤★★★, W : 6.5 mi by B 3237 and B 3248 – Morwenstow (Church★, cliffs★★), SW : 11.5 mi by A 39

Red Lion

The Quay ✉ EX39 5TF – ☎ (01237) 431 237 – www.clovelly.co.uk
11 rm – †£ 84/89 ††£ 131/142 **Rest** – *(dinner only)* Menu £ 30
♦ Cosy little hotel/inn on the quayside; a superb location. All rooms enjoy sea and harbour views and are dressed in soft, understated colours, providing a smart resting place. Simple dining room looks out to harbour.

CLOWS TOP – Worcestershire – pop. 1 164 18 B2

London 141 mi – Bewdley 6 mi – Stourport-on-Seven 10 mi

The Colliers Arms

Tenbury Rd, East : 0.5 mi on A 456 ✉ DY14 9HA – ☎ (01299) 832 242 – www.colliersarms.com – Closed Sunday dinner
Rest – Menu £ 15 (dinner Monday-Thursday) – Carte £ 15/20
♦ Cosy, well-run pub with lovely rear terrace. Classical cooking is hearty, unfussy and flavoursome. Produce comes from within 10 miles; eggs and veg are from their hens and garden out back.

CLUN – Shropshire – 503 K26 18 A2

London 173 mi – Church Stretton 16 mi – Ludlow 16 mi

Birches Mill without rest

Northwest : 3 mi by A 488, Bicton rd, Mainstone rd and Burlow rd ✉ SY7 8NL – ☎ (01588) 640 409 – www.birchesmill.co.uk – April-October
3 rm – †£ 74 ††£ 90
♦ High quality comforts in remote former corn mill: interior has characterful 17C/18C structures. Flagged lounge with lovely inglenook. Simple but tastefully decorated rooms.

COBHAM – Surrey – 504 S30 – pop. 1 586 7 D1

London 24 mi – Guildford 10 mi

Plan : see Greater London (South-West) 5

The Old Bear

Riverhill ✉ KT11 3DX – ☎ (01932) 862 116 – www.theoldbearcobham.co.uk
Rest – Carte £ 24/35
♦ Enlarged 17C coaching inn at the south end of the high street. Rustic bar; separate dining area. Staff wear butcher's aprons – appropriate as the highlights of the menu are game and offal.

ENGLAND

COCKERMOUTH – Cumbria – 501 J20 – pop. 7 446 — 21 A2

London 306 mi – Carlisle 25 mi – Keswick 13 mi

Town Hall, Market St ☎ (01900) 822634, cockermouthtic@co-net.com

Embleton, ☎ (017687) 76 223

at Lorton Southeast : 4.25 mi by B 5292 – ✉ Cockermouth

Winder Hall Country House

on B 5289 ✉ CA13 9UP – ☎ (01900) 85 107 – www.winderhall.co.uk – Closed January

7 rm – †£ 82/140 ††£ 145/185

Rest – *(dinner only) (booking essential for non-residents)* Menu £ 34 **s**

◆ Part-Jacobean manor house with mullioned windows and tranquil garden. Comfortable lounge and high quality bedrooms retain rich history of house and include two four-posters. Oak panelled dining room overlooks garden. Local produce well-used in homemade dishes. Relaxed, friendly service.

New House Farm

South : 1.25 mi on B 5289 ✉ CA13 9UU – ☎ (01900) 85 404 – www.newhouse-farm.com

5 rm – †£ 60/85 ††£ 120/170 **Rest** – Menu £ 30

◆ Very well appointed, richly decorated guesthouse with hot tub in garden. Sumptuous bedrooms; one with double jacuzzi, two with four-posters. Fine furnishings and roll-top baths. Aga-cooked breakfasts and home-cooked evening meals. Tea rooms just next door.

The Old Vicarage

Church Ln., North : 0.5 mi by B 5289 on Lorton Church rd ✉ CA13 9UN – ☎ (01900) 85 656 – www.oldvicarage.co.uk

8 rm – †£ 78/125 ††£ 125 **Rest** – Menu £ 29

◆ Well-kept Victorian house in beautiful countryside spot. Comfortable lounge and hospitable owners. Sympathetically modernised bedrooms; four-postered Room 1 is the best. Dining room offers lovely fell views and home-cooked, local produce.

COCKLEFORD – Gloucestershire – ✉ Cheltenham — 4 C1

London 95 mi – Bristol 48 mi – Cheltenham 7 mi

The Green Dragon Inn with rm

✉ GL53 9NW – ☎ (01242) 870 271 – www.green-dragon-inn.co.uk

9 rm – †£ 70 ††£ 95 **Rest** – *(booking essential)* Carte £ 25/35

◆ Characterful stone pub with huge open fires and carved mice hidden in the woodwork – the hallmark of designer Robert 'Mouseman' Thompson. Hearty lunches; unusual starters; generous, meaty mains. Simple, modern bedrooms; one boasts a super king-sized bed.

COGGESHALL – Essex – 504 W28 – pop. 3 919 – ✉ Colchester — 13 C2

London 49 mi – Braintree 6 mi – Chelmsford 16 mi – Colchester 9 mi

Baumanns Brasserie

4-6 Stoneham St ✉ CO6 1TT – ☎ (01376) 561 453 – www.baumannsbrasserie.co.uk – Closed first 2 weeks January, Monday and Tuesday

Rest – Menu £ 20/23 – Carte £ 24/35

◆ Characterful 16C building, its walls packed with pictures and prints. Tasty cooking, made using local produce, brings out classic flavour combinations. Speedy service.

at Pattiswick Northwest : 3 mi by A 120 (Braintree Rd) – ✉ Coggeshall

The Compasses at Pattiswick

Compasses Rd ✉ CM77 8BG – ☎ (01376) 561 322 – www.thecompassesatpattiswick.co.uk

Rest – Carte £ 22/35

◆ Smart, rural pub with cheery service. Cooking is simple and honest, with plenty of effort put into sourcing local ingredients. Pheasant is from local shoots and venison from the woods behind.

ENGLAND

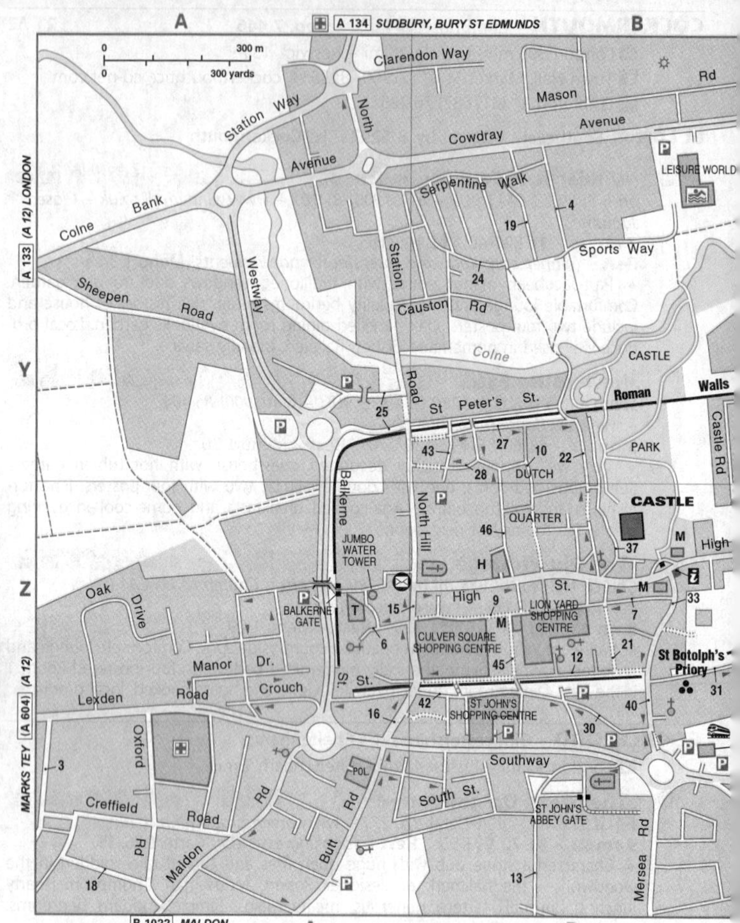

COLCHESTER – Essex – 504 W28 – pop. 104 390 Great Britain **13** D2

London 52 mi – Cambridge 48 mi – Ipswich 18 mi – Luton 76 mi

Visitor Information Centre, 1 Queens Street ✆ (01206) 282920, vic@colchester.gov.uk

Birch Grove Layer Rd, ✆ (01206) 734 276

Castle and Museum★ **AC** BZ

Rose and Crown

♿ rm, 🚭 📶 🏃 P VISA 🔘

East St ✉ CO1 2TZ – ✆ (01206) 866 677
– www.rose-and-crown.com CZ**d**

39 rm – †£ 99/109 ††£ 109/120, ☕ £ 10.95

Rest – Carte £ 17/23

◆ Part-15C coaching inn with period features and original stained glass. Bedrooms vary from family to business, to four-poster with a whirlpool bath. Characterful bar serves traditional pub fare. Contemporary restaurant offers classics with the odd Asian touch.

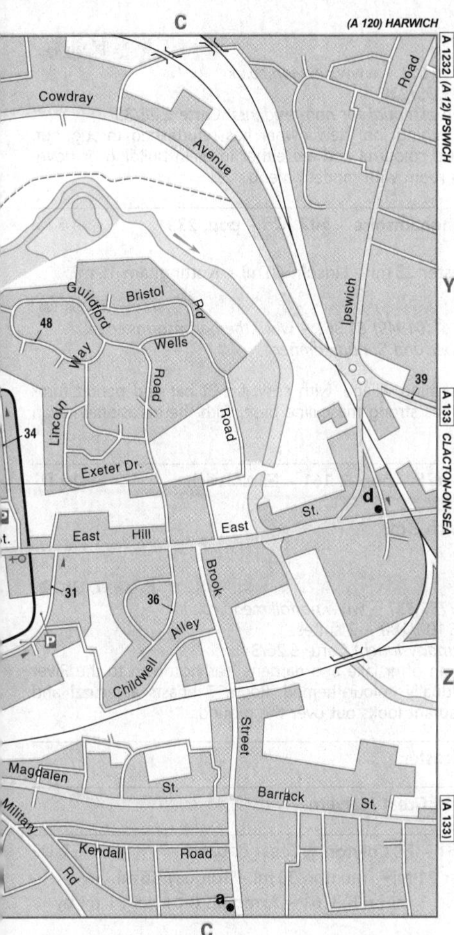

COLCHESTER

Street	Grid	No.
Beverley Rd	AZ	3
Catchpool Rd	BY	4
Church St	AZ	6
Culver Square Shopping Centre	BZ	
Culver St East	BZ	7
Culver St West	BZ	9
East Stockwell St	BYZ	10
Eld Lane	BZ	12
Flagstaff Rd	BZ	13
Headgate	ABZ	16
Head St	BZ	15
High St	BZ	
Inglis Rd	AZ	18
Kings Meadow Rd	BY	19
Lion Yard Shopping Centre	BZ	
Long Wyre St	BZ	21
Maidenburgh St	BYZ	22
Margaret Rd	BY	24
Middleborough	AY	25
Northgate St	BY	27
Nunn's Rd	BY	28
Osborne St	BZ	30
Priory St	BCZ	31
Queen St	BZ	33
Roman Rd	CY	34
Rosebery Ave	CY	36
Ryegate Rd	BYZ	37
St Andrews Ave	CY	39
St Botolph's St	BZ	40
St John's Shopping Centre	BZ	
St John's St	BZ	42
Short Cut Rd	BY	43
Trinity St	BZ	45
West Stockwell St	BYZ	46
Worcester Rd	CY	48

ENGLAND

Red House without rest
29 Wimpole Rd ✉ *CO1 2DL*
– ✆ *(01206) 509 005* CZ**a**
3 rm – †£ 50/60 ††£ 70/80

◆ Red-brick Victorian house away from main centre. Original fittings include stained glass and ornate plasterwork on ceiling in sitting room. Ample bedrooms; personal touches.

COLERNE – **Wilts.** – **503** M29 – **see Bath (Bath & North East Somerset)**

COLLYWESTON – **Northants.** – **502** S26 – **see Stamford**

COLN ST ALDWYNS – **Gloucestershire** – **503** O28 – **pop. 260** **4** D1
– ✉ **Cirencester**

London 101 mi – Bristol 53 mi – Gloucester 20 mi – Oxford 28 mi

New Inn At Coln
✉ *GL7 5AN – ✆ (01285) 750 651 – www.new-inn.co.uk*
13 rm – £ 85/130 £ 95/210
Rest – *(bar lunch) (booking essential for non-residents)* Carte £ 28/35
◆ Pretty 16C Cotswold coaching inn. New owner has refurbished throughout; bedrooms are now bold and colourful and are either in main building or dovecote to rear. Stylish dining room with modern menu.

COLSTON BASSETT – Nottinghamshire – 502 R25 – pop. 239 — 16 B2
– ✉ Nottingham

London 129 mi – Leicester 23 mi – Lincoln 40 mi – Nottingham 15 mi

The Martins Arms
School Ln ✉ NG12 3FD – ✆ (01949) 81 361 – www.themartinsarms.co.uk – Closed dinner 25 December and Sunday dinner
Rest – Carte £ 21/32
◆ Creeper-clad pub in charming village, with cosy, fire-lit bar and period furnished dining rooms. Menu has strong masculine base, with the occasional Italian influence or global flavour.

COLTISHALL – Norfolk – 504 Y25 – pop. 2 161 – ✉ Norwich — 15 D1
Great Britain

London 133 mi – Norwich 8 mi
Norfolk Broads★

ENGLAND

Norfolk Mead
✉ *NR12 7DN – ✆ (01603) 737 531 – www.norfolkmead.co.uk*
11 rm – £ 80/95 £ 100/180 – 2 suites
Rest – *(dinner only and Sunday lunch)* Carte £ 26/34
◆ Restful 18C manor with an otter lake and gardens leading down to the River Bure. Bedrooms are individually colour-themed. Room 7 boasts a jacuzzi and lovely views. Candlelit restaurant looks out over the grounds.

COLTON – N. Yorks. – see Tadcaster

COLWALL – Herefordshire – see Great Malvern

COLYFORD – Devon – 503 K31 – ✉ Colyton Great Britain — 2 D2

London 168 mi – Exeter 21 mi – Taunton 30 mi – Torquay 46 mi
Colyton★ (Church★), N : 1 mi on B 3161 – Axmouth (★), S : 1 mi by A 3052 and B 3172

Swallows Eaves
✉ *EX24 6QJ – ✆ (01297) 553 184 – www.swallowseaves.co.uk*
8 rm – £ 50/65 £ 95/118
Rest ***Reeds*** – *(closed Sunday) (dinner only)* Menu £ 28
◆ Unusual grey shale-coated 1920s house, with views from some rooms over the Axe Valley: listen out for birdsong on the marshes. Fully refurbished guest areas – bedrooms and bathrooms to follow. Menus feature locally sourced meats, fish and vegetables.

COMBE HAY – Bath & North East Somerset – see Bath

CONEYTHORPE – North Yorkshire – see Knaresborough

Guesthouses don't provide the same level of service as hotels. They are often characterised by a warm welcome and a decor which reflects the owner's personality. Those shown in red are particularly pleasant.

CONGLETON – Cheshire – 502 N24 – pop. 25 400 Great Britain **20** B3

London 183 mi – Liverpool 50 mi – Manchester 25 mi – Sheffield 46 mi

Town Hall, High St ✆ (01260) 271095, congletontic@cheshireeast.gov.uk

Biddulph Rd, ✆ (01260) 273 540

Little Moreton Hall★★ **AC**, SW : 3 mi by A 34

XX **Pecks**

Newcastle Rd, Moreton, South : 2.75 mi on A 34 ✉ CW12 4SB – ✆ (01260) 275 161 – www.pecksrest.co.uk – Closed 25-31 December, Sunday dinner and Monday

Rest – Menu £ 40 (dinner) – Carte lunch £ 28/38

♦ Airy, modish restaurant with unique style. À la carte lunch; monthly changing 5/7 course set dinner at 8pm sharp. Traditional homemade dishes use good produce and arrive in generous portions.

X **L'Endroit**

70-72 Lawton St ✉ CW12 1RS – ✆ (01260) 299 548 – www.lendroit.co.uk – Closed 2 weeks February,1 week June,1 week September, Sunday, Monday and lunch Saturday

Rest – French – Carte £ 21/37

♦ Welcoming restaurant with warm décor, upmarket bistro-style and small patio. Seasonally changing à la carte displays tasty, well-done dishes with strong French undertones. Good value lunch.

CONSTABLE BURTON – N. Yorks. – 502 O21 – see Leyburn

CONSTANTINE BAY – Cornwall – 503 E32 – see Padstow

COOKHAM – Windsor and Maidenhead – 504 R29 – pop. 5 304 **11** C3

– ✉ Maidenhead Great Britain

London 32 mi – High Wycombe 7 mi – Oxford 31 mi – Reading 16 mi

to Marlow, Maidenhead and Windsor (Salter Bros. Ltd) (summer only)

Stanley Spencer Gallery★ **AC**

The White Oak

Pound Ln ✉ SL6 9QE – ✆ (01628) 523 043 – www.thewhiteoak.co.uk – Closed Sunday dinner

Rest – Menu £ 15/19 – Carte £ 22/39

♦ Smart, contemporary pub with neutral hues and lovely terrace. Straightforward pub-style dishes feature quality meats and unfussy accompaniments, and include tasty sharing boards and assiettes.

COOKHAM DEAN – Windsor and Maidenhead Great Britain **11** C3

London 32 mi – High Wycombe 7 mi – Oxford 31 mi – Reading 16 mi

Windsor Castle★★★, Eton★★ and Windsor★, S : 5 mi by B 4447, A 4 (westbound) and A 308

XX **Sanctum on the Green** with rm

The Old Cricket Common ✉ SL6 9NZ – ✆ (01628) 482 638 – www.sanctumonthegreen.com

9 rm – †£ 120 ††£ 160

Rest – *(booking essential)* Carte £ 28/38

♦ Part-timbered, beamed inn boasting rustic bar, two dining rooms, airy conservatory and delightful patio terrace. Classically based dishes display modern touches. Individually furnished bedrooms are split between the inn and the annexe; one has a jacuzzi bath.

ENGLAND

CORBRIDGE – Northumberland – 501 N19 – pop. 2 800 Great Britain 24 A2

London 300 mi – Hexham 3 mi – Newcastle upon Tyne 18 mi

Hill St ✆ (01434) 632815, corbridgetic@btconnect.com

Hadrian's Wall★★, N : 3 mi by A 68 – Corstopitum★ AC, NW : 0.5 m

at Great Whittington North : 5.5 mi by A 68 off B 6318 – ✉ Corbridge

Queens Head Inn P VISA

✉ NE19 2HP – ✆ (01434) 672 267 – www.the-queens-head-inn.co.uk – Closed 25 December

Rest – Carte £ 17/28

◆ Dating from 1615, with cosy bar and bric à brac filled dining room. Menu offers everything from stotties to duck spring rolls, with lamb and beef from farm next door. Friendly service.

Don't confuse the couvert rating ✗ with the stars ✿! Couverts defines comfort and service, while stars are awarded for the best cuisine across all categories of comfort.

CORFE CASTLE – Dorset – 503 N32 – pop. 1 335 – ✉ Wareham 4 C3

London 129 mi – Bournemouth 18 mi – Weymouth 23 mi

Castle★ (≤★★) AC

Mortons House rm, P VISA

45 East St ✉ BH20 5EE – ✆ (01929) 480 988 – www.mortonshouse.co.uk

19 rm – †£ 75/100 ††£ 140/155 – 2 suites

Rest – Menu £ 35 – Carte £ 35/48

◆ Elizabethan manor built in the shape of an "E" in the Queen's honour. Wood-panelled drawing room. Range of different bedrooms, some themed: the Victoria room boasts an original Victorian bath. Traditional, formal dining room offers views out over the courtyard.

CORNHILL-ON-TWEED – Northumberland – 501 N17 – pop. 317 24 A1

Scotland

London 345 mi – Edinburgh 49 mi – Newcastle upon Tyne 59 mi

Ladykirk (Kirk o'Steil★), NE : 6 mi by A 698 and B 6470

Tillmouth Park ≤ P VISA

Northeast : 2.5 mi on A 698 ✉ TD12 4UU – ✆ (01890) 882 255 – www.tillmouthpark.co.uk – Closed 2 January-4 April

14 rm – †£ 75/195 ††£ 215

Rest *The Library* – Menu £ 22/37

◆ Traditional 19C country house in 15 acres of grounds; set in prime shooting/-fishing country. Welcoming interior with characterful stained glass and grand staircases. Spacious bedrooms boast modern bathrooms. Wood-panelled restaurant serves seasonal, local produce.

Coach House rm, P VISA

Crookham, East : 4 mi on A 697 ✉ TD12 4TD – ✆ (01890) 820 293 – www.coachhousecrookham.com – Closed December

11 rm – †£ 45/85 ††£ 75/110

Rest – *(dinner only) (booking essential for non-residents)* Menu £ 23

◆ Keenly run, small hotel set around a courtyard, converted from a collection of old farm buildings, including a 1680s dower house. Lounge with honesty bar in stable block; where the bedrooms are larger and more modern. Cosy breakfast/-dining room in original house.

CORSE LAWN – Worcs. – see Tewkesbury (Glos.)

CORSHAM – Wiltshire – **504** N29 – pop. 11 318 **4** C2

London 107 mi – Bristol 22 mi – Chippenham 5 mi

Heatherly Cottage without rest

Ladbrook Ln, Gastard, Southeast : 1.25 mi by B 3353 ✉ SN13 9PE – ☎ (01249) 701 402 – www.heatherlycottage.co.uk – April-October

3 rm – †£ 55/58 ††£ 76/78

♦ Part 17C stone cottage set down a quiet country road close to small village. Three very good value rooms: spacious, individually furnished and with good facilities.

CORTON DENHAM – Somerset – **504** M31 – pop. 210 – ✉ Sherborne **4** C3

London 123 mi – Bristol 36 mi – Cardiff 110 mi – Southampton 84 mi

The Queens Arms with rm

✉ DT9 4LR – ☎ (01963) 223 017 – www.thequeensarms.com

5 rm – †£ 70/85 ††£ 85/130 **Rest** – *(booking advisable)* Carte £ 20/28

♦ Charming 18C stone pub run by an enthusiastic owner, who takes care not to out-price the locals. Lunch focuses on one or two hearty courses, while the evening menu offers a more formal three course selection. Bedrooms are charming, well-appointed and good value.

COTTERED – Hertfordshire – **504** T28 – pop. 1 788 **12** B2

London 46 mi – Luton 24 mi – Cambridge 29 mi – Watford 43 mi

The Bull of Cottered

✉ SG9 9QP – ☎ (01763) 281 243

Rest – *(booking essential)* Carte £ 25/35

♦ Homely village pub with flower displays, sunny garden and warming fires in winter. Food is unfussy and unpretentious, with tasty light bites at lunch and hearty, wholesome dishes at dinner.

COVENTRY – West Midlands – **503** P26 – pop. 303 475 Great Britain **19** D2

London 100 mi – Birmingham 18 mi – Bristol 96 mi – Leicester 24 mi

St Michael's Tower, Priory Street ☎ (024) 7622 7264, tic@cvone.co.uk

Windmill Village Allesley Birmingham Rd, ☎ (024) 7640 4041

Sphinx Sphinx Drive, ☎ (024) 7645 1361

City★ - Cathedral★★★ **AC** AV – Old Cathedral★ AV **B** – Museum of British Road Transport★ **AC** AV **M2**

Plans on following pages

at Shilton Northeast : 6.75 mi by A 4600 - BX - on B 4065 – ✉ Coventry

Barnacle Hall without rest

Shilton Ln. , West : 1 mi by B 4029 following signs for garden centre ✉ CV7 9LH – ☎ (024) 7661 2629 – www.barnaclehall.co.uk – closed 24 December-2 January

3 rm – †£ 45 ††£ 75

♦ Interesting part 16C farmhouse in rural location. Westerly facing 18C stone façade; remainder 16/17C. Beamed rooms have countryside outlook and farmhouse style furnishings.

at Balsall Common West : 6.75 mi by B 4101 - AY – ✉ Coventry

The White Horse

Kenilworth Rd ✉ CV7 7DT – ☎ (01676) 533 207 – www.thewhitehorseatbc.co.uk

Rest – Menu £ 13 (lunch) – Carte £ 22/28

♦ Striking black and white timbered pub with decked terrace, spacious modern interior and paved rear dining area. Easy-to-read menus display British pub classics and some Mediterranean influences.

COVENTRY

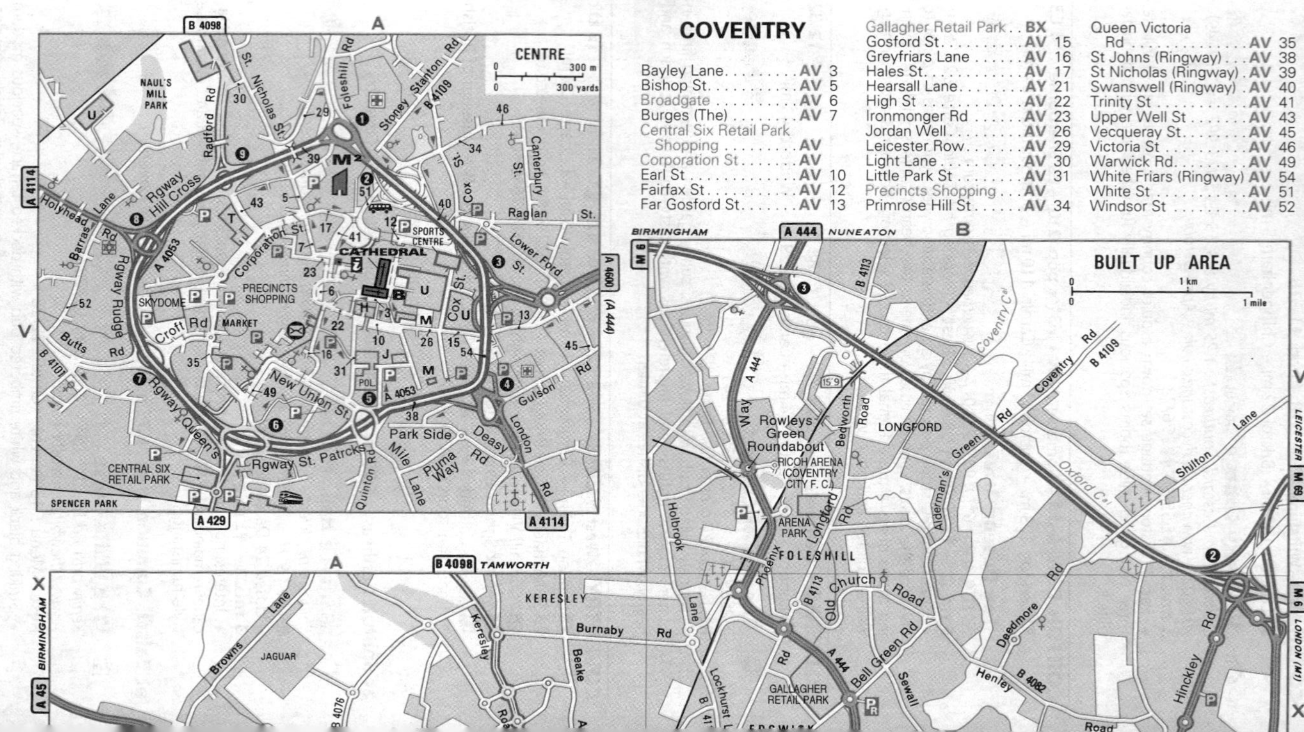

CENTRE
300 m
300 yards
NAUL'S MILL PARK
St. Nicholas St.
Radford Rd
Foleshill Rd
Stoney Stanton Rd
B 4109
Canterbury St.
Raglan St.
Lower Ford St.
Cox St.
Holyhead Rd
Barras Lane
Rgway Hill Cross
Rgway Rudge
A 4053
Corporation St.
CATHEDRAL
SPORTS CENTRE
PRECINCTS SHOPPING
SKYDOME
MARKET
Croft Rd
Butts Rd
New Union St.
Rgway Queen's
Rgway St. Patrcks
Quinton Rd
Park Side
Mile Lane
Puma Way
Deasy Rd
London Rd
Gulson Rd
CENTRAL SIX RETAIL PARK
SPENCER PARK
B 4098
A 4114
A 4600
(A 444)
A 429
B 4101
BUILT UP AREA
1 km
1 mile
BIRMINGHAM
A 444
NUNEATON
M 6
B 4113
Coventry Cal
Coventry Rd
LONGFORD
Bedworth Road
Rowleys Green Roundabout
RICOH ARENA (COVENTRY CITY F. C.)
ARENA PARK
Longford Rd
Alderman's Green Rd
Oxford Cal
Shilton Lane
LEICESTER
M 69
LONDON (M1)
Holbrook Lane
Phoenix Way
FOLESHILL
Old Church Road
Bell Green Rd
Sewall
Deedmore Rd
Henley Road
B 4082
Hinckley Rd
GALLAGHER RETAIL PARK
Lockhurst Lane
KERESLEY
Keresley
Burnaby Rd
Beake
B 4098
TAMWORTH
Browns Lane
JAGUAR
B 4076
A 45

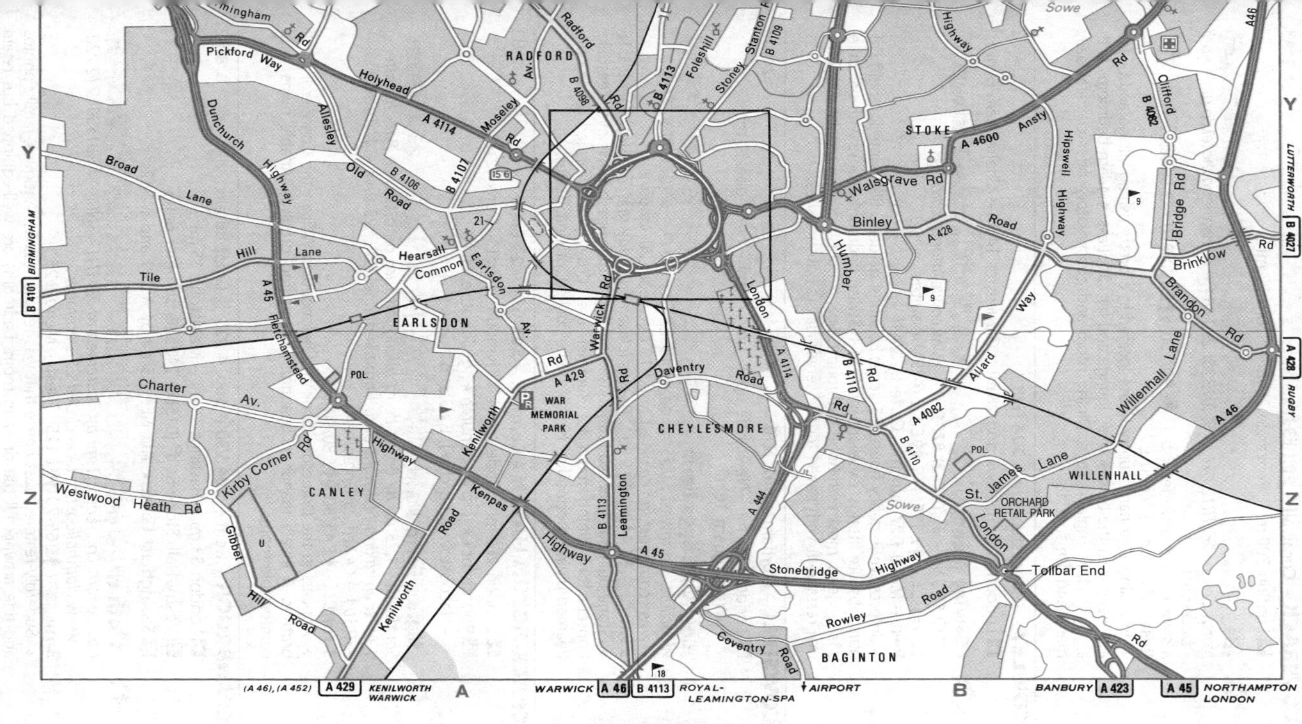

Pickford Way
Holyhead Rd
A 4114
Moseley Av.
Rd
RADFORD
Radford Rd
B 4098
B 4113
Foleshill Rd
Stoney Stanton Rd
B 4109
Dunchurch Highway
Allesley Old Road
B 4106
B 4107
Broad Lane
Hill Lane
Tile Hill
Hearsall Common
Earlsdon Av.
EARLSDON
A 45
Fletchamstead Highway
POL.
Charter Av.
Kirby Corner Rd
Westwood Heath Rd
Gibbet Hill Road
CANLEY
Kenilworth Road
Kenpas Highway
Warwick Rd
A 429
WAR MEMORIAL PARK
Daventry Road
CHEYLESMORE
B 4113
Leamington Rd
London Road
A 4114
A 444
STOKE
A 4600
Ansty Rd
Walsgrave Rd
Binley Road
A 428
Humber Rd
Hipswell Highway
Clifford
B 4082
Bridge Rd
Brinklow Rd
Brandon Rd
Allard Way
A 4082
B 4110
Willenhall Lane
A 46
St. James Lane
WILLENHALL
ORCHARD RETAIL PARK
London Road
Sowe
Stonebridge Highway
Tollbar End
Rowley Road
Coventry Road
BAGINTON
B 4101 BIRMINGHAM
LUTTERWORTH B 4027
A 428 RUGBY
(A 46), (A 452) A 429 KENILWORTH WARWICK
WARWICK A 46
B 4113 ROYAL-LEAMINGTON-SPA
AIRPORT
BANBURY A 423
A 45 NORTHAMPTON LONDON
A
B
Y
Z

COVERACK – Cornwall – **503** E33 **1** A3

London 300 mi – Penzance 25 mi – Truro 27 mi

Bay rm,

North Corner ✉ TR12 6TF – ✆ (01326) 280 464 – www.thebayhotel.co.uk – April - December

13 rm (dinner included) – £ 90/150 £ 190/230 – 2 suites

Rest – *(bar lunch)* Menu £ 29

♦ Imposing Victorian country house located in a pretty fishing village and boasting views over the bay. Homely lounge and bar. Spotless, modern bedrooms with a slight New England style. Dining room and conservatory offer classical daily menu and fish specials.

COWLEY – Gloucestershire – **504** N28 **4** C1

London 105 mi – Swindon 28 mi – Gloucester 14 mi – Cheltenham 6 mi

Cowley Manor

✉ GL53 9NL – ✆ (01242) 870 900 – www.cowleymanor.com

22 rm – £ 175/475 £ 175/475 – 8 suites

Rest – Menu £ 27 (lunch) – Carte £ 28/44

♦ Impressive Regency house. 55 acres; beautiful gardens. Retro interior, bold colours, obscure fittings, excellent mod cons. Stylish bedrooms, some with balconies/lake views, most with huge bathrooms. Spa, 2 pools and sun terrace. Semi-formal restaurant with paved terrace serves classic British dishes.

ENGLAND

COWSHILL – Durham – **502** N19 **24** A3

London 295 mi – Newcastle upon Tyne 42 mi – Stanhope 10 mi – Wolsingham 16 mi

Low Cornriggs Farm

Weardale, Northwest : 0.75 mi on A 689 ✉ DL13 1AQ – ✆ (01388) 537 600 – www.cornriggsfarm.co.uk – Closed 19 December-20 January

3 rm – £ 44/46 £ 66 **Rest** – *(closed Saturday and Tuesday)* Menu £ 18

♦ Stone-built 300 year-old farmhouse boasting some superb views over Teesdale. Conservatory dining room for summer use. Cosy, pine-furnished bedrooms. Beamed dining room offers hearty, home-cooked, organic dishes.

CRACKINGTON HAVEN – Cornwall – **503** G31 – ✉ **Bude** **1** B2

London 262 mi – Bude 11 mi – Plymouth 44 mi – Truro 42 mi

Poundstock★ (★★, church★, guildhouse★), NE : 5.5 mi by A 39 – Jacobstow (Church★), E : 3.5 m

Manor Farm without rest

Southeast : 1.25 mi by Boscastle rd taking left turn onto Church Park Rd after 1 mi then taking first right onto unmarked lane. ✉ EX23 0JW – ✆ (01840) 230 304 – Closed 25 December

3 rm – £ 45/50 £ 80/90

♦ Appears in the Domesday Book and belonged to William the Conqueror's half brother. A lovely manor in beautifully manicured grounds. Affable owner and comfortable rooms.

CRANBROOK – Kent – **504** V30 – **pop. 4 225** Great Britain **8** B2

London 53 mi – Hastings 19 mi – Maidstone 15 mi

Vestry Hall, Stone St ✆ (01580) 712538 (summer only)

Sissinghurst Castle★ **AC**, NE : 2.5 mi by A 229 and A 262

Cloth Hall Oast

Coursehorn Ln. , East : 1 mi by Tenterden rd ✉ TN17 3NR – ✆ (01580) 712 220 – www.clothhalloast.co.uk – closed 25 December

3 rm – £ 65/70 £ 125 **Rest** – Menu £ 25

♦ Superbly restored oast house that was rebuilt in 2001. Antiques, family photos and fine artwork fill the drawing room. Bedrooms are well-equipped but retain some original character; one boasts a splendid four-poster bed. Communal breakfasts and dinners at an antique table, set below restored rafters in the main hall.

Apicius (Tim Johnson)
23 Stone St ✉ TN17 3HE – ☎ (01580) 714 666 – www.restaurant-apicius.co.uk – Closed 2 weeks summer, 2 weeks Christmas-New Year, Saturday lunch, Sunday dinner, Monday and Tuesday
Rest – Menu £ 27/32
Spec. Brixham crab panna cotta, radish salad and Parmesan tuile. Saddle of rabbit with broad beans and girolles. Glazed chocolate torte, poached cherries and pistachio ice cream.
◆ Named after Roman author of world's first cookbook. Cosy interior mixes original features with modern style. Passionate, well balanced, precise cooking uses local ingredients.

at Sissinghurst Northeast : 1.75 mi by B 2189 on A 262 – ✉ Cranbrook

Rankins
The Street, on A 262 ✉ TN17 2JH – ☎ (01580) 713 964 – www.rankinsrestaurant.com – Closed 1 week September, Monday, Tuesday and bank holidays
Rest – *(dinner only and Sunday lunch) (booking essential)* Carte £ 27/34
◆ Well-run village restaurant, immaculately kept by knowledgeable, personable owners. Concise set menus display hearty, traditional dishes with the odd Mediterranean touch. Desserts a speciality.

CRAYKE – N. Yorks. – see Easingwold

CRICKLADE – Wiltshire – **503** 029 **4** D1
London 89 mi – Birmingham 86 mi – Bristol 54 mi – Cardiff 87 mi

The Red Lion with rm
74 High St ✉ SN6 6DD – ☎ (01793) 750 776 – Closed Monday
5 rm – †£ 75 ††£ 75
Rest – *(booking essential)* Menu £ 15/20 – Carte £ 18/31
◆ Very charming 17C pub off the Thames path. 9 real ales and 30 speciality beers in the low-beamed bar; beer pairings for every dish in the airy dining room. Classical cooking; extremely local produce. Comfy bedrooms are in the old stables.

CROCKERTON – Wiltshire – see Warminster

CROFT-ON-TEES – Durham – **502** P20 – see Darlington

CROMER – Norfolk – **504** X25 – pop. 8 836 **15** D1
London 132 mi – Norwich 23 mi
Louden Rd ☎ (0871) 2003071, cromertic@north-norfolk.gov.uk
Royal Cromer Overstrand Rd, ☎ (01263) 512 884

at Overstrand Southeast : 2.5 mi by B 1159 – ✉ Cromer

Sea Marge
16 High St. ✉ NR27 0AB – ☎ (01263) 579 579 – www.mackenziehotels.com
25 rm – †£ 93/146 ††£ 168/178 – 3 suites
Rest – *(bar lunch)* Menu £ 21 – Carte £ 19/37
◆ Mock Elizabethan house built in 1908; gardens lead down to beach. Interior features panelled bar, minstrel gallery. Most bedrooms have sea views; newer ones with colonial feel. Restaurant offers views from a large leaded window.

CROPSTON – Leicestershire – **502** Q25 **16** B2
London 106 mi – Birmingham 49 mi – Sheffield 67 mi – Leicester 6 mi

Horseshoe Cottage Farm
Roecliffe Rd, Hallgates, Northwest : 1 mi on Woodhouse Eaves rd ✉ LE7 7HQ – ☎ (0116) 235 00 38 – www.horseshoecottagefarm.com
3 rm – †£ 63 ††£ 95 **Rest** – Menu £ 25
◆ Extended farmhouse in pleasant countryside location beside Bradgate Country Park. Comfortable lounge; homely touches in spacious, traditional bedrooms. Home-cooked food in communal dining room; local produce well used, including some from the vegetable garden.

ENGLAND

CROSTHWAITE – Cumbria – 502 L21 – see Kendal

CRUDWELL – Wilts. – 503 N29 – see Malmesbury

CUCKFIELD – West Sussex – 504 T30 – pop. 3 266 **7** D2

London 40 mi – Brighton 15 mi

Ockenden Manor

Ockenden Lane ✉ RH17 5LD – ✆ (01444) 416 111 – www.ockenden-manor.co.uk

19 rm – †£ 115 ††£ 405 – 3 suites

Rest – *(booking essential at lunch)* Menu £ 29 (lunch)/54 – Carte £ 54/75

Spec. Caramelised calves sweetbreads with fricassé of chicken oysters. Sliced saddle and breast of Ditching lamb. Pistachio crème brûlée with raspberry sorbet

♦ Secluded part 16C manor; heritage is on display in antique furnished bedrooms, many named after previous owners. Ideal for golfers, historians and the romantic. Appealing seasonal cooking, with a superb balance of flavours, served in formal yet relaxed surroundings. Impeccable service.

Cuckoo

1 Broad St ✉ RH17 5LJ – ✆ (01444) 414 184 – www.cuckoorestaurant.co.uk – Closed 1 week July, 25 December, Sunday dinner and Monday

Rest – Menu £ 15/20 – Carte dinner Saturday £ 25/30

♦ Charming 17C cottage in heart of pretty village, with log fire, fresh flowers, personable owner and informal ambience. Tasty, modern British cooking uses fresh, seasonal produce.

CUDDINGTON – Buckinghamshire – 503 M24 Great Britain **11** C2

London 48 mi – Aylesbury 6 mi – Oxford 17 mi

Waddesdon Manor★★ **AC**, NE : 6 mi via Cuddington Hill, Cannon's Hill, Waddesdon Hill and A 41

The Crown

Aylesbury Rd ✉ HP18 0BB – ✆ (01844) 292 222 – www.thecrowncuddington.co.uk – Closed Sunday dinner

Rest – Menu £ 17 (lunch) – Carte £ 21/28

♦ Attractive thatched pub with traditional styling, welcoming atmosphere and friendly team. Seasonal menus display hearty comfort food in the winter and lighter dishes in the summer.

CULLINGWORTH – W. Yorks. – 502 O22 – see Haworth

CUTNALL GREEN – Worcs. – 503 N27 – see Droitwich Spa

CUXHAM – Oxfordshire – 504 Q29 **11** C2

London 49 mi – Hillingdon 32 mi – Reading 18 mi – Milton Keynes 61 mi

The Half Moon

✉ OX49 5NF – ✆ (01491) 614 151 – www.thehalf-moon.com – Closed Sunday dinner September-May and Monday

Rest – Carte £ 16/30

♦ Thatched 17C pub blends rustic beams with contemporary furnishings. Menu focuses on local produce, with vegetables and herbs from the garden. Homemade chutneys and jams for sale.

DALTON – N. Yorks. – 502 O20 – see Richmond

DANEHILL – East Sussex Great Britain **8** A2

London 53 mi – Brighton 21 mi – East Grinstead 7 mi

Sheffield Park Garden★, S : 3 mi on A 275

Coach & Horses

School Ln, Northeast: 3.5 mi on Chelwood Common rd. ✉ RH17 7JF – ✆ (01825) 740 369 – www.coachandhorses.danehill.biz – Closed 26 December and Sunday dinner except summer

Rest – Carte £ 22/27

♦ Small, characterful stone pub with two cosy bars, a rustic dining room, pleasant garden and 'child free' terrace. Menus offer light lunches, hearty classics and tasty, locally inspired dinners.

DARGATE – Kent – see Faversham

DARLEY – North Yorkshire – 502 O21 22 B2

London 217 mi – Harrogate 8 mi – Ripon 16 mi

Cold Cotes

Cold Cotes Rd, Felliscliffe, South : 2 mi by Kettlesing rd, going straight over crossroads and on Harrogate rd ✉ HG3 2LW – ✆ (01423) 770 937 – www.coldcotes.com

6 rm – †£ 60/70 ††£ 88/98 **Rest** – Menu £ 25

◆ Remotely set farmhouse in mature gardens; welcoming hosts and well-kept bedrooms, split between the house and the barn conversion. Dining room with pleasant country views; tasty home-cooking makes use of produce from the garden.

DARLEY ABBEY – Derbs. – 502 P25 – see Derby

DARLINGTON – Darlington – 502 P20 – pop. 86 082 22 B1

London 251 mi – Leeds 61 mi – Middlesbrough 14 mi – Newcastle upon Tyne 35 mi

Teesside Airport : ✆ (08712) 242426, E : 6 mi by A 67

The Dolphin Centre, Horsemarket ✆ (01325) 388666, tic@darlington.gov.uk

Blackwell Grange Briar Close, ✆ (01325) 464 458

Stressholme Snipe Lane, ✆ (01325) 461 002

at Croft-on-Tees South : 4.25 mi on A 167 – ✉ Darlington

Clow Beck House

Monk End Farm, West : 0.75 mi by A 167 off Barton rd ✉ DL2 2SW – ✆ (01325) 721 075 – www.clowbeckhouse.co.uk – Closed 24 December-2 January

13 rm – †£ 88 ††£ 140

Rest – *(dinner only) (residents only)* Carte £ 27/41 **s**

◆ Collection of converted farm buildings not far from the River Tees. Welcoming owners and homely interior. Immaculately kept, tastefully furnished bedrooms come with iPod docks, bathrobes and chocolates. Home-cooked dinners with a puzzle supplied while you wait.

at Hurworth-on-Tees South : 5.5 mi by A 167

Rockliffe Hall

✉ DL2 2DU – ✆ (01325) 729 999 – www.rockliffehall.com

60 rm – †£ 255 ††£ 270

Rest ***Kenny Atkinson at The Orangery*** – see restaurant listing

Rest ***Waterhouse Bistro*** – Menu £ 25 **s** – Carte £ 25/32 **s**

◆ Extended red-brick building in peaceful location, with championship golf course and state-of-the-art leisure facilities. Spacious, stylish, well-equipped bedrooms with superb bathrooms. Bright, modern bistro offers golf course views and brasserie menu.

Kenny Atkinson at The Orangery – at Rockliffe Hall Hotel

✉ DL2 2DU – ✆ (01325) 729 999 – www.rockliffehall.com – Closed Sunday

Rest – *(dinner only)* Menu £ 55/70 **s**

◆ Restored Victorian orangery with pitched glass roof. Classically based menus offer locally influenced dishes, with a personal touch. Linen-clad tables; structured, formal service.

The Bay Horse

45 The Green ✉ DL2 2AA – ✆ (01325) 720 663 – www.thebayhorsehurworth.com – Closed Sunday dinner

Rest – Menu £ 15 (weekday lunch) – Carte £ 22/38

◆ Smart village pub with pleasant terrace and gardens. Wide-ranging menu offers largely hearty classics; presentation ranges from simple and rustic to more modern and intricate.

ENGLAND

at Headlam Northwest : 8 mi by A 67 – ✉ Gainford

Headlam Hall
✉ DL2 3HA – ☎ (01325) 730 238 – www.headlamhall.co.uk
– Closed 24-26 December
38 rm – †£ 95 ††£ 120 – 2 suites
Rest – Menu £ 17 (lunch) – Carte £ 26/38
♦ Part Georgian, part Jacobean manor house in delightful, secluded countryside with charming walled gardens. Period interior furnishings and antiques. Good leisure facilities. Country house restaurant in four distinctively decorated rooms.

DARTMOUTH – Devon – 503 J32 – pop. 5 512 2 C3

London 236 mi – Exeter 36 mi – Plymouth 35 mi
The Engine House, Mayor's Ave ☎ (01803) 834224, holidays@discoverdartmouth.com
Town★★ (<★) - Old Town - Butterwalk★ - Dartmouth Castle (<★★★) AC
Start Point (<★), S : 13 mi (including 1 mi on foot)

Dart Marina
Sandquay ✉ TQ6 9PH – ☎ (01803) 832 580 – www.dartmarina.com
49 rm – †£ 95/185 ††£ 185/255
Rest *River Restaurant* – *(dinner only and Sunday lunch)* Menu £ 16/32
Rest *Wildfire* – ☎ (01803) 837 180 – Carte £ 31/43
♦ Lovely location with excellent views over the Dart Marina. The hotel has smart, comfy bedrooms, many with balconies. Welcoming, bright, modern public areas. Stylish River Restaurant; terrace overlooks river. Modern, informal Wildfire offers eclectic menus.

Royal Castle
11 The Quay ✉ TQ6 9PS – ☎ (01803) 833 033 – www.royalcastle.co.uk
25 rm – †£ 95/105 ††£ 145/199 **Rest** – Menu £ 16/23 – Carte £ 30/36
♦ Modernised 15C coaching inn: once two buildings, now joined by a smart glass atrium. Boldly coloured bedrooms with good comforts – some have jacuzzi baths. Two bars: one for drinkers only, one serving all-day dishes. Restaurant offers modern takes on old classics.

The New Angel Rooms
51 Victoria Rd ✉ TQ6 9RT – ☎ (01803) 839 425 – www.thenewangel.co.uk – Closed January
6 rm – †£ 135/165 ††£ 135/165
Rest *The New Angel* – see restaurant listing
♦ Characterful townhouse towards the edge of town with snug lounge and smart breakfast room. Immensely charming, individually designed bedrooms boast bold designs and a real sense of quality.

The New Angel
2 South Embankment ✉ TQ6 9BH – ☎ (01803) 839 425 – www.thenewangel.co.uk – Closed January, Sunday and Monday
Rest – *(booking essential)* Menu £ 25/40
♦ Split over two floors, with open-plan kitchen, pleasant estuary views and funky cocktail lounge. Classical cooking with French undertones. Bedrooms available a short walk away.

Seahorse
5 South Embankment ✉ TQ6 9BH – ☎ (01803) 835 147 – www.seahorserestaurant.co.uk – Closed 25 December, Sunday and Monday
Rest – Seafood – *(booking essential)* Menu £ 20 (lunch) – Carte £ 27/43
♦ Picturesque location overlooking estuary/harbour; some al fresco tables. Classic bistro dishes with strong seafood slant; cooked in charcoal oven. Twice daily menu; simplicity is key.

ENGLAND

Jan and Freddies Brasserie
10 Fairfax Pl ✉ TQ6 9AD – ✆ (01803) 832 491 – www.janandfreddiesbrasserie.co.uk – Closed 3-28 January and Sunday
Rest – *(dinner only and lunch June to October) (booking advisable)*
Carte £ 26/33
◆ Bright, stylish brasserie in the town centre, with welcoming service and a personal touch. Menus are classically based, with dishes crafted from local, seasonal produce.

at Kingswear East : via lower ferry – ✉ Dartmouth

Nonsuch House
Church Hill, from lower ferry take first right onto Church Hill before Steam Packet Inn ✉ TQ6 0BX – ✆ (01803) 752 829 – www.nonsuch-house.co.uk
4 rm – £ 100/145 £ 125/170
Rest – *(closed Tuesday, Wednesday and Saturday) (dinner only) (residents only)*
Menu £ 35 **s**
◆ Charming Edwardian house run by friendly, hands-on owners; and boasting lovely views over the castle, town and sea. Bright Mediterranean style décor blends nicely with original features. Spacious, well-appointed bedrooms – one has a small balcony. Local, seasonal cooking in conservatory dining room.

at Strete Southwest : 4 mi on A 379 – ✉ Dartmouth

The Kings Arms
Dartmouth Rd ✉ TQ6 0RW – ✆ (01803) 770 377 – www.kingsarms-dartmouth.co.uk
Rest – Carte £ 22/35
◆ Dour exterior hides gem of a pub serving wide-ranging menu with focus on seafood; locally caught, simply cooked and very tasty. Delightful rear garden with fantastic coastal views.

ENGLAND

DATCHWORTH – Hertfordshire – 504 T28 — 12 B2

London 31 mi – Luton 15 mi – Stevenage 6 mi

Coltsfoot Country Retreat
Coltsfoot Ln., Bulls Grn., South : 0.75 mi by Bramfield Rd ✉ SG3 6SB – ✆ (01438) 212 800 – www.coltsfoot.com
15 rm – £ 138 £ 165
Rest – *(closed Sunday) (dinner only) (booking essential)* Menu £ 33 – Carte £ 28/41
◆ Stylish hotel, once a working farm, in 40 rural acres. Lounge bar with log-burning stove. Highly individual rooms around courtyard have vaulted ceilings and rich furnishings. Main barn houses restaurant: concise modern menus employ good seasonal produce.

The Tilbury
Watton Rd ✉ SG3 6TB – ✆ (01438) 815 550 – www.thetilbury.co.uk – Closed Sunday dinner
Rest – Menu £ 18/23 – Carte £ 24/35
◆ Local, seasonal produce leads the way at Paul Bloxham's pub. Menus change regularly and feature a real mix of dishes, from classical steaks to adventurous stuffed lobster and scallop sea bass.

DAVENTRY – Northamptonshire – 504 Q27 – pop. 21 731 — 16 B3

London 79 mi – Coventry 23 mi – Leicester 31 mi – Northampton 13 mi
9 Norton Rd, ✆ (01327) 702 829
27 Hellidon Lakes H. & C.C. Hellidon, ✆ (01327) 262 550
18 Staverton Park Staverton, ✆ (01327) 302 000

Fawsley Hall

Fawsley, South : 6.5 mi by A 45 off A 361 ✉ *NN11 3BA – ☎ (01327) 892 000 – www.fawsleyhall.com*

53 rm – †£ 175 ††£ 325 – 5 suites

Rest *Equilibrium* – *(Closed Sunday-Wednesday) (dinner only) (booking essential)* Menu £ 59

Rest *Bess's Brasserie* – Carte £ 23/39

◆ Set in 2,000 peaceful acres, a luxurious Tudor manor house boasting Georgian/-Victorian wings, a grand hall and exclusive leisure club and spa. Well-appointed bedrooms: most characterful in main house; more contemporary in annexe. Ambitious, innovative menu in intimate Equilibrium. Brasserie classics in Bess's.

at Staverton Southwest : 2.75 mi by A 45 off A 425 – ✉ Daventry

Colledges House

Oakham Ln, off Glebe Ln ✉ *NN11 6JQ – ☎ (01327) 702 737 – www.colledgeshouse.co.uk*

4 rm – †£ 68/80 ††£ 98/106 **Rest** – Menu £ 32

◆ Part 17C house in a quiet village. Full of charm with antiques, curios, portraits and an inglenook fireplace. Homely bedrooms are in the main house and an adjacent cottage. Evening meals served at elegant oak table.

DAYLESFORD Glos – Gloucestershire – **503** O28 – See Stow-on-the-Wold

---

DEAL – Kent – **504** Y30 – pop. 29 248 **9** D2

London 78 mi – Canterbury 19 mi – Dover 8 mi – Margate 16 mi

The Landmark Centre, 129 High St ☎ (01304) 369576, info@deal.gov.uk

Walmer & Kingsdown Kingsdown The Leas, ☎ (01304) 373 256

Dunkerley's

19 Beach St ✉ *CT14 7AH – ☎ (01304) 375 016 – www.dunkerleys.co.uk*

16 rm – †£ 70/80 ††£ 100/150

Rest *Restaurant* – see restaurant listing

◆ The hotel faces the beach and the Channel. Bedrooms are comfortably furnished and the principal rooms have jacuzzis. Comfortable bar offers a lighter menu than the restaurant.

Number One without rest

1 Ranelagh Rd ✉ *CT14 7BG – ☎ (01304) 364 459 – www.numberonebandb.co.uk*

4 rm – †£ 80 ††£ 90

◆ Former boarding house close to the promenade, refurbished in a contemporary style. Understated bedrooms boast bold feature wallpaper, luxury bathrooms, fine bed linen and stimulating art.

Restaurant – at Dunkerley's Hotel

19 Beach St ✉ *CT14 7AH – ☎ (01304) 375 016 – www.dunkerleys.co.uk – Closed Sunday dinner and Monday*

Rest – Seafood – Menu £ 16/28

◆ With views of the Channel, the restaurant is best known for preparing locally caught seafood, although non-seafood options are also available. Wide ranging wine list.

at Worth Northwest : 5 mi by A 258

Solley Farm House without rest

The Street ✉ *CT14 0DG – ☎ (01304) 613 701 – www.solleyfarmhouse.co.uk – Closed 25-26 December*

3 rm – †£ 90 ††£ 120

◆ 300 year old house, overlooking the village pond and church. Full of character and charm, with a very welcoming owner. Organic breakfasts served on the terrace in summer.

DEDDINGTON - Oxfordshire - 503 Q28 - pop. 1 595 — 10 B1

London 72 mi - Birmingham 46 mi - Coventry 33 mi - Oxford 18 mi

Deddington Arms

Horsefair ✉ OX15 0SH - ✆ (01869) 338 364 - www.oxfordshire-hotels.co.uk

27 rm - †£ 65/90 ††£ 90/130 **Rest** - Menu £ 20 (dinner) - Carte £ 29/33

◆ Traditional coaching inn with a smart, modish ambience, on the market place. Spacious modern bedrooms in rear extension. Stylish rooms, two four-postered, in the main house. The restaurant is decorated in a warm and contemporary style.

The Old Post House without rest

New St, on A4260 ✉ OX15 0SP - ✆ (01869) 338 978 - www.oldposthouse.co.uk

3 rm - †£ 55 ††£ 85

◆ Charming 17C sandstone house with mullioned windows and beautiful walled garden. Comfy, open-fired lounge and spacious, classically styled bedrooms. Outdoor pool by prior arrangement. Tea and cake on arrival; tasty Aga-cooked breakfasts and homemade preserves.

DEDHAM - Essex - 504 W28 - pop. 1 847 - ✉ Colchester — 13 D2

Great Britain

London 63 mi - Chelmsford 30 mi - Colchester 8 mi - Ipswich 12 mi

Stour Valley★ - Flatford Mill★, E : 6 mi by B 1029, A 12 and B 1070

Maison Talbooth

Stratford Rd, West : 0.5 mi ✉ C07 6HP - ✆ (01206) 323 150 - www.milsomhotels.com

12 rm - †£ 120 ††£ 350

Rest *Le Talbooth* - see restaurant listing

◆ Quiet, Victorian country house with intimate atmosphere, lawned gardens and views over river valley. Some rooms are smart and contemporary, others more traditional in style.

Milsoms

Stratford Rd, West : 0.75 mi ✉ CO7 6HW - ✆ (01206) 322 795 - www.milsomhotels.com

15 rm - †£ 95/180 ††£ 115/180, £ 15

Rest - *(bookings not accepted)* Carte £ 22/40

◆ Modern hotel overlooking Constable's Dedham Vale with attractive garden and stylish lounge. Bright, airy and welcoming rooms feature unfussy décor and modern colours. Likeably modish, wood-floored bistro.

Le Talbooth

Stratford Rd., West : 0.5 mi ✉ C07 6HP - ✆ (01206) 323 150 - www.milsomhotels.com - Closed Sunday dinner October-June

Rest - Menu £ 23/28 (lunch) - Carte £ 38/54

◆ Part Tudor house in attractive riverside setting. Exposed beams and real fires contribute to the traditional atmosphere. Menus combine the classic and the more modern. Well chosen wine list.

Fountain House & Dedham Hall with rm

Brook St ✉ CO7 6AD - ✆ (01206) 323 027 - www.dedhamhall.co.uk - Closed Christmas-New Year, Sunday and Monday

5 rm - †£ 65 ††£ 110 **Rest** - *(dinner only) (booking essential)* Menu £ 33

◆ In a quiet, country house dating back to 15C with traditional, uncluttered ambience. Weekly changing traditionally based set menu. Comfortable bedrooms also available.

The Sun Inn with rm

High St ✉ CO7 6DF - ✆ (01206) 323 351 - www.thesuninndedham.com - Closed 25-26 December

5 rm - †£ 70 ††£ 75/150 **Rest** - Menu £ 14 - Carte £ 18/30

◆ Sunny-coloured pub in idyllic village location. Italian-themed à la carte features simple, tasty dishes. Bar board menu offers sandwiches, terrines and tarts. Contemporary bedrooms.

DENBURY - Devon 2 C2

London 193 mi – Plymouth 31 mi – Torbay 10 mi – Exeter 21 mi

The Union Inn

The Green ✉ *TQ12 6DQ* – ✆ *(01803) 812 595 – www.theunioninndenbury.co.uk*

Rest – Menu £ 17 (Monday-Thursday dinner) – Carte £ 19/32

♦ Characterful village pub overlooking the green. Menus feature tasty classics prepared in a fresh, modern manner; good value tasting menu at certain times. Regular pie, steak and curry nights.

DENHAM - Buckinghamshire - 504 S29 - pop. 2 269 Great Britain 11 D3

London 20 mi – Buckingham 42 mi – Oxford 41 mi

Windsor Castle★★★, Eton★★ and Windsor★, S : 10 mi by A 412

The Swan Inn

Village Rd ✉ *UB9 5BH* – ✆ *(01895) 832 085 – www.swaninndenham.co.uk – Closed 25-26 December*

Rest – *(booking essential)* Carte £ 20/27

♦ Wisteria-clad, red-brick Georgian pub with pleasant terrace and gardens. Menus change with the seasons and offer plenty of interest; sides are appealing and pudding is a must.

ENGLAND

DERBY - Derby - 502 P25 - pop. 229 407 Great Britain 16 B2

London 132 mi – Birmingham 40 mi – Coventry 49 mi – Leicester 29 mi

Nottingham East Midlands Airport, Castle Donington : ✆ (0871) 919 9000, SE : 12 mi by A 6 X

Assembly Rooms, Market Pl ✆ (01332) 255802, tourism@derby.gov.uk

18 Sinfin Wilmore Rd, ✆ (01332) 766 323

18 Mickleover Uttoxeter Rd, ✆ (01332) 516 011

18 Kedleston Park Quardon Kedlston, ✆ (01332) 840 035

36 Breadsall Priory H. & C.C. Morley Moor Rd, ✆ (01332) 836 106

18 Allestree Park Allestree Hall, ✆ (01332) 550 616

City★ – Museum and Art Gallery★ (Collection of Derby Porcelain★) YZ **M1** – Royal Crown Derby Museum★ **AC** Z **M2**

Kedleston Hall★★ **AC**, NW : 4.5 mi by Kedleston Rd X

Cathedral Quarter

16 St. Marys Gate ✉ *DE1 3JR* – ✆ *(01332) 546 080 – www.finessecollection.com* Yx

38 rm – †£ 110/130 ††£ 140

Rest *Opulence* – *(closed Sunday dinner and Monday)* Menu £ 16 (lunch) – Carte dinner £ 27/41

♦ Boutique-style hotel retaining original features like mosaic floors and marble pillars. Bedrooms vary in size but all are furnished in a contemporary style with pastel shades. First floor Opulence boasts wood panelling and a 10-seater chef's table. Modern menus.

at Darley Abbey North : 2.5 mi off A 6 - X - ✉ Derby

Darleys

Darley Abbey Mill ✉ *DE22 1DZ* – ✆ *(01332) 364 987 – www.darleys.com – Closed 25 December-15 January, Sunday dinner and bank holidays*

Rest – *(booking advisable)* Menu £ 19 (lunch) – Carte dinner £ 33/37

♦ Popular weir-side restaurant with river views. Attractive terrace, modern bar-lounge and traditional dining room. Great value lunches and more ambitious modern European dishes in the evening.

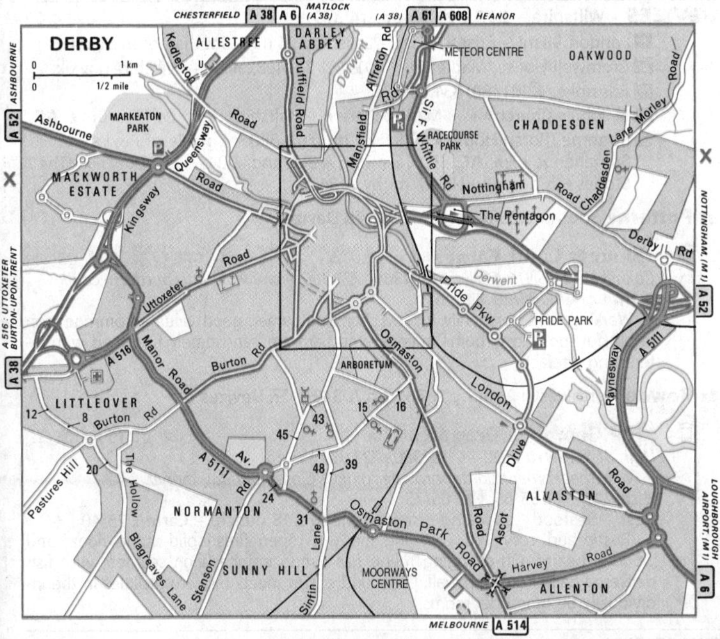

DERBY

CHESTERFIELD A 38 A 6 MATLOCK (A 38) (A 38) A 61 A 608 HEANOR

0 1 km
0 1/2 mile

ALLESTREE
DARLEY ABBEY
METEOR CENTRE
OAKWOOD
MARKEATON PARK
CHADDESDEN
RACECOURSE PARK
MACKWORTH ESTATE
The Pentagon
PRIDE PARK
ARBORETUM
LITTLEOVER
NORMANTON
ALVASTON
SUNNY HILL
MOORWAYS CENTRE
ALLENTON
Ashbourne Road
Kedleston Road
Duffield Road
Alfreton Rd
Mansfield Rd
Sir F. Whittle Rd
Nottingham Road
Chaddesden Lane
Morley Road
Derby Rd
Queensway
Kingsway
Uttoxeter Road
Derwent
Pride Pkw
Raynesway
A 5111
A 516
Manor Road
Burton Rd
Osmaston
London Road
Drive
Ascot
Road
Osmaston Park Road
Harvey Road
A 5111 Av.
Rd
Pastures Hill
The Hollow
Blagreaves Lane
Stenson
Sinfin Lane
ASHBOURNE A 52
A 516 : UTTOXETER BURTON-UPON-TRENT A 38
NOTTINGHAM, (M 1) A 52
LOUGHBOROUGH AIRPORT, (M 1) A 6
MELBOURNE A 514
X

ENGLAND

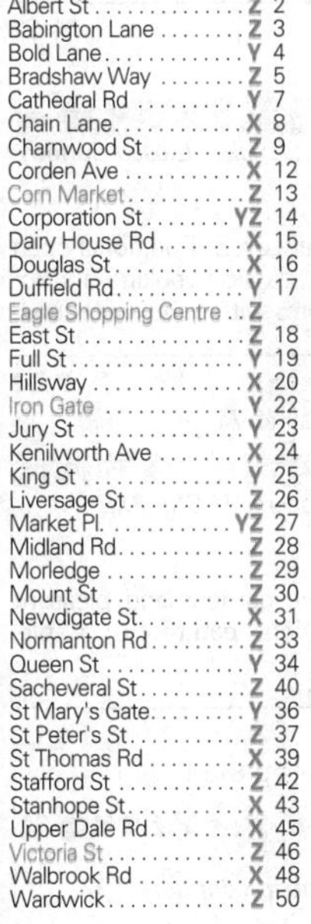

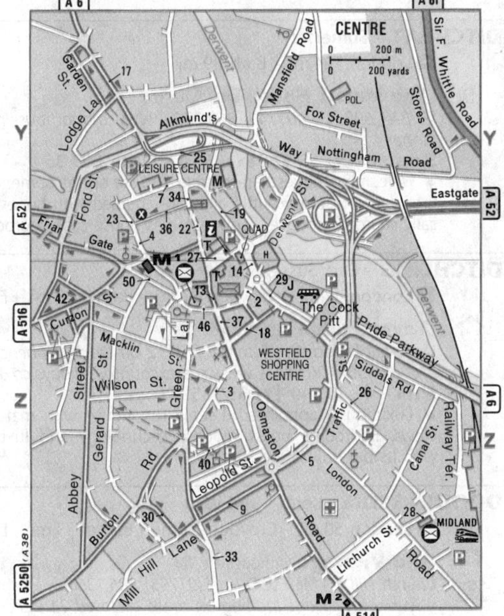

DEVIZES – Wiltshire – 503 O29 – pop. 14 379 — 4 C2

London 98 mi – Bristol 38 mi – Salisbury 25 mi – Southampton 50 mi
Cromwell House, Market Pl ✆ (01380) 729408, all.tic's@wiltshire.gov.uk
Erlestoke, ✆ (01380) 831 069
St John's Church★★ – Market Place★ – Wiltshire Heritage Museum★ **AC**
Potterne (Porch House★★) S : 2.5 mi by A 360 – E : Vale of Pewsey★. Stonehenge★★★ **AC**, SE : 16 mi by A 360 and A 344 – Avebury★★ (The Stones★, Church★) NE : 7 mi by A 361

at Potterne South : 2.25 mi on A 360 – ✉ Devizes

Blounts Court Farm without rest

Coxhill Ln ✉ SN10 5PH – ✆ (01380) 727 180 – www.blountscourtfarm.co.uk
3 rm – ♦£ 55/80 ♦♦£ 80
◆ Working farm personally run by charming owner: good value accommodation in blissful spot. Cosy rooms in converted barn are handsomely furnished with interesting artefacts.

at Rowde Northwest : 2 mi by A 361 on A 342 – ✉ Devizes

The George & Dragon with rm

High St ✉ SN10 2PN – ✆ (01380) 723 053 – www.thegeorgeanddragonrowde.co.uk – Closed Sunday dinner
3 rm – ♦£ 55/65 ♦♦£ 65/75
Rest – Seafood – *(booking essential)* Menu £ 18 (lunch) – Carte £ 25/40
◆ Rustic and cosy 16C coaching inn with open fires, solid stone floors and wooden beams. Oft-changing menu has strong emphasis on seafood, with fish delivered daily from Cornwall. Old-world charm meets modern facilities in the individually designed bedrooms.

ENGLAND

DIDSBURY – Gtr Manchester – 502 N23 – see Manchester

DITCHEAT – Somerset — 4 C2

London 124 mi – Bath 29 mi

The Manor House Inn with rm

✉ BA4 6RB – ✆ (01749) 860 276 – www.manorhouseinn.co.uk – Closed Sunday dinner
3 rm – ♦£ 55 ♦♦£ 85 **Rest** – Carte £ 23/36
◆ Welcoming, equestrian-themed pub set on the Somerset Levels. Traditional open fires and a restored skittle alley are coupled with honest classical cooking and locally sourced produce. Former stables house cosy bedrooms with good mod cons.

DITCHLING – East Sussex – 504 T31 — 7 D2

London 47 mi – Croydon 37 mi – Barnet 89 mi – Ealing 71 mi

Tovey Lodge without rest

Underhill Ln, South : 1 mi by B 2112 off Ditchling beacon rd ✉ BN6 8XE – ✆ (08456) 120 544 – www.sussexcountryholidays.co.uk
5 rm – ♦£ 70/140 ♦♦£ 85/155
◆ Luxuriously appointed, keenly run house with mature gardens and pleasant views. Bedrooms boast modern technology and luxurious bathrooms; Maple, with its balcony, is the best.

DODDINGTON – Kent – 504 W30 — 9 C2

London 50 mi – Croydon 51 mi – Barnet 73 mi – Ealing 87 mi

Old Vicarage without rest

Church Hill ✉ ME9 0BD – ✆ (01795) 886 136 – www.oldvicaragedoddington.co.uk – Closed 24 December-3 January
5 rm – ♦£ 55/65 ♦♦£ 79/85
◆ Restored house which blends period features with modern furnishings. Tastefully decorated bedrooms. Breakfast at impressive antique dining table with pleasant countryside views.

DOGMERSFIELD – Hampshire 7 C1

London 44 mi – Farnham 6 mi – Fleet 2 mi

Four Seasons

Dogmersfield Park, Chalky Ln ✉ RG27 8TD – ✆ (01252) 853 000 – www.fourseasons.com/hampshire

111 rm – †£ 225/334 ††£ 225/334, ☕ £ 27 – 22 suites

Rest *Seasons* – *(closed Sunday dinner and Monday) (dinner only and Sunday lunch)* Carte £ 41/65

♦ Part Georgian splendour in extensive woodlands; many original features in situ. Superb spa facilities: vast selection of leisure pursuits. Luxurious, highly equipped bedrooms. Restaurant has thoroughly modish, relaxing feel.

DONCASTER – South Yorkshire – 502 Q23 – pop. 67 977 23 C3

London 173 mi – Kingston-upon-Hull 46 mi – Leeds 30 mi – Nottingham 46 mi

Robin Hood Airport : ✆ (0871) 220 2210, SE : 7m off A638

38-40 High St ✆ (01302) 734309, touristi.nformation@doncaster.gov.uk

Doncaster Town Moor Belle Vue Bawtry Rd, ✆ (01302) 533 778

Crookhill Park Conisborough, ✆ (01709) 862 979

Wheatley Amthorpe Rd, ✆ (01302) 831 655

Owston Park Owston Owston Lane, Carcroft, ✆ (01302) 330 821

Mount Pleasant

rm, rest,

Great North Rd, Southeast : 6 mi on A 638 ✉ DN11 0HW – ✆ (01302) 868 696 – www.mountpleasant.co.uk

54 rm ☕ – †£ 79/99 ††£ 99/119 – 2 suites

Rest *Garden* – Carte £ 23/41 **s**

♦ Well-run, privately owned hotel with spacious inner. Comfortable, individually styled bedrooms: one with a five-poster bed; some with jacuzzi baths or saunas. Pleasant wellness centre and treatment rooms. Large formal dining room offers extensive, classical menu.

DONHEAD-ST-ANDREW – Wiltshire – 503 N30 4 C3

London 115 mi – Bournemouth 34 mi – Poole 32 mi – Bath 37 mi

Forester Inn

Lower St ✉ SP7 9EE – ✆ (01747) 828 038 – www.theforesterdonheadstandrews.co.uk – Closed Sunday dinner

Rest – Menu £ 18 – Carte £ 20/30

♦ Gloriously rustic 13C thatched pub. Menus display a strong seafood base, with constantly changing Brixham fish and a set 3 course selection. Charcuterie and tapas dishes on offer in the bar.

DORCHESTER – Dorset – 503 M31 – pop. 16 171 4 C3

London 135 mi – Bournemouth 27 mi – Exeter 53 mi – Southampton 53 mi

11 Antelope Walk ✆ (01305) 267992, dorchester.tic@westdorset-dc.gov.uk

Came Down, ✆ (01305) 813 494

Town★ - Dorset County Museum★ **AC**

Maiden Castle★★ (≤★) SW : 2.5 mi – Puddletown Church★, NE : 5.5 mi by A 35. Moreton Church★★, E : 7.5 mi – Bere Regis★ (St John the Baptist Church★ - Roof★★) NE : 11 mi by A 35 – Athelhampton House★ **AC**, NE : 6.5 mi by A 35 - Cerne Abbas★, N : 7 mi by A 352 – Milton Abbas★, NE : 12 mi on A 354 and by-road

Yalbury Cottage

Lower Bockhampton, East : 3.75 mi by A 35 ✉ DT2 8PZ – ✆ (01305) 262 382 – www.yalburycottage.com – Closed 3-24 January

8 rm ☕ – †£ 65/83 ††£ 95/115

Rest – *(closed Sunday dinner and Monday) (dinner only)* Menu £ 26/35

♦ Welcoming thatched cottage with a small garden, set in a quiet hamlet. Characterful beamed lounge with a gas-fire. Modern, comfortable bedrooms are located in the extension. Linen-clad dining room offers a set menu; most produce is sourced from within nine miles.

Little Court without rest 
5 Westleaze, Charminster, North : 1 mi by A 37, turning right at Loders garage ✉ DT2 9PZ – ☎ (01305) 261 576 – www.littlecourt.net – Closed 25 December-1 January
8 rm ☕ – 🚹£ 89 🚹🚹£ 99/139
♦ Lutyens style house boasting Edwardian wood/brickwork, leaded windows and mature gardens with a pool and tennis court. Bedrooms display original features and modern furnishings; one four-poster.

Sienna (Russell Brown) AC VISA MC
36 High West St ✉ DT1 1UP – ☎ (01305) 250 022 – www.siennarestaurant.co.uk – Closed 2 weeks spring, 2 weeks autumn, Sunday and Monday
Rest – *(booking essential)* Menu £ 27/41
Spec. Veal with white beans and pickled carrots. Sea bass with scallops, tomato and basil. Selvatica chocolate tasting plate.
♦ Small high street restaurant with frosted glass façade, intimate interior and smartly laid tables. Choice of concise à la carte or 6 course tasting menu. Precise cooking uses top quality local produce and classic flavour combinations. Polite, measured service.

at Winterbourne Steepleton **West : 4.75 mi by B 3150 and A 35 on B 3159 – ✉ Dorchester**

Old Rectory without rest 
✉ DT2 9LG – ☎ (01305) 889 468 – www.theoldrectorybandb.co.uk – Closed 1 week Christmas
4 rm ☕ – 🚹£ 60 🚹🚹£ 100
♦ Attractive house in pretty village; cross the brook and enter mature gardens. Comfy lounge and conservatory breakfast room. Immaculate bedrooms with homely, modern décor and smart bathrooms.

ENGLAND

DORRIDGE – West Midlands – 503 O26 – ✉ Birmingham 19 C2

London 109 mi – Birmingham 11 mi – Warwick 11 mi

The Forest with rm AC rest, P VISA MC AE
25 Station Approach ✉ B93 8JA – ☎ (01564) 772 120 – www.forest-hotel.com – Closed 25 December and Sunday dinner
12 rm – 🚹£ 95/110 🚹🚹£ 120/140, ☕ £ 10
Rest – Menu £ 16 (weekday dinner) – Carte £ 21/29
♦ Attractive red-brick and timber former pub with a busy ambience. Food is its backbone: modern classics served in stylish bar and restaurant. Cool, modern bedrooms.

DOUGLAS – Isle of Man – 502 G21 – see Man (Isle of)

DOVER – Kent – 504 Y30 – pop. 34 087 Great Britain 9 D2

London 76 mi – Brighton 84 mi
to France (Calais) (P & O Stena Line) frequent services daily (1 h 15 mn) – to France (Calais) (SeaFrance S.A.) frequent services daily (1 h 30 mn) – to France (Boulogne) (SpeedFerries) 3-5 daily (50 mn)
The Old Town Gaol, Biggin ☎ (01304) 205108, tic@doveruk.com
Castle★★ **AC** Y
White Cliffs, Langdon Cliffs, NE : 1 mi on A 2 Z and A 258

at St Margaret's at Cliffe **Northeast : 4 mi by A 258 - Z – ✉ Dover**

Wallett's Court Country House P VISA MC AE
West Cliffe, Northwest : 0.75 mi on Dover rd ✉ CT15 6EW – ☎ (01304) 852 424 – www.wallettscourt.com – Closed 25-26 December
17 rm ☕ – 🚹£ 90/120 🚹🚹£ 150/190
Rest ***The Restaurant*** – Menu £ 25/40 – Carte dinner £ 40/50
♦ Heavily beamed 17C country house with characterful lounge and comfy bar. Four-poster bedrooms in main house; rustic rooms in annexes; most luxurious rooms above pleasant spa. Atmospheric restaurant with smartly laid tables offers ambitious, original, modern menu.

DOVER

DOWNTON – Hants. – **503** P31 – see Lymington

DROITWICH SPA – Worcestershire – **503** N27 – pop. 22 585 **19** C3

London 129 mi – Birmingham 20 mi – Bristol 66 mi – Worcester 6 mi

St Richard's House, Victoria Sq ✆ (01905) 774312, heritage@droitwichspa.gov.uk

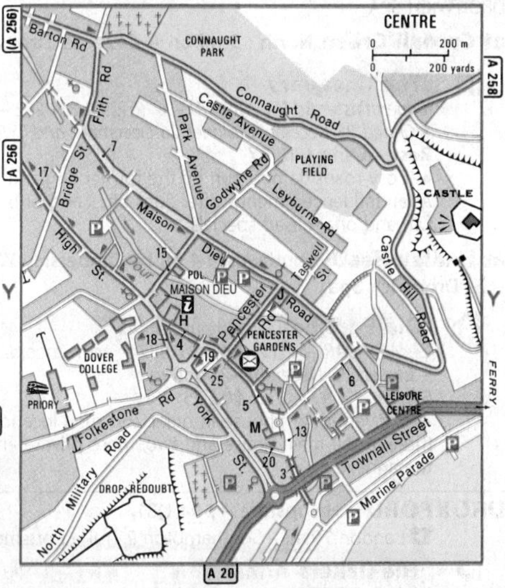

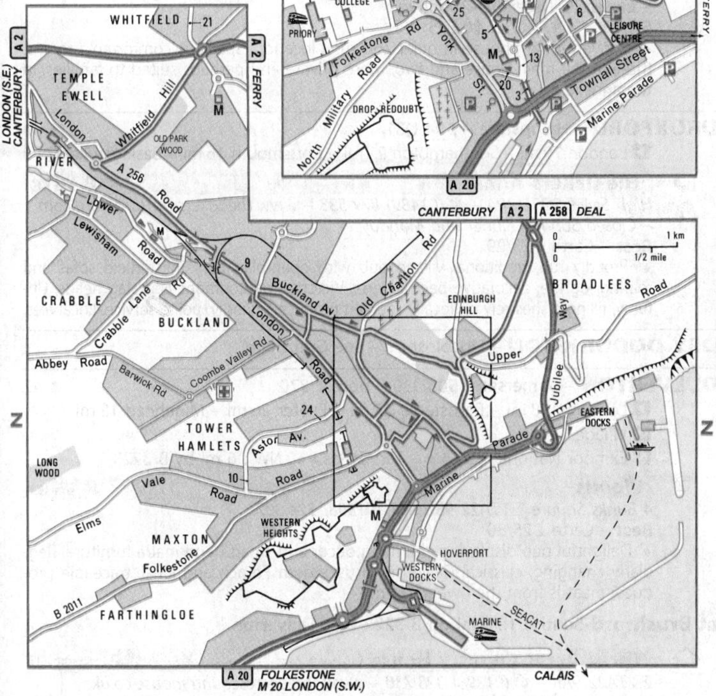

Droitwich G. & C.C. Ford Lane, ✆ (01905) 774 344

Large towns and cities include detailed plans locating hotels and restaurants. Use the given coordinates (ex.: **12**BMe) to find them easily.

at Cutnall Green North : 3 mi on A 442 – ✉ Droitwich Spa

The Chequers

Kidderminster Rd ✉ WR9 0PJ – ☎ (01299) 851 292 – www.chequerscutnallgreen.co.uk – Closed 25 December, dinner 26 December and 1 January

Rest – Carte £ 18/27

◆ Cosy roadside pub, run by the former England football team chef and his wife. Asian-influenced menus offer light bites and pub classics, with more adventurous fish and offal-based specials.

at Hadley Heath Southwest : 4 mi by Ombersley Way, A 4133 and Ladywood rd – ✉ Droitwich Spa

Old Farmhouse without rest

✉ WR9 0AR – ☎ (01905) 620 837 – www.theoldfarmhouse.uk.com – Closed 25 December-2 January

5 rm ☕ – †£ 40/45 ††£ 75

◆ Converted farmhouse in quiet and rural location. Spacious comfortable rooms, three in the main house and two, more private and perhaps suited to families, in the annexe.

DROXFORD – Hampshire – 504 Q31 — 6 B2

London 79 mi – Southampton 21 mi – Portsmouth 16 mi – Basingstoke 37 mi

The Bakers Arms

High St ✉ SO32 3PA – ☎ (01489) 877 533 – www.thebakersarmsdroxford.com – Closed Sunday dinner and Monday

Rest – Carte £ 23/29

◆ Proudly run, traditional village pub with open-plan bar, Chesterfield sofas and roaring log fire; decorative beer adverts, Victorian photographs and stag heads. Unfussy, filling dishes rely on locally sourced produce. Friendly, polite service. Local ales.

DRY DODDINGTON – Lincolnshire – see Grantham

DULVERTON – Somerset – 503 J30 – pop. 1 870 — 3 A2

London 198 mi – Barnstaple 27 mi – Exeter 26 mi – Minehead 18 mi

Village★

Exmoor National Park★★ - Tarr Steps★★, NW : 6 mi by B 3223

Woods

4 Banks Square ✉ TA22 9BU – ☎ (01398) 324 007

Rest – Carte £ 25/30

◆ Delightful pub displaying charming décor and smart hand-made furniture. Regularly changing, classical Gallic menu uses both French and local, traceable produce; meat is from the owner's farm.

at Brushford South : 1.75 mi on B 3222 – ✉ Dulverton

Three Acres Country House without rest

✉ TA22 9AR – ☎ (01398) 323 730 – www.threeacrescountryhouse.co.uk

6 rm ☕ – †£ 75 ††£ 120

◆ Remotely set guesthouse boasting nearly 3 acres of mature gardens/parkland. Comfy lounge, small bar, pine-furnished breakfast room and pleasant terrace. Large, cosy bedrooms with country views.

DUNSTER – Somerset – 503 J30 – pop. 848 — 3 A2

London 185 mi – Minehead 3 mi – Taunton 23 mi

Town★★ - Castle★★ AC (upper rooms ≤★) - Water Mill★ AC - St George's Church★ - Dovecote★

Exmoor House without rest

12 West St ✉ TA24 6SN – ☎ (01643) 821 268 – www.exmoorhousedunster.co.uk

6 rm ☕ – †£ 50 ††£ 75

◆ Terraced Georgian house on the main street of a historic town; run by warm, welcoming owners. Comfy, chintzy lounge and spacious pine-furnished breakfast room. Cosy, well-kept bedrooms.

ENGLAND

DURHAM – Durham – **501** P19 – **pop. 42 939** Great Britain **24** B3

London 267 mi – Leeds 77 mi – Middlesbrough 23 mi – Newcastle upon Tyne 20 mi

2 Millennium Pl ✆ (0191) 384 3720, touristinfo@durhamcity.gov.uk

Mount Oswald South Rd, ✆ (0191) 386 7527

City★★★ - Cathedral★★★ (Nave★★★, Chapel of the Nine Altars★★★, Sanctuary Knocker★) B – Oriental Museum★★ **AC** (at Durham University by A 167) B – City and Riverside (Prebends' Bridge ≤★★★ A , Framwellgate Bridge ≤★★ B) – Monastic Buildings (Cathedral Treasury★, Central Tower ≤★) B – Castle★ (Norman chapel★) **AC** B

Hartlepool Historic Quay★, SE : 14 mi by A 181, A 19 and A 179

Fallen Angel

rm, AC, VISA, MC, AE

34 Old Elvet ✉ *DH1 3HN* – ✆ *(0191) 384 10 37 – www.fallenangelhotel.com* **Bc**

9 rm – ♦£ 110/160 ♦♦£ 110/160 – 1 suite

Rest – Carte £ 25/37

♦ A one-off: luxurious, individually themed bedrooms include 'Sci-Fi', which comes with Dalek and Tardis and the indulgent, red velvet 'Le Boudoir'. The garden rooms have terraces, hot tubs and a Rolls Royce. Accessible menu in informal conservatory restaurant.

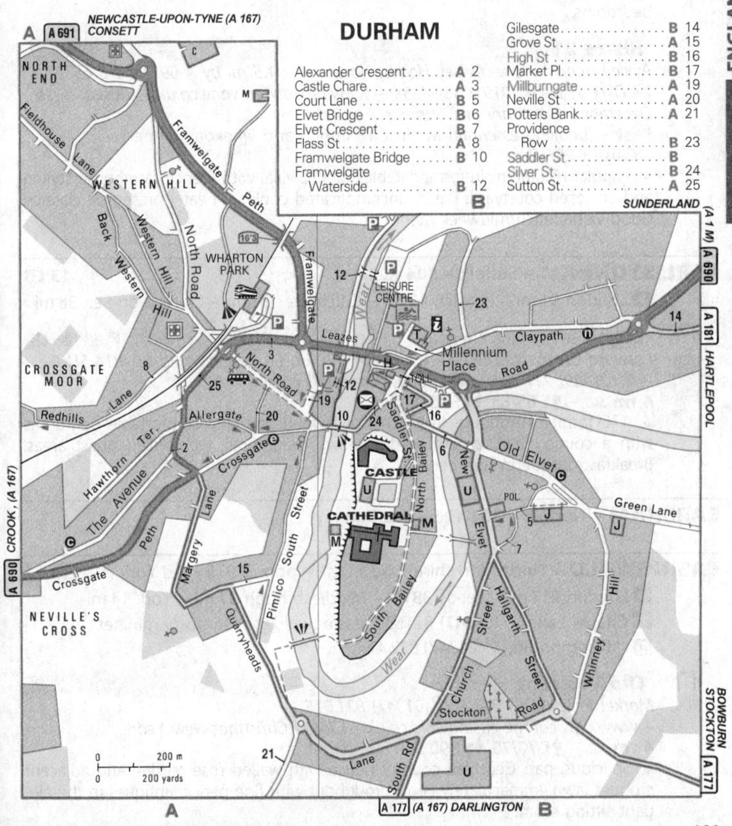

ENGLAND

Farnley Tower

The Avenue ✉ DH1 4DX – ☎ (0191) 375 0011 – www.farnley-tower.co.uk – Closed first 2 weeks January and 25-26 December. Ac

13 rm – £ 55/70 £ 75/90

Rest *Gourmet Spot* – ☎ (0191) 384 6655 *(closed Sunday and Monday) (dinner only)* Carte £ 30/40

◆ Spacious Victorian house in quiet residential area close to city centre. Modern, airy, well-equipped bedrooms with a good degree of comfort. Gourmet Spot, stylish and slick in black granite and leather, serves original, modern cuisine.

Cathedral View Town House without rest

212 Lower Gilesgate ✉ DH1 1QN – ☎ (0191) 386 9566 – www.cathedralview.com Bn

6 rm – £ 60/90 £ 75/100

◆ Alluring Georgian townhouse with terraced garden in older part of the city near the centre. Attractive breakfast room with good views. Spacious, individually named rooms.

Castle View without rest

4 Crossgate ✉ DH1 4PS – ☎ (0191) 386 8852 – www.castle-view.co.uk – Closed 2 weeks Christmas-New Year Ae

6 rm – £ 55/60 £ 80

◆ Attractive Georgian townhouse off steep cobbled hill, reputedly once the vicarage to adjacent church. Breakfast on terrace in summer. Individually furnished bedrooms.

Bistro 21

Aykley Heads House, Aykley Heads, Northwest : 1.5 mi by A 691 and B 6532 ✉ DH1 5TS – ☎ (0191) 384 4354 – www.bistrotwentyone.co.uk – Closed 25-26 December, 1 January and Sunday

Rest – *(booking essential)* Menu £ 18 (lunch and weekday dinner) – Carte £ 25/40

◆ Popular restaurant in former stables of 17C villa, with French farmhouse styling and enclosed courtyard. Fresh, uncomplicated cooking; neatly presented classics. Good value lunch/midweek menu.

ENGLAND

EARL STONHAM – Suffolk – 504 X27 15 C3

London 91 mi – Ipswich 12 mi – Colchester 33 mi – Clacton-on-Sea 38 mi

Bays Farm without rest

Forward Green, Northwest : 1 mi by A1120 on Broad Green Rd ✉ IP14 5HU – ☎ (01449) 711 286 – www.baysfarmsuffolk.co.uk

4 rm – £ 65/85 £ 75/110

◆ 17C former farmhouse in 4 acres of lawned gardens. Comfortable bedrooms with a country feel, 2 with garden views. Traditional, wood-filled guest areas. Breakfast outside in summer.

EARSHAM – Norfolk – 504 Y26 – see Bungay

EASINGWOLD – North Yorkshire – 502 Q21 – pop. 3 975 – ✉ York 23 C2

London 217 mi – Leeds 38 mi – Middlesbrough 37 mi – York 14 mi

Chapel Lane ☎ (01347) 821530, easingwold.touristinfo@virgin.net

Stillington Rd, ☎ (01347) 822 474

Old Vicarage without rest

Market Pl ✉ YO61 3AL – ☎ (01347) 821 015 – www.oldvicarage-easingwold.co.uk – Closed Christmas-New Year

4 rm – £ 70/75 £ 90/95

◆ Spacious, part Georgian country house with walled rose garden and adjacent croquet lawn. Immaculately kept throughout with fine period antiques in the elegant sitting room.

at Crayke East : 2 mi on Helmsley Rd – ✉ York

The Durham Ox with rm
Westway ✉ *YO61 4TE* – ✆ *(01347) 821 506* – *www.thedurhamox.com*
5 rm – †£ 80 ††£ 150 **Rest** – *(booking essential)* Carte £ 27/37
♦ 300 year old, family run pub set in a sleepy hamlet. Regularly changing à la carte features hearty dishes of fresh seafood, local meats, Crayke game and tasty spit-roast chicken. Bedrooms are set in old farm cottages; some are suites, some have jacuzzis.

EAST ALLINGTON – Devon 2 C3

London 210 mi – Plymouth 24 mi – Torbay 18 mi – Exeter 38 mi

Fortescue Arms
✉ *TQ9 7RA* ✆ *(01548) 521 215* – *www.fortescue-arms.co.uk* – *Closed Monday lunch*
Rest – Carte £ 18/32
♦ Ivy-clad building; formerly part of the Fallapit estate. Choice of small beamed bar serving pub classics and blackboard specials or more formal dining room offering a concise à la carte.

EASTBOURNE – East Sussex – 504 U31 – pop. 106 562 Great Britain 8 B3

London 68 mi – Brighton 25 mi – Dover 61 mi – Maidstone 49 mi
Cornfield Rd ✆ (01323) 415450, tic@eastbourne.gov.uk
Royal Eastbourne Paradise Drive, ✆ (01323) 744 045
Eastbourne Downs East Dean Rd, ✆ (01323) 720 827
Eastbourne Golfing Park Lottbridge Drove, ✆ (01323) 520 400
Seafront★
Beachy Head★★★, SW : 3 mi by B 2103 Z

Plan on next page

The Grand rm,
King Edward's Par. ✉ *BN21 4EQ* – ✆ *(01323) 412 345* – *www.grandeastbourne.com*
131 rm – †£ 165/510 ††£ 195/540 – 10 suites Zx
Rest *Mirabelle* – see restaurant listing
Rest *Garden Restaurant* – Menu £ 21/37 – Carte £ 11/23
♦ Built in 1871 and offering all its name promises. Retains many original features, including ornate plasterwork, column-lined corridors and a Great Hall. Classical bedrooms; pay the extra for a sea view. Lavish lounges, smart cocktail bar and formal restaurant.

Brayscroft
13 South Cliff Ave ✉ *BN20 7AH* – ✆ *(01323) 647 005* – *www.brayscrofthotel.co.uk*
6 rm – †£ 36/65 ††£ 72/80 **Rest** – Menu £ 15 Zn
♦ Spacious Edwardian house – now a small hotel – located close to the seafront, gardens and pier. Traditional lounge and dining room display antiques and Italian artwork. Comfortable, classically styled bedrooms. Evening meals by daily arrangement; tailored to each guest they feature fresh, local, free range ingredients.

Mirabelle – at The Grand Hotel
King Edward's Par. ✉ *BN21 4EQ* – ✆ *(01323) 435 066*
– Closed first 2 weeks January, Sunday and Monday Zx
Rest – *(booking essential)* Menu £ 23/39 – Carte £ 39/66
♦ Plush fabrics and linen-laid tables with monogrammed silverware; formal dress code and professional team. Seasonal classics or 6 course tasting menu at dinner. Rich, well-executed cooking.

at Jevington Northwest : 6 mi by A 259 - Z - on Jevington Rd – ✉ Polegate

Hungry Monk
The Street ✉ *BN26 5QF* – ✆ *(01323) 482 178* – *www.hungrymonk.co.uk* – *Closed 24-26 December, Monday and bank holidays*
Rest – *(booking essential)* Menu £ 17 (weekday lunch)/36
♦ Charming 14C cottages with terrace, cosy lounges, traditional main room and several private rooms. Country style cooking with modern European edge. Allegedly the birthplace of banoffee pie.

EASTBOURNE

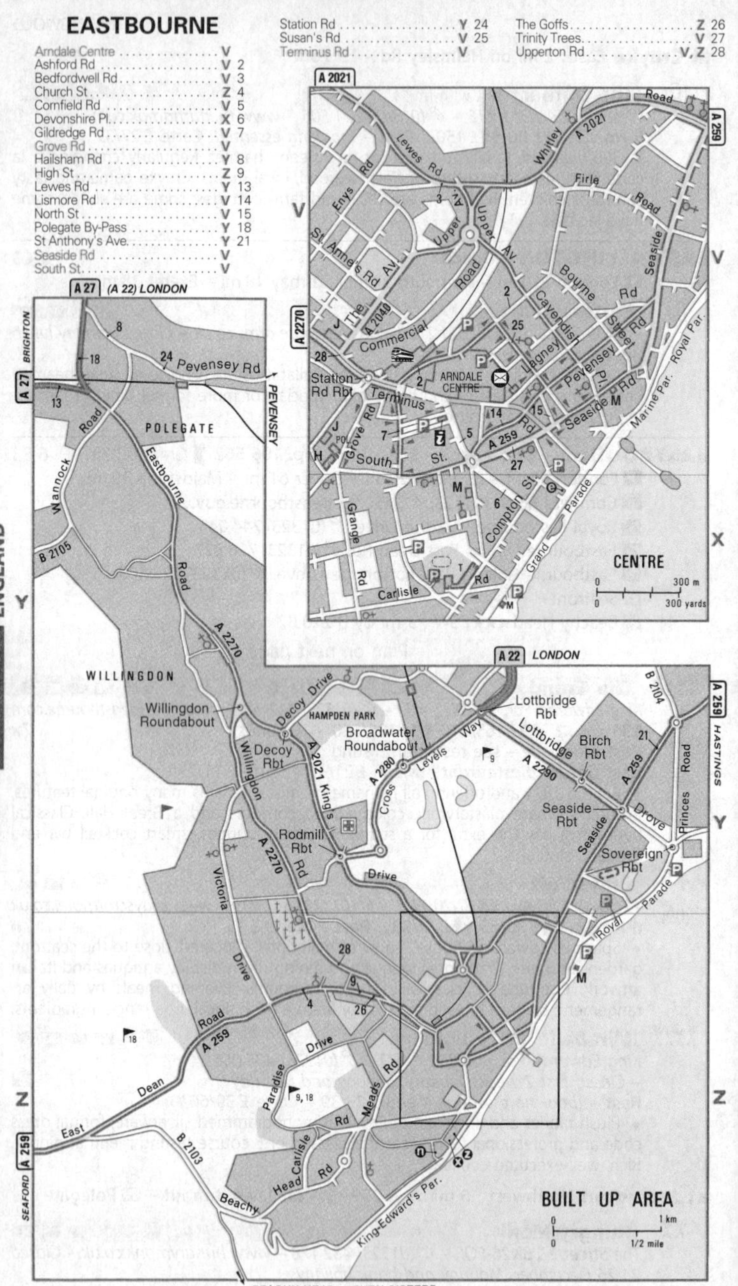

A 2021
A 259
A 2270
A 27
(A 22) LONDON
BRIGHTON
PEVENSEY
POLEGATE
Pevensey Rd
Wannock
Eastbourne Road
WILLINGDON
Willingdon Roundabout
Decoy Drive
Decoy Rbt
HAMPDEN PARK
Broadwater Roundabout
Lottbridge Rbt
Birch Rbt
Seaside Rbt
Sovereign Rbt
Rodmill Rbt
A 22 LONDON
HASTINGS
SEAFORD
BEACHY HEAD. SEVEN SISTERS
Lewes Rd
Upper Av.
St. Anne's Rd
Commercial Road
Station Rd Rbt
Terminus
ARNDALE CENTRE
Grove Rd
South St.
Cavendish
Bourne
Seaside Rd
Pevensey Rd
Marine Par.
Royal Par.
Grand Parade
Compton St.
Carlisle Rd
Grange Rd
Whitley Road
Firle Road
CENTRE
0 300 m
0 300 yards
BUILT UP AREA
0 1 km
0 1/2 mile
ENGLAND

EAST CHILTINGTON – E. Sussex – see Lewes

EAST CHISENBURY – Wiltshire **4** D2

London 92 mi – Bristol 51 mi – Southampton 53 mi – Reading 51 mi

Red Lion Freehouse

SN9 6AQ – (01980) 671 124 – www.redlionfreehouse.com – Closed 2 weeks January, Sunday dinner and Monday

Rest – *(booking advisable)* Menu £ 15 (weekday lunch) – Carte £ 25/35

♦ Delightful thatched pub with exposed beams, wood burner and a pretty garden. Enthusiastic owners cook pleasingly down-to-earth dishes, precisely composed and packed with flavour. Daily changing, seasonal à la carte, great value lunch menu and Sunday roasts.

EAST END – Hampshire – see Lymington

EAST GARSTON – West Berkshire – see Lambourn

EASTGATE – Durham – **502** N19 **24** A3

London 288 mi – Bishop Auckland 20 mi – Newcastle upon Tyne 35 mi – Stanhope 3 mi

Horsley Hall

Southeast : 1 mi by A 689 DL13 2LJ – (01388) 517 239 – www.horsleyhall.co.uk – Closed 23 December-3 January

7 rm – £ 65/85 ££ 120/160

Rest – *(closed Sunday) (booking essential for non residents)* Menu £ 19/29

♦ Attractive ivy-clad former hunting lodge with 14C origins, built for the Bishop of Durham. Impressive hall; superb stained glass; mix of simple, cosy bedrooms – two with Edwardian bathrooms. Baronial style dining room boasts impressive ornate ceiling.

EAST GRINSTEAD – West Sussex – **504** T30 – **pop. 26 222** **7** D2

London 48 mi – Brighton 30 mi – Eastbourne 32 mi – Lewes 21 mi

Copthorne Borers Arm Rd, (01342) 712 508

Gravetye Manor

Vowels Ln., Southwest : 4.5 mi by B 2110 taking second turn left towards West Hoathly RH19 4LJ – (01342) 810 567 – www.gravetyemanor.co.uk – closed 2 January-1 February

18 rm – ££ 354/426, £ 18 **Rest** – *(booking essential)* Carte £ 29/43

♦ Elizabethan manor house surrounded by 35 acres of gardens and 1,000 acres of forestry land. Wood-panelled guest areas display heavy fabrics. Traditionally appointed bedrooms boast large beds. Afternoon tea and all day dining in lounges. Classical dining room.

EAST HOATHLY – East Sussex – **504** U31 – **pop. 1 206** **8** B3

London 60 mi – Brighton 16 mi – Eastbourne 13 mi – Hastings 25 mi

Old Whyly

London Rd, Northwest : 0.5 mi, turning right after post box on right, taking centre gravel drive after approx. 400 metres BN8 6EL – (01825) 840 216 – www.oldwhyly.co.uk

3 rm – £ 75 ££ 90/135 **Rest** – Menu £ 30

♦ Charming, secluded Georgian manor house decorated with antiques, oils and watercolours. Airy bedrooms individually styled. Delightful owner. Warm, informal dining room.

EAST KENNETT – Wiltshire – see Marlborough

EAST LAVANT – W. Sussex – see Chichester

EASTON – Devon – **503** I31 – see Chagford

EASTON – Somerset – see Wells

EAST WITTON – North Yorkshire – 502 O21 – ✉ Leyburn **22** B1

London 238 mi – Leeds 45 mi – Middlesbrough 30 mi – York 39 mi

The Blue Lion with rm

✉ DL8 4SN – ✆ (01969) 624 273 – www.thebluelion.co.uk – Closed 25 December

15 rm – †£ 68 ††£ 140 **Rest** – *(booking essential)* Carte £ 22/43

♦ Charming, characterful countryside pub. Daily-changing menu features a tasty mix of classic and modern dishes, all with seasonality and traceability at their core. Bedrooms – in the pub and outbuildings – are warm and cosy.

EBRINGTON – Gloucestershire – 504 O27 – see Chipping Campden

ECCLESTON – Lancashire – 502 L23 – pop. 4 708 **20** A2

London 219 mi – Birmingham 103 mi – Liverpool 29 mi – Preston 11 mi

Parr Hall Farm without rest

Parr Ln. ✉ PR7 5SL – ✆ (01257) 451 917 – www.parrhallfarm.com

10 rm – †£ 40 ††£ 70

♦ Welcoming, red-brick former farmhouse. Low-beamed, pine-furnished breakfast room. Bedrooms, located in the adjacent barn conversion, boast country style fabrics and modern bathrooms.

ECKINGTON – Derbyshire – 502 P24 – pop. 16 684 **16** B1

London 155 mi – Leeds 49 mi – Sheffield 10 mi – Manchester 58 mi

The Inn at Troway

Snowdon Ln, Southeast : 7.5 mi by A 6135, B 6052 and B 6056 ✉ S21 5RU – ✆ (01246) 270 751 – www.relaxeatanddrink.co.uk – Closed 25 December

Rest – *(booking advisable)* Menu £ 12 – Carte £ 15/25

♦ Early Victorian pub in picturesque location with delightful countryside views. Hearty, satisfying dishes on wide-ranging menu. Fine selection of local ales; helpful local staff.

ECKINGTON – Worcestershire – 504 N27 – see Pershore

EGHAM – Surrey – 504 S29 – pop. 27 666 **7** C1

London 29 mi – Reading 21 mi

Great Fosters

Stroude Rd, South : 1.25 mi by B 388 ✉ TW20 9UR – ✆ (01784) 433 822 – www.greatfosters.co.uk

41 rm – †£ 130/175 ††£ 175, £ 19.50 – 3 suites

Rest *The Oak Room* – see restaurant listing

♦ Elizabethan mansion built as a hunting lodge for Henry VIII. Charming inner with original features; spacious guest areas offer lovely garden views. Medieval-style bedrooms boast feature beds.

Monsoon

20 High St ✉ TW20 9DT – ✆ (01784) 432 141 – www.monsoonrestaurant.co.uk

Rest – Indian – Menu £ 15 – Carte £ 16/25

♦ Smart, stylish restaurant that prides itself on immaculate upkeep and personable service. Contemporary artwork enlivens the walls. Freshly cooked, authentic Indian dishes.

The Oak Room – at Great Fosters Hotel

Stroude Rd, South : 1.25 mi by B 388 ✉ TW20 9UR – ✆ (01784) 433 822 – www.greatfosters.co.uk

Rest – *(closed Saturday lunch)* Menu £ 25 – Carte dinner approx. £ 49

♦ Spacious 16C oak-framed dining room with cosy bar and delightful terrace. Charming period features, immaculately laid tables and formal service. Skilful, modern cooking; complex combinations.

ELDERSFIELD – Worcestershire – see Tewkesbury

ELLAND – West Yorkshire – 502 O22 – pop. 14 554 – ✉ Halifax **22** B3

London 204 mi – Bradford 12 mi – Burnley 29 mi – Leeds 17 mi

Hullen Edge Hammerstones Leach Lane, ✆ (01422) 372 505

ENGLAND

La Cachette

31 Huddersfield Rd ✉ HX5 9AW – ✆ (01422) 378 833 – www.lacachette-elland.com – Closed 2 weeks August, 27 December-7 January, Sunday and bank holidays

Rest – Menu £ 22 (dinner) – Carte £ 24/36

◆ Long-standing, well-run bistro. Spacious bar and dining rooms display Gallic décor and memorabilia. Extensive choice from daily/weekly menus and specials. Classical, seasonal French cooking.

ELSTOW – Beds. – **504** S27 – see Bedford

ELTISLEY – Cambridgeshire – **507** T27 — 14 A3

London 70 mi – Leicester 62 mi

The Eltisley

2 The Green ✉ PE19 6TG – ✆ (01480) 880 308 – www.theeltisley.co.uk – Closed Sunday dinner and Monday except July-September

Rest – Carte £ 23/33

◆ Chic and stylish gastropub beside a village green. Simple, unfussy cooking relies on quality, local produce to speak for itself; everything from starters to desserts is homemade.

ELTON – Cambridgeshire – **504** S26 — 14 A2

London 84 mi – Peterborough 11 mi – Bedford 40 mi – Kettering 24 mi

The Crown Inn with rm

8 Duck St ✉ PE8 6RQ – ✆ (01832) 280 232 – www.thecrowninn.org – Closed 1-7 January, Sunday dinner and Monday lunch

5 rm – †£ 60 ††£ 90/120 **Rest** – Menu £ 15 (lunch) – Carte £ 15/30

◆ 17C honey-stone pub in a delightful country parish, with thatched roof, cosy inglenook and laid-back feel. Extensive menus offer British classics and some Mediterranean influences. Smart, individually styled bedrooms – some with feature beds or roll-top baths.

ENGLAND

ELY – Cambridgeshire – **504** U26 – pop. 13 954 Great Britain — 14 B2

London 74 mi – Cambridge 16 mi – Norwich 60 mi

Oliver Cromwell's House, 29 St Mary's St ✆ (01353) 662062, tic@eastcambs.gov.uk

107 Cambridge Rd, ✆ (01353) 662 751

Cathedral★★ **AC**

Wicken Fen★, SE : 9 mi by A 10 and A 1123

The Boathouse

5-5A Annesdale ✉ CB7 4BN – ✆ (01353) 664 388 – www.theboathouseely.co.uk – Closed Christmas

Rest – *(booking essential)* Menu £ 16 (except Sunday) – Carte £ 23/32

◆ A riverside setting makes for a charming ambience: bag a terrace table if you can. Airy, dark wood interior where worldwide menus benefit from numerous creative touches.

at Little Thetford South : 2.75 mi by A 10 – ✉ Ely

Springfields without rest

Ely Rd, North : 0.5 mi on A 10 ✉ CB6 3HJ – ✆ (01353) 663 637 – Closed Christmas

3 rm – †£ 55 ††£ 75

◆ Welcoming, bric-a-brac-filled bungalow in pleasant gardens: a perfect home from home. Comfy lounge with wood burning stove; immaculately kept bedrooms. Courtyard breakfast when weather allows.

at Sutton Gault West : 8 mi by A 142 off B 1381 – ✉ Ely

The Anchor Inn with rm

✉ CB6 2BD – ✆ (01353) 778 537 – www.anchor-inn-restaurant.co.uk – Closed dinner 25-26 December and 1 January

4 rm – †£ 60 ††£ 130 **Rest** – Menu £ 16 (lunch) – Carte £ 20/30

◆ Riverside pub dating back to 1650 and the creation of the Hundred Foot Wash. Tempting main menu complemented by daily fish specials and occasionally oxen and zebra from the nearby estate. Neat, pine furnished bedrooms. Two suites; one with river views.

EMSWORTH - Hampshire - 504 R31 - pop. 18 310 **6** B2

London 75 mi - Brighton 37 mi - Portsmouth 10 mi - Southampton 22 mi

36 on the Quay (Ramon Farthing) with rm

47 South St, The Quay ✉ PO10 7EG - ✆ (01243) 375 592 - www.36onthequay.co.uk - Closed 2 weeks January, 1 week May, 1 week November, Sunday and Monday

6 rm - †£ 70 ††£ 95/110

Rest - *(booking essential)* Menu £ 27/49

Spec. Red mullet with tomato caponata and anchovy beignet. Veal with dauphinoise potatoes and shallot cream. Iced peanut parfait with doughnuts and coffee cream.

♦ Long-standing quayside restaurant run by experienced chef-owner. Elegant bar-lounge and intimate linen-laid restaurant in neutral hues. Concise à la carte of well-executed, classical dishes in flavoursome, tried-and-tested combinations. Contemporary bedrooms with good comforts; be ready to order breakfast at check-in.

Fat Olives

30 South St ✉ PO10 7EH - ✆ (01243) 377 914 - www.fatolives.co.uk - Closed 2 weeks June, 2 weeks Christmas, Sunday and Monday

Rest - *(booking essential)* Menu £ 19 (lunch) - Carte £ 32/43

♦ Small terraced house with a welcoming ambience. Simply decorated with wood floor and rough plaster walls. Tasty modern British menu and, yes, fat olives are available!

EPSOM - Surrey - 504 T30 - pop. 64 493 **7** D1

London 17 mi - Guildford 16 mi

Longdown Lane South Epsom Downs, ✆ (01372) 721 666

Horton Park G & C.C. Hook Rd, ✆ (020) 8393 8400

Chalk Lane

Chalk Ln., Southwest : 0.5 mi by A 24 and Woodcote Rd ✉ KT18 7BB - ✆ (01372) 721 179 - www.chalklanehotel.com

22 rm - †£ 85/185 ††£ 100/185

Rest - Menu £ 18 (weekday lunch) - Carte dinner £ 31/43

♦ At the foot of the Epsom Downs and near to the racecourse. Quality furnishings throughout; the neatly kept bedrooms are most comfortable. Smart, modern dining room.

Le Raj

211 Fir Tree Rd, Epsom Downs, Southeast : 2.25 mi by B 289 and B 284 on B 291 ✉ KT17 3LB - ✆ (01737) 371 371 - www.lerajrestaurant.co.uk - Closed Christmas

Rest - Bangladeshi - Menu £ 10 (lunch) - Carte £ 27/46

♦ Original, interesting menu makes good use of fresh ingredients and brings a modern style to traditional Bangladeshi cuisine. Smart, vibrant, contemporary interior décor.

ERMINGTON - Devon - 503 I32 **2** C2

London 216 mi - Plymouth 11 mi - Salcombe 15 mi

Plantation House with rm

Totnes Rd, Southwest : 0.5 mi on A 3121 ✉ PL21 9NS - ✆ (01548) 831 100 - www.plantationhousehotel.co.uk - Closed Christmas

9 rm - †£ 70/95 ††£ 170

Rest - *(dinner only) (booking essential for non-residents)* Menu £ 35/39 **s**

♦ Appealing, converted Georgian rectory with smart gardens and terraced seating area. Personally run. Sound cooking of locally sourced ingredients. Individually styled bedrooms.

ESHER - Surrey - 504 S29 - pop. 46 599 **7** D1

London 20 mi - Portsmouth 58 mi

Thames Ditton & Esher Portsmouth Rd, ✆ (020) 8398 1551

Moore Place Portsmouth Rd, ✆ (01372) 463 533

Cranfield Golf at Sandown More Lane, ✆ (01372) 468 093

Plan : see Greater London (South-West) 5

XX **George**

104 High St ✉ KT10 9QJ – ✆ (01372) 471 500 – www.george-esher.com – Closed lunch Saturday and dinner Sunday-Monday BZ**x**

Rest – Carte £ 15/30

♦ Spacious brasserie-style restaurant with dark wood bar and lower level main dining room. Smart, unfussy tableware. Constantly evolving, modern brasserie menu relies on quality ingredients.

ETTINGTON – **Warwickshire** – **504** P27 – **pop. 953** **19** C3

London 95 mi – Birmingham 41 mi – Leicester 48 mi – Coventry 23 mi

The Chequers Inn

91 Banbury Rd ✉ CV37 7SR – ✆ (01789) 740 387 – www.the-chequers-ettington.co.uk – Closed Sunday dinner and Monday

Rest – Carte £ 20/27

♦ Chandeliers, brushed velvet furniture and Regency chairs set at chequered tables mean that this is not your typical pub. Cooking is classical in style, with well-matching flavours.

EVERSHOT – **Dorset** – **503** M31 – **pop. 225** – ✉ **Dorchester** **4** C3

London 149 mi – Bournemouth 39 mi – Dorchester 12 mi – Salisbury 53 mi

Summer Lodge

9 Fore St ✉ DT2 0JR – ✆ (01935) 482 000 – www.summerlodgehotel.com

20 rm – †£ 375/495 ††£ 400/520 – 4 suites

Rest *The Restaurant* – *(booking essential to non residents)* Menu £ 28 (lunch) – Carte dinner £ 48/66

♦ Attractive former dower house in mature gardens. Country house style guest areas display heavy fabrics and antiques. Individually designed bedrooms boast quality furnishings and marble bathrooms. Exclusive glass-built wellness centre. Formal dining room and conservatory offer classical cuisine. Smart, effective service.

The Acorn Inn

28 Fore St ✉ DT2 0JW – ✆ (01935) 83 228 – www.acorn-inn.co.uk

10 rm – †£ 75/90 ††£ 130/140 **Rest** – Menu £ 23 (lunch) – Carte £ 18/33

♦ Historic inn mentioned in 'Tess of the d'Urbervilles'. Individually styled bedrooms boast fabric-covered walls, good facilities and modern bathrooms. Guest areas include a characterful residents' lounge, a locals bar with skittle alley and a classical restaurant.

Wooden Cabbage

East Chelborough, West : 3.25 mi by Beaminter rd, Chelborough rd on East Chelborough rd ✉ DT2 0QA – ✆ (01935) 83 362 – www.woodencabbage.co.uk – Restricted opening in winter

3 rm – †£ 75 ††£ 100/110 **Rest** – Carte approx. £ 30

♦ Attractive former gamekeeper's cottage. Spacious guest areas include a cosy dining room used in winter and an airy conservatory used in summer. Pretty bedrooms boast good facilities and lovely countryside views. Meals (by arrangement) feature home-grown produce.

EXETER – **Devon** – **503** J31 – **pop. 106 772** **2** D2

London 201 mi – Bournemouth 83 mi – Bristol 83 mi – Plymouth 46 mi

Exeter Airport : ✆ (01392) 367433, E : 5 mi by A 30 V

Dixs Field, Princesshay ✆ (01392) 665700, evit@exeter.gov.uk

Downes Crediton Hookway, ✆ (01363) 773 025

City★★ - Cathedral★★ Z – Royal Albert Memorial Museum★ Y

Killerton★★ **AC**, NE : 7 mi by B 3181 V – Ottery St Mary★ (St Mary's★) E : 12 mi by B 3183 - Y - A 30 and B 3174 – Crediton (Holy Cross Church★), NW : 9 mi by A 377

Plans pages 208, 209

Abode Exeter

Cathedral Yard ✉ *EX1 1HD* – ✆ *(01392) 319 955*
– *www.abodehotels.co.uk* Yz
52 rm – 🯅£ 145 🯅🯅£ 145, ☕ £ 13.50 – 1 suite
Rest *Michael Caines* – see restaurant listing
◆ Georgian-style frontage; located on the doorstep of the cathedral. Boutique style hotel with a very modern, stylish interior. Understated bedrooms feature good mod cons.

The Queens Court

Bystock Terr. ✉ *EX4 4HY* – ✆ *(01392) 272 709*
– *www.queenscourt-hotel.co.uk*
– *Closed 1 week Christmas* Yn
18 rm ☕ – 🯅£ 120 🯅🯅£ 120
Rest *Olive Tree* – *(closed Sunday lunch)* Carte £ 30/35
◆ A town house hotel located close to Central train station. Bright public areas decorated in a clean, modern style. Well-equipped, tidily furnished and co-ordinated bedrooms. Brightly painted, clean-lined restaurant.

Silversprings without rest

12 Richmond Rd ✉ *EX4 4JA* – ✆ *(01392) 494 040*
– *www.silversprings.co.uk*
– *Closed 20 December to 4 January* Ya
10 rm ☕ – 🯅£ 55/80 🯅🯅£ 80/100
◆ Cream coloured Georgian terraced house in Roman part of town. Warm and friendly, with immaculately kept public areas. Varied palettes and cathedral views distinguish rooms.

ENGLAND

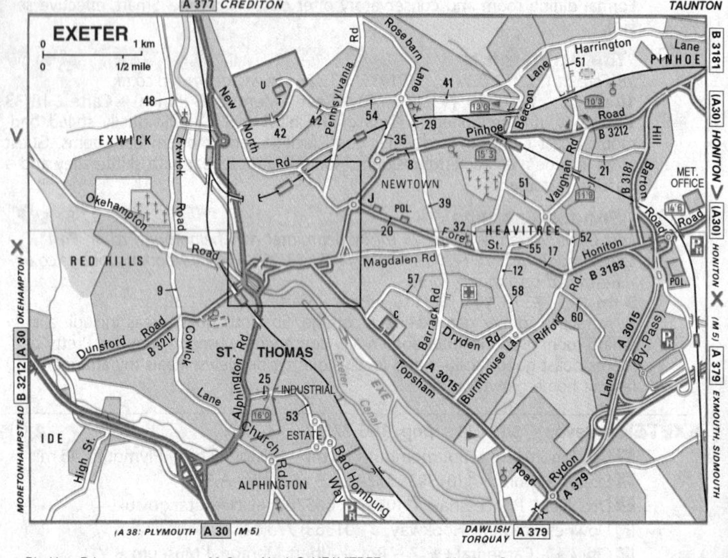

XX Angela's

VISA MC

38 New Bridge St ✉ EX4 3AH – ✆ (01392) 499 038
– www.angelasrestaurant.co.uk – Closed 1 week spring, 1 week summer, 1 week winter, lunch Tuesday, Sunday and Monday **Za**

Rest – Menu £ 19 (lunch) – Carte £ 32/42

♦ Neighbourhood restaurant with welcoming feel. Plain décor with oils and prints; large well spaced tables. Extensive menu of local, seasonal fare; plenty of meat, fish and vegetarian choices.

XX Michael Caines – at Abode Exeter Hotel

A/C VISA MC AE D

Cathedral Yard ✉ EX1 1HD – ✆ (01392) 223 638 – www.michaelcaines.com

Rest – *(closed Sunday)* Menu £ 20 (lunch) – Carte £ 46/52 **Yz**

♦ Comfortable, contemporarily stylish restaurant overlooking Cathedral. Menu has good choice of well-balanced and confident modern British cooking. Pleasant, efficient service.

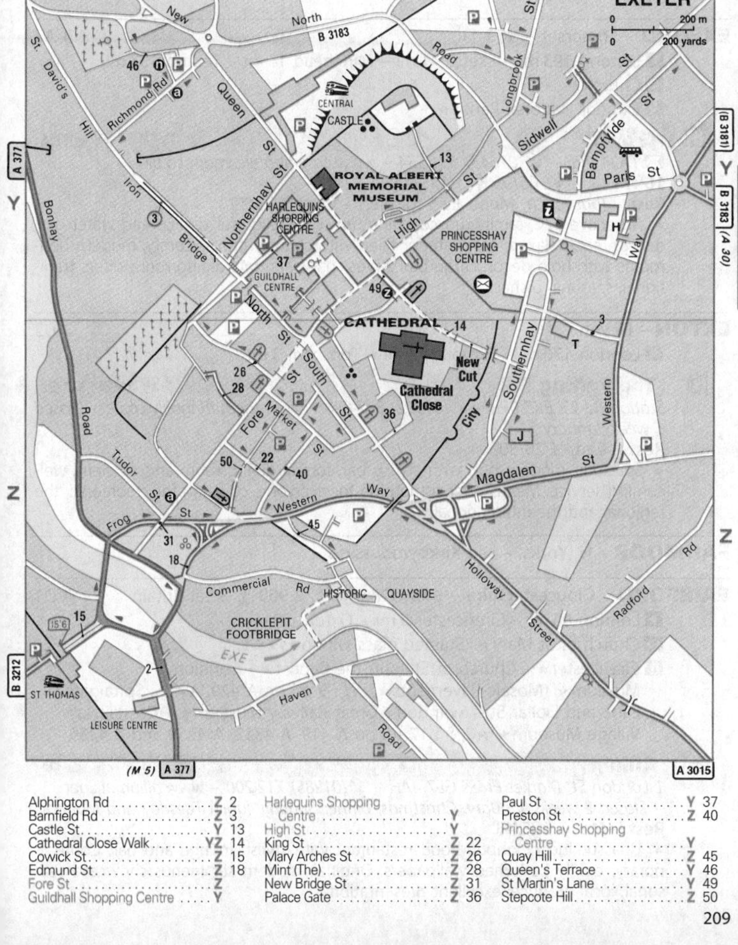

Alphington Rd . . . . Z 2
Barnfield Rd . . . . Z 3
Castle St . . . . Y 13
Cathedral Close Walk . . . . . . YZ 14
Cowick St . . . . Z 15
Edmund St . . . . Z 18
Fore St . . . . Z
Guildhall Shopping Centre . . . . . Y
Harlequins Shopping Centre . . . . . Y
High St . . . . Y
King St . . . . Z 22
Mary Arches St . . . . Z 26
Mint (The) . . . . Z 28
New Bridge St . . . . Z 31
Palace Gate . . . . Z 36
Paul St . . . . Y 37
Preston St . . . . Z 40
Princesshay Shopping Centre . . . . . Y
Quay Hill . . . . Z 45
Queen's Terrace . . . . Y 46
St Martin's Lane . . . . Y 49
Stepcote Hill . . . . Z 50

at Rockbeare East : 7.5 mi by A 30 - V – ✉ Exeter

Jack in the Green Inn

London Rd ✉ EX5 2EE – ✆ (01404) 822 240 – www.jackinthegreen.uk.com – Closed 25 December-6 January

Rest – Menu £ 25 – Carte £ 26/40

◆ Unassuming whitewashed pub with warm, welcoming interior. They support local producers and cooking is taken seriously. Extensive menus feature fresh fish specials; and bread, veg and water are satisfyingly free of charge. Jazz evenings take place in summer.

at Kenton Southeast : 7 mi by A 3015 - X - on A 379 – ✉ Exeter

XX **Rodean**

The Triangle ✉ EX6 8LS – ✆ (01626) 890 195 – www.rodeanrestaurant.co.uk – Closed 2 weeks early August, Sunday dinner and Monday

Rest – *(dinner only and Sunday lunch) (booking advisable)* Menu £ 19 – Carte £ 30/40

◆ Family run early 20C butchers shop in pretty spot. Bar area for pre-prandials. Restaurant in two rooms with beams and local photos. Menus employ good use of local ingredients.

EXFORD – Somerset – **503** J30 **3** A2

London 193 mi – Exeter 41 mi – Minehead 14 mi – Taunton 33 mi

Church★

Exmoor National Park★★

Crown

✉ TA24 7PP – ✆ (01643) 831 554 – www.crownhotelexmoor.co.uk

16 rm – †£ 65/95 ††£ 125/145

Rest – *(bar lunch)* Menu £ 33 (dinner) – Carte £ 23/32

◆ Attractive 17C, family-run coaching inn with delightful terrace and water garden to rear. Relaxed, cosy interior filled with country prints. Comfy, modern bedrooms with bold décor. Large bar serves snacks. Formal dining room offers traditional, seasonal dishes.

EXTON – Devon **2** D2

London 176 mi – Exmouth 4 mi – Topsham 3 mi

The Puffing Billy

Station Rd ✉ EX3 0PR – ✆ (01392) 877 888 – www.thepuffingbilly.co.uk – Closed 1 week January

Rest – Carte £ 20/30

◆ Spacious, modern pub with stylish bar, formal dining room and efficient, welcoming service. Menus offer something for everyone, covering the traditional, the regional and the international.

FADMOOR – N. Yorks. – see Kirkbymoorside

FAIRFORD – Gloucestershire – **503** O28 – **pop. 2 960** Great Britain **4** D1

London 88 mi – Cirencester 9 mi – Oxford 29 mi

Church of St Mary★ (Stained glass windows★★)

Cirencester★ - Church of St John the Baptist★ - Corinium Museum★ (Mosaic Pavements★), W : 9 mi on A 429, A 435, Spitalgate Lane and Dollar St – Swindon - Great Railway Museum★ **AC** - Railway Village Museum★ **AC**, S : 17 mi on A 419, A 4312, A 4259 and B 4289

XXX **Allium**

1 London St, Market Pl ✉ GL7 4AH – ✆ (01285) 712 200 – www.allium.uk.net – Closed 2 weeks January, Christmas, dinner Sunday, lunch Tuesday and Monday

Rest – Menu £ 25/43

◆ Unassuming neighbourhood restaurant with stylish lounge and bar. Contemporary, boldly patterned wallpapers. Original, modern set menus showcase seasonal, local produce; excellent presentation.

ENGLAND

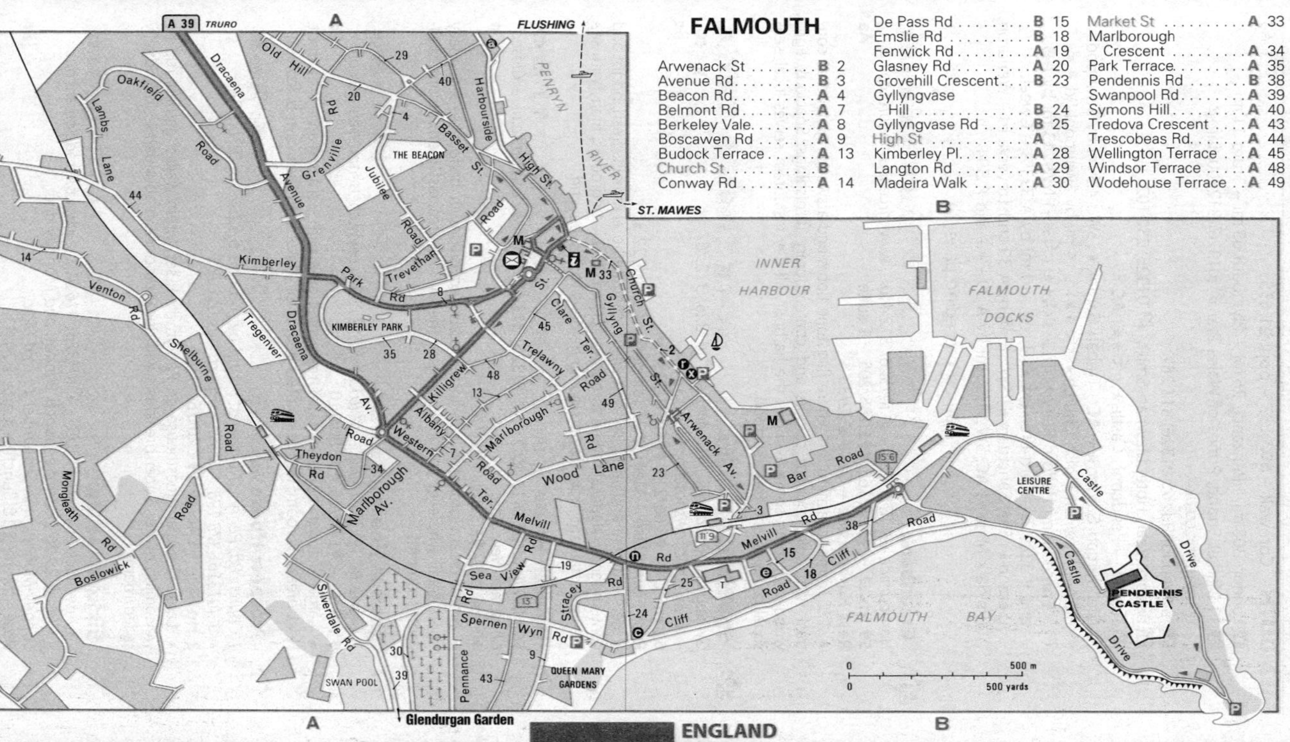
FALMOUTH
Arwenack St . . . . B 2
Avenue Rd. . . . . B 3
Beacon Rd. . . . . A 4
Belmont Rd . . . . A 7
Berkeley Vale. . . . . A 8
Boscawen Rd . . . . A 9
Budock Terrace . . . . . . A 13
Church St. . . . . B
Conway Rd . . . . A 14
De Pass Rd . . . . B 15
Emslie Rd . . . . B 18
Fenwick Rd . . . . A 19
Glasney Rd . . . . A 20
Grovehill Crescent . . . . B 23
Gyllyngvase Hill . . . . . . B 24
Gyllyngvase Rd . . . . . . B 25
High St . . . . A
Kimberley Pl. . . . . A 28
Langton Rd . . . . A 29
Madeira Walk . . . . A 30
Market St . . . . A 33
Marlborough Crescent . . A 34
Park Terrace. . . . . A 35
Pendennis Rd . . . . B 38
Swanpool Rd. . . . . A 39
Symons Hill. . . . . A 40
Tredova Crescent . . . . A 43
Trescobeas Rd. . . . . . . A 44
Wellington Terrace . . . A 45
Windsor Terrace . . . . . A 48
Wodehouse Terrace . . A 49
A 39 TRURO
FLUSHING
ST. MAWES
Glendurgan Garden
PENRYN RIVER
INNER HARBOUR
FALMOUTH DOCKS
FALMOUTH BAY
THE BEACON
KIMBERLEY PARK
LEISURE CENTRE
PENDENNIS CASTLE
QUEEN MARY GARDENS
SWAN POOL
0 500 m
0 500 yards
A
B

FALMOUTH – Cornwall – 503 E33 – pop. 21 635 1 A3

London 308 mi – Penzance 26 mi – Plymouth 65 mi – Truro 11 mi

11 Market Strand, Prince of Wales Pier ☎ (01326) 312300, info@falmouthtic.co.uk

Swanpool Rd, ☎ (01326) 311 262

Budock Vean Hotel Mawnan Smith, ☎ (01326) 252 102

Town★ – Pendennis Castle★ (≤★★) AC B

Glendurgan Garden★★ AC - Trebah Garden★, SW : 4.5 mi by Swanpool Rd A – Mawnan Parish Church★ (≤★★) S : 4 mi by Swanpool Rd A – Cruise along Helford River★. Trelissick★★ (≤★★) NW : 13 mi by A 39 and B 3289 A – Carn Brea (≤★★) NW : 10 mi by A 393 A – Gweek (Setting★, Seal Sanctuary★) SW : 8 mi by A 39 and Treverva rd – Wendron (Poldark Mine★) AC, SW : 12.5 mi by A 39 - A - and A 394

Plan on preceding page

Greenbank

Harbourside ✉ TR11 2SR – ☎ (01326) 312 440 – www.greenbank-hotel.co.uk

59 rm – ♦£ 99/165 ♦♦£ 185/205 – 1 suite **Aa**

Rest *Harbourside* – Carte £ 22/33

♦ 17C former coaching inn where flagstone floors and a sweeping staircase contrast with bold, modern colours and contemporary furnishings. Spacious, light wood bedrooms; some overlook the harbour. All day restaurant serves local, seasonal produce and fresh seafood.

St Michael's H & Spa

Gyllyngvase Beach ✉ TR11 4NB – ☎ (01326) 312 707 – www.stmichaelshotel.co.uk **Bc**

61 rm – ♦£ 66/219 ♦♦£ 131/219

Rest *Flying Fish* – Menu £ 27 (dinner) – Carte £ 22/36

♦ Reinvestment and refurbishment ensure that the hotel remains fresh, bright and contemporary. Nautical theme throughout. Comfortable bedrooms, many with sea views. Restaurant looks down sloping gardens to bay beyond.

Dolvean House without rest

50 Melvill Rd ✉ TR11 4DQ – ☎ (01326) 313 658 – www.dolvean.co.uk – Closed Christmas-New Year **Bn**

10 rm – ♦£ 39/65 ♦♦£ 77/98

♦ Smart cream property with local books and guides in parlour: exceptionally good detail wherever you look. Elegant, neatly laid breakfast room. Bright, well-kept bedrooms.

Chelsea House without rest

2 Emslie Rd ✉ TR11 4BG – ☎ (01326) 212 230 – www.chelseahousehotel.com

9 rm – ♦£ 50/65 ♦♦£ 80/110 **Be**

♦ Large Victorian house in quiet residential area with partial sea-view at front. Neat breakfast room; well-appointed bedrooms, three with their own balconies.

Prospect House without rest

1 Church Rd, Penryn, Northwest : 2 mi by A 39 on B 3292 ✉ TR10 8DA – ☎ (01326) 373 198 – www.prospecthouse.co.uk

3 rm – ♦£ 40/45 ♦♦£ 70/75

♦ Large Georgian guesthouse on Penryn river, set within walled garden, run by welcoming owner. Super breakfasts with local produce in abundance. Individually styled rooms.

Bistro de la Mer

28 Arwenack St ✉ TR11 3JB – ☎ (01326) 316 509 – www.bistrodelamer.com – Closed 25-26 December, lunch Sunday and Monday and Sunday-Monday mid-September to mid-May **Br**

Rest – Menu £ 18 (lunch) – Carte £ 24/41

♦ Modest bistro with a subtle Mediterranean feel, set over two floors and decorated in sunny seaside colours of yellow and blue. Extensive seafood-oriented menu; honest cooking.

ENGLAND

Samphire
36 Arwenack St ✉ TR11 3JF – ✆ (01326) 210 759 – www.samphire-falmouth.co.uk – Closed 2 weeks January and Monday in winter **Bx**
Rest – Carte £ 20/27
◆ Informal restaurant with downstairs cocktail bar, situated in the heart of town. Appealing seasonal menu includes plenty of fresh local seafood and Sunday roasts. Attentive service.

at Mylor Bridge North : 4.5 mi by A 39 - A - and B 3292 on Mylor rd – ✉ Falmouth

Pandora Inn
Restronguet Creek, Northeast : 1 mi by Passage Hill off Restronguet Hill ✉ TR11 5ST – ✆ (01326) 372 678 – www.pandorainn.com – Closed 25 December
Rest – Carte £ 20/32
◆ Characterful 13C inn in scenic spot, with its own pontoon. Seasonally changing menus feature fish, seafood and salads in summer; with casseroles, stews and game in winter.

at Maenporth Beach South : 3.75 mi by Pennance Rd

Cove
Maenporth Beach ✉ TR11 5HN – ✆ (01326) 251 136 – www.thecovemaenporth.co.uk
Rest – Carte £ 23/35
◆ Within a modern building overlooking the beach and cove. Concise menu with daily specials; bright, unfussy cooking, with the occasional Asian note. Young, enthusiastic service.

FARNBOROUGH – Hants. – 504 R30 – pop. 57 147 **7 C1**

London 41 mi – Reading 17 mi – Southampton 44 mi – Winchester 33 mi

Southwood Ively Rd, ✆ (01252) 548 700

Aviator
Farnborough Rd, Southwest : 1 mi on A 325 ✉ GU14 6EL – ✆ (01252) 555 890 – www.aviatorfarnborough.co.uk
169 rm – †£ 175/245 ††£ 175/245, ☕ £ 16
Rest *Brasserie* – *(Closed Saturday lunch)* Menu £ 21 (lunch) – Carte £ 32/44
◆ Eye-catching hotel overlooking Farnborough Airport, with smart lounge/bar and unusual circular atrium. Sleek, good-sized bedrooms feature light wood, modern facilities and fully tiled bathrooms. Stylish, contemporary ground floor brasserie looks out over airfield.

FARNHAM – Dorset – 503 N31 – see Blandford Forum

FARNINGHAM – Kent – 504 U29 **8 B1**

London 22 mi – Dartford 7 mi – Maidstone 20 mi

Beesfield Farm without rest
Beesfield Lane, off A 225 ✉ DA4 0LA – ✆ (01322) 863 900 – www.beesfieldfarm.co.uk – Closed 15 December-1 January
3 rm ☕ – †£ 55/65 ††£ 75/80
◆ Peaceful valley setting, with attractive garden. Exudes character: oldest part is 400 year-old Kentish longhouse. Comfy sitting room; bedrooms boast beams and garden outlook.

FAR SAWREY – Cumbria – 502 L20 – see Hawkshead

FAVERSHAM - Kent - **504** W30 - pop. 18 222 **9** C1

London 52 mi - Dover 26 mi - Maidstone 21 mi - Margate 25 mi

Fleur de Lis Heritage Centre, 13 Preston St ✆ (01795) 534542, ticfaversham@btconnect.com

Read's (David Pitchford) with rm

Macknade Manor, Canterbury Rd, East : 1 mi on A 2 ✉ ME13 8XE – ✆ (01795) 535 344 – www.reads.com – Closed Christmas, first week January, Sunday and Monday

6 rm – ♀£ 125/185 ♀♀£ 165/195 **Rest** – Menu £ 24/55

Spec. Terrine of ham hock with piccalilli. Fillet of beef on potato and shallot galette with confit beetroot. Lemon tart with sorbet and glazed meringue.

◆ Elegant red-brick house with beautiful grounds and traditionally furnished dining rooms. Confident, well-presented, classically based dishes make the best of local produce, including fruit, vegetables and herbs from the walled garden. Comfortable, well-kept bedrooms, tastefully decorated in a country house style.

at Dargate East : 6 mi by A 2 off A 299 – ✉ Kent

The Dove

Plum Pudding Ln ✉ ME13 9HB – ✆ (01227) 751 360 – Closed Sunday dinner and Monday

Rest – *(booking advisable at weekends)* Carte £ 18/34

◆ Attractive Victorian pub with well-tended gardens and cosy rooms. Weekday menus offer enticing nibbles, pub classics and specials. Concise Friday and Saturday menus are much more ambitious.

at Oare Northwest : 2.5 mi by A2 off B2045 – ✉ Kent

Three Mariners

2 Church Rd ✉ ME13 0QA – ✆ (01795) 533 633 – www.thethreemarinersoare.co.uk – Closed Sunday dinner and Monday

Rest – Menu £ 11/20 – Carte £ 22/32

◆ Welcoming 500 year old pub set by a small marina in a sleepy hamlet, boasting pleasant marsh views. Constantly evolving menus offer an appealing mix of carefully prepared, flavoursome dishes.

FERMAIN BAY - C.I. - **503** L33 - see Channel Islands (Guernsey)

FERRENSBY - N. Yorks. - see Knaresborough

FLAUNDEN - Hertfordshire - pop. 5 468 **12** A2

London 35 mi - Reading 43 mi - Luton 23 mi - Milton Keynes 42 mi

The Bricklayers Arms

Hogpits Bottom ✉ HP3 0PH – ✆ (01442) 833 322 – www.bricklayersarms.com

Rest – Carte £ 24/35

◆ Smart pub tucked away in a small hamlet. There are no snacks on offer, just traditional, hearty, French-inspired dishes. Meat and fish are smoked in-house and old-school puddings follow.

FLETCHING - East Sussex - **504** U30/3 - pop. 1 722 **8** A2

London 45 mi - Brighton 20 mi - Eastbourne 24 mi - Maidstone 20 mi

The Griffin Inn with rm

✉ TN22 3SS – ✆ (01825) 722 890 – www.thegriffininn.co.uk – Closed 25 December

13 rm – ♀£ 70/80 ♀♀£ 130/160

Rest – *(meals in bar Sunday dinner)* Menu £ 30 (Sunday lunch) – Carte £ 25/36

◆ Hugely characterful brick coaching inn, under the same ownership for over 30 years. Various rooms and sizeable garden/terrace with wood burning oven for summer BBQs. British and Italian classics. Individually decorated bedrooms accessed via narrow, sloping corridors.

ENGLAND

FOLKESTONE - Kent - **504** X30 - **pop. 45 273** Great Britain **9** D2

London 76 mi – Brighton 76 mi – Dover 8 mi – Maidstone 33 mi

Access Channel Tunnel : Eurotunnel information and reservations ✆ (08705) 353535

Bouverie Place Shopping Centre ✆ (01303) 258594, cckirkham@gmail.com

The Leas★ (≤★) Z

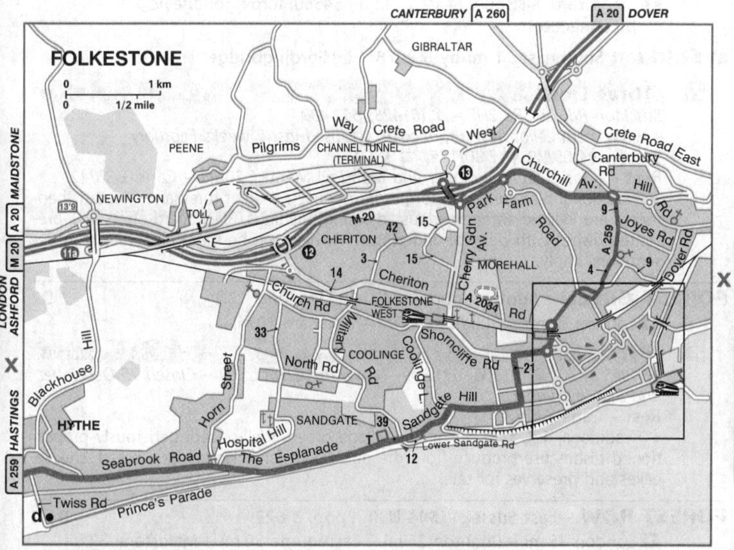

ENGLAND

FOLKESTONE

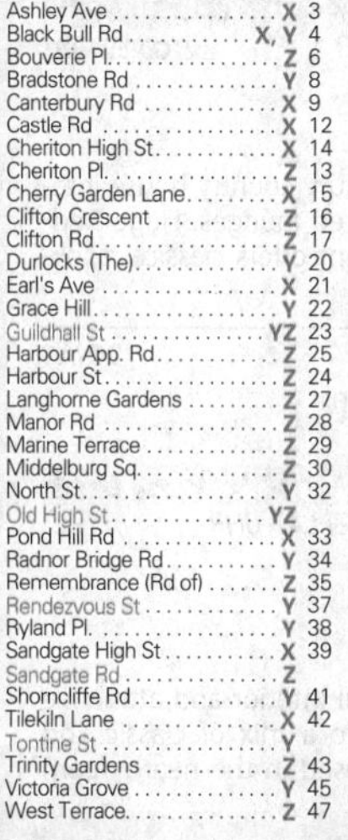

Ashley Ave . . . . . X 3
Black Bull Rd . . . . . X, Y 4
Bouverie Pl. . . . . . Z 6
Bradstone Rd . . . . . Y 8
Canterbury Rd . . . . . X 9
Castle Rd . . . . . X 12
Cheriton High St. . . . . X 14
Cheriton Pl. . . . . Z 13
Cherry Garden Lane. . . . . X 15
Clifton Crescent . . . . . Z 16
Clifton Rd. . . . . Z 17
Durlocks (The). . . . . Y 20
Earl's Ave . . . . . X 21
Grace Hill. . . . . Y 22
Guildhall St . . . . . YZ 23
Harbour App. Rd. . . . . Z 25
Harbour St. . . . . Z 24
Langhorne Gardens . . . . . Z 27
Manor Rd . . . . . Z 28
Marine Terrace . . . . . Z 29
Middelburg Sq. . . . . . Z 30
North St. . . . . Y 32
Old High St. . . . . YZ
Pond Hill Rd . . . . . X 33
Radnor Bridge Rd. . . . . Y 34
Remembrance (Rd of) . . . . . Z 35
Rendezvous St . . . . . Y 37
Ryland Pl. . . . . . Y 38
Sandgate High St . . . . . X 39
Sandgate Rd. . . . . Z
Shorncliffe Rd . . . . . Y 41
Tilekiln Lane . . . . . X 42
Tontine St . . . . . Y
Trinity Gardens . . . . . Z 43
Victoria Grove . . . . . Y 45
West Terrace. . . . . Z 47

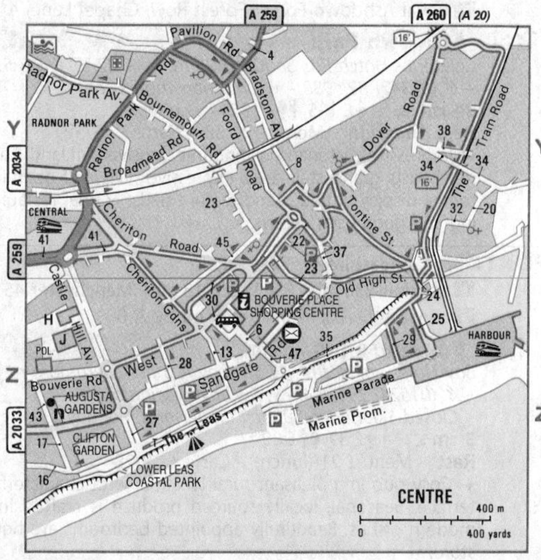

The Relish without rest
4 Augusta Gardens ✉ CT20 2RR – ☎ (01303) 850 952 – www.hotelrelish.co.uk – Closed 22 December-2 January, minimum 2 night stay at weekends
10 rm ☕ – 🚹£ 69/85 🚹🚹£ 105/145 **Zn**
◆ Large Regency townhouse overlooking private parkland. Stylish black canopy to entrance; modish furnishings. Handy food and drink area at foot of stairs. Light, airy rooms.

FORDINGBRIDGE – Hampshire – 503 O31 – pop. 5 755 6 A2

London 101 mi – Bournemouth 17 mi – Salisbury 11 mi – Southampton 22 mi

Kings Yard, Salisbury St ☎ (01425) 654560, fordingbridgevic@btconnect.com

at Stuckton Southeast : 1 mi by B 3078 – ✉ Fordingbridge

Three Lions
Stuckton Rd. ✉ SP6 2HF – ☎ (01425) 652 489 – www.thethreelionsrestaurant.co.uk – Closed last 2 weeks February
7 rm – 🚹£ 69/79 🚹🚹£ 80/125, ☕ £ 7.95
Rest – *(Closed Sunday dinner and Monday)* Menu £ 20/25 – Carte £ 33/42
◆ Traditional pine-furnished former farmhouse on quiet rural lane. Pleasant bedrooms are located among various adjoining buildings. Blackboard offers well-presented dishes with classical undertones – which can be more elaborate than descriptions imply.

FOREST GREEN – Surrey – pop. 1 843 – ✉ Dorking 7 D2

London 34 mi – Guildford 13 mi – Horsham 10 mi

Parrot Inn
✉ RH5 5RZ – ☎ (01306) 621 339 – www.theparrot.co.uk – Closed 25 December and Sunday dinner
Rest – Carte £ 18/28
◆ Traditional 17C pub set on the village green. Well-priced, generously proportioned dishes use produce from the pub's own farm. Homemade bread, cheese, cakes and preserves for sale.

FOREST ROW – East Sussex – 504 U30 – pop. 3 623 8 A2

London 35 mi – Brighton 26 mi – Eastbourne 30 mi – Maidstone 32 mi

Royal Ashdown Forest Forest Row, Chapel Lane, ☎ (01342) 822 018

Ashdown Park
Colemans Hatch Rd., South : 3.25 mi by A 22 ✉ RH18 5JR – ☎ (01342) 824 988 – www.ashdownpark.com
94 rm ☕ – 🚹£ 195 🚹🚹£ 195 – 5 suites
Rest *Anderida* – Menu £ 24/38 – Carte £ 45/52
◆ Impressive Victorian building in extensive parkland. Luxury country house interior boasts grand staircases, impressive halls and open-fired lounges. Huge bedrooms display antiques and feature beds. Formal restaurant offers classical cooking and good estate views.

FORTON – Lancashire Great Britain 20 A1

London 236 mi – Blackpool 18 mi – Manchester 45 mi

Lancaster - Castle★, N : 5.5 mi by A 6

Bay Horse Inn with rm
Bay Horse Ln, North : 1.25 mi by A 6 on Quernmore rd ✉ LA2 0HR – ☎ (01524) 791 204 – www.bayhorseinn.com – Closed 1 January, Sunday dinner and Monday
3 rm ☕ – 🚹£ 89 🚹🚹£ 89
Rest – Menu £ 21 (lunch) – Carte £ 18/28
◆ Cosy pub in a pleasant rural location, with characterful interior and attractive terrace. Seasonal, locally sourced produce is crafted into a mix of classic and modern dishes. Beautifully appointed bedrooms are housed in the nearby corn store.

FOTHERINGHAY Northants – NTH – 504 S26 – see Oundle

FOWEY – Cornwall – 503 G32 – pop. 2 064 — 1 B2

London 277 mi – Newquay 24 mi – Plymouth 34 mi – Truro 22 mi

5 South St (01726) 833616, info@fowey.co.uk

Town★★

Gribbin Head (≤★★) 6 mi rtn on foot – Bodinnick (≤★★) - Lanteglos Church★, E : 5 mi by ferry – Polruan (≤★★) SE : 6 mi by ferry – Polkerris★, W : 2 mi by A 3082

Fowey Hall

VISA AE

Hanson Drive, West : 0.5 mi off A 3082 ✉ PL23 1ET – (01726) 833 866 – www.foweyhallhotel.co.uk

25 rm – †£ 135/235 ††£ 150/235 – 11 suites

Rest – *(light lunch Monday-Saturday)* Carte £ 23/40

◆ Striking 19C manor house overlooking town, with ornate library and period-furnished lounge/billiard room. Mix of traditional and modern bedrooms. Families well-catered for; trendy, informal feel pervades. Oak-panelled restaurant for adults. Conservatory for those with children. Classical à la carte has modern touches.

Old Quay House

VISA AE

28 Fore St ✉ PL23 1AQ – (01726) 833 302 – www.theoldquayhouse.com – Closed 14 November-22 December

11 rm – †£ 170/240 ††£ 200/270

Rest – Carte £ 39/49

◆ Friendly boutique hotel, run by experienced owner. Stylish interior has black and white theme; great outlook from terrace. Bedrooms range from small standard to penthouse - some have balconies and water views. Chic, informal bar-cum-restaurant with modern menu.

The Bistro at Tiffins

A/C VISA

24 Fore St. ✉ PL23 1AQ – (01726) 832 322 – www.tiffinsbistro.co.uk – Closed 25 December and 1 January

Rest – Menu £ 17 (lunch) – Carte £ 20/31

◆ Former deli; now a relaxed, cosy, all day eatery. Upstairs restaurant open in evening. Modern European dishes range from sandwiches and pizza to bouillabaisse and beef Bourguignon.

at Golant North : 3 mi by B 3269 – ✉ Fowey

Cormorant

VISA

✉ PL23 1LL – (01726) 833 426 – www.cormoranthotel.co.uk – Closed January

14 rm – †£ 90/200 ††£ 150/200

Rest – *(booking essential for non residents)* Carte £ 33/44

◆ Well-run hotel in superb waterside position. At only one room deep, all its bedrooms overlook the estuary; superior rooms boast balconies. Lounge, bar and formal, linen-laid restaurant. Appealing seasonal menus feature local meats and interesting seafood dishes.

FREATHY – Cornwall – see Millbrook

FRESSINGFIELD – Suffolk – 504 X26 — 15 D2

London 104 mi – Ipswich 34 mi – Lowestoft 27 mi

Fox & Goose Inn

VISA

Church Rd ✉ IP21 5PB – (01379) 586 247 – www.foxandgoose.net – Closed 27-30 December, 2 weeks mid-January and Monday

Rest – *(booking advisable)* Menu £ 18 (lunch) – Carte £ 28/35

◆ Attractive 16C pub with rustic inner and pleasant terrace; opposite the green and duck pond. Classic pub dishes and good value lunch in bar; more sophisticated, modern offerings in restaurant.

FRILSHAM – Newbury – see Yattendon

FRISTON – Suffolk – see Aldeburgh

FRITHSDEN – Herts. – see Hemel Hempstead

FRITTON – Norfolk 15 D2

London 133 mi – Great Yarmouth 8 mi – Norwich 19 mi

Fritton House

Church Ln ✉ NR31 9HA – ✆ (01493) 484 008 – www.adnams.co.uk

8 rm – †£ 120/160 ††£ 120/160 – 1 suite

Rest – Menu £ 30 (dinner) – Carte £ 19/30

♦ Attractive 15C former coaching inn with period features, at the heart of the Somerleyton Estate. Cosy drawing room. Stylish bedrooms with old beams and modern bathrooms. Rustic bar and dining area with terrace. Pub dishes at lunch; restaurant fare at dinner.

FROGGATT EDGE – Derbyshire – 502 P24 16 A1

London 167 mi – Bakewell 6 mi – Sheffield 11 mi

The Chequers Inn with rm

on A 625 ✉ S32 3ZJ – ✆ (01433) 630 231 – www.chequers-froggatt.com – Closed 25 December

5 rm – †£ 75/100 ††£ 75/100 **Rest** – Carte £ 18/29

♦ Traditional 16C inn built right into the stone boulders of Froggat Edge and boasting a direct path up to the peak. Cooking is unfussy, tasty and largely classical, with more imaginative specials. Bedrooms are comfy; the one to the rear is quietest and best.

FROME – Somerset – 503 M/N30 – pop. 24 171 4 C2

London 118 mi – Bristol 24 mi – Southampton 52 mi – Swindon 44 mi

Babington House

Babington, Northwest : 6.5 mi by A 362 on Vobster rd

✉ BA11 3RW – ✆ (01373) 812 266 – www.babingtonhouse.co.uk

32 rm – †£ 220/720 ††£ 220/720, £ 14.50

Rest *Orangery* – Carte £ 31/43

♦ Country house with a vivid difference: Georgian exterior; cool, fashionable inner, with a laid-back, bohemian feel. Good health club, children's play area and even a cinema. Modern, understated bedrooms. Large conservatory dining room with solid stone floor; appealing Mediterranean menu.

FUNTINGTON – W. Sussex – 504 R31 – see Chichester

FYFIELD – Oxfordshire – see Oxford

GALMPTON 2 C2

London 199 mi – Plymouth 32 mi – Torbay 5 mi – Exeter 27 mi

Old Mill Farm without rest

Greenway, South : 1 mi by Greenway Rd turning right into no-through road. ✉ TQ5 OER – ✆ (01803) 842 344 – www.oldmillfarm-dart.co.uk – Closed January

3 rm – †£ 130 ††£ 140

♦ Lovingly restored corn mill in delightful spot at the edge of the River Dart. Bedrooms have a fresh, airy feel; Kingfisher is the largest with a window-side bath. Charming owners.

GATESHEAD – Tyne and Wear – 501 P19 – pop. 78 403 Great Britain 24 B2

London 282 mi – Durham 16 mi – Middlesbrough 38 mi – Newcastle upon Tyne 1 mi

Access Tyne Tunnel (toll)

Central Library, Prince Consort Rd ✆ (0191) 433 8420, ctouristinformationcentre@gateshead.gov.uk BX - The Sage, St Mary's Sq, Gateshead Quays ✆ (0191) 478 4222, tourism@gateshead.gov.uk AX

Ravensworth Wrekenton Angel View, Long Bank, ✆ (0191) 487 6014

Heworth Gingling Gate, ✆ (0191) 469 9832

Beamish : North of England Open Air Museum★★ **AC**, SW : 6 mi by A 692 and A 6076 BX

Plan : see Newcastle upon Tyne

Stables Lodge without rest

South Farm, Lamesley, Southwest : 5 mi by A 167 and Belle Vue Bank on A 692 ✉ NE11 0ET – ✆ (0191) 492 17 56 – www.thestableslodge.co.uk

3 rm – ♦£ 74/138 ♦♦£ 74/138

♦ Rustic and cosy former farmhouse, just off the A1. Individually decorated, very comfortable bedrooms; the Red Room is the most luxurious; the Garden Room has its own hot tub.

Six

Baltic Centre for Contemporary Art, Gateshead Quays, South Shore Rd ✉ NE8 3BA – ✆ (0191) 440 49 48 – www.sixbaltic.com – Closed 25-26 December, 1 January and Sunday dinner BX**x**

Rest – Menu £ 18 (lunch and early dinner) – Carte £ 28/44

♦ Fantastic location on top floor of Baltic Centre; floor to ceiling windows afford views of city's skyline, the Tyne and the Millennium bridge. Modern brasserie, with a menu to match.

at Low Fell South : 2 mi on A 167 - BX – ✉ Gateshead

Eslington Villa

8 Station Rd, West : 0.75 mi by Belle Vue Bank, turning left at T junction, right at roundabout then taking first turn right ✉ NE9 6DR – ✆ (0191) 487 6017 – www.eslingtonvilla.co.uk – Closed bank holidays

18 rm – ♦£ 70/80 ♦♦£ 85/95

Rest – *(closed Saturday lunch and Sunday dinner)* Menu £ 20/25

♦ Well-run, stylish, privately owned hotel 10 minutes' drive from city centre. Nicely furnished lounge bar leads from smart reception. Attractively styled, modern bedrooms. Classical dining room and conservatory; wide-ranging, traditional menu with modern twists.

GEORGE GREEN – Buckinghamshire 11 D3

London 23

Pinewood

Wexham Park Lane, Uxbridge Rd, on A412 ✉ SL3 6AP – ✆ (01753) 896 400 – www.pinewoodhotel.co.uk – Closed 24-28 December

49 rm – ♦£ 69/159 ♦♦£ 89/169

Rest *Eden* – Carte £ 20/34

♦ Located on the A412 close to Slough; ideal for those on business or on a trip to Legoland. Functional, modern rooms with some flair. Modern dishes with a twist in Eden.

GILLINGHAM – Dorset – 503 N30 – pop. 8 630 4 C3

London 116 mi – Bournemouth 34 mi – Bristol 46 mi – Southampton 52 mi

Stourhead★★★ **AC**, N : 9 mi by B 3092, B 3095 and B 3092

Stock Hill Country House rm, VISA MC

Stock Hill, West : 1.5 mi on B 3081 ✉ SP8 5NR – ✆ (01747) 823 626 – www.stockhillhouse.co.uk

9 rm (dinner included) – †£ 125/175 ††£ 260/320

Rest – *(booking essential)* Menu £ 30/45

◆ Well-run Georgian country house with later extensions, in attractive, mature grounds. Classical lounges boast heavy fabrics and antiques. Bedrooms, in the main house and stables, are a mix of cottagey and contemporary country house styles. All have good facilities. Formal, two-roomed restaurant with own kitchen garden.

GISBURN – Lancashire – 502 N22 — 20 B2

London 242 mi – Bradford 28 mi – Skipton 12 mi

La Locanda VISA MC AE

Main St ✉ BB7 4HH – ✆ (01200) 445 303 – www.lalocanda.co.uk – Closed 25 December-1 January and Monday except bank holidays

Rest – Italian – *(dinner only) (booking essential)* Menu £ 14 (weekdays) – Carte £ 17/28

◆ Charming low-beamed, flag-floored cottage, run by passionate Italian owners. Large, seasonal menu features local and imported produce. Homemade ice cream and ravioli are specialities. Authentic, rustic cooking comes in generous portions. Polite, helpful service.

ENGLAND

GITTISHAM – Devon – 503 K31 – see Honiton

GODSHILL – Isle of Wight – 504 Q32 – see WIGHT (Isle of)

GOLANT Cornwall – Cornwall – 503 G32 – see Fowey

GOLDSBOROUGH – North Yorkshire – see Whitby

GOODNESTONE – Kent – ✉ Wingham — 9 D2

London 73 mi – Croydon 75 mi – Bromley 67 mi – Lewisham 66 mi

The Fitzwalter Arms VISA MC

The Street ✉ CT3 1PJ – ✆ (01304) 840 303 – www.thefitzwalterarms.co.uk – Closed 25 December, 1 January, Sunday dinner and Tuesday

Rest – Menu £ 16 (lunch) – Carte £ 20/25

◆ Unusual brick building with castellated exterior, mullioned windows and shabby yet characterful feel. Concise blackboard menu features tasty country dishes with some modern European influences.

GOREY – C.I. – 503 P33 – see Channel Islands (Jersey)

GORING – Oxfordshire – 503 Q29 – pop. 4 193 Great Britain — 10 B3

London 56 mi – Oxford 16 mi – Reading 12 mi

Ridgeway Path★★

Leatherne Bottel P VISA MC AE

The Bridleway, North : 1.5 mi by B 4009 ✉ RG8 0HS – ✆ (01491) 872 667 – www.leathernebottel.co.uk – Closed Sunday dinner

Rest – *(booking essential)* Menu £ 19 (lunch)/30 (Sunday) – Carte £ 36/44

◆ Delightful Thameside restaurant with lovely summer terrace. Menus fuse traditional recipes with interesting, modern combinations. Tasting menu at dinner; leaves/herbs picked fresh from garden.

GOSFORTH – Tyne and Wear – 501 P18 – see Newcastle upon Tyne

GOVETON – Devon – 503 I33 – see Kingsbridge

GRANGE-OVER-SANDS – Cumbria – 502 L21 – pop. 4 835 — 21 A3

Great Britain

London 268 mi – Kendal 13 mi – Lancaster 24 mi

Victoria Hall, Main St (015395) 34026, grangetic@southlakeland.gov.uk

Meathop Rd, (015395) 33 180

Cartmel Priory★, NW : 3 mi

Netherwood

rest,

Lindale Rd LA11 6ET – (015395) 32 552 – www.netherwood-hotel.co.uk

34 rm – £ 60/120 £ 100/200

Rest – Menu £ 18/32

♦ Impressive castellated mansion on the hillside, affording lovely bay views. Traditional guest areas display wood panelling and original features. Simple, well-maintained bedrooms; more contemporary rooms in outbuildings. Formal dining comes with great outlook.

Clare House

rm,

Park Rd LA11 7HQ – (015395) 33 026 – www.clarehousehotel.co.uk – 28 March to 19 November

18 rm (dinner included) – £ 85/156 £ 170/178

Rest – *(dinner only) (booking essential for non-residents)* Menu £ 34

♦ Family-run Victorian house set in lovely gardens, overlooking Morecambe Bay. Two classical sitting rooms. Stylish, boldly coloured bedrooms in main house; smaller, simpler rooms with balconies in wing. Smart, modern dining room offers traditional daily menus.

at Cartmel Northwest : 3 mi – Grange-Over-Sands

L'Enclume (Simon Rogan) with rm

rest,

Cavendish St LA11 6PZ – (015395) 36 362 – www.lenclume.co.uk

12 rm – £ 118 £ 188

Rest – *(closed lunch Monday-Tuesday) (booking essential)* Menu £ 25 (lunch) – Carte £ 65/80

Spec. Sugar 'snax' and carrots with ham fat and nasturtiums. Suckling pig with sweet onion and mugwort. Wineberries and sweet cheese with lemon balm and milk skin.

♦ Stone-built former smithy's in busy little village. Small lounge and plain, wood-floored restaurant. Knowledgeable staff. Refined, original cooking uses modern techniques and is underpinned by a classical style. Flavours are clean and combinations, sublime. Choice of 8/13 courses. Smart, traditionally styled bedrooms.

Rogan and Company

The Square LA11 6QD – (015395) 35 917 – www.roganandcompany.co.uk

Rest – Carte £ 25/32

♦ Converted cottage by lovely stream; informal cousin to L'Enclume. Stylish, split-level interior with sofas, polished tables and high bar seating. Extensive menus of locally sourced produce.

GRANTHAM – Lincolnshire – 502 S25 – pop. 34 592 Great Britain — 17 C2

London 113 mi – Leicester 31 mi – Lincoln 29 mi – Nottingham 24 mi

The Guildhall Arts Centre, St Peter's Hill (01476) 406166, granthamtic@southkesteven.gov.uk

Belton Park Londonthorpe Rd, Belton Lane, (01476) 567 399

De Vere Belton Woods H., (01476) 593 200

St Wulfram's Church★

Belton House★ **AC**, N : 2.5 mi by A 607. Belvoir Castle★★ **AC**, W : 6 mi by A 607

ENGLAND

at Hough-on-the-Hill **North : 6.75 mi by A 607 – ✉ Grantham**

XX **Brownlow Arms** with rm — rest, P VISA

High Rd ✉ NG32 2AZ – ☎ (01400) 250 234
4 rm ☕ – 🚹£ 65/70 🚹🚹£ 96/110
Rest – *(Closed Monday and Sunday dinner) (dinner only and Sunday lunch)*
Menu £ 25 (lunch) – Carte £ 28/39

♦ Attractive part 17/19C inn in heart of rural Lincolnshire. Wood-panelled bar with deep armchairs. Formal dining: well executed modern British dishes. Very tasteful bedrooms.

at Harlaxton **Southwest : 2.5 mi on A 607 – ✉ Grantham**

The Gregory — P VISA

The Drift, Southwest : 2 mi by A 607 ✉ NG32 1AD – ☎ (01476) 577 076 – www.thegregory.co.uk – Closed dinner 25-26 December and 1 January
Rest – Carte £ 20/35 **s**

♦ Roadside community pub with spacious dining room and smaller lounge, both with very modern feel. Pub classics dominate the menu, with steaks, pies and old-fashioned puddings.

at Woolsthorpe-by-Belvoir **West : 7.5 mi by A 607 – ✉ Grantham**

The Chequers with rm — P VISA AE

Main St ✉ NG32 1LU – ☎ (01476) 870 701 – www.chequersinn.net – Closed dinner 25-26 December and 1 January lunch
4 rm ☕ – 🚹£ 50 🚹🚹£ 70
Rest – Menu £ 17 – Carte £ 21/33

♦ Cosy, open-fired pub in a quaint village owned by Belvoir Estate; backing onto the local cricket pitch. Simple homemade and local offerings at lunch, supplemented by steaks and game at dinner. Crisply furnished, modern bedrooms are located in the old stables.

ENGLAND

at Great Gonerby **Northwest : 2 mi on B 1174 – ✉ Grantham**

XX **Harry's Place** — P VISA

17 High St ✉ NG31 8JS – ☎ (01476) 561 780 – Closed Christmas and New Year, Sunday and Monday
Rest – *(booking essential)* Carte £ 55/66

♦ Long-standing, intimate restaurant consisting of just three tables; run by dedicated and delightful husband and wife team. Warm, welcoming feel, with fresh flowers, candles and antiques. Classically based, hand-written menus offer two choices per course.

at Dry Doddington **Northwest : 11 mi by B 1174 and A 1**

Wheatsheaf Inn — P VISA

Main St ✉ NG23 5HU – ☎ (01400) 281 458 – www.wheatsheaf-pub.co.uk – Closed Monday and lunch Tuesday
Rest – Menu £ 14 (lunch) – Carte £ 21/30

♦ Smartly kept pub overlooking a pretty green, with cosy bar, laid-back restaurant and small courtyard. Simple, unfussy light bites lunch menu; more ambitious à la carte with evening specials.

GRASMERE – **Cumbria** – **502** K20 – ✉ **Ambleside** Great Britain — **21** A2

London 282 mi – Carlisle 43 mi – Kendal 18 mi

Dove Cottage★ **AC** AY **A**

Lake Windermere★★, SE : by A 591 AZ

Plans : see Ambleside

Rothay Garden
Broadgate ✉ *LA22 9RJ – ☏ (01539) 435 334 – www.rothaygarden.com*
30 rm (dinner included) – ♦£ 138/143 ♦♦£ 235/245 AY**s**
Rest – Menu 43 (dinner) **s** – Carte £ 31/42 **s**
♦ Old Lakeland house with gardens leading to river and stylish, contemporary inner. Boldly coloured lounges. Contemporary bedrooms with good facilities: choose those with patios or the loft suites. Neat, linen-laid dining room has lovely outlook and modern menu.

Moss Grove Organic without rest
✉ *LA22 9SW – ☏ (015394) 35 251 – www.mossgrove.com*
– Closed 24-25 December BZ**s**
11 rm – ♦£ 95/110 ♦♦£ 175/195
♦ Large house with stylish, modern interior, which features some reclaimed furnishings. Sizeable bedrooms boast feature walls: several have four-posters; one has a hot tub. Organic breakfasts.

Grasmere
Broadgate ✉ *LA22 9TA – ☏ (015394) 35 277 – www.grasmerehotel.co.uk*
– Closed January BZ**r**
13 rm – ♦£ 50/60 ♦♦£ 110/126 – 1 suite
Rest – *(dinner only) (booking essential for non-residents)* Menu £ 30 **s**
♦ Small Victorian house close to the village centre, with the River Rothay running through the garden. Traditionally styled lounge and bar. Similarly classical bedrooms, with colourful fabrics adding a modern touch. Pine-roofed dining room overlooks the garden.

Lake View Country House without rest
Lake View Dr ✉ *LA22 9TD – ☏ (015394) 35 384 – www.lakeview-grasmere.com*
4 rm – ♦£ 94 ♦♦£ 114 BZ**c**
♦ Traditional country house run by an enthusiastic owner. Cosy, homely bedrooms display some antiques; two rooms have spa baths. Linen-laid breakfast room. Yoghurts and compotes are homemade.

ENGLAND

GRASSINGTON – North Yorkshire – 502 O21 – pop. 1 102 — 22 A2
– ✉ Skipton

London 240 mi – Bradford 30 mi – Burnley 28 mi – Leeds 37 mi

National Park Centre, Colvend, Hebden Rd ☏ (01756) 751690, grassington@yorkshiredales.org.uk

Ashfield House
Summers Fold, off Main St ✉ *BD23 5AE – ☏ (01756) 752 584*
– www.ashfieldhouse.co.uk
8 rm – ♦£ 65/75 ♦♦£ 95/200
Rest – *(closed Wednesday and Sunday) (dinner only) (booking essential for non-residents)* Menu £ 35 **s**
♦ Bright, cheery hotel with larger-than-life owner. Cosy beams and flag floors blend well with Mediterranean colours in the bedrooms. Split-level rear cottage boasts spiral staircase and terrace. Modern menus rely on local produce; vegetarian dishes a speciality.

Grassington Lodge without rest
8 Wood Ln ✉ *BD23 5LU – ☏ (01756) 752 518 – www.grassingtonlodge.co.uk*
12 rm – ♦£ 60/75 ♦♦£ 80/160
♦ Georgian stone house set on a cobbled street close to the square. Fresh, modern inner with comfy lounge, bar and smart terrace. Neat bedrooms: those in the eaves are the best. Good extras.

Grassington House with rm
5 The Sq. ✉ *BD23 5AQ – ☏ (01756) 752 406 – www.grassingtonhousehotel.co.uk*
9 rm – ♦£ 80 ♦♦£ 90/130 **Rest** – Menu £ 14 (lunch) – Carte £ 26/37 **s**
♦ Georgian house with large bar-lounge and two-roomed restaurant; one a conservatory with grand piano. Delightful service. Classical menu displays Mediterranean touches and includes home-bred pork. Smart, modern bedrooms. Breakfast offers home-cured bacon/sausages.

GREAT DUNMOW – Essex – **504** V28 – pop. 5 943 **13** C2

London 42 mi – Cambridge 27 mi – Chelmsford 13 mi – Colchester 24 mi

Starr with rm

Market Pl ✉ *CM6 1AX* – ✆ *(01371) 874 321* – *www.the-starr.co.uk* – *Closed 27 December-7 January, Sunday dinner and Monday*

8 rm – †£ 90 ††£ 130/160 **Rest** – Menu £ 40 (dinner) – Carte £ 32/47

♦ Former 15C pub with rustic bar and fire. Characterful restaurant has exposed beams and conservatory. Strong, interesting cooking, traditionally inspired. Smart bedrooms.

Square 1

15 High St ✉ *CM6 1AB* – ✆ *(01371) 859 922* – *www.square1restaurant.co.uk* – *Closed 25-26 December, 1 January and Sunday dinner*

Rest – Carte £ 22/37

♦ Modern family-run restaurant in 14C monastic reading room. Stylish interior with vibrant artwork and open plan kitchen. Contemporary menu with subtle Mediterranean feel.

at Great Easton North : 2.75 mi by B 184

The Green Man

Mile End Green, Northeast : 1 mi by B 184 on Mile End Green rd ✉ *CM6 2DN* – ✆ *(01371) 852 285* – *www.thegreenmanrestaurant.com* – *Closed two weeks in January, Sunday dinner and Monday*

Rest – Carte £ 26/36

♦ Contemporary, minimalist-style pub, 20 minutes from Stansted Airport. Ambitious cooking, classic desserts and attentive, assured service. Terrace and garden overlooking fields.

at Aythorpe Roding Southwest : 5.5 mi on B 184

Axe & Compasses

Dunmow Rd ✉ *CM6 1PP* – ✆ *(01279) 876 648* – *www.theaxeandcompasses.co.uk* – *Closed 26 December*

Rest – Carte £ 22/25

♦ Characterful, cottage style pub complete with part-thatched roof and white picket fence. Tasty, attractively presented food; hearty pub favourites with their roots in the region.

GREAT EASTON – Essex – **504** U28 – see Great Dunmow

GREAT GONERBY – Lincs. – **502** S25 – see Grantham

GREAT HALLINGBURY – Essex – see Bishop's Stortford

GREAT MALVERN – Worcestershire – **503** N27 – pop. 35 588 **18** B3

London 127 mi – Birmingham 34 mi – Cardiff 66 mi – Gloucester 24 mi

21 Church St ✆ (01684) 892289, malvern.tic@malvernhills.gov.uk

Bredon House without rest

34 Worcester Rd. ✉ *WR14 4AA* – ✆ *(01684) 566 990* – *www.bredonhouse.co.uk*

10 rm – †£ 45/70 ††£ 85/105 B**a**

♦ Elegant, Grade II listed Regency house with spectacular views. Personable owners make breakfast a special event. Most of the individually styled rooms enjoy the fine vista.

The Cotford

51 Graham Rd ✉ *WR14 2HU* – ✆ *(01684) 572 427* – *www.cotfordhotel.co.uk*

15 rm – †£ 69/85 ††£ 125 B**s**

Rest – *(dinner only and Sunday lunch)* Menu £ 30

♦ Recently refurbished Victorian gothic stone building in landscaped gardens; built in 1851 for the Bishop of Worcester. Modern but homely guest areas; cosy bedrooms. Contemporary dining room with garden views; seasonal menu of local, organic produce.

GREAT MALVERN

Street	Map	No.
Albert Rd South	B	3
Blackmore Park Rd	A	5
Church St	B	
Clerkenwell Crescent	B	6
Cockshot Rd	B	8
Court Rd	B	12
Croft Bank	A	13
Happy Valley off St Ann's Rd	B	15
Imperial Rd	B	16
Jubilee Drive	A	17
Lygon Bank	B	18
Madresfield Rd	B	20
Moorlands Rd	B	22
North Malvern Rd	B	23
Orchard Rd	B	24
Richmond Rd	B	25
Townsend Way	A	26
Upper Welland Rd	A	27
Walwyn Rd	A	29
Wells Rd	A, B	30
Zetland Rd	B	31

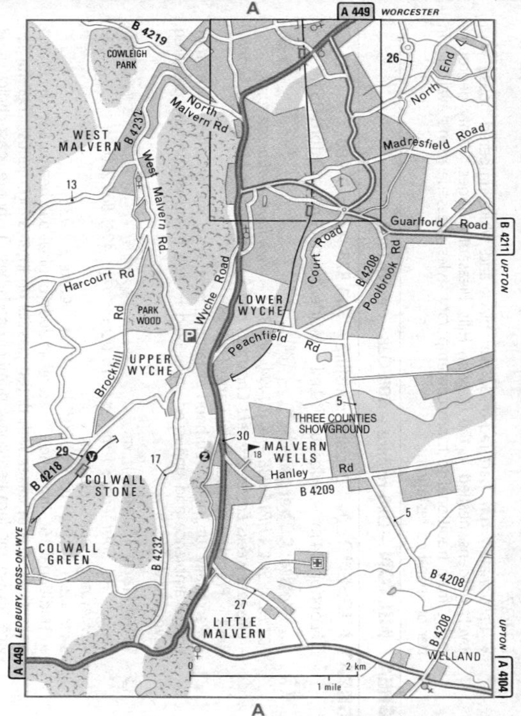

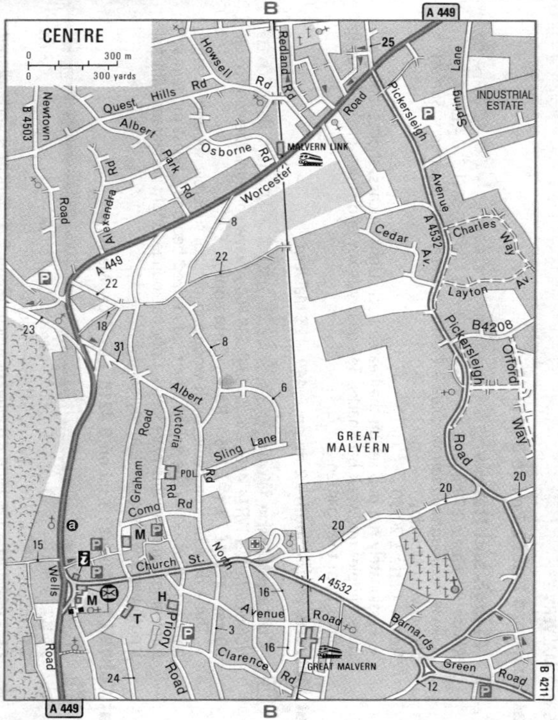

at Guarlford East : 2.5 mi on B 4211

Plough and Harrow

Rhydd Rd, East : 0.5 mi on B 4211 ✉ WR13 6NY – ☎ (01684) 310 453 – www.theploughandharrow.co.uk – Closed 25 December, 1 January, Sunday dinner and Monday

Rest – Carte £ 20/30

◆ Passionately run pub set off the beaten track. Light lunches; short evening à la carte; simpler midweek bar snacks. Seasonality is key and much of the fruit/veg comes from their garden.

at Malvern Wells South : 2 mi on A 449 – ✉ Malvern

Cottage in the Wood

rest,

Holywell Rd ✉ WR14 4LG – ☎ (01684) 588 860 – www.cottageinthewood.co.uk

30 rm – †£ 79 ††£ 195 **Rest** – Carte approx. £ 28 s Az

◆ Three detached properties with woodland behind, superbly set and boasting amazing views down the valley. Smart, good-sized bedrooms boast modern soft furnishings; most rooms have views. Cosy bar-lounge. Bright restaurant with full-length windows and modern menu.

at Colwall Southwest : 3 mi on B 4218 – ✉ Great Malvern

Colwall Park

rm,

✉ WR13 6QG – ☎ (01684) 540 000 – www.colwall.co.uk Av

21 rm – †£ 89/105 ††£ 129/135 – 1 suite

Rest *Seasons* – *(booking essential at lunch)* Menu £ 20 (lunch) – Carte dinner £ 22/37

◆ Passionately run, part red-brick, part black and white timbered house with lovely gardens, nestled in the Malvern Hills. Pleasant lounges. Comfy bedrooms range from traditional to more contemporary styles. Brasserie menu available in bar or linen-laid restaurant.

ENGLAND

GREAT MILTON – Oxfordshire – 503 Q28 – see Oxford

GREAT MISSENDEN – Buckinghamshire – 504 R28 – pop. 7 980 11 C2

London 34 mi – Aylesbury 10 mi – Maidenhead 19 mi – Oxford 35 mi

La Petite Auberge

107 High St ✉ HP16 0BB – ☎ (01494) 865 370 – www.lapetiteauberge.co.uk – Closed 2 weeks Easter, 2 weeks Christmas and Sunday (except Mothering Sunday)

Rest – French – *(dinner only)* Carte £ 30/38

◆ Personally run, neighbourhood restaurant; neat, crisp and candlelit, with an intimate ambience and unhurried style. Bold French menu of carefully prepared, flavourful dishes.

The Nags Head with rm

London Rd, Southeast : 1 mi ✉ HP16 0DG – ☎ (01494) 862 200 – www.nagsheadbucks.com

5 rm – †£ 90/110 ††£ 90/110 **Rest** – Carte £ 25/35

◆ Traditional 15C inn whose features include original oak beams and thick brick walls. Gallic charm mixes with British classics on interesting menus. Cheerful service. Stylish, modern bedrooms; number one is best. Tasty breakfast choice.

GREAT WHITTINGTON – Northd. – 501 O18 – see Corbridge

GREAT WOLFORD – Warwickshire – 503 P27 19 C3

London 84 mi – Birmingham 37 mi – Cheltenham 26 mi

The Fox & Hounds Inn with rm

✉ CV36 5NQ – ☎ (01608) 674 220 – www.thefoxandhoundsinn.com – Closed 6-20 January for meals, Sunday dinner and Monday

3 rm – †£ 50 ††£ 80 **Rest** – Carte £ 26/40

◆ Cosy, characterful, family-run country inn with traditional interior, low beams, hop bines and a large inglenook. Daily blackboard menus display rustic pub dishes of local, seasonal produce. Simple, pine-furnished bedrooms offer pleasant country views.

GREAT YARMOUTH – Norfolk – **504** Z26 – pop. 58 032 **15** D2

Great Britain

London 126 mi – Cambridge 81 mi – Ipswich 53 mi – Norwich 20 mi

25 Marine Parade ✆ (01493) 846345, tourism@great-yarmouth.gov.uk

Gorleston Warren Rd, ✆ (01493) 661 911

Beach House Caister-on-Sea, Great Yarmouth & Caister, ✆ (01493) 728 699

Norfolk Broads★

XX Andover House with rm

28-30 Camperdown ✉ NR30 3JB – ✆ (01493) 843 490 – www.andoverhouse.co.uk

16 rm – †£ 69/95 ††£ 85/105 – 4 suites

Rest – *(residents only Sunday and Monday)* Carte £ 27/48 **s**

◆ Modernised, listed Victorian property with a crisp, chic style. Accessible menu of classics served in stylish bar. Constantly evolving à la carte of modern, well-presented and accomplished dishes, with the occasional Asian touch. Simple, modern bedrooms.

XX Seafood

85 North Quay ✉ NR30 1JF – ✆ (01493) 856 009 – www.theseafood.co.uk – Closed 2 weeks Christmas, last week in May, first week in June, Saturday lunch, Sunday and bank holidays

Rest – Seafood – Carte £ 28/49

◆ Long-standing restaurant on the edge of town, run by friendly owners. Traditional interior boasts intimate booths, a lobster tank and fresh fish display. Reliable, classical seafood dishes.

GREEN ISLAND – **503** P33 – see Channel Islands (Jersey)

GRETA BRIDGE – Durham – **502** O20 – see Barnard Castle

GRIMSTON – Norfolk – **504** V25 – see King's Lynn

GRINDLETON – Lancashire – **502** M22 – see Clitheroe

GRINSHILL – Shrops. – **503** L25 – see Shrewsbury

GROUVILLE – C.I. – **503** M33 – see Channel Islands (Jersey)

GUARLFORD – Worcestershire – see Great Malvern

GUERNSEY – C.I. – **503** O/P33 – see Channel Islands

GUILDFORD – Surrey – **504** S30 – pop. 69 400 Great Britain **7** C1

London 33 mi – Brighton 43 mi – Reading 27 mi – Southampton 49 mi

14 Tunsgate ✆ (01483) 444333, tic@guildford.gov.uk Y

Clandon Park★★, E : 3 mi by A 246 Z – Hatchlands Park★, E : 6 mi by A 246 Z. Painshill★★, Cobham, NE : 10 m – Polesden Lacey★, E : 13 mi by A 246 Z and minor rd

Plan on next page

at Shere East : 6.75 mi by A 246 off A 25 - Z – ✉ Guildford

XX Kinghams

Gomshall Ln ✉ GU5 9HE – ✆ (01483) 202 168 – www.kinghams-restaurant.co.uk – Closed 25 December-5 January, Sunday dinner and Monday

Rest – *(booking essential)* Menu £ 24 (weekday lunch) – Carte £ 32/37

◆ Popular restaurant in 17C cottage in appealing village. Daily blackboard and fish specials are particularly good value. Adventurous modern menus with bold combinations.

GUILDFORD

Bedford Rd . . . . Y 2
Bridge St . . . . Y 3
Castle St. . . . . Y 5
Chertsey St . . . . Y 6
Commercial Rd . . . . Y 8
Eastgate Gardens . . . . Y 9
Friary Bridge. . . . . Y 12
Friary Centre . . . . Y
High St. . . . . Y
Ladymead . . . . Z 13
Leapale Lane . . . . Y 15
Leapale Rd. . . . . Y 16
Leas Rd . . . . Y 17
Market St. . . . . Y 18
Mary Rd . . . . Y 19
Middle Rd. . . . . Z 20
Millbrook . . . . Y 21
New Inn Lane . . . . Z 22
North St . . . . Y
One Tree Hill Rd. . . . . Z 24
Onslow St . . . . Y 25
Park St . . . . Y 27
Quarry St . . . . Y 28
Stoughton Rd. . . . . Z 30
Trood's Lane. . . . . Z 31
Tunsgate . . . . Y 33
Tunsgate Shopping Centre . . . . . . Y
Warwick's Bench . . . . Y 34
Woodbridge Rd . . . . Z 37

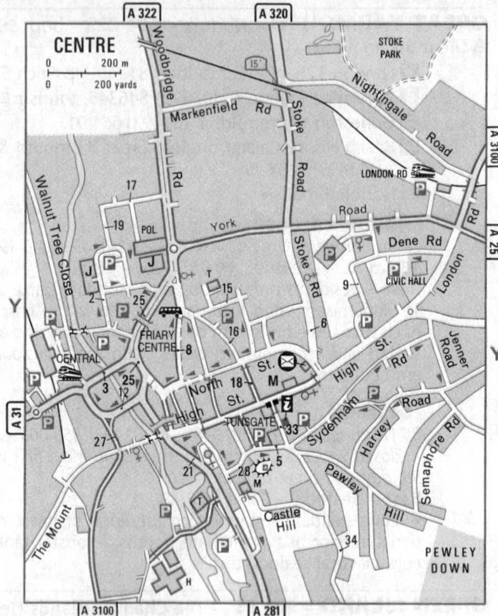

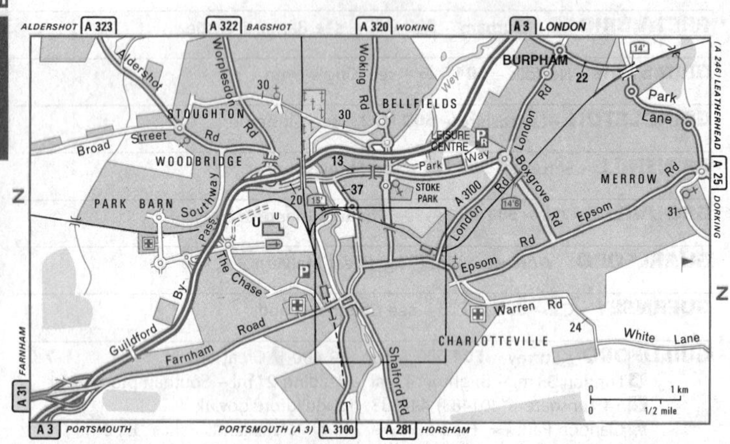

GULVAL – Cornwall – **503** D33 – see Penzance

GULWORTHY – Devon – **503** H32 – see Tavistock

HADLEIGH – Suffolk – **504** W27 – **pop. 7 124** **15** C3

London 72 mi – Cambridge 49 mi – Colchester 17 mi – Ipswich 10 mi

Hadleigh Library, 29 High St ✆ (01473) 823778, hadleigh.library@suffolk.co.uk

Edge Hall without rest

2 High St. ✉ IP7 5AP – ✆ (01473) 822 458 – www.edgehall.co.uk

6 rm – †£ 58/100 ††£ 85/125

◆ One of the oldest houses in the town (1590), with a Georgian façade. Spacious, comfy bedrooms are traditionally furnished, as are the communal areas. Very well-kept gardens.

ENGLAND

HADLEY HEATH - Worcs. - see Droitwich Spa

HALAM - Nottinghamshire Great Britain 16 B1

London 134 mi - Derby 8 mi - Nottingham 8 mi

Southwell Minster★★ **AC**, E : 2 mi on Mansfield Rd, Halam Hill, Market Pl and A 612

Waggon and Horses

The Turnpike, Mansfield Rd. ✉ NG22 8AE - ✆ (01636) 813 109 - www.thewaggonathalam.co.uk - Closed Sunday dinner and Monday

Rest - Menu £ 15 (weekdays) - Carte £ 20/38

◆ Fresh, unfussy pub offering daily blackboard menu of fresh fish and local meats, with complimentary sides of veg. OAP discount Tuesday-Sunday; interesting ales and slick, cheery serving team.

HALFORD - Warwickshire - 503 P27 - pop. 301 19 C3

London 94 mi - Oxford 43 mi - Stratford-upon-Avon 8 mi

Old Manor House without rest

Queens St ✉ CV36 5BT - ✆ (01789) 740 264 - www.oldmanor-halford.co.uk - Closed 25 December

3 rm - †£ 55/65 ††£ 100

◆ Characterful house in quiet residential area, well located for Stratford and the Cotswolds. Spacious garden next to River Stour. Well appointed drawing room and atmospheric bedrooms with rich fabrics.

The Halford Bridge with rm

Fosse Way ✉ CV36 5BN - ✆ (01789) 740 636 - www.thehalfordbridge.co.uk - Closed Sunday dinner

10 rm - †£ 70 ††£ 85

Rest - Menu £ 14 (Monday-Thursday) - Carte £ 21/28

◆ Imposing stone-built former coaching inn set on the Fosse Way. Classic combinations with a personal twist on seasonally changing menu. Atmospheric bar and enthusiastic service. Modern bedrooms with nutty names and original wood beams.

HALFWAY BRIDGE - W. Sussex - 504 R31 - see Petworth

HALIFAX - West Yorkshire - 502 O22 - pop. 83 570 22 B2

London 205 mi - Bradford 8 mi - Burnley 21 mi - Leeds 15 mi

Visitor Centre & Art Gallery, Piece Hall ✆ (01422) 368725, halifax@ytbtic.co.uk

18 Halifax Bradley Hall Holywell Green, ✆ (01422) 374 108

18 Halifax West End Highroad Well Paddock Lane, ✆ (01422) 341 878

9 Ryburn Sowerby Bridge Norland, ✆ (01422) 831 355

9 Lightcliffe Knowle Top Rd, ✆ (01422) 202 459

18 Ogden Union Lane, ✆ (01422) 244 171

Design House

Dean Clough (Gate 5) ✉ HX3 5AX - ✆ (01422) 383 242 - www.designhouserestaurant.co.uk - Closed 26 December-10 January, Saturday lunch, Sunday and bank holidays

Rest - Menu £ 15 (dinner) - Carte £ 27/45

◆ Long-standing restaurant in converted mill complex. Striking interior with subtle blue hues; smart team offer warm welcome. Extensive menus of precise, tasty, classical and more modern dishes.

Shibden Mill Inn with rm

Shibden Mill Fold ✉ HX3 7UL - ✆ (01422) 365 840 - www.shibdenmillinn.com

11 rm - †£ 72/79 ††£ 105/111 **Rest** - Carte £ 16/40

◆ Charming whitewashed country inn - formerly a corn mill - set in the valley. Extensive menu ranges from the traditional to the more modern. Events include fortnightly 'guinea pig' nights. Individually appointed bedrooms are comfy and cosy.

ENGLAND

HALTWHISTLE – Northumberland – 501 M19 – pop. 3 811 Great Britain 24 A2

London 335 mi – Carlisle 22 mi – Newcastle upon Tyne 37 mi

Railway Station, Station Rd (01434) 322002, haltwhistletic@btconnect.com

Wallend Farm Greenhead, (01697) 747 367

Hadrian's Wall★★, N : 4.5 mi by A 6079 – Housesteads★★ **AC**, NE : 6 mi by B 6318 – Roman Army Museum★ **AC**, NW : 5 mi by A 69 and B 6318 – Vindolanda (Museum★) **AC**, NE : 5 mi by A 69 – Steel Rig (★) NE : 5.5 mi by B 6318

Centre of Britain

Main St NE49 0BH – (01434) 322 422 – www.centre-of-britain.org.uk

12 rm – †£ 59/79 ††£ 110 **Rest** – Menu £ 18 (lunch) – Carte £ 19/33

♦ Attractive hotel on busy main street. Oldest part, a pele tower, dates from 15C. Comfortable modern décor, including bedrooms, incorporates original architectural features. Glass-roofed restaurant with light, airy feel.

Ashcroft without rest

Lantys Lonnen NE49 0DA – (01434) 320 213 – www.ashcroftguesthouse.co.uk – Closed 25 December

8 rm – †£ 60/88 ††£ 88

♦ Imposing Victorian house, formerly a vicarage, with beautifully kept gardens. Family run and attractively furnished throughout creating a welcoming atmosphere. Large bedrooms.

HAMBLE-LE-RICE – Hampshire – 503 Q31 – see Southampton

HAMBLETON – Rutland – see Oakham

HAMPTON IN ARDEN – West Midlands – 504 O26 – pop. 1 655 19 C2

London 113 mi – Birmingham 15 mi – Leicester 39 mi – Coventry 11 mi

Hampton Manor

Shadowbrook Ln B92 0EN – (01675) 446 080 – www.hamptonmanor.eu – closed 3-7 January and 26 December

11 rm – †£ 140 ††£ 140, £ 15.95 – 1 suite

Rest *Peel's* – see restaurant listing

♦ Early Victorian manor house in 45 acres; built for grandson of Sir Robert Peel. Contemporary décor blends with characterful plasterwork and wood panelling; bedrooms boast mod cons.

XX Peel's – at Hampton Manor

Shadowbrook Ln B92 0EN – (01675) 446 080 – www.peelsrestaurant.co.uk – closed 3-7 January and 26 December

Rest – Menu £ 15/39

♦ Contemporary dining room situated in former stable courtyard, with slate floor, glass roof and floor-to-ceiling windows. Modern style menus; bold, gutsy flavours. Formal service.

HARDWICK – Cambs. – see Cambridge

HARLAXTON – Lincs. – 502 S25 – see Grantham

HAROME – N. Yorks. – see Helmsley

HARPENDEN – Hertfordshire – 504 S28 – pop. 28 452 12 A2

London 32 mi – Luton 6 mi

Harpenden Common East Common, (01582) 711 320

Hammonds End, (01582) 712 580

XX Bean Tree

20A Leyton Rd AL5 2HU – (01582) 460 901 – www.thebeantree.com – Closed Saturday lunch, Sunday dinner and Monday

Rest – Menu £ 20 (weekdays) – Carte £ 25/53

♦ Converted red-brick cottage with bean tree and smart terrace. Intimate, softly lit restaurant with sage green palette. Carefully sought ingredients; precise modern cooking.

ENGLAND

HARROGATE – North Yorkshire – 502 P22 – pop. 66 178

Great Britain

London 211 mi – Bradford 18 mi – Leeds 15 mi – Newcastle upon Tyne 76 mi

Royal Baths, Crescent Rd (01423) 537300, tic@harrogate.gov.uk

Forest Lane Head, (01423) 863 158

Pannal Follifoot Rd, (01423) 872 628

Oakdale, (01423) 567 162

Crimple Valley Hookstone Wood Rd, (01423) 883 485

Town★

Fountains Abbey★★★ **AC** :- Studley Royal **AC** (≤★ from Anne Boleyn's Seat) - Fountains Hall (Fa 0.5ade★), N : 13 mi by A 61 and B 6265 AY – Harewood House★★ (The Gallery★) **AC**, S : 7.5 mi by A 61 BZ

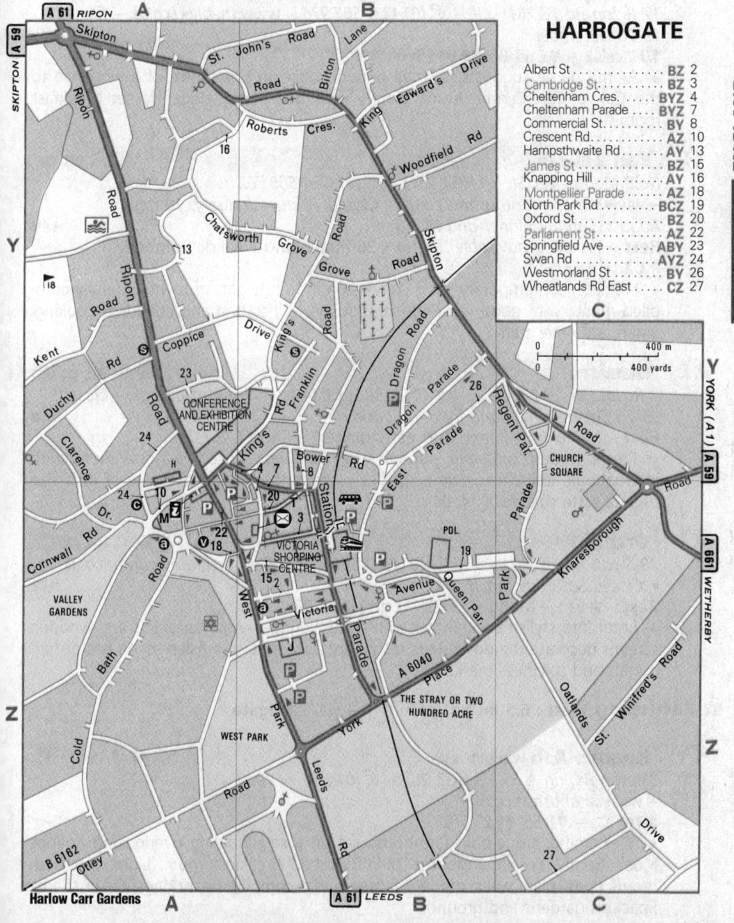

ENGLAND

Hotel du Vin
Prospect Pl ✉ *HG1 1LB – ☎ (01423) 856 800 – www.hotelduvin.com* BZa
48 rm – ♦£ 95/110 ♦♦£ 120/165, ☕ £ 13.95
Rest ***Bistro*** – Carte £ 27/35
♦ Terrace of Georgian houses overlooking pleasant green. Individually appointed bedrooms with wine-themed décor and modern facilities. Buzzy, modern, stylish French bistro and private dining rooms. Good menu of Gallic influenced dishes.

Brookfield House without rest
5 Alexandra Rd ✉ *HG1 5JS – ☎ (01423) 506 646 – www.brookfieldhousehotel.co.uk* BYs
6 rm ☕ – ♦£ 65/85 ♦♦£ 95
♦ Family owned Victorian property in a quiet, residential location close to the town centre. Homely feel in communal areas and comfortable bedrooms with a mix of styles.

The Bijou without rest
17 Ripon Rd ✉ *HG1 2JL – ☎ (01423) 567 974 – www.thebijou.co.uk – Closed 19-26 December* AYs
10 rm ☕ – ♦£ 65/85 ♦♦£ 115
♦ As the name suggests, a small period house, in the centre of town close to the Convention Centre. Immaculately kept bedrooms; elegantly set breakfast room.

ENGLAND

Van Zeller
No.8 Montpellier St. ✉ *HG1 2TQ – ☎ (01423) 508 762 – www.vanzellerrestaurants.co.uk – Closed 10 days January, 10 days August, Sunday dinner and Monday* AZv
Rest – *(booking advisable)* Menu £ 20 (lunch and weekday dinner) – Carte £ 33/54
♦ Intimate, contemporary shop conversion in trendy part of town. Carefully compiled menu, with good value lunch; unfussy, well-crafted and confident cooking. Smart, attentive staff.

Quantro
3 Royal Par ✉ *HG1 2SZ – ☎ (01423) 503 034 – www.quantro.co.uk – Closed 25-26 December, 1 January and Sunday* AZa
Rest – Menu £ 14 (lunch and early dinner) – Carte £ 25/32
♦ Fresh, modern brasserie; popular with all. Keenly priced, seasonal menu with international influences. Some smaller plates at lunch and a choice of dish size on à la carte suits local workers.

Orchid
28 Swan Rd ✉ *HG1 2SE – ☎ (01423) 560 425 – www.orchidrestaurant.co.uk – Closed Saturday lunch* AZc
Rest – Asian – Menu £ 13/22 – Carte £ 22/38
♦ Enter into stylish cocktail bar with comfy lounges. Asian artefacts and wooden screens decorate the downstairs restaurant. Extensive pan-Asian menu has dishes' origins and spiciness marked.

at Kettlesing West : 6.5 mi by A 59 - AY – ✉ Harrogate

Knabbs Ash without rest
Skipton Rd, on A 59 ✉ *HG3 2LT – ☎ (01423) 771 040 – www.knabbsash.co.uk*
3 rm ☕ – ♦£ 55 ♦♦£ 75/80
♦ Welcoming, stone-built farmhouse set on a smallholding overlooking Knabbs Moor. Comfy, cosy lounge and pine-furnished breakfast room. Light, airy bedrooms boast plain walls, modern fabrics and a complimentary decanter of sherry. Spacious gardens and grounds.

HARTINGTON – Derbyshire – **502** O24 – pop. 1 604 – ✉ Buxton **16** A1

London 168 mi – Derby 36 mi – Manchester 40 mi – Sheffield 34 mi

Biggin Hall

Biggin, Southeast : 2 mi by B 5054 ✉ SK17 ODH – ☎ (01298) 84 451 – www.bigginhall.co.uk

20 rm – £ 60/115 £ 126/136

Rest – *(booking essential)* Menu £ 12/20 **s** – Carte (lunch) approx. £ 16 **s**

♦ Characterful house with traditional, rustic appeal. Many guests follow the Tissington Trail: bike storage and picnics are offered. Classical, low-beamed bedrooms in main house; brighter rooms in the barns. Pleasant garden views from dining room. Homely cooking.

HARTLAND – Devon – **503** G31 **1** B1

London 221 mi – Bude 15 mi – Clovelly 4 mi

Golden Park without rest

Southwest : 5 mi following signs for Elmscott and Bude ✉ EX39 6EP – ☎ (01237) 441 254 – www.goldenpark.co.uk – Closed 25 December and restricted opening in winter

3 rm – £ 75 £ 90

♦ Walk to the North Devon coast from this delightfully set part 17C farmhouse. Style and character prevail, particularly in guests' lounge and beamed, smartly decorated rooms.

The Hart Inn

The Square ✉ EX39 6BL – ☎ (01237) 441 474 – www.thehartinn.com – Closed 25 December, Sunday dinner and Monday

Rest – Carte £ 14/26

♦ Part 14 and 16C coaching inn with rustic, homely interior. Regularly changing menu features some Scandinavian influences but produce remains seasonal and local; generous portions.

ENGLAND

HARWELL – Oxfordshire – **503** Q29 – pop. 2 015 **10** B3

London 64 mi – Oxford 16 mi – Reading 18 mi – Swindon 22 mi

Kingswell

rm,

Reading Rd, East : 0.75 mi on A 417 ✉ OX11 0LZ – ☎ (01235) 833 043 – www.kingswell-hotel.com – Closed 24-30 December

20 rm – £ 110 £ 130 **Rest** – Menu £ 24/28 – Carte £ 23/38

♦ Large red-brick hotel located on the south Oxfordshire Downs. Convenient for Didcot rail and Oxford. Spacious, uniform, traditional bedrooms and pubby public areas. Classic menus served in traditional dining room.

HARWICH – Essex – **504** X28 – pop. 20 130 **13** D2

London 78 mi – Chelmsford 41 mi – Colchester 20 mi – Ipswich 23 mi

to Denmark (Esbjerg) (DFDS Seaways A/S) 3-4 weekly (20 h) – to The Netherlands (Hook of Holland) (Stena Line) 2 daily (3 h 30 mn)

Iconfield Park, Parkeston ☎ (01255) 506139, harwichtic@btconnect.com

Parkeston Station Rd, ☎ (01255) 503 616

Pier at Harwich

The Quay ✉ CO12 3HH – ☎ (01255) 241 212 – www.milsomhotels.com

14 rm – £ 80/140 £ 185/210

Rest *Harbourside* – Seafood – Carte £ 35/56

Rest *Ha'Penny* – Carte £ 21/32

♦ Bright Victorian building located on the quayside giving many bedrooms views of the area's busy sea lanes. Décor is comfortably stylish and contemporary with a nautical theme. Seafood restaurant with North Sea outlook. Informal bistro.

HASTINGS and ST LEONARDS – East Sussex – **504** V31 – pop. 85 828 **8** B3

London 65 mi – Brighton 37 mi – Folkestone 37 mi – Maidstone 34 mi

Town Hall, Queen's Sq, Priory Meadow ☎ (0845) 2741001, hic@hastings.gov.uk

Beauport Park Golf Course St Leonards-on-Sea Battle Rd, ☎ (01424) 854 245

HASTINGS ST. LEONARDS

Albert Rd . . . . **BZ** 3
Bourne (The). . . . . **BY** 4
Cambridge Gardens . . . . . . **BZ** 5
Castle Hill Rd . . . . **BZ** 8
Castle St . . . . **BZ** 7
Cornwallis Gardens. . . . . . . **BZ** 9
Cornwallis Terrace . . . . **BZ** 10
Denmark Pl. . . . . **BZ** 13
Dorset Pl. . . . . **BZ** 15
Gensing Rd. . . . . **AZ** 16
George St . . . . **BY** 18
Grosvenor Crescent . . . . . **AY** 19
Harold Pl. . . . . **BZ** 20
Havelock Rd . . . . **BZ** 21
King's Rd . . . . **AZ** 22
London Rd . . . . **AZ**
Marine Court . . . . **AZ** 23
Middle St . . . . **BZ** 24
Norman Rd. . . . . **AZ**
Priory Meadow Shopping Centre . . . . **BZ**
Queen's Rd. . . . . **BZ**
Robertson St . . . . **BZ** 27
Rock-a-Nore Rd . . . . **BY** 30
St Helen's Park Rd . . . . . . **BY** 31
Sedlescombe Rd South . . **AY** 32
Silchester Rd . . . . **AZ** 33
Warrior Square . . . . **AZ** 34
Wellington Pl. . . . . **BZ** 35
Wellington Square . . . . . . **BZ** 36
White Rock Road . . . . **BZ** 38

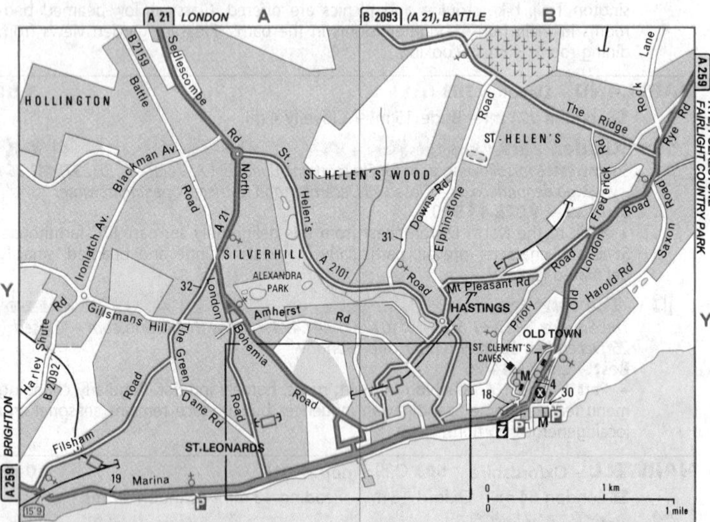

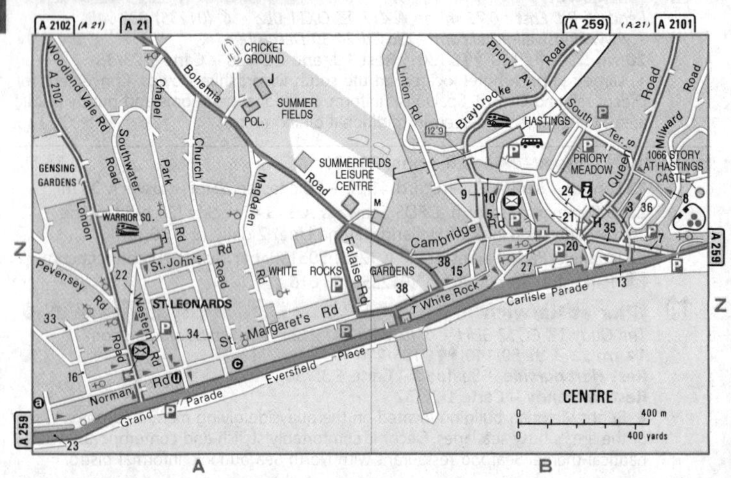

Zanzibar without rest
9 Eversfield Pl ✉ TN37 6BY – ✆ (01424) 460 109 – www.zanzibarhotel.co.uk
9 rm – †£ 99/229 ††£ 109/239 AZ**c**
◆ Contemporary guesthouse with slightly unusual design. Bedrooms are named after countries and continents; South America is largest, with feature whirlpool bath and seaview.

Hastings House without rest
9 Warrior Sq. ✉ TN37 6BA – ✆ (01424) 422 709
– www.hastingshouse.co.uk AZ**u**
7 rm – £ 70/100 £ 99/135
◆ Stylish, modern and very comfortable guesthouse just off the promenade; personally run by hospitable owners. Rooms 3, 5 and 7 are the best choice for their size and sea views.

Webbe's Rock-a-Nore
1 Rock-a-Nore ✉ TN34 3DW – ✆ (01424) 721 650
– www.webbesrestaurants.co.uk – Closed 4-11 January BY**x**
Rest – Seafood – Carte £ 20/28
◆ Bright, contemporary restaurant with horseshoe counter and open kitchen, in an enviable position across the beach from the fishing Stade. Unsurprisingly fresh fish and seafood.

St Clements
3 Mercatoria, St Leonards on Sea ✉ TN38 0EB – ✆ (01424) 200 355
– www.stclementsrestaurant.co.uk – Closed Sunday dinner and Monday
Rest – Menu £ 16/27 – Carte £ 30/35 AZ**a**
◆ Pleasant neighbourhood restaurant with striking local artwork hung on plain walls. Comprehensive à la carte and concise, good value lunch and midweek menus. Tasty modern European cooking is unfussy with a rustic edge. Fresh fish from Hastings plays a key role.

HATCH BEAUCHAMP – Somerset – 503 K30 – see Taunton

HATFIELD HEATH – Essex – 504 U28 – see Bishop's Stortford (Herts.)

HATFIELD PEVEREL – Essex – 504 V28 – pop. 3 258 Great Britain 13 C2

London 39 mi – Chelmsford 8 mi – Maldon 12 mi
Colchester - Castle and Museum★, E : 13 mi by A 12

Blue Strawberry Bistrot
The Street ✉ CM3 2DW – ✆ (01245) 381 333 – www.bluestrawberrybistrot.co.uk
– Closed 26 December, Saturday lunch and Sunday dinner
Rest – Menu £ 17/24 – Carte (dinner only Friday-Saturday) £ 19/35
◆ Busy, brick-built former pub, which inside resembles a traditional French neighbourhood brasserie. Keenly priced bistro-style dishes and old-school desserts. Polite service.

HATHERSAGE – Derbyshire – 502 P24 – pop. 1 582 16 A1
– ✉ Sheffield (s. Yorks.)

London 177 mi – Derby 39 mi – Manchester 34 mi – Sheffield 11 mi
Sickleholme Bamford, ✆ (01433) 651 306

The George
✉ S32 1BB – ✆ (01433) 650 436 – www.george-hotel.net
22 rm – £ 96/119 £ 152/167
Rest ***George's*** – Menu £ 37
◆ Keenly run, 14C stone coaching inn displaying exposed brick walls and wooden beams. Comfy, open-fired lounge and small cocktail bar. Smart, pastel-hued bedrooms with bright, modern fabrics. Formal restaurant offers modern British menu with some global influences.

The Walnut Club
Unit 6, The Square, Main Rd ✉ S32 1BB
– ✆ (01433) 651 155 – www.thewalnutclub.com
– Closed Monday except Bank Holidays
Rest – *(dinner only and lunch Friday-Sunday)* Carte £ 23/31
◆ Modern eatery with large bar counter and funky wallpaper – a piece of the city in a traditional stone-built village. Menus mix classic British and international dishes. Live jazz at weekends.

ENGLAND

HAWES – North Yorkshire – **502** N21 – pop. 1 117 **22** A1

London 253 mi – Kendal 27 mi – Leeds 72 mi – Newcastle upon Tyne 76 mi

Dales Countryside Museum, Station Yard ✆ (01969) 666210, hawes@yorkshiredales.org.uk

Stone House

Sedbusk, North : 1 mi by Muker rd ✉ DL8 3PT – ✆ (01969) 667 571 – www.stonehousehotel.com – Closed January and mid-week in December

23 rm – £ 51/121 £ 171 – 1 suite **Rest** – *(dinner only)* Menu £ 33

♦ Built in 1908 as a family home. Interior decorated in traditional style; public areas include billiard room and oak panelled lounge. Some rooms with private conservatories. Dining room has exposed beams and wooden tables.

HAWKSHEAD – Cumbria – **502** L20 – pop. 570 – ✉ Ambleside **21** A2

Great Britain

London 283 mi – Carlisle 52 mi – Kendal 19 mi

Main Street ✆ (015394) 36946 (summer only), enquiries@hawksheadtouristinfo.org.uk

Village★

Lake Windermere★★ – Coniston Water★ (Brantwood★, on east side), SW : by B 5285

at Far Sawrey Southeast : 2.5 mi on B 5285 – ✉ Ambleside

West Vale without rest

✉ LA22 0LQ – ✆ (015394) 42 817 – www.westvalecountryhouse.co.uk – Closed 24-26 December and 4 January-7 February

7 rm – £ 85/120 £ 120/130

♦ Welcoming slate house boasting lovely countryside views; run by keen owners. Two comfy lounges and a smart country house style room for hearty breakfasts. Good-sized bedrooms with warm, comfy, boutique style. Tea and cake on arrival, and plenty of extra touches.

HAWNBY – North Yorkshire – **502** Q21 – ✉ Helmsley **23** C1

London 245 mi – Middlesbrough 27 mi – Newcastle upon Tyne 69 mi – York 30 mi

The Inn at Hawnby

✉ YO62 5QS – ✆ (01439) 798 202 – www.innathawnby.co.uk – Closed 25 December

9 rm – £ 79 £ 99

Rest – *(Closed Monday and Tuesday February and March)* Carte £ 23/32

♦ Homely inn set in a very rural spot in prime walking and shooting country. Classically styled bedrooms are split between the house and barn, and boast good linens and home comforts. Simplicity is key. Pub-style dishes at lunch; more substantial, classical dinners.

at Laskill Northeast : 2.25 mi by Osmotherley rd – ✉ Hawnby

Laskill Country House

Easterside ✉ YO62 5NB – ✆ (01439) 798 265 – www.laskillcountryhouse.co.uk

3 rm – £ 45/60 £ 100 **Rest** – Menu £ 25

♦ Delightful manor-style house in popular shooting/walking area. Comfy lounge; small function suite. Good-sized bedrooms with countryside views. Communal dining; wholesome home-cooked meals, with meat from the family's farms.

HAWORTH – West Yorkshire – **502** O22 – pop. 6 078 – ✉ Keighley **22** A2

Great Britain

London 213 mi – Burnley 22 mi – Leeds 22 mi – Manchester 34 mi

2-4 West Lane ✆ (01535) 642329, haworth@ytbtic.co.uk

Bront£ Parsonage Museum **AC**

Ashmount Country House without rest
Mytholmes Ln ✉ BD22 8EZ – ☎ (01535) 645 726
– www.ashmounthaworth.co.uk
10 rm – †£ 95 ††£ 235
◆ Built in 1870 by the physician to the Brontë sisters, this refurbished guesthouse has extremely comfortable, period-furnished bedrooms and state-of-the-art bathrooms; some rooms even have their own outdoor hottubs.

Old Registry without rest
4 Main St ✉ BD22 8DA – ☎ (01535) 646 503 – www.theoldregistryhaworth.co.uk
– Closed 24-26 December
9 rm – †£ 55/100 ††£ 100/120
◆ Stone former registrar's office on cobbled main street. Individually themed bedrooms boast rich fabrics and antiques: 5 are feature rooms; some have four-posters. Breakfast of local produce.

Weaver's with rm
rest,
15 West Ln ✉ BD22 8DU – ☎ (01535) 643 822 – www.weaversmallhotel.co.uk
– Closed 26 December-6 January
3 rm – †£ 65/75 ††£ 110
Rest – *(Closed Sunday, Monday and lunch Saturday)* Menu £ 22 (weekdays) – Carte £ 22/33
◆ Charming former weavers' cottages at the top of a cobbled street. Characterful, cluttered lounge with ornaments, artefacts and informal atmosphere. Wide-ranging menus have a strong northern base. Warm, welcoming bedrooms.

HAYDON BRIDGE – **Northd.** – **501** N19 – **see Hexham**

HAYLING ISLAND – **Hampshire** – **504** R31 – **pop. 14 842** **6** B3

London 77 mi – Brighton 45 mi – Southampton 28 mi
Beachlands, Seven Seafront ☎ (023) 9246 7111, tourism@havant.gov.uk
Links Lane, ☎ (023) 9246 4446

Cockle Warren Cottage without rest
36 Seafront ✉ PO11 9HL – ☎ (023) 9246 4961 – www.cocklewarren.co.uk
6 rm – †£ 49/59 ††£ 65/80
◆ Pleasant cottage with welcoming owner, set just across the road from the beach. Comfortable, well-kept bedrooms; 1 and 4 have sea views. Conservatory breakfast room and terrace overlook pool.

HAYWARDS HEATH – **West Sussex** – **504** T31 – **pop. 29 110** **7** D2
Great Britain

London 41 mi – Brighton 16 mi
Lindfield East Mascalls Lane, ☎ (01444) 484 467
Sheffield Park Garden★, E : 5 mi on A 272 and A 275

Jeremy's at Borde Hill
Borde Hill Gdns, North : 1.75 mi by B 2028 on Balcombe Rd ✉ RH16 1XP
– ☎ (01444) 441 102 – www.jeremysrestaurant.com – Closed 1-14 January,
Sunday dinner and Monday
Rest – Menu £ 25 (weekdays) – Carte £ 29/42
◆ Converted 19C stables with delightful views to Victorian walled garden. Contemporary interior with modern art. Confident, vibrant cooking in a light Mediterranean style.

HEADLAM – **Durham** – **502** O20 – **see Darlington**

HEATHROW AIRPORT – **Middx.** – **504** S29 – **see Hillingdon (Greater London)**

HEBDEN BRIDGE – **West Yorkshire** – **502** N22 – **pop. 4 086** **22** A2
– ✉ **West Yorkshire**

London 223 mi – Burnley 13 mi – Leeds 24 mi – Manchester 25 mi
1 Bridge Gate ☎ (01422) 843831
Great Mount Wadsworth, ☎ (01422) 842 896

Holme House without rest
New Road ✉ HX7 8AD – ✆ (01422) 847 588
– www.holmehousehebdenbridge.co.uk
3 rm – †£ 65 ††£ 78/90
♦ Late Georgian house in town centre with gated parking and neat garden. Smart, comfortable, well furnished rooms. Bedrooms boast excellent facilities and spacious bathrooms.

HEDDON ON THE WALL – Northumberland 24 A2

London 288 mi – Blaydon 7 mi – Newcastle upon Tyne 8 mi

Close House
Southwest : 2.25 mi by B 6528 ✉ NE15 0HT – ✆ (01661) 852 255
– www.closehouse.co.uk – Closed January
19 rm – †£ 118 ††£ 175
Rest *Bewickes* – ✆ (01661) 835 099 – Menu £ 22 (lunch) – Carte dinner £ 31/41
♦ Stunning Georgian mansion in 300 acres of mature grounds that stretch to the river. Original features blend with modern décor; front bedrooms have views, those to rear are more contemporary. Stylish restaurant offers interesting modern cooking and intimate air.

HEDLEY ON THE HILL – Northumberland 24 A2

London 293 mi – Newcastle upon Tyne 16 mi – Sunderland 26 mi – South Shields 26 mi

The Feathers Inn
✉ NE43 7SW – ✆ (01661) 843 607 – www.thefeathers.net
– Closed first 2 weeks in January and Monday lunch
Rest – Carte £ 16/25
♦ Traditional stone inn set on a steep hill, offering daily changing menu of hearty British classics, cooked using carefully sourced, regional produce. Relaxed, friendly atmosphere.

HELMSLEY – North Yorkshire – 502 Q21 – pop. 1 559 Great Britain 23 C1

London 239 mi – Leeds 51 mi – Middlesbrough 28 mi – York 24 mi

Helmsley Castle, Castlegate ✆ (01439) 770173, helmsley.tic@english-heritage.org.uk

Ampleforth College Castle Drive, Gilling East, ✆ (01439) 788 212

Rievaulx Abbey★★ **AC**, NW : 2.5 mi by B 1257

Black Swan
Market Pl ✉ YO62 5BJ – ✆ (01439) 770 466 – www.blackswan-helmsley.co.uk
39 rm – †£ 105/235 ††£ 175/275 – 3 suites
Rest *The Rutland Room* – *(dinner only and Sunday lunch)* Menu £ 33 (Sunday lunch) – Carte £ 33/48
♦ Part 16C coaching inn in a historic market town; indeed it overlooks the market. Charming rustic interior with exposed beams. Many bedrooms with period fittings and features. Formal dining in classically furnished restaurant.

Feversham Arms
on B 1257 ✉ YO62 5AG – ✆ (01439) 770 766 – www.fevershamarmshotel.com
33 rm (dinner included) – †£ 195 ††£ 245 – 16 suites
Rest *Conservatory* – Menu £ 36 (dinner) – Carte £ 36/50
♦ Former coaching inn; its stone façade concealing a surprisingly modern interior. Muted colours and quality fabrics feature throughout. Comfortable bedrooms have a quiet, restful nature; some overlook the swimming pool. Superb spa facility. Warm, red décor in airy, glass-roofed restaurant; modern brasserie-style menu.

No.54 without rest
54 Bondgate ✉ YO62 5EZ – ☎ (01439) 771 533 – www.no54.co.uk – Closed Christmas and New Year
3 rm – £ 55/65 £ 90/110
◆ Victorian terraced cottage, formerly the village vet's. Charming owner. Bedrooms are strong point: set around flagged courtyard, they're airy, bright and very well-equipped.

Carlton Lodge without rest
Bondgate ✉ YO62 5EY – ☎ (01439) 770 557 – www.carlton-lodge.com – Closed 2 weeks January
8 rm – £ 50/68 £ 85/100
◆ Late 19C house set just out of town. Homely and traditional air to the décor in the communal areas and the bedrooms, some of which have period features. Cosy breakfast room.

at Harome Southeast : 2.75 mi by A 170 – ✉ York

Pheasant
✉ YO62 5JG – ☎ (01439) 771 241 – www.thepheasanthotel.com
12 rm – £ 75/115 £ 150 – 2 suites
Rest – *(booking essential for non residents)* Menu £ 30/35 – Carte £ 36/44
◆ Ivy-clad hotel in picturesque hamlet with a duck pond and mill stream close by. Under the same ownership as The Star Inn. Charmingly decorated public areas; comfy, up-to-date bedrooms. Formal restaurant and conservatory; choose from array of fresh, modern menus.

Cross House Lodge at The Star Inn
✉ YO62 5JE – ☎ (01439) 770 397 – www.thestaratharome.co.uk – Closed 1 January
11 rm – £ 240
Rest *The Star Inn* – see restaurant listing
Rest *Wheelhouse* – *(booking essential) (residents only set menu only and lunch by arrangement)* Menu £ 65 **s**
◆ Converted farm buildings set opposite a pub, in a pretty village. Open-plan, split-level lounge. Ultra-stylish, super-smart bedrooms in either the main building or local cottages. Communal dining and breakfast for residents in the Wheelhouse.

The Star Inn
High St ✉ YO62 5JE – ☎ (01439) 770 397 – www.thestaratharome.co.uk – Closed Monday lunch and Sunday dinner
Rest – *(booking essential)* Carte £ 25/45 **s**
◆ Charming 14C thatched pub with cosy bar and two dining rooms: one traditional; one more modern and boasting a chef's table. Pub-style dishes are rooted in tradition but use modern techniques. Herbs and vegetables come straight from the kitchen garden.

at Ampleforth Southwest : 4.5 mi by A 170 off B 1257 – ✉ Helmsley

Shallowdale House
West : 0.5 mi ✉ YO62 4DY – ☎ (01439) 788 325 – www.shallowdalehouse.co.uk – Closed Christmas-New Year
3 rm – £ 90 £ 120 **Rest** – Menu £ 38
◆ Modern guesthouse affording spectacular views of the Howardian Hills; an area of outstanding beauty. Spacious rooms boast large picture windows to make the most of the scenery. A warm, relaxed atmosphere pervades. 4 course, home-cooked evening meals.

at Byland Abbey Southwest : 6.5 mi by A 170 – ✉ Helmsley

The Abbey Inn with rm
✉ YO61 4BD – ☎ (01347) 868 204 – www.theappletree.org – Closed Tuesday
3 rm – £ 100/200 £ 100/200
Rest – *(booking essential)* Menu £ 16 (lunch) – Carte £ 16/32
◆ Historic inn in stunning location across from the ruins of the Byland Abbey. Breakfast, morning coffee and afternoon tea available, as well as local, seasonal cooking at lunch and dinner. Spacious, high quality bedrooms boast luxurious bathrooms to match.

ENGLAND

at Oldstead Southwest : 7.5 mi by A 170

Black Swan with rm — rest, P VISA MC

✉ *YO61 4BL – ☎ (01347) 868 387 – www.blackswanoldstead.co.uk – Closed lunch Monday- Wednesday*

4 rm – †£ 125 ††£ 150/180 **Rest** – Carte £ 25/40

◆ Owned by a family who've lived and farmed here for generations. Top-rate bar meals in characterful beamed bar; more ambitious dishes in upstairs restaurant. Cooking is modern and highly skilled but satisfyingly unpretentious. Bedrooms boast modern fabrics, antiques, luxurious bathrooms and private patios.

at Scawton West : 8.5 mi by A 170 – ✉ Helmsley

Hare Inn — P VISA MC AE

✉ *YO7 2HG – ☎ (01845) 597 769 – www.thehareinn.co.uk – Closed Sunday dinner and Monday*

Rest – Carte £ 30/40

◆ Warm, inviting and busy pub, parts of which date from 13C; in a remote setting, close to Rievaulx Abbey. Satisfying local food, with meat from Masham and poultry from Pateley Bridge.

HELSTON – Cornwall – 503 E33 – pop. 10 578 — 1 A3

London 306 mi – Falmouth 13 mi – Penzance 14 mi – Truro 17 mi

The Flora Day Furry Dance★★

Lizard Peninsula★ - Gunwalloe Fishing Cove★, S : 4 mi by A 3083 and minor rd - Culdrose (Flambards Village Theme Park★), SE : 1 mi - Wendron (Poldark Mine★), NE : 2.5 mi by B 3297 – Gweek (Seal Sanctuary★), E : 4 mi by A 394 and minor rd

Nansloe Manor — AC rest, rm, P VISA MC AE

Meneage Rd, South : 1.5 mi on A 3083 ✉ TR13 OSB – ☎ (01326) 558 400 – www.nansloe-manor.co.uk – Closed 2 weeks January

15 rm – †£ 171/226 ††£ 190/250

Rest – *(closed Sunday and Monday)* Menu £ 25 (lunch) – Carte £ 28/39

◆ Restored Georgian Manor House set in 4 acres. Handmade French furniture, pastel décor and airy, continental feel. Subtly elegant bedrooms; some with balcony/terrace/views. Menus make use of produce from garden; classic combinations are presented in a contemporary style.

at Trelowarren Southeast : 4 mi by A 394 and A 3083 on B 3293 – ✉ Helston

New Yard — P VISA MC

Trelowarren Estate ✉ TR12 6AF – ☎ (01326) 221 595 – www.trelowarren.com – Closed Monday September-May and Sunday dinner

Rest – *(booking advisable at dinner)* Menu £ 20/25 – Carte £ 27/57

◆ Converted stable yard adjoining a craft gallery. Large, simply furnished dining room opens onto a terrace. Dinner offers elaborate seasonal menus of locally inspired dishes; lunch is simpler.

HEMEL HEMPSTEAD – Hertfordshire – 504 S28 – pop. 83 118 — 12 A2

Great Britain

London 30 mi – Aylesbury 16 mi – Luton 10 mi – Northampton 46 mi

Little Hay Golf Complex Bovingdon Box Lane, ☎ (01442) 833 798

Boxmoor 18 Box Lane, ☎ (01442) 242 434

Whipsnade Wild Animal Park★

Restaurant 65 — VISA MC AE

65 High St (Old Town) ✉ HP1 5AL – ☎ (01442) 239 010 – www.restaurant65.co.uk – Closed 1 week January, Saturday lunch, Sunday dinner and Monday

Rest – *(booking advisable)* Menu £ 20/28

◆ Charming 17C building in old part of town; snug restaurant with white walls, black beams and homely, relaxed feel. Well executed modern British cooking with a classical base.

at Frithsden **Northwest : 4.5 mi by A 4146 – ✉ Hemel Hempstead**

The Alford Arms

✉ HP1 3DD – ✆ (01442) 864 480 – www.alfordarmsfrithsden.co.uk – Closed 25-26 December

Rest – Carte £ 20/27

◆ Attractive Victorian pub overlooking the village green. Traditional British menu follows the seasons: salads and fish in summer, game and comfort dishes in winter. Good classical desserts.

HEMINGFORD GREY – Cambs. – 504 T27 – see Huntingdon

HENFIELD – West Sussex – 504 T31 – pop. 4 527 **7** D2

London 47 mi – Brighton 10 mi – Worthing 11 mi

The Ginger Fox

Albourne, Southwest 3 mi on A281 ✉ BN6 9EA – ✆ (01273) 857 888 – www.gingermanrestaurants.com – Closed 25 December

Rest – Carte £ 20/30

◆ Characterful 17C inn with thatched roof, wooden beams and open fires. Cooking is skilful, with a real country flavour. Tasty, unfussy dishes and popular vegetarian tasting plate. Favoured by families, with children's menu, spacious garden and slides.

at Wineham **Northeast : 3.5 mi by A 281 and B 2116 on Wineham Lane – ✉ Henfield**

Frylands without rest

West : 0.25 mi taking left turn at telephone box ✉ BN5 9BP – ✆ (01403) 710 214 – www.frylands.co.uk – Closed 20 December-1 January and 3-10 July

3 rm – †£ 38/40 ††£ 60/65

◆ Part Elizabethan farmhouse in 250 acres with woodlands and fishing. Fresh home-cooked breakfasts. Bedrooms exude charm and character with homely furnishings and original features. Charming owner.

HENLADE – Somerset – see Taunton

HENLEY – West Sussex – see Midhurst

HENLEY-IN-ARDEN – Warwickshire – 503 O27 – pop. 2 797 **19** C3

London 104 mi – Birmingham 15 mi – Stratford-upon-Avon 8 mi – Warwick 8 mi

The Crabmill

Claverdon, East : 1 mi on A 4189 ✉ B95 5EE – ✆ (01926) 843 342 – www.thecrabmill.co.uk – Closed Sunday dinner

Rest – *(booking essential)* Carte £ 25/30

◆ Characterful timbered pub with various beamed rooms and peaceful terrace and garden. Good-sized menu offers modern Mediterranean-influenced dishes, with lighter bites available during the day.

at Tanworth-in-Arden **Northwest : 4.5 mi by A 3400 on Tanworth Rd – ✉ Henley-In-Arden**

The Bell Inn with rm

The Green ✉ B94 5AL – ✆ (01564) 742 212 – www.thebellattanworthinarden.co.uk

9 rm – †£ 41/76 ††£ 72/122 **Rest** – Carte £ 19/26

◆ Traditional-looking whitewashed pub concealing a small shop and post office. Exposed beams and wood floors are offset by bold décor and contemporary furnishings. Classical pub cooking, with fish a particular strength. Bedrooms continue the stylish, modern theme.

ENGLAND

HENLEY-ON-THAMES – Oxfordshire – **504** R29 – pop. 10 513 — **11** C3

London 40 mi – Oxford 23 mi – Reading 9 mi

to Reading (Salter Bros. Ltd) (summer only) daily (2 h 15 mn) – to Marlow (Salter Bros. Ltd) (summer only) daily (2 h 15 mn)

Town Hall, Market Place ✆ (01491) 578034, info@henleytowncouncil.gov.uk

Huntercombe Nuffield, ✆ (01491) 641 207

Hotel du Vin
rm, rm, VISA MC AE
New St ✉ RG9 2BP – ✆ (01491) 848 400 – www.hotelduvin.com
38 rm – †£ 125/195 ††£ 125/195, ☕ £ 13.95 – 2 suites
Rest *Bistro* – Carte £ 23/34
◆ Former brewery premises; now an easy-going, designer styled boutique hotel. Stunning rooms: studios with outdoor terrace and bath tub or airy doubles with great amenities. Bistro with resolutely Gallic style, French influenced menus and excellent wine list.

Falaise House without rest
VISA MC
37 Market Pl ✉ RG9 2AA – ✆ (01491) 573 388 – www.falaisehouse.com
6 rm ☕ – †£ 85 ††£ 115
◆ Very well located 18C house boasting stylish, luxury bedrooms; some with chaises longues. Good breakfast choice includes homemade preserves and smoked salmon, cooked to order.

Luscombes at The Golden Ball
VISA MC
Lower Assendon, Northwest : 0.75 mi by A 4130 on B 480 ✉ RG9 6AH – ✆ (01491) 574 157 – www.luscombes.co.uk
Rest – Carte £ 24/44
◆ Cosy restaurant, popular with locals, serving modern menu of tasty, simply cooked dishes. Smiley, attentive service. Lighter lunches, homemade preserves and afternoon cream teas.

Three Tuns
VISA MC
5 Market Pl. ✉ RG9 2AA – ✆ (01491) 411 588 – www.thethreetunshenley.com – Closed,1 week August, Christmas, Sunday, Monday and bank holidays
Rest – Carte £ 26/36
◆ Characterful market place pub with cosy, wood-panelled front bar. Restaurant-style dishes show classic roots, with a touch of modernity. Superb value two course lunch menu.

at Lower Shiplake South : 2 mi by A 4155 – ✉ Henley-On-Thames

Crowsley House
VISA MC
Crowsley Rd ✉ RG9 3JT – ✆ (01189) 406 708 – www.crowsleyhouse.co.uk
3 rm ☕ – †£ 75/95 ††£ 95/125
Rest – Menu £ 25
◆ Discreet guest house in secluded conservation area; two lively cats come as part of the family. Pristine, well-equipped bedrooms boast contemporary bathrooms. Breakfast is an extensive continental affair, with freshly baked pastries. Gourmet meals by arrangement.

at Shiplake Row 3.5mi South by A 4155 on Peppard and Binfield Heath rd

Orwells
VISA MC
✉ RG9 4DP – ✆ (01189) 403 673 – www.orwellsatshiplake.co.uk – Closed 5 days Christmas-New Year, 2 weeks early January, 2 weeks early September, Sunday dinner and Monday
Rest – Menu £ 16 (Tuesday-Thursday) – Carte £ 20/38
Rest *The Room* – (dinner only) – Carte £ 38/48
◆ Dating from the 18C and named after George Orwell, who spent his childhood in the area. Contemporary interior divided into three: the bar, conservatory and 'fine dining' room. Modern cooking, with a 'use local' ethos. More elaborate dishes at dinner in The Room.

ENGLAND

London 133 mi – Birmingham 51 mi – Cardiff 56 mi
1 King St ✆ (01432) 268430, tic-hereford@herefordshire.gov.uk
Raven's Causeway Wormsley, ✆ (01432) 830 219
Belmont Lodge Belmont Ruckhall Lane, ✆ (01432) 352 666
Hereford Municipal Holmer Rd, ✆ (01432) 344 376
Burghill Valley Burghill Tillington Rd, ✆ (01432) 760 456
City★ - Cathedral★★ (Mappa Mundi★) A **A** – Old House★ A **B**
Kilpeck (Church of SS. Mary and David★★) SW : 8 mi by A 465 B

Brandon Lodge without rest
Ross Rd, South : 1.75 mi on A 49 ✉ HR2 8BH – ✆ (01432) 355 621 – www.brandonlodge.co.uk
10 rm – †£ 45/50 ††£ 60/70
◆ A good value hotel with 18C origins, charmingly overseen by owner. Bedrooms in main building or adjacent annexe: all are spacious, boasting a cheery warmth and good facilities.

Stewing Pot VISA
17 Church St ✉ HR1 2LR – ✆ (01432) 265 233 – www.stewingpot.co.uk – Closed 25-26 December, Sunday and Monday Aa
Rest – *(booking essential at dinner)* Menu £ 18/23 – Carte £ 24/34
◆ Neighbourhood eatery tucked away down a narrow street, with plain décor and simple, homely furnishings. Taking on a bistro style, cooking is classical and reliably tasty.

at Winforton Northwest : 15 mi on A 438 – ✉ Hereford

Winforton Court without rest
✉ HR3 6EA – ✆ (01544) 328 498 – www.winfortoncourt.co.uk – Closed 23-28 December
3 rm – †£ 70 ††£ 85/105
◆ Wonderfully characterful 16C house used as a circuit court by "Hanging" Judge Jeffries. Exudes personality with exposed beams, thick walls and uneven floors. Rustic bedrooms.

ENGLAND

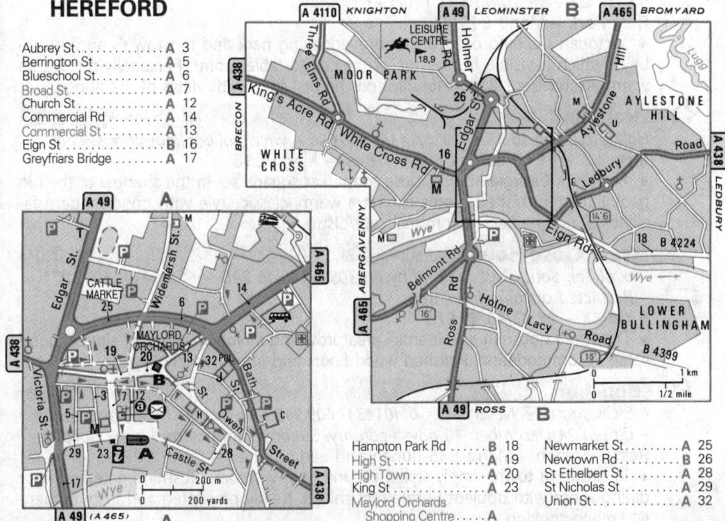

HERM – C.I. – 503 P33 – see Channel Islands

HERSTMONCEUX – East Sussex – 504 U31 – pop. 3 898 — 8 B3

London 63 mi – Eastbourne 12 mi – Hastings 14 mi – Lewes 16 mi

XXX Sundial

Gardner St ✉ BN27 4LA – ✆ (01323) 832 217 – www.sundialrestaurant.co.uk – Closed 7-14 January, Sunday dinner and Monday

Rest – French – Menu £ 24 – Carte £ 35/48

◆ Converted 16C cottage retaining leaded windows and beamed ceiling. Comfy dining room. Seasonal menus offer rich, classical French dishes; the chateaubriand for two must be booked in advance.

at Wartling Southeast : 3.75 mi by A 271 on Wartling rd – ✉ Herstmonceux

Wartling Place

✉ BN27 1RY – ✆ (01323) 832 590 – www.wartlingplace.co.uk

4 rm – ♦£ 78/85 ♦♦£ 125/160 **Rest** – Menu £ 35

◆ Part Georgian house with three acres of gardens, sited in the village. Pleasantly furnished, with some antiques; two of the rooms have four-poster beds. Breakfast is taken communally at an antique table in the dining room. Dinner by arrangement.

HESSLE – Kingston-upon-Hull – 502 S22 – see Kingston-upon-Hull

HETTON – North Yorkshire – 502 N21 – see Skipton

HEXHAM – Northumberland – 501 N19 – pop. 10 682 Great Britain — 24 A2

London 304 mi – Carlisle 37 mi – Newcastle upon Tyne 21 mi

Wentworth Car Park ✆ (01434) 652220

Spital Park, ✆ (01434) 603 072

De Vere Slaley Hall Slaley, ✆ (01434) 673 154

Tynedale Tyne Green, ✆ (01434) 608 154

Abbey★ (Saxon Crypt★★, Leschman chantry★)

Hadrian's Wall★★, N : 4.5 mi by A 6079. Housesteads★★, NW : 12.5 mi by A 6079 and B 6318

Beaumont

Beaumont St ✉ NE46 3LT – ✆ (01434) 602 331 – www.bw-beaumonthotel.co.uk

35 rm – ♦£ 70/90 ♦♦£ 110/190

Rest *Park* – Menu £ 13/23

◆ Victorian building of local stone overlooking park and the town's ancient abbey - which is visible from some of the comfortable rooms. Personally run with a warm atmosphere. Park restaurant on the first floor with views of the abbey.

Hallbank

Hallgate ✉ NE46 1XA – ✆ (01434) 606 656 – www.hallbankguesthouse.com

8 rm – ♦£ 60/80 ♦♦£ 80/90 **Rest** – Menu £ 18

◆ Red-brick Georgian house close to market square, set in the shadow of the old gaol. Fully refurbished rooms exhibit a warm, classic style with good modern facilities. Dine in adjacent, informal café/bistro.

West Close House without rest

Hextol Ter, Southwest : 0.5 mi by B 6305 ✉ NE46 2AD – ✆ (01434) 603 307 – Restricted opening in winter.

3 rm – ♦£ 32/45 ♦♦£ 65

◆ Detached house in a residential area providing a high standard of simple, good value accommodation. Polished wood floors and immaculately kept.

XX Bouchon

4-6 Gilesgate ✉ NE46 3NJ – ✆ (01434) 609 943 – www.bouchonbistrot.co.uk – Closed 24 December, 10 days February, Sunday, Monday and bank holidays

Rest – French – Menu £ 15 (lunch and early dinner) – Carte £ 22/33

◆ In centre of town: simply styled ground floor with bar; plush intimate first floor dining room with opulent purple furnishings. Neatly presented and tasty authentic French cooking.

The Rat Inn

Anick, Northeast : 1.45 mi signposted off A 69 roundabout ✉ NE46 4LN – ☎ (01434) 602 814 – www.theratinn.com – Closed Sunday dinner and Monday

Rest – Carte £ 18/30

♦ Traditional pub with an open range and pleasant Tyne Valley views. Daily changing blackboard menu features wholesome pub classics, as well as some more ambitious dishes – including some for two.

at Slaley Southeast : 5.5 mi by B 6306 – ✉ Hexham

Slaley Hall

Southeast : 2.25 mi ✉ NE47 0BY – ☎ (01434) 673 350 – www.devere.co.uk

133 rm – †£ 79/199 ††£ 149/199 – 9 suites

Rest *Duke's Grill* – *(dinner only and Sunday lunch)* Menu £ 25 – Carte £ 25/46

Rest *Hadrian's Brasserie* – *(Closed Sunday dinner)* Carte £ 28/39

Rest *Claret Jug* – *(Easter - October)* Carte £ 23/31

♦ Spacious countryside leisure oasis boasting numerous recreational facilities, including a spa and two golf courses. Unwind in stylish guest areas and contemporary bedrooms; a few remain in classic style. Dishes from Josper Grill in opulent Duke's. Modern brasserie fare in Hadrian's. British classics in The Claret Jug.

at Haydon Bridge West : 7.5 mi on A 69 – ✉ Hexham

Langley Castle

Langley-on-Tyne, South : 2 mi by A 69 on A 686 ✉ NE47 5LU – ☎ (01434) 688 888 – www.langleycastle.com

27 rm – †£ 115 ††£ 165 **Rest** – Menu £ 20/40

♦ Stunning 14C castle in 12 acres. Stone walls, tapestries and heraldic shields give baronial feel. Luxurious bedrooms exhibit period features; some have window seats or four-posters. Stable rooms are simpler. Dining room offers adventurous, seasonally influenced menu.

HEYTESBURY – Wilts. – 503 N30 – see Warminster

HIGH WYCOMBE – Buckinghamshire – 504 R29 – pop. 77 178 11 C2

Great Britain

London 34 mi – Aylesbury 17 mi – Oxford 26 mi – Reading 18 mi

The Library, 5 Eden Place ☎ (01494) 421892, tourism_enquiries@wycombe.gov.uk

Hazlemere G & C.C. Hazlemere Penn Rd, ☎ (01494) 719 300

Wycombe Heights Loudwater Rayners Ave, ☎ (01494) 816 686

Chiltern Hills★

Eat-Thai

14-15 Easton St ✉ HP11 1NT – ☎ (01494) 532 888 – www.eat-thai.co.uk

Rest – Thai – Menu £ 12/25 – Carte £ 23/31

♦ Modern restaurant with wood floors and well-spaced tables. Three distinct areas serving fresh, tasty dishes with ingredients flown regularly from Thailand. Attentive service.

HIGHCLERE – Hampshire – 503 P29 – pop. 2 409 – ✉ Newbury 6 B1

London 69 mi – Newbury 5 mi – Reading 25 mi

The Yew Tree with rm

Hollington Cross, Andover Rd., South : 1 mi on A 343 ✉ RG20 9SE – ☎ (01635) 253 360 – www.theyewtree.net – Closed dinner 25-26 December

7 rm – †£ 110 ††£ 110

Rest – Menu £ 16 (Sunday supper)/23 – Carte £ 30/50

♦ Characterful 17C whitewashed inn with wood-furnished terrace, rustic beamed interior, three linen-laid dining rooms and a marble-topped bar. Classical cooking mixes pub and restaurant style dishes. Service is structured. Smart, modern bedrooms boast wet rooms.

HIGHCLIFFE - Dorset - 503 O31 4 D3

London 112 mi - Bournemouth 10 mi - Salisbury 21 mi - Southampton 26 mi

Lord Bute

179-185 Lymington Rd ✉ BH23 4JS - ✆ (01425) 278 884 - www.lordbute.co.uk
11 rm - †£ 78/98 ††£ 115 - 2 suites
Rest - *(Closed Sunday dinner and Monday)* Menu £ 17/33 **s** - Carte £ 27/37 **s**

◆ Modern, purpose-built property with a warm, contemporary style. Light, airy conservatory lounge with terrace. Comfortable, well-appointed bedrooms boast bold colours, safes and spa baths. Smart, formal restaurant hosts occasional cabaret or jazz evenings.

HIGH CROSBY - Cumbria - see Carlisle

HIGHER BURWARDSLEY - Ches. - see Tattenhall

HINDON - Wiltshire - 503 N30 - pop. 493 4 C2

London 103 mi - Shaftesbury 7 mi - Warminster 10 mi

The Lamb Inn with rm

High St ✉ SP3 6DP - ✆ (01747) 820 573 - www.lambathindon.co.uk
19 rm - †£ 50/90 ††£ 80/115 **Rest** - Carte £ 19/29

◆ Scottish-themed 13C inn with cosy, characterful rooms featuring deep red walls, inglenook fireplaces and antique furniture. Appealing menu blends local produce and traditional Scottish dishes with a few Mediterranean specials. Smart bedrooms; some four-posters.

ENGLAND

HINDRINGHAM - Norfolk 15 C1

London 118 mi - Fakenham 8 mi - Holt 8 mi

Field House without rest

Moorgate Rd ✉ NR21 0PT - ✆ (01328) 878 726 - www.fieldhousehindringham.co.uk - Closed 20 December to 1 February
3 rm - †£ 70/75 ††£ 90/100

◆ Well-kept flint stone house with pretty garden and summer house. Pristine lounge with books and magazines. Extensive breakfast menus. Carefully co-ordinated rooms with extras.

HINTLESHAM - Suffolk - 504 X27 - see Ipswich

HINTON ST GEORGE - Somerset 3 B3

London 138 mi - Taunton 21 mi - Weymouth 41 mi - Yeovil 13 mi

Lord Poulett Arms with rm

High St ✉ TA17 8SE - ✆ (01460) 73 149 - www.lordpoulettarms.com - Closed 25-26 December and 1 January
4 rm - †£ 65 ††£ 95 **Rest** - Carte £ 22/32

◆ Charming pub with lavender-framed terrace, boules pitch, secret garden and detailed, candlelit country interior. Local, seasonal produce informs an interesting menu that's rooted firmly in the Med. Smart, stylish bedrooms boast roll-top or slipper baths.

HISTON - Cambs. - 504 U27 - see Cambridge

HOCKLEY HEATH - West Midlands - 503 O26 - pop. 1 525 - ✉ Solihull 19 C2

London 117 mi - Birmingham 11 mi - Coventry 17 mi

Nuthurst Grange Country House

Nuthurst Grange Lane, South : 0.75 mi by A 3400 ✉ B94 5NL - ✆ (01564) 783 972 - www.nuthurst-grange.com
19 rm - †£ 100/129 ††£ 125/165
Rest *Kingswood* - see restaurant listing

◆ Part Edwardian manor house, overlooking M40 and convenient for Birmingham Airport. Classic English country décor throughout. Spacious rooms with high level of comfort.

XXX **Kingswood** – at Nuthurst Grange Country House Hotel
Nuthurst Grange Ln, South : 0.75 mi by A 3400 ✉ B94 5NL – ✆ (01564) 783 972 – www.nuthurst-grange.co.uk
Rest – *(closed Sunday dinner)* Menu £ 20/30 – Carte £ 30/39
◆ Thoroughly traditional tone in the dining room's décor which contributes to a formal ambience. Seasonal menu draws on British and French traditions.

HOLBEACH – Lincolnshire – 502 U25 – pop. 7 247 — 17 D2

London 117 mi – Kingston-upon-Hull 81 mi – Norwich 62 mi – Nottingham 60 mi

Pipwell Manor without rest
Washway Rd, Saracen's Head, Northwest : 1.5 mi by A 17 ✉ PE12 8AY – ✆ (01406) 423 119
4 rm – †£ 40 ††£ 60
◆ Charming Georgian manor built on the site of an old Cistercian Grange, close to the solitude of the Wash. Garden railway for train spotters. Traditional country style bedrooms display fresh, modern touches. Complimentary tea and cake served on arrival.

HOLFORD – Somerset – 503 K30 – pop. 307 – ✉ Bridgwater — 3 B2

Great Britain

London 171 mi – Bristol 48 mi – Minehead 15 mi – Taunton 22 mi
Stogursey Priory Church★★, W : 4.5 mi

Combe House
Southwest : 0.75 mi by Youth Hostel rd ✉ TA5 1RZ – ✆ (01278) 741 382 – www.combehouse.co.uk
19 rm – †£ 85/115 ††£ 165/175
Rest – Menu £ 20 (lunch) – Carte dinner £ 31/39
◆ Smart country house with lovely garden, in a secluded wooded valley. Stylish, modern interior boasts a pleasant spa. Bright bedrooms feature contemporary fabrics and white furniture. Split-level restaurant offers classical cooking with a modern edge.

HOLKHAM – Norfolk – 504 W25 — 15 C1

London 124 mi – King's Lynn 32 mi – Norwich 39 mi

The Victoria
Park Rd. ✉ NR23 1RG – ✆ (01328) 711 008 – www.holkham.co.uk
10 rm – †£ 90/240 ††£ 90/240
Rest *The Restaurant* – see restaurant listing
◆ Extended flint farmhouse boasting country outlook and large lawned gardens. Characterful, shabby-chic interior with individually styled bedrooms; some furniture from Indian sub-continent.

XX **The Restaurant** – at The Victoria Hotel
Park Rd ✉ NR23 1RG – ✆ (01328) 711 008 – www.holkham.co.uk
Rest – Menu £ 23 (lunch) – Carte £ 23/39
◆ Choice of 2 colonial-style dining rooms, conservatory or wood-furnished terrace. Seasonally evolving menus have unfussy, brasserie style: local produce to the fore. Friendly, attentive service.

HOLMFIRTH – West Yorkshire – 502 O23 – pop. 21 979 — 22 B3

London 187 mi – Leeds 35 mi – Sheffield 32 mi – Manchester 25 mi

Sunnybank without rest
78 Upperthong Ln, West : 0.5 mi by A6024 ✉ HD9 3BQ – ✆ (01484) 684 857 – www.sunnybankguesthouse.co.uk
5 rm – †£ 70/80 ††£ 90/100
◆ Attractive Victorian house in mature gardens with smart bedrooms, good facilities and a modern edge; 2 rooms have great country views. Breakfast room boasts cushioned window seats.

ENGLAND

The Butchers Arms
38 Towngate, East : 1 mi by B 6106 ✉ HD9 1TE – ✆ (01484) 682 361 – www.thebutchersarms.co.uk – Closed 2 weeks in January
Rest – *(booking essential)* Menu £ 15 (lunch) – Carte £ 15/42
◆ Stone inn with delightful terraces, hidden on the fringes of a sleepy hamlet. A huge array of menus offer robust, country dishes. All produce is from within 75 miles; most from even closer.

HOLT – Norfolk – 504 X25 – pop. 3 550 **15** C1

London 124 mi – King's Lynn 34 mi – Norwich 22 mi

Byfords
Shirehall Plain ✉ NR25 6BG – ✆ (01263) 711 400 – www.byfords.org.uk
16 rm – 🚹£ 105/115 🚹🚹£ 140/198 **Rest** – Carte £ 22/29
◆ Flint-fronted Grade II listed house that boasts something different: a well-stocked deli; rustic cellar café; and stunning rooms, with great bathrooms and under-floor heating.

Plantation House without rest
Old Cromer Rd, East 1.25 mi by A148 on Kelling Hospital rd ✉ NR25 6AJ – ✆ (01263) 710 121 – www.plantation-house.net – Closed 20 October-5 November and 22-31 December
4 rm – 🚹£ 62/72 🚹🚹£ 92
◆ Brick-built cottage just out of town, in exceptional mature gardens. Colonial style with heavy fabrics and objets d'art. Individually styled bedrooms with extra touches; most overlook garden.

HOLT – Wilts. – 503 – see Bradford-on-Avon

HONITON – Devon – 503 K31 – pop. 11 213 **2** D2

London 186 mi – Exeter 17 mi – Southampton 93 mi – Taunton 18 mi

Lace Walk Car Park ✆ (01404) 43716, honitontic@btconnect.com

All Hallows Museum★ **AC**

Ottery St Mary★ (St Mary's★) SW : 5 mi by A 30 and B 3177. Faraway Countryside Park (≤★) **AC**, SE : 6.5 mi by A 375 and B 3174

The Holt
178 High St ✉ EX14 1LA – ✆ (01404) 47 707 – www.theholt-honiton.com – Closed 25-26 December, Sunday and Monday
Rest – Carte £ 20/27
◆ Rustic family-run pub providing a 'distinctive and sustainable taste of Devon'. Regularly changing menu of regional and homemade produce; local ales from the family brewery.

The Railway
Queen St ✉ EX14 1HE – ✆ (01404) 47 976 – www.therailwayhoniton.co.uk – Closed Sunday and Monday
Rest – Carte £ 24/29
◆ Smart, modern town centre pub offering authentic Italian cooking at affordable prices, including homemade pasta, brick-fired pizzas and steaks. Eclectic wine list. Weekly film club.

at Gittisham Southwest : 3 mi by A 30 – ✉ Honiton

Combe House
✉ EX14 3AD – ✆ (01404) 540 400 – www.combehousedevon.com – Closed last 2 weeks January
13 rm – 🚹£ 159/179 🚹🚹£ 179/199 – 3 suites
Rest – *(booking essential for non-residents)* Menu £ 35/45
◆ Listed Elizabethan mansion set in glorious Devon countryside. Impressive Great Hall. Individually designed, stylish bedrooms with fine antiques and roaring fires. Unfussy cooking makes good use of local produce. Friendly service.

ENGLAND

HOOK – Hampshire – 504 R30 – pop. 6 471 – ✉ Basingstoke 6 B1

London 47 mi – Oxford 39 mi – Reading 13 mi – Southampton 31 mi

Tylney Hall

Rotherwick , Northwest : 2.5 mi by A30 and Newnham rd on Ridge Ln
✉ RG27 9AZ – ☎ (01256) 764 881 – www.tylneyhall.co.uk
103 rm – †£ 180 ††£ 210/280 – 9 suites
Rest *Oak Room* – Menu £ 25/38 – Carte £ 38/48
◆ Grand and beautifully restored 19C mansion in delightful, extensive Gertrude Jekyll gardens. Country house rooms, some with private conservatories or suites over two floors. Classically English dining room with oak panelling and garden views.

The Hogget

London Rd, at the junction of A 30 and A 287 ✉ RG27 9JJ – ☎ (01256) 763 009 – www.hogget.co.uk – Closed 25-26 December and Sunday dinner
Rest – Carte £ 23/28
◆ Located at junction of A30 and A287. Wholesome, honest cooking; sensibly priced dishes, made using local produce: pie and mash or steak and chips through to crab cake or calves liver.

HOPE – Derbyshire – 502 O23 – ✉ Sheffield 16 A1

London 180 mi – Derby 50 mi – Manchester 31 mi – Sheffield 15 mi

Losehill House

Lose Hill Ln, Edale Rd, North : 1 mi by Edale Rd ✉ S33 6AF – ☎ (01433) 621 219 – www.losehillhouse.co.uk
21 rm – †£ 130/165 ††£ 150/250 **Rest** – Menu £ 15/35
◆ Comfortable, well-kept hotel with a bright, airy, modern feel. Open-plan lounge and bar. Small pool, sauna and outdoor hot tub. Bedrooms all have a view. Formally laid restaurant with superb views up to Win Hill; modern-style dishes, with cheese a speciality.

Underleigh House without rest

Losehill Ln, Hope Valley, North : 1 mi by Edale Rd ✉ S33 6AF – ☎ (01433) 621 372 – www.underleighhouse.co.uk – Closed Christmas, New Year and January
5 rm – †£ 70 ††£ 90/105
◆ Converted Victorian property, rurally located and personally run; well situated for the Peak District. Countryside views and a welcoming country ambience.

HORLEY – Surrey – 504 T30 – pop. 22 582 7 D2

London 27 mi – Brighton 26 mi – Royal Tunbridge Wells 22 mi

Langshott Manor

Langshott, North : 0.5 mi by A 23 turning right at Chequers H. onto Ladbroke Rd ✉ RH6 9LN – ☎ (01293) 786 680 – www.langshottmanor.com
21 rm – †£ 135/230 ††£ 179/340 – 1 suite
Rest *Mulberry* – *(booking essential)* Menu £ 21 (lunch)/44 – Carte £ 20/55
◆ Part Elizabethan manor house set amidst gardens of roses, vines and ponds. For centuries the home of aristocrats, now a refined and harmonious country house hotel. Formal dining room offers intimate ambience.

HORNCASTLE – Lincolnshire – 502 T24 – pop. 6 090 17 C1

London 143 mi – Lincoln 22 mi – Nottingham 62 mi
The Library, Wharf Rd ☎ (01507) 601111, horncastleinfo@e-lindsey.gov.uk

Magpies

71-75 East St ✉ LN9 6AA – ☎ (01507) 527 004 – Closed 27 December-15 January, Monday and Tuesday
Rest – Menu £ 40 (dinner) – Carte lunch £ 29/32
◆ Renowned, family-run restaurant in a converted 18C house. Snug, comfortable, beamed interior. Local ingredients are used in accomplished, refined dishes that take on a modern style.

HORNDON-ON-THE-HILL – Thurrock – 504 V29 – pop. 1 612 13 C3

London 25 mi – Chelmsford 22 mi – Maidstone 34 mi – Southend-on-Sea 16 mi

The Bell with rm rm, VISA

High Rd ✉ SS17 8LD – ✆ (01375) 642 463 – www.bell-inn.co.uk – Closed 25-26 December and Bank Holiday Mondays

15 rm ☕ – 🚹£ 70/110 🚹🚹£ 70/119

Rest – Carte £ 22/33

◆ 15C coaching inn, run by the same family for 50 years. Cooking is a step above your usual pub fare, displaying classically based dishes with some modern touches. Pub bedrooms are styled after Victorian mistresses; those in Hill House display thoughtful extras.

HORNINGSEA – Cambs. – see Cambridge

HORNINGSHAM – Wiltshire – 504 N30 – see Warminster

HORN'S CROSS – Devon – 503 H31 – ✉ Bideford ▮ Great Britain 2 C1

London 222 mi – Barnstaple 15 mi – Exeter 46 mi

Clovelly★★, W : 6.5 mi on A 39 and B 3237 – Bideford : Bridge★★ - Burton Art Gallery★ **AC** - Lundy Island★★ (by ferry), NE : 7 mi on a 39 and B 3235 – Hartland : Hartland Church★ - Hartland Quay★ (✱★★) - Hartland Point ⋞★★★, W : 9 mi on A 39 and B 3248 – Great Torrington (Dartington Crystal★ **AC**), SE : 15 mi on A 39 and A 386 – Rosemoor★, SE : 16 mi on A 39, A 386 and B 3220

The Roundhouse without rest VISA

West : 1 mi on A 39 ✉ EX39 5DN – ✆ (01237) 451 687 – www.the-round-house.co.uk

3 rm ☕ – 🚹£ 40/50 🚹🚹£ 60/65

◆ Located on site of 13C corn mill, this friendly guesthouse offers cream teas on arrival. Spacious lounge and good quality breakfasts. Comfy, clean, well-kept bedrooms.

HORRINGER – Suffolk – 504 W27 – see Bury St Edmunds

HORSHAM – West Sussex – 504 T30 – pop. 47 804 7 D2

London 39 mi – Brighton 23 mi – Guildford 20 mi – Lewes 25 mi

9 Causeway ✆ (01403) 211661, tourist.information@horsham.gov.uk

Mannings Heath Fullers, Hammerpond Rd, Mannings Heath, ✆(01403) 210 228

South Lodge VISA

Brighton Rd, Lower Beeding, Southeast : 5 mi on A 281 ✉ RH13 6PS – ✆ (01403) 891 711 – www.exclusivehotels.co.uk

85 rm – 🚹£ 250 🚹🚹£ 250, ☕ £ 16 – 4 suites

Rest *Camellia Country Kitchen* – *(booking essential for non-residents)* Menu £ 20 (lunch) – Carte £ 33/53

Rest *The Pass* – *(closed Monday-Tuesday)* Menu £ 28/60

◆ Victorian mansion in 93 acres, with period furnishings, heavy panelled walls and corporate feel. Traditional bedrooms in main house; more contemporary rooms in wing – some suites have jacuzzis/terraces. Informal dining with South Downs views in Camellia. Live kitchen action and elaborate, intricate cooking in The Pass.

Restaurant Tristan VISA

Stans Way, off East St ✉ RH12 1HU – ✆ (01403) 255 688 – www.restauranttristan.co.uk – Closed 25-31 December, 1-7 January, 2 weeks late July-early August, Sunday and Monday

Rest – Menu £ 17/37

◆ First floor restaurant in characterful 16C beamed house. Cooking is seasonal but also elaborate in style and the kitchen is a fan of modern techniques. Service is smooth and effective.

ENGLAND

at Rowhook **Northwest : 4 mi by A 264 and A 281 off A 29 – ✉ Horsham**

The Chequers Inn
✉ RH12 3PY – ✆ (01403) 790 480
– Closed 25 December and Sunday dinner
Rest – Carte £ 25/35
♦ Part-15C inn with a charming open-fired, stone-floored bar and unusual corrugated dining room extension. Chef-owner grows, forages for or shoots the majority of his produce. Classical menus.

HOUGH-ON-THE-HILL – **Lincs. – see Grantham**

HOVE – **Brighton and Hove** – **504** T31 – **see Brighton and Hove**

HOVERINGHAM – **Nottinghamshire – pop. 308** **16** B2

London 135 mi – Birmingham 77 mi – Leeds 74 mi – Sheffield 57 mi

The Reindeer Inn
Main St ✉ NG14 7JR – ✆ (01159) 663 629
– www.thereindeerinn.com
– Closed 2 weeks mid May, Monday and lunch Tuesday
Rest – Menu £ 7 (lunch) – Carte £ 19/34
♦ Characterful country inn set next to a cricket pitch, with beams, open fire and a cosy, relaxed atmosphere. Popular with locals. Well-priced menus offer mainly classical dishes.

Don't confuse the couvert rating with the stars!
Couverts defines comfort and service, while stars are awarded for the best cuisine across all categories of comfort.

ENGLAND

HUDDERSFIELD – **West Yorkshire** – **502** O23 – **pop. 146 234** **22** B3

London 191 mi – Bradford 11 mi – Leeds 15 mi – Manchester 25 mi
Huddersfield Library, Princes Alexandra Walk ✆ (01484) 223200, huddersfield.information@kirklees.gov.uk
27 Bradley Park Bradley Rd, ✆ (01484) 223 772
18 Woodsome Hall Fenay Bridge, ✆ (01484) 602 971
18 Outlane Slack Lane, Off New Hey Rd, ✆ (01422) 374 762
18 Meltham Thick Hollins Hall, ✆ (01484) 850 227
18 Fixby Hall Lightridge Rd, ✆ (01484) 426 203
18 Crosland Heath Felks Stile Rd, ✆ (01484) 653 216

Plans pages 252, 253

at Thunder Bridge **Southeast : 5.75 mi by A 629 - B – ✉ Huddersfield**

Woodman Inn with rm
✉ HD8 0PX – ✆ (01484) 605 778
– www.woodman-inn.co.uk
– Closed dinner 25 December
12 rm – †£ 48 ††£ 60
Rest – Menu £ 16/19 – Carte approx. £ 29
♦ Traditional 19C pub set in a small hamlet in the valley. The classic British menus are extensive and change with the seasons. Lunch is simple and hearty, dinner more ambitious. Nearby cottage bedrooms are simple but well-kept.

Street	Grid	No.	Street	Grid	No.	Street	Grid	No.
Acre St	AB	3	Haeton Rd	B	48	Pike Low Rd	A	111
Armitage Rd	B	4	Halifax Old Rd	B	49	Quarmby Rd	A	114
Ashes Lane	B	6	Halifax Rd	B	51	Reinwood Rd	A	121
Balmoral Ave	B	7	Helme Lane	A	54	Rochdale Rd	A	123
Bolstermoor Rd	A	12	Hey Lane	B	55	St John's Rd	B	124
Brighouse Rd	AB	15	Huddersfield Rd	B	58	St Thomas Rd	B	126
Butternab Rd	B	16	Kaye Lane	B	61	Scar Lane	A	128
Church Lane	B	19	King's Mill ln	B	64	Scotgate Rd	B	129
Clough Rd	A	24	Knowl Rd	A	66	Slades Lane	A	130
Crosland Factory Lane	A	27	Leymoor Rd	A	72	Station Rd	A	138
Dog Kennel Bank	B	28	Lindley Moor	A	73	Swallow Lane	A	139
East St	A	31	Lockwood Rd	B	75	Udget St	A	142
Edgerton Rd	B	33	Lockwood Scar	B	76	Vicarage Rd	A	147
Fartown Green Rd	B	36	Longwood Gate	A	78	Waingate	B	150
Gillroyd Lane	A	40	Manchester Rd	B	84	Walpde Rd	B	154
Glead Rd	A	42	New Mill Rd	B	97	West Bourne Rd	B	157
Gleholt Rd	B	43	Norttgate	B	106	Whitehead Lane	B	160
Grimescar Rd	B	46	Pack Rd	B	109	Woodhead Rd	B	163

at Shelley Southeast : 6.25 mi by A 629 - B - on B 6116 – ✉ Huddersfield

Three Acres rest,

Roydhouse, Northeast : 1.5 mi on Flockton rd ✉ HD8 8LR
– ☎ (01484) 602 606 – www.3acres.com
– *Closed 1 January*
14 rm – £ 83/105 £ 125 – 2 suites
Rest – *(booking essential)* Carte £ 30/41

◆ Well-established stone inn, set in a pleasant rural location. Two smart meeting rooms. Bedrooms are warm, modern and comfortable; those in the annexe are the most spacious. Agreeably busy restaurant with open fires: fish dishes prepared at open seafood bar.

HUDDERSFIELD

Chapel Hill . . . . **C** 18
Claremont St . . . . **C** 21
Fitzwilliam St . . . . **C** 37
Gaswoors St . . . . **C** 39
Great Northern St . . . . **C** 45
Imperial Arcade . . . . **C** 60
Kingsgate Shopping Centre . . . . **C**
King St . . . . **C** 63
Lower Fitzwilliam St . . . . . **C** 79
Manchester Rd . . . . **C** 84
Market Pl. . . . . **C** 85
Market St . . . . **C** 87
Merton St. . . . . **C** 91
New North Rd . . . . **C** 100
Northumberland St . . . . . . **C** 105
Outcote Bank . . . . **C** 108
Piazza Shopping Centre . . **C**
Portland St . . . . **C** 112
Queen St . . . . **C** 115
Queen St South. . . . . **C** 117
Railway St . . . . **C** 120
St Peter's St. . . . . **C** 125
Springwood Ave . . . . **C** 136
Spring St . . . . **C** 133
Trinity St. . . . . **C** 141
Venn St. . . . . **C** 145
Victoria Lane . . . . **C** 148
Wakefield Rd. . . . . **C** 151
Water St. . . . . **C** 156

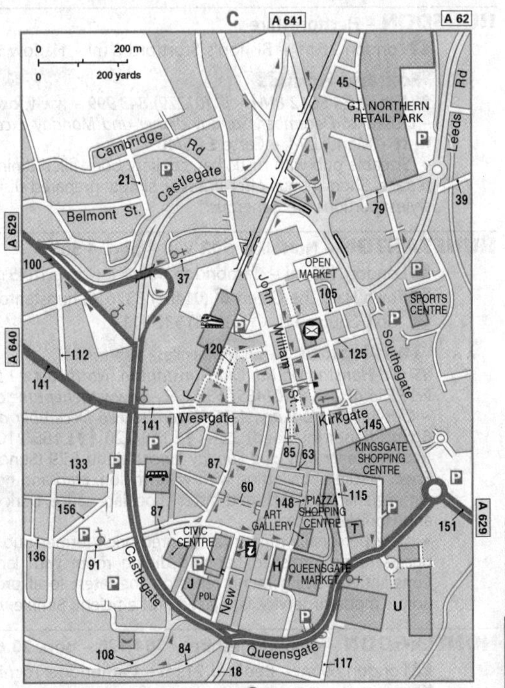

ENGLAND

HUNGERFORD – West Berkshire – **503** P29 – pop. 4 938 **10** A3

London 74 mi – Bristol 57 mi – Oxford 28 mi – Reading 26 mi

Savernake Forest★★ (Grand Avenue★★★), W : 7 mi by A 4 – Crofton Beam Engines★, SW : 8 mi by A 338 and minor roads

Fishers Farm without rest

Shefford Woodlands, North : 4 mi by A 4 and A 338 on B 4000
RG17 7AB – (01488) 648 466
– www.fishersfarm.co.uk
3 rm – £ 45/60 £ 65/90

◆ Attractive red-brick farmhouse in a rural spot on a working farm. Well-appointed sitting room. Breakfast served family style. Individually styled rooms with country views.

at Lambourn Woodlands North : 6 mi by A 338 on B 4000

XX Hare

RG17 7SD – (01488) 71 386
– www.theharerestaurant.co.uk
– Closed 2 weeks January-February, 2 weeks July-August, Sunday dinner and Monday
Rest – *(booking essential)* Menu £ 26 (lunch) – Carte (dinner) £ 30/42

◆ Attractive former pub with lawned garden, paved terrace, small lounge and three characterful dining rooms. Concise but interesting menus of flavoursome modern dishes crafted from local produce.

HUNSDON – Hertfordshire **12** B2

London 26 mi – Bishop's Stortford 8 mi – Harlow 7 mi

Fox and Hounds

2 High St ✉ SG12 8NH – ✆ (01279) 843 999 – www.foxandhounds-hunsdon.co.uk – Closed 26 December, Sunday dinner and Monday except bank holiday lunch

Rest – Menu £ 14 – Carte £ 25/40

◆ Sizeable pub with rustic bar, cookery book filled dining room, large garden and terrace. Short menus offer unfussy, simply prepared dishes in a range of different styles; portions are generous.

HUNSTANTON – Norfolk – **502** V25 – **pop. 4 505** **14** B1

London 120 mi – Cambridge 60 mi – Norwich 45 mi

Town Hall, The Green ✆ (01485) 532610, hunstanton.tic@west-norfolk.gov.uk

Golf Course Rd, ✆ (01485) 532 811

The Neptune (Kevin Mangeolles) with rm

85 Old Hunstanton Rd, Old Hunstanton, Northeast : 1.5 mi on A 149 ✉ PE36 6HZ – ✆ (01485) 532 122 – www.theneptune.co.uk – Closed 1-21 January, 1-15 November, 26 December and Monday

6 rm (dinner included) – £ 110/120 £ 185/210

Rest – *(dinner only and Sunday lunch)* Menu £ 29 (Sunday lunch) – Carte £ 44/51

Spec. Mackerel ballottine with watermelon, crab and horseradish salad. Hare loin with celeriac tart, ceps and bitter chocolate sauce. Dark chocolate mousse, praline and Horlicks ice cream.

◆ Very personally run, attractive, red-brick former pub. New England style inner boasts rattan-furnished bar and dining room with large nautical photographs. Constantly evolving menu relies on the latest local produce available. Presentation is modern; service is relaxed and efficient. Simple, comfortable bedrooms.

ENGLAND

HUNTINGDON – Cambridgeshire – **504** T26 – **pop. 20 600** **14** A2

London 69 mi – Bedford 21 mi – Cambridge 16 mi

Pathfinder HOuse, St. Mary's St ✆ (01480) 388588, hunts.tic@huntsdc.gov.uk

Hemingford Abbots Cambridge Rd, New Farm Lodge, ✆ (01480) 495 000

Old Bridge

1 High St ✉ PE29 3TQ – ✆ (01480) 424 300 – www.huntsbridge.com

24 rm – £ 99/115 £ 195

Rest ***Terrace*** – see restaurant listing

◆ Long-standing, family-owned riverside hotel with small wine shop in reception: one owner is a Master of Wine. Contemporary bedrooms feature plenty of fabrics and spacious bathrooms.

Terrace – at Old Bridge Hotel

1 High St ✉ PE29 3TQ – ✆ (01480) 424 300 – www.huntsbridge.com

Rest – Menu £ 20 (lunch) – Carte £ 32/39

◆ Choose between formal wood-panelled dining room and more casual conservatory with terrace. Menus change every two days and feature traditional dishes with some Mediterranean influences.

at Hemingford Grey Southeast : 5 mi by A 1198 off A 14 – ✉ Huntingdon

The Willow without rest

45 High St ✉ PE28 9BJ – ✆ (01480) 494 748 – www.thewillowguesthouse.co.uk – Closed 25-26 December, 31 December and 1 January

7 rm – £ 49/65 £ 75

◆ Simple, well-kept guesthouse with pleasant courtyard – set right next door to 'The Cock' pub. Comfortable, unfussy bedrooms; the two in the eaves are reached via an outside staircase.

The Cock

47 High St ✉ PE28 9BJ – ✆ (01480) 463 609 – www.cambscuisine.com

Rest – Menu £ 16 (lunch Monday-Saturday) – Carte £ 22/31

◆ Homely 17C country pub with spacious dining room, run by an experienced team. Tried-and-tested pub cooking offers good value lunches, daily fish specials and a mix and match sausage board.

HUNWORTH – Norfolk 15 C1

London 129 mi – Norwich 25 mi – East Dereham 17 mi – Taverham 19 mi

Hunny Bell

The Green ✉ NR24 2AA – ✆ (01263) 712 300 – www.hunnybell.co.uk – Closed 25 December

Rest – Carte £ 20/30

◆ Sympathetically renovated 18C whitewashed pub with smart country interior. Appealing menu of sophisticated pub classics crafted from local, seasonal produce; even the bar snacks are homemade.

HURLEY – Windsor and Maidenhead – pop. 1 712 11 C3

London 35 mi – Maidenhead 5 mi – Reading 18 mi

Black Boys Inn with rm

Henley Rd, Southwest : 1.5 mi on A 4130 ✉ SL6 5NQ – ✆ (01628) 824 212 – www.blackboysinn.co.uk – Closed Sunday dinner

8 rm – †£ 85 ††£ 85/120 **Rest** – Carte £ 26/38

◆ Rustic restaurant in 16C former pub with exposed beams and wood burning stove. Experienced owners are avid Francophiles and the concise, traditional French menu reflects this. Polite service. Clean, unfussy bedrooms with thoughtful extras such as reading books.

HURSTBOURNE TARRANT – Hampshire – 503 P30 – pop. 700 6 B1
– ✉ Andover

London 77 mi – Bristol 77 mi – Oxford 38 mi – Southampton 33 mi

Esseborne Manor

Northeast : 1.5 mi on A 343 ✉ SP11 0ER – ✆ (01264) 736 444 – www.esseborne-manor.co.uk

19 rm – †£ 110 ††£ 125/180

Rest – Menu £ 16/28 **s** – Carte (dinner) £ 19/28 **s**

◆ 100 year old country house in attractive grounds with herb garden. Smart, well-appointed bedrooms, some in the garden cottages. Ferndown room boasts a spa bath and private patio. Long, narrow dining room with large windows.

HURWORTH-ON-TEES – Darlington – 502 P20 – see Darlington

HUTTON-LE-HOLE – North Yorkshire – 502 R21 – pop. 162 23 C1

London 244 mi – Scarborough 27 mi – York 33 mi

Burnley House without rest

✉ YO62 6UA – ✆ (01751) 417 548 – www.burnleyhouse.co.uk – April-October

6 rm – †£ 55/65 ††£ 95/100

◆ Attractive part 16C, part Georgian house, Grade II listed in a picturesque Moors village. Brown trout in beck winding through garden. Simple, individually styled bedrooms.

HUTTON MAGNA – Durham – see Barnard Castle

ICKLESHAM – East Sussex – 504 V/W31 9 C3

London 66 mi – Brighton 42 mi – Hastings 7 mi

Manor Farm Oast

Windmill Ln, South : 0.5 mi ✉ TN36 4WL – ✆ (01424) 813 787 – www.manorfarmoast.co.uk – Closed Christmas-New Year and 9-16 January

3 rm – †£ 65/105 ††£ 105 **Rest** – Menu £ 30

◆ 19C former oast house retaining original features and surrounded by orchards. Welcoming beamed lounge with open fire. One of the comfy bedrooms is completely round. Home-cooked menus in circular dining room.

ILFRACOMBE – Devon – 503 H30 – pop. 10 508 Great Britain 2 C1

London 218 mi – Barnstaple 13 mi – Exeter 53 mi

Mortehoe★★ : St Mary's Church - Morte Point★, SW : 5.5 mi on B 3343 – Lundy Island★★ (by ferry). Braunton : St Brannock's Church★, Braunton Burrows★, S : 8 mi on A 361 – Barnstaple★ : Bridge★, S : 12 mi on A 3123, B 3230, A 39, A 361 and B 3233

ENGLAND

XX **Quay**
11 The Quay ✉ EX34 9EQ – ✆ (01271) 868 090 – www.11thequay.co.uk – 26 April to October
Rest – Menu £ 12/17 – Carte £ 25/37
◆ Smart, three-floored restaurant packed with Damien Hirst artwork and surprisingly set in an old fishing port. Same menu served throughout, with seafood and local produce to the fore.

ILKLEY – West Yorkshire – 502 O22 – pop. 13 472 — 22 B2

London 210 mi – Bradford 13 mi – Harrogate 17 mi – Leeds 16 mi
Town Hall, Station Rd ✆ (01943) 602319, ilkleytic@bradford.gov.uk
Myddleton, ✆ (01943) 607 277

XXX ✿ **Box Tree** (Simon Gueller)
37 Church St, on A 65 ✉ LS29 9DR – ✆ (01943) 608 484 – www.theboxtree.co.uk – Closed 1-7 January, Monday and Sunday dinner
Rest – *(dinner only - lunch Friday-Sunday)* Menu £ 30 (lunch)/35 – Carte £ 46/61
Spec. Roast scallops, cauliflower purée, Alsace bacon. Fillet of local beef, celeriac mash, bourgogne garnish, roast foie gras. Hot apricot soufflé, Grand Marnier sauce.
◆ Iconic restaurant in a charming 18C sandstone cottage. Plush sitting area with semi-gilded ceiling and fine antiques. Two main dining rooms laid with quality tableware. Confident, classical cooking is precise and skilful, with a strong French bias. Preparations are straightforward and let the ingredients shine through.

ILMINGTON – Warwickshire – 504 O27 Great Britain — 19 C3

London 91 mi – Birmingham 31 mi – Oxford 34 mi – Stratford-upon-Avon 9 mi
Hidcote Manor Garden★★, SW : 2 mi by minor rd – Chipping Campden★★, SW : 4 mi by minor rd

Folly Farm Cottage rm,
Back St ✉ CV36 4LJ – ✆ (01608) 682 425 – www.follyfarm.co.uk
3 rm – †£ 65 ††£ 130 **Rest** – Carte approx. £ 19
◆ Cosy, characterful cottage in small village, with friendly owners and lovely garden. Beams and heavy drapes abound. Some bedrooms have four-posters or whirlpool baths; two have small kitchens. Simple home-cooked dinners.

The Howard Arms with rm rest,
Lower Green ✉ CV36 4LT – ✆ (01608) 682 226 – www.howardarms.com
8 rm – †£ 90/110 ††£ 110/145 **Rest** – Carte £ 15/25
◆ Delightful 17C Cotswold stone inn, on a peaceful village green. Choice of beamed bar with inglenook fireplace, raised-level dining room and lovely terrace. Dishes are hearty and British-based. Warm, cosy bedrooms; those in the extension are more contemporary.

INGHAM – Norfolk — 15 D1

London 139 mi – Norwich 25 mi – Ipswich 65 mi – Lowestoft 30 mi

The Ingham Swan
Sea Palling Rd ✉ NR12 9AB – ✆ (01692) 581 099 – www.theinghamswan.co.uk – Closed Sunday dinner and Monday lunch
Rest – *(booking essential at dinner)* Menu £ 16/20 – Carte £ 20/38
◆ Cosy, attractive, thatched 14C pub in the shadow of an 11C church; equally characterful beamed interior. Quite complex dishes use plenty of ingredients, albeit in classic combinations.

INGLETON – North Yorkshire – 502 M21 – pop. 1 641 — 22 A2

– ✉ Carnforth (lancs.)
London 266 mi – Kendal 21 mi – Lancaster 18 mi – Leeds 53 mi
The Community Centre ✆ (015242) 41049, ingleton@ytbtic.co.uk

Riverside Lodge rm,
24 Main St ✉ LA6 3HJ – ✆ (015242) 41 359 – www.riversideingleton.co.uk – Closed 24-25 December
7 rm – †£ 47 ††£ 64 **Rest** – *(Closed Sunday)* Menu £ 17 (dinner) **s**
◆ Pleasant 19C house close to famous pot-holing caves. Informal gardens. Cosy sitting room and homely bedrooms. Conservatory dining room with great views across Yorkshire Dales.

IPSWICH

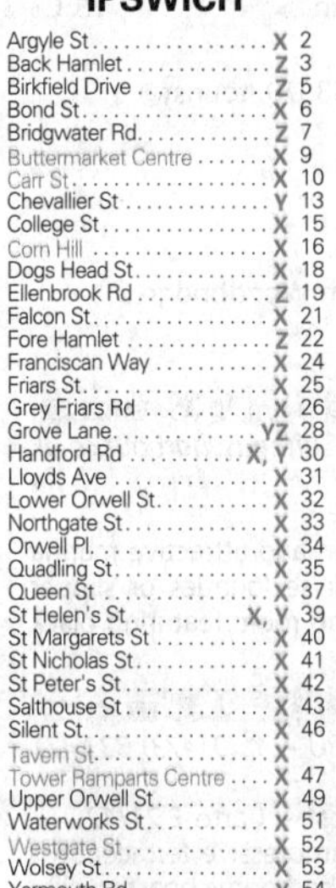

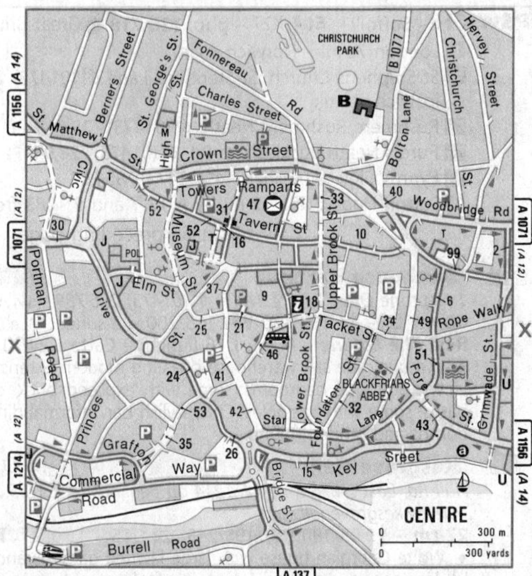

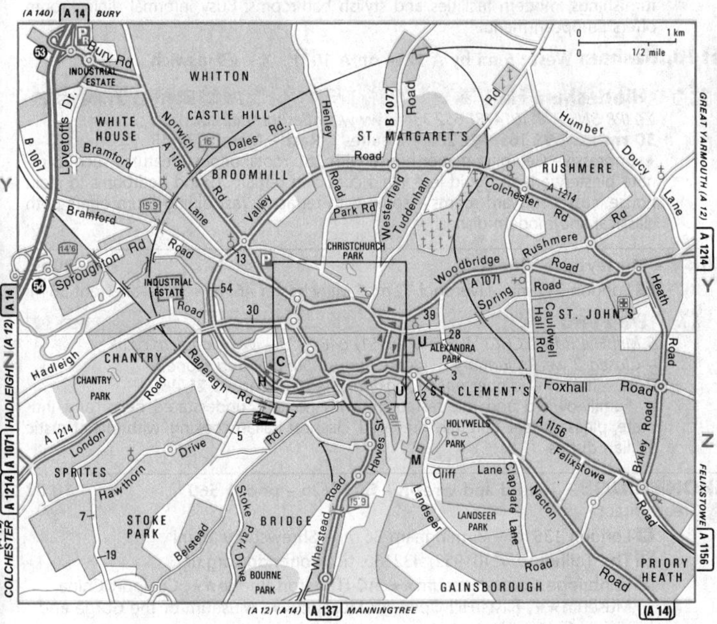

ENGLAND

IPSWICH – Suffolk – 504 X27 – pop. 138 718 Great Britain 15 C3

London 76 mi – Norwich 43 mi

St Stephens Church, St Stephens Lane (01473) 258070, tourist@ipswich.gov.uk

Rushmere Rushmere Heath, (01473) 725 648

Purdis Heath Bucklesham Rd, (01473) 728 941

Fynn Valley Witnesham, (01473) 785 267

Sutton Hoo★, NE : 12 mi by A 12 Y and B 1083 from Woodbridge

Plan on preceding page

Salthouse Harbour

1 Neptune Quay IP4 1AX – (01473) 226 789 – www.salthouseharbour.co.uk

68 rm – £ 100/170 £ 115/200 – 2 suites Xa

Rest *The Eaterie* – Menu £ 16 (lunch) – Carte £ 24/41

♦ Old quayside salt warehouse boasting modern extension and attractive marina views. Boutique bedrooms: some with exposed brick, chaise longues or slipper baths, some with balconies. Chic, stylish bar. Informal dining room featuring black booths and modern menu.

Kesgrave Hall

Hall Rd, East : 4.75 mi by A 1214 on Bealings rd IP5 2PU – (01473) 333 471 – www.kesgravehall.com

22 rm – £ 95/180 £ 195/245, £ 15 – 1 suite **Rest** – Carte £ 21/42

♦ White Georgian house with large lawned gardens and impressive terrace. Stylish lounges have relaxed, urban-chic feel. Large, luxurious bedrooms boast quality furnishings, modern facilities and stylish bathrooms. Busy informal dining room offers European menu.

ENGLAND

at Hintlesham West : 5 mi by A 1214 on A 1071 - Y – Ipswich

Hintlesham Hall

IP8 3NS – (01473) 652 334 – www.hintleshamhall.com

30 rm – £ 165 £ 205 – 3 suites **Rest** – Menu £ 34/45

♦ Impressive Georgian manor house with 16C roots; original features such as ornate plasterwork and gold leaf inlaid cornicing remain. Grand bedrooms in main house; cosy courtyard rooms – some with terraces. Vast dining room offers both classical and modern dishes.

IRBY – Merseyside – 502 K23 20 A3

London 212 mi – Liverpool 12 mi – Manchester 46 mi – Stoke-on-Trent 56 mi

Da Piero

5 Mill Hill Rd CH61 4UB – (0151) 648 7373 – www.dapiero.co.uk – Closed 2 weeks January, 2 weeks August, Sunday and Monday

Rest – Italian – *(dinner only) (booking essential)* Carte £ 21/46

♦ Family-owned and run restaurant with homely, understated décor and intimate, pleasant feel. Carefully prepared, classical Italian cooking, with lots of rustic Sicilian dishes.

IRONBRIDGE – Telford and Wrekin – 503 M26 – pop. 1 560 18 B2

Great Britain

London 135 mi – Birmingham 36 mi – Shrewsbury 18 mi

The Tollhouse (01952) 432166, tic@ironbridge.org.uk

Ironbridge Gorge Museum★★ **AC** (The Iron Bridge★★, Coalport China Museum★★, Blists Hill Open Air Museum★★, Museum of the Gorge and Visitor Centre★)

The Library House without rest

11 Severn Bank TF8 7AN – (01952) 432 299 – www.libraryhouse.com – Closed 24-28 December

4 rm – £ 65/75 £ 90

♦ Nicely hidden, albeit tricky to find, guesthouse with rear terrace. Homely sitting room. Cottage style breakfast room. Compact, comfy rooms, with a touch of style about them.

XX **Restaurant Severn**

33 High St. ✉ TF8 7AG – ✆ (01952) 432 233 – www.restaurantsevern.co.uk – Closed 2 weeks January, 1 week summer, bank holidays, Sunday dinner, Monday and Tuesday

Rest – *(dinner only and Sunday lunch) (booking essential)* Menu £ 19 (lunch) – Carte £ 26/28

◆ Close to the Severn and world heritage site 'Ironbridge'. Pleasant, light and airy dining room with a real family feel. Experienced owners cook tasty, classically based dishes.

X **da Vinci**

26 High St ✉ TF8 7AD – ✆ (01952) 432 250 – www.davincisironbridge.co.uk – Closed Christmas-New Year, Sunday and Monday

Rest – Italian – *(dinner only) (booking essential)* Carte £ 17/32

◆ Keenly run osteria in conservation village. Split-level dining with warm décor and simple, rustic style. Italian chef sources produce from his homeland. Authentic cooking; Tuscan specialities.

ISLE OF MAN – I.O.M. – 502 G21 – see Man (Isle of)

ITTERINGHAM – Norfolk – 504 X25 – ✉ Aylsham — 15 C1

London 126 mi – Cromer 11 mi – Norwich 17 mi

Walpole Arms

The Common ✉ NR11 7AR – ✆ (01263) 587 258 – www.thewalpolearms.co.uk – Closed 25 December and Sunday dinner

Rest – Carte £ 21/28

◆ 18C inn with characterful beamed bar and more formal restaurant. Interesting, Mediterranean-influenced menu is made up of generous, well-prepared dishes and appealing daily specials. The pork belly with Mediterranean vegetables is a firm favourite with the locals.

IVYCHURCH – Kent – 504 W30 Great Britain — 9 C2

London 67 mi – Ashford 11 mi – Rye 10 mi

Rye Old Town★★ : Mermaid St★ - St Mary's Church (≤★), SW : 9 mi on A 2070 and A 259

Olde Moat House without rest

Northwest : 0.75 mi on B 2070 ✉ TN29 0AZ – ✆ (01797) 344 700 – www.oldemoathouse.co.uk

3 rm – †£ 60/70 ††£ 70/95

◆ Blissfully characterful guesthouse with 15C origins, set in over three acres, encircled by small moat. Beamed sitting room with inglenook. Individual, homely styled rooms.

IWERNE MINSTER – Dorset – 504 N31 – see Blandford Forum

IXWORTH – Suffolk – 504 W27 – see Bury St Edmunds

JERSEY – C.I. – 503 O/P33 – see Channel Islands

JEVINGTON – E. Sussex – 504 U31 – see Eastbourne

KEGWORTH – Leicestershire – 502 Q25 – pop. 3 338 Great Britain — 16 B2

London 123 mi – Leicester 18 mi – Loughborough 6 mi – Nottingham 13 mi

Calke Abbey★, SW : 7 mi by A 6 (northbound) and A 453 (southbound) – Derby★ - Museum and Art Gallery★, Royal Crown Derby Museum★, NW : 9 mi by A 50 – Nottingham Castle Museum★, N : 11 mi by A 453 and A 52

Kegworth House without rest

42 High St ✉ DE74 2DA – ✆ (01509) 672 575 – www.kegworthhouse.co.uk

11 rm – †£ 52/160 ††£ 93/195

◆ Georgian manor house in village, secluded in walled garden. Fine interior with original decorative features. Individually-decorated bedrooms of charm and character.

KELSALE – Suffolk – 504 Y27 – pop. 1 309 – ✉ Saxmundham — 15 D3

London 103 mi – Cambridge 68 mi – Ipswich 23 mi – Norwich 37 mi

Mile Hill Barn without rest

North Green, North : 1.5 mi on A 12 ✉ IP17 2RG – ☎ (01728) 668 519 – www.mile-hill-barn.co.uk

3 rm – †£ 65/75 ††£ 90/100

◆ Traditional 15C Suffolk barn in landscaped gardens. Tea on arrival in impressive raftered lounge. Bedrooms boast feature beds and modern bathrooms. Cosy breakfast room; Aga-cooked breakfasts.

KELVEDON – Essex – 504 W28 – pop. 4 593 — 13 C2

London 56 mi

George & Dragon

Coggleshall Rd, Northwest : 2 mi on B 1024 ✉ CO5 9PL – ☎ (01376) 561 797 – www.georgeanddragonkelvedon.co.uk – Closed 24-31 December, Sunday and Monday

Rest – Carte £ 24/28

◆ Clean, bright, welcoming restaurant with a sleek, ultra-modern style, encompassing topiary planters, marble tiled floors, antique mirrors and art deco pictures and statuettes. Simple, well-priced menu with locally caught fish specials. Pretty terrace.

KENDAL – Cumbria – 502 L21 – pop. 28 030 Great Britain — 21 B2

London 270 mi – Bradford 64 mi – Burnley 63 mi – Carlisle 49 mi

Town Hall, Highgate ☎ (01539) 797516, kendaltic@southlakeland.gov.uk

The Heights, ☎ (01539) 723 499

Levens Hall and Garden★ **AC**, S : 4.5 mi by A 591, A 590 and A 6. Lake Windermere★★, NW : 8 mi by A 5284 and A 591

Beech House without rest

40 Greenside, by All Hallows Lane ✉ LA9 4LD – ☎ (01539) 720 385 – www.beechhouse-kendal.co.uk – Closed Christmas

6 rm – †£ 60/75 ††£ 80/100

◆ Pretty three-storey Georgian house set just out of town. Small honesty bar. Modern, open-plan lounge with comfy sofas and communal breakfast tables. Bright, airy, pine-furnished bedrooms come with complimentary cake and up-to-date bathrooms. Welcoming owners.

at Sizergh Southwest : 3 mi by A 591 – ✉ Kendal

The Strickland Arms

✉ LA8 8DZ – ☎ (01539) 561 010 – www.thestricklandarms.com – Closed 25 December

Rest – Carte £ 20/30

◆ Former coach house for next door Sizergh Castle. Sizeable interior with characterful, shabby-chic feel. Menus feature classical pub dishes, with daily specials on the board. Regular events.

at Crosthwaite West : 5.25 mi by All Hallows Lane – ✉ Kendal

The Punch Bowl Inn with rm

✉ LA8 8HR – ☎ (01539) 568 237 – www.the-punchbowl.co.uk

9 rm – †£ 95/120 ††£ 140/310 **Rest** – Carte £ 30/40

◆ Charming 17C inn set in the picturesque Lyth Valley, boasting cosy fires, exposed wooden beams and trailing hop bines. Choice of rustic bar or formal restaurant, which offer interesting takes on old favourites at lunch and more ambitious dishes at dinner. Luxury bedrooms boast quality linens and roll-top baths.

KENILWORTH – Warwickshire – 503 P26 – pop. 22 218 Great Britain — 19 C2

London 102 mi – Birmingham 19 mi – Coventry 5 mi – Leicester 32 mi

The Library, 11 Smalley Pl ☎ (01926) 748900, kenilworthlibrary@warwickshire.gov.uk

Castle★ **AC**

Victoria Lodge without rest
180 Warwick Rd ✉ CV8 1HU – ✆ (01926) 512 020
– www.victorialodgekenilworth.co.uk – Closed 2 weeks Christmas
10 rm – †£ 49/62 ††£ 80
• Keenly run, red-brick house with comfy lounge and linen-laid breakfast room. Immaculately kept, colourful bedrooms; some with balconies or patios. Complimentary bottled water; great breakfasts.

Petit Gourmand
101-103 Warwick Rd ✉ CV8 1HL – ✆ (01926) 864 567
– www.petit-gourmand.co.uk – Closed Christmas and Sunday dinner
Rest – Carte £ 22/37
• Boasts contemporary feel, typified by striking mirrors and artwork. Good value, hearty, classically based dishes supplemented by tried-and-tested daily specials.

Bosquet
97a Warwick Rd ✉ CV8 1HP – ✆ (01926) 852 463
– www.restaurantbosquet.co.uk – Closed 10 days August and Christmas
Rest – French – *(dinner only lunch by arrangement)* Menu £ 31 – Carte £ 36/40
• Contemporary feel to this established restaurant with wooden floors, well-spaced tables and stylish leather chairs. Confident, well-informed cooking displays a classical French base.

KENTON – Exeter – 503 J31 – see Exeter

KERNE BRIDGE – Herefordshire – 503 M28 – see Ross-on-Wye

KESSINGLAND – Suffolk – 504 26 – pop. 4 211 15 D2

London 126 mi – Norwich 28 mi – Ipswich 40 mi – Colchester 66 mi

Old Rectory
157 Church Rd ✉ NR33 7SQ – ✆ (01502) 742 188 – www.bandblowestoft.co.uk
– Closed 20 December-2 January
3 rm – †£ 54/62 ††£ 78/94 **Rest** – Menu £ 22
• 1834 rectory retaining original character, a short walk from the beach. Individually furnished bedrooms boast antique furniture and feature beds. Beautiful gardens. Choice of dishes offered at dinner; locally sourced produce includes their own vegetables and eggs.

KESWICK – Cumbria – 502 K20 – pop. 4 984 Great Britain 21 A2

London 294 mi – Carlisle 31 mi – Kendal 30 mi
Moot Hall, Market Sq. ✆ (017687) 72645, keswicktic@lake-district.gov.uk
Threlkeld Hall, ✆ (017687) 79 324
Derwentwater★ X – Thirlmere (Castlerigg Stone Circle★), E : 1.5 mi X **A**

Plan on next page

Lairbeck
Vicarage Hill ✉ CA12 5QB – ✆ (017687) 73 373
– www.lairbeckhotel-keswick.co.uk X**a**
14 rm – †£ 59/103 ††£ 150
Rest – *(dinner only)* Menu £ 28 **s**
• Attractive Victorian house in the suburbs, its mature garden boasting a huge Sequoia Redwood. Original barley-twist staircase, galleried landing and comfy bar-lounge. Bedrooms come in a mix of styles; some have lovely views. Daily menu in pleasant dining room.

Morrel's
34 Lake Rd ✉ CA12 5DQ – ✆ (017687) 72 666 – www.morrels.co.uk
Rest – *(dinner only and Sunday lunch)* Carte £ 20/31 Z**x**
• Popular local eatery with scrubbed wood flooring, etched glass dividers and large, colourful canvasses. Seasonally changing dishes have subtle Mediterranean influences; some come in two sizes.

ENGLAND

KESWICK

Bank St . . . . Z 2
Borrowdale Rd . . . . . Z 3
Brackenrigg Drive . . Z 5
Brundholme Rd . . . . X 6
Chestnut Hill . . . . . . X 8
Church St . . . . Z 10
Crosthwaite Rd . . . . X 12
Derwent St . . . . Z 13
High Hill . . . . Z 14
Main St . . . . Z
Manor Brow . . . . X 17
Market Square . . . . . Z 18
Museum Square . . . Z 19
Otley Rd . . . . Z 20
Park Horse Yard . . . . Z 21
Police Station Court . Z 22
Ratcliffe Pl. . . . . Z 23
St Herbert St . . . . . . Z 24
Standish St . . . . Z 25
Station St . . . . Z 26
The Crescent . . . . . . Z 27
The Hawthorns . . . . . Y 29
The Headlands . . . . . Z 31
Tithebarn St . . . . Z 32

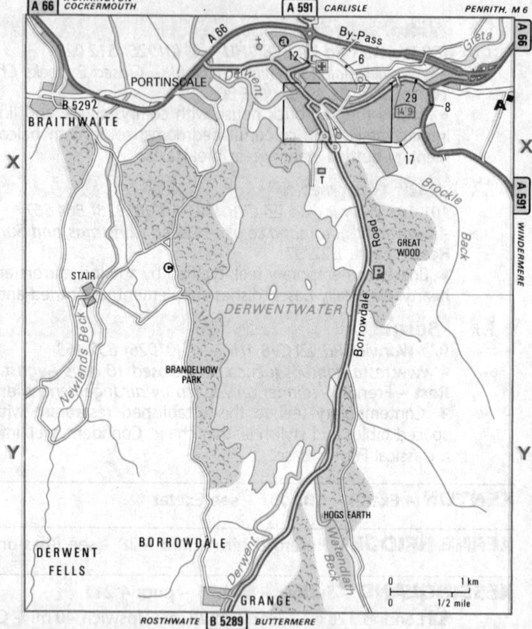

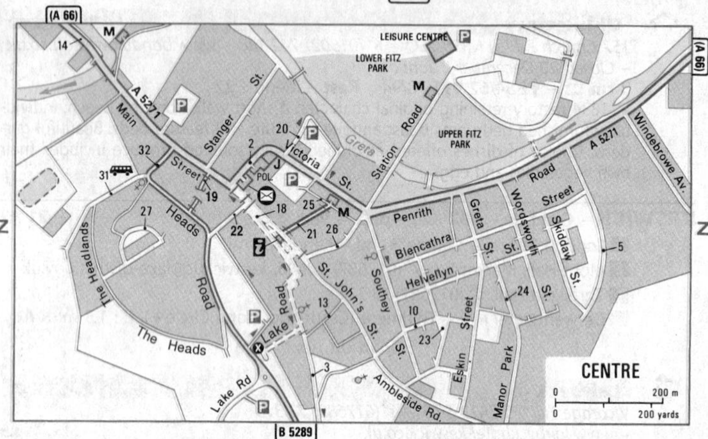

at Braithwaite West : 2 mi by A 66 - X - on B 5292 – ✉ Keswick

Cottage in the Wood

Magic Hill, Whinlatter Forest, Northwest : 1.75 mi on B 5292 ✉ CA12 5TW – ☎ (017687) 78 409 – www.thecottageinthewood.co.uk – Closed January

10 rm – £ 75/98 £ 160

Rest – *(closed Sunday and Monday) (dinner only)* Menu £ 26/32 **s**

◆ 17C whitewashed property in mountainside forest, affording excellent views down the valley. Beamed lounge filled with books/ornaments. Smart, pine-furnished bedrooms and up-to-date bathrooms. Traditional menus in restaurant; airy extension offers superb outlook.

at Portinscale West : 1.5 mi by A 66 – ✉ Keswick

Swinside Lodge
Newlands, South : 1.5 mi on Grange Rd ✉ CA12 5UE – ☎ (017687) 72 948 – www.swinsidelodge-hotel.co.uk – closed Christmas Xc
7 rm (dinner included) – †£ 126/146 ††£ 232/272
Rest – *(dinner only) (booking essential for non-residents)* Menu £ 45 **s**
◆ Immaculately whitewashed house in countryside location, boasting lovely views over the fells. Local info in reception. Two small, traditional country house lounges filled with books and antiques. Bedrooms are more modern in style. Formal, linen-laid dining room offers classical daily menus and house party atmosphere.

KETTLESING – **N. Yorks.** – **502** P21 – **see Harrogate**

KETTLEWELL – **North Yorkshire** – **502** N21 – **pop. 297** **22** A2
London 246 mi – Darlington 42 mi – Harrogate 30 mi – Lancaster 42 mi

Littlebeck without rest
The Grn., take turning at the Old Smithy shop by the bridge ✉ BD23 5RD – ☎ (01756) 760 378 – www.little-beck.co.uk
3 rm – †£ 45/50 ††£ 75
◆ Neatly kept house in fresh, neutral tones. Large, book-filled lounge with wood burning stove; rear terrace overlooks stream. Comfy, unfussy bedrooms boast lovely views. Aga-cooked breakfasts.

KEYSTON – **Cambridgeshire** – **504** S26 – **pop. 257** – ✉ **Huntingdon** **14** A2
London 75 mi – Cambridge 29 mi – Northampton 24 mi

The Pheasant
Village Loop Rd. ✉ PE28 0RE – ☎ (01832) 710 241 – www.thepheasant-keyston.co.uk – Closed Sunday dinner
Rest – *(booking essential)* Menu £ 20 (lunch) – Carte £ 28/32
◆ Charming thatched 'destination dining' pub set in a sleepy hamlet. Seasonal daily menu features both the classics and some more international flavours – and a good selection of offal.

KIBWORTH BEAUCHAMP – **Leicestershire** – **504** Q/R26 – **pop. 3 550** – ✉ **Leicester** **16** B2
London 85 mi – Birmingham 49 mi – Leicester 6 mi – Northampton 17 mi

Firenze
9 Station St ✉ LE8 0LN – ☎ (0116) 279 6260 – www.firenze.co.uk – Closed Christmas, New Year, Sunday and bank holidays
Rest – Italian – *(booking essential)* Menu £ 23 (lunch)/23 (weekday dinner) – Carte £ 23/41
◆ Smart neighbourhood restaurant displaying colourful modern fabrics and Mediterranean artwork. Extensive à la carte and tasting menus offer authentic Italian dishes; good value lunch.

KIBWORTH HARCOURT **Leics.** – **Leicestershire** – **504** R26 **16** B2
London 101 mi – Leicester 9 mi – Coventry 36 mi – Nottingham 41 mi

Boboli
88 Main St ✉ LE8 0NQ – ☎ (0116) 279 3303 – www.bobolirestaurant.co.uk – Closed Christmas-New Year, Monday and Sunday dinner
Rest – Italian – Menu £ 17 (weekday lunch) – Carte £ 18/31
◆ Stylish Italian restaurant named after gardens in Florence. Fresh, simple and seasonally-changing cooking with bold flavours. Affordable wines and cheery, prompt service.

KIDDERMINSTER – **Worcestershire** – **503** N26 – **pop. 55 348** **18** B2
London 139 mi – Birmingham 17 mi – Shrewsbury 34 mi – Worcester 15 mi

ENGLAND

at Chaddesley Corbett Southeast : 4.5 mi by A 448 – ✉ Kidderminster

Brockencote Hall
on A 448 ✉ DY10 4PY – ✆ (01562) 777 876 – www.brockencotehall.com
17 rm – †£ 85/145 ††£ 120/190 **Rest** ***Restaurant*** – see restaurant listing
◆ Keenly run, 19C mansion with long driveway leading past a lake, croquet lawn and grazing sheep. Classic guest areas. Spacious, well-equipped bedrooms: some in annexe; some with great park views.

Restaurant – at Brockencote Hall Hotel
on A 448 ✉ DY10 4PY – ✆ (01562) 777 876 – www.brockencotehall.com
Rest – Menu £ 22 (lunch) **s** – Carte £ 37/54 **s**
◆ Well-run restaurant with cocktail bar and conservatory. Large, airy dining room with French windows opening onto a terrace. Skilfully prepared, flavoursome modern dishes have a classical base.

KINGHAM – Oxfordshire – 503 P28 – pop. 1 434 — 10 A1

London 81 mi – Gloucester 32 mi – Oxford 25 mi

Mill House
✉ OX7 6UH – ✆ (01608) 658 188 – www.millhousehotel.co.uk
23 rm – †£ 85 ††£ 120/160 **Rest** – Menu £ 13 (lunch)/28 – Carte £ 24/28
◆ Privately run house in 10 acres of lawned gardens with brook flowing through grounds. Spacious lounge with comfortable armchairs and books. Country house style bedrooms. Modern décor suffuses restaurant.

Moat End without rest
The Moat, by West St ✉ OX7 6XZ – ✆ (01608) 658 090 – www.moatend.co.uk – Closed Christmas and New Year
3 rm – †£ 60/70 ††£ 75
◆ Cosy converted barn with garden, ponies and countryside views; luxury breakfasts include eggs from own hens. Neatly kept, compact rooms. Friendly owner has wealth of local knowledge.

The Kingham Plough with rm
The Green ✉ OX7 6YD – ✆ (01608) 658 327 – www.thekinghamplough.co.uk
7 rm – †£ 70/125 ††£ 85/125 **Rest** – Carte £ 20/44
◆ Rustic, laid-back pub and restaurant located on the green in an unspoilt Cotswold village; run by a friendly team and experienced chef-owner. Menus mix modern, gutsy pub dishes with a few more ambitious offerings, and evolve as new ingredients arrive. Comfy bedrooms await: 2 and 4, in the main building, are best.

The Tollgate Inn with rm
Church St ✉ OX7 6YA – ✆ (01608) 658 389 – www.thetollgate.com – Closed first week in January and Monday
9 rm – †£ 70 ††£ 110 **Rest** – Carte £ 22/35
◆ Grade II listed inn in centre of unspoiled village. Easy-going lunch menu; more ambitious evening à la carte. Comfy seating and inglenooks, plus popular front terrace. Immaculately kept bedrooms have a warm, bright feel.

KINGSBRIDGE – Devon – 503 I33 – pop. 5 521 — 2 C3

London 236 mi – Exeter 36 mi – Plymouth 24 mi – Torquay 21 mi
The Quay ✆ (01548) 853195, advice@kingsbridgeinfo.co.uk
Thurlestone, ✆ (01548) 560 405
Town★ – Boat Trip to Salcombe★★ **AC**
Prawle Point (← ★★★) SE : 10 mi around coast by A 379

at Goveton Northeast : 2.5 mi by A 381 – ✉ Kingsbridge

Buckland-Tout-Saints
Goveton, Northeast : 2.5 mi by A 381 ✉ TQ7 2DS – ✆ (01548) 853 055 – www.tout-saints.co.uk – closed 3-19 January
14 rm – †£ 99/169 ††£ 99/169 – 2 suites **Rest** – Menu £ 19/37
◆ Immaculate, impressive Queen Anne mansion with neat lawned gardens in rural location. Wood panelled lounge; all other areas full of antiques. Well-furnished bedrooms. Accomplished cooking in beautiful wood-panelled country house restaurant.

ENGLAND

KINGSKERSWELL – Devon – 503 J32 – pop. 4 624 – ✉ Torquay 2 C2

London 199 mi – Exeter 18 mi – Torquay 4 mi

Bickley Mill Inn with rm

Stoneycombe, West : 2 mi by Stoneycombe rd. ✉ TQ12 5LN – ℘ (01803) 873 201 – www.bickleymill.co.uk – Closed 26-28 December and 1 January

12 rm – †£ 68 ††£ 80/90

Rest – Menu £ 15 (lunch Monday-Saturday) – Carte £ 17/21

♦ Modern-looking former flour mill with huge decked terrace and gardens built into the rocks. Menus are simple, traditional and keenly priced; Brixham market fish features in the specials. Individually designed bedrooms are bold and stylish; two are in the eaves.

KING'S LYNN – Norfolk – 502 V25 – pop. 40 921 Great Britain 14 B1

London 103 mi – Cambridge 45 mi – Leicester 75 mi – Norwich 44 mi

The Custom House, Purfleet Quay ℘ (01553) 763044, kings-lynn.tic@west-norfolk.gov.uk

Eagles Tilney All Saints School Rd, ℘ (01553) 827 147

Houghton Hall★★ **AC**, NE : 14.5 mi by A 148 – Four Fenland Churches★ (Terrington St Clement, Walpole St Peter, West Walton, Walsoken) SW : by A 47

Bankhouse

King's Staithe Sq ✉ PE30 1RD – ℘ (01553) 660 492 – www.thebankhouse.co.uk

11 rm – †£ 80/110 ††£ 120

Rest – Carte £ 22/31

♦ Grade II listed Georgian house by the River Ouse. Comfortable bedrooms in various shapes and sizes: all have good facilities and excellent bathrooms; some have a pleasant outlook. Stylish, contemporary bar and brasserie.

at Grimston East : 6.25 mi by A 148 – ✉ King'S Lynn

Congham Hall

Lynn Rd. ✉ PE32 1AH – ℘ (01485) 600 250 – www.conghamhallhotel.co.uk

23 rm – †£ 110/310 ††£ 125/350 – 2 suites

Rest *Orangery* – Menu £ 21 (lunch) – Carte £ 40/48

♦ Part-Georgian country house with neat lawns and formal flower garden. Comfy lounges and small bar with terrace. Well-appointed bedrooms offer pleasant views. Currently undergoing an extension project. Good service from smartly attired staff. Restaurant offers classical menu; kitchen and herb garden produce features.

KINGS MILLS – C.I. – see Channel Islands (Guernsey)

KINGSTON BAGPUIZE – Oxon. – 503 P28 – see Oxford

KINGSTON BLOUNT – Oxon. – see Chinnor

KINGSTON-UPON-HULL – City of Kingston upon Hull – 502 S22 – pop. 301 416 Great Britain 23 D2

London 183 mi – Leeds 61 mi – Nottingham 94 mi – Sheffield 68 mi

Access Humber Bridge (toll)

Humberside Airport : ℘ (01652) 688456, S : 19 mi by A 63

to The Netherlands (Rotterdam) (P & O North Sea Ferries) daily (11 h) – to Belgium (Zeebrugge) (P & O North Sea Ferries) 3-4 weekly (13 h 45 mn)

1 Paragon St ℘ (01482) 223559, hull.tic@vhey.co.uk

Springhead Park Willerby Rd, ℘ (01482) 656 309

Sutton Park Salthouse Rd, ℘ (01482) 374 242

Burton Constable★ **AC**, NE : 9 mi by A 165 and B 1238 Z

Plan on next page

ENGLAND

KINGSTON-UPON-HULL

A 1079
Beverley Road
Waterloo St.
Barmston Street
Wincolmlee
Lockwood St.
Cleveland Street
B 1237
Jenning St.
St. Mark St.
Cannon St.
Caroline St.
Scott St.
Lime Street
Norfolk St.
Liddell St.
Charles St.
Freetown Way
Street
Witham
Great Union St.
A 165
Prospect
Albion St.
George
PROSPECT CENTRE
ST. STEPHENS SHOPPING CENTRE
Guildhall Road
POL.
Alfred Gelder
Carr La.
Anlaby Rd
Osborne St
PRINCES QUAY
High
Hull
Garrison Rd
A 63
A 1105
Castle St.
Hessle Road
TIDAL SURGE BARRIER
Humber St.
KINGSTON RETAIL PARK
Kingston St.
Wellington St. West
English Street
HULL ARENA
THE DEEP
HUMBER
CENTRE
0 400 m
0 400 yards
X
Y

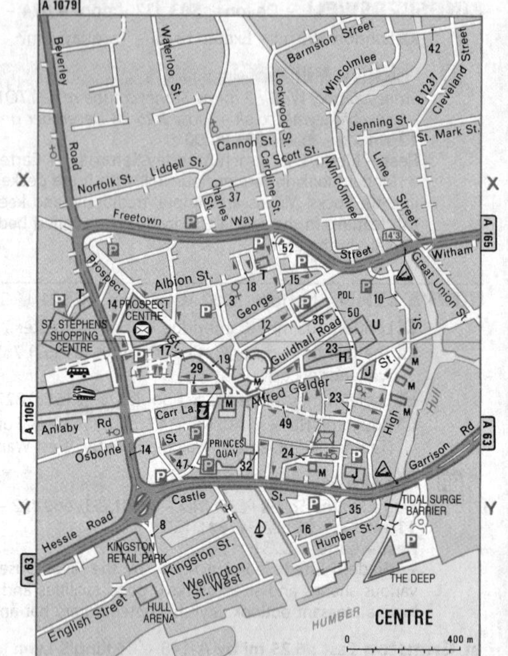

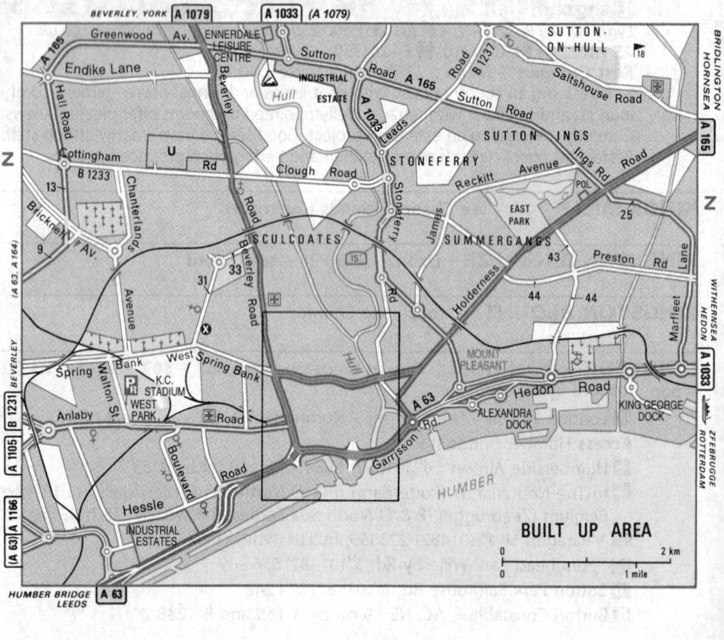

BEVERLEY, YORK
A 1079
A 1033 (A 1079)
Greenwood Av.
ENNERDALE LEISURE CENTRE
Sutton Road
A 165
Endike Lane
Hall Road
INDUSTRIAL ESTATE
Hull
B 1237
SUTTON-ON-HULL
Saltshouse Road
Sutton Road
SUTTON INGS
Leads
Cottingham Rd
B 1233
Clough Road
STONEFERRY
Reckitt Avenue
Ings Rd
Road
POL.
EAST PARK
Chanterlands Avenue
Bricknell Av.
SCULCOATES
Beverley Road
Stoneferry Rd
James
SUMMERGANGS
Preston Rd
Lane
Holderness
Marfleet
Spring Bank
West Spring Bank
K.C. STADIUM
WEST PARK
Walton St.
Anlaby Road
Boulevard
Hessle Road
INDUSTRIAL ESTATES
MOUNT PLEASANT
Hedon Road
A 63
Garrisson Rd.
ALEXANDRA DOCK
KING GEORGE DOCK
HUMBER
BRIDLINGTON HORNSEA
WITHERNSEA HEDON
ZEEBRUGGE ROTTERDAM
A 1033
(A 63, A 164)
BEVERLEY
B 1231
A 1105
A 1166
(A 63)
HUMBER BRIDGE LEEDS
A 63
BUILT UP AREA
0 2 km
0 1 mile
Z

ENGLAND

Boars Nest
22-24 Princes Ave, Northwest : 1 mi by Ferensway off West Spring Bank Rd
✉ HU5 3QA – ✆ (01482) 445 577 – www.theboarsnesthull.com
– Closed 31 December and 1 January Z**x**
Rest – Menu £ 10 (lunch)/23 – Carte £ 24/34
◆ Rustic restaurant, formerly part-butcher's shop, with tiles/meats hooks still in situ. 3 main dining areas and upstairs lounge. Simple, classical English dishes use local, seasonal produce.

at Hessle **Southwest : 2 mi by A 63 – ✉ Kingston-Upon-Hull**

Artisan
22 The Weir ✉ HU13 0RU – ✆ (01482) 644 906 – www.artisanrestaurant.com
– Closed 1 week Easter, 1 week early August, 1 week Christmas, Sunday and Monday
Rest – *(dinner only set menu Friday and Saturday) (booking essential) (lunch by arrangement)* Menu £ 25/50
◆ Intimate restaurant with plush, homely interior; run by passionate husband and wife team. Classical French and Italian influenced cooking; local ingredients to the fore. Set menu only Fri/Sat.

KINGSWEAR – Devon – 503 J32 – see Dartmouth

KINGTON – County of Herefordshire – 503 K27 – pop. 2 597 18 A3

London 152 mi – Birmingham 61 mi – Hereford 19 mi – Shrewsbury 54 mi

at Titley **Northeast : 3.5 mi on B 4355 – ✉ Kington**

The Stagg Inn (Steve Reynolds) with rm
✉ HR5 3RL – ✆ (01544) 230 221 – www.thestagg.co.uk
– Closed 2 weeks between January and February, first 2 weeks in November, 25-26 December, 1 January, Sunday dinner and Monday
6 rm – †£ 70/100 ††£ 130
Rest – *(booking essential)* Carte £ 25/34
Spec. Scallops on parsnip purée. Fillet of beef with béarnaise sauce. 3 crème brûlées of vanilla, cardamom and coffee.
◆ Part-medieval, part-Victorian pub with delightfully cosy interior. Straightforward cooking uses classically based recipes and relies on careful preparation and top quality produce. Menus are short, simple and to the point; dishes are truly satisfying. Bedrooms in the pub can be noisy; opt for one in the old vicarage.

KIRKBY LONSDALE – Cumbria – 502 M21 – pop. 2 076 21 B3
– ✉ Carnforth (lancs.)

London 259 mi – Carlisle 62 mi – Kendal 13 mi – Lancaster 17 mi
Scaleber Lane Barbon, ✆ (015242) 76 366
Casterton Sedbergh Rd, ✆ (015242) 71 592

Hipping Hall with rm
Southeast : 2.5 mi on A 65 ✉ LA6 2JJ
– ✆ (015242) 71 187 – www.hippinghall.com
– Closed 3-7 January
9 rm (dinner included) – †£ 150/248 ††£ 200/330
Rest – *(dinner only and Friday-Sunday lunch)* Menu £ 30/50
◆ Charming part-15/16C house set in mature grounds; with attractive medieval-style restaurant, minstrels gallery and well-spaced tables laid with quality tableware. Concise, modern menus; polite service. Comfy, boldly papered lounges and well-appointed, stark white bedrooms featuring thick carpets and modern bathrooms.

ENGLAND

Sun Inn with rm

6 Market St ✉ LA6 2AU – ✆ (015242) 71 965 – www.sun-inn.info – Closed Monday lunch

11 rm – †£ 70/130 ††£ 100/150

Rest – Carte £ 24/31

◆ 17C inn in busy market town with lively locals bar and rustically refurbished restaurant. Tempting bar nibbles and tasty, seasonal dishes made with locally sourced produce. Good quality linen in modern, immaculately kept bedrooms.

at Lupton Northwest : 4.75 mi on A 65 – **502** L21

Plough

Cow Brow ✉ LA6 1PJ – ✆ (015395) 67 700 – www.punchbowlinns.co.uk

Rest – Carte £ 17/31

◆ Cosy, welcoming pub featuring oak beams, antique furniture, wood burning stoves and wine caves. Tasty choices include small plates and interesting side dishes. Smart, cheery staff.

KIRKBYMOORSIDE – North Yorkshire – 502 R21 – pop. 2 595 — 23 C1

London 244 mi – Leeds 61 mi – Scarborough 26 mi – York 33 mi

Manor Vale, ✆ (01751) 431 525

ENGLAND

Brickfields Farm without rest

Kirby Mills, East : 0.75 mi by A 170 on Kirby Mills Industrial Estate rd ✉ YO62 6NS – ✆ (01751) 433 074 – www.brickfieldsfarm.co.uk

7 rm – †£ 125 ††£ 125

◆ Attractive red-brick farmhouse with most of its bedrooms in converted out-buildings; one boasts a four-poster. Simple, modern comforts and traditional character. Conservatory breakfast room.

Cornmill

Kirby Mills, East : 0.5 mi by A 170 ✉ YO62 6NP – ✆ (01751) 432 000 – www.kirbymills.demon.co.uk

5 rm – †£ 68/70 ††£ 105/110

Rest – *(Closed Sunday)* Menu £ 30 (dinner)

◆ Charming 18C cornmill with pleasant courtyard. Spacious, rustic bedrooms set in the old farmhouse and stables. Characterful dining room with mill race running beneath a glass panel. Seasonal produce from the kitchen garden and fish from the river inform the menu.

at Fadmoor Northwest : 2.25 mi – ✉ **Kirkbymoorside**

Plough Inn

Main St ✉ YO62 7HY – ✆ (01751) 431 515 – www.theploughfadmoor.co.uk – Closed 25 December, Sunday dinner, Monday except bank holidays and Tuesday

Rest – Carte £ 16/25

◆ 18C inn delightfully set by the village green. The cooking, like the décor, is traditional in style; with classic dishes like steak and mushroom suet pudding and treacle tart.

KIRKBY STEPHEN – Cumbria – 502 M20 – pop. 1 832 — 21 B2

London 296 mi – Carlisle 46 mi – Darlington 37 mi – Kendal 28 mi

Augill Castle

Northeast : 4.5 mi by A 685 ✉ CA17 4DE – ✆ (01768) 341 937 – www.stayinacastle.com

12 rm – †£ 80 ††£ 160/240 **Rest** – *(dinner only)* Menu £ 40 **s**

◆ Carefully restored Victorian folly in neo-Gothic style with extensive gardens; fine antiques and curios abound. Comfy music room and library. Individually decorated bedrooms. Expansive dining room with ornate ceiling and Spode tableware.

at Ravenstonedale Southwest : 5 mi by A 685

The Black Swan with rm
✉ CA17 4NG – ☎ (01539) 623 204 – www.blackswanhotel.com – Closed 25 December
15 rm – †£ 47 ††£ 75/125 **Rest** – Carte £ 17/26
◆ Set in a remote village, a part-Victorian, family-run pub with a huge garden and babbling beck. Menus feature filling pub classics, supplemented by restaurant-style specials in the evening. Cosy, antique-furnished bedrooms; one is more modern and boasts a four-poster.

KIRKWHELPINGTON – Northumberland – 501 N/O18 – pop. 353 — 24 A2
– ✉ Morpeth Great Britain

London 305 mi – Carlisle 46 mi – Newcastle upon Tyne 20 mi
Wallington House★ AC, E : 3.5 mi by A 696 and B 6342

Shieldhall
Wallington, Southeast : 2.5 mi by A 696 on B 6342 ✉ *NE61 4AQ – ☎ (01830) 540 387 – www.shieldhallguesthouse.co.uk – Closed December-February*
4 rm – †£ 60/80 ††£ 100 **Rest** – Menu £ 28
◆ Early 17C farmhouse and outbuildings, where Capability Brown's uncle once lived. Mix of rustic and country house guest areas; library-lounge boasts garden views. Individually styled bedrooms with furniture handmade by the owner. Beamed, flag-floored dining room offers classical British dishes and Aga-cooked breakfasts.

KIRTLINGTON – Oxfordshire – 503 Q28 — 10 B2

London 70 mi – Bicester 11 mi – Oxford 16 mi

Dashwood rm,
South Green, Heyford Rd ✉ *OX5 3HJ – ☎ (01869) 352 707 – www.thedashwood.co.uk*
12 rm – †£ 85 ††£ 115
Rest – *(closed Monday lunch and Sunday dinner)* Menu £ 11 (lunch)/25 – Carte approx. £ 25
◆ Grade II listed 16C building in local soft stone. Lounge with comfy leather armchairs. Bedrooms, boasting super contemporary décor, divided between main building and barn. Exposed stone dining room: impressive menus with modern European slant.

KNARESBOROUGH – North Yorkshire – 502 P21 – pop. 13 380 — 22 B2

London 217 – Bradford 21 – Harrogate 3 – Leeds 18
9 Castle Courtyard, Market Pl ☎ (01423) 866886 (limited winter opening, Nov- Mar), kntic@harrogate.gov.uk
Boroughbridge Rd, ☎ (01423) 862 690

Newton House without rest
5-7 York Pl ✉ *HG5 0AD – ☎ (01423) 863 539 – www.newtonhouseyorkshire.com – Closed Christmas*
11 rm – †£ 50/65 ††£ 115
◆ Extended mid-18C house boasts homely lounge with soft suites and smart, comfortable, individually decorated bedrooms; those on the first floor and in the annexe are larger.

at Ferrensby Northeast : 3 mi on A 6055

General Tarleton Inn with rm
Boroughbridge Rd ✉ *HG5 0PZ – ☎ (01423) 340 284 – www.generaltarleton.co.uk*
13 rm – †£ 75 ††£ 129/150 **Rest** – Menu £ 15 (lunch) – Carte £ 25/33
◆ This 18C coaching inn has several dining areas inside and out. The menu has a strong seasonal Yorkshire base and features well-priced, tasty dishes and classics aplenty. Bedrooms are comfortable and well-kept.

at Coneythorpe Northeast : 4.75 mi by A 59

The Tiger Inn

✉ HG5 0RY – ✆ (01423) 863 632 – www.tiger-inn.co.uk

Rest – *(booking advisable)* Menu £ 19 – Carte £ 19/23

♦ Popular, family-owned pub with bustling atmosphere, particularly in the front bar. Monthly changing menu of pub classics, supplemented by fish specials; hearty, substantial cooking.

KNOWSTONE – Devon – see South Molton

KNUTSFORD – Cheshire – 502 M24 – pop. 12 656 — 20 B3

London 187 mi – Chester 25 mi – Liverpool 33 mi – Manchester 18 mi

Council Offices, Toft Rd ✆ (01565) 632611, ktic@cheshireeast.gov.uk

Belle Epoque Brasserie with rm

60 King St ✉ *WA16 6DT* – ✆ *(01565) 633 060* – *www.thebelleepoque.com*
– *Closed 25-26 December*

7 rm – †£ 95 ††£ 115

Rest – *(closed Sunday dinner)* Menu £ 19 – Carte £ 31/37

♦ Bustling brasserie with art nouveau décor. Traditional and modern dishes with international touches use local produce. Contemporary style bedrooms boast modern facilities.

at Mobberley Northeast : 2.5 mi by A 537 on B 5085 – ✉ Knutsford

Hinton

Town Lane, on B 5085 ✉ *WA16 7HH* – ✆ *(01565) 873 484*
– *www.thehinton.co.uk*

6 rm – †£ 48 ††£ 62 **Rest** – *(by arrangement)* Menu £ 18

♦ Welcoming cream-washed guesthouse on the main road through the village. Traditional sitting room with velvet sofas. Comfy, well-kept bedrooms have a homely style and offer good facilities. Neat dining room with individual linen-clad tables; meals by arrangement.

at Lower Peover Southwest : 3.25 mi by A 50 on B 5081

The Bells of Peover

The Cobbles ✉ *WA16 9PZ* – ✆ *(01565) 722 269*

Rest – Carte £ 19/34

♦ Refurbished 16C former coaching inn whose regulars once included Generals Eisenhower and Patton. Offers a range of options: from appealing snacks in the bar, to 'fine dining' upstairs.

at Lach Dennis Southwest : 7 mi by A 50 and B 5081 on B 5082 – ✉ Knutsford

Duke of Portland

Penny's Ln ✉ *CW9 8SY* – ✆ *(01606) 46 264*
– *www.dukeofportland.com*

Rest – Menu £ 16 (lunch and Monday-Thursday dinner)) – Carte £ 22/35

♦ Village inn on main road; most popular place to dine is smart, contemporary room housing stag's head. Lengthy menu offers simply prepared dishes of carefully sourced, local produce.

KYNASTON – Herefordshire – see Ledbury

LACH DENNIS – Ches. – see Knutsford

LACOCK – Wiltshire – 503 N29 – pop. 1 068 – ✉ Chippenham — 4 C2

London 109 mi – Bath 16 mi – Bristol 30 mi – Chippenham 3 mi

Village★★ - Lacock Abbey★ **AC** – High St★, St Cyriac★, Fox Talbot Museum of Photography★ **AC**

ENGLAND

At The Sign of the Angel

6 Church St ✉ SN15 2LB – ✆ (01249) 730 230 – www.lacock.co.uk – Closed Christmas
11 rm – †£ 82 ††£ 120/145
Rest – *(Closed Monday lunch)* Menu £ 18/22 – Carte £ 22/36
♦ Delightful 15C inn with beamed ceilings and open fires, located in charming 15C National Trust village. Traditional, antique-furnished bedrooms offer modern amenities; Room 5 is particularly pleasant and light. Classic country cooking uses home-grown produce.

LA HAULE – C.I. – **503** L33 – see Channel Islands (Jersey)

LAMBOURN – West Berkshire – pop. 2 955 **10** A3

London 71 mi – Bristol 60 mi – Coventry 95 mi

at East Garston Southeast : 3 mi on Newbury Rd

Queen's Arms with rm

✉ RG17 7ET – ✆ (01488) 648 757 – www.queensarmshotel.co.uk – Closed 25 December
8 rm – †£ 95 ††£ 130
Rest – British – Menu £ 20 (Monday-Saturday) – Carte £ 24/32
♦ A quintessentially English inn with an atmospheric, antique-furnished bar, which celebrates country pursuits. Rustic British dishes might include shepherd's pie or rib-eye steak; the lunch menu is particularly good value. Superb bedrooms and a generous breakfast.

ENGLAND

LAMBOURN WOODLANDS – Berks. – see Hungerford

LANCASTER – Lancashire – **502** L21 – pop. 45 952 Great Britain **20** A1

London 252 mi – Blackpool 26 mi – Bradford 62 mi – Burnley 44 mi
The Storey, Meeting House Lane ✆ (01524) 582394, lancastervic@lancaster.gov.uk
18 Ashton Hall Ashton-with-Stodday, ✆ (01524) 752 090
9 Lansil Caton Rd, ✆ (01524) 39 269
Castle★ **AC**

The Ashton

Wyresdale Rd, Southeast : 1.25 mi by A 6 on Clitheroe rd ✉ LA1 3JJ – ✆ (01524) 68 460 – www.theashtonlancaster.com
5 rm – †£ 98 ††£ 118/168 **Rest** – Menu £ 30
♦ Georgian house in lawned gardens; personally run by friendly owner. Good-sized bedrooms are decorated in bold colours and feature a blend of modern and antique furniture. Small, informal dining room; home-cooked comfort food makes good use of local produce.

The Borough

3 Dalton Sq ✉ LA1 1PP – ✆ (01524) 64 170 – www.theboroughlancaster.co.uk – Closed 25 December
Rest – Carte £ 18/35
♦ Characterful pub set on cobbled square. Hearty, filling dishes use regional produce; DIY deli boards are popular. Local bitters and some unusual bottled beers. Regular comedy nights.

LANGAR – Nottinghamshire – **502** R25 **16** B2

London 132 mi – Boston 45 mi – Leicester 25 mi – Lincoln 37 mi

Langar Hall

✉ NG13 9HG – ✆ (01949) 860 559 – www.langarhall.co.uk
11 rm – †£ 88/125 ††£ 140/195 – 1 suite
Rest – Menu £ 18/23 – Carte £ 25/38
♦ Georgian manor in pastoral setting, next to early English church; overlooks park, medieval fishponds. Antique filled rooms named after people featuring in house's history. Elegant, candlelit, pillared dining room.

LANGHO – Lancs. – 502 M22 – see Blackburn

LANGPORT – Somerset – 503 L30 – pop. 2 851 — 3 B3

London 134 mi – Weston-super-Mare 31 mi – Taunton 15 mi – Yeovil 16 mi

The Parsonage

Mulchelney, South : 2 mi on Muchelney Pottery rd ✉ *TA10 0DL* – ✆ *(01458) 259 058 – www.parsonagesomerset.co.uk – Closed Christmas and New Year*

3 rm – †£ 53 ††£ 95 **Rest** – Menu £ 30

◆ Traditional Somerset longhouse in charming setting with airy, well-kept country bedrooms and lovely rear garden. Delightful hosts dine with their guests at family style meals crafted from fresh, local ingredients. Al fresco breakfast in summer.

LANGTHWAITE – N. Yorks. – 502 O20 – see Reeth

LA PULENTE – C.I. – 503 P33 – see Channel Islands (Jersey)

LAPWORTH – Warwickshire — 19 C2

London 108 mi – Birmingham 23 mi – Leicester 47 mi – Coventry 19 mi

The Boot Inn

Old Warwick Rd ✉ *B94 6JU* – ✆ *(01564) 782 464 – www.lovelypubs.co.uk*

Rest – *(booking essential)* Carte £ 20/26

◆ Buzzy pub by the Grand Union and Stratford-upon-Avon canal junction, boasting a large terrace, traditional bar and modern restaurant. Dishes vary from simple bar snacks to sophisticated specials.

LASKILL N. Yorks – North Yorkshire – 502 Q21 – see Hawnby

LASTINGHAM – North Yorkshire – 502 R21 – pop. 87 – ✉ York — 23 C1

London 244 mi – Scarborough 26 mi – York 32 mi

Lastingham Grange

✉ *YO62 6TH* – ✆ *(01751) 417 345 – www.lastinghamgrange.com – mid March to mid November*

11 rm – †£ 100/150 ††£ 150/200

Rest – *(light lunch Monday-Saturday)* Menu £ 40 – Carte £ 23/31

◆ A delightfully traditional country house atmosphere prevails throughout this extended, pleasantly old-fashioned, 17C farmhouse. Lovely gardens; well-appointed bedrooms. Dining room with rustic fare and rose garden view.

LAVENHAM – Suffolk – 504 W27 – pop. 1 231 – ✉ Sudbury — 15 C3

Great Britain

London 66 mi – Cambridge 39 mi – Colchester 22 mi – Ipswich 19 mi

Lady St ✆ (01787) 248207, lavenhamtic@babergh.gov.uk

Town★★ – Church of St Peter and St Paul★

Swan

High St ✉ *CO10 9QA* – ✆ *(01787) 247 477 – www.theswanatlavenham.co.uk*

42 rm – †£ 85/145 ††£ 170/190 – 3 suites

Rest *Gallery* – Menu £ 19/36

◆ Characterful, 15C former coaching inn with superbly atmospheric baronial bar. Beamed, individually decorated bedrooms boast a subtle contemporary style. The Gallery, with its timbered roof and minstrels' gallery, offers a modern British menu. Live piano at weekends.

Lavenham Priory without rest

Water St. ✉ *CO10 9RW* – ✆ *(01787) 247 404 – www.lavenhampriory.co.uk – Closed 25 December to 2 January*

6 rm – †£ 87 ††£ 164

◆ A Jacobean oak staircase and Elizabethan wall paintings are just two elements of this part 13C former priory, bursting with character. Bedrooms are stylishly furnished with antiques.

ENGLAND

The Great House with rm

Market Pl. ✉ CO10 9QZ – ☎ (01787) 247 431 – www.greathouse.co.uk – Closed January, 2 weeks summer, Sunday dinner, Monday and lunch Tuesday

3 rm – †£ 90/120 ††£ 190, ☐ £ 15 – 2 suites

Rest – French – Menu £ 19/32 – Carte dinner £ 29/46

♦ Impressive Georgian façade conceals 14C timbered house with eye-catching modern art and heated rear terrace. Classical French cooking displays modern twists. Service is well-paced and attentive. Contemporary, country house bedrooms boast old beams and modern hues.

LEAMINGTON SPA – Warks. – 503 P27 – see Royal Leamington Spa

LECHLADE – Gloucestershire – 503 O28 – pop. 2 415 Great Britain 4 D1

London 84 mi – Cirencester 13 mi – Oxford 25 mi

Fairford : Church of St Mary★ (stained glass windows★★), W : 4.5 mi on A 417

at Southrop Northwest : 3 mi on Eastleach rd – ✉ Lechlade

The Swan

✉ GL7 3NU – ☎ (01367) 850 205 – www.theswanatsouthrop.co.uk – Closed 25 December and Sunday dinner

Rest – Menu £ 16 – Carte £ 25/30

♦ Ex-London restaurateur combines Italian-influenced cooking with pub classics at this delightful creeper-clad inn, set in a picture perfect Cotswold village. Charming service.

LEDBURY – County of Herefordshire – 503 M27 – pop. 8 491 18 B3

London 119 mi – Hereford 14 mi – Newport 46 mi – Worcester 16 mi

Feathers

High St ✉ HR8 1DS – ☎ (01531) 635 266 – www.feathers-ledbury.co.uk

19 rm ☐ – †£ 90/125 ††£ 135/185 – 3 suites

Rest *Quills* – *(dinner only Friday- Saturday and Sunday lunch)* Carte £ 24/34

Rest *Fuggles* – Carte £ 24/34

♦ Modernised 16C black and white timbered coaching inn; a clever blend of old and new. Comfortable bedrooms; Lanark House suites more contemporary in style. Linen-clad Quills boasts chandeliers. Fuggles is more informal. Modern, seasonally changing menus.

at Kynaston West : 6.5 mi by A 449, A 4172 and Aylton rd on Much Marcle rd. – ✉ Ledbury

Hall End without rest

✉ HR8 2PD – ☎ (01531) 670 225 – www.hallendhouse.com – Closed Christmas and New Year

3 rm ☐ – †£ 65 ††£ 100/120

♦ Lovingly restored, personally run, part Georgian home and livery stable in the countryside. Relax in the orangery and, suitably reposed, retire to lavishly furnished bedrooms.

at Trumpet Northwest : 3.25 mi on A 438 – ✉ Ledbury

Verzon House

Hereford Rd ✉ HR8 2PZ – ☎ (01531) 670 381 – www.verzonhouse.com – Closed first 2 weeks January

8 rm ☐ – †£ 105/175 ††£ 165/195

Rest – *(light lunch)* Menu £ 20 (weekdays) – Carte approx. £ 36

♦ Pleasantly restored Georgian house with delightful terrace. Modern bedrooms are named after cider apples; most have countryside views. There is a midweek, set price 4 course Italian menu and an à la carte of modern, mostly English dishes. Tapas only at lunchtime.

C. Labonne/MICHELIN

LEEDS

County: West Yorkshire
Michelin regional map: **502** P22
London 204 mi – Liverpool 75 mi
– Manchester 43 mi
– Newcastle upon Tyne 95 mi

Population: 443 247
Great Britain
Map reference: **22** B2

PRACTICAL INFORMATION

Tourist Information

The Arcade, City Station ✆ (0113) 242 5242, tourinfo@leeds.gov.uk

Airport

Leeds-Bradford Airport : ✆ (0113) 250 9696, NW : 8 mi by A 65 and A 658 BT

Golf Courses

36 Temple Newsam Halton Temple Newsam Rd, ✆ (0113) 264 5624

18 Gotts Park Armley Armley Ridge Rd, ✆ (0113) 234 2019

18 Middleton Park Middleton Ring Rd, Beeston Park, ✆ (0113) 270 0449

27 Moor Allerton Wike Coal Rd, ✆ (0113) 266 1154

18 Howley Hall Morley Scotchman Lane, ✆ (01924) 350 100

9 Roundhay Park Lane, ✆ (0113) 266 2695

SIGHTS

In town

City★ - Royal Armouries Museum★★★ GZ - City Art Gallery★ **AC** GY **M**

On the outskirts

Kirkstall Abbey★ **AC**, NW : 3 mi by A 65 GY – Temple Newsam★ (decorative arts★) **AC**, E : 5 mi by A 64 and A 63 CU **D**

In the surrounding area

Harewood House★★ (The Gallery★) **AC**, N : 8 mi by A 61 CT – Nostell Priory★, SE : 18 mi by A 61 and A 638 – Yorkshire Sculpture Park★, S : 20 mi by M 1 to junction 38 and 1 mi north off A 637 – Brodsworth Hall★, SE : 25 mi by M 1 to junction 40, A 638 and minor rd (right) in Upton

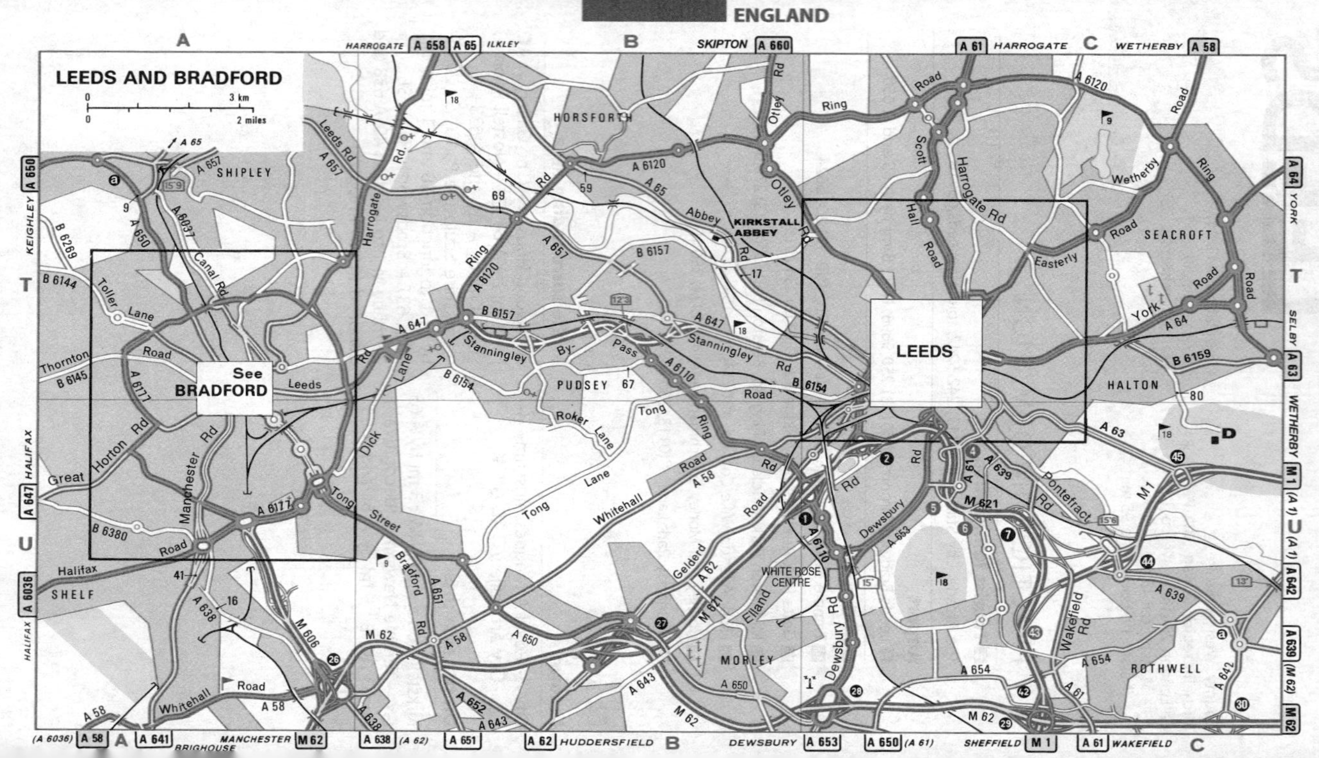

LEEDS AND BRADFORD
0 3 km
0 2 miles
HARROGATE A 658 A 65 ILKLEY
SKIPTON A 660
A 61 HARROGATE
WETHERBY A 58
A 64 YORK
SELBY A 63
WETHERBY M 1 (A 1) U (A 1) A 642
A 639 (M 62) M 62
KEIGHLEY A 650
HALIFAX A 647
HALIFAX A 6036
(A 6036) A 58 A 641 BRIGHOUSE
MANCHESTER M 62
A 638 (A 62) A 651
A 62 HUDDERSFIELD
DEWSBURY A 653
A 650 (A 61)
SHEFFIELD M 1
A 61 WAKEFIELD
LEEDS
See BRADFORD
SHIPLEY
HORSFORTH
KIRKSTALL ABBEY
SEACROFT
HALTON
PUDSEY
WHITE ROSE CENTRE
MORLEY
ROTHWELL
SHELF
Ring Road
Harrogate Rd
Scott Hall Road
Easterly Road
York Road
Wetherby Road
Otley Rd
Abbey Rd
Stanningley Rd
Stanningley By-Pass
Tong Road
Tong Lane
Roker Lane
Whitehall Road
Dewsbury Rd
Elland Road
Gelderd Rd
Pontefract Rd
Wakefield Rd
Leeds Rd
Harrogate Rd.
Dick Lane
Tong Street
Bradford Rd
Canal Rd
Toller Lane
Thornton Road
Horton Rd
Great Horton Road
Manchester Rd
Halifax Road
Leeds Road

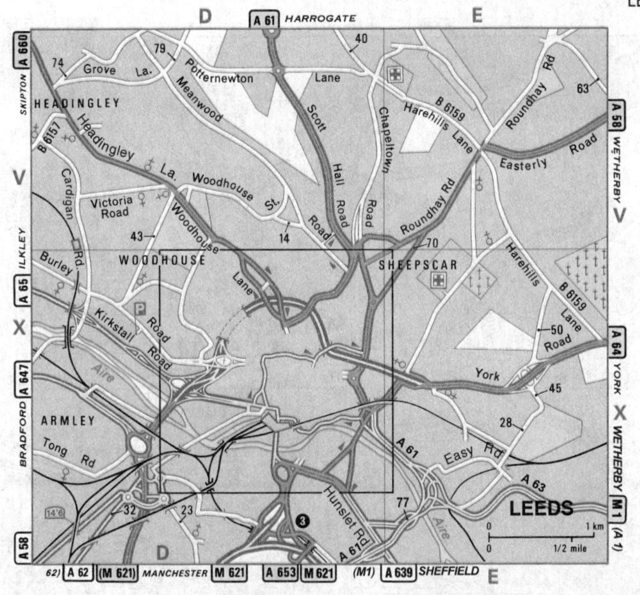

Bradford Rd . . . . AT 9
Cambridge Rd . . . . DV 14
Cleckheaton Rd . . . . AU 16
Commercial Rd . . . . BT 17
Domestic St . . . . DX 23
East Park Parade . . . . . EX 28
Gelderd Rd . . . . DX 32
Harrogate Rd . . . . DV 40
Huddersfield Rd . . . . . . AU 41
Hyde Park Rd . . . . AV 43
Ivy St . . . . EX 45
Lupton Ave . . . . EX 51
New Rd Side . . . . BT 59
Oakwood Lane . . . . EV 63
Pudsey Rd . . . . BT 67
Rodley Lane . . . . BV 69
Roseville Rd . . . . EVX 70
Shaw Lane . . . . DV 74
South Accommodation Rd . . . . EX 77
Stainbeck Rd . . . . DV 79
Templenewsam Rd . . . . CT 80
White Rose Centre . . . . . CU

Malmaison

rm,

1 Swinegate ✉ *LS1 4AG – ℰ (0113) 398 1000 – www.malmaison-leeds.com* GZ**n**

100 rm – £ 79/170 £ 79/170, £ 14.50 – 1 suite

Rest – Menu £ 15 – Carte £ 28/46

♦ Relaxed, contemporary hotel hides behind imposing Victorian exterior. Vibrantly and individually decorated rooms are stylishly furnished, with modern facilities to the fore. Dine in modern interpretation of a French brasserie.

Quebecs without rest

9 Quebec St ✉ *LS1 2HA – ℰ (0113) 244 8989 – www.theetoncollection.com – Closed 23 December-4 January* FZ**a**

43 rm – £ 149 £ 149, £ 10 – 2 suites

♦ 19C former Liberal Club, now a modish, intimate boutique hotel. Original features include oak staircase and stained glass window depicting Yorkshire cities. Stylish bedrooms.

42 The Calls

42 The Calls ✉ *LS2 7EW – ℰ (0113) 244 0099 – www.42thecalls.co.uk – Closed 3 days Christmas* GZ**z**

38 rm – £ 89/190 £ 125/225, £ 14.50 – 3 suites

Rest *Brasserie Forty 4* – see restaurant listing

♦ Converted 18C quayside grain mill retaining many of its original workings. Well-equipped, comfortable bedrooms offer a host of extras; those facing the river are the best.

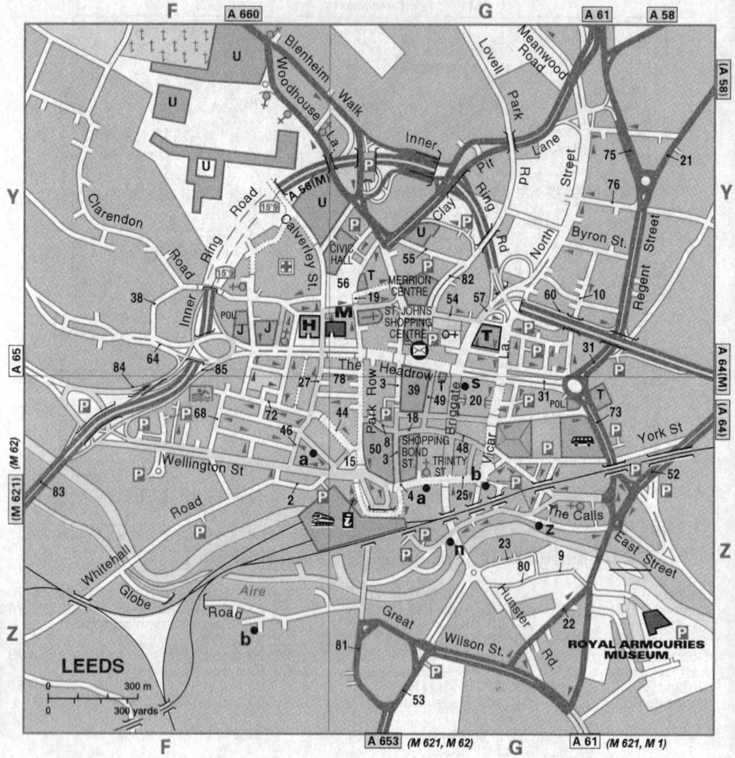

Street	Grid	No.
Aire St	FZ	2
Albion St	GZ	3
Boar Lane	GZ	4
Bond St	GZ	8
Bowman Lane	GZ	9
Bridge St	GY	10
Briggate	GZ	
City Square	GZ	15
Commercial St	GZ	18
Cookridge St	GY	19
County Arcade	GZ	20
Cross Stamford St	GY	21
Crown Point Rd	GZ	22
Dock St	GZ	23
Duncan St	GZ	25
Eastgate	GZ	31
East Parade	FGZ	27
Hanover Way	FY	38
Headrow Centre	GZ	39
Headrow (The)	GY	
Infirmary St	GZ	44
King St	FZ	46
Kirkgate	GZ	48
Lands Lane	GZ	49
Leeds Shopping Plaza	GZ	50
Marsh Lane	GZ	52
Meadow Lane	GZ	53
Merrion Centre	GY	
Merrion St	GY	54
Merrion Way	GY	55
Millennium Square	GY	56
New Briggate	GY	57
New York Rd	GY	60
Park Lane	FY	64
Queen St	FZ	68
St John's Centre	GY	
St Paul's St	FZ	72
St Peter's St	GZ	73
Sheepscar St South	GY	75
Skinner Lane	GY	76
South Parade	FGZ	78
Trinity St Shopping Centre	GZ	
Victoria Rd	GZ	81
Wade Lane	GY	82
Waterloo St	GZ	80
Wellington Rd	FZ	83
Westgate	FZ	85
West St	FZ	84

XXX **Anthony's**

19 Boar Lane ✉ LS1 6EA – ✆ (0113) 245 5922 – www.anthonysrestaurant.co.uk – Closed Christmas-New Year, Sunday and Monday GZ**a**

Rest – *(booking essential)* Menu £ 24/45

◆ Family-run, basement restaurant offering immaculately laid tables and formal service from a well-versed team. Creative cooking features modern techniques and some interesting combinations.

XX **Brasserie Forty 4** – at 42 The Calls Hotel

44 The Calls ✉ LS2 7EW – ✆ (0113) 234 3232 – www.brasserie44.com – Closed Sunday and Bank Holidays except Good Friday GZ**z**

Rest – Menu £ 23 (early dinner) – Carte £ 27/29

◆ Former riverside warehouse with minimalist dining room and stylish bar which exudes atmosphere of buzzy informality. Smokehouse and chargrilled options in an eclectic range of dishes.

XX **Piazza by Anthony**

The Corn Exchange ✉ LS1 7BR – ✆ (0113) 247 0995 – www.anthonysrestaurant.co.uk – Closed 25-26 December and 1 January

Rest – Carte £ 22/37 GZ**b**

◆ Located on the ground floor of the historic former Corn Exchange; large open dining room in the centre, with meeting rooms, private dining areas and artisanal food shops surrounding. Wide-ranging menu of tasty European dishes. Outstanding breads in the bakery.

XX **Foundry**

1 Saw Mill Yard, Round Foundry ✉ LS11 5WH – ✆ (0113) 245 0390 – www.thefoundrywinebar.co.uk – Closed Saturday lunch and Sunday

Rest – Menu £ 16 (lunch) – Carte £ 29/39 FZ**b**

◆ Set in a building once joined to the foundry and mills, with vaulted ceiling, ornate bar and French bistro feel. Classical menus feature hearty, robust comfort dishes and extensive daily specials.

XX **Fourth Floor** – at Harvey Nichols

107-111 Briggate ✉ LS1 6AZ – ✆ (0113) 204 8000 – www.harveynichols.com – closed 25 December, 1 January and dinner Sunday-Monday GZ**s**

Rest – Menu £ 20 – Carte £ 25/30

◆ Bright, contemporary dining room on the top floor of this chic store; watch the chefs prepare tasty, modern, globally influenced dishes. Pleasant service from a smartly attired team.

LEICESTER – Leicester – **502** Q26 – pop. 330 574 Great Britain **16** B2

London 107 mi – Birmingham 43 mi – Coventry 24 mi – Nottingham 26 mi

East Midlands Airport, Castle Donington : ✆ (0871) 9199000 NW : 22 mi by A 50 - AX - and M 1

7-9 Every St, Town Hall Sq ✆ (0844) 888 5181(calls charged), info@goleicestershire.com

18 Leicestershire Evington Lane, ✆ (0116) 273 8825

18 Western Park Scudamore Rd, ✆ (0116) 287 5211

18 Humberstone Heights Gipsy Lane, ✆ (0116) 299 5570

18 Oadby Leicester Road Racecourse, ✆ (0116) 270 0215

9 Blaby Lutterworth Rd, ✆ (0116) 278 4804

Guildhall★ BY **B** – Museum and Art Gallery★ CY **M3** – St Mary de Castro Church★ BY **D**

National Space Centre★ N : 2 mi by A 6 - AX - turning east into Corporation Rd and right into Exploration Drive

Plans pages 280, 281

Leicester Marriott

Smith Way, Grove Park, Enderby, Southwest : 4 mi by A 5460 off A 563 at junction 21 of M1 ✉ LE19 1SW – ✆ (0116) 282 0100 – www.leicestermarriott.co.uk

226 rm – †£ 129 ††£ 129 – 1 suite AY**z**

Rest – Menu £ 22 (dinner) – Carte £ 24/34

◆ Sleekly designed, comfortable hotel in useful location by junction 21 of M1. Coffee shop and bar. State-of-the-art gym. Standard and executive bedrooms. East meets west in contemporary restaurant; choice of buffet and eclectic à la carte.

Belmont

De Montfort St ✉ LE1 7GR – ✆ (0116) 254 4773 – www.belmonthotel.co.uk – Closed 24-26 December CY**c**

74 rm – †£ 79/89 ††£ 99 – 1 suite

Rest *Cherry's* – *(Closed Saturday lunch, Sunday dinner and August)* Menu £ 16 – Carte £ 21/28

◆ Friendly, family run hotel in city suburb, made up of a collection of houses – each with its own classical style. Bedrooms vary in shape and size: all have modern touches and good facilities. Contemporary bar with snack menu; formal restaurant offering traditional fare.

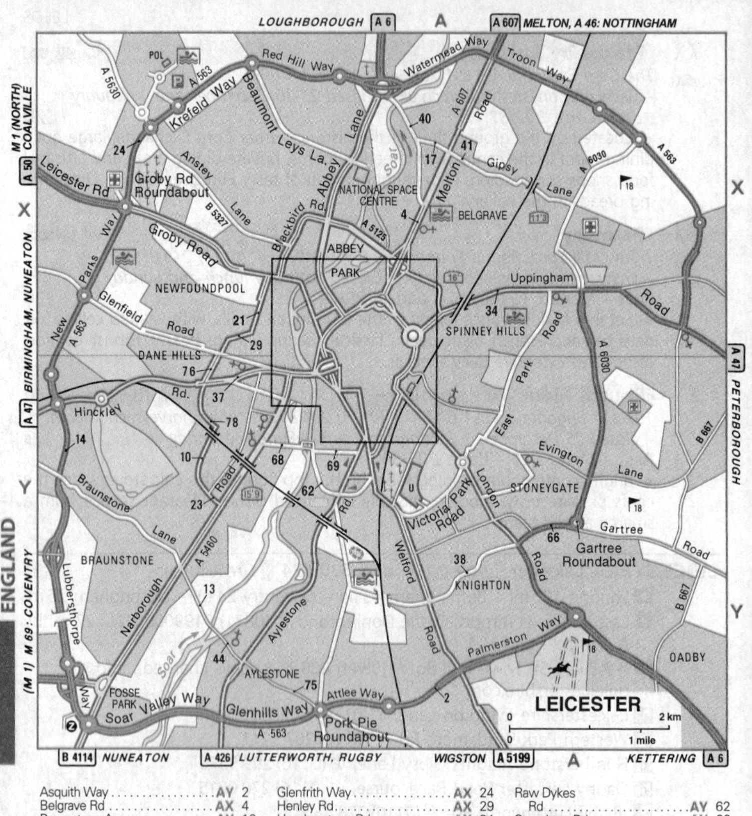

Asquith Way	AY	2	Glenfrith Way	AX	24	Raw Dykes Rd	AY	62
Belgrave Rd	AX	4	Henley Rd	AX	29	Stoughton Rd	AY	66
Braunstone Ave	AY	10	Humberstone Rd	AX	34	Upperton Rd	AY	68
Braunstone Lane East	AY	13	King Richards Rd	AY	37	Walnut St	AY	69
Braunstone Way	AY	14	Knighton Rd	AY	38	Wigston Lane	AY	75
Checketts Rd	AX	17	Loughborough Rd	AX	40	Woodville Rd	AY	76
Fosse Rd North	AX	21	Marfitt St	AX	41	Wyngate Drive	AY	78
Fullhurst Ave	AY	23	Middleton St	AY	44			

Hotel Maiyango

13-21 St. Nicholas Pl ✉ LE1 4LD – ☎ (0116) 251 88 98
– www.maiyango.com BY**a**
13 rm – †£ 145 ††£ 145, ☕ £ 7.95
– 1 suite
Rest – *(Closed Sunday lunch)* Menu £ 19/28
◆ Stylish city centre hotel in converted shoe factory. Spacious rooms feature heavy wood furniture and modern facilities; 3rd floor bar overlooks rooftops. Ground floor restaurant with colonial feel serves well presented Mediterranean/Asian influenced cooking.

Boot Room

26-29 Millstone Ln. ✉ LE1 5JN – ☎ (0116) 262 2555
– www.thebootroomeaterie.co.uk
– Closed Christmas-New Year, Sunday and Monday BY**x**
Rest – Menu £ 14 (lunch) – Carte £ 25/32
◆ Sizeable restaurant located in former shoe factory, with industrial style, relaxed ambience and friendly service. Simple, straightforward British cooking with European touches.

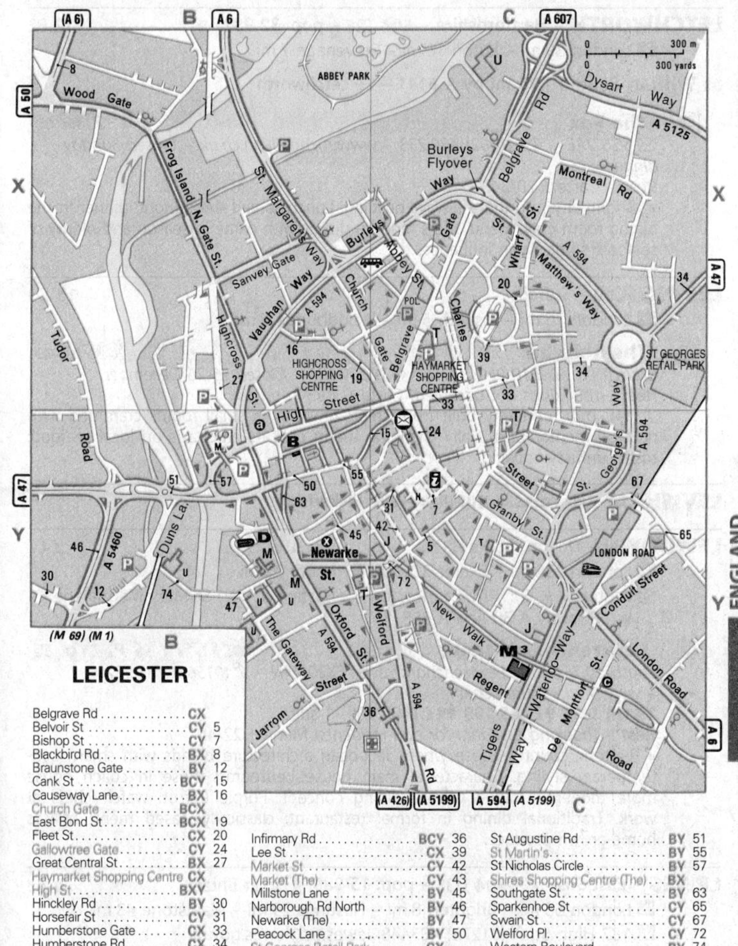

LEICESTER

Street	Grid	No.
Belgrave Rd	CX	
Belvoir St	CY	5
Bishop St	CY	7
Blackbird Rd	BX	8
Braunstone Gate	BY	12
Cank St	BCY	15
Causeway Lane	BX	16
Church Gate	BCX	
East Bond St	BCX	19
Fleet St	CX	20
Gallowtree Gate	CY	24
Great Central St	BX	27
Haymarket Shopping Centre	CX	
High St	BXY	
Hinckley Rd	BY	30
Horsefair St	CY	31
Humberstone Gate	CX	33
Humberstone Rd	CX	34
Infirmary Rd	BCY	36
Lee St	CX	39
Market St	CY	42
Market (The)	CY	43
Millstone Lane	BY	45
Narborough Rd North	BY	46
Newarke (The)	BY	47
Peacock Lane	BY	50
St Georges Retail Park	CX	
St Augustine Rd	BY	51
St Martin's	BY	55
St Nicholas Circle	BY	57
Shires Shopping Centre (The)	BX	
Southgate St	BY	63
Sparkenhoe St	CY	65
Swain St	CY	67
Welford Pl.	CY	72
Western Boulevard	BY	74

LEIGH-ON-SEA – Southend-on-Sea – 504 W29 — 13 C3

▶ London 37 mi – Brighton 85 mi – Dover 86 mi – Ipswich 57 mi

XX Bank

1470 London Rd ✉ SS9 2UR – ☎ (01702) 719 000 – www.thebankonline.co.uk – Closed Sunday dinner and Monday

Rest – Menu £ 19/20 – Carte £ 30/37

◆ Former bank set in parade of shops. Spacious restaurant with small terrace and bar, high ceilings and intimate lighting. Wide menu of classic '80s cooking displays fresh, neat flavours.

X The Sandbar & Seafood Co. Ltd

71 Broadway ✉ SS9 1PE – ☎ (01702) 480 067 – www.sandbarandseafood.co.uk

Rest – *(booking essential)* Carte £ 21/37

◆ Light and airy split-level restaurant with casual lower floor and striking black canopied terrace. Traditional cooking with some Mediterranean influences; tasty old-school puddings.

LETCHWORTH – Hertfordshire – 504 T28 – pop. 32 932 12 B2

London 39 mi – Luton 18 mi – Stevenage 7 mi

at Willian South : 1.75 mi by A 6141 – ✉ Letchworth

The Fox

✉ SG6 2AE – ☎ (01462) 480 233 – www.foxatwillian.co.uk – Closed Sunday dinner

Rest – Carte £ 20/34

♦ Bright, airy pub that's always bustling. Lunch served throughout; dinner in the dining room only. Menu offers modern dishes with game in season and plenty of seafood; some Asian influences.

LEVINGTON – Suffolk 15 D3

London 75 mi – Ipswich 5 mi – Woodbridge 8 mi

The Ship Inn

Church Ln ✉ IP10 0LQ – ☎ (01473) 659 573 – Closed 25-26 December

Rest – *(bookings not accepted)* Carte £ 20/30

♦ 14C pub reputedly built from ships' timbers; its small rooms crammed with nautical memorabilia. Daily changing menu puts its emphasis on local seafood; rustic, unfussy cooking.

LEVISHAM – N. Yorks. – 502 R21 – see Pickering

LEWDOWN – Devon – 503 H32 2 C2

London 238 mi – Exeter 37 mi – Plymouth 29 mi

Lydford★★, E : 4 m. Launceston★ - Castle★ (<★) St Mary Magdalene★, W : 8 mi by A 30 and A 388

Lewtrenchard Manor

South : 0.75 mi by Lewtrenchard rd ✉ EX20 4PN – ☎ (01566) 783 222 – www.lewtrenchard.co.uk

13 rm – †£ 105/190 ††£ 140/220 – 1 suite

Rest – *(booking essential for non-residents)* Menu £ 22/45

♦ Historic country house where Jacobean architecture blends with smart, contemporary styling. Characterful main house bedrooms; those in coach house more modern. Unique private dining concept, Purple Carrot: watch chefs at work. Traditional dining in formal restaurant; classically based menu utilises home-grown produce.

LEWES – East Sussex – 504 U31 – pop. 15 988 Great Britain 8 A3

London 53 mi – Brighton 8 mi – Hastings 29 mi – Maidstone 43 mi

187 High St ☎ (01273) 483448, lewes.tic@lewes.gov.uk

Chapel Hill, ☎ (01273) 473 245

Town★ (High St★, Keere St★) – Castle (<★) **AC**

Sheffield Park Garden★ **AC**, N : 9.5 mi by A 275

Shelleys

High St ✉ BN7 1XS – ☎ (01273) 472 361 – www.the-shelleys.co.uk

18 rm – †£ 98/155 ††£ 180/265 – 1 suite

Rest – Menu £ 21 (lunch) – Carte (dinner) £ 27/33

♦ Formerly an inn, and before that, a private house dating back to 1577 – owned by the great poet's family. Spacious, classically styled bedrooms include a four-poster and suite with garden views. Smart restaurant overlooks the lawns.

Millers without rest

134 High St ✉ BN7 1XS – ☎ (01273) 475 631 – www.millersbedandbreakfast.com – Closed 4-6 November, and 22 December-5 January

3 rm – †£ 85 ††£ 95

♦ Characterful, small family home in a row of 16C houses that lead to the high street. Appealing personal feel in the individual bedrooms with books, trinkets and knick-knacks.

ENGLAND

The Real Eating Company

18 Cliffe High St ✉ BN7 2AJ – ☎ (01273) 402 650 – www.real-eating.co.uk – closed 25 December, Sunday and Monday dinner
Rest – Carte £ 21/30
◆ Light lunches in buzzy atmosphere; more intimate at dinner. Fresh seasonal, local produce cooked in unfussy style to create honest, tasty dishes, including plenty of British favourites.

at East Chiltington **Northwest : 5.5 mi by A 275 and B 2116 off Novington Lane – ✉ Lewes**

The Jolly Sportsman

Chapel Ln ✉ BN7 3BA – ☎ (01273) 890 400 – www.thejollysportsman.com
Rest – *(booking essential)* Menu £ 16 (weekday lunch) – Carte £ 22/29
◆ Set in a small hamlet, a grey clapperboard pub that's popular with the locals. Plenty of choice, including interesting bar bites, good value set menus and a rustic, European-based à la carte.

LEYBURN – North Yorkshire – 502 O21 – pop. 1 844 — 22 B1

London 251 mi – Darlington 25 mi – Kendal 43 mi – Leeds 53 mi
4 Central Chambers, Railway St ☎ (01748) 828747, tic.leyburn@richmondshire.gov.uk

Clyde House without rest

5 Railway St. ✉ DL8 5AY – ☎ (01969) 623 941 – www.clydehouseleyburn.co.uk
6 rm – †£ 40/50 ††£ 75
◆ 18C former coaching inn, refurbished to a high standard, with fresh, bright, modern styling. Bedrooms are spacious with high ceilings; those in former stables are smaller but boast exposed beams. Hearty Yorkshire breakfasts served in smart, open-plan kitchen.

The Sandpiper Inn with rm

Market Pl ✉ DL8 5AT – ☎ (01969) 622 206 – www.sandpiperinn.co.uk – Closed Monday and restricted opening on Tuesday in winter
2 rm – †£ 65/70 ††£ 75/80
Rest – Carte £ 22/34
◆ Charming 16C inn just off the square in busy market town. Frequently changing blackboard menus feature fine local produce; simpler dishes and sandwiches at lunchtime. Pleasant bedrooms have a homely feel.

at Constable Burton **East : 3.5 mi on A 684 – ✉ Leyburn**

Wyvill Arms with rm

✉ DL8 5LH – ☎ (01677) 450 581 – www.thewyvillarms.co.uk
3 rm – †£ 60 ††£ 75 **Rest** – Carte £ 20/35
◆ Intimate, ivy-clad stone pub with pleasant gardens, formerly an 18C farmhouse. Menus offer plenty of choice and feature local, traceable produce in carefully prepared, classical dishes. Simple, well-kept bedrooms.

LICHFIELD – Staffordshire – 502 O25 – pop. 28 435 Great Britain — 19 C2

London 128 mi – Birmingham 16 mi – Derby 23 mi – Stoke-on-Trent 30 mi
Lichfield Garrick, Castle Dyke ☎ (01543) 412112, info@visitlichfield.com
Lichfield Golf and Country Club Elmhurst, ☎ (01543) 417 333
City★ - Cathedral★★ **AC**

Chandlers Grande Brasserie

Corn Exchange, Conduit St ✉ WS13 6JU – ☎ (01543) 416 688 – www.chandlersrestaurant.co.uk – Closed 1 and 30 May, 29 August, 26 December and Sunday
Rest – Menu £ 14/18 – Carte £ 25/36
◆ Hexagonal building in heart of the city, with spacious, wood-floored restaurant and mezzanine floor for more intimate dining. Menus offer a mix of classic and Mediterranean dishes.

LICKFOLD – W. Sussex – see Petworth

LIFTON – Devon – 503 H32 – pop. 964 2 C2

London 238 mi – Bude 24 mi – Exeter 37 mi – Launceston 4 mi

Launceston★ - Castle★ (≤★) St Mary Magdalene★, W : 4.5 mi by A 30 and A 388

Arundell Arms

Fore St ✉ PL16 0AA – ✆ (01566) 784 666 – www.arundellarms.com – Closed 24-26 December

21 rm – †£ 98/118 ††£ 175

Rest – Menu £ 23/40 – Carte £ 36/50

◆ Roadside former coaching inn with access to 20 miles of the Tamar River for fishing. Comfortable, characterful bedrooms. Smart bar and restaurant; the latter with views over the garden and terrace. Light lunches available in bar. Classic menus in restaurant.

LINCOLN – Lincolnshire – 502 S24 – pop. 85 963 Great Britain 17 C1

London 140 mi – Bradford 81 mi – Cambridge 94 mi – Kingston-upon-Hull 44 mi

Humberside Airport : ✆ (01652) 688456, N : 32 mi by A 15 - Y - M 180 and A 18

9 Castle Hill ✆ (01522) 873213, tourism@lincoln.gov.uk

Carholme Carholme Rd, ✆ (01522) 523 725

City★★ - Cathedral and Precincts★★★ **AC** Y – High Bridge★★ Z **9** – Usher Gallery★ **AC** YZ **M1** – Jew's House★ Y – Castle★ **AC** Y

Doddington Hall★ **AC**, W : 6 mi by B 1003 - Z - and B 1190. Gainsborough Old Hall★ **AC**, NW : 19 mi by A 57 - Z - and A 156

Charlotte House

The Lawns, Union Rd ✉ LN1 3BJ – ✆ (01522) 541 000 – www.charlottehouselincoln.com Y**v**

14 rm – †£ 145 ††£ 195, £ 9.50 – 6 suites

Rest – *(dinner only and Sunday lunch)* Menu £ 25 – Carte £ 23/41

◆ Set next to a castle, a stylish and contemporary converted Georgian building with 8 acres of grounds, super-cool, comfy bedrooms and luxurious bathrooms. Free town transfers. Dine at linen-laid tables in smart, glass-fronted restaurant.

Bailhouse without rest

34 Bailgate ✉ LN1 3AP – ✆ (01522) 541 000 – www.bailhouse.co.uk Y**c**

10 rm – ††£ 175, £ 9.50

◆ Beautiful 14C building with 19C additions. Intimate, relaxing feel enhanced by unobtrusive service, enclosed garden, and rooms oozing charm, some with 14C exposed beams.

St Clements Lodge without rest

21 Langworthgate ✉ LN2 4AD – ✆ (01522) 521 532 – www.stclementslodge.co.uk Y**u**

3 rm – †£ 50 ††£ 68

◆ A good value house in a convenient location, a short walk from the sights. Run by hospitable owners who keep three large, pleasantly decorated bedrooms.

Wig & Mitre

30-32 Steep Hill ✉ LN2 1LU – ✆ (01522) 535 190 – www.wigandmitre.com Y**r**

Rest – Menu £ 15/20 – Carte £ 21/29

◆ Well-established pub with a cosy bar, period dining rooms and an airy beamed restaurant. Classical dishes display some global influences; breakfasts are hearty. Over 50 wines by the glass.

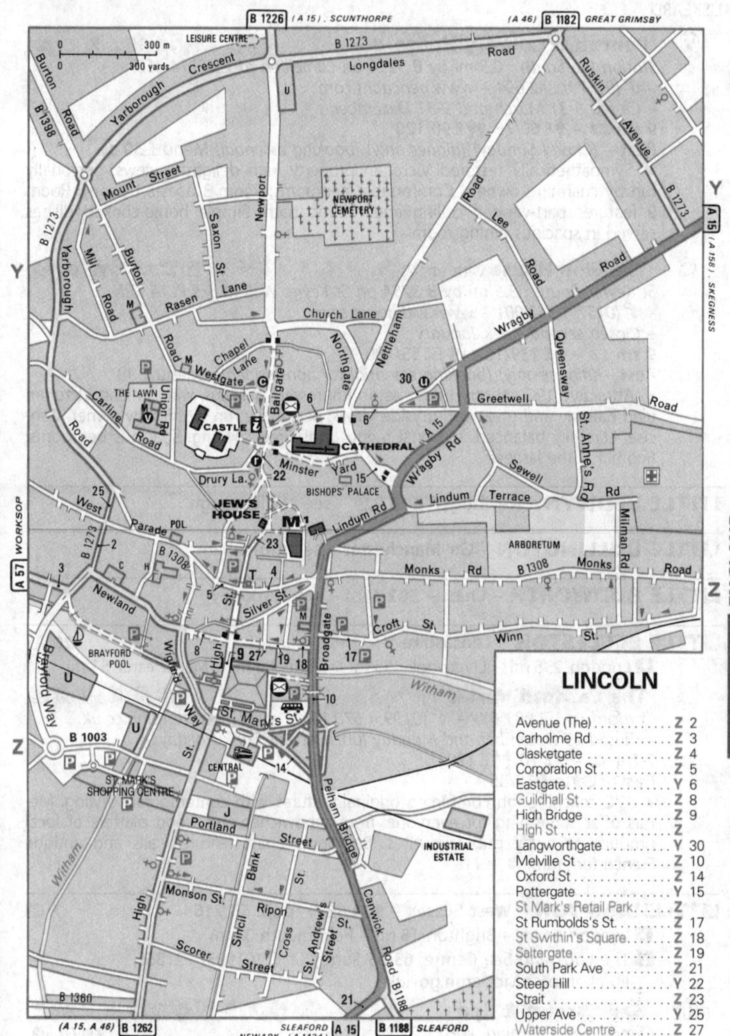

LISKEARD – Cornwall – **503** G32 – pop. 8 478 **1** B2

London 261 mi – Exeter 59 mi – Plymouth 19 mi – Truro 37 mi

Church★

Lanhydrock★★, W : 11.5 mi by A 38 and A 390 – NW : Bodmin Moor★★ - St Endellion Church★★ - Altarnun Church★ - St Breward Church★ - Blisland★ (church★) - Camelford★ – Cardinham Church★ - Michaelstow Church★ - St Kew★ (church★) - St Mabyn Church★ – St Neot★ (Parish Church★★) - St Sidwell's, Laneast★ - St Teath Church★ - St Tudy★ – Launceston★ - Castle★ (≤★) St Mary Magdalene★, NE : 19 mi by A 390 and A 388

Pencubitt Country House

Station Rd, South : 0.5 mi by B 3254 on Lamellion rd ✉ PL14 4EB – ✆ (01579) 342 694 – www.pencubitt.com – Closed 8-31 March and 9-31 December

9 rm – †£ 60/75 ††£ 90/120

Rest – *(Closed Sunday) (dinner only) (booking essential)* Menu £ 30 **s**

◆ Sympathetically restored Victorian property with delightful views, personally run by charming owners. Comfortable bedrooms; Room 3 boasts balcony; Room 9 features part-vaulted ceiling and roll-top bath. Simple home-cooked dishes served in spacious dining room.

The Well House with rm

St Keyne, South : 3.5 mi by B 3254 on St Keyne Well rd. ✉ PL14 4RN – ✆ (01579) 342 001 – www.wellhouse.co.uk – Closed second week January

9 rm – †£ 139/162 ††£ 155/180

Rest – *(dinner only) (booking essential for non-residents)* Menu £ 38

◆ Attractive 19C country house set in impressive gardens, with striking Victorian tiled hallway and great countryside views; personally run by friendly owner. Concise, carefully balanced, seasonal menu of assured cooking. Spacious bedrooms; Room 1 is the largest.

LITTLE BEDWYN – Newbury – 503 P29 – see Marlborough

LITTLE BOLLINGTON – Gtr Manchester – see Altrincham

LITTLE BUDWORTH – Ches. – 502 M24 – see Tarporley

LITTLE ECCLESTON – Lancashire — 20 A2

London 238 mi – Liverpool - 55 mi – Leeds 83 mi – Manchester 51 mi

The Cartford Inn with rm

Cartford Ln ✉ PR3 0YP – ✆ (01995) 670 166 – www.thecartfordinn.co.uk – Closed 25 December and Monday lunch except Bank Holidays

7 rm – †£ 70 ††£ 120

Rest – Carte £ 19/35

◆ 17C coaching inn combining original features with contemporary styling. Menus offer something for everyone; from sandwiches and wood platters of local produce to gutsy pub favourites. Bedrooms boast feature walls and antique French furniture.

LITTLEHAMPTON – West Sussex – 504 S31 – pop. 55 716 — 7 C3

London 64 mi – Brighton 18 mi – Portsmouth 31 mi

The Look and Sea Centre, 63-65 Surrey St ✆ (01903) 721866, littlehampton.vic@arun.gov.uk

Bailiffscourt & Spa

Climping St, Climping, West : 2.75 mi by A 259 ✉ BN17 5RW – ✆ (01903) 723 511 – www.hshotels.co.uk

39 rm (dinner included) – †£ 245/355 ††£ 330/455

Rest – Menu £ 20/48 – Carte approx. £ 48

◆ Charming, reconstructed medieval manor in immaculate gardens. Bedrooms are split between the house and outbuildings; the newer rooms in the grounds are more suited to families. Beautiful spa facility. Classic country house cooking served in formal dining room.

Amberley Court without rest

Crookthorn Ln, Climping, West : 1.75 mi by B 2187 off A 259 ✉ BN17 5SN – ✆ (01903) 725 131 – Closed 16-23 December and 27 December-3 January

5 rm – †£ 50/79 ††£ 89/105

◆ Converted farm barn with a tidy, homely atmosphere. Exposed beams, flourishing plants and a warm welcome. Clean, modern, simply decorated bedrooms; some are in the grounds.

ENGLAND

LITTLE LANGDALE – Cumbria – **502** K20 – see Ambleside

LITTLE LANGFORD – Wilts. – see Salisbury

LITTLE MARLOW – Buckinghamshire – see Marlow

LITTLE PETHERICK – Cornwall – **503** F32 – see Padstow

LITTLE SHELFORD – Cambs. – **504** U27 – see Cambridge

LITTLE THETFORD – Cambs. – see Ely

LITTLE WILBRAHAM – Cambs. – see Cambridge

C. Labonne/MICHELIN

LIVERPOOL

County: Merseyside
Michelin regional map: **502** L23
London 219 mi
– Birmingham 103 mi – Leeds 75 mi
– Manchester 35 mi

Population: 469 017
Great Britain
Map reference: **20** A3

PRACTICAL INFORMATION

Tourist Information

08 Place, 36-38 Whitechapel, (0151) 233 2459, 08place@liverpool.gov.uk

Airport

Liverpool John Lennon Airport: (0871) 521 8484, SE: 6 mi by A 561 BX

Ferries and Shipping Lines

to Birkenhead and Wallasey (Mersey Ferries) frequent services daily.

to Isle of Man (Douglas) (Isle of Man Steam Packet Co. Ltd) 2 daily (2h 30 mn) - to Dublin (P & O Irish Sea) 1-2 daily (8h).

Tunnel

Mersey Tunnels (toll) AX

Golf Courses

Allerton Municipal Allerton Rd, (0151) 428 1046

Liverpool Municipal Kirby Ingoe Lane, (0151) 546 5435

Bowring Roby Rd, Bowring Park, (0151) 489 1901

SIGHTS

In town

City★ – The Walker★★ DY **M3** – Liverpool Cathedral★★ (Lady Chapel★) EZ – Metropolitan Cathedral of Christ the King★★ EY – Albert Dock★ CZ (Merseyside Maritime Museum★ **AC** **M2** - Tate Liverpool★)

In the surrounding area

Speke Hall★ **AC**, SE : 8 mi by A 561 BX

ENGLAND

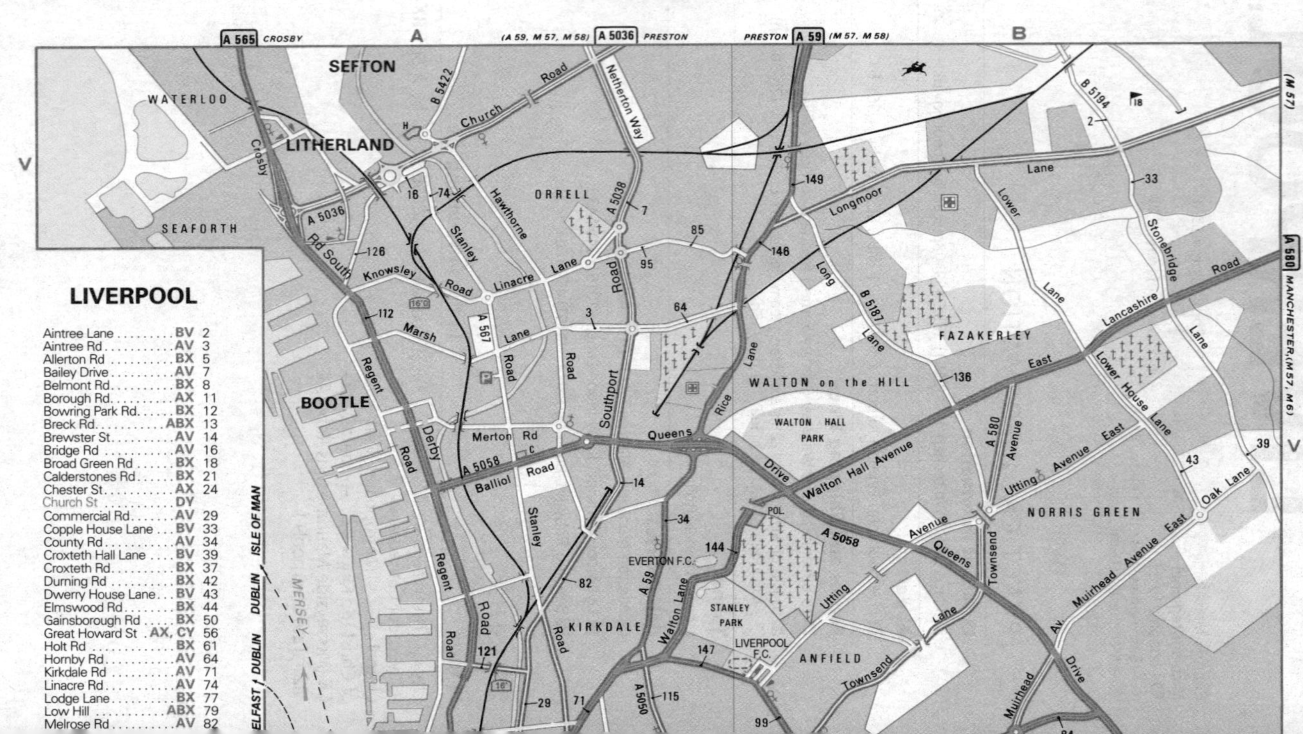

LIVERPOOL

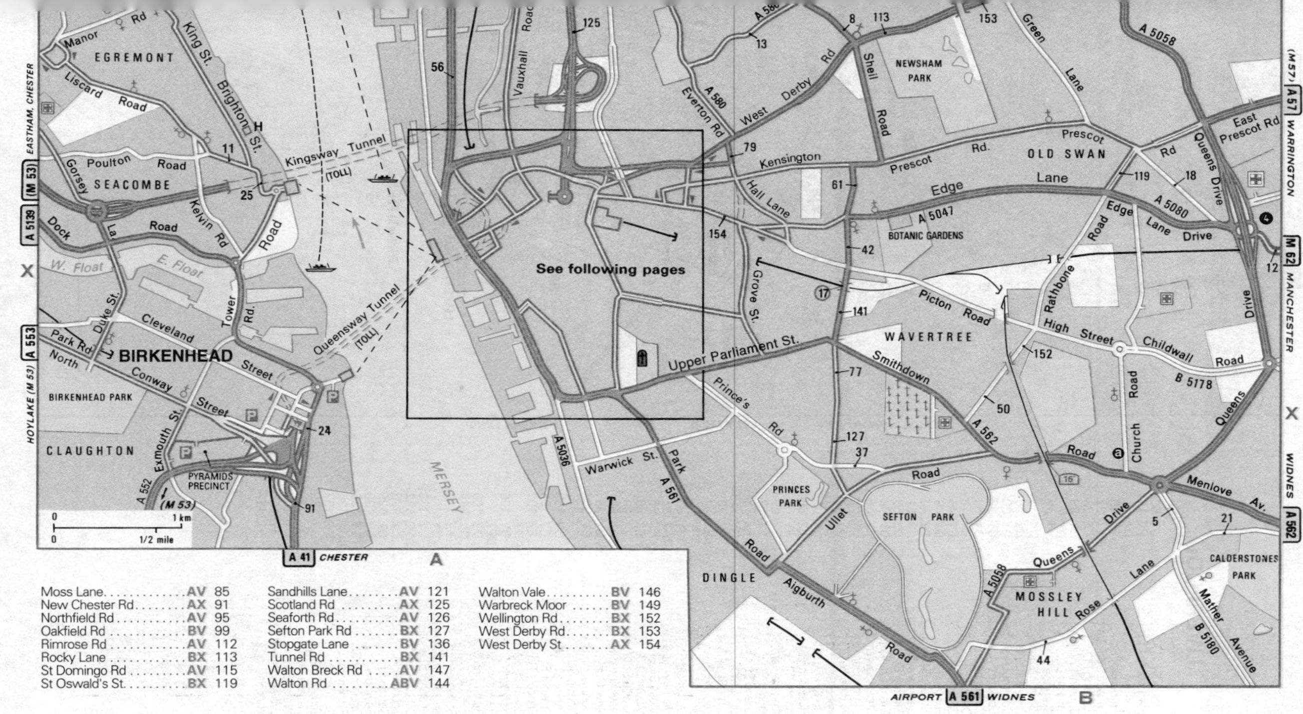

Street	Grid	No.	Street	Grid	No.	Street	Grid	No.
Moss Lane	AV	85	Sandhills Lane	AV	121	Walton Vale	BV	146
New Chester Rd	AX	91	Scotland Rd	AX	125	Warbreck Moor	BV	149
Northfield Rd	AV	95	Seaforth Rd	AV	126	Wellington Rd	BX	152
Oakfield Rd	BV	99	Sefton Park Rd	BX	127	West Derby Rd	BX	153
Rimrose Rd	AV	112	Stopgate Lane	BV	136	West Derby St	AX	154
Rocky Lane	BX	113	Tunnel Rd	BX	141			
St Domingo Rd	AV	115	Walton Breck Rd	AV	147			
St Oswald's St	BX	119	Walton Rd	ABV	144			

ENGLAND

LIVERPOOL

Argyle St . . . . DZ 6
Blackburne Pl. . . . . EZ 10
Bold St. . . . . DZ
Brunswick Rd . . . . EY 19
Canada Boulevard . . . . CYZ 22
Canning Pl. . . . . CZ 23
Churchill Way . . . . DY 26
Church St . . . . DY
Clarence St. . . . . EYZ 27
Clayton Square Shopping Centre DY
College Lane. . . . . DZ 28
Commutation Row . . . . DY 30
Cook St . . . . CY 32
Crosshall St. . . . . DY 36
Daulby St. . . . . EY 40
Erskine St . . . . EY 45
Fontenoy St . . . . DY 48
Forrest St . . . . DZ 49
George's Dock Lane . . . . CY 51
Grafton St . . . . DZ 53
Great Charlotte St . . . . DY 54
Great Howard St . . . . CY 56
Hatton Garden . . . . DY 57
Haymarket . . . . DY 58
Hood St. DY 62
Houghton St. . . . . DY 65
Huskisson St. . . . . EZ 66
James St. . . . . CY 68
King Edward St. . . . . CY 69
Knight St . . . . EZ 72
Leece St . . . . EZ 73
Lime St . . . . DY
Liver St . . . . CZ 76
London Rd . . . . DEY
Lord St . . . . CDY
Mansfield St. . . . . DEY 80
Mathew St. . . . . CDY 81
Moss St. EY 86
Mount St . . . . EZ 88
Myrtle St . . . . EZ 89
Newington St . . . . DZ 92
New Quay. . . . . CY 93
North John St . . . . CY 96
Norton St. . . . . EY 97
Parker St . . . . DY 103
Prescot St . . . . EY 105
Prince's Rd . . . . EZ 107
Queen Square . . . . DY
Ranelagh St . . . . DY 108
Renshaw St . . . . DEZ
Richmond St. . . . . DY 109
Roe St . . . . DY 114
St James Pl. . . . . EZ 117
St John's Centre. . . . . DY
St John's Lane . . . . DY 118
School Lane . . . . DYZ 122
Scotland Pl. . . . . DY 123
Sefton St . . . . DZ 129
Seymour St . . . . EY 130
Skelhorne St . . . . DY 133
Stanley St. . . . . CDY 135
Suffolk St. . . . . DZ 137
Tarleton St. . . . . DY 139
Victoria St . . . . DY 143
Water St . . . . CY 150
William Brown St . . . . DY 156
York St. DZ 157

ENGLAND

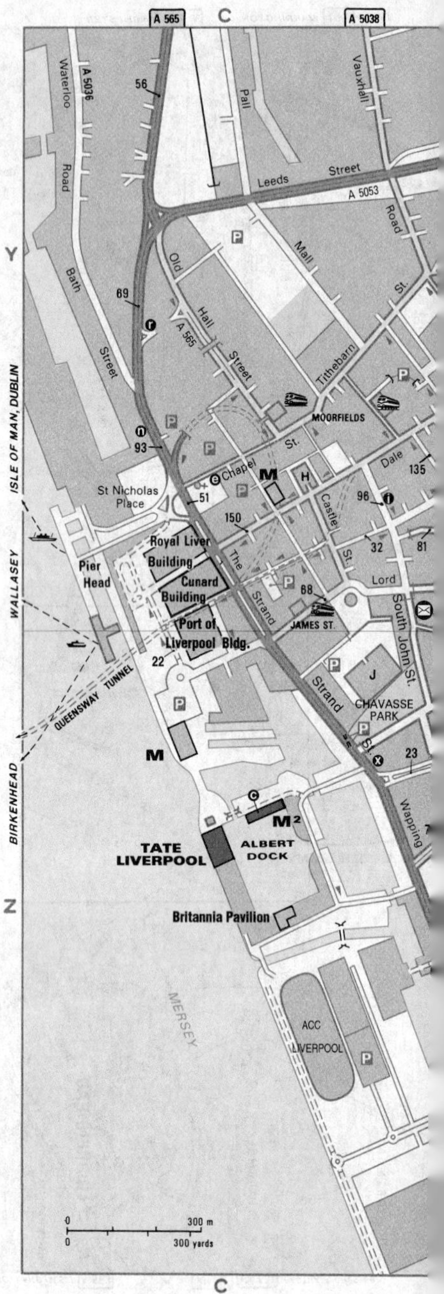

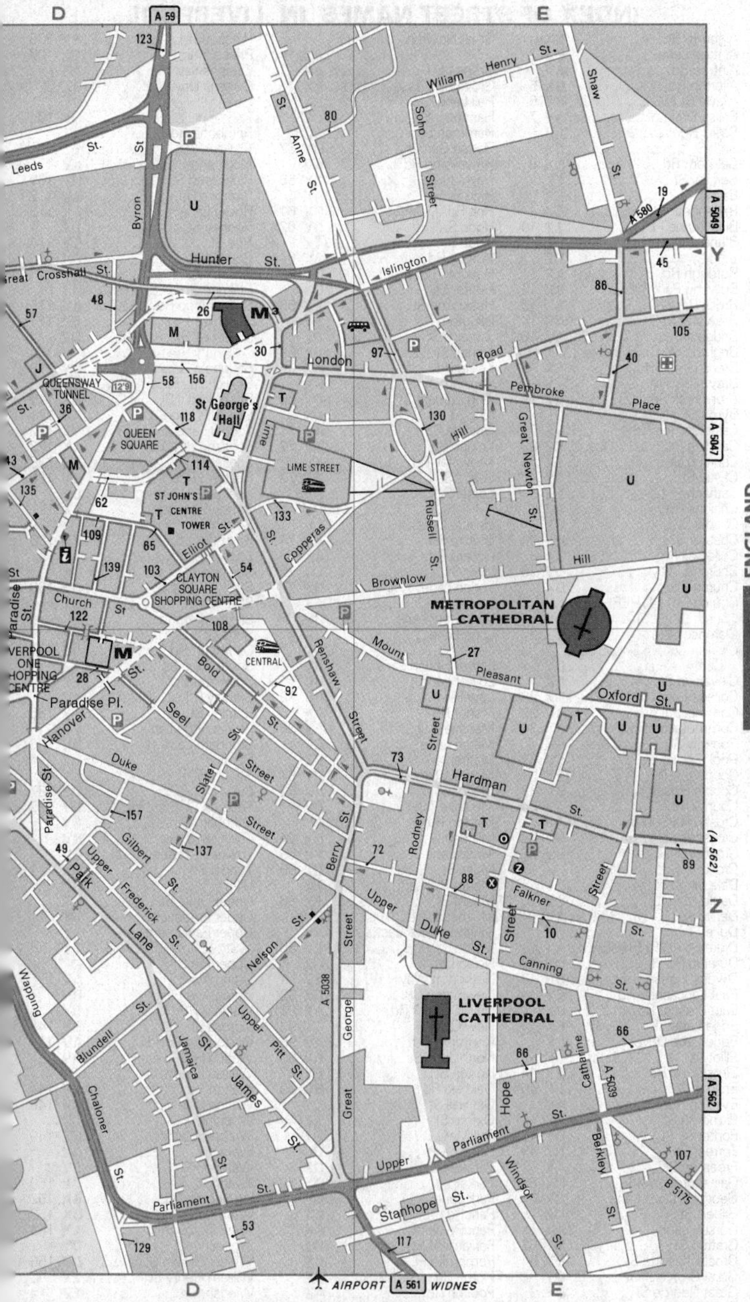

METROPOLITAN CATHEDRAL
LIVERPOOL CATHEDRAL
St George's Hall
QUEEN SQUARE
ST JOHN'S CENTRE TOWER
CLAYTON SQUARE SHOPPING CENTRE
LIVERPOOL ONE SHOPPING CENTRE
QUEENSWAY TUNNEL
LIME STREET
CENTRAL
AIRPORT A 561 WIDNES

ENGLAND

INDEX OF STREET NAMES IN LIVERPOOL

ENGLAND

Hilton

3 Thomas Steers Way ✉ L1 8LW – ✆ (0151) 708 4200
– www.hilton.co.uk/liverpool CZ**x**
204 rm – †£ 99/149 ††£ 109/159, ☕ £ 14.95
– 11 suites
Rest *Exchange* – Menu £ 15/25 – Carte £ 17/43
◆ Spacious, light-filled hotel in waterfront location, with the latest in modern styling and facilities. Floor to ceiling windows in bedrooms. Trendy cocktail bar, good conference facilities and well-equipped gym. Accessible menu of international dishes in Exchange.

Malmaison

7 William Jessop Way, Princes Dock ✉ L3 1QZ – ✆ (0151) 229 5000
– www.malmaison-liverpool.com CY**n**
130 rm – †£ 170 ††£ 170, ☕ £ 13.95
– 2 suites
Rest *The Brasserie* – *(Closed Saturday lunch)* Menu £ 15
– Carte £ 26/37
◆ Contemporary waterfront hotel, with striking façade and stylish, comfortable bedrooms decorated in sensuous purple/orange tones. Football themed suites, The Kop and The Toffee. Sexy, sophisticated 'Plum' bar. Classic brasserie dishes in industrial style restaurant.

Hope Street

40 Hope St ✉ L1 9DA – ✆ (0151) 709 3000
– www.hopestreethotel.co.uk EZ**o**
89 rm – †£ 160 ††£ 160, ☕ £ 16.50
– 9 suites
Rest *The London Carriage Works* – see restaurant listing
◆ Former carriage works; now a modern, boutique hotel. Stylish, minimalist bedrooms boast stark white walls and underfloor heating; top floor loft suites have stunning skyline views. Trendy bar open Thurs-Sat.

Hard Days Night

Central Buildings, North John St ✉ L2 6RR – ✆ (0151) 236 19 64
– www.harddaysnighthotel.com CY**i**
110 rm – †£ 110/275 ††£ 110/275, ☕ £ 15.95
– 2 suites
Rest *Blakes* – *(Closed Sunday and Monday)* Menu £ 14 (lunch) **s**
– Carte £ 34/49 **s**
◆ Unique Beatles themed hotel; their story recounted in artwork from doorstep to rooftop, with every room featuring original works. Suites styled around Lennon and McCartney. Blakes, named after designer of Sgt. Pepper album cover, features modern brasserie menu.

Racquet Club

Hargreaves Buildings, 5 Chapel St ✉ L3 9AG – ✆ (0151) 236 6676
– www.racquetclub.org – Closed 25 December, first week January and bank holidays CY**e**
8 rm – †£ 100/160 ††£ 100/160, ☕ £ 12
Rest *Ziba* – *(Closed Sunday and Saturday lunch)* Carte £ 18/28 **s**
◆ Ornate Victorian building – a former Shipping Agency office – with a bohemian ambience. Bedrooms differ greatly in style and size; most feature artwork and antique furniture. Dine at clothed tables in high-ceilinged Ziba; the eclectic menu offers mainly English dishes.

Don't confuse the couvert rating ✗ with the stars ✿!
Couverts defines comfort and service, while stars are awarded for the best cuisine across all categories of comfort.

ENGLAND

Panoramic

West Tower, 34th floor, ✉ L3 9PJ – ✆ (0151) 236 55 34
– www.panoramicliverpool.com
– Closed bank holidays CY**r**
Rest – Menu £ 20 (lunch)
– Carte dinner £ 39/55
◆ On 34th floor of city's highest building; a stylish glass skyscraper with 360° views. Clothed tables, formal service; intimate dinners. Creative, ambitious cooking; excellent value lunch.

60 Hope Street

60 Hope St ✉ L1 9BZ – ✆ (0151) 707 6060
– www.60hopestreet.com
– Closed bank holidays, Saturday lunch and Sunday dinner EZ**x**
Rest – Menu £ 25 – Carte dinner £ 33/51
◆ Attractive Grade II listed Georgian house concealing well-established modern brasserie with bold feature walls and informal basement wine bar. Interesting regional dishes provide good value.

The London Carriage Works – at Hope Street Hotel

40 Hope St ✉ L1 9DA – ✆ (0151) 705 2222
– www.thelondoncarriageworks.co.uk EZ**o**
Rest – Menu £ 20 (lunch)
– Carte approx. £ 54
◆ Spacious, open-plan brasserie dominated by impressive glass sculpture, with long bar, squashy sofas and relaxed ambience. Modern European brasserie dishes focus on local ingredients.

ENGLAND

Spire

1 Church Rd ✉ L15 9EA – ✆ (0151) 734 5040
– www.spirerestaurant.co.uk
– Closed 1-14 January, Sunday, and lunch Monday and Saturday BX**a**
Rest – Menu £ 10/14 (midweek)
– Carte dinner £ 28/34
◆ Simple neighbourhood restaurant set in the Penny Lane area of the city. Good value, understated menus offer regional and modern European dishes. Tasty modern cooking; friendly service.

Host

31 Hope St ✉ L1 9HX – ✆ (0151) 708 5831
– www.ho-st.co.uk
– closed 25-26 December EZ**z**
Rest – South-East Asian
– Carte £ 17/22
◆ Lively place with trendy bar and informal dining area of refectory-style tables. Wide range of Asian-inspired dishes, including Chinese, Japanese, Thai and Vietnamese. Good desserts.

Maritime Dining Room

Merseyside Maritime Museum, (4th Floor) ✉ L3 4AQ
– ✆ (0151) 478 4056 – www.liverpoolmuseums.org.uk
– Closed 25 December and 1 January CZ**c**
Rest – *(lunch only)* Menu £ 15
– Carte £ 19/23
◆ Located on top floor of the superb maritime museum, with views over the famous Albert Dock. Seasonally changing menu of hearty, rustic British classics, with the occasional modern twist.

Guesthouses ⌂ don't provide the same level of service as hotels. They are often characterised by a warm welcome and a décor which reflects the owner's personality. Those shown in red ⌂ are particularly pleasant.

LIZARD – Cornwall – 503 E34 1 A3

London 326 mi – Penzance 24 mi – Truro 29 mi

Lizard Peninsula★ - Mullion Cove★★ (Church★) - Kynance Cove★★ - Cadgwith★ - Coverack★ – Cury★ (Church★) - Gunwalloe Fishing Cove★ - St Keverne (Church★) - Landewednack★ (Church★) – Mawgan-in-Meneage (Church★) - Ruan Minor (Church★) - St Anthony-in-Meneage★

Landewednack House

Church Cove, East : 1 mi by A 3083 ✉ TR12 7PQ – ☎ (01326) 290 877 – www.landewednackhouse.com

5 rm – †£ 55/85 ††£ 190 **Rest** – Menu £ 35

◆ Part 17C former rectory and garden, overlooking Church Cove. Smart interiors stylishly furnished with antiques. Diners encouraged to discuss menus: best local produce to hand.

C. Eymenier/MICHELIN

LONDON

Map reference: **12** B3

PRACTICAL INFORMATION

Tourist Information

Britain & London Visitor Centre, Thames Tower, Black Rd, W6 ✆ (020) 8846 9000, bvlcenquiry@visitlondon.com

Airports

Heathrow ✆ 0844 335 1801 **12** AX Terminal: Bus and Coach services run regularly, each day from Victoria. By Rail: Heathrow Express and Connect from Paddington Underground, daily every 20 minutes.

Gatwick ✆ 0844 335 1802 **13**: by A23 EZ and M23 - Terminal: Coach services from Victoria Coach Station run regularly each day. By Rail: Gatwick Express from Victoria Underground, daily every 15 minutes. Southern Trains every 15 minutes from Victoria, London Bridge and Clapham Junction

London City Airport ✆ (020) 7646 0088 **11** HV

Stansted, at Bishop's Stortford ✆ 0844 335 1803, NE: 34m **11** by M11 JT and A12O.

British Airways, Ticket sales and reservations, Paddington Station London, W2, ✆08700 8509 8500 **36** BX

Banks

Open, generally 9.30 am to 4.30 pm weekdays (except public holidays). You need ID (passport) for cashing cheques. Banks levy smaller commissions than hotels. Many 'Bureaux de Change' around Piccadilly open 7 days.

Medical Emergencies

To contact a doctor for first aid, emergency medical advice and chemists night service: ✆ 07000 372255.

Accident & Emergency: dial 999 for Ambulance, Police or Fire Services.

Post Offices

Open Monday to Friday 9am to 5.30 pm. Late collections made from Leicester Square.

Shopping

Most stores are found in Oxford Street (Selfridges, M & S), Regent Street (Hamleys, Libertys) and Knightsbridge (Harrods, Harvey Nichols). Open usually Monday to Saturday 9 am to 6 pm. Some open later (8 pm) once a week; Knightsbridge Wednesday, Oxford Street and Regent Street Thursday. Other areas worth visiting include Jermyn Street and Savile Row (mens outfitters), Bond Street (jewellers and haute couture).

Theatres

The "West End" has many major theatre performances and can generally be found around Shaftesbury Avenue. Most daily newspapers give details of performances. A half-price ticket booth is located in Leicester Square and is open Monday to Saturday 1 pm to 6.30 pm, Sunday and matinée days 12 noon to 6.30 pm. Restrictions apply.

Tipping

When a service charge is included in a bill it is not necessary to tip extra. If service is not included a discretionary 10% is normal.

Travel

As driving in London is difficult, it is advisable to take the Underground, a bus or taxi. Taxis can be hailed when the amber light is illuminated.

Congestion Charging

The congestion charge is £ 8 per day on all vehicles (except motor cycles and exempt vehicles) entering the central zone between 7.00 am and 6.00 pm - Monday to Friday except on Bank Holldays.

Payment can be made in advance, on the day, by post, on the Internet, by telephone (0845 900 1234) or at retail outlets.

A charge of up to £ 100 will be made for non-payment.

Further information is available on the Transport for London website - www.tfl.gov.uk

Localities outside the Greater London limits are listed alphabetically throughout the guide.

SIGHTS

Historical Buildings and Monuments

Palace of Westminster★★★: House of Lords★★, Westminster Hall★ (hammerbeam roof★★★), Robing Room★, Central Lobby★, House of Commons★, Big Ben★, Victoria Tower★ 39 ALX - Tower of London★★★ (Crown Jewels★★★, White Tower or Keep★★★, St John's Chapel★★) - British Airways London Eye (views★★★) 32 AMV.
Banqueting House★★ 31 ALV - Buckingham Palace★★ (Changing of the Guard, Royal Mews★★, Queen's Gallery★★) 38 AIX - Kensington Palace★★ 27 ABV - Lincoln's Inn★★ 32 AMT - Lloyds Building★★ 34 ARU - Royal Hospital Chelsea★★ 37 AGZ - St James's Palace★★ 30 AJV - Somerset House★★ 32 AMU - South Bank Arts Centre★★ (Royal Festival Hall★, National Theatre Royal★, County Hall★) 32 AMV - Spencer House★★ 30 AIV - The Temple★★ (Middle Temple Hall★★) 32 ANU - Tower Bridge★★ 34 ASV.
Albert Memorial★ 36 ADX - Apsley House★ 30 AHV - Burlington House★ 30 AIV - Charterhouse★ 19 UZD - George Inn★, Southwark 33 AQV - Gray's Inn★ 32 AMV - Guildhall★ (Lord Mayor's Show) 33 AQT - Shakespeare's Globe★ 33 APV - Dr Johnson's House★ 32 ANT - Leighton House★ 35 AAX - Linley Sambourne House★ 35 AAX - London Bridge★ 34 ARV - Mansion House★ (plate and insignia★★) 33 AQV - The Monument★ (✻★) 34 ARU - Old Admiralty★ 31 AKV - Royal Albert Hall★ 36 ADX - Royal Exchange★ 34 ARU - Royal Opera House★ (Covent Garden) 31 ALU - Staple Inn★ 32 ANT - Theatre Royal★ (Haymarket) 31 AKV - Westminster Bridge★ 39 ALX.

Churches

The City Churches

St Paul's Cathedral★★★ (Dome ⋞★★★) 33 APU.
St Bartholomew the Great★★ (choir★) 33 APT - St Dunstan-in-the-East★ (Tower★) 34 ARU - St Mary-at-Hill★★ (plan★) 34 ARU - Temple Church★★ 32 ANU.
All Hallows-by-the-Tower (font cover★★, brasses★) 34 ARU - Christ Church★ 33 APT - Cole Abbey Presbyterian Church (spire★) 33 APU - St Andrew Undershaft (monuments★) 34 ARU - St Bride★ (steeple★★) 32 ANU - St Clement Eastcheap (pulpit★) 34 ARU - St Edmund the King and Martyr (spire★) 34 ARU - St Giles Cripplegate★ 33 AQT - St Helen Bishopsgate★ (monuments★★) 34 ART - St James Garlickhythe (spire★, sword rests★) 33 AQU - St Magnus the Martyr (tower★, sword rest★) 34 ARU - St Margaret Lothbury★ (spire★, woodwork★, screen★, font★) 33 AQT - St Margaret Pattens (spire★, woodwork★) 34 ARU - St Martin-within-Ludgate (spire★, door cases★) 33 APU - St Mary Abchurch★ (reredos★★, spire★, dome★) 33 AQU - St Mary-le-Bow (steeple★★) 33 AQU - St Michael Paternoster Royal (spire★) 35 AQU - St Olave★ 34 ARU - St Peter upon Cornhill (screen★) 34 ARU - St Stephen Walbrook★ (steeple★, dome★) 33 AQU.

Other Churches

Westminster Abbey★★★ (Henry VII Chapel★★★, Chapel of Edward the Confessor★★, Chapter House★★, Poets' Corner★) 39 ALX.
Southwark Cathedral★★ 33 AQV.
Queen's Chapel★ 39 AJV - St Clement Danes★ 32 AMU - St James's★ 30 AJV - St Margaret's★ 39 ALX - St Martin-in-the-Fields★ 31 ALV - St Paul's★ (Covent Garden) 31 ALU - Westminster Roman Catholic Cathedral★ 39 ALX.

Parks

Regent's Park★★★ (terraces★★, Zoo★★) 11 QZC.
Hyde Park 29 AFV - Kensington Gardens★★ 28 ACV (Orangery★) 27 ABV - St James's Park★★31 AKV.

Streets and Squares

The City★★★ 33 AQT.
Bedford Square★★ 31 AKT - Belgrave Square★★ 37 AGX - Burlington Arcade★ 30 AIV - Covent Garden★★ (The Piazza★★) 31 ALU - The Mall★★ 31 AKV - Piccadilly★ 30 AIV - Trafalgar Square★★ 31 AKV - Whitehall★★ (Horse Guards★) 31 ALV.
Barbican★ 33 AQT - Bond Street★ 30 AIU - Canonbury Square★ 13 UZB - Carlton House Terrace★ 31 AKV - Cheyne Walk★ 23 PZG - Fitzroy Square★ 18 RZD - Jermyn Street★ 30 AJV - Leicester Square★ 31 AKU - Merrick Square★ 19 VZE - Montpelier Square★ 37 AFX - Neal's Yard★ 31 ALU - Piccadilly Arcade★ 30 AIV - Piccadilly Circus★ 31 AKU - Portman Square★ 29 AGT - Regent Street★ 30 AIU - Royal Opera Arcade★ 31 AKV - St James's Square★ 31 AJV - St James's Street★ 30 AIV - Shepherd Market★ 30 AHV - Trinity Church Square★ 19 VZE - Victoria Embankment Gardens★ 31 ALV - Waterloo Place★ 31 AKV.

Museums

British Museum★★★ 31 AKL - Imperial War Museum★★★ 40 ANY - National Gallery★★★ 31 AKV - Science Museum★★★ 36 ADX - Tate Britain★★★ 39 ALY - Victoria and Albert Museum★★★ 36 ADY - Wallace Collection★★★ 29 AGT.
Courtauld Institute Galleries★★ (Somerset House) 32 AMU - Gilbert Collection★★ (Somerset House) 32 AMU - Museum of London★★ 33 APT - National Portrait Gallery★★ 31 AKU - Natural History Museum★★ 36 ADY - Sir John Soane's Museum★★ 32 AMT - Tate Modern★★ (views★★★ from top floors) 33 APV.
Clock Museum★ (Guildhall) 33 AQT - London's Transport Museum★ 31 ALU - Madame Tussaud's Waxworks★ 17 QZD - National Army Museum★ 37 AGZ - Percival David Foundation of Chinese Art★ 18 SZD - Wellington Museum★ (Apsley House) 30 AHV.

Outer London

Blackheath 8 HX terraces and houses★, Eltham Palace★ **A**
Brentford 5 BX Syon Park★★, gardens★
Bromley 7 GXY The Crystal Palace Park★
Chiswick 6 CV Chiswick Mall★★, Chiswick House★ **D**, Hogarth's House★ **E**
Dulwich 11 Picture Gallery★ FX **X**
Greenwich 7 and 8 GHV Cutty Sark★★ GV **F**, Footway Tunnel (≤ ★★), Fan Museum★ 10 GV **A**, National Maritime Museum★★ (Queen's House★★) GV **M²** Royal Naval College★★ (Painted Hall★, the Chapel★) GV **G**, The Park and Old Royal Observatory★ (Meridian Building: collection★★) HV **K**, Ranger's House★ (Wernher Collection) GX **N**
Hampstead Kenwood House★★ (Adam Library★★, paintings★★) 2 EU **P**, Fenton House★★ 11 PZA
Hampton Court 5 BY (The Palace★★★, gardens★★★, Fountain Court★, The Great Vine★)
Kew 6 CX Royal Botanic Gardens★★★: Palm House★★, Temperate House★, Kew Palace or Dutch House★★, Orangery★, Pagoda★, Japanese Gateway★
Hendon★ 2 Royal Air Force Museum★★ CT **M³**
Hounslow 5 BV Osterley Park★★
Lewisham 7 GX Horniman Museum★ **M⁴**
Richmond 5 and 6 CX Richmond Park★★, ✻★★★ CX, Richmond Hill✻★★ CX, Richmond Bridge★★ BX **R**, Richmond Green★★ BX **S**, (Maids of Honour Row★★, Trumpeter's House★), Asgill House★ BX **B**, Ham House★★ BX **V**
Shoreditch 14 XZ Beffrye Museum★ **M**
Tower Hamlets 7 GV Canary Wharf★★ B, Isle of Dogs★ St Katharine Dock★ 34 ASV
Twickenham 5 BX Marble Hill House★ **Z**, Strawberry Hill★ **A**

The maps in this section of the Guide are based upon the Ordnance Survey of Great Britain with the permission of the Controller of Her Majesty's Stationery Office.

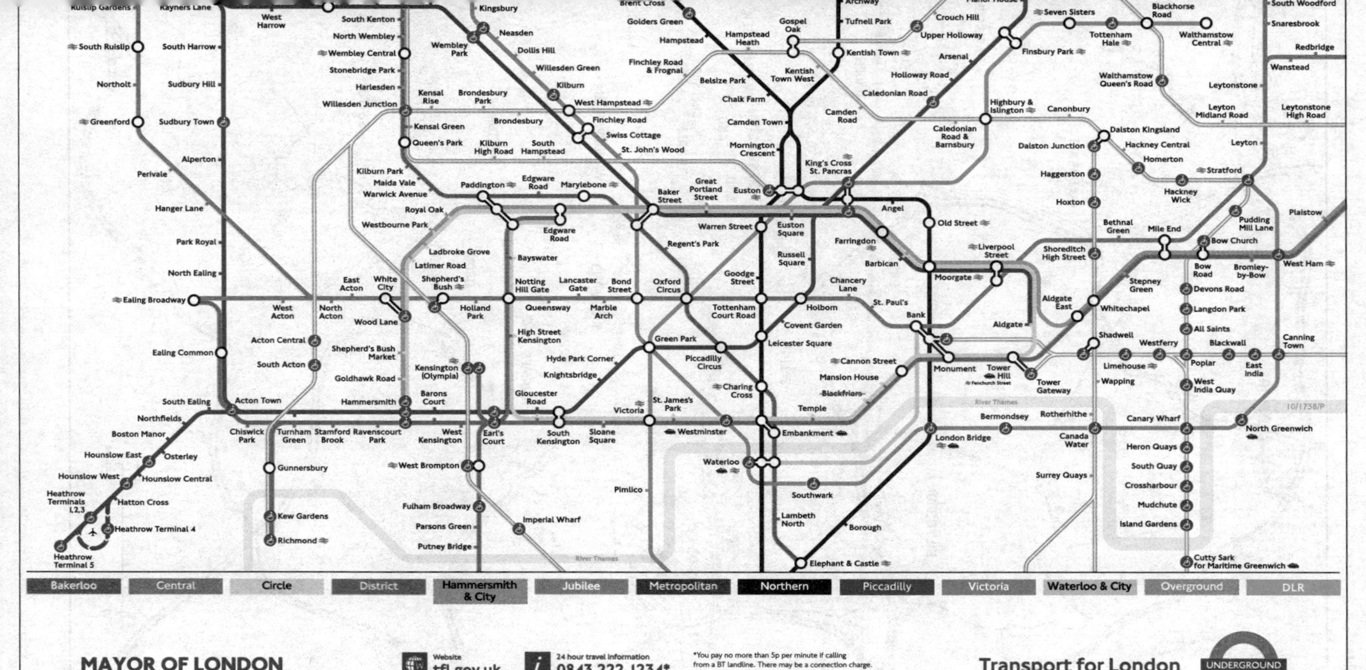

 Reg. user No. 10/1738/P Version C 02.2010 Improvement works may affect your journey, please check before you travel Correct at time of going to print

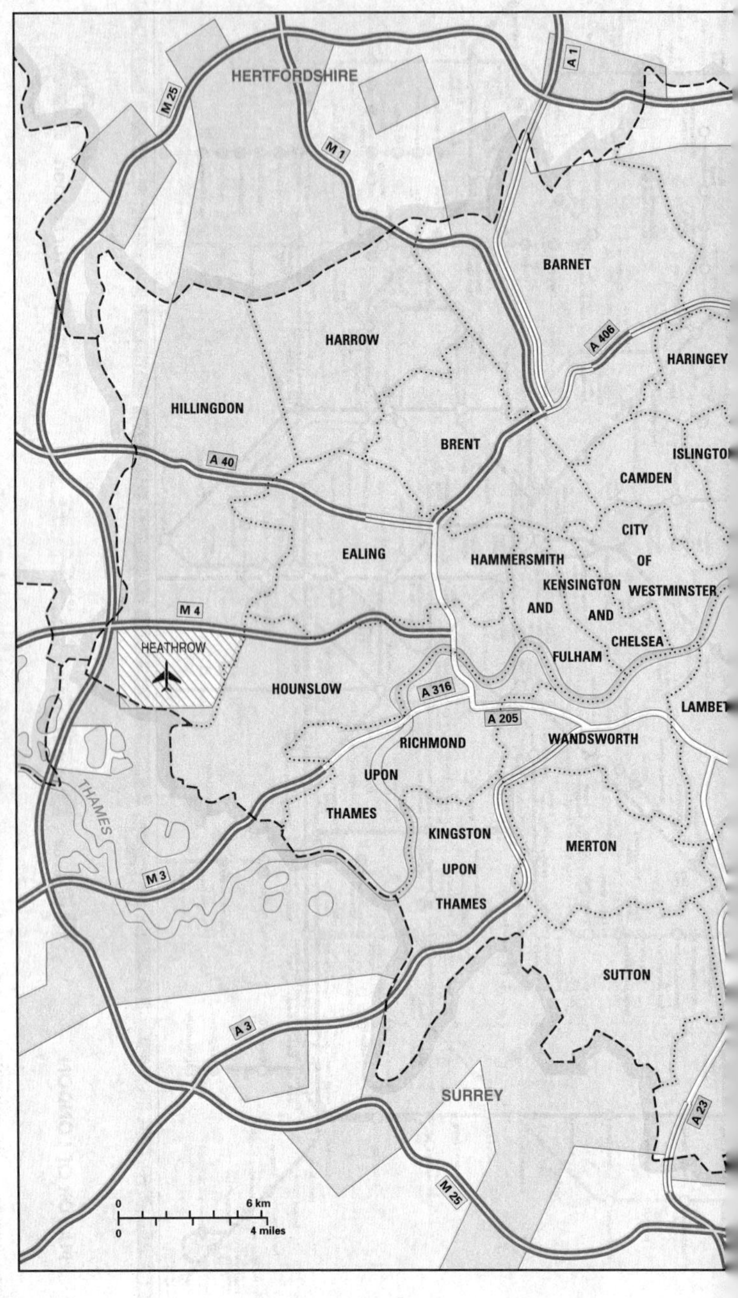
HERTFORDSHIRE
M 25
M 1
A 1
BARNET
A 406
HARINGEY
HARROW
HILLINGDON
BRENT
A 40
ISLINGTO
CAMDEN
CITY
OF
WESTMINSTER
EALING
HAMMERSMITH
AND
FULHAM
KENSINGTON
AND
CHELSEA
M 4
HEATHROW
HOUNSLOW
A 316
A 205
LAMBET
RICHMOND
UPON
THAMES
WANDSWORTH
THAMES
KINGSTON
UPON
THAMES
MERTON
M 3
SUTTON
A 3
SURREY
A 23
M 25
0
6 km
0
4 miles

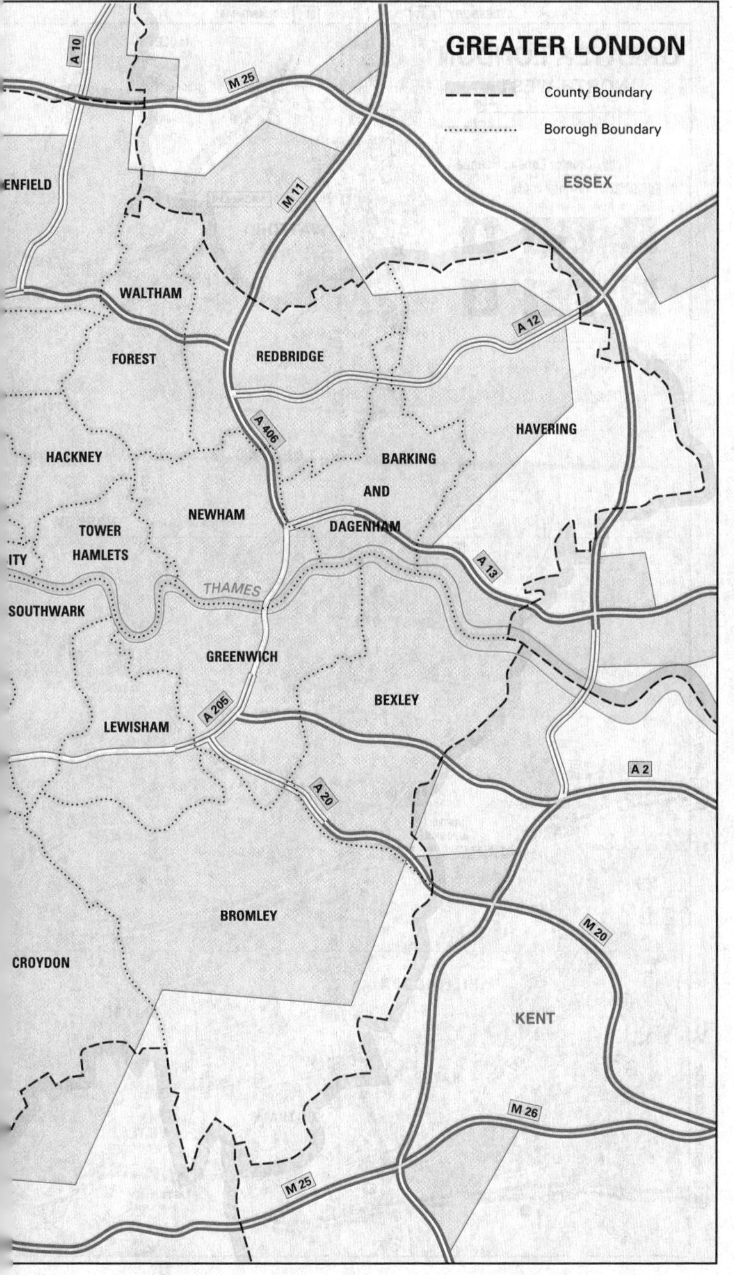
GREATER LONDON
County Boundary
Borough Boundary
ESSEX
ENFIELD
WALTHAM
FOREST
REDBRIDGE
HAVERING
HACKNEY
BARKING
AND
DAGENHAM
NEWHAM
TOWER
HAMLETS
ITY
THAMES
SOUTHWARK
GREENWICH
BEXLEY
LEWISHAM
BROMLEY
CROYDON
KENT
A 10
M 25
M 11
A 12
A 406
A 13
A 205
A 20
A 2
M 20
M 26

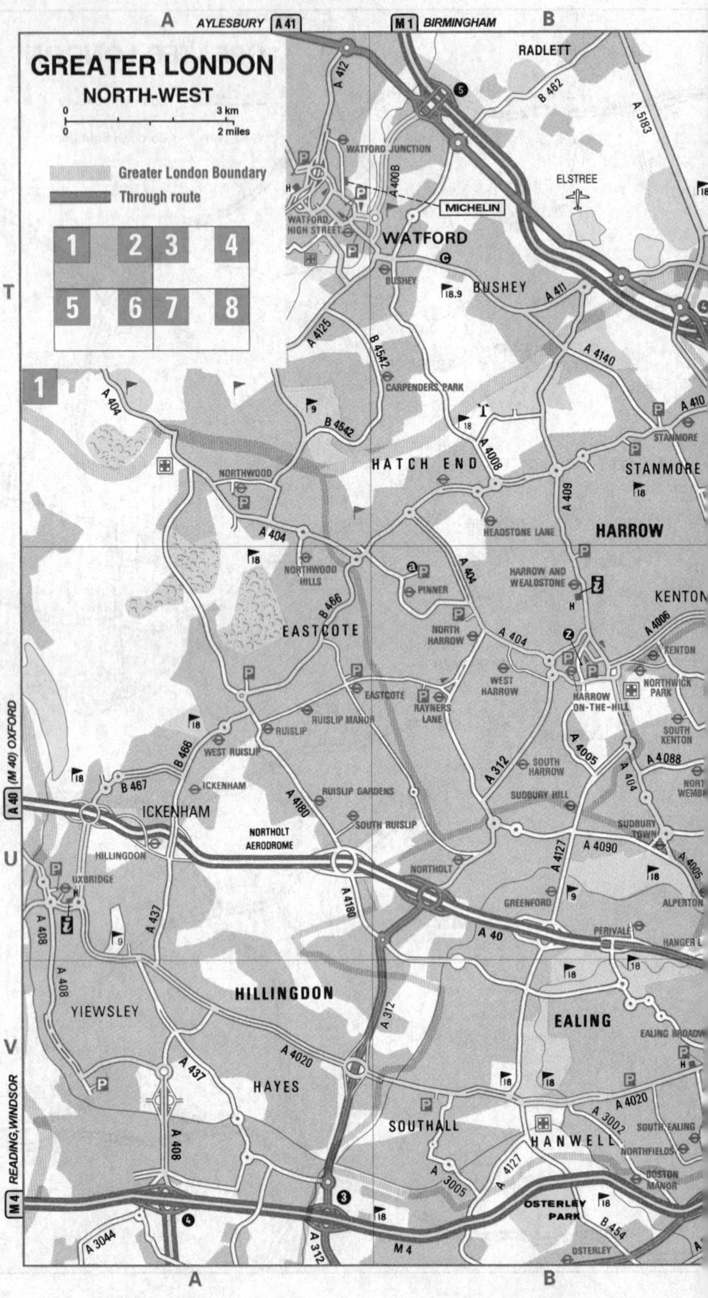
GREATER LONDON
NORTH-WEST
0 3 km
0 2 miles
Greater London Boundary
Through route
AYLESBURY A 41
M 1 BIRMINGHAM
RADLETT
WATFORD JUNCTION
ELSTREE
MICHELIN
WATFORD HIGH STREET
WATFORD
BUSHEY
CARPENDERS PARK
HATCH END
NORTHWOOD
STANMORE
HARROW
HEADSTONE LANE
NORTHWOOD HILLS
PINNER
HARROW AND WEALDSTONE
KENTON
EASTCOTE
NORTH HARROW
WEST HARROW
RAYNERS LANE
HARROW ON-THE-HILL
NORTHWICK PARK
RUISLIP MANOR
RUISLIP
WEST RUISLIP
SOUTH HARROW
SOUTH KENTON
ICKENHAM
RUISLIP GARDENS
SUDBURY HILL
SOUTH RUISLIP
SUDBURY TOWN
NORTHOLT AERODROME
HILLINGDON
NORTHOLT
UXBRIDGE
GREENFORD
ALPERTON
PERIVALE
HILLINGDON
YIEWSLEY
EALING
EALING BROADW
HAYES
SOUTHALL
HANWELL
SOUTH EALING
NORTHFIELDS
BOSTON MANOR
OSTERLEY PARK
OSTERLEY
A 40 (M 40) OXFORD
M 4 READING, WINDSOR
LONDON

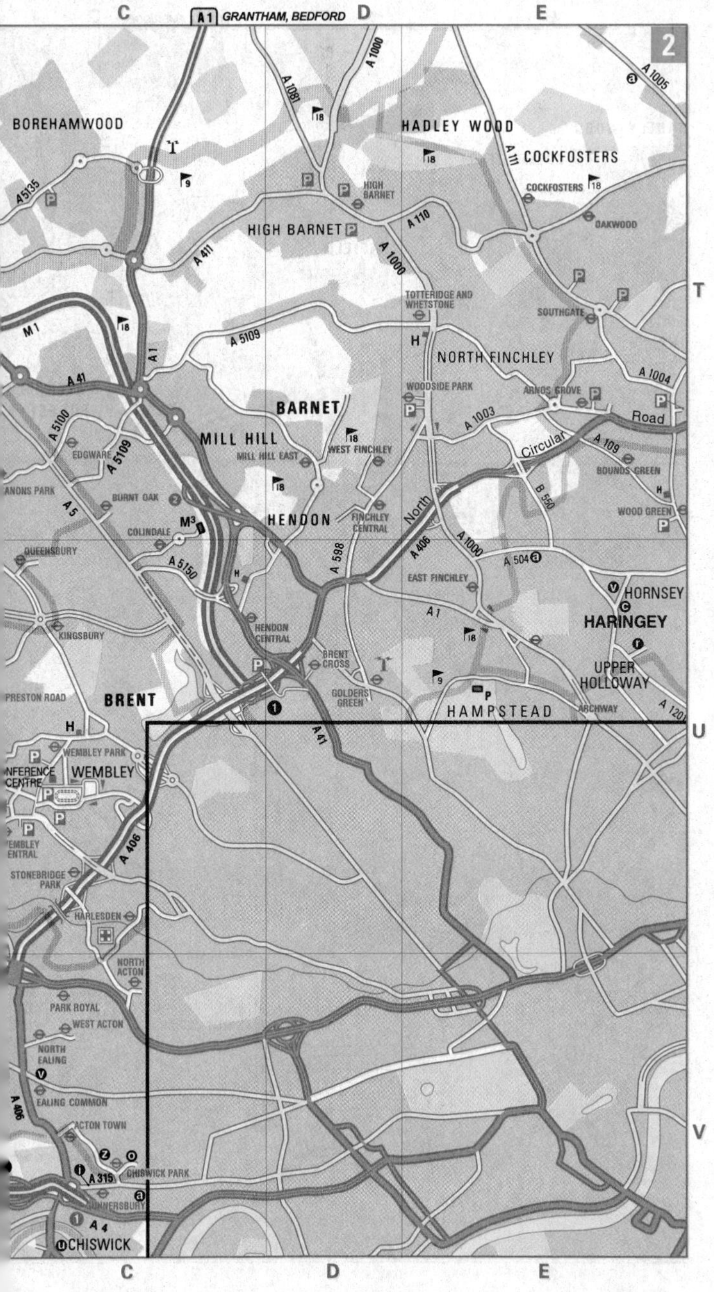
C
D
E
A1 GRANTHAM, BEDFORD
2
BOREHAMWOOD
HADLEY WOOD
COCKFOSTERS
HIGH BARNET
TOTTERIDGE AND WHETSTONE
SOUTHGATE
OAKWOOD
NORTH FINCHLEY
WOODSIDE PARK
ARNOS GROVE
BARNET
MILL HILL
MILL HILL EAST
WEST FINCHLEY
EDGWARE
BURNT OAK
COLINDALE
HENDON
FINCHLEY CENTRAL
North Circular Road
BOUNDS GREEN
WOOD GREEN
QUEENSBURY
EAST FINCHLEY
HORNSEY
HARINGEY
KINGSBURY
HENDON CENTRAL
BRENT CROSS
GOLDERS GREEN
UPPER HOLLOWAY
PRESTON ROAD
BRENT
HAMPSTEAD
ARCHWAY
WEMBLEY PARK
WEMBLEY
STONEBRIDGE PARK
HARLESDEN
NORTH ACTON
PARK ROYAL
WEST ACTON
NORTH EALING
EALING COMMON
ACTON TOWN
CHISWICK PARK
GUNNERSBURY
CHISWICK
T
U
V
LONDON

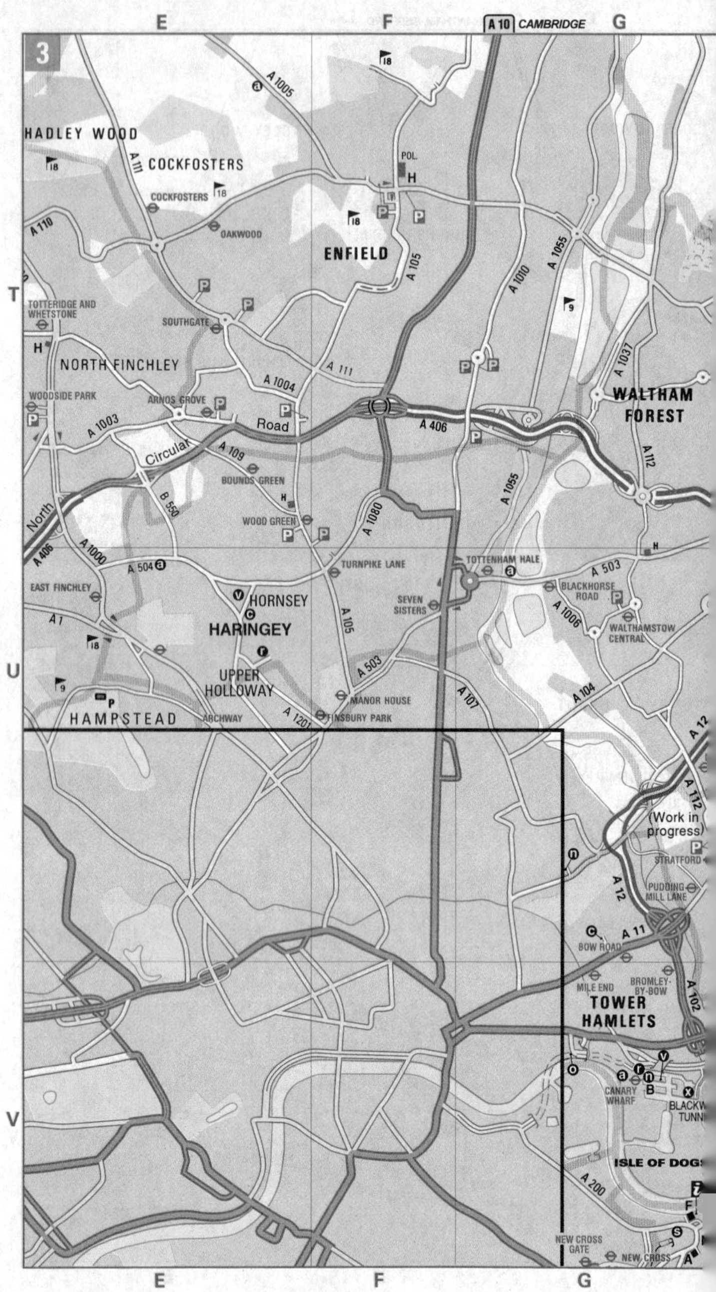

E
F
A 10 CAMBRIDGE
G
3
A 1005
HADLEY WOOD
COCKFOSTERS
A 111
POL.
ENFIELD
A 105
A 1010
A 1055
A 110
OAKWOOD
TOTTERIDGE AND WHETSTONE
SOUTHGATE
NORTH FINCHLEY
A 111
A 1004
A 1037
WALTHAM FOREST
WOODSIDE PARK
ARNOS GROVE
A 1003
Road
A 406
Circular
A 109
A 112
BOUNDS GREEN
B 550
North
WOOD GREEN
A 1080
A 1055
A 406
A 1000
A 504
TURNPIKE LANE
TOTTENHAM HALE
A 503
EAST FINCHLEY
HORNSEY
SEVEN SISTERS
BLACKHORSE ROAD
A 1006
A 1
HARINGEY
A 105
WALTHAMSTOW CENTRAL
UPPER HOLLOWAY
A 503
A 107
A 104
HAMPSTEAD
ARCHWAY
A 1201
MANOR HOUSE
FINSBURY PARK
A 12
A 112
(Work in progress)
STRATFORD
A 12
PUDDING MILL LANE
A 11
BOW ROAD
MILE END
BROMLEY-BY-BOW
A 102
TOWER HAMLETS
CANARY WHARF
ISLE OF DOGS
A 200
NEW CROSS GATE
NEW CROSS
T
U
V
LONDON

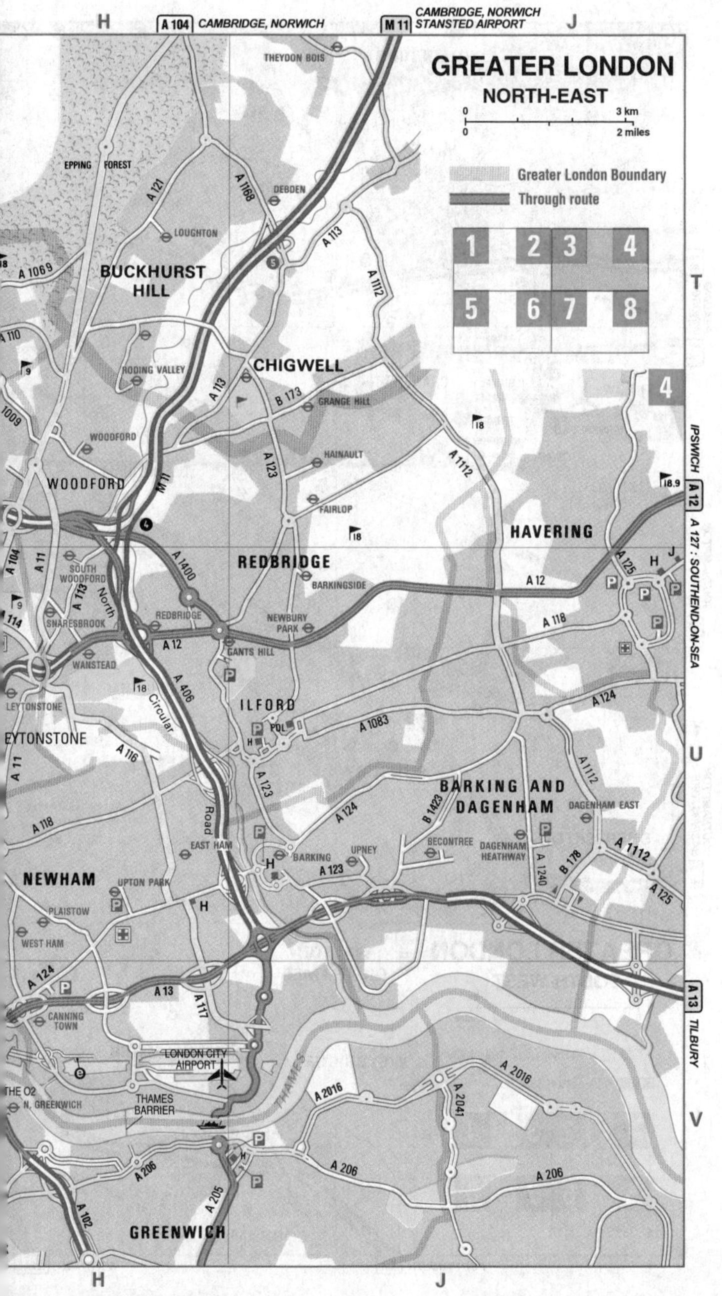
GREATER LONDON
NORTH-EAST
0 3 km
0 2 miles
Greater London Boundary
Through route
A 104 CAMBRIDGE, NORWICH
M 11 CAMBRIDGE, NORWICH STANSTED AIRPORT
THEYDON BOIS
EPPING FOREST
DEBDEN
LOUGHTON
BUCKHURST HILL
CHIGWELL
RODING VALLEY
GRANGE HILL
WOODFORD
HAINAULT
FAIRLOP
HAVERING
REDBRIDGE
SOUTH WOODFORD
BARKINGSIDE
SNARESBROOK
REDBRIDGE
NEWBURY PARK
GANTS HILL
WANSTEAD
North Circular Road
ILFORD
LEYTONSTONE
BARKING AND DAGENHAM
DAGENHAM EAST
EAST HAM
BECONTREE
DAGENHAM HEATHWAY
BARKING
UPNEY
NEWHAM
UPTON PARK
PLAISTOW
WEST HAM
CANNING TOWN
LONDON CITY AIRPORT
THE O2
N. GREENWICH
THAMES BARRIER
THAMES
GREENWICH
IPSWICH A 12
A 127 : SOUTHEND-ON-SEA
A 13 TILBURY
LONDON

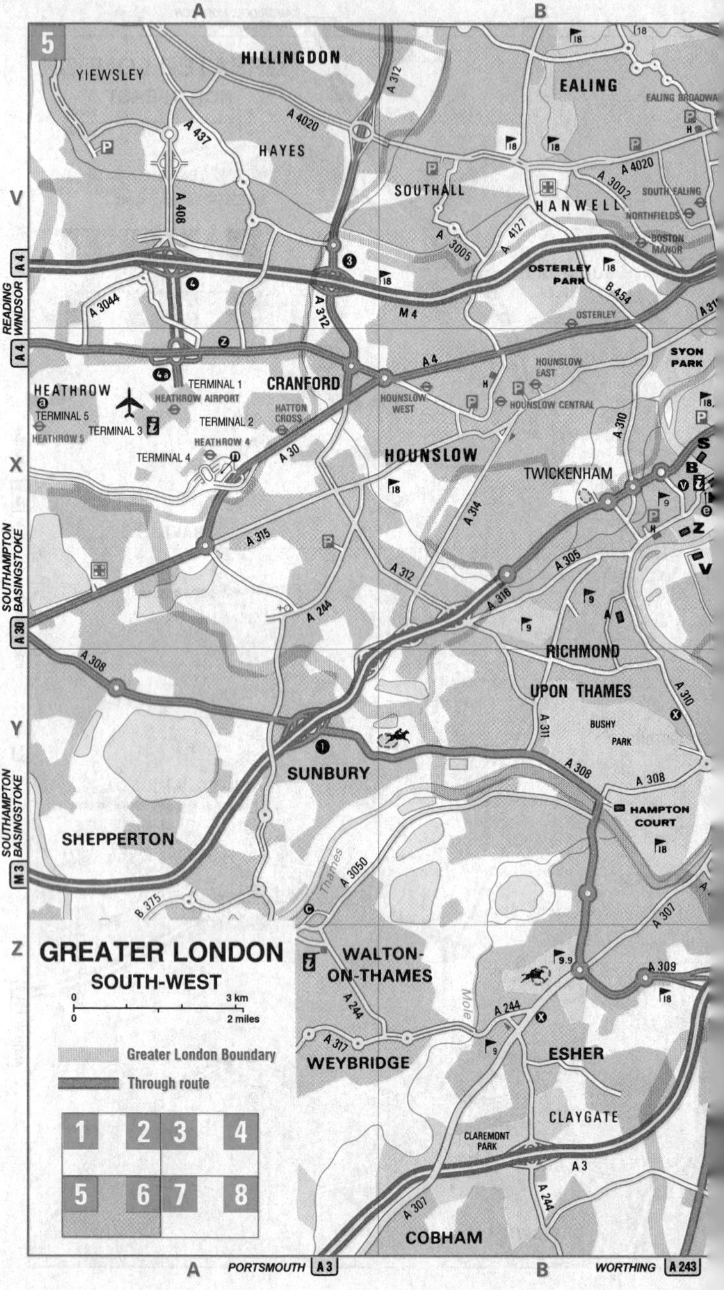

GREATER LONDON
SOUTH-WEST

0 — 3 km
0 — 2 miles

Greater London Boundary

Through route

1 2 3 4
5 6 7 8

A B
5
V X Y Z

HILLINGDON
YIEWSLEY
HAYES
EALING
EALING BROADWAY
SOUTHALL
HANWELL
SOUTH EALING
NORTHFIELDS
BOSTON MANOR
OSTERLEY PARK
OSTERLEY
SYON PARK
HOUNSLOW EAST
HOUNSLOW WEST
HOUNSLOW CENTRAL
HOUNSLOW
CRANFORD
HEATHROW
HEATHROW AIRPORT
TERMINAL 1
TERMINAL 2
TERMINAL 3
TERMINAL 4
TERMINAL 5
HEATHROW 4
HEATHROW 5
HATTON CROSS
TWICKENHAM
RICHMOND UPON THAMES
BUSHY PARK
HAMPTON COURT
SUNBURY
SHEPPERTON
WALTON-ON-THAMES
WEYBRIDGE
ESHER
CLAYGATE
CLAREMONT PARK
COBHAM
Thames
Mole

M 4, A 4, A 30, A 312, A 4020, A 437, A 408, A 3044, A 3005, A 4127, A 3002, B 454, A 310, A 314, A 315, A 305, A 316, A 244, A 308, A 311, A 3050, B 375, A 307, A 309, A 317, A 3, A 243, M 3

READING WINDSOR A 4
SOUTHAMPTON BASINGSTOKE A 30
SOUTHAMPTON BASINGSTOKE M 3
PORTSMOUTH A 3
WORTHING A 243

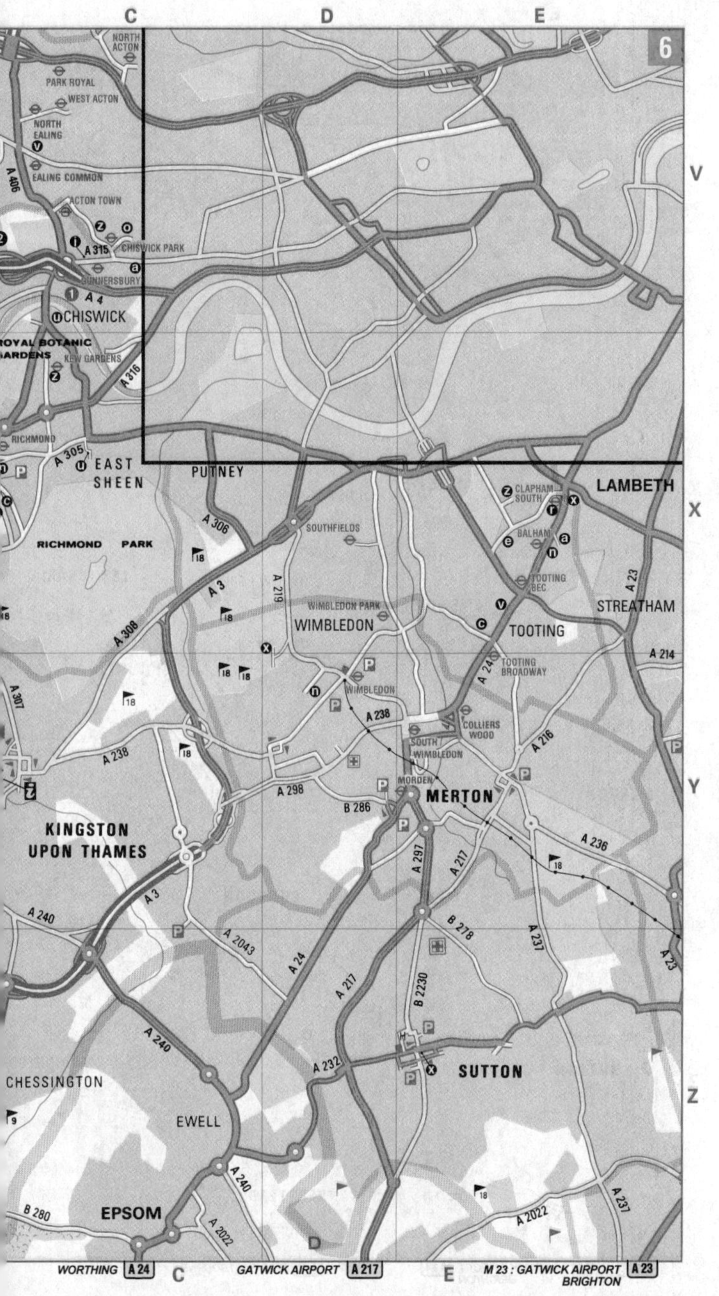
C
D
E
6
V
X
Y
Z
NORTH ACTON
PARK ROYAL
WEST ACTON
NORTH EALING
EALING COMMON
ACTON TOWN
CHISWICK PARK
GUNNERSBURY
CHISWICK
ROYAL BOTANIC GARDENS
KEW GARDENS
RICHMOND
EAST SHEEN
PUTNEY
LAMBETH
CLAPHAM SOUTH
BALHAM
RICHMOND PARK
SOUTHFIELDS
TOOTING BEC
STREATHAM
WIMBLEDON PARK
WIMBLEDON
TOOTING
TOOTING BROADWAY
COLLIERS WOOD
SOUTH WIMBLEDON
MORDEN
MERTON
KINGSTON UPON THAMES
CHESSINGTON
EWELL
SUTTON
EPSOM
A 406
A 315
A 4
A 316
A 305
A 306
A 3
A 308
A 219
A 24
A 23
A 214
A 307
A 238
A 216
A 298
B 286
A 297
A 217
A 236
A 240
A 2043
B 278
A 237
B 2230
A 232
B 280
A 2022
WORTHING A 24
GATWICK AIRPORT A 217
M 23 : GATWICK AIRPORT BRIGHTON A 23
LONDON

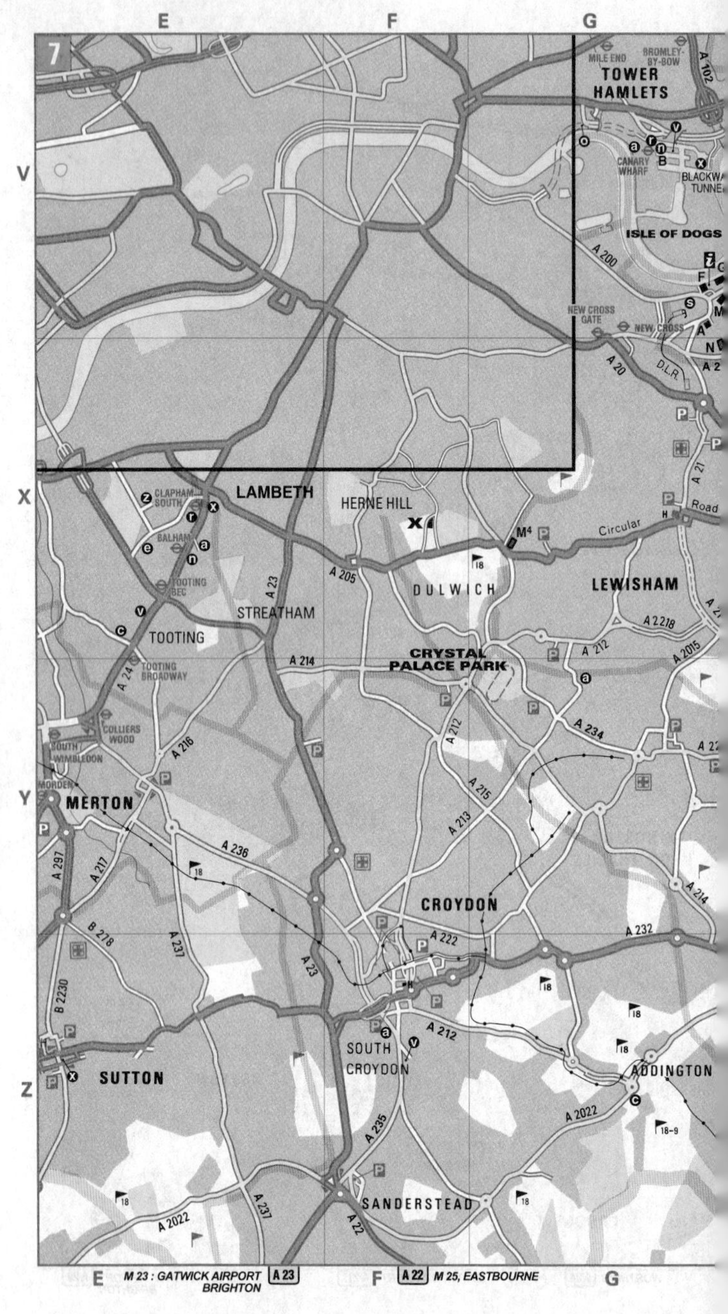
E
F
G
7
V
X
Y
Z
LONDON
MILE END
BROMLEY-BY-BOW
TOWER HAMLETS
A 102
CANARY WHARF
BLACKWALL TUNNEL
ISLE OF DOGS
A 200
NEW CROSS GATE
NEW CROSS
D.L.R.
A 20
A 21
LAMBETH
HERNE HILL
CLAPHAM SOUTH
BALHAM
TOOTING BEC
A 23
A 205
STREATHAM
DULWICH
Circular Road
LEWISHAM
A 2218
A 212
A 2015
TOOTING
TOOTING BROADWAY
A 214
CRYSTAL PALACE PARK
A 24
A 234
COLLIERS WOOD
SOUTH WIMBLEDON
A 216
MORDEN
MERTON
A 215
A 213
A 236
A 297
A 217
CROYDON
B 278
A 237
A 222
A 232
B 2230
A 212
SOUTH CROYDON
SUTTON
ADDINGTON
A 2022
A 235
SANDERSTEAD
A 22
M 23 : GATWICK AIRPORT BRIGHTON
A 23
A 22
M 25, EASTBOURNE

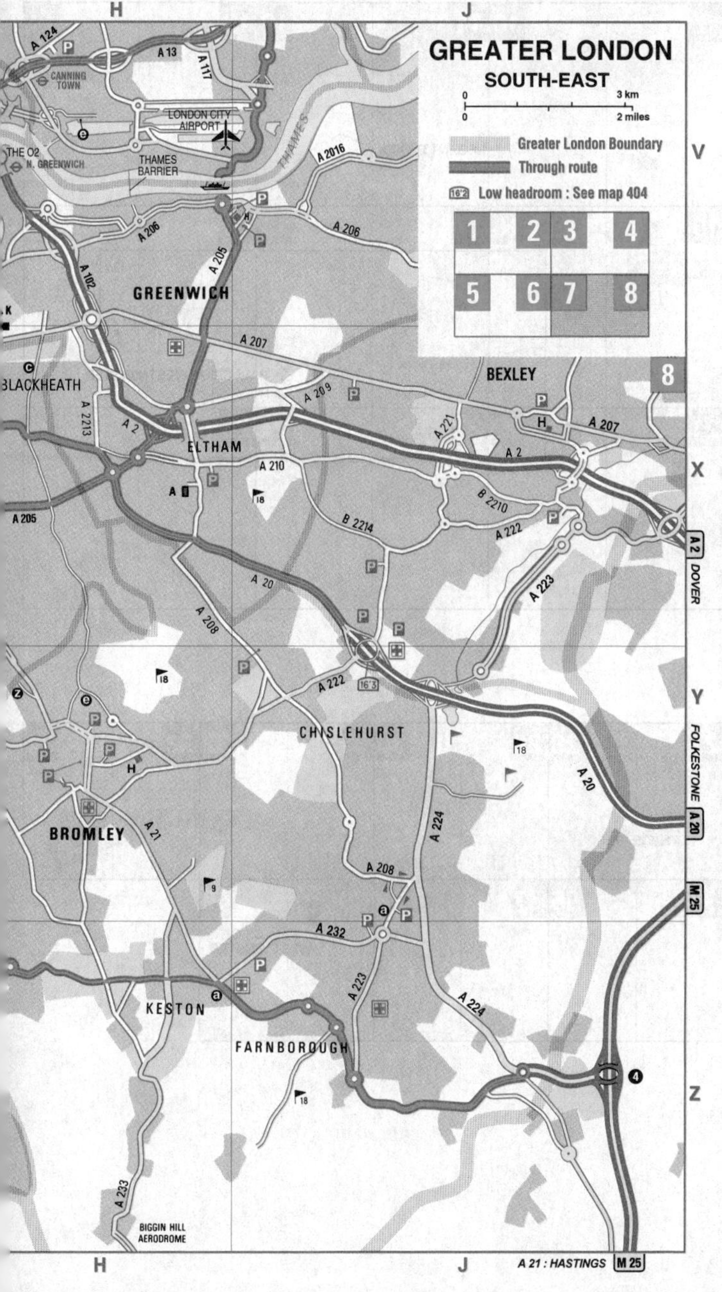
GREATER LONDON
SOUTH-EAST
0 3 km
0 2 miles
Greater London Boundary
Through route
Low headroom : See map 404
1 2 3 4
5 6 7 8
GREENWICH
BLACKHEATH
ELTHAM
BEXLEY
CHISLEHURST
BROMLEY
KESTON
FARNBOROUGH
CANNING TOWN
LONDON CITY AIRPORT
THE O2
N. GREENWICH
THAMES BARRIER
THAMES
BIGGIN HILL AERODROME
A 2 DOVER
FOLKESTONE A 20
M 25
A 21 : HASTINGS M 25
H
J
V
X
Y
Z
8

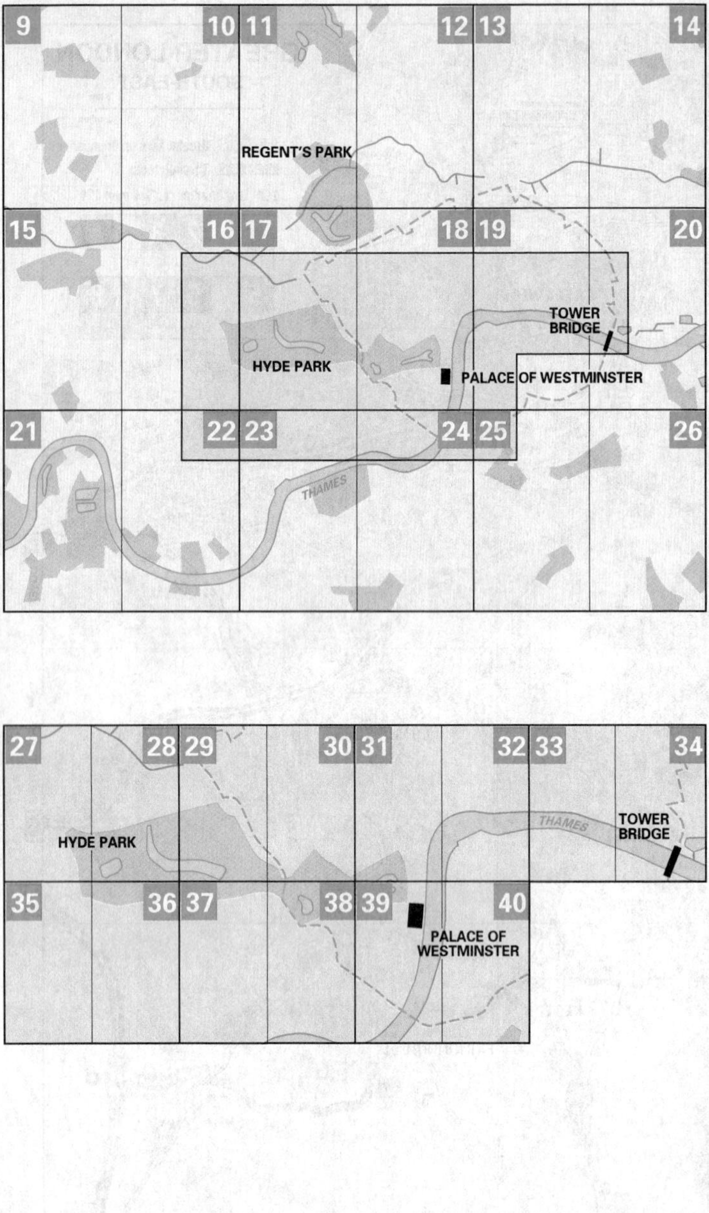

9 10 11 12 13 14
REGENT'S PARK
15 16 17 18 19 20
TOWER BRIDGE
HYDE PARK
PALACE OF WESTMINSTER
21 22 23 24 25 26
THAMES

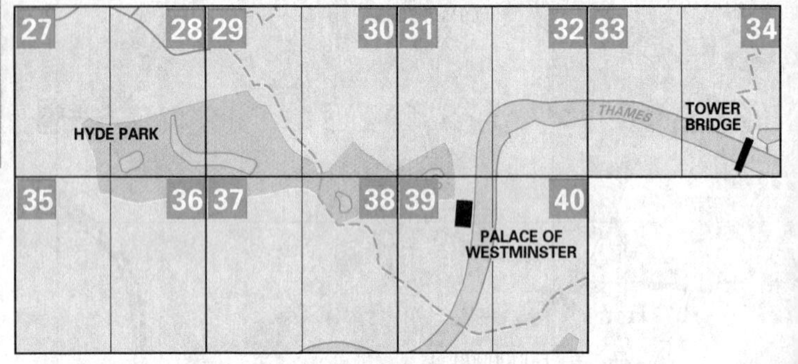

INDEX OF STREET NAMES IN LONDON CENTRE

LONDON

Street	Plan	Grid	No.
Oxford Gardens	16	MZD	
Royal Crescent	16	MZE	371
St Ann's Rd	16	MZE	
St Mark's Rd	16	MZD	
Shirland Rd	16	NZD	
Sinclair Rd	16	MZE	
Sixth Ave	16	MZC	
Sutherland Ave	16	NZD	
Walterton Rd	16	NZD	347
Warwick Ave	16	OZD	
West Cross Route	16	MZE	

PLAN 17

Street	Plan	Grid	No.
Allsop Pl.	17	QZD	4
Blomfield Rd	17	OZD	
Broadley St	17	PZD	
Clifton Gardens	17	PZD	
Frampton St	17	PZD	
Hall Rd	17	PZC	
Lisson Grove	17	PZD	
Maida Ave	17	PZD	
North Carriage Drive	17	PZE	
Park Rd	17	QZD	
Rossmore Rd	17	QZD	
St John's Wood Rd	17	PZD	
Warrington Crescent	17	OZD	348

PLAN 18

Street	Plan	Grid	No.
Bernard St	18	SZD	25
Chester Rd	18	RZC	
Euston Rd	18	RZD	
Fitzroy Square	18	RZD	
Great Ormond St	18	SZD	
Guilford St	18	SZD	
Herbrand St	18	SZD	218
Hunter St	18	SZD	233
Judd St	18	SZC	
Park Crescent	18	RZD	28
Robert St	18	RZC	
Russell Square	18	SZD	
Sidmouth St	18	SZD	385
Tavistock Pl.	18	SZD	
Tavistock Square	18	SZD	409
Upper Woburn Pl.	18	SZD	432
Woburn Pl.	18	SZD	

PLAN 19

Street	Plan	Grid	No.
Bath St	19	VZC	
Beech St	19	VZD	
Borough Rd	19	UZE	
Bowling Green Lane	19	UZD	43
Bunhill Row	19	VZD	
Calthorpe St	19	TZD	65
Central St	19	VZC	
Chiswell St	19	VZD	
City Rd	19	VZC	
Clerkenwell Rd	19	UZD	474
Corporation Row	19	UZD	110
Dufferin St	19	VZD	141
Elephant and Castle Shopping Centre	19	UZF	
Falmouth Rd	19	VZE	
Fann St	19	VZD	166
Goswell Rd	19	UZC	
Great Dover St	19	VZE	
Harper Rd	19	VZE	
King's Cross Rd	19	TZC	
Lever St	19	VZC	
Lloyd Baker St	19	UZC	265
Long Lane SOUTHWARK	19	VZE	
Merrick Square	19	VZE	
Moreland St	19	VZC	293
Myddelton St	19	UZC	296
Newington Causeway	19	VZE	307
New Kent Rd	19	VZF	
Old St	19	VZD	
Paul St	19	VZD	
Percival St	19	UZD	
Pilgrimage St	19	VZE	349
Rosebery Ave	19	UZD	
St John St	19	UZC	
Suffolk St	19	VZE	
Tabard St	19	VZE	408
Trinity Church Square	19	VZE	
Trinity St	19	VZE	
Whitecross St	19	VZD	
Worship St	19	VZD	

PLAN 20

Street	Plan	Grid	No.
Abbey St	20	XZE	
Appold St	20	XZD	5
Back Church Rd	20	XZD	
Bermondsey St	20	XZE	
Bethnal Green Rd	20	XZD	
Bigland St	20	YZD	
Brady St	20	YZD	
Brick Lane	20	XZD	
Brunel Rd	20	YZE	
Cable St	20	YZD	
Cambridge Heath Rd	20	YZD	
Cannon Street Rd	20	YZD	
Cavell St	20	YZD	
Cephas St	20	YZD	
Cheshire St	20	XZD	
Christian St	20	YZD	
Clements Rd	20	YZE	
Club Row	20	XZD	
Commercial Rd	20	YZD	
Curtain Rd	20	XZD	126
Dock St	20	XZD	
Drummond Rd	20	YZE	
Fielgate St	20	XZD	
Globe Rd	20	YZC	
Grange Rd	20	XZE	
Great Eastern St	20	XZD	192
Highway (The)	20	YZE	
Jamaica Rd	20	XZE	
Jublilee St	20	YZD	
Lower Rd	20	YZE	
Luke St	20	XZD	
Mile End Rd	20	YZD	
New Rd	20	YZD	
Old Montague St	20	XZD	
Pages Walk	20	XZF	
Redman's Rd	20	YZD	
Roman Rd	20	YZC	
Rovel Rd	20	XZE	75
Salter Rd	20	YZE	
Sclater St	20	XZD	470
Shoreditch High St	20	XZD	384
Sidney St	20	YZD	
Spa Rd	20	XZE	
Stepney Way	20	YZD	
Surrey Quay's Rd	20	YZE	377
Tarling St	20	YZD	
Thomas Moore St	20	XZE	365
Turin St	20	XZC	
Vallance Rd	20	YZD	
Vaughan Way	20	XZE	
Wapping High St	20	YZE	
Wapping Lane	20	YZE	
Wapping Wall	20	YZE	
Whitechapel Rd	20	XZD	

PLAN 21

Street	Plan	Grid	No.
Banin St	21	LZF	
Barnes High St	21	KZH	404
Bath Rd	21	KZF	
Brook Green	21	LZF	
Burlington Lane	21	KZG	
Castelnau	21	LZG	
Chancellor's Rd	21	LZG	21
Chiswick High Rd	21	KZG	
Chiswick Lane	21	KZG	
Chiswick Mall	21	KZG	
Church Rd RICHMOND UPON THAMES	21	KZH	
Dailing Rd	21	LZF	13
Devonshire Rd	21	KZG	
Dorchester Grove	21	KZG	402
Dover House Rd	21	LZH	
Erpingham Rd	21	LZH	
Ferry Rd	21	KZG	
Glenthorne Rd	21	LZF	
Great West Rd	21	KZG	
Gwendolen Ave	21	LZH	
Hammersmith Bridge	21	LZG	
Hammersmith Bridge Rd	21	LZG	431
Hertford Ave	21	KZH	
Hotham Rd	21	LZH	
Howards Lane	21	LZH	
King St HAMMERSMITH	21	KZG	
Lonsdale Rd	21	KZG	
Lower Richmond Rd	21	LZH	
Mill Hill Rd	21	KZH	
Prebend Gardens	21	KZF	
Priory Lane	21	KZH	
Queen's Ride Lower	21	LZH	
Rainville Rd	21	LZG	
Rannoch Rd	21	LZG	
Rocks Lane	21	LZH	
Roehampton Lane	21	KZH	
Station Rd	21	KZH	
Stevenage Rd	21	LZG	
Suffolk Rd	21	KZG	
Talgarth Rd	21	LZG	
Terrace (The)	21	KZH	
Turnham Green Terrace	21	KZG	389
Upper Richmond Rd	21	LZH	
Upper Richmond Rd West	21	KZH	
Verdun Rd	21	KZG	
Vine Rd	21	KZH	
White Hart Lane	21	KZH	

PLAN 22

Street	Plan	Grid	No.
Armoury Way	22	NZH	7
Bagley's Lane	22	OZH	
Baron's Court Rd	22	MZG	
Bishops Rd	22	NZG	
Bishop's Park Rd	22	MZH	
Broomhouse Lane	22	NZH	
Carnwath Rd	22	NZH	
Charlwood Rd	22	MZH	
Clancarty Rd	22	NZH	
Crabtree Lane	22	MZG	164
Dawes Rd	22	MZG	
Disraeli Rd	22	MZH	
Edith Rd	22	MZG	
Estcourt Rd	22	MZG	203
Fairfield St	22	OZH	165
Fawe Park Rd	22	MZH	
Filmer Rd	22	MZG	
Finlay St	22	MZH	
Fulham High St	22	MZH	172
Fulham Palace Rd	22	MZG	
Gliddon Rd	22	MZG	182
Greyhound Rd	22	MZG	
Gunterstone Rd	22	MZG	
Halford Rd	22	NZG	
Hammersmith Rd	22	MZG	
Harwood Rd	22	NZG	
Hugon Rd	22	NZH	
Hurlingham Rd	22	NZH	
Munster Rd	22	MZG	
Musard Rd	22	MZG	
New King's Rd	22	NZH	
Oakhill Rd	22	NZH	

LONDON

Street	Plan	Grid	No.
Oxford Rd WANDSWORTH	22	MZH	
Parsons Green Lane	22	NZG	
Peterborough Rd	22	NZH	
Putney Bridge	22	MZH	
Putney Bridge Rd	22	MZH	
Putney High St	22	MZH	
Putney Hill	22	MZH	358
Queensmill Rd	22	MZG	450
Rylston Rd	22	MZG	
St Dunstan's Rd	22	MZG	
Star Rd	22	MZG	
Stephendale Rd	22	OZH	
Studdridge St	22	NZH	
Swandon Way	22	OZH	
Vanston Pl.	22	NZG	207
Wandsworth Bridge	22	OZH	437
Wandsworth Bridge Rd	22	NZH	
West Cromwell Rd	22	NZG	
Woodlaw Rd	22	MZG	

PLAN 23

Street	Plan	Grid	No.
Albert Bridge	23	QZB	
Albert Bridge Rd	23	QZG	
Avenue (The)	23	QZH	
Battersea Bridge	23	PZG	
Battersea Bridge Rd	23	PZG	
Battersea Church Rd	23	PZG	
Battersea Park Rd	23	QZH	
Battersea Rise	23	PZH	
Cambridge Rd BATTERSEA	23	QZH	449
Carriage Drive East	23	QZG	
Carriage Drive North	23	QZG	
Carriage Drive South	23	QZG	
Cheyne Walk	23	PZG	
Clapham Common West Side	23	QZH	92
East Hill	23	PZH	155
Edith Grove	23	PZG	
Elspeth Rd	23	QZH	
Falcon Rd	23	PZH	
Gowrie Rd	23	QZH	
Gunter Grove	23	OZG	202
Imperial Rd	23	OZG	
Latchmere Rd	23	QZH	
Lavender Hill	23	QZH	
Lombard Rd	23	PZH	266
Lots Rd	23	OZG	
Marney Rd	23	QZH	
Northcote Rd	23	QZH	
North Side	23	PZH	316
Parade (The)	23	QZG	
Parkgate Rd	23	QZG	
Plough Rd	23	PZH	
Prince of Wales Drive	23	QZH	
St John's Hill	23	PZH	
St John's Rd	23	QZH	
Surrey Lane	23	PZH	
Townmead Rd	23	OZH	
Trinity Rd	23	PZH	441
Vicarage Crescent	23	PZH	433
Westbridge Rd	23	PZG	
York Rd WANDSWORTH	23	PZH	

PLAN 24

Street	Plan	Grid	No.
Acre Lane	24	SZH	
Bedford Rd	24	SZH	
Binfield Rd	24	SZH	
Bridgefoot	24	SZG	49
Cedars Rd	24	RZH	
Clapham Common North Side	24	RZH	428
Clapham High St	24	SZH	
Clapham Manor St	24	SZH	
Clapham Park Hill	24	SZH	
Crescent Lane	24	SZH	
Fentiman Rd	24	TZG	
Jeffrey's Rd	24	SZH	
King's Ave	24	SZH	
Landor Rd	24	SZH	
Landsdowne Way	24	SZG	
Larkhall Lane	24	SZH	
Lingham St	24	SZH	
Long Rd	24	RZH	
Miles St	24	SZG	290
North St	24	RZH	
Old Town	24	RZH	426
Park Rd LAMBETH	24	SZH	
Queenstown Rd	24	RZH	
Queen's Circus	24	RZG	361
Rectory Grove	24	RZH	
Silverthorne Rd	24	RZH	
Triangle Place	24	SZH	
Union Rd	24	SZH	
Voltaire Rd	24	SZH	436
Wandsworth Rd	24	SZG	
Wilkinson St	24	TZG	420

PLAN 25

Street	Plan	Grid	No.
Akerman Rd	25	UZH	
Albany Rd	25	VZG	
Angell Drive	25	UZH	
Atlantic Rd	25	UZH	
Barrington Rd	25	UZH	
Benhill Rd	25	VZG	
Brixton Hill	25	UZH	
Brixton Rd	25	UZH	
Calais St	25	UZG	
Caldwell St	25	UZG	
Camberwell Grove	25	VZH	
Camberwell New Rd	25	UZG	
Camberwell Rd	25	VZG	
Carew St	25	VZH	
Champion Park	25	VZH	
Chapter Rd	25	UZG	
Church St Camberwell	25	VZG	
Clapham Rd	25	TZH	
Coldharbour Lane	25	UZH	
Comber Grove	25	VZG	
Denmark Hill	25	VZH	
Denmark Rd	25	VZH	
Dorset Rd	25	TZG	
East St	25	VZG	
Edmund St	25	VZG	
Effra Rd	25	UZH	
Elephant Rd	25	VZF	163
Elmington Rd	25	VZG	
Fawnbrake Ave	25	VZH	
Ferndene Rd	25	VZH	
Flint St	25	VZG	
Flodden Rd	25	VZG	
Foxley Rd	25	UZG	
Groveway	25	UZH	
Grove Lane	25	VZH	
Harleyford St	25	UZG	211
Herne Hill	25	VZH	
Herne Hill Rd	25	VZH	
Heygate St	25	VZF	
John Ruskin St	25	VZG	
Kellett Rd	25	UZH	
Knatchbull Rd	25	UZH	
Lilford Rd	25	UZH	
Lomond Grove	25	VZG	
Lothian Rd	25	UZG	
Loughborough Rd	25	UZH	
Manor Pl.	25	VZG	
Milkwood Rd	25	VZH	
Minet Rd	25	UZH	
Mostyn Rd	25	UZH	
Newington Butts	25	UZF	306
New Church Rd	25	VZG	
Penton Pl.	25	UZG	
Portland St	25	VZG	
Railton Rd	25	UZH	
Red Post Hill	25	VZH	
Rodney Rd	25	VZF	
Shakespeare Rd	25	UZH	
Sidney Rd	25	TZH	
Southampton Way	25	VZG	
Stocwell Park Rd	25	TZH	
Stocwell Rd	25	TZH	
Sunray Ave	25	VZH	
Thurlow St	25	VZG	
Vassall Rd	25	UZG	
Walworth Rd	25	VZG	
Warner Rd	25	VZH	
Wells Way	25	VZG	
Wiltshire Rd	25	UZH	
Wyndham Rd	25	VZG	

PLAN 26

Street	Plan	Grid	No.
Ady's Rd	26	XZH	
Asylum Rd	26	YZG	
Avondale Rise	26	XZH	
Avonley Rd	26	YZG	
Barry Rd	26	YZH	
Bellenden Rd	26	XZH	
Bird In Bush Rd	26	YZG	
Carlton Grove	26	YZG	
Catlin St	26	YZG	
Cheltenham Rd	26	YZH	
Clayton Rd	26	YZH	
Clifton Way	26	YZG	
Cobourg Rd	26	XZG	
Commercial Way	26	XZG	
Consort Rd	26	YZH	
Coopers Rd	26	XZG	
Copeland Rd	26	YZH	
Crystal Palace Rd	26	XZH	
Dalwood St	26	XZG	
Dog Kennel Hill	26	XZH	
Dunton Rd	26	XZG	
East Dulwich Grove	26	XZH	
East Dulwich Rd	26	XZH	
Evelina Rd	26	YZH	
Galleywall Rd	26	YZG	
Glengall Rd	26	XZG	
Grove Hill Rd	26	XZH	
Grove Vale	26	XZH	
Hanover Park	26	XZH	
Havil St	26	XZG	
Heaton Rd	26	YZH	
Hollydale Rd	26	YZH	
Ilderton Rd	26	YZG	
Kender St	26	YZG	
Lausanne Rd	26	YZH	
Linden Grove	26	YZH	
Lordship Lane	26	XZH	
Lyndhurst Grove	26	XZH	
Lyndhurst Way	26	XZH	
Lynton Rd	26	YZG	
Mandela Way	26	XZF	
Marlborough Grove	26	XZG	
Mc Neil Rd	26	XZH	
Meeting House Lane	26	YZG	
Melbourne Grove	26	XZH	
Naylord Rd	26	YZG	
Neate St	26	XZG	
Nunhead Grove	26	YZH	
Nunhead Lane	26	YZH	
Oglander Rd	26	XZH	
Old Kent Rd	26	XZG	
Peckham Hill St	26	XZH	
Peckham Park Rd	26	XZG	
Peckham Rd	26	XZH	
Peckham Rye	26	YZH	
Pomeroy St	26	YZG	
Pytchley Rd	26	XZH	
Queens Rd	26	YZH	
Raymouth Rd	26	YZF	
Reverdy Rd	26	XZG	
Rolls Rd	26	XZG	

Street	Plan	Grid	No.
Rotherhithe New Rd	26	YZG	
Rye Lane	26	XZH	
St George's Way	26	XZG	
St James Rd	26	YZG	
Shenley Rd	26	XZH	
Southwark Park Rd	26	XZF	
Stuart Rd	26	YZH	
Summer Rd	26	XZG	
Surrey Canal Rd	26	YZG	
Trafalgar Ave	26	XZG	
Verney Rd	26	YZG	
Willowbrook Rd	26	XZG	
Willow Walk	26	XZF	
Yaldind Rd	26	XZF	369

PLAN 27

Street	Plan	Grid	No.
Artesian Rd	27	AAU	
Aubrey Walk	27	AAV	
Bark Pl.	27	ABU	
Bayswater Rd	27	ABV	
Bedford Gardens	27	AAV	
Bishop's Bridge Rd.	27	ABT	
Bourne Terrace	27	ABT	
Broad Walk (The)	27	ABV	
Campden Grove	27	AAV	
Campden Hill Rd.	27	AAV	
Campden Hill Square	27	AAV	
Chepstow Crescent	27	AAU	84
Chepstow Pl.	27	AAU	
Chepstow Rd	27	AAT	
Chepstow Villas	27	AAU	
Colville Rd	27	AAU	
Colville Terrace	27	AAU	
Dawson Pl.	27	AAU	
Garway Rd	27	ABU	
Gloucester Terrace	27	ABT	
Great Western Rd	27	AAT	
Harrow Rd.	27	ABT	
Hereford Rd	27	ABU	
Holland Park Ave	27	AAV	
Inverness Terrace	27	ABU	
Kensington Church St	27	AAV	
Kensington Gardens Square	27	ABU	
Kensington Palace Gardens	27	ABV	
Kensington Park Rd	27	AAU	
Kensington Pl.	27	AAV	
Ladbroke Rd	27	AAV	
Ladbroke Square	27	AAV	
Ledbury Rd	27	AAT	
Leinster Square	27	ABU	
Linden Gardens	27	AAU	
Moscow Rd	27	ABU	
Newton Rd	27	ABT	
Notting Hill Gate	27	AAV	
Orme Court	27	ABU	328
Ossington St	27	ABU	
Palace Court	27	ABU	
Palace Gardens Terrace	27	ABV	
Palace Green	27	ABV	
Pembridge Crescent	27	AAU	
Pembridge Gardens	27	AAU	
Pembridge Rd.	27	AAU	
Pembridge Square	27	AAU	
Pembridge Villas	27	AAU	
Porchester Gardens	27	ABU	
Porchester Rd	27	ABT	
Porchester Square	27	ABT	197
Portobello Rd	27	AAU	
Queensborough Terrace	27	ABU	
Queensway	27	ABU	
St Luke's Rd	27	AAT	
St Petersburgh Pl.	27	ABU	
Sheffield Terrace	27	AAV	
Talbot Rd	27	AAT	
Tavistock Rd	27	AAT	
Uxbridge St	27	AAV	
Westbourne Gardens	27	ABT	
Westbourne Grove	27	AAU	
Westbourne Park Rd	27	AAT	
Westbourne Park Villas	27	ABT	

PLAN 28

Street	Plan	Grid	No.
Chilworth St	28	ACU	
Church St	28	ADT	
Cleveland Square	28	ACU	
Cleveland Terrace	28	ACT	
Craven Hill	28	ACU	
Craven Rd	28	ACU	
Craven Terrace	28	ACU	
Devonshire Terrace	28	ACU	136
Eastbourne Terrace	28	ACT	
Edgware Rd	28	ADT	
Gloucester Square	28	ADU	
Hyde Park Gardens	28	ADU	
Lancaster Gate	28	ACU	
Lancaster Terrace	28	ADU	257
Leinster Gardens	28	ACU	
Leinster Terrace	28	ACU	
London St	28	ADT	
Norfolk Pl.	28	ADT	
North Wharf Rd	28	ADT	
Orsett Terrace	28	ACT	
Porchester Terrace	28	ACU	
Praed St.	28	ADU	
Queen Anne's Gate	28	ACU	94
Queen's Gardens	28	ACU	
Radnor Pl.	28	ADT	
Ring (The)	28	ADV	
Sale Place	28	AET	
South Wharf Rd	28	ADT	
Spring St	28	ADU	
Stanhope Terrace	28	ADU	158
Sussex Gardens	28	ADU	
Sussex Pl.	28	ADU	
Sussex Square	28	ADU	
Westbourne Crescent	28	ADU	448
Westbourne St	28	ADU	
Westbourne Terrace.	28	ACT	
Westbourne Terrace Rd	28	ACT	452

PLAN 29

Street	Plan	Grid	No.
Albion St	29	AFU	
Aybrook St	29	AGT	
Baker St.	29	AGT	
Bell St	29	AET	
Blandford St	29	AGT	
Bryanston Pl.	29	AFT	
Bryanston Square	29	AFT	14
Bryanston St	29	AFU	
Cambridge Square	29	AET	67
Chapel St.	29	AET	
Chiltern St	29	AGT	
Clarendon Pl.	29	AEU	93
Connaught Square	29	AFU	
Connaught St	29	AFU	
Crawford Pl.	29	AFT	
Crawford St.	29	AFT	
Culross St	29	AGU	
Dorset St.	29	AGT	
Dunraven St	29	AGU	149
Enford St	29	AFT	
George St	29	AFT	
Gloucester Pl.	29	AGT	
Granville Pl.	29	AGU	476
Great Cumberland Pl.	29	AFT	
Green St	29	AGU	
Harcourt St	29	AFT	
Harrowby St	29	AFT	
Hyde Park Square	29	AEU	
Hyde Park St	29	AEU	
Kendal St	29	AFU	
Lees Pl.	29	AGU	
Manchester Square	29	AGT	281
Manchester St	29	AGT	
Marble Arch	29	AGU	
Marylebone Rd	29	AFT	
Montagu Pl.	29	AFT	
Montagu Square	29	AGT	90
Mount St	29	AGV	
Norfolk Crescent	29	AFT	
North Audley St	29	AGU	314
North Row	29	AGU	
Old Marylebone Rd	29	AFT	
Orchard St	29	AGU	
Oxford Square	29	AFU	332
Oxford St	29	AGU	
Paddington St	29	AGT	
Park Lane	29	AGU	
Park St MAYFAIR	29	AGU	
Portman Square	29	AGT	
Portman St	29	AGU	
Reeves Mews	29	AGV	103
Rotten Row	29	AEV	
Serpentine Rd	29	AFV	
Seymour St	29	AFU	
Shouldham St	29	AFT	
Southwick St	29	AET	156
Stanhope Pl.	29	AFU	400
Upper Berkeley St	29	AFU	
Upper Brook St	29	AGU	
Upper Grosvenor St	29	AGU	
Upper Montagu St	29	AFT	
Wigmore St	29	AGU	
Woods Mews	29	AGU	
York St	29	AFT	

PLAN 30

Street	Plan	Grid	No.
Adam's Row	30	AHU	
Albemarle St	30	AIU	225
Aldford St	30	AHV	2
Argyll St	30	AIU	
Arlington St	30	AIV	6
Avery Row	30	AHU	12
Beak St	30	AIU	
Berkeley Square	30	AHU	
Berkeley St	30	AIV	
Binney St	30	AHU	
Bolton St	30	AIV	
Brick St	30	AHV	
Brook St	30	AHU	
Brook's Mews	30	AHU	
Bruton St	30	AIU	
Burlington Arcade	30	AIV	
Bury St	30	AIV	
Carlos Pl.	30	AHU	35
Carnaby St	30	AIU	
Cavendish Square	30	AHT	
Chandos St	30	AIT	36
Charles St	30	AHV	
Cleveland St	30	AIT	
Clifford St	30	AIU	38
Conduit St	30	AIU	
Cork St	30	AIU	
Curzon St	30	AHV	
Davies St	30	AHU	
Deanery St	30	AHV	132
Devonshire St	30	AHT	48
Dover St	30	AIV	
Duke St	30	AHU	
Duke St ST. JAMES	30	AIV	
Eastcastle St	30	AIT	
Farm St MAYFAIR	30	AHV	
Foley St	30	AIT	
Gilbert St	30	AHU	
Grafton St	30	AIU	62
Great Castle St	30	AIT	189
Great Marlborough St	30	AIU	

LONDON

PLAN 33

PLAN 34

PLAN 35

PLAN 36

LONDON

Gloucester Rd 36 ACX
Grenville Pl. 36 ACY
Harcourt Terrace 36 ACZ 477
Harrington Gardens 36 ACY
Harrington Rd 36 ADY
Hollywood Rd 36 ACZ
Hyde Park Gate 36 ACX
Kensington Gore 36 ACX
King's Rd 36 ADZ
Launceston Pl. 36 ACX 259
Little Boltons (The) 36 ACZ
Manresa Rd 36 ADZ
Neville Terrace 36 ADZ 300
Old Church St 36 ADZ
Onslow Gardens 36 ADZ
Onslow Square 36 ADY
Palace Gate 36 ACX
Park Walk 36 ACZ
Pelham St 36 ADY
Prince Consort Rd 36 ADX
Prince's Gardens 36 ADX 356
Queensberry Pl. 36 ADY 360
Queen's Gate 36 ACX
Queen's Gate Gardens 36 ACY 198
Queen's Gate Pl. 36 ACY 363
Queen's Gate Terrace 36 ACX
Redcliffe Rd 36 ACZ
Roland Gardens 36 ACZ
South Parade 36 ADZ
Stanhope Gardens 36 ACY
Sumner Pl. 36 ADY
Sydney Pl. 36 ADY 405
Thurloe Pl. 36 ADY
Thurloe Square 36 ADY
Tregunter Rd 36 ACZ
Vale (The) 36 ADZ
Victoria Grove 36 ACX
Victoria Rd KENSINGTON 36 ACX
Wetherby Gardens 36 ACY

PLAN 37

Basil St 37 AFX
Beauchamp Pl. 37 AFX
Belgrave Square 37 AGX
Bourne St 37 AGY
Bray Pl. 37 AFY 45
Britten St 37 AEZ
Brompton Rd 37 AFX
Cadogan Gardens 37 AGY 23
Cadogan Gate 37 AGY 220
Cadogan Pl. 37 AGY
Cadogan Square 37 AGY
Cadogan St 37 AFY
Carriage Rd (The) 37 AFX
Chelsea Bridge Rd 37 AGZ
Chelsea Embankment 37 AGZ
Chelsea Manor St 37 AFZ
Cheltenham Terrace 37 AGZ
Chesham Pl. 37 AGX
Chesham St 37 AGY
Chester Row 37 AGY
Cheval Pl. 37 AFX
Christchurch St 37 AFZ
Draycott Ave 37 AFY
Draycott Pl. 37 AFY
Eaton Pl. 37 AGY
Egerton Gardens 37 AFY 160
Egerton Gardens Mews 37 AFY 162
Egerton Terrace 37 AFY 161
Elystan Pl. 37 AFZ
Elystan St 37 AEY
Ennismore Gardens 37 AEX
Flood St 37 AFZ
Franklin's Row 37 AGZ
Glebe Pl. 37 AEZ
Grosvenor Crescent 37 AGX
Hans Crescent 37 AFX
Hans Pl. 37 AFX
Hans Rd 37 AFX
Harriet St 37 AGX 214
Hasker St 37 AFY
Holbein Mews 37 AGZ 223
Holbein Pl. 37 AGY
Ixworth Pl. 37 AEY
Jubilee Pl. 37 AFZ
Knightsbridge 37 AFX
Lennox Gardens 37 AFY
Lennox Gardens Mews 37 AFY 263
Lower Sloane St 37 AGY
Lowndes Square 37 AGX
Lowndes St 37 AGX
Lyall St 37 AGY
Markham St 37 AFZ
Milner St 37 AFY
Montpelier Square 37 AFX
Montpelier St 37 AFX
Moore St 37 AFY
Mossop St 37 AFY
Oakley St 37 AEZ
Ormonde Gate 37 AGZ 329
Pimlico Rd 37 AGZ
Pont St 37 AFY
Radnor Walk 37 AFZ
Rawlings St 37 AFY
Redesdale St 37 AFZ 367
Royal Hospital Rd 37 AFZ
Rutland Gate 37 AEX
St Leonard's Terrace 37 AGZ
Shawfield St 37 AFZ
Sloane Ave 37 AFY
Sloane Square 37 AGY
Sloane St 37 AGX
Smith St 37 AFZ
South Terrace 37 AEY
Sydney St 37 AEZ
Symons St 37 AGY 407
Tedworth Square 37 AFZ
Tite St 37 AFZ
Trevor Pl. 37 AFX
Trevor Square 37 AFX
Walton St 37 AFY
West Halkin St 37 AGX
Whiteheads 37 AFY
William St 37 AGX 468
Wilton Pl. 37 AGX

PLAN 38

Alderney St 38 AIY
Belgrave Pl. 38 AHX
Belgrave Rd 38 AIY
Birdcage Walk 38 AIX
Bressenden Pl. 38 AIX
Buckingham Gate 38 AIX
Buckingham Palace Rd 38 AHY
Carlisle Pl. 38 AIY
Castle Lane 38 AIX
Chapel St BELGRAVIA 38 AHX
Charlwood St 38 AIZ
Chelsea Bridge 38 AHZ
Chester Square 38 AHY
Chester St 38 AHX
Churchill Gardens Rd 38 AIZ
Clarendon St 38 AIZ
Constitution Hill 38 AHX
Cumberland St 38 AIZ
Denbigh St 38 AIZ
Duke of Wellington Pl. 38 AHX 142
Eaton Square 38 AHY
Ebury Bridge 38 AHZ
Ebury Bridge Rd 38 AHZ
Ebury St 38 AHY
Eccleston Bridge 38 AHY 157
Eccleston Square 38 AIY
Eccleston St 38 AHY
Elizabeth St 38 AHY
Francis St 38 AIY
Gillingham St 38 AIY
Gloucester St 38 AIZ
Grosvenor Gardens 38 AHX
Grosvenor Pl. 38 AHX
Grosvenor Rd 38 AHZ
Guildhouse St 38 AIY 201
Halkin St 38 AHX
Hobart Pl. 38 AHX
Hudson's Pl. 38 AIY
Hugh St 38 AIY
Lower Belgrave St 38 AHY
Lower Grosvenor Pl. 38 AIX 274
Lupus St 38 AIZ
Palace St 38 AIX
St George's Drive 38 AIY
South Eaton Pl. 38 AHY
Sutherland St 38 AHZ
Terminus Pl. 38 AIY 412
Upper Belgrave St 38 AHX
Vauxhall Bridge Rd 38 AIY
Victoria St 38 AIX
Warwick Square 38 AIY
Warwick Way 38 AHZ
Wilton Rd 38 AIY
Wilton St 38 AHX

PLAN 39

Abingdon St 39 AKY
Albert Embankment 39 ALY
Artillery Row 39 AKX 8
Atterbury St 39 ALZ
Aylesford St 39 AKZ
Bessborough Gardens 39 AKZ
Bessborough St 39 AKZ 30
Bridge St 39 ALX
Broad Sanctuary 39 ALX 52
Caxton St 39 AKX
Chichester St 39 AJZ
Claverton St 39 AJZ
Dolphin Square 39 AJZ
Douglas St 39 AKY
Erasmus St 39 AKY
Glasshouse St LAMBETH 39 ALZ 108
Great College St 39 ALX
Great George St 39 AKX 193
Great Peter St 39 AKY
Great Smith St 39 AKX
Greencoat Pl. 39 AJY
Greycoat Pl. 39 AKY 200
Greycoat St 39 AKY
Horseferry Rd 39 AKY
Howick Pl. 39 AJY
John Islip St 39 AKZ
King Charles St 39 AKX
Lambeth Bridge 39 ALY
Marsham St 39 AKY
Millbank 39 ALZ
Monck St 39 AKY
Montpelier Walk 37 AFX
Moreton St 39 AJZ
Nine Elms Lane 39 AKZ
Old Pye St 39 AKX
Page St 39 AKY
Palmer St 39 AKX
Parlament Square 39 ALX
Parliament St 39 ALX
Parry St 39 ALZ 341
Petty France 39 AJX
Ponsonby Pl. 39 AKZ
Rampayne St 39 AKZ

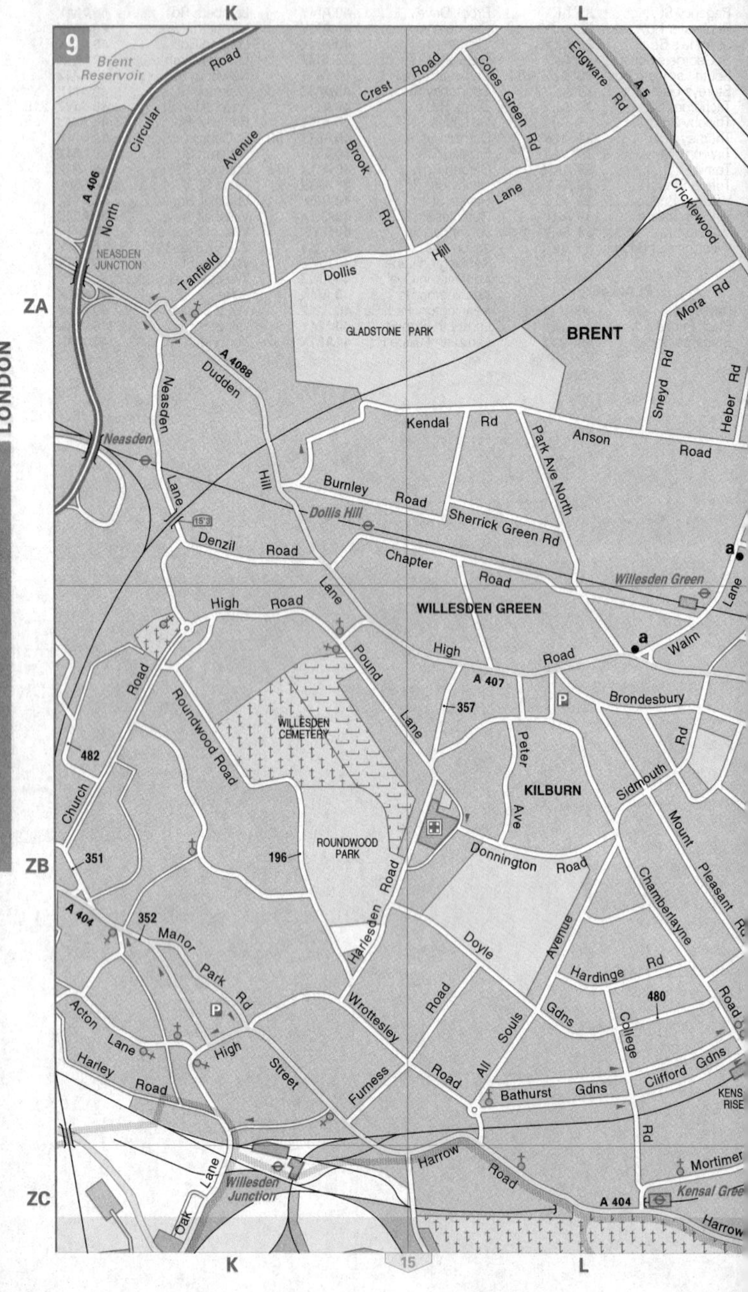
K
L
9
Brent Reservoir
North Circular Road
A 406
NEASDEN JUNCTION
Crest Road
Coles Green Rd
Edgware Rd
A 5
Avenue
Brook Rd
Lane
Cricklewood
Tanfield
Dollis Hill
GLADSTONE PARK
BRENT
Mora Rd
Sneyd Rd
Heber Rd
A 4088
Dudden Hill
Neasden Lane
Neasden
Kendal Rd
Park Ave North
Anson Road
Burnley Road
Sherrick Green Rd
Dollis Hill
Denzil Road
Chapter Road
Willesden Green
Lane
a
High Road
WILLESDEN GREEN
Walm
Pound Lane
A 407
Brondesbury Rd
Roundwood Road
WILLESDEN CEMETERY
357
Peter Ave
KILBURN
Sidmouth
Mount Pleasant Rd
482
Church Road
ROUNDWOOD PARK
196
351
Donnington Road
Harlesden Road
Chamberlayne Road
A 404
352
Manor Park Rd
Doyle Road
Avenue
Hardinge Rd
480
Acton Lane
Wrottesley Road
All Souls
Gdns
College Rd
Harley Road
High Street
Furness
Bathurst Gdns
Clifford Gdns
KENS RISE
Harrow Road
Mortimer
Oak Lane
Willesden Junction
Kensal Gree
A 404
Harrow
ZA
ZB
ZC
15
LONDON

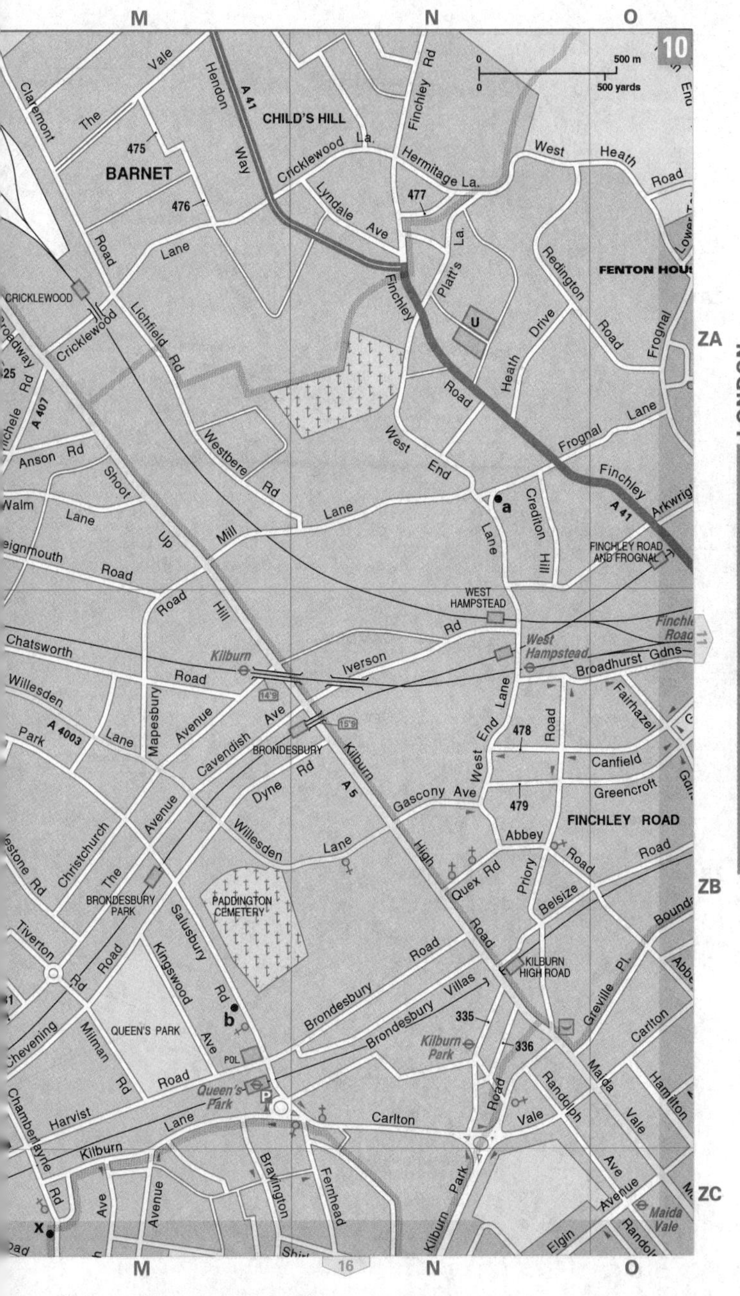
M
N
O
10
500 m
500 yards
CHILD'S HILL
BARNET
Hendon Way
A 41
Finchley Rd
Cricklewood La.
Hermitage La.
West Heath Road
Lyndale Ave
Platt's La.
FENTON HOUSE
Redington Road
Frognal
Heath Drive
Frognal Lane
CRICKLEWOOD
Cricklewood Broadway
Lichfield Rd
A 407
Anson Rd
Shoot Up Hill
Westbere Rd
West End Lane
Mill Lane
Crediton Hill
Finchley Road
FINCHLEY ROAD AND FROGNAL
WEST HAMPSTEAD
West Hampstead
Kilburn
Chatsworth Road
Iverson Rd
Broadhurst Gdns
Fairhazel
Willesden Lane
A 4003
Mapesbury Road
Cavendish Ave
BRONDESBURY
Kilburn High Road
A 5
Dyne Rd
Gascony Ave
Canfield
Greencroft
FINCHLEY ROAD
Abbey Road
Priory
Quex Rd
Belsize Road
Christchurch Avenue
BRONDESBURY PARK
Salusbury Rd
PADDINGTON CEMETERY
KILBURN HIGH ROAD
Brondesbury Road
Brondesbury Villas
Kilburn Park
Greville Pl.
Carlton
Kingswood Ave
QUEEN'S PARK
Milman Rd
Queen's Park
Harvist Road
Kilburn Lane
Chamberlayne Rd
Bravington
Fernhead
Kilburn Park Road
Randolph
Maida Vale
Hamilton
Elgin Avenue
Maida Vale
475
476
477
478
479
335
336
a
b
x
ZA
ZB
ZC
16
11
LONDON

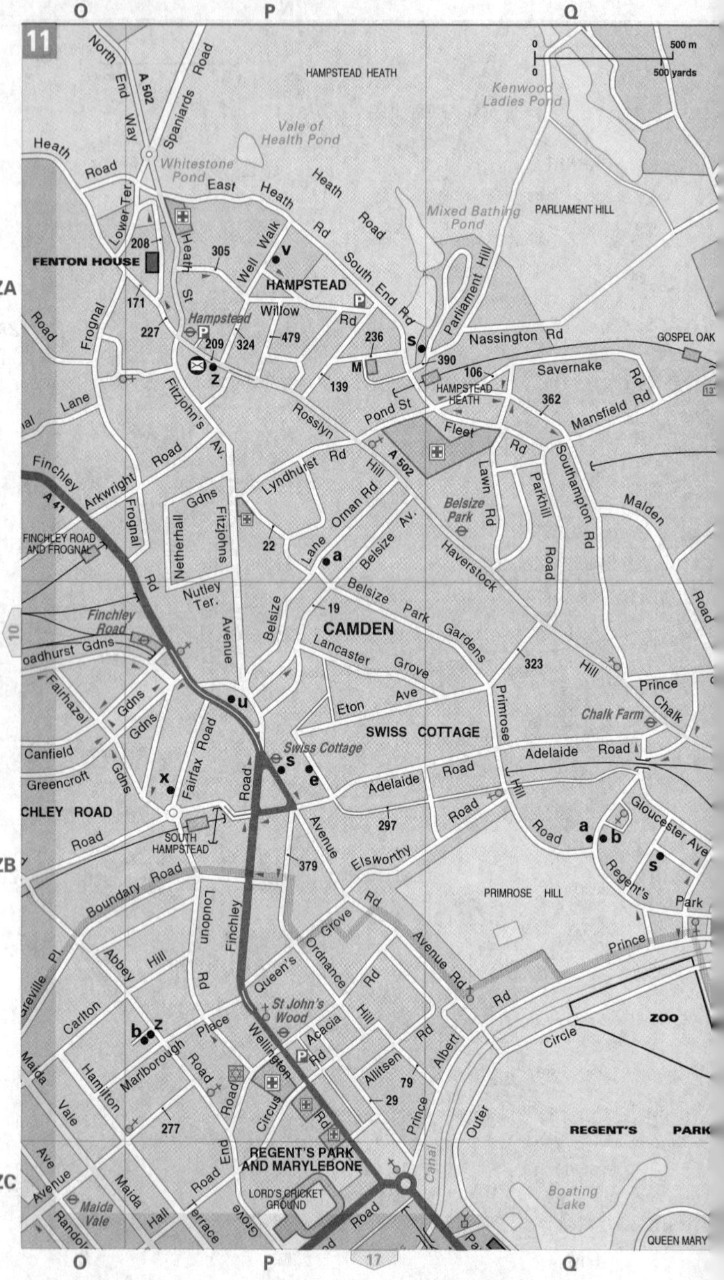
O
P
Q
11
0
500 m
0
500 yards
HAMPSTEAD HEATH
Kenwood Ladies Pond
Vale of Health Pond
Whitestone Pond
Mixed Bathing Pond
PARLIAMENT HILL
North End Way
A 502
Spaniards Road
Heath Road
Lower Ter.
East Heath Rd
Heath Road
Heath St
Well Walk
South End Rd
Parliament Hill
208
FENTON HOUSE
305
HAMPSTEAD
ZA
Road
Frognal
171
227
Hampstead
Willow Rd
209
324
479
236
Nassington Rd
GOSPEL OAK
390
106
Savernake Rd
M
139
HAMPSTEAD HEATH
Pond St
Lane
Fitzjohn's Av.
Rosslyn Hill
362
Mansfield Rd
Fleet Rd
A 502
Finchley Road
Arkwright Road
Lyndhurst Rd
Lawn Rd
Parkhill Road
Southampton Rd
Malden Road
A 41
Frognal
Netherhall Gdns
Fitzjohns Avenue
Belsize Park
Belsize Lane
Belsize Av.
Haverstock Hill
FINCHLEY ROAD AND FROGNAL
22
Nutley Ter.
Belsize Park Gardens
10
Finchley Road
Belsize
19
CAMDEN
Lancaster Grove
323
Road
oadhurst Gdns
Fairhazel Gdns
Eton Ave
Primrose Hill
Prince
Chalk
Chalk Farm
SWISS COTTAGE
Canfield Gdns
Fairfax Road
Swiss Cottage
Adelaide Road
Greencroft Gdns
Road
Adelaide Road
Road
CHLEY ROAD
SOUTH HAMPSTEAD
297
Gloucester Ave
Road
Avenue
Elsworthy
379
Regent's Park
ZB
Boundary Road
Loudoun Rd
Finchley
Grove
Rd
PRIMROSE HILL
Greville Pl.
Abbey Hill
Ordnance Hill
Queen's
Avenue Rd
Prince
Rd
Carlton
St John's Wood
ZOO
Circle
Place
Wellington
Acacia
Hill Rd
Albert
Maida Vale
Hamilton
Marlborough
Road
Rd
Allitsen
79
29
277
Circus Rd
Prince
Outer
REGENT'S PARK
Road
End
REGENT'S PARK AND MARYLEBONE
Canal
ZC
Avenue
Ave
Maida Vale
Maida
Hall
Terrace
Grove
LORD'S CRICKET GROUND
Road
Boating Lake
Randol
QUEEN MARY
O
P
17
Q

R
S
T
12
Archway
Holloway
Road
UPPER HOLLOWAY
A 1
Hornsey
Tollington
Park
Tollington Way
Road
Sisters
Swains
Lane
DARTMOUTH PARK
Dartmouth
Park
Hill
Junction
Chetwynd Road
Highgate Rd
Tufnell Park
Tufnell
Park
Road
Holloway
Seven
Hornsey
A 503
ZA
Dalmeny Rd
Dalmeny Ave
Carleton Rd
Parkhurst
Road
Caledonian
Road
Hillmarton Road
Camden
Hungerford Road
ISLING
Fortess
Road
Lady Margaret Rd
Highgate
Rd
Leighton Rd
Kentish Town
A 400
Islip Street
Busby Place
Torriano Ave
Caledonian Road
North
Road
Gaisford Street
Patshull Road
Spring Place
Willes Road
KENTISH TOWN
Road
Wales
16
Market
Road
York
Way
Mackenzie
Roman
A 503
A 5200
Brewery
Road
A 5203
Caledonian
CALEDONIAN AND BARNSB
13
Town
St
Pancras
Camden
Road
Agar
Grove
Farm
CAMDEN ROAD
366
Way
Offord
15'0
15'
15'6
Richmo
ZB
Kentish
Road
Camden Town
Camden
Rd
Royal
St
Pancras
Way
College
St
Parkway
Pratt
St
Street
Camden High St
York
Copenhagen
St
Road
Delancey St
Outer
Park
Village
East
Albany
Crowndale Rd
Pancras
Rd
Mornington Crescent
Hampstead
Road
Eversholt
Street
M
455
KING'S CROSS
Way
Caledonian
Calshot St
Pentonville
Pancras
Rd
ST PANCRAS
BRITISH LIBRARY
Midland Rd
Ossulston St
Road
King's
417
ZC
TERRACES
REGENT'S PARK
Circle
Robert Street
Chester Rd
St
EUSTON
P
P
Euston
Judd
H
Gra
Cross
18
LONDON

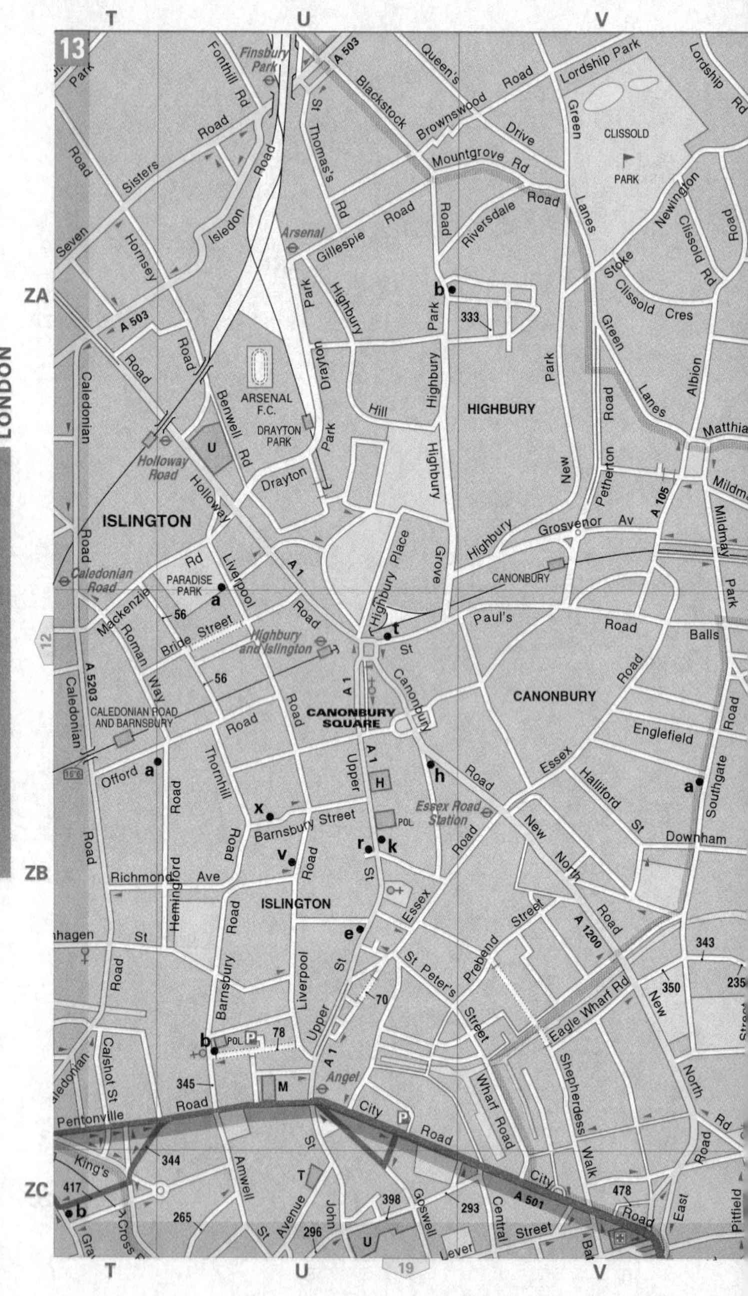
T
U
V
13
ZA
ZB
ZC
LONDON
Finsbury Park
Arsenal
Holloway Road
Caledonian Road
Highbury and Islington
Essex Road Station
Angel
ARSENAL F.C.
DRAYTON PARK
ISLINGTON
HIGHBURY
CANONBURY
CANONBURY SQUARE
CLISSOLD PARK
PARADISE PARK
CALEDONIAN ROAD AND BARNSBURY
CANONBURY
Seven Sisters Road
Fonthill Rd
Hornsey Road
Isledon Road
Blackstock Road
St Thomas's Rd
Queen's Drive
Brownswood Road
Lordship Park
Lordship Rd
Mountgrove Rd
Riversdale Road
Gillespie Road
Highbury Park
Highbury Hill
Drayton Park
Benwell Rd
Holloway Road
Green Lanes
Stoke Newington Road
Clissold Rd
Clissold Cres
Albion Road
Petherton Road
New Park
Highbury Grove
Highbury Place
Grosvenor Av
Matthias
Mildmay
Mildmay Park
Caledonian Road
Liverpool Rd
Mackenzie Rd
Roman Way
Bride Street
Paul's Road
St Paul's Road
Balls Pond Road
Canonbury Road
Englefield Road
Essex Road
Halliford St
Southgate Road
Downham
New North Road
Offord Road
Thornhill Road
Barnsbury Street
Upper St
Richmond Ave
Hemingford Road
Barnsbury Road
Copenhagen St
Liverpool Road
St Peter's Street
Prebend Street
Eagle Wharf Rd
Wharf Road
Shepherdess Walk
New North Rd
East Road
Pitfield
Pentonville Road
Calshot St
King's Cross
Amwell St
St John St
Goswell
City Road
Central Street
Lever
A 503
A 1
A 5203
A 105
A 1200
A 501
12
19
56
70
78
333
343
344
345
350
235
265
293
296
398
417
478
a
b
e
h
k
r
t
v
x
H
POL.
P
M
U
T

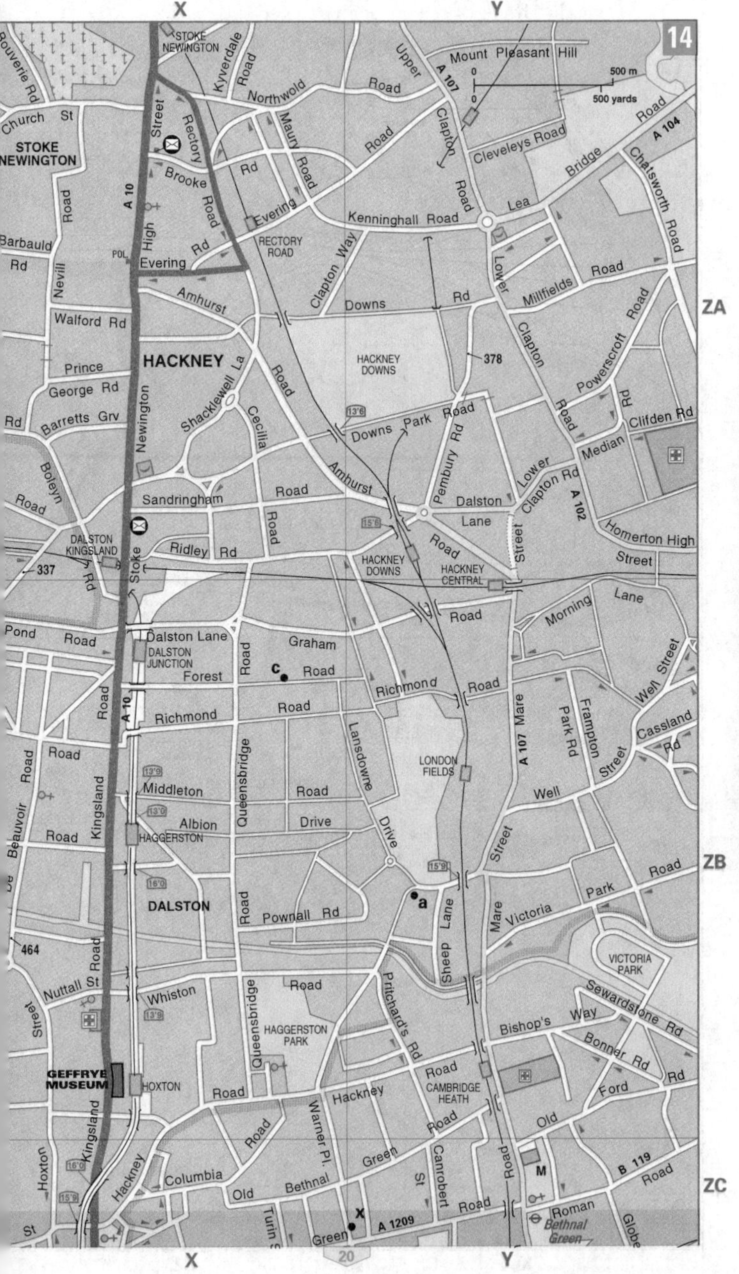
X
Y
14
STOKE NEWINGTON
Kyverdale Road
Northwold Road
Upper Clapton Road
Mount Pleasant Hill
A 107
0
500 m
500 yards
Rouverie Rd
Church St
STOKE NEWINGTON
Stoke Newington High Street
Rectory Road
Brooke Rd
Maury Road
Cleveleys Road
Lea Bridge Road
A 104
Chatsworth Road
A 10
Evering Rd
Kenninghall Road
RECTORY ROAD
Clapton Way
Barbauld Rd
Nevill Road
POL
Lower Clapton Road
Millfields Road
Amhurst Road
Downs Rd
ZA
Walford Rd
HACKNEY DOWNS
378
Powerscroft Road
Prince George Rd
HACKNEY
Shacklewell La
Cecilia Road
Barretts Grv
Clifden Rd
Median Road
Downs Park Road
Pembury Rd
Boleyn Road
Sandringham Road
Dalston Lane
A 102
Homerton High Street
DALSTON KINGSLAND
Ridley Rd
HACKNEY DOWNS
HACKNEY CENTRAL
337
Morning Lane
Pond Road
Dalston Lane
Graham Road
DALSTON JUNCTION
Forest Road
Queensbridge Road
Richmond Road
Well Street
Cassland Rd
Frampton Park Rd
Mare Street
Beauvoir Road
Kingsland Road
Middleton Road
Lansdowne Drive
LONDON FIELDS
Albion Drive
HAGGERSTON
ZB
DALSTON
Pownall Rd
Sheep Lane
Victoria Park Road
VICTORIA PARK
464
Nuttall St
Whiston Road
Pritchard's Rd
Sewardstone Rd
Bishop's Way
Bonner Rd
HAGGERSTON PARK
GEFFRYE MUSEUM
HOXTON
Hackney Road
CAMBRIDGE HEATH
Ford Rd
Old Ford Road
Warner Pl.
Cambrobert St
Columbia Road
Old Bethnal Green Road
B 119
ZC
Roman Road
Bethnal Green
Turin St
A 1209
Globe Rd
20
LONDON

K
L
9
15
ZC
ZD
ZE
ZF
Willesden Junction
Kensal Green
KENSAL GREEN CEMETERY
Mortimer
Harrow Road
A 404
Grand Union Canal
A 219
Old Oak Lane
Victoria Rd
WORMWOOD SCRUBS
Scrubs Lane
Barlby
St Quintin
Highlever Road
Wood Lane
Wulfstan Street
East Acton
The Fairway
Brassie Ave
Western Ave
Du Cane Road
Westway
A 40
East Acton Lane
Old Oak Road
Yew Tree Rd
Bryony Road
Bloemfontein Road
South Africa Road
White City
BBC
Wood Lane
WHITE CITY
WESTFIELD SHOPPING CENTRE
Bromyard Avenue
Ashfield Rd
Steventon Rd
Wormholt Road
Sawley Road
LOFTUS ROAD STADIUM
SHEPHERD'S BUSH
EALING
The Vale
Uxbridge Road
A 4020
a
Shepherd's Bush Market
Larden Road
Askew Road
Percy Road
Coningham Road
Lime Grove
454
Cobbold Road
462
Goldhawk Road
Goldhawk Road
A 402
Emlyn Road
Abinger Rd
The Blenheim Rd
Avenue
387
463
c
Paddenswick Rd
Brackenbury Rd
Hammersmith Grove
Bath Road
Prebend Gdns
Stamford Brook
Goldhawk Road
RAVENSCOURT PARK
Ravenscourt Park
13
Banim St
b
HAMMERSMITH
Glenthorne Rd
e
Hammersmith
Turnham Green
Shepherd's Bush Road
500 m
500 yards
21
LONDON

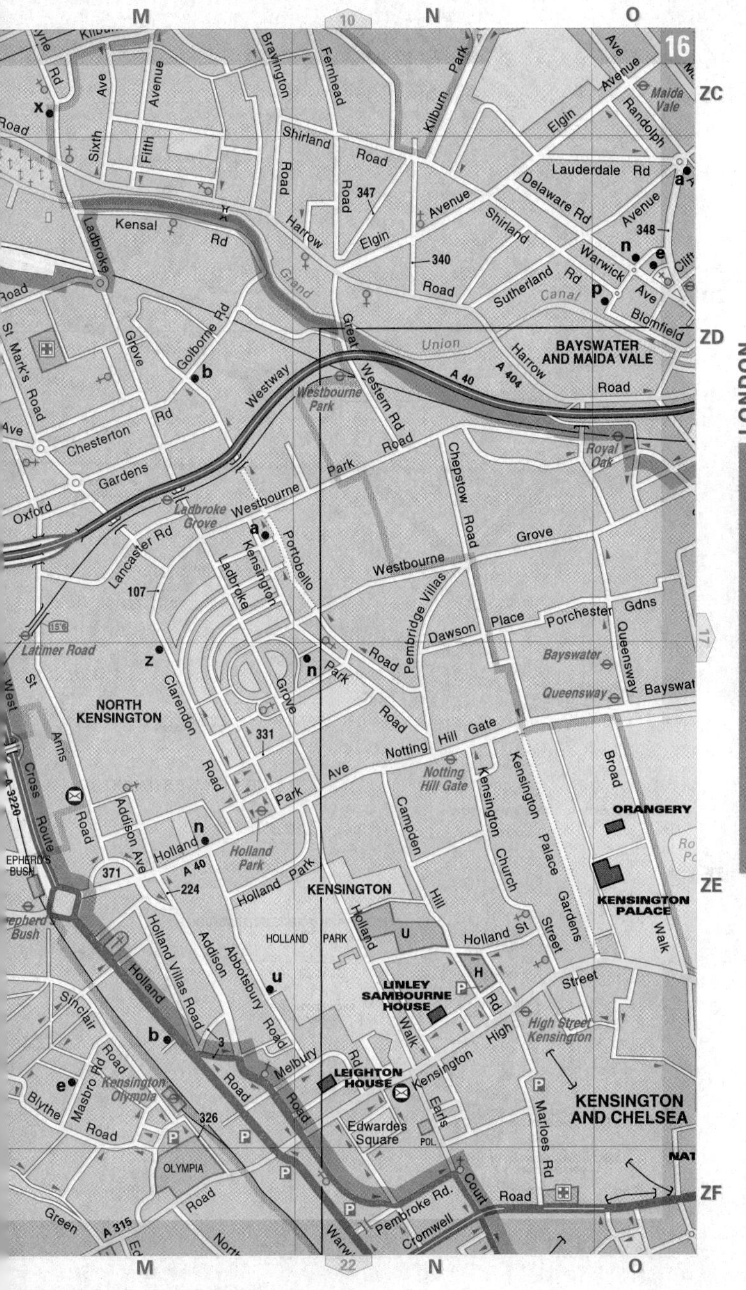
M
N
O
10
16
ZC
ZD
ZE
ZF
22
17
LONDON
Maida Vale
Randolph
Elgin
Avenue
Lauderdale Rd
Delaware Rd
Shirland Road
Kilburn Park
Fernhead
Bravington
Sixth Ave
Fifth Avenue
Kensal Rd
Ladbroke
Harrow Road
Elgin Avenue
347
340
348
Warwick Ave
Sutherland
Grand Union Canal
Blomfield
BAYSWATER AND MAIDA VALE
Harrow Road
A 40
A 404
Westway
Westbourne Park
Great Western Rd
Golborne Rd
Grove
St Mark's Road
Chesterton Rd
Gardens
Oxford
Ave
Royal Oak
Chepstow Road
Westbourne Park Road
Ladbroke Grove
Westbourne Grove
Lancaster Rd
Kensington Park Road
Portobello
Ladbroke Grove
107
Pembridge Villas
Dawson Place
Porchester Gdns
Queensway
Bayswater
Latimer Road
NORTH KENSINGTON
Clarendon Road
St Anns Road
West Cross Route
A 3220
331
Notting Hill Gate
Holland Park Ave
Campden Hill
Kensington Church Street
Kensington Palace Gardens
Broad Walk
ORANGERY
KENSINGTON PALACE
Addison Ave
Holland Rd
Holland Park
371
224
Shepherd's Bush
KENSINGTON
Holland Park
HOLLAND PARK
Holland Walk
Holland St
Holland Villas Road
Addison Road
Abbotsbury Road
LINLEY SAMBOURNE HOUSE
High Street Kensington
Kensington High Street
Sinclair Road
Melbury Rd
LEIGHTON HOUSE
Earls Court Road
Marloes Rd
KENSINGTON AND CHELSEA
Masbro Rd
Blythe Road
Kensington Olympia
326
Edwardes Square
POL.
OLYMPIA
Pembroke Rd.
Cromwell Road
Green
A 315

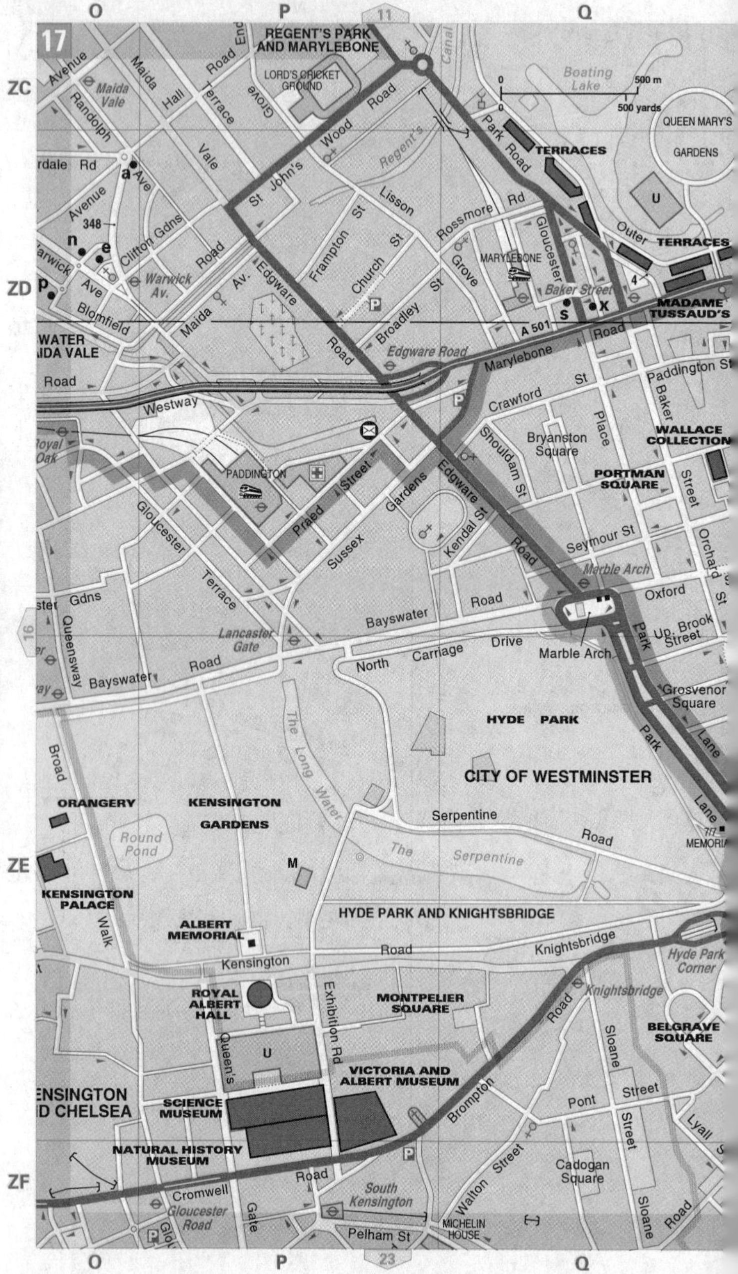

O
P
Q
11
17
ZC
ZD
ZE
ZF
REGENT'S PARK AND MARYLEBONE
LORD'S CRICKET GROUND
Boating Lake
0
500 m
500 yards
QUEEN MARY'S GARDENS
TERRACES
Outer
TERRACES
U
Avenue
Maida Vale
Maida
Hall
Road
End
Terrace
Grove
Road
Wood
St John's
Regent's
Canal
Park Road
Randolph
rdale Rd
a
Ave
Vale
Avenue
348
n
e
Clifton Gdns
arwick
Warwick Av.
Road
Ave
Blomfield
Maida
Av.
Edgware
Frampton
St
Church
St
Lisson
Rossmore
Rd
Grove
MARYLEBONE
Gloucester
Baker Street
4
S
X
MADAME TUSSAUD'S
Broadley
St
Road
A 501
Road
WATER
IDA VALE
Road
Edgware Road
Marylebone
Paddington St
Westway
Crawford
St
Place
Baker
WALLACE COLLECTION
Royal Oak
PADDINGTON
Street
Praed
Gardens
Shouldham St
Bryanston Square
PORTMAN SQUARE
Street
Gloucester
Sussex
Edgware
Kendal St
Road
Seymour St
Orchard
St
Marble Arch
Oxford
Terrace
ster Gdns
16
Queensway
Lancaster Gate
Bayswater
Road
Drive
Marble Arch
Park
Up. Brook Street
Bayswater
Road
North
Carriage
Grosvenor Square
HYDE PARK
Park
Lane
The Long Water
Broad
CITY OF WESTMINSTER
ORANGERY
KENSINGTON GARDENS
Serpentine
Road
Lane
MEMORIA
Round Pond
The Serpentine
M
KENSINGTON PALACE
Walk
HYDE PARK AND KNIGHTSBRIDGE
ALBERT MEMORIAL
Road
Knightsbridge
Hyde Park Corner
Kensington
ROYAL ALBERT HALL
Exhibition Rd
MONTPELIER SQUARE
Knightsbridge
Road
BELGRAVE SQUARE
Sloane
U
Queen's
VICTORIA AND ALBERT MUSEUM
Street
Pont
ENSINGTON
D CHELSEA
SCIENCE MUSEUM
Brompton
Street
Lyall
NATURAL HISTORY MUSEUM
Street
Cadogan Square
Road
Cromwell
South Kensington
Walton
Gloucester Road
Gate
Sloane
Road
MICHELIN HOUSE
Pelham St
23
O
P
Q

LONDON

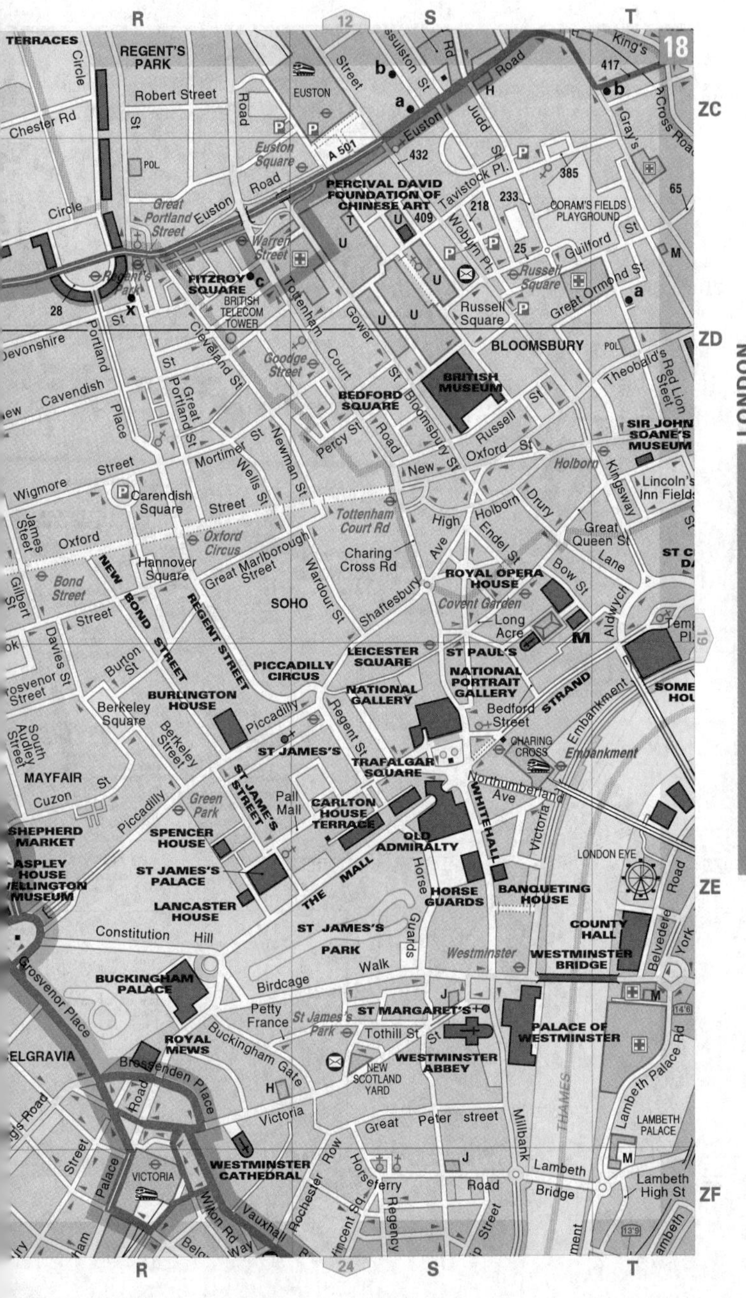
REGENT'S PARK
EUSTON
PERCIVAL DAVID FOUNDATION OF CHINESE ART
CORAM'S FIELDS PLAYGROUND
FITZROY SQUARE
BRITISH TELECOM TOWER
BLOOMSBURY
BRITISH MUSEUM
BEDFORD SQUARE
SIR JOHN SOANE'S MUSEUM
Cavendish Square
Oxford Circus
Tottenham Court Rd
SOHO
ROYAL OPERA HOUSE
Covent Garden
LEICESTER SQUARE
PICCADILLY CIRCUS
NATIONAL GALLERY
NATIONAL PORTRAIT GALLERY
BURLINGTON HOUSE
ST JAMES'S
TRAFALGAR SQUARE
CHARING CROSS
MAYFAIR
Green Park
CARLTON HOUSE TERRACE
SHEPHERD MARKET
SPENCER HOUSE
OLD ADMIRALTY
ST JAMES'S PALACE
LONDON EYE
HORSE GUARDS
BANQUETING HOUSE
LANCASTER HOUSE
ST JAMES'S PARK
COUNTY HALL
WESTMINSTER BRIDGE
BUCKINGHAM PALACE
ST MARGARET'S
PALACE OF WESTMINSTER
ROYAL MEWS
WESTMINSTER ABBEY
NEW SCOTLAND YARD
THAMES
LAMBETH PALACE
WESTMINSTER CATHEDRAL
VICTORIA
LONDON

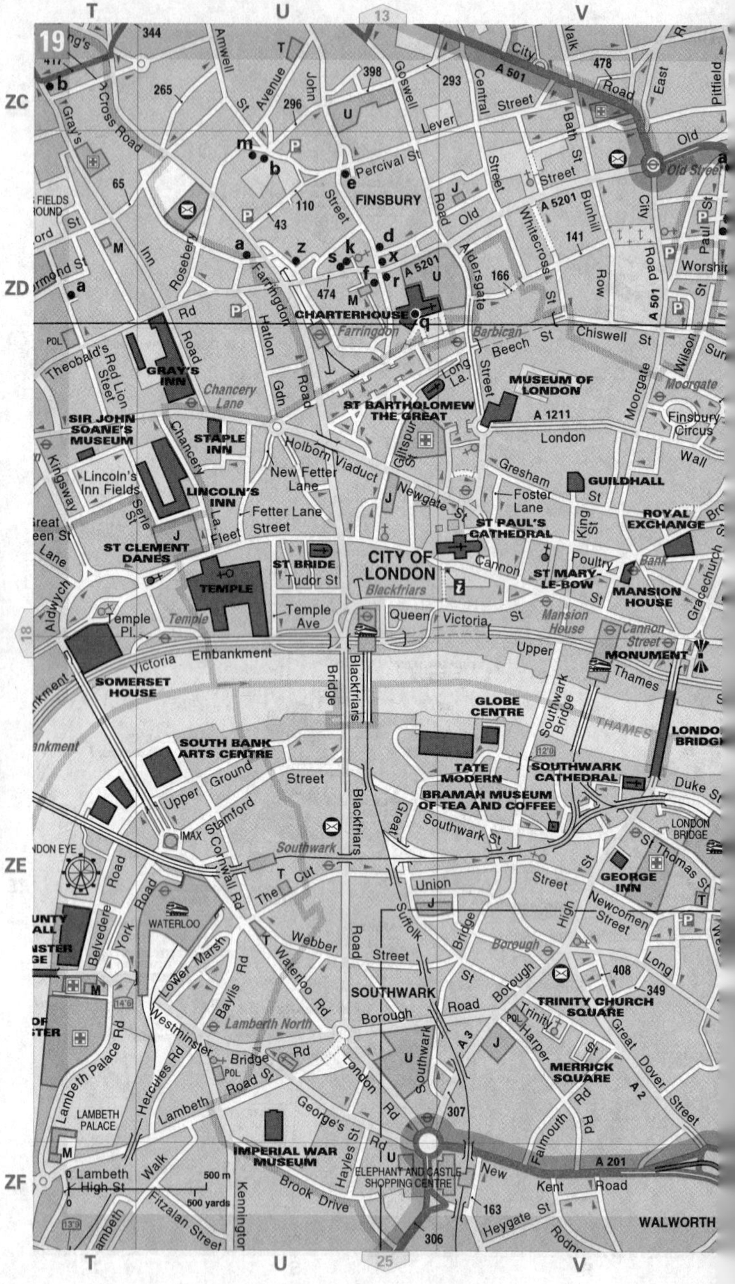

19

T U V

ZC ZD ZE ZF

FINSBURY

CHARTERHOUSE

GRAY'S INN

SIR JOHN SOANE'S MUSEUM

STAPLE INN

LINCOLN'S INN

ST BARTHOLOMEW THE GREAT

MUSEUM OF LONDON

GUILDHALL

ROYAL EXCHANGE

ST PAUL'S CATHEDRAL

ST CLEMENT DANES

TEMPLE

ST BRIDE

CITY OF LONDON

ST MARY-LE-BOW

MANSION HOUSE

MONUMENT

SOMERSET HOUSE

GLOBE CENTRE

LONDON BRIDGE

SOUTH BANK ARTS CENTRE

TATE MODERN

SOUTHWARK CATHEDRAL

BRAMAH MUSEUM OF TEA AND COFFEE

GEORGE INN

WATERLOO

SOUTHWARK

TRINITY CHURCH SQUARE

MERRICK SQUARE

LAMBETH PALACE

IMPERIAL WAR MUSEUM

ELEPHANT AND CASTLE SHOPPING CENTRE

WALWORTH

500 m

500 yards

T U V

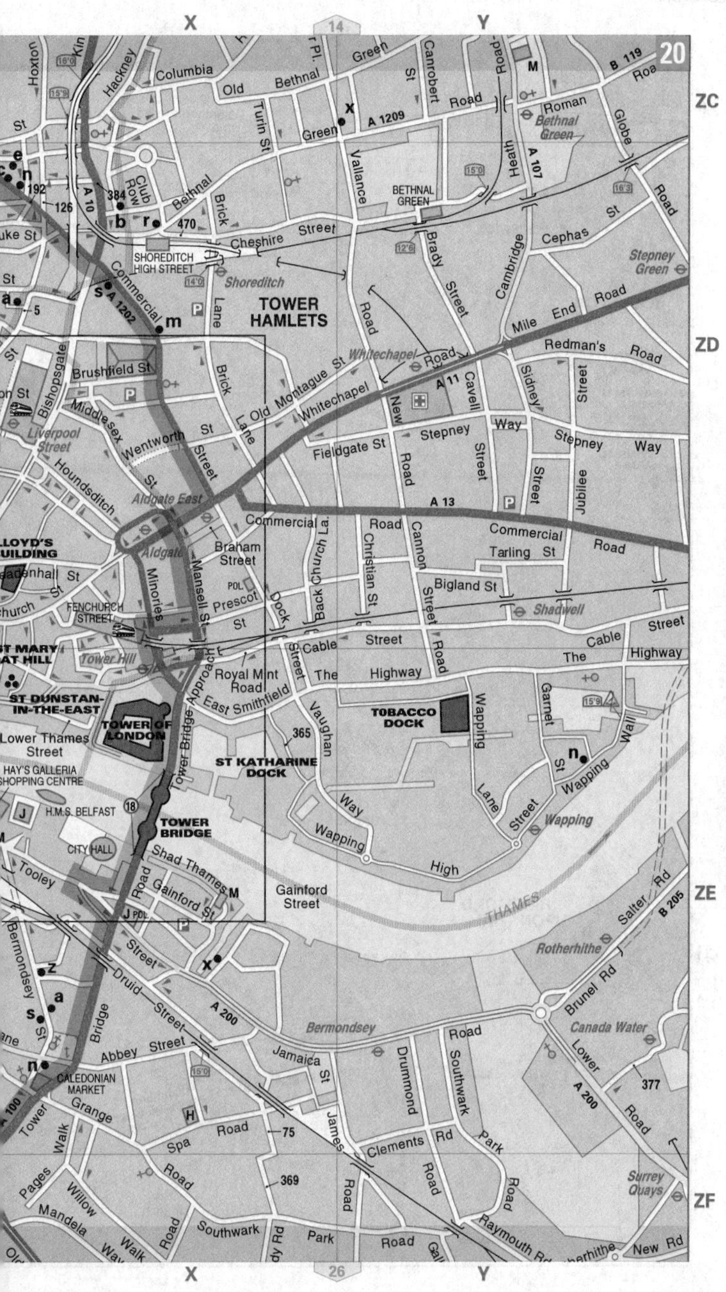

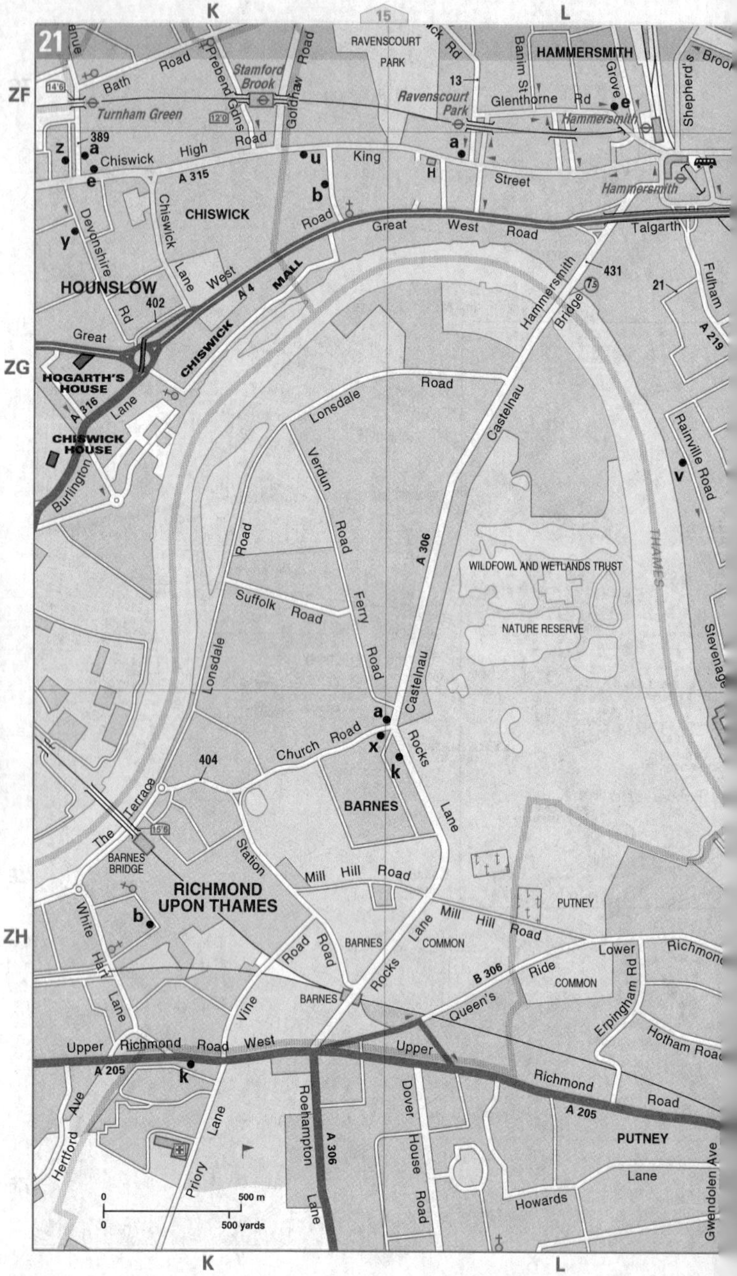

K 15 L

21

ZF

ZG

ZH

RAVENSCOURT PARK

HAMMERSMITH

Bath Road

Stamford Brook

Prebend Gdns

Goldhawk Road

Banim St

Grove

Shepherd's Bush

Turnham Green

Ravenscourt Park

Glenthorne Rd

Hammersmith

13

389

z a

Chiswick High Road

u

King Street

a

H

e

A 315

b

Hammersmith

CHISWICK

Road

Great West Road

Talgarth

y

Devonshire Rd

Chiswick Lane

West

A 4

MALL

CHISWICK

Hammersmith Bridge

431

21

Fulham

HOUNSLOW

402

A 219

Great

HOGARTH'S HOUSE

A 316

Lane

Road

Lonsdale

Castelnau

CHISWICK HOUSE

Burlington

Verdun Road

Rainville Road

v

Road

A 306

THAMES

WILDFOWL AND WETLANDS TRUST

Suffolk Road

Ferry Road

NATURE RESERVE

Stevenage

Lonsdale

Castelnau

a

Church Road

x

Rocks

k

404

The Terrace

BARNES

Lane

15'6

BARNES BRIDGE

Station

Mill Hill Road

RICHMOND UPON THAMES

PUTNEY

b

White Hart Lane

Mill Hill Road

Road Road

BARNES

Lane

COMMON

Lower Richmond

Ride

B 306

COMMON

Erpingham Rd

BARNES

Rocks

Vine

Queen's

Hotham Road

Upper Richmond Road West

Upper

A 205

k

Richmond Road

A 205

Hertford Ave

Priory Lane

Roehampton Lane

A 306

Dover House Road

PUTNEY

Lane

Howards

Gwendolen Ave

0 500 m

0 500 yards

K L

LONDON

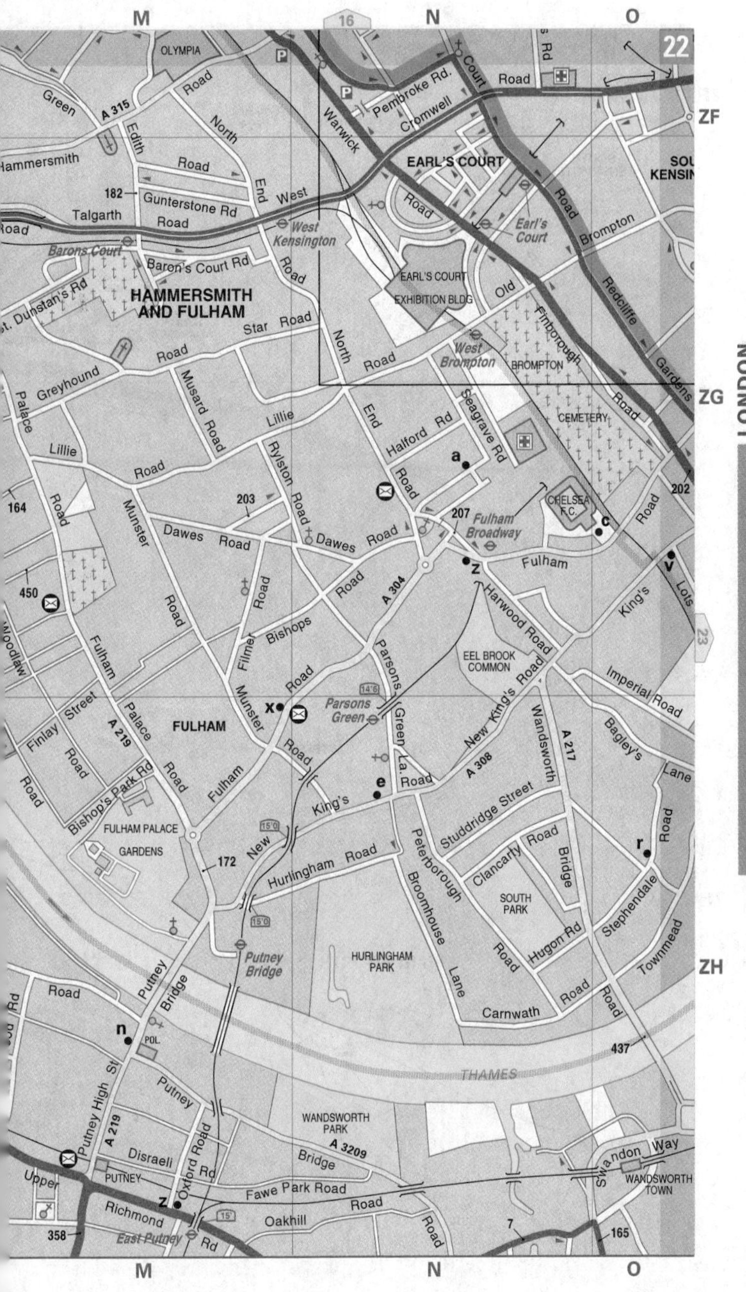
M
N
O
16
22
ZF
ZG
ZH
OLYMPIA
Pembroke Rd.
Cromwell
Warwick
EARL'S COURT
SOU
KENSIN
Hammersmith
Edith
North
End
West
Gunterstone Rd
Talgarth
Road
West Kensington
Earl's Court
Brompton
Redcliffe
Gardens
Barons Court
Baron's Court Rd
St. Dunstan's Rd
HAMMERSMITH AND FULHAM
EARL'S COURT EXHIBITION BLDG
Old
Finborough
Star Road
West Brompton
BROMPTON
CEMETERY
Greyhound
Musard Road
Lillie
Palace
Halford Rd
Seagrave Rd
Rylston Road
Munster
Dawes Road
Fulham Broadway
CHELSEA F.C.
Fulham
King's
Lots
Harwood Road
EEL BROOK COMMON
Imperial Road
Bishops
Filmer
Parsons
Parsons Green
New King's Road
Wandsworth
Bagley's
Lane
Finlay
Street
FULHAM
Green La.
Studdridge Street
Woodlaw
Bishop's Park Rd
FULHAM PALACE GARDENS
Clancarty Road
Bridge
Hurlingham Road
Peterborough
Broomhouse
SOUTH PARK
Stephendale
Hugon Rd
Townmead
Putney Bridge
HURLINGHAM PARK
Lane
Carnwath
THAMES
POL.
Putney High St
WANDSWORTH PARK
Disraeli Rd
Oxford Road
Swandon Way
WANDSWORTH TOWN
Upper Richmond Rd
PUTNEY
Fawe Park Road
Oakhill Road
East Putney
A 315
A 304
A 219
A 308
A 217
A 3209
182
203
164
450
207
202
172
437
358
7
165
LONDON

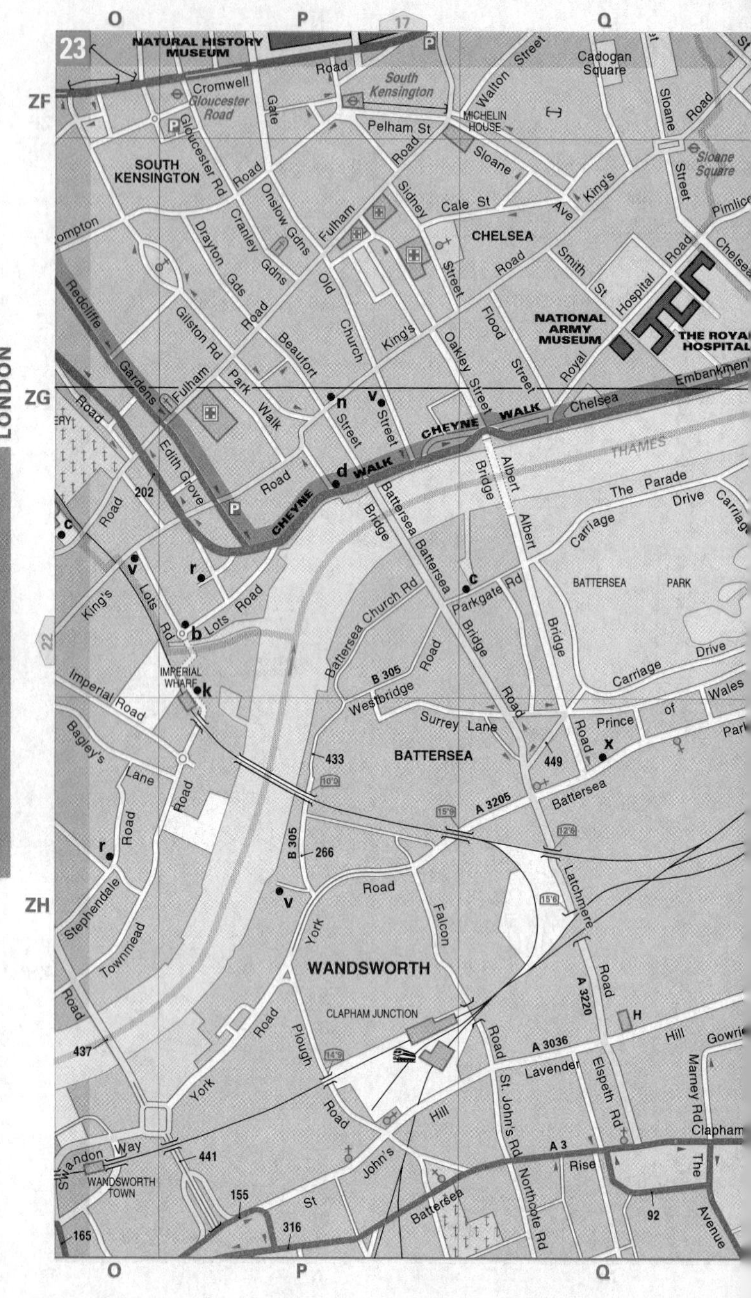
NATURAL HISTORY MUSEUM
South Kensington
Gloucester Road
Cromwell
SOUTH KENSINGTON
Cadogan Square
MICHELIN HOUSE
Pelham St
Sloane Square
CHELSEA
NATIONAL ARMY MUSEUM
THE ROYAL HOSPITAL
CHEYNE WALK
THAMES
Albert Bridge
Battersea Bridge
BATTERSEA PARK
Carriage Drive
IMPERIAL WHARF
Imperial Road
Lots Road
King's Road
Westbridge Road
Surrey Lane
Prince of Wales
BATTERSEA
Battersea Park Road
Latchmere Road
WANDSWORTH
CLAPHAM JUNCTION
Lavender Hill
St. John's Rd
Northcote Rd
Elspeth Rd
WANDSWORTH TOWN
Swandon Way
York Road
Plough Road
Falcon Road
Stephendale
Townmead
Bagley's Lane
Edith Grove
Redcliffe Gardens
Fulham Road
Old Church Street
Oakley Street
Flood Street
Sloane Street
King's Road
Royal Hospital Road
Chelsea Embankment
A 3205
A 3220
A 3036
A 3
B 305
O
P
Q
ZF
ZG
ZH
23
17
22
LONDON

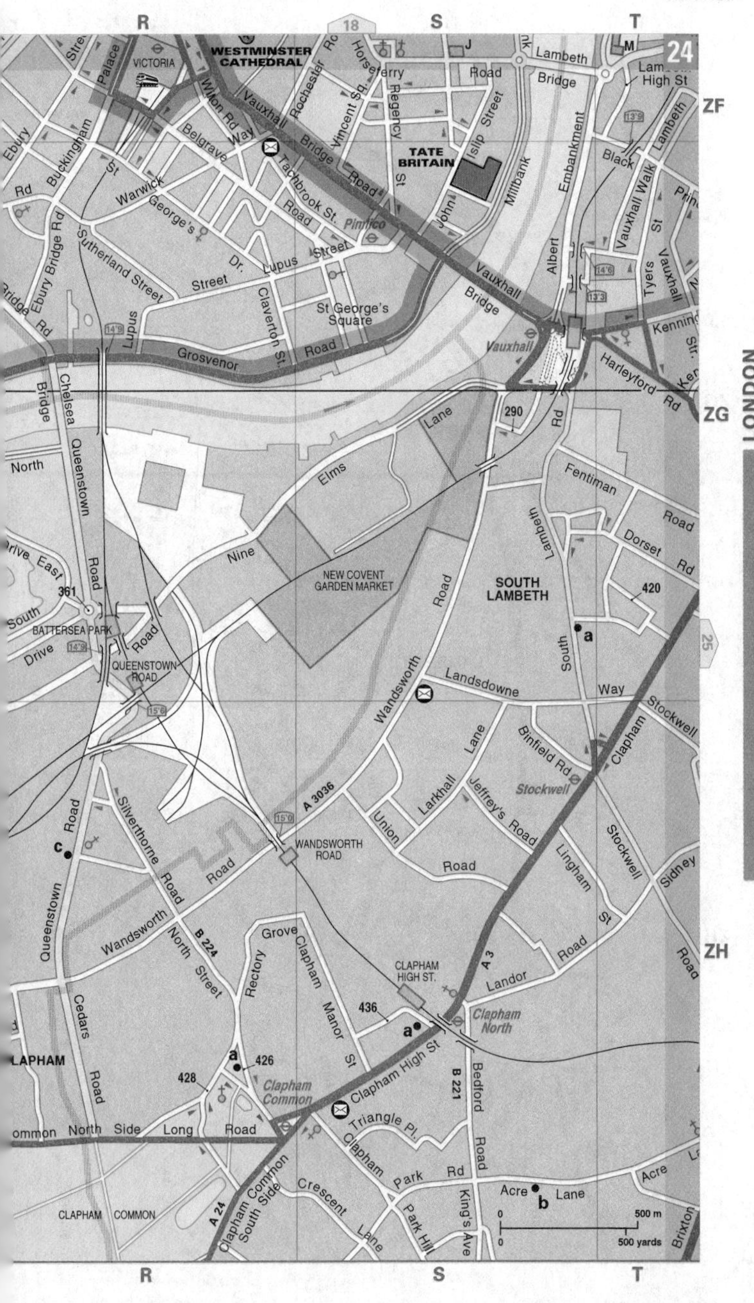
WESTMINSTER CATHEDRAL
VICTORIA
TATE BRITAIN
Pimlico
Vauxhall
St George's Square
NEW COVENT GARDEN MARKET
SOUTH LAMBETH
BATTERSEA PARK
QUEENSTOWN ROAD
WANDSWORTH ROAD
Stockwell
CLAPHAM HIGH ST.
Clapham North
Clapham Common
CLAPHAM COMMON
Vauxhall Bridge Road
Grosvenor Road
Nine Elms Lane
Wandsworth Road
Landsdowne Way
Clapham High St
Clapham Common North Side
Long Road
Clapham Common South Side
Bedford Road
Acre Lane
LONDON
500 m
500 yards

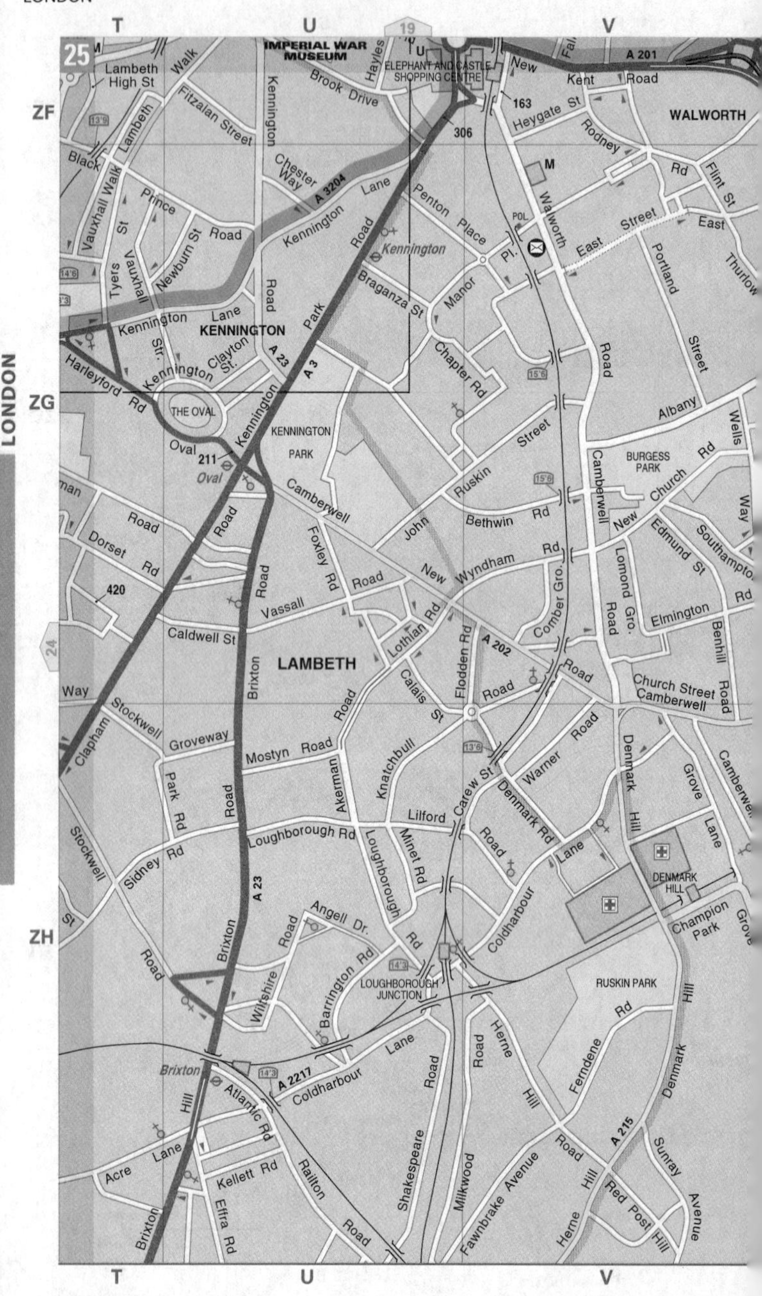
IMPERIAL WAR MUSEUM
ELEPHANT AND CASTLE SHOPPING CENTRE
WALWORTH
KENNINGTON
THE OVAL
KENNINGTON PARK
BURGESS PARK
LAMBETH
DENMARK HILL
LOUGHBOROUGH JUNCTION
RUSKIN PARK
Kennington
Oval
Brixton
Lambeth High St
Lambeth Walk
Fitzalan Street
Kennington Road
Brook Drive
Chester Way
Kennington Lane
Penton Place
Braganza St
Manor Pl.
Chapter Rd
Walworth Road
East Street
Portland Street
Albany Rd
Heygate St
Rodney Rd
Flint St
New Kent Road
Harleyford Rd
Clayton St.
Kennington Park Road
Camberwell Road
Camberwell New Road
John Ruskin Street
Bethwin Rd
Wyndham Rd
Comber Gro.
Lomond Gro.
Elmington Rd
Edmund St
Southampton Way
Dorset Rd
Caldwell St
Vassall Road
Foxley Rd
Lothian Rd
Flodden Rd
Calais St
Church Street Camberwell
Benhill Road
Brixton Road
Stockwell Road
Clapham Road
Groveway
Mostyn Road
Akerman Road
Knatchbull Road
Lilford Road
Loughborough Rd
Minet Rd
Carew St
Denmark Rd
Warner Road
Coldharbour Lane
Grove Lane
Champion Park
Sidney Rd
Angell Dr.
Barrington Rd
Wiltshire Road
Atlantic Rd
Acre Lane
Kellett Rd
Effra Rd
Railton Road
Shakespeare Road
Milkwood Road
Herne Hill
Ferndene Rd
Fawnbrake Avenue
Red Post Hill
Sunray Avenue
Denmark Hill
A 3204
A 23
A 3
A 202
A 2217
A 215
A 201

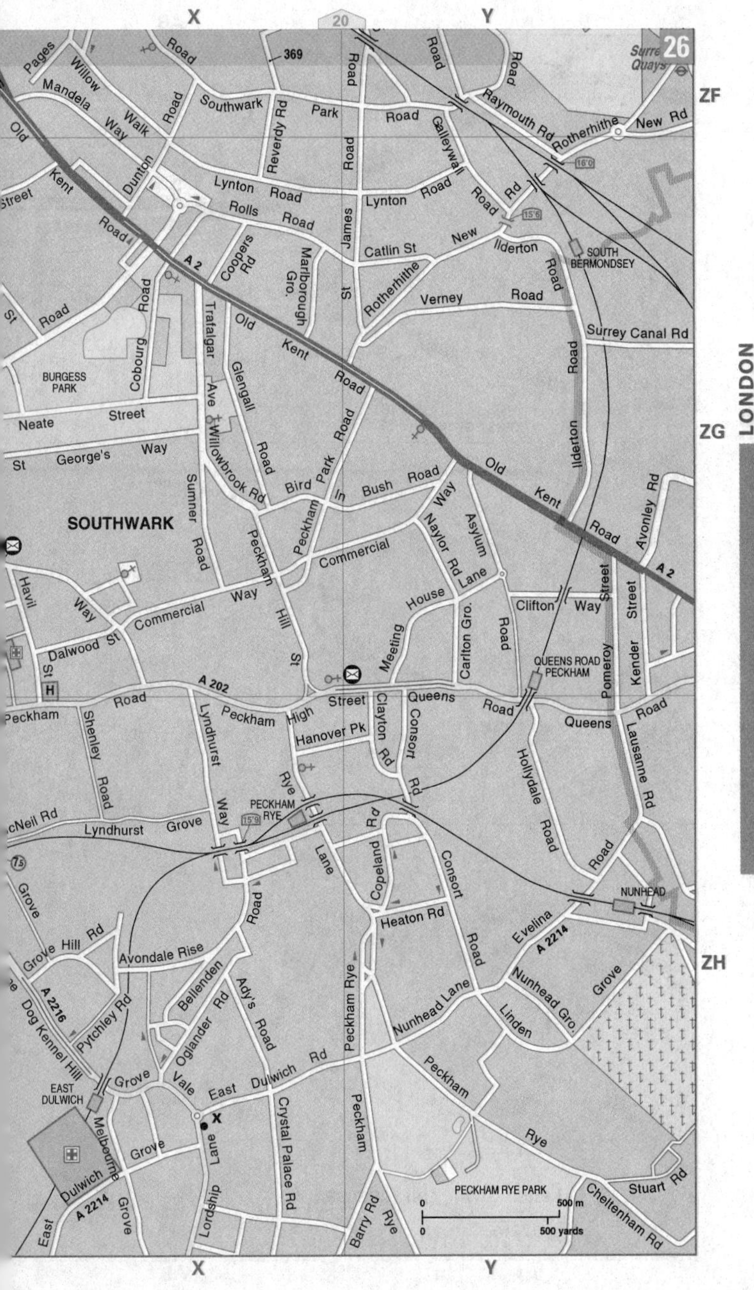
X
Y
20
26
ZF
ZG
ZH
LONDON
SOUTHWARK
BURGESS PARK
SOUTH BERMONDSEY
QUEENS ROAD PECKHAM
PECKHAM RYE
NUNHEAD
EAST DULWICH
PECKHAM RYE PARK
Surrey Quays
Old Kent Road
A 2
A 202
A 2214
A 2216
369
Southwark Park Road
Lynton Road
Rolls Road
Raymouth Rd
Rotherhithe New Rd
Galleywall Road
Ilderton Road
Verney Road
Surrey Canal Rd
Catlin St
St James Road
Neate Street
St George's Way
Commercial Way
Peckham Road
Peckham High Street
Queens Road
Peckham Hill St
Peckham Park Road
Bird in Bush Road
Asylum Road
Clifton Way
Pomeroy Street
Kender Street
Avonley Rd
Lyndhurst Grove
Lyndhurst Way
Rye Lane
Peckham Rye
Nunhead Lane
East Dulwich Rd
Crystal Palace Rd
Lordship Lane
Grove Vale
Dog Kennel Hill
Evelina Road
Hollydale Road
Lausanne Rd
Linden Grove
Cheltenham Rd
Stuart Rd
Barry Rd
Heaton Rd
Copeland Rd
Consort Road
Avondale Rise
Bellenden Rd
Ady's Road
Oglander Rd
Pytchley Rd
Grove Hill Rd
Melbourne Grove
Dulwich Grove
Sumner Road
Trafalgar Ave
Glengall Road
Willowbrook Rd
Cobourg Road
Dunton Road
Mandela Way
Willow Walk
Pages
Coopers Rd
Marlborough Gro.
Reverdy Rd
Naylor Rd
Carlton Gro.
Meeting House Lane
Clayton Rd
Hanover Pk
Shenley Road
Dalwood St
Havil Way
McNeil Rd
Nunhead Gro.
15'6
15'9
16'0
500 m
500 yards
0

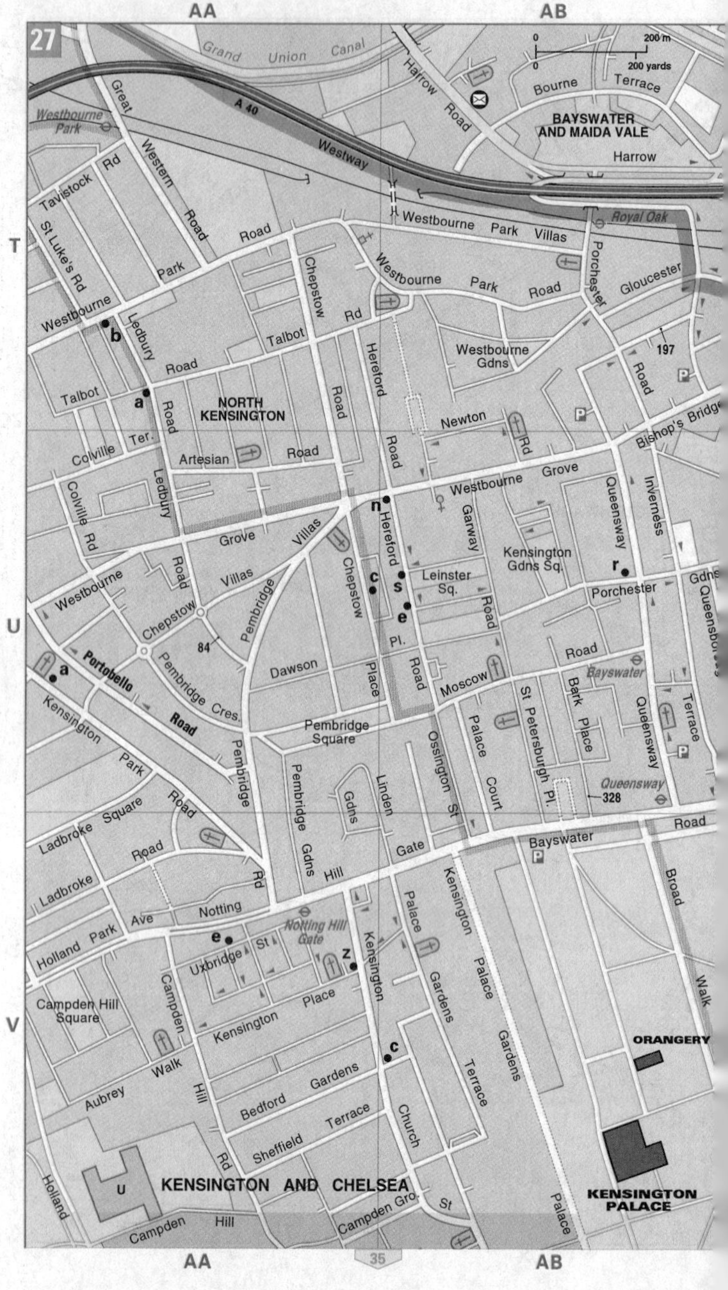
AA
AB
27
Grand Union Canal
Westbourne Park
A 40
Westway
Harrow Road
Bourne Terrace
BAYSWATER AND MAIDA VALE
Harrow
Royal Oak
Great Western Road
Tavistock Rd
St Luke's Rd
Westbourne Park Road
Westbourne Park Villas
Westbourne Park Road
Porchester
Gloucester
Chepstow Rd
Talbot Road
Ledbury Road
Hereford Road
Westbourne Gdns
197
NORTH KENSINGTON
Talbot
Colville Ter.
Artesian Road
Newton Rd
Bishop's Bridge
Westbourne Grove
Colville Rd
Westbourne Grove
Queensway
Inverness
Garway Road
Kensington Gdns Sq.
Grove Villas
Chepstow Villas
Hereford
Leinster Sq.
Porchester
Gdns
Queensborough
Westbourne
Chepstow
Pembridge Villas
Chepstow Pl.
Road
84
Portobello Road
Pembridge Cres.
Dawson Place
Moscow Road
Bayswater
Kensington Park Road
Pembridge Square
Pembridge Road
Pembridge Gdns
Gdns
Linden Gate
Ossington St
Palace Court
St Petersburgh Pl.
Bark Place
Queensway
Terrace
Queensway
328
Ladbroke Square
Road
Rd
Bayswater Road
Ladbroke Road
Hill
Notting
Notting Hill Gate
Holland Park Ave
Uxbridge St
Kensington Church
Palace Gardens
Kensington Palace Gardens
Broad Walk
Campden Hill Square
Campden Hill Rd
Kensington Place
Aubrey Walk
Bedford Gardens
Sheffield Terrace
Church
Terrace
ORANGERY
KENSINGTON AND CHELSEA
Holland
Campden Hill
Campden Gro.
St
Palace
KENSINGTON PALACE
T
U
V
a
b
n
c
s
e
r
z
U
0
200 m
200 yards
LONDON
35

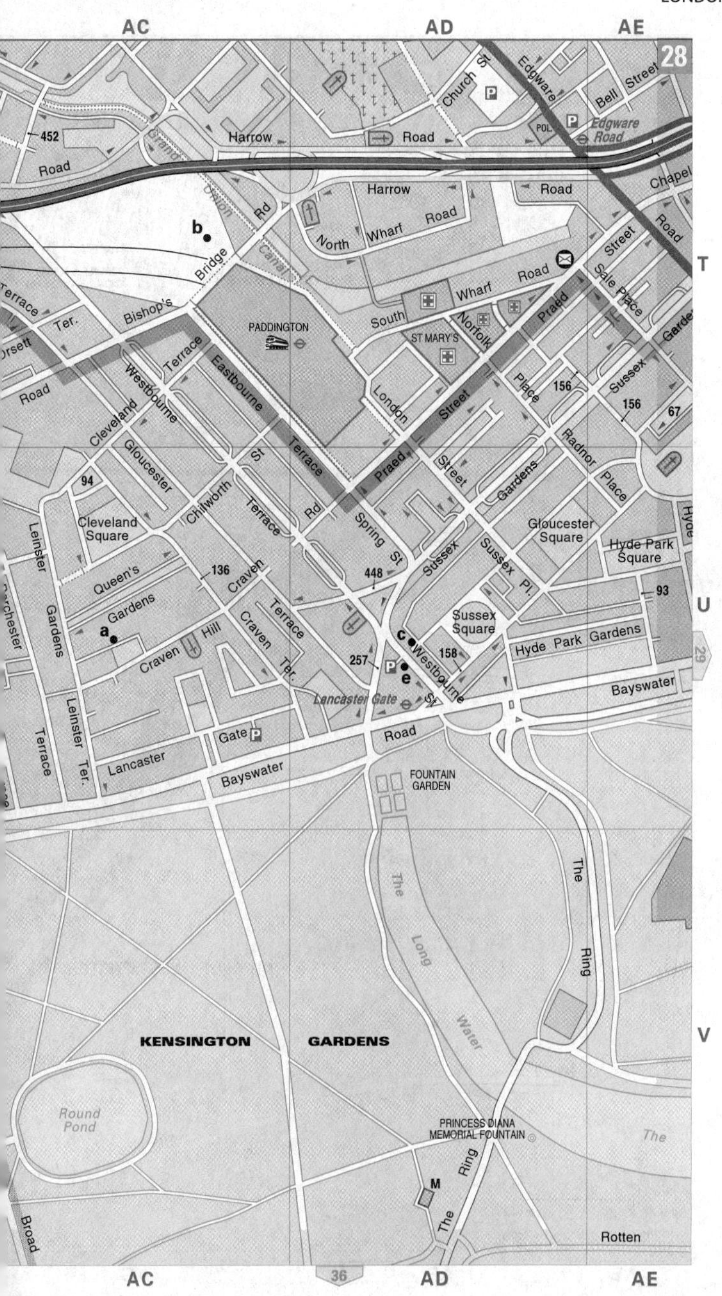
AC
AD
AE
28
Harrow
Road
Church St
Edgware
Bell
Street
Edgware Road
POL
452
Road
Grand Union Canal
Rd
Harrow
Road
North
Wharf
Road
Chapel
b
Bridge
Street
Road
Wharf
Road
South
Wharf
Sale Place
Terrace
Bishop's
Ter.
PADDINGTON
ST MARY'S
Norfolk
Praed
Orsett
Terrace
Eastbourne
London
Sussex
Gardens
Road
Westbourne
Street
Place
156
156
67
Cleveland
Gloucester
St
Terrace
Praed
Street
Radnor
Place
94
Chilworth
Terrace
Rd
Gardens
Gloucester
Square
Hyde
Cleveland
Square
Leinster
Spring
St
Sussex
Sussex
Pl.
Hyde Park
Square
Queen's
136
Craven
448
93
Gardens
Terrace
Sussex
Square
a
Craven
Hill
c
Westbourne
Hyde Park Gardens
Chester
Gardens
Craven
257
158
29
Craven
Ter.
e
St
Bayswater
Lancaster Gate
Leinster
Ter.
Terrace
Gate
Road
Lancaster
Bayswater
FOUNTAIN GARDEN
The
Long
Water
The
Ring
KENSINGTON
GARDENS
Round
Pond
PRINCESS DIANA MEMORIAL FOUNTAIN
The
Ring
The
M
Broad
Rotten
36
T
U
V
LONDON

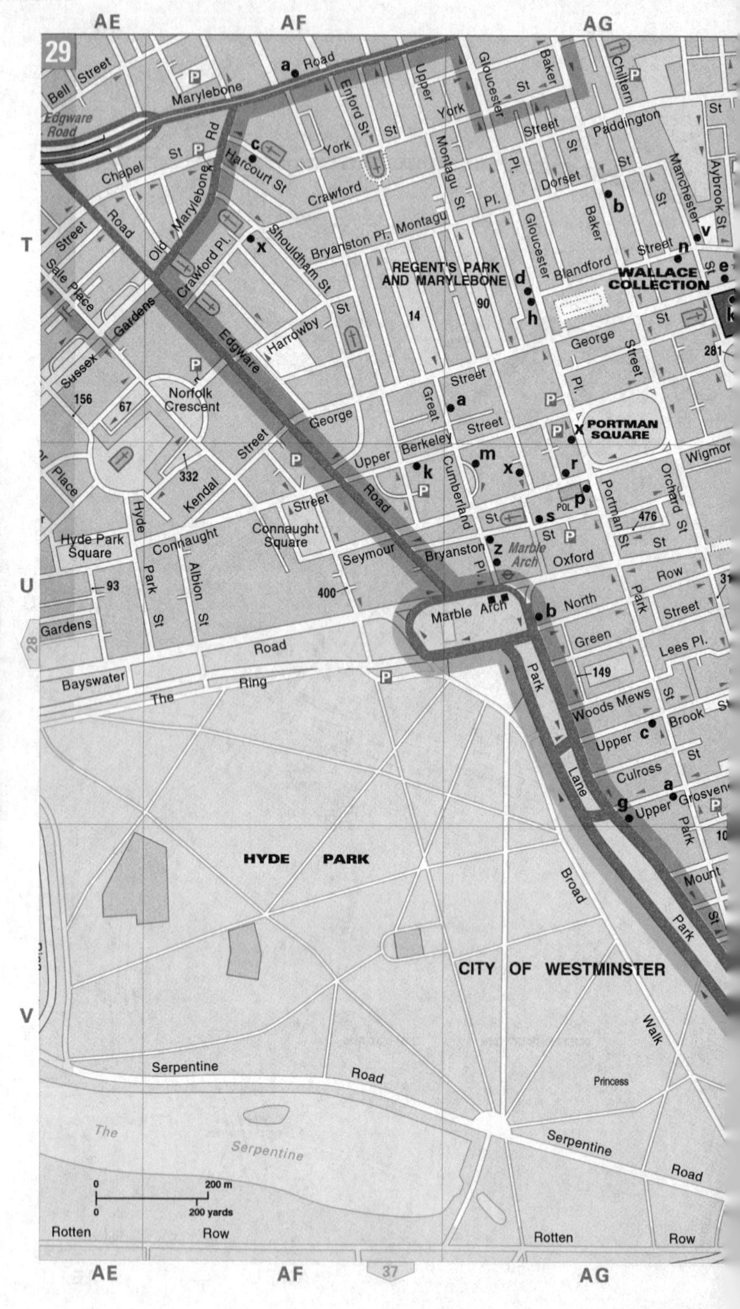
AE
AF
AG
29
T
U
V
28
37
REGENT'S PARK AND MARYLEBONE
WALLACE COLLECTION
PORTMAN SQUARE
HYDE PARK
CITY OF WESTMINSTER
Marble Arch
Edgware Road
Marylebone Road
Bell Street
Chapel St
Harcourt St
Crawford St
Shouldham St
Bryanston Pl.
Montagu Pl.
York St
Enford St
Upper
Gloucester Pl.
Baker St
Dorset St
Blandford Street
Paddington St
Chiltern St
Manchester St
Aybrook St
George St
Portman Square
Great Cumberland Pl.
Upper Berkeley Street
Seymour Street
Connaught Square
Connaught Street
Hyde Park Square
Hyde Park St
Albion St
Kendal Street
Norfolk Crescent
Sussex Gardens
Sale Place
Oxford St
Bryanston St
North Row
Park Street
Green Street
Lees Pl.
Woods Mews
Upper Brook St
Culross St
Upper Grosvenor St
Mount St
Park Lane
Orchard St
Portman St
Wigmore St
Bayswater Road
The Ring
Broad Walk
Serpentine Road
The Serpentine
Princess
Rotten Row
0
200 m
200 yards
LONDON

AH
AI
AJ
30
T
U
V
31
38
LONDON
BRITISH TELECOM TOWER
Cavendish Sq.
Oxford Circus
Hannover Sq.
MAYFAIR
Grosvenor Square
Berkeley Square
Golden Sq.
BURLINGTON HOUSE
BURLINGTON ARCADE
PICCADILLY ARCADE
ST JAMES SQUARE
SHEPHERD MARKET
SPENCER HOUSE
QUEEN'S CHAPEL
ST JAMES PALACE
LANCASTER HOUSE
GREEN PARK
Green Park
Bond St
APSLEY HOUSE WELLINGTON MUSEUM
PICCADILLY
REGENT ST
NEW BOND ST
OLD BOND ST
JERMYN ST
ST JAMES'S ST
Oxford St
Wigmore St
Marylebone High St
Harley Street
Wimpole St
Portland Place
Great Portland St
Regent St
Mortimer St
Margaret St
Great Marlborough St
Carnaby St
Conduit St
Savile Row
Bruton Street
Brook St
Grosvenor St
Mount St
Curzon St
Berkeley St
Dover St
Albemarle St
Vigo St
Sackville St
King St
Pall Mall
Duke St
Charlotte St
Goodge St
Cleveland St
Wells St
Berner's St
Newman St
Eastcastle St
Poland St
Noel St
D'Arblay St
Broadwick St
Lexington St
Marshall St
Kingly St
Maddox St
Hanover St
Princes St
Henrietta Pl.
Vere St
Holles St
Cavendish St
Weymouth St
New Cavendish Street
Welbeck St
Queen Anne Street
Langham St
Titchfield St
Foley St
Great Titchfield St
Argyll St
South Molton St
Davies St
Gilbert St
Binney St
James St
Duke St
Brook's Mews
Grosvenor Street
Mount Row
Adam's Row
South Audley St
Farm Street
Hay's Mews
Charles Street
Hill St
Bolton Street
Queen's Walk
Hertford St
Brick St
Old Park La.
Curzon Street
Park Lane
Cork St
Bury St
Beak St
Golden Sq.
Brewer St

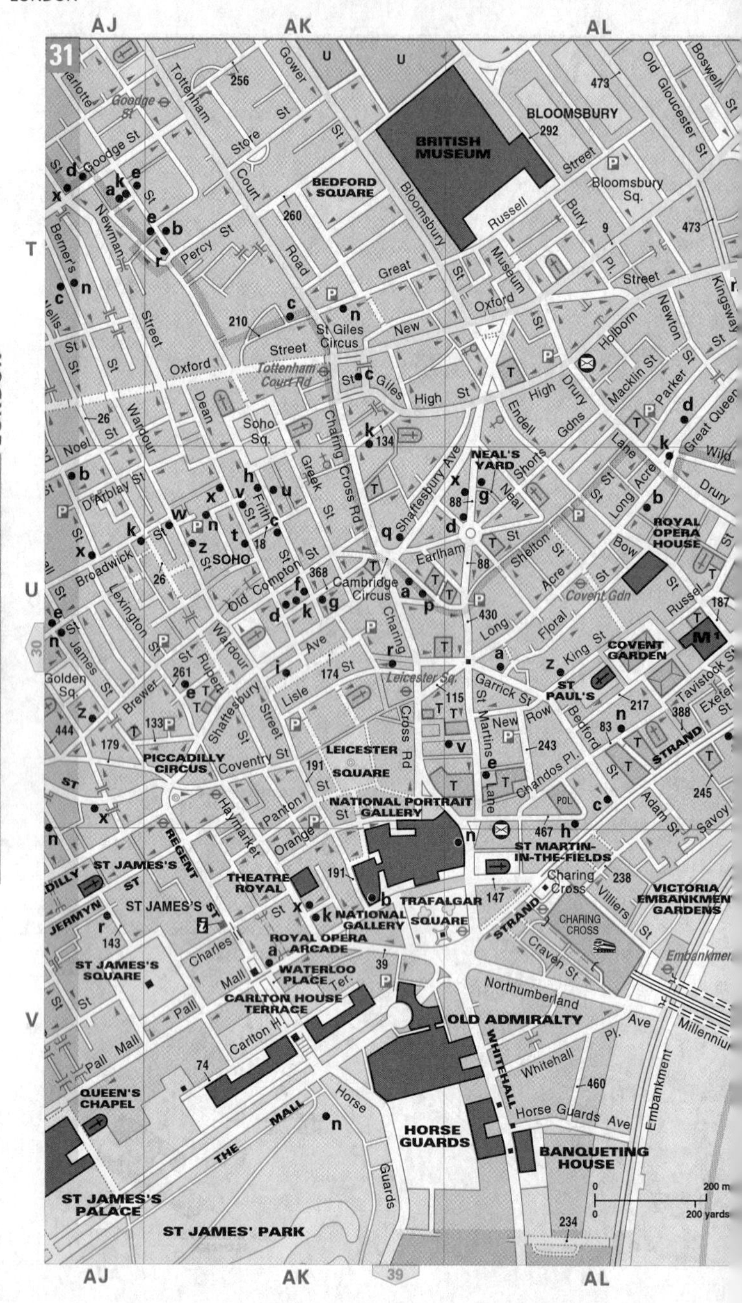
AJ
AK
AL
31
T
U
V
30
39
BRITISH MUSEUM
BLOOMSBURY
BEDFORD SQUARE
Bloomsbury Sq.
St Giles Circus
Tottenham Court Rd
Goodge St
Soho Sq.
SOHO
NEAL'S YARD
ROYAL OPERA HOUSE
Covent Gdn
COVENT GARDEN
ST PAUL'S
Cambridge Circus
Leicester Sq.
LEICESTER SQUARE
Golden Sq.
PICCADILLY CIRCUS
NATIONAL PORTRAIT GALLERY
ST MARTIN-IN-THE-FIELDS
THEATRE ROYAL
TRAFALGAR SQUARE
NATIONAL GALLERY
ROYAL OPERA ARCADE
WATERLOO PLACE
CARLTON HOUSE TERRACE
Charing Cross
CHARING CROSS
VICTORIA EMBANKMENT GARDENS
OLD ADMIRALTY
WHITEHALL
HORSE GUARDS
BANQUETING HOUSE
ST JAMES'S
ST JAMES'S SQUARE
QUEEN'S CHAPEL
ST JAMES'S PALACE
ST JAMES' PARK
THE MALL
STRAND
REGENT ST
JERMYN ST
Oxford Street
New Oxford St
Great Russell Street
Tottenham Court Road
Gower St
Store St
Goodge St
Percy St
Newman St
Berner's St
Wardour St
Dean St
Greek St
Frith St
Old Compton St
Charing Cross Rd
Shaftesbury Ave
St Giles High St
Endell St
Drury Lane
Long Acre
Floral St
King St
Garrick St
Bedford St
Chandos Pl.
Haymarket
Pall Mall
Charles II St
Coventry St
Lisle St
Northumberland Ave
Whitehall
Horse Guards Ave
Horse Guards
Craven St
Villiers St
Adam St
Savoy
Embankment
Kingsway
Great Queen St
Holborn
Broadwick St
Lexington St
D'Arblay St
Noel St
Brewer St
Rupert St
Earlham St
Shelton St
Bow St
Russell St
Tavistock St
Exeter St
Bury Pl.
Museum St
Bloomsbury St
Old Gloucester St
Boswell St
Newton St
Macklin St
Parker St
Orange St
Panton St
Carlton H. Ter.
Millennium
Embankment
0
200 m
200 yards

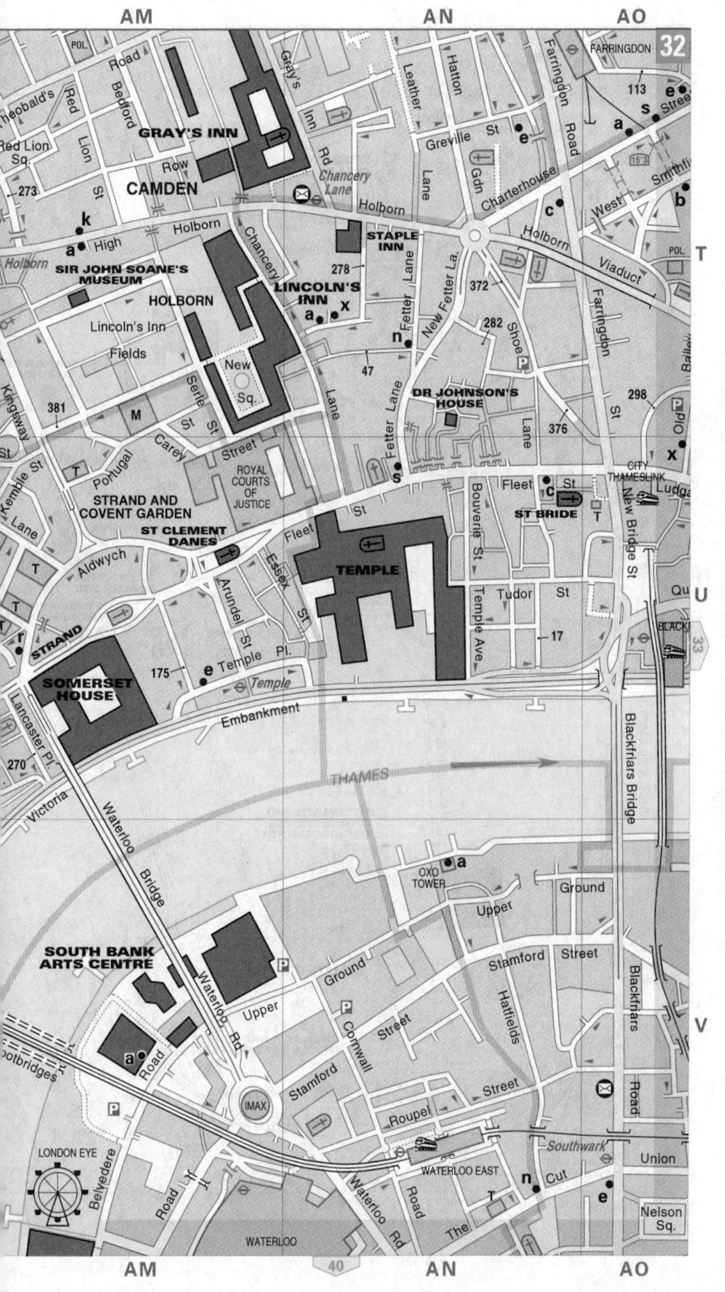
AM
AN
AO
32
GRAY'S INN
CAMDEN
STAPLE INN
LINCOLN'S INN
SIR JOHN SOANE'S MUSEUM
HOLBORN
Lincoln's Inn Fields
DR JOHNSON'S HOUSE
ROYAL COURTS OF JUSTICE
STRAND AND COVENT GARDEN
ST CLEMENT DANES
ST BRIDE
TEMPLE
STRAND
SOMERSET HOUSE
THAMES
OXO TOWER
SOUTH BANK ARTS CENTRE
LONDON EYE
WATERLOO EAST
WATERLOO
CITY THAMESLINK
FARRINGDON
T
U
V
33
40
LONDON

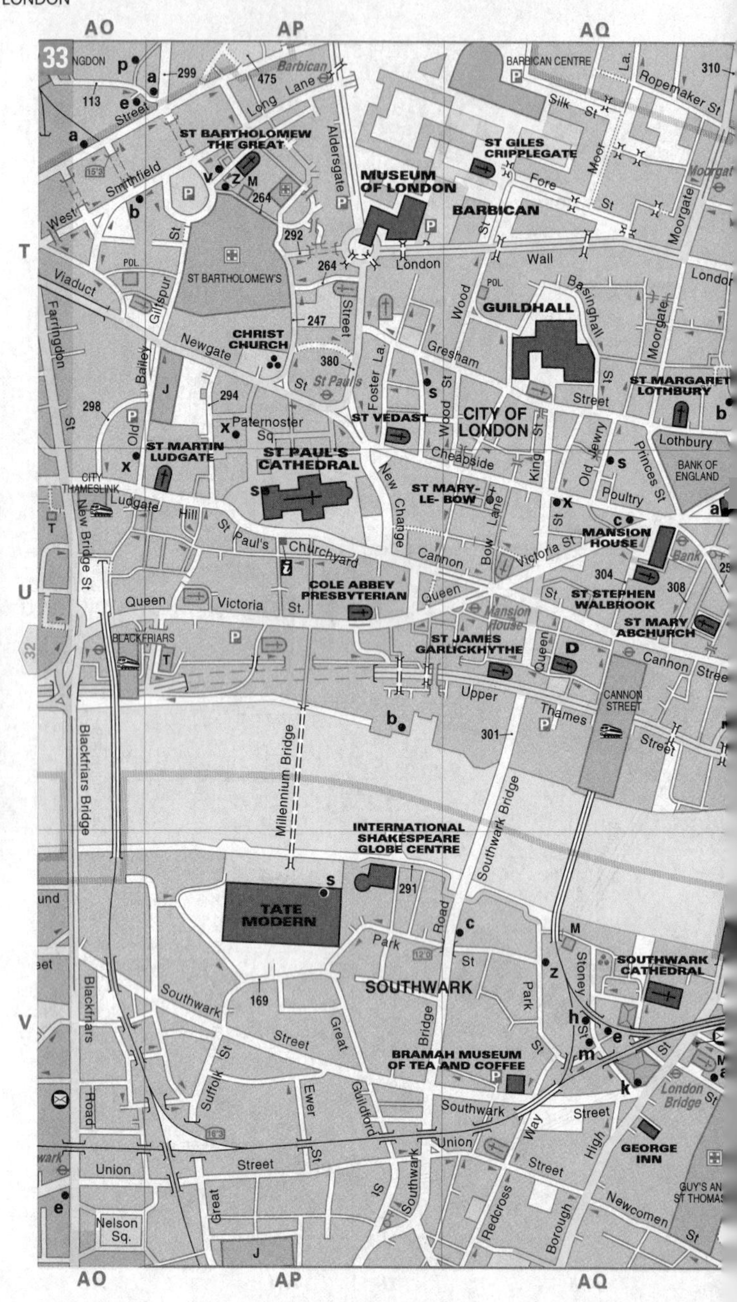

AO
AP
AQ
33
T
U
V
ST BARTHOLOMEW THE GREAT
MUSEUM OF LONDON
BARBICAN
BARBICAN CENTRE
ST GILES CRIPPLEGATE
ST BARTHOLOMEW'S
CHRIST CHURCH
GUILDHALL
ST MARGARET LOTHBURY
CITY OF LONDON
ST VEDAST
ST MARTIN LUDGATE
ST PAUL'S CATHEDRAL
BANK OF ENGLAND
ST MARY-LE- BOW
MANSION HOUSE
COLE ABBEY PRESBYTERIAN
ST STEPHEN WALBROOK
ST MARY ABCHURCH
ST JAMES GARLICKHYTHE
BLACKFRIARS
CITY THAMESLINK
CANNON STREET
INTERNATIONAL SHAKESPEARE GLOBE CENTRE
TATE MODERN
SOUTHWARK
SOUTHWARK CATHEDRAL
BRAMAH MUSEUM OF TEA AND COFFEE
GEORGE INN
Millennium Bridge
Southwark Bridge
Blackfriars Bridge

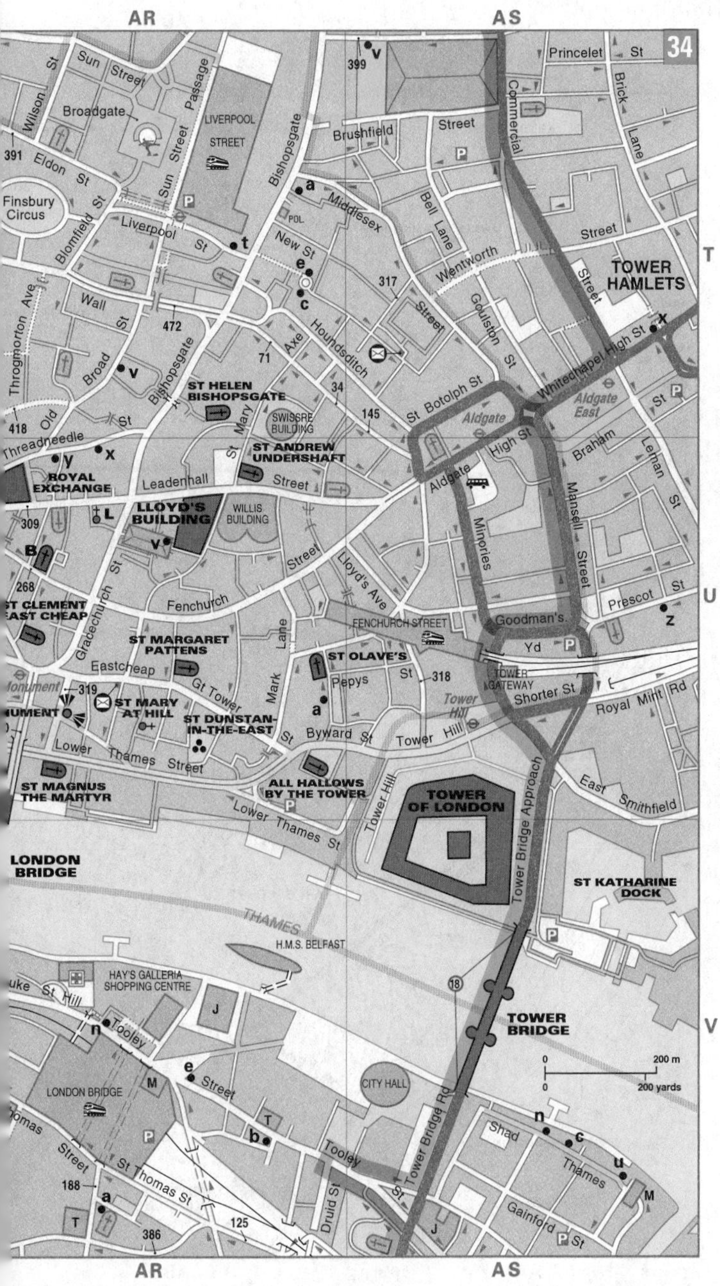

AR
AS
34
T
U
V
LONDON
Sun Street
Wilson St
Broadgate
Sun Street Passage
LIVERPOOL STREET
Bishopsgate
Eldon St
Finsbury Circus
Blomfield St
Liverpool St
Wall
Throgmorton Ave
Old Broad St
Threadneedle St
ROYAL EXCHANGE
Leadenhall Street
LLOYD'S BUILDING
WILLIS BUILDING
ST HELEN BISHOPSGATE
SWISS RE BUILDING
ST ANDREW UNDERSHAFT
St Mary Axe
Houndsditch
Middlesex Street
New St
Brushfield Street
Bell Lane
Wentworth Street
Goulston St
Commercial Street
Princelet St
Brick Lane
TOWER HAMLETS
Whitechapel High St
Aldgate East
Aldgate
St Botolph St
Aldgate High St
Braham St
Leman St
Mansell Street
Minories
Prescot St
Goodman's Yd
Fenchurch Street
FENCHURCH STREET
Lloyd's Ave
Gracechurch St
ST CLEMENT EAST CHEAP
ST MARGARET PATTENS
Eastcheap
Monument
MONUMENT
ST MARY AT HILL
Gt Tower St
ST DUNSTAN-IN-THE-EAST
Mark Lane
ST OLAVE'S
Pepys St
Byward St
Tower Hill
TOWER GATEWAY
Shorter St
Royal Mint Rd
Lower Thames Street
ST MAGNUS THE MARTYR
ALL HALLOWS BY THE TOWER
TOWER OF LONDON
Tower Bridge Approach
East Smithfield
ST KATHARINE DOCK
LONDON BRIDGE
THAMES
H.M.S. BELFAST
HAY'S GALLERIA SHOPPING CENTRE
Duke St Hill
Tooley Street
TOWER BRIDGE
CITY HALL
Tower Bridge Rd
Shad Thames
Gainford St
St Thomas St
Thomas Street
Druid St
200 m
200 yards

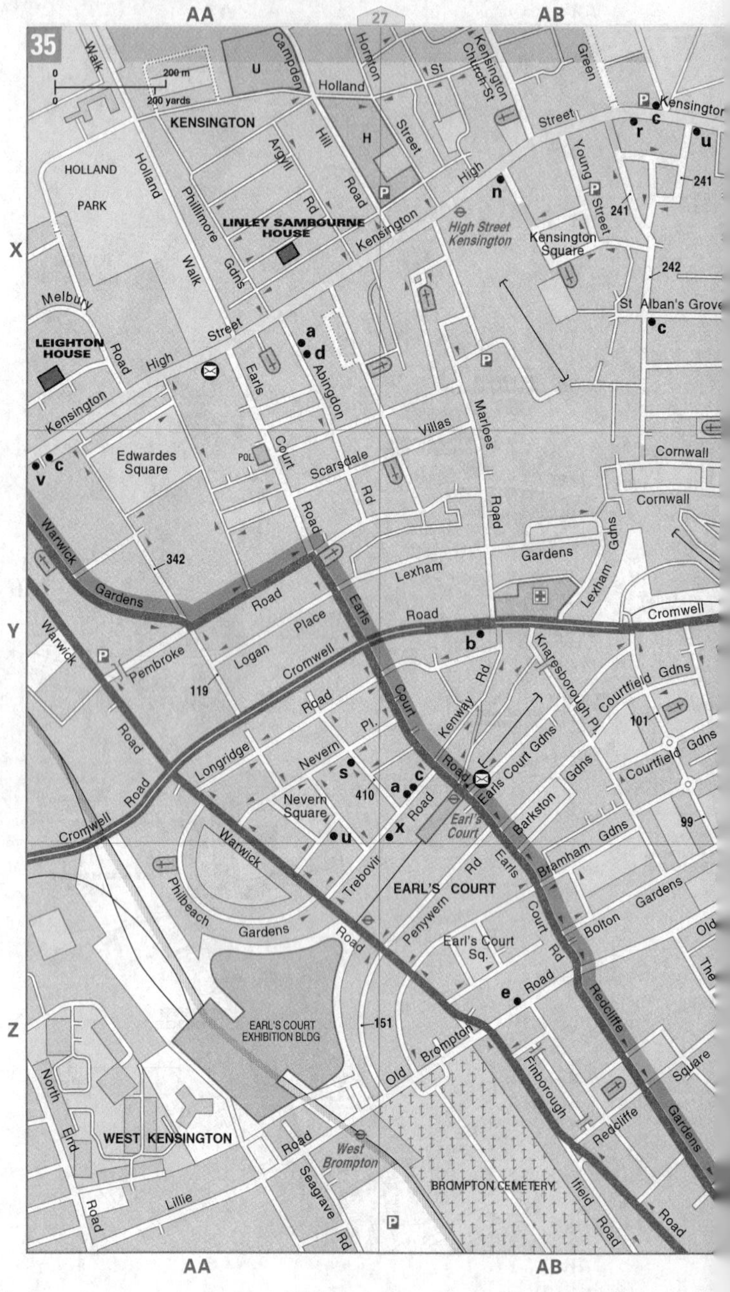
AA
AB
27
35
KENSINGTON
HOLLAND PARK
LINLEY SAMBOURNE HOUSE
LEIGHTON HOUSE
High Street Kensington
Kensington Square
Edwardes Square
Nevern Square
EARL'S COURT
Earl's Court
Earl's Court Sq.
EARL'S COURT EXHIBITION BLDG
WEST KENSINGTON
West Brompton
BROMPTON CEMETERY
X
Y
Z
LONDON

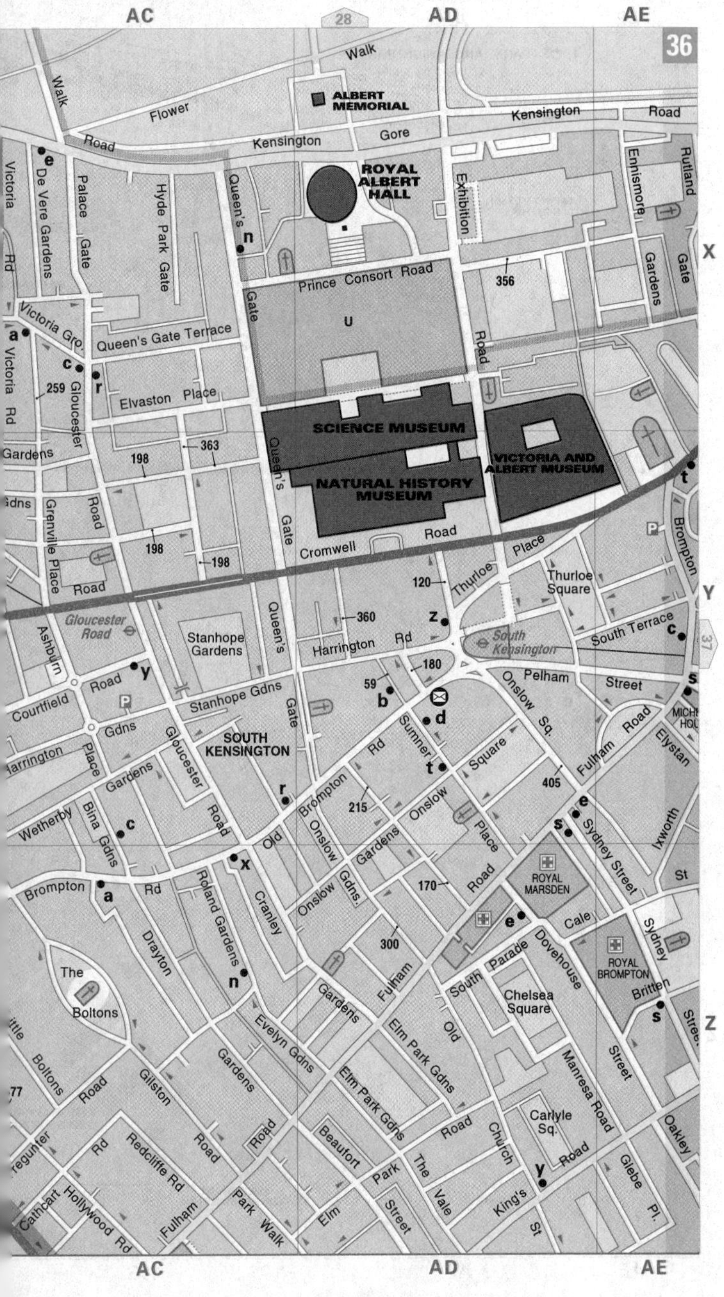
AC
28
AD
AE
36
Walk
ALBERT MEMORIAL
Flower
Kensington
Road
Gore
Road
ROYAL ALBERT HALL
Exhibition
Ennismore
Rutland
De Vere Gardens
Victoria Rd
Palace Gate
Hyde Park Gate
Queen's Gate
Prince Consort Road
356
Gardens
Gate
X
U
Victoria Gro.
Queen's Gate Terrace
Road
LONDON
Victoria Rd
259
Gloucester
Elvaston Place
363
198
SCIENCE MUSEUM
VICTORIA AND ALBERT MUSEUM
NATURAL HISTORY MUSEUM
Gardens
Grenville Place
Road
198
198
Cromwell Road
Place
Thurloe
Thurloe Square
Brompton
120
Y
Gloucester Road
Ashburn
Stanhope Gardens
360
Harrington Rd
South Kensington
South Terrace
37
180
59
Pelham Street
Onslow Sq.
Courtfield Road
Stanhope Gdns
Gdns
Sumner
Road
Harrington
Place
Gloucester
SOUTH KENSINGTON
Gate
Rd
Fulham
Square
Elystan
Gardens
Brompton
215
405
Wetherby
Bina Gdns
Road
Old
Onslow
Onslow
Place
Sydney Street
Ixworth
Gardens
Onslow Gdns.
170
Road
Brompton Rd
Roland Gardens
Cranley
ROYAL MARSDEN
St
Cale
Sydney
Drayton
300
Dovehouse
ROYAL BROMPTON
The Boltons
South Parade
Fulham
Chelsea Square
Britten
Gardens
Old
Street
Z
Evelyn Gdns
Elm Park Gdns
Manresa Road
Boltons
Gilston
Gardens
Road
Elm Park Gdns
Road
Carlyle Sq.
Oakley
Road
Redcliffe Rd
Road
Road
Beaufort
The Vale
Church
Road
Glebe Pl.
Cathcart
Hollywood Rd
Fulham
Park Walk
Elm
Park Street
King's St
AC
AD
AE

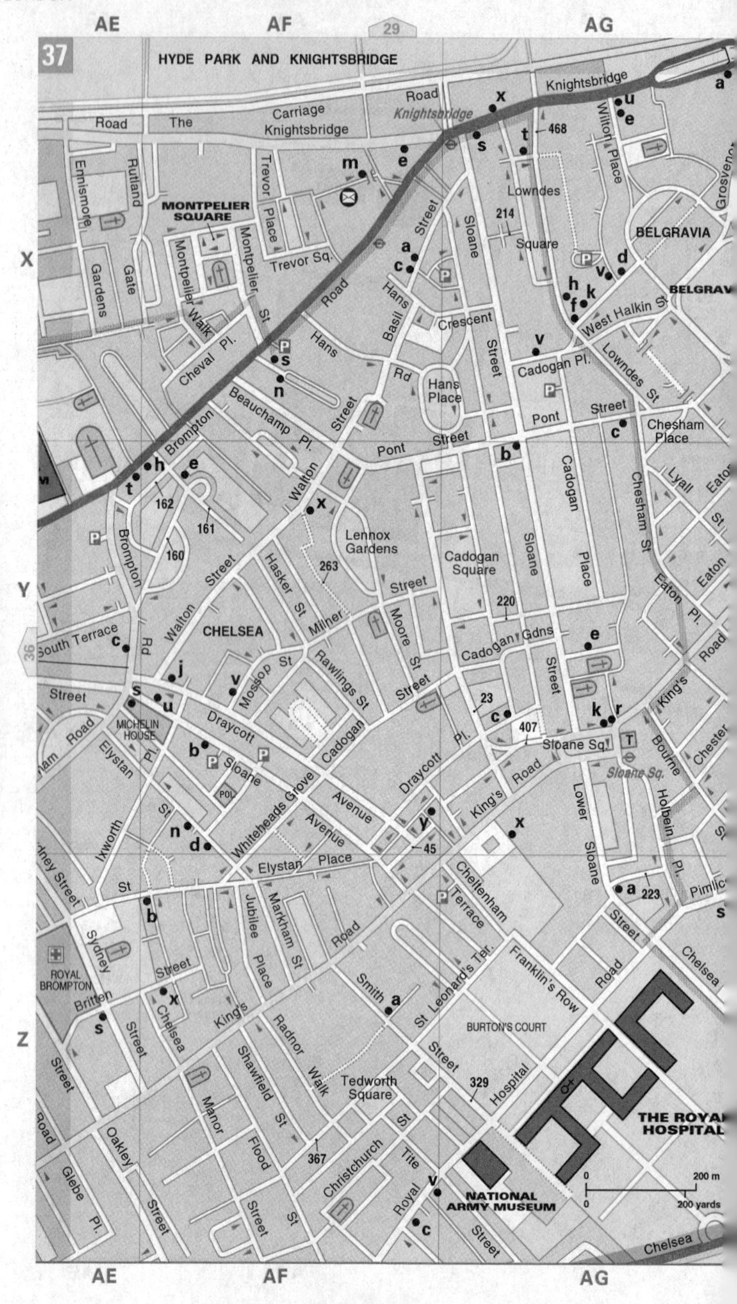
37
HYDE PARK AND KNIGHTSBRIDGE
AE
AF
AG
X
Y
Z
LONDON
MONTPELIER SQUARE
BELGRAVIA
CHELSEA
MICHELIN HOUSE
ROYAL BROMPTON
BURTON'S COURT
THE ROYAL HOSPITAL
NATIONAL ARMY MUSEUM
Knightsbridge
Carriage Road
Lowndes Square
Sloane Street
Cadogan Square
Lennox Gardens
Hans Place
Sloane Sq.
King's Road
Brompton Road
Walton Street
Tedworth Square
200 m
200 yards

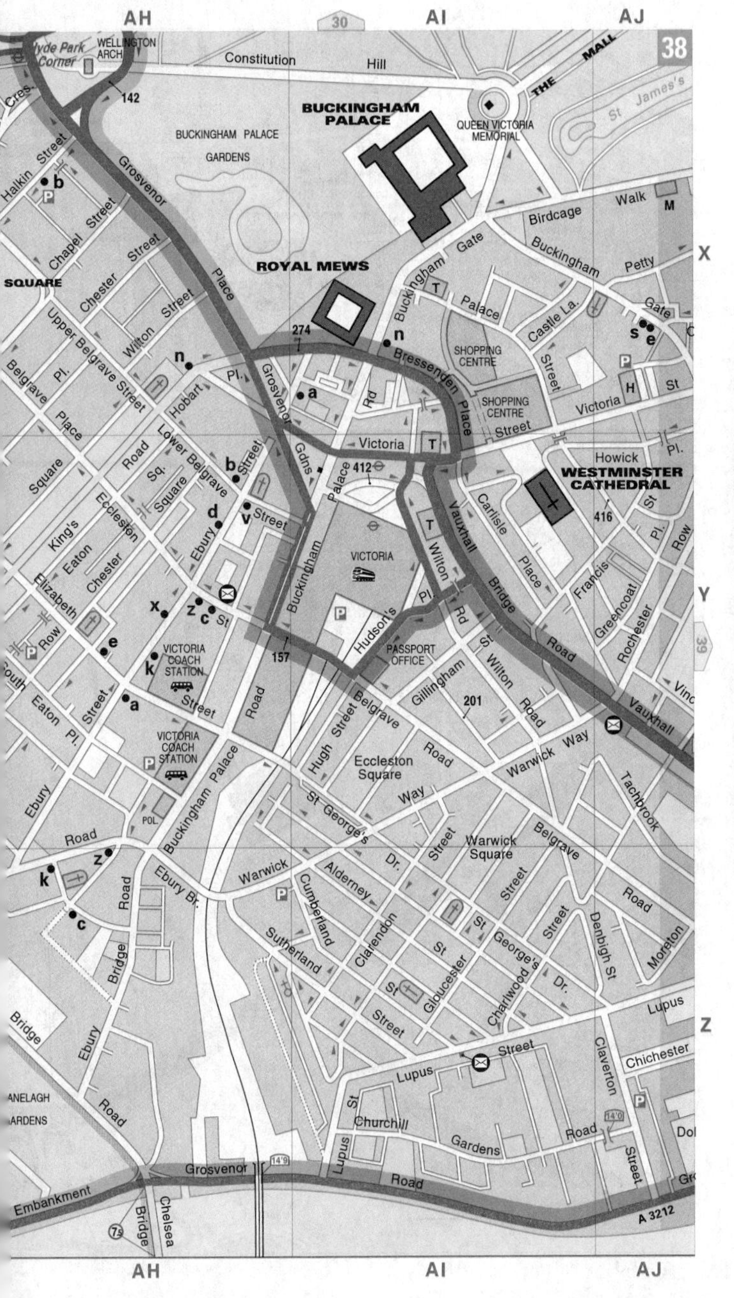
AH
AI
AJ
30
38
39
X
Y
Z
Hyde Park Corner
WELLINGTON ARCH
Constitution Hill
THE MALL
BUCKINGHAM PALACE
BUCKINGHAM PALACE GARDENS
QUEEN VICTORIA MEMORIAL
St James's
ROYAL MEWS
Birdcage Walk
Buckingham Gate
Petty France
Grosvenor Place
Halkin Street
Chapel Street
Chester Street
Wilton Street
Upper Belgrave Street
Belgrave Place
Hobart Pl.
Lower Belgrave Street
Bressenden Place
Buckingham Palace Rd
SHOPPING CENTRE
Castle La.
Victoria Street
Howick Pl.
WESTMINSTER CATHEDRAL
Grosvenor Gdns
Palace St
VICTORIA
Vauxhall Bridge Road
Carlisle Place
Francis St
Greencoat Row
Rochester Row
Wilton Rd
Hudson's Pl.
PASSPORT OFFICE
Eccleston Square
Eaton Square
Chester Square
Ebury Street
Elizabeth Street
VICTORIA COACH STATION
Belgrave Road
Gillingham St
Warwick Way
Tachbrook Street
Hugh Street
Eccleston Street
St George's Dr.
Warwick Square
Alderney Street
Cumberland Street
Sutherland Street
Clarendon Street
Gloucester Street
Charlwood Street
Denbigh St
Moreton Street
Lupus Street
Chichester Street
Claverton Street
Churchill Gardens Road
Grosvenor Road
Embankment
Chelsea Bridge
Ebury Bridge Road
Ebury Br.
RANELAGH GARDENS
A 3212
142
274
412
416
157
201
SQUARE

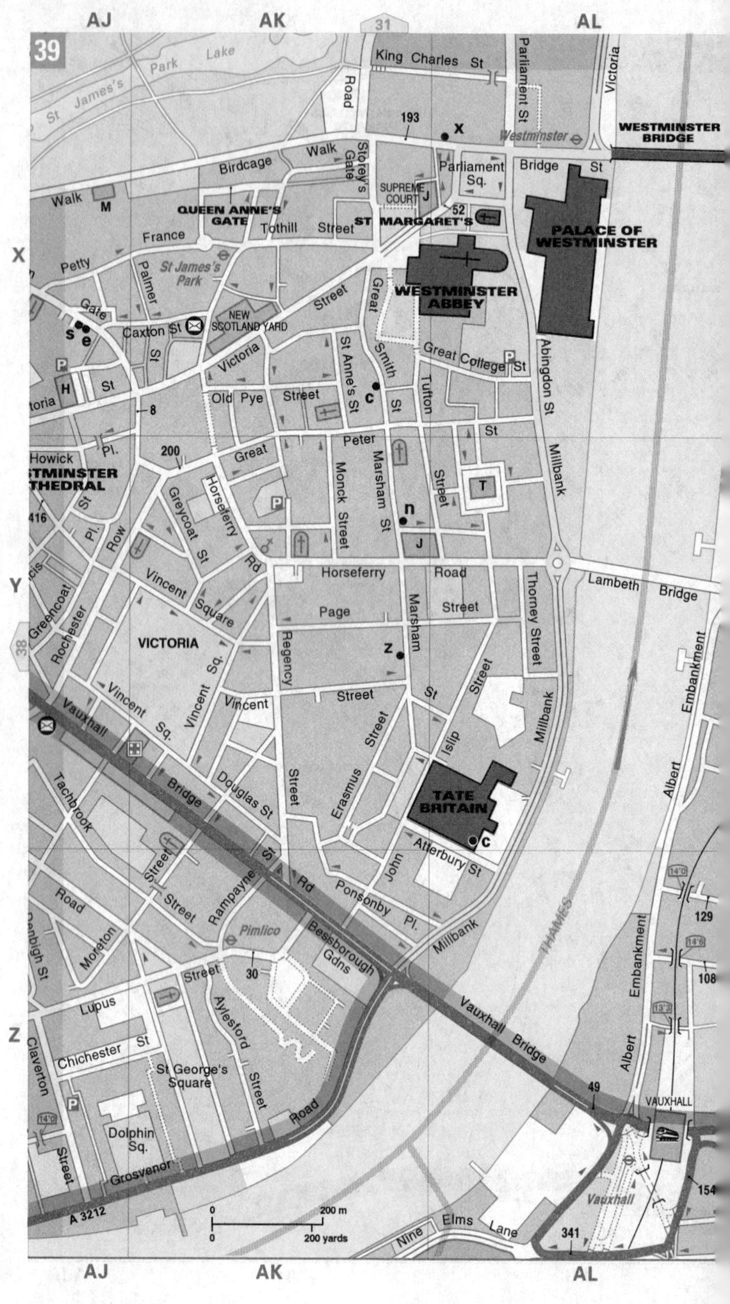
AJ
AK
AL
31
39
X
Y
Z
38
St James's Park Lake
King Charles St
Parliament St
Victoria
Road
193
Westminster
WESTMINSTER BRIDGE
Birdcage Walk
Storey's Gate
Parliament Sq.
Bridge St
SUPREME COURT
QUEEN ANNE'S GATE
Tothill Street
ST MARGARET'S
52
PALACE OF WESTMINSTER
France
Petty
St James's Park
Palmer
Gate
WESTMINSTER ABBEY
Great Smith St
NEW SCOTLAND YARD
Caxton St
Victoria Street
Great College St
Abingdon St
St Anne's St
Tufton St
Old Pye Street
8
Peter St
Howick Pl.
200
Great Peter St
Marsham St
Millbank
WESTMINSTER CATHEDRAL
Horseferry Rd
Greycoat St
Monck Street
416
Row
Horseferry Road
Lambeth Bridge
Vincent Square
Greencoat
Rochester
Page Street
Thorney Street
VICTORIA
Regency
Marsham St
Vincent Sq.
Vincent Street
Islip
Vauxhall Bridge
Tachbrook Street
Douglas St
Erasmus Street
TATE BRITAIN
Atterbury St
John
Rampayne St
Ponsonby Pl.
Road
Street
Pimlico
Bessborough Gdns
Millbank
THAMES
Albert Embankment
129
108
Denbigh St
Moreton
30
Lupus
Aylesford Street
Chichester St
Claverton Street
St George's Square
Vauxhall Bridge
49
VAUXHALL
Dolphin Sq.
Grosvenor Road
A 3212
0 200 m
0 200 yards
Nine Elms Lane
Vauxhall
341
154
LONDON

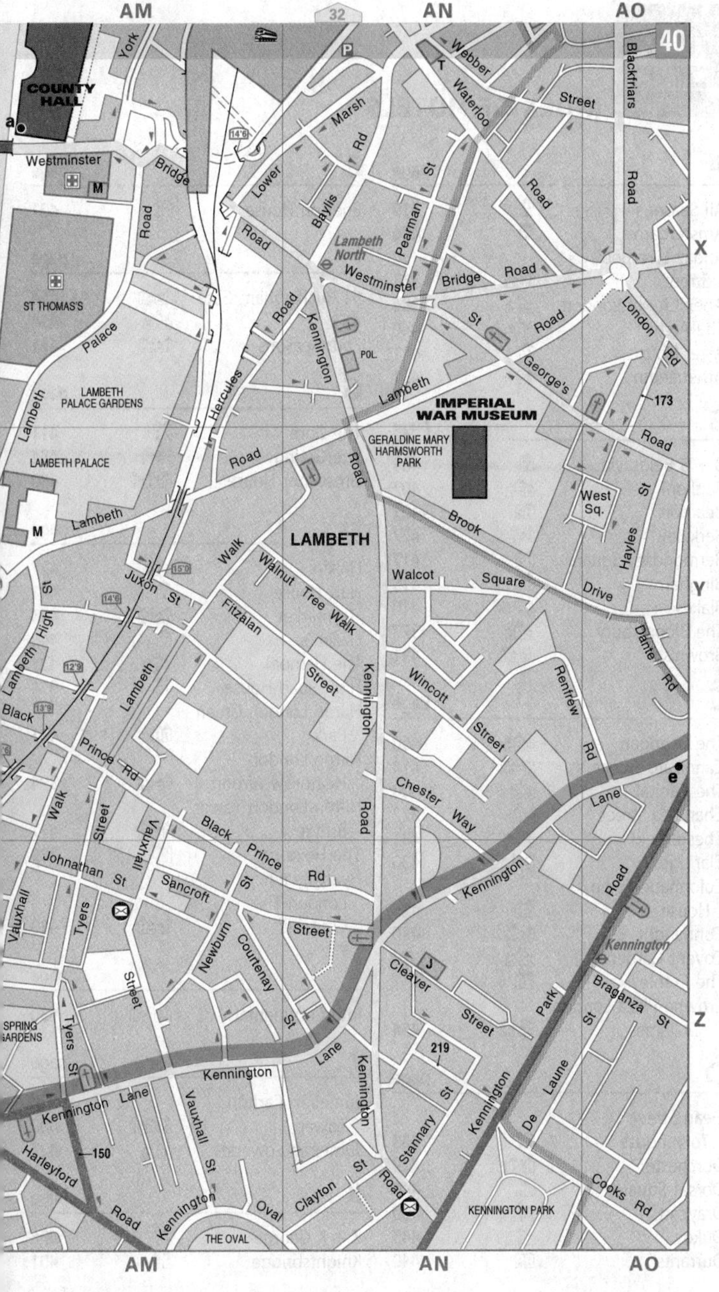
AM
AN
AO
32
40
COUNTY HALL
Westminster
Bridge
Road
York
ST THOMAS'S
Palace
LAMBETH PALACE GARDENS
Lambeth
LAMBETH PALACE
Lambeth
Hercules
Road
Lower
Marsh
Rd
Baylis
Lambeth North
Westminster
Bridge
Road
Pearman
St
Waterloo
Webber
Street
Blackfriars
Road
Road
London
Rd
St
George's
Road
Kennington
POL.
Lambeth
IMPERIAL WAR MUSEUM
GERALDINE MARY HARMSWORTH PARK
Road
Brook
West Sq.
St
Hayles
Drive
Dante
Rd
LAMBETH
Walk
Walnut Tree Walk
Walcot
Square
Juxon
St
Fitzalan
Street
Kennington
Road
Wincott
Street
Renfrew
Rd
Lambeth High St
Lambeth
Black
Prince
Rd
Chester
Way
Lane
Walk
Street
Vauxhall
Black
Prince
Rd
Johnathan
St
Sancroft
St
Kennington
Road
Vauxhall
Tyers
Street
Newburn
Courtenay
St
Street
Cleaver
Street
J
Kennington
Braganza
St
Park
St
SPRING GARDENS
Tyers
St
Kennington
Lane
Kennington
Lane
Kennington
219
St
Stannary
Kennington
De
Laune
Harleyford
Road
Vauxhall
St
Kennington
Oval
Clayton
St
Road
KENNINGTON PARK
Cooks
Rd
THE OVAL
173
150
X
Y
Z
LONDON

INDEX OF HOTELS

LONDON

INDEX OF RESTAURANTS

A

B

LONDON

LONDON

STARRED RESTAURANTS

BIB GOURMAND

Good food at moderate prices

PARTICULARLY PLEASANT HOTELS

PARTICULARLY PLEASANT RESTAURANTS

RESTAURANTS BY CUISINE TYPE

Eastern European

French

Indian

Innovative

International

Italian

Italian influences

Italian vegetarian

Japanese

LONDON

LONDON

Moroccan

North African

Polish

Scottish

Seafood

Spanish

Thai

Traditional

Turkish

Vegetarian

Vietnamese

OUTSIDE DINING

RESTAURANTS OPEN LATE

Time of last orders in brackets

LONDON

Boroughs and areas

Greater London is divided, for administrative purposes, into 32 boroughs plus **the City:** these sub-divide naturally into minor areas, usually grouped around former villages or quarters, which often maintain a distinctive character.

BRENT – Greater London – pop. 263 464 **12** A3

Kensal Green

Paradise by way of Kensal Green
19 Kilburn Ln ✉ W10 4AE ⊖ Kensal Green. – ☎ (020) 8969 0098 – www.theparadise.co.uk **10**MZC**x**
Rest – British – Menu £ 25/30 – Carte £ 28/40
◆ Great fun, with music, film and comedy nights. Share terrific snacks in the bar; dine on satisfyingly robust British classics in the restaurant or 'host your own roast' with friends.

Queen's Park

Salusbury
50-52 Salusbury Rd ✉ NW6 6NN ⊖ Queens Park. – ☎ (020) 7328 3286 – Closed 25-26 December, 1 January and Monday lunch **10**MZB**b**
Rest – Menu £ 22/25
◆ Pleasingly down-to-earth pub, more shabby than chic. Italian influenced menu is a model of understatement; skilled kitchen produces generously sized dishes with plenty of flavour.

Willesden Green

Sushi-Say
33B Walm Ln. ✉ NW2 5SH ⊖ Willesden Green – ☎ (020) 8459 2971 – Closed 21 February-8 March, 2 weeks August, 25-26 December, 1 January, Monday and Tuesday **9**LZB**a**
Rest – Japanese – *(dinner only and lunch Saturday-Sunday)* Menu £ 19/40 – Carte £ 17/43
◆ Very popular with the locals, attracted by sweet service and an extensive selection of Japanese food. Sit at the counter to watch the skill of the owner as he prepares the sushi.

Queensbury
110 Walm Ln ✉ NW2 4RS ⊖ Willesden Green. – ☎ (020) 8452 0171 – www.thequeensbury.net **9**LZA**a**
Rest – Carte £ 20/30
◆ Formerly called The Green, this reinvigorated pub has a brightly styled dining room beyond the bar and offers an appealing menu covering all bases. Weekend brunch and occasional live music.

BROMLEY – Greater London – pop. 280 305 **12** B3

27 Orpington Golf Centre Sandy Lane, St Paul's Cray, ☎ (01689) 839 677
9 Magpie Hall lane Magpie Hall lane

Farnborough

Chapter One
Farnborough Common, Locksbottom ✉ BR6 8NF – ☎ (01689) 854 848 – www.chaptersrestaurants.com – Closed first week January **8**HZ**a**
Rest – Modern European – Menu £ 19 (lunch) – Carte £ 32/42
Spec. Raviolo of lobster with a butter sauce. Veal rump with gratin potatoes. Poached plum with quark mousse, lavender and honey ice cream.
◆ The skilled kitchen produces assured and precisely executed, modern European cooking at a fair price. The mock Tudor exterior belies the contemporary styling of the restaurant and bar within.

Orpington

Xian
324 High St. ✉ BR6 0NG – ✆ (01689) 871 881 – Closed 2 weeks April, 25-26 December, Sunday lunch and Monday **8JYa**
Rest – Chinese – Menu £ 10/17 – Carte £ 18/25
◆ Modern, marbled interior with oriental artefacts make this personally run Chinese restaurant a firm favourite with locals. Look out for the Peking specialities.

Sundridge Park

Crown
46 Plaistow Ln ✉ BR1 3PA Sundridge Park ⊖ Sundridge Park (rail). – ✆ (020) 8466 1313 – www.thecrownsundridgepark.co.uk – Closed Sunday dinner and Monday **HYe**
Rest – Menu £ 20 – Carte £ 23/33
◆ This handsome, sizeable Victorian pub was gutted and transformed into a contemporary dining pub. Pub classics during the week; more adventurous cooking at weekends. Over 300 bottles on wine list.

CAMDEN – Greater London – pop. 198 020 — 12 B3

Belsize Park

XO
29 Belsize Ln. ✉ NW3 5AS ⊖ Belsize Park – ✆ (020) 7433 0888 – www.rickerrestaurants.com/xo – Closed 25-26 December and 1 January
Rest – Asian – Menu £ 15 (lunch) – Carte £ 23/44 **11PZAa**
◆ Stylish dining room with banquettes, revolving lights and mirrors. Vibrant atmosphere; popular with locals. Japanese, Korean, Thai and Chinese cooking; dishes are best shared.

Bloomsbury

Covent Garden
10 Monmouth St. ✉ WC2H 9HB ⊖ Covent Garden – ✆ (020) 7806 1000 – www.firmdalehotels.com **31ALUx**
56 rm – †£ 288 ††£ 408, ☕ £ 21 – 2 suites
Rest *Brasserie Max* – *(booking essential)* Menu £ 25 – Carte £ 34/54
◆ Individually designed and stylish bedrooms, with CDs and DVDs discreetly concealed. Boasts a very comfortable first floor oak-panelled drawing room with its own honesty bar. Busy, warm and relaxed restaurant also offers afternoon tea.

Charlotte Street
15 Charlotte St. ✉ W1T 1RJ ⊖ Goodge Street – ✆ (020) 7806 2000 – www.firmdalehotels.com **31AKTe**
48 rm – †£ 276 ††£ 384, ☕ £ 20 – 4 suites
Rest *Oscar* – ✆ (020) 7907 4005 – Menu £ 25 – Carte £ 33/50
◆ Interior designed with a charming and understated English feel. Impeccably kept and individually decorated bedrooms. In-house screening room. Bright restaurant with large bar and European menu.

Montague on the Gardens
15 Montague St. ✉ WC1B 5BJ ⊖ Holborn – ✆ (020) 7637 1001 – www.montaguehotel.com **31ALTa**
94 rm – †£ 145/230 ††£ 165/230, ☕ £ 16.50 – 6 suites
Rest *The Blue Door Bistro* – Menu £ 25 – Carte £ 29/51
◆ Cosy British feel to this period townhouse. Clubby bar and conservatory overlooking a secluded garden. Individually decorated bedrooms. Bistro divided into two small, pretty rooms.

The Bloomsbury
16-22 Gt Russell St ✉ WC1B 3NN ⊖ Tottenham Court Road – ✆ (020) 7347 1000 – www.doylecollection.com/bloomsbury **31AKTn**
153 rm – †£ 138/334 ††£ 138/334, ☕ £ 21
Rest *Landseer* – *(bar lunch)* Carte £ 30/42 **s**
◆ Refurbished in 2009. Neo-Georgian building by Edward Lutyens, built for YMCA in 1929. Smart comfortable interior, from the lobby to the bedrooms. Restaurant with mostly British menu.

XXX ✿✿ **Pied à Terre** (Shane Osborn)

34 Charlotte St ✉ W1T 2NH ⊖ Goodge Street – ☎ (020) 7636 1178 – www.pied-a-terre.co.uk – Closed last week December, first week January, Saturday lunch, Sunday and bank holidays **31**AJT**e**

Rest – Innovative – Menu £ 30/72

Spec. Foie gras in Sauternes consommé, smoked bacon and red onion. Pigeon with liquorice purée, caramelised endive and caramel. Honey poached apricot, almond financier and vanilla ice cream.

◆ David Moore made the best of limited space to create a stylish and intimate restaurant that is very well established and professionally run. Shane Osborn's cooking is expertly rendered and elaborate in style but with clear flavours.

XX ✿ **Hakkasan**

8 Hanway Pl. ✉ W1T 1HD ⊖ Tottenham Court Road – ☎ (020) 7927 7000 – www.hakkasan.com – Closed 24-25 December **31**AKT**c**

Rest – Chinese – Carte £ 43/95

Spec. Crispy duck salad with pine nuts and shallots. Grilled sea bass with honey. 'Chocolate textures'.

◆ Cool and seductive subterranean restaurant, with an air of exclusivity. Innovation and originality have been added to the Cantonese base to create dishes with zip and depth. Lunchtime dim sum is a highlight.

XX **Mon Plaisir**

19-21 Monmouth St. ✉ WC2H 9DD ⊖ Covent Garden – ☎ (020) 7836 7243 – www.monplaisir.co.uk – Closed Christmas and New Year, Sunday and bank holidays **31**ALU**g**

Rest – French – Menu £ 17 (lunch) – Carte £ 29/38

◆ This proud French institution opened in the 1940s. Enjoy satisfyingly authentic classics in any of the four contrasting rooms, full of Gallic charm; the bar was salvaged from a Lyonnais brothel.

XX **Incognico**

117 Shaftesbury Ave. ✉ WC2H 8AD ⊖ Tottenham Court Road – ☎ (020) 7836 8866 – www.incognico.com **31**AKU**q**

Rest – Modern European – Menu £ 20/25 – Carte £ 31/38

◆ Comfortable, smartly dressed restaurant with dark wood and brown leather lending a masculine, clubby feel. Influences from France and Italy inform the cooking from a capable kitchen.

XX **Roka**

37 Charlotte St ✉ W1T 1RR ⊖ Goodge Street – ☎ (020) 7580 6464 – www.rokarestaurant.com – Closed 24- 26 December and 1 January

Rest – Japanese – Carte approx. £ 38 **31**AJT**k**

◆ Bright, atmospheric interior of teak and oak; bustling and trendy feel. Contemporary touches added to Japanese dishes; try specialities from the on-view Robata grill. Capable and chatty service.

XX **Fino**

33 Charlotte St. (entrance on Rathbone St.) ✉ W1T 1RR ⊖ Goodge Street – ☎ (020) 7813 8010 – www.finorestaurant.com – Closed Saturday lunch and Sunday **31**AJT**a**

Rest – Spanish – Menu £ 18 (lunch) – Carte £ 28/44

◆ Seafood is handled especially well in this lively, quite smart and smoothly run basement tapas restaurant. Sensibly divided menu, with dishes designed for sharing. Youthful, helpful service.

XX **Sardo**

45 Grafton Way ✉ W1T 5DQ ⊖ Warren Street – ☎ (020) 7387 2521 – www.sardo-restaurant.com – Closed Christmas, Saturday lunch and Sunday

Rest – Italian – Carte £ 26/34 **18**RZD**c**

◆ Expect a warm and welcoming atmosphere at this simply decorated Italian restaurant, with plenty of regulars and friendly service. Sardinian specialities and seasonal specials are the highlights.

XX **Archipelago**

110 Whitfield St. ✉ W1T 5ED ⊖ Goodge Street – ✆ (020) 7383 3346 – www.archipelago-restaurant.co.uk – Closed Saturday lunch, Sunday and bank holidays **18**RZD**c**

Rest – Innovative – Carte £ 27/40

♦ Eccentrically decorated in the style of an overflowing bazaar. Asian influence to the equally exotic and highly unusual menu which could include crocodile, zebra, wildebeest and even scorpion.

XX **Rasa Samudra**

5 Charlotte St. ✉ W1T 1RE ⊖ Goodge Street – ✆ (020) 7637 0222 – www.rasarestaurants.com – Closed 25 December, 1 January and Sunday lunch **31**AKT**r**

Rest – Indian – Menu £ 23 (lunch)/30 – Carte £ 18/29

♦ Its bright pink hue makes it easy to spot. Specialises in the southwest region of Kerala so expect fish, vegetarian dishes and plenty of coconut and have the pre-meal snacks. Well meaning service.

X **Mennula**

10 Charlotte St. ✉ W1T 2LT ⊖ Goodge Street – ✆ (020) 7363 2833 – www.mennula.com – Closed Saturday lunch and bank holidays **31**AKT**b**

Rest – Italian – Menu £ 20 (lunch) – Carte £ 27/43

♦ Sicilian specialities provide the highlights at this enthusiastically run Italian restaurant, whose name means 'almond'. Compact but bright, crisply decorated room; ask for one of the booths.

X **Paramount**

Centre Point, 101-103 New Oxford St., (31st Floor) ✉ WC1A 1DD ⊖ Tottenham Court Road – ✆ (020) 7420 2900 – www.paramount.uk.net – Closed 25 December and Sunday **31**AKT**b**

Rest – Modern European – Menu £ 24 (lunch) – Carte £ 35/51

♦ Worth the palaver of getting into this Grade II listed building: the views are terrific and this is a fun, keenly run restaurant. Ambitious and quite elaborate cooking; champagne bar one floor up.

X **Giaconda Dining Room**

9 Denmark St. ✉ WC2H 8LS ⊖ Tottenham Court Road – ✆ (020) 7240 3334 – www.giacondadining.com – Closed 2 weeks August, Easter, Saturday, Sunday and bank holidays **31**AKT**k**

Rest – Modern European – *(booking essential)* Carte £ 24/28

♦ Aussie owners run a small, fun and very busy place in an unpromising location. The very well priced menu offers an appealing mix of gutsy, confident, no-nonsense food, with French and Italian influences.

X **Salt Yard**

54 Goodge St. ✉ W1T 4NA ⊖ Goodge Street – ✆ (020) 7637 0657 – www.saltyard.co.uk – Closed Christmas and New Year, Saturday lunch, Sunday and bank holidays **31**AJT**d**

Rest – Mediterranean – Carte £ 25/35

♦ Ground floor bar and buzzy basement restaurant specialising in good value plates of tasty Italian and Spanish dishes, ideal for sharing; charcuterie a speciality. Super wine list.

X **Cigala**

54 Lamb's Conduit St. ✉ WC1N 3LW ⊖ Russell Square – ✆ (020) 7405 1717 – www.cigala.co.uk – Closed 24-26 December and Easter **19**TZD**a**

Rest – Spanish – *(booking essential)* Menu £ 18 (lunch) – Carte £ 21/43

♦ Spanish restaurant on corner of attractive street. Simply furnished; open-plan kitchen. Robust Iberian cooking, with some dishes designed for sharing; interesting drinks list.

Tsunami

93 Charlotte St. ✉ W1T 4PY ⊖ Goodge Street – ✆ (020) 7637 0050 – www.tsunamirestaurant.co.uk – Closed 24-26 December, 1 January, Saturday lunch and Sunday **30**AIT**n**

Rest – Japanese – Menu £ 15 (lunch) – Carte £ 21/40

◆ Sister to the original in Clapham. Sweet, pretty place, with lacquered walls, floral motif and moody lighting. Contemporary Japanese cuisine is carefully prepared and sensibly priced.

Acorn House

69 Swinton St. ✉ WC1X 9NT ⊖ King's Cross – ✆ (020) 7812 1842 – www.acornhouserestaurant.com – Closed Saturday lunch and bank holidays

Rest – Modern European – Menu £ 25 (dinner) – Carte £ 22/32 **18**TZC**b**

◆ Eco-friendly training restaurant with a bright and appealing café-style feel and helpful service. Dishes are healthy, seasonal and generously proportioned, using organic ingredients.

Barrica

62 Goodge St ✉ W1T 4NE ⊖ Goodge Street – ✆ (020) 7436 9448 – www.barrica.co.uk – Closed Sunday and bank holidays **31**AJT**x**

Rest – Spanish – *(booking essential)* Carte £ 20/23

◆ Lively, noisy and warmly decorated tapas bar, with a busy front bar. Authentic dishes come with plenty of flavour and are complemented by a thoughtfully compiled Spanish wine list.

CAMDEN TOWN

York & Albany with rm

127-129 Parkway ✉ NW1 7PS ⊖ Camden Town – ✆ (020) 7388 3344 – www.gordonramsay.com/yorkandalbany **12**RZB**s**

10 rm – †£ 186/222 ††£ 282/690, ☕ £ 12.50

Rest – Modern European – *(booking essential)* Menu £ 21 (lunch and early dinner) – Carte £ 36/52

◆ 1820s John Nash former coaching inn, now part of Gordon Ramsay's empire. Smart bar and informal dining; lower level offers kitchen views. Cooking is refined without being fussy, and influences are European. Comfortable, individually decorated bedrooms.

Market

43 Parkway ✉ NW1 7PN ⊖ Camden Town – ✆ (020) 7267 9700 – www.marketrestaurant.co.uk – Closed Christmas and New Year, Sunday dinner and bank holidays **12**RZB**x**

Rest – British – *(booking essential)* Carte £ 23/30

◆ Market fresh produce used to create satisfying and refreshingly matter of fact British dishes, at excellent prices that entice plenty of passers-by. Appealing décor of exposed brick walls, old school chairs and zinc-topped tables.

DARTMOUTH PARK

Bull and Last

168 Highgate Rd ✉ NW5 1QS ⊖ Tufnell Park – ✆ (020) 7267 3641 – www.thebullandlast.co.uk – Closed 25 December **12**RZA**a**

Rest – *(booking essential)* Carte £ 25/32

◆ Bright, breezy and enthusiastically run pub opposite Parliament Hill. Cooking is robust, generous and satisfying, with sourcing taken seriously; game and charcuterie the specialities.

EUSTON

Novotel London St. Pancras

100-110 Euston Rd. ✉ NW1 2AJ ⊖ Euston – ✆ (020) 7666 9000 – www.novotel.com **18**SZC**a**

309 rm – †£ 295 ††£ 295, ☕ £ 14.95 – 3 suites

Rest – *(bar lunch Saturday, Sunday and bank holidays)* Menu £ 19/23 – Carte £ 26/42

◆ Halfway between Euston and Kings Cross, this hotel has good-sized bedrooms for a London hotel and those on the higher floors enjoy views over the city. Good business amenities. International menu and buffet breakfast.

XX **Snazz Sichuan**

37 Chalton St ✉ NW1 1JD ⊖ Euston – ✆ (020) 7388 0808 – www.newchinaclub.co.uk **12**SZC**b**

Rest – Chinese – Carte £ 10/40

♦ Authentic Sichuan atmosphere and cooking, with gallery and traditional tea room. Menu split into hot and cold dishes; the fiery Sichuan pepper helps heat you from inside out.

HAMPSTEAD

X **Goldfish**

82 Hampstead High St. ✉ NW3 1RE ⊖ Hampstead – ✆ (020) 7794 6666 – www.goldfish-restaurant.co.uk – Closed 24-25 December **11**PZA**z**

Rest – Asian – Carte £ 20/28

♦ Sweet little place, divided into three differently decorated rooms. Mix of Chinese and other Asian countries; chef also adds own creations. Well-priced lunch menu, including popular weekend dim sum.

Wells

30 Well Walk ✉ NW3 1BX ⊖ Hampstead. – ✆ (020) 7794 3785 – www.thewellshampstead.co.uk **11**PZA**v**

Rest – Carte £ 28/38

♦ Part country pub, part city sophisticate; busy ground floor, with more sedate upstairs restaurant. Cooking is hearty in flavour and sophisticated in look, with a pleasing British edge.

Magdala

2A South Hill Park ✉ NW3 2SB ⊖ Belsize Park. – ✆ (020) 7435 2503 – www.the-magdala.com **11**PZA**s**

Rest – Carte £ 19/28

♦ Uncomplicated pub food but prepared with care; some dishes designed for sharing. Relaxed, locals pub on the edge of the Heath, with countryside feel. Upstairs room used at weekends.

HATTON GARDEN

XX **Bleeding Heart**

Bleeding Heart Yard, off Greville St. ✉ EC1N 8SJ ⊖ Farringdon – ✆ (020) 7242 8238 – www.bleedingheart.co.uk – Closed 24 December-4 January, Saturday and Sunday **32**ANT**e**

Rest – French – *(booking essential)* Carte £ 26/41

♦ Dickensian Yard plays host to this atmospheric, candlelit restaurant; popular with those from The City. Classic French cuisine is the draw, with service that's formal but has personality.

HOLBORN

Renaissance Chancery Court

252 High Holborn ✉ WC1V 7EN ⊖ Holborn – ✆ (020) 7829 9888 – www.renaissancechancerycourt.com **32**AMT**a**

354 rm – †£ 264/366 ††£ 264/366, ☕ £ 24.50 – 2 suites

Rest ***Pearl*** – see restaurant listing

♦ Striking building built in 1914, now an imposing place to stay. Impressive marbled lobby and grand central courtyard. Very large bedrooms with comprehensive modern facilities.

XXX **Pearl** – at Renaissance Chancery Court Hotel

252 High Holborn ✉ WC1V 7EN ⊖ Holborn – ✆ (020) 7829 7000 – www.pearl-restaurant.com – Closed last 2 weeks August, Christmas, Saturday lunch, Sunday and bank holidays **32**AMT**a**

Rest – French – Menu £ 29/58

♦ Impressive former banking hall, with walls clad in Italian marble and Corinthian columns. Waiters provide efficient service at well-spaced tables; cooking shows originality.

XX **Asadal**

227 High Holborn ✉ WC1V 7DA ⊖ Holborn – ☎ (020) 7430 9006 – www.asadal.co.uk – Closed 25-26 December, 1 January and Sunday lunch
Rest – Korean – Menu £ 12 (lunch) – Carte £ 13/20 **31**ALT**n**
◆ Sharing is the key in this busy basement, where you'll be oblivious to its unprepossessing location. Hotpots and barbecues the highlights from the easy-to-follow menu. Swift service.

XX **Moti Mahal**

45 Great Queen St. ✉ WC2B 5AA ⊖ Holborn – ☎ (020) 7240 9329 – www.motimahal-uk.com – Closed 25-27 December, 1-2 January, Saturday lunch and Sunday **31**ALU**k**
Rest – Indian – Carte £ 43/58
◆ Restaurant is split between a bright, busy ground floor and more intimate basement. Specialities follow the Grand Trunk Road, stretching from Bengal to the North West and the Pakistan border.

X **Great Queen Street**

32 Great Queen St ✉ WC2B 5AA ⊖ Holborn – ☎ (020) 7242 0622 – Closed Christmas, New Year, Sunday dinner and bank holidays **31**ALT**d**
Rest – British – *(booking essential)* Carte £ 25/32
◆ The menu is a model of British understatement; the cooking, confident and satisfying with laudable prices and generous portions. Lively atmosphere and enthusiastic service.

X **Villandry Kitchen**

95-97 High Holborn ✉ WC1V 6LF ⊖ Holborn – ☎ (020) 7242 4580 – www.villandry.com – Closed 25-26 December and 1 January **32**AMT**k**
Rest – French – Carte £ 21/34
◆ Open all day and offering everything from breakfast and afternoon tea to pizza, charcuterie and comforting French classics. Large, animated room with rustic feel and friendly service.

Primrose Hill

XX **Odette's**

130 Regent's Park Rd. ✉ NW1 8XL ⊖ Chalk Farm – ☎ (020) 7586 8569 – www.odettesprimrosehill.com – Closed Christmas and Monday **11**QZB**b**
Rest – Modern European – Menu £ 20 (lunch and early dinner) – Carte £ 31/44
◆ A local institution that has recently lightened up. Warm and inviting interior, with chatty but organised service. Robust and flavoursome cooking, with plenty of choice available.

XX **Sardo Canale**

42 Gloucester Ave. ✉ NW1 8JD ⊖ Chalk Farm – ☎ (020) 7722 2800 – www.sardocanale.com – Closed 25 December and Monday **12**RZB**a**
Rest – Italian – Menu £ 13 (lunch) – Carte £ 25/34
◆ A series of five snug but individual dining rooms in conservatory style; delightful terrace with 200 year old olive tree. Appealing Italian menus with strong Sardinian accent.

X **L'Absinthe**

40 Chalcot Rd ✉ NW1 8LS ⊖ Chalk Farm – ☎ (020) 7483 4848 – Closed 1 week Christmas and Monday **11**QZB**s**
Rest – French – Menu £ 13 (lunch) – Carte £ 19/29
◆ Lively and enthusiastically run French bistro, with tightly packed tables, spread over two floors. All the favourites, from Lyonnais salad to duck confit. Commendably priced French wine list.

Engineer

65 Gloucester Ave ✉ NW1 8JH ⊖ Chalk Farm. – ☎ (020) 7722 0950 – www.the-engineer.com **11**QZB**s**
Rest – Carte £ 24/32
◆ Grade II listed pub with Italianate façade. Divided between bar and restaurant, with a popular garden terrace at the back. Confident, wholesome cooking; suppliers name-checked on the menu.

Swiss Cottage

XX **Bradley's**

25 Winchester Rd. ✉ NW3 3NR ⊖ Swiss Cottage – ✆ (020) 7722 3457 – www.bradleysnw3.co.uk – Closed Christmas, Saturday lunch and Sunday dinner **11**PZB**e**

Rest – Modern European – Menu £ 17/24 – Carte £ 30/40

◆ A stalwart of the local dining scene and ideal for visitors to the nearby Hampstead Theatre. The thoughtfully compiled and competitively priced set menus of mostly classical cooking draw in plenty of regulars.

XX **Singapore Garden**

83 Fairfax Rd. ✉ NW6 4DY ⊖ Swiss Cottage – ✆ (020) 7328 5314 – www.singaporegarden.co.uk – Closed Christmas **11**PZB**x**

Rest – Asian – Menu £ 20/30 – Carte £ 30/45

◆ A smart, bright and comfortable room, with endearingly enthusiastic service. Your best bet is to pick vibrant and zesty dishes from the list of Singaporean and Malaysian specialities.

XX **Eriki**

4-6 Northways Par., Finchley Rd. ✉ NW3 5EN ⊖ Swiss Cottage – ✆ (020) 7722 0606 – www.eriki.co.uk – Closed Christmas, 1 January and Saturday

Rest – Indian – Menu £ 11/20 – Carte £ 23/34 **11**PZB**u**

◆ The menu offers an invigorating gastronomic tour of all parts of India; vegetarians will be in clover. Vividly coloured, comfortable room with well-meaning service and lots of regulars.

Tufnell Park

Junction Tavern

101 Fortess Rd ✉ NW5 1AG ⊖ Tufnell Park. – ✆ (020) 7485 9400 – www.junctiontavern.co.uk – Closed 24-26 December and 1 January

Rest – Carte £ 23/30 **12**RZA**x**

◆ Sizeable pub with striking matt black façade. Dining room on one side, along with conservatory and busy bar. Well-balanced menu; flavoursome cooking. Interesting and regularly changing guest beers.

West Hampstead

X **Walnut**

280 West End Ln., Fortune Grn. ✉ NW6 1LJ ⊖ West Hampstead – ✆ (020) 7794 7772 – www.walnutwalnut.com – Closed Monday **10**NZA**a**

Rest – Traditional – *(dinner only)* Carte £ 23/34

◆ Eco-aware chef-owner in his raised, open kitchen offers classical cooking, where game and fish are the specialities. Relaxed and informal corner restaurant, with plenty of local regulars.

CITY OF LONDON – Greater London – pop. 7 172 091 — 12 B3

Andaz Liverpool Street

Liverpool St. ✉ EC2M 7QN ⊖ Liverpool Street – ✆ (020) 7961 1234 – www.andaz.com **34**ART**t**

264 rm – †£ 270/378 ††£ 300/408, ☕ £ 20 – 3 suites

Rest *1901* – see restaurant listing

Rest *Catch* – Seafood – ✆ (020) 7618 7200 *(closed Saturday and Sunday)* Carte £ 34/81

Rest *Miyako* – Japanese – ✆ (020) 7618 7100 *(closed Saturday lunch and Sunday) (booking essential)* Carte £ 15/46

◆ A contemporary and stylish interior hides behind the classic Victorian façade. Part of Hyatt group. Bright and spacious bedrooms with state-of-the-art facilities. Seafood at Catch, based within original hotel lobby. Miyako is a compact Japanese restaurant.

LONDON

LONDON

Threadneedles

5 Threadneedle St. ✉ *EC2R 8AY* ⊖ *Bank* – ✆ *(020) 7657 8080 – www.theetoncollection.com* **34**ARU**y**
68 rm – †£ 414 ††£ 546, ☕ £ 19.50 – 1 suite
Rest *Bonds* – see restaurant listing
◆ A converted bank, dating from 1856, with a stunning stained-glass cupola in the lounge. Rooms are very stylish and individual featuring CD players and Egyptian cotton sheets.

Apex City of London

No 1, Seething Ln. ✉ *EC3N 4AX* ⊖ *Tower Hill* – ✆ *(020) 7702 2020 – www.apexhotels.co.uk* **34**ARU**a**
179 rm – †£ 384 ††£ 384, ☕ £ 18
Rest *Addendum* – ✆ (020) 7977 9500 – Menu £ 20 (dinner) – Carte £ 24/41
◆ Tucked away behind Tower of London, overlooking leafy square. Smart meeting facilities and well-equipped gym. Comfortable bedrooms and sleek bathrooms. Easy-going style in Addendum.

Rhodes Twenty Four

24th floor, Tower 42, 25 Old Broad St. ✉ *EC2N 1HQ* ⊖ *Liverpool Street – ✆ (020) 7877 7703 – www.rhodes24.co.uk – Closed 24 December-4 January, Saturday, Sunday and bank holidays* **34**ART**v**
Rest – British – Carte £ 37/61
Spec. Sardines on toast with tomato and cucumber dressing. Steamed mutton and onion suet pudding with carrots. Bread and butter pudding.
◆ Prepare for security checks at Tower 42 before taking the lift up to its 24th floor; the views will be worth it. The unmistakeable signature of Gary Rhodes is writ large on the menu: seasonal dishes of a pleasingly British persuasion.

Coq d'Argent

1 Poultry ✉ *EC2R 8EJ* ⊖ *Bank* – ✆ *(020) 7395 5000 – www.coqdargent.co.uk – Closed Christmas, bank holidays, Saturday lunch and Sunday dinner*
Rest – French – *(booking essential)* Menu £ 28 (lunch) – Carte £ 44/58 **33**AQU**c**
◆ Resembling the bow of a ship; with a busy bar, terrace and formal garden providing commanding views over the Square Mile. Slick, well run, modern restaurant; appealing shellfish counter.

1901 – at Andaz Liverpool Street Hotel

Liverpool St. ✉ *EC2M 7QN* ⊖ *Liverpool Street* – ✆ *(020) 7618 7000 – www.andaz.com – Closed Saturday lunch, Sunday and bank holidays*
Rest – French – Menu £ 22 – Carte £ 36/47 **34**ART**t**
◆ An impressive and imposing room, with an eye-catching cupola, cocktail bar and cheese and wine room. Kitchen makes proud use of British ingredients in refined and skilled cooking.

Bonds – at Threadneedles Hotel

5 Threadneedle St. ✉ *EC2R 8AY* ⊖ *Bank* – ✆ *(020) 7657 8088 – www.theetoncollection.com – Closed Saturday and Sunday* **34**ARU**y**
Rest – Modern European – Menu £ 18/20 – Carte £ 27/53
◆ Former banking hall from the 1850s, with pillars, marble and panelling. Experienced kitchen produced dishes with bold flavours; fish from Newhaven and slow-cooked meats the specialities.

Lutyens

85 Fleet St. ✉ *EC4Y 1AE* ⊖ *St Paul's* – ✆ *(020) 7583 8385 – www.lutyens-restaurant.com – Closed 24 December-4 January and bank holidays* **32**ANU**c**
Rest – Modern European – Menu £ 40 (dinner) – Carte £ 38/57
◆ The unmistakable hand of Sir Terence Conran: timeless and understated good looks mixed with functionality and an appealing Anglo-French menu with plenty of classics that include fruits de mer.

XX **Club Gascon** (Pascal Aussignac) AC VISA MC AE
57 West Smithfield ✉ EC1A 9DS ⊖ Barbican – ☎ (020) 7796 0600 – www.clubgascon.com – Closed Christmas and New Year, Saturday lunch, Sunday and bank holidays **33**APT**z**
Rest – French – *(booking essential)* Menu £ 28 (lunch) – Carte £ 37/57
Spec. White pudding gnocchi with asparagus and sea urchin jus. Coconut glazed black cod with white port and winkle risotto. Rhubarb and custard sweet foie gras with vanilla.
♦ The gastronomy of Gascony and France's southwest are the starting points but the assured and intensely flavoured cooking also pushes at the boundaries. Marble and huge floral displays create suitably atmospheric surroundings.

XX **The Chancery** AC VISA MC AE
9 Cursitor St ✉ EC4A 1LL ⊖ Chancery Lane – ☎ (020) 7831 4000 – www.thechancery.co.uk – Closed 24-27 and 31 December, Saturday lunch and Sunday **32**ANT**a**
Rest – Modern European – Menu £ 35
♦ Near Law Courts, a small restaurant with basement bar. Contemporary interior with intimate style. Quality ingredients put to good use in accomplished, modern dishes.

XX **Mint Leaf Lounge** AC VISA MC AE
12 Angel Ct., Lothbury ✉ EC2R 7HB ⊖ Bank – ☎ (020) 7600 0992 – www.mintleaflounge.com – Closed 25-26 December, Saturday, Sunday and bank holidays **33**AQT**b**
Rest – Indian – Menu £ 18 (lunch) – Carte £ 30/45
♦ Sister branch to the original in St James's. Slick and stylish, with busy bar. Well paced service of carefully prepared contemporary Indian food, with many of the influences from the south.

XX **Vivat Bacchus** AC VISA MC AE
(basement) 47 Farringdon St ✉ EC4A 4LL ⊖ Farringdon – ☎ (020) 7353 2648 – www.vivatbacchus.co.uk – Closed 24 December-5 January, Saturday and Sunday **32**ANT**c**
Rest – Traditional – Menu £ 15/18 – Carte £ 20/42
♦ Platters and tapas served in the large bar; more intimate basement restaurant for meat dishes and South African specialities. Hugely impressive wine list with five cellars of wine.

XX **Vanilla Black** AC VISA MC AE
17-18 Tooks Ct. ✉ EC4A 1LB ⊖ Chancery Lane – ☎ (020) 7242 2622 – www.vanillablack.co.uk – Closed Christmas and New Year, Saturday lunch, Sunday and bank holidays except Good Friday **32**ANT**x**
Rest – Vegetarian – Menu £ 23/30
♦ Proving that vegetarian food can be flavoursome and satisfying, with a menu that is varied and imaginative. This is a well run, friendly restaurant with understated décor, run by a husband and wife team.

XX **Cinnamon Kitchen** AC VISA MC AE
9 Devonshire Sq. ✉ EC2M 4YL ⊖ Liverpool Street – ☎ (020) 7626 5000 – www.cinnamon-kitchen.com – Closed 1 January, Saturday lunch, Sunday and bank holidays **34**ART**e**
Rest – Indian – Menu £ 18 (lunch)/19 – Carte £ 23/33
♦ Sister to The Cinnamon Club. Contemporary Indian cooking, with punchy flavours and arresting presentation. Sprightly service in large, modern surroundings. Watch the action from the Tandoor Bar.

XX **Kenza** AC VISA MC AE
10 Devonshire Sq. ✉ EC2M 4YP ⊖ Liverpool Street – ☎ (020) 7929 5533 – www.kenza-restaurant.com – Closed Saturday lunch, Sunday and bank holidays **34**ART**c**
Rest – Lebanese – Menu £ 12 – Carte £ 26/37
♦ Exotic basement restaurant, with lamps, carvings, pumping music and nightly belly dancing. Lebanese and Moroccan cooking are the menu influences and the cooking is authentic and accurate.

LONDON

XX **Devonshire Terrace**

Devonshire Sq. ✉ EC2M 4WY ⊖ Liverpool Street – ☎ (020) 7256 3233 – www.devonshireterrace.co.uk – Closed Saturday, Sunday and bank holidays **34**ART**c**

Rest – Modern European – Carte £ 28/41

◆ Brasserie-style cooking, where you choose the sauce and side dish to accompany your main course. Bright and busy restaurant with open kitchen and choice of two terraces, one within large atrium.

XX **Sauterelle**

The Royal Exchange ✉ EC3V 3LR ⊖ Bank – ☎ (020) 7618 2483 – www.restaurantsauterelle.com – Closed Christmas and New Year, bank holidays, Saturday and Sunday **33**AQU**a**

Rest – French – Menu £ 24 – Carte £ 31/54

◆ Impressive location on the mezzanine floor of The Royal Exchange; ask for a table looking down over the Grand Café. A largely French inspired contemporary menu makes good use of luxury ingredients.

XX **The Mercer**

34 Threadneedle St ✉ EC2R 8AY ⊖ Bank – ☎ (020) 7628 0001 – www.themercer.co.uk – Closed 24 December-2 January, Saturday, Sunday and bank bolidays **34**ARU**x**

Rest – Modern European – Carte £ 28/42

◆ Converted bank, with airy feel thanks to high ceilings and large windows. Brasserie style menu with appealing mix of classics and comfort food. Huge choice of wines available by glass or carafe.

XX **Boisdale of Bishopsgate**

Swedeland Ct, 202 Bishopsgate ✉ EC2M 4NR ⊖ Liverpool Street – ☎ (020) 7283 1763 – www.boisdale.co.uk – Closed 23 December-2 January, Saturday, Sunday and bank holidays **34**ART**a**

Rest – Scottish – Carte £ 27/55

◆ Through ground floor bar, serving oysters and champagne, to brick vaulted basement with red and tartan décor. Menu featuring Scottish produce. Live jazz most evenings.

XX **The White Swan**

108 Fetter Lane ✉ EC4A 1ES ⊖ Chancery Lane – ☎ (020) 7242 9696 – www.thewhiteswanlondon.com – Closed 25-26 December **32**ANT**n**

Rest – Modern European – Carte £ 30/40

◆ Smart dining room above pub just off Fleet Street: mirrored ceilings, colourful paintings on wall. Modern, daily changing menus, are good value for the heart of London.

XX **Manicomio**

6 Gutter Ln. ✉ EC2V 8AS ⊖ St Paul's – ☎ (020) 7726 5010 – www.manicomio.co.uk – Closed 24 December-3 January, Saturday, Sunday and bank holidays **33**APT**s**

Rest – Italian – Menu £ 20 (early dinner) – Carte £ 33/51

◆ Second branch to follow the first in Chelsea. Regional Italian fare, with top-notch ingredients. Bright and fresh first floor restaurant, with deli-café on the ground floor and bar on top floor.

XX **Luc's Brasserie**

17-22 Leadenhall Market ✉ EC3V 1LR ⊖ Bank – ☎ (020) 7621 0666 – www.lucsbrasserie.com – Closed 25 December-4 January, Friday-Monday dinner, Saturday-Sunday and Bank Holidays **34**ARU**v**

Rest – French – *(booking essential at lunch)* Menu £ 19 – Carte £ 29/41

◆ Looks down on the Victorian splendour of Leadenhall Market. First appeared in 1890 but re-invigorated in 2006. The menu is a paean to all things French and every classic dish is there.

High Timber

8 High Timber St. ✉ EC4V 3PA ⊖ Mansion House – ✆ (020) 7248 1777 – www.hightimber.com – Closed 25-26 December, Saturday, Sunday and bank holidays **33**APU**b**

Rest – Modern European – Menu £ 19 (lunch) – Carte £ 24/51

♦ Rustic look to the room, despite being in a modern block, with river views. Great wine cellar, with large choice from South Africa, owners' homeland. Cumbrian steaks the speciality.

Goodman City

11 Old Jewry ✉ EC2R 8DU ⊖ Bank – ✆ (020) 7600 8220 – www.goodmanrestaurants.com – Closed Saturday and Sunday **33**AQU**s**

Rest – Beef specialities – Menu £ 18 (lunch) – Carte £ 26/63

♦ Steaks, cut to order, are the stars of the show at this sister to the Mayfair original. Choose corn-fed, wet-matured USDA beef or Scottish and Irish grass fed; plenty of side dishes available too.

Amico Bio

44 Cloth Fair ✉ EC1A 7JQ ⊖ Barbican – ✆ (0207) 600 77 78 – www.amicobio.co.uk – Closed 25 December, Saturday lunch, Sunday and bank holidays **33**APT**v**

Rest – Italian vegetarian – Carte £ 17/21 **s**

♦ Simple little place owned by an experienced chef and his cousin; the organic produce comes from the family farm in Capua and the combination of flavours remain true to their upbringing in Campania.

Terranostra

27 Old Bailey ✉ EC4M 7HS ⊖ St Paul's – ✆ (020) 3201 0077 – www.terranostrafood.co.uk – Closed Saturday lunch and Sunday

Rest – Italian – *(booking advisable at lunch)* Carte £ 23/30 **33**AOU**x**

♦ Its informal, relaxed feel and sweet-natured service provides the ideal respite from bustle of The City and the trauma of the Old Bailey. Light, fresh food, with Sardinian leanings.

Paternoster Chop House

Warwick Ct., Paternoster Sq. ✉ EC4M 7DX ⊖ St Paul's – ✆ (020) 7029 9400 – www.paternosterchophouse.com – Closed 24 December-1 January, Saturday, Sunday dinner and bank holidays **33**APT**x**

Rest – British – Menu £ 27 – Carte £ 29/45

♦ Appropriately British menu in a restaurant lying in the shadow of St Paul's Cathedral. Large, open room with full-length windows; busy bar attached. Kitchen uses thoughtfully sourced produce.

28°-50°

140 Fetter Ln ✉ EC4A 1BT ⊖ Temple – ✆ (020) 7242 8877 – www.2850.co.uk – Closed Christmas-New Year , Saturday and Sunday **32**ANU**s**

Rest – French – Menu £ 22 (lunch) – Carte £ 25/29

♦ Subterranean wine bar and informal restaurant, from the same owners as Texture. Robust, mostly French dishes accompany a thoughtfully assembled wine list, with much choice by the glass.

Restaurant at St Paul's Cathedral

St Paul's Churchyard ✉ EC4M 8AD ⊖ St. Paul's – ✆ (020) 7248 2469 – www.restaurantatstpauls.co.uk **33**APU**s**

Rest – British – *(lunch only) (booking advisable)* Menu £ 24

♦ Tucked away in a corner of the crypt of Sir Christopher Wren's 17C masterpiece. The kitchen prepares everything from scratch and celebrates all things British, including drinks.

Goldfish City

46 Gresham St ✉ EC2V 7AY ⊖ Bank – ✆ (020) 7726 0308 – www.goldfish-resaturant.co.uk – Closed Saturday, Sunday and bank holidays

Rest – Asian – *(booking advisable)* Menu £ 23/30 – Carte £ 23/37 **33**AQU**x**

♦ Busy at lunch thanks to the selection of well-priced steamed dim sum. Balanced main menu mixes the classic with the modern. Spread over three floors, with discreet décor and helpful service.

CROYDON – Greater London – pop. 316 283 — 12 B3

ADDINGTON

XX **Planet Spice**

88 Selsdon Park Rd. ✉ CR2 8JT – ✆ (020) 8651 3300 – www.planet-spice.com – Closed 26 December **7GZc**

Rest – Indian – Carte £ 20/34

♦ Brasserie style Indian restaurant with fresh, vibrant décor and a modern feel. Attentive and helpful service. Traditional cooking with some innovative touches.

SOUTH CROYDON

XX **Cassoulet**

18 Selsdon Rd. ✉ CR2 6PA – ✆ (020) 8633 1818 – www.lecassoulet.co.uk – Closed 25-26 December and 1 January **7FZv**

Rest – French – Menu £ 17/28

♦ Evolving, seasonal set menus offer a range of traditional and more modern French dishes, with wider choice at dinner. Chic and elegant interior; carefully run, with attentive service.

X **Fish and Grill**

48-50 South End ✉ CR0 1DP – ✆ (020) 8774 4060 – www.fishandgrill.co.uk – Closed 25 December **7FZa**

Rest – Seafood – Menu £ 15 (lunch) – Carte £ 26/34

♦ Stylish and vibrant brasserie, with well-organised service and a bustling atmosphere. Appealing menu, with assorted seafood and grilled meats the specialities; good homemade desserts.

EALING – Greater London – pop. 300 948 — 12 A3

West Middlesex Southall Greenford Rd, ✆ (020) 8574 3450

Horsenden Hill Woodland Rise

EALING

X **Charlotte's Place**

16 St Matthew's Rd. ✉ W5 3JT ⊖ Ealing Common – ✆ (020) 8567 7541 – www.charlottes.co.uk – Closed 26 December-4 January **2CVc**

Rest – Modern European – Menu £ 15 (weekday lunch) – Carte £ 24/34

♦ Warmly run neighbourhood restaurant opposite the Common; divided between bright ground floor room and cosier downstairs. Menu is a mix of largely British and Mediterranean influences.

X **Kiraku**

8 Station Par., Uxbridge Rd. ✉ W5 3LD ⊖ Ealing Common – ✆ (020) 8992 2848 – www.kiraku.co.uk – Closed Christmas and New Year, 10 days August, Tuesday following bank holidays and Monday **2CVv**

Rest – Japanese – Carte £ 15/33

♦ The name of this cute little Japanese restaurant means 'relax and enjoy'; easy with such charming service. Extensive menu includes zensai, skewers, noodles, rice dishes and assorted sushi.

ACTON GREEN

XX **Le Vacherin**

76-77 South Par. ✉ W4 5LF ⊖ Chiswick Park – ✆ (020) 8742 2121 – www.levacherin.com – Closed Monday lunch and bank holidays **6CVo**

Rest – French – Menu £ 17/33 – Carte dinner £ 34/43

♦ Authentic feel to this comfortable brasserie, with its brown leather banquette seating, mirrors and belle époque prints. French classics from snails to duck confit; beef is a speciality.

Bollo

13-15 Bollo Ln ✉ W4 5LR ⊖ Chiswick Park. – ✆ (020) 8994 6037 – www.thebollohouse.co.uk **6CVz**

Rest – Carte £ 20/30

♦ Large Victorian pub with original glass cupola and oak panelling. Menu is a mix of generous pub classics and dishes with a southern Mediterranean influence. Look out for quiz nights and promotions.

Duke of Sussex

75 South Par ✉ W4 5LF ⊖ Chiswick Park. – ✆ (020) 8742 8801 – Closed Monday lunch **6**CV**o**

Rest – Carte £ 20/28

◆ A grand Victorian pub with ornate décor. Appealingly rustic Spanish influences in the daily changing menu, with stews and cured meats a speciality; some dishes designed for sharing.

GREENWICH – Greater London – pop. 219 263 **12** B3

Greenwich

Rivington Grill

178 Greenwich High Rd. ✉ SE10 8NN ⊖ Greenwich (DLR) – ✆ (020) 8293 9270 – www.rivingtongreenwich.co.uk – Closed 25 December, Monday and lunch Tuesday and Wednesday **7**GV**s**

Rest – British – Carte £ 21/39

◆ Part of the Picturehouse complex; 21C rustic interior with closely set tables. Firmly English menus in bar and galleried restaurant. Banquets and market breakfasts on offer.

LONDON

HACKNEY – Greater London – pop. 202 824 **12** B3

Hackney

Empress of India

130 Lauriston Rd, Victoria Park ✉ E9 7LH ⊖ Mile End. – ✆ (020) 8533 5123 – www.theempressofindia.com – Closed 25 December **3**GU**n**

Rest – Carte £ 24/35

◆ Dating from 1880 with a large central bar; mosaics, murals and photos commemorate Queen Victoria and the British Raj. Go for the speciality: spit-roasted rare breed meats, poultry and seasonal game.

Cat & Mutton

76 Broadway Mkt ✉ E8 4QJ ⊖ Bethnal Green. – ✆ (020) 7254 5599 – www.catandmutton.co.uk – Closed 25-26 December **14**YZB**a**

Rest – British – Carte £ 20/31

◆ The pub's lived-in look, music and relaxed vibe attract a young, local crowd. Satisfying pub food, from a weekly changing menu, delivers on flavour. Regular quiz nights and art classes.

Prince Arthur

95 Forest Rd ✉ E8 3BH ⊖ Bethnal Green. – ✆ (020) 7249 9996 – www.theprincearthurlondonfields.com – Closed 25 December and Monday-Thursday lunch **14**XZB**c**

Rest – Carte £ 22/32

◆ An intimate local pub for local people, with plenty of character. Unpretentious and heart-warming menu, with classics like a pint of prawns and cottage pie; filling puddings.

Hoxton

The Hoxton

rm, VISA AE

81 Great Eastern St ✉ EC2A 3HU ⊖ Old Street – ✆ (020) 7550 1000 – www.hoxtonhotels.com **20**XZD**x**

205 rm – †£ 59/199 ††£ 59/199, ☕ £ 10

Rest *Hoxton Grill* – Menu £ 16 – Carte £ 26/37

◆ Urban lodge: industrial styled, clean lined modernism. "No ripoffs" mantra: cheap phone rate, free internet, complimentary 'lite Pret' breakfast. Carefully considered rooms. Cooking style: New York deli meets French brasserie.

Great Eastern Dining Room

54 Great Eastern St. ✉ EC2A 3QR ⊖ Old Street – ✆ (020) 7613 4545 – www.rickerrestaurants.com – Closed Saturday lunch, Sunday and bank holidays **20**XZD**n**

Rest – Asian – Menu £ 15 (lunch and early dinner) – Carte £ 17/38

◆ Half the place is a bar that's heaving in the evening. Dining area has candle-lit tables, contemporary chandeliers, and carefully prepared, seriously tasty pan-Asian cooking.

X **Fifteen London**
13 Westland Pl ✉ N1 7LP ⊖ Old Street – ✆ (0871) 330 15 15 – www.fifteen.net
Rest – Italian – *(booking essential)* Menu £ 28 (weekday lunch)/60 – Carte £ 36/42 **13**VZC**c**
◆ Original branch of Jamie Oliver's charitable restaurants; run by trainees alongside full-time staff. Buzzy ground floor trattoria; more formal basement restaurant. Tasty, seasonal Italian food.

SHOREDITCH

XXX **Boundary** with rm
2-4 Boundary St. ✉ E2 7DD ⊖ Old Street – ✆ (020) 7729 1051 – www.theboundary.co.uk – Closed Sunday dinner, lunch Monday and Saturday
12 rm – †£ 168/240 ††£ 168/240, ☕ £ 13 – 5 suites **20**XZD**b**
Rest – French – Menu £ 25 (lunch) – Carte £ 33/54
◆ Sir Terence Conran has taken a warehouse and created a 'caff' with a bakery and shop, a rooftop terrace and a stylish, good-looking French restaurant serving plenty of cross-Channel classics. Comfy and individual bedrooms.

XXX **L' Anima**
1 Snowden St. ✉ EC2A 2DQ ⊖ Liverpool Street – ✆ (0207) 422 7000 – www.lanima.co.uk – Closed Saturday lunch, Sunday and bank holidays
Rest – Italian – *(booking essential)* Menu £ 29 (lunch) – Carte £ 29/48 **20**XZD**a**
◆ Very handsome room, with limestone and leather creating a sophisticated, glamorous environment. Precisely executed dishes with the emphasis on flavour; smooth but personable service.

XX **Lena**
66 Great Eastern St. ✉ EC2A 3JT ⊖ Old Street – ✆ (020) 7739 5714 – www.lenarestaurant.com – Closed 26-29 December and Sunday **20**XZD**c**
Rest – Italian – Menu £ 14 (weekdays) – Carte £ 30/45
◆ Named after the owner's mother and eclectically decorated using leather, wood, plastic and ceramics. Menu looks to southern Italy for influences. Live jazz in the stylish bar at weekends.

X **Rivington Grill**
28-30 Rivington St. ✉ EC2A 3DZ ⊖ Old Street – ✆ (020) 7729 7053 – www.rivingtongrill.co.uk – Closed 24-26 December and 1 January
Rest – British – Menu £ 19 (weekend lunch) – Carte £ 25/49 **20**XZD**e**
◆ Very appealing 'back to basics' British menu, with plenty of comforting classics including a section 'on toast'. This converted warehouse is popular with the local community of artists.

Princess of Shoreditch
76-78 Paul St ✉ EC2A 4NE ⊖ Old Street. – ✆ (020) 7729 9270 – www.theprincessofshoreditch.com – Closed 25-26 December **19**VZD**a**
Rest – Menu £ 20 – Carte £ 25/35
◆ Pies and platters in the busy ground floor bar; more ambitious but still flavoursome European-influenced cooking in the calmer upstairs room. Friendly service a feature.

HAMMERSMITH and FULHAM – Greater London – pop. 165 242 12 B3

FULHAM

XX **Mao Tai**
58 New Kings Rd., Parsons Green ✉ SW6 4LS ⊖ Parsons Green – ✆ (020) 7731 2520 – www.maotai.co.uk – Closed 25-27 December **22**NZH**e**
Rest – Chinese – *(dinner only and Sunday lunch)* Carte £ 38/54
◆ Influences from across China inform the modern menu of this stylish, long-standing Chinese restaurant. Divided into two rooms; the front section with the cocktail bar is the more animated.

XX **Manson**

676 Fulham Rd. ✉ SW6 5FA ⊖ Parsons Green – ✆ (020) 7384 9559 – www.mansonrestaurant.co.uk **22**MZH**x**

Rest – Modern European – *(booking advisable)* Menu £ 16 (lunch) – Carte £ 29/38

◆ Slight Left Bank aesthetic, with smoked mirrors and 1930s French street lamps. Pleasant, breezy service. Cooking also has a French bias and displays more sophistication than one expects.

XX **Blue Elephant**

4-6 Fulham Broadway ✉ SW6 1AA ⊖ Fulham Broadway – ✆ (020) 7385 6595 – www.blueelephant.com – Closed 25 December and 1 January **22**NZG**z**

Rest – Thai – *(booking essential)* Menu £ 15/35 – Carte £ 32/50

◆ A London institution, with a gloriously unrestrained décor of plants, streams and bridges. Carefully prepared dishes from across Thailand. Curries are a strength and service is well-meaning.

Harwood Arms

Walham Grove ✉ SW6 1QP ⊖ Fulham Broadway. – ✆ (020) 7386 1847 – www.harwoodarms.com – Closed 24-28 December, 1 January and Monday lunch

Rest – British – Carte £ 28/32 **22**NZG**a**

Spec. Herefordshire snails with oxtail and stout. Braised beef cheeks and celeriac purée. Camp coffee ice cream.

◆ A proper, busy London pub that happens to serve exceedingly good food. Flavours are appropriately robust and the kitchen uses great seasonal produce. Prices are down-to-earth, service is warm and the place is as refreshingly uncomplicated as it looks.

Sands End

135-137 Stephendale Rd ✉ SW6 2PR ⊖ Fulham Broadway. – ✆ (020) 7731 7823 – www.thesandsend.co.uk **22**OZH**r**

Rest – *(booking advisable)* Menu £ 13 (lunch) – Carte £ 24/30

◆ Busy and warmly run pub with junkshop-chic, country-comes-to-the-city feel. Appealing bar snacks; a concise, balanced menu produces carefully prepared and attractively presented dishes.

HAMMERSMITH

XX **River Café** (Ruth Rogers)

Thames Wharf, Rainville Rd ✉ W6 9HA ⊖ Barons Court – ✆ (020) 7386 4200 – www.rivercafe.co.uk – Closed 25 December-1 January, Sunday dinner and bank holidays **21**LZG**r**

Rest – Italian – *(booking essential)* Carte £ 49/78

Spec. Wood-roasted langoustines with chilli and lemon. Slow roast veal shin with sage, polenta and Parmesan. Panna cotta with grappa and raspberries.

◆ The open kitchen let the superlative ingredients shine on the twice-daily changing menu; pasta a real highlight. Wood-fired oven dominates the stylish riverside room, with its contagiously effervescent atmosphere, helped along by charming, friendly service.

XX **Indian Zing**

236 King St. ✉ W6 0RF ⊖ Ravenscourt Park – ✆ (020) 8748 5959 – www.indianzing.co.uk **21**LZG**a**

Rest – Indian – Menu £ 15 (lunch) – Carte £ 20/30

◆ Proud and enthusiastic chef-owner is keen to satisfy his diners. Flavoursome and quite refined Indian cooking from across the continent. Colourful surroundings, with closely set tables.

X **Azou**

375 King St. ✉ W6 9NJ ⊖ Stamford Brook – ✆ (020) 8563 7266 – www.azou.co.uk – Closed 25-26 December **21**KZG**u**

Rest – North African – *(dinner only)* Menu £ 15 – Carte £ 20/32

◆ Silks, lanterns and rugs add to the atmosphere of this personally run, North African restaurant. Most come for the excellent tajines, with triple steamed couscous. Much is designed for sharing.

Anglesea Arms

35 Wingate Rd ✉ W6 0UR ⊖ Ravenscourt Park. – ☎ (020) 8749 1291 – www.anglesea-arms.com – Closed 25 December **15**LZE**c**

Rest – *(bookings not accepted)* Carte £ 17/46

♦ Busy wood-panelled bar; brighter, calmer rear dining room with part-glass roof and exposed kitchen. Regularly changing blackboard menu; expect robust cooking with a strong British bias.

Havelock Tavern

57 Masbro Rd, Brook Grn ✉ W14 0LS ⊖ Kensington Olympia. – ☎ (020) 7603 5374 – www.thehavelocktavern.com – Closed 25 December **16**MZE**e**

Rest – *(bookings not accepted)* Carte £ 21/26

♦ Warm, friendly and atmospheric pub with easygoing service and pleasantly mixed clientele. Blackboard menu offers robust, satisfying pub food. Arrive early if you don't want to wait for a table.

Carpenter's Arms

91 Black Lion Ln ✉ W6 9BG ⊖ Stamford Brook. – ☎ (020) 8741 8386 – www.carpentersarmsw6.co.uk **21**KZG**b**

Rest – *(booking essential)* Menu £ 16 (lunch) – Carte £ 30/55

♦ This is a civilised sort of pub and one that makes a virtue of its pared down simplicity. Good efforts are made with the service and the menu has something for all tastes and appetites.

Dartmouth Castle

26 Glenthorne Rd ✉ W6 0LS ⊖ Hammersmith. – ☎ (020) 8748 3614 – www.thedartmouthcastle.co.uk – Closed 24 December to 1 January and 2nd Monday in August **21**LZF**e**

Rest – Carte £ 18/30

♦ The Mediterranean exerts quite an influence on the large menu at this popular, welcoming and traditional pub. Spread over two levels but the ground floor is the more atmospheric.

Shepherd's Bush

Princess Victoria

217 Uxbridge Rd ✉ W12 9DH ⊖ Shepherd's Bush. – ☎ (020) 8749 5886 – www.princessvictoria.co.uk – Closed 2 weeks at Christmas **15**KZE**a**

Rest – Menu £ 15 (lunch) – Carte £ 22/32

♦ Magnificent Victorian gin palace, with original plasterwork. The kitchen knows its butchery; pork board, homemade sausages and terrines all feature. Excellent wine list, with over 350 bottles.

HARINGEY – Greater London – pop. 216 507 **12** B3

Crouch End

Bistro Aix

54 Topsfield Par, Tottenham Ln. ✉ N8 8PT – ☎ (020) 8340 6346 – www.bistroaix.co.uk – Closed 26 December, 1 January and Monday

Rest – French – Menu £ 15 (weekday dinner) – Carte £ 20/34 **3**EU**v**

♦ Dressers, cabinets and contemporary artwork lend an authentic Gallic edge to this bustling bistro. Traditionally prepared French classics are the highlights of an extensive menu.

Queens Pub and Dining Room

26 Broadway Par ✉ N8 9DE – ☎ (020) 8340 2031 – www.thequeenscrouchend.co.uk **3**EU**c**

Rest – Carte approx. approx. £ 25

♦ Striking example of a classic Victorian pub, from the original mahogany panelling to the stained glass windows and ornate ceiling. The menu is a mix of pub classics and Mediterranean influences.

Fortis Green

Clissold Arms

115 Fortis Green ✉ N2 9HR ⊖ East Finchley. – ✆ (020) 8444 4224 – Closed 1 January **3**EU**a**

Rest – Carte £ 22/35

♦ Reputedly the venue for The Kinks' first gig. Now modernised throughout, with a large rear terrace. Interesting menus, with terrines, whole sea bass and 28-day aged steaks the specialities.

Highgate

Rose and Crown

86 Highgate High St. ✉ N6 5HX ⊖ Archway – ✆ (020) 8340 0770 – www.roseandcrownhighgate.co.uk – Closed 2-7 January, Sunday dinner and Monday lunch **2**EU**i**

Rest – Modern European – Carte £ 27/36

♦ Converted pub, smartly kitted out but not overly formal thanks to genial staff. Seasonally changing, European-influenced cooking, with competitively priced weekly-changing set menu.

Tottenham

Lock

Heron House, Hale Wharf, Ferry Ln. ✉ N17 9NF ⊖ Tottenham Hale – ✆ (020) 8885 2829 – www.thelockrestaurant.com – Closed 26 December-4 January and Monday **3**GU**a**

Rest – Modern European – Menu £ 17 (lunch) – Carte dinner £ 22/48

♦ Unpromising location for this starkly decorated restaurant. But the service is affable and the Mediterranean-influenced food is prepared with care and flair and represents value for money.

HARROW – Greater London – pop. 206 643 **12** A3

Harrow on the Hill

Incanto

41 High St. ✉ HA1 3HT ⊖ Harrow on the Hill – ✆ (020) 8426 6767 – www.incanto.co.uk – Closed Sunday dinner and Monday **1**BU**z**

Rest – Italian – Menu £ 20/23 – Carte £ 31/38

♦ Within Grade II former post office; split-level restaurant to rear of well stocked deli. Well paced service; Southern Italian bias to the rustic cooking, with quality produce to the fore.

Pinner

Friends

11 High St. ✉ HA5 5PJ ⊖ Pinner – ✆ (020) 8866 0286 – www.friendsrestaurant.co.uk – Closed Sunday dinner, Monday and bank holidays **1**BU**a**

Rest – Modern European – Menu £ 24/32

♦ Pretty beamed cottage, with some parts dating back 400 years. Inside, a welcoming glow from the log fire; personal service from owners and a fresh, regularly-changing menu.

HILLINGDON – Greater London – pop. 242 755 **12** A3

Haste Hill Northwood The Drive, ✆ (01923) 825 224

Heathrow Airport

Sofitel

Terminal 5, Heathrow Airport ✉ TW6 2GD – ✆ (020) 8757 7777 – www.sofitel.com **5**AX**a**

578 rm – †£ 114/396 ††£ 114/396, ☕ £ 21.50 – 27 suites

Rest *Brasserie Roux* – French – Menu £ 20 – Carte £ 27/39

Rest *Vivre* – Menu £ 25 (dinner) – Carte £ 25/38

♦ Smart and well-run contemporary hotel, opened in 2008. Designed around a series of atriums, with direct access to T5. Crisply decorated, comfortable bedrooms with luxurious bathrooms. French brasserie classics. International menu in large Vivre.

Hilton London Heathrow Airport
Terminal 4 ✉ TW6 3AF – ✆ (020) 8759 7755 – www.hilton.co.uk/heathrow **5AXn**
355 rm – †£ 153/377 ††£ 153/377, ☕ £ 21.95 – 5 suites
Rest *Aromi* – *(Closed lunch Saturday, Sunday and bank holidays) (buffet lunch)* Menu £ 33 – Carte £ 29/38
Rest *Zen Oriental* – ✆ (020) 8564 9609 – Menu £ 33 – Carte £ 34/63
◆ Group hotel with a striking modern exterior and linked to Terminal 4 by a covered walkway. Good-sized bedrooms, with contemporary styled suites. Spacious Aromi in vast atrium. Zen Oriental offers formal Chinese experience.

London Heathrow Marriott
Bath Rd, Hayes ✉ UB3 5AN – ✆ (020) 8990 1100 – www.londonheathrowmarriott.co.uk **5AXz**
391 rm – †£ 227 ††£ 227, ☕ £ 16.95 – 2 suites
Rest *Tuscany* – Italian – *(closed Sunday) (dinner only)* Menu £ 39 – Carte £ 32/45
Rest *Allie's grille* – Carte £ 25/38
◆ Built at the end of 20C, this modern, comfortable hotel is centred around a large atrium, with comprehensive business facilities: there is an exclusive Executive floor. Italian cuisine in bright and convivial Tuscany. Grill favourites in Allie's.

LONDON

HOUNSLOW – Greater London – pop. 212 341 **12 A3**

The Treaty Centre, High St ✆ (0845) 456 2929, leisureshop-hct@lang.com
Wyke Green Isleworth Syon Lane, ✆ (020) 8560 8777
Airlinks Southall Lane, ✆ (020) 8561 1418
Hounslow Heath, Staines Rd, ✆ (020) 8570 5271

CHISWICK

Moran
626 Chiswick High Rd. ✉ W4 5RY ⊖ Gunnersbury – ✆ (020) 8996 5200 – www.moranhotels.com **6CVi**
123 rm – †£ 90/225 ††£ 90/225, ☕ £ 10
Rest *Napa* – *(bar lunch Saturday)* Menu £ 17/22 – Carte £ 25/36
◆ Converted office block with all-glass exterior, midway between Heathrow and West End. Decorated in a restrained contemporary style with bright and airy bedrooms. Two-tiered restaurant with terrace and modern menu.

High Road House
162 Chiswick High Rd ✉ W4 1PR ⊖ Turnham Green – ✆ (020) 8742 1717 – www.highroadhouse.co.uk **21KZGe**
14 rm – †£ 105 ††£ 115/125, ☕ £ 10
Rest *High Road Brasserie* – see restaurant listing
◆ Cool, sleek hotel and club, the latter a slick place to lounge around or play games. Light, bright bedrooms with crisp linen. A carefully appointed, fairly-priced destination.

La Trompette
5-7 Devonshire Rd. ✉ W4 2EU ⊖ Turnham Green – ✆ (020) 8747 1836 – www.latrompette.co.uk – Closed 24-25 December and 1 January **21KZGy**
Rest – Modern European – *(booking essential)* Menu £ 24/40
Spec. Pithiviers of quail and mushroom with sauce Soubise. Cod with shrimp vol-au-vent, celery and chives. White chocolate tart with raspberries and honeycomb.
◆ Enthusiastically run and smart neighbourhood restaurant, sister to Chez Bruce. Small front terrace and light, comfortable interior. Balanced menu and confident kitchen produce robust, spirited dishes. Wine list varied in price and geography.

Michael Nadra
6-8 Elliott Rd. ✉ W4 1PE ⊖ Turnham Green – ✆ (020) 8742 0766 – www.restaurant-michaelnadra.co.uk **21KZGz**
Rest – Modern European – Menu £ 16 (lunch) – Carte £ 32/40
◆ Enough regulars now appreciate the chef-owner's well-judged cooking for him to finally put his own name above the door of this intimate, friendly restaurant. Balanced and sensibly priced menu.

Charlotte's Bistro

6 Turnham Green Terr. ✉ W4 1QP ⊖ Turnham Green – ✆ (020) 8742 3590 – www.charlottes.co.uk – Closed 26 December **21**KZG**a**

Rest – *(booking advisable)* Menu £ 15 – Carte £ 22/28

♦ A pleasant, unpretentious bistro; run by a friendly team, with a well-priced menu of flavoursome, well prepared dishes of largely European provenance. Little sister to Charlotte's Place in Ealing.

High Road Brasserie – at High Road House Hotel

162 Chiswick High Rd ✉ W4 1PR ⊖ Turnham Green – ✆ (020) 8742 7474 – www.highroadhouse.co.uk **21**KZG**e**

Rest – Traditional – *(Closed 25 December) (booking essential)* Carte £ 21/42

♦ Authentic brasserie, with mirrors, panelling and art deco lighting. Despite the high volume of customers, the classic dishes are prepared with care and staff cope well with being busy.

Sam's Brasserie

11 Barley Mow Passage ✉ W4 4PH ⊖ Turnham Green – ✆ (020) 8987 0555 – www.samsbrasserie.co.uk – Closed 24-28 December **2**CV**a**

Rest – Mediterranean – Menu £ 17/18 – Carte £ 29/39

♦ Bustling and fun brasserie with large bar, in former Sanderson wallpaper mill. Appealing menu leans towards the Med; cooking is flavoursome. Service is young and keen and the wine affordable.

LONDON

ISLINGTON – Greater London – pop. 175 797 **12** B3

ARCHWAY

500

782 Holloway Rd ✉ N19 3JH ⊖ Archway – ✆ (020) 7272 3406 – www.500restaurant.co.uk – Closed first 2 weeks in August, 21-31 December, Sunday lunch and Monday **12**SZA**y**

Rest – Italian – *(booking essential)* Carte £ 20/25

♦ Small, fun and well-priced Italian that's always busy. Good pastas and bread; the veal chop and rabbit are specialities. The passion of the ebullient owner and keen chef are evident.

St John's Tavern

91 Junction Rd ✉ N19 5QU ⊖ Archway. – ✆ (020) 7272 1587 – www.stjohnstavern.com – Closed 25-26 December and lunch Monday-Thursday **12**RZA**s**

Rest – Carte £ 23/30

♦ Daily changing menu in the dining room at the back of the pub. Cosy atmosphere, with dark colours and fireplace. Rustic cooking from open kitchen and blackboard menu.

BARNSBURY

Morgan M

489 Liverpool Rd. ✉ N7 8NS ⊖ Highbury and Islington – ✆ (020) 7609 3560 – www.morganm.com – Closed 24-30 December, Sunday dinner, Monday and lunch Tuesday and Saturday **13**UZA**a**

Rest – French – Menu £ 28/41

♦ Classic, full flavoured French dishes, seasonal specialities and a separate vegetarian menu ensures a loyal crowd of regulars at this formally run restaurant, set within a converted pub.

Fig

169 Hemingford Rd. ✉ N1 1DA ⊖ Caledonian Road – ✆ (020) 7609 3009 – www.fig-restaurant.co.uk – Closed 23 December-6 January and Sunday

Rest – Modern European – *(dinner only)* Carte £ 31/36 **13**UZB**a**

♦ Well-travelled Danish chef-owner uses Scandinavian influences and other world cuisines to create light, fresh and flavoursome dishes. Warm, cosy and inviting neighbourhood feel.

Canonbury

Trullo

300-302 St Paul's Rd. ✉ N1 2LH ⊖ Highbury and Islington – ✆ (020) 7226 2733 – www.trullorestaurant.com – Closed Sunday dinner and Monday **13UZBt**

Rest – Italian – *(dinner only and lunch Saturday and Sunday) (booking essential)* Menu £ 25 (lunch) – Carte £ 14/34

◆ Great value Italian food that delivers on flavour ensures that this friendly and relaxed restaurant is always full of contented diners. Terrific antipasti and the charcoal grill dishes are favourites.

House

63-69 Canonbury Rd ✉ N1 2DG ⊖ Highbury and Islington. – ✆ (020) 7704 7410 – www.thehouse.islington.com – Closed Monday lunch **13UZBh**

Rest – Menu £ 18 (lunch) – Carte £ 26/35

◆ A smart looking pub with an attractive terrace; but one that still feels like a genuine local. The cooking is crisp and confident and there's an emphasis on good quality, organic ingredients.

LONDON

Clerkenwell

Malmaison

18-21 Charterhouse Sq ✉ EC1M 6AH ⊖ Barbican – ✆ (020) 7012 3700 – www.malmaison.com **19UZDq**

97 rm – †£ 306/378 ††£ 306/378, ☕ £ 17.95

Rest *Brasserie* – *(closed Saturday lunch)* Menu £ 18 – Carte £ 29/40

◆ Striking early 20C red-brick building overlooking pleasant square. Stylish, comfy public areas. Bedrooms in vivid, bold colours, with plenty of extra touches. Modern brasserie employing meats from Smithfield.

The Rookery without rest

12 Peters Lane, Cowcross St ✉ EC1M 6DS ⊖ Barbican – ✆ (020) 7336 0931 – www.rookeryhotel.com – Closed 24-26 December **33AOTp**

32 rm – †£ 210/276 ††£ 276, ☕ £ 10.95 – 1 suite

◆ A row of charmingly restored 18C houses. Wood panelling, stone-flagged flooring, open fires and antique furniture. Highly individual bedrooms, with Victorian bathrooms.

Portal

88 St John St. ✉ EC1M 4EH ⊖ Farringdon – ✆ (020) 7253 6950 – www.portalrestaurant.com – Closed Christmas, Easter, Saturday lunch, Sunday and bank holidays **19UZDr**

Rest – Mediterranean – Carte £ 33/49

◆ Portugal and southern Europe are the main influences, with fish and pork dishes the house specialities. Busy front bar and a chic, semi-industrial feel to the rear restaurant. Helpful service.

The Larder

91-93 St John St. ✉ EC1M 4NU ⊖ Farringdon – ✆ (020) 7608 1558 – www.thelarderrestaurant.com – Closed 23 December-3 January and Sunday

Rest – Modern European – Menu £ 18 (lunch) – Carte £ 25/37 **19UZDf**

◆ Large, glass-fronted restaurant with stark, noisy, industrial feel and own bakery selling breads and pastries. Unfussy food has an English accent with some European influences.

St John

26 St John St. ✉ EC1M 4AY ⊖ Barbican – ✆ (020) 7251 0848 – www.stjohnrestaurant.com – Closed Christmas and New Year, Easter, Saturday lunch, Sunday dinner and bank holidays, **33APTc**

Rest – British – *(booking essential)* Carte £ 28/53

Spec. Potted beef and pickled beetroot. Poached rabbit with carrots and borlotti beans. Damson jelly and shortbread.

◆ 'Nose to tail eating' is how they describe their cooking at this busy, bright, converted 19C smokehouse. Strong on offal, game and unusual cuts; gloriously British, highly seasonal, appealingly simple and very satisfying.

Comptoir Gascon

61-63 Charterhouse St. ✉ EC1M 6HJ ⊖ Farringdon – ✆ (020) 7608 0851 – www.comptoirgascon.com – Closed Christmas and New Year, Sunday and Monday **33**AOT**a**

Rest – French – *(booking essential)* Carte £ 15/30

◆ Buzzy restaurant; sister to Club Gascon. Rustic and satisfying specialities from the SW of France include wine, cheese, bread and especially duck. Further produce on display to take home.

Hix Oyster and Chop House

36-37 Greenhill Rents ✉ EC1M 6BN ⊖ Farringdon – ✆ (0207) 017 1930 – www.hixoysterandchophouse.co.uk – Closed 25-26 December, 1 January, Saturday lunch and bank holidays **33**AOT**e**

Rest – British – Carte £ 29/60

◆ Appropriately utilitarian surroundings put the focus on seasonal and often underused British ingredients. Cooking is satisfying and unfussy, with plenty of oysters and aged beef served on the bone.

Vinoteca

7 St John St. ✉ EC1M 4AA ⊖ Farringdon – ✆ (020) 7253 8786 – www.vinoteca.co.uk – Closed 24 December-1 January and Sunday

Rest – Modern European – Carte £ 21/31 **33**APT**a**

◆ This cosy and passionately run 'bar and wine shop' is always busy and full of life. Thrilling wine list is constantly evolving; the classic and vibrant dishes are the ideal accompaniment.

Coach & Horses

26-28 Ray St ✉ EC1R 3DJ ⊖ Farringdon. – ✆ (020) 7837 1336 – www.thecoachandhorses.com – Closed 24 December-3 January, Easter, Saturday lunch, Sunday dinner and bank holidays **19**UZD**a**

Rest – Menu £ 16 (Sunday lunch) – Carte £ 20/29

◆ Cosy, warm feel to this restored Victorian pub, with traditional wood panelling and engraved windows. British dishes at the heart of the menu and appealing snacks in the bar.

FINSBURY

Zetter

St John's Sq., 86-88 Clerkenwell Rd. ✉ EC1M 5RJ ⊖ Farringdon – ✆ (020) 7324 4444 – www.thezetter.com **19**UZD**s**

59 rm – †£ 222 ††£ 222, ☕ £ 9.50

Rest *Bistrot Bruno Loubet* – see restaurant listing

◆ Discreetly trendy modern design in the well-equipped bedrooms and rooftop studios of a converted 19C warehouse: pleasant extras from old paperbacks to flat screen TV/DVDs.

Bistrot Bruno Loubet – at Zetter Hotel

St John's Sq., 86-88 Clerkenwell Rd. ✉ EC1M 5RJ ⊖ Farringdon – ✆ (020) 7324 4455 – www.bistrotbrunoloubet.com **19**UZD**s**

Rest – French – *(booking advisable)* Carte £ 26/36

◆ Having made his name in the early '90s, Bruno Loubet's London return was much anticipated. His flavoursome regional French cooking proves a good fit for this busy, bright restaurant at the Zetter hotel.

Moro

34-36 Exmouth Market ✉ EC1R 4QE ⊖ Farringdon – ✆ (020) 7833 8336 – www.moro.co.uk – Closed Christmas and New Year, Easter and bank holidays **19**UZD**b**

Rest – Mediterranean – *(booking essential)* Carte £ 28/40

◆ Daily changing menu an eclectic mix of Mediterranean, Moroccan and Spanish. Friendly T-shirted staff. Informal surroundings with bare tables and a large zinc bar.

LONDON

Medcalf

40 Exmouth Mkt. ✉ EC1R 4QE ⊖ Farringdon – ✆ (020) 7833 3533 – www.medcalfbar.co.uk – Closed 24 December-1 January, Sunday dinner and bank holidays **19**UZD**b**

Rest – British – *(booking essential)* Carte £ 26/37

♦ Bustling, no-frills former butcher's shop with lively atmosphere. Satisfying robust cooking, with the emphasis on seasonal, British ingredients. Good range of beer and wine by the glass.

Cicada

132-134 St John St. ✉ EC1V 4JT ⊖ Farringdon – ✆ (020) 7608 1550 – www.rickerrestaurants.com **19**UZD**d**

Rest – Asian – Menu £ 18/30 – Carte £ 23/50

♦ Set in a culinary hotbed, this buzzy restaurant and vibrant bar is spacious, lively and popular for its south east Asian dishes. You can even just pop in for one course and a beer.

LONDON

The Modern Pantry

47-48 St John's Sq. ✉ EC1V 4JJ ⊖ Farringdon – ✆ (020) 7553 9210 – www.themodernpantry.co.uk – Closed 25-26 December **19**UZD**k**

Rest – International – *(booking advisable)* Carte £ 27/40

♦ Fusion cooking that uses complementary flavours to create vibrant, zesty dishes. The simple, crisp ground floor of this Georgian building has the buzz; upstairs is more intimate. Clued-up service.

Morito

32 Exmouth Market ✉ EC1R 4QE ⊖ Farringdon – ✆ (020) 7278 7007 – Closed Sunday and Monday lunch **19**UZD**m**

Rest – Spanish – Carte £ 20/25

♦ From the owners of next door Moro comes this authentic and appealingly down to earth little tapas bar. Seven or eight dishes between two should suffice but over-ordering is easy and won't break the bank.

Green

29 Clerkenwell Gn ✉ EC1R 0DU ⊖ Farringdon. – ✆ (020) 7490 8010 – www.thegreenec1.co.uk **19**UZD**z**

Rest – Carte £ 21/30

♦ The building dates from 1580 and became a tavern in 1720. Appetising and imaginative bar snacks on the ground floor; intimate upstairs dining room for fresh, seasonal and unfussy cooking.

Peasant

240 St John St ✉ EC1V 4PH ⊖ Farringdon. – ✆ (020) 7336 7726 – www.thepeasant.co.uk – Closed 25 December to 2 January **19**UZD**e**

Rest – *(booking essential)* Menu £ 35 – Carte £ 18/38

♦ This handsome Victorian pub was at the vanguard of the gastropub movement. Busy bar with its tiles and mosaics; upstairs for a less frantic environment and wholesome British cooking.

Well

180 St John St ✉ EC1V 4JY ⊖ Farringdon. – ✆ (020) 7251 9363 – www.downthewell.com **19**UZD**x**

Rest – Carte £ 30/60

♦ Compact pub with sliding glass doors and popular pavement benches. Modern dishes range from potted shrimps to foie gras and chicken liver parfait. Classic puddings; splendid cheeses.

HIGHBURY

Au Lac

82 Highbury Park ✉ N5 2XE ⊖ Arsenal – ✆ (020) 7704 9187 **13**UZA**b**

Rest – Vietnamese – *(dinner only and lunch Thursday and Friday)* Carte £ 8/21

♦ Cosy Vietnamese restaurant, with brightly coloured walls and painted fans. Large menus with authentic dishes usefully highlighted. Fresh flavours; good value.

ISLINGTON

XX **Almeida**

30 Almeida St. ✉ N1 1AD ⊖ Angel – ✆ (020) 7354 4777 – www.almeida-restaurant.co.uk – Closed 26 December, 1 January, Sunday dinner and Monday lunch **13**UZB**r**

Rest – French – Menu £ 16/33 – Carte lunch £ 21/37

♦ Crisply decorated restaurant dating from 1891. Classically inspired menus with plenty of choice; good value lunch. Interesting French regional wines. Overwhelmingly busy pre/post theatre.

XX **Metrogusto**

13 Theberton St ✉ N1 0QY ⊖ Angel – ✆ (020) 7226 9400 – www.metrogusto.co.uk – Closed 25 December, 1 January, Monday and bank holidays **13**UZB**e**

Rest – Italian – *(dinner only and lunch Saturday-Sunday)* Menu £ 19 – Carte £ 24/33

♦ A gem amongst all the chain restaurants in Islington. Warm hospitality and competitively priced, seasonal and contemporary Italian cooking with daily specials. Lively, eye-catching artwork.

X **Ottolenghi**

287 Upper St. ✉ N1 2TZ ⊖ Highbury and Islington – ✆ (020) 7288 1454 – www.ottolenghi.co.uk – Closed 25-26 December, 1 January and Sunday dinner

Rest – Mediterranean – *(booking essential)* Carte £ 20/35 **13**UZB**k**

♦ This attractive deli morphs into a little restaurant at night, with communal tables and chatty service. Fresh, flavoursome dishes with influences from across all parts of the Med.

The Drapers Arms

44 Barnsbury St ✉ N1 1ER ⊖ Highbury and Islington. – ✆ (020) 7619 0348 – www.thedrapersarms.com **13**UZB**x**

Rest – British – Carte £ 22/29

♦ Handsome Georgian pub, revived and re-opened in 2009. The food is all about seasonality and flavour; 'proper' British dishes and less familiar cuts. Same menu in the bar and upstairs dining room.

Compass

58 Penton St ✉ N1 9PZ ⊖ Angel. – ✆ (020) 7837 3891 – www.thecompassn1.co.uk – Closed lunch Monday and Tuesday **13**UZB**b**

Rest – Carte £ 22/30

♦ Victorian pub rescued from a life of seedy anonymity and turned into a lively local known for its food. Plenty of accurately cooked British pub classics alongside others of more European provenance.

Barnsbury

209-211 Liverpool Rd ✉ N1 1LX ⊖ Highbury and Islington. – ✆ (020) 7607 5519 – www.thebarnsbury.co.uk – Closed 24-26 December, 1 January and Monday lunch **13**UZB**v**

Rest – Carte £ 25/35

♦ Expect generous portions of gutsy cooking at this genuine neighbourhood pub, with friendly and attentive service. Sit in the more atmospheric bar rather than in the dining area at the back.

Northgate

113 Southgate Rd ✉ N1 3JS ⊖ Dalston Kingsland (rail). – ✆ (020) 7359 7392 – Closed 25 December **13**VZB**a**

Rest – *(dinner only and lunch Saturday and Sunday)* Carte £ 20/27

♦ Cavernous corner pub; busy front bar with tables laid for dining at the back. Large blackboard menu lists mostly Mediterranean-influenced dishes with the emphasis on flavour. Relaxed service.

LONDON

King's Cross

Fellow

24 York Way ✉ N1 9AA ⊖ King's Cross. – ✆ (020) 7833 4395 – www.thefellow.co.uk – Closed Sunday dinner **12**SZB**x**

Rest – Modern European – Carte £ 27/32

♦ Busy, atmospheric pub close to the station with a youthful, local clientele. Confident cooking on the ground floor displays a lightness of touch; boisterous upstairs cocktail bar.

KENSINGTON and CHELSEA (Royal Borough of) – Greater London – pop. 158 439 **12** B3

Chelsea

Jumeirah Carlton Tower

Cadogan Pl. ✉ SW1X 9PY ⊖ Knightsbridge – ✆ (020) 7235 1234 – www.jumeirah.com **37**AGX**v**

190 rm – †£ 264/750 ††£ 264/750, ☕ £ 37 – 30 suites

Rest *Rib Room* – Menu £ 30 (lunch) – Carte approx. £ 63

♦ Imposing international hotel overlooking a leafy square. Well-equipped rooftop health club has great views. Generously proportioned rooms boast every conceivable facility. Rib Room restaurant has a clubby atmosphere.

Wyndham Grand

Chelsea Harbour ✉ SW10 0XG ⊖ Imperial Wharf – ✆ (020) 7823 3000 – www.wyndhamgrandlondon.co.uk **23**PZG**k**

158 suites – ††£ 219, ☕ £ 24 **Rest** – Menu £ 25/30 – Carte £ 35/41

♦ Modern, all-suite hotel within an exclusive marina and retail development. Many of the spacious and well-appointed rooms have balconies and views across the Thames. Modern restaurant overlooks the harbour.

Sheraton Park Tower

101 Knightsbridge ✉ SW1X 7RN ⊖ Knightsbridge – ✆ (020) 7235 8050 – www.luxurycollection.com/parktowerlondon – Closed 25-26 December and 1 January **37**AGX**t**

275 rm – †£ 570 ††£ 570, ☕ £ 25 – 5 suites

Rest *One-O-One* – see restaurant listing

♦ Built in the 1970s in a unique cylindrical shape. Well-equipped bedrooms are all identical in size. Top floor executive rooms have commanding views of Hyde Park and City.

The Capital

22-24 Basil St. ✉ SW3 1AT ⊖ Knightsbridge – ✆ (020) 7589 5171 – www.capitalhotel.co.uk **37**AFX**a**

49 rm – †£ 276/366 ††£ 366, ☕ £ 19.50 – 8 suites

Rest – *(booking essential)* Menu £ 35 (lunch) – Carte £ 48/66

♦ In 2011, this thoroughly British hotel celebrates 40 years under the same private ownership. Immaculately kept bedrooms, a discreet atmosphere and conscientious, attentive service are the hallmarks. Elegant and formal dining offers a menu of classic British dishes.

Draycott without rest

26 Cadogan Gdns ✉ SW3 2RP ⊖ Sloane Square – ✆ (020) 7730 6466 – www.draycotthotel.com **37**AGY**c**

35 rm – †£ 156/312 ††£ 251/312, ☕ £ 20.95 – 11 suites

♦ Charming, discreet 19C house with elegant sitting room overlooking tranquil garden for afternoon tea. Bedrooms are individually decorated in a country house style and are named after writers or actors.

The Cadogan

75 Sloane St ✉ SW1X 9SG ⊖ Knightsbridge – ✆ (020) 7235 7141 – www.cadogan.com **37**AGY**b**

63 rm – †£ 275/325 ††£ 325, ☕ £ 22.50

Rest *Langtry's* – *(closed Sunday dinner)* Menu £ 20 – Carte £ 31/46

♦ An Edwardian townhouse, made famous by two former residents – Oscar Wilde and Lillie Langtry. Quiet drawing room for afternoon tea; bedrooms are varied and comfortable. Discreet restaurant; traditional menu.

LONDON

Knightsbridge
10 Beaufort Gdns ✉ SW3 1PT ⊖ Knightsbridge – ✆ (020) 7584 6300 – www.knightsbridgehotel.com **37**AFX**s**
44 rm – †£ 204 ††£ 372, ☕ £ 17.50
Rest – *(room service only)*
♦ Attractively furnished townhouse with a very stylish, discreet feel. Every bedroom is immaculately appointed and has an individuality of its own; fine detailing throughout.

Egerton House
17-19 Egerton Ter. ✉ SW3 2BX ⊖ South Kensington – ✆ (020) 7589 2412 – www.egertonhousehotel.com **37**AFY**e**
27 rm – †£ 282/318 ††£ 306/390, ☕ £ 25 – 1 suite
Rest – *(room service only)* Carte £ 35/55
♦ Discreet, compact but comfortable townhouse in a good location, recently refurbished throughout and owned by Red Carnation group. High levels of personal service make the hotel stand out.

The Levin
28 Basil St. ✉ SW3 1AS ⊖ Knightsbridge – ✆ (020) 7589 6286 – www.thelevinhotel.co.uk **37**AFX**c**
12 rm ☕ – †£ 342 ††£ 438
Rest ***Le Metro*** – *(closed Sunday dinner)* Menu £ 20 – Carte £ 22/35
♦ Impressive façade, contemporary interior and comfortable bedrooms in subtle art deco style, boasting marvellous champagne mini bars. Sister to The Capital hotel. Informal brasserie includes blackboard menu and pies of the week.

Beaufort without rest
33 Beaufort Gdns ✉ SW3 1PP ⊖ Knightsbridge – ✆ (020) 7584 5252 – www.thebeaufort.co.uk **37**AFX**n**
29 rm – †£ 173/253 ††£ 322/334, ☕ £ 19.50
♦ A vast collection of English floral watercolours adorn this 19C townhouse in a useful location. Modern and co-ordinated rooms. Tariff includes all drinks and afternoon tea.

Sydney House without rest
9-11 Sydney St. ✉ SW3 6PU ⊖ South Kensington – ✆ (020) 7376 7711 – www.sydneyhousechelsea.com – Closed 25-29 December **36**ADY**s**
21 rm – †£ 145/215 ††£ 175/295, ☕ £ 10.95
♦ Stylish, discreet and compact Georgian townhouse made brighter through mirrors and light wood. Thoughtfully designed bedrooms; Room 43 has its own terrace. Part of Abode group.

The Sloane Square
7-12 Sloane Sq. ✉ SW1W 8EG ⊖ Sloane Square – ✆ (020) 7896 9988 – www.sloanesquarehotel.co.uk – Closed Christmas **37**AGY**k**
102 rm – †£ 187/310 ††£ 332, ☕ £ 6.50
Rest ***Chelsea Brasserie*** – see restaurant listing
♦ Red-brick hotel opened in 2007, boasts bright, contemporary décor. Stylish, co-ordinated bedrooms, with laptops; library of DVDs and games available. Rooms at back slightly quieter.

XXXX ✿✿✿ **Gordon Ramsay**
68-69 Royal Hospital Rd. ✉ SW3 4HP ⊖ Sloane Square – ✆ (020) 7352 4441 – www.gordonramsay.com – Closed Christmas, Saturday and Sunday
Rest – French – *(booking essential)* Menu £ 45/90 **37**AFZ**c**
Spec. Butter poached lobster with morels, asparagus and wild garlic. Pigeon with polenta, shallots, beetroot and date sauce. Strawberry and lemon balm Eton mess with vanilla ice cream wafer.
♦ Head Chef Clare Smyth has brought a lighter, more instinctive style to the cooking while still delivering on the Gordon Ramsay classics. The elegant simplicity of the room exudes calmness; service is equally composed and well-organised.

XXX **Tom Aikens** A/C VISA MC AE
✿ *43 Elystan St. ✉ SW3 3NT ⊖ South Kensington – ✆ (020) 7584 2003 – www.tomaikens.co.uk – Closed 24-29 December, 1-3 January, Saturday lunch, Sunday and bank holidays* **37**AFY**n**
Rest – Innovative – Carte £ 53/89
Spec. Sheep's cheese gazpacho with chervil cannelloni and honey. Lamb with aligot potato and anchovy beignet. Truffle and vanilla panna cotta with black pepper and white chocolate.
♦ Neat and elegant dining room, with well co-ordinated service. Seasonal ingredients, largely from the British Isles, are used in dishes that show plenty of originality and skill, with fish the kitchen's strength.

XXX **Bibendum** A/C VISA MC AE
Michelin House, 81 Fulham Rd. ✉ SW3 6RD ⊖ South Kensington – ✆ (020) 7581 5817 – www.bibendum.co.uk – Closed 24-26 December and 1 January
Rest – French – Menu £ 30 – Carte £ 40/61 **37**AEY**s**
♦ Has maintained a loyal following for over 20 years, with its French food that comes with a British accent. Located on the 1st floor of a London landmark – Michelin's former HQ, dating from 1911.

LONDON

XXX **Fifth Floor** – at Harvey Nichols A/C VISA MC AE
109-125 Knightsbridge ✉ SW1X 7RJ ⊖ Knightsbridge – ✆ (020) 7235 5250 – www.harveynichols.com – Closed Sunday dinner **37**AGX**s**
Rest – Modern European – Menu £ 25/40
♦ Modern cooking with influences kept mostly from within Europe. Stylish and elegant, tent-like room with sophisticated bar attached; reached via its own elevator. Prompt service.

XXX **Toto's** VISA MC AE
Walton House, Walton St ✉ SW3 2JH ⊖ Knightsbridge – ✆ (020) 7589 0075 – Closed 25-27 December **37**AFY**x**
Rest – Italian – *(booking essential at dinner)* Menu £ 27 (lunch) – Carte £ 33/51
♦ A long standing Chelsea institution, with old school service and plenty of local regulars who add to the discreet atmosphere. Familiar and satisfying dishes, with homemade pasta the highlight.

XXX **Awana** A/C VISA MC AE
85 Sloane Ave. ✉ SW3 3DX ⊖ South Kensington – ✆ (020) 7584 8880 – www.awana.co.uk – Closed 25 December and 1 January **37**AFY**b**
Rest – Malaysian – *(booking essential)* Menu £ 15 (lunch) – Carte £ 27/54
♦ Smart and stylish restaurant showcasing Malaysia's rich culinary diversity. The 'Malaysian Journey' menu provides a good introduction. If without a booking, consider sitting at the Satay Bar.

XXX **Chutney Mary** A/C VISA MC AE
535 King's Rd. ✉ SW10 0SZ ⊖ Fulham Broadway – ✆ (020) 7351 3113 – www.realindianfood.com – Closed dinner 25 December **22**OZG**v**
Rest – Indian – *(dinner only and lunch Saturday-Sunday)* Menu £ 22 – Carte £ 37/47
♦ Soft lighting and sepia etchings hold sway at this forever popular restaurant. Extensive menu of specialities from all corners of India. Complementary wine list.

XXX **One-O-One** – at Sheraton Park Tower Hotel A/C VISA MC AE
101 Knightsbridge ✉ SW1X 7RN ⊖ Knightsbridge – ✆ (020) 7290 7101 – www.oneoonerestaurant.com **37**AGX**t**
Rest – Seafood – Menu £ 19/42 – Carte £ 50/66
♦ Smart ground floor restaurant; lacking a little in atmosphere but the seafood is good. Much of the produce from Brittany and Norway; don't miss the King crab legs. Small tasting plates also offered.

A red **Rest** mention denotes an establishment with an award for culinary excellence, ✿ (star) or ☺ (Bib Gourmand).

XX **Rasoi** (Vineet Bhatia)
10 Lincoln St. ✉ SW3 2TS ⊖ Sloane Square – ✆ (020) 7225 1881 – www.rasoirestaurant.co.uk – Closed Saturday lunch **37**AFY**y**
Rest – Indian – Menu £ 26 (lunch) – Carte £ 58/83
Spec. Seafood medley with soft-shell crab chutney and gun powder prawn. Charcoal roasted lamb chops with chilli and roasted peanut khichdi. Spiced caramelised pineapple.
◆ Innovative and creative Indian cuisine in the incongruous setting of a typical Chelsea townhouse. Ring the doorbell and you'll be greeted by an exotic aroma that hints of what's to follow.

XX **Le Colombier**
145 Dovehouse St. ✉ SW3 6LB ⊖ South Kensington – ✆ (020) 7351 1155 – www.le-colombier-restaurant.co.uk **36**ADZ**e**
Rest – French – Menu £ 26 (lunch) – Carte £ 31/50
◆ Proudly Gallic corner restaurant in an affluent residential area. Attractive enclosed terrace. Bright and cheerful surroundings and service of traditional French cooking.

XX **Racine**
239 Brompton Rd ✉ SW3 2EP ⊖ South Kensington – ✆ (020) 7584 4477 – www.racine-restaurant.com – Closed 25 December **37**AEY**t**
Rest – French – Menu £ 18/20 – Carte £ 28/44
◆ An authentic feel to this French brasserie, with dark leather seats, wood floors and mirrors. The menu provides a roll-call of classic regional specialities, from steak tartare to fruits de mer.

XX **Daphne's**
112 Draycott Ave. ✉ SW3 3AE ⊖ South Kensington – ✆ (020) 7589 4257 – www.daphnes-restaurant.co.uk – Closed 25-26 December and 1 January
Rest – Italian – *(booking essential)* Menu £ 19 (lunch and early dinner) – Carte £ 29/48 **37**AFY**j**
◆ Established over 40 years ago and a Chelsea institution with 'celebrity' following. Reliable formula of tired and tested Italian classics in a room with a warm, Tuscan feel.

XX **Poissonnerie de l'Avenue**
82 Sloane Ave. ✉ SW3 3DZ ⊖ South Kensington – ✆ (020) 7589 2457 – www.poissonneriedelavenue.com – Closed 24-26 December **37**AFY**u**
Rest – Seafood – Menu £ 28 (lunch) – Carte £ 25/39
◆ A smart, personally run, wood-panelled Chelsea institution since 1946. Its extensive choice of carefully prepared, traditional seafood dishes attracts a smart and loyal following.

XX **Caraffini**
61-63 Lower Sloane St. ✉ SW1W 8DH ⊖ Sloane Square – ✆ (020) 7259 0235 – www.caraffini.co.uk – Closed 25 December, Easter, Sunday and bank holidays
Rest – Italian – *(booking essential)* Carte £ 23/41 **37**AGZ**a**
◆ The omnipresent and ebullient owner oversees the friendly service in this attractive neighbourhood restaurant. Authentic and robust Italian cooking; informal atmosphere.

XX **Eight over Eight**
392 King's Rd ✉ SW3 5UZ ⊖ Gloucester Road – ✆ (020) 7349 9934 – www.rickerrestaurants.com – Closed Sunday lunch **23**PZG**n**
Rest – Asian – Menu £ 17 – Carte £ 28/39
◆ Reopened in 2010 after a fire, with a slightly plusher feel; still as popular as ever with the fashionable crowds. Influences stretch across South East Asia and dishes are designed for sharing.

XX **Bluebird**
350 King's Rd. ✉ SW3 5UU ⊖ Sloane Square – ✆ (020) 7559 1000 – www.bluebirdchelsea.com **23**PZG**n**
Rest – British – Menu £ 21 – Carte £ 26/73
◆ Former industrial space incorporates everything from a wine store to a private members club. Large, buzzy restaurant champions British produce in an appealing menu that has something for everyone.

XX **Le Cercle**

1 Wilbraham Pl ✉ SW1X 9AE ⊖ Sloane Square – ✆ (020) 7901 9999 – www.lecercle.co.uk – Closed Christmas - New Year, Sunday and Monday

Rest – French – Menu £ 20/35 – Carte £ 20/35 **37**AGY**e**

◆ Deep basement location made into a fashionable spot, with drapes and high ceilings; comes alive more at dinner. Order three or four small plates of the delicate French cooking per person.

XX **Painted Heron**

112 Cheyne Walk ✉ SW10 0DJ ⊖ Gloucester Road – ✆ (020) 7351 5232 – www.thepaintedheron.com – closed 25 December, 1 January **23**PZG**d**

Rest – Indian – *(dinner only and lunch Saturday-Sunday)* Menu £ 35 (dinner) – Carte £ 31/42

◆ Well-supported locally and quite formally run Indian restaurant. Nooks and crannies create an intimate atmosphere. Fish and game dishes are the highlight of the contemporary cooking.

XX **Marco**

Stamford Bridge, Fulham Rd. ✉ SW6 1HS ⊖ Fulham Broadway – ✆ (020) 7915 2929 – www.marcorestaurant.org – Closed 24 July-8 August, Sunday and Monday except match days **22**OZG**c**

Rest – Traditional – *(dinner only)* Menu £ 22/45 – Carte £ 35/59

◆ Marco Pierre White's restaurant at Chelsea Football Club offers an appealing range of classics, from British favourites to satisfying French and Italian fare. Comfortable and well-run room.

XX **Carpaccio**

4 Sydney St. ✉ SW3 6PP ⊖ South Kensington – ✆ (020) 7352 3435 – www.carpacciorestaurant.co.uk – Closed Christmas, Sunday, Monday lunch and bank holidays **36**ADY**e**

Rest – Italian – Carte £ 26/42

◆ Lively local Italian with an animated service crew; blokey decoration courtesy of stills from Bond movies and Ayrton Senna's cockpit. All-encompassing menu ranges from pizza to carpaccio.

XX **Good Earth**

233 Brompton Rd. ✉ SW3 2EP ⊖ Knightsbridge – ✆ (020) 7584 3658 – www.goodearthgroup.co.uk – Closed 23-31 December **37**AFY**h**

Rest – Chinese – Menu £ 14/30 – Carte £ 28/37

◆ The basement is busier and more popular than the ground floor. Extensive menu makes good use of quality ingredients and offers appealing choice between classic and more unusual dishes.

XX **The Botanist**

7 Sloane Sq ✉ SW1W 8EE ⊖ Sloane Square – ✆ (020) 7730 0077 – www.thebotanistonsloanesquare.com – Closed 25-26 December, Saturday, Sunday and bank holidays **37**AGY**r**

Rest – Modern European – Menu £ 29 – Carte £ 26/33

◆ Pass through the busy bar to get to the stylish and comfortable restaurant with its warm and vibrant atmosphere. Appealing and accessible menu delivers unfussy and satisfying dishes.

XX **Chelsea Brasserie** – at The Sloane Square Hotel

7-12 Sloane Sq. ✉ SW1W 8EG ⊖ Sloane Square – ✆ (020) 7896 9988 – www.sloanesquarehotel.co.uk – Closed Christmas **37**AGY**k**

Rest – French – *(closed Sunday dinner)* Menu £ 25 (weekday dinner) – Carte £ 34/40

◆ You pass through the busy bar to get to the smartly lit brasserie, with exposed brick, mirrors and tiles. Cooking has a strong French base. Good value theatre menu and brisk service.

X **Bibendum Oyster Bar** VISA MC AE

Michelin House, 81 Fulham Rd. ✉ *SW3 6RD* ⊖ *South Kensington – ✆ (020) 7589 1480 – www.bibendum.co.uk – Closed 24-26 December and 1 January*

Rest – Seafood – *(bookings not accepted)* Carte £ 20/33 **37**AEY**s**

◆ Oysters, potted shrimps and a shared plateau de fruits de mer are the highlights at this continental-style café, with its mosaic floor and colourful ceramic tiles. Wine list includes 460ml pots.

X **Foxtrot Oscar** AC VISA MC AE

79 Royal Hospital Rd. ✉ *SW3 4HN* ⊖ *Sloane Square – ✆ (020) 7352 4448 – www.gordonramsay.com – Closed 25 December* **37**AFZ**v**

Rest – Traditional – *(booking essential)* Menu £ 22 (lunch) – Carte £ 25/37

◆ Gordon Ramsay's least known restaurant has a relaxed, local feel and is decorated with burgundy walls and photos. Bistro cooking, with the Foxtrot Burger being a highlight.

X **Manicomio** AC VISA MC AE

85 Duke of York Sq., King's Rd. ✉ *SW3 4LY* ⊖ *Sloane Square – ✆ (020) 7730 3366 – www.manicomio.co.uk – Closed 25-26 December and 1 January*

Rest – Italian – Carte £ 34/40 **37**AGY**x**

◆ Modern, busy Italian, popular with shoppers and visitors to the Saatchi Gallery; the simplest dishes are the best ones. The terrific terrace fills quickly. Next door is their café and deli.

LONDON

X **Aubaine** AC VISA MC AE DC

260-262 Brompton Rd. ✉ *SW3 2AS* ⊖ *South Kensington – ✆ (020) 7052 0100 – www.aubaine.co.uk – Closed 25 December* **37**AEY**c**

Rest – French – Carte £ 28/41

◆ 'Boulangerie, patisserie, restaurant'. Pass the bakery aromas to an all-day eatery with 'distressed' country feel. Well-judged menus range from croque monsieur to coq au vin.

X **Tom's Kitchen** VISA MC AE

27 Cale St. ✉ *SW3 3QP* ⊖ *South Kensington – ✆ (020) 7349 0202 – www.tomskitchen.co.uk – Closed 25-26 December* **37**AFZ**b**

Rest – French – Carte £ 34/60

◆ A converted pub, whose white tiles and mirrors help to give it an industrial feel. Appealing and wholesome dishes come in man-sized portions. The eponymous Tom is Tom Aikens.

Admiral Codrington AC VISA MC AE

17 Mossop St ✉ *SW3 2LY* ⊖ *South Kensington. – ✆ (020) 7581 0005 – www.theadmiralcodrington.com* **37**AFY**v**

Rest – Carte £ 24/30

◆ A Chelsea institution, with popular bar in the evenings and a separate, smart restaurant with retractable roof. The menu covers all bases and mixes British classics with European influences.

Chelsea Ram AC VISA MC

32 Burnaby St ✉ *SW10 0PL* ⊖ *Fulham Broadway. – ✆ (020) 7351 4008 – Closed Sunday dinner* **23**PZG**r**

Rest – Carte £ 18/30

◆ A warm, welcoming and relaxed pub surrounded by residential streets, with a loyal local following. Expect proper 'pub grub' where the portions are generous and the prices fair.

Cadogan Arms AC VISA MC AE

298 King's Rd ✉ *SW3 5UG* ⊖ *South Kensington. – ✆ (020) 7352 6500 – www.thecadoganarmschelsea.com – Closed 25-26 December* **36**ADZ**y**

Rest – *(booking advisable at dinner)* Carte £ 24/37

◆ Part of the Martin Brothers bourgeoning pub group. This is a proper pub, with billiard tables upstairs and a gusty, full-on menu. Stuffed and mounted animals stare down as you eat.

Builders Arms

13 Britten St ✉ SW3 3TY ⊖ South Kensington. – ✆ (020) 7349 9040 – www.geronimo-inns.co.uk – Closed 25-26 December **37**AFZ**x**

Rest – *(bookings not accepted)* Carte £ 25/30

♦ Lively and busy pub, popular with the locals. Rustic and satisfying cooking, with blackboard daily specials; the popular peri-peri chicken dish is for sharing. Regular wine promotions.

Pig's Ear

35 Old Church St ✉ SW3 5BS ⊖ Sloane Square. – ✆ (020) 7352 2908 – www.thepigsear.com – Closed 2 weeks at Christmas and Sunday dinner

Rest – Carte £ 22/35 **23**PZG**v**

♦ Honest pub, with rough-and-ready ground floor bar for lunch; more intimate, wood-panelled upstairs dining room for dinner. Robust, confident and satisfying cooking with a classical bent.

LONDON

Phoenix

23 Smith St ✉ SW3 4EE ⊖ Sloane Square. – ✆ (020) 7730 9182 – www.geronimo-inns.co.uk – Closed 25-26 December **37**AFZ**a**

Rest – Carte £ 23/30

♦ Friendly, conscientiously run Chelsea local, where satisfying and carefully prepared pub classics are served in the roomy, civilised bar or in the warm, comfortable dining room at the back.

Lots Road Pub & Dining Room

114 Lots Rd ✉ SW10 0RJ ⊖ Fulham Broadway. – ✆ (020) 7352 6645 – www.lotsroadpub.com **23**PZG**b**

Rest – Carte £ 20/31

♦ Lively semicircular shaped pub, close to Chelsea Harbour. Hearty and satisfying classics, from mussels to Perthshire côte de boeuf and a tart of the day. Service keeps it bright and cheery.

Earl's Court

K + K George

1-15 Templeton Pl. ✉ SW5 9NB ⊖ Earl's Court – ✆ (020) 7598 8700 – www.kkhotels.com **35**AAY**s**

154 rm ☕ – 🚹£ 264 🚹🚹£ 264/336 **Rest** – Carte £ 23/34

♦ Five converted 19C houses overlooking large rear garden. Scandinavian-style rooms with low beds, white walls and light wood furniture. Breakfast room has the garden view. Informal dining in the bar.

Twenty Nevern Square without rest

20 Nevern Sq. ✉ SW5 9PD ⊖ Earl's Court – ✆ (020) 7565 9555 – www.twentynevernsquare.co.uk **35**AAY**u**

20 rm – 🚹£ 119/156 🚹🚹£ 167/215, ☕ £ 10

♦ In an attractive Victorian garden square, an individually designed, privately owned townhouse. Original pieces of furniture and some rooms with their own terrace.

Mayflower without rest

26-28 Trebovir Rd. ✉ SW5 9NJ ⊖ Earl's Court – ✆ (020) 7370 0991 – www.mayflowerhotel.co.uk **35**ABY**x**

43 rm – 🚹£ 107/144 🚹🚹£ 138/180, ☕ £ 10 – 4 suites

♦ Conveniently placed, friendly establishment with a secluded rear breakfast terrace and basement breakfast room. Individually styled rooms with Asian influence.

Amsterdam without rest

7-9 Trebovir Rd. ✉ SW5 9LS ⊖ Earl's Court – ✆ (020) 7370 2814 – www.amsterdam-hotel.com **35**ABY**c**

19 rm – 🚹£ 96/125 🚹🚹£ 118/128 – 8 suites

♦ Basement breakfast room and a small secluded garden. The brightly decorated bedrooms are light and airy. Some have smart wood floors; some boast their own balcony.

Rushmore without rest
11 Trebovir Rd. ✉ SW5 9LS ⊖ Earl's Court – ☎ (020) 7370 3839 – www.rushmore-hotel.co.uk **35**ABY**a**
22 rm – †£ 71/96 ††£ 90/152
◆ Behind its Victorian façade lies an hotel popular with tourists. Individually decorated bedrooms in a variety of shapes and sizes. Piazza-style conservatory breakfast room.

Langan's Coq d'Or
254-260 Old Brompton Rd. ✉ SW5 9HR ⊖ Earl's Court – ☎ (020) 7259 2599 – www.langansrestaurants.co.uk – Closed 25-26 December **35**ABZ**e**
Rest – Traditional – Menu £ 27
◆ Sit in the glass-enclosed front section which opens onto the street in summer or in the warm main room whose walls are covered with pictures and photos. A menu of satisfying brasserie classics.

KENSINGTON

Royal Garden rm,
2-24 Kensington High St. ✉ W8 4PT ⊖ High Street Kensington – ☎ (020) 7937 8000 – www.royalgardenhotel.co.uk **35**ABX**c**
374 rm – †£ 215/310 ††£ 263/335, ☕ £ 21.50 – 22 suites
Rest *Min Jiang* – see restaurant listing
Rest *Park Terrace* – ☎ (020) 7361 0602 – Menu £ 20/31 – Carte £ 22/33
◆ A tall, modern hotel with many of its rooms enjoying enviable views over the adjacent Kensington Gardens. All the modern amenities and services, with well-drilled staff. Bright, spacious Park Terrace offers British, Asian and modern European cuisine.

The Milestone
1-2 Kensington Ct. ✉ W8 5DL ⊖ High Street Kensington – ☎ (020) 7917 1000 – www.milestonehotel.com **35**ABX**u**
57 rm – †£ 282/336 ††£ 318/372, ☕ £ 29 – 6 suites
Rest *Cheneston's* – *(booking essential for non-residents)* Menu £ 27 – Carte £ 29/78
◆ Elegant hotel with decorative Victorian façade and English feel. Charming oak-panelled lounge and snug bar. Meticulously decorated bedrooms with period detail. Panelled dining room with charming little oratory for privacy seekers.

Baglioni
60 Hyde Park Gate ✉ SW7 5BB ⊖ High Street Kensington – ☎ (020) 7368 5700 – www.baglionihotels.com **36**ACX**e**
52 rm – †£ 335/474 ††£ 384/474, ☕ £ 28 – 15 suites
Rest *Brunello* – ☎ (020) 7368 5900 – Menu £ 22/27 – Carte £ 46/61
◆ Opposite Kensington Palace, this hotel boasts an ornate interior and a trendy basement bar. Small gym/sauna. Stylish bedrooms come in cool shades and boast impressive facilities. Restaurant specialises in rustic Italian cooking.

Launceston Place
1a Launceston Pl. ✉ W8 5RL ⊖ Gloucester Road – ☎ (020) 7937 6912 – www.launcestonplace-restaurant.co.uk – Closed 25 December, 1 January, Monday lunch and bank holidays **36**ACX**a**
Rest – Modern European – Menu £ 20/48
◆ Relaunched and reinvigorated, with dark walls and moody lighting, but still with that local feel. Cooking is original and deftly executed and uses ingredients largely from the British Isles.

Belvedere
Holland House, off Abbotsbury Rd. ✉ W8 6LU ⊖ Holland Park – ☎ (020) 7602 1238 – www.belvedererestaurant.co.uk – Closed 1 January **16**MZE**u**
Rest – French – Menu £ 20 (lunch) – Carte £ 28/44
◆ Former 19C orangery in a delightful position in the middle of the park. On two floors with a bar and balcony terrace. Huge vases of flowers. Modern take on classic dishes.

XXX **Min Jiang** – at Royal Garden Hotel

Royal Garden Hotel, 10th Floor, 2-24 Kensington High St. ✉ W8 4PT
⊖ High Street Kensington – ☎ (020) 7361 1988 – www.minjiang.co.uk
Rest – Chinese – Menu £ 15/48 – Carte £ 34/119 **35**ABX**c**

◆ A comfortable Chinese restaurant looking down over Kensington Gardens from its 10th floor location. Most provinces of China are represented on the menu but the main speciality is the Beijing duck.

XX **Kitchen W8**

11-13 Abingdon Rd. ✉ W8 6AH ⊖ High Street Kensington – ☎ (020) 7937 0120 – www.kitchenw8.com – Closed bank holidays **35**AAX**a**
Rest – Modern European – Menu £ 20 (lunch) – Carte £ 32/41
Spec. Smoked eel and mackerel with sweet mustard dressing. Cod with Parmesan gnocchi and girolles. Salted chocolate parfait with honeycomb ice cream.

◆ Smart, comfortable restaurant which is not as casual as its name implies, but which does have a pleasant, neighbourhood feel. Skilled kitchen produces balanced dishes free of showiness, with the emphasis on flavour.

XX **Babylon** – at The Roof Gardens

99 Kensington High St (entrance on Derry St) ✉ W8 5SA
⊖ High Street Kensington – ☎ (020) 7368 3993 – www.roofgardens.virgin.com – Closed 25-30 December and Sunday dinner **35**ABX**n**
Rest – Modern European – Menu £ 22 (lunch) – Carte £ 44/56

◆ Situated on the roof of this pleasant London building affording attractive views of the London skyline. Stylish modern décor in keeping with the contemporary, British cooking.

XX **Clarke's**

124 Kensington Church St. ✉ W8 4BH ⊖ Notting Hill Gate – ☎ (020) 7221 9225 – www.sallyclarke.com – Closed Christmas, Sunday dinner and bank holidays
Rest – Modern European – Menu £ 40 (dinner) – Carte £ 37/41 **27**ABV**c**

◆ Forever popular restaurant, now serving a choice of dishes boasting trademark fresh, seasonal ingredients and famed lightness of touch. Loyal following for over 20 years.

XX **Zaika**

1 Kensington High St ✉ W8 5NP ⊖ High Street Kensington – ☎ (020) 7795 6533 – www.zaika-restaurant.co.uk – Closed 25-26 December, 1-2 January and Monday lunch **35**ABX**r**
Rest – Indian – Menu £ 25 (lunch) – Carte £ 31/48

◆ A converted bank, sympathetically restored, with original features and Indian artefacts adding plenty of colour. Well-organised service of modern and quite innovative Indian dishes.

XX **Whits**

21 Abingdon Rd. ✉ W8 6AH ⊖ High Street Kensington – ☎ (020) 7938 1122 – www.whits.co.uk – Closed Christmas, New Year, Sunday and Monday
Rest – Modern European – Menu £ 19/24 – Carte dinner £ 31/39 **35**AAX**d**

◆ Run by friendly owner. Bar runs length of lower level. Most diners migrate upstairs with its modish artwork and intimate tables. Modern cooking with generous portions.

XX **Memories of China**

353 Kensington High St ✉ W8 6NW ⊖ High Street Kensington – ☎ (020) 7603 6951 – www.memoriesofchinaken.co.uk – Closed 25-26 December and 1 January **35**AAY**v**
Rest – Chinese – *(booking essential)* Menu £ 20 – Carte £ 32/59

◆ Subtle lighting and brightly coloured high-back chairs add to the modern feel of this Chinese restaurant. Screens separate the tables. Plenty of choice from extensive menu.

Take note of the classification: you should not expect the same level of service in a X or 🏠 as in a XXXXX or 🏠🏠🏠🏠.

XX **Timo** A/C VISA MC AE

343 Kensington High St. ✉ W8 6NW ⊖ High Street Kensington – ✆ (020) 7603 3888 – www.timorestaurant.net – Closed Christmas, Sunday and bank holidays **35**AAY**c**

Rest – Italian – Menu £ 14 (lunch and early dinner) – Carte £ 30/44

♦ Modern, personally run restaurant with unadorned walls and comfortable seating in brown suede banquettes. Italian menus of contemporary dishes and daily changing specials.

X **Kensington Place** A/C VISA MC AE

201-209 Kensington Church St. ✉ W8 7LX ⊖ Notting Hill Gate – ✆ (020) 7727 3184 – www.kensingtonplace-restaurant.co.uk **27**AAV**z**

Rest – Modern European – Menu £ 19/23

♦ Opened in 1987 as a big, boisterous, brasserie; these days a little less noisy but it remains well run. Competitively priced set menu offers a wide choice of modern European dishes.

X **Cibo** VISA MC AE

3 Russell Gdns ✉ W14 8EZ ⊖ Kensington Olympia – ✆ (020) 7371 6271 – www.ciborestaurant.net – Closed 1 week Christmas, Sunday dinner and bank holidays **16**MZE**b**

Rest – Italian – Carte £ 23/37

♦ Long-standing neighbourhood Italian with local following. More space at the back of the room. Robust, satisfying cooking; the huge grilled shellfish and seafood platter a speciality.

X **Malabar** A/C VISA MC AE

27 Uxbridge St. ✉ W8 7TQ ⊖ Notting Hill Gate – ✆ (020) 7727 8800 – www.malabar-restaurant.co.uk – Closed 24-27 December **27**AAV**e**

Rest – Indian – *(buffet lunch Sunday)* Menu £ 23 **s** – Carte £ 19/33 **s**

♦ Opened in 1983 in a residential street, but keeps up its appearance, remaining fresh and good-looking. Balanced menu of carefully prepared and well-priced Indian dishes, including excellent breads. Courteous service.

X **Wódka** VISA MC AE

12 St Albans Grove ✉ W8 5PN ⊖ High Street Kensington – ✆ (020) 7937 6513 – www.wodka.co.uk **35**ABX**c**

Rest – Polish – *(dinner only and lunch Wednesday-Friday)* Menu £ 18 (lunch and early dinner) – Carte £ 23/33

♦ Warmly run, long-standing neighbourhood Polish restaurant. Robust and satisfying dishes, with plenty of game, alongside heartening soups; but desserts also reveal a lightness of touch.

North Kensington

The Portobello without rest VISA MC AE

22 Stanley Gdns. ✉ W11 2NG ⊖ Notting Hill Gate – ✆ (020) 7727 2777 – www.portobellohotel.co.uk – Closed Christmas **16**NZE**n**

21 rm – †£ 168 ††£ 228, ☕ £ 17

♦ An attractive Victorian townhouse in an elegant terrace. Original and theatrical décor. Circular beds, half-testers, Victorian baths: no two bedrooms are the same.

XXX **The Ledbury** A/C VISA MC AE

✿✿ *127 Ledbury Rd. ✉ W11 2AQ ⊖ Notting Hill Gate – ✆ (020) 7792 9090 – www.theledbury.com – Closed 24-26 December, August bank holiday and Monday lunch* **27**AAT**a**

Rest – French – Menu £ 28/65

Spec. Scallop ceviche with seaweed and horseradish. Roe deer baked in Douglas Fir with beetroot and bone marrow. Honey and gingerbread soufflé with thyme ice cream.

♦ Elegant, understated surroundings with professional, well-organised service but it still has a neighbourhood feel. Highly skilled kitchen with an inherent understanding of flavour; great ingredients, especially game in season.

LONDON

XX **Notting Hill Brasserie**
92 Kensington Park Rd ✉ W11 2PN ⊖ Notting Hill Gate – ✆ (020) 7229 4481 – www.nottinghillbrasserie.com **27**AAU**a**
Rest – French – Menu £ 24/27 – Carte £ 40/53
♦ Modern, comfortable restaurant with quiet, formal atmosphere, set over four small rooms. Authentic African artwork on walls. Contemporary dishes with European influence.

XX **Edera**
148 Holland Park Ave. ✉ W11 4UE ⊖ Holland Park – ✆ (020) 7221 6090 – www.londonfinediningroup.com – Closed Christmas and Easter **16**MZE**n**
Rest – Italian – Carte £ 36/46
♦ Warm and comfortable neighbourhood restaurant with plenty of local regulars and efficient, well-marshalled service. Robust cooking has a subtle Sardinian accent and comes in generous portions.

XX **E&O**
14 Blenheim Cres. ✉ W11 1NN ⊖ Ladbroke Grove – ✆ (020) 7229 5454 – www.rickerrestaurants.com – Closed 25-26 December and August bank holiday
Rest – Asian – Menu £ 19 (weekday lunch) – Carte £ 27/50 **16**MZD**a**
♦ Mean, moody and cool: does that describe the surroundings or the A-list diners? Minimalist chic meets high sound levels. Menus scour Far East, with dishes meant for sharing.

X **Bumpkin**
209 Westbourne Park Rd ✉ W11 1EA ⊖ Westbourne Park – ✆ (020) 7243 9818 – www.bumpkinuk.com – Closed 1 January, 29 August and 25-26 December
Rest – British – Carte £ 28/40 **27**AAT**b**
Rest *Brasserie* – Carte £ 29/40
♦ Converted pea-green pub with casual, clubby feel and wholesome philosophy of cooking seasonal, carefully sourced and organic food. Whisky tasting and private dining on top floors. First floor restaurant offers modern Mediterranean menu.

Fat Badger
310 Portobello Rd ✉ W10 5TA ⊖ Ladbroke Grove. – ✆ (020) 8969 4500 – www.thefatbadger.com **16**MZD**b**
Rest – British – Menu £ 25 (lunch) – Carte £ 20/29
♦ Large rustic pub with old sofas, chandeliers, upstairs dining room with intriguing wallpaper. Seasonal and earthy British food, with whole beasts delivered to the kitchen.

SOUTH KENSINGTON

The Pelham
15 Cromwell Pl. ✉ SW7 2LA ⊖ South Kensington – ✆ (020) 7589 8288 – www.pelhamhotel.co.uk **36**ADY**z**
51 rm – †£ 182 ††£ 299/322, ☕ £ 17.50 – 1 suite
Rest *Bistro Fifteen* – *(Closed 25 December)* Menu £ 19/23 – Carte £ 35/46
♦ Immaculately kept, with willing staff and a discreet atmosphere. A mix of English country house and city town house; with panelled sitting room and library. Colourful all day bistro; candlelit at dinner, with European menu.

Blakes rest,
33 Roland Gdns. ✉ SW7 3PF ⊖ Gloucester Road – ✆ (020) 7370 6701 – www.blakeshotels.com **36**ACZ**n**
33 rm – †£ 180/318 ††£ 390/450, ☕ £ 25 – 8 suites **Rest** – Carte £ 40/76
♦ Behind the Victorian façade lies one of London's first 'boutique' hotels. Dramatic, bold and eclectic décor, with oriental influences and antiques from around the globe. Fashionable restaurant with bamboo and black walls.

Number Sixteen without rest
16 Sumner Pl ✉ SW7 3EG ⊖ South Kensington – ✆ (020) 7589 5232 – www.numbersixteenhotel.co.uk **36**ADY**d**
42 rm – †£ 144 ††£ 336, ☕ £ 17.50
♦ Enticingly refurbished 19C town houses in smart area. Discreet entrance, comfy sitting room and charming breakfast terrace. Bedrooms in English country house style.

LONDON

The Cranley without rest
10 Bina Gardens ✉ SW5 0LA ⊖ Gloucester Road – ☏ (020) 7373 0123 – www.cranley.franklynhotels.com **36**ACY**c**
38 rm – ♦£ 138/276 ♦♦£ 161/305, ☕ £ 25 – 1 suite
♦ Delightful Regency townhouse combines charm and period details with modern comforts and technology. Individually styled bedrooms; some with four-posters. Room service available.

The Rockwell
181-183 Cromwell Rd. ✉ SW5 0SF ⊖ Earl's Court – ☏ (020) 7244 2000 – www.therockwell.com **35**ABY**b**
40 rm – ♦£ 120/165 ♦♦£ 180/190, ☕ £ 12.50
Rest – Menu £ 35 – Carte £ 30/39
♦ Two Victorian houses with open, modern lobby and secluded, south-facing garden terrace. Bedrooms come in bold warm colours; 'Garden rooms' come with their own patios. Small dining room offers easy menu of modern European staples.

The Gore
190 Queen's Gate ✉ SW7 5EX ⊖ Gloucester Road – ☏ (020) 7584 6601 – www.gorehotel.com **36**ACX**n**
50 rm – ♦£ 207 ♦♦£ 242, ☕ £ 16.95
Rest ***190 Queensgate*** – *(booking essential)* Menu £ 20/24 – Carte £ 26/42
♦ Idiosyncratic Victorian house, with lobby covered with pictures and prints. Individually styled bedrooms have discreet mod cons and charming bathrooms. Informal bistro with European menu.

Aster House without rest
3 Sumner Pl. ✉ SW7 3EE ⊖ South Kensington – ☏ (020) 7581 5888 – www.asterhouse.com **36**ADY**t**
13 rm ☕ – ♦£ 96/216 ♦♦£ 240/300
♦ End of terrace Victorian house with a pretty little rear garden and first floor conservatory. Ground floor rooms available. Useful location for visiting many tourist attractions.

Bombay Brasserie
Courtfield Rd. ✉ SW7 4QH ⊖ Gloucester Road – ☏ (020) 7370 4040 – www.bombaybrasserielondon.com – Closed 25-26 December **36**ACY**y**
Rest – Indian – *(booking advisable at dinner)* Menu £ 22 (weekday lunch buffet) – Carte £ 31/43
♦ Plush new look for this well-run, well-known and comfortable Indian restaurant; very smart bar and conservatory with a show kitchen. More creative dishes now sit alongside the more traditional.

L'Etranger
36 Gloucester Rd. ✉ SW7 4QT ⊖ Gloucester Road – ☏ (020) 7584 1118 – www.circagroupltd.co.uk – Closed Saturday lunch **36**ACX**c**
Rest – Innovative – *(booking essential)* Menu £ 20 (lunch) – Carte £ 32/101
♦ Silks and lilacs create a stylish, atmospheric feel; ask for a corner table. Interesting menus incorporate techniques and flavours from Japanese cooking. Impressive wine and sake lists.

Pasha
1 Gloucester Rd ✉ SW7 4PP ⊖ Gloucester Road – ☏ (020) 7589 7969 – www.pasha-restaurant.co.uk – Closed 24-25 December **36**ACX**r**
Rest – Moroccan – Menu £ 15/30 – Carte £ 26/32
♦ Relax over ground floor cocktails, then descend to mosaic floored restaurant where the rose-petal strewn tables are the ideal accompaniment to tasty Moroccan home cooking.

Bistro K
117-119 Old Brompton Rd. ✉ SW7 3RN ⊖ Gloucester Road – ☏ (020) 7373 7774 – www.bistro-k.co.uk – Closed Christmas and New Year, 2 weeks August, Monday and bank holidays **36**ACZ**x**
Rest – French – Menu £ 15/25 (early dinner) – Carte £ 29/44
♦ More formal than the name would suggest and the cooking is more delicate and sophisticated. The surroundings are bright and contemporary and the front terrace is an appealing spot.

XX **Cambio de Tercio**

163 Old Brompton Rd ✉ SW5 0LJ ⊖ Gloucester Road – ✆ (020) 7244 8970 – www.cambiodetercio.co.uk **36**ACZ**a**

Rest – Spanish – Carte £ 30/54

♦ Good ingredients and authentic Spanish flavours; desserts are more contemporary. Choose tapas or regular menu. Service improves the more you visit. Owner also has tapas bar across the road.

X **Bumpkin**

102 Old Brompton Rd ✉ SW7 3RD ⊖ Gloucester Road – ✆ (020) 7341 0802 – www.bumpkinuk.com **36**ACY**r**

Rest – British – Carte £ 28/40

♦ Sister to the Notting Hill original with the same pub-like informality and friendly service. The kitchen champions British seasonal produce; the simpler dishes are the best ones.

X **Bangkok**

9 Bute St ✉ SW7 3EY ⊖ South Kensington – ✆ (020) 7584 8529 – www.bankokrestaurant.co.uk – Closed Christmas-New Year and Sunday

Rest – Thai – Carte £ 22/29 **36**ADY**b**

♦ This simple Thai bistro has been a popular local haunt for nearly 40 years. Guests can watch the chefs at work, preparing inexpensive and authentic dishes from the succinct menu.

LONDON

KINGSTON UPON THAMES – Greater London – pop. 146 873 — 12 A3

18 Hampton Court Palace Hampton Wick, ✆ (020) 8977 2423

Surbiton

XX **The French Table**

85 Maple Rd ✉ KT6 4AW – ✆ (020) 8399 2365 – www.thefrenchtable.co.uk – Closed 25 December-6 January, 2 weeks August, Sunday dinner and Monday **6**CY**a**

Rest – Mediterranean – Menu £ 20 (lunch) – Carte dinner £ 33/39

♦ Run by a husband and wife team; a narrow room with a lively, local atmosphere. Gutsy and satisfying French-Mediterranean cooking. Saturday morning cookery lessons. Private dining room upstairs.

LAMBETH – Greater London – pop. 267 785 — 12 B3

Brixton

XX **Upstairs**

89b Acre Ln. ✉ SW2 5TN ⊖ Clapham North – ✆ (020) 7733 8855 – www.upstairslondon.com – Closed 24 December-7 January, 17-26 April, 14-30 August, Sunday and Monday **24**SZH**b**

Rest – Modern European – *(dinner only)* Menu £ 30

♦ Uncomplicated, easy to eat and flavoursome cooking from a concise but balanced and well-priced set menu. First floor bar, second floor dining room – look for the buzzer next to Opus coffee shop.

Clapham Common

XX **Trinity**

4 The Polygon ✉ SW4 0JG ⊖ Clapham Common – ✆ (020) 7622 1199 – www.trinityrestaurant.co.uk – Closed 23-29 December, 2 January, Monday lunch and Sunday dinner **24**RZH**a**

Rest – Innovative – Menu £ 25 (weekdays) – Carte dinner £ 28/51

♦ Smartly decorated and smoothly run neighbourhood restaurant; ask for a table by the windows in summer. Sophisticated cooking displays some innovative combinations. Good value lunch menu.

X **Tsunami**

Unit 3, 5-7 Voltaire Rd ✉ SW4 6DQ ⊖ Clapham North – ☎ (020) 7978 1610 – www.tsunamirestaurant.co.uk – Closed 24-26 December and 1 January **24**SZH**a**

Rest – Japanese – *(dinner only and lunch Saturday-Sunday)* Menu £ 11 (lunch) – Carte £ 18/41

♦ Stylish and lively surroundings in which to enjoy innovative and original modern Japanese cooking, with large, local following. A second branch now in Charlotte Street.

East Dulwich

Palmerston

91 Lordship Ln ✉ SE22 8EP ⊖ East Dulwich (rail) – ☎ (020) 8693 1629 – www.thepalmerston.net **26**XZH**x**

Rest – Menu £ 15 (lunch) – Carte £ 22/29

♦ Full of atmosphere and attracting a range of ages, thanks to its young, engaging staff and good food. Menus evolve monthly and mix classics with the more modern. Well-priced weekday menu.

Kennington

X **Lobster Pot**

3 Kennington Ln. ✉ SE11 4RG ⊖ Kennington – ☎ (020) 7582 5556 – www.lobsterpotrestaurant.co.uk – Closed 25 December-4 January, Sunday and Monday **40**AOY**e**

Rest – French – Carte £ 38/50

♦ Family-run, with exuberant décor of fish tanks, portholes and even the sound of seagulls. Classic seafood menu with fruits de mer, plenty of oysters and daily specials. Good crêpes too.

Southbank

London Marriott H. County Hall rm,

Westminster Bridge Rd ✉ SE1 7PB ⊖ Westminster – ☎ (020) 7928 5200 – www.marriottcountyhall.com **40**AMX**a**

195 rm – †£ 448 ††£ 448, ☐ £ 20.95 – 5 suites

Rest *County Hall* – ☎ (020) 7902 8000 *(closed 26 December)* Menu £ 28 – Carte £ 32/43

♦ Occupying the historic County Hall building. Many of the spacious and comfortable bedrooms enjoy river and Parliament outlook. Impressive leisure facilities. World famous views from restaurant.

XXX **Skylon**

1 Southbank Centre, Belvedere Rd ✉ SE1 8XX ⊖ Waterloo – ☎ (020) 7654 7800 – www.skylonrestaurant.co.uk – Closed 25 December and Sunday dinner **32**AMV**a**

Rest – Modern European – Menu £ 28/45

♦ Ask for a window table here at the Royal Festival Hall. Informal grill-style operation on one side, a more formal and expensive restaurant on the other, with a busy cocktail bar in the middle.

Stockwell

Canton Arms

177 South Lambeth Rd ✉ SW8 1XP ⊖ Stockwell. – ☎ (020) 7582 8710 – www.cantonarms.com – Closed 25-26 December, 31 December, 1 January, Monday lunch, Sunday dinner and bank holidays **24**SZG**a**

Rest – Carte £ 20/26

♦ An appreciative crowd of all ages come for the earthy, robust and seasonal British dishes which suit the relaxed environment of this pub so well. Staff are attentive and knowledgeable.

LONDON

LEWISHAM – Greater London – pop. 248 922 — 12 B3

BLACKHEATH

XX **Chapters**
43-45 Montpelier Vale ✉ SE3 0TJ – ✆ (020) 8333 2666 – www.chaptersrestaurants.com — **8**HX**c**
Rest – Modern European – Carte £ 18/45
♦ A contemporary and bustling all day brasserie and bar at the top of town. Large, appealingly priced menu with British and Mediterranean influences, with meats cooked over charcoal a speciality.

LONDON HEATHROW AIRPORT – see Hillingdon, London p. 393

MERTON – Greater London – pop. 187 908 — 12 B3

WIMBLEDON

Cannizaro House
West Side, Wimbledon Common ✉ SW19 4UE ⊖ Wimbledon – ✆ (020) 8879 1464 – www.cannizarohouse.com — **6**DXY**x**
44 rm – †£ 210/570 ††£ 210/570 – 2 suites
Rest – Menu £ 29 (dinner - except Sunday) – Carte £ 34/41
♦ Part-Georgian mansion in charming spot overlooking Wimbledon Common. Modern bedrooms; funky suites; 'Sophia Johnson' has lovely balcony overlooking the park. Local artists' work decorates. Contemporary, glass-fronted bar leads to restaurant with modern menu.

X **Light House**
75-77 Ridgway ✉ SW19 4ST ⊖ Wimbledon – ✆ (020) 8944 6338 – www.lighthousewimbledon.com – Closed 25-26 December, 1 January and Sunday dinner — **6**DY**n**
Rest – International – Menu £ 15 (lunch) – Carte £ 24/34
♦ The robust and flavoursome Italian dishes provide the highlights of the menu. This large, well lit room attracts plenty of locals and the service remains calm and cheery.

RICHMOND-UPON-THAMES – Greater London – pop. 172 335 — 12 B3

Old Town Hall, Whittaker Ave 020 8940 9125, info@visitrichmond.co.uk
Richmond Park Roehampton Gate, ✆ (020) 8876 3205
Sudbrook Park

BARNES

XX **Sonny's**
94 Church Rd ✉ SW13 0DQ – ✆ (020) 8748 0393 – www.sonnys.co.uk – Closed Sunday dinner and bank holidays — **21**KZH**x**
Rest – Modern European – Menu £ 16/19 – Carte £ 28/32
♦ Long-established neighbourhood spot which successfully combines its role as deli, café and restaurant. The latter's menus are full of seasonal goodness and the service is warm and attentive.

XX **Indian Zilla**
2-3 Rocks Ln. ✉ SW13 0DB – ✆ (020) 8878 3989 – www.indianzilla.co.uk
Rest – Indian – Menu £ 15 (lunch) – Carte £ 19/35 — **21**LZH**k**
♦ Bright, and contemporary restaurant with attentive, friendly service. Modern menu includes a few classics; the authentic, fully-flavoured dishes display a lightness of touch.

X **Riva**
169 Church Rd. ✉ SW13 9HR – ✆ (020) 8748 0434 – Closed Christmas and New Year, 3 weeks August, 1 week Easter, Saturday lunch and bank holidays
Rest – Italian – Carte £ 31/47 **s** — **21**LZH**a**
♦ A restaurant built on customer loyalty; the regulars are showered with attention from the eponymous owner. Gutsy, no-nonsense dishes, full of flavour. Interesting all-Italian wine list.

Brown Dog

28 Cross St ✉ SW13 0AP ⊖ Barnes Bridge (Rail). – ✆ (020) 8392 2200 – www.thebrowndog.co.uk – Closed 25-26 December **21**KZH**b**

Rest – Carte £ 20/30

◆ Pretty Victorian pub with a genuine neighbourhood feel; snug bar, intimate dining room and a look that combines the traditional with the modern. Concise, balanced menu delivers commendably priced dishes that display a deft touch.

East Sheen

Mango & Silk

199 Upper Richmond Rd. West ✉ SW14 8 QT – ✆ (020) 8876 6220 – www.mangoandsilk.co.uk – Closed Monday **21**KZH**k**

Rest – Indian – *(dinner only and Sunday lunch)* Carte £ 18/23

◆ An air of calm pervades the restaurant, thanks to the charming owner. Udit Sarkhel is the chef and his cooking is as expertly crafted as ever. The generous prices make over-ordering the easy option.

Victoria with rm

10 West Temple Sheen ✉ SW14 7RT ⊖ Mortlake (Rail). – ✆ (020) 8876 4238 – www.thevictoria.net – Closed 2 days between Christmas and New Year

7 rm – †£ 112/132 ††£ 128/148 **6**CX**u**

Rest – British – Carte £ 25/35

◆ Beautifully restored pub, eat in the relaxed bar or more formal conservatory overlooking the terrace; this is a genuine local that plays its part in the community and the kitchen takes its sourcing seriously. Simple bedrooms available.

Kew

The Glasshouse

14 Station Par. ✉ TW9 3PZ ⊖ Kew Gardens – ✆ (020) 8940 6777 – www.glasshouserestaurant.co.uk – Closed 24-26 December and 1 January

Rest – Modern European – Menu £ 24/40 **6**CX**z**

Spec. Ravioli of rabbit with spring greens and thyme. Monkfish and octopus with fennel and sauce antiboise. Crème fraîche parfait with strawberry sorbet.

◆ Bright and relaxed interior, with a palpable sense of neighbourhood. Balanced and seasonally informed dishes are full of flavour, from a varied and appealing menu influenced mostly by Europe. Service is pleasant and unflappable.

Kew Grill

10b Kew Grn. ✉ TW9 3BH ⊖ Kew Gardens – ✆ (020) 8948 4433 – www.awtrestaurants.com – Closed 25-26 December and Monday lunch

Rest – Beef specialities – *(booking essential)* Menu £ 15 (lunch) – Carte £ 25/38 **6**CV**u**

◆ Just off Kew Green, this long, narrow restaurant has a Mediterranean style and feel. Grilled specialities employ top-rate ingredients: the beef is hung for 35 days.

Richmond

Petersham

Nightingale Ln. ✉ TW10 6UZ – ✆ (020) 8940 7471 – www.petershamhotel.co.uk

59 rm – †£ 70/160 ††£ 170 – 1 suite **6**CX**c**

Rest *The Restaurant at The Petersham* – see restaurant listing

◆ Extended over the years, a fine example of Victorian Gothic architecture. Impressive Portland stone, self-supporting staircase. Most comfortable rooms overlook the Thames.

Bingham

61-63 Petersham Rd. ✉ TW10 6UT – ✆ (020) 8940 0902 – www.thebingham.co.uk – Closed first week January **6**CX**a**

15 rm – †£ 140/190 ††£ 250/285, £ 15

Rest *Bingham Restaurant* – see restaurant listing

◆ A pair of conjoined and restored Georgian townhouses; a short walk from Richmond centre. Ask for a room overlooking the river and garden. Contemporary styled bedrooms; some with four-posters.

LONDON

XXX **The Restaurant at The Petersham** – at Petersham Hotel

Nightingale Ln. ✉ *TW10 6UZ – ☎ (020) 8940 7471 – www.petershamhotel.co.uk – Closed 24-26 December* **6**CX**c**

Rest – French – Menu £ 25 (lunch) – Carte dinner £ 29/45

♦ Tables by the window have spectacular views across royal parkland and the winding Thames. Formal surroundings in which to enjoy classic and modern cooking. See the cellars.

XX **Bingham Restaurant** – at Bingham Hotel

✿ *61-63 Petersham Rd.* ✉ *TW10 6UT – ☎ (020) 8940 0902 – www.thebingham.co.uk – Closed first week January and Sunday dinner*

Rest – Modern European – Menu £ 23/45 **6**CX**a**

Spec. Calves sweetbreads with caper and raisin vinaigrette. Suckling pig with fennel, apple and pistachio. Passion fruit curd with blood orange sorbet.

♦ On a summer's day, sit on the balcony terrace overlooking the garden and the Thames. Well-meaning and courteous service in a comfortable, boldly decorated room. Cooking is accomplished and precise; delicate in presentation but assured in flavour.

LONDON

X **Petersham Nurseries Café**

✿ *Church Ln (off Petersham Rd)* ✉ *TW10 7AG – ☎ (020) 8605 3627 – www.petershamnurseries.com – Closed 23 December-12 January, Monday and Tuesday* **6**CX**x**

Rest – Italian influences – *(lunch only) (booking advisable)* Carte £ 38/46

Spec. Halibut brandade with polenta and basil. Beef fillet with white beans, chard and salsa verde. Almond tart with roasted peaches.

♦ The Café is outside on sunny days and in a greenhouse the rest of the time; leave your best shoes at home! The food's all about natural flavours and fresh, vibrant ingredients; its earthiness seems so right when you're eating among plants and flowers.

X **Swagat**

86 Hill Rise ✉ *TW10 6UB ⊖ Richmond – ☎ (0208) 940 7557 – www.swagatindiancuisine.co.uk – Closed 25-26 December and 1 January*

Rest – Indian – *(dinner only)* Menu £ 30 – Carte £ 22/34 **6**CX**i**

♦ Well-meaning service and an appealing menu have made this Indian restaurant popular with locals so it's worth booking. Plenty of classics and vegetarian choices; try the less familiar.

X **Matsuba**

10 Red Lion St ✉ *TW9 1RW – ☎ (020) 8605 3513 – Closed 25-26 December, 1 January and Sunday* **6**CX**n**

Rest – Japanese – Carte approx. £ 35

♦ Family-run Japanese restaurant with just 11 tables; understated but well-kept appearance. Extensive menu offers wide range of Japanese dishes, along with bulgogi, a Korean barbecue dish.

TEDDINGTON

X **Simply Thai**

196 Kingston Rd. ✉ *TW11 9JD – ☎ (020) 8943 9747 – www.simplythai-restaurant.co.uk – Closed 25 December and Monday*

Rest – Thai – *(dinner only)* Menu £ 25 – Carte £ 28/33 **5**BY**x**

♦ Extremely busy local Thai restaurant; the owner does all the cooking and her passion is clear. New creations sit alongside classics on the large menu. Prices are fair; service can sometimes struggle to keep up.

TWICKENHAM

XX **A Cena**

418 Richmond Rd. ✉ *TW1 2EB ⊖ Richmond – ☎ (020) 8288 0108 – www.acena.co.uk – Closed 24-26 December, 1 January, Sunday dinner and Monday lunch* **5**BX**e**

Rest – Italian – Carte £ 19/37

♦ Rustic and quite intimate feel to this well-run neighbourhood Italian restaurant. Appealing, seasonal menu covers most of Italy and the generously sized dishes are full of flavour.

Tangawizi
406 Richmond Rd., Richmond Bridge ✉ TW1 2EB ⊖ Richmond – ✆ (020) 8891 3737 – www.tangawizi.co.uk – Closed 25 December **5**BX**e**
Rest – Indian – *(dinner only)* Carte £ 15/30
◆ Name means Ginger in Swahili. Sleek décor in warm purple with subtle Indian touches. Well-priced, nicely balanced, slowly evolving menus take their influence from north India.

Brula
43 Crown Rd., St Margarets ✉ TW1 3EJ – ✆ (020) 8892 0602 – www.brula.co.uk – Closed Christmas and Sunday dinner **5**BX**v**
Rest – French – *(booking essential)* Menu £ 18 (lunch) – Carte £ 28/38
◆ French brasserie in look, with mirrors and chandeliers. Good value, well-crafted cooking is largely French but now comes with other European influences. Friendly service and popular with locals.

SOUTHWARK – Greater London – pop. 243 749 **12** B3

Level 2, Tate Modern, Bankside ✆ (020) 7401 5266, tourismino@southwark.gov.uk

BERMONDSEY

Hilton London Tower Bridge rm,
5 More London, Tooley St. ✉ SE1 2BY ⊖ London Bridge – ✆ (020) 3002 4300 – www.hilton.co.uk/towerbridge **34**ARV**e**
245 rm – †£ 418 ††£ 418, ☕ £ 19.95
Rest – Menu £ 22 (dinner) – Carte £ 32/35
◆ Usefully located new-style Hilton hotel with boldly decorated open-plan lobby. Contemporary bedrooms boast well-designed features; 4 floors of executive rooms. Dine on classics and comfort food in restaurant with outdoor seating.

Bermondsey Square rm,
Bermondsey Sq, Tower Bridge Rd ✉ SE1 3UN ⊖ London Bridge – ✆ (0207) 378 2450 – www.bermondseysquarehotel.co.uk **20**XZE**n**
79 rm – †£ 129/219 ††£ 139/219, ☕ £ 10.95
Rest *Alfie's* – English – ✆ (0870) 111 2525 – Menu £ 15/17 – Carte approx. £ 26
◆ Opened in 2009 in hip, regenerated square. Cleverly designed hotel, with subtle 60's influence and fun feel. Well-equipped rooms, including four loft suites. English menu in Alfie's makes good use of local food markets.

London Bridge rm,
8-18 London Bridge St. ✉ SE1 9SG ⊖ London Bridge – ✆ (020) 7855 2200 – www.londonbridgehotel.com **33**AQV**a**
138 rm – †£ 344 ††£ 344, ☕ £ 16.95 – 3 suites
Rest *Londinium* – *(dinner only)* Carte £ 26/40
◆ In one of the oldest parts of London, independently owned with an ornate façade dating from 1915. Modern interior with classically decorated bedrooms and an impressive gym. Londinium for brasserie dining.

Le Pont de la Tour
36d Shad Thames, Butlers Wharf ✉ SE1 2YE ⊖ London Bridge – ✆ (020) 7403 8403 – www.lepontdelatour.co.uk **34**ASV**c**
Rest – French – Menu £ 32/43
◆ Elegant and stylish room commanding spectacular views of the Thames and Tower Bridge. Formal and detailed service. Modern menu with an informal bar attached.

Vivat Bacchus London Bridge
4 Hays Ln. ✉ SE1 2HB ⊖ London Bridge – ✆ (0207) 234 0891 – www.vivatbacchus.co.uk – Closed 24 December-3 January, bank holidays and Sunday **34**ARV**n**
Rest – Traditional – Menu £ 12/20 – Carte £ 26/36
◆ South African element to both the menu and the very impressive wine list. International platters in ground floor wine bar; robust cooking in the basement restaurant, with its great cheese room.

LONDON

XX **Magdalen**

152 Tooley St. ✉ SE1 2TU ⊖ London Bridge – ✆ (020) 7403 1342 – www.magdalenrestaurant.co.uk – Closed Christmas and New Year, 2 weeks August, Saturday lunch, Sunday and bank holidays **34**ARV**b**

Rest – British – Menu £ 19 (lunch) – Carte £ 28/36

♦ Confident and satisfying British cooking with big flavours, using carefully sourced ingredients. Divided between two floors; upstairs is more convivial, downstairs more intimate.

X **Zucca**

184 Bermondsey St ✉ SE1 3TQ ⊖ Borough – ✆ (020) 7378 6809 – www.zuccalondon.com – Closed 24 December-10 January, Sunday dinner and Monday **20**XZE**s**

Rest – Italian – *(booking essential at dinner)* Carte £ 18/24

♦ Bright and buzzy modern room, where the informed Italian cooking is driven by the fresh ingredients, the prices are more than generous and the service is sweet and responsive. The appealing antipasti is great for sharing.

X **Blueprint Café**

Design Museum, Shad Thames, Butlers Wharf ✉ SE1 2YD ⊖ London Bridge – ✆ (020) 7378 7031 – www.danddlondon.com – Closed Sunday dinner

Rest – Modern European – Menu £ 20 – Carte £ 22/36 **34**ASV**u**

♦ Champions British produce in dishes using simple, but informed, techniques. Bright, retro feel; located above the Design Museum, with retractable windows and binoculars on each table.

X **Village East**

171-173 Bermondsey St. ✉ SE1 3UW ⊖ London Bridge – ✆ (020) 7357 6082 – www.villageeast.co.uk – Closed 25-26 December **20**XZE**a**

Rest – Modern European – Carte £ 29/37

♦ In a glass-fronted block sandwiched by Georgian townhouses, this trendy restaurant has two loud, buzzy bars and dining areas serving ample portions of modern British fare.

X **Cantina Del Ponte**

36c Shad Thames, Butlers Wharf ✉ SE1 2YE ⊖ London Bridge – ✆ (020) 7403 5403 – www.cantina.co.uk – Closed 25-27 December **34**ASV**c**

Rest – Italian – Menu £ 15/19 – Carte £ 27/38

♦ An Italian stalwart, refurbished late in 2007. Simple menu offers an appealing mix of classic dishes, with a good value set menu until 7pm. Riverside setting with pleasant terrace.

X **Butlers Wharf Chop House**

36e Shad Thames, Butlers Wharf ✉ SE1 2YE ⊖ London Bridge – ✆ (020) 7403 3403 – www.chophouse.co.uk – Closed 1-2 January **34**ASV**n**

Rest – British – Menu £ 22 (lunch) – Carte £ 28/43

♦ Grab a table on the terrace in summer and dine in the shadow of Tower Bridge. Rustic feel to the interior; noisy and fun. The menu focuses on traditional English ingredients and dishes.

X **Champor-Champor**

62-64 Weston St. ✉ SE1 3QJ ⊖ London Bridge – ✆ (020) 7403 4600 – www.champor-champor.com – Closed 1 week Easter, 1 week Christmas, Sunday and Bank Holidays **34**ARV**a**

Rest – Asian – *(dinner only)* Menu £ 32

♦ Choice of two beguiling and colourful rooms: ask for the second as it has even more character, better lighting and a mezzanine. Food is rooted in Malay traditions with a hint of modernity.

Garrison

99-101 Bermondsey St ✉ SE1 3XB ⊖ London Bridge. – ✆ (020) 7089 9355 – www.thegarrison.co.uk **20**XZE**z**

Rest – *(booking essential at dinner)* Menu £ 14 (early dinner) – Carte £ 30/40

♦ Known for its vintage look, booths and sweet-natured service, The Garrison boasts a warm, relaxed vibe. Open from breakfast until dinner where a Mediterranean-led menu pulls in the crowd.

LONDON

SOUTHWARK

All Seasons
47 Southwark Bridge Rd ✉ SE1 9HH ⊖ London Bridge – ✆ (020) 7015 1480 – www.all-seasons-hotels.com **33**AQV**c**
78 rm – †£ 195 ††£ 195, ☕ £ 5 – 6 suites
Rest – *(dinner only)* Carte £ 18/28 **s**
◆ Purpose-built budget hotel south of the City, near the Globe Theatre. Uniform style, reasonably spacious bedrooms with writing desks. Top floor dining room with bar.

Oxo Tower
Oxo Tower Wharf (8th floor), Barge House St. ✉ *SE1 9PH* ⊖ *Southwark – ✆ (020) 7803 3888 – www.harveynichols.com* **32**ANV**a**
Rest – Modern European – Menu £ 35 (lunch) – Carte £ 46/64
Rest *Oxo Tower Brasserie* – see restaurant listing
◆ Top of a converted factory, providing stunning views of the Thames and beyond. Stylish, minimalist interior with huge windows. Modern, mostly European, cuisine.

Roast
The Floral Hall, Borough Mkt. ✉ *SE1 1TL* ⊖ *London Bridge – ✆ (0845) 034 7300 – www.roast-restaurant.com – Closed 26 and 31 December, 1 January and Sunday dinner* **33**AQV**e**
Rest – British – *(booking essential)* Menu £ 26 (lunch) – Carte £ 39/54
◆ Set into the roof of Borough Market's Floral Hall. Extensive cocktail list in bar; split-level restaurant has views to St Paul's. Robust English cooking uses market produce.

Baltic
74 Blackfriars Rd ✉ *SE1 8HA* ⊖ *Southwark – ✆ (020) 7928 1111 – www.balticrestaurant.co.uk – Closed 24-26 December* **33**AOV**e**
Rest – Eastern European – *(booking advisable at dinner)* Menu £ 15/18 – Carte £ 22/34
◆ Celebrates 10 years in 2011. Set in a Grade II listed 18C former coach house. Enjoy big portions of authentic and hearty east European food. Interesting vodkas; live jazz on Sundays.

Oxo Tower Brasserie
Oxo Tower Wharf (8th floor), Barge House St. ✉ *SE1 9PH* ⊖ *Southwark – ✆ (020) 7803 3888 – www.harveynichols.com* **32**ANV**a**
Rest – Modern European – Carte £ 37/57
◆ Same views but less formal and more fun than the restaurant. Open-plan kitchen produces a modern, easy to eat and quite light menu. In summer, try to secure a table on the terrace.

Cantina Vinopolis
No.1 Bank End ✉ *SE1 9BU* ⊖ *London Bridge – ✆ (020) 7940 8333 – www.cantinavinopolis.com – Closed 25-26 December* **33**AQV**z**
Rest – International – Menu £ 30 – Carte £ 23/39
◆ Large, solid brick vaulted room under Victorian railway arches, with an adjacent wine museum. Modern menu with a huge selection of wines by the glass.

Tate Modern (Restaurant)
Tate Modern (7th floor), Bankside ✉ *SE1 9TG* ⊖ *Southwark – ✆ (020) 7887 8888 – www.tate.org.uk/modern/eatanddrink – Closed 24-26 December* **33**APV**s**
Rest – British – (lunch only and dinner Friday-Saturday) Carte £ 30/36
◆ 7th floor restaurant with floor to ceilings windows on two sides and large mural. Appealing mix of light and zesty dishes, with seasonal produce. Good choice of wines and non-alcoholic drinks.

Tapas Brindisa

18-20 Southwark St., Borough Market ✉ SE1 1TJ ⊖ London Bridge – ✆ (020) 7357 8880 – www.brindisatapaskitchens.com – Closed 25-28 December and 1 January **33**AQV**k**

Rest – Spanish – *(bookings not accepted)* Carte £ 19/27

♦ Prime quality Spanish produce sold in owner's shops and this bustling eatery on edge of Borough Market. Freshly prepared, tasty tapas: waiters will assist with your choice.

Wright Brothers

11 Stoney St., Borough Market ✉ SE1 9AD ⊖ London Bridge – ✆ (020) 7403 9554 – www.wrightbrothers.co.uk – Closed Christmas-New Year and bank holidays **33**AQV**m**

Rest – Seafood – *(booking advisable)* Carte £ 23/40

♦ Originally an oyster wholesaler; now offers a wide range of oysters along with porter, as well as fruits de mer, daily specials and assorted pies. It fills quickly and an air of contentment reigns.

Brew Wharf

Brew Wharf Yard, Stoney St ✉ SE1 9AD ⊖ London Bridge – ✆ (020) 7378 6601 – www.brewwharf.com – Closed Christmas-New Year, Sunday and bank holidays **33**AQV**h**

Rest – Traditional – Menu £ 24 – Carte £ 22/33

♦ A busy bar, microbrewery and restaurant; come in a group to enjoy the sports screen and vast selection of beers and ales. The gutsy food and shared platters are the perfect match for the beer.

Anchor & Hope

36 The Cut ✉ SE1 8LP ⊖ Southwark. – ✆ (020) 7928 9898 – Closed 2 weeks at Christmas, Easter, May and August bank holidays, Sunday dinner and Monday lunch **32**ANV**n**

Rest – British – *(bookings not accepted)* Menu £ 30 (lunch Sunday) – Carte £ 22/35

♦ As popular as ever thanks to its congenial feel and lived-in looks but mostly because of the appealingly seasonal menu and the gutsy, bold cooking that delivers on flavour. No reservations so be prepared to wait at the bar.

SUTTON – Gtr London **12** B3

SUTTON – Surrey – ✉

27 Oak Sports Centre Carshalton Woodmansterne Rd, ✆ (020) 8643 8363

Brasserie Vacherin

12 High St ✉ SM1 1HN – ✆ (020) 8722 0180 – www.brasserievacherin.co.uk – Closed 25 December **7**EZ**x**

Rest – French – Menu £ 17 (lunch) – Carte £ 23/36

♦ Relaxed, modern French brasserie with tiled walls, art nouveau posters and deep red banquettes. Good value midweek set price menu and à la carte of French classics. Diligent service.

TOWER HAMLETS – Greater London – pop. 196 106 **12** B3

BETHNAL GREEN

Town Hall

Patriot Sq. ✉ E2 9NF ⊖ Bethnal Green – ✆ (020) 7871 0460 – www.townhallhotel.com **20**YZC**x**

97 rm – †£ 174/348 ††£ 174/348, ☐ £ 9 – 1 suite

Rest *Viajante* – see restaurant listing

♦ Edwardian, former council offices converted into a hotel in 2010. Its period character is balanced with modernity, with individually decorated, understated bedrooms and frequently changing art.

LONDON

XX **Viajante** – at Town Hall Hotel
Patriot Sq., ((entrance on Cambridge Heath Rd)) ✉ E2 9NF ⊖ Bethnal Green – ✆ (020) 7871 0461 – www.viajante.co.uk **20YZCx**
Rest – Innovative – *(closed lunch Monday and Tuesday) (booking essential)* Menu £ 25/60
Spec. Scallop, pickled cucumber and celery juice. Iberico pig neck, langoustine and broth. Panna cotta ice cream with basil and apple.
◆ Highly innovative and original cooking in the form of 6, 9 or 12 delicate courses. A converted Victorian town hall is the unlikely setting for this inventive cooking; ask to sit in the front room to watch the chefs at work.

Bow

Morgan Arms
43 Morgan St ✉ E3 5AA ⊖ Bow Road. – ✆ (020) 8980 6389 – www.geronimo-inns.co.uk – Closed 25-26 December **3GUc**
Rest – *(bookings not accepted)* Carte £ 19/35
◆ Characterful pub with mismatch of furniture and shabby-chic appeal. Constantly evolving menu offers robust cooking, using some unusual and sometimes unfamiliar ingredients.

Canary Wharf

Four Seasons
Westferry Circus ✉ E14 8RS ⊖ Canary Wharf – ✆ (020) 7510 1999 – www.fourseasons.com/canarywharf **3GVa**
128 rm – †£ 456/516 ††£ 456/516, ☐ £ 25 – 14 suites
Rest *Quadrato* – see restaurant listing
◆ Professionally run international hotel geared primarily to the local corporate market; whose deluxe rooms boast impressive views across the river. Leisure facilities housed in an adjacent club.

XXX **Quadrato** – at Four Seasons Hotel
Westferry Circus ✉ E14 8RS ⊖ Canary Wharf – ✆ (020) 7510 1999 – www.fourseasons.com/canarywharf **3GVa**
Rest – Italian – Carte £ 33/53
◆ Smart, spacious restaurant on the ground floor of the Four Seasons, with river-facing terrace. Luxury ingredients used in dishes that cover all parts of Italy. Knowledgeable service.

XXX **Dockmaster's House**
1 Hertsmere Rd ✉ E14 8JJ ⊖ Canary Wharf – ✆ (020) 7345 0345 – www.dockmastershouse.com – Closed 25 December-1 January, Saturday lunch and Sunday **3GVr**
Rest – Indian – *(booking advisable)* Menu £ 19 (lunch and early dinner) – Carte £ 29/39
◆ A contemporary overhaul of a three storey Georgian house in the shadow of Canary Wharf's skyscrapers has created this slick operation. Elaborate Indian cooking, although sometimes a little pretentious.

XX **Plateau**
Canada Place (4th floor), Canada Square ✉ E14 5ER ⊖ Canary Wharf – ✆ (020) 7715 7100 – www.plateaurestaurant.co.uk – Closed 25-26 December, 1 January, Saturday, Sunday and Bank Holidays **3GVn**
Rest – Modern European – Menu £ 18/27 – Carte £ 35/44
◆ Impressive open-plan space with dramatic glass walls and ceilings and striking 1970s design. Rotisserie meats in the Grill; globally-influenced dishes in formal restaurant.

XX **Roka Canary Wharf**
Ist Floor,4 Park Pavilion ✉ E14 5FW ⊖ Canary Wharf – ✆ (020) 7636 5228 – www.rokarestaurant.com – Closed 25 December, 1 January, Sunday and bank holidays **3GVv**
Rest – Japanese – *(booking essential)* Carte approx. £ 38
◆ You'll be hit by a wall of sound at this large and perennially busy operation in the shadow of Canary Wharf Tower. The meats cooked on the robata grill are highlights of the Japanese menu.

Gun

27 Coldharbour ✉ E14 9NS ⊖ Blackwall (DLR). – ✆ (020) 7515 5222 – www.thegundocklands.com – Closed 25 December **7**GV**x**

Rest – Carte £ 21/30

♦ Despite its 21C makeover, this 18C pub, with links to Lord Nelson, hasn't forgotten its roots. Smart dining room; menu a mix of classic and modern. Always busy, especially the large decked area.

LIMEHOUSE

Narrow

44 Narrow St ✉ E14 8DP ⊖ Limehouse (DLR). – ✆ (020) 7592 7950 – www.gordonramsay.com **3**GV**o**

Rest – *(booking essential)* Menu £ 22 – Carte £ 21/27

♦ Grade II listed former dockmaster's house on the river; part of Gordon Ramsay's group. Menu specialises in British favourites, from shrimps to sardines, braised beef to trifle.

LONDON

SPITALFIELDS

Galvin La Chapelle

35 Spital Sq. ✉ E1 6DY ⊖ Liverpool Street – ✆ (020) 7299 0400 – www.galvinrestaurants.com – Closed 25-26 December and 1 January

Rest – French – Menu £ 25 (lunch)/29 (early dinner) – Carte £ 37/56 **34**AST**v**

Spec. Lasagne of crab with velouté of girolles. Tagine of pigeon with aubergine purée and harissa sauce. Tarte tatin with crème fraîche.

♦ The Victorian splendour of St. Botolph's Hall, with its vaulted ceiling, arched windows and marble pillars, lends itself perfectly to its new role as a glamorous restaurant. The food is bourgeois French with a sophisticated edge and is bound to satisfy.

Les Trois Garcons

1 Club Row ✉ E1 6JX ⊖ Shoreditch – ✆ (020) 7613 1924 – www.lestroisgarcons.com – Closed 16-31 August, 23 December-10 January, Sunday and Bank Holidays **20**XZD**r**

Rest – French – *(dinner only and lunch in December)* Menu £ 46

♦ Extraordinarily eccentric, with stuffed animals, twinkling beads, assorted chandeliers and ceiling handbags. The French food is more traditional and governed by the seasons.

Hawksmoor

157 Commercial St. ✉ E1 6BJ ⊖ Shoreditch – ✆ (020) 7247 7392 – www.thehawksmoor.com – Closed Christmas, Sunday dinner and bank holidays

Rest – Beef specialities – *(booking advisable)* Carte £ 34/51 **20**XZD**s**

♦ Unremarkable surroundings and ordinary starters and puds but no matter: this is all about great British beef, hung for 35 days, from Longhorn cattle in the heart of the Yorkshire Moors.

Galvin Café a Vin

35 Spital Sq. (entrance on Bishops Sq.) ✉ E1 6DY ⊖ Liverpool Street – ✆ (020) 7299 0404 – www.galvinrestaurants.com – Closed 25-26 December and 1 January **34**AST**v**

Rest – Menu £ 15 (lunch) – Carte £ 23/33

♦ In the same building as La Chapelle is this simpler but equally worthy operation from the Galvin brothers. The room may not have the grandeur of next door but what it does offer is classic French bistro food at very appealing prices.

St John Bread and Wine

94-96 Commercial St ✉ E1 6LZ ⊖ Shoreditch – ✆ (020) 7251 0848 – www.stjohnbreadandwine.com – Closed Christmas-New Year and bank holidays

Rest – British – Carte £ 24/27 **20**XZD**m**

♦ Part-wine shop/bakery and local restaurant. Highly seasonal and appealing menu changes twice a day; cooking is British, uncomplicated and very satisfying. Try the less familiar dishes.

Wapping

Wapping Food

Wapping Wall ✉ E1W 3SG ⊖ Wapping – ☎ (020) 7680 2080 – www.thewappingproject.com – Closed 24 December-3 January, Sunday dinner and bank holidays **20**YZE**n**

Rest – Modern European – Carte £ 30/54

♦ This striking Victorian former hydraulic power station houses an atmospheric restaurant and art gallery. Sit among the old turbines and enjoy robust, straightforward dishes based on what's in season.

Whitechapel

Cafe Spice Namaste

16 Prescot St. ✉ E1 8AZ ⊖ Tower Hill – ☎ (020) 7488 9242 – www.cafespice.co.uk – Closed Saturday lunch, Sunday and bank holidays

Rest – Indian – Menu £ 30/65 – Carte £ 23/29 **34**ASU**z**

♦ Fresh, vibrant and fairly priced Indian cuisine from Cyrus Todiwala, served in a colourfully decorated room that was once a magistrate's court. Engaging service from an experienced team.

Whitechapel Gallery Dining Room

77-82 Whitechapel High St. ✉ E1 7QX ⊖ Aldgate East – ☎ (020) 7522 7896 – www.whitechapelgallery.com – Closed Christmas and New Year, Monday and dinner Sunday and Tuesday **34**AST**x**

Rest – Mediterranean – *(booking advisable)* Menu £ 23 (lunch) – Carte (dinner) £ 27/34

♦ The Gallery was founded in 1901 and expanded in 2009 with the creation of this sweet, tightly packed restaurant. Concise seasonal menu; British produce with Mediterranean flavours.

WANDSWORTH – Greater London – pop. 259 881 **12** B3

Balham

Brasserie James

47 Balham Hill ✉ SW12 9DR ⊖ Clapham South – ☎ (020) 8772 0057 – www.brasseriejames.com – Closed 23-31 December **6**EX**x**

Rest – Modern European – Menu £ 15/17 – Carte £ 26/36

♦ Crisp and neat brasserie owned and run by former Conran/D&D chef. Something for everyone on the seasonal menu, from moules to pasta. Weekend brunches; good value set menus; wines by carafe.

Lamberts

2 Station Par. ✉ SW12 9AZ ⊖ Balham – ☎ (020) 8675 2233 – www.lambertsrestaurant.com – Closed Sunday dinner and Monday **6**EX**n**

Rest – Traditional – *(dinner only and lunch Saturday-Sunday)* Menu £ 20/30

♦ Locals come for the relaxed surroundings, hospitable service and tasty, seasonal food. Sunday lunch is very popular. The enthusiasm of the eponymous owner has rubbed off on his team.

Harrison's

15-19 Bedford Hill ✉ SW12 9EX ⊖ Balham – ☎ (020) 8675 6900 – www.harrisonsbalham.co.uk – Closed 25-26 December **6**EX**a**

Rest – Mediterranean – Menu £ 16/18 (weekdays) – Carte £ 22/36

♦ Sister to Sam's Brasserie in Chiswick. Open all day, with an appealing list of favourites, from fishcakes to Cumberland sausages. Weekend brunches; kids' menu; good value weekday set menus.

Avalon

16 Balham Hill ✉ SW12 9EB ⊖ Clapham South. – ☎ (020) 8675 8613 – www.theavalonlondon.com **6**EX**r**

Rest – *(booking advisable)* Menu £ 18 – Carte £ 20/25

♦ Fully renovated pub that has a suitably mythical edge to its aesthetic. Tiled rear dining room with plenty of bustle. Menu combines British and Mediterranean influences in no-nonsense cooking.

LONDON

Battersea

Chada

208-210 Battersea Park Rd. ✉ SW11 4ND – ✆ (020) 7622 2209 – www.chadathai.com – Closed bank holidays and Sunday **23**QZH**x**

Rest – Thai – *(dinner only)* Carte £ 19/47

◆ Going strong after 20 years; its striking façade stands out in an otherwise unremarkable street. The welcome is warm, the service polite and the Thai food appealing and keenly priced.

Ransome's Dock

35-37 Parkgate Rd. ✉ SW11 4NP – ✆ (020) 7223 1611 – www.ransomesdock.co.uk – Closed 25-26 December, August bank holiday and Sunday dinner **23**QZG**c**

Rest – British – Carte £ 23/38

◆ Husband and wife team run a brasserie-style operation in a converted warehouse, with a canal-side terrace. Careful sourcing underpins the cooking. Thoughtful, varied and sensibly priced wine list.

Tom Ilić

123 Queenstown Rd. ✉ SW8 3RH – ✆ (020) 7622 0555 – www.tomilic.com – Closed Christmas, 1 week August, dinner Sunday, lunch Tuesday and Monday

Rest – Traditional – *(booking essential)* Menu £ 17/22 – Carte £ 27/36 **24**RZH**c**

◆ Spacious, simply decorated neighbourhood restaurant offering an appealing offal-based menu, with plenty of pork. Skilled, intricate cooking with bold, gutsy flavours to the fore.

Butcher & Grill

39-41 Parkgate Rd ✉ SW11 4NP – ✆ (020) 7924 3999 – www.thebutcherandgrill.com – Closed 25-26 December, dinner Sunday and Bank Holidays **23**QZG**c**

Rest – Traditional – Menu £ 15 (weekdays) – Carte £ 17/43

◆ Former warehouse converted into butcher's-cum-deli-cum-steakhouse. Tables on two levels; comes alive in the evenings. Quality raw ingredients, from lamb burgers and cutlets to rib-eyes and T-bones.

Bolingbroke

174 Northcote Rd ✉ SW11 6RE ⊖ Clapham Junction (Rail). – ✆ (020) 7228 4040 – www.thebolingbroke.com **6**EX**z**

Rest – Menu £ 19 – Carte £ 25/33

◆ Smart, locally popular pub whose more diminutive size adds extra charm. Glass-roofed dining room sees flavoursome dishes with a mostly British accent; more choice at dinner. Child friendly.

Battersea Heliport

Verta

Bridges Wharf ✉ SW11 3BE – ✆ (020) 7801 3500 – www.hotelverta.co.uk

68 rm – †£ 210/294 ††£ 210/294, ☕ £ 19.50 – 2 suites **23**PZH**v**

Rest *Patrisey* – Carte £ 33/44

◆ Built in 2010, in a unique riverside location with a heliport. Well-equipped bedrooms; those without views are bigger than those with. Impressive spa facilities. Choose from a wide-ranging menu, while watching the helicopters land.

Putney

Enoteca Turi

28 Putney High St. ✉ SW15 1SQ ⊖ Putney Bridge – ✆ (020) 8785 4449 – www.enotecaturi.com – Closed 25-26 December, 1 January, lunch bank holidays and Sunday **22**MZH**n**

Rest – Italian – Menu £ 19/30 – Carte £ 26/38

◆ A long-standing owner-run Italian restaurant. Earthy cooking focuses on the northerly regions of Italy. Interesting wine list, with plenty by the glass and carafe.

Prince of Wales

138 Upper Richmond Rd ✉ SW15 2SP ⊖ East Putney. – ✆ (020) 8788 1552 – www.princeofwalesputney.co.uk **22**MZH**z**

Rest – British – Carte £ 30/40

◆ Warmly run Victorian pub; eat in the busy bar or in lavishly decorated baronial style dining room. Seasonality to the fore, with game a speciality. Spit-roast chickens feature on Sunday lunchtimes.

TOOTING

Kastoori

188 Upper Tooting Rd ✉ SW17 7EJ ⊖ Tooting Bec – ✆ (020) 8767 7027 – www.kastoorirestaurant.com – Closed 25-26 December and lunch Monday and Tuesday **6**EX**v**

Rest – Indian – Carte £ 14/19

◆ The family proudly celebrate their Gujarati heritage by offering a wide selection of vegetarian dishes. Enthusiastic service makes up for the modest look of this long-standing restaurant.

WANDSWORTH

Chez Bruce (Bruce Poole)

2 Bellevue Rd ✉ SW17 7EG ⊖ Tooting Bec – ✆ (020) 8672 0114 – www.chezbruce.co.uk – Closed 24-26 December and 1 January **6**EX**e**

Rest – French – *(booking essential)* Menu £ 28 (weekday lunch)/45

Spec. Hake with courgette flower, escabèche of mackerel and coriander. Pork with choucroute, crispy belly and boudin blanc. Apricot and almond tart with amaretto ice cream.

◆ Simply decorated neighbourhood restaurant serving confident classical French cooking with a touch of the Mediterranean. Animated, informal atmosphere; well-organised service.

WESTMINSTER (City of) – Greater London – pop. 181 766 — 12 B3

BAYSWATER AND MAIDA VALE

Lancaster London

Lancaster Ter. ✉ W2 2TY ⊖ Lancaster Gate – ✆ (020) 7262 6737 – www.lancasterlondon.com **28**ADU**e**

394 rm – †£ 191/372 ††£ 191/372, ☕ £ 20 – 22 suites

Rest *Nipa* – see restaurant listing

Rest *Island* – Modern European – ✆ (020) 7551 6070 – Menu £ 19 (early dinner) – Carte £ 24/48

◆ Formerly called the Royal Lancaster. Imposing 1960s purpose-built hotel overlooking Hyde Park. Extensive conference facilities. Well-equipped bedrooms are decorated in traditional style. Modern, stylish restaurant with buzzy open kitchen. Full length windows allow good views of adjacent Hyde Park. Seasonally based, modern menus with wide range of dishes.

The Hempel

31-35 Craven Hill Gdns. ✉ W2 3EA ⊖ Queensway – ✆ (020) 7298 9000 – www.the-hempel.co.uk – Closed 24-28 December **28**ACU**a**

44 rm – †£ 219/334 ††£ 219/334, ☕ £ 21.50 – 6 suites

Rest *No.35* – *(closed Sunday) (dinner only)* Carte £ 32/47

◆ A crisp, minimalist environment in a blizzard of white; room 110 has a suspended bed. Basement art gallery also used for private parties. Zen garden in the Square opposite. Bright, ground floor dining room has a British menu. Trendy restaurant with European menu.

Colonnade Town House without rest

2 Warrington Cres ✉ W9 1ER ⊖ Warwick Avenue – ✆ (020) 7286 1052 – www.theetoncollection.co.uk **17**OZD**e**

43 rm – †£ 144/288 ††£ 144/288, ☕ £ 12.50

◆ Former hospital in quiet yet central location. Bedrooms range in size according to grade; all are comfy and classically furnished with good amenities. Tapas served in bar/on pleasant terrace.

LONDON

LONDON

New Linden without rest

59 Leinster Sq. ✉ W2 4PS ⊖ Bayswater – ✆ (020) 7221 4321 – www.mayflower-group.co.uk **27**ABU**e**

50 rm – †£ 110/144 ††£ 156/180

♦ Smart four storey white stucco façade. Basement breakfast room with sunny aspect. Bedrooms are its strength: flat screen TVs and wooden floors; two split-level family rooms.

Le Café Anglais

8 Porchester Gdns. ✉ W2 4BD ⊖ Bayswater – ✆ (020) 7221 1415 – www.lecafeanglais.co.uk – Closed 25-26 December and 1 January

Rest – Modern European – Menu £ 22/25 – Carte £ 26/46 **27**ABU**r**

♦ Big, bustling and contemporary brasserie with art deco styling, within Whiteley's shopping centre. Large and very appealing selection of classic brasserie food; the rotisserie is the centrepiece.

Angelus

4 Bathurst St. ✉ W2 2SD ⊖ Lancaster Gate – ✆ (020) 7402 0083 – www.angelusrestaurant.co.uk – Closed 24 December-2 January **28**ADU**c**

Rest – French – Menu £ 30 (lunch) – Carte £ 34/56

♦ Hospitable owner has created an attractive French brasserie within a 19C former pub, with a warm and inclusive feel. Satisfying and honest French cooking uses seasonal British ingredients.

Nipa – at Lancaster London Hotel

Lancaster Ter. ✉ W2 2TY ⊖ Lancaster Gate – ✆ (020) 7551 6039 – www.niparestaurant.co.uk – Closed Saturday lunch and Sunday **28**ADU**e**

Rest – Thai – Menu £ 29/32 – Carte £ 26/37

♦ On the 1st floor and overlooking Hyde Park. Authentic and ornately decorated restaurant offers subtly spiced Thai cuisine. Keen to please staff in traditional silk costumes.

Pearl Liang

8 Sheldon Sq., Paddington Central ✉ W2 6EZ ⊖ Paddington – ✆ (020) 7289 7000 – www.pearlliang.co.uk **28**ACT**b**

Rest – Chinese – Menu £ 25 – Carte £ 25/44

♦ Spacious, business-orientated Chinese restaurant within a corporate development. Extensive choice from a variety of set menus; try the more unusual dishes like jellyfish or pig's trotter.

Hereford Road

3 Hereford Rd. ✉ W2 4AB ⊖ Bayswater – ✆ (020) 7727 1144 – www.herefordroad.org – Closed 25-26 December and 1 January **27**ABU**s**

Rest – British – *(booking essential)* Menu £ 16 (weekday lunch) – Carte £ 23/29

♦ Converted butcher's shop specialising in tasty British dishes without frills, using first rate, seasonal ingredients; offal a highlight. Booths for six people are the prized seats. Friendly and relaxed feel.

Assaggi

39 Chepstow Pl., (above Chepstow pub) ✉ W2 4TS ⊖ Bayswater – ✆ (020) 7792 5501 – www.assaggi.com – Closed 2 weeks Christmas, Sunday and bank holidays **27**AAU**c**

Rest – Italian – *(booking essential)* Carte approx. £ 47

♦ Pared-down simplicity to this room above a pub, where regulars are given fulsome welcomes. Cooking relies on the quality of the ingredients and the wine list is exclusively Italian.

El Pirata De Tapas

115 Westbourne Grove ✉ W2 4UP ⊖ Bayswater – ✆ (020) 7727 5000 – www.elpiratadetapas.co.uk **27**ABU**n**

Rest – Spanish – Menu £ 10 (lunch) – Carte approx. £ 25

♦ Contemporary yet warm Spanish restaurant with a genuine neighbourhood feel. Authentic flavours from a well-priced and appealing selection of tapas, ideal for sharing with friends.

Prince Alfred & Formosa Dining Room

5A Formosa St ✉ W9 1EE ⊖ Warwick Avenue. – ✆ (020) 7286 3287
– www.theprincealfred.com **17**OZD**n**

Rest – Carte £ 21/35

◆ Characterful and classic Victorian pub, with a large, more modern dining room in side extension. Open kitchen and a mix of British specialities and European classics. Friendly service.

Warrington

93 Warrington Cres ✉ W9 1EH ⊖ Maida Vale. – ✆ (020) 7592 7960
– www.gordonramsay.com – Closed lunch Monday-Wednesday **17**OZD**a**

Rest – Menu £ 22 (lunch and early dinner) – Carte £ 20/30

◆ Wood panelling, mosaics and friezes add to the atmosphere in the ground floor of this Gordon Ramsay pub. Go upstairs to the restaurant if you want a more sophisticated menu of mostly British produce.

Waterway

54 Formosa St ✉ W9 2JU ⊖ Warwick Avenue. – ✆ (020) 7266 3557
– www.thewaterway.co.uk **17**OZD**p**

Rest – Menu £ 17 (lunch) – Carte £ 30/45

◆ Terrific decked terrace by the canal its most appealing feature. Contemporary interior with busy cocktail bar; menu in separate dining room mixes the classics with more ambitious dishes.

LONDON

Belgravia

Berkeley

Wilton Pl. ✉ SW1X 7RL ⊖ Knightsbridge – ✆ (020) 7235 6000
– www.the-berkeley.co.uk **37**AGX**e**

189 rm – †£ 588/708 ††£ 708, ☕ £ 29 – 25 suites

Rest ***Marcus Wareing at The Berkeley and Koffmann's*** – see restaurant listing

◆ Discreet and rejuvenated hotel with rooftop pool and opulently decorated bedrooms. Relax in the gilded and panelled Caramel Room or have a drink in the cool Blue Bar.

Lanesborough

Hyde Park Corner ✉ SW1X 7TA ⊖ Hyde Park Corner – ✆ (020) 7259 5599
– www.lanesborough.com **37**AGX**a**

86 rm – †£ 450/594 ††£ 594, ☕ £ 30 – 10 suites

Rest ***Apsleys*** – see restaurant listing

◆ Converted in the 1990s from 18C St George's Hospital. Butler service offered. Regency-era inspired decoration; lavishly appointed rooms with impressive technological extras.

Halkin

5 Halkin St ✉ SW1X 7DJ ⊖ Hyde Park Corner – ✆ (020) 7333 1000
– www.halkin.como.bz **38**AHX**b**

35 rm – †£ 348/600 ††£ 348/600, ☕ £ 27.50 – 6 suites

Rest ***Nahm*** – see restaurant listing

◆ Opened in 1991 as London's first boutique hotel and still looking sharp today. Thoughtfully conceived bedrooms with silk walls and marbled bathrooms; everything at the touch of a button. Abundant Armani-clad staff. Small, discreet bar.

Jumeirah Lowndes

21 Lowndes St ✉ SW1X 9ES ⊖ Knightsbridge – ✆ (020) 7823 1234
– www.jumeirahlowndeshotel.com **37**AGX**h**

87 rm – ††£ 598, ☕ £ 27 – 14 suites

Rest ***Mimosa*** – Menu £ 18 (lunch) – Carte approx. £ 33

◆ Compact yet friendly modern corporate hotel within this exclusive residential area. Good levels of personal service offered. Close to the famous shops of Knightsbridge. Modern restaurant opens onto street terrace.

Marcus Wareing at The Berkeley
Wilton Pl. SW1X 7RL Knightsbridge – (020) 7235 1200 – www.marcus-wareing.com – Closed Saturday lunch and Sunday **37**AGX**e**
Rest – French – Menu £ 38/75
Spec. Sweetbread, ginger and pineapple gastrique. Halibut with lobster, asparagus and almonds. Basil parfait with lemon caramel and sherbet.
♦ Marcus Wareing's cooking is creative, sophisticated and backed by sound classical techniques. The restaurant is sumptuously appointed, and service is smooth and well-organised. The chef's table is one of the best in town.

Apsleys – at Lanesborough Hotel
Hyde Park Corner SW1X 7TA Hyde Park Corner – (020) 7333 7254 – www.apsleys.co.uk **37**AGX**a**
Rest – Italian – Menu £ 28/35 – Carte £ 51/80
Spec. Potato agnolotti with lobster. Pigeon with pearl onions and mustard seed sauce. Chocolate dome with mint and sea salt ice cream.
♦ Under the guidance of celebrated chef Heinz Beck from Rome's La Pergola. Exquisite and precise Italian cooking, in a grand, eye-catching but far from intimidating room, designed by Adam Tihany. The serving team are polished and the atmosphere upbeat.

LONDON

Pétrus
1 Kinnerton St. SW1X 8EA Knightsbridge – (020) 7592 1609 – www.gordonramsay.com/petrus – Closed 25 December and Sunday
Rest – Modern European – Menu £ 25/55 **37**AGX**v**
Spec. Langoustine tail with watercress soup and confit potato. Beef fillet and shin with celeriac and Barolo sauce. Chocolate sphere with milk ice cream and honeycomb.
♦ Elegant Gordon Ramsay restaurant, opened in 2010, in tones of silver, oyster and – as a nod to the name – claret. Immaculately laid tables; experienced service team with personality. Elaborate French-based cooking uses top quality ingredients.

Amaya
Halkin Arcade, 19 Motcomb St SW1X 8JT Knightsbridge – (020) 7823 1166 – www.realindianfood.com – Closed 25 December **37**AGX**k**
Rest – Indian – Menu £ 25/39 – Carte £ 32/68
Spec. Tarragon and turmeric chicken tikka. Duck grilled wtih tamarind glaze. Rose petal crème brûlée.
♦ Order a selection of small dishes from the tawa griddle, tandoor or sigri grill and finish with a curry or biryani. Dishes are aromatic and satisfying and the cooking skilled and consistent. The busy restaurant is suitably bright and colourful.

Zafferano
15 Lowndes St SW1X 9EY Knightsbridge – (020) 7235 5800 – www.zafferanorestaurant.com – Closed Christmas-New Year **37**AGX**f**
Rest – Italian – *(booking essential)* Carte £ 36/65
Spec. Cured pork in figs, mozzarella in carrozza. Pappardelle with lamb ragu and pecorino cheese. Chocolate fondant with gianduia chocolate ice cream.
♦ Pasta is the star of the show at this perennially busy Italian restaurant. The cooking is reliable and assured and the menus balanced. The stylish surroundings are comfortable but also full of bustle; the bar is an appealing adjunct.

Koffmann's – at Berkeley Hotel
Wilton Pl. SW1X 7RL Knightsbridge – (020) 7235 1010 – www.the-berkeley.co.uk **37**AGX**u**
Rest – French – Menu £ 23 (lunch) – Carte £ 46/77
♦ Pierre Koffmann, one of London's most fêted chefs, was enticed out of retirement to open this smart, comfortable and spacious restaurant. Expect plenty of gutsy flavours true to his Gascon roots.

Nahm – at Halkin Hotel
5 Halkin St. SW1X 7DJ Hyde Park Corner – (020) 7333 1234 – www.halkin.como.bz – Closed lunch Saturday and Sunday **38**AHX**b**
Rest – Thai – *(booking advisable)* Menu £ 25/60 – Carte £ 40/50
♦ An appealing mix of copper tones, wood and candlelight, along with an understated hint of Asian design, gives the room a warm feel. The Thai cuisine served here is based on Royal Thai traditions.

XX **Noura Brasserie**

16 Hobart Pl. ✉ SW1W 0HH ⊖ Victoria – ✆ (020) 7235 9444 – www.noura.co.uk **38**AHX**n**

Rest – Lebanese – Menu £ 18/45 – Carte £ 24/39

♦ Dine in either the bright bar or the comfortable, contemporary restaurant. Authentic, modern Lebanese cooking specialises in chargrilled meats and meze.

Pantechnicon Rooms

10 Motcomb St ✉ SW1X 8LA ⊖ Knightsbridge – ✆ (020) 7730 6074 – www.thepantechnicon.com **37**AGX**d**

Rest – Carte £ 30/45

♦ Urbane, enthusiastically run pub with a busy ground floor and altogether more formal upstairs dining room. Traditional dishes are given a modern twist; oysters and Scottish steaks are perennials.

Hyde Park and Knightsbridge

Mandarin Oriental Hyde Park

66 Knightsbridge ✉ SW1X 7LA ⊖ Knightsbridge – ✆ (020) 7235 2000 – www.mandarinoriental.com/london **37**AGX**x**

173 rm – †£ 666/750 ††£ 666/750, ☕ £ 29 – 25 suites

Rest ***Bar Boulud*** – see restaurant listing

♦ Built in 1889 this classic hotel, with striking façade, remains one of London's grandest. Many of the luxurious and impeccably kept bedrooms enjoy views of Hyde Park. Heston Blumenthal due to open as we went to print.

XX **Zuma**

5 Raphael St ✉ SW7 1DL ⊖ Knightsbridge – ✆ (020) 7584 1010 – www.zumarestaurant.com – Closed 25-26 December-1 January **37**AFX**m**

Rest – Japanese – Carte £ 60/90

♦ Eye-catching design that blends East with West. Bustling atmosphere; fashionable clientele; popular sushi bar. Varied and interesting contemporary Japanese food.

XX **Bar Boulud** – at Mandarin Oriental Hyde Park Hotel

66 Knightsbridge ✉ SW1X 7LA ⊖ Knightsbridge – ✆ (020) 7201 3899 – www.barboulud.com/barbouludlondon **37**AGX**x**

Rest – French – Menu £ 20 (lunch and early dinner) – Carte £ 29/48

♦ Daniel Boulud's London outpost is fashionable, fun and frantic. His hometown is Lyon but he built his considerable reputation in New York, so charcuterie, sausages and burgers are the highlights.

XX **Mr Chow**

151 Knightsbridge ✉ SW1X 7PA ⊖ Knightsbridge – ✆ (020) 7589 7347 – www.mrchow.com – Closed 24-26 December, 1 January and Monday lunch

Rest – Chinese – Carte £ 39/63 **37**AFX**e**

♦ Long-standing Chinese restaurant, opened in 1968. Smart clientele, stylish and comfortable surroundings and prompt service from Italian waiters. Carefully prepared and satisfying food.

Mayfair

Dorchester

Park Ln. ✉ W1K 1QA ⊖ Hyde Park Corner – ✆ (020) 7629 8888 – www.thedorchester.com **30**AHV**a**

196 rm – †£ 258/906 ††£ 318/906, ☕ £ 31.50 – 54 suites

Rest ***Alain Ducasse at The Dorchester and China Tang*** – see restaurant listing

Rest ***The Grill*** – Menu £ 26/30 – Carte £ 44/90

♦ A sumptuously decorated, luxury hotel offering every possible facility. Impressive marbled and pillared promenade. Rooms quintessentially English in style. Exemplary levels of service. Exuberant tartan décor in The Grill.

LONDON

Claridge's

Brook St ✉ *W1K 4HR* ⊖ *Bond Street* – ✆ *(020) 7629 8860*
– *www.claridges.co.uk* **30**AHU **c**

143 rm – †£ 732 ††£ 732, ☕ £ 29 – 60 suites

Rest *Gordon Ramsay at Claridge's* – see restaurant listing

♦ Rightly celebrated for its art deco and one of London's finest hotels. Exceptionally well-appointed and sumptuous bedrooms, all with butler service. Magnificent Foyer for afternoon tea.

Connaught

Carlos Pl. ✉ *W1K 2AL* ⊖ *Bond Street* – ✆ *(020) 7499 7070*
– *www.the-connaught.co.uk* **30**AHU **e**

95 rm – †£ 660 ††£ 780, ☕ £ 30 – 26 suites

Rest *Hélène Darroze at The Connaught* – see restaurant listing

Rest *Espelette* – ✆ (020) 3147 7100 – Carte £ 39/77

♦ Restored and renovated but still retaining an elegant British feel. Now this famous London hotel offers a choice between contemporary and classic bedrooms. Two stylish bars. Espelette an all-day venue for classic French and British dishes.

InterContinental

1 Hamilton Pl, Park Ln. ✉ *W1J 7QY* ⊖ *Hyde Park Corner* – ✆ *(020) 7409 3131*
– *www.london.intercontinental.com* **30**AHV **k**

399 rm – †£ 275/475 ††£ 275/475, ☕ £ 26.50 – 48 suites

Rest *Theo Randall* – see restaurant listing

Rest *Cookbook Café* – Carte £ 29/61

♦ International hotel relaunched in 2007 after major refit. English-style bedrooms with hi-tech equipment and large, open-plan lobby. Cookbook Café invites visiting chefs to showcase their talents.

London Hilton

22 Park Ln. ✉ *W1K 1BE* ⊖ *Hyde Park Corner* – ✆ *(020) 7493 8000*
– *www.hilton.co.uk/londonparklane* **30**AHV **e**

397 rm – †£ 246/660 ††£ 246/660, ☕ £ 26.50 – 56 suites

Rest *Galvin at Windows* – see restaurant listing

Rest *Trader Vics* – ✆ (020) 7208 4113 *(closed 25-26 December)*
Carte £ 33/53

Rest *Podium* – ✆ (020) 7208 4022 – Menu £ 21
– Carte £ 28/50

♦ This 28 storey tower is one of the city's tallest hotels, providing impressive views from the upper floors. Club floor bedrooms are particularly comfortable. Exotic Trader Vics with bamboo and plants. Modern European food in Podium.

Grosvenor House

Park Ln. ✉ *W1K 7TN* ⊖ *Marble Arch* – ✆ *(020) 7499 6363*
– *www.londongrosvenorhouse.co.uk* **29**G3

378 rm – †£ 299/395 ††£ 299/395, ☕ £ 28 – 52 suites

Rest *JW Steakhouse* – ✆ (020) 7399 8460
– Carte £ 35/70

♦ Refurbished hotel in commanding position by Hyde Park. Uniform, comfortable bedrooms in classic Marriott styling. Boasts the largest ballroom in Europe. JW Steakhouse serves prime, hand-cut beef and fresh seafood.

Westbury

Bond St. ✉ *W1S 2YF* ⊖ *Bond Street* – ✆ *(020) 7629 7755*
– *www.westburymayfair.com* **30**AIU **a**

232 rm – †£ 238/561 ††£ 298/618, ☕ £ 26 – 13 suites

Rest – *(closed Saturday lunch and Sunday dinner)* Menu £ 30/58

♦ Caused a commotion with its New York styling when it opened in the 1950s; now fully refurbished. Smart, comfortable bedrooms; art deco suites. Elegant, well-known Polo bar. Bright, fresh restaurant; extensive private dining facilities.

LONDON

Brown's
Albemarle St. ✉ *W1S 4BP* ⊖ *Green Park* – ✆ *(020) 7493 6020 – www.roccofortecollection.com* **30**AIV**d**
105 rm – †£ 312/474 ††£ 354/540, ☕ £ 27 – 12 suites
Rest *HIX at The Albemarle* – British – ✆ (020) 7518 4004 – Menu £ 30 – Carte £ 28/64
♦ This urbane hotel with an illustrious past offers a swish bar featuring Terence Donovan prints, up-to-the minute bedrooms and a quintessentially English sitting room for tea. Wood panelled dining room with traditional British cooking.

London Marriott H. Park Lane
140 Park Lane ✉ *W1K 7AA* ⊖ *Marble Arch* – ✆ *(020) 7493 7000 – www.londonmarriott.parklane.co* **29**AGU**b**
148 rm – †£ 419 ††£ 419, ☕ £ 25 – 9 suites
Rest *140 Park Lane* – Menu £ 22 – Carte £ 31/48
♦ This international hotel is usefully located close to the shops of Oxford Street and Hyde Park. Well-kept basement health club. Smart, generously sized bedrooms are well-equipped. Attractive restaurant overlooks Marble Arch.

Metropolitan
Old Park Ln ✉ *W1K 1LB* ⊖ *Hyde Park Corner* – ✆ *(020) 7447 1000 – www.metropolitan.como.bz – Closed 25 December and 1 January* **30**AHV**c**
147 rm – †£ 468 ††£ 468, ☕ £ 28 – 3 suites
Rest *Nobu* – see restaurant listing
♦ Minimalist interior and a voguish reputation has made this hotel and its Met Bar the favoured choice of pop stars and celebrities. Sleek design and fashionably attired staff set it apart.

Athenaeum
116 Piccadilly ✉ *W1J 7BJ* ⊖ *Hyde Park Corner* – ✆ *(020) 7499 3464 – www.athenaeumhotel.com* **30**AHV**g**
145 rm – †£ 390 ††£ 516, ☕ £ 27 – 11 suites
Rest *Damask* – Menu £ 19/27 – Carte £ 43/63
♦ A new look for this 1920s building, with its stylish bedrooms which come in cool pastel shades and have floor to ceiling windows. 'Living Wall' a striking feature, along with whisky-stocked bar. Bright restaurant offers plenty of classics.

Chesterfield
35 Charles St. ✉ *W1J 5EB* ⊖ *Green Park* – ✆ *(020) 7491 2622 – www.chesterfieldmayfair.com* **30**AHV**f**
103 rm – †£ 222/402 ††£ 246/402, ☕ £ 22.50 – 4 suites
Rest – Menu £ 30 (lunch) – Carte £ 37/59
♦ An assuredly English feel to this Georgian house. Discreet lobby leads to a clubby bar and wood panelled library. Individually decorated bedrooms, with some antique pieces. Intimate and pretty restaurant.

London Marriott H. Grosvenor Square
Grosvenor Sq. ✉ *W1K 6JP* ⊖ *Bond Street* – ✆ *(020) 7493 1232 – www.marriottgrosvenorsquare.com* **30**AHU**s**
226 rm – †£ 275/430 ††£ 275/430, ☕ £ 22 – 11 suites
Rest *Maze Grill* – see restaurant listing
♦ A well-appointed international group hotel that benefits from an excellent location in the heart of Mayfair. Many of the bedrooms specifically equipped for the business traveller.

Hilton London Green Park
Half Moon St. ✉ *W1J 7BN* ⊖ *Green Park* – ✆ *(020) 7629 7522 – www.hilton.co.uk/greenpark* **30**AIV**a**
162 rm – †£ 114/305 ††£ 137/317, ☕ £ 19.95
Rest – *(bar lunch Saturday and Sunday)* Menu £ 20 **s** – Carte £ 31/36 **s**
♦ A row of sympathetically adjoined townhouses in the heart of Mayfair, dating from the 1730s. Bedrooms vary in size and shape; those on the first and fifth floors have been refurbished in a bright, contemporary style. Modern menu served in airy restaurant.

LONDON

Alain Ducasse at The Dorchester

Park Ln. ✉ W1K 1QA ⊖ Hyde Park Corner – ✆ (020) 7629 8866 – www.alainducasse-dorchester.com – Closed 25 December dinner until dinner 31 December, 22-25 April, 7-30 August, Saturday lunch, Sunday and Monday **30**AHV**a**

Rest – French – Menu £ 50/78

Spec. Roasted chicken and lobster with sweetbreads. Fillet of beef and foie gras Rossini with'sacristain' potatoes. 'Baba like in Monte-Carlo'.

♦ Luxury and extravagance are the hallmarks of this Alain Ducasse outpost. Dining room is elegant without being staid; food is modern and refined yet satisfying and balanced. Service is formal and well-organised.

Hélène Darroze at The Connaught

Carlos Pl. ✉ W1K 2AL ⊖ Bond Street – ✆ (020) 3147 7200 – www.the-connaught.co.uk – Closed 2 weeks August, 1 week January, Saturday lunch, Sunday and Monday **30**AHU**e**

Rest – French – *(booking essential)* Menu £ 35/75

Spec. Foie gras with mild spices and dried fruit chutney. Scallops with tandoori spices and lemongrass. Strawberry and bay leaf panna cotta with lemon jelly.

♦ Landes and the SW of France inform Hélène Darroze's exquisite cooking, although international influences also play a part. The dining room is elegant and comfortable, with original mahogany wood panelling. Service is courteous and professional.

Le Gavroche (Michel Roux Jnr)

43 Upper Brook St. ✉ W1K 7QR ⊖ Marble Arch – ✆ (020) 7408 0881 – www.le-gavroche.co.uk – Closed Christmas-New Year, Sunday and bank holidays **29**AGU**c**

Rest – French – *(booking essential)* Menu £ 49 (lunch) – Carte £ 60/107

Spec. Soufflé Suissesse. Roast black-leg chicken with morels and madeira sauce. Chocolate and praline indulgence with gold leaf.

♦ Classic and indulgent French cuisine is the draw at Michel Roux's renowned London institution. The large, smart basement room has a clubby, masculine feel; service is formal and structured.

Square (Philip Howard)

6-10 Bruton St. ✉ W1J 6PU ⊖ Green Park – ✆ (020) 7495 7100 – www.squarerestaurant.com – Closed 25 December, 1 January and lunch Saturday, Sunday and bank holidays, **30**AIU**v**

Rest – French – Menu £ 35/75

Spec. Langoustine with Parmesan gnocchi and truffle. Saddle of hare with tarte fine of celeriac and pear. Brillat-Savarin cheesecake with passion fruit and mango.

♦ Confident and accomplished kitchen which understands the importance of sound techniques, prime ingredients and clarity of flavour. The room is comfortable and the buoyant atmosphere prevents things becoming too formal. Good cheeseboard.

Sketch (The Lecture Room & Library)

9 Conduit St., (First Floor) ✉ W1S 2XG ⊖ Oxford Street – ✆ (020) 7659 4500 – www.sketch.uk.com – Closed 25-30 December, last 2 weeks August, Saturday lunch, Sunday, Monday and bank holidays **30**AIU**h**

Rest – French – *(booking essential)* Menu £ 35 (lunch) – Carte £ 70/129

Spec. Langoustines 'addressed in five ways'. Lamb with aubergine, tomato, ewe's milk cheese and spinach. Pierre Gagnaire's 'grand dessert'.

♦ Pierre Gagnaire's London operation is found within a striking 18C townhouse which is full of colour, energy and vitality. The menus offer plenty of choice; cooking is ambitious and elaborate, and dishes arrive artfully presented.

XXXX ✿ **Galvin at Windows** – at London Hilton Hotel

22 Park Ln. ✉ W1K 1BE ⊖ Hyde Park Corner – ✆ (020) 7208 4021 – www.galvinatwindows.com – Closed 25 December, Saturday lunch, Sunday dinner and bank holidays **30**AHV**e**

Rest – French – Menu £ 27/65

Spec. Scallop, cuttlefish and chorizo paella. Spiced pigeon with foie gras boudin and macaroni gratin. Rum baba with crème Chantilly.

♦ Spectacular views from the 28th floor of the Hilton are not the only draw: the room is contemporary and cleverly laid out, service is attentive and efficient and the cooking is confident, detailed, balanced and satisfying.

XXXX **Gordon Ramsay at Claridge's**

Brook St. ✉ W1K 4HR ⊖ Bond Street – ✆ (020) 7499 0099 – www.gordonramsay.com/claridges **30**AHU**c**

Rest – Modern European – *(booking essential)* Menu £ 30/70

♦ Grand and impressive room within the elegant surroundings of Claridge's hotel. Service is ceremonial and structured and the cooking is classically based. Popular chef's table in the kitchen.

XXXX **China Tang** – at Dorchester Hotel

Park Ln. ✉ W1A 2HJ ⊖ Hyde Park Corner – ✆ (020) 7629 9988 – www.thedorchester.com – Closed 25 December **30**AHV**a**

Rest – Chinese – Menu £ 15 (lunch) – Carte £ 40/70

♦ Sir David Tang's atmospheric, art deco-inspired Chinese restaurant is always abuzz with activity. The kitchen is a model of conservatism and concentrates on traditional Cantonese specialities.

XXX ✿✿ **Hibiscus** (Claude Bosi)

29 Maddox St. ✉ W1S 2PA ⊖ Oxford Circus – ✆ (020) 7629 2999 – www.hibiscusrestaurant.co.uk – Closed 23 December-3 January, Sunday and Monday **30**AIU**s**

Rest – Innovative – Menu £ 30/75

Spec. Smoked sweetbreads with lettuce velouté and brown butter. Lobster with pork 'san choi bau' and hollandaise. Chocolate tart with basil ice cream.

♦ Claude Bosi's cooking is creative and bold, but with a sound, classical base; desserts are a real highlight. Attractive room combines French oak with Welsh slate as a reminder of his previous restaurant in Ludlow. Formal and conscientious service.

XXX ✿ **Greenhouse**

27a Hay's Mews ✉ W1J 5NY ⊖ Hyde Park Corner – ✆ (020) 7499 3331 – www.greenhouserestaurant.co.uk – Closed 24 December-4 January, Saturday lunch, Sunday and bank holidays **30**AHV**m**

Rest – Innovative – Menu £ 29/70

Spec. Calves sweetbreads with wild garlic and leeks. Lamb with artichokes, quinoa and lemon cream. "Snix" - chocolate, salted caramel and peanuts.

♦ Smart, elegant restaurant broken up into sections by glass screens. Innovative selection of elaborately presented dishes, underpinned with sound French culinary techniques.

XXX ✿ **Murano** (Angela Hartnett)

20 Queen St. ✉ W1J 5PP ⊖ Green Park – ✆ (020) 7495 1127 – www.angela-hartnett.com – Closed 24 December until dinner 31 December and Sunday **30**AHV**b**

Rest – Italian influences – Menu £ 30/60

Spec. Apple, black pudding and octopus salad with chorizo oil. Lamb with celery and olive pureé, artichokes and garlic. Chocolate mousse with raspberry sorbet.

♦ Now wholly owned by chef Angela Hartnett, this bright and stylishly decorated restaurant provides a luminous setting for her refined and balanced cooking, with its strong Italian influences. The best tables are at the front, by the window.

LONDON

XXX **Maze**

10-13 Grosvenor Sq. ✉ W1K 6JP ⊖ Bond Street – ✆ (020) 7107 0000 – www.gordonramsay.com **30**AHU**z**

Rest – Innovative – Menu £ 23 (lunch) – Carte £ 29/33

Spec. Terrine of foie gras and smoked eel with apple and celery. Roast duck with pickled red endive and beetroot. Rice pudding with chocolate and an orange and thyme marmalade.

◆ Choose a variety of small but expertly formed dishes at this sleek and stylish contemporary restaurant. The cooking is innovative, balanced and precise; service is well-organised.

XXX **Kai**

65 South Audley St. ✉ W1K 2QU ⊖ Hyde Park Corner – ✆ (020) 7493 8988 – www.kaimayfair.co.uk – Closed 25-26 December and 1 January **30**AHV**n**

Rest – Chinese – *(booking essential)* Menu £ 19 (lunch) – Carte £ 40/75

Spec. Wasabi prawns with mango and basil seeds. Sea bass with chickpeas, shallots and ginger. Rice dumplings with ginger and honey wafers.

◆ Carefully prepared Chinese food, from a menu that mixes the classics with more innovative dishes; flavours are clean and assured. Spread over two floors, with sweet natured service and smart surroundings.

XXX **Benares** (Atul Kochhar)

12a Berkeley Square House ✉ W1J 6BS ⊖ Green Park – ✆ (020) 7629 8886 – www.benaresrestaurant.com – Closed 25 December and 1 January

Rest – Indian – Menu £ 25 (lunch) – Carte £ 45/83 **30**AIU**q**

Spec. Tandoor roasted pigeon with vanilla and beetroot. Tiger prawns with asparagus and spring onions. Strawberry jelly with black pepper and yoghurt parfait.

◆ Modern techniques are added to a classical base to create contemporary Indian cuisine that continues to evolve. The smart first-floor surroundings match the food in their sophistication. Popular and stylish Chef's Table.

XXX **Tamarind**

20 Queen St. ✉ W1J 5PR ⊖ Green Park – ✆ (020) 7629 3561 – www.tamarindrestaurant.com – Closed 25-27 December, 1 January, lunch Saturday and bank holidays **30**AHV**h**

Rest – Indian – Menu £ 19 (weekday lunch) – Carte £ 48/72

Spec. Spiced chickpeas and whole-wheat crisps with mint chutney. Lamb cutlets marinated with garlic, papaya and fennel. Mango kulfi.

◆ Makes the best use of its basement location, with smoked mirrors, gilded columns and a somewhat exclusive feel. Appealing and balanced Indian cooking; kebabs and curries are the specialities, complemented by carefully prepared vegetable dishes.

XXX **Umu**

14-16 Bruton Pl ✉ W1J 6LX ⊖ Bond Street – ✆ (020) 7499 8881 – www.umurestaurant.com – Closed 24 December-6 January, Saturday lunch, Sunday and bank holidays **30**AIU**k**

Rest – Japanese – Menu £ 25 (lunch) – Carte £ 33/48

Spec. Langoustine with amber tomato jelly, vinaigrette and caviar. Pigeon with radish and egg yolk sauce. Japanese tiramisu with macha tea and sake.

◆ Stylish, discreet interior using natural materials, with central sushi bar. Extensive choice of Japanese dishes; choose one of the seasonal kaiseki menus for the full experience. Over 160 different labels of sake.

XXX **Scott's**

20 Mount St ✉ W1K 2HE ⊖ Bond Street – ✆ (020) 7495 7309 – www.scotts-restaurant.com – Closed dinner 24, 25-26 December and 1 January

Rest – Seafood – Carte £ 33/64 **30**AHU**d**

◆ A landmark London institution reborn. Stylish yet traditional; oak panelling juxtaposed with vibrant artwork from young British artists. Top quality seafood, kept simple.

LONDON

XXX **Cecconi's**
5a Burlington Gdns ✉ W1S 3EP ⊖ Green Park – ✆ (020) 7434 1500 – www.cecconis.com – Closed 25 December **30**AIU**d**
Rest – Italian – *(booking essential)* Carte £ 27/45
♦ Branches of this fashionable restaurant are now opening up around the world. Regulars pop in for a bite at the bar; the restaurant prepares the classic dishes with care. Open from breakfast onwards; popular for weekend brunches.

XXX **Corrigan's Mayfair**
28 Upper Grosvenor St. ✉ W1K 7EH ⊖ Marble Arch – ✆ (020) 7499 9943 – www.corrigansmayfair.com – Closed 25-26 December, 1 January and Saturday lunch **29**AGU**a**
Rest – British – Menu £ 27 (lunch) – Carte £ 43/73
♦ Richard Corrigan's flagship celebrates British and Irish cooking, with game a speciality. The room is comfortable, clubby and quite glamorous and feels as though it has been around for years.

XXX **Bentley's (Grill)**
11-15 Swallow St. ✉ W1B 4DG ⊖ Piccadilly Circus – ✆ (020) 7734 4756 – www.bentleys.org – Closed 25-26 December, 1 January, Saturday lunch and Sunday **30**AJU**n**
Rest – British – Carte £ 35/90
♦ Entrance into striking bar; panelled staircase to richly decorated restaurant. Carefully sourced seafood or meat dishes enhanced by clean, crisp cooking. Unruffled service.

XXX **Theo Randall** – at Intercontinental Hotel
1 Hamilton Pl, Park Ln. ✉ W1J 7QY ⊖ Hyde Park Corner – ✆ (020) 7318 8747 – www.theorandall.com – Closed Saturday lunch, Sunday and Bank Holidays **30**AHV**k**
Rest – Italian – Menu £ 27 (lunch) – Carte £ 45/55
♦ Daily changing seasonal menu of comforting Italian dishes, served in the smart and spacious surroundings of an international hotel. Wood oven a feature; produce imported directly from Italy.

XXX **Sartoria**
20 Savile Row ✉ W1S 3PR ⊖ Green Park – ✆ (020) 7534 7000 – www.sartoriabar.com – Closed 24-25 December, Sunday, Saturday lunch and bank holidays **30**AIU**b**
Rest – Italian – Menu £ 24 – Carte £ 34/44
♦ In the street renowned for English tailoring, a coolly sophisticated restaurant to suit those looking for classic Italian cooking with modern touches.

XXX **Avista**
Millennium Mayfair Hotel, 39 Grosvenor Sq ✉ W1K 2HP ⊖ Bond Street – ✆ (020) 7596 3399 – www.avistarestaurant.com – Closed Saturday lunch and Sunday **30**AHU**x**
Rest – Italian – Menu £ 23 (lunch) – Carte £ 28/66
♦ A large room, softened by neutral shades, within the Millennium Hotel. The menu traverses Italy and the cooking marries the rustic with the more refined. Pasta dishes are a highlight.

XX ✿ **Wild Honey**
12 St George St. ✉ W1S 2FB ⊖ Oxford Circus – ✆ (020) 7758 9160 – www.wildhoneyrestaurant.co.uk – Closed 25-26 December and 1 January **30**AIU**w**
Rest – Modern European – Menu £ 20 (lunch) – Carte £ 33/46
Spec. Belly pork with snails, garlic and parsley. Veal with gnocchi and young vegetables. Wild honey ice cream with crushed honeycomb.
♦ Skilled kitchen uses seasonal ingredients at their peak to create dishes full of flavour and free from ostentation. Attractive oak-panelled room, with booth seating for larger groups. Personable and unobtrusive service.

LONDON

XX ✿ **Semplice** (Marco Torri) A/C VISA MC AE

9-10 Blenheim St. ✉ *W1S 1LJ* ⊖ *Bond Street* – ✆ *(020) 7495 1509 – www.ristorantesemplice.com – Closed 2 weeks Christmas, Easter, Saturday lunch and Sunday* **30**AHU**k**

Rest – Italian – *(booking essential at dinner)* Menu £ 30 (lunch) – Carte £ 34/53

Spec. Veal served with tonnata sauce. Rabbit with glazed carrots and artichoke sauce. Domori chocolate fondant

♦ Plenty of regulars are always in evidence in this comfortable and stylish restaurant, decorated with ebony, leather and gold. The enthusiasm of the young owners is palpable; the kitchen uses small, specialist suppliers in unfussy, flavoursome dishes.

XX ✿ **Nobu Berkeley St** A/C VISA MC AE

15 Berkeley St. ✉ *W1J 8DY* ⊖ *Green Park* – ✆ *(020) 7290 9222 – www.noburestaurants.com/berkeley – Closed 25-26 December, Saturday, Sunday and bank holidays* **30**AIV**b**

Rest – Japanese – *(booking essential)* Carte £ 65/85

Spec. King crab claw tempura with butter ponzu. Black cod with miso. Chocolate tart with sake kasu ice cream and chocolate sauce.

♦ Offers all the innovative Nobu favourites, along with specialities from the wood oven. Large, lively but smoothly run first floor operation with plenty of glamour; ground floor destination bar. Helpful, well-informed service.

XX **Maze Grill** – at London Marriott H. Grosvenor Square A/C VISA MC AE ⓓ

10-13 Grosvenor Sq. ✉ *W1K 6JP* ⊖ *Bond Street* – ✆ *(020) 7495 2211 – www.gordonramsay.com* **30**AHU**s**

Rest – Beef specialities – Menu £ 21 (lunch) – Carte £ 30/47

♦ An addendum to Maze, with a menu specialising in steaks, from Hereford grass-fed to Wagyu 9th grade; all appealingly served on wooden boards, with a variety of sauces and side dishes.

XX **Bellamy's** A/C VISA MC AE

18 Bruton Pl. ✉ *W1J 6LY* ⊖ *Bond Street* – ✆ *(020) 7491 2727 – www.bellamysrestaurant.co.uk – Closed Saturday lunch, Sunday and bank holidays,* **30**AIU**c**

Rest – French – Menu £ 29 – Carte £ 43/57

♦ French deli/brasserie tucked down a smart mews. Go past the caviar and cheeses into the restaurant proper for a very traditional, but well-executed, range of Gallic classics.

XX **Patterson's** A/C ⇔ VISA MC AE ⓓ

4 Mill St. ✉ *W1S 2AX* ⊖ *Oxford Street* – ✆ *(020) 7499 1308 – www.pattersonsrestaurant.com – Closed 25-26 December, Saturday lunch and Sunday* **30**AIU**p**

Rest – Modern European – Menu £ 23/45

♦ Stylish modern interior in black and white. Elegant tables and attentive service. Modern British cooking with concise wine list and sensible prices.

XX **Alloro** A/C ⇔ VISA MC AE

19-20 Dover St. ✉ *W1S 4LU* ⊖ *Green Park* – ✆ *(020) 7495 4768 – www.alloro-restaurant.co.uk – Closed Christmas-New Year, Saturday lunch and Sunday* **30**AIV**r**

Rest – Italian – Menu £ 33/35

♦ Confidently run and smartly dressed Italian with an appealing and sensibly priced menu of easy-to-eat dishes. All breads and pasta made in-house. Boisterous and busy adjacent baretto.

XX **Goodman** A/C VISA MC AE

26 Maddox St. ✉ *W1S 1QH* ⊖ *Oxford Circus* – ✆ *(020) 7499 3776 – www.goodmanrestaurants.com – Closed Sunday and bank holidays*

Rest – Beef specialities – *(booking essential)* Menu £ 18 (lunch) – Carte £ 26/51 **30**AIU**u**

♦ A worthy attempt at recreating a New York steakhouse; all leather and wood and macho swagger. Beef is dry or wet aged in house and comes with a choice of four sauces; rib-eye the speciality.

XX **Dolada**

13 Albemarle St. ✉ W1S 4HJ ⊖ Green Park
– ☎ (020) 7409 1011 – www.dolada.co.uk
– Closed 23 December-6 January, Saturday lunch and Sunday **30**AIV**x**

Rest – Italian – Menu £ 23 (lunch) – Carte £ 22/46

♦ Smart basement restaurant lightened by confident and thoughtful service. Dishes from across Italy; the deconstructed spaghetti carbonara a speciality. Even more originality in the tasting menu.

XX **Hush**

8 Lancashire Ct., Brook St. ✉ W1S 1EY ⊖ Bond Street
– ☎ (020) 7659 1500 – www.hush.co.uk
– Closed 25-26 December, 1 January and Sunday **30**AHU**v**

Rest – Modern European – *(booking essential)* Carte £ 25/47

♦ Accessible brasserie-style menu served in a large, busy room; smart destination bar upstairs and plenty of private dining. Tucked away in a charming courtyard, with a summer terrace.

XX **Fakhreldine**

85 Piccadilly ✉ W1J 7NB ⊖ Green Park – ☎ (020) 7493 3424
– www.fakhreldine.co.uk **30**AIV**e**

Rest – Lebanese – Menu £ 14/29 – Carte £ 28/42

♦ Long-standing restaurant with great view of Green Park. Large selection of classic meze dishes and more modern European-style menu of original Lebanese dishes.

XX **Nobu** – at The Metropolitan Hotel

✿ 19 Old Park Ln. ✉ W1Y 1LB ⊖ Hyde Park Corner
– ☎ (020) 7447 4747 – www.noburestaurants.com
– Closed 25-26 December and 1 January **30**AHV**c**

Rest – Japanese – *(booking essential)* Carte £ 37/68

Spec. Tuna sashimi salad with matsuhisa dressing. Black cod with miso. Chocolate bento box with green tea ice cream.

♦ Its celebrity clientele ensure this remains one of the more glamorous spots. Staff are fully conversant in the innovative menu that adds South American influences to Japanese cooking. Has spawned many imitators.

XX **Tempo**

54 Curzon St. ✉ W1J 8PG ⊖ Green Park – ☎ (020) 7629 2742
– www.tempomayfair.co.uk – Closed 24 December-3 January, Sunday and bank holidays **30**AIV**m**

Rest – Italian – Menu £ 22 (lunch) – Carte £ 29/50

♦ The hands-on owner is a reassuring presence in this cosy restaurant, which re-opened in 2010 after a full revamp. The menu covers all Italian regions and includes cicchetti, or small plates.

XX **Sumosan**

26 Albemarle St. ✉ W1S 4HY ⊖ Green Park – ☎ (020) 7495 5999
– www.sumosan.com – Closed bank holidays, lunch Saturday and Sunday

Rest – Japanese – Carte £ 53/97 **30**AIU**e**

♦ Aims to attract the smart set, with its cocktail list, modern interpretations of Japanese flavours and too-cool-to-smile service. Skilled kitchen deftly executes a wide-ranging menu.

XX **Mews of Mayfair**

10-11 Lancashire Ct., Brook St. , (first floor) ✉ W1S 1EY ⊖ Bond Street
– ☎ (020) 7518 9388 – www.mewsofmayfair.com – Closed 25-26 December, Sunday dinner and bank holidays **30**AHU**a**

Rest – Modern European – Menu £ 19 (lunch) – Carte £ 29/47

♦ This pretty restaurant, bright in summer and warm in winter, is on the first floor of a mews house, once used as storage rooms for Savile Row. Seasonal menus offer something for everyone.

XX **Chor Bizarre**

16 Albemarle St. ✉ W1S 4HW ⊖ Green Park – ✆ (020) 7629 9802 – www.chorbizarre.com **30**AIV**s**

Rest – Indian – Carte £ 32/47

♦ Eccentric and colourful décor of trinkets, curios and antiques; the name translates as 'thieves' market'. The menu is long and chatty; dishes from more northerly parts of India are the highlight.

XX **Sketch (The Gallery)**

9 Conduit St. ✉ W1S 2XG ⊖ Oxford Street – ✆ (020) 7659 4500 – www.sketch.uk.com – Closed 25-26 December, Sunday and bank holidays **30**AIU**h**

Rest – International – *(dinner only) (booking essential)* Carte £ 35/63

♦ Art gallery during the day morphs into a noisy brasserie at night, when aphorisms are projected onto the white walls. Menu is international in its scope; the cocktail list is equally popular.

XX **Cocoon**

65 Regent St. ✉ W1B 4EA ⊖ Piccadilly Circus – ✆ (020) 7494 7600 – www.cocoon-restaurants.com **30**AJU**x**

Rest – Asian – Menu £ 25/50 – Carte £ 31/44

♦ Trendy restaurant, based on a prime Regent Street site. Silk nets cleverly divide long, winding room. Bold, eclectic menus cover a wide spectrum of Asian dishes.

XX **Momo**

25 Heddon St. ✉ W1B 4BH ⊖ Oxford Circus – ✆ (020) 7434 4040 – www.momoresto.com – Closed 25 December and Sunday lunch **30**AIU**n**

Rest – Moroccan – Menu £ 19 (lunch) – Carte £ 31/47

♦ Lanterns, rugs, trinkets and music contribute to the authentic Moroccan atmosphere; come in a group to better appreciate it. The more traditional dishes are the kitchen's strength.

XX **Veeraswamy**

Victory House, 99 Regent St., (entrance on Swallow St.) ✉ W1B 4RS ⊖ Piccadilly Circus – ✆ (020) 7734 1401 – www.realindianfood.com – Closed dinner 25 December **30**AIU**t**

Rest – Indian – Menu £ 21 (lunch and early dinner) – Carte £ 34/49

♦ May have opened back in 1926 but feels fresh and is awash with vibrant colours and always full of bustle. Skilled kitchen cleverly mixes the traditional with more contemporary creations.

XX **La Petite Maison**

54 Brooks Mews ✉ W1K 4EG ⊖ Bond Street – ✆ (020) 7495 4774 – www.lpmlondon.co.uk – Closed 25-26 December **30**AHU**f**

Rest – French – Carte £ 32/65 **s**

♦ Open-plan restaurant; sister to the eponymous Nice original. Healthy French Mediterranean cooking with a seafood slant. 20 starters to choose from; sharing is encouraged.

XX **Cafe at Sotheby's**

34-35 New Bond St. ✉ W1A 2AA ⊖ Bond Street – ✆ (020) 7293 5077 – www.sothebys.com – Closed 24 December-4 January, Saturday , Sunday ,and bank hoildays **30**AIU**y**

Rest – Modern European – *(lunch only) (booking essential)* Carte £ 26/35 **s**

♦ Occupying a cosy space just off the foyer of the famous auction house. The appealing lunch menu changes weekly; the lobster sandwich is a perennial favourite. Service is discreet.

XX **Kiku**

17 Half Moon St. ✉ W1J 7BE ⊖ Green Park – ✆ (020) 7499 4208 – www.kikurestaurant.co.uk – Closed 25 December, 1 January, lunch Sunday and bank holidays **30**AIV**g**

Rest – Japanese – Menu £ 20 (lunch) – Carte £ 29/55

♦ Bright and fresh feel thanks to minimalistic décor of stone and natural wood. A plethora of menus, a fierce adherence to seasonality and an authentic emphasis on presentation.

Bar Trattoria Semplice

22 Woodstock St. ✉ W1C 2AR ⊖ Bond Street – ☎ (020) 7491 8638 – www.bartrattoriasemplice.com – Closed 25-26 December, Easter and bank holidays **30**AHU**m**

Rest – Italian – Menu £ 17 (lunch) – Carte £ 23/36

◆ Baby sister to Semplice a few yards away, offering simpler, well-priced cooking in a relaxed and fun room. Specialities from a different region of Italy are featured each month. All-day menu in bar.

Chisou

4 Princes St. ✉ W1B 2LE ⊖ Oxford Circus – ☎ (020) 7629 3931 – www.chisou.co.uk – Closed Christmas-New Year, Sunday and bank holidays

Rest – Japanese – Menu £ 15 (lunch) – Carte £ 25/43 **30**AIU**m**

◆ In Mayfair's Japanese quarter; simple slate flooring and polished wood tables. Cosy sushi bar to rear. Elaborate menus of modern/classic Japanese dishes. Gets very busy.

Bentley's (Oyster Bar)

11-15 Swallow St. ✉ W1B 4DG ⊖ Piccadilly Circus – ☎ (020) 7734 4756 – www.bentleys.org – Closed 25 December and 1 January **30**AJU**n**

Rest – Seafood – Carte £ 29/85

◆ Sit at the counter to watch white-jacketed staff open oysters by the bucket load. Interesting seafood menus feature tasty fish pies; lots of daily specials on blackboard.

Aubaine

4 Heddon St. ✉ W1B 4BS ⊖ Oxford Circus – ☎ (020) 7440 2510 – www.aubaine.co.uk – Closed Sunday dinner **30**AIU**d**

Rest – Menu £ 19 (lunch) – Carte approx. £ 28

◆ Sister to the Chelsea original but this time without the boulangerie. The look is of a farmhouse as imagined by a townie; the accessible menu wouldn't look out of place in a bistro.

Automat

33 Dover St. ✉ W1S 4NF ⊖ Green Park – ☎ (020) 7499 3033 – www.automat-london.com – Closed 25-26 December and 1 January

Rest – American – Carte £ 39/50 **30**AIV**r**

◆ Buzzing New York style brasserie in three areas: a café, a 'dining car' with deep leather banquettes, and actual brasserie itself. Classic dishes from burgers to cheesecake.

Le Boudin Blanc

5 Trebeck St. ✉ W1J 7LT ⊖ Green Park – ☎ (020) 7499 3292 – www.boudinblanc.co.uk – Closed 24-26 December **30**AHV**q**

Rest – French – Menu £ 15 (lunch and early dinner) – Carte £ 32/44

◆ Appealing, lively French bistro in Shepherd Market, spread over two floors. Satisfying French classics and country cooking is the draw, along with authentic Gallic service. Good value lunch menu.

Only Running Footman

5 Charles St ✉ W1J 5DF ⊖ Green Park. – ☎ (020) 7499 2988 – www.therunningfootmanmayfair.com **30**AHV**x**

Rest – Carte £ 26/35

◆ Busy ground floor bar with its appealing menu of pub classics doesn't take bookings. By contrast, upstairs is formal and its menu more European and ambitious but simpler dishes still the best.

Regent's Park and Marylebone

The Landmark London

222 Marylebone Rd ✉ NW1 6JQ ⊖ Edgware Rd – ☎ (020) 7631 8000 – www.landmarklondon.co.uk **29**AFT**a**

291 rm – †£ 312/660 ††£ 312/660, ☕ £ 28 – 9 suites

Rest *Winter Garden* – Carte £ 35/74

◆ Imposing Victorian Gothic building with a vast glass-enclosed atrium, overlooked by many of the modern, well-equipped bedrooms. Winter Garden popular for afternoon tea.

LONDON

Hyatt Regency London-The Churchill rm,
30 Portman Sq. W1H 7BH Marble Arch
– (020) 7486 5800 – www.london.churchill.hyatt.com **29**AGT**x**
404 rm – £ 240/480 £ 240/480, £ 27.50 – 40 suites
Rest *The Montagu* – (020) 7299 2037 – Menu £ 26 – Carte £ 37/53
◆ Smart property overlooking attractive square. Elegant marbled lobby. Well-appointed and recently refurbished rooms have the international traveller in mind. Restaurant provides popular Sunday brunch entertainment.

Langham rm,
1c Portland Pl., Regent St. W1B 1JA Oxford Circus – (020) 7636 1000
– www.langhamhotels.com **29**AGT**n**
359 rm – £ 192/225 £ 446/675, £ 30 – 21 suites
Rest *Landau* – (020) 7965 0165 *(Closed Saturday lunch and Sunday)*
Menu £ 29 (lunch) – Carte £ 51/60
◆ Opened in 1865 and relaunched in 2009 following a major refurbishment. Impressive art deco Palm Court; comfortable bedrooms and notable leisure facilities. The Landau is an eye-catching and ornate room, with a wide-ranging menu.

Montcalm rm,
34-40 Great Cumberland Pl. W1H 7TW Marble Arch – (020) 7402 4288
– www.montcalm.co.uk **29**AGU**m**
126 rm – £ 420 £ 420/1020, £ 19.95 – 17 suites
Rest *Vetro* – Italian – *(closed Sunday dinner)* Carte £ 29/45
◆ Named after an 18C French general, The Montcalm forms part of a crescent of townhouses with a Georgian façade. A top-to-toe refurbishment has created smart and contemporary bedrooms in lively colours. Classic Italian dishes in Vetro.

The Arch rm,
50 Great Cumberland Pl. W1H 7FD Marble Arch – (020) 7724 4700
– www.thearchlondon.com **29**AGT**a**
80 rm – £ 294 £ 360/540, £ 18.95 – 2 suites
Rest *Hunter 486* – (020) 7725 4825 – Menu £ 20 (lunch) – Carte £ 23/53
◆ Fashioned out of a row of seven terrace houses and two mews cottages. Plenty of extras and thoughtful touches are found in the comfortable bedrooms. Interesting pieces of art throughout. Relaxed restaurant doubles as a champagne bar.

Sanderson
50 Berners St W1T 3NG Oxford Circus – (020) 7300 1400
– www.morganshotelgroup.com **31**AJT**c**
150 rm – £ 414/627 £ 414/627, £ 25
Rest *Suka* – Carte £ 35/45
◆ Designed by Philipe Starck and still attracting a suitably fashionable crowd. Purple Bar dark and moody; Long Bar bright and stylish. Pure white bedrooms with idiosyncratic design touches. Malaysian dishes designed for sharing in Suka.

Dorset Square without rest
39 Dorset Sq NW1 6QN Marylebone – (020) 7723 7874
– www.dorsetsquare.co.uk **17**QZD**s**
37 rm – £ 120/240 £ 174/336, £ 15
◆ Converted Regency townhouses in a charming square which was the site of the original Lord's cricket ground. A warm and welcoming country house in the city with individually decorated rooms.

Durrants rest,
26-32 George St. W1H 5BJ Bond Street – (020) 7935 8131
– www.durrantshotel.co.uk **29**AGT**e**
92 rm – £ 125 £ 175, £ 18 – 4 suites
Rest – *(Closed dinner 25 December)* Carte £ 31/41
◆ Traditional, privately owned hotel with friendly, long-standing staff. Newly refurbished bedrooms are brighter in style but still English in character. Clubby dining room for mix of British classics and lighter, European dishes.

LONDON

Mandeville

Mandeville Pl. ✉ *W1U 2BE* ⊖ *Bond Street* – ✆ *(020) 7935 5599 – www.mandeville.co.uk* **30**AHT**x**

140 rm – †£ 383 ††£ 407, ☕ £ 22.50 – 2 suites

Rest *de Ville* – *(closed Sunday)* Menu £ 30 – Carte £ 27/36 **s**

◆ Usefully located hotel with marbled reception leading into a very colourful and comfortable bar. Stylish rooms have flatscreen TVs and make good use of the space available. Modern British cuisine served in bright de Ville restaurant.

No.Ten Manchester Street without rest

✉ *W1U 4DG* ⊖ *Baker Street* – ✆ *(020) 7317 5900 – www.tenmanchesterstreethotel.com* **29**AGT**v**

44 rm – †£ 167 ††£ 263, ☕ £ 15.50 – 1 suite

◆ Converted Edwardian house in an appealing, central location. Discreet entrance leads into stylish little lounge; semi-enclosed cigar bar also a feature. Neat and well-kept bedrooms.

The Sumner without rest

54 Upper Berkeley St ✉ *W1H 7QR* ⊖ *Marble Arch* – ✆ *(020) 7723 2244 – www.thesumner.com* **29**AFU**k**

20 rm ☕ – †£ 200 ††£ 200

◆ Two Georgian terrace houses in central location. Comfy, stylish sitting room; basement breakfast room. Largest bedrooms, 101 and 201, benefit from having full-length windows.

Hart House without rest

51 Gloucester Pl. ✉ *W1U 8JF* ⊖ *Marble Arch* – ✆ *(020) 7935 2288 – www.harthouse.co.uk* **29**AGT**d**

15 rm ☕ – †£ 89/135 ††£ 125/150

◆ Within an attractive Georgian terrace and run by the same family for over 35 years. Warm and welcoming service; well-kept, competitively priced bedrooms over three floors.

St George without rest

49 Gloucester Pl. ✉ *W1U 8JE* ⊖ *Marble Arch* – ✆ *(020) 7486 8586 – www.stgeorge-hotel.net* **29**AGT**h**

18 rm – †£ 85/145 ††£ 110/195, ☕ £ 5

◆ Terraced house on a busy street, usefully located within walking distance of many attractions. Offers a warm welcome and comfortable bedrooms which are spotlessly maintained.

Rhodes W1 (Restaurant)

Cumberland Hotel, Great Cumberland Pl. ✉ *W1H 7DL* ⊖ *Marble Arch* – ✆ *(020) 7616 5930 – www.rhodesw1.com – Closed 2 weeks in summer, Saturday lunch, Sunday and Monday* **29**AGU**z**

Rest – French – *(booking advisable)* Menu £ 25/50

Spec. Scallops with braised oxtail and blood orange. Pigeon with foie gras, chicory and pickled blackberries. Pistachio cake with apricot and tarragon ice cream.

◆ Just 12 tables in a warm and textured room designed by Kelly Hoppen. Influences are more European than usual for a Gary Rhodes restaurant but with the same emphasis on clear, uncluttered flavours.

Locanda Locatelli

8 Seymour St. ✉ *W1H 7JZ* ⊖ *Marble Arch* – ✆ *(020) 7935 9088 – www.locandalocatelli.com – Closed 25-26 December* **29**AGU**r**

Rest – Italian – Carte £ 41/60

Spec. Chestnut tagliatelle with wild mushrooms. Veal saltimbocca. Degustation of Amedei chocolate.

◆ Slick and dapper-looking Italian with a celebrity following and a sophisticated atmosphere. Plenty of interest on the extensive menu, with cooking that is confident, balanced and expertly rendered; pastas and desserts are the stand-out courses.

LONDON

XXX **Latium**

AC VISA MC AE D

21 Berners St. ✉ W1T 3LP ⊖ Oxford Circus – ☎ (020) 7323 9123 – www.latiumrestaurant.com – Closed 10 days Christmas, Saturday lunch, Sunday and bank holidays **31**AJT**n**

Rest – Italian – Menu £ 20/33

◆ Bright and contemporary surroundings but with warm and welcoming service. Owner-chef from Lazio but dishes come from across Italy, often using British produce. Ravioli is the house speciality.

XX ✿ **Texture** (Agnar Sverrisson)

AC VISA MC AE

34 Portman St. ✉ W1H 7BY ⊖ Marble Arch – ☎ (020) 7224 0028 – www.texture-restaurant.co.uk – Closed Christmas-New Year, 2 weeks August, Sunday and Monday **29**AGU**p**

Rest – Innovative – Menu £ 22 (lunch) – Carte £ 43/51

Spec. Salmon graflax with horseradish and rye bread. Icelandic salted cod with barley and shellfish jus. White chocolate mousse with cucumber and dill.

◆ Technically skilled but light and invigorating cooking from Icelandic chef-owner, who uses ingredients from home. Bright restaurant with high ceiling and popular adjoining champagne bar. Pleasant service from keen staff, ready with a smile.

LONDON

XX ✿ **L'Autre Pied** (Marcus Eaves)

AC VISA MC AE

5-7 Blandford St. ✉ W1U 3DB ⊖ Bond Street – ☎ (020) 7486 9696 – www.lautrepied.co.uk **30**AHT**k**

Rest – Modern European – Menu £ 21 (lunch) – Carte £ 39/60

Spec. Raviolo of veal and chorizo with shellfish bisque. Roast pork with croquette of spiced pig's head. Baked Alaska, elderflower and vanilla ice cream

◆ A more informal sibling to Pied à Terre, with red leather seating, closely set tables and relaxed atmosphere. But cooking is just as ambitious: it is original, creative and technically adroit.

XX **Galvin Bistrot de Luxe**

AC VISA MC AE

66 Baker St. ✉ W1U 7DJ ⊖ Baker Street – ☎ (020) 7935 4007 – www.galvinrestaurants.com – Closed 25-26 December and 1 January

Rest – French – Menu £ 18 (lunch)/20 (early dinner) – Carte £ 32/51 **29**AGT**b**

◆ Firmly established modern Gallic bistro with ceiling fans, globe lights and wood panelled walls. Satisfying and precisely cooked classic French dishes from the Galvin brothers.

XX **Zayna**

AC VISA MC AE

25 New Quebec St. ✉ W1H 7SF ⊖ Marble Arch – ☎ (020) 7723 2229 – www.zaynarestaurant.co.uk **29**AGU**x**

Rest – Indian – Menu £ 25/30 – Carte £ 30/40

◆ Enthusiastically run, elegant restaurant spread over two floors, with keen owner. Interesting north Indian and Pakistani delicacies; kitchen only uses halal meat and free-range chicken.

XX **Ozer**

AC VISA MC AE

5 Langham Pl., Regent St. ✉ W1B 3DG ⊖ Oxford Circus – ☎ (020) 7323 0505 – www.ozer.co.uk **30**AIT**z**

Rest – Turkish – Menu £ 19/23 – Carte £ 21/42

◆ The large front bar is always busy but go through to the equally popular but comfortable restaurant to enjoy authentic Turkish food. Wide range of appealing hot and cold meze is the draw.

XX **Rhodes W1 Brasserie**

AC VISA MC AE

Great Cumberland Pl. ✉ W1H 7DL ⊖ Marble Arch – ☎ (020) 7616 5930 – www.rhodesw1.com **29**AGU**z**

Rest – Modern European – Menu £ 21 (lunch) – Carte £ 27/44

◆ Large brasserie on the ground floor of the Cumberland hotel, with keen, helpful service and equally big bar. Expect Gary Rhodes' signature dishes, alongside others of a more European persuasion.

XX **Colony**

8 Paddington St ✉ W1U 5QH ⊖ Baker Street – ☎ (020) 7935 3353 – www.colonybarandgrill.com **30**AHT**d**

Rest – Indian – Menu £ 20 – Carte £ 26/42

♦ Courtesy of Atul Kochhar, of Benares fame: small tasting plates, lunchtime thalis and grazing menus with mostly Indian influences are served at this relaxed lounge bar with a dining area.

XX **Iberica**

195 Great Portland St ✉ W1W 5PS ⊖ Great Portland St – ☎ (020) 7636 8650 – www.ibericalondon.co.uk – Closed Sunday dinner **18**RZD**x**

Rest – Spanish – *(booking advisable at dinner)* Menu £ 22 (weekday lunch) – Carte £ 15/32

♦ These large premises pay homage to Spain's food and culture. Punchy flavoured tapas in the ground floor bar; more intimate upstairs. Wander through the deli to appreciate the quality of ingredients.

XX **The Providores**

109 Marylebone High St. ✉ W1U 4RX ⊖ Bond Street – ☎ (020) 7935 6175 – www.theprovidores.co.uk – Closed Christmas-New Year **30**AHT**y**

Rest – Innovative – Carte £ 36/57

♦ Packed ground floor for tapas; upstairs for innovative fusion cooking, with spices and ingredients from around the world, including Australasia. Starter-sized dishes at dinner allow for greater choice.

XX **Cafe Luc**

50 Marylebone High St ✉ W1U 5HN ⊖ Regent's Park – ☎ (020) 7258 8595 – www.cafeluc.com **30**AHT**b**

Rest – Modern European – Menu £ 16 – Carte £ 24/35

♦ Spacious, grand and keenly run brasserie with smart leather banquette seating and clusters of lights. The menu offers a host of brasserie and continental classics to suit all tastes.

XX **La Porte des Indes**

32 Bryanston St ✉ W1H 7EG ⊖ Marble Arch – ☎ (020) 7224 0055 – www.laportedesindes.com – Closed 25-26 December and 1 January

Rest – Indian – Menu £ 36 – Carte £ 36/56 **29**AGU**s**

♦ Don't be fooled by the discreet entrance: inside there is a spectacularly unrestrained display of palm trees, murals and waterfalls. French-influenced Indian cuisine.

XX **Levant**

Jason Ct., 76 Wigmore St. ✉ W1U 2SJ ⊖ Bond Street – ☎ (020) 7224 1111 – www.levant.co.uk – Closed 23-29 December and 1 January **30**AHT**c**

Rest – Lebanese – *(dinner only and lunch Saturday-Sunday)* Carte £ 20/40

♦ Belly dancing, lanterns and a low-slung bar all add up to an exotic dining experience. The Lebanese food is satisfying and authentic, carefully prepared and ideal for sharing in groups.

XX **Villandry**

170 Great Portland St ✉ W1W 5QB ⊖ Regent's Park – ☎ (020) 7631 3131 – www.villandry.com – Closed Christmas, New Year and Sunday dinner

Rest – French – Carte £ 25/47 **30**AIT**s**

♦ The senses are heightened by passing through the well-stocked deli to the dining room behind. Bare walls, wooden tables and a menu offering simple, tasty dishes.

XX **L'Aventure**

3 Blenheim Ter ✉ NW8 0EH ⊖ St John's Wood – ☎ (020) 7624 6232 – Closed first week January, last 2 weeks August, Saturday lunch and Sunday

Rest – French – Menu £ 20/40 **11**PZB**b**

♦ Behind the pretty tree-lined entrance you'll find a charming neighbourhood restaurant. Relaxed atmosphere and service by personable owner. Authentic French cuisine.

LONDON

XX **Phoenix Palace**

5 Glentworth St. ✉ NW1 5PG ⊖ Baker Street – ✆ (020) 7486 3515 – www.phoenixpalace.co.uk **17**QZD**x**

Rest – Chinese – *(booking advisable at dinner)* Menu £ 25 – Carte approx. £ 28

♦ Huge restaurant offering a plethora of menus but the cooking is still good. Dim sum during the day and Cantonese dishes and rotisserie meats at night draw in the groups of families and friends.

XX **Vineria**

1 Blenheim Ter. ✉ NW8 0EH ⊖ St John's Wood – ✆ (020) 7328 5014 – www.vineria.it – Closed Monday **11**PZB**z**

Rest – Italian – Menu £ 20 (lunch) – Carte £ 27/37

♦ Pleasant enclosed front terrace; conservatory section and white walls ensure a bright interior. Undemanding menu covers all parts of Italy, with pasta dishes the kitchen's strength.

X **Trishna**

15-17 Blandford St. ✉ W1U 3DG ⊖ Baker Street – ✆ (020) 7935 5624 – www.trishnalondon.com – Closed 25-29 December and 1-4 January

Rest – Indian – Menu £ 16/35 – Carte £ 29/39 **29**AGT**r**

♦ A franchise of the celebrated Mumbai restaurant. Specialises in fish and seafood dishes, with brown crab with butter garlic being a highlight. Bright surroundings allow the focus to be the food.

X **Hix (Selfridges)**

Mezzanine Fl, Selfridges, 400 Oxford St ✉ W1A 1AB ⊖ Bond St – ✆ (020) 7499 5400 – www.hixatselfridges.co.uk **30**AHU**p**

Rest – Modern European – Carte £ 25/40

♦ On the mezzanine floor of the famous store; open from breakfast onwards, with a popular champagne bar to refuel shoppers. Menu is lighter and more European than at the other Hix restaurants.

X **The Wallace**

Hertford House, Manchester Sq ✉ W1U 3BN ⊖ Bond Street – ✆ (020) 7563 9505 – www.thewallacerestaurant.com – Closed 24-27 December

Rest – French – *(lunch only and dinner Friday-Saturday)* **29**AGT**k**

Carte £ 26/35

♦ Large glass-roofed courtyard on the ground floor of Hertford House and the splendid Wallace Collection. French-influenced menu, with fruits de mer section; terrines are the house speciality.

X **Caffé Caldesi**

118 Marylebone Ln.(1st floor) ✉ W1U 2QF ⊖ Bond Street – ✆ (020) 7487 0754 – www.caldesi.com – Closed 25-26 December and 1 January **30**AHT**s**

Rest – Italian – Menu £ 17 (lunch) – Carte £ 26/40

♦ Converted pub with a simple modern interior in which to enjoy tasty, uncomplicated Italian dishes. Downstairs is a lively bar with a deli counter serving pizzas and pastas.

X **Dinings**

22 Harcourt St. ✉ W1H 4HH ⊖ Marylebone – ✆ (020) 7723 0666 – www.dinings.co.uk – Closed lunch Saturday and Sunday **29**AFT**c**

Rest – Japanese – *(booking essential)* Carte £ 31/43

♦ Resembles an after-work Japanese izakaya, or pub, with chummy atmosphere and loud music. Food is a mix of small plates of delicate dishes, a blend of modern and the more traditional.

X **Il Baretto**

43 Blandford St. ✉ W1U 7HF ⊖ Baker Street – ✆ (020) 7486 7340 – www.ilbaretto.co.uk – Closed 24-26 December **29**AGT**n**

Rest – Italian – Carte £ 21/46

♦ The wood-fired oven is the star of the show at this neighbourhood Italian. The extensive menu has something for everyone, although prices vary a lot. The basement room has a lively atmosphere.

Chada Chada

16-17 Picton Pl. ✉ W1U 1BP ⊖ Bond Street – ☎ (020) 7935 8212 – www.chadathai.com – Closed Sunday and bank holidays **30**AHU**b**

Rest – Thai – Carte £ 19/47

♦ Authentic and fragrant Thai cooking; the good value menu offers some interesting departures from the norm. Service is eager to please in the compact and cosy rooms.

Larrik

32 Crawford Pl ✉ W1H 5NN ⊖ Edgware Rd. – ☎ (020) 7723 0066 – www.thelarrik.com – Closed 25 December **29**AFT**x**

Rest – Carte £ 20/27

♦ The front section of this traditional looking pub is brighter and more fun. The kitchen is well-grounded in the basics and reliable, whether making a salad or burger. Regularly changing real ales.

St James's

The Ritz

150 Piccadilly ✉ W1J 9BR ⊖ Green Park – ☎ (020) 7493 8181 – www.theritzlondon.com **30**AIV**c**

116 rm – †£ 300/954 ††£ 420/954, ☕ £ 35 – 17 suites

Rest ***The Ritz Restaurant*** – see restaurant listing

♦ World famous hotel, opened 1906 as a fine example of Louis XVI architecture and decoration. Elegant Palm Court famed for its afternoon tea. Many of the lavishly appointed and luxurious rooms and suites overlook the park.

Sofitel St James London

6 Waterloo Pl. ✉ SW1Y 4AN ⊖ Piccadilly Circus – ☎ (020) 7747 2200 – www.sofitelstjames.com **31**AKV**a**

180 rm ☕ – †£ 450/510 ††£ 528 – 6 suites

Rest ***Brasserie Roux*** – see restaurant listing

♦ Grade II listed building in smart Pall Mall location. Classically English interiors include floral Rose Lounge and clubby bar. Comfortable, well-fitted bedrooms and impressive spa.

Haymarket

1 Suffolk Pl. ✉ SW1Y 4HX ⊖ Piccadilly Circus – ☎ (020) 7470 4000 – www.firmdalehotels.com **31**AKV**d**

47 rm – †£ 396 ††£ 396, ☕ £ 19.50 – 3 suites

Rest ***Brumus*** – Menu £ 22 – Carte £ 32/48

♦ Smart, spacious hotel in John Nash Regency building, with stylish blend of modern and antique furnishings. Large, comfortable bedrooms in soothing colours. Impressive pool. Brumus bar and restaurant puts focus on Italian cooking.

Dukes

35 St James's Pl. ✉ SW1A 1NY ⊖ Green Park – ☎ (020) 7491 4840 – www.dukeshotel.com **30**AIV**f**

84 rm – †£ 234/530 ††£ 414/689, ☕ £ 22 – 6 suites

Rest – Menu £ 19/21 – Carte £ 30/44

♦ The most recent redecoration retained the discreet, traditionally British feel of this hotel in a central but quiet location. Dukes bar famous for its martinis. Elegant bedrooms with country house feel. Discreet dining room.

Stafford

16-18 St James's Pl. ✉ SW1A 1NJ ⊖ Green Park – ☎ (020) 7493 0111 – www.kempinski.com/london **30**AIV**u**

73 rm – †£ 492/528 ††£ 528, ☕ £ 25 – 15 suites

Rest – *(closed Saturday lunch and bank holidays)* Menu £ 30 (lunch) – Carte dinner £ 34/65

♦ A genteel atmosphere prevails in this discreet 'country house in the city'. Bedrooms divided between main house, converted 18C stables and newer Mews. Traditional and intimate dining room.

LONDON

St James's Hotel and Club
7-8 Park Pl. ✉ SW1A 1LS ⊖ Green Park – ✆ (020) 7316 1600 – www.stjameshotelandclub.com **30**AIV**k**
50 rm – †£ 282/414 ††£ 282/522, ☕ £ 22 – 10 suites
Rest ***Seven Park Place*** – see restaurant listing
♦ 1890s house in cul-de-sac, formerly a private club, reopened as a hotel in 2008. Modern, boutique-style interior with over 200 paintings. Fine finish to compact, but well-equipped bedrooms.

The Ritz Restaurant – at The Ritz Hotel
150 Piccadilly ✉ W1J 9BR ⊖ Green Park – ✆ (020) 7493 8181 – www.theritzlondon.com **30**AIV**c**
Rest – Traditional – Menu £ 39 (lunch)/48 – Carte £ 64/87 **s**
♦ Grand and lavish restaurant, with Louis XVI decoration, trompe l'oeil and ornate gilding. Delightful terrace over Green Park. Structured, formal service. Classic, traditional dishes are the highlight of the menu. Jacket and tie required.

The Wolseley
160 Piccadilly ✉ W1J 9EB ⊖ Green Park – ✆ (020) 7499 6996 – www.thewolseley.com – Closed dinner 24 and 31 December, 25 December and August bank holiday **30**AIV**q**
Rest – Modern European – *(booking essential)* Carte £ 21/51
♦ Feels like a grand European coffee house, with pillars and high vaulted ceiling. Appealing menus range from caviar to a hot dog. Open from breakfast and boasts a celebrity following.

Seven Park Place – at St James's Hotel and Club
7-8 Park Pl. ✉ SW1A 1LS ⊖ Green Park – ✆ (020) 7316 1614 – www.stjameshotelandclub.com **30**AIV**k**
Rest – Modern European – *(closed Sunday and Monday) (booking essential)* Menu £ 30/45
Spec. Foie gras with roasted peaches and gingerbread. Lamb with garlic purée and rosemary jus. White chocolate parfait with cherries.
♦ Small restaurant concealed somewhat within St. James's Hotel and divided between two rooms; ask for the gilded back room. The accomplished food has a French base, displays confidence and clarity and uses quality British ingredients.

Sake No Hana
23 St James's St ✉ SW1A 1HA ⊖ Green Park – ✆ (020) 7925 8988 – www.sakenohana.com – Closed 24-25 December and Sunday lunch **30**AIV**n**
Rest – Japanese – Carte £ 20/60
♦ Stylish first floor restaurant reached by elevator, where cedar wood décor goes some way to disguising an ugly '60s building. Mix of traditional and modern Japanese food; ground floor sushi bar.

Brasserie Roux – at Sofitel St James London
8 Pall Mall ✉ SW1Y 5NG ⊖ Piccadilly Circus – ✆ (020) 7968 2900 – www.brasserieroux.com **31**AKV**a**
Rest – French – Menu £ 20 – Carte £ 21/45
♦ Informal, smart, classic brasserie style with large windows making the most of the location. Extensive choice of French classics. Restaurant concept to change mid 2011.

Le Caprice
Arlington House, Arlington St. ✉ SW1A 1RJ ⊖ Green Park – ✆ (020) 7629 2239 – www.le-caprice.co.uk – Closed 24-26 December and 1 January **30**AIV**h**
Rest – Modern European – Menu £ 20 (dinner) – Carte £ 29/53
♦ Still attracting a fashionable clientele and as busy as ever. Dine at the bar or in the smoothly run restaurant. Food combines timeless classics with modern dishes.

XX **Franco's**

61 Jermyn St. ✉ SW1Y 6LX ⊖ Green Park – ✆ (020) 7499 2211 – www.francoslondon.com – Closed Sunday and bank holidays **30**AIV**i**

Rest – Italian – *(booking essential)* Menu £ 26 (lunch) – Carte £ 37/52

◆ Open from breakfast until late, with café at the front leading into smart, clubby restaurant. Menu covers all parts of Italy and includes popular grill section and plenty of classics.

XX **Avenue**

7-9 St James's St. ✉ SW1A 1EE ⊖ Green Park – ✆ (020) 7321 2111 – www.theavenue-restaurant.co.uk – Closed 25-26 December, Saturday lunch and Sunday **30**AIV**y**

Rest – Modern European – Menu £ 25 – Carte £ 28/57

◆ Large, brash restaurant, with sheer white décor and a very popular bar. All-encompassing menu, with everything from caviar to burgers. Service comes with an urgency not always required.

XX **Matsuri - St James's**

15 Bury St. ✉ SW1Y 6AL ⊖ Green Park – ✆ (020) 7839 1101 – www.matsuri-restaurant.com – Closed 25 December and 1 January **30**AIV**w**

Rest – Japanese – Menu £ 25 (lunch and early dinner) – Carte £ 25/44

◆ Sweet natured service at this traditional Japanese stalwart. Teppan-yaki is their speciality, with Scottish beef the highlight; sushi counter also available. Good value lunch menus.

XX **Quaglino's**

16 Bury St ✉ SW1Y 6AL ⊖ Green Park – ✆ (020) 7930 6767 – www.quaglinos.co.uk – Closed 25 December, Sunday and Bank Holidays **30**AIV**j**

Rest – Modern European – *(booking essential)* Menu £ 20 – Carte £ 33/46

◆ This big, bold restaurant achieved iconic status on reopening in the early '90s. No longer quite so glamorous but it still offers a good night out and a easy menu, with fruits de mer the highlight.

XX **Mint Leaf**

Suffolk Pl. ✉ SW1Y 4HX ⊖ Piccadilly Circus – ✆ (020) 7930 9020 – www.mintleafrestaurant.com – Closed 25-26 December, 1 January, lunch Saturday and Sunday **31**AKV**k**

Rest – Indian – Menu £ 18/20 – Carte £ 29/37

◆ Cavernous and moodily lit basement restaurant incorporating trendy bar with lounge music and extensive cocktail list. Contemporary Indian cooking with curries the highlight.

X **Al Duca**

4-5 Duke of York St. ✉ SW1Y 6LA ⊖ Piccadilly Circus – ✆ (020) 7839 3090 – www.alduca-restaurant.co.uk – Closed 24 December-4 January and Sunday

Rest – Italian – Menu £ 18/28 **31**AJV**r**

◆ Cooking which focuses on flavour continues to draw in the regulars at this warm and spirited Italian restaurant. Prices are keen when one considers the central location and service is brisk and confident.

X **Inn the Park**

St James's Park ✉ SW1A 2BJ ⊖ Charing Cross – ✆ (020) 7451 9999 – www.innthepark.com – Closed 25 December **31**AKV**n**

Rest – British – Carte £ 26/36

◆ Oliver Peyton's eco-friendly restaurant in the middle of the park, with a terrific terrace. British menu uses many small suppliers. Cooking is straightforward and wholesome.

X **Portrait**

National Portrait Gallery, 3rd Floor, St Martin's Pl ✉ WC2H 0HE ⊖ Charing Cross – ✆ (020) 7312 2490 – www.searcys.co.uk – Closed 24-26 December **31**ALV**n**

Rest – Modern European – *(lunch only and dinner Thursday-Saturday) (booking essential)* Menu £ 25 – Carte £ 29/37

◆ On the top floor of National Portrait Gallery with rooftop local landmark views: a charming spot for lunch. Modern British/European dishes; weekend brunch.

LONDON

The National Dining Rooms

Sainsbury Wing, The National Gallery, Trafalgar Sq ✉ WC2N 5DN
⊖ Charing Cross – ☎ (020) 7747 2525 – www.thenationaldiningrooms.co.uk
– Closed 25-26 December and 1 January **31**AKV**b**
Rest – British – *(lunch only and dinner Friday)* Menu £ 28 – Carte approx. £ 25
♦ Set on the East Wing's first floor, you can tuck into cakes in the bakery or grab a prime corner table in the restaurant for great views and proudly seasonal British menus.

Soho

Soho

4 Richmond Mews ✉ W1D 3DH ⊖ Tottenham Court Road – ☎ (020) 7559 3000
– www.sohohotel.com **31**AKU**n**
89 rm – †£ 348 ††£ 432, ☕ £ 19.50 – 2 suites
Rest *Refuel* – ☎ (020) 7559 3007 – Menu £ 23 – Carte £ 32/48
♦ Stylish and very fashionable hotel boasts two screening rooms, comfy drawing room and up-to-the-minute bedrooms, some vivid, others more muted, all boasting hi-tech extras. Contemporary bar and restaurant.

Sanctum Soho

20 Warwick St ✉ W1B 5NF ⊖ Piccadilly Circus – ☎ (020) 7292 6100
– www.sanctumsoho.com **30**AIU**a**
30 rm – †£ 276/516 ††£ 276/516, ☕ £ 15
Rest *No. 20* – Modern – *(Closed Sunday dinner)* Menu £ 20 – Carte £ 27/39
♦ Plenty of glitz and bling at this funky, self-styled rock 'n' roll hotel, with some innovative touches such as TVs behind mirrors. Rooftop lounge and hot tub. Relaxed and comfortable dining with plenty of classic dishes.

Dean Street Townhouse

69-71 Dean St. ✉ W1D 3SE ⊖ Tottenham Court Road – ☎ (0207) 434 17 75
– www.deanstreettownhouse.com **31**AKU**t**
39 rm – †£ 120/270 ††£ 120/270, ☕ £ 15
Rest *Dean Street Townhouse Restaurant* – see restaurant listing
♦ In the heart of Soho where bedrooms range from tiny to bigger; the latter have roll-top baths in the room. All are well designed and come with a good range of extras. Cosy ground floor lounge.

Hazlitt's without rest

6 Frith St ✉ W1D 3JA ⊖ Tottenham Court Road – ☎ (020) 7434 1771
– www.hazlittshotel.com **31**AKU**u**
29 rm – †£ 149/230 ††£ 169/230 – 3 suites
♦ Three adjoining early 18C townhouses and former home of the eponymous essayist. Idiosyncratic bedrooms, many with antique furniture and Victorian baths; ask for one of the newer ones.

Gauthier - Soho

21 Romilly St ✉ W1D 5AF ⊖ Leicester Square – ☎ (020) 7494 3111
– www.gauthiersoho.co.uk – Closed 21-30 August, Sunday, lunch Saturday and bank holidays **31**AKU**k**
Rest – French – Menu £ 25/35
Spec. Truffle risotto with brown butter and Parmesan. Roast red deer with pear and celeriac. Goose egg soufflé with chocolate custard.
♦ Professionally run restaurant with an intimate and somewhat secretive feel, spread over three floors of an 18C townhouse. The refined and elegant cooking emphasises the natural flavours of the quality ingredients.

Quo Vadis

26-29 Dean St. ✉ W1D 3LL ⊖ Tottenham Court Road – ☎ (020) 7437 9585
– www.quovadis.co.uk – Closed Sunday from 30 April-1 October and bank holidays **31**AKU**v**
Rest – British – Menu £ 20 (lunch) – Carte £ 29/33
♦ Dating from the 1920s and renewed in 2008; a veritable Soho institution with an art deco feel. Instantly appealing menu of carefully prepared classics, from grilled Hereford beef to assorted seafood.

XXX **Aqua Nueva**

240 Regent St., (entrance on Argyll St.) ✉ W1F 7EB ⊖ Oxford Circus – ✆ (020) 7478 0540 – www.aqua-london.com – Closed 25-26 December, 1 January and Sunday **30**AIU**x**

Rest – Spanish – Menu £ 20 (lunch) – Carte £ 30/52

♦ Large operation on the 5th floor of a former department store. Choose between the elegant main dining room or the more buzzy but equally stylish tapas bar. Spanish food interpreted in a modern style.

XXX **Red Fort**

77 Dean St. ✉ W1D 3SH ⊖ Tottenham Court Road – ✆ (020) 7437 2525 – www.redfort.co.uk – Closed 25 December, lunch Saturday, Sunday and bank holidays **31**AKU**x**

Rest – Indian – *(booking advisable at dinner)* Menu £ 20/40 – Carte £ 33/40

♦ Smart, stylish restaurant with modern water feature and glass ceiling to rear. Seasonally changing menus of authentic dishes handed down over generations.

XX **Dean Street Townhouse Restaurant**

69-71 Dean St. ✉ W1D 3SE ⊖ Tottenham Court Road – ✆ (0207) 434 17 75 – www.deanstreettownhouse.com **31**AKU**t**

Rest – British – *(booking essential)* Carte £ 22/40

♦ Georgian house now home to a fashionable and very busy bar and restaurant; the Parlour is the less hectic area. Appealingly classic British food includes some retro dishes and satisfying puddings.

XX **Yauatcha**

15 Broadwick St ✉ W1F 0DL ⊖ Tottenham Court Road – ✆ (020) 7494 8888 – www.yauatcha.com – Closed 24-25 December **31**AJU**k**

Rest – Chinese – Carte £ 27/59

Spec. Scallop shu mai with tobiko caviar. Spicy king soya wagyu beef. Chocolate and raspberry delice with vanilla ice cream.

♦ Refined, delicate and delicious dim sum; ideal for sharing in a group. Stylish surroundings spread over two floors: the lighter, brighter ground floor or the darker, more atmospheric basement. Afternoon teas also a speciality.

XX **Aqua Kyoto**

240 Regent St., (entrance on Argyll St.) ✉ W1F 7EB ⊖ Oxford Circus – ✆ (020) 7478 0540 – www.aqua-london.com – Closed 25-26 December, 1 January and Sunday **30**AIU**x**

Rest – Japanese – Menu £ 17 (lunch) – Carte £ 34/54

♦ The more boisterous of the two large restaurants on the 5th floor of Aqua London, along with a busy bar. Ideally suited to larger groups, as the contemporary Japanese food is designed for sharing.

XX **Bob Bob Ricard**

1 Upper James St ✉ W1F 9DF ⊖ Oxford Circus – ✆ (020) 3145 1000 – www.bobbobricard.com – Closed 25-26 December **31**AJU**n**

Rest – Modern European – Carte £ 26/49

♦ Enigmatically decorated and flamboyant grand café, with a menu that offers everything from caviar and jelly, to beef Wellington or a bowl of cornflakes. Open from early to very late.

XX **Floridita**

100 Wardour St ✉ W1F 0TN ⊖ Tottenham Court Road – ✆ (020) 7314 4000 – www.floriditalondon.com – Closed 25-26 December, 1 January, Sunday, Monday and Bank Holidays **31**AKU**z**

Rest – Latin American – *(dinner only and lunch in December)* Menu £ 39 – Carte £ 28/60

♦ Mediterranean tapas on the ground floor; the huge downstairs for live music, dancing and Latin American specialities, from Cuban spice to Argentinean beef. Great cocktails and a party atmosphere.

LONDON

XX **Benja**

17 Beak St ✉ W1F 9RW ⊖ Oxford Circus – ✆ (020) 7287 0555 – www.benjarestaurant.com – Closed Sunday **30**AIU**j**

Rest – Thai – Carte £ 25/39

♦ Soho townhouse divided into three sleek and colourful floors including an intimate basement bar. Thai food is carefully prepared and full of punchy flavours. Service is very charming.

XX **Vasco and Piero's Pavilion**

15 Poland St ✉ W1F 8QE ⊖ Oxford Circus – ✆ (020) 7437 8774 – www.vascosfood.com – Closed Saturday lunch, Sunday and bank holidays

Rest – Italian – *(booking essential at lunch)* Menu £ 20 (early dinner) – Carte lunch £ 27/38 **31**AJU**b**

♦ Celebrating forty years in 2011; its longevity down to its twice-daily changing menu and the simple but effective Umbrian-influenced cooking. The bright room attracts a high proportion of regulars.

XX **La Trouvaille**

12A Newburgh St. ✉ W1F 7RR ⊖ Oxford Circus – ✆ (020) 7287 8488 – www.latrouvaille.co.uk – Closed Monday dinner, Sunday and bank holidays

Rest – French – Menu £ 21/35 **30**AIU**g**

♦ In a charming cobbled street and keenly run by two northern Frenchmen. Ground floor for cheese, charcuterie and wine; upstairs for set menus of classic French cooking. Wines are largely organic.

XX **Plum Valley**

20 Gerrard St ✉ W1D 6JQ ⊖ Leicester Square – ✆ (020) 7494 4366 – Closed 24-25 December **31**AKU**i**

Rest – Chinese – Menu £ 38 – Carte £ 19/30

♦ Its striking black façade make this modern Chinese restaurant easy to spot in Chinatown. Mostly Cantonese cooking, with occasional forays into Vietnam and Thailand; dim sum is the strength.

X **Arbutus**

63-64 Frith St. ✉ W1D 3JW ⊖ Tottenham Court Road – ✆ (020) 7734 4545 – www.arbutusrestaurant.co.uk – Closed 25-26 December and 1 January

Rest – Modern European – *(booking advisable)* Menu £ 17 (lunch) – Carte £ 28/37 **31**AKU**h**

Spec. Braised pigs head, ravioli of caramelised onions. Rabbit with braised celery and shoulder cottage pie. Crème caramel.

♦ It takes a lot of work and experience to make it all look so easy. Bubbly and enthusiastic service; relaxed, sociable surroundings and bistro-style dishes packed with flavour from a highly skilled kitchen. Terrific, affordable wine list.

X **Bocca di Lupo**

12 Archer St. ✉ WID 7BB ⊖ Piccadilly Circus – ✆ (020) 7734 2223 – www.boccadilupo.com – Closed Christmas-New Year and Sunday dinner

Rest – Italian – *(booking essential)* Carte £ 19/39 **31**AKU**e**

♦ Deservedly busy and great fun; but atmosphere, food and service are all best when sitting at the marble counter, watching the chefs. Specialities from across Italy are available in large or small sizes; they're full of flavour and vitality.

X **Polpo**

41 Beak St. ✉ W1F 9SB ⊖ Oxford Circus – ✆ (0207) 734 4479 – www.polpo.co.uk – Closed 25 December-1 January, Sunday dinner and bank holidays

Rest – Italian – Carte £ 12/20 **30**AJU**e**

♦ A fun and lively Venetian bacaro, with a stripped-down, faux-industrial look. The small plates, from arancini and prosciutto to fritto misto and Cotechino sausage, are so well priced that waiting for a table is worth it.

X **Dehesa**

25 Ganton St. ✉ W1F 9BP ⊖ Oxford Circus – ✆ (020) 7494 4170 – www.dehesa.co.uk – Closed Christmas and Sunday dinner **30**AIU**i**

Rest – Mediterranean – Carte £ 20/30

♦ Repeats the success of its sister restaurant, Salt Yard, by offering tasty, good value Spanish and Italian tapas. Unhurried atmosphere in appealing corner location. Terrific drinks list too.

Hix

66-70 Brewer St. ✉ WIF 9UP ⊖ Piccadilly Circus – ✆ (020) 7292 3518 – www.hixsoho.co.uk – Closed 25-26 December **30**AJU**z**

Rest – British – Carte £ 27/55

◆ The exterior hints at exclusivity but the enormous interior is fun and sociable and comes decorated with the works of eminent British artists. Expect classic British dishes and ingredients.

Tierra Brindisa

46 Broadwick St. ✉ W1F 7AF ⊖ Tottenham Court Rd – ✆ (020) 7534 1690 – www.brindisatapaskitchens.com – Closed Sunday **31**AJU**x**

Rest – Spanish – *(booking essential at dinner)* Carte £ 18/30

◆ Sister to Tapas Brindisa in Borough Market; this is a slightly more structured affair but still as busy and enjoyable. Focus is on natural flavours, uncluttered plates and quality Spanish produce.

Barrafina

54 Frith St. ✉ W1D 3SL ⊖ Tottenham Court Road – ✆ (020) 7813 8016 – www.barrafina.co.uk – Closed bank holidays **31**AKU**c**

Rest – Spanish – *(bookings not accepted)* Carte £ 30/45 **s**

◆ Centred around a counter with seating for 20, come here if you want authentic Spanish tapas served in a buzzy atmosphere. Seafood is a speciality and the Jabugo ham a must.

LONDON

Barshu

28 Frith St. ✉ W1D 5LF ⊖ Leicester Square – ✆ (020) 7287 8822 – www.bar-shu.co.uk – Closed 24-25 December **31**AKU**g**

Rest – Chinese – *(booking advisable)* Carte £ 24/35

◆ The fiery and authentic flavours of China's Sichuan Province are the draw here; help is at hand as menu has pictures. It's decorated with carved wood and lanterns; downstairs is better for groups.

Imli

167-169 Wardour St ✉ W1F 8WR ⊖ Tottenham Court Road – ✆ (020) 7287 4243 – www.imli.co.uk – Closed 25-26 December and 1 January

Rest – Indian – Menu £ 9 (weekday lunch)/13 – Carte £ 20/30 **31**AKU**w**

◆ Long, spacious interior is a busy, buzzy place. Good value, fresh and tasty Indian tapas-style dishes prove a popular currency. Same owners as Tamarind.

Polpetto

46 Dean St, (1st floor) ✉ W1D 5BG ⊖ Leicester Square – ✆ (020) 7734 1969 – www.polpetto.co.uk – Closed 25 December to 1 January, Sunday and bank holidays **31**AKU**d**

Rest – Italian – Carte £ 16/22

◆ Baby sister to Polpo is located, incongruously, above the iconic French House pub. It's just one small but thoughtfully designed room; order a number of the small, keenly priced plates.

Ba Shan

24 Romilly St. ✉ W1D 5AH ⊖ Leicester Square – ✆ (020) 7287 3266 – Closed Christmas **31**AKU**f**

Rest – Chinese – *(booking advisable)* Carte £ 16/26 **s**

◆ 3-4 tables in each of the five rooms. Open all day, serving a mix of 'snack' and 'home-style' dishes, some with Sichuan leanings, others from northern areas and Henan province.

Baozi Inn

25 Newport Court ✉ WC2H 7JS ⊖ Leicester Square – ✆ (020) 7287 6877 – Closed 24-25 December **31**AKU**r**

Rest – Chinese – Carte £ 19/25

◆ Baozi, or steamed filled buns, are a good way to start, followed by some fiery Sichuan specialities. Simple, honest and friendly restaurant, just off the main strip of Chinatown.

Strand and Covent Garden

Savoy

Strand ✉ *WC2R 0EU* ⊖ *Charing Cross* – ✆ *(020) 7836 4343 – www.fairmont.com/savoy* **31**ALU**s**

221 rm – †£ 654/714 ††£ 1074, ☕ £ 30 – 47 suites

Rest *River Room* – Menu £ 29 – Carte £ 44/56

◆ The grande dame of London hotels dazzles once again! Reopened in 2010 following a 3 year restoration, its luxurious bedrooms and stunning suites come in an Edwardian or art deco style. Thames Foyer is the hotel's heart; choose the famous American Bar or new Beaufort Bar. River Room now has a more contemporary feel.

One Aldwych

1 Aldwych ✉ *WC2B 4RH* ⊖ *Temple* – ✆ *(020) 7300 1000 – www.onealdwych.com*

93 rm – †£ 468/583 ††£ 468/583, ☕ £ 23 – 12 suites **32**AMU**r**

Rest *Axis* – see restaurant listing

Rest *Indigo* – Menu £ 20 – Carte £ 31/43

◆ Former 19C bank, now a stylish hotel with lots of artwork; the lobby changes its look seasonally and doubles as a bar. Stylish, contemporary bedrooms with the latest mod cons; the deluxe rooms and suites are particularly desirable. Impressive leisure facilities. Light, accessible menu at Indigo.

Swissôtel The Howard

Temple Pl ✉ *WC2R 2PR* ⊖ *Temple* – ✆ *(020) 7836 3555 – www.swissotel.com/london* **32**AMU**e**

187 rm – †£ 140/260 ††£ 180/280, ☕ £ 23.50 – 2 suites

Rest *12 Temple Place* – ✆ (020) 7300 1700 *(Closed 1 January, dinner 24 December, 25, 31 December, Saturday lunch, Sunday and bank holidays)* Menu £ 21 (lunch) – Carte £ 32/45

◆ Discreet elegance is the order of the day at this handsomely appointed hotel. Many of the comfortable rooms enjoy balcony views of the Thames. Attentive service. Large terrace to restaurant serving modern European dishes.

St Martins Lane

45 St Martin's Ln ✉ *WC2N 3HX* ⊖ *Charing Cross* – ✆ *(020) 7300 5500 – www.morganshotelgroup.com* **31**ALU**e**

202 rm – †£ 246/594 ††£ 246/594, ☕ £ 25 – 2 suites

Rest *Asia de Cuba* – Menu £ 60 – Carte £ 50/118

◆ The unmistakable hand of Philippe Starck evident at this most contemporary of hotels. Unique and stylish, from the starkly modern lobby to the state-of-the-art rooms. 350 varieties of rum and tasty Asian dishes at fashionable Asia de Cuba.

The Ivy

1-5 West St ✉ *WC2H 9NQ* ⊖ *Leicester Square* – ✆ *(020) 7836 4751 – www.the-ivy.co.uk – Closed 24-26 December and 1 January* **31**AKU**p**

Rest – International – Carte £ 27/52

◆ One of the original celebrity hang-out restaurants; still pulling them in. Appealing menu, from shepherd's pie to fishcakes and nursery puddings. Staff go about their business with alacrity.

Axis – at One Aldwych Hotel

1 Aldwych ✉ *WC2B 4RH* ⊖ *Temple* – ✆ *(020) 7300 0300 – www.onealdwych.com – Closed Sunday and Monday* **31**AMU**r**

Rest – Modern European – Menu £ 20 – Carte £ 32/42

◆ A spiral marble staircase leading down to this impressively high-ceilinged restaurant adds to the expectation. The menu is a combination of British classics and lighter European choices.

J. Sheekey

28-32 St Martin's Ct. ✉ *WC2 4AL* ⊖ *Leicester Square* – ✆ *(020) 7240 2565 – www.j-sheekey.co.uk – Closed 25-26 December and 1 January* **31**ALU**v**

Rest – Seafood – *(booking essential)* Menu £ 26 (weekend lunch) – Carte £ 19/64

◆ Festooned with photographs of actors and linked to the theatrical world since opening in 1890. Wood panels and alcove tables add famed intimacy. Accomplished seafood cooking.

LONDON

XX **Rules**

35 Maiden Ln. ✉ *WC2E 7LB* ⊖ *Leicester Square – ☎ (020) 7836 5314 – www.rules.co.uk – Closed 4 days Christmas* **31**ALU**n**

Rest – British – *(booking essential)* Carte £ 34/58

◆ London's oldest restaurant boasts a fine collection of antique cartoons, drawings and paintings. Tradition continues in the menu, specialising in game from its own estate.

XX **Clos Maggiore**

33 King St ✉ *WC2E 8JD* ⊖ *Leicester Square – ☎ (020) 7379 9696 – www.closmaggiore.com – Closed lunch 24 December-26 December*

Rest – French – Menu £ 20 (lunch) – Carte £ 29/34 **31**ALU**z**

◆ Well-dressed restaurant with poised service; ask for a table in the enchanting little rear conservatory, whose roof opens in summer. Sophisticated cooking from a largely French repertoire. Exceptional value lunch and pre-theatre menus.

XX **Forge**

14 Garrick St ✉ *WC2E 9BJ* ⊖ *Leicester Square – ☎ (020) 7379 1432 – www.theforgerestaurant.co.uk – Closed 24 December and Bank Holidays*

Rest – Modern European – Menu £ 17 (lunch)/28 – Carte £ 31/38 **31**ALU**a**

◆ Décor mixes the old with the new; the front area is more intimate, the back more fun. Extensive menu offers something for everyone, from pasta to Dover Sole, tournedos Rossini to a hamburger.

XX **Le Deuxième**

65a Long Acre ✉ *WC2E 9JH* ⊖ *Covent Garden – ☎ (020) 7379 0033 – www.ledeuxieme.com – Closed 24-25 December* **31**ALU**b**

Rest – Modern European – Menu £ 17 (lunch) – Carte £ 33/38

◆ Caters well for theatregoers: opens early, closes late. Buzzy eatery, simply decorated in white with subtle lighting. International menu but emphasis within Europe.

X **L'Atelier de Joël Robuchon**

13-15 West St ✉ *WC2H 9NE* ⊖ *Leicester Square – ☎ (020) 7010 8600 – www.joelrobuchon.co.uk* **31**AKU**a**

Rest – French – *(closed 25-26 December, 1 January, Sunday and bank holidays)* Carte £ 45/100

Rest *La Cuisine* – French – *(Closed 25-26 December, 1 January, Sunday and bank holidays)* Menu £ 27 (early dinner) – Carte £ 43/85

Spec. Crispy langoustine fritters with basil pistou. Rib of veal with girolles, fondant potatoes and braised sucrine. Cointreau soufflé with milk chocolate ice cream.

◆ Wonderfully precise, creative and occasionally playful cooking; dishes may look delicate but pack a punch. Ground floor Atelier with counter seating and chefs on view. More structured La Cuisine. Cool top floor bar.

X **J. Sheekey Oyster Bar**

33-34 St Martin's Ct. ✉ *WC2 4AL* ⊖ *Leicester Square – ☎ (020) 7240 2565 – www.j-sheeky.co.uk – Closed 25-26 December and 1 January* **31**ALU**v**

Rest – Seafood – Carte £ 23/35

◆ An addendum to J. Sheekey restaurant. Sit at the bar to watch the chefs prepare the same quality seafood as next door but at slightly lower prices; fish pie and fruits de mer are the popular choices. Open all day.

X **Terroirs**

5 William IV St ✉ *WC2N 4DW* ⊖ *Charing Cross – ☎ (020) 7036 0660 – www.terroirswinebar.com* **31**ALU**h**

Rest – French – *(Closed 24-27, 31 December, 1 January, Sunday and bank holidays)* Carte £ 20/33

◆ Eat in the ground floor bistro/wine bar or two floors below at 'Downstairs at Terriors' where the menu is a little more substantial. Flavoursome French cooking, with extra Italian and Spanish influences. Thoughtfully compiled wine list.

LONDON

Bedford & Strand

1a Bedford St WC2E 9HH Charing Cross – (020) 7836 3033 – www.bedford-strand.com – Closed 24 December-3 January, Sunday and bank holidays
Rest – British – *(booking essential)* Carte £ 27/38 **31**ALU**c**
◆ They call themselves a 'wine room and bistro' which neatly sums up both the philosophy and the style of the place – interesting wines, reassuringly familiar food and relaxed basement surroundings.

VICTORIA

The Goring

15 Beeston Pl, Grosvenor Gdns SW1W 0JW Victoria – (020) 7396 9000 – www.thegoring.com **38**AIX**a**
65 rm – £ 492/570 £ 550, £ 25 – 6 suites
Rest – British – *(Closed Saturday lunch)* Menu £ 35 (lunch)/48
◆ Celebrated its centenary in 2010; this very English hotel is still owned and run by the Goring family who built it - the fourth generation is now at the helm. Many of the attractive rooms overlook a peaceful garden. Elegantly appointed restaurant with an appropriately British menu.

LONDON

Crowne Plaza London - St James

45 Buckingham Gate SW1E 6AF St James's Park – (020) 7834 6655 – www.london.crowneplaza.com **39**AJX**e**
321 rm – £ 426 £ 426, £ 18.50 – 19 suites
Rest *Quilon and Bank* – see restaurant listing
Rest *Bistro 51* – Carte £ 33/47
◆ Built in 1897 as serviced accommodation for visiting aristocrats. Behind the impressive Edwardian façade lies an equally elegant interior. Quietest rooms overlook courtyard. Bright and informal café-style restaurant.

51 Buckingham Gate without rest

51 Buckingham Gate SW1E 6AF St James's Park – (020) 7769 7766 – www.51-buckinghamgate.com **39**AJX**s**
89 suites – £ 702, £ 22.50
◆ In the courtyard of the Crowne Plaza but offering greater levels of comfort and service. Contemporary in style, suites range from one to seven bedrooms. Butler service available. Restaurants located in adjacent hotel.

41 without rest

41 Buckingham Palace Rd. SW1W 0PS Victoria – (020) 7300 0041 – www.41hotel.com **38**AIX**n**
29 rm – £ 275/395 £ 287/419, £ 25 – 1 suite
◆ Smart and discreet addendum to The Rubens hotel next door. Attractively decorated and quiet lounge where breakfast is served; comfortable bedrooms boast fireplaces and plenty of extras.

The Rubens at The Palace

39 Buckingham Palace Rd SW1W 0PS Victoria – (020) 7834 6600 – www.rubenshotel.com **38**AIX**n**
160 rm – £ 155/311 £ 167/311, £ 18.50 – 1 suite
Rest *Old Masters* – *(Closed lunch Saturday and Sunday)* Menu £ 28
Rest *Library* – *(dinner only)* Menu £ 35 – Carte £ 42/59
Rest *bbar* – (020) 7958 7000 *(Closed Saturday, Sunday and bank holidays)* Menu £ 21 – Carte £ 25/47
◆ Discreet, comfortable hotel in great location for visitors to London. Constant reinvestment ensures bright and contemporary bedrooms. Old Masters for grills. Fine dining in cosy Library. Casual dining in bbar.

Tophams without rest

24-32 Ebury St SW1W 0LU Victoria – (020) 7730 3313 – www.tophamshotel.com **38**AHY**d**
48 rm – £ 95/375 £ 109/375, £ 14.95
◆ A row of five pretty terraced houses, in a good spot for tourists and recently refurbished. Neat bedrooms with large bathrooms and good mod cons. Comfortable breakfast room.

B + B Belgravia without rest

64-66 Ebury St ✉ SW1W 9QD ⊖ Victoria – ✆ (020) 7259 8570 – www.bb-belgravia.com **38**AHY**x**

17 rm ☕ – 🚹£ 99 🚹🚹£ 170

◆ Two houses, three floors, and, considering the location, representing good value accommodation. Sleek, clean-lined bedrooms. Breakfast overlooking little garden terrace.

Lord Milner without rest

111 Ebury Street ✉ SW1W 9QU ⊖ Victoria – ✆ (020) 7881 9880 – www.lordmilner.com **38**AHY**k**

10 rm – 🚹£ 100/165 🚹🚹£ 115/165, ☕ £ 14 – 1 suite

◆ A four storey terraced house, with individually decorated bedrooms, three with four-poster beds and all with marble bathrooms. Garden Suite the best room, with its own patio. No public areas.

XXX ✿ **Quilon** – at Crowne Plaza London - St James Hotel

41 Buckingham Gate ✉ SW1E 6AF ⊖ St James's Park – ✆ (020) 7821 1899 – www.quilon.co.uk – Closed Saturday lunch **39**AJX**e**

Rest – Indian – Menu £ 22 (lunch)/39 – Carte dinner £ 34/57

Spec. Spiced oysters and lentils with onion relish. Koondapur halibut curry and tamarind gravy. Spiced dark chocolate and hazelnut mousse

◆ Vibrant and well-balanced Indian dishes, many of which originate from the south west coast of India but are given a 'Western' twist . Skilled use of spices, appealing seafood specialities and well-organised service.

LONDON

XXX **Roux at Parliament Square**

RICS, Parliament Sq. ✉ SW1P 3AD ⊖ Westminster – ✆ (020) 7334 3737 – www.rouxatparliamentsquare.co.uk – Closed Christmas-New Year, Saturday and Sunday **39**ALX**x**

Rest – French – Menu £ 30/55

◆ Light floods through the Georgian windows of this comfortable Westminster restaurant, popular with MPs and surveyors. French base to the food, which is intricate but also light and contemporary.

XXX **Roussillon**

16 St Barnabas St ✉ SW1W 8PE ⊖ Sloane Square – ✆ (020) 7730 5550 – www.roussillon.co.uk – Closed Christmas to New Year, Saturday lunch and Sunday

Rest – French – Menu £ 35 (lunch)/60 ⚘ **38**AHZ**c**

◆ A longstanding neighbourhood restaurant, with a comfortable, discreet and grown up feel. Expect quite formal service and a creative style of cooking.

XXX **The Cinnamon Club**

30-32 Great Smith St ✉ SW1P 3BU ⊖ St James's Park – ✆ (020) 7222 2555 – www.cinnamonclub.com – Closed 1 January, Sunday and bank holidays

Rest – Indian – Menu £ 22 – Carte £ 29/45 **39**AKX**c**

◆ Housed in former Westminster Library: exterior has ornate detail, interior is stylish and modern. Walls are lined with books. New Wave Indian cooking with plenty of choice.

XXX **Santini**

29 Ebury St ✉ SW1W 0NZ ⊖ Victoria – ✆ (020) 7730 4094 – www.santini-restaurant.com – Closed 1 January , Easter, 23-27 December, lunch Saturday and Sunday **38**AHY**v**

Rest – Italian – Menu £ 25 (dinner) – Carte £ 29/54

◆ Smart, crisp and cool Italian restaurant, with a large, impressive terrace and old-school service. Menu has subtle Venetian accent but is not inexpensive; pastas and desserts are good.

XXX **Shepherd's**

Marsham Ct., Marsham St. ✉ SW1P 4LA ⊖ Pimlico – ✆ (020) 7834 9552 – www.langansrestaurants.co.uk – Closed bank holidays **39**AKY**z**

Rest – British – *(booking essential)* Menu £ 38

◆ A truly English restaurant where game and traditional puddings are a highlight. Popular with those from Westminster – the booths offer a degree of privacy.

XX **Il Convivio**

143 Ebury St ✉ SW1W 9QN ⊖ Sloane Square – ✆ (020) 7730 4099 – www.etruscarestaurants.com – Closed Christmas-New Year, Sunday and Bank Holidays **38**AHY**a**

Rest – Italian – Carte £ 34/50

◆ Handsome Georgian house, with a retractable roof and Dante's poetry embossed on the walls. All pasta is made on the top floor of the house. Dishes are artfully presented and flavoursome.

XX **Tinello**

87 Pimlico Rd ✉ SW1W 8PH ⊖ Sloane Square – ✆ (020) 7730 3663 – www.tinello.co.uk – Closed 24 December-2 January and Sunday **37**AGZ**s**

Rest – Italian – *(booking essential at dinner)* Carte £ 32/37

◆ Sleekly designed Italian restaurant run by two brothers, both alumni of Locanda Locatelli. Their native Tuscany informs the cooking; the antipasti or 'small eats' section is very appealing.

XX **Boisdale**

15 Eccleston St ✉ SW1W 9LX ⊖ Victoria – ✆ (020) 7730 6922 – www.boisdale.co.uk – Closed 1 week Christmas, Saturday lunch and Sunday

Rest – Scottish – Menu £ 20 – Carte £ 30/64 **38**AHY**c**

◆ A proudly Scottish restaurant with acres of tartan and a charmingly higgledy-piggledy layout. Stand-outs are the smoked salmon and the 28-day aged Aberdeenshire cuts of beef. Live nightly jazz.

XX **Rex Whistler**

Tate Britain, Millbank ✉ SW1P 4RG ⊖ Pimlico – ✆ (020) 7887 8825 – www.tate.org.uk/britain/eatanddrink – Closed 24-26 December **39**ALY**c**

Rest – British – *(lunch only) (booking essential)* Menu £ 20 – Carte £ 33/40

◆ As with upstairs, it celebrates Britain, with a daily catch from Newlyn and fruity desserts the specialities. Comfortable room, with striking Rex Whistler mural. Terrific wine list.

XX **Bank** – at Crowne Plaza London-St James Hotel

45 Buckingham Gate ✉ SW1E 6BS ⊖ St James's Park – ✆ (020) 7630 6644 – www.bankrestaurants.com – Closed Saturday lunch, Sunday and bank holidays **39**AJX**e**

Rest – Modern European – *(booking essential at lunch)* Carte £ 34/49

◆ Behind the understated entrance lies a vibrant and busy interior. Pass through one of Europe's longest bars to reach the conservatory restaurant, where you'll find a varied, accessible menu.

XX **Osteria Dell' Angolo**

47 Marsham St. ✉ SW1P 3DR ⊖ St. James's Park – ✆ (020) 3268 1077 – www.osteriadellangolo.co.uk – Closed 24-31 December, Saturday lunch, Sunday and bank holidays **39**AKY**n**

Rest – Italian – Menu £ 15 (lunch)/20 – Carte £ 29/42

◆ Expert restaurateur Claudio Pulze opened this sunny Italian restaurant opposite the Home Office in 2009. Tuscan element to the cooking, along with some creativity; service is keen and friendly.

X **Olivo**

21 Eccleston St ✉ SW1W 9LX ⊖ Victoria – ✆ (020) 7730 2505 – www.olivorestaurant.com – Closed lunch Saturday and Sunday and bank holidays **38**AHY**z**

Rest – Italian – Menu £ 25 (lunch) – Carte dinner £ 33/38

◆ Carefully prepared, authentic Sardinian specialities are the highlight at this popular Italian restaurant. Simply decorated in blues and yellows, with an atmosphere of bonhomie.

X **Olivomare**

10 Lower Belgrave St ✉ SW1W 0LJ ⊖ Victoria – ✆ (020) 7730 9022 – www.olivorestaurants.com – Closed bank holidays **38**AHY**b**

Rest – Seafood – Carte £ 36/39

◆ Understated and stylish piscatorial decoration and seafood with a Sardinian base. Fortnightly changing menu, with high quality produce, much of which is available in shop next door.

Ebury
11 Pimlico Rd ✉ SW1W 8NA ⊖ Sloane Square. – ☎ (020) 7730 6784 – www.theebury.co.uk – Closed 25-26 December **38**AHZ**z**
Rest – Menu £ 20 (lunch and early dinner) – Carte £ 30/45
♦ Smart and stylish room, with an appealing menu ranging from burgers to black bream. Low-slung tables around popular central bar; efficient service. Upstairs is used for private parties.

Thomas Cubitt
44 Elizabeth St ✉ SW1W 9PA ⊖ Sloane Square. – ☎ (020) 7730 6060 – www.thethomascubitt.co.uk **38**AHY**e**
Rest – *(booking essential)* Carte £ 30/45
♦ A pub of two halves: choose the busy ground floor bar with its accessible menu or upstairs for more ambitious, quite elaborate cooking with courteous service and a less frenetic environment.

Orange with rm
37-39 Pimlico Rd ✉ SW1W 8NE ⊖ Sloane Square. – ☎ (020) 7881 9844 – www.theorange.co.uk **38**AHZ**k**
4 rm – †£ 189/212 ††£ 189/212 **Rest** – Carte £ 23/26
♦ Family-friendly pub with laid-back atmosphere and slight colonial feel. Pizza from the wood-fired oven in the bar or rustic cooking in the upstairs dining room. Film nights on Monday. Bedrooms named after local streets.

LONDON

LONG COMPTON – Warks. – see Shipston-on-Stour

LONG CRENDON – Buckinghamshire – 504 Q/R28 – pop. 2 383 – ✉ Aylesbury **11** C2

London 50 mi – Aylesbury 11 mi – Oxford 15 mi

Angel with rm
47 Bicester Rd ✉ HP18 9EE – ☎ (01844) 208 268 – www.angelrestaurant.co.uk – Closed 1-7 January and Sunday dinner
4 rm – †£ 70 ††£ 95 **Rest** – Menu £ 16/20 – Carte £ 28/41
♦ Comfortable, characterful former pub with low ceilings, leather-furnished lounge/bar and airy conservatory. Wide-ranging menus offer tasty, globally influenced dishes. Well-chosen wine list. Stylish bedrooms, all individually decorated; Room 4 is the biggest.

LONGHORSLEY – Northd. – 501 – see Morpeth

LONG MELFORD – Suffolk – 504 W27 – pop. 2 734 Great Britain **15** C3

London 62 mi – Cambridge 34 mi – Colchester 18 mi – Ipswich 24 mi
Melford Hall★ AC

Black Lion
Church Walk, The Green ✉ CO10 9DN – ☎ (01787) 312 356 – www.blacklionhotel.net
9 rm – †£ 102 ††£ 173 – 1 suite **Rest** – Carte £ 29/32
♦ 17C Georgian inn overlooking village green. Named after wines, bedrooms are smart, stylish and individually designed; good facilities and traditional bathrooms. Formal restaurant with enclosed rear terrace features extensive, popular menu.

Scutchers
Westgate St, on A 1092 ✉ CO10 9DP – ☎ (01787) 310 200 – www.scutchers.com – Closed Christmas, New Year, Sunday, Monday and Bank Holidays
Rest – Menu £ 28 – Carte £ 34/49
♦ Former medieval hall house set in pleasant rural village: now a smart, split-level, personally run restaurant. Traditional dishes use quality ingredients; good value set menu.

LONGRIDGE – Lancashire – **502** M22 – **pop. 7 491** — **20** A2

London 241 mi – Blackburn 12 mi – Burnley 18 mi

XX The Longridge Restaurant

104-106 Higher Rd, Northeast : 0.5 mi by B 5269 following signs for Jeffrey Hill ✉ PR3 3SY – ✆ (01772) 784 969 – www.heathcotes.co.uk – Closed 3-7 January, Monday, Tuesday and bank holidays

Rest – Menu £ 19 (weekday lunch)/25 – Carte £ 36/58

◆ Stylish, subtly hued restaurant with changing character: bright by day and intimate at night. Seasonal, regional cooking uses quality ingredients to create appealing, flavoursome dishes.

LONGSTOCK – Hampshire – **503** P30 – **see Stockbridge**

LONG SUTTON – Somerset – **503** L30 – ✉ **Langport** — **3** B3

London 132 mi – Bridgwater 16 mi – Yeovil 10 mi

The Devonshire Arms with rm

✉ TA10 9LP – ✆ (01458) 241 271 – www.thedevonshirearms.com – Closed 25-26 December and 1 January

9 rm – †£ 70/120 ††£ 85/130 **Rest** – Carte £ 22/29

◆ Spacious Grade II listed hunting lodge set on village green; contemporary interior, with relaxing, open-plan bar and formal dining room. Locally sourced produce used in seasonal European dishes. Comfortable bedrooms boast excellent quality linen and toiletries.

LONGTOWN – Cumbria – **502** L18 — **21** A1

London 326 mi – Carlisle 9 mi – Newcastle upon Tyne 61 mi

Bessiestown Farm

Catlowdy, Northeast : 8 mi by Netherby St on B 6318 ✉ CA6 5QP – ✆ (01228) 577 219 – www.bessiestown.co.uk – Closed 24-26 December

6 rm – †£ 57 ††£ 85/90 **Rest** – Menu £ 18

◆ Immaculately kept converted farmhouse in rural location. Traditional, homely lounge with pleasant conservatory overlooking garden. Friendly owner. Spacious bedrooms; Dovecote is the largest. Bright, airy dining room; home-cooked meals available Thurs-Sat.

LOOE – Cornwall – **503** G32 – **pop. 5 280** — **1** B2

London 264 mi – Plymouth 23 mi – Truro 39 mi

The Guildhall, Fore St ✆ (01503) 262072, looetic@btconnect.com

Bin Down, ✆ (01503) 240 239

Whitsand Bay Hotel Torpoint Portwrinkle, ✆ (01503) 230 276

Town★ – Monkey Sanctuary★ **AC**

Barclay House

St Martins Rd, East Looe, East : 0.5 mi by A 387 on B 3253 ✉ PL13 1LP – ✆ (01503) 262 929 – www.barclayhouse.co.uk

11 rm – †£ 55/132 ††£ 145/175 – 1 suite

Rest *Restaurant* – see restaurant listing

◆ Imposing, whitewashed Victorian house in elevated position; most bedrooms come with a view. Room 7 is contemporary with superb estuary vista; 9 boasts a balcony and whirlpool bath.

XX Restaurant – at Barclay House Hotel

St Martins Rd, East Looe, East : 0.5 mi by A 387 on B 3253 ✉ PL13 1LP – ✆ (01503) 262 929 – www.barclayhouse.co.uk

Rest – *(closed Sunday dinner) (dinner only and Sunday lunch June-October)* Menu £ 25 – Carte £ 28/42

◆ Light, modern restaurant featuring abstract local art and with extensive views of the estuary. Dishes make use of local, seasonal produce, including seafood from the day boats.

Trawlers on the Quay
The Quay, East Looe ✉ PL13 1AH – ✆ (01503) 263 593 – www.trawlers-restaurant.co.uk
Rest – Seafood – Carte £ 19/30
♦ Bright, contemporary restaurant, perched on the edge of the quay; ask for a window table. The menu focuses on seafood and ranges from light lunches up to the full three courses.

LORTON – **Cumbria** – **502** K20 – **see Cockermouth**

LOUGHBOROUGH – **Leicestershire** – **502** – **pop. 55 258** **16** B2
London 117 mi – Birmingham 41 mi – Leicester 11 mi – Nottingham 15 mi
Town Hall, Market Pl ✆ (01509) 231914, tic@charnwoodbc.gov.uk
Lingdale Woodhouse Eaves Joe Moore's Lane, ✆ (01509) 890 703

at Belton **West : 6 mi by A 6 on B 5324 – ✉ Loughborough**

The Queen's Head with rm
2 Long St ✉ LE12 9TP – ✆ (01530) 222 359 – www.thequeenshead.org – Closed 25-26 December and Sunday dinner
6 rm – £ 70 £ 80/100 **Rest** – Menu £ 16/23
♦ Modern, minimalist pub in the village centre, with comfy bar-lounge and more formal restaurant. Menus offer plenty of choice, with several dishes available in two sizes. Brunch served on Sundays. Individually designed, modern bedrooms offer good facilities.

at Woodhouse Eaves **South : 4.5 mi by A 6 via Woodhouse – ✉ Loughborough**

The Woodhouse
43 Maplewell Rd ✉ LE12 8RG – ✆ (01509) 890 318 – www.thewoodhouse.co.uk – Closed Saturday lunch, Sunday dinner and Monday
Rest – Menu £ 16/19 – Carte approx. £ 35
♦ Smart village restaurant with comfy lounge, bold modern colours and eye-catching art. Concise, understated menu relies on quality local produce: classical combinations have a personal twist.

LOUTH – **Lincolnshire** – **502** T/U23 – **pop. 15 930** **17** D1
London 156 mi – Boston 34 mi – Great Grimsby 17 mi – Lincoln 26 mi
Town Hall, Cannon St. ✆ (01507) 601111, louthinfo@e-lindsey.gov.uk

Brackenborough rest,
Cordeaux Corner, Brackenborough, North : 2 mi by A 16 ✉ LN11 0SZ – ✆ (01507) 609 169 – www.oakridgehotels.co.uk
24 rm – £ 82 £ 97 **Rest** – Menu £ 17/20 – Carte £ 25/38
♦ Contemporary, family-owned hotel with relaxed feel and warm, personal style. Spacious, individually designed bedrooms boast all mod cons; executive rooms include jacuzzi baths. Sexy cocktail bar. Lounge/bar and conservatory for all-day dining. Formal restaurant.

LOVINGTON – **Somerset** – **503** M30 – **see Castle Cary**

LOW FELL – **Tyne and Wear** – **see Gateshead**

LOW ROW – **North Yorkshire** – **502** N20 – **see Reeth**

LOWER FROYLE – **Hampshire** – **see Alton**

LOWER HARDRES – **Kent** – **504** X30 – **see Canterbury**

LOWER ODDINGTON – **Glos.** – **see Stow-on-the-Wold**

LOWER PEOVER – **City of Chester and West Cheshire** – **see Knutsford**

LOWER SHIPLAKE – **Oxfordshire** – **504** R29 – **see Henley-on-Thames**

LOWER SLAUGHTER – Glos. – 503 – see Bourton-on-the-Water

LOWER SWELL – Glos. – see Stow-on-the-Wold

LOWER VOBSTER – Somerset – pop. 2 222 – ✉ Radstock 4 C2

London 119 mi – Bath 16 mi – Frome 5 mi

The Vobster Inn with rm

✉ BA3 5RJ – ✆ (01373) 812 920 – www.vobsterinn.co.uk – Closed Sunday dinner and Monday

3 rm – †£ 60/68 ††£ 95 **Rest** – Carte £ 18/28

◆ Solid stone pub with homely, traditional inner, featuring exposed beams and open fires. Seasonal, Mediterranean-inspired menu reflects owners' Spanish heritage. Popular theme evenings. Cosy, well-equipped bedrooms; the family room overlooks the garden.

LOWESTOFT – Suffolk – 504 Z26 – pop. 68 340 Great Britain 15 D2

London 116 mi – Ipswich 43 mi – Norwich 30 mi

East Point Pavillion, Royal Plain ✆ (01502) 533600, touristinfo@waveny.gov.uk

Rookery Park Carlton Colville, ✆ (01502) 509 190

Norfolk Broads★

Britten House without rest

21 Kirkley Cliff Rd ✉ NR33 0DB – ✆ (01502) 573 950 – www.brittenhouse.co.uk – Closed 24-25 December

7 rm – †£ 60/70 ††£ 75/95 – 1 suite

◆ Fine brick-built Victorian house overlooking the promenade; birthplace of Benjamin Britten in 1913. Classically furnished bedrooms named after composers; choose a front-facing room with sea view.

LUDFORD – Lincolnshire 17 C1

London 174 mi – Sheffield 74 mi – Kingston upon Hull 43 mi – Nottingham 59 mi

The Black Horse Inn

Magna Mile ✉ LN8 6AJ – ✆ (01507) 313 645 – Closed Sunday dinner and Monday

Rest – Carte £ 17/31

◆ Slightly worn but well-loved pub with homely décor, simple furnishings and welcoming open fires. Concise menus feature good old-fashioned classics, including game, pies and stews in winter.

LUDLOW – Shropshire – 503 L26 – pop. 9 548 Great Britain 18 B2

London 162 mi – Birmingham 39 mi – Hereford 24 mi – Shrewsbury 29 mi

Castle St ✆ (01584) 875053, ludlow.tourism@shropshire.gov.uk

Town★ Z – Castle★ **AC** – Feathers Hotel★ – St Laurence's Parish Church★ (Misericords★) **S**

Stokesay Castle★ **AC**, NW : 6.5 mi by A 49

Overton Grange

Old Hereford Rd, South : 1.75 mi by B 4361 ✉ SY8 4AD – ✆ (01584) 873 500 – www.overtongrangehotel.com

14 rm – †£ 95/140 ††£ 140/240

Rest – *(booking essential for non-residents)* Menu £ 33/43

◆ Well-maintained Edwardian country house boasting subtle modern touches alongside original features. Bedrooms feature modern facilities and smart bathrooms. Superb pool. Dining rooms offer immaculately laid tables and countryside views; cooking has a French base.

Dinham Hall

Dinham ✉ SY8 1EJ – ✆ (01584) 876 464 – www.dinhamhall.com Z**b**

13 rm – †£ 95/140 ††£ 140/240 **Rest** – Menu £ 15/35

◆ 18C manor house, with pretty walled garden, situated by Ludlow Castle in the heart of charming medieval town. Period furnishings and individual rooms. Informal dining with crisp, bright décor.

ENGLAND

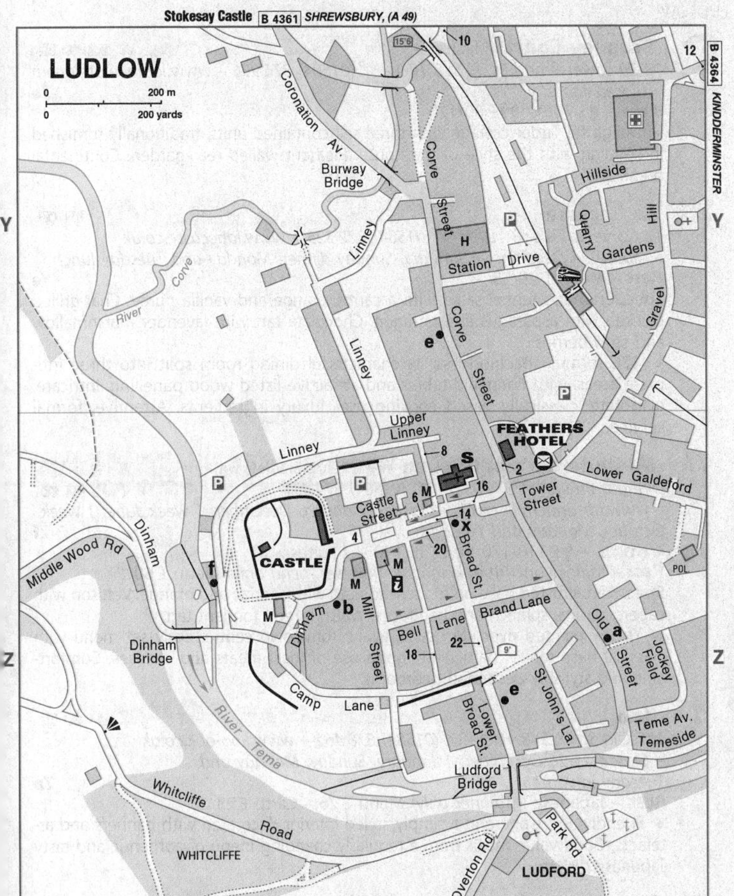

Bull Ring	Z 2	Fishmore Rd	Y 10	Lower Raven Lane	Z 18
Castle Square	Z 4	Henley Rd	Y 12	Market St	Z 20
Church St	Z 6	High St	Z 14	Silk Mill	Z 22
College St	Z 8	King St	Z 16		

Fishmore Hall

rest, VISA MC AE

Fishmore Rd, North : 1.5 mi off A 4117 ✉ SY8 3DP – ✆ (01584) 875 148 – www.fishmorehall.co.uk

15 rm – £ 105 £ 225 **Rest** – Menu £ 25/49 – Carte £ 26/36

◆ Elegantly restored Georgian house – a former boys' school – set out of town in half an acre of land. Very modern, designer bedrooms, boasting bold wallpaper and flat screen TVs. Two smart dining rooms serve modern British menus.

De Grey's Town House without rest

VISA MC

Broad St ✉ SY8 1NG – ✆ (01584) 872 764 – www.degreys.co.uk – Closed 24-26, 31 December and 1 January Zx

9 rm – £ 65 £ 110/190

◆ Dating back to 1570 this building retains all its good old English style and charm. Bedrooms are spacious, very individual and feature quality hand made oak furniture.

Bromley Court without rest
18-20 Lower Broad St ✉ SY8 1PQ – ☎ (01584) 876 996 – www.ludlowhotels.com – Closed January **Ze**
3 rm – ♦£ 70/90 ♦♦£ 80/120
♦ Delightful Tudor cottage with three self-contained units, traditionally furnished in keeping with the style of the house. Pleasant walled rear garden. Continental breakfasts.

La Bécasse
17 Corve St ✉ SY8 1DA – ☎ (01584) 872 325 – www.labecasse.co.uk – Closed 24 December-6 January, Sunday dinner, Monday and Tuesday lunch
Rest – Menu £ 29/55 **Ye**
Spec. Crab and fennel salad with a carrot, orange and vanilla purée. Char-grilled chicken with asparagus and tarragon. Chocolate tart with lavender marshmallow and strawberries.
♦ 17C former coaching inn; its characterful dining room split into three intimate areas, with linen-laid tables and attractive listed wood panelling. Intricate, elaborate, classically based cooking uses luxury ingredients. Attentive, formal service.

Mr Underhill's at Dinham Weir (Chris Bradley) with rm
Dinham Bridge ✉ SY8 1EH – ☎ (01584) 874 431 – www.mr-underhills.co.uk – Closed 25 and 26 December, 1 week June, 1 week October, Monday and Tuesday **Zf**
4 rm – ♦£ 110/170 ♦♦£ 135/170 – 2 suites
Rest – *(dinner only) (booking essential) (set menu only)* Menu £ 60
Spec. Herb crusted hake on fondant tomato with chorizo and orange. Venison with capers, raisins, spinach and beetroots. Welsh rarebit fondant tart.
♦ Yellow painted riverside house, away from town centre. Daily set menu with classical base makes particularly good use of local meats and cheeses. Comfortable and stylishly decorated bedrooms.

Koo
127 Old St ✉ SY8 1NU – ☎ (01584) 878 462 – www.koo-ook.co.uk – Closed 25-26 December, 1 January, Sunday, Monday and Tuesday in winter **Za**
Rest – Japanese – *(dinner only)* Menu £ 26 – Carte £ 23/25
♦ Friendly atmosphere in a simply styled interior decorated with banners and artefacts. Good value meals from a regularly changing menu of authentic and tasty Japanese dishes.

at Woofferton South : 4 mi by B 4361 - Z - on A 49 – ✉ Ludlow

Ravenscourt Manor without rest
on A 49 ✉ SY8 4AL – ☎ (01584) 711 905 – April-October
3 rm – ♦£ 55/60 ♦♦£ 80
♦ Characterful black and white timbered 16C manor house in two and a half acres of lawned gardens. Friendly welcome; comfy lounge. Individually decorated, period style rooms.

at Bromfield Northwest : 2.5 mi on A 49 - Y – ✉ Ludlow

Clive with rm
✉ SY8 2JR – ☎ (01584) 856 565 – www.theclive.co.uk – Closed 25-26 December
15 rm – ♦£ 65/90 ♦♦£ 90/115
Rest – *(booking essential at dinner)* Carte £ 22/31
♦ Large converted pub with modern décor in vivid colours. Restaurant, bar, café and bistro areas. Menu of internationally inspired traditional dishes. Very good modern bedrooms.

LUPTON – Cumbria – **502** L21 – see Kirkby Lonsdale

LUTON – Luton – 504 S28 – pop. 185 543 Great Britain 12 A2

London 35 mi – Cambridge 36 mi – Ipswich 93 mi – Oxford 45 mi

Luton International Airport : ✆ (01582) 405100, E : 1.5 mi X

Central Library, St George's Sq ✆ (01582) 401579, tourist.information@luton.gov.uk

Stockwood Park London Rd, ✆ (01582) 413 704

Whipsnade Wild Animal Park★, West : 8 mi by B 489, signed from M 1 (junction 9) and M 25 (junction 21) X

Luton Hoo

The Mansion House, Southeast : 2.5 mi by A 505 on A 1081 ✉ LU1 3TQ – ✆ (01582) 734 437 – www.lutonhoo.com

207 rm – †£ 230 ††£ 230 – 21 suites

Rest *Wernher* – *(closed Saturday lunch)* Menu £ 30/43 – Carte approx. £ 32

Rest *Adam's Brasserie* – *(Closed lunch Monday and Tuesday)* Menu £ 25/30 (dinner) – Carte approx. £ 25

◆ Stunning 18C house set in over 1,000 acres of gardens, some designed by Capability Brown. Main mansion boasts numerous comfortable sitting rooms and characterful bedrooms. Formal, marble-filled Wernher restaurant offers traditional menu. Geared towards families, Adam's brasserie is simpler.

Good food at moderate prices? Look for the Bib Gourmand.

LUXBOROUGH – Somerset – 503 J30 – ✉ Watchet 3 A2

London 205 mi – Exeter 42 mi – Minehead 9 mi – Taunton 25 mi

Royal Oak Inn of Luxborough with rm

Exmoor National Park ✉ TA23 0SH – ✆ (01984) 640 319 – www.theroyaloakinnluxborough.co.uk – Closed 25 December

11 rm – †£ 65 ††£ 100

Rest – Carte £ 16/32

◆ Red sandstone pub in an extremely beautiful location; well used by the community. Seasonal menu offers substantial dishes of classically prepared, boldly flavoured foods, with an international edge. Bedrooms are compact but charming; Room 14 has its own terrace.

LYDDINGTON – Rutland – see Uppingham

LYDFORD – Devon – 503 H32 – pop. 1 734 – ✉ Okehampton 2 C2

London 234 mi – Exeter 33 mi – Plymouth 25 mi

Village★★

Dartmoor National Park★★

The Dartmoor Inn with rm

Moorside, East : 1 mi on A 386 ✉ EX20 4AY – ✆ (01822) 820 221 – www.dartmoorinn.com – Closed Sunday dinner and Monday lunch

3 rm – †£ 85/95 ††£ 100/125

Rest – Menu £ 21 – Carte £ 21/38

◆ Lovely pub on the edge of Dartmoor National Park, close to Lydford Gorge and the White Lady waterfall. Shabby-chic, French farmhouse styling. Set and à la carte menus feature tasty modern dishes; the mixed grill of sea fish is popular. Spacious bedrooms and some unusual, yet appealing, breakfast choices.

LYME REGIS – Dorset – 503 L31 – pop. 4 406 3 B3

London 160 mi – Dorchester 25 mi – Exeter 31 mi – Taunton 27 mi

Guildhall Cottage, Church St ✆ (01297) 442138, lymeregis.tic@westdorset-dc.gov.uk

Timber Hill, ✆ (01297) 442 963

Town★ – The Cobb★

Alexandra

Pound St ✉ DT7 3HZ – ☎ (01297) 442 010 – www.hotelalexandra.co.uk – Closed I9 December-27 January

24 rm (dinner included) – †£ 95/195 ††£ 225/255

Rest – Menu £ 38 (dinner) – Carte £ 22/36

◆ Smart, extended 18C house in lawned gardens, superbly located with magnificent views out to sea. Family-run, the hotel features a comfortable lounge, a south-facing conservatory and modern bedrooms. Room 12 has a large bow window. Tasty, home-cooked menus.

Hix Oyster and Fish House

Lister Gdns. ✉ DT7 3JP – ☎ (01297) 446 910 – www.restaurantsetcltd.co.uk – Closed 25-26 December and 1 January

Rest – Seafood – *(booking essential)* Menu £ 21 (lunch) – Carte £ 26/67

◆ Small restaurant in a terrace by the new gardens; superb views over the bay and Cobb. Rustic, simple and understated. Daily seafood menu with a real understanding of less is more.

LYMINGTON – Hampshire – 504 P31 – pop. 14 227 — 6 A3

London 103 mi – Bournemouth 18 mi – Southampton 19 mi – Winchester 32 mi

to the Isle of Wight (Yarmouth) (Wightlink Ltd) frequent services daily (30 mn)

St Barb Museum and Visitor Centre, New St (01590) 689000, information@nfdc.gov.uk

ENGLAND

Stanwell House

14-15 High St ✉ SO41 9AA – ☎ (01590) 677 123 – www.stanwellhouse.com

23 rm – †£ 99 ††£ 138 – 6 suites

Rest *Bistro* – Menu £ 13/27 – Carte £ 30/41 **s**

Rest *Seafood at Stanwells* – Menu £ 13/27 – Carte £ 28/42

◆ Well-run, centrally located former coaching inn. Comfortable, individually decorated bedrooms include some four-posters; those in the original house are more characterful. Informal bistro overlooks terrace. Fresh seafood and attentive service in Stanwells.

The Mill at Gordleton

rest,

Silver St, Hordle, Northwest : 3.5 mi by A 337 off Sway Rd ✉ SO41 6DJ – ☎ (01590) 682 219 – www.themillatgordleton.co.uk – Closed 25 December

6 rm – †£ 95/115 ††£ 175 – 1 suite

Rest – Menu £ 16/25 – Carte £ 33/44

◆ Delightfully located part-17C water mill in well-kept gardens. Comfortable, traditional interior with a pubby bar and country house lounge. Homely, individually styled bedrooms. Formal restaurant offers classic British cooking, with terrace for alfresco dining.

at East End East : 3 mi by B3054

East End Arms with rm

Lymington Rd ✉ SO41 5SY – ☎ (01590) 626 223 – www.eastendarms.co.uk – Closed Sunday dinner

5 rm – †£ 68 ††£ 95/115

Rest – Carte £ 19/27

◆ Traditional country pub owned by John Illsley of Dire Straits. Shabby locals bar and classical pine-furnished dining room; great display of music-based photos. Concise menus of satisfying British dishes. Modern, cottage-style bedrooms provide a smart contrast.

at Downton West : 3 mi on A 337 – ✉ Lymington

The Olde Barn without rest
Christchurch Rd, East : 0.5 mi on A 337 ✉ SO41 0LA – ✆ (01590) 644 939 – www.theoldebarn.co.uk
3 rm – †£ 50/60 ††£ 70/75
◆ Converted 17C barn with small, traditional lounge and communal breakfast room. Bedrooms in the barn annexe – a converted dairy – are spotlessly kept, with a homely, cottagey style.

LYMM – Warrington – **502** M23 – **pop. 9 554** **20** B3
London 190 mi – Liverpool 26 mi – Leeds 62 mi – Sheffield 68 mi

The Church Green
Higher Ln, on A 56 ✉ WA13 0AP – ✆ (01925) 752 068 – www.thechurchgreen.co.uk – Closed 25 December
Rest – *(booking essential)* Menu £ 25 (lunch) – Carte £ 30/38
◆ Double gable-fronted Victorian pub beside Lymm Dam. Smart, modern interior with conservatory, attractive terrace and kitchen garden. Simple pub-style bar dishes; more ambitious evening menu.

LYNDHURST – Hampshire – **503** – **pop. 2 281** Great Britain **6** A2
London 95 mi – Bournemouth 20 mi – Southampton 10 mi – Winchester 23 mi
New Forest Museum and Visitor Centre, Main Car Park ✆ (023) 8028 2269
Dibden Golf Centre Main Rd, ✆ (023) 8020 7508
New Forest Southampton Rd, ✆ (023) 8028 2752
New Forest★★ (Bolderwood Ornamental Drive★★, Rhinefield Ornamental Drive★★)

Lime Wood
Beaulieu Rd, Southeast : 1 mi by A 35 on B 3056 ✉ SO43 7FZ – ✆ (023) 8028 7177 – www.limewoodhotel.co.uk
15 rm – †£ 245/295 ††£ 325/375, £ 16.50 – 14 suites – ††£ 375/725
Rest *Dining Room* – ✆ (023) 8028 7167 – Menu £ 30/50
Rest *Scullery* – ✆ (023) 8028 7168 – Carte £ 23/48
◆ Impressive extended Georgian mansion set in large grounds in the New Forest. Stylish, contemporary and beautifully furnished bedrooms; many with forest views. Luxurious bathrooms. Stunning spa. Smart, formal Dining Room offers refined, classic dishes and attentive, friendly service. Relaxed, all-day dining in Scullery.

LYNMOUTH – Devon – **503** I30 – see Lynton

LYNTON – Devon – **503** I30 – **pop. 1 870** **2** C1
London 206 mi – Exeter 59 mi – Taunton 44 mi
Town Hall, Lee Rd ✆ (01598) 752225, info@lyntourism.co.uk
Town★ (<★)
Valley of the Rocks★, W : 1 mi – Watersmeet★, E : 1.5 mi by A 39. Exmoor National Park★★ – Doone Valley★, SE : 7.5 mi by A 39 (access from Oare on foot)

Hewitt's - Villa Spaldi without rest
North Walk ✉ EX35 6HJ – ✆ (01598) 752 293 – www.hewittshotel.com – 15 February-15 October
7 rm – †£ 70/90 ††£ 180/240, £ 8.50 – 1 suite
◆ Splendid 19C Arts and Crafts house in tranquil wooded cliffside setting. Stained glass window by Burne Jones and library filled with antiques. Stylish rooms with sea views.

ENGLAND

Victoria Lodge without rest
30-31 Lee Rd ✉ EX35 6BS – ✆ (01598) 753 203 – www.victorialodge.co.uk – mid April - October
8 rm – †£ 119 ††£ 140
♦ Large 19C house decorated with period photographs, prints and Victoriana. Traditional décor in communal areas and bedrooms which are comfortable and inviting.

St Vincent
Market St, Castle Hill ✉ EX35 6JA – ✆ (01598) 752 244 – www.st-vincent-hotel.co.uk – Easter-October
5 rm – †£ 75 ††£ 75/80 **Rest** – Menu £ 27
♦ Grade II listed Georgian House with charming Belgian owners, set 200 metres from the coastal path. Lovely fire-lit lounge, fresh, uncluttered bedrooms and smart bathrooms. Cloth-clad dining room; homely Belgian/Mediterranean menus, with plenty of seafood in summer.

at Lynmouth East : 1 mi

Shelley's without rest
8 Watersmeet Rd ✉ EX35 6EP – ✆ (01598) 753 219 – www.shelleyshotel.co.uk – March-November
11 rm – †£ 70 ††£ 110
♦ Centrally located hotel named after eponymous poet who honeymooned here in 1812. Stylish public areas. Very comfortable bedrooms with good views of picturesque locale.

The Heatherville
Tors Park, by Tors Rd ✉ EX35 6NB – ✆ (01598) 752 327 – www.heatherville.co.uk – March-November
6 rm – †£ 75 ††£ 100 **Rest** – Menu £ 25
♦ Victorian house perched above the town. Well kept throughout with bright, warm décor. Rooms with bold fabrics and woodland views: room 6 has the best outlook. Home-cooked meals employ fresh, local produce.

at Martinhoe West : 4.25 mi via Coast rd (toll) – ✉ Barnstaple

Old Rectory
✉ EX31 4QT – ✆ (01598) 763 368 – www.oldrectoryhotel.co.uk – Restricted opening in winter
10 rm (dinner included) – †£ 170/205 ††£ 215/250
Rest – *(dinner only) (residents only)* Menu £ 34
♦ Built in 19C for rector of Martinhoe's 11C church, this quiet country retreat is set in a charming spot, with a well-tended three acre garden and cascading brook. Fresh, bright bedrooms are modern, yet retain period touches: Heddon and Paddock are two of the best. Comfortable dining room; simple home-cooking.

LYTHAM – Lancashire – 502 L22 – see Lytham St Annes

LYTHAM ST ANNE'S – Lancashire – 502 L22 – pop. 41 327 — 20 A2

London 237 mi – Blackpool 7 mi – Liverpool 44 mi – Preston 13 mi
Town Hall, St Annes Rd West ✆ (01253) 725610, touristinfo@flyde.gov.uk
Fairhaven Ansdell, Oakwood Avenue, ✆ (01253) 736 741
St Annes Old Links Highbury Rd, ✆ (01253) 723 597

at Lytham

Rooms without rest
35 Church Rd ✉ FY8 5LL – ✆ (01253) 736 000 – www.theroomslytham.com
5 rm – †£ 95/130 ††£ 120/175
♦ Boutique-style guesthouse with striking, contemporary décor. Good-sized bedrooms boast modern facilities, including iPod docks and large flat screen TVs. Extensive breakfasts.

XX **Hastings**
26 Hastings Pl. ✉ FY8 5LZ – ✆ (01253) 732 400 – www.hastingslytham.co.uk – Closed Monday
Rest – Carte £ 27/43
♦ Red-brick restaurant with modern bar, intimate ground floor dining room and brighter mezzanine, featuring exposed rafters and glass skylight. Wide-ranging menu with a regional slant.

at St Anne's

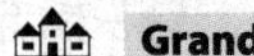
Grand
South Promenade ✉ FY8 1NB – ✆ (01253) 721 288 – www.the-grand.co.uk – Closed 24-25 December
55 rm – †£ 111 ††£ 169, ☕ £ 6.50
Rest *Café Grand* – ✆ (01253) 643 413 – Carte £ 23/31
♦ Impressive, turreted Victorian hotel on promenade. Stylish, contemporary guest areas. Variously sized bedrooms, most with good views; turret rooms are the most spacious, and have particularly good aspects. Laid-back, stylish Café Grand offers accessible menu.

MADINGLEY – Cambs. – 504 U27 – see Cambridge

MAENPORTH BEACH – Cornwall – see Falmouth

MAIDEN BRADLEY – Wiltshire – 503 N30 – pop. 335 4 C2

London 114 mi – Bristol 36 mi – Cardiff 77 mi – Southampton 75 mi

The Somerset Arms with rm
Church St ✉ BA12 7HW – ✆ (01985) 844 207 – www.thesomersetarms.co.uk – Closed Sunday dinner and Monday; restricted opening in January
5 rm ☕ – †£ 80/95 ††£ 100/120 **Rest** – Carte £ 16/35
♦ Proudly run pub, with polite, well-paced service; popular with locals. Oft-changing menu uses local produce, including eggs from their own hens and veg from the garden. Flavourful, rustic cooking; steaks a speciality. Contemporary bedrooms; one with free-standing bath.

MAIDENCOMBE – Devon – 503 J32 – see Torquay

MAIDENHEAD – Windsor and Maidenhead – 504 R29 – pop. 58 848 11 C3

London 33 mi – Oxford 32 mi – Reading 13 mi
to Marlow, Cookham and Windsor (Salter Bros. Ltd) (summer only) (3 h 45 mn)
The Library, St Ives Rd ✆ (01628) 796502, maidenhead.tic@rbwm.gov.uk
Bird Hills Hawthorn Hill Drift Rd, ✆ (01628) 771 030
Shoppenhangers Rd, ✆ (01628) 624 693

Plan on next page

Fredrick's
Shoppenhangers Rd ✉ SL6 2PZ – ✆ (01628) 581 000 – www.fredricks-hotel.co.uk – Closed 25-29 December X**c**
36 rm – †£ 109/275 ††£ 149/285, ☕ £ 23.50 – 1 suite
Rest *Fredrick's* – see restaurant listing
♦ Redbrick former inn with well-equipped spa facilities. Ornate, marble reception with smoked mirrors. Conservatory with wicker chairs. Very comfy, individually styled rooms.

XXX **Fredrick's** – at Fredrick's Hotel
Shoppenhangers Rd ✉ SL6 2PZ – ✆ (01628) 581 000 – www.fredricks-hotel.co.uk – Closed 25-29 December X**c**
Rest – Menu £ 25/39 – Carte £ 41/54
♦ Ornate paintings, smoked mirrors and distressed pine greet diners in this large restaurant. Chandeliers, full-length windows add to classic feel. Elaborate British menus.

ENGLAND

MAIDENHEAD

- Bad Godesberg Way . . . . . Y 2
- Belmont Park Ave . . . . Y 3
- Blackamoor Lane . . . . V 5
- Boyn Hill Ave . . . . Z 6
- Braywick Rd . . . . Z 7
- Bridge St . . . . Y 9
- College Rd . . . . V 13
- Cookham Rd . . . . Y 14
- Crescent (The) . . . . Y 15
- Ferry Rd . . . . X 17
- Frascati Way . . . . YZ 18
- Furze Platt Rd . . . . V 20
- Grenfell Pl. . . . . Z 21
- Gringer Hill . . . . V 22
- Harrow Lane . . . . V 24
- High St . . . . Y
- High St BRAY-ON-THAMES . . . . X 25
- King's Grove . . . . Z 27
- Linden Ave . . . . V 28
- Lower Cookham Rd . . . . . V 29
- Manor Lane . . . . X 31
- Market St . . . . Y 32
- Nicholson's Walk Shopping Centre . . . . . YZ
- Norreys Drive . . . . X 35
- Oldfield Rd . . . . V 36
- Ray Mill Rd West . . . . V 39
- Ray St . . . . V 38
- St Ives Rd . . . . Y 41
- St Mark Rd . . . . V 42
- Stafferton Way . . . . Z 43
- Upper Bray Rd . . . . X 45

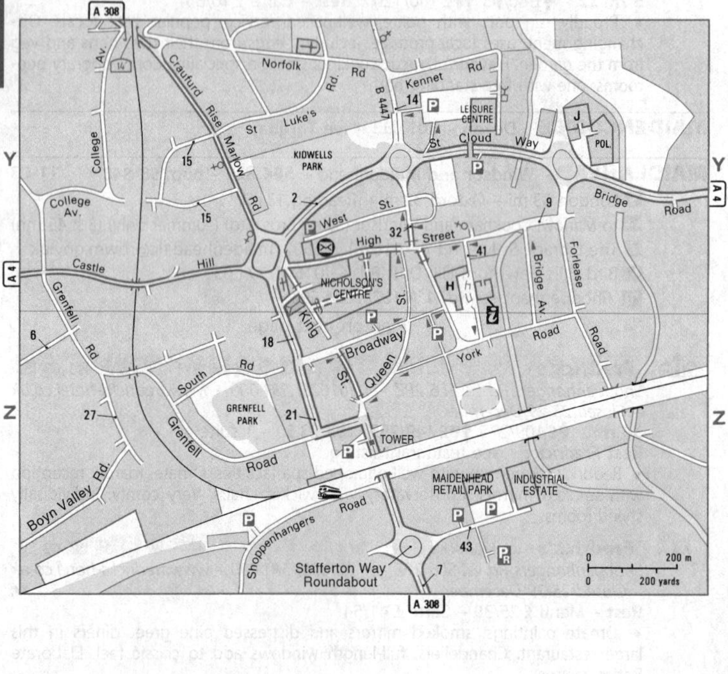

ENGLAND

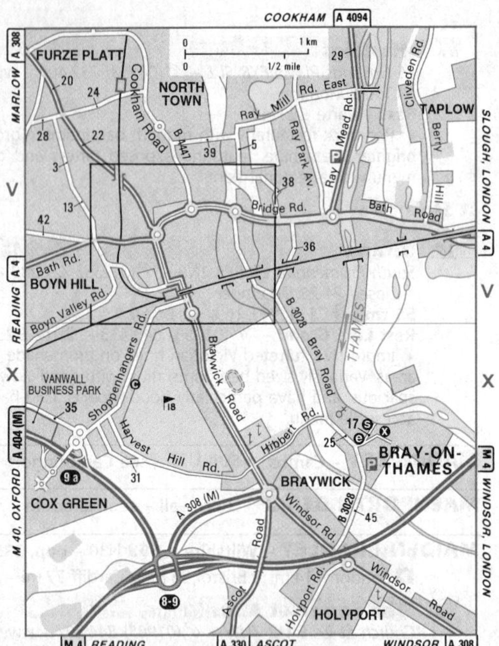

A 308
Y
Z
Craufurd Rise
Marlow Rd
College
College Av.
Norfolk Rd
St Luke's Rd
Kennet Rd
B 4447
LEISURE CENTRE
KIDWELLS PARK
St Cloud Way
POL.
Bridge Road
A 4
West St.
High Street
Castle Hill
A 4
NICHOLSON'S CENTRE
King St.
Bridge Av.
Forlease Road
Grenfell Rd
Broadway
Queen St.
York Road
South Rd
GRENFELL PARK
Grenfell Road
TOWER
Boyn Valley Rd.
MAIDENHEAD RETAIL PARK
INDUSTRIAL ESTATE
Shoppenhangers Road
Stafferton Way Roundabout
0 200 m
0 200 yards
A 308

at Burchett's Green West : 3 mi by A 4 off A 404

Crown

Burchetts Green Rd ✉ SL6 6QZ – ✆ (01628) 826 184
– Closed first 2 weeks January, Sunday dinner and Monday
Rest – Carte £ 19/26
♦ Simple country pub with friendly atmosphere. Daily changing menus focus on well-sourced, quality produce, including veg and herbs from the garden. Good value, tasty, rustic cooking; try the homemade bread. Interesting wine list. Polite, friendly service.

MAIDENSGROVE – Oxfordshire – pop. 1 572 – ✉ Henley-On-Thames 11 C3

London 43 mi – Oxford 23 mi – Reading 15 mi

The Five Horseshoes

✉ RG9 6EX – ✆ (01491) 641 282 – www.thefivehorseshoes.co.uk
– Closed Monday dinner October-February
Rest – Menu £ 15 (weekdays) – Carte £ 20/40
♦ Walkers' paradise: a charming part-17C inn boasting characterful beamed bar and suntrap restaurant with countryside views. Doorstop sandwiches, comforting classics and homely desserts.

MAIDSTONE – Kent – 504 V30 – pop. 89 684 Great Britain 8 B2

London 36 mi – Brighton 64 mi – Cambridge 84 mi – Colchester 72 mi
Town Hall, High St ✆ (01622) 602169, tourism@maidstone.gov.uk
Tudor Park Hotel Bearsted Ashford Rd, ✆ (01622) 734 334
Cobtree Manor Park Boxley Chatham Rd, ✆ (01622) 753 276
Leeds Castle★ **AC**, SE : 4.5 mi by A 20 and B 2163

at Bearsted East : 3 mi by A 249 off A 20 – ✉ **Maidstone**

Fish On The Green

Church Ln. ✉ ME14 4EJ
– ✆ (01622) 738 300 – www.fishonthegreen.com
– Closed 26 December-26 January, Sunday dinner and Monday
Rest – Seafood – Menu £ 13 (lunch) – Carte £ 29/43
♦ Well-run, contemporary restaurant with pleasant terrace, tucked away in corner of the green. Focus on fresh fish, with a few local meat dishes. Good value lunch menu; friendly service.

MALMESBURY – Wiltshire – 503 N29 – pop. 5 094 4 C2

London 108 mi – Bristol 28 mi – Gloucester 24 mi – Swindon 19 mi
Town Hall, Cross Hayes ✆ (01666) 823748, tic@malmesbury.gov.uk
Town★ – Market Cross★★ – Abbey★

Whatley Manor

Easton Grey, West : 2.25 mi on B 4040 ✉ SN16 0RB – ✆ (01666) 822 888
– www.whatleymanor.com
15 rm – †£ 295 ††£ 295/495 – 8 suites
Rest *Le Mazot* – see restaurant listing
Rest *The Dining Room* – *(dinner only) (booking essential for non-residents)*
Menu £ 73/90 **s**
Spec. Smoked and roasted scallops with almond purée and white shellfish foam. Taste of veal with hazelnut purée and Madeira juices. Chicory mousse with bitter coffee and mascarpone cream.
♦ Cotswold stone buildings set in beautiful gardens. Chic, contemporary, luxurious bedrooms; sumptuous bathrooms. Stunning spa, top class business centre and cinema. The Dining Room offers comfortable surroundings in which to enjoy technically-skilled and innovative cooking, with charming service.

ENGLAND

The Old Bell

Abbey Row ✉ SN16 0BW – ✆ (01666) 822 344
– www.oldbellhotel.com
33 rm – †£ 90/99 ††£ 115/275
Rest ***The Restaurant*** – see restaurant listing
◆ Hugely characterful part-13C former abbots' hostel in pleasant gardens, set next to the abbey. Intimate bar. Mix of bedroom styles: bold and fashionable in main house, more classical in annexe.

Le Mazot – (at Whatley Manor Hotel)

Easton Grey, West : 2.25 mi on B 4040 ✉ SN16 0RB – ✆ (01666) 822 888
– www.whatleymanor.com
Rest – Menu £ 22 (lunch) **s** – Carte £ 33/40 **s**
◆ Unusual gold wood Swiss chalet restaurant within delightful country house, offering casual dining on comfy banquettes. Cooking is refined, light and skilled. Polite, careful service.

The Restaurant – at The Old Bell Hotel

Abbey Row ✉ SN16 0BW – ✆ (01666) 822 344 – www.oldbellhotel.com – Closed Sunday and Monday dinner
Rest – *(booking essential at dinner)* Menu £ 40 (dinner)
– Carte lunch £ 25/40
◆ Imposing, richly coloured dining room displaying old portraits and fine china. Skilled kitchen offers brasserie-style lunch and fine dining in evening. Refined, artful dishes; attentive service.

ENGLAND

at Crudwell **North : 4 mi on A 429 – ✉ Malmesbury**

Rectory

✉ *SN16 9EP – ✆ (01666) 577 194 – www.therectoryhotel.com*
12 rm – †£ 95/105 ††£ 175/185
Rest – *(dinner only)* Carte approx. £ 28
◆ 17C stone-built former Rectory with formal garden. A little quirky but personally run. Comfortable, individually-styled bedrooms with many modern extras, some with spa baths. Airy oak-panelled dining room; modern seasonal cooking.

The Potting Shed

The Street ✉ SN16 9EW – ✆ (01666) 577 833
– www.thepottingshedpub.com
Rest – Carte £ 24/29
◆ Spacious, light-filled pub with contemporary décor, exposed beams and a relaxing feel. Monthly changing menus offer wholesome, satisfying dishes, with vegetables and herbs from their garden.

MALPAS – Cheshire – 502 L24 – pop. 3 684 — 20 A3

London 177 mi – Birmingham 60 mi – Chester 15 mi – Shrewsbury 26 mi

at Tilston **Northwest : 3 mi on Tilston Rd – ✉ Malpas**

Tilston Lodge without rest

✉ *SY14 7DR – ✆ (01829) 250 223*
3 rm – †£ 50/55 ††£ 90
◆ Large, red-brick former Victorian hunting lodge with neat gardens and mature grounds. Homely bedrooms boast good facilities and country views. Charming owner is Lord Mayor of Chester.

MALVERN WELLS – Worcs. – 503 N27 – see Great Malvern

Fancy a last minute break?
Check hotel websites to take advantage of price promotions.

MAN (Isle of) – I.O.M. – **502** G21 – **pop. 80 058** Great Britain **20** B1

from Douglas to Belfast (Isle of Man Steam Packet Co. Ltd) (summer only) (2 h 45 mn)
– from Douglas to Republic of Ireland (Dublin) (Isle of Man Steam Packet Co. Ltd) (2 h 45 mn/4 h)
– from Douglas to Heysham (Isle of Man Steam Packet Co.) (2 h/3 h 30 mn)
– from Douglas to Liverpool (Isle of Man Steam Packet Co. Ltd) (2 h 30 mn/4 h)

Laxey Wheel★★ - Snaefell★ (✳★★★) - Cregneash Folk Museum★

DOUGLAS – Douglas – **pop. 26 218** **20** B1

Ronaldsway Airport : ✆ (01624) 821600, SW : 7 mi
Sea Terminal Buildings ✆ (01624) 686766, tourism@gov.im
Douglas Pulrose Park, ✆ (01624) 675 952
King Edward Bay Onchan Groudle Rd, ✆ (01624) 620 430

Sefton rm, VISA AE
Harris Promenade ✉ IM1 2RW – ✆ (01624) 645 500 – www.seftonhotel.co.im
90 rm – †£ 85/105 ††£ 135 – 12 suites
Rest *The Gallery* – *(bar lunch)* Carte £ 35/65 **s**
◆ Victorian-fronted promenade hotel, built around unique atrium water garden. Bedrooms may have balconies, look out to sea or have water garden views. Impressive apartment suites. The Gallery, with its boldly coloured Manx art, offers speciality flambé dishes.

The Regency VISA AE
Queens Promenade ✉ IM2 4NN – ✆ (01624) 680 680 – www.regency.im
34 rm – †£ 75/110 ††£ 119/155 – 4 suites
Rest *Five Continents* – *(dinner only)* Menu £ 24 – Carte £ 31/42
◆ Perfect for business travellers: mobile phone loan, PCs with free internet in every bedroom and special office suites, combined with traditional seaside styling and Douglas Bay views. Oak panelled restaurant boasts original collection of Island pictures.

Penta without rest VISA AE
Queens Promenade ✉ IM9 4NE – ✆ (01624) 680 680 – www.regency.im
22 rm – †£ 49/90 ††£ 59/100
◆ Set on the promenade, with views over Douglas Bay. Large, functional, well-equipped bedrooms feature computers with free internet access. Wine-themed, Mediterranean-style breakfast room.

Birchfield House VISA
York Rd, via The Promenade taking first left after the Gaiety Theatre. ✉ IM2 3BN – ✆ (01624) 673 000 – www.birchfieldhouse.com
3 rm – †£ 195 ††£ 195, £ 15
Rest – Menu £ 40 – Carte £ 40/60
◆ Professionally run, boutique-style guesthouse set just back from the promenade. Very comfortable lounge with honesty bar. Stylish bedrooms boast Egyptian cotton, iPod docks and flat screen TVs. Wood-furnished dining room, with option of eating communally. Menus designed around guests' tastes use organic, local produce.

Ciappelli's VISA AE
King Edward Bay Golf and Country Club, Groudle Rd, Onchan, Northeast : 2.5 mi by The Promenade and Harbour Rd ✉ IM3 2JR – ✆ (01624) 677 442 – www.ciappellis.com – Closed Sunday dinner
Rest – Italian influences – Menu £ 22 (lunch) – Carte £ 33/51
◆ Keenly run restaurant set in golf club. Flavoursome cooking based on classic combinations, with Italian and Mediterranean influences. Efficient, formal service. Good value lunch menu.

ENGLAND

XXX **JAR**

Admirals House, 12-13 Loch Promenade ✉ IM1 2LX – ☎ (01624) 663 553 – www.jar.co.im

Rest – Menu £ 25 (lunch) – Carte £ 29/44

◆ Set on ground floor of hotel, with comfy, leather-furnished lounge and pleasant coastal outlook from front tables. Italian-influenced menus; clean, unfussy, flavoursome cooking.

XX **Macfarlane's**

24 Duke St ✉ IM1 2AY – ☎ (01624) 624 777 – www.macfarlanes.im – Closed 2 weeks August, 1 week Christmas, Saturday lunch, Sunday and Monday

Rest – *(booking essential)* Carte £ 27/46

◆ Small, simple restaurant in heart of town, with leather-topped tables and high-sided booths. Unfussy, regularly changing menu relies on fresh local produce, with fish to the fore.

PORT ERIN – Port Erin – pop. 3 575 — 20 B1

Rowany Cottier without rest

Spaldrick ✉ IM9 6PE – ☎ (01624) 832 287 – www.rowanycottier.com

5 rm – †£ 47/75 ††£ 80/94

◆ Large, purpose-built house set by Bradda Glen. Pleasant guest areas with views over Port Erin and Calf of Man. Simple, well-kept bedrooms. Locally sourced breakfast; homemade bread.

PORT ST MARY – Port St Mary – pop. 1 913 — 20 B1

Ballahane House without rest

Truggan Rd, West : 0.75 mi by Cregneish rd ✉ IM9 5LD – ☎ (01624) 834 238 – www.ballahane.co.uk

3 rm – †£ 65/80 ††£ 104/110

◆ Hidden behind farm buildings on a country lane, with views of Bradda Head. Stylish, modern interior; bedrooms are named after their colours: pink, blue and oyster. Organic island breakfasts.

Aaron House without rest

The Promenade ✉ IM9 5DE – ☎ (01624) 835 702 – www.aaronhouse.co.uk – Closed Christmas-New Year

6 rm – †£ 49/108 ††£ 98/128

◆ Charming, antique-furnished guesthouse with bay/harbour views and strong Victorian feel. Comfy, traditional bedrooms. Afternoon tea on arrival. Interesting breakfast choices.

RAMSEY – Ramsey – pop. 7 309 — 20 B1

The River House without rest

North : 0.25 mi by A 9 turning left immediately after bridge ✉ IM8 3DA – ☎ (01624) 816 412 – Closed Christmas

3 rm – †£ 60 ††£ 110/130

◆ Attractive Georgian country house with pleasant gardens. Tastefully furnished throughout, with comfy drawing room, antiques and objets d'art. Traditional, cottage-style bedrooms.

C. Labonne/MICHELIN

MANCHESTER

County: Greater Manchester
Michelin regional map: 502 N23
London 202 mi – Birmingham 86 mi – Glasgow 221 mi – Leeds 43 mi

Population: 394 269
Great Britain
Map reference: 20 B2

PRACTICAL INFORMATION

Tourist Information

Manchester Visitor Centre, Town Hall Extension, Lloyd St ✆ (0871) 222 8223, touristinformation@visitmanchester.co.uk

Salford T.I.C., Pier 8, Salford Quays ✆ (0161) 848 8601, tic@salford.gov.uk

Airport

Manchester International Airport : ✆ (08712) 710 711, S : 10 mi by A 5103 - AX - and M 56

Golf Courses

Heaton Park Prestwich, ✆(0161) 654 9899

Houldsworth Park Stockport Houldsworth St, Reddish, ✆(0161) 442 1712

Chorlton-cum-Hardy Barlow Hall Rd, Barlow Hall, ✆(0161) 881 3139

William Wroe Flixton Pennybridge Lane, ✆(0161) 748 8680

SIGHTS

See

City★ - Castlefield Heritage Park★ CZ – Town Hall★ CZ – Manchester Art Gallery★ CZ **M2** – Cathedral★ (stalls and canopies★) CY – Museum of Science and Industry★ CZ **M** – Urbis★ CY – Imperial War Museum North★, Trafford Park AX **M**

Env.

Whitworth Art Gallery★, S : 1.5 m

Exc.

Quarry Bank Mill★, S : 10 mi off B 5166, exit 5 from M 56

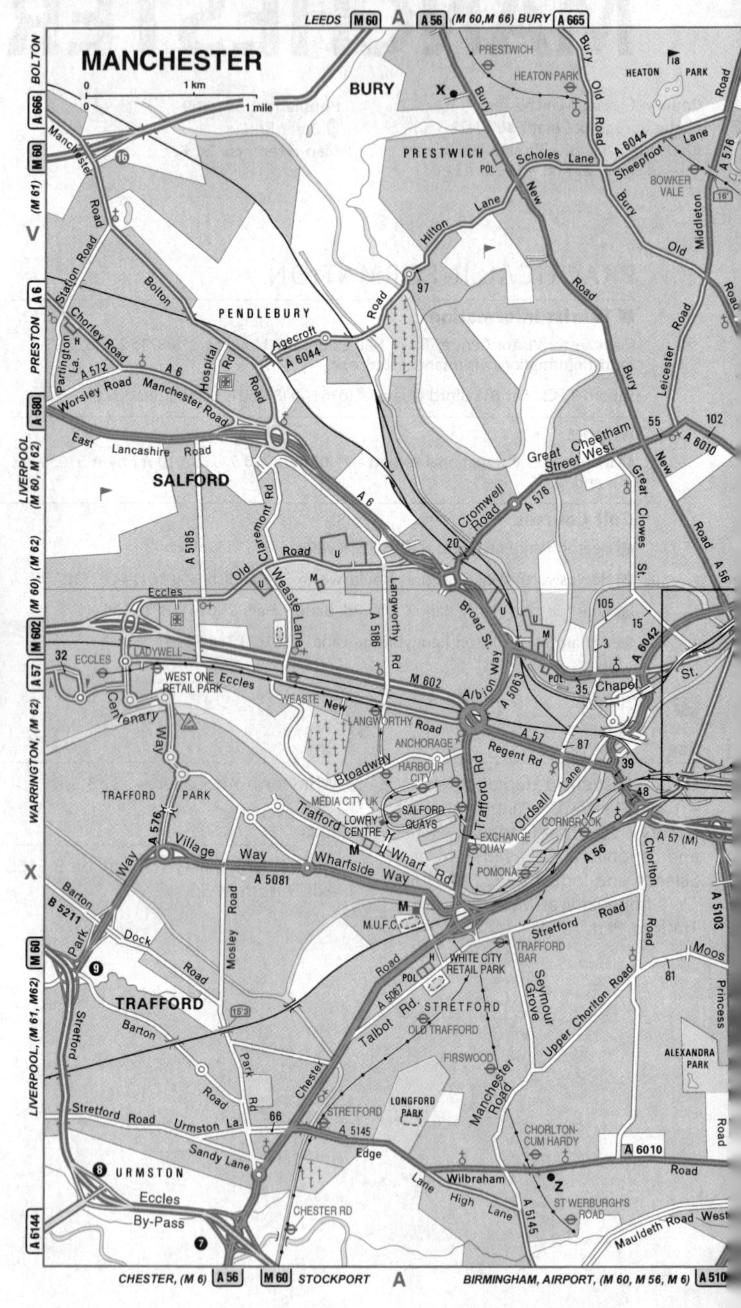
MANCHESTER
LEEDS M 60
A
A 56 (M 60, M 66) BURY A 665
BOLTON A 666
M 60
(M 61)
V
PRESTON A 6
LIVERPOOL (M 60, M 62) A 580
(M 60), (M 62)
M 602
A 57
WARRINGTON, (M 62)
X
LIVERPOOL, (M 61, M62) M 60
A 6144
CHESTER, (M 6) A 56
M 60 STOCKPORT
A
BIRMINGHAM, AIRPORT, (M 60, M 56, M 6)
BURY
PRESTWICH
HEATON PARK
HEATON PARK
PENDLEBURY
SALFORD
ECCLES
TRAFFORD PARK
TRAFFORD
URMSTON
STRETFORD
BOWKER VALE
WEST ONE RETAIL PARK
MEDIA CITY UK
SALFORD QUAYS
LOWRY CENTRE
EXCHANGE QUAY
POMONA
CORNBROOK
M.U.F.C.
WHITE CITY RETAIL PARK
OLD TRAFFORD
FIRSWOOD
LONGFORD PARK
CHORLTON-CUM HARDY
ST WERBURGH'S ROAD
CHESTER RD
ALEXANDRA PARK
TRAFFORD BAR
ANCHORAGE
HARBOUR CITY
LANGWORTHY
WEASTE
LADYWELL
Bury Old Road
Bury New Road
Scholes Lane
Hilton Lane
Sheepfoot Lane
Middleton Old Road
Leicester Road
Great Cheetham Street West
Cromwell Road
Great Clowes St.
Broad St.
Albion Way
Chapel St.
Regent Rd
Ordsall Lane
Trafford Rd
Chorlton Road
Stretford Road
Upper Chorlton Road
Seymour Grove
Princess Road
Moss
Manchester Road
Talbot Rd.
Chester Road
Wilbraham Road
Mauldeth Road West
High Lane
Edge Lane
Sandy Lane
Urmston La.
Stretford Road
Barton Road
Park Rd
Mosley Road
Barton Dock Road
Park Way
Village Way
Wharfside Way
Wharf Rd
Trafford Road
Broadway
New Langworthy Road
Eccles New Road
Centenary Way
Weaste Lane
Langworthy Rd
Claremont Rd
Old Road
Eccles Old Road
East Lancashire Road
Worsley Road
Manchester Road
Chorley Road
Partington La.
Station Road
Bolton Road
Manchester Road
Hospital Rd
Agecroft Road
Eccles By-Pass
A 6044
A 576
A 6010
A 6042
A 5063
A 57
A 57 (M)
A 5103
A 5081
A 5067
A 5145
A 6010
A 5185
A 5186
A 572
A 6
B 5211
M 602
POL.
H
M
U
X
Z
97
102
55
20
105
15
3
35
87
39
48
81
66
32
16
18
1 km
1 mile
0
ENGLAND

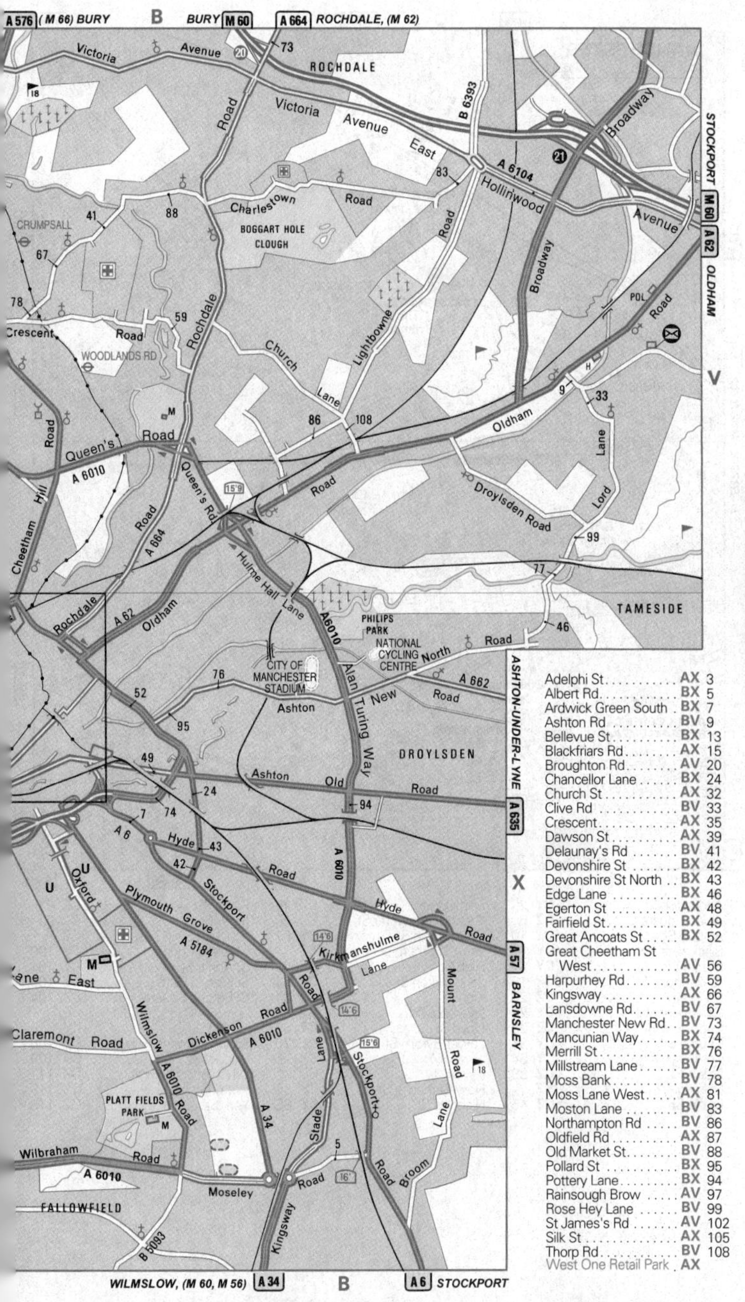

Street	Grid	No.
Adelphi St	AX	3
Albert Rd	BX	5
Ardwick Green South	BX	7
Ashton Rd	BV	9
Bellevue St	BX	13
Blackfriars Rd	AX	15
Broughton Rd	AV	20
Chancellor Lane	BX	24
Church St	AX	32
Clive Rd	BV	33
Crescent	AX	35
Dawson St	AX	39
Delaunay's Rd	BV	41
Devonshire St	BX	42
Devonshire St North	BX	43
Edge Lane	BX	46
Egerton St	AX	48
Fairfield St	BX	49
Great Ancoats St	BX	52
Great Cheetham St West	AV	56
Harpurhey Rd	BV	59
Kingsway	AX	66
Lansdowne Rd	BV	67
Manchester New Rd	BV	73
Mancunian Way	BX	74
Merrill St	BX	76
Millstream Lane	BV	77
Moss Bank	BV	78
Moss Lane West	AX	81
Moston Lane	BV	83
Northampton Rd	BV	86
Oldfield Rd	AX	87
Old Market St	BV	88
Pollard St	BX	95
Pottery Lane	BX	94
Rainsough Brow	AV	97
Rose Hey Lane	BV	99
St James's Rd	AV	102
Silk St	AX	105
Thorp Rd	BV	108
West One Retail Park	AX	

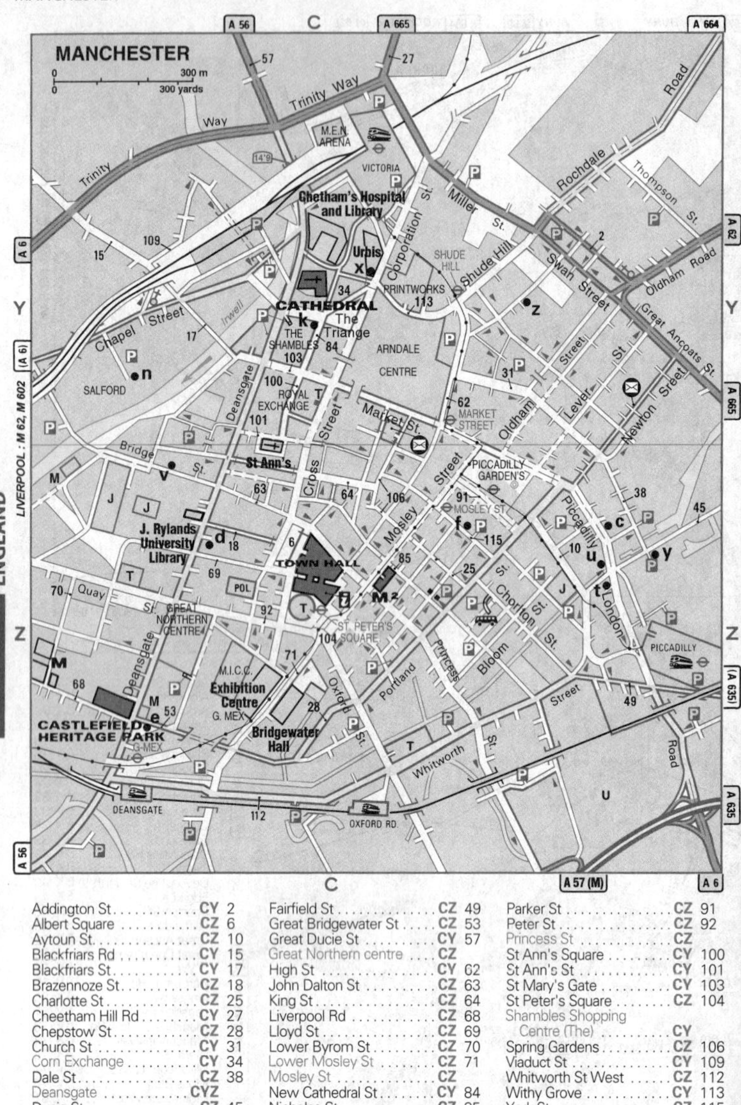

Addington St . . . CY 2	Fairfield St . . . CZ 49	Parker St . . . CZ 91
Albert Square . . . CZ 6	Great Bridgewater St . . . CZ 53	Peter St . . . CZ 92
Aytoun St . . . CZ 10	Great Ducie St . . . CY 57	Princess St . . . CZ
Blackfriars Rd . . . CY 15	Great Northern centre . . . CZ	St Ann's Square . . . CY 100
Blackfriars St . . . CY 17	High St . . . CY 62	St Ann's St . . . CY 101
Brazennoze St . . . CZ 18	John Dalton St . . . CZ 63	St Mary's Gate . . . CY 103
Charlotte St . . . CZ 25	King St . . . CZ 64	St Peter's Square . . . CZ 104
Cheetham Hill Rd . . . CY 27	Liverpool Rd . . . CZ 68	Shambles Shopping Centre (The) . . . CY
Chepstow St . . . CZ 28	Lloyd St . . . CZ 69	Spring Gardens . . . CZ 106
Church St . . . CY 31	Lower Byrom St . . . CZ 70	Viaduct St . . . CY 109
Corn Exchange . . . CY 34	Lower Mosley St . . . CZ 71	Whitworth St West . . . CZ 112
Dale St . . . CZ 38	Mosley St . . . CZ	Withy Grove . . . CY 113
Deansgate . . . CYZ	New Cathedral St . . . CY 84	York St . . . CZ 115
Ducie St . . . CZ 45	Nicholas St . . . CZ 85	

Lowry

50 Dearmans Pl, Chapel Wharf, Salford ✉ *M3 5LH – ☎ (0161) 827 4000 – www.roccofortecollection.com* CY**n**

158 rm – †£ 350 ††£ 350/385, ☕ £ 18.50 – 7 suites

Rest *The River* – see restaurant listing

◆ Modern and hugely spacious, with excellent facilities, impressive spa and minimalist feel: art displays and exhibitions feature throughout. Stylish bedrooms with oversized windows; some river views.

Hilton

303 Deansgate ✉ *M3 4LQ – ☎ (0161) 870 16 00 – www.hilton.co.uk/manchesterdeansgate* CZ**e**

275 rm – †£ 349 ††£ 349, ☕ £ 10 – 5 suites

Rest *Podium* – Menu £ 17/25 – Carte £ 28/76

◆ 23 floors of a striking glass skyscraper. Smart atrium lobby with elevated walkways; glass bottomed pool above. Comfortable, contemporary bedrooms with views. Superb 360° outlook from Cloud bar. Stylish Podium restaurant offers modern brasserie menu of European dishes.

Malmaison

Piccadilly ✉ *M1 3AQ – ☎ (0161) 278 1000 – www.malmaison-manchester.com* CZ**u**

166 rm – †£ 170/190 ††£ 190, ☕ £ 13.95 – 1 suite

Rest *Brasserie* – ☎ (0161) 278 1001 – Menu £ 18 – Carte £ 24/37

◆ Former cotton warehouse and dolls hospital boasting seductive red and black Moulin Rouge style décor and sensuous spa. Comfy bedrooms. Uniquely designed suites include Man Utd theme and mini cinema dark room. Cocktails in bar; tasty classics in brasserie.

ENGLAND

Abode

107 Piccadilly ✉ *M1 2DB – ☎ (0161) 247 77 44 – www.abodehotels.co.uk* CZ**c**

61 rm – †£ 79/160 ††£ 79/160, ☕ £ 13.50

Rest *Michael Caines* – see restaurant listing

◆ Late Victorian cotton merchant's former head office with iron columns and girders still in situ. Relaxed boutique ambience with modern, trendy open-plan rooms and stylish bathrooms.

City Inn

One Piccadilly Place, 1 Auburn Street ✉ *M1 3DG – ☎ (0161) 242 10 00 – www.cityinn.com* CZ**t**

284 rm – †£ 225 ††£ 225, ☕ £ 12.95 – 1 suite

Rest *Elements* – ☎ (0161) 242 10 20 – Menu £ 16 – Carte £ 17/30

◆ Contemporary glass building with spacious, airy interior and local art on display. Modern bedrooms boast pale hues, iMac computers and excellent entertainment facilities. Showers only. Smart, stylish restaurant with appealing, wide ranging menu.

The River – at The Lowry Hotel

50 Dearmans Pl, Chapel Wharf, Salford ✉ *M3 5LH – ☎ (0161) 827 4000 – www.roccofortecollection.com* CY**n**

Rest – Menu £ 15 – Carte £ 37/47

◆ Airy first-floor restaurant with river views; vast mirrors, modern artwork and decorative plates fill the walls. Modern presentation of classic combinations with regional ingredients to the fore.

Wings

1 Lincoln Sq ✉ *M2 5LN – ☎ (0161) 834 9000 – www.wingsrestaurant.co.uk* CZ**d**

Rest – Chinese – Menu £ 30 – Carte £ 24/63

◆ Well-run restaurant off busy square. Narrow room with linen-clad tables, comfy booths, terracotta army replicas and Hong Kong skyline murals. Extensive menu of authentic Cantonese dim sum.

XX **Second Floor - Restaurant** – at Harvey Nichols

21 New Cathedral St ✉ M1 1AD – ✆ (0161) 828 8898 – www.harveynichols.com – Closed 25 December, 1 January, Easter Sunday, Sunday dinner and Monday

Rest – Menu £ 40 – Carte £ 30/60 CY**k**

◆ Smart restaurant with stylish, colour-changing lighting and oversized windows offering big wheel and city views. Elaborate modern European menu with interesting twists; good presentation.

XX **Michael Caines** – at Abode Hotel

107 Piccadilly ✉ M1 2DB – ✆ (0161) 247 77 44 – www.abodehotels.co.uk – Closed 25 December, 1 January and Sunday CZ**c**

Rest – Menu £ 20 (lunch and early dinner) – Carte approx. £ 39

◆ Modern restaurant in hotel basement, featuring subdued lighting and a sophisticated style. Contemporary British cooking, with some Mediterranean influences. Tasting menu and matching wines.

XX **Grado**

New York St ✉ M1 4BD – ✆ (0161) 238 97 90 – www.heathcotes.co.uk – Closed 25-26 December, 1 January, Sunday and bank holiday Monday May-August

Rest – Spanish – Menu £ 17 (lunch) – Carte £ 28/45 CZ**f**

◆ Set in an office block in heart of the city, with long bar for tapas dining or tables for à la carte. Menus offer classic Spanish dishes and a daily-changing charcoal oven special.

XX **The Modern**

URBIS, Floor 5-6, Cathedral Gardens ✉ M4 3BG – ✆ (0161) 605 82 82 – www.themodernmcr.co.uk – Closed 25-26 December and Sunday dinner

Rest – Menu £ 15 (lunch and early dinner) – Carte £ 23/33 CY**x**

◆ Set on 5th floor of impressive glass building, with beautiful views. Seasonal, modern British dishes use local produce where possible; good value set lunch/-early evening menu.

X **Luso**

63 Bridge St ✉ M3 3BQ – ✆ (0161) 839 55 50 – www.lusorestaurant.co.uk – Closed 25-31 December, Sunday and bank holidays CZ**v**

Rest – Portuguese – Carte £ 31/39

◆ Inspired by the Roman name for Portugal – Lusitania – the owner's homeland. The menu reflects this heritage and includes dishes from former Portuguese provinces; tapas style 'Pesticos' at lunch.

X **Second Floor - Brasserie** – at Harvey Nichols

21 New Cathedral St ✉ M1 1AD – ✆ (0161) 828 8898 – www.harveynichols.com – Closed 25 December, 1 January, Easter Sunday, Sunday dinner and Monday

Rest – Carte £ 24/32 CY**k**

◆ Relaxed, minimalist brasserie and bar, with colour-changing strip lighting and buzzy atmosphere. Extensive menu of modern British dishes, with some lighter meals available. Popular with shoppers.

X **Northern Quarter**

108 High St ✉ M4 1HQ – ✆ (0161) 832 7115 – www.tnq.co.uk CY**z**

Rest – *(booking essential at dinner)* Menu £ 14 – Carte £ 22/36

◆ Friendly, modern restaurant with floor to ceiling windows. Keenly priced, seasonal menus offer classic dishes presented in a modern style. Popular, bi-monthly themed evenings.

at Didsbury South : 5.5 mi by 5103 - AX - on A 5145 – ✉ Manchester

Didsbury House

Didsbury Pk, South : 1.5 mi on A 5145 ✉ M20 5LJ – ✆ (0161) 448 2200 – www.didsburyhouse.com

23 rm – 🚹£ 70/140 🚹🚹£ 175/250, ☕ £ 14.50 – 4 suites

Rest – *(room service only)* Carte approx. £ 24

◆ Cream-washed Victorian villa – now a boutique townhouse; original features include an impressive stained glass window. Bedrooms are comfortable and stylish with a contemporary edge; some boast hot tubs. Small basement dining room; accessible, all-day menu.

ENGLAND

Eleven Didsbury Park

11 Didsbury Pk, South : 1.5 mi by A 5145 ✉ M20 5LH – ☎ (0161) 448 7711 – www.elevendidsburypark.com

20 rm – †£ 70/140 ††£ 175/250, ☕ £ 14.50 – 1 suite

Rest – *(room service only)* Carte approx. £ 24

◆ Comfortable, boutique-style townhouse in pleasant residential setting, with simply furnished breakfast room overlooking delightful garden. Stylish, contemporary bedrooms with warm décor and good facilities; many have tubs in the rooms. Informal all-day menu.

Café Jem&I

1c School Ln ✉ M20 6RD – ☎ (0161) 445 3996 – jemandirestaurant.co.uk – Closed bank holidays except 25 December

Rest – Carte £ 22/32

◆ Simple, unpretentious cream-coloured building tucked away off the high street. Open-plan kitchen; homely, bistro feel. Good value, modern European menus. Polite, friendly service.

at West Didsbury **South : 5.5 mi by A 5103 - AX - on A 5145 – ✉ Manchester**

Rhubarb

167 Burton Rd ✉ M20 2LN – ☎ (0161) 448 8887 – www.rhubarbrestaurant.co.uk – Closed 25 December and 1 January

Rest – *(dinner only and Sunday lunch)* Menu £ 16 (weekday dinner) – Carte £ 22/33

◆ Suburban eatery with small pavement terrace, where neutral hues are offset by large canvasses and a colourful feature wall. Large, seasonally changing menus display an eclectic mix of dishes.

at Chorlton-Cum-Hardy **Southwest : 4 mi . by A 5103 - AX - on A 6010 – ✉ Manchester**

Abbey Lodge without rest

501 Wilbraham Rd ✉ M21 0UJ – ☎ (0161) 862 9266 – www.abbey-lodge.co.uk

4 rm – †£ 50/60 ††£ 70, ☕ £ 7.50 AX**z**

◆ Attractive Edwardian house boasting many original features including stained glass windows. Owner provides charming hospitality and pine fitted rooms are immaculately kept.

at Manchester International Airport **South : 9 mi by A 5103 - AX - off M 56 – ✉ Manchester**

Moss Nook

Ringway Rd, Moss Nook, East : 1.25 mi on Cheadle rd ✉ M22 5NA – ☎ (0161) 437 4778 – www.manchesterairportrestaurant.co.uk – Closed 1-11 January, Sunday and Monday

Rest – Menu £ 21/38 – Carte £ 38/46

◆ Established restaurant in red-brick house: entrance to rear past garden and pergola-covered terrace. Traditional décor, rich fabrics, wood panelling and stained glass. Classical French cooking.

at Prestwich **Northwest : 5 mi on A 56**

Aumbry

2 Church Ln ✉ M25 1AJ – ☎ (0161) 798 58 41 – www.aumbryrestaurant.co.uk – Closed 2 weeks early January, 25 December, Monday, Tuesday and dinner Sunday AV**x**

Rest – *(booking essential)* Menu £ 19 (lunch) – Carte £ 23/38

◆ Intimate neighbourhood restaurant offering small à la carte or 9 course tasting menu. Precise cooking with a good combination of flavours; local, seasonal produce well used.

MANCHESTER INTERNATIONAL AIRPORT **Gtr Manchester – Greater Manchester – 503** N23 – **see Manchester**

MANSFIELD – Nottinghamshire – 502 Q24 – pop. 69 987 — 16 B1

London 143 mi – Chesterfield 12 mi – Worksop 14 mi

XX No.4 Wood Street

4 Wood St ✉ NG18 1QA – ☎ (01623) 424 824 – www.4woodstreet.co.uk – Closed 26 December, 1 January, Saturday lunch, Sunday dinner and Monday

Rest – Menu £ 15 – Carte £ 22/47

◆ Solid brick restaurant hidden away in town centre. Relax in lounge bar with comfy armchairs before enjoying well-executed, modern, seasonal dishes in rustic dining room.

XX Lambs at the Market

Cattle Market House, Nottingham Rd ✉ NG18 1BD – ☎ (01623) 424 880 – www.lambsatthemarket.co.uk – Closed 1 week January and 1 week July

Rest – *(dinner only and Sunday lunch)* Menu £ 18 (weekday dinner) – Carte £ 24/35

◆ Family-run restaurant in attractive Victorian building, with a more contemporary interior. Modern European cooking has a British bias; portions are generous and flavours, clear.

MARAZION – Cornwall – 503 D33 – pop. 1 381 – ✉ Penzance — 1 A3

London 318 mi – Penzance 3 mi – Truro 26 mi

Praa Sands Penzance, ☎ (01736) 763 445

St Michael's Mount★★ (≤★★) – Ludgvan★ (Church★) N : 2 mi by A 30 – Chysauster Village★, N : 2 mi by A 30 – Gulval★ (Church★) W : 2.5 m – Prussia Cove★, SE : 5.5 mi by A 30 and minor rd

Mount Haven

Turnpike Rd, East : 0.25 mi ✉ TR17 0DQ – ☎ (01736) 710 249 – www.mounthaven.co.uk – Closed mid-December-mid-February

18 rm – ♦£ 85/105 ♦♦£ 130/210 **Rest** – *(bar lunch)* Carte £ 27/36

◆ Small hotel overlooking St Michael's Bay. Spacious bar and lounge featuring Indian crafts and fabrics. Contemporary rooms with modern amenities, most with balcony and view. Bright attractive dining room; menu mixes modern and traditional.

at Perranuthnoe Southeast : 1.75 mi by A 394 – ✉ Penzance

Ednovean Farm without rest

✉ TR20 9LZ – ☎ (01736) 711 883 – www.ednoveanfarm.co.uk – Closed Christmas-New Year

3 rm – ♦£ 100/110 ♦♦£ 110

◆ Very spacious, characterful converted 17C granite barn offering peace, tranquillity and Mounts Bay views. Fine choice at breakfast on oak table. Charming, individual rooms.

Victoria Inn with rm

✉ TR20 9NP – ☎ (01736) 710 309 – www.victoriainn-penzance.co.uk – Closed 1 week January, 25-26 December, 1 January, Sunday dinner and Monday in winter

2 rm – ♦£ 45 ♦♦£ 70 **Rest** – Carte £ 20/35

◆ Characterful, pink-washed pub in the heart of the village, with a cosy, homely feel and a suntrap terrace. Short menu of wholesome dishes showcases local produce and is supplemented by blackboard of seafood specials. Simple, nautically themed bedrooms.

at St Hilary East : 2.5 mi by Turnpike Rd on B 3280 – ✉ Penzance

Ennys without rest

Trewhella Ln ✉ TR20 9BZ – ☎ (01736) 740 262 – www.ennys.co.uk

5 rm – ♦£ 80/135 ♦♦£ 95/145

◆ A beautiful and delightfully remote guesthouse, its lovingly restored interior simply furnished in light colours, with Indian artefacts from the charming owner's travels. Grass tennis court and pool set in secluded part of the garden. Complimentary afternoon tea.

MARCHAM – Oxfordshire – 503 P29 – see Abingdon

MARGATE – Kent – 504 Y29 – pop. 58 465 — 9 D1

London 74 mi – Canterbury 17 mi – Dover 21 mi – Maidstone 43 mi

12-13 The Parade ☎ (0872) 646111

The Ambrette

44 King St ✉ CT9 1QE – ✆ (01843) 231 504 – www.theambrette.co.uk – closed Monday

Rest – Indian – Menu £ 20 (lunch) – Carte £ 17/34

◆ Quirky Indian restaurant in modest surroundings. Concise, seasonal menu showcases Kentish produce in an original style; freshly prepared dishes offer well-balanced flavours and subtle spicing.

MARKET DRAYTON – Shropshire – 502 M25 – pop. 10 407 18 B1

London 159 mi – Nantwich 13 mi – Shrewsbury 21 mi

Goldstone Hall

Goldstone, South : 4.5 mi by A 529 ✉ TF9 2NA – ✆ (01630) 661 202 – www.goldstonehall.com

12 rm – †£ 85/92 ††£ 145 **Rest** – Menu £ 25 (lunch) **s** – Carte £ 33/54 **s**

◆ 16C red-brick country house that's been extensively added to over the ages. Five acres of formal garden: PG Wodehouse enjoyed its shade! Modern rooms with huge beds. Contemporary twists on daily changing menus.

MARKET HARBOROUGH – Leicestershire – 504 R26 – pop. 20 127 16 B3

London 88 mi – Birmingham 47 mi – Leicester 15 mi – Northampton 17 mi

Council Offices, Adam and Eve St ✆ (01858) 828282

Great Oxendon Rd, ✆ (01858) 463 684

at Thorpe Langton North : 3.75 mi by A 4304 and Great Bowden rd – ✉ Market Harborough

The Bakers Arms

Main St ✉ LE16 7TS – ✆ (01858) 545 201 – www.thebakersarms.co.uk – Closed Sunday dinner and Monday

Rest – *(dinner only and Saturday-Sunday lunch) (booking essential)* Carte £ 22/28

◆ Thatched, yellow-washed pub with characterful interior. Blackboard menu evolves constantly throughout the day, displaying pub classics, reliable combinations and comforting desserts.

MARLBOROUGH – Wiltshire – 503 O29 – pop. 7 713 4 D2

London 84 mi – Bristol 47 mi – Southampton 40 mi – Swindon 12 mi

The Library, High St ✆ (01225) 774 222, all.tic's@kennet.gov.uk

The Common, ✆ (01672) 512 147

Town★

Savernake Forest★★ (Grand Avenue★★★), SE : 2 mi by A 4 – Whitehorse (<★), NW : 5 m – West Kennett Long Barrow★, Silbury Hill★, W : 6 mi by A 4. Ridgeway Path★★ – Avebury★★ (The Stones★, Church★), W : 7 mi by A 4 – Crofton Beam Engines★ **AC**, SE : 9 mi by A 346 – Wilton Windmill★ **AC**, SE : 9 mi by A 346, A 338 and minor rd

Coles

27 Kingsbury Hill ✉ SN8 1JA – ✆ (01672) 515 004 – www.colesrestaurant.co.uk – Closed 25 December, Sunday and bank holidays

Rest – Carte £ 25/31

◆ Shots of 70s film stars adorn a busy, bay-windowed former pub which retains its firelit bar. Friendly staff and elaborate but robust cuisine with an array of daily specials.

at Ramsbury Northeast : 7.25 mi by A 346 – ✉ Marlborough

The Bell

The Square ✉ SN8 2PE – ✆ (01672) 520 230 – www.thebellramsbury.com – Closed 25 December, dinner Sunday and bank holiday

Rest – Menu £ 15/20 – Carte £ 22/30

◆ Whitewashed Victorian pub with an atmospheric bar and pleasant dining room. A constantly evolving menu offers pub classics with the odd modern touch and tempting, locally sourced steaks.

ENGLAND

at Little Bedwyn East : 9.5 mi by A 4 – ✉ Marlborough

XX ✿ **Harrow at Little Bedwyn** (Roger Jones)
✉ SN8 3JP – ☎ (01672) 870 871 – www.theharrowatlittlebedwyn.co.uk
– *Closed 10 days Christmas and Sunday-Tuesday*
Rest – Menu £ 30 (lunch) – Carte £ 42/52
Spec. Langoustine fish finger, ketchup and chips. Wild sea bass with mushroom risotto. Deconstructed lemon meringue pie.
◆ Former pub with smartly laid tables and an intimate atmosphere. Flavourful, seasonal cooking is presented in a modern style, whilst retaining its classical base. Top quality produce; fish plays an important role. Comprehensive wine list and regular wine evenings.

at East Kennett West : 5.25 mi by A4

Old Forge without rest
✉ SN8 4EY – ☎ (01672) 861 686 – www.theoldforge-avebury.co.uk
4 rm – †£ 60 ††£ 70
◆ Converted former smithy with a relaxing, homely feel. Comfortable bedrooms have classic country house style; the family room has pleasant countryside views. Communal breakfast.

ENGLAND

MARLDON – Devon – 503 J32 – pop. 1 798 — 2 C2

London 193 mi – Newton Abbott 7 mi – Paignton 3 mi

Church House Inn
Village Rd ✉ *TQ3 1SL – ☎ (01803) 558 279*
– www.churchhousemarldon.com
Rest – Carte £ 21/33
◆ Charming inn of huge character displaying original Georgian windows. Fresh and simple décor. Menu leans towards the Mediterranean with some North African and Asian influences.

MARLOW – Buckinghamshire – 504 R29 – pop. 17 522 — 11 C3

London 35 mi – Aylesbury 22 mi – Oxford 29 mi – Reading 14 mi
to Henley-on-Thames (Salter Bros. Ltd) (summer only) (2 h 15 mn) – to Maidenhead, Cookham and Windsor (Salter Bros. Ltd) (summer only)
31 High St ☎ (01628) 483597, tourism_enquiries@wycombe.gov.uk

Danesfield House rest,
Henley Rd, Southwest : 2.5 mi on A 4155 ✉ *SL7 2EY*
– ☎ (01628) 891 010 – www.danesfieldhouse.co.uk
84 rm – †£ 195/245 ††£ 245/345, £ 10.50
Rest *Adam Simmonds at Danesfield House* – see restaurant listing
Rest *Orangery* – Menu £ 22 (lunch) – Carte £ 27/34
◆ Stunning house and gardens in Italian Renaissance style, with breathtaking views of the Thames. Grand lounge with country house feel, comfy bedrooms, cocktail bar and state-of-art health spa. Charming, informal terrace brasserie.

Compleat Angler
Marlow Bridge, Bisham Rd ✉ *SL7 1RG – ☎ (0844) 879 9128*
– www.macdonaldhotels.co.uk/compleatangler
61 rm – †£ 130/250 ††£ 140/260 – 3 suites
Rest *Aubergine at the Compleat Angler* – ☎ (01628) 405 405 *(closed Monday and Tuesday)* Menu £ 25/50
Rest *Bowaters* – *(closed Sunday dinner)* Menu £ 25 – Carte £ 31/43
◆ Smart riverside hotel boasting superb views, set in enviable location between bridge and weir. Bedrooms mix classical furnishings with contemporary fabrics: some have waterfront balconies; feature rooms are best. Ambitious French menu in Aubergine. More traditional British fare in contemporary Bowaters.

Adam Simmonds at Danesfield House

Henley Rd, Southwest : 2.5 mi on A 4155 ✉ SL7 2EY – ✆ (01628) 891 010 – www.danesfieldhouse.co.uk – Closed 2 weeks Christmas, 2 weeks late August, Sunday and Monday

Rest – *(dinner only and lunch Friday-Saturday)* Menu £ 55

Spec. Langoustines with yoghurt panna cotta and cucumber. Poached turbot with wild garlic leaf, peas and morels. Chocolate, banana and rum millefeuille.

♦ Elegant, very intimate fine dining restaurant with a huge fireplace, panelled walls, linen-laid tables and a relaxed air. Creative, flavourful, intricate cooking uses modern techniques, making skilful use of excellent quality, seasonal ingredients. Formal service.

Vanilla Pod

31 West St ✉ SL7 2LS – ✆ (01628) 898 101 – www.thevanillapod.co.uk – Closed 24 December-6 January, Sunday, Monday and bank holidays

Rest – *(booking essential)* Menu £ 20/40 **s**

♦ Discreet, well-established address with plush furnishings and just a few tables; formerly home to T. S. Elliot. Ambitious cooking boasts French foundations, original touches and artistic flair.

The Hand and Flowers (Tom Kerridge) with rm

126 West St ✉ SL7 2BP – ✆ (01628) 482 277 – www.thehandandflowers.co.uk – Closed 24-26 December, 1 January dinner and Sunday dinner

4 rm – †£ 140 ††£ 190 **Rest** – *(booking essential)* Carte £ 31/42

Spec. Moules marinière with warm stout and brown bread. Slow braised shin of beef with glazed carrot, red wine and beef marrow. Lavender panna cotta with heather honey, whiskey jelly and honeycomb.

♦ Softly lit pub with low beamed ceilings, flagstone floors and a characterful dining area. Formal, French-accented team serve refined, flavoursome dishes created using classical techniques. Ingredients marry perfectly and the simple is turned into the sublime. Charming cottage bedrooms; some boasting outdoor jacuzzis.

The Royal Oak

Frieth Rd, Bovingdon Green, West : 1.25 mi by A 4155 ✉ SL7 2JF – ✆ (01628) 488 611 – www.royaloakmarlow.co.uk – Closed 25-26 December

Rest – Carte £ 20/27

♦ Part-17C, country-chic pub with herb garden, petanque pitch and pleasant terrace. Set close to the M40 and M4: an ideal London getaway. Largely British menu with the odd Asian influence.

at Little Marlow East : 3 mi on A 4155

The Queens Head

Pound Ln ✉ SL7 3SR – ✆ (01628) 482 927 – www.marlowslittlesecret.co.uk – Closed 25 and 26 December

Rest – Carte £ 22/32

♦ 16C pub popular with walkers. Lunch menu offers ploughman's and fish and chips; dinner menu raises bar with duck liver parfait and pan-fried sea bass. Poised, friendly service.

MARPLE – Greater Manchester – 502 N23 – pop. 18 475 — 20 B3

London 190 mi – Chesterfield 35 mi – Manchester 11 mi

Springfield without rest

99 Station Rd ✉ SK6 6PA – ✆ (0161) 449 0721 – www.springfieldhotelmarple.co.uk

7 rm – †£ 57 ††£ 79

♦ Personally run, part-Victorian house with sympathetic extensions and pleasant rural views. Bright breakfast room; individually styled bedrooms. Useful for visits to the Peak District.

ENGLAND

MARSDEN – West Yorkshire – 502 O23 – pop. 3 499 – ✉ Huddersfield 22 A3

London 195 mi – Leeds 22 mi – Manchester 18 mi – Sheffield 30 mi

Olive Branch with rm

✉ HD7 6LU – ☎ (01484) 844 487 – www.olivebranch.uk.com

3 rm – ♦£ 73 ♦♦£ 93/105

Rest – *(dinner only and Sunday lunch)* Menu £ 19 – Carte £ 26/46

♦ Characterful drovers' inn with stone floors, rustic walls, secluded garden and pleasant views from terrace. Classical, French-influenced menu supplemented by fish specials. Good choice of wines by the glass. Bedrooms are modern, cosy and individually themed.

MARSTON MEYSEY – Wiltshire 4 D1

London 91 mi – Birmingham 82 mi – Bristol 56 mi – Coventry 85 mi

The Old Spotted Cow with rm

The Street ✉ SN6 6LQ – ☎ (01285) 810 264 – www.theoldspottedcow.co.uk – Closed Monday except bank holidays

1 rm – ♦£ 70 ♦♦£ 90 **Rest** – Carte £ 18/25

♦ Enthusiastically run country pub serving seasonal, rustic cooking, which combines hearty British classics with worldly spices. Sunday roasts, summer barbecues and monthly spice nights. One comfortable, contemporary bedroom.

MARTINHOE – Devon – see Lynton

MARTON – Shropshire Great Britain 18 A1

London 174 mi – Birmingham 57 mi – Shrewsbury 16 mi

Powis Castle★★★, NW : 7 mi by B 4386 and A 490

The Sun Inn

✉ SY21 8JP – ☎ (01938) 561 211 – www.suninn.org.uk – Closed Sunday dinner and Monday except bank holidays, and lunch Tuesday

Rest – Carte £ 20/30

♦ Welcoming, family-run country pub on the English-Welsh border. Pub snacks in the cosy fire-lit bar; regularly changing à la carte of classic dishes in the bright restaurant.

MASHAM – North Yorkshire – 502 P21 – pop. 1 171 – ✉ Ripon 22 B1

London 231 mi – Leeds 38 mi – Middlesbrough 37 mi – York 32 mi

Swinton Park

Swinton, Southwest : 1 mi ✉ HG4 4JH – ☎ (01765) 680 900 – www.swintonpark.com

26 rm (dinner included) – ♦♦£ 245/360 – 4 suites

Rest *Samuels* – Menu £ 45 – Carte £ 23/30

♦ 17C castle with Georgian and Victorian additions, on a 20,000 acre estate and deer park. Luxurious, antique filled lounges. Very comfortable, individually styled bedrooms. Grand dining room with ornate gold leaf ceiling and garden views.

Bank Villa

on A 6108 ✉ HG4 4DB – ☎ (01765) 689 605 – www.bankvilla.com

6 rm – ♦£ 55/75 ♦♦£ 55/125 **Rest** – Menu £ 24 **s**

♦ Stone-built Georgian villa with Victorian additions. Two lounges and conservatory; delightful, sun-trap stepped garden. Cosy, cottagey rooms: some are in the eaves. Home-cooked menus in pastel dining room/tea room.

Vennell's

7 Silver St ✉ HG4 4DX – ☎ (01765) 689 000 – www.vennellsrestaurant.co.uk – closed 1 week in January, 1 week late June, Sunday dinner and Monday

Rest – *(dinner only and Sunday lunch) (booking essential)* Menu £ 28 **s**

♦ Local art for sale at this personally run local eaterie with comfy basement bar. Bold, confident cooking executed with care and precision. Popular annual 'lobster week'.

ENGLAND

MATFEN – Northumberland – 501 O18 – pop. 500 — 24 A2

London 309 mi – Carlisle 42 mi – Newcastle upon Tyne 24 mi

Matfen Hall

✉ *NE20 0RH* – *☎ (01661) 886 500* – *www.matfenhall.com*

53 rm – †£ 60/185 ††£ 90/185

Rest ***Library and Print Room*** – *(dinner only and Sunday lunch)* Menu £ 30 **s** – Carte £ 30/50 **s**

◆ 19C country mansion built by Thomas Ruckman, master of Gothic design. Set in 500 acres with superb Grand Hall, fine paintings, plush drawing room and mix of bedroom styles. Characterful Library dining room has display of original books.

MATLOCK – Derbyshire – 502 P24 – pop. 11 265 Great Britain — 16 B1

London 153 mi – Derby 17 mi – Manchester 46 mi – Nottingham 24 mi

Crown Sq ☎ (01629) 583388, matlockinfo@derbyshiredales.gov.uk

Hardwick Hall★★ **AC**, E : 12.5 mi by A 615 and B 6014 – Crich Tramway Village★ **AC**, S : 12 mi by A 6 and B 5036

at Birchover Northwest : 7.5 mi by A 6 – ✉ Matlock

The Druid Inn

Main St ✉ *DE4 2BL* – *☎ (01629) 650 302* – *www.thedruidinn.co.uk* – *Closed Sunday dinner*

Rest – Menu £ 13 (weekdays) – Carte £ 20/30

◆ Remotely set stone inn with cosy bar, small wine cave and contemporary two-tier dining room. Cooking is kept simple and in a classical vein, featuring hearty steaks, pies and in winter, stews.

MAWGAN PORTH – Cornwall – 503 E32 – see Newquay

MEDBOURNE – Leicestershire – 504 R26 — 16 B2

London 93 mi – Corby 9 mi – Leicester 16 mi

Homestead House without rest

Ashley Rd ✉ *LE16 8DL* – *☎ (01858) 565 724* – *www.homesteadhouse.co.uk*

3 rm – †£ 35 ††£ 55

◆ Personally run, spotlessly kept guest house with comfortable, leather-furnished lounge and traditionally styled, homely bedrooms; two with a pleasant country-side outlook.

MELLOR – Lancs. – see Blackburn

MELTON MOWBRAY – Leicestershire – 502 R25 – pop. 25 554 — 16 B2

London 113 mi – Leicester 15 mi – Northampton 45 mi – Nottingham 18 mi

Council Offices, Nottingham Rd ☎ (01664) 480992, customerservices@melton.gov.uk

Thorpe Arnold Waltham Rd, ☎ (01664) 562 118

Stapleford Park

East : 5 mi by B 676 on Stapleford rd ✉ *LE14 2EF* – *☎ (01572) 787 000* – *www.staplefordpark.com*

55 rm – †£ 220 ††£ 288

Rest ***Grinling Gibbons Dining Room*** – *(booking essential)* Menu £ 24/47

◆ Astoundingly beautiful stately home in 500 glorious acres, exuding a grandeur rarely surpassed. Extensive leisure facilities; uniquely designed rooms of sumptuous elegance. Ornate rococo dining room a superb example of master craftsman's work.

at Stathern North : 8 mi by A 607 – ✉ Melton Mowbray

Red Lion Inn

2 Red Lion St ✉ *LE14 4HS* – *☎ (01949) 860 868* – *www.theredlioninn.co.uk* – *Closed Sunday dinner*

Rest – *(booking essential)* Menu £ 19 (lunch) – Carte £ 22/32

◆ Large, whitewashed village pub. Menus offer straightforward cooking and refined pub classics with the odd international twist. Produce is sourced from their allotment and local suppliers.

ENGLAND

MEVAGISSEY – Cornwall – 503 F33 – pop. 2 221 1 B3

London 287 mi – Newquay 21 mi – Plymouth 44 mi – Truro 20 mi

Town★★

NW : Lost Gardens of Heligan★

Trevalsa Court

School Hill, East : 0.5 mi on B 3273 (St Austell rd) ✉ PL26 6TH – ☎ (01726) 842 468 – www.trevalsa-hotel.co.uk – Closed January and December

14 rm – †£ 75/160 ††£ 210/235 **Rest** – *(dinner only)* Menu £ 30

◆ Charming Arts and Crafts style house combines dark wood panelling with bright modern art and bold soft furnishings. Well-appointed bedrooms; most with coastal views. Oak-panelled dining room looks onto terrace and garden; short, set price dinner menu.

MICKLETON – Glos. – 503 O27 – see Chipping Campden

MIDDLEHAM – North Yorkshire – 502 O21 – pop. 754 22 B1

London 233 mi – Kendal 45 mi – Leeds 47 mi – Newcastle upon Tyne 63 mi

at Carlton-in-Coverdale Southwest : 4.5 mi by Coverham rd – ✉ Leyburn

Abbots Thorn without rest

✉ DL8 4AY – ☎ (01969) 640 620 – www.abbotsthorn.co.uk – Closed January and December

3 rm – †£ 44/64 ††£ 64/78

◆ Well priced, comfortable, quiet guesthouse in attractive rural village. Handy for visits to Moors. Cosy sitting room. Sizeable bedrooms which are homely and well-kept.

MIDDLETON-IN-TEESDALE – Durham – 502 N20 – pop. 1 143 24 A3

London 447 mi – Carlisle 91 mi – Leeds 124 mi – Middlesbrough 70 mi

10 Market Pl ☎ (01833) 641001, tic@middletonplus.myzen.co.uk

Grove Lodge

Hude, Northwest : 0.5 mi on B 6277 ✉ DL12 0QW – ☎ (01833) 640 798 – www.grovelodgeteesdale.co.uk

3 rm – †£ 52 ††£ 82 **Rest** – Menu £ 23

◆ Victorian former shooting lodge perched on a hill where the two front facing rooms have the best views. Neat and friendly house, traditionally decorated. Home-cooked dinners are proudly served.

MIDHURST – West Sussex – 504 R31 – pop. 6 120 7 C2

London 57 mi – Brighton 38 mi – Chichester 12 mi – Southampton 41 mi

North St ☎ (01730) 817322, midtic@chichester.gov.uk

Spread Eagle

South St ✉ GU29 9NH – ☎ (01730) 816 911 – www.hshotels.co.uk

38 rm – †£ 120/145 ††£ 230/260 – 2 suites **Rest** – Menu £ 21/40 **s**

◆ 15C hotel retaining plenty of character in the form of antiques, gleaming brass and inglenook fireplaces. Traditional bedrooms; good leisure facilities. Formally laid restaurant offers good value set price menus; classic dishes presented in a modern style.

at Henley North : 4.5 mi by A286

Duke of Cumberland

✉ GU27 3HQ – ☎ (01428) 652 280 – www.dukeofcumberland.com – Closed Sunday dinner and Monday

Rest – Carte £ 23/35

◆ Hidden gem with delightful, low-beamed interior, huge fireplace and tiered gardens with babbling brooks. Appealing, daily changing menu of carefully prepared, seasonal dishes. Charming service.

at Bepton Southwest : 2.5 mi by A 286 on Bepton rd – ✉ Midhurst

Park House
✉ *GU29 0JB* – ☎ *(01730) 819 000* – *www.parkhousehotel.com*
– *Closed 25-26 December*
14 rm – †£ 120/256 ††£ 150/320 – 1 suite
Rest – *(booking essential at lunch)* Menu £ 26/36
◆ Comfortable country house with light, modern style and smart spa and leisure facilities. Spacious bedrooms in neutral shades; most have views of well-tended gardens and golf course; some in separate two-storey house. Stylish restaurant/-conservatory offers modern menus.

at Redford West : 3 mi by A272 then following signs for Redford

Redford Cottage without rest
✉ *GU29 0QF* – ☎ *(01428) 741 242* – *Closed Christmas-New Year*
5 rm – †£ 65 ††£ 95
◆ Charming 15C cottage in delightful gardens. Uniquely styled, attractively furnished bedrooms; china, books and pictures abound. Hearty breakfast from the Aga can be taken on the terrace.

at Trotton West : 3.25 mi on A 272

The Keepers Arms
✉ *GU31 5ER* – ☎ *(01730) 813 724* – *www.keepersarms.co.uk*
– *Closed 25-26 December*
Rest – Carte £ 23/30
◆ Cheery, welcoming neighbourhood inn with many regular diners and a family feel. Low ceilings, an open fire and a host of quirky tables. Good value, honest cooking and an oft-changing wine list.

ENGLAND

MID LAVANT – West Sussex – 504 R31 – see Chichester

MIDSOMER NORTON – Bath and North East Somerset – 503 M30 — 4 C2

London 125 mi – Bath 11 mi – Wells 12 mi

The Moody Goose at the Old Priory with rm
Church Sq ✉ *BA3 2HX* – ☎ *(01761) 416 784*
– *www.theoldpriory.co.uk* – *Closed Christmas and Sunday*
6 rm – †£ 85/95 ††£ 120/145
Rest – Menu £ 29/33 – Carte dinner £ 39/45
◆ 12C former priory, by a church, with an enviable walled garden. Impressive interior with open bar and smart dining room, featuring solid stone floors, beams and vast fireplaces. Classical French cooking utilises quality seasonal ingredients. Warm, comfy bedrooms.

MILFORD-ON-SEA – Hampshire – 503 P31 – pop. 4 229 — 6 A3
– ✉ Lymington

London 109 mi – Bournemouth 15 mi – Southampton 24 mi
– Winchester 37 mi

Westover Hall
Park Ln. ✉ *SO41 0PT* – ☎ *(01590) 643 044* – *www.westoverhallhotel.com*
11 rm (dinner included) – †£ 100/130 ††£ 220/280 – 4 suites
Rest *Vista Bistro* – Carte £ 25/36
Rest *One Park Lane* – *(dinner only)* Menu £ 42
◆ Characterful 19C mansion in delightful spot overlooking the coast. Impressive hall and minstrels gallery, comfortable sitting room and contemporary bedrooms. Informal Vista offers classic bistro menus. Wood-panelled One Park Lane has a formal, elegant feel.

MILLBROOK – Cornwall – 503 H32 **2** C2

London 235 mi – Liskeard 16 mi – Plymouth 23 mi

at Freathy **West : 3 mi by B 3247, Whitsand Bay Rd on Treninnow Cliff Rd** – ✉ Millbrook

The View

East : 1 mi ✉ PL10 1JY – ☎ (01752) 822 345 – www.theview-restaurant.co.uk – Restricted opening November-January. Closed February, Monday except bank holidays and Tuesday.

Rest – Carte £ 25/32 **s**

◆ Charming and informal converted café perched on a cliff, with coastal views. Relaxed daytime vibe; more atmospheric in the evening. Assured, confident cooking and friendly service. Plenty of seafood; generous portions. Try the rustic homemade bread.

MILTON KEYNES

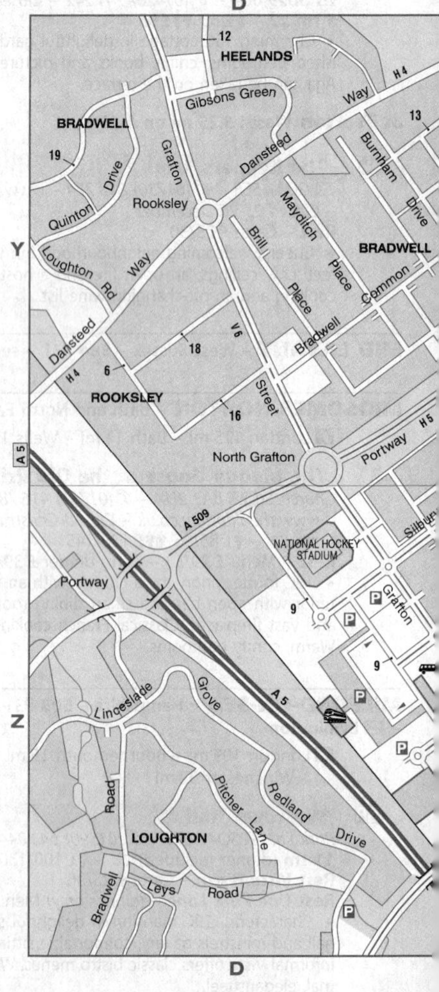

ENGLAND

MILSTEAD – Kent – see Sittingbourne

MILTON – Oxon. – see Banbury

MILTON ABBOT – Devon – 503 H32 – see Tavistock

MILTON KEYNES – Milton Keynes – 504 R27 – pop. 156 148 11 C1

London 56 mi – Bedford 16 mi – Birmingham 72 mi – Northampton 18 mi

The Chapel, The Knoll, Newport Pagnell (01908) 614 638, info@destinationmiltonkeynes.co.uk

18 Abbey Hill Two Mile Ash Monks Way, (01908) 563 845

18 Tattenhoe Bletchley Tattenhoe Lane, (01908) 631 113

27 Wavendon Golf Centre Wavendon Lower End Rd, (01908) 281 811

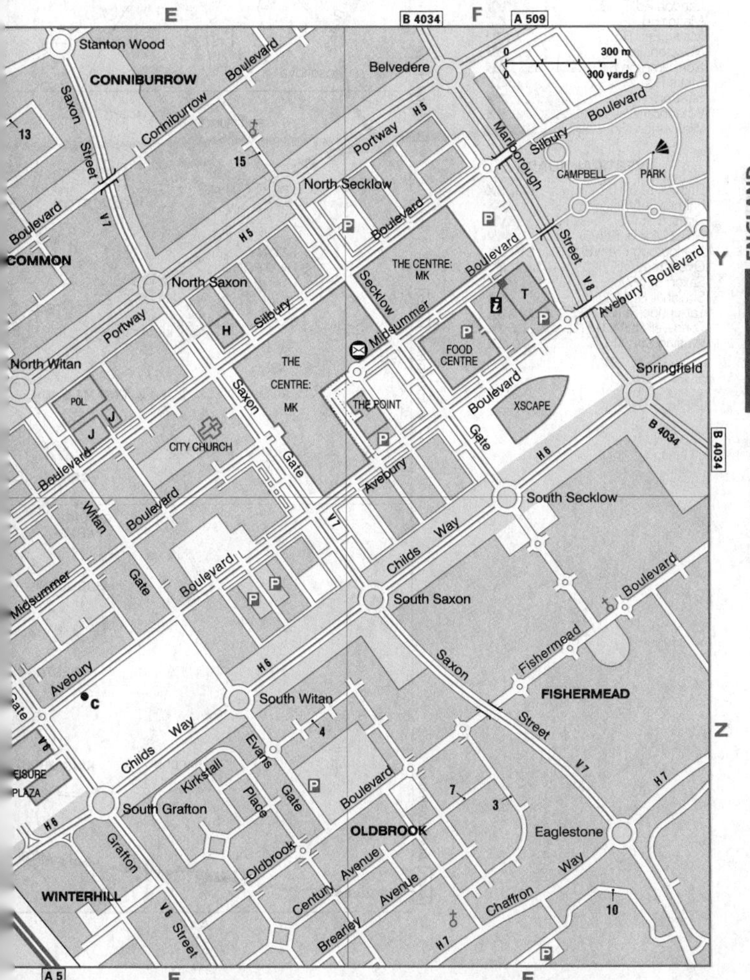

HORIZONTAL ROADS

Bletcham Way (H10) .... **CX**
Chaffron Way (H7) .... **BX, CV**
Childs Way (H6) .... **BX, CV**
Dansteed Way (H4) .... **ABV**
Groveway (H9) .... **CVX**
Millers Way (H2) .... **AV**
Monks Way (H3) .... **ABV**
Portway (H5) .... **BCV**
Ridgeway (H1) .... **AV**
Standing Way (H8) .... **BX, CV**

MILTON KEYNES

Buckingham Rd .... **BX**
London Rd .... **CUV**
Manor Rd .... **CX**
Marsh End Rd .... **CU**
Newport Rd .... **BV**
Northampton Rd .... **AU**
Stoke Rd .... **CX**
Stratford Rd .... **AV**
Whaddon Way .... **BX**
Wolverton Rd .... **BU**

VERTICAL ROADS

Brickhill St (V10) .... **BU, CX**
Fulmer St (V3) .... **ABX**
Grafton St (V6) .... **BVX**
Great Monks St (V5) .... **AV**
Marlborough St (V8) .... **BV, CX**
Overstreet (V9) .... **BV**
Saxon St (V7) .... **BVX**
Snelshall St (V1) .... **BX**
Tattenhoe St (V2) .... **ABX**
Tongwell St (V11) .... **CVX**
Watling St (V4) .... **AV, BX**

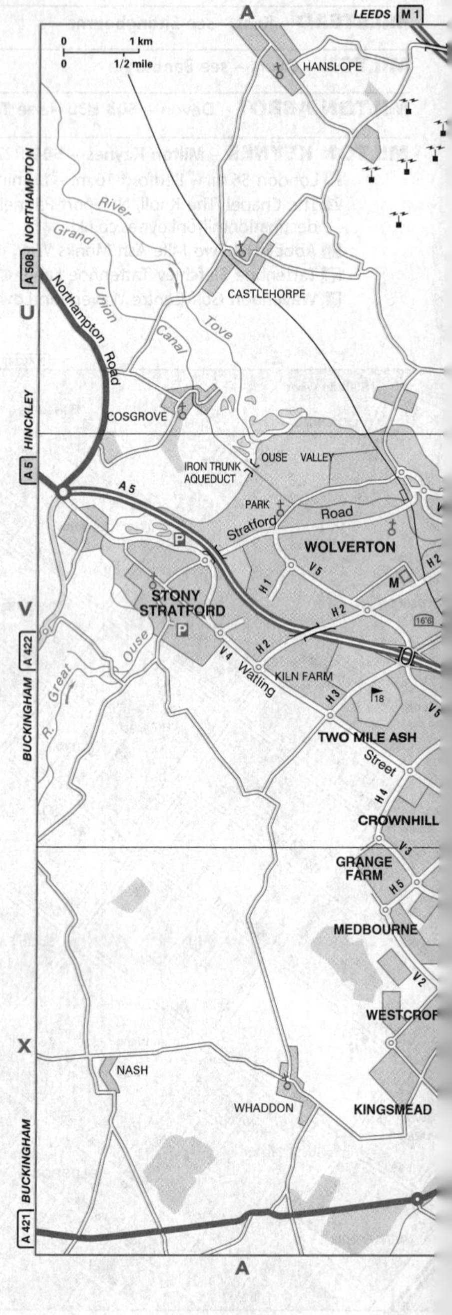

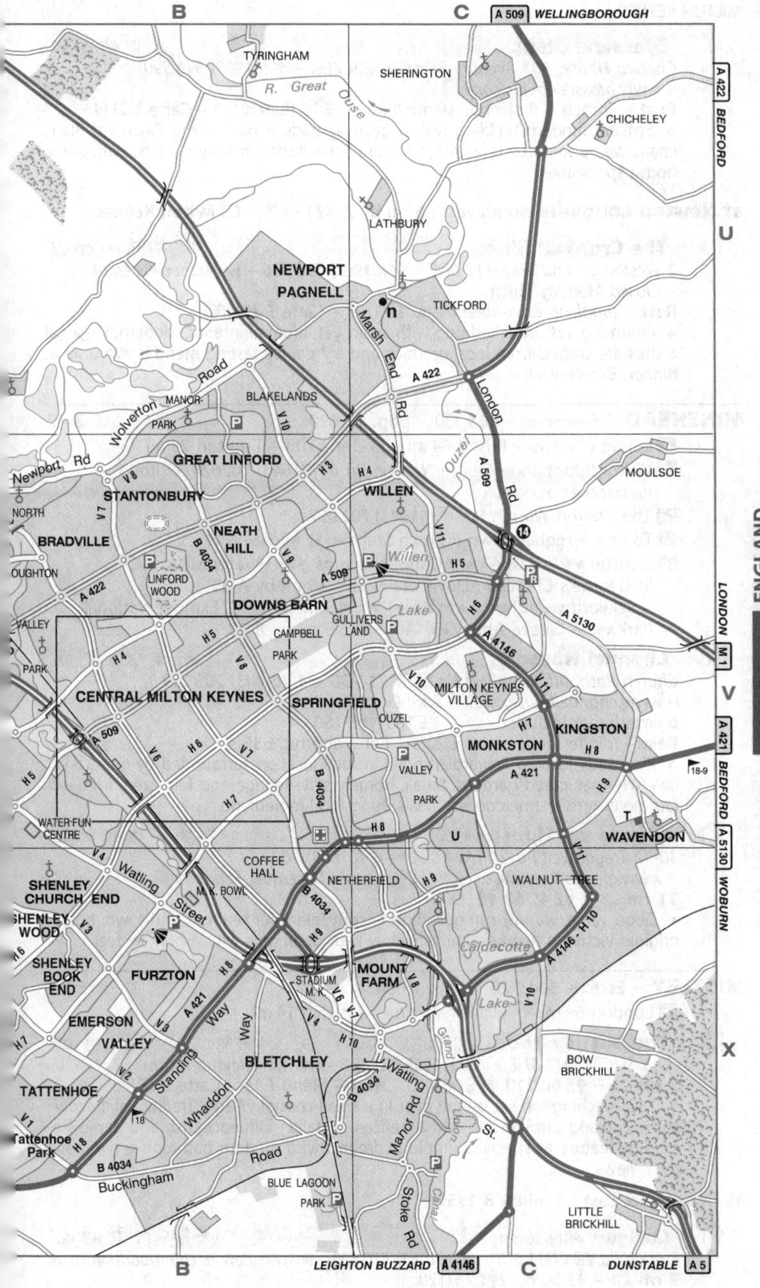

B
C
A 509 WELLINGBOROUGH
TYRINGHAM
SHERINGTON
R. Great Ouse
A 422 BEDFORD
CHICHELEY
LATHBURY
U
NEWPORT PAGNELL
TICKFORD
Marsh End Rd
London Rd
A 422
Wolverton Road
MANOR PARK
BLAKELANDS
V 10
Newport Rd
GREAT LINFORD
H 3
H 4
WILLEN
Ouzel
A 509
MOULSOE
STANTONBURY
V 8
V 7
NORTH
BRADVILLE
NEATH HILL
B 4034
V 9
V 11
Willen
H 5
OUGHTON
LINFORD WOOD
A 422
A 509
DOWNS BARN
Lake
H 6
A 5130
LONDON M 1
VALLEY
PARK
GULLIVERS LAND
CAMPBELL PARK
A 4146
CENTRAL MILTON KEYNES
SPRINGFIELD
MILTON KEYNES VILLAGE
OUZEL
V 10
V
A 509
V 6
H 6
V 7
H 7
KINGSTON
MONKSTON
H 8
A 421 BEDFORD
18-9
VALLEY PARK
A 421
H 9
H 5
WATER-FUN CENTRE
B 4034
H 8
U
WAVENDON
A 5130 WOBURN
V 4
Watling Street
COFFEE HALL
NETHERFIELD
H 9
WALNUT TREE
SHENLEY CHURCH END
M. K. BOWL
SHENLEY WOOD
V 3
B 4034
H 9
A 4146 - H 10
Caldecotte
SHENLEY BOOK END
FURZTON
H 8
STADIUM M. K.
MOUNT FARM
V 8
Lake
V 10
EMERSON VALLEY
A 421
Way
Way
V 3
V 6
V 7
V 4
H 10
Grand
X
H 7
VALLEY
BLETCHLEY
BOW BRICKHILL
Standing
Watling
TATTENHOE
V 2
Whaddon
B 4034
Manor Rd
Union
St.
V 1
18
Tattenhoe Park
H 8
B 4034
Road
Buckingham
BLUE LAGOON PARK
Stoke Rd
Canal
LITTLE BRICKHILL
B
LEIGHTON BUZZARD A 4146
C
DUNSTABLE A 5
ENGLAND

Brasserie Blanc

Chelsea House, 301 Avebury Blvd ✉ MK9 2GA – ✆ (01908) 546 590 – www.brasserieblanc.com EZ **c**

Rest – French – *(booking essential)* Menu £ 15 (lunch)/19 – Carte £ 21/46

◆ Striking modern building with a bustling trade – part of the Raymond Blanc chain. Menu features refined French brasserie dishes, mainly classics, with some house specialities.

at Newton Longville Southwest : 6 mi by A 421 - AX – ✉ Milton Keynes

The Crooked Billet

2 Westbrook End ✉ MK17 0DF – ✆ (01908) 373 936 – www.thebillet.co.uk – Closed Monday lunch

Rest – *(booking advisable)* Menu £ 21/23 – Carte £ 25/40

◆ Charming 17C thatched pub with smart yet informal interior. Modern, seasonal dishes are crafted from local produce and a 7 course tasting menu is available at dinner. Excellent wine list.

MINEHEAD – Somerset – 503 J30 – pop. 11 699 — 3 A2

London 187 mi – Bristol 64 mi – Exeter 43 mi – Taunton 25 mi

Visitor Information Centre, Warren Rd ✆ (01643) 702624, visitor@westsomerset.gov.uk

The Warren Warren Rd, ✆ (01643) 702 057

Town★ - Higher Town (Church Steps★, St Michael's★)

Dunster★★ - Castle★★ **AC** (upper rooms ≤★) Water Mill★ **AC**, St George's Church★, Dovecote★, SE : 2.5 mi by A 39 – Selworthy★ (Church★, ≤★★) W : 4.5 mi by A 39. Exmoor National Park★★ – Cleeve Abbey★★ **AC**, SE : 6.5 mi by A 39

Channel House

Church Path, off Northfield Dr ✉ TA24 5QG – ✆ (01643) 703 229 – www.channelhouse.co.uk – April-October

8 rm (dinner included) – †£ 105 ††£ 180

Rest – *(dinner only)* Menu £ 20 **s** – Carte approx. £ 35 **s**

◆ Pleasantly located Edwardian hotel in rural location surrounded by mature yet carefully manicured gardens. Small, homely style lounge and fair sized, immaculate bedrooms. Home-cooked meals using local ingredients.

Glendower House without rest

30-32 Tregonwell Rd ✉ TA24 5DU – ✆ (01643) 707 144 – www.glendower-house.co.uk – Closed mid December-February

11 rm – †£ 45/60 ††£ 90

◆ Good value, warmly run guesthouse, convenient for seafront and town; boasts original Victorian features. Immaculately kept bedrooms with a homely feel.

MISTLEY – Essex – 504 X28 – pop. 1 684 — 13 D2

London 69 mi – Colchester 11 mi – Ipswich 14 mi

The Mistley Thorn with rm

High St ✉ CO11 1HE – ✆ (01206) 392 821 – www.mistleythorn.com

5 rm – †£ 60/110 ††£ 60/110 **Rest** – Menu £ 15 – Carte £ 18/26

◆ 18C coaching inn set by the river in a small coastal village. Traditional, flavoursome cooking displays the odd American or Italian influence; fish and game frequently feature as specials. Simple bedrooms with modern bathrooms; two have river views.

at Bradfield East : 2 mi by B 1352

Curlews without rest

Station Rd ✉ CO11 2UP – ✆ (01255) 870 890 – www.curlewsaccommodation.co.uk

7 rm – †£ 50/60 ††£ 75/120

◆ Homely guest house where traditional bedrooms boast modern bathrooms; one is self contained disabled suite; others have balconies with splendid views over farmland and the Stour Estuary.

MITTON – Lancs. – 502 M22 – see Whalley

MOBBERLEY – Ches. – 502 N24 – see Knutsford

MOCCAS – County of Herefordshire – 503 L27 18 A3

London 171 mi – Hereford 13 mi – Cwmbrân 45 mi – Great Malvern 36 mi

Moccas Court

HR2 9LH – (01981) 500 019 – www.moccas-court.co.uk – Closed 25-26 December and midweek in winter

5 rm – £ 105/168 £ 117/187

Rest – *(closed Sunday and Monday) (dinner only)* Menu £ 45

◆ Breathtakingly beautiful Grade I listed Georgian house in 100 acres of grounds on terraced banks over the Wye. Antique filled interior; bedrooms furnished to high standard. Estate sourced produce served in ornate Round Room.

MONKS ELEIGH – Suffolk – 504 W27 15 C3

London 72 mi – Cambridge 47 mi – Colchester 17 mi – Ipswich 16 mi

The Swan

The Street IP7 7AU – (01449) 741 391 – www.monkseleigh.com – Closed 25-26 December, Sunday dinner and Monday

Rest – *(booking essential in summer)* Menu £ 18 – Carte £ 19/30

◆ Thatched pub with fresh, bright interior. Frequently changing, seasonal menu of generous, flavourful dishes, with the occasional Italian influence; all homemade from local produce.

MONKTON COMBE – Bath and North East Somerset – see Bath

MORECAMBE – Lancashire – 502 L21 – pop. 49 569 20 A1

London 247 mi – Preston 27 mi – Blackpool 39 mi – Blackburn 34 mi

Midland

Marine Road West LA4 4BU – (01524) 424 000 – www.elh.co.uk

43 rm – £ 93/120 £ 126/180 – 1 suite **Rest** – Carte £ 26/41

◆ Iconic 1933 hotel set in a stunning location, with views of Morecambe Bay and the mountains. Art deco styling; original features include a listed staircase. Variously sized, starkly decorated, contemporary bedrooms. Modern restaurant offers superb outlook.

MORETONHAMPSTEAD – Devon – 503 I32 – pop. 1 380 2 C2
– Newton Abbot

London 213 mi – Exeter 13 mi – Plymouth 30 mi

Bovey Castle North Bovey, (01647) 445 009

Dartmoor National Park★★

White Hart

The Square TQ13 8NF – (01647) 441 340 – www.whitehartdartmoor.co.uk

28 rm – £ 60/75 £ 90/110

Rest – Carte £ 22/31

◆ 17C Grade II listed former coaching inn in the town; bright and comfortable, with a cosy lounge and pleasant locals bar. Simply furnished bedrooms have modern touches; the newer ones are in the annexe. Open-style, wood-floored dining room offers classic dishes.

The White Horse Inn

7 George St TQ13 8PG – (01647) 440 267 – www.whitehorsedevon.co.uk – Closed Sunday, Monday and lunch in winter

Rest – Carte £ 19/30

◆ Pub with rustic, flag-floored rooms and a sunny, Mediterranean-style courtyard. Tasty, unfussy dishes offer more than a hint of Italy. Thin crust pizzas baked in a custom-built oven.

ENGLAND

MORETON-IN-MARSH – Gloucestershire – 503 O28 – pop. 3 198 4 D1

Great Britain

London 86 mi – Birmingham 40 mi – Gloucester 31 mi – Oxford 29 mi

Chastleton House★★, SE : 5 mi by A 44

Manor House

rest,

High St ✉ GL56 0LJ – ✆ (01608) 650 501 – www.cotswold-inns-hotels.co.uk/manor

35 rm – †£ 120/160 ††£ 155/260

Rest *Mulberry* – *(dinner only)* Menu £ 38

◆ Part-16C Cotswold stone house hides chic, stylish interior with vibrant furnishings. Numerous comfy guest areas; beautiful grounds. Quirky, individually decorated bedrooms ooze style. Relaxed brasserie and bar for afternoon tea and cocktails; sophisticated Mulberry for dinner.

The Old School without rest

Little Compton, East : 4 mi on A 44 ✉ GL56 0SL – ✆ (01608) 674 588 – www.theoldschoolbedandbreakfast.com

4 rm – †£ 70/96 ††£ 96/125

◆ Attractive, well kept Victorian building with large, neat garden. Period features such as A-frame ceilings and stained glass windows are complemented by modern furnishings.

at Bourton-on-the-Hill West : 2 mi on A 44 – ✉ Moreton-In-Marsh

Horse & Groom with rm

✉ GL56 9AQ – ✆ (01386) 700 413 – www.horseandgroom.info – Closed Sunday dinner except at bank holidays

5 rm – †£ 80 ††£ 160

Rest – *(booking essential)* Carte £ 20/35

◆ Grade II listed yellow-stone building with a friendly atmosphere. Menu features hearty, unfussy cooking and ranges from classic pub dishes to more restaurant style offerings. Modern bedrooms, each individually styled.

ENGLAND

MORPETH – Northumberland – 501 O18 – pop. 13 555 24 B2

London 301 mi – Edinburgh 93 mi – Newcastle upon Tyne 15 mi

The Chantry, Bridge St ✆ (01670) 500700, morpeth.tic@northumberland.gov.uk

The Clubhouse, ✆ (01670) 504 942

Black Door Bar & Dining Rooms

59 Bridge St ✉ NE61 1PQ – ✆ (01670) 516 200 – www.blackdoorgroup.co.uk – Closed Sunday dinner

Rest – Carte £ 18/22

◆ Informal dining and bar on rustic ground floor; fashionable first floor room with feature walls in chocolate flock. Smart private room above. Appealing menu of classic dishes.

at Longhorsley Northwest : 6.5 mi by A 192 on A 697 – ✉ Morpeth

Thistleyhaugh Farm

Northwest : 3.75 mi by A 697 and Todburn rd taking first right turn ✉ NE65 8RG – ✆ (01665) 570 629 – www.thistleyhaugh.co.uk – Closed 20 December-February

5 rm – †£ 50/75 ††£ 80

Rest – Menu £ 20

◆ Attractive Georgian farmhouse on working farm in a pleasant rural area. The River Coquet flows through the grounds. Comfortable, cosy bedrooms in traditional style. Communal dining overlooking garden.

MORSTON – Norfolk – see Blakeney

MORTEHOE – Devon – 503 H30 – see Woolacombe

MOULSFORD - Oxfordshire - pop. 491 10 B3

London 53 mi – Newbury 16 mi – Reading 13 mi

XX **The Beetle & Wedge Boathouse** with rm

Ferry Ln ✉ OX10 9JF – ✆ (01491) 651 381 – www.beetleandwedge.co.uk

3 rm – †£ 75 ††£ 90

Rest – *(booking essential)* Menu £ 22 (weekdays) – Carte £ 27/35

◆ Busy Thameside restaurant with charming terrace; dine in light conservatory or more rustic char grill. Classic menu with plenty of choice, including dishes from the grill. Comfortable bedrooms in Ferryman's Cottage; one has his-and-hers roll-top baths.

MOULTON - North Yorkshire - 502 P20 - pop. 197 - ✉ Richmond 22 B1

London 243 mi – Leeds 53 mi – Middlesbrough 25 mi – Newcastle upon Tyne 43 mi

XX **Black Bull Inn**

✉ DL10 6QJ – ✆ (01325) 377 289 – www.blackbullmoulton.com – Closed Sunday dinner

Rest – Seafood – Menu £ 20 (weekdays) – Carte £ 31/39

◆ Set in heart of rural village; dine in bar, conservatory, beamed dining room or Brighton Belle Pullman carriage from 1932. Seafood based menu and traditional desserts. Refurbishment underway.

MOUSEHOLE - Cornwall - 503 D33 - ✉ Penzance 1 A3

London 321 mi – Penzance 3 mi – Truro 29 mi

Village★

Penwith★★ – Lamorna (The Merry Maidens and The Pipers Standing Stone★) SW : 3 mi by B 3315. Land's End★ (cliff scenery★★★) W : 9 mi by B 3315

Old Coastguard

The Parade ✉ TR19 6PR – ✆ (01736) 731 222 – www.oldcoastguardhotel.co.uk – Closed 7 January-11 February and 24-27 December

14 rm – †£ 90/158 ††£ 120/210

Rest – Carte £ 18/30

◆ Creamwash hotel in unspoilt village with good views of Mounts Bay. Spacious lounge has sun terrace overlooking water. Modern rooms: Premier variety are best for the vista. Gutsy, unfussy dishes of local produce served in modern, open-plan restaurant.

X **Cornish Range** with rm

6 Chapel St ✉ TR19 6SB – ✆ (01736) 731 488 – www.cornishrange.co.uk – Closed 2 weeks January-February

3 rm – ††£ 80/110

Rest – Seafood – *(booking essential)* Carte £ 23/35

◆ Converted 18C pilchard processing cottage hidden away in narrow street. Cottagey inner filled with Cornish artwork. Excellent local seafood dishes. Very comfortable bedrooms.

X **2 Fore Street**

2 Fore St ✉ TR19 6PF – ✆ (01736) 731 164 – www.2forestreet.co.uk – Closed 4 January-10 February, and Monday in November and February

Rest – Seafood – *(booking essential at dinner)* Carte £ 25/31

◆ Cosy, bright bistro in pretty harbourside setting; popular with locals and tourists. Menu based on the best of the day's catch; simple, unfussy preparation. Casual, friendly service.

A good night's sleep without spending a fortune? Look for Bib Hotel.

MUCH WENLOCK – Shropshire – 502 M26 – pop. 1 959 — 18 B2

Great Britain

London 154 mi – Birmingham 34 mi – Shrewsbury 12 mi – Worcester 37 mi

The Museum, High St ✆ (01952) 727679, muchwenlock.tourism@shropshire.gov.uk

Priory★ **AC**

Ironbridge Gorge Museum★★ **AC** (The Iron Bridge★★ - Coalport China Museum★★ - Blists Hill Open Air Museum★★ – Museum of the Gorge and Visitor Centre★) NE : 4.5 mi by A 4169 and B 4380

at Brockton Southwest : 5 mi on B 4378 – ✉ Much Wenlock

The Feathers at Brockton with rm

✉ TF13 6JR – ✆ (01746) 785 202 – www.feathersatbrockton.co.uk – Closed Monday and lunch Tuesday

4 rm – †£ 50 ††£ 75

Rest – Menu £ 18 – Carte £ 20/40

◆ Rustic 16C pub in prime walking country, with snug, characterful inner and relaxing atmosphere. Traditional British dishes made using local produce. Comfortable, country style bedrooms.

The sun's out? Then enjoy eating outside on the terrace:

ENGLAND

MURCOTT – Oxfordshire – pop. 1 293 – ✉ Kidlington — 10 B2

London 70 mi – Oxford 14 mi – Witney 20 mi

The Nut Tree (Mike North)

Main St ✉ OX5 2RE – ✆ (01865) 331 253 – www.nuttreeinn.co.uk – Closed Sunday dinner in winter and Monday

Rest – Menu £ 18 (weekdays except Friday dinner) – Carte £ 29/45

Spec. Home-smoked salmon with horseradish and salmon skin biscuit. Confit of Nut Tree raised pork with celeriac purée. Hot chocolate fondant and Cornish sea salt caramel with peanut butter ice cream.

◆ Traditional thatched village pub owned by a local and his wife; its unassuming interior a real contrast to the quality cuisine. Menus change constantly, relying on seasonal ingredients that arrive at the door: produce is organic, free range or wild where possible. Rare breed pigs and Dexter cattle are raised out back.

MYLOR BRIDGE – Cornwall – 503 E33 – see Falmouth

NAILSWORTH – Glos. – 503 N28 – pop. 5 276 — 4 C1

London 110 mi – Bristol 30 mi – Swindon 28 mi

Wild Garlic

3 Cossack Sq ✉ GL6 0DB – ✆ (01453) 832 615 – www.wild-garlic.co.uk – Closed 1-12 January, Sunday dinner and lunch Monday-Tuesday

Rest – Carte £ 27/32

◆ Relaxed, friendly restaurant decorated with foodie photos. Produce sourced from within 30 miles where possible. Everything made in-house, including excellent garlic-infused bread.

NANTWICH – Cheshire – 502 M24 – pop. 13 447 — 20 A3

London 176 mi – Chester 20 mi – Liverpool 45 mi – Manchester 40 mi

Nantwich Civic Hall, Market St ✆ (01270) 610983, Nantwich.tic@cheshireeast.gov.uk

Alvaston Hall Middlewich Rd, ✆ (01270) 628 473

Rookery Hall

Worleston, North : 2.5 mi by A 51 on B 5074 ✉ CW5 6DQ – ✆ (01270) 610 016 – www.handpicked.co.uk

68 rm – ♦£ 97/123 ♦♦£ 107/169 – 2 suites

Rest – *(dinner only and Sunday lunch) (booking essential)* Carte £ 30/44 **s**

♦ 19C property set in pleasant grounds, with considerable extensions. Main building offers characterful, country house bedrooms. More modern bedrooms in purpose-built rear wing. Smart impressive spa. Formal, two-roomed, wood-panelled dining room overlooking gardens.

NETHER BURROW – ✉ Kirkby Lonsdale — 20 B1

London 257 mi – Liverpool 73 mi – Leeds 101 mi – Manchester 68 mi

The Highwayman

✉ LA6 2RJ – ✆ (01524) 273 338 – www.highwaymaninn.co.uk – Closed 25 December

Rest – Carte £ 16/30

♦ Sizeable 18C coaching inn with open-fired, stone-floored bar and lovely terrace. Extensive menu offers hearty, rustic cooking with a familiar, comforting feel. Very seasonal, local ethos.

NETLEY MARSH – Hampshire – 503 P31 – see Southampton

NETTLEBED – Oxfordshire – 504 R29 — 11 C3

London 44 mi – Oxford 20 mi – Reading 10 mi

White Hart

28 High St ✉ RG9 5DD – ✆ (01491) 641 245 – www.whitehartnettlebed.com

12 rm – ♦£ 65/150 ♦♦£ 115/250

Rest – Carte £ 21/36

♦ Recently refurbished part 17C inn boasts spacious, modern bedrooms, all uniquely styled with a certain "designer" appeal, some in original hotel, others in adjacent new block. Minimalist Bistro.

ENGLAND

NEWARK-ON-TRENT – Nottinghamshire – 502 R24 – pop. 35 454 — 17 C1

Great Britain

London 127 mi – Lincoln 16 mi – Nottingham 20 mi – Sheffield 42 mi

Coddington, Newark, ✆ (01636) 626 282

St Mary Magdalene★

Grange

73 London Rd, South : 0.5 mi on Grantham rd (B 6326) ✉ NG24 1RZ – ✆ (01636) 703 399 – www.grangenewark.co.uk – Closed 24 December-5 January

19 rm – ♦£ 85/95 ♦♦£ 120/160

Rest *Cutlers* – *(closed Sunday dinner) (dinner only and Sunday lunch)* Carte £ 25/33

♦ Small, personally run hotel with tranquil landscaped garden, set in residential area not far from the town. Traditional bedrooms vary in size but all are cosy and comfy; some have four-posters. Classical menu served in restaurant, amongst antique china and cutlery.

at Caunton Northwest : 7 mi by A 616 – ✉ Newark-On-Trent

Caunton Beck

Main St ✉ NG23 6AB – ✆ (01636) 636 793 – www.wigandmitre.com

Rest – Menu £ 15 – Carte £ 23/28

♦ Modern looking pub with tan coloured bricks, a wrought iron pergola and large front terrace. Menus offer gutsy masculine cooking, with the odd global influence. Open from 8am for breakfast.

NEWBIGGIN – Cumbria – **502** L19 – see Penrith

NEWBURY – West Berkshire – **503** Q29 – **pop. 32 675** **10** B3

London 67 mi – Bristol 66 mi – Oxford 28 mi – Reading 17 mi
The Wharf ✆ (01635) 30267, tourism@westberks.gov.uk
Newbury and Crookham Greenham Common Bury's Bank Rd, ✆ (01635) 40 035
Donnington Valley Donnington Snelsmore House, Snelsmore Common, ✆ (01635) 568 140

The Vineyard at Stockcross

Stockcross, Northwest : 2 mi by A 4 on B 4000
✉ RG20 8JU – ✆ (01635) 528 770
– www.the-vineyard.co.uk AVb

34 rm – †£ 189 ††£ 316, ☕ £ 19.50 – 15 suites – ††£ 316/622
Rest – Menu £ 46 – Carte £ 70/99

◆ Extended, bay-windowed former hunting lodge with striking fire and water feature. Some bedrooms have a country house style; others are more contemporary – all boast marble bathrooms. Smart, split-level restaurant with immaculately dressed tables and professional service. French-rooted menus; intricate, detailed cooking.

NEWBURY

Almond Ave .... BY 3
Andover Rd .... BZ 4
Bartholomew St .... BZ 6
Bone Lane .... BZ 10
Carnegie Rd .... BZ 13
Castle Grove .... BY 15
Cheap St .... BZ 16
Chesterfield Rd .... BZ 18
Craven Rd .... BZ 24
Dolman Rd .... BY 25
Donnington Link .... BY 27
Greenham Hill .... BZ 31
Greenham Rd .... BZ 33
Hambridge Rd .... BZ 36
Kennett Shopping Centre .... BZ
Kiln Rd .... BY 40
Kings Rd .... BZ
London Rd .... BY
Love Lane .... BY
Maple Crescent .... BY 43
Market St .... BZ 45
Mill Lane .... BZ
Newtown Rd .... BZ 48
New Rd .... BZ 46
Northbrook St .... BYZ
Northcroft Lane .... BZ
Old Bath Rd .... BY
Oxford Rd .... BY
Park Way .... BYZ 50
Pound St .... BZ
Queens Rd .... BZ
Racecourse Rd .... BZ
Rockingham Rd .... BZ 52
St Johns Rd .... BZ
Sandleford Link .... BZ 54
Shaw Hill .... BY
Shaw Rd .... BY
Station Rd .... BZ
Strawberry Hill .... BY 58
Western Ave .... BY
West St .... BZ 66
Wharf St .... BZ 67

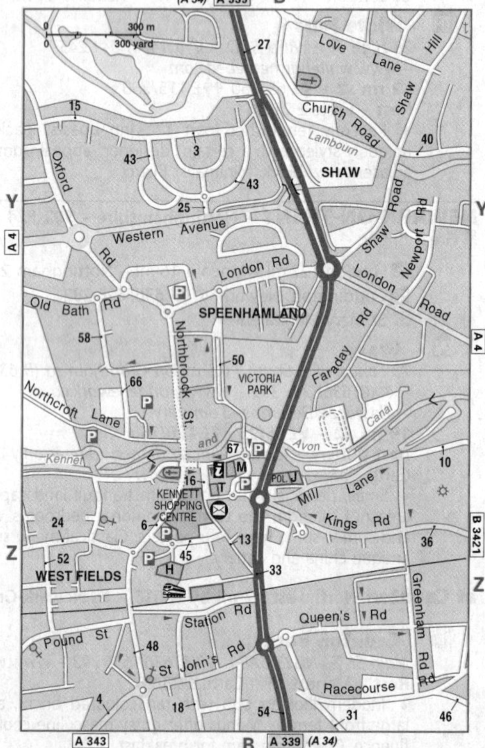

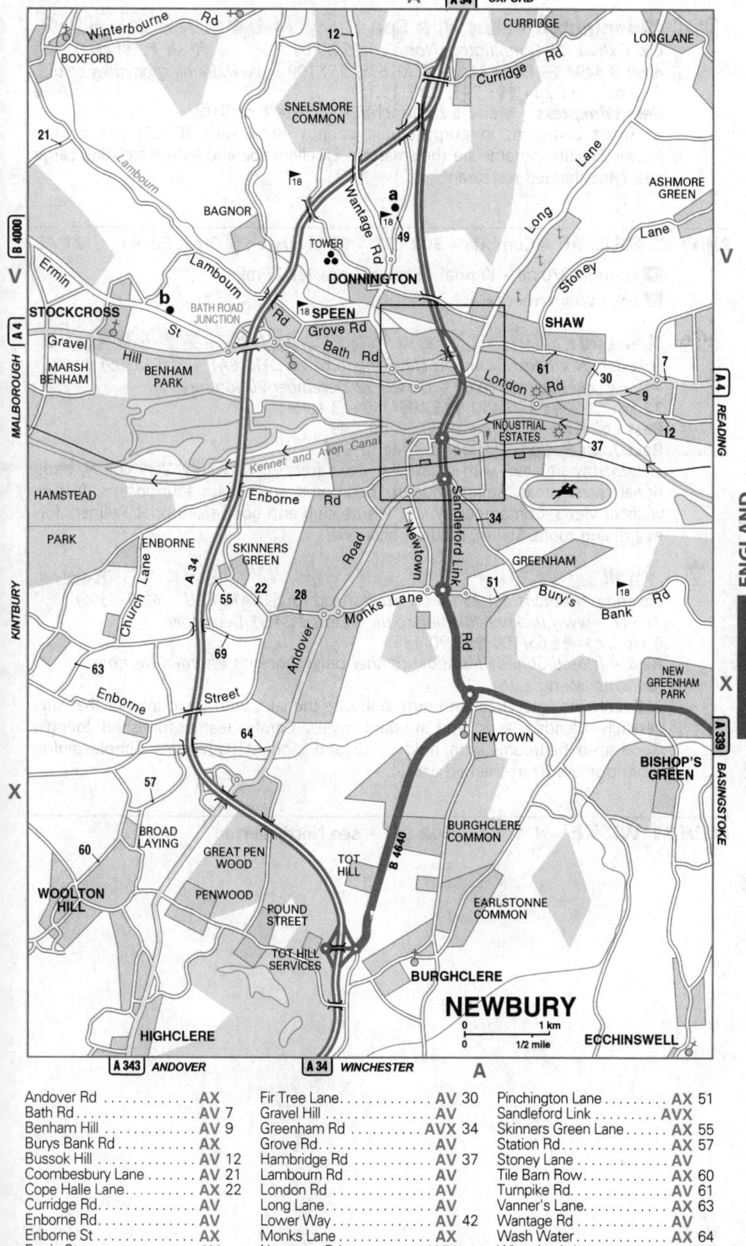
OXFORD
A 34
CURRIDGE
LONGLANE
BOXFORD
Winterbourne Rd
Curridge Rd
SNELSMORE COMMON
Lambourn
ASHMORE GREEN
BAGNOR
Wantage Rd
Long Lane
TOWER
DONNINGTON
Stoney Lane
STOCKCROSS
BATH ROAD JUNCTION
SPEEN
SHAW
Lambourn Rd
Grove Rd
Bath Rd
Gravel Hill
MARSH BENHAM
BENHAM PARK
London Rd
INDUSTRIAL ESTATES
Kennet and Avon Canal
HAMSTEAD
Enborne Rd
PARK
ENBORNE
SKINNERS GREEN
Church Lane
Road
Newtown
Sandleford Link
GREENHAM
Monks Lane
Andover
Bury's Bank Rd
Enborne Street
NEW GREENHAM PARK
NEWTOWN
BISHOP'S GREEN
BROAD LAYING
GREAT PEN WOOD
BURGHCLERE COMMON
TOT HILL
B 4640
WOOLTON HILL
PENWOOD
POUND STREET
EARLSTONNE COMMON
TOT HILL SERVICES
BURGHCLERE
NEWBURY
HIGHCLERE
ECCHINSWELL
A 343 ANDOVER
A 34 WINCHESTER
A 4 READING
A 339 BASINGSTOKE
B 4000
A 4 MALBOROUGH
KINTBURY
ENGLAND
1 km
1/2 mile

Donnington Valley H. & Spa
Old Oxford Rd, Donnington, North : 1.75 mi by A 4 off B 4494 ✉ RG14 3AG – ✆ (01635) 551 199 – www.donningtonvalley.co.uk
AVa
111 rm – †£ 204 ††£ 245, ☕ £ 15.15
Rest *Winepress* – Menu £ 23 (lunch)/29 – Carte £ 30/51
◆ Smart bedrooms in purpose-built country hotel with 18-hole golf course. Newer Executive rooms are the smartest. Excellent spa and leisure facilities. Large bar. Wine-themed restaurant.

NEWBY BRIDGE – Cumbria – 502 L21 – ✉ Ulverston ▮ Great Britain 21 A3

London 270 mi – Kendal 16 mi – Lancaster 27 mi

Lake Windermere★★

Lakeside
Lakeside, Northeast : 1 mi on Hawkshead rd ✉ LA12 8AT – ✆ (015395) 30 001 – www.Lakesidehotel.co.uk – Closed 22 December-20 January
72 rm ☕ – †£ 125/450 ††£ 195/450 – 3 suites
Rest *Lakeview* – *(dinner only)* Menu £ 49
Rest *John Ruskins Brasserie* – Menu £ 39
◆ Superbly situated, with great lake views from conservatory. Very comfy, traditional guest areas. Smart, modern bedrooms: some with four-posters, feature walls or views. Contemporary spa, leisure club and good-sized pool. Refined, formal dining room. Stylish, modern brasserie.

ENGLAND

Knoll
Lakeside, Northeast : 1.25 mi on Hawkshead rd ✉ LA12 8AU – ✆ (015395) 31 347 – www.theknoll-lakeside.co.uk – Closed 24-31 December
8 rm ☕ – †£ 65/100 ††£ 90/135
Rest – *(closed Sunday-Monday) (dinner only) (booking essential for non-residents)* Menu £ 26
◆ Keenly run, late Victorian house opposite the lake, with smart interior that successfully blends classic and modern styles. Comfy, leather-furnished lounge. Good-sized bedrooms with bold décor and modern bathrooms. Simple dining room displays heart-themed art.

NEWBY WISKE – N. Yorks. – 502 P21 – see Northallerton

Steve Wright/Fotolia.com

NEWCASTLE UPON TYNE

County: Tyne and Wear
Michelin regional map: 501
London 276 mi – Edinburgh 105 mi – Leeds 95 mi

Population: 189 863
Great Britain
Map reference: 24 B2

PRACTICAL INFORMATION

Tourist Information

8-9 Central Arcade (0191) 277 8000, tourist.info@newcastle.gov.uk

Guild Hall Visitors Centre, Quayside (0191) 277 2444

Airport

Newcastle Airport : (0871) 882 1121, NW : 5 mi by A 696 AV

Ferries and Shipping Lines

to Norway (Bergen, Haugesund and Stavanger) (Fjord Line) (approx 26 h) – to The Netherlands (Amsterdam) (DFDS Seaways A/S) daily (15 h)

Tunnel

Tyne Tunnel (toll)

Golf Courses

Broadway East Gosforth, (0191) 285 0553

City of Newcatle Gosforth Three Mill Bridge, (0191) 285 1775

Wallsend Bigges Main Rheydt Ave,, NE : by A1058, (0191) 262 1973

Whickham Fellside Rd, Hollinside Park, (0191) 488 1576

SIGHTS

In town

City★ – Grey Street★ CZ – Quayside★ CZ : Composition★, All Saints Church★ (interior★) – Castle Keep★ **AC** CZ – Laing Art Gallery and Museum★ **AC** CY **M1** – Museum of Antiquities★ CY **M2** – LIFE Interactive World★ CZ – Gateshead Millennium Bridge★ CZ

On the outskirts

Hadrian's Wall★★, W : by A 69 AV

In the surrounding area

Beamish : North of England Open-Air Museum★★ **AC**, SW : 7 mi by A 692 and A 6076 AX – Seaton Delaval Hall★ **AC**, NE : 11 mi by A 189 - BV - and A 190

NEWCASTLE-UPON-TYNE

Street	Grid	No.
Adelaide Terrace	AX	2
Atkinson Rd	AX	3
Bath St	BX	4
Bensham Rd	AX	6
Benton Bank	BV	8
Buddle St	BV	13
Byker Bridge	BV	15
Church Ave	AV	16
Church Rd	AV	18
Clayton Rd	BV	21
Coldwell Lane	BX	22
Coldwell St	BX	24
Condercum Rd	AX	26
Fossway	BV	31
Haddrick's Mill Rd	BV	36
High St West	BV	37
Jesmond Dene Rd	BV	39
Killingworth Rd	BV	42
Lobley Hill Rd	AX	45
Matthew Bank	BV	49
Neptune Rd	BV	51
Redheugh Bridge	AX	62
Red Hall Drive	BV	61
Saltwell Rd	BX	69
Shipdon Rd	AX	71
Springfield Rd	AV	72
Station Rd	BX	73
Stephenson Rd	BV	74
Sunderland Rd	BX	76
Sutton St	BV	77
Swalwell Bank	ABX	79
Waverdale Ave	BV	83
West Farm Ave	BV	87
Whickham Bank	AX	89
Windy Nook Rd	BX	91

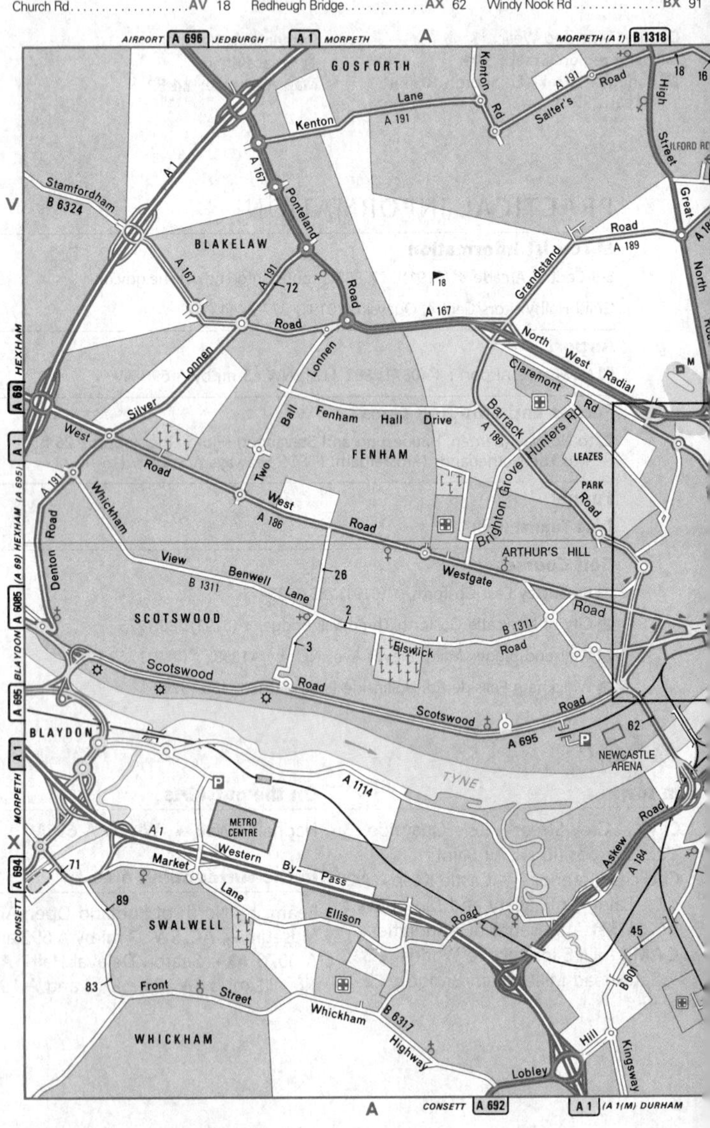

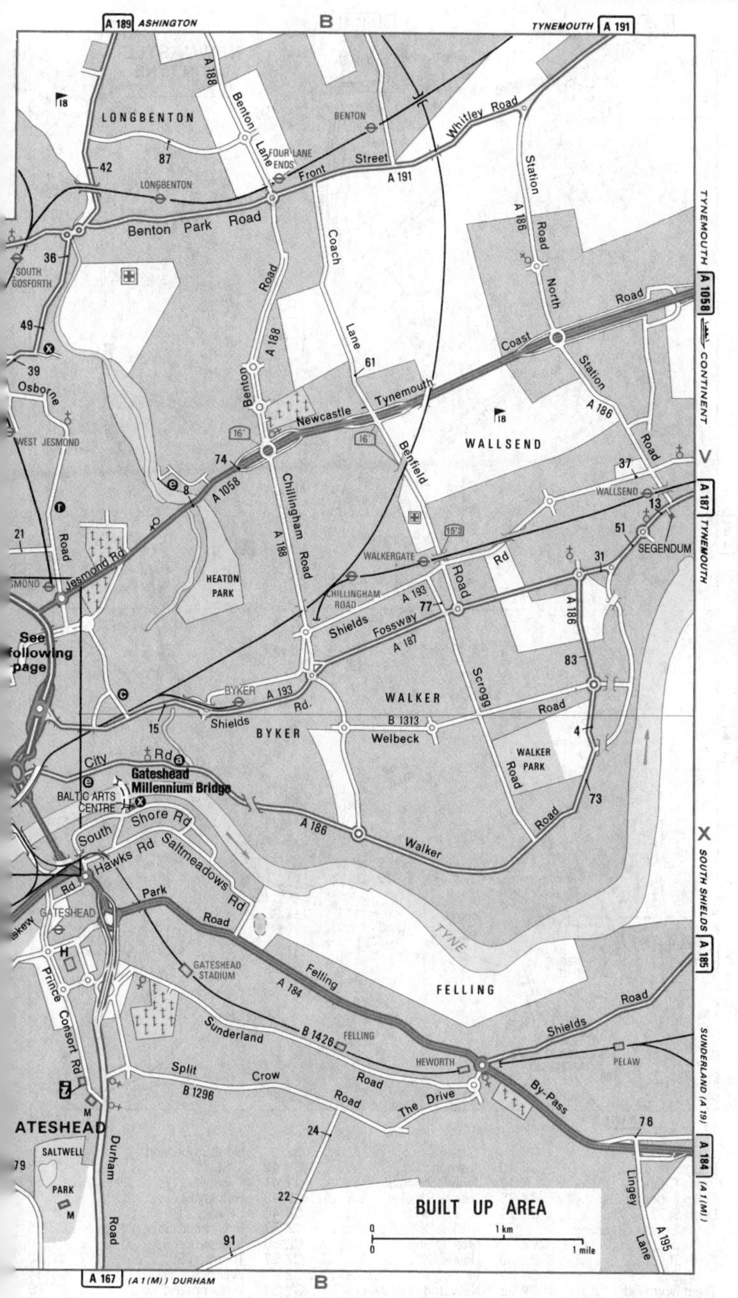
A 189 ASHINGTON
B
TYNEMOUTH A 191
LONGBENTON
BENTON
FOUR LANE ENDS
Whitley Road
Front Street
A 191
Benton Park Road
Coach Lane
Station Road
A 186
North Road
Coast Road
Newcastle - Tynemouth
WALLSEND
Benfield
Chillingham Road
A 188
Benton Road
A 1058
WEST JESMOND
SOUTH GOSFORTH
Osborne
Jesmond Rd
HEATON PARK
WALKERGATE
CHILLINGHAM ROAD
Shields Fossway
A 193
A 187
BYKER
WALKER
Scrogg Road
B 1313
Welbeck
Shields Rd.
City Rd
Gateshead Millennium Bridge
BALTIC ARTS CENTRE
South Shore Rd
Hawks Rd
Saltmeadows Rd
Walker Road
A 186
WALKER PARK
SEGENDUM
WALLSEND
TYNE
Park Road
Felling A 184
GATESHEAD
GATESHEAD STADIUM
FELLING
Sunderland B 1426
FELLING
HEWORTH
PELAW
Shields Road
By-Pass
Split Crow Road
B 1296
The Drive
Prince Consort Rd
ATESHEAD
SALTWELL PARK
Durham Road
Lingey Lane
A 195
BUILT UP AREA
1 km
1 mile
See following page
A 167 (A 1(M)) DURHAM
TYNEMOUTH A 1058
CONTINENT
A 187 TYNEMOUTH
SOUTH SHIELDS A 185
SUNDERLAND (A 19)
A 184 (A 1(M))
ENGLAND

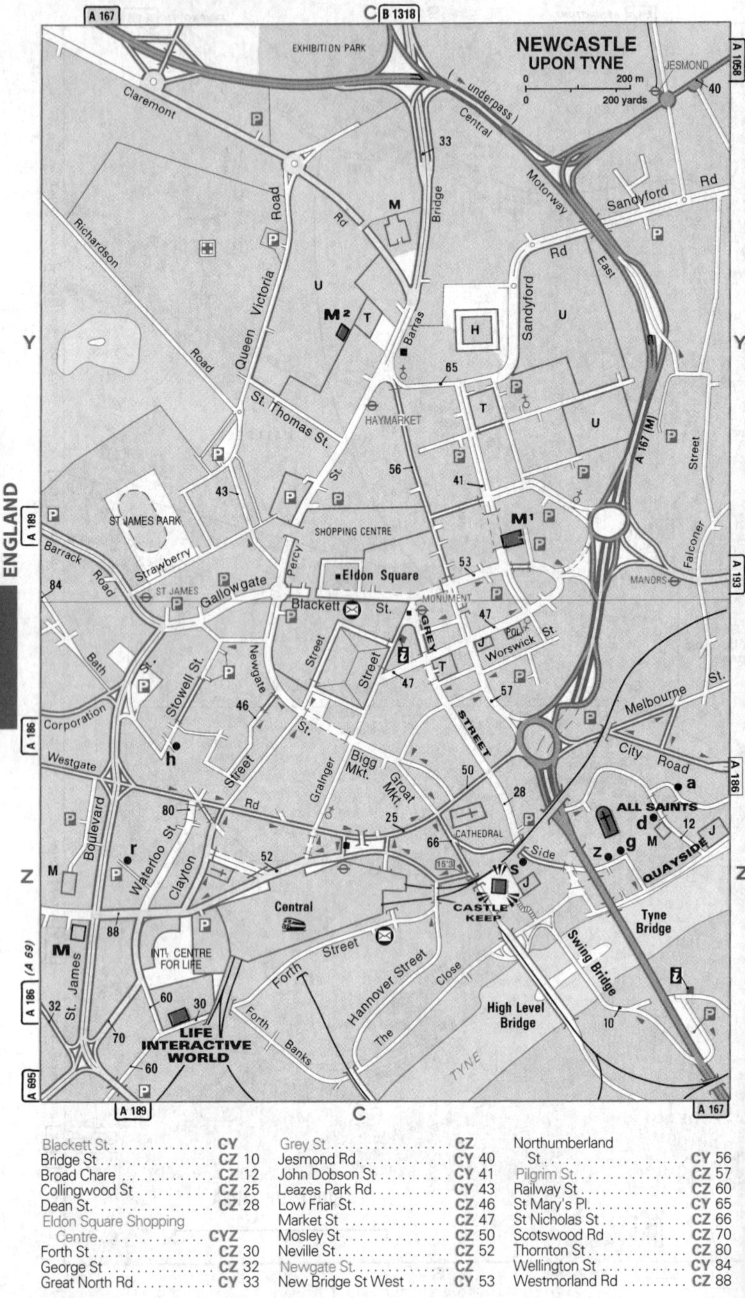

Blackett St.	CY	Grey St	CZ	Northumberland St	CY 56
Bridge St	CZ 10	Jesmond Rd	CY 40	Pilgrim St.	CZ 57
Broad Chare	CZ 12	John Dobson St	CY 41	Railway St	CZ 60
Collingwood St	CZ 25	Leazes Park Rd	CY 43	St Mary's Pl.	CY 65
Dean St.	CZ 28	Low Friar St.	CZ 46	St Nicholas St	CZ 66
Eldon Square Shopping Centre	CYZ	Market St	CZ 47	Scotswood Rd	CZ 70
Forth St	CZ 30	Mosley St	CZ 50	Thornton St	CZ 80
George St	CZ 32	Neville St	CZ 52	Wellington St	CY 84
Great North Rd	CY 33	Newgate St.	CZ	Westmorland Rd	CZ 88
		New Bridge St West	CY 53		

Jesmond Dene House

Jesmond Dene Rd, Northeast : 1.5 mi by B 1318 off A 189 ✉ NE2 2EY – ☎ (0191) 212 3000 – www.jesmonddenehouse.co.uk BV**x**

40 rm – †£ 161/181 ††£ 187/207

Rest – Menu £ 23 (lunch) – Carte dinner £ 46/57

◆ 19C house attractively located in a tranquil dene. Subtle modern touches blend with period features to create a cosy atmosphere. Well-appointed bedrooms differ in décor and outlook. Carefully judged modern cooking is crafted from regional ingredients.

Hotel du Vin

Allan House, City Rd ✉ NE1 2BE – ☎ (0191) 229 22 00 – www.hotelduvin.com

42 rm – †£ 135/170 ††£ 135/170, ☕ £ 14.50 BX**a**

Rest *Bistro* – Carte £ 22/43

◆ Former home of the Tyne Tees Steam Shipping Co., overlooking the river and decorated with photos of ship building scenes. Stylish, chic bedrooms have wine themes; some have feature baths, others boast terraces. Classic brasserie dishes and impressive wine list in Bistro.

Malmaison

104 Quayside ✉ NE1 3DX – ☎ (0191) 245 5000 – www.malmaison.com

120 rm – †£ 105/180 ††£ 105/180, ☕ £ 14.50 – 2 suites BX**e**

Rest *Brasserie* – *(dinner only and Sunday lunch)* Carte £ 26/43

◆ Unstuffy and contemporary hotel hides within this quayside former Co-operative building. Vibrantly and individually decorated rooms; some overlook Millennium Bridge. Brasserie has modern interpretation of French style.

Fisherman's Lodge

Jesmond Dene, Jesmond ✉ NE7 7BQ – ☎ (0191) 281 3281 – www.fishermanslodge.co.uk – Closed Christmas, 1 January and Sunday dinner

Rest – Menu £ 20/22 (weekday dinner) – Carte £ 36/52 BV**e**

◆ Attractive Victorian house secreted in a narrow wooded valley yet close to city centre. Series of well-appointed, stylish rooms. Modern British cooking with seafood bias.

Café 21

Trinity Gardens ✉ NE1 2HH – ☎ (0191) 222 0755 – www.cafetwentyone.co.uk – Closed 25-26 December, 1 January and Easter Monday CZ**a**

Rest – Menu £ 20 (lunch) – Carte £ 34/50

◆ Stylish, open-plan brasserie where subtle greys contrast with bold floral fabrics. Appealing classics display French undertones; best value menus at lunch/early dinner. Efficient service.

Amer's

34 Osborne Rd, Jesmond ✉ NE2 2AJ – ☎ (0191) 281 5377 www.jesmondhotel.co.uk – Closed 2 weeks Christmas, Monday, and Sunday dinner

Rest – *(booking essential)* Menu £ 11/22 – Carte £ 14/26 BV**r**

◆ Small ground floor restaurant with cosy bar, set in the heart of Jesmond. Tasty, modern cooking uses simple, locally sourced ingredients. Good value midweek fixed price menu.

Brasserie Black Door

The Biscuit Factory, 16 Stoddart St ✉ NE2 1AN – ☎ (0191) 260 5411 – www.blackdoorgroup.co.uk – Closed 25 December, 1 January and Sunday dinner

Rest – Menu £ 13/19 – Carte £ 22/28 BV**c**

◆ Art gallery restaurant set in a 1930s former biscuit factory. Through modish lounge to airy dining space with industrial ambience, wall art and recognisable brasserie dishes.

Rasa

27 Queen St ✉ NE1 3UG – ☎ (0191) 232 77 99 – www.rasarestaurants.com – Closed 25 December, Sunday and Bank Holidays CZ**g**

Rest – Indian – Menu £ 22 – Carte £ 16/23

◆ Extensive menu of authentic Keralan cooking; friendly, knowledgeable staff are happy to explain dishes. Vegetarians particularly well catered for. Very good value lunch menus.

ENGLAND

X **Pan Haggerty**
21 Queen St ✉ NE1 3UG – ✆ (0191) 221 09 04 – www.panhaggerty.com – Closed 25-26 December and Sunday dinner CZ**z**
Rest – Menu £ 16 (lunch) – Carte dinner £ 30/35
◆ Situated on the quayside; modern and stylish, with a rustic edge. Mix of regional and British dishes made with locally sourced ingredients; well presented, with precise flavours.

X **Caffé Vivo**
29 Broad Chare ✉ NE1 3DQ – ✆ (0191) 232 13 31 – www.caffevivo.co.uk – Closed 25-26 December, 1 January, Sunday and Monday CZ**d**
Rest – Italian – Menu £ 18 (weekdays) – Carte £ 18/37
◆ Housed within a quayside warehouse, along with a theatre. Simpler café during the day gives way to a bustling dinner. Much of the produce imported from Italy; the cooking is simple and satisfying.

X **Barn Asia**
Waterloo Square, St James's Boulevard ✉ NE1 4DN – ✆ (0191) 221 10 00 – www.barnasia.com – Closed Sunday and Monday CZ**r**
Rest – South-East Asian – *(dinner only and Friday lunch)* Carte £ 23/30
◆ Stark furnishings vibrantly decorated with interesting artwork and bright lanterns. Wide-ranging SE Asian menu offers dishes from Vietnamese classics to some Thai and Japanese.

X **Blackfriars**
Friars St ✉ NE1 4XN – ✆ (0191) 261 5945 – www.blackfriarsrestaurant.co.uk – Closed Christmas, Sunday dinner and bank holidays CZ**h**
Rest – Menu £ 15 (lunch) **s** – Carte £ 19/39 **s**
◆ Late 13C stone built monks' refectory still serving food in a split level beamed restaurant. Relaxed atmosphere with friendly informal service. Interesting and original menu.

at Gosforth North : 2.5 mi by B 1318 - AV – ✉ Newcastle Upon Tyne

Newcastle Marriott H. Gosforth Park
High Gosforth Park, North : 2 mi on B 1318 at junction with A 1056 ✉ NE3 5HN – ✆ (0191) 236 4111 – www.marriott.co.uk/nclgf
173 rm – †£ 120/130 ††£ 130 – 5 suites
Rest *Plate* – *(bar lunch Monday-Saturday)* Menu £ 27
◆ Set next to the renowned racecourse; the most famous hotel in the city. Large, angular building with traditional styling, extensive conference/leisure facilities and bedrooms boasting good mod cons. Equestrian-themed restaurant offers classical à la carte.

at Ponteland Northwest : 8.25 mi by A 167 on A 696 - AV – ✉ Newcastle Upon Tyne

X **Cafe Lowrey**
33-35 Broadway, Darras Hall Estate, Southwest : 1.5 mi by B 6323 off Darras Hall Estate rd ✉ NE20 9PW – ✆ (01661) 820 357 – www.cafelowrey.co.uk – Closed 25 December, Sunday dinner and Monday
Rest – *(dinner only and lunch Saturday and Sunday) (booking essential)* Menu £ 17 (dinner) – Carte £ 27/35
◆ Small restaurant in shopping parade with wooden chairs and cloth-laid tables. Blackboard menus offering modern British cooking using local produce.

NEWICK – East Sussex – 504 U31 – pop. 2 129 — 8 A2

▶ London 57 mi – Brighton 14 mi – Eastbourne 20 mi – Hastings 34 mi

Newick Park
Southeast : 1.5 mi following signs for Newick Park ✉ BN8 4SB – ✆ (01825) 723 633 – www.newickpark.co.uk – Closed 31 December-6 January
15 rm – †£ 125 ††£ 165/285 – 1 suite
Rest – *(booking essential for non-residents)* Carte £ 26/39
◆ Georgian manor in 200 acres; views of Longford river and South Downs. Stately hallway and lounge. Unique rooms, some with original fireplaces, all with Egyptian cotton sheets. Dine in relaxed formality on high-back crimson chairs.

NEW MILTON – Hampshire – 503 P31 – pop. 24 324 6 A3

London 106 mi – Bournemouth 12 mi – Southampton 21 mi – Winchester 34 mi

Barton-on-Sea Milford Rd, (01425) 615 308

Chewton Glen

Christchurch Rd, West : 2 mi by A 337 and Ringwood Rd on Chewton Farm Rd ✉ BH25 6QS – (01425) 275 341 – *www.chewtonglen.com*

48 rm – †£ 385/440 ††£ 385/440, ☕ £ 25 – 10 suites

Rest *Marryat Room and Conservatory* – Menu £ 25/65 **s**

◆ 19C country house in 130 acres of New Forest parkland. Luxurious bedrooms and grand suites blend the classic with the contemporary; most have terraces/-balconies. Impressive leisure facilities include croquet, archery and clay pigeon shooting. Conservatory dining room offers accomplished cooking.

NEWPORT PAGNELL – Milton Keynes – 504 R27 – pop. 14 739 11 C1

London 57 mi – Bedford 13 mi – Luton 21 mi – Northampton 15 mi

Plan : see Milton Keynes

Robinsons

18-20 St John St ✉ MK16 8HJ – (01908) 611 400 – www.robinsonsrestaurant.co.uk – Closed Sunday, Saturday lunch and bank holidays CU**n**

Rest – Menu £ 14/20 – Carte £ 30/38

◆ Smart restaurant combining exposed brick and wood floors with neutral hues and contemporary furnishings. Great value, seasonal menus display an interesting mix of British/European dishes.

ENGLAND

NEWQUAY – Cornwall – 503 E32 – pop. 19 562 1 A2

London 291 mi – Exeter 83 mi – Penzance 34 mi – Plymouth 48 mi

Newquay Airport : (01637) 860600 Y

Municipal Offices, Marcus Hill (01637) 854020, newquay.tic@cornwall.gov.uk

Tower Rd, (01637) 872 091

Treloy, (01637) 878 554

Merlin Mawgan Porth, (01841) 540 222

Penhale Point and Kelsey Head★ (≤★★), SW : by A 3075 Y – Trerice★ **AC**, SE : 3.5 mi by A 392 - Y - and A 3058. St Agnes - St Agnes Beacon★★ (✲★★), SW : 12.5 mi by A 3075 - Y - and B 3285

Plan on next page

at Watergate Bay Northeast : 3 mi by A 3059 on B 3276 – ✉ Newquay

Fifteen Cornwall

On The Beach ✉ TR8 4AA – (01637) 861 000 – www.fifteencornwall.co.uk

Rest – Italian – *(booking essential)* Menu £ 26/55 – Carte (lunch) £ 30/45

◆ Phenomenally successful converted café in a golden idyll. Jamie Oliver's academy youngsters offer Cornwall-meets-Italy menus in a cavernous room bathed in West Coast hues. Dinner is 5 course tasting menu.

at Mawgan Porth Northeast : 6 mi by A 3059 on B 3276

Scarlet

Tredragon Rd ✉ TR8 4DQ – (01637) 861 800 – www.scarlethotel.co.uk – Closed 2 January-3 February

37 rm ☕ – †£ 175/270 ††£ 320/415

Rest *Restaurant* – Menu £ 20/40 – Carte (lunch) £ 20/28

◆ Stunning location to this eco-friendly and decidedly cool hotel: there's a path to the beach and every room has a terrace and sea views. Bedrooms in natural tones with organic bedding. Great spa. Kitchen makes intelligent use of local produce.

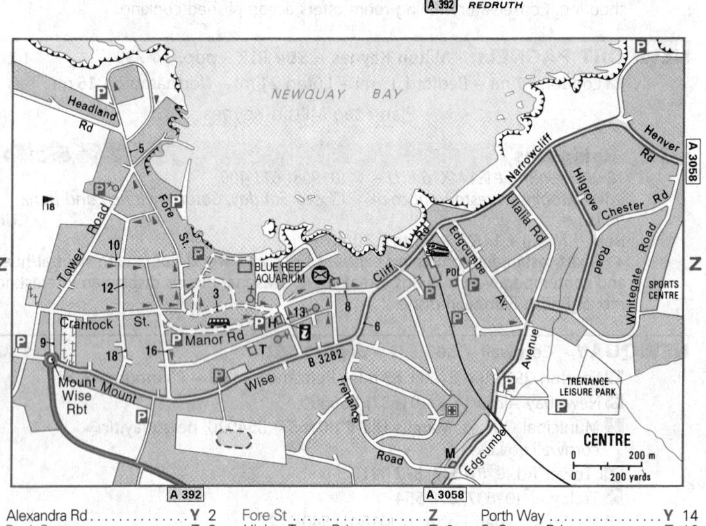

NEW ROMNEY – Kent – 504 W31 9 C2

London 71 mi – Brighton 60 mi – Folkestone 17 mi – Maidstone 36 mi

Romney Bay House

Coast Rd, Littlestone, East : 2.25 mi by B 2071 ✉ *TN28 8QY* – ✆ *(01797) 364 747* – *www.romneybayhousehotel.co.uk* – *Closed 1 week Christmas and 1 week early January*

10 rm – †£ 69/95 ††£ 164

Rest – *(closed Sunday, Monday and Thursday) (dinner only) (booking essential for non-residents) (set menu only)* Menu £ 45

◆ Beach panorama for late actress Hedda Hopper's house, built by Portmeirion architect Clough Williams-Ellis. Individual rooms; sitting room with telescope and bookcases. Enjoy drinks on terrace before conservatory dining.

NEWTON LONGVILLE – Bucks. – 504 R28 – see Milton Keynes

NEWTON-ON-OUSE – North Yorkshire – 502 Q22 – see York

NEWTON POPPLEFORD – Devon – 503 K31 – see Sidmouth

NITON – Isle of Wight – 504 Q32 – see Wight (Isle of)

NOMANSLAND – Hampshire – 503 P31 — 4 D3

London 96 mi – Bournemouth 26 mi – Salisbury 13 mi – Southampton 14 mi

Les Mirabelles

Forest Edge Rd ✉ SP5 2BN – ☎ (01794) 390 205 – www.lesmirabelles.co.uk – Closed 25 December-mid January, 1-7 May, Sunday and Monday

Rest – French – Menu £ 20 – Carte £ 27/41

◆ Bright, modern restaurant overlooking the common, enthusiastically run by a welcoming Frenchman. Well-balanced menu of classic Gallic dishes; superb wine list. Friendly atmosphere.

NORTHALLERTON – North Yorkshire – 502 P20 – pop. 15 517 — 22 B1

London 238 mi – Leeds 48 mi – Middlesbrough 24 mi – Newcastle upon Tyne 56 mi

Applegarth ☎ (01609) 776864

at Staddlebridge Northeast : 7.5 mi by A 684 on A 19 at junction with A 172 – ✉ Northallerton

McCoys Bistro at The Tontine with rm

on southbound carriageway (A 19) ✉ DL6 3JB – ☎ (01609) 882 671 – www.mccoystontine.co.uk – Closed 25-26 December and 1 January

7 rm – £ 115 £ 175

Rest – *(booking essential)* Menu £ 17 (lunch) – Carte £ 25/49

◆ Yorkshire meets France in long-standing restaurant with mirrors, wood panelling, framed memorabilia. Snug bar to plot coups in. Large bedrooms, unique in decorative style.

at Newby Wiske South : 2.5 mi by A 167 – ✉ Northallerton

Solberge Hall

Northwest : 1.25 mi on Warlaby rd ✉ DL7 9ER – ☎ (01609) 779 191 – www.solbergehall.co.uk

22 rm – £ 55/85 £ 95/105 – 2 suites

Rest – Menu £ 17 (lunch) – Carte (dinner) £ 24/40

◆ Tranquil grounds surround this graceful Georgian house, situated in the heart of the countryside. Popular for weddings; bedrooms in main house or stable block. Local ingredients well employed in flavoursome menus.

NORTHAMPTON – Northamptonshire – 504 R27 – pop. 189 474 — 16 B3

Great Britain

London 69 mi – Cambridge 53 mi – Coventry 34 mi – Leicester 42 mi

The Royal and Derngate Theatre Foyer, Guildhall Rd ☎ (01604) 622677, northampton.tic@northamptonshireenterprise.ltd.uk

Delapre Nene Valley Way, Eagle Drive, ☎ (01604) 764 036

Collingtree Park Windingbrook Lane, ☎ (01604) 700 000

All Saints, Brixworth★, N : 7 mi on A 508 Y

Plan on next page

Dang's

205 Wellingborough Rd ✉ NN1 4ED – ☎ (01604) 607 060 – www.dangs.ws – Closed 25-26 December and 1 January Z**n**

Rest – Vietnamese – *(dinner only)* Carte £ 20/35 **s**

◆ Immaculately furnished, contemporary Vietnamese restaurant. Passionately run, food is fresh, tasty, good value and mostly homemade. Noodle bowls are a speciality.

NORTHAMPTON

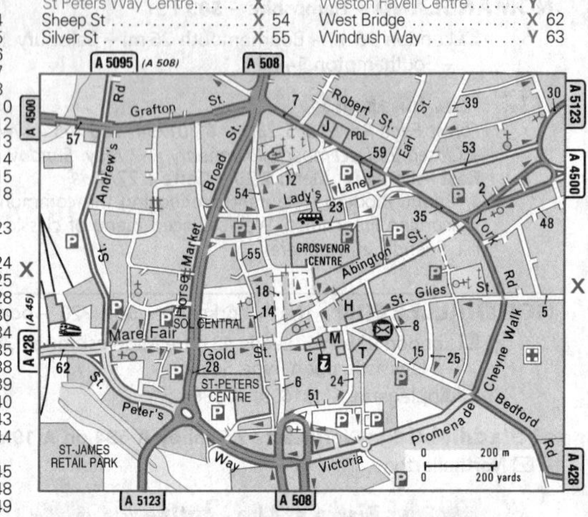

LEICESTER A 5199 · A 508 MARKET HARBOROUGH · KETTERING A 43
(A 45) WELLINGBOROUGH · A 4500 · A 45 WELLINGBOROUGH · A 428 BEDFORD
A 428 (M 1) RUGBY · A 4500 (M 1) DAVENTRY
A 43 OXFORD · A 45 (M 1) MILTON KEYNES

Red House Road
MOULTON PARK
Talavera Way
Holly Lodge Drive
Harborough Rd
Welford Road
Boughton Green Rd
KINGSTHORPE
Kettering Road
A 5123
Booth Lane
Lumbertubs
WESTON FAVELL CENTRE
Mill Lane
Kingsthorpe Rd
Balfour Rd
Kingsley Rd
Harlestone Road
DUSTON
DALLINGTON
A 428
Weston Favell
Road
Way
ABINGTON PARK
A 4500
Wellingborough Road
Billing Road
Billing Rd East
Valley Way
A 4500
Weedon Rd
SIXFIELDS STADIUM
E. Mobs Way
Grand Union Canal
Bedford Rd
A 428
Nene
C
THE LAKES
Upton Way
Danes Camp Way
Towcester Rd
London Rd
FAR COTTON
BRACKMILLS
Nene Valley Way
Road
High St.
GREAT HOUGHTON
A 45
HARDINGSTONE
Mere Way
B 526
1 km
1 mile

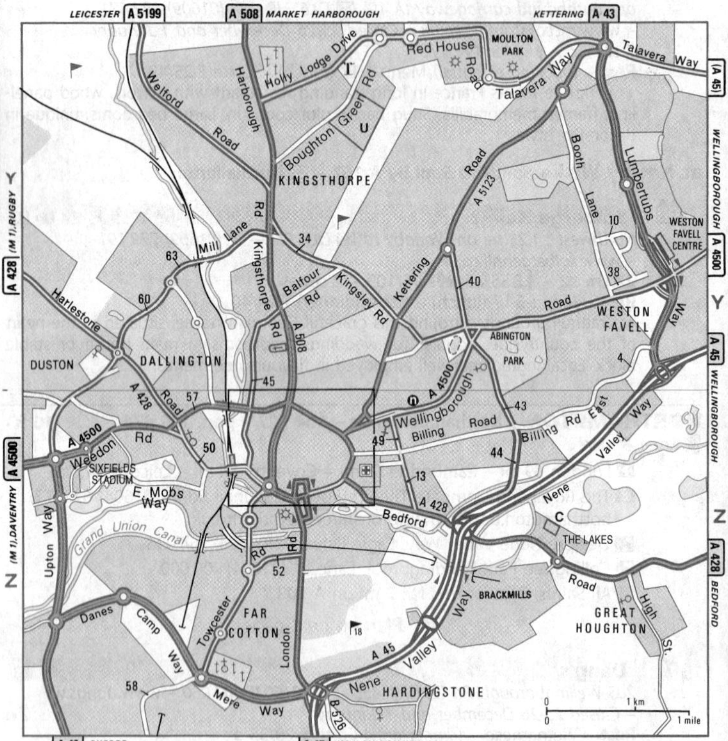

ENGLAND

NORTHAW – Hertfordshire – 504 T28 **12** B2

London 22 mi

The Sun at Northaw

1 Judges Hill ✉ EN6 4NL – ✆ (01707) 655 507 – www.thesunatnorthaw.co.uk – Closed Sunday dinner and Monday

Rest – Carte £ 25/35

♦ Whitewashed 16C inn by village green; dine in bar or either dining room. Hearty, traditional, flavoursome cooking: dishes use East of England produce, and a map points out suppliers.

NORTH BOVEY – Devon – 503 I32 – pop. 254 – ✉ Newton Abbot **2** C2

London 214 mi – Exeter 13 mi – Plymouth 34 mi – Torquay 21 mi

Dartmoor National Park★★

Bovey Castle

Northwest : 2 mi by un-marked single track road.

✉ TQ13 8RE – ✆ (01647) 445 000 – www.boveycastle.com

60 rm – †£ 149/239 ††£ 179/334 – 4 suites

Rest *The Edwardian* – *(dinner only and Sunday lunch)* Carte £ 32/55

Rest *Castle Bistro* – Carte £ 16/30

♦ Opulent castle and sporting estate in a beautiful location on Dartmoor, offering a relaxed, homely feel and a high degree of comfort. Bedrooms feature contemporary touches while retaining a classic edge. The Edwardian has a grill-style menu. The all day bistro with its superb decked terrace offers modern, pubby fare.

Gate House without rest

just off village green, past "Ring of Bells" public house ✉ TQ13 8RB – ✆ (01647) 440 479 – www.gatehouseondartmoor.com – Closed 24-26 December

3 rm – †£ 52 ††£ 80

♦ 15C white Devon hallhouse; picturebook pretty with thatched roof, pink climbing rose. Country style rooms; some have views of moor. Large granite fireplace in sitting room.

NORTH CHARLTON – Northd. – 501 O17 – see Alnwick

NORTH HINKSEY – Oxon. – 504 Q28 – see Oxford

NORTH KILWORTH – Leicestershire – 502 Q26 **16** B3

London 95 mi – Leicester 20 mi – Market Harborough 9 mi

Kilworth House

Lutterworth Rd, West : 0.5 mi on A 4304 ✉ LE17 6JE – ✆ (01858) 880 058 – www.kilworthhouse.co.uk

41 rm – †£ 165/225 ††£ 165/225 – 3 suites

Rest *The Wordsworth* – *(dinner only)* Menu £ 40

Rest *The Orangery* – Carte £ 26/38

♦ 19C extended house set in 38 acres of parkland, with original staircase, stained glass windows and open air theatre. Individually appointed rooms, some with commanding views. Ornate Wordsworth with courtyard vista. Light meals in beautiful Orangery.

NORTHLEACH – Gloucestershire – 503 O28 – pop. 1 923 **4** D1

London 87 mi – Birmingham 73 mi – Bristol 54 mi – Coventry 47 mi

The Wheatsheaf Inn

West End ✉ GL50 3EZ – ✆ (01451) 860 244 – www.cotswoldswheatsheaf.com

Rest – Menu £ 13 (lunch) – Carte £ 13/45

♦ Characterful 17C former coaching inn set in historic village, with stone-floored bar and open fires. Daily changing menus offer mostly pub classics; refined, flavoursome cooking.

NORTH LEIGH – Oxfordshire – 504 P28 – see Witney

NORTH LOPHAM – Norfolk – 504 W26 — 15 C2

London 98 mi – Norwich 34 mi – Ipswich 31 mi – Bury Saint Edmunds 20 mi

Church Farm House

Church Rd ✉ IP22 2LP – ✆ (01379) 687 270 – www.churchfarmhouse.org – Closed January

3 rm – †£ 50/60 ††£ 100 **Rest** – Menu £ 30

◆ Characterful thatched farmhouse with lovely garden, simple facilities, homely feel and personal touches. Individually styled bedrooms look to the church. Home cooked meals use local produce, with breakfast served outside in summer.

NORTH MOLTON – Devon – 503 I30 — 2 C1

London 192 mi – Cardiff 118 mi – Plymouth 87 mi – Swansea 153 mi

Heasley House

Heasley Mill, Northwest : 1.25 mi by Heasley Mill rd. ✉ EX36 3LE – ✆ (01598) 740 213 – www.heasley-house.co.uk – Closed Christmas and February

8 rm – †£ 105 ††£ 140

Rest – *(dinner only) (booking essential for non residents)* Menu £ 30

◆ Former Georgian Dower House in remote Devon village bordering Exmoor National Park. Clean, fresh style with whitewashed walls, rush matting and quirky modern artwork. Hands-on owners. Tea and cakes on arrival. Simple, wholesome cooking.

NORTH WALSHAM – Norfolk – 503 Y25 – pop. 11 845 — 15 D1

Great Britain

London 125 mi – Norwich 16 mi

Blicking Hall★★ **AC**, W : 8.5 mi by B 1145, A 140 and B 1354

Beechwood

20 Cromer Rd ✉ NR28 0HD – ✆ (01692) 403 231 – www.beechwood-hotel.co.uk

17 rm – †£ 82 ††£ 90/160

Rest – *(dinner only and Sunday lunch)* Menu £ 36

◆ Privately owned, peacefully set, part 19C hotel where Agatha Christie once stayed. Thoughtfully appointed bedrooms; newer ones are larger. Attentive service. Handsome dining room with flowers.

NORTON ST PHILIP – Somerset – 503 N30 – pop. 820 – ✉ Bath — 4 C2

London 113 mi – Bristol 22 mi – Southampton 55 mi – Swindon 40 mi

Plaine without rest

✉ BA2 7LT – ✆ (01373) 834 723 – www.theplaine.co.uk

3 rm – †£ 75/95 ††£ 110/125

◆ 16C stone cottages opposite George Inn on site of original market place. Beams, stone walls denote historic origins. Fresh and brighter interior, thanks to keen new owners.

NORWICH – Norfolk – 504 Y26 – pop. 174 047 Great Britain — 15 D2

London 109 mi – Kingston-upon-Hull 148 mi – Leicester 117 mi – Nottingham 120 mi

Norwich Airport : ✆ (0844) 748 0112, N : 3.5 mi by A 140 V

The Forum, Millennium Plain ✆ (01603) 213999, tourism@norwich.gov.uk

Royal Norwich Hellesdon Drayton High Rd, ✆ (01603) 425 712

Marriott Sprowston Manor Hotel Wroxham Rd, ✆ (0870) 400 72 29

Costessy Park Costessey, ✆ (01603) 746 333

Bawburgh Marlingford Rd, Glen Lodge, ✆ (01603) 740 404

City★★ - Cathedral★★ Y – Castle (Museum and Art Gallery★ **AC**) Z – Market Place★ Z

Sainsbury Centre for Visual Arts★ **AC**, W : 3 mi by B 1108 X. Blicking Hall★★ **AC**, N : 11 mi by A 140 - V - and B 1354 – NE : Norfolk Broads★

Plans pages 517, 518

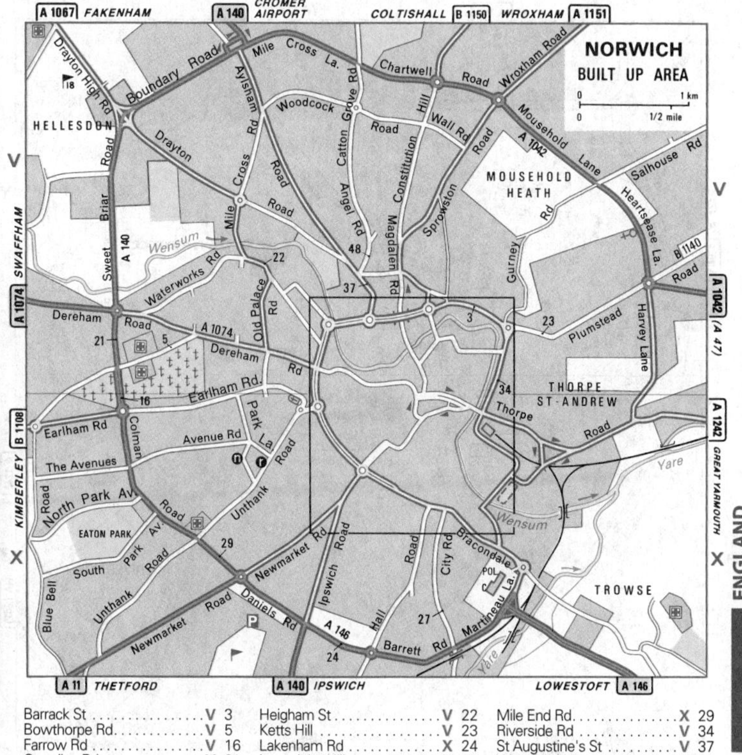

St Giles House

rm, AC rest, P VISA AE

41-45 St Giles St ✉ NR2 1JR – ✆ (01603) 275 180
– www.stgileshousehotel.com YZ**o**

23 rm – †£ 120 ††£ 130 – 1 suite

Rest – Menu £ 20 – Carte (dinner) £ 25/37

◆ Stylish, centrally located hotel with impressive façade, columns and wood panelling. Luxurious 'Deluxe' front suites. Rear bedrooms are quieter and more contemporary. Open-plan lounge/bar/dining room with pleasant terrace serves modern brasserie classics.

Catton Old Hall without rest

P VISA

Lodge Ln., Old Catton, North : 3.5 mi by Catton Grove Rd. off St Faiths Rd.
✉ NR6 7HG – ✆ (01603) 419 379 – www.catton-hall.co.uk

7 rm – †£ 70/85 ††£ 75/150

◆ Attractive 17C house with characterful interior. Individually designed bedrooms include 5 feature rooms; Anna Sewell, with exposed rafters and a vast four-poster, is the best.

XX Roger Hickman's

AC VISA

79 Upper St Giles St ✉ NR2 1AB – ✆ (01603) 633 522
– www.rogerhickmansrestaurant.com – Closed 1 week August, 1 week Christmas, Sunday and Monday Z**c**

Rest – Menu £ 19/35

◆ Traditionally styled restaurant with plenty of romantic corners. Classic combinations of ingredients presented in a distinctly contemporary style. Tasting menu available at dinner.

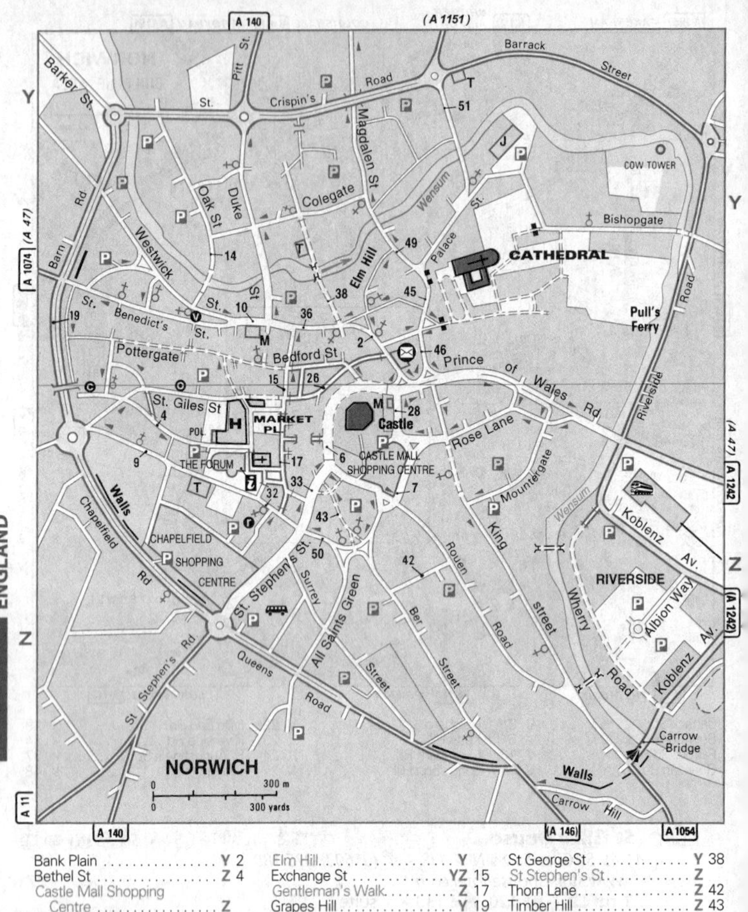

St Benedicts

9 St Benedicts St. ✉ NR2 4PE – ✆ (01603) 765 377 – www.rafflesrestaurants.co.uk – Closed 25 December-1 January, Sunday and Monday Y**v**

Rest – Menu £ 12/17 – Carte £ 12/24

♦ Attractive high street eatery in fashionable area. Simple bistro-style interior with green panelled walls and friendly service. Neatly presented, tasty cooking; good value midweek menus.

Mackintosh's Canteen

Unit 410, Chaplefield Plain ✉ NR2 1SZ – ✆ (01603) 305 280 – www.mackintoshscanteen.co.uk Z**r**

Rest – Menu £ 20 (lunch) – Carte £ 24/32

♦ Smart modern brasserie boasting full length windows, combined with an all day terraced café: a shoppers' haven. Friendly, efficient team serve tasty, freshly prepared modern dishes.

103

103 Unthank Rd ✉ NR2 2PE – ✆ (01603) 610 047 – www.103unthank.com – Closed 24-27 December, 1 January, Sunday dinner and bank holidays

Rest – *(bookings not accepted)* Carte £ 21/27 X**r**

◆ Popular deli/restaurant in the heart of the Golden Triangle, with open-plan kitchen, deli counter and heated pavement terrace. Daily changing menus; Mediterranean and Asian influences.

Mad Moose Arms

2 Warwick St., off Dover St. ✉ NR2 3LD – ✆ (01603) 627 687 – www.madmoose.co.uk – Closed 25 December X**n**

Rest – Menu £ 28 (dinner) – Carte £ 20/30 **s**

◆ Attractive neighbourhood pub with busy, buzzy atmosphere and blackboard of pub favourites. More formal upstairs restaurant offers ambitious, classically based dishes with modern presentation.

at Stoke Holy Cross South : 5.75 mi by A 140 - X – ✉ Norwich

Wildebeest Arms

82-86 Norwich Rd ✉ NR14 8QJ – ✆ (01508) 492 497 – www.thewildebeest.co.uk – Closed 25-26 December

Rest – *(booking essential)* Menu £ 17/22 – Carte £ 25/33

◆ Attractive pub with tree trunk tables, wild animal artefacts, a smartly furnished front terrace and a warm, friendly feel. Good value set menus and daily changing à la carte with a strong Mediterranean slant; accomplished, seasonal cooking. Well-organised service.

NOSS MAYO – Devon – 503 H33 2 C3

London 242 mi – Plymouth 12 mi – Yealmpton 3 mi

Saltram House★★, NW : 7 mi by B 3186 and A 379 – Plymouth★, NW : 9 mi by B 3186 and A 379

The Ship Inn

✉ PL8 1EW – ✆ (01752) 872 387 – www.nossmayo.com

Rest – Carte £ 21/32

◆ Large, busy, well run pub with wonderful waterside views from its peaceful spot on the Yealm Estuary. Appealing menu of pub classics, with desserts from the tried-and-tested stable.

NOTTINGHAM – City of Nottingham – 502 Q25 – pop. 249 584 16 B2

Great Britain

London 135 mi – Birmingham 50 mi – Leeds 74 mi – Leicester 27 mi

Nottingham East Midlands Airport, Castle Donington : ✆ (0871) 9199000 SW : 15 mi by A 453 AZ

1-4 Smithy Row ✆ (08444) 775678, touristinfo@nottinghamcity.gov.uk

18 Bulwell Forest Hucknall Rd, ✆ (0115) 977 0576

18 Wollaton Park, ✆ (0115) 978 7574

18 Mapperley Central Ave, Plains Rd, ✆ (0115) 955 6672

18 Nottingham City Bulwell Norwich Gardens, ✆ (0115) 927 2767

18 Beeston Fields Beeston, ✆ (0115) 925 7062

18 Ruddington Grange Ruddington Wilford Rd, ✆ (0115) 984 6141

18 Edwalton Wellin Lane, ✆ (0115) 923 4775

27 Cotgrave Place G. & C.C. Stragglethorpe Cotgrave, Nr Cotgrave Village, ✆ (0115) 933 3344

Castle Museum★ (alabasters★) **AC**, CZ **M**

Wollaton Hall★ **AC**, W : 2.5 mi by Ilkeston Rd, A 609 AZ **M**. Southwell Minster★★, NE : 14 mi by A 612 BZ - Newstead Abbey★ **AC**, N : 11 mi by A 60, A 611 - AY - and B 683 – Mr Straw's House★, Worksop, N : 20 mi signed from B 6045 (past Bassetlaw Hospital) – St Mary Magdalene★, Newark-on-Trent, NE : 20 mi by A 612 BZ

Plans on following pages

ENGLAND

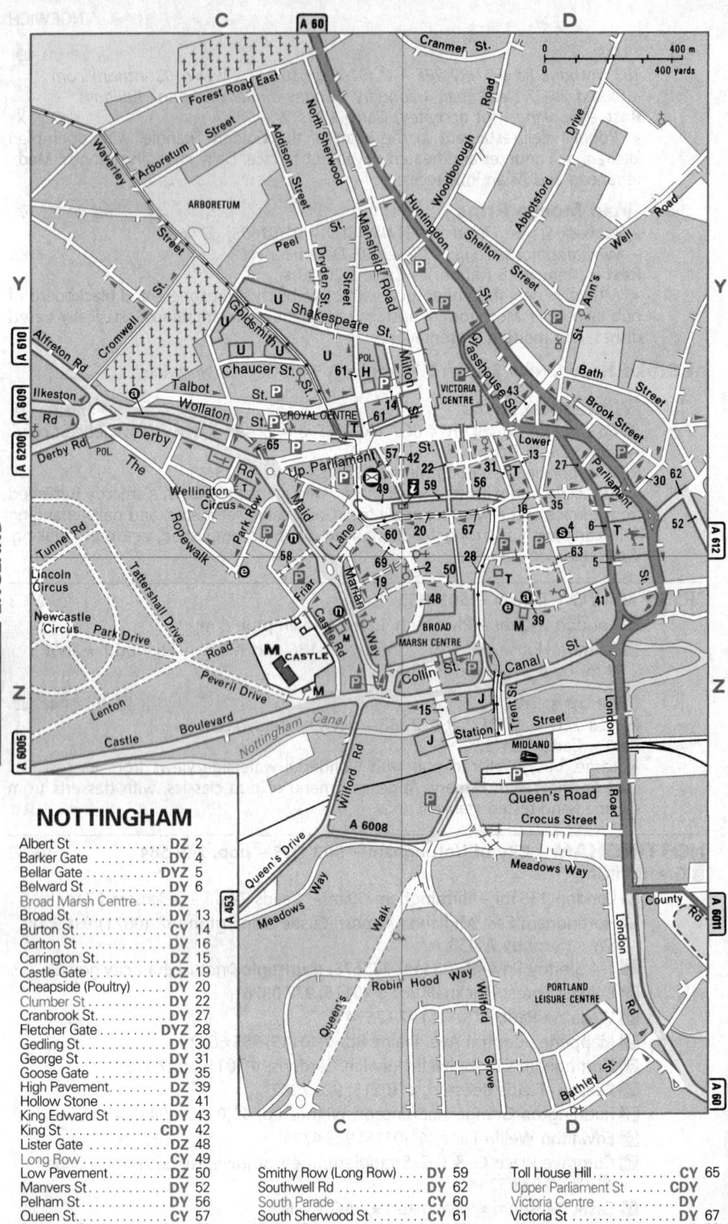

NOTTINGHAM

Street	Grid	No.
Albert St	DZ	2
Barker Gate	DY	4
Bellar Gate	DYZ	5
Belward St	DY	6
Broad Marsh Centre	DZ	
Broad St	DY	13
Burton St	CY	14
Carlton St	DY	16
Carrington St	DZ	15
Castle Gate	CZ	19
Cheapside (Poultry)	DY	20
Clumber St	DY	22
Cranbrook St	DY	27
Fletcher Gate	DYZ	28
Gedling St	DY	30
George St	DY	31
Goose Gate	DY	35
High Pavement	DZ	39
Hollow Stone	DZ	41
King Edward St	DY	43
King St	CDY	42
Lister Gate	DZ	48
Long Row	CY	49
Low Pavement	DZ	50
Manvers St	DY	52
Pelham St	DY	56
Queen St	CY	57
St James St	CYZ	58
Smithy Row (Long Row)	DY	59
Southwell Rd	DY	62
South Parade	CY	60
South Sherwood St	CY	61
Stoney St	DYZ	63
Toll House Hill	CY	65
Upper Parliament St	CDY	
Victoria Centre	DY	
Victoria St	DY	67
Wheeler Gate	CYZ	69

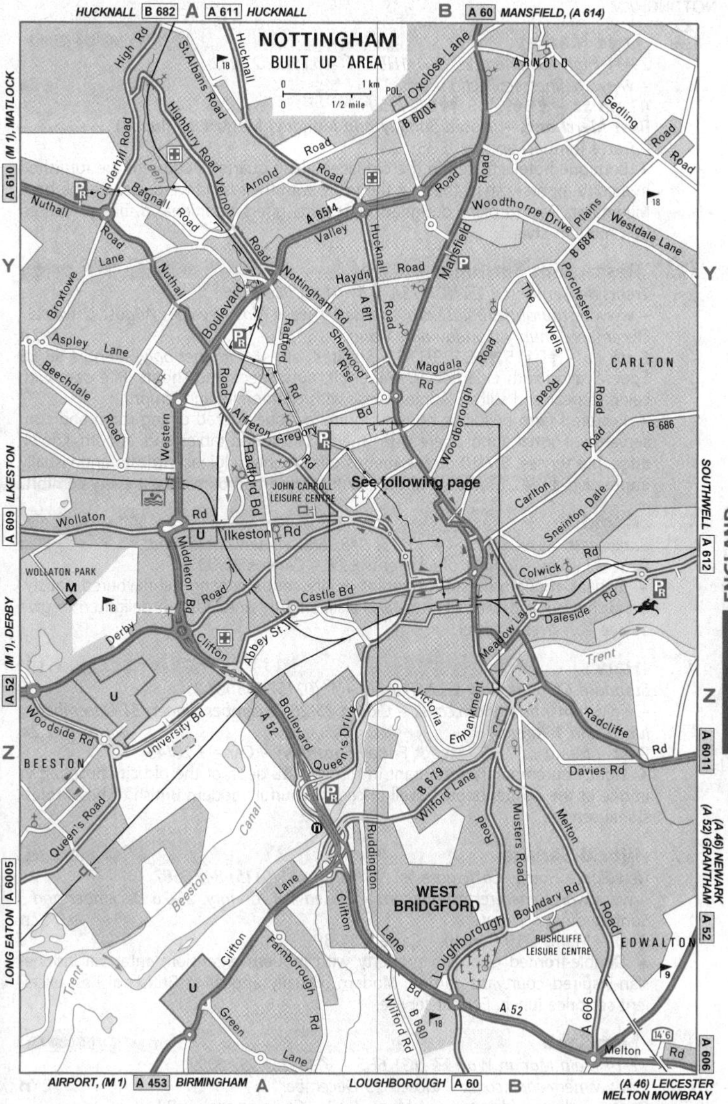

HUCKNALL B 682 A A 611 HUCKNALL B A 60 MANSFIELD, (A 614)

NOTTINGHAM
BUILT UP AREA

0 1 km
0 1/2 mile

A 610 (M 1), MATLOCK
A 609 ILKESTON
A 52 (M 1), DERBY
LONG EATON A 6005
SOUTHWELL A 612
A 6011
(A 46) NEWARK (A 52) GRANTHAM A 52
A 606

Y Y
Z Z

High Rd
St. Albans Road
Hucknall
Highbury Road
Vernon
Cinderhill Road
Leen
Bagnall Road
Nuthall
Road
Lane
Nuthall
Broxtowe
Aspley Lane
Beechdale Road
Western Boulevard
Arnold Road
A 6514 Valley Road
Nottingham Rd
Hucknall Road
Haydn Road
A 611
Radford Rd
Sherwood Rise
Alfreton Road
Gregory Bd
Radford Bd
Road
POL.
Oxclose Lane
B 6004
ARNOLD
Gedling Road
Road
Road
Mansfield Road
Woodthorpe Drive
Plains
Westdale Lane
B 684
Porchester Road
The Wells Road
Magdala Rd
Woodborough Road
CARLTON
B 686
Carlton Road
Sneinton Dale
See following page
JOHN CARROLL LEISURE CENTRE
Wollaton
Rd
U
Ilkeston Rd
Middleton Bd
Road
WOLLATON PARK
M
Castle Bd
Colwick Rd
Daleside Rd
Derby
Clifton
Abbey St.
Meadow La
Trent
Woodside Rd
U
University Bd
A 52
Boulevard
Queen's Drive
Victoria Embankment
Radcliffe Rd
Davies Rd
BEESTON
Queen's Road
Canal
B 679
Wilford Lane
Road
Musters Road
Melton Road
Ruddington Lane
Beeston
Lane
Clifton
WEST BRIDGFORD
Boundary Rd
Loughborough Rd
RUSHCLIFFE LEISURE CENTRE
EDWALTON
Trent
U
Clifton
Farnborough Rd
Green Lane
Wilford Rd
B 680
A 52
A 606
Melton Rd
14'6

AIRPORT, (M 1) A 453 BIRMINGHAM A LOUGHBOROUGH A 60 B (A 46) LEICESTER MELTON MOWBRAY

ENGLAND

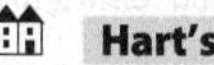

Hart's

Standard Hill, Park Row ✉ *NG1 6FN*
– ✆ *(0115) 988 1900*
– *www.hartsnottingham.co.uk* CZe

30 rm – †£ 125 ††£ 175, ☕ £ 14.50 – 2 suites
Rest *Hart's* – see restaurant listing

◆ Sophisticated, boutique-style hotel built on the ramparts of a medieval castle. Bedrooms boast superb linen and modern bathrooms; Garden Rooms come with a view. Small bar/lounge.

Lace Market
29-31 High Pavement ✉ NG1 1HE – ☎ (0115) 852 3232 – www.thefinessecollection.com DZ**a**
42 rm – †£ 69/159 ††£ 89/159
Rest *Merchants* – *(closed Sunday and Monday)* Menu £ 15 (lunch) – Carte (dinner) approx. £ 33
◆ Boutique hotel situated in the old lacemaking quarter. Bedrooms are furnished in a contemporary style; those at the front, with their large windows, are the best. Minimalist, David Collins designed Merchants offers traditional dishes presented in a modern style.

Restaurant Sat Bains with rm
rest,
Trentside, Lenton Ln ✉ NG7 2SA – ☎ (0115) 986 6566 – www.restaurantsatbains.com – Closed 1 week May, 2 weeks August, 2 weeks December-January, Sunday and Monday AZ**n**
5 rm – †£ 115 ††£ 129/175 – 3 suites **Rest** – *(dinner only)* Menu £ 58/88
Spec. Scallop with elderflower, grapefruit, nuts, seeds and shoots. Roe deer with celeriac, pear and stilton. Apple muesli with chamomile and lemon.
◆ Restored farm buildings housing intimate stone-floored dining room and conservatory. Formal atmosphere with smartly laid round tables and smooth, knowledgeable service. 5/7/10 course menus offer highly original, intricate and visually impressive dishes. Modern, individually furnished bedrooms boast every comfort.

ENGLAND

Anoki
Barkergate ✉ NG1 1JU – ☎ (0115) 948 3888 – www.anoki.co.uk DY**s**
Rest – Indian – *(dinner only)* Menu £ 27 – Carte £ 25/33
◆ Elegant, modern Indian restaurant in city centre serving full flavoured, satisfying dishes cooked with vibrancy and skill. Smartly dressed staff delighted to give advice – or even a taster.

Hart's
Standard Ct., Park Row ✉ NG1 6GN – ☎ (0115) 988 1900 – www.hartsnottingham.co.uk – Closed 25-26 December dinner, 31 December lunch and 1 January CZ**e**
Rest – Menu £ 17/25 (except Friday-Saturday) – Carte £ 28/43
◆ Light, contemporary restaurant in former A&E dept. of the old city hospital; sit in one of the central booths. Well-priced, flavourful, modern British dishes. Professional service.

World Service
Newdigate House, Castlegate ✉ NG1 6AF – ☎ (0115) 847 5587 – www.worldservicerestaurant.com – Closed 1-8 January, 25-26 December and Sunday dinner CZ**n**
Rest – Menu £ 19 (lunch) – Carte £ 31/39
◆ Double-fronted Georgian property with modern extension; enter via Indonesian-inspired courtyard garden. Modern, visually appealing British dishes; excellent set price lunch. Formal service.

MemSaab
12-14 Maid Marian Way ✉ NG1 6HS – ☎ (0115) 957 0009 – www.mem-saab.co.uk – Closed 25 December CY**n**
Rest – Indian – *(dinner only)* Menu £ 17 – Carte approx. £ 27
◆ Spacious restaurant dominated by a wooden copy of the Gateway of India, with some striking portraits on the walls. Authentic Indian cooking: dishes might include locally farmed ostrich.

1877
128 Derby Rd ✉ NG1 5FB – ☎ (0115) 958 8008 – www.restaurant1877.com – Closed Sunday dinner and Monday CY**a**
Rest – *(dinner only and lunch Saturday-Sunday)* Menu £ 10 – Carte £ 10/32
◆ Keenly run, contemporary restaurant set on corner site, with elegant private first floor dining room. Wholesome, tasty, modern English dishes made from seasonal, local produce.

Iberico World Tapas

High Pavement ✉ NG1 1HN – ✆ (0115) 941 0410 – www.ibericotapas.com – Closed 25-26 December, 1 January and Sunday DZ**e**

Rest – Menu £ 10 (lunch) – Carte £ 18/21

◆ Lively restaurant in basement of former city jail and law courts, with vaulted ceiling and colourful Moorish tiles and fretwork. Tasty tapas menu with 'Spanish' and 'World' sections.

at Plumtree **Southeast : 5.75 mi by A 60 - BZ - off A 606 – ✉ Nottingham**

Perkins

Old Railway Station, Station Rd ✉ NG12 5NA – ✆ (0115) 937 3695 – www.perkinsrestaurant.co.uk – Closed Sunday dinner

Rest – Menu £ 15/22 – Carte £ 27/33

◆ Former railway station; now a light, modern, airy restaurant; sit in the conservatory and watch the trains. Classically based menus include sharing boards and tureens; local produce features.

at Stapleford **Southwest : 5.5 mi by A 52 - AZ - ✉ Nottingham**

Crème

12 Toton Ln ✉ NG9 7HA – ✆ (0115) 939 7422 – www.cremerestaurant.co.uk – Closed 26 December-5 January, Monday, Saturday lunch and Sunday dinner

Rest – Menu £ 15/17

◆ Smart, well run restaurant offering well-presented, modern British cooking served by friendly staff. Long lounge area with comfy sofas; airy, formally-laid dining room.

at Sherwood Business Park **Northwest : 10 mi by A 611 - AY - off A 608 – ✉ Nottingham**

Dakota

rm,

Lakeview Dr ✉ NG15 0DA – ✆ (01623) 727 670 – www.dakotanottingham.co.uk

92 rm – †£ 79/129 ††£ 79/129, ☐ £ 12.50

Rest ***Grill*** – Carte £ 26/38 **s**

◆ Situated close to the M1, in the heart of the business park. Spacious bedrooms feature exposed brickwork, king-sized beds and all mod cons; bathrooms have walk-in showers. Spacious restaurant with bar/lounge. Seasonal classics on grill-style menu.

NUNEATON – Warwickshire – **503** P26 – pop. 70 721 **19** D2

London 102 mi – Birmingham 25 mi – Coventry 17 mi

Leathermill Grange

Leathermill Lane, Caldecote, Northwest : 3.5 mi by B 4114 on B 4111 ✉ CV10 0RX – ✆ (01827) 714 637 – www.leathermillgrange.co.uk – Closed Christmas-New Year

4 rm ☐ – †£ 70 ††£ 90 **Rest** – Menu £ 25

◆ Imposing Victorian farmhouse in peaceful rural spot. Spacious, spotless bedrooms - one four poster. Homebaking and tea on arrival. Guest lounge and conservatory with garden view. Meals homecooked on Aga use fruit and vegetables grown in garden. Fine tableware.

OAKHAM – Rutland – **502** R25 – pop. 9 620 Great Britain **17** C2

London 103 mi – Leicester 26 mi – Northampton 35 mi – Nottingham 28 mi

Rutland County Museum, Catmose St ✆ (01572) 758441, museum@rutland.gov.uk

Oakham Castle★

Rutland Water★, E : by A 606 – Normanton Church★ **AC**, SE : 5 mi by A 603 and minor road East

ENGLAND

Barnsdale Lodge
The Avenue, Rutland Water, East : 2.5 mi on A 606 ✉ LE15 8AH – ☎ (01572) 724 678 – www.barnsdalelodge.co.uk
45 rm – †£ 90/105 ††£ 105/130
Rest *Restaurant* – Carte £ 28/35
◆ Privately owned, converted farmhouse with mature gardens. Ample, modern rooms, a large bar flagged in York stone and extensive meeting facilities in renovated stables. Flavours of the season to fore in the Restaurant.

Lord Nelson's House and Nicks Restaurant with rm
Market Pl ✉ LE15 6DT – ☎ (01572) 723 199 – www.nicksrestaurant.co.uk – Closed 25-26 December, 1 January, Sunday and Monday
4 rm – †£ 60/89 ††£ 115 **Rest** – Menu £ 17/20 – Carte (dinner) £ 23/39
◆ 17C townhouse in corner of busy market square. Two wood-furnished dining rooms: one with inglenook; one overlooking the marketplace. Choose from informal brasserie or fine dining menus. Characterful, individually styled first-floor bedrooms. Traditional guest areas.

at Hambleton East : 3 mi by A 606 – ✉ Oakham

Hambleton Hall
✉ LE15 8TH – ☎ (01572) 756 991 – www.hambletonhall.com
16 rm – †£ 190/210 ††£ 220/385, £ 16.50 – 1 suite
Rest – Menu £ 27/46 – Carte £ 58/76
Spec. Assiette of duck with orange and Earl Grey. Whissendine veal with sweetbread raviolo and morel mushrooms. Tastes of Pimms.
◆ Looking over Rutland Water, a beautiful Victorian manor house with gardens, still run by its founding family. Charming period interiors and immaculate, antique filled bedrooms. Cooking is confident and continues to evolve; it is based on classic techniques but with modern touches.

Finch's Arms with rm
Oakham Rd ✉ LE15 8TL – ☎ (01572) 756 575 – www.finchsarms.co.uk
6 rm – †£ 75 ††£ 95 **Rest** – Menu £ 15/19 – Carte £ 25/35
◆ Attractive 17C sandstone inn boasting contemporary Mediterranean-style rooms and a large terrace with beautiful Rutland Water views. Menus feature both classic and modern British dishes. Bedrooms are exceedingly stylish.

OAKSEY – Wiltshire – 503 N29 — 4 C1

London 98 mi – Cirencester 8 mi – Stroud 20 mi

The Wheatsheaf at Oaksey
Wheatsheaf Ln ✉ SN16 9TB – ☎ (01666) 577 348 – www.thewheatsheafatoaksey.co.uk – Closed Sunday dinner and Monday
Rest – Carte £ 20/35
◆ Community pub with traditional fire-lit bar and more modern dining room. Blackboard menu of wholesome dishes with the occasional Thai influence. Appealing nursery puddings.

OARE – Kent – 504 W30 – see Faversham

OBORNE – Dorset – 503 M31 – see Sherborne

OCKLEY – Surrey – 504 S30 — 7 D2

London 31 mi – Brighton 32 mi – Guildford 23 mi – Lewes 36 mi
Gatton Manor Hotel G. & C.C. Standon Lane, ☎ (01306) 627 555

Bryce's
Old School House, Stane St, on A 29 ✉ RH5 5TH – ☎ (01306) 627 430 www.bryces.co.uk – Closed 25-26 December, 1 January, and Sunday dinner in winter
Rest – Seafood – Menu £ 15 (weekdays) – Carte £ 34/40
◆ Smart dining pub offering fresh seafood from the South Coast day boats. Choice of cheaper, simpler bar menu or more adventurous offerings and blackboard specials in the linen-laid dining room.

ENGLAND

ODIHAM – Hampshire – 504 R30 – pop. 2 908 – ✉ Hook **7 C1**

London 51 mi – Reading 16 mi – Southampton 37 mi – Winchester 25 mi

XX St John

83 High St ✉ RG29 1LB – ✆ (01256) 702 697 – www.stjohn-restaurant.co.uk – Closed 26-29 December and Sunday

Rest – Menu £ 25 (lunch) – Carte £ 26/44

◆ Eclectically furnished eatery – a mix between neighbourhood brasserie and formal restaurant. Linen-laid tables and leather seating. Good-sized, seasonal menus of classical, gutsy dishes.

OLD BURGHCLERE – Hampshire – 504 Q29 – ✉ Newbury **6 B1**

London 77 mi – Bristol 76 mi – Newbury 10 mi – Reading 27 mi

XX Dew Pond

✉ RG20 9LH – ✆ (01635) 278 408 – www.dewpond.co.uk – Closed 2 weeks Christmas-New Year, Sunday and Monday

Rest – *(dinner only)* Carte approx. £ 32

◆ Long-standing, personally run restaurant with attractive country views. Homely lounge; two dining rooms display local art for sale. Classical cooking with French influences. Friendly service.

OLD WARDEN – Beds. – 504 S27 – see Biggleswade

OLDHAM – Greater Manchester – 502 N23 – pop. 103 544 **20 B2**

London 212 mi – Leeds 36 mi – Manchester 7 mi – Sheffield 38 mi

v (0161) 777 3064, tourist@oldham.gov.uk

Crompton and Royton Royton High Barn, ✆ (0161) 624 2154

Werneth Garden Suburb Green Lane, ✆ (0161) 624 1190

Lees New Rd, ✆ (0161) 624 4986

Plan : see Manchester

The White Hart Inn with rm

51 Stockport Rd, Lydgate ✉ OL4 4JJ – ✆ (01457) 872 566 – www.thewhitehart.co.uk – Closed 26 December and 1 January

12 rm – †£ 95 ††£ 128 **Rest** – Carte £ 22/35

◆ Stone-built inn overlooking Saddleworth Moor, boasting a large dark wood bar, exposed beams, open fires and photos of the owner's mountain travels. Good-sized menus display modern, brasserie-style dishes and a few pub classics – and at very reasonable prices. Individually styled bedrooms are furnished with antiques.

OLDSTEAD – North Yorkshire – 502 Q21 – see Helmsley

OLTON – W. Mids. – 502 O26 – see Solihull

OMBERSLEY – Worcestershire – 503 N27 – pop. 2 089 **18 B3**

London 148 mi – Birmingham 42 mi – Leominster 33 mi

Bishopswood Rd, ✆ (01905) 620 747

XX Venture In

Main St ✉ WR9 0EW – ✆ (01905) 620 552 – Closed 2 weeks February, 2 weeks August, 1 week Christmas, Sunday dinner and Monday

Rest – Menu £ 27/37 – Carte approx. £ 37

◆ Charming, restored Tudor inn, traditional from its broad inglenook to its fringed Victorian lights. Modern, flavourful menu, well judged and locally sourced. Friendly staff.

ENGLAND

ORFORD – Suffolk – 504 Y27 – pop. 1 153 – ✉ Woodbridge 15 D3

London 103 mi – Ipswich 22 mi – Norwich 52 mi

Crown and Castle

✉ *IP12 2LJ – ✆ (01394) 450 205 – www.crownandcastle.co.uk*
18 rm (dinner included) – ♦£ 100 ♦♦£ 220 – 1 suite
Rest ***The Trinity*** – see restaurant listing
♦ Refreshingly well-run, mock-Tudor style house with relaxed yet professional service; set next to the 12C castle. Smart guest areas. Modern, individually designed bedrooms with good comforts and stylish bathrooms; some have terraces, others boast distant sea views.

Trinity – at Crown and Castle Hotel

✉ *IP12 2LJ – ✆ (01394) 450 205 – www.crownandcastle.co.uk*
Rest – *(booking essential at dinner)* Carte £ 25/34
♦ Relaxed dining room with red banquettes, eclectic art and chic, modern bar-lounge. Wide-ranging lunches and more sophisticated dinners; classical British puddings. Simple yet precise cooking relies on quality, seasonal ingredients. Friendly, efficient service.

OSMOTHERLEY – North Yorkshire – 502 Q20 – pop. 1 217 – ✉ Northallerton 22 B1

London 245 mi – Darlington 25 mi – Leeds 49 mi – Middlesbrough 20 mi

Golden Lion with rm

6 West End ✉ DL6 3AA – ✆ (01609) 883 526 – www.goldenlionosmotherley.co.uk – Closed 25 December, lunch Monday and Tuesday
3 rm – ♦£ 80 ♦♦£ 90 **Rest** – Carte £ 20/24
♦ Set in a delightful village, with a warm, rustic, fire-lit interior. Staff make you feel instantly at ease; unpretentious, classic cooking leaves you relaxed, sated and satisfied. Modern bedrooms have good showers.

OSWESTRY – Shropshire – 502 K25 – pop. 16 660 18 A1

London 182 mi – Chester 28 mi – Shrewsbury 18 mi
Mile End Services ✆ (01691) 662488, oswestrytourism@shropshire.gov.uk
Aston Park, ✆ (01691) 610 535
Llanymynech Pant, ✆ (01691) 830 983

Walls

Welsh Walls ✉ SY11 1AW – ✆ (01691) 670 970 – www.the-walls.co.uk – Closed 1 January
Rest – Carte £ 23/31
♦ Built in 1841 as a school; now a buzzy restaurant. High ceiling with wooden rafters; original wood flooring. Friendly atmosphere. Varied menu offers some adventurous options.

at Rhydycroesau West : 3.25 mi on B 4580 – ✉ Oswestry

Pen-Y-Dyffryn Country H.

✉ *SY10 7JD – ✆ (01691) 653 700 – www.peny.co.uk*
12 rm – ♦£ 86/89 ♦♦£ 130/172
Rest – *(dinner only) (booking essential for non-residents)* Menu £ 37
♦ Peaceful 19C listed rectory in five-acre informal gardens near Offa's Dyke. Cosy lounge, friendly ambience; good-sized, individually styled rooms, four in the coach house. Home-cooked dishes utilising organic ingredients.

OUNDLE – Northamptonshire – 504 S26 – pop. 5 219 – ✉ Peterborough 17 C3

London 89 mi – Leicester 37 mi – Northampton 30 mi
14 West St ✆ (01832) 274333, oundletic@east-northamptonshire.gov.uk
Benefield Rd, ✆ (01832) 273 267

at Fotheringhay North : 3.75 mi by A 427 off A 605 – ✉ Peterborough (cambs.)

Castle Farm without rest

✉ PE8 5HZ – ☎ (01832) 226 200 – www.castlefarm-guesthouse.co.uk
5 rm – †£ 45/47 ††£ 80/85
◆ Large 19C wisteria-clad former farmhouse, with lawned gardens leading down to the river. Comfy open-fired lounge with country views and traditionally styled bedrooms; two are in the wing.

The Falcon Inn

✉ PE8 5HZ – ☎ (01832) 226 254 – www.thefalcon-inn.co.uk
Rest – Menu £ 16 – Carte £ 28/35
◆ Attractive ivy-clad inn with neat garden and terrace, set in a pretty village. Good-sized menus include unusual combinations and some interesting modern takes on traditional dishes.

OVERSTRAND – Norfolk – **504** Y25 – see Cromer

OXFORD – Oxfordshire – **503** Q28 – pop. 143 016 Great Britain **10** B2

London 59 mi – Birmingham 63 mi – Brighton 105 mi – Bristol 73 mi
Access Swinford Bridge (toll)
to Abingdon Bridge (Salter Bros. Ltd) (summer only) daily (2 h)
15-16 Broad St ☎ (01865) 252200, tic@oxford.gov.uk
City★★★ - Christ Church★★ (Hall★★ **AC**, Tom Quad★, Tom Tower★, Cathedral★ **AC** - Choir Roof★) BZ – Merton College★★ **AC** BZ - Magdalen College★★ BZ – Ashmolean Museum★★ BY **M1** – Bodleian Library★★ (Ceiling★★, Lierne Vaulting★) **AC** BZ **A1** – St John's College★ BY - The Queen's College★ BZ – Lincoln College★ BZ - Trinity College (Chapel★) BY – New College (Chapel★) **AC**, BZ – Radcliffe Camera★ BZ **P1** – Sheldonian Theatre★ **AC**, BZ **T** – University Museum of National History★ BY **M4** – Pitt Rivers Museum★ BY **M3**
Iffley Church★ AZ **A**. Woodstock : Blenheim Palace★★★ (Park★★★) **AC**, NW : 8 mi by A 4144 and A 34 AY

Plans on following pages

Randolph

Beaumont St ✉ *OX1 2LN – ☎ (0844) 879 91 32 – www.macdonaldhotels.co.uk*
142 rm – †£ 140/290 ††£ 160/300, £ 17.50 – 9 suites BY**n**
Rest *The Restaurant at the Randolph* – ☎ (0870) 400 82 00 *(dinner only and lunch Saturday-Sunday)* Menu £ 30 – Carte £ 34/45
◆ Grand Victorian edifice. Lounge bar: deep burgundy, polished wood and chandeliers. Handsome rooms in a blend of rich fabrics; some, more spacious, have half-tester beds. Spacious, linen-clad Restaurant.

Malmaison

3 Oxford Castle ✉ *OX1 1AY – ☎ (01865) 268 400 – www.malmaison.com*
91 rm – †£ 155/265 ††£ 155/265, £ 13.95 – 3 suites BZ**a**
Rest *Brasserie* – Carte £ 28/42
◆ Unique accommodation by castle: this was a prison from 13C to 1996! Former visitors' room now moody lounge. Stunning rooms in converted cells or former house of correction! Brasserie in old admin area: modern British menu with fine French edge.

Old Bank

92-94 High St ✉ *OX1 4BN – ☎ (01865) 799 599 – www.oldbank-hotel.co.uk*
41 rm – †£ 128/250 ††£ 172/340, £ 13.95 – 1 suite BZ**s**
Rest *Quod* – ☎ (01865) 202 505 – Menu £ 15 (lunch) – Carte £ 24/38
◆ Elegantly understated, clean-lined interiors and the neo-Classical façade of the city's first bank - an astute combination. Rooms in modern wood and leather with CD players. Lively Italian-influenced brasserie.

ENGLAND

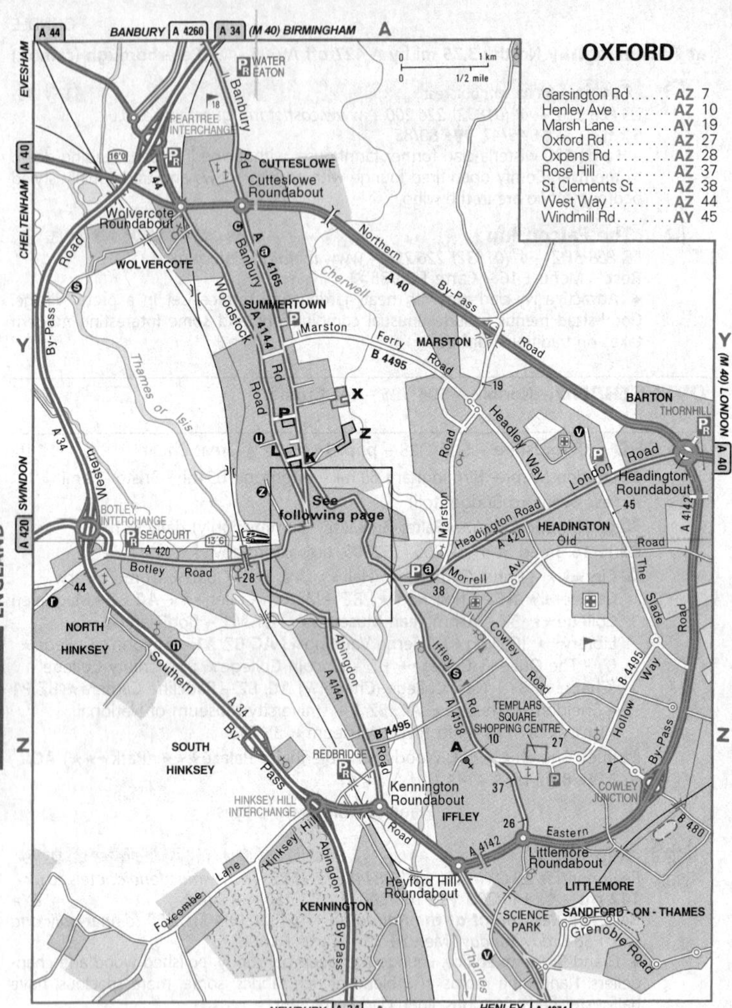

ENGLAND

Old Parsonage

1 Banbury Rd ✉ OX2 6NN – ✆ (01865) 310 210 – www.oldparsonage-hotel.co.uk

30 rm – †£ 128/250 ††£ 172/265, ☕ £ 12.95 **BYe**

Rest – Menu £ 17 (lunch and early dinner) – Carte £ 34/39

♦ Discreet address with airy, minimalist feel. Characterful guest areas include a library, richly coloured bar-lounge and terrace. Some of the stylish bedrooms boast balconies/gardens. Afternoon tea is followed by contemporary Mediterranean dinner: jazz on Fridays.

Remont without rest

367 Banbury Rd ✉ OX2 7PL – ✆ (01865) 311 020 – www.remont-oxford.co.uk – Closed 15 December-8 January **AYc**

25 rm ☕ – †£ 64/84 ††£ 92/138

♦ Stylish hotel on outskirts of city. Crisp, contemporary bedrooms; superior rooms have sofas; rear room quietest. Light, airy breakfast room with buffet counter overlooks garden.

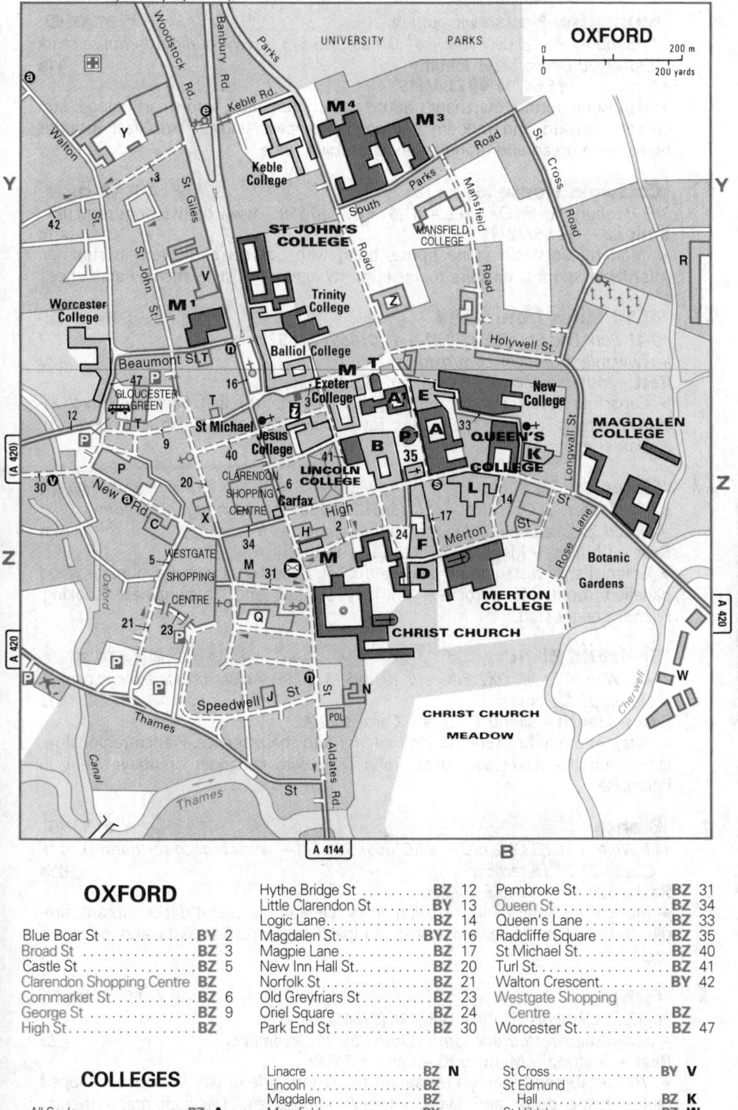

OXFORD

- Blue Boar St . . . . BY 2
- Broad St . . . . BZ 3
- Castle St . . . . BZ 5
- Clarendon Shopping Centre BZ
- Cornmarket St . . . . BZ 6
- George St . . . . BZ 9
- High St . . . . BZ
- Hythe Bridge St . . . . BZ 12
- Little Clarendon St . . . . BY 13
- Logic Lane . . . . BZ 14
- Magdalen St . . . . BYZ 16
- Magpie Lane . . . . BZ 17
- New Inn Hall St . . . . BZ 20
- Norfolk St . . . . BZ 21
- Old Greyfriars St . . . . BZ 23
- Oriel Square . . . . BZ 24
- Park End St . . . . BZ 30
- Pembroke St . . . . BZ 31
- Queen St . . . . BZ 34
- Queen's Lane . . . . BZ 33
- Radcliffe Square . . . . BZ 35
- St Michael St . . . . BZ 40
- Turl St . . . . BZ 41
- Walton Crescent . . . . BY 42
- Westgate Shopping Centre . . . . BZ
- Worcester St . . . . BZ 47

COLLEGES

- All Souls . . . . BZ A
- Balliol . . . . BY
- Brasenose . . . . BZ B
- Christ Church . . . . BZ
- Corpus Christi . . . . BZ D
- Exeter . . . . BZ
- Hertford . . . . BZ E
- Jesus . . . . BZ
- Keble . . . . BY
- Lady Margaret Hall . . . . AY Z
- Linacre . . . . BZ N
- Lincoln . . . . BZ
- Magdalen . . . . BZ
- Mansfield . . . . BY
- Merton . . . . BZ
- New . . . . BZ
- Nuffield . . . . BZ P
- Oriel . . . . BZ F
- Pembroke . . . . BZ Q
- Queen's . . . . BZ
- St Anne's . . . . AY K
- St Anthony's . . . . AY L
- St Catherine's . . . . BY R
- St Cross . . . . BY V
- St Edmund Hall . . . . BZ K
- St Hilda's . . . . BZ W
- St Hugh's . . . . AY P
- St John's . . . . BY
- St Peter's . . . . BZ X
- Sommerville . . . . BY Y
- Trinity . . . . BY
- University . . . . BZ L
- Wadham . . . . BY Z
- Wolfson . . . . AY X
- Worcester . . . . BY

Burlington House without rest
374 Banbury Rd ✉ OX2 7PP – ✆ (01865) 513 513 – www.burlington-house.co.uk – Closed 20 December-4 January AY**a**
12 rm – †£ 64/94 ††£ 84/119
♦ Handsome former merchant's house dating from 1889, with smart lounge, Japanese courtyard and modern bedrooms (compact singles). Breakfast includes homemade bread and granola, served on blue china.

Cotswold House without rest
363 Banbury Rd ✉ OX2 7PL – ✆ (01865) 310 558 – www.cotswoldhouse.co.uk
8 rm – †£ 55/72 ††£ 90/95 AY**c**
♦ Modern, Cotswold stone house, hung with baskets of flowers in summer. Affordable, spotless en suite rooms in pretty, traditional style; friendly ambience.

4550 Miles from Delhi
40-41 Park End St. ✉ OX1 1JD – ✆ (01865) 244 922 – www.milesfromdelhi.com/oxford BZ**v**
Rest – Indian – Menu £ 20 (lunch) – Carte £ 16/35
♦ Capacious restaurant with open kitchen and friendly staff. Fantastic choice includes sizzling Tandoori specialities, Tawa dishes from the Punjab and good vegetarian selection.

Shanghai 30's
82 St Aldates ✉ OX1 1RA – ✆ (01865) 242 230 – www.shanghai30s.com – Closed 20 December-8 January and Monday lunch BZ**n**
Rest – Chinese – Menu £ 12/23 – Carte £ 18/46
♦ Colonial-style restaurant in characterful 15C building; sit in more intimate wood panelled room. Menu focuses on fiery Sichuan and Shanghainese cooking. Friendly, eager staff.

Brasserie Blanc
71-72 Walton St ✉ OX2 6AG – ✆ (01865) 510 999 – www.brasserieblanc.com – Closed 25 December AY**z**
Rest – French – Menu £ 15/19 – Carte £ 22/42
♦ Busy, informal brasserie; striking interior and sharp service; French regional recipes with the new-wave touch: John Dory with coriander or ribeye steak in béarnaise.

Branca
111 Walton St ✉ OX2 6AJ – ✆ (01865) 556 111 – www.branca-restaurants.com – Closed 25-26 December BY**a**
Rest – Italian – Carte £ 20/26
♦ Modern restaurant with casual, friendly feel and minimalist décor. Vibrant, simple, fresh Italian influenced dishes: antipasti taster plates, pasta and pizza are specialities.

Fishers
36-37 St Clements ✉ OX4 1AB – ✆ (01865) 243 003 – www.fishers-restaurant.com – Closed 25-26 December AZ**a**
Rest – Seafood – Menu £ 20 – Carte £ 24/29
♦ Well-established seafood restaurant on eastern side of city, with paper-topped tables, rustic décor and lively, informal atmosphere. Daily changing menus; friendly service.

The Magdalen Arms
243 Iffley Rd ✉ OX4 1SJ – ✆ (01865) 243 159 – Closed Monday, Sunday dinner and Tuesday lunch AZ**s**
Rest – Carte £ 20/28
♦ Battleship-grey pub that's a hit with the locals, boasting quirky standard lamps, eclectic 1920s posters, board games and a bar billiards table. Tasty, good value dishes rely on seasonal local produce. Delicious fresh juices and homemade lemonade.

The Anchor
2 Hayfield Rd, Walton Manor ✉ OX2 6TT – ✆ (01865) 510 282
– www.theanchoroxford.com – Closed 25-26 December AY**u**
Rest – Menu £ 19 (lunch) – Carte £ 22/30
◆ Striking art deco pub with real community feel: host to a breakfast club and regular quiz nights. Chef promotes local, seasonal ingredients and creates tasty, gutsy, carefully presented dishes.

The Black Boy
91 Old High St, Headington ✉ OX3 9HT – ✆ (01865) 741 137
– www.theblackboy.uk.com AY**v**
Rest – Carte £ 17/26
◆ Sizeable pub just off Headington village serving sensibly priced pub classics with a French edge. Homemade breads and pizzas; popular Sunday roasts. Thursday jazz night.

at Sandford-on-Thames Southeast : 5 mi by A 4158 – ✉ Oxford

Oxford Thames Four Pillars rm, rest,
Henley Rd ✉ OX4 4GX – ✆ (01865) 334 444
– www.four-pillars.co.uk AZ**v**
62 rm – †£ 140/190 ††£ 180/240
Rest ***The River Room*** – *(closed Saturday lunch)* Menu £ 15 – Carte £ 20/33 **s**
◆ Modern sandstone hotel set in 30 acres of peaceful parkland leading to the Thames. Bright Connoisseur rooms are the best; some have garden views and balconies. Lovely pool. Great outlook from The River Room, which serves both light and elaborate dishes.

at Toot Baldon Southeast : 5.5 mi by B 480 - AZ – ✉ Oxford

The Mole Inn
✉ OX44 9NG – ✆ (01865) 340 001 – www.themoleinn.com
Rest – Carte £ 23/30
◆ Popular pub with pleasant terrace and beautiful landscaped gardens. Appealing menu suits all tastes and appetites. Sourcing is taken seriously, so when ingredients are gone, they're gone.

at Great Milton Southeast : 12 mi by A 40 off A 329 - AY – ✉ Oxford

Le Manoir aux Quat' Saisons (Raymond Blanc)
Church Rd ✉ OX44 7PD – ✆ (01844) 278 881
– www.manoir.com
25 rm – †£ 460/520 ††£ 580/640, £ 16 – 7 suites
Rest – French – Menu £ 53 (weekday lunch) **s** – Carte £ 98/105 **s**
Spec. Plancha seared Cornish lobster with red pepper and cardamom jus. Roast Aylesbury duck breast with lavender honey, pickled radish and blackcurrants. Croustade of caramelised apples with honey and ginger ice cream.
◆ Majestic property providing the ultimate guest experience: service levels are unparalleled. Sumptuous, open-fired lounges and lovely terrace. Luxurious bedrooms. Cosy restaurant and conservatory offer French-inspired cuisine using seasonal garden produce. Dishes are prepared with skill, clarity and a lightness of touch.

at North Hinksey Southwest : 3.5 mi by A 420 – ✉ Oxford

Gables without rest
6 Cumnor Hill ✉ OX2 9HA – ✆ (01865) 862 153 – www.gables-guesthouse.co.uk
– Closed 21 December - 2 January AZ**r**
5 rm – †£ 50/70 ††£ 80/90
◆ Proudly run guest house with welcoming owner and thoughtful touches in its immaculately kept rooms. Relaxing conservatory looks out onto pretty garden. Flexible arrival times.

The Fishes
✉ OX2 0NA – ✆ (01865) 249 796 – www.fishesoxford.co.uk AZ**n**
Rest – Carte £ 20/40
◆ Lively, family-friendly pub with pretty riverside garden, perfect for picnics. Food is fresh, free range and available all day. Wednesday is steak night; Sunday means a roast.

ENGLAND

at Fyfield Southwest : 6.5 mi by A 420 AZ – ✉ Abingdon

The White Hart
Main Rd ✉ OX13 5LW – ✆ (01865) 390 585 – www.whitehart-fyfield.com
– Closed Sunday dinner and Monday except Bank Holidays
Rest – Menu £ 18 (weekday lunch) – Carte £ 25/32
♦ 15C former chantry house with impressive flag-floored, vaulted dining room. Menus display honest British cooking, internationally influenced sharing boards and excellent desserts.

at Kingston Bagpuize Southwest : 7 mi by A 420 AZ – ✉ Oxford

Fallowfields Country House
Faringdon Rd ✉ OX13 5BH – ✆ (01865) 820 416 – www.fallowfields.com
10 rm – †£ 105/120 ††£ 150/170
Rest – Menu £ 18 (lunch) – Carte £ 21/39
♦ 19C manor house with lawned garden and fire-lit lounge. Spacious, individually styled bedrooms boast lovely views; most have spa baths. The elephant emblem appears throughout. Modern menus list the miles or yards the produce has travelled; much is home-grown.

at Wolvercote Northwest : 2.5 mi by A 4144 (Woodstock Rd) on Godstow Rd

The Trout Inn
195 Godstow Rd ✉ OX2 8PN – ✆ (01865) 510 930
– www.thetroutoxford.co.uk AY**s**
Rest – *(booking advisable)* Carte £ 16/30
♦ Idyllically set Cotswold stone inn with delightful riverside terrace. Menus display strong Italian influences, as well as more international dishes. Popular in summer, when booking is a must.

OXHILL – Warwickshire – **503** P27 – **pop. 303** **19** C3

London 90 mi – Banbury 11 mi – Birmingham 37 mi

Oxbourne House
✉ CV35 0RA – ✆ (01295) 688 202 – www.oxbournehouse.com
3 rm – †£ 50/65 ††£ 70/90 **Rest** – Menu £ 25
♦ Late 20C house oozing charm, individuality and fine rural views; splendid gardens. Antiques abound, complemented by the finest soft furnishings. Stylishly appointed bedrooms. Spacious dining room: plenty of ingredients grown in house grounds.

PADSTOW – Cornwall – **503** F32 – **pop. 2 449** **1** B2

London 288 mi – Exeter 78 mi – Plymouth 45 mi – Truro 23 mi

Red Brick Building, North Quay ✆ (01841) 533449, padstowtic@btconnect.com

Trevose Constantine Bay, ✆ (01841) 520 208

Town★ - Prideaux Place★

Trevone (Cornwall Coast Path★★) W : 3 mi by B 3276 – Trevose Head★ (≤★★) W : 6 mi by B 3276. Bedruthan Steps★, SW : 7 mi by B 3276 – Pencarrow★, SE : 11 mi by A 389

Metropole
Station Rd ✉ PL28 8DB – ✆ (01841) 532 486 – www.the-metropole.co.uk
58 rm – †£ 92/170 ††£ 144/226 BY**a**
Rest – *(bar lunch Monday-Saturday)* Menu £ 30 – Carte approx. £ 30
♦ Grand 19C hotel perched on a cliff above the old railway station, just a short walk from town. Characterful, well-appointed guest areas. Smart, contemporary bedrooms; No.6 boasts great harbour and estuary views. Simply prepared lunches; more elaborate dinners.

ENGLAND

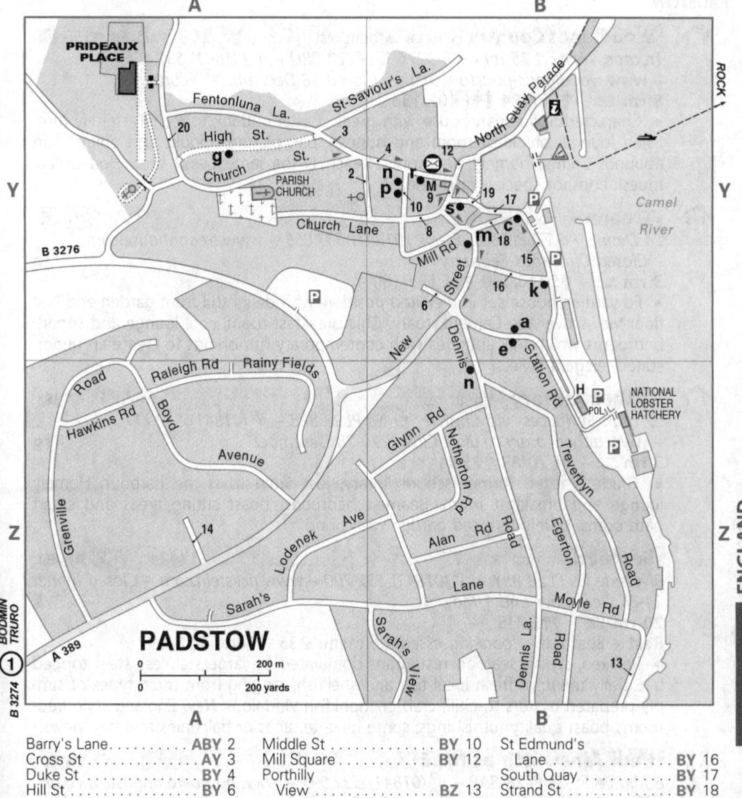

Old Custom House Inn

South Quay ✉ *PL28 8BL*
– ✆ *(01841) 532 359*
– *oldcustomhousepadstow.co.uk* BY**c**
21 rm ☕ – ††£ 120/140
Rest *Pescadou* – Seafood – *(booking essential)* Menu £ 12 (lunch)
– Carte £ 29/33

♦ Well-run, slate hotel; formerly a grain store and exciseman's house. Smart beauty studio and ice cream parlour. Nautically themed bedrooms feature good mod cons – some have roll-top baths or harbour/estuary views. Traditional bar and open-plan seafood restaurant.

Treverbyn House without rest

Station Rd ✉ *PL28 8DA*
– ✆ *(01841) 532 855*
– *www.treverbynhouse.com*
– *Closed 20 December-7 February* BY**e**
5 rm ☕ – †£ 100 ††£ 120

♦ Charming Edwardian house built for a wine merchant. Comfortable bedrooms boast polished floors and interesting furniture from local sale rooms – one has a huge roll-top bath; some have harbour views. Breakfast in the garden or lovely dining room. Delightful owner.

Woodlands Country House without rest

Treator, West : 1.25 mi on B 3276 ✉ PL28 8RU – ✆ (01841) 532 426 – www.woodlands-padstow.co.uk – Closed 18 December-1 February

8 rm – £ 76/84 £ 102/136

◆ Characterful Victorian house with great coastal outlook to rear. Tastefully furnished lounge, breakfast room and honesty bar; pictures, books and objets d'art abound. Comfy, homely bedrooms; Beach is the largest and best. Homemade muesli and hot specials at breakfast.

Treann without rest

24 Dennis Rd ✉ PL28 8DE – ✆ (01841) 533 855 – www.treannhouse.com – Closed Christmas-February BZ**n**

3 rm – £ 110/160 £ 130/180

◆ Edwardian house set in elevated position, with delightful front garden and first floor views over the Camel Estuary. Chic breakfast room, cool lounge and superb bedrooms which mix antiques with contemporary furnishings to create an understated, elegant style.

Althea Library without rest

27 High St, (access via Church St.) ✉ PL28 8BB – ✆ (01841) 532 717 – www.althealibrary.co.uk – Closed 20-28 December AY**g**

3 rm – £ 70/88 £ 94

◆ Grade II listed former school library, just 5min from the harbour. Homely lounge and breakfast room. Beamed bedrooms boast sitting areas and smart bathrooms. Lovely terraced garden with pond.

Seafood with rm

rest,

Riverside ✉ PL28 8BY – ✆ (01841) 532 700 – www.rickstein.com – Closed dinner 24-26 December and 1 May BY**k**

20 rm – £ 235

Rest – Seafood – *(booking essential)* Menu £ 35 – Carte £ 38/65

◆ Relaxed, stylish seafood restaurant dominated by large stainless steel topped bar. Daily menu of fresh local fish and shellfish, ranging from three types of simply prepared oysters to chilli crab or monkfish vindaloo. New England style bedrooms boast quality furnishings; some have terraces or balconies and bay views.

Paul Ainsworth at No.6

6 Middle St ✉ PL28 8AP – ✆ (01841) 532 093 – www.number6inpadstow.co.uk – Closed 8 January-1 February, 24-26 December, Sunday-Monday February-May and Monday May-November BY**n**

Rest – Menu £ 15 (lunch) **s** – Carte £ 31/36 **s**

◆ Delightful Georgian townhouse on a harbour backwater. Small library where tea and local scones are served; L-shaped bar and restaurant with black & white floor tiles. Relaxed air and friendly service. Precise, modern, seasonal cooking with artistic presentation.

St Petroc's with rm

4 New St ✉ PL28 8EA – ✆ (01841) 532 700 – www.rickstein.com – Closed dinner 24 December-26 December and 1 May BY**m**

10 rm – £ 270 – 2 suites

Rest – Seafood – *(booking essential)* Carte £ 33/39

◆ Attractive house on a steep hill, with pine-furnished bistro and terrace running down one side. Unfussy, largely seafood-based menu offers simply prepared, old-fashioned favourites. Smart, well-appointed bedrooms in house/annexe; small lounge and quiet library.

Custard

1A The Strand ✉ PL28 8AJ – ✆ (01841) 532 565 – www.custardpadstow.com – Closed 2-18 January, 31 October-11 November, 25-28 December, Sunday-Tuesday September-Easter and Sunday Easter-June BY**s**

Rest – Carte £ 22/34

◆ Homely little eatery with kitsch touches that evoke childhood memories. Flexible all-day menu ranges from afternoon tea and light snacks to 3 courses. Simple, flavoursome cooking uses local ingredients. British comfort dishes and old-fashioned classics feature.

Rick Stein's Café with rm

10 Middle St ✉ PL28 8AP – ✆ (01841) 532 700 – www.rickstein.com – Closed dinner 25-26 December and 2 May BY**p**

3 rm – ♦£ 145 ♦♦£ 145

Rest – *(booking essential at dinner)* Menu £ 22 – Carte £ 26/32

♦ Deceptively large café hidden behind a tiny shop front on a small side street. Concise, seasonally changing menu of tasty, unfussy cooking with influences from Thailand, Morocco and the Med. Homemade bread to start; great value set menus. Comfy, simply furnished bedrooms. Breakfast in café or small courtyard garden.

Margot's

11 Duke St ✉ PL28 8AB – ✆ (01841) 533 441 – Closed January, 24-31 December, Sunday and Monday BY**r**

Rest – *(booking essential at dinner)* Menu £ 23/30

♦ Small yellow and blue bistro with relaxed atmosphere and loyal local following. Daily menu features the latest seasonal produce. Dinner also offers a good value set selection and tasting menu.

at Little Petherick South : 3 mi on A 389 – ✉ Wadebridge

Molesworth Manor without rest

✉ PL27 7QT – ✆ (01841) 540 292 – www.molesworth.co.uk – Restricted opening in winter

9 rm – ♦£ 75 ♦♦£ 95/110

♦ Part 17C and 19C former rectory. Charming individual establishment with inviting country house atmosphere amid antique furniture and curios. Rooms furnished in period style.

at St Issey South : 3.5 mi on A 389 – ✉ Wadebridge

Higher Trevorrick Country House

Northwest : 0.75 mi by Burgois rd on Sea Mills and Trevorrick rd. ✉ PL27 7QH ✆ (01841) 540 943 – www.higher-trevorrick.co.uk – Closed 16 December-31 January

3 rm – ♦£ 66/112 ♦♦£ 119/150 **Rest** – Menu £ 25

♦ Restored property with spectacular first floor views out over Camel Estuary and towards Rock. Spacious, well-kept bedrooms. Experienced, personable owners. No children policy. Daily changing menu served in pleasant conservatory overlooking garden.

at St Merryn West : 2.5 mi by A 389 on B 3276 – **503** F32 – ✉ Padstow

Rosel & Co.

The Dog House ✉ PL28 8NF – ✆ (01841) 521 289 – www.roselandco.co.uk – March-October. Closed Sunday and Monday

Rest – *(dinner only)* Menu £ 32

♦ Simply styled, brightly lit restaurant with chunky wooden tables, open kitchen and warm, relaxed ambience. Concise menu of precise, flavourful cooking: well-sourced ingredients used to create classic combinations with interesting modern twists.

The Cornish Arms

Churchtown ✉ PL28 8ND – ✆ (01841) 520 288 – www.rickstein.com

Rest – Carte £ 16/30

♦ A real locals pub, surprisingly leased by Rick Stein. Sound, sensibly priced cooking offer typical pub dishes and a few fish specials; and doesn't exclude the regulars. Smart terrace.

at Constantine Bay West : 4 mi by B 3276 – ✉ Padstow

Treglos rm, rest,

✉ PL28 8JH – ✆ (01841) 520 727 – www.tregloshotel.com – April-October

38 rm – ♦£ 65/149 ♦♦£ 150/199 – 4 suites

Rest – *(bar lunch Monday-Saturday)* Menu £ 29

♦ An extensive, family run building surrounded by garden. Facilities include games rooms, children's play area and a lounge bar. Consistently decorated, bright, neat bedrooms. Smart attire the code in very comfortable dining room.

ENGLAND

PAINSWICK – Gloucestershire – 503 N28 – pop. 1 666 Great Britain 4 C1

London 107 mi – Bristol 35 mi – Cheltenham 10 mi – Gloucester 7 mi

Town★

Cotswolds 88

Kemps Ln ✉ GL6 6YB – ✆ (01452) 813 688 – www.cotswolds88hotel.com

17 rm – ♦£ 165/185 ♦♦£ 250/450

Rest – Menu £ 15 – Carte approx. £ 40

◆ Stone Regency style house with neat garden and terrace. Bold stylish colours, quirky furnishings and striking fixtures abound. Eclectic bedrooms; modern bathrooms. Restaurant offers modern menu of organic produce.

PANGBOURNE – West Berkshire – 504 Q29 10 B3

London 51 mi – Hillingdon 38 mi – Reading 14 mi – Oxford 23 mi

Elephant

Church Rd ✉ RG8 7AR – ✆ (0118) 984 22 44 – www.elephanthotel.co.uk

22 rm – ♦£ 100/120 ♦♦£ 160

Rest – Menu £ 10 (lunch) – Carte (dinner) £ 27/44

◆ Smart, stylish hotel with subtle colonial feel and pleasant rear garden. Individually decorated bedrooms have excellent facilities; some annexe rooms have terraces. Dark wood furnished restaurant boasts modern, internationally influenced brasserie menu.

PATELEY BRIDGE – North Yorkshire – 502 O21 – pop. 2 504 22 B2
– ✉ Harrogate Great Britain

London 225 mi – Leeds 28 mi – Middlesbrough 46 mi – York 32 mi

18 High St ✆ (01423) 711147, pbtic@harrogate.gov.uk

Fountains Abbey★★★ **AC** - Studley Royal **AC** (≤★ from Anne Boleyn's Seat) - Fountains Hall (Fa 0.5ade★), NE : 8.5 mi by B 6265

at Ramsgill-in-Nidderdale Northwest : 5 mi by Low Wath Rd – ✉ Harrogate

Yorke Arms (Frances Atkins) with rm

✉ HG3 5RL – ✆ (01423) 755 243 – www.yorke-arms.co.uk

12 rm – ♦£ 100/150 ♦♦£ 180 – 1 suite

Rest – *(closed Sunday dinner to non-residents)* Menu £ 30 (lunch) – Carte (dinner) £ 34/58

Spec. Pigeon with blackcurrant jelly, foie gras and broad beans. Salmon with cucumber, caviar and mixed grains. Salted caramel with vanilla praline fruits.

◆ Enthusiatically run, charming part 17C former shooting lodge with antiques, beamed ceilings and open fires. Measured and accomplished cooking from a classically-based, seasonal menu. Lavishly furnished bedrooms.

PATRICK BROMPTON – North Yorkshire – 502 P21 – ✉ Bedale 22 B1

London 242 mi – Newcastle upon Tyne 58 mi – York 43 mi

Elmfield House without rest

Arrathorne, Northwest : 2.25 mi by A 684 on Richmond rd ✉ DL8 1NE – ✆ (01677) 450 558 – www.elmfieldhouse.co.uk

7 rm – ♦£ 71 ♦♦£ 72/86

◆ Spacious, uncluttered guest house set in peaceful farmland, with nearby fishing lake and 14 acre forest. Neat, classically styled bedrooms with modern touches; some four-posters.

Mill Close Farm without rest

Patrick Brompton ✉ DL8 1JY – ✆ (01677) 450 257 – www.millclose.co.uk – Closed January and December

3 rm – ♦£ 60/65 ♦♦£ 80/95

◆ Modernised farmhouse with walled garden and summerhouse. Bedrooms blend contemporary furnishings with traditional features and have an uncluttered, homely feel; two boast whirlpool baths.

PATTISWICK – Essex – see Coggeshall

PAULERSPURY – Northants. – 503 R27 – see Towcester

PAXFORD – Gloucestershire – 504 O27 – see Chipping Camden

PENN – Buckinghamshire – 504 R/S29 – pop. 3 779 — 11 D2

London 31 mi – High Wycombe 4 mi – Oxford 36 mi

The Old Queens Head

Hammersley Ln ✉ HP10 8EY – ✆ (01494) 813 371
– www.oldqueensheadpenn.co.uk – Closed 25-26 December
Rest – Carte £ 20/27
◆ Lively pub with characterful rustic feel, part-dating back to 1666; head for the old barn. Menus offer generous, hearty dishes and some appealing sides. Home-made puddings are a must.

PENRITH – Cumbria – 501 L19 – pop. 14 471 — 21 B2

London 290 mi – Carlisle 24 mi – Kendal 31 mi – Lancaster 48 mi
Robinsons School, Middlegate ✆ (01768) 867466, pen.tic@eden.gov.uk
- Rheged, Redhills, Penrith ✆ (01768) 860034, tic@rheged.com
Salkeld Rd, ✆ (01768) 891 919

Brooklands without rest

2 Portland Pl ✉ CA11 7QN – ✆ (01768) 863 395
– www.brooklandsguesthouse.com – Closed 2 weeks Christmas and New Year
6 rm – £ 38/60 £ 75/85
◆ Victorian terraced house located close to the town centre; run by warm, welcoming owners. Traditional, antique-furnished hall and smart breakfast room with marble-topped tables. Homely, pine-furnished bedrooms boast good modern facilities; one has a four-poster.

at Temple Sowerby East : 6.75 mi by A 66 – ✉ Penrith

Temple Sowerby House

✉ CA10 1RZ – ✆ (01768) 361 578 – www.templesowerby.com
– Closed 19-29 December
12 rm – £ 90/95 £ 145/160
Rest – *(dinner only) (booking essential to non residents)* Menu £ 38
◆ Attractive, red-brick Georgian mansion with spacious, classically styled guest areas. Traditional country house bedrooms boast antique furnishings and contemporary facilities. Modern menus of local, seasonal produce served overlooking enclosed, lawned gardens.

at Clifton Southeast : 3 mi on A 6

George and Dragon with rm

✉ CA10 2ER – ✆ (01768) 865 381 – www.georgeanddragonclifton.co.uk
10 rm – £ 67/102 £ 89/135
Rest – Carte £ 20/30
◆ 18C coaching inn belonging to local landowners, the Lowther family. Simple, effective cooking; organic meats, seasonal game and vegetables come fresh from the surrounding estate. Comfortable, modern bedrooms are decorated in bold colours.

at Newbiggin West : 3.5 mi by A 66 – ✉ Penrith

Old School

✉ CA11 0HT – ✆ (01768) 483 709 – www.theold-school.com – Closed 2 weeks June and 1 week Christmas
3 rm – £ 38/55 £ 75/80
Rest – Menu £ 20
◆ Grey-stone Victorian schoolhouse in a small village. Compact, traditionally styled guest areas. Classical bedrooms named after the colour of their décor – red, green and blue – the latter is the largest, with the best outlook. Home-cooked meals from a set menu.

ENGLAND

PENZANCE – Cornwall – 503 D33 – pop. 20 255 **1** A3

London 319 mi – Exeter 113 mi – Plymouth 77 mi – Taunton 155 mi

Access Access to the Isles of Scilly by helicopter, British International Heliport ☎ (01736) 364296, Fax (01736) 363871

to the Isles of Scilly (Hugh Town) (Isles of Scilly Steamship Co. Ltd) (summer only) (approx. 2 h 40 mn)

Station Rd ☎ (01736) 362 207, penzancetic@cornwall.gov.uk

Town★ - Outlook★★★ – Western Promenade (←★★★) YZ – National Lighthouse Centre★ **AC** Y – Chapel St★ Y – Maritime Museum★ **AC** Y **M1** – Penlee House Gallery and Museum★, **AC**

St Buryan★★ (church tower★★), SW : 5 mi by A 30 and B 3283 - Penwith★★ – Trengwainton Garden★★, NW : 2 mi – Sancreed - Church★★ (Celtic Crosses★★) - Carn Euny★, W : 3.5 mi by A 30 Z – St Michael's Mount★★ (←★★), E : 4 mi by B 3311 - Y - and A 30 – Gulval★ (Church★), NE : 1 mi - Ludgvan★ (Church★), NE : 3.5 mi by A 30 - Chysauster Village★, N : 3.5 mi by A 30, B 3311 and minor rd – Newlyn★ - Pilchard Works★, SW : 1.5 mi by B 3315 Z - Lanyon Quoit★, NW : 3.5 mi by St Clare Street – Men-an-Tol★, NW : 5 mi by B 3312 - Madron Church★, NW : 1.5 mi by St Clare Street Y. Morvah (←★★), NW : 6.5 mi by St Clare Street Y – Zennor (Church★), NW : 6 mi by B 3311 Y – Prussia Cove★, E : 8 mi by B 3311 - Y - and A 394 – Land's End★ (cliff scenery★★★), SW : 10 mi by A 30 Z – Porthcurno★, SW : 8.5 mi by A 30, B 3283 and minor rd

ENGLAND

Hotel Penzance

Britons Hill ✉ TR18 3AE – ☎ (01736) 363 117 – www.hotelpenzance.com – Closed 3-17 January Y**c**

25 rm – †£ 80/145 ††£ 180/190

Rest ***Bay*** – see restaurant listing

◆ Adjoining Edwardian merchants' houses, overlooking the bay and St Michael's Mount. Several lounges, pleasant garden terrace and outdoor pool. Mix of classic and contemporary bedrooms.

Abbey without rest

Abbey St ✉ TR18 4AR – ☎ (01736) 366 906 – www.theabbeyonline.co.uk – Closed January-February Y**u**

6 rm – †£ 90/150 ††£ 150/200 – 2 suites

◆ 17C country house in powder blue, with tranquil walled gardens. Relaxed, slightly quirky atmosphere with shabby-chic charm. Lovely antique-filled sitting room and bright, well-kept bedrooms.

Beachfield

The Promenade ✉ TR18 4NW – ☎ (01736) 362 067 – www.beachfield.co.uk – Closed 2 weeks Christmas Z**a**

18 rm – †£ 60/90 ††£ 130/160

Rest – *(closed Sunday) (dinner only)* Menu £ 28 **s**

◆ Classic seaside hotel with good views. Well-kept public areas include traditional lounge. Comfy bedrooms are well maintained and have a neat, bright feel. Traditional, varied menus, featuring fish specials.

Chy-An-Mor without rest

15 Regent Terr ✉ TR18 4DW – ☎ (01736) 363 441 – www.chyanmor.co.uk – 16 April-14 November Y**e**

9 rm – †£ 40/70 ††£ 84/90

◆ Terraced guesthouse overlooking the promenade. Lounge displays various artefacts from the charming owners' travels. Bedrooms boast lovely soft furnishings; some have 6ft iron beds.

The Summer House

Cornwall Ter ✉ TR18 4HL – ☎ (01736) 363 744 – www.summerhouse-cornwall.com – April-October Z**s**

5 rm – †£ 110/125 ††£ 150 **Rest** – Menu £ 35

◆ There's a friendly atmosphere to this listed Regency House in bright blues and yellows. Pleasant patio garden. Residents can enjoy Mediterranean influenced cooking.

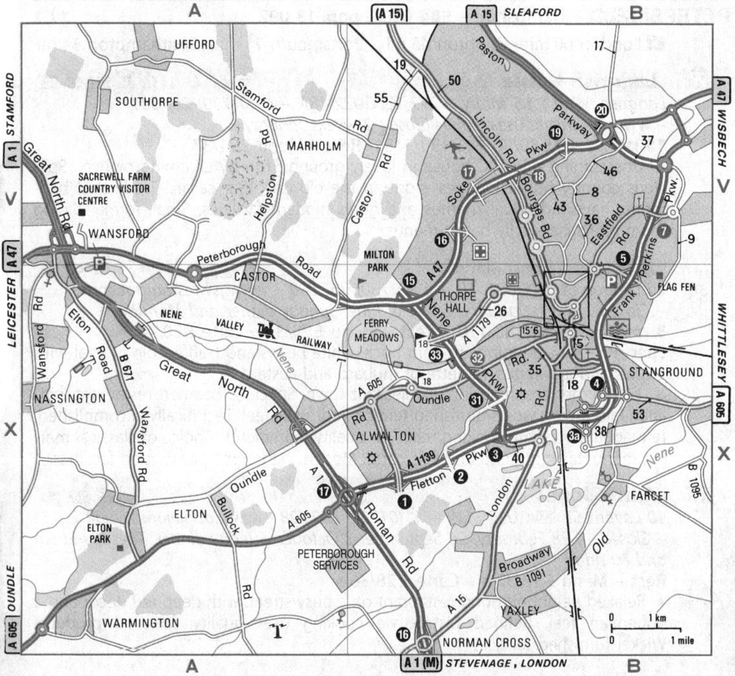

A B

(A 15) A 15 SLEAFORD

UFFORD SOUTHORPE MARHOLM Stamford Rd Helpston Rd Castor Rd Paston Parkway Lincoln Rd Pkw Soke Bourges Bd Eastfield Rd Frank Perkins Pkw. 17 19 20 37 46 8 43 36 9 50 55

A 1 STAMFORD Great North Rd SACREWELL FARM COUNTRY VISITOR CENTRE WANSFORD A 47 WISBECH

A 47 LEICESTER Peterborough Road CASTOR MILTON PARK THORPE HALL FLAG FEN 26 5 7 15 16 18

Wansford Rd Elton Road B 671 NENE VALLEY RAILWAY Nene FERRY MEADOWS A 1179 Nene Pkw 18 33 32 Rd. 35 Rd 15 15 6 STANGROUND WHITTLESEY

NASSINGTON Great North Rd A 605 Oundle Rd 18 31 4 53 A 605

X ALWALTON A 1139 Fletton Pkw 3 40 2 1 38 3a Nene X

Wansford Rd Oundle A 1 17 LAKE FARCET B 1095

ELTON PARK ELTON Bullock Rd A 605 PETERBOROUGH SERVICES Roman Rd London Old Broadway B 1091 ENGLAND

OUNDLE A 605 WARMINGTON A 15 YAXLEY NORMAN CROSS 16 0 1 km 0 1 mile

A A 1 (M) STEVENAGE, LONDON B

PETERBOROUGH

- Bridge St . . . . Z
- Cattle Market Rd . . . . Y 2
- Church St . . . . YZ
- City Rd . . . . Y 3
- Cowgate . . . . Y 5
- Cross St . . . . Z 6
- Dogsthorpe Rd . . . . BV 8
- Edgerley Drain Rd . . . . BV 9
- Embankment Rd . . . . Z 12
- Exchange St . . . . Y 13
- Fletton Ave . . . . BX 15
- Geneva St . . . . Y 16
- Guntons Rd . . . . BV 17
- High St . . . . BX 18
- Hurn Rd . . . . BV 19
- Longthorpe Parkway . . . . . . BX 26
- Long Causeway . . . . Y 25
- Market Way . . . . Y 28
- Midgate . . . . Y 29
- New Rd . . . . BX 35
- Park Rd . . . . BV 36
- Paston Parkway . . . . BV 37
- Peterborough Rd . . . . BX 38
- Phorpres Way . . . . BX 40
- Queensgate Shopping Centre . . . . Y
- Rivergate . . . . Z 42
- Rivergate Shopping Centre . . . . Z
- St Paul's Rd . . . . BV 43
- Thorpe Rd . . . . Y 45
- Welland Rd . . . . BV 46
- Wentworth St . . . . Z 48
- Werrington Parkway . . . . . . BV 50
- Wheelyard . . . . Y 52
- Whittlesey Rd . . . . BX 53
- Woodcroft Rd . . . . BV 55

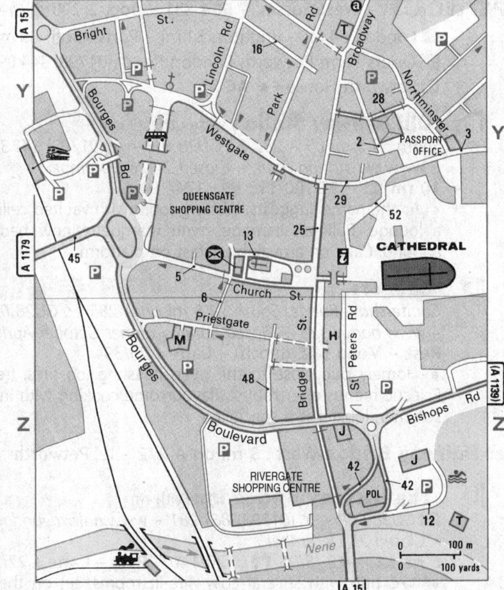

PETERSFIELD – Hampshire – 504 R30 – pop. 13 092 7 C2

London 60 mi – Brighton 45 mi – Portsmouth 21 mi – Southampton 34 mi

Langrish House

Langrish, West : 3.5 mi by A 272 ✉ GU32 1RN – ✆ (01730) 266 941 – www.langrishhouse.co.uk – Closed 2 weeks January

13 rm – £ 80/90 £ 130/145 **Rest** – Menu £ 21/37

♦ Unassuming mid-17C house in lovely grounds; run by charming owners. Spacious country house lounges – one in the old Civil War cellars. Traditional bedrooms have individual themes and good modern facilities. Small formal dining room offers classically based menus.

JSW (Jake Watkins) with rm

20 Dragon St ✉ GU31 4JJ – ✆ (01730) 262 030 – www.jswrestaurant.com – Closed 2 weeks January, 2 weeks June, Sunday dinner and Monday

3 rm – £ 65 £ 85/110 **Rest** – Menu £ 25/37 – Carte £ 30/48

Spec. Pheasant boudin with ham hock, white beans and truffle. Loin of veal with morels and asparagus. Assiette of rhubarb and custard.

♦ 17C former coaching inn, in pleasant town. Spacious beamed restaurant with linen-laid tables, wood-furnished terrace and rustic feel. Technically accomplished, refined, flavoursome cooking relies on quality ingredients. Choice of classical market menu, tasting menu and à la carte. Modern bedrooms boast good facilities.

Annie Jones

10 Lavant St. ✉ GU32 3EW – ✆ (01730) 262 728 – www.anniejones.co.uk – Closed 14-28 February, 26 September-3 October, Sunday dinner, Tuesday lunch and Monday

Rest – Menu £ 18/32 **s** – Carte £ 28/36 **s**

♦ Relaxed neighbourhood restaurant on a busy street, with deep red décor and a bohemian feel. Refined bistro-style cooking uses quality seasonal produce. Wicker-furnished terrace.

ENGLAND

PETWORTH – West Sussex – 504 S31 – pop. 2 298 Great Britain 7 C2

London 54 mi – Brighton 31 mi – Portsmouth 33 mi

Osiers Farm Petworth London Rd, ✆ (01798) 344 097

Petworth House★★ **AC**

Old Railway Station without rest

South : 1.5 mi by A 285 ✉ GU28 0JF – ✆ (01798) 342 346 – www.old-station.co.uk – Closed 24-26 December

10 rm – £ 100/118 £ 174/194

♦ As the name suggests. Waiting room with vaulted ceiling and ticket office now a lounge, Pullman carriages with marquetry now bedrooms; original features abound. Cake on arrival; breakfast on platform.

Badgers

Coultershaw Bridge, South : 1.5 mi on A 285 ✉ GU28 0JF – ✆ (01798) 342 651 – www.badgers.cc – Closed Sunday dinner October-April

Rest – Menu £ 15 (lunch) – Carte £ 20/39

♦ Homely pub close to the river, boasting log fires, fresh flowers and candles. Eclectic menus offer robust, flavoursome cooking with international influences. In summer, lobster is a speciality.

at Halfway Bridge West : 3 mi on A 272 – ✉ Petworth

The Halfway Bridge Inn with rm

✉ GU28 9BP – ✆ (01798) 861 281 – www.halfwaybridge.co.uk – Closed 25 December

6 rm – £ 75/95 £ 120/140 **Rest** – Carte £ 22/37

♦ 17C pub with several cosy, fire-lit rooms, set on the edge of Cowdray Park. Lunchtime baguettes, traditional pub dishes and nursery puddings. Bedrooms are set in converted stables and, like the pub, blend rustic charm with modern fittings and facilities.

at Lickfold Northwest : 6 mi by A 272 – ✉ Petworth

The Lickfold Inn

✉ *GU28 9EY* – ✆ *(01798) 861 285* – *www.evanspubs.co.uk*

Rest – Carte £ 25/34

♦ Rurally set 15C inn with a charming feel, typified by cosy seating and open fires. Appealing menu of straightforward pub dishes; popular starter and antipasti boards; interesting cheeses.

PICKERING – North Yorkshire – **502** R21 – **pop. 6 616** **23** C1

London 237 mi – Middlesborough 43 mi – Scarborough 19 mi – York 25 mi

The Ropery ✆ (01751) 473791, pickeringtic@btconnect.com

White Swan Inn

Market Pl ✉ *YO18 7AA* – ✆ *(01751) 472 288* – *www.white-swan.co.uk*

20 rm – †£ 115/135 ††£ 150/180 – 1 suite **Rest** – Carte £ 25/46

♦ Well-run former coaching inn, with bar and lounges in modern hues. Appealing bedrooms boast good mod cons and smart bathrooms: those in the outbuildings have heated stone floors; one has a bath in the lounge. Brasserie-style restaurant offers classical menus.

17 Burgate without rest

17 Burgate ✉ *YO18 7AU* – ✆ *(01751) 473 463* – *www.17burgate.co.uk* – *Closed 3 weeks spring, 1 week autumn and Christmas*

5 rm – †£ 79/100 ††£ 80/110

♦ Restored 17C townhouse with colourful gardens; run by charming, experienced couple. Lounge boasts honesty bar and large inglenook; breakfast room has Mackintosh-style chairs. Spacious bedrooms furnished in comfy, modern style: two have a subtle oriental theme.

Bramwood without rest

19 Hall Garth ✉ *YO18 7AW* – ✆ *(01751) 474 066* – *www.bramwoodguesthouse.co.uk*

8 rm – †£ 50/65 ††£ 80

♦ Georgian townhouse with pretty gardens, set close to town. Cosy, homely interior with fire-lit lounge and tea on arrival. Breakfast in large kitchen, beside china-filled dressers, or in more formal dining room. Comfy, cottagey bedrooms. Owners go the extra mile.

at Levisham Northeast : 6.5 mi by A 169 – ✉ Pickering

Moorlands Country House

✉ *YO18 7NL* – ✆ *(01751) 460 229* – *www.moorlandslevisham.co.uk* – *March-November, minimum 2 night stay*

4 rm – †£ 130/160 ††£ 140/160

Rest – Menu £ 25 – Carte £ 17/25

♦ 19C restored vicarage in the heart of the national park, boasting superb views down the valley. Spacious, well-maintained interior with a classically decorated lounge and flowery wallpapers. Comfortable bedrooms boast rich colour schemes; one has a four-poster bed. Traditional three course dinners. Menu changes daily.

at Sinnington Northwest : 4 mi by A 170 – ✉ York

Fox and Hounds with rm

Main St ✉ *YO62 6SQ* – ✆ *(01751) 431 577* – *www.thefoxandhoundsinn.co.uk* – *Closed 25-26 December*

10 rm – †£ 59/79 ††£ 90/110 **Rest** – Carte £ 21/32

♦ Handsome and sturdy 18C coaching inn in pretty village; substantial interior has plenty of charm. Flexible menus, with local specialities the popular choice. Comfortable, cottagey bedrooms are popular at weekends.

PICKHILL – North Yorkshire – 502 P21 – pop. 412 – ✉ Thirsk 22 B1

London 229 mi – Leeds 41 mi – Middlesbrough 30 mi – York 34 mi

Nags Head Country Inn

✉ YO7 4JG – ✆ (01845) 567 391 – www.nagsheadpickhill.co.uk
– Closed 25 December

14 rm – †£ 75 ††£ 95/105 **Rest** – Carte £ 19/31

♦ Atmospheric 300 year old inn in an ancient hamlet, an easy drive to Thirsk and Ripon races. Neat rooms in soft floral fabrics. Over 800 ties on display in the rustic bar. Rural restaurant adorned with bookshelves and patterned rugs.

PIDDLETRENTHIDE – Dorset – 503 M31 – pop. 691 4 C3

London 129 mi – Bristol 54 mi – Cardiff 120 mi – Southampton 55 mi

The European Inn with rm

South : 0.5 mi on B 3143 ✉ DT2 7QT – ✆ (01300) 348 308
– www.european-inn.co.uk – Closed Monday

3 rm – †£ 75 ††£ 100 **Rest** – *(booking advisable)* Carte £ 20/29

♦ Relaxing inn loved by the locals. Concise menu of unfussy dishes which make good use of Dorset produce, including fish from the south coast day boats; simple, skilled cooking. Stylish bedrooms boast feature walls; those at the back offer countryside views.

PILLERTON PRIORS – Warks. – 503 P27 – see Stratford-upon-Avon

PLUMTREE – Notts. – see Nottingham

ENGLAND

PLYMOUTH – Plymouth – 503 H32 – pop. 243 795 2 C2

London 242 mi – Bristol 124 mi – Southampton 161 mi

Access Tamar Bridge (toll) AY

Plymouth City (Roborough) Airport : ✆ (01752) 204090, N : 3.5 mi by A 386 ABY

to France (Roscoff) (Brittany Ferries) 1-3 daily (6 h) – to Spain (Santander) (Brittany Ferries) 2 weekly (approx 24 h)

Plymouth Mayflower, 3-5 The Barbican ✆ (01752) 306330, barbicantic@plymouth.gov.uk

Staddon Heights Plymstock, ✆ (01752) 402 475

Elfordleigh Hotel G. & C.C. Plympton Colebrook, ✆ (01752) 348 425

Town★ - Smeaton's Tower (≤★★) **AC** BZ **T1** – Plymouth Dome★ **AC** BZ – Royal Citadel (ramparts ≤★★) **AC** BZ – City Museum and Art Gallery★ BZ **M1**

Saltram House★★ **AC**, E : 3.5 mi BY **A** - Tamar River★★ – Anthony House★ **AC**, W : 5 mi by A 374 – Mount Edgcumbe (≤★) **AC**, SW : 2 mi by passenger ferry from Stonehouse AZ. NE : Dartmoor National Park★★ – Buckland Abbey★★ **AC**, N : 7.5 mi by A 386 ABY

Plans pages 545, 546

Bowling Green without rest

9-10 Osborne Pl, Lockyer St, The Hoe ✉ PL1 2PU – ✆ (01752) 209 090
– www.thebowlinggreenplymouth.com BZ**r**

12 rm – †£ 45/60 ††£ 68/72

♦ Georgian house, half overlooking Hoe, near site of Drake's legendary game. High-ceilinged rooms in pine and modern fabrics; some have power showers. Stroll to promenade.

Tanners

Prysten House, Finewell St ✉ PL1 2AE – ✆ (01752) 252 001
– www.tannersrestaurant.com – Closed 24 December-18 January, Sunday and Monday BZ**n**

Rest – *(booking essential)* Menu £ 15 – Carte £ 32/41

♦ Characterful 15C house, reputedly Plymouth's oldest building: mullioned windows, tapestries, exposed stone and an illuminated water well. Modern, interesting cooking.

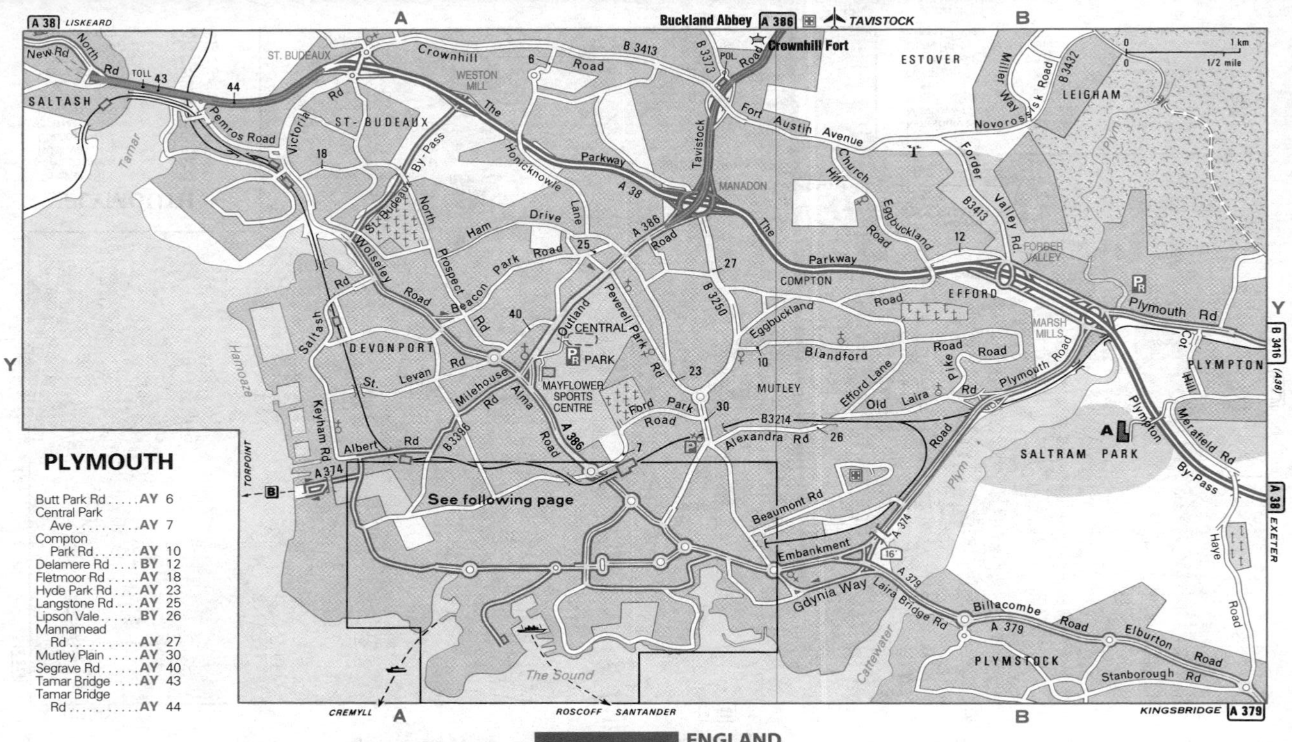

A 38 LISKEARD
Buckland Abbey
A 386
TAVISTOCK
Crownhill Fort
B 3416 (A38)
A 38 EXETER
KINGSBRIDGE A 379
TORPOINT
CREMYLL
ROSCOFF SANTANDER
SALTASH
ST. BUDEAUX
WESTON MILL
ESTOVER
LEIGHAM
MANADON
FORDER VALLEY
COMPTON
EFFORD
MARSH MILLS
PLYMPTON
DEVONPORT
MUTLEY
SALTRAM PARK
PLYMSTOCK
CENTRAL PARK
MAYFLOWER SPORTS CENTRE
Hamoaze
Tamar
Plym
Cattewater
The Sound
See following page
1 km
1/2 mile

PLYMOUTH

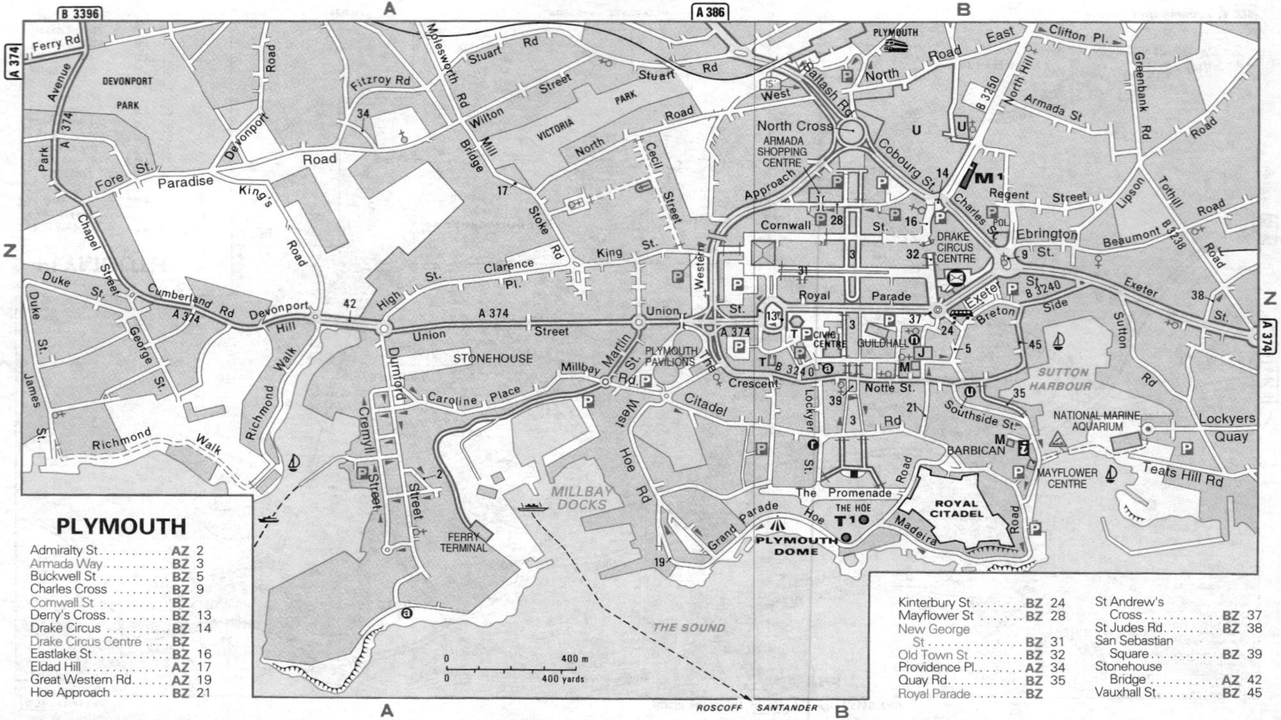

PLYMOUTH

Street	Square	No.
Admiralty St	AZ	2
Armada Way	BZ	3
Buckwell St	BZ	5
Charles Cross	BZ	9
Cornwall St	BZ	
Derry's Cross	BZ	13
Drake Circus	BZ	14
Drake Circus Centre	BZ	
Eastlake St	BZ	16
Eldad Hill	AZ	17
Great Western Rd	AZ	19
Hoe Approach	BZ	21
Kinterbury St	BZ	24
Mayflower St	BZ	28
New George St	BZ	31
Old Town St	BZ	32
Providence Pl	AZ	34
Quay Rd	BZ	35
Royal Parade	BZ	
St Andrew's Cross	BZ	37
St Judes Rd	BZ	38
San Sebastian Square	BZ	39
Stonehouse Bridge	AZ	42
Vauxhall St	BZ	45

XX **Artillery Tower**

Firestone Bay ✉ PL1 3QR – ✆ (01752) 257 610 – www.artillerytower.co.uk – Closed 10 days at Christmas, 10 days in August, Sunday and Monday

Rest – *(booking essential at lunch)* Menu £ 25/35 AZ**a**

◆ Uniquely located in 500 year-old circular tower, built to defend the city. Courteous service of mostly well executed local dishes: blackboard fish specialities.

XX **Barbican Kitchen**

Black Friars Distillery, 60 Southside St ✉ PL1 2LQ – ✆ (01752) 604 448 – www.barbicankitchen.com – Closed 25-26 December and dinner 31 December

Rest – *(booking advisable)* Carte £ 18/31 BZ**u**

◆ Fun, informal eatery set in the Plymouth Gin Distillery. Two long, industrial style rooms decorated in vibrant fuschia and lime. Brasserie menus offer a good selection of simply cooked dishes.

XX **Chloe's**

Gill Akaster House, Princess St ✉ PL1 2EX – ✆ (01752) 201 523 – www.chloesrestaurant .co.uk – Closed Sunday and Monday BZ**a**

Rest – Menu £ 19 – Carte £ 19/40

◆ Airy, open plan restaurant with simple neighbourhood feel, neutral décor and hanging Hessian lights. Tasty dishes display a classical French base. Live pianist every night.

at Plympton St Maurice East : 6 mi by A 374 on B 3416 - BY – ✉ **Plymouth**

St Elizabeth's House

Longbrook St ✉ PL7 1NJ – ✆ (01752) 344 840 – www.stelizabeths.co.uk – Closed 25-26 December

13 rm – †£ 139 ††£ 179 – 1 suite

Rest – Menu £ 15 (lunch) – Carte (dinner) £ 20/36

◆ Immaculate cream-washed former convent, now a stylish boutique hotel; lounge is dressed in period décor while light bedrooms are contemporary, with up-to-date facilities. Formal dining room offers classically based cooking with a modern twist.

PLYMPTON SAINT MAURICE Devon – Plymouth – 503 H32 – see Plymouth

POLPERRO – Cornwall – 503 G33 – ✉ Looe 1 B2

London 271 mi – Plymouth 28 mi

Village★

Trenderway Farm without rest

Northeast: 2 mi by A 387 ✉ PL13 2LY – ✆ (01503) 272 214 – www.trenderwayfarm.co.uk

8 rm – †£ 85/155 ††£ 100/175

◆ 16C farmhouse and outbuildings in 206 acres of working farmland. Well-appointed bedrooms in mix of styles; some with seating areas and kitchenettes. Cream tea on arrival; Aga-cooked breakfasts.

PONTELAND – Tyne and Wear – 501 O19 – see Newcastle upon Tyne

POOLE – Poole – 503 O31 – pop. 144 800 4 C3

London 116 mi – Bournemouth 4 mi – Dorchester 23 mi – Southampton 36 mi

to France (Cherbourg) (Brittany Ferries) 1-2 daily May-October (4 h 15 mn) day (5 h 45 mn) night – to France (St Malo) (Brittany Ferries) daily (8 h) – to France (St Malo) (Condor Ferries Ltd)

Welcome Centre, Enefco House, Poole Quay ✆ (01202) 253253, info@poole.gov.uk

Parkstone Links Rd, ✆ (01202) 707 138

Bulbury Woods Lytchett Minster Bulberry Lane, ✆ (01929) 459 574

Town★ (Waterfront **M1** , Scaplen's Court **M2**)

Compton Acres★★, (English Garden ≤★★★) **AC**, SE : 3 mi by B 3369 BX (on Bournemouth town plan) – Brownsea Island★ (Baden-Powell Stone ≤★★) **AC**, by boat from Poole Quay or Sandbanks BX (on Bournemouth town plan)

Plan of Built up Area : see Bournemouth BX

Plan on next page

ENGLAND

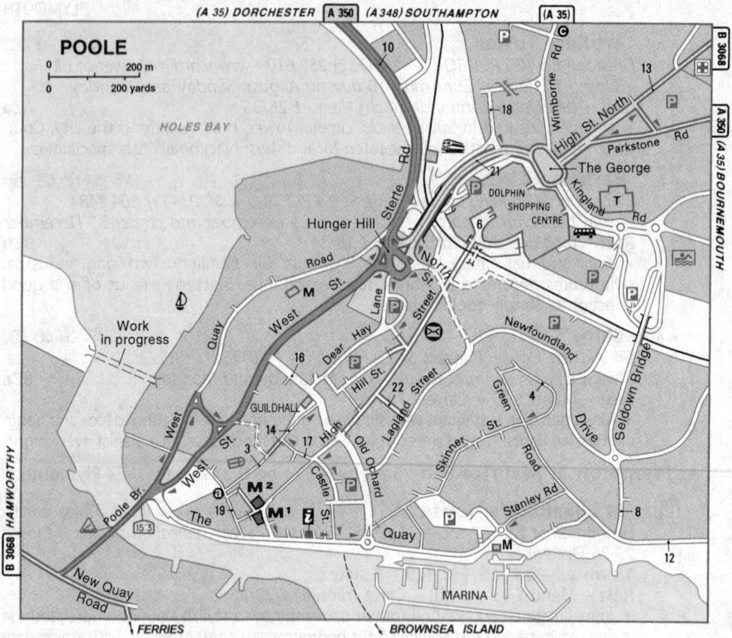

POOLE

Church St	3	Furnell Rd	8	New Orchard	16
Dolphin Quay Shopping Centre		High St		New St	17
Emerson Rd	4	Holes Bay Rd	10	Serpentine Rd	18
Falkland Square	6	Labrador Drive	12	Thames St	19
Fishermans Rd	7	Longfleet Rd	13	Towngate Bridge	21
		Market St	14	Westons Lane	22

Hotel du Vin

7-11 Thames St. ✉ *BH15 1JN – ✆ (01202) 785 570 – www.hotelduvin.com* **a**

38 rm ☕ – 🛉£ 190/210 🛉🛉£ 200/400

Rest ***Bistro*** – Carte £ 24/45

♦ Striking Queen Anne property in the heart of the old town. Smart guest areas boast colourful, eye-catching murals; stylish, modern bedrooms display a strong wine theme. Large French bistro offers a 300 bin wine list. Superb wine tasting room completes the picture.

Harbour Heights

Haven Rd, Sandbanks, Southeast : 3 mi by B 3369 ✉ *BH13 7LW – ✆ (01202) 707 272 – www.fjbhotels.co.uk* BX**n**

38 rm ☕ – 🛉£ 135/225 🛉🛉£ 350/440

Rest ***Habar Bistro*** – Menu £ 27/29 **s** – Carte £ 24/61 **s**

♦ Refurbished 1920s whitewashed hotel perched on the hillside; overlooking the bay and Brownsea Island. Modern lounge-bar boasts superb three-tiered terrace. Contemporary bedrooms come with good mod cons and smart bathrooms. Open-plan restaurant serves modern menu.

Cranborne House without rest

45 Shaftesbury Rd ✉ *BH15 2LU – ✆ (01202) 685 200 – www.cranborne-house.co.uk* **c**

5 rm ☕ – 🛉£ 49/69 🛉🛉£ 69/89

♦ Victorian house on the main road; run by friendly owners. Small, homely lounge-cum-breakfast room. Bedrooms – in modern extension – boast quality handmade furniture and good modern facilities.

The Cow

58 Station Rd, Ashley Cross ✉ *BH14 8UD – ✆ (01202) 749 569 – www.thecowpub.co.uk – Closed Sunday dinner* BX**a**

Rest – Carte £ 22/32

♦ Smart, modern pub next to the railway station. Light lunch menu of pub favourites. Evening à la carte steps things up a gear, but is only available in the French-style bistro.

POOLEY BRIDGE – Cumbria – 501 L20 – see Ullswater

PORLOCK – Somerset – 503 J30 – pop. 1 395 – ✉ Minehead 3 A2

London 190 mi – Bristol 67 mi – Exeter 46 mi – Taunton 28 mi

Village★ - Porlock Hill (≤★★) – St Dubricius Church★

Dunkery Beacon★★★ (≤★★★), S : 5.5 mi – Exmoor National Park★★ - Selworthy★ (≤★★, Church★), E : 2 mi by A 39 and minor rd - Luccombe★ (Church★), E : 3 mi by A 39 – Culbone★ (St Beuno), W : 3.5 mi by B 3225, 1.5 mi on foot – Doone Valley★, W : 6 mi by A 39, access from Oare on foot

Oaks

✉ *TA24 8ES – ✆ (01643) 862 265 – www.oakshotel.co.uk – April-October and Christmas-New Year*

8 rm (dinner included) – †£ 150 ††£ 220

Rest – *(dinner only) (booking essential for non-residents)* Menu £ 35 **s**

♦ Imposing Edwardian house boasting great views over the weir and Porlock Bay. Antique-filled entrance hall with beautiful parquet floor. Cake on arrival in snug lounge. Large, comfy bedrooms come with fresh fruit bowls, good mod cons and smart bathrooms. Dining room offers classical daily menu and views from every table.

ENGLAND

PORT ERIN – Isle of Man – 502 F21 – see Man (Isle of)

PORTGATE – Devon – pop. 1 453 2 C2

London 211 mi – Launceston 8 mi – Plymouth 34 mi

The Harris Arms

✉ *EX20 4PZ – ✆ (01566) 783 331 – www.theharrisarms.co.uk – Closed 26 December, Sunday dinner and Monday*

Rest – Menu £ 17 (Sunday lunch) – Carte £ 20/27

♦ Simple exterior hides classical rooms, a large terrace and lovely rear views. Concise menus offer fresh, tried-and-tested dishes, supplemented by tasty daily specials. Excellent wine list.

PORTHLEVEN – Cornwall – pop. 3 190 1 A3

London 284 mi – Helston 3 mi – Penzance 12 mi

Kota with rm

Harbour Head ✉ *TR13 9JA – ✆ (01326) 562 407 – www.kotarestaurant.co.uk – Closed 1 January-10 February, 25 December, Monday except high season and Sunday*

2 rm – †£ 50/80 ††£ 80/95

Rest – *(dinner only and lunch Friday-Saturday)* Menu £ 14 (lunch) – Carte £ 24/33

♦ Cottagey converted 18C harbourside granary. Characterful restaurant - thick walls, tiled floors - serves modern Asian inspired dishes with local fish specials. Simple rooms.

PORTINSCALE – Cumbria – see Keswick

PORTSCATHO – Cornwall – 503 F33 – ✉ Truro 1 B3

London 298 mi – Plymouth 55 mi – Truro 16 mi

St Just-in-Roseland Church★★, W : 4 mi by A 3078 – St Anthony-in-Roseland (≤★★) S : 3.5 m

Rosevine

Rosevine, North : 2 mi by A 3078 ✉ TR2 5EW – ☎ (01872) 580 206 – www.rosevine.co.uk – Closed January and 2 weeks November
15 suites – ††£ 150/350, ☕ £ 7
Rest – *(closed Sunday dinner) (bar lunch)* Carte £ 21/40
◆ Dramatically refurbished and extended country house overlooking the sea. Cool, contemporary, neutrally hued inner. Stylish, modern bedrooms boast kitchenettes. Strongly family orientated services; kids have their own lounge. All-day brasserie uses local produce.

Driftwood

Rosevine, North : 2 mi by A 3078 ✉ TR2 5EW – ☎ (01872) 580 644 – www.driftwoodhotel.co.uk – Closed 6 December-4 February
15 rm ☕ – †£ 200/221 ††£ 260
Rest – *(dinner only) (booking essential)* Menu £ 42
◆ Stylish décor and a neutral, contemporary feel make this an enviable spot to lay one's head. Attractive decking affords fine sea views. Smart bedrooms with pristine style. Distinctive modern dining room with fine vistas.

PORTSMOUTH and SOUTHSEA – Portsmouth – 503 Q31 — 6 B3

– pop. 187 056 Great Britain

London 78 mi – Brighton 48 mi – Salisbury 44 mi – Southampton 21 mi

to the Isle of Wight (Ryde) (Wightlink Ltd) frequent services daily (15 mn) – from Southsea to the Isle of Wight (Ryde) (Hovertravel Ltd) frequent services daily (10 mn)

to France (St Malo) (Brittany Ferries) daily (8 h 45 mn) day (10 h 45 mn) night – to France (Caen) (Brittany Ferries) 2-4 daily (6 h) day (6 h 45 mn) night – to France (Cherbourg) (Brittany Ferries) 2 daily (5 h) day, (7 h) night – to France (Le Havre) (LD Lines) daily (5 h 30 mn/7 h 30 mn) – to France (Cherbourg) (Brittany Ferries) 1-2 daily (2 h 45 mn) – to France (Caen) (Brittany Ferries) 2-4 daily (3 h 45 mn) – to Spain (Bilbao) (P & O European Ferries Ltd) 1-2 weekly (35 h) – to Guernsey (St Peter Port) and Jersey (St Helier) (Condor Ferries Ltd) daily except Sunday (10 hrs) – to the Isle of Wight (Fishbourne) (Wightlink Ltd) frequent services daily (35 mn)

Clarence Esplanade, Southsea ☎ (023) 9282 6722, vis@portsmouthcc.gov.uk

Southsea Burrfields Rd, ☎ (023) 9266 8667

Crookhorn Lane Waterlooville Widley, ☎ (023) 9237 2210

Southwick Park Southwick Pinsley Drive, ☎ (023) 9238 0131

City★ – Naval Portsmouth BY : H.M.S. Victory★★★ **AC**, The Mary Rose★★, Royal Naval Museum★★ **AC** – Old Portsmouth★ BYZ : The Point (≤★★) - St Thomas Cathedral★ – Southsea (Castle★ **AC**) AZ – Royal Marines Museum, Eastney★ **AC**, AZ **M1**

Portchester Castle★ **AC**, NW : 5.5 mi by A 3 and A 27 AY

Plans pages 551, 552

The Clarence

Clarence Rd. ✉ PO5 2LQ – ☎ (023) 9287 6348 – www.theclarencehotel.co.uk – Closed 24 December-3 January AZ**c**
8 rm ☕ – †£ 85/145 ††£ 99/225
Rest – *(dinner only) (residents only)* Carte £ 26/33
◆ Red-brick, bay windowed house a short walk from the sea. Variously sized bedrooms feature contemporary décor, a good level of facilities, superb modern bathrooms and pleasing extra touches. Appealing menu of modern British cooking served in cosy restaurant.

The Retreat without rest

35 Grove Rd South, Southsea ✉ PO5 3QS – ☎ (023) 9235 3701 – www.theretreatguesthouse.co.uk CZ**e**
4 rm ☕ – †£ 75 ††£ 105
◆ Grade II listed Arts and Crafts house; originally built for the mayor. Original terrazzo floors and stained glass. Relaxed, spacious inner with stylish, understated décor. One four-poster room.

ENGLAND

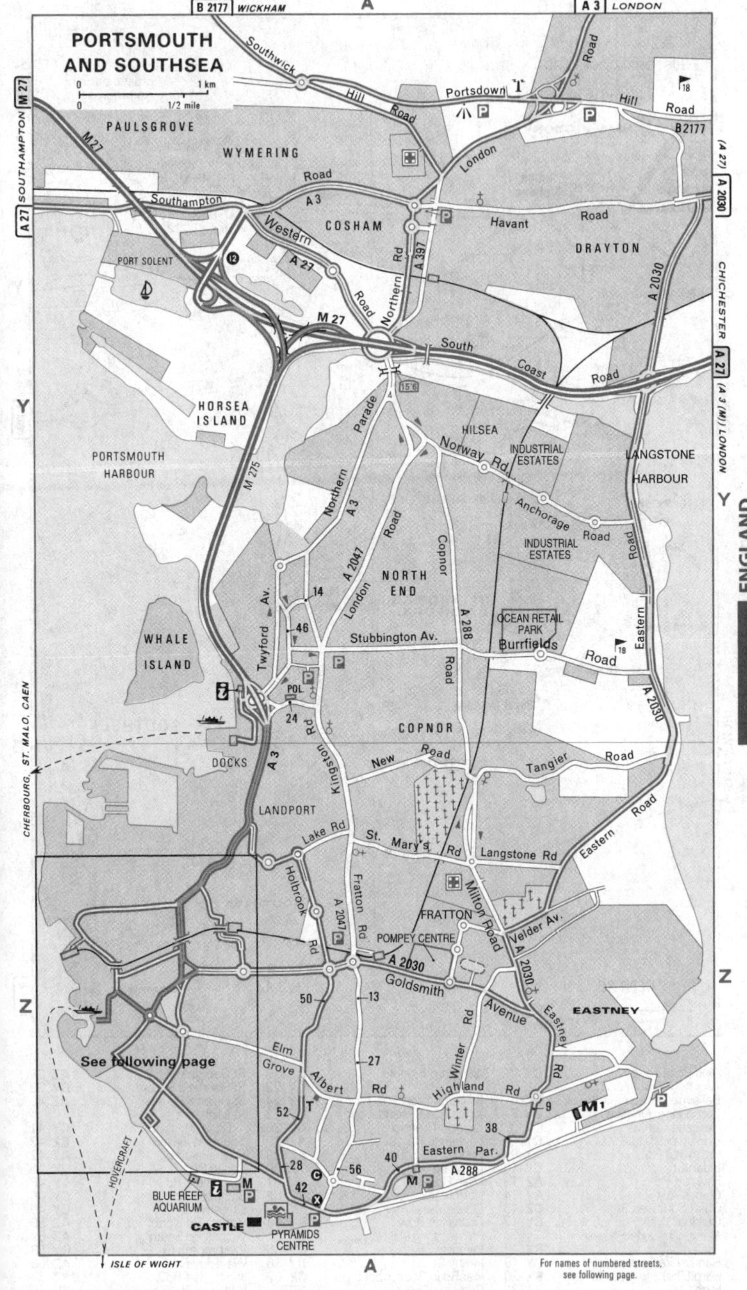

For names of numbered streets, see following page.

ENGLAND

CENTRE

Alec Rose Lane . . . . CY 2
Arundel St . . . . CY 5
Bellevue Terrace . . . . CZ 6
Cambridge Junction . . . . BY 7
Cascade Centre . . . . CY
Commercial Rd . . . . CY
Cromwell Rd . . . . AZ 9
Eldon St . . . . CY 10
Fawcett Rd . . . . AZ 13
Gladys Ave . . . . AY 14
Great Southsea St . . . . CZ 15
Guildhall Walk . . . . CY 17
Gunwharf Quay Shopping Centre . . . . BY
Hampshire Terrace . . . . CY 18
Hard (The) . . . . BY 20
High St . . . . BYZ 21
Isambard Brunel Rd . . . . CY 22
Kingston Crescent . . . . AY 24
Kings Road Roundabout . . . . . . CY 23
Landport Terrace . . . . CY 25
Lawrence Rd . . . . AZ 27
Lennox Rd South . . . . AZ 28
Lombard St . . . . BYZ 29
Main Rd . . . . BY 31
Norfolk St . . . . CYZ 32
Ocean Retail Park . . . . AY
Ordnance Row . . . . BY 34
Palmerston Rd . . . . CZ
Paradise St . . . . CY 35
Penny St . . . . BZ 36
Pier Road Roundabout . . . . CZ 37
Pompey Centre . . . . AZ
St George's Rd . . . . AZ 38
St George's Square . . . . BY 39
St Helen's Parade . . . . AZ 40
St Michael's Rd . . . . CY 41
Southsea Terrace . . . . CZ 43
South Parade . . . . AZ 42
Spring St . . . . CY 45
Stamshaw Rd . . . . AY 46
Stanhope Rd . . . . CY 48
Unicorn Rd . . . . CY 49
Victoria Rd North . . . . AZ 50
Victoria Rd South . . . . AZ 52
Warblington St . . . . BY 53
Waverley Rd . . . . AZ 56
White Hart Rd . . . . BYZ 57
Wiltshire St . . . . CY 59

Restaurant 27
27a South Par, Southsea ✉ PO5 2JF – ✆ (023) 9287 6272 – www.restaurant27.com – Closed Sunday dinner, Monday and Tuesday AZ**x**
Rest – *(dinner only and Sunday lunch) (booking advisable)* Menu £ 25/37
◆ Keenly run, open-plan restaurant with lounge area for aperitifs and canapés. Cooking is skilful with creative touches. Attentive, knowledgeable service from smart young team.

Montparnasse
103 Palmerston Rd, Southsea ✉ PO5 3PS – ✆ (023) 9281 6754 – www.bistromontparnasse.co.uk – Closed 25-26 December, Sunday and Monday
Rest – Menu £ 35 CZ**a**
◆ Keenly run, suburban restaurant with shabby-chic styling. Set lunch and dinner menus. Ambitious cooking features original, sometimes unusual, combinations. Refined appearance but hearty to eat.

Brasserie Blanc
1 Gunwharf Quays ✉ PO1 3FR – ✆ (023) 9289 1320 – www.brasserieblanc.com – Closed 25 December BY**x**
Rest – French – Menu £ 15/18 – Carte £ 21/36
◆ Bustling brasserie on ground floor of 'The Lipstick', serving well-priced, tasty classics prepared with care. Comfy seating, well-spaced tables, open kitchen and super terrace.

PORT ST MARY – I.O.M. – 502 F/G21 – see Man (Isle of)

PORT SUNLIGHT – Merseyside – 502 L23 20 A3

London 206 mi – Liverpool 6 mi – Bolton 42 mi – St Helens 20 mi

Leverhulme H. & Spa
Lodge Ln, Central Rd ✉ CH62 5EZ – ✆ (0151) 644 55 55 – www.leverhulmehotel.co.uk
15 rm – †£ 145/260 ††£ 160/395
Rest *Paesano* – ✆ (0151) 644 66 55 – Menu £ 15 (lunch) – Carte £ 26/34
◆ Originally the cottage hospital for a Victorian conservation village. Now a hotel with personality, whose bright interior mixes contemporary design with art deco. Restaurant has glass-topped tables and international cuisine.

POSTBRIDGE – Devon – 503 I32 2 C2

London 207 mi – Exeter 21 mi – Plymouth 21 mi

Lydgate House
✉ PL20 6TJ – ✆ (01822) 880 209 – www.lydgatehouse.co.uk
7 rm – †£ 60 ††£ 130
Rest – *(closed Sunday and Monday) (dinner only)* Menu £ 28
◆ In an idyllic secluded location high up on the moors within woodland and overlooking the East Dart River. Comfortable sitting room with log fires and neat, snug bedrooms. Candlelit conservatory dining room.

POTTERNE – Wilts. – 503 O29 – see Devizes

PRESTBURY – Cheshire – 502 N24 – pop. 3 269 20 B3

London 184 mi – Liverpool 43 mi – Manchester 17 mi – Stoke-on-Trent 25 mi
Mottram Hall Hotel Mottram St Andrews Wilmslow Rd, ✆ (01625) 820 064

White House Manor without rest
New Road ✉ SK10 4HP – ✆ (01625) 829 376 – www.thewhitehousemanor.co.uk – Closed 25-26 December
12 rm – †£ 60/125 ††£ 110/150, £ 11.50
◆ Attractive Georgian house with mature lawned garden and sheltered terrace. Nicely furnished lounge boasts an honesty bar. Beautifully appointed bedrooms display quality furnishings and extras.

PRESTON – Lancashire – 502 L22 20 A2

London 226 mi – Blackpool 18 mi – Burnley 22 mi – Liverpool 30 mi
The Guildhall, Lancaster Rd ✆ (01772) 253731, tourism@preston.gov.uk
Fulwood Fulwood Hall Lane, ✆ (01772) 700 011
Ingol Tanterton Hall Rd, ✆ (01772) 734 556
Ashton & Lea Lea Tudor Ave, Blackpool Rd, ✆ (01772) 735 282
Penwortham Blundell Lane, ✆ (01772) 744 630

XX Inside Out

100 Higher Walton Rd, Walton-le-Dale, Southeast : 1.75 mi by A 6 on A 675 ✉ PR5 4HR – ✆ (01772) 251 366 – www.insideoutrestaurant.co.uk – Closed first week January and Monday
Rest – Menu £ 15 – Carte £ 22/33
♦ Inside - a chic and stylish restaurant; 'out' - a lovely decked terrace with heaters overlooking a garden. Well sourced, quality ingredients assembled with love and flair.

PRESTON CANDOVER 6 B2

London 59 mi – Croydon 67 mi – Barnet 72 mi – Ealing 54 mi

Purefoy Arms

✉ RG25 2EJ – ✆ (01256) 389 777 – www.thepurefoyarms.co.uk
Rest – Carte £ 19/25
♦ Dating from the 1860s, this once crumbling pub was thoughtfully restored and is run by a charming, young but experienced couple. There are hints of Spain on the menu, especially in the bar nibbles; prices are very competitive and the focus is on flavour.

ENGLAND

PRESTWICH – Greater Manchester – 503 N23 – see Manchester

PULHAM MARKET – Norfolk – 504 X26 – pop. 919 – ✉ Diss 15 C2

London 106 mi – Cambridge 58 mi – Ipswich 29 mi – Norwich 16 mi

Old Bakery without rest

Church Walk ✉ IP21 4SL – ✆ (01379) 676 492 – www.theoldbakery.net – Closed 2 weeks Christmas-New Year
4 rm – †£ 65 ††£ 85
♦ Pretty 16C former bakery just off the village green. Characterful interior features exposed beams and inglenooks: homely lounge and breakfast room; good-sized bedrooms with modern facilities.

PURTON – Wiltshire – 503 O29 – pop. 3 328 – ✉ Swindon 4 D2

London 94 mi – Bristol 41 mi – Gloucester 31 mi – Oxford 38 mi

Pear Tree at Purton

Church End, South : 0.5 mi by Church St on Lydiard Millicent rd ✉ SN5 4ED – ✆ (01793) 772 100 – www.peartreepurton.co.uk
15 rm – †£ 110/150 ††£ 150 – 2 suites **Rest** – Menu £ 20/35 **s**
♦ Personally run, extended 16C sandstone vicarage in mature seven-acre garden. Spacious flower-filled lounge. Rooms with traditional comforts and thoughtful extras. Conservatory restaurant overlooks wild flower borders.

RADNAGE – Bucks. – see Stokenchurch

RAINHAM – Medway – 504 U29 9 C1

London 14 mi – Basildon 16 mi – Dartford 9 mi

XX The Barn

507 Lower Rainham Rd, North : 1.75 mi by Station Rd ✉ ME8 7TN – ✆ (01634) 361 363 – www.thebarnrestaurantrainham.co.uk – Closed 23 December-4 January, Monday, lunch Saturday and Sunday, and bank holidays
Rest – Menu £ 17/23 – Carte £ 17/37
♦ Black and white timbered, 18C Essex barn, reconstructed on this site. Heavily beamed, rustic dining room and upstairs lounge. Good choice of menus. Elaborate cooking comes in generous portions.

RAMSBOTTOM – Greater Manchester – **502** N23 – **pop. 17 352** **20** B2

London 223 mi – Blackpool 39 mi – Burnley 12 mi – Leeds 46 mi

ramsons

18 Market Pl ✉ BL0 9HT – ✆ (01706) 825 070 – www.ramsons-restaurant.com – Closed 26 December, 1 January, Monday and Tuesday

Rest – Italian influences – *(booking essential)* Menu £ 30/38 – Carte £ 30/56

◆ Intimate, two-roomed restaurant run by passionate owner. Array of menus includes 6/10 course tasting options. Clean, refined, Italian-influenced cooking mixes quality local/imported produce.

RAMSBURY – Wilts. – **503** P29 – see Marlborough

RAMSEY – Isle of Man – **502** G21 – see Man (Isle of)

RAMSGATE – Kent – **504** Y30 – **pop. 37 967** **9** D1

London 77 mi – Southend-on-Sea 89 mi – Ipswich 128 mi

Age & Sons

Charlotte Court ✉ CT11 8HE – ✆ (01843) 851 515 – www.ageandsons.co.uk – Closed 4-24 January, Monday and Sunday dinner

Rest – Carte £ 19/26

◆ Attractive converted wine warehouse in centre of town. Sexy basement bar; rustic ground floor café; more formal 1st floor restaurant and lovely terrace. Interesting modern menu of gutsy, flavourful cooking. Charming service.

Eddie Gilberts

32 King St. ✉ CT11 8NT – ✆ (01843) 852 123 – www.eddiegilberts.com – Closed Sunday dinner

Rest – Seafood – Carte £ 17/31

◆ High street fish shop; head upstairs to light, airy restaurant, with fishing nets and piscatorial pictures. Extensive array of fresh fish; well presented in generous portions.

RAMSGILL-IN-NIDDERDALE – N. Yorks. – **502** O21 – see Pateley Bridge

RANTON GREEN – Staffordshire – **502** N25 **19** C1

London 150 mi – Birmingham 36 mi – Stoke-on-Trent 19 mi – Wolverhampton 32 mi

Hand and Cleaver

Butt Ln ✉ ST18 9JZ – ✆ (01785) 822 367 – www.handandcleaver.co.uk – Closed Monday

Rest – Carte £ 20/30

◆ Huge pub with pleasant garden, spacious lounge and dining room with booths. Menus offer extensive choice, from tasty nibbles to carefully crafted, satisfying classics; offal is a favourite.

RAVENSTONEDALE – Cumbria – **502** M20 – see Kirkby Stephen

RAYLEIGH – Essex – **504** V29 – **pop. 30 629** **13** C3

London 35 mi – Chelmsford 13 mi – Southend-on-Sea 6 mi

at Thundersley South : 1.25 mi on A 129 – ✉ Rayleigh

The Woodmans Arms

Rayleigh Rd ✉ SS7 3TA – ✆ (01268) 775 799 – www.thewoodmansarms.co.uk

Rest – Carte £ 18/28

◆ Comfy sofas for drinkers; smart restaurant for diners. Seasonal cooking is hearty and flavourful; traditional in the main with lighter choices at lunch. A cheerful young team.

READING – Reading – **503** Q29 – **pop. 232 662** **11** C3

London 43 mi – Brighton 79 mi – Bristol 78 mi – Croydon 47 mi

Access Whitchurch Bridge (toll)

to Henley-on-Thames (Salter Bros. Ltd) (summer only)

Calcot Park Calcot Bath Rd, ✆ (0118) 942 7124

Plan on next page

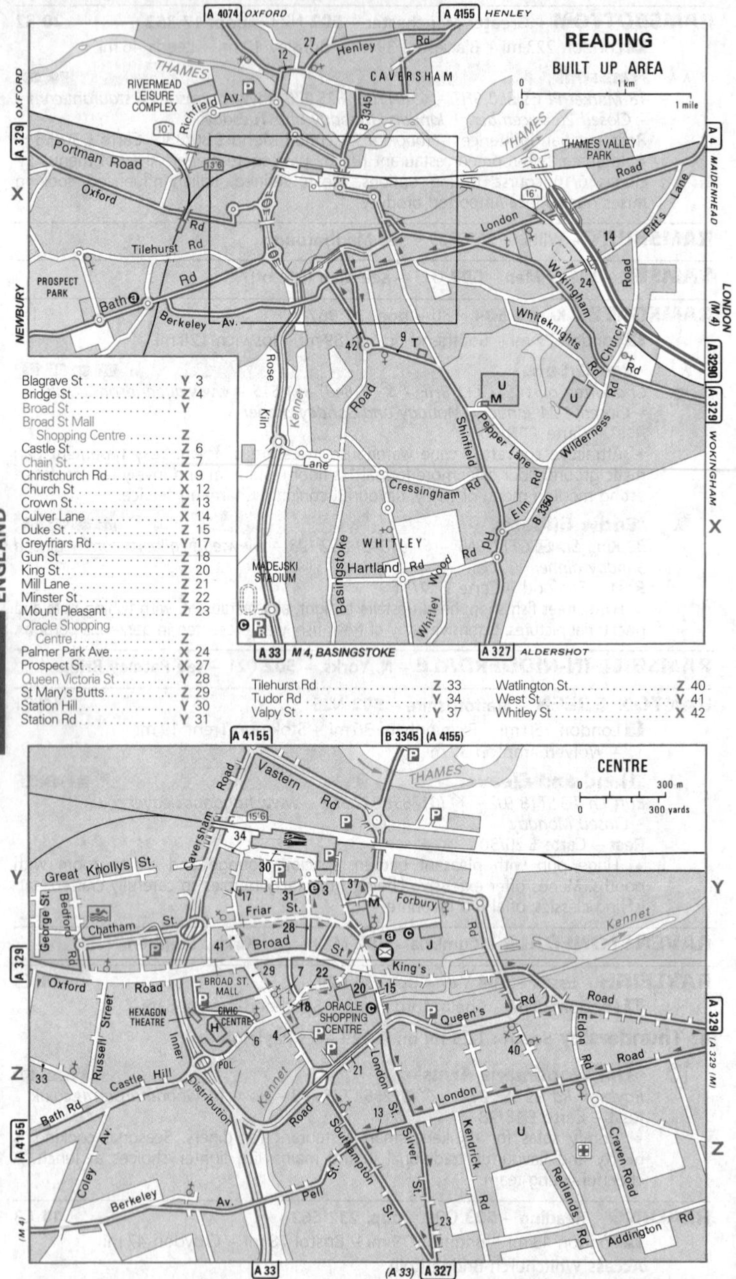
READING
BUILT UP AREA
CENTRE
A 4074 OXFORD
A 4155 HENLEY
A 329 OXFORD
NEWBURY
A 4 MAIDENHEAD
LONDON (M 4)
A 3290
A 329 WOKINGHAM
A 33 M 4, BASINGSTOKE
A 327 ALDERSHOT
CAVERSHAM
RIVERMEAD LEISURE COMPLEX
THAMES VALLEY PARK
PROSPECT PARK
WHITLEY
MADEJSKI STADIUM
THAMES
Kennet
Blagrave St . . . . . Y 3
Bridge St . . . . . Z 4
Broad St . . . . . Y
Broad St Mall Shopping Centre . . . . . Z
Castle St . . . . . Z 6
Chain St . . . . . Z 7
Christchurch Rd . . . . . X 9
Church St . . . . . X 12
Crown St . . . . . Z 13
Culver Lane . . . . . X 14
Duke St . . . . . Z 15
Greyfriars Rd . . . . . Y 17
Gun St . . . . . Z 18
King St . . . . . Z 20
Mill Lane . . . . . Z 21
Minster St . . . . . Z 22
Mount Pleasant . . . . . Z 23
Oracle Shopping Centre . . . . . Z
Palmer Park Ave . . . . . X 24
Prospect St . . . . . X 27
Queen Victoria St . . . . . Y 28
St Mary's Butts . . . . . Z 29
Station Hill . . . . . Y 30
Station Rd . . . . . Y 31
Tilehurst Rd . . . . . Z 33
Tudor Rd . . . . . Y 34
Valpy St . . . . . Y 37
Watlington St . . . . . Z 40
West St . . . . . Y 41
Whitley St . . . . . X 42
A 4155
B 3345 (A 4155)
HEXAGON THEATRE
CIVIC CENTRE
BROAD ST. MALL
ORACLE SHOPPING CENTRE
A 329 (M)
A 33
(A 33) A 327
ENGLAND

Forbury

26 The Forbury ✉ RG1 3EJ – ✆ (0118) 952 7770 – www.theforburyhotel.co.uk Yc

23 rm – †£ 95/260 ††£ 135/280, ☕ £ 17

Rest *Cerise* – ✆ (0800) 078 9789 – Carte £ 34/48

◆ Former civic hall overlooking Forbury Square Gardens; now a very stylish town house hotel. Eye-catching artwork features in all the stunningly individualistic bedrooms. Stylish basement cocktail bar/restaurant where clean, crisp, modern cooking holds sway.

Malmaison

Great Western House, 18-20 Station Rd ✉ RG1 1JX – ✆ (0118) 956 2300 – www.malmaison.com Ye

75 rm – †£ 190 ††£ 190, ☕ £ 14.50

Rest *Brasserie* – *(closed Saturday lunch)* Menu £ 25 – Carte £ 29/37

◆ Modernised Victorian railway hotel with contemporary furnishings, busy cafe and smart bar. Spacious, stylish bedrooms boast high level of facilities. Railway theme throughout. Industrial feel Brasserie serves contemporary, French influenced cooking.

Beech House without rest

60 Bath Rd ✉ RG30 2AY – ✆ (0118) 959 1901 – www.beechhousehotel.com

15 rm ☕ – †£ 75/85 ††£ 85/95 Xa

◆ Red brick Victorian house with neat garden, terrace and summer house. Traditionally furnished with antiques and period ornaments. Pleasant, well equipped bedrooms with showers.

Forbury's

1 Forbury Sq ✉ RG1 3BB – ✆ (0118) 957 4044 – www.forburys.com – Closed 26 December, 1 January and Sunday Ya

Rest – Menu £ 17/21 – Carte £ 35/46

◆ Modern eatery near law courts. Relaxing area of comfy leather seats. Spacious dining room enhanced by bold prints of wine labels. Eclectic menus with Gallic starting point.

LSQ2

Lime Sq., 220 South Oak Way, Green Park, South : 2 mi by A 33 ✉ RG2 6UP – ✆ (0118) 987 3702 – www.lsq2.co.uk – Closed Christmas-New Year, Saturday and Sunday Xc

Rest – Menu £ 13 (lunch) – Carte £ 24/34

◆ Bright, airy restaurant with full length windows and terrace, set in suburban business park. Flavoursome cooking mixes British classics with modern Asian and international brasserie dishes.

London Street Brasserie

2-4 London St ✉ RG1 4PN – ✆ (0118) 950 5036 – www.londonstbrasserie.co.uk – Closed 25 December Zc

Rest – *(booking essential)* Menu £ 19 – Carte £ 26/36

◆ Lively and modern: a polite, friendly team serve appetising British classics and international dishes. Deck terrace and first-floor window tables overlook the river Kennett.

at Shinfield South : 4.25 mi on A 327 - X – ✉ Reading

L'Ortolan

Church Lane ✉ RG2 9BY – ✆ (0118) 988 8500 – www.lortolan.com – Closed 24 December-7 January, Sunday and Monday

Rest – Menu £ 29 (lunch)/49 (dinner midweek) – Carte £ 29/65

Spec. Duck liver terrine with cherries, salted caramel jelly. Sea bass with scallops, fennel and sauce vierge. Raspberry tasting plate.

◆ Red brick former vicarage with lawned gardens and stylish lounge and conservatory. Bright, comfortable dining room; classically based cooking with some original touches and pretty presentation. Smart, busy private dining rooms.

at Sonning-on-Thames Northeast : 4.25 mi by A 4 on B 4446

XXX **French Horn** with rm

✉ RG4 6TN – ✆ (0118) 969 2204 – www.thefrenchhorn.co.uk
– Closed 25-31 December

16 rm – †£ 135 ††£ 170 **Rest** – *(booking essential)* Carte £ 35/59 **s**

♦ Long-standing family owned restaurant in pretty riverside setting. Bay windowed dining room overlooks lovely garden and offers classical French menus crafted from seasonal ingredients. Comfy, traditional bedrooms; some in an annexe, some with views.

REDDITCH – Worcestershire – 503 O27 – pop. 74 803 — 19 C2

London 111 mi – Birmingham 15 mi – Cheltenham 33 mi – Stratford-upon-Avon 15 mi

Palace Theatre, Alcester St ✆ (01527) 60806, info.centre@redditchbc.gov.uk

Abbey Hotel G. & C.C. Dagnell End Rd, ✆ (01527) 406 600

Lower Grinsty Callow Hill Green Lane, ✆ (01527) 543 079

Pitcheroak Plymouth Rd, ✆ (01527) 541 054

Old Rectory

Ipsley Lane, Ipsley ✉ *B98 0AP – ✆ (01527) 523 000*
– www.theoldrectory-hotel.co.uk

10 rm – †£ 129 ††£ 159

Rest – *(closed Friday-Sunday) (booking essential for non-residents)*
Menu £ 15/25

♦ Converted early Georgian rectory surrounded by pleasant mature gardens creating a quiet and secluded haven. Smart, traditional interior décor and individually styled rooms. Charming Georgian style conservatory restaurant.

REDFORD – West Sussex – see Midhurst

REETH – North Yorkshire – 502 O20 – pop. 939 – ✉ Richmond — 22 B1

London 253 mi – Leeds 53 mi – Middlesbrough 36 mi – Newcastle upon Tyne 61 mi

Hudson House, The Green ✆ (01748) 884059,reeth@yorkshiredales.org.uk

The Burgoyne

On The Green ✉ *DL11 6SN – ✆ (01748) 884 292 – www.theburgoyne.co.uk*
– Closed 2 January-11 February

8 rm – †£ 120/144 ††£ 138/191 – 1 suite

Rest – *(dinner only) (booking essential for non-residents)* Menu £ 35

♦ Late Georgian hotel overlooking the green with views of the Dales. A charming, personally run, traditionally furnished house with well-appointed, individually styled rooms. Deep green dining room complements surrounding fells.

at Low Row West : 4 mi on B 6270

The Punch Bowl Inn with rm

✉ *DL11 6PF – ✆ (01748) 886 233 – www.pbinn.co.uk – Closed 25 December*

11 rm – †£ 98/120 ††£ 98/120 **Rest** – Carte £ 18/25

♦ Popular with walkers, this traditional 17C stone-built inn has a modernised, shabby-chic interior. Classic dishes are listed on mirrors above the fireplace. Supremely comfortable bedrooms, decorated in a fresh, modern style; all with views over Swaledale.

at Langthwaite Northwest : 3.25 mi on Langthwaite rd – ✉ Reeth

The Charles Bathurst Inn with rm

✉ *DL11 6EN – ✆ (01748) 884 567 – www.cbinn.co.uk – Closed 25 December*

19 rm – †£ 105/120 ††£ 105/120 **Rest** – Carte £ 23/34

♦ Characterful 18C hostelry set in a peaceful hillside village, boasting commanding rural views. The daily menu, inscribed on a mirror, offers refined yet hearty classical British dishes. Bedrooms are spacious and extremely comfy.

ENGLAND

REIGATE – Surrey – 504 T30 – pop. 47 602 7 D2

London 26 mi – Brighton 33 mi – Guildford 20 mi – Maidstone 38 mi

XX Tony Tobin @ The Dining Room

59a High St ✉ RH2 9AE – ✆ (01737) 226 650 – www.tonytobinrestaurants.co.uk – Closed 23 December-3 January, Saturday lunch, Sunday dinner and bank holidays

Rest – Menu £ 22 (weekdays) – Carte £ 37/52

◆ Contemporary first floor restaurant with pale hues and comfy lounge/bar above. Classical set lunch, more modern à la carte and 5 course tasting menu; the latter with wine recommendations.

X Westerly

2-4 London Rd ✉ RH2 9AN – ✆ (01737) 222 733 – www.thewesterly.co.uk – Closed 25 December-5 January, 2 weeks August, Sunday, Monday, Tuesday and lunch Saturday

Rest – *(booking essential at dinner)* Menu £ 25 (lunch) – Carte dinner £ 29/34

◆ Popular, two-roomed restaurant on the corner of a busy road. Concise menus follow the seasons; well-executed dishes are a mix of traditional preparations and modern interpretations of classics.

X Barbe

71 Bell St ✉ RH2 7AN – ✆ (01737) 241 966 – www.labarbe.co.uk – Closed Saturday lunch, Sunday dinner and bank holidays

Rest – French – Menu £ 25/32

◆ Long-standing French bistro with cheery owner and huge local following. Two main dining areas strewn with Gallic memorabilia. Simply laid, tightly packed tables. Classical, bi-monthly menu.

RETFORD – Nottinghamshire – 502 R24 – pop. 20 679 16 B1

London 148 mi – Lincoln 23 mi – Nottingham 31 mi – Sheffield 27 mi

40 Grove St (01777) 860780, retford.tourist@bassettlaw.gov.uk

The Barns without rest

Morton Farm, Babworth, Southwest : 2.25 mi by A 6420 ✉ DN22 8HA – ✆ (01777) 706 336 – www.thebarns.co.uk – Closed Christmas and New Year

6 rm – †£ 39/45 ††£ 63/75

◆ Privately owned and run converted part 18C farmhouse on a quiet country road. Informal, old-fashioned, cottage décor throughout. Beams within and lawned gardens without.

RHYDYCROESAU – Shrops. – 502 K25 – see Oswestry

RICHMOND – North Yorkshire – 502 O20 – pop. 8 178 Great Britain 22 B1

London 243 mi – Leeds 53 mi – Middlesbrough 26 mi – Newcastle upon Tyne 44 mi

Friary Gardens, Victoria Rd ✆ (01748) 828 742, richmond@ytbtic.co.uk

Bend Hagg, ✆ (01748) 825 319

Catterick Leyburn Rd, ✆ (01748) 833 268

Town★ - Castle★ **AC** – Georgian Theatre Royal and Museum★

The Bowes Museum★, Barnard Castle, NW : 15 mi by B 6274, A 66 and minor rd (right) – Raby Castle★, NE : 6 mi of Barnard Castle by A 688

Millgate House without rest

3 Millgate ✉ DL10 4JN – ✆ (01748) 823 571 – www.millgatehouse.com

3 rm – †£ 95/145 ††£ 145

◆ Georgian townhouse with fine elevated views of river Swale and Richmond Castle. Award winning terraced garden. Antique furnished interior. Bedrooms are tastefully restrained.

at Dalton Northwest : 6.75 mi by Ravensworth rd and Gayles rd – ✉ Richmond

Travellers Rest

✉ DL11 7HU – ☎ (01833) 621 225 – *Closed 25-26 December, 1 January, dinner Sunday and Monday*

Rest – *(dinner only and Sunday lunch)* Carte £ 18/30

♦ Community pub serving remote village. Blackboard menus offer fresh, home-made dishes, including tasty terrines, fishcakes and the popular duck with orange sauce. Friendly service.

RINGWOOD – Hampshire – 503 O31 – pop. 13 387 6 A2

London 102 mi – Bournemouth 11 mi – Salisbury 17 mi – Southampton 20 mi

The Furlong ☎ (01425) 470896, information@nfdc.gov.uk

Moortown Lodge without rest

244 Christchurch Rd, South : 1 mi on B 3347 ✉ *BH24 3AS* – ☎ *(01425) 471 404 – www.moortownlodge.co.uk*

7 rm – †£ 70 ††£ 96

♦ Welcoming Georgian hunting lodge, on a busy road at the edge of the forest. Large room with soft seating and neatly laid breakfast tables. Comfy bedrooms; some larger, with feature beds.

RIPLEY – North Yorkshire – 502 P21 – pop. 193 – ✉ Harrogate 22 B2

London 213 mi – Bradford 21 mi – Leeds 18 mi – Newcastle upon Tyne 79 mi

Boar's Head

✉ *HG3 3AY* – ☎ *(01423) 771 888 – www.boarsheadripley.co.uk*

25 rm – †£ 75/105 ††£ 125/150

Rest *Restaurant* – *(closed Sunday dinner)* Carte £ 20/32

Rest *Bistro* – Carte £ 20/32

♦ 18C coaching inn within estate village of Ripley Castle, reputedly furnished from castle's attics. Comfy, stylish, unique rooms are individually furnished; some in courtyard or adjacent house. Classically based, seasonal dishes in The Restaurant. More informal dining in The Bistro.

RIPLEY – Surrey – 504 S30 – pop. 2 041 7 C1

London 28 mi – Guildford 6 mi

Talbot Inn

High St. ✉ *GU23 6BB* – ☎ *(01483) 225 188 – www.thetalbotinn.com*

39 rm – †£ 60/110 ††£ 80/110, £ 5.95

Rest – *(closed Sunday dinner)* Carte £ 24/40

♦ Historic coaching inn dating back to the 15C. Characterful bedrooms in the main house; more uniform rooms in the courtyard. Charming lounge and bar with low beams and open fires. Brasserie-style dining room offers a mix of classic pub and more modern dishes.

Drake's (Steve Drake)

The Clock House, High St ✉ *GU23 6AQ* – ☎ *(01483) 224 777 – www.drakesrestaurant.co.uk – Closed 2 weeks January, 2 weeks August, Sunday, Monday and lunch Tuesday-Wednesday*

Rest – Menu £ 26/52

Spec. Rabbit with carrot, tarragon cream and Parma ham. Brill with turmeric, piccalilli, chorizo and creamed cauliflower. Raspberry with pineapple ravioli, white pepper and raspberry air.

♦ Georgian restaurant's red brick façade dominated by large clock. Intimate lounges and relaxing, open plan dining room with local gallery art on walls. Simple, seasonal menu; kitchen makes use of modern techniques and interesting combinations. Well-established team provide formal service.

RIPON – North Yorkshire – **502** P21 – pop. 16 468 Great Britain **22** B2

London 222 mi – Leeds 26 mi – Middlesbrough 35 mi – York 23 mi

Minster Rd ☎ (01765) 604625, ripontic@harrogate.gov.uk

Ripon City Palace Rd, ☎ (01765) 603 640

Town★ - Cathedral★ (Saxon Crypt) **AC**

Fountains Abbey★★★ **AC** :- Studley Royal **AC** (≤★ from Anne Boleyn's Seat) - Fountains Hall (Fa 0.5ade★), SW : 2.5 mi by B 6265 – Newby Hall (Tapestries★) **AC**, SE : 3.5 mi by B 6265

Old Deanery

Minster Rd ✉ HG4 1QS – ☎ (01765) 600 003 – www.theolddeanery.co.uk – Closed 25 December and 1-7 January

10 rm – †£ 80/95 ††£ 150

Rest – *(closed Sunday dinner)* Menu £ 16 (lunch) – Carte £ 13/36

◆ Eponymously named hotel opposite cathedral. Stylish interior blends seamlessly with older charms. Afternoon tea in secluded garden. 18C oak staircase leads to modern rooms. Appealing seasonal cooking in spacious dining room.

Sharow Cross House

Dishforth Rd, Sharow, Northeast : 1.75 mi by A 61 on Sharow rd ✉ HG4 5BQ – ☎ (01765) 609 866 – www.sharowcrosshouse.com – Closed Christmas-New Year

3 rm – †£ 60/70 ††£ 80/90 **Rest** – Menu £ 25

◆ Late Victorian villa, originally a country residence for a soap manufacturer. Characterful interior with spacious, light-filled rooms; tea served in comfy lounge on arrival. Tastefully furnished bedrooms with thoughtful extras; master room offers cathedral views. Set dinners – choose in advance from a series of seven.

at Aldfield Southwest : 3.75 mi by B 6265 – ✉ Ripon

Bay Tree Farm

✉ HG4 3BE – ☎ (01765) 620 394 – www.baytreefarm.co.uk

6 rm – †£ 50/60 ††£ 90 **Rest** – *(closed Sunday dinner)* Menu £ 18

◆ 18C sandstone barn with rural views, set on a working farm. Lounge with wood burning stove and French windows opening into garden; bright, spacious bedrooms with modern bathrooms. Homely food could include beef from the farm.

RISHWORTH – W. Yorks. – see Sowerby Bridge

ROADE – Northamptonshire – **504** R27 – pop. 2 254 **16** B3

London 66 mi – Coventry 36 mi – Leicester 42 mi – Northampton 5 mi

Roade House with rm

16 High St ✉ NN7 2NW – ☎ (01604) 863 372 – www.roadehousehotel.co.uk – Closed 26-31 December, Saturday lunch and Sunday dinner

10 rm – †£ 65/150 ††£ 75/150 **Rest** – Menu £ 23 (lunch) – Carte £ 28/38

◆ Personally run, former village pub and schoolhouse, with two lounges and a simple linen-laid dining room. Crafted from local produce, monthly set menus offer classical cooking with modern touches. Pleasant bedrooms are furnished in pine.

ROCHDALE – Greater Manchester – **502** N23 – pop. 95 796 **20** B2

London 224 mi – Blackpool 40 mi – Burnley 11 mi – Leeds 45 mi

Touchstones, The Esplanade ☎ (01706) 924928, tic@link4life.org

Bagslate Edenfield Rd, ☎ (01706) 643 818

Marland Bolton Rd, Springfield Park, ☎ (01706) 649 801

Castle Hawk Castleton Chadwick Lane, ☎ (01706) 640 841

Nutters

Edenfield Rd, Norden, West : 3.5 mi on A 680 ✉ OL12 7TT – ☎ (01706) 650 167 – www.nuttersrestaurant.com – Closed 27-28 December, 2-3 January and Monday

Rest – Menu £ 17 (weekday lunch)/38 – Carte £ 26/38

◆ Views of the lyrical gardens contrast with a menu of often complex modern British dishes with international twists and influences. Best views at either end of the room.

ENGLAND

ROCK – Cornwall – 503 F32 – pop. 4 593 – ✉ Wadebridge **1 B2**

London 266 mi – Newquay 24 mi – Tintagel 14 mi – Truro 32 mi

Pencarrow★, SE : 8.5 mi by B 3314 and A 389

St Enodoc

✉ *PL27 6LA – ✆ (01208) 863 394 – www.enodoc-hotel.co.uk*
– Closed 13 December-11 February

16 rm – £ 95/185 £ 130/235 – 4 suites

Rest ***Restaurant Nathan Outlaw and Seafood and Grill*** – see restaurant listing

◆ Beautifully located hotel boasting stunning bay views. Strong New England theme throughout with pastel painted woodwork and stripy sofas. Comfy guest areas and modern, well-appointed bedrooms.

Restaurant Nathan Outlaw – at the St Enodoc Hotel

✉ *PL27 6LA – ✆ (01208) 863 394 – www.nathan-outlaw.com*
– Closed 13 December-11 February, Sunday and Monday

Rest – *(dinner only) (booking essential)* Menu £ 55/65

Spec. Cod, tartare sauce, peas and clams. Sea bass with crab and sea vegetables. Elderflower jelly with gooseberries and lemon sorbet.

◆ Intimate fine dining restaurant of just 9 tables, featuring pale colours and modern art. Clean, precise cooking showcases the finest local, seasonal ingredients and focuses on fresh, quality seafood. Choose between two 6 course menus and one vegetarian option.

Seafood and Grill – at the St Enodoc Hotel

✉ *PL27 6LA – ✆ (01208) 863 394 – www.nathan-outlaw.com*
– Closed 13 December-11 February

Rest – Menu £ 23 – Carte £ 25/40

◆ All day, split-level restaurant and bar overlooking the Camel Estuary and opening out onto a lovely rear terrace. Menus feature light offerings and simply executed steak and seafood dishes.

at Trebetherick North : 1 mi by Trewint Lane

St Moritz

✉ *PL27 6SD – ✆ (01208) 862 242 – www.stmoritzhotel.co.uk*

30 rm – £ 75/142 £ 99/220 – 15 suites – £ 189/309

Rest – *(dinner only)* Carte £ 28/40

◆ Art deco style hotel with leisure club, indoor and outdoor swimming pools and a 6 room spa. Smartly furnished bedrooms; spacious bathrooms. Suites have a lounge, kitchen and estuary views. Restaurant displays a simple, flavoursome menu of unfussy dishes.

ROCKBEARE – Devon – see Exeter

ROECLIFFE – North Yorkshire – see Boroughbridge

ROGATE – West Sussex – 504 R30 – pop. 1 785 – ✉ Petersfield (hants.) **7 C2**

London 63 mi – Brighton 42 mi – Guildford 29 mi – Portsmouth 23 mi

Mizzards Farm without rest

Southwest : 1 mi by Harting rd ✉ *GU31 5HS – ✆ (01730) 821 656 – Closed Christmas and New Year. Minimum 2 night stay*

3 rm – £ 60 £ 90

◆ 17C farmhouse with delightful landscaped gardens, which include a lake, bordered by river Rother. Views of woods and farmland. Fine fabrics and antiques in appealing rooms.

ROMALDKIRK – Durham – 502 N20 – see Barnard Castle

ROMSEY – Hampshire – 503 P31 – pop. 17 386 Great Britain 6 A2

London 82 mi – Bournemouth 28 mi – Salisbury 16 mi – Southampton 8 mi

13 Church St ✆ (01794) 512987, romseytic@testvalley.gov.uk

Dunwood Manor Awbridge Danes Rd, ✆ (01794) 340 549

Nursling, ✆ (023) 8073 4637

Wellow East Wellow Ryedown Lane, ✆ (01794) 322 872

Abbey★ (interior★★)

Broadlands★ **AC**, S : 1 m

Ranvilles Farm House without rest

Ower, Southwest : 2 mi on A 3090 (southbound carriageway) ✉ SO51 6AA – ✆ (023) 8081 4481 – www.ranvilles.com

5 rm – †£ 30/40 ††£ 60/70

◆ Attractive part-16C former farmhouse in mature grounds. Spacious beamed interior has a cottagey, country house feel. Comfy lounge with antique breakfast table and good-sized, homely bedrooms.

ROSS-ON-WYE – County of Herefordshire – 503 M28 – pop. 10 085 18 B3

Great Britain

London 118 mi – Gloucester 15 mi – Hereford 15 mi – Newport 35 mi

Swan House, Edde Cross St ✆ (01989) 562768, tic-ross@herefordshire.gov.uk

Market House★ – Yat Rock (<★)

SW : Wye Valley★ – Goodrich Castle★ **AC**, SW : 3.5 mi by A 40

Wilton Court

Wilton Ln, Wilton, West : 0.75 mi by B 4260 (A 49 Hereford) ✉ HR9 6AQ – ✆ (01989) 562 569 – www.wiltoncourthotel.com – Closed 2-15 January

10 rm – †£ 90/135 ††£ 125/165

Rest *Mulberry* – Menu £ 19 (lunch) – Carte £ 28/41

◆ Attractive, part-Elizabethan house on the banks of the river Wye. 16C wood panelling in situ in bar and two of the bedrooms: others have a distinctly William Morris influence. Light, airy conservatory restaurant boasts Lloyd Loom furniture and garden views.

The Bridge at Wilton with rm

Wilton, West : 0.75 mi by B 4260 (A 49 Hereford) ✉ HR9 6AA – ✆ (01989) 562 655 – www.bridge-house-hotel.com

9 rm – †£ 80 ††£ 98/120 **Rest** – Menu £ 16 (lunch) – Carte £ 29/41

◆ On the banks of the Wye, boasting a kitchen garden supplying ingredients for the owners' passionate belief in home cooking. Also, a homely bar and well-maintained bedrooms.

The Lough Pool at Sellack

Sellack, Northwest : 3.25 mi by B 4260 and A 49 on Hoarwithy rd ✉ HR9 6LX – ✆ (01989) 730 236 – www.loughpool.co.uk – Closed 25 December, Easter, Sunday dinner and Monday except Bank Holidays

Rest – Menu £ 16 (Sunday lunch) – Carte £ 20/28

◆ Characterful black and white timbered inn set in a beautiful, rural location. Seasonally changing menu offers wide range of dishes with British, Mediterranean and Asian influences.

at Kerne Bridge South : 3.75 mi on B 4234 – ✉ Ross-On-Wye

Lumleys without rest

✉ HR9 5QT – ✆ (01600) 890 040 – www.thelumleys.co.uk

3 rm – †£ 50 ††£ 70

◆ Double-fronted brick house with colourful gardens; formerly the village pub, now a cosy, characterful guesthouse run with love and care. Cluttered, homely bedrooms, comfy lounge, and drying room for walkers. Well-located for the Wye Valley and Forest of Dean.

at Walford South: 3.75 mi on B 4234

Mill Race
HR9 5QS – (01989) 562 891 – www.millrace.info
Rest – Carte £ 18/30
◆ Surprisingly modern-looking pub in a small country village. Regulars gather at the bar and families are welcome. Cooking is simple and lets the locally sourced ingredients speak for themselves.

ROTHBURY – **Northumberland** – **501** O18 – **pop. 1 963** – **Morpeth** **24** A2
Great Britain

London 311 mi – Edinburgh 84 mi – Newcastle upon Tyne 29 mi
Coquetdale Centre, Church St (01669) 620887, tic.rothbury@nnpa.org.uk
Cragside House★ (interior★) **AC**

Farm Cottage without rest
Thropton, West : 2.25 mi on B 6341 NE65 7NA – (01669) 620 831 – www.farmcottageguesthouse.co.uk – Closed 1 week Christmas-New Year
5 rm – £ 60/65 £ 76/90
◆ 18C stone cottage and gardens; owner was actually born here. Two comfy lounges filled with family prints and curios. Individually styled rooms with plenty of extra touches.

Thropton Demesne Farmhouse without rest
Thropton, West : 2.25 mi on B 6341 NE65 7LT – (01669) 620 196 – www.throptondemesne.co.uk – April-October
4 rm – £ 60 £ 70
◆ Early 19C stone-built former farmhouse; unbroken Coquet Valley views. Lounge defined by quality décor. Artwork on walls by owner. Individually styled rooms with lovely vistas.

ROWDE – **Wilts.** – **503** N29 – **see Devizes**

ROWHOOK – **W. Sussex** – **see Horsham**

ROWSLEY – **Derbyshire** – **502** P24 – **pop. 451** – **Matlock** Great Britain **16** A1

London 157 mi – Derby 23 mi – Manchester 40 mi – Nottingham 30 mi
Chatsworth★★★ (Park and Garden★★★) **AC**, N : by B 6012

East Lodge
DE4 2EF – (01629) 734 474 – www.eastlodge.com
12 rm – £ 80/160 £ 80/160 **Rest** – Menu £ 24/38
◆ 17C hunting lodge in 10 acres of landscaped gardens. Elegant, well-appointed guest areas. Smart bedrooms – several with four-posters – have good views and state-of-the-art bathrooms; some with TVs. Fresh cooking. Everything made in-house; simpler dishes at lunch.

Peacock
Bakewell Rd DE4 2EB – (01629) 733 518 – www.thepeacockatrowsley.com – Closed 24-26 December
16 rm – £ 95/125 £ 185/250, £ 6.95
Rest – *(closed Sunday dinner and bank holiday Mondays)* Menu £ 26 (lunch) – Carte £ 47/54
◆ Characterful 17C house with gardens leading down to the river. Bold modern colours sit alongside fine art and period furnishings in both the guest areas and bedrooms. Charming bar boasts stone walls, large fireplace and snack menu. Restaurant offers modern dishes.

ROYAL LEAMINGTON SPA – **Warwickshire** – **503** P27 – **pop. 61 595** **19** D3

London 99 mi – Birmingham 23 mi – Coventry 9 mi – Leicester 33 mi
The Royal Pump Rooms, The Parade (01926) 742762, leamingtontic@shakespeare-country.co.uk
Leamington and County Whitnash Golf Lane, (01926) 425 961

ROYAL LEAMINGTON SPA

Adelaide Rd V
Avenue Rd. . . . . V 2
Bath St. . . . . V 3
Beauchamp Ave . . . . . U
Beauchamp Hill. . . . . U 4
Binswood St . . . . . U 6
Brandon Parade . . . . . U 10
Church Hill . . . . . UV 16
Clarendon Ave. . . . . U
Clarendon Pl. . . . . U 18
Dale St . . . . . UV
Hamilton Terrace. . . . . V 21
High St . . . . . V 22
Holly Walk . . . . . U
Kenilworth Rd . . . . . U
Leam Terrace. V
Leicester St. . . . . U
Lillington Ave. . . . . U
Lillington Rd. . . . . U
Lower Ave . . . . . V 28
Newbold Terrace. . . . . V 30
Northumberland Rd . . . . . U 33
Old Warwick Rd V
Parade. . . . . UV
Priory Terrace. . . . . V 37
Radford Rd V
Regent Grove. . . . . UV 40
Regent St. . . . . UV
Royal Priors Shopping Centre . . . . . U
Rugby Rd. . . . . U
Russell Terrace V
Spencer St. . . . . V 44
Tachbrook Rd. . . . . V 47
Victoria Terrace . . . . . V 49
Warwick St . . . . . U
Willes Rd . . . . . UV

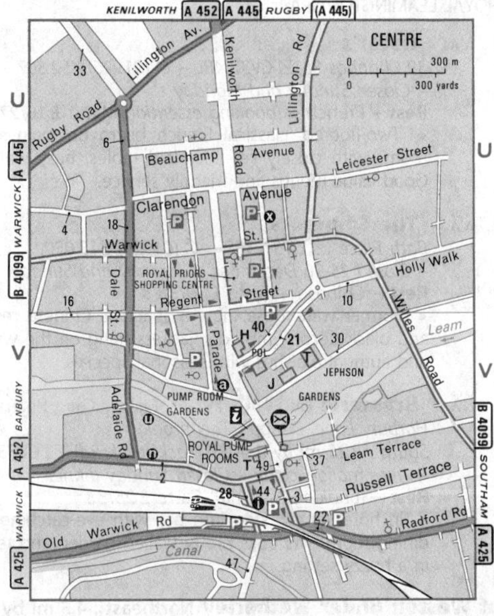

Mallory Court

Harbury Lane, Bishop's Tachbrook, South : 2.25 mi by B 4087 (Tachbrook Rd)
✉ CV33 9QB – ✆ (01926) 330 214 – www.mallory.co.uk
30 rm – 🚹£ 95/375 🚹🚹£ 149/450
Rest *The Brasserie at Mallory* – see restaurant listing
Rest *The Dining Room* – *(closed Saturday lunch) (booking essential)*
Menu £ 30/58
Spec. Dressed crab, roasted scallop, apple and wasabi sorbet. Beef fillet, braised oxtail, morels, Madeira sauce. Chocolate hazelnut rocher.

◆ Part Edwardian country house in Lutyens style; extensive landscaped gardens. Finest quality antiques and furnishings throughout public areas and individually styled bedrooms. Refined, classically-based cooking in elegant, panelled restaurant; formal and well-organised service.

Adams without rest

22 Avenue Rd ✉ CV31 3PQ – ✆ (01926) 450 742 – www.adams-hotel.co.uk – Closed Christmas-New Year V**n**
14 rm – 🚹£ 70/85 🚹🚹£ 90/95

◆ Delightful house of the Regency period with plenty of charm and character: original features include ceiling mouldings. Immaculate and similarly attractive bedrooms.

York House without rest

9 York Rd ✉ CV31 3PR – ✆ (01926) 424 671 – www.yorkhousehotel.biz – Closed 22 December-1 January V**u**
8 rm – 🚹£ 40/58 🚹🚹£ 70/75

◆ Victorian house on a pleasant parade, retains characterful fittings such as stained glass windows. Views of River Leam. Simply furnished rooms in period style.

Restaurant 23

23 Dormer Place ✉ CV32 5AA – ✆ (01926) 422 422 – www.restaurant23.co.uk – Closed 25-26 December, 2 weeks January, last 2 weeks August, Sunday and Monday V**a**
Rest – Menu £ 20/23 – Carte £ 38/48

◆ Ever spoken to a working chef in a restaurant? You can here, in elegantly appointed surroundings, where classically based, seasonal, modern dishes are concocted by the owner.

XX **Oscar's** VISA AE

39 Chandos St ✉ CV32 4RL – ✆ (01926) 452 807 – www.oscarsfrenchbistro.co.uk – Closed Sunday and Monday Ux

Rest – French – *(booking essential)* Menu £ 16/27

◆ Two-floored, classical French bistro on main shopping street. Three dining rooms with closely set linen-laid tables, busy walls and plenty of atmosphere. Good value menus and friendly service.

XX **The Emperors** AC VISA AE

Bath Place ✉ CV31 3BP – ✆ (01926) 313 030 – Closed 25-26 December, 1 January and Sunday Vi

Rest – Chinese – Carte £ 19/38 **s**

◆ Former warehouse, now a spacious Chinese restaurant with smart red, gold and black décor. Emperors' jackets hang on the walls. Large menus mix popular and authentic dishes with seasonal specials.

XX **Brasserie at Mallory** – at Mallory Court Hotel AC P VISA AE

Harbury Lane, Bishop's Tachbrook, South : 2.25 mi by B 4087 (Tachbrook Rd) ✉ CV33 9QB – ✆ (01926) 453 939 – www.mallory.co.uk – Closed Sunday dinner

Rest – *(booking essential)* Carte £ 25/38

◆ In hotel annex; step into bar with eye-catching Art Deco style. Conservatory dining room overlooks pretty walled garden and terrace. Modern British cooking in a buzzy setting.

ENGLAND

at Weston under Wetherley Northeast : 4.5 mi by A 445 on B 4453 – ✉ Royal Leamington Spa

Wethele Manor Farm without rest P VISA AE

✉ CV33 9BZ – ✆ (01926) 831 772 – www.wethelemanor.com

9 rm – †£ 65/90 ††£ 80/120

◆ 16C farmhouse with large garden, patio and water feature, set in 250 acres of working farm. Comfy lounge in old dairy; wood-furnished breakfast room complete with well. Classical bedrooms.

ROYAL TUNBRIDGE WELLS – Kent – 504 U30 – pop. 60 095 8 B2

Great Britain

London 36 mi – Brighton 33 mi – Folkestone 46 mi – Hastings 27 mi

The Old Fish Market, The Pantiles ✆ (01892) 515675, touristinformationcentre@tunbridgewells.gov.uk

Langton Rd, ✆ (01892) 523 034

The Pantiles★ B **26** – Calverley Park★ B

Hotel du Vin AC P VISA AE

Crescent Rd ✉ TN1 2LY – ✆ (01892) 526 455 – www.hotelduvin.com

34 rm – †£ 115/300 ††£ 115/300, £ 13.95 Bc

Rest *Bistro* – *(booking essential)* Carte £ 25/41

◆ Attractive 19C property in the town centre, boasting good southerly views over the park. Wine-themed interior with comfy lounge, clubby bar and contemporary bedrooms named after vineyards. Bistro offers concise menu of classic British and international dishes.

Brew House rm, AC P VISA AE

1 Warwick Pk. ✉ TN2 5TA – ✆ (01892) 520 587 – www.brewhousehotel.com

15 rm – †£ 199 ††£ 199 Bx

Rest *One* – Carte £ 21/31

◆ Former brewhouse and Subbuteo factory; now a boutique hotel. Bedrooms – 3 of which have balconies – boast a clean, minimalist style; bathrooms have glass walls which turn opaque at the touch of a button. Stylish restaurant decorated in vivid pinks and stark whites.

ROYAL TUNBRIDGE WELLS

Benhall Mill Rd . . . . **A** 3
Bishop's Down . . . . **A** 4
Calverley Rd . . . . **B**
Crescent Rd . . . . **B** 9
Fir Tree Rd . . . . **A** 10
Grosvenor Rd . . . . **B** 12
Hall's Hole Rd . . . . **A** 13
High Rocks Lane . . . . **A** 16
High St . . . . **B** 14
Hungershall Park Rd . . . . . . **A** 17
Lansdowne Rd . . . . **B** 18
Lower Green Rd . . . . **A** 20
Major York's Rd . . . . **A** 21
Monson Rd . . . . **B** 22
Mount Ephraim . . . . **A, B** 23
Mount Ephraim Rd . . . . **B** 24
Mount Pleasant Rd . . . . **B** 25
Pantiles (The) . . . . **B** 26
Prospect Rd . . . . **A** 27
Royal Victoria Pl. Shopping Centre . . . . **B**
Rusthall Rd . . . . **A** 28
St John's Rd . . . . **B** 29
Tea Garden Lane . . . . **A** 30
Vale Rd . . . . **B** 33
Victoria Rd . . . . **B** 34
Warwick Park . . . . **B** 35

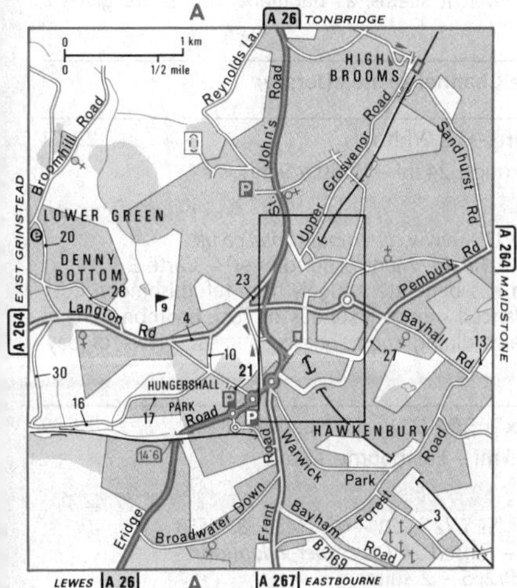

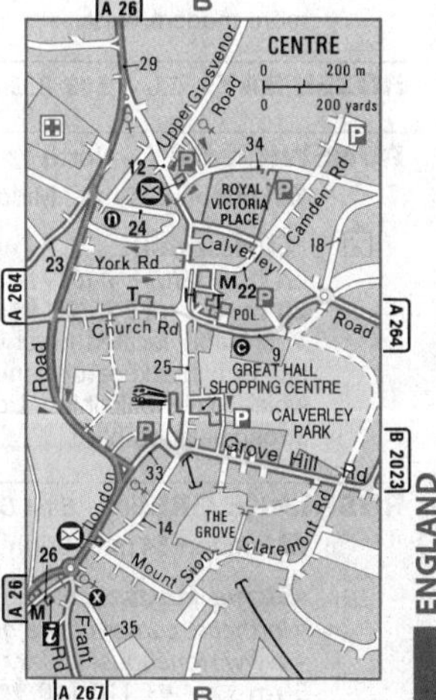

ENGLAND

Danehurst without rest

41 Lower Green Rd, Rusthall, West : 1.75 mi by A 264 ✉ TN4 8TW – ✆ (01892) 527 739 – www.danehurst.net – Closed Christmas and 2 weeks mid-March — Ae

3 rm – ♦£ 70/90 ♦♦£ 119/129

♦ Quiet Victorian house with terrace and koi carp pond. Quality furnishings and good attention to detail in bedrooms. Comfy lounge, library and conservatory breakfast room with homemade bread/jam.

Thackeray's

85 London Rd ✉ TN1 1EA – ✆ (01892) 511 921 – www.thackerays-restaurant.co.uk – Closed Sunday dinner and Monday — Bn

Rest – Menu £ 18/27 – Carte £ 38/52

♦ Attractive clapperboard house; former residence of the author Thackeray. Lovely terrace, lounge and two dining rooms with bold art. Classical cooking uses good ingredients; modern presentation.

at Speldhurst **Northwest : 3.5 mi by A 26 - A**

George & Dragon

Speldhurst Hill ✉ TN3 0NN – ✆ (01892) 863 125 – www.speldhurst.com – Closed 1 January and Sunday dinner

Rest – Carte £ 20/28

♦ Impressive and hugely characterful Wealden Hall house dating back to 1212. Generous cooking uses local, organic produce. Lunch offers pub classics; the evening menu is more elaborate.

ROYSTON – Hertfordshire – **504** T27 – **pop. 14 570** — **12** B1

London 48 mi

The Cabinet at Reed

High St, South : 3 mi by A 10 ✉ SG8 8AH – ✆ (01763) 848 366 – www.thecabinetatreed.co.uk – Closed 26 December, 1 January and Monday

Rest – Menu £ 15/25 – Carte £ 25/45

♦ White clapperboard pub with pleasant restaurant and delightful snug. Cooking is flavoursome but not always what it seems, as traditional dishes are given a more modern twist.

ROZEL BAY – C.I. – **503** P33 – see Channel Islands (Jersey)

RUNSWICK BAY – North Yorkshire – ✉ Whitby — **23** C1

London 285 mi – Middlesbrough 24 mi – Whitby 9 mi

Cliffemount

✉ TS13 5HU – ✆ (01947) 840 103 – www.cliffemounthotel.co.uk

20 rm – †£ 75/85 ††£ 170 **Rest** – Menu £ 30 (dinner) – Carte £ 30/41

♦ Enviably located hotel which has benefitted hugely from refurbishment. Cosy bar with blackboard menu. Balanced mix of luxurious or cosy bedrooms, 10 of which have balconies. Light, airy dining room boasts fantastic views of bay. Strong seafood base.

ENGLAND

RUSHLAKE GREEN – East Sussex – **504** U31 – ✉ Heathfield — **8** B2

London 54 mi – Brighton 26 mi – Eastbourne 13 mi

Stone House

(Northeast corner of the green.) ✉ TN21 9QJ – ✆ (01435) 830 553 – www.stonehousesussex.co.uk – Closed 24 December-2 January

5 rm – †£ 110/140 ††£ 199/265 – 2 suites

Rest – *(dinner only and lunch May-August) (residents only)* Menu £ 28 – Carte £ 21/25

♦ Impressive gates and beautiful gardens lead to charming, part-15C house; personally run and still in the same family. Country house interior with original staircases, wood-panelling and antiques. Individually decorated bedrooms feature period furnishings and some four-posters. Classical menus use kitchen garden produce.

RYE – East Sussex – **504** W31 – **pop. 3 708** Great Britain — **9** C2

London 61 mi – Brighton 49 mi – Folkestone 27 mi – Maidstone 33 mi

4/5 Lion St ✆ (01797) 229049, ryetic@tourismse.com

Old Town★★ : Mermaid Street★, St Mary's Church (★)

The George in Rye

98 High St. ✉ TN31 7JT – ✆ (01797) 222 114 – www.thegeorgeinrye.com

24 rm – †£ 130 ††£ 175 **Rest** – Carte £ 25/46

♦ Part 16C coaching inn; appealing mix of contemporary design and original features. Variously-sized bedrooms have state-of-the-art TVs and quality linen. Pleasant courtyard. Trendy restaurant offers Mediterranean dishes made with locally sourced produce and good choice of wines by glass.

Mermaid Inn

Mermaid St. ✉ TN31 7EY – ✆ (01797) 223 065 – www.mermaidinn.com

31 rm – †£ 90/180 ††£ 180/250 **Rest** – Menu £ 26/41 – Carte £ 44/55

♦ Historic inn dating from 15C. Immense character from the timbered exterior on a cobbled street to the heavily beamed, antique furnished interior warmed by roaring log fires. Two dining options: both exude age and character.

Jeake's House without rest

Mermaid St. ✉ TN31 7ET – ✆ (01797) 222 828 – www.jeakeshouse.com

11 rm – †£ 70/79 ††£ 104/138

♦ Down a cobbled lane, a part 17C house, once a wool store and a Quaker meeting place. Welcoming atmosphere amid antiques, sloping floors and beams. Pretty, traditional rooms.

Oaklands without rest
Udimore Rd, Southwest : 1.25 mi on B 2089 ✉ TN31 6AB – ☏ (01797) 229 734 – www.oaklands-rye.co.uk
3 rm – ♦£ 65 ♦♦£ 95/100
♦ Friendly Edwardian house with town/coast/white cliff views. Guest areas feature souvenirs from owner's time abroad – breakfast table is an Omani front door. Well-kept bedrooms; 2 four-posters.

Willow Tree House without rest
113 Winchelsea Rd., South : 0.5 mi on A 259 ✉ TN31 7EL – ☏ (01797) 227 820 – www.willow-tree-house.com
6 rm – ♦£ 75 ♦♦£ 90/130
♦ Lovingly restored 18C house close to harbour. Light colours and modern fabrics sit beside exposed brickwork and original fireplaces. Bedrooms boast excellent bathrooms with power showers. Good breakfasts.

Webbe's at The Fish Café
17 Tower St. ✉ TN31 7AT – ☏ (01797) 222 226 – www.webbesrestaurants.co.uk – Closed 1 week January
Rest – Seafood – Carte £ 22/31
♦ Relaxed café in former antiques warehouse, with terracotta-coloured brick walls, open-plan kitchen and small counter. Extensive menu of simply prepared seafood from Rye/Hastings day boats.

The Ship Inn with rm
The Strand ✉ TN31 7DB – ☏ (01797) 222 233 – www.theshipinnrye.co.uk
10 rm – ♦£ 70 ♦♦£ 100 **Rest** – Carte £ 16/30
♦ 16C former warehouse with shabby, slightly wacky styling and extremely laid-back feel. Carefully prepared, rustic dishes arrive in generous, flavoursome portions and ingredients are well-sourced. Compact bedrooms boast unusual feature walls and bold styling.

SAFFRON WALDEN – Essex – 504 U27 – pop. 14 313 — 12 B1

London 43 mi – Bishop's Stortford 12 mi – Cambridge 18 mi

the restaurant
Victoria House, 2 Church St ✉ CB10 1JW – ☏ (01799) 526 444 – www.trocs.co.uk – Closed 1 week spring, 2 weeks summer, Sunday and Monday
Rest – *(dinner only)* Menu £ 17 (weekdays) – Carte £ 22/34
♦ Cosy basement restaurant in town centre, displaying stone floors, exposed brick and modern art. Stylishly presented dishes boast well-defined flavours and some interesting Mediterranean touches.

Dish
13a King St ✉ CB10 1HE – ☏ (01799) 513 300 – www.dishrestaurant.co.uk – Closed 25-26 December, 1 January and Sunday dinner
Rest – Menu £ 19/20 – Carte (dinner Friday-Saturday) £ 28/32
♦ First floor restaurant within characterful beamed house in town centre. Modern oil paintings exude jazzy theme. Classically based dishes take on adventurous note at dinner.

ST ALBANS – Hertfordshire – 504 T28 – pop. 82 429 Great Britain — 12 A2

London 27 mi – Cambridge 41 mi – Luton 10 mi
Town Hall, Market Pl ☏ (01727) 864511, tic@stalbans.gov.uk
Batchwood Hall Batchwood Drive, ☏ (01727) 833 349
Redbourn Kinsbourne Green Lane, ☏ (01582) 793 493
City★ - Cathedral★ BZ – Verulamium★ (Museum★ **AC** AY)
Hatfield House★★ **AC**, E : 6 mi by A 1057

Plans on following pages

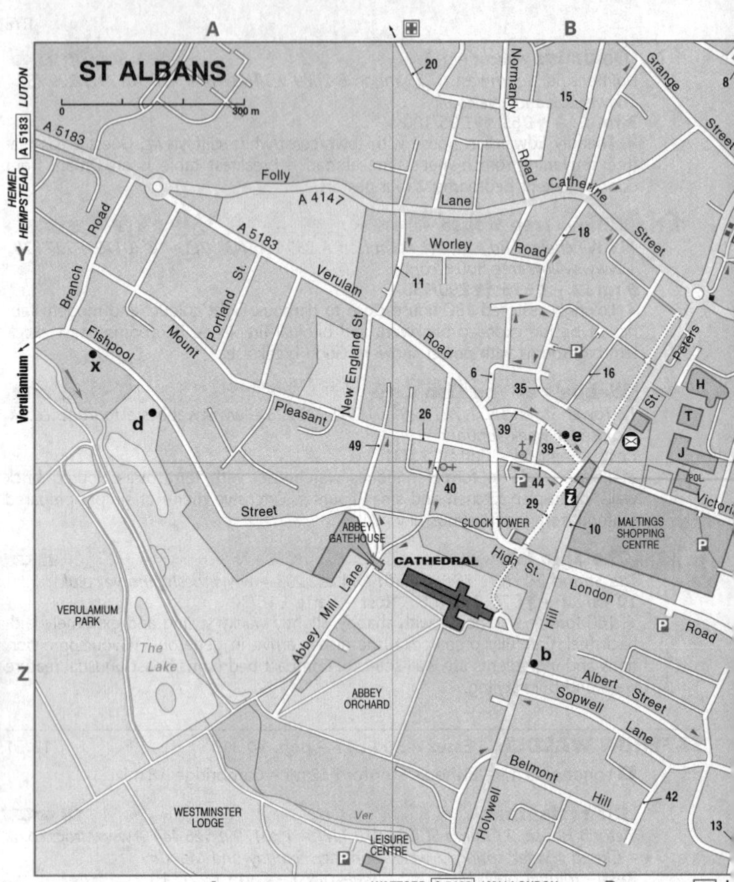

St Michael's Manor

rm,

St Michael's Village, Fishpool St ✉ AL3 4RY – ✆ (01727) 864 444
– www.stmichaelsmanor.com AY**d**

29 rm – †£ 125/180 ††£ 260
– 1 suite

Rest *The Lake* – *(closed dinner 25 December)* Menu £ 17/21 (weekdays)
– Carte £ 29/43

◆ This part 16C, part William and Mary manor house overlooks a lake. Elegant bedrooms are named after trees; some are suites with sitting rooms, all are luxurious and stylish. Conservatory dining room with splendid vistas.

Ardmore House

54 Lemsford Rd ✉ AL1 3PR – ✆ (01727) 859 313
– www.ardmorehousehotel.co.uk CY**a**

40 rm – †£ 63/95 ††£ 85/135

Rest *Belvedere* – Italian – ✆ (01727) 841 444 *(closed Sunday dinner)*
Menu £ 15/22 – Carte approx. £ 22

◆ Two part-Edwardian, part-Victorian properties in quiet residential road. Traditional guest areas and terrace overlook gardens. Simple, well-kept bedrooms have bright, airy feel and good desk space. Spacious Italian-themed conservatory restaurant.

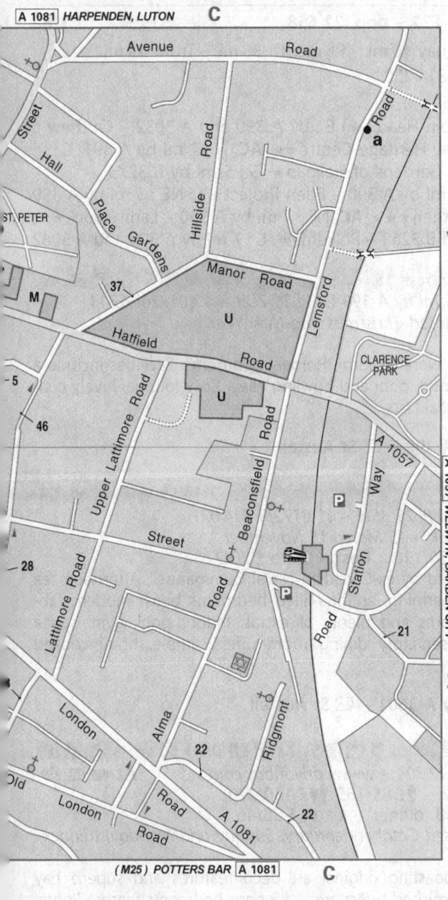

Abbey Mill Lane . . . . **AZ**
Albert St. . . . . **BZ**
Alma Rd. . . . . **CZ**
Avenue Rd . . . . **CY**
Beaconsfield Rd . . . . **CYZ**
Belmont Hill. . . . . **BZ**
Branch Rd . . . . **AY**
Bricket Rd . . . . **BCYZ** 5
Britton Ave . . . . **BY** 6
Carlisle Ave. . . . . **BCY** 8
Catherine St . . . . **BY**
Chequer St . . . . **BZ** 10
Church Crescent . . . . **ABY** 11
Cottonmill Lane . . . . **BCZ** 13
Dalton St . . . . **BY** 15
Drovers Way . . . . **BY** 16
Etna Rd . . . . **BY** 18
Fishpool St . . . . **AYZ**
Folly Ave . . . . **BY** 20
Folly Lane . . . . **ABY**
Grange St . . . . **BY**
Grimston Rd . . . . **CZ** 21
Grosvenor Rd . . . . **CZ** 22
Hall Pl. Gardens . . . . **CY**
Hatfield Rd . . . . **CY**
High St. . . . . **BZ**
Hillside Rd . . . . **CY**
Holywell Hill. . . . . **BZ**
Lattimore Rd . . . . **CZ**
Lemsford Rd. . . . . **CY**
London Rd . . . . **BCZ**
Lower Dagnall St . . . . **BYZ** 26
Maltings Shopping Centre. . . **BZ**
Manor Rd . . . . **CY**
Market Pl. . . . . **BZ** 29
Marlborough Rd . . . . **CZ** 28
Mount Pleasant. . . . . **AY**
New England St . . . . **AY**
Normandy Rd . . . . **BY**
Old London Rd . . . . **CZ**
Portland St. . . . . **AY**
Ridgemont Rd. . . . . **CZ**
Russell Ave. . . . . **BY** 35
St Peter's Rd. . . . . **CY** 37
St Peter's St. . . . . **BCY**
Sopwell Lane . . . . **BZ**
Spencer St . . . . **BY** 39
Spicer St College . . . . **BYZ** 40
Station Way. . . . . **CZ**
Thorpe Rd . . . . **BZ** 42
Upper Dagnall St . . . . **BYZ** 44
Upper Lattimore Rd . . . . **CYZ**
Upper Marlborough Rd . . . . **CYZ** 46
Verulam Rd . . . . **ABY**
Victoria St . . . . **BCZ**
Watson's Walk . . . . **CZ** 48
Welclose St . . . . **AYZ** 49
Worley Rd. . . . . **BY**

ENGLAND

Sukiyaki

VISA MC AE

6 Spencer St ✉ AL3 5EG – ☎ (01727) 865 009
– Closed 2 weeks in summer, 1 week Christmas, Sunday, Monday and Tuesday lunch BY**e**

Rest – Japanese – Menu £ 9/22 – Carte £ 17/20

◆ A pared-down style, minimally decorated restaurant with simple, precise helpings of Japanese food. No noodles or sushi, expect instead sukiyaki (a beef dish), and tempura.

Blue Anchor

P VISA MC

145 Fishpool St ✉ AL3 4RY – ☎ (01727) 855 038
– www.theblueanchorstalbans.co.uk – Closed Sunday dinner and Monday

Rest – Carte £ 20/29 AY**x**

◆ Smart pub with bistro-style interior and riverside garden. The chef is passionate about local, seasonal produce; menus display top notch ingredients, homemade and home-smoked products.

ST ANNE'S – **Lancs.** – **502** K22 – **see Lytham St Anne's**

ST AUBIN – **C.I.** – **503** P33 – **see Channel Islands (Jersey)**

ST AUSTELL – Cornwall – **503** F32 – pop. 22 658 **1** B2

London 281 mi – Newquay 16 mi – Plymouth 38 mi – Truro 14 mi

Carlyon Bay, ☎ (01726) 814 250

Holy Trinity Church★

St Austell Bay★★ (Gribbin Head★★) E : by A 390 and A 3082 – Carthew : Wheal Martyn China Clay Heritage Centre★★ **AC**, N : 2 mi by A 391 – Mevagissey★★ - Lost Gardens of Heligan★, S : 5 mi by B 3273 – Charlestown★, SE : 2 mi by A 390 – Eden Project★★, NE : 3 mi by A 390 at St Blazey Gate. Trewithen★★★ **AC**, NE : 7 mi by A 390 – Lanhydrock★★, NE : 11 mi by A 390 and B 3269 – Polkerris★, E : 7 mi by A 390 and A 3082

Poltarrow Farm without rest

St Mewan, Southwest : 1.75 mi by A 390 ✉ PL26 7DR – ☎ (01726) 67 111 – www.poltarrow.co.uk – Closed Christmas and New Year

5 rm – †£ 50 ††£ 80

◆ Appealing 19C house on working farm. Homely bedrooms. Facilities include a snooker table, badminton court, pool and bowling alley. Cosy lounge; lovely conservatory for Aga-cooked breakfasts.

at Tregrehan East : 2.5 mi by A 390 – ✉ St Austell

Anchorage House

Nettles Corner, Boscundle ✉ PL25 3RH – ☎ (01726) 814 071 – www.anchoragehouse.co.uk – 15 March-15 November

5 rm – †£ 75/80 ††£ 120/130 **Rest** – Carte £ 20/22

◆ Modern guesthouse owned by ex-Canadian Naval Commander. Afternoon tea served in comfy lounge. Charming, antique-filled bedrooms boast modern fabrics, state-of-the-art bathrooms and plenty of extras. Indoor pool, gym, sauna and chill out lounge. Conservatory dining room offers simple, home-cooked dishes. Lovely owners.

ENGLAND

at Carlyon Bay East : 2.5 mi by A 3601 – ✉ St Austell

Carlyon Bay

rest,

✉ PL25 3RD – ☎ (01726) 812 304 – www.carlyonbay.com

86 rm (dinner included) – †£ 85/165 ††£ 150/220

Rest *Bay View* – Menu £ 38 (dinner) – Carte £ 38/46

Rest *Fusion* – Asian – *(closed October-February, Sunday and Monday) (dinner only)* Carte approx. £ 30

◆ Imposing 1920s hotel boasting original art deco features and superb bay views. Large, traditionally furnished guest areas. Modern bedrooms feature lightly hued fabrics: rear rooms are bright; front rooms have views. Bay View serves unfussy classics. Fusion offers Asian-influenced fare.

Austell's

10 Beach Rd. ✉ PL25 3PH – ☎ (01726) 813 888 – www.austells.net – closed 1-14 January, 25-26 December and Monday

Rest – *(dinner only and lunch Friday-Saturday)* Menu £ 35

◆ Keenly run restaurant with relaxed, stylish interior. Small bar and open-plan kitchen. Modern, seasonal menu showcases local produce and features original touches. More casual weekend lunches.

ST BRELADE'S BAY – C.I. – **503** P33 – see Channel Islands (Jersey)

ST HELIER – C.I. – **503** P33 – see Channel Islands (Jersey)

ST HILARY – Cornwall – see Marazion

ST ISSEY – Cornwall – **503** F32 – see Padstow

ST IVES – Cornwall – **503** D33 – **pop. 9 866** **1** A3

London 319 mi – Penzance 10 mi – Truro 25 mi

The Guildhall, Street-an-Pol ✆ (01736) 796297, stivestic@cornwall.gov.uk

Tregenna Castle H., ✆ (01736) 795 254

West Cornwall Lelant, ✆ (01736) 753 401

Town★★ - Barbara Hepworth Museum★★ **AC** Y **M1** – Tate St Ives★★ (≤★★) - St Nicholas Chapel (≤★★) Y – Parish Church★ Y **A**

S : Penwith★★ Y. St Michael's Mount★★ (≤★★) S : 10 mi by B 3306 - Y - B 3311, B 3309 and A 30

Garrack

Burthallan Ln ✉ TR26 3AA – ✆ (01736) 796 199 – www.garrack.com – Closed 5 days Christmas Y**a**

18 rm ☐ – †£ 60/202 ††£ 130/202

Rest – *(dinner only and Sunday lunch)* Menu £ 16/27 – Carte approx. £ 28

♦ Well-established hotel with pleasant gardens close to Tate. Plenty of homely touches. Spacious pool and sauna. Individually designed bedrooms, many with feature beds. Very popular dining room serves Cornish specialities.

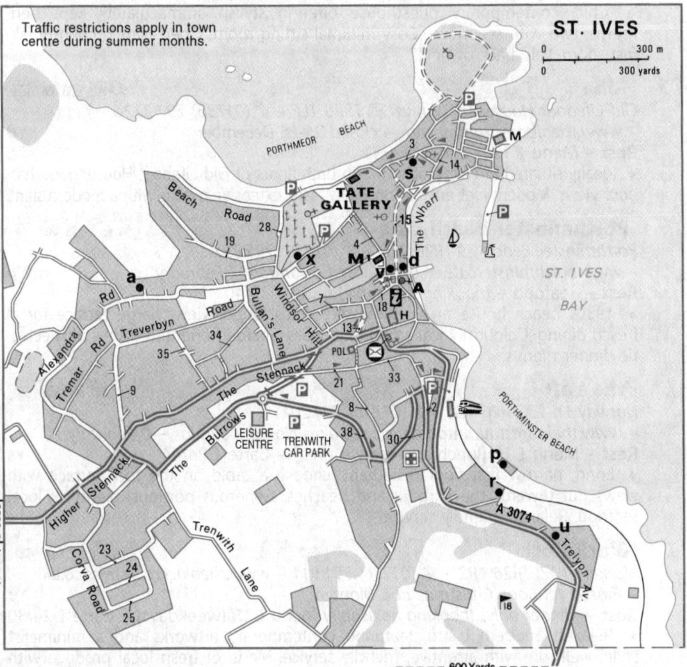

Traffic restrictions apply in town centre during summer months.

ST. IVES

ENGLAND

Albert Rd	Y	2	Porthia Crescent	Y	24
Back Rd West	Y	3	Porthia Rd	Y	25
Barnoon Hill	Y	4	Porthmeor Hill	Y	28
Bedford Rd	Y	7	Porthrepta Rd	Z	29
Bishop's Rd	Y	8	Talland Rd	Y	30
Carnellis Rd	Y	9	Tregenna Terrace	Y	33
Chapel St	Y	13	Trelawney Rd	Y	34
Fish St	Y	14	Trerice Rd	Y	35
Fore St	Y	15	Trewidden Rd	Y	38
High St	Y	18	Wheal Whidden	Z	40
Orange Lane	Y	19			
Parc Owles	Z	20			
Park Ave	Y	21			
Penwith Rd	Y	23			

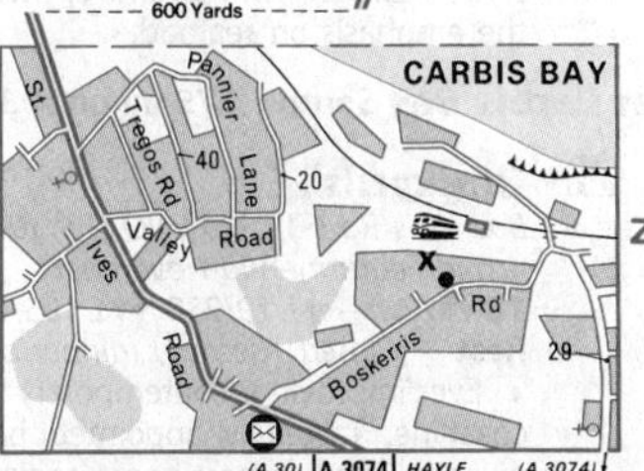

Blue Hayes without rest
Trelyon Ave ✉ TR26 2AD – ☎ (01736) 797 129 – www.bluehayes.co.uk – March-October Yu
6 rm – †£ 100/130 ††£ 210/230
◆ 19C house with super view from terrace over the harbour; access to coast path from garden. Hi-tech interior. Single course supper available. Well-appointed bedrooms.

Primrose Valley without rest
Porthminster Beach ✉ TR26 2ED – ☎ (01736) 794 939 – www.primroseonline.co.uk – Closed 19-27 December and 3-27 January
10 rm – †£ 90/155 ††£ 135/165 Yr
◆ Edwardian villa with unrivalled proximity to beach. Stylish café bar and lounge; relaxing front patio. Local suppliers ensure good breakfast choice. Individually styled rooms.

abode st ives without rest
1 Fern Glen ✉ TR26 1QP – ☎ (01736) 799 047 – www.abodestives.co.uk – closed 1 week Christmas Yx
4 rm – †£ 105 ††£ 130
◆ Chic, contemporary guesthouse offering stylish, immaculately kept bedrooms; two with sea views. Cosy minimal sitting room. Open-plan kitchen/breakfast room. Laid-back owners.

ENGLAND

XX **Alba**
Old Lifeboat House, The Wharf ✉ TR26 1LF – ☎ (01736) 797 222 – www.thealbarestaurant.com – closed 25-26 December Yd
Rest – Menu £ 17 – Carte £ 24/31
◆ Ideally situated in centre of town, on both floors of Old Lifeboat House; good harbour views. Modern feel; artwork on walls. Tasty, extensive menus with a modern slant.

X **Porthminster Beach Cafe**
Porthminster Beach ✉ TR26 2EB – ☎ (01736) 795 352 – www.porthminstercafe.co.uk – Closed 3 January-7 February Yp
Rest – Seafood – *(booking advisable)* Carte £ 32/40
◆ 1930s beach house on Porthminster sands. Super views: large terrace for al fresco dining. Colourful local artwork on walls. Seafood oriented dishes plus eclectic dinner menus.

X **The Loft**
Norway Ln ✉ TR26 1LZ – ☎ (01736) 794 204 – www.theloftrestaurantandterrace.co.uk – closed 2 January-10 February
Rest – Menu £ 16 (lunch and early dinner) – Carte £ 24/44 Ys
◆ Long, narrow first floor restaurant; choose a table on the roof terrace with views out towards the harbour and beaches. Generous portions; plenty of local seafood. Relaxed, friendly service.

X **Black Rock**
Market Pl ✉ TR26 1RZ – ☎ (01736) 791 911 – www.theblackrockstives.co.uk – Closed January, Christmas and Monday Yv
Rest – *(dinner only) (booking advisable)* Menu £ 18 (weekdays) – Carte £ 24/30
◆ Relaxed, modern bistro, featuring contemporary artworks and a minimalist style; well run, with attentive, friendly service. Menu of fresh local produce with the emphasis on seafood.

at Carbis Bay South : 1.75 mi on A 3074 – ✉ St Ives

Boskerris
Boskerris Rd ✉ TR26 2NQ – ☎ (01736) 795 295 – www.boskerrishotel.co.uk – mid-February-mid-November Zx
15 rm – †£ 79/230 ††£ 105/230
Rest – *(Closed Tuesday) (dinner only)* Carte £ 28/32 **s**
◆ Ever-improving, contemporary hotel with panoramic views of Carbis Bay and coastline. Tastefully appointed bedrooms; relaxing lounge. Enthusiastic young owners. Good, honest home-cooking.

ST JUST – Cornwall – 503 C33 – pop. 1 890 1 A3

London 325 mi – Penzance 7 mi – Truro 35 mi

Cape Cornwall G. & C.C., ☎ (01736) 788 611

Church★

Penwith★★ – Sancreed - Church★★ (Celtic Crosses★★), SE : 3 mi by A 3071 – St Buryan★★ (Church Tower★★), SE : 5.5 mi by B 3306 and A 30 – Land's End★ (cliff scenery★★★), S : 5.5 mi by B 3306 and A 30 – Cape Cornwall★ (≤★★), W : 1.5 mi - Morvah (≤★★), NE : 4.5 mi by B 3306 – Geevor Tin Mine★ **AC**, N : 3 mi by B 3306 – Carn Euny★, SE : 3 mi by A 3071 - Wayside Cross★ - Sennen Cove★ (≤★), S : 5.5 mi by B 3306 and A 30. Porthcurno★, S : 9.5 mi by B 3306, A 30 and B 3315

Boscean Country House without rest

Northwest : 0.5 mi by Boswedden Rd ✉ TR19 7QP – ☎ (01736) 788 748 – www.bosceancountryhouse.co.uk – Easter-October

12 rm – †£ 65/95 ††£ 110/125

◆ Stunning Arts and Crafts house set in three acres of walled gardens. Lovely wood panelled guest areas. Comfy, antique-furnished bedrooms; some with wrought iron beds and original fireplaces.

ST KEVERNE – Cornwall – 503 E33 – pop. 1 843 1 A3

London 302 mi – Penzance 26 mi – Truro 28 mi

Old Temperance House without rest

The Square ✉ TR12 6NA – ☎ (01326) 280 986 – www.oldtemperancehouse.co.uk

4 rm – †£ 55 ††£ 82

◆ Pretty pink-washed cottage framed by olive trees. Immaculately kept, contemporary interior; bright bedrooms display thoughtful touches. Fresh fruit and produce from local butcher for breakfast.

The Greenhouse

6 High St. ✉ TR12 6NN – ☎ (01326) 280 800 – www.tgor.co.uk – Closed 3 weeks January, Sunday lunch at bank holidays and Mother's Day

Rest – *(dinner only and Sunday lunch)* Carte £ 18/33

◆ Simply furnished eatery with open kitchen, set in a sleepy little village. Daily blackboard menu is centred around local, organic and gluten free produce. Cooking is unfussy and flavoursome.

ST KEW – Cornwall – See Wadebridge

ST LAWRENCE – C.I. – 503 P33 – see Channel Islands (Jersey)

ST MARGARET'S AT CLIFFE – Kent – 504 Y30 – see Dover

ST MARTIN'S – Cornwall – 503 B34 – see Scilly (Isles of)

ST MARY'S – Cornwall – 503 B34 – see Scilly (Isles of)

ST MAWES – Cornwall – 503 E33 – ✉ Truro 1 B3

London 299 mi – Plymouth 56 mi – Truro 18 mi

Town★ - Castle★ **AC** (≤★)

St Just-in-Roseland Church★★, N : 2.5 mi by A 3078

Tresanton

27 Lower Castle Rd ✉ TR2 5DR – ☎ (01326) 270 055 – www.tresanton.com – Closed 3-13 January

27 rm – †£ 225/365 ††£ 225/365 – 2 suites

Rest – *(booking essential for non-residents)* Menu £ 35/42

◆ Series of adjoining houses, formerly a yachtsman's club and cinema, offering valet parking and stunning bay views. Family friendly with homely lounges, small movie room, well-equipped bedrooms and mosaic-floored bathrooms. Superb service. Bright restaurant opens onto large terrace. Popular Sunday BBQs and jazz band.

ST MERRYN – Cornwall – 503 F32 – see Padstow

ST OSYTH – Essex – **504** X28 – see Clacton-on-Sea

ST PETER PORT – C.I. – **503** P33 – see Channel Islands (Guernsey)

ST SAVIOUR – Guernsey – **503** P33 – see Channel Islands (Guernsey)

ST SAVIOUR – Saint Saviour – **503** P33 – see Channel Islands (Jersey)

SALCOMBE – Devon – 503 I33 – pop. 1 893 — 2 C3

London 243 mi – Exeter 43 mi – Plymouth 27 mi – Torquay 28 mi

Council Hall, Market St ✆ (01548) 843927, info@salcombeinformation.co.uk

Sharpitor (Overbecks Museum and Garden★) (≤★★) **AC**, S : 2 mi by South Sands Z. Prawle Point (≤★★★) E : 16 mi around coast by A 381 - Y - and A 379

South Sands

Bolt Head ✉ TQ8 8LL – ✆ (01548) 859 000 – www.southsands.com

22 rm – †£ 205/295 ††£ 205/295 – 5 suites — Z**x**

Rest – Menu £ 20 (lunch and early dinner) – Carte £ 24/39

◆ Stylish hotel by the water's edge, with subtle New England theme and stunning spiral staircase. Subtle, tasteful bedrooms; go for one at the front with a balcony. Large, airy restaurant with delightful decked terrace; menus place their emphasis on fresh seafood.

at Soar Mill Cove Southwest : 4.25 mi by A 381 - Y - via Malborough village – ✉ Salcombe

Soar Mill Cove

✉ *TQ7 3DS – ✆ (01548) 561 566 – www.soarmillcove.co.uk – February-November*

22 rm – †£ 99/180 ††£ 140/240

Rest – Menu £ 29 (dinner) – Carte lunch £ 18/28

◆ Family-run hotel built from local slate and stone; delightfully set by the water's edge in a secluded cove. Good range of leisure facilities. Spacious bedrooms in bright, contemporary styles; half have sea views. Smart champagne bar. Classically based modern menu.

ENGLAND

SALCOMBE

- Allenhayes Rd .... Y 2
- Bonaventure Rd...... Y 3
- Buckley St .... Y 4
- Camperdown Rd..... Y 7
- Church St........... Y 8
- Coronation Rd .... Y 9
- Devon Rd........... Y 13
- Fore St .... Y
- Fortescue Rd .... Z 14
- Grenville Rd .... Y 15
- Herbert Rd .... Z 18
- Knowle Rd .... Y 19
- Moult Rd .... Z 20
- Newton Rd.......... Y 23
- Sandhills Rd .... Z 24
- Shadycombe Rd ..... Y 25

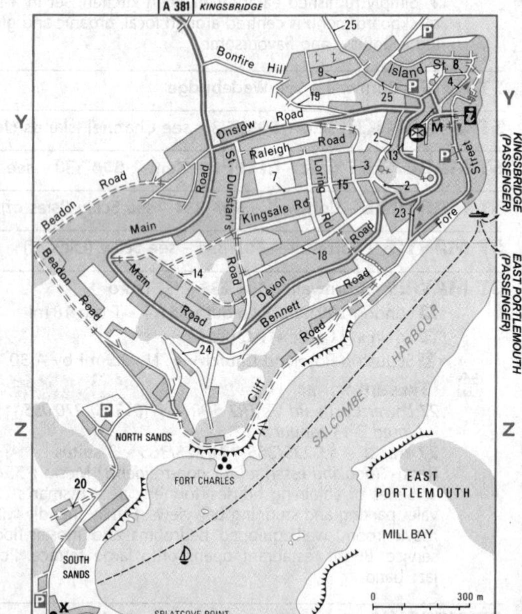

SALE – Greater Manchester – 502 N23 – pop. 55 234 – ✉ Manchester 20 B3

London 212 mi – Liverpool 36 mi – Manchester 6 mi – Sheffield 43 mi

Sale Lodge Golf Rd, ✆ (0161) 973 1638

Cornerstones without rest

230 Washway Rd, (on A 56) ✉ M33 4RA – ✆ (0161) 283 6909 – www.cornerstonesguesthouse.com

9 rm – £ 30/42 £ 56/60, £ 6.50

◆ Substantial red-brick Victorian house with neat garden, in leafy suburban location. Slightly wacky interior with bohemian-style lounge and breakfast room. Bedrooms range from retro to modern.

SALISBURY – Wiltshire – 503 O30 – pop. 43 355 4 D3

London 91 mi – Bournemouth 28 mi – Bristol 53 mi – Southampton 23 mi

Fish Row ✆ (01722) 334956, visitorinfo@wiltshire.gov.uk

Salisbury & South Wilts. Netherhampton, ✆ (01722) 742 645

High Post Great Durnford, ✆ (01722) 782 356

City★★ - Cathedral★★★ **AC** Z – Salisbury and South Wiltshire Museum★ **AC** Z **M2** – Close★ Z : Mompesson House★ **AC** Z **A** – Sarum St Thomas Church★ Y **B** – Redcoats in the Wardrobe★ Z **M1**

Wilton Village★ (Wilton House★★ **AC**, Wilton Carpet Factory★ **AC**), W : 3 mi by A 30 Y – Old Sarum★ **AC**, N : 2 mi by A 345 Y – Woodford (Heale House Garden★) **AC**, NW : 4.5 mi by Stratford Rd Y. Stonehenge★★★ **AC**, NW : 10 mi by A 345 Y and A 303 – Wardour Castle★ **AC**, W : 15 mi by A 30 Y

Plan on next page

Cricket Field House without rest

Wilton Rd, West : 1.25 mi on A 36 ✉ SP2 9NS – ✆ (01722) 322 595 – www.cricketfieldhouse.co.uk

14 rm – £ 50/75 £ 85/99

◆ Personally run extended house overlooking the County Cricket Ground. Bedrooms are prettily decorated with pictures and floral touches; majority of rooms are in the annex.

2 Park Lane without rest

2 Park Lane, North : 1.25 mi by A 345 ✉ SP1 3NP – ✆ (01722) 321 001 – www.2parklane.co.uk – closed Christmas-New Year

6 rm – £ 65/70 £ 70/85

◆ Fine Victorian house hidden away on a private road. Pleasant entranceway with original tiled floor; smart period breakfast room. Comfortable, modern bedrooms come in light, understated hues.

St Anns House without rest

32-34 St Ann St ✉ SP1 2DP – ✆ (01722) 335 657 – www.stannshouse.co.uk – Closed 20 December-2 January Z**e**

8 rm – £ 54/74 £ 79/110, £ 8.50

◆ Traditional Georgian townhouse with immaculate bedrooms, sash windows and original fireplaces. Large breakfast menu offers well sourced options. Honesty bar and private dining available.

Anokaa

60 Fisherton St ✉ SP2 7RB – ✆ (01722) 414 142 – www.anokaa.com

Rest – Indian – *(buffet lunch)* Menu £ 9/24 – Carte £ 20/30 Y**e**

◆ Lives up to being "something out of the ordinary", with eye-catching interior and staff in silky full-length gowns. Indian dishes mix modern and classical styles with aplomb.

at Burcombe West : 5.25 mi by A 36 - Y - off A 30 – ✉ Salisbury

The Ship Inn

Burcombe Ln ✉ SP2 0EJ – ✆ (01722) 743 182 – www.theshipburcombe.co.uk

Rest – Carte £ 23/31

◆ Charming 17C pub with open fire, low ceilings and oak beams. Seasonal à la carte and twice-daily changing specials offer satisfying portions of traditional dishes. Delightful riverside garden.

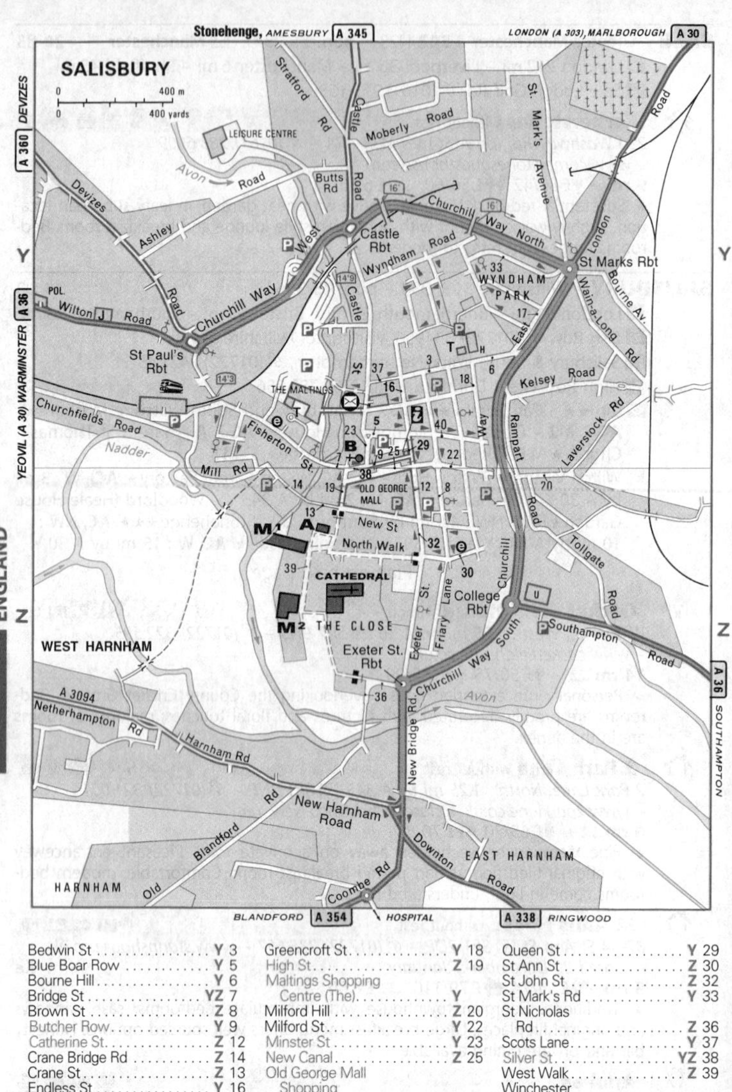

Bedwin St . . . . Y 3
Blue Boar Row . . . . Y 5
Bourne Hill . . . . Y 6
Bridge St . . . . YZ 7
Brown St . . . . Z 8
Butcher Row . . . . Y 9
Catherine St . . . . Z 12
Crane Bridge Rd . . . . Z 14
Crane St . . . . Z 13
Endless St . . . . Y 16
Estcourt Rd . . . . Y 17
Greencroft St . . . . Y 18
High St . . . . Z 19
Maltings Shopping Centre (The) . . . . Y
Milford Hill . . . . Z 20
Milford St . . . . Y 22
Minster St . . . . Y 23
New Canal . . . . Z 25
Old George Mall Shopping Centre . . . . Z
Queen St . . . . Y 29
St Ann St . . . . Z 30
St John St . . . . Z 32
St Mark's Rd . . . . Y 33
St Nicholas Rd . . . . Z 36
Scots Lane . . . . Y 37
Silver St . . . . YZ 38
West Walk . . . . Z 39
Winchester St . . . . Y 40

at Teffont West : 10.25 mi by A 36 - Y - and A 30 on B 3089 – ✉ Salisbury

Howard's House

Teffont Evias ✉ SP3 5RJ – ✆ (01722) 716 392 – www.howardshousehotel.co.uk – Closed Christmas

9 rm – †£ 110 ††£ 195

Rest – *(booking essential for non-residents)* Menu £ 28/29 – Carte dinner £ 30/46

◆ Personally run, part 17C dower house boasting fine gardens in a quaint, quiet village. Comfortable lounge and pleasant bedrooms with village or garden vistas. Garden herbs and vegetables grace accomplished cooking.

at Little Langford Northwest : 8 mi by A 36 - Y - and Great Wishford rd – ✉ Salisbury

Little Langford Farmhouse without rest
✉ *SP3 4NP – ✆ (01722) 790 205 – www.littlelangford.co.uk*
3 rm – †£ 60/75 ††£ 80/85
◆ Unusual Victorian gothic farmhouse boasting a turret, crenellations and lancet windows; set amidst rolling farmland. Original features include a fine tile-floored entranceway and stripped oak furnishings. Spacious, double aspect bedrooms have a classical style.

at Upper Woodford North : 6.75 mi by A 360

The Bridge Inn
✉ *SP4 6NU – ✆ (01722) 782 323 – www.thebridgewoodford.co.uk – Closed Sunday dinner January-February*
Rest – Carte £ 23/31
◆ Light, airy pub on banks of the River Avon, its garden an alfresco delight. Light bites lunch menu and classic à la carte; fresh, tasty dishes neatly presented on wood or slate.

SANDFORD-ON-THAMES – Oxon. – see Oxford

SANDIWAY – Cheshire – **502** M24 – pop. 4 299 – ✉ Northwich **20** A3

London 191 mi – Liverpool 34 mi – Manchester 22 mi – Stoke-on-Trent 26 mi

Nunsmere Hall
Tarporley Rd, Southwest : 1.5 mi by A 556 on A 49 ✉ CW8 2ES – ✆ (01606) 889 100 – www.nunsmere.co.uk
36 rm – †£ 135 ††£ 135
Rest *The Crystal* – Menu £ 22/30 – Carte dinner £ 41/51
◆ Secluded, on a wooded peninsular, originally built in 1900. Deep-seated sofas and sumptuous drawing rooms. Tasteful, individually furnished bedrooms exude quality and comfort. Dine in the classical style on imaginative and accomplished cuisine.

SANDSEND – N. Yorks. – **502** R/S20 – see Whitby

SANDWICH – Kent – **504** Y30 – pop. 4 398 Great Britain **9** D2

London 72 mi – Canterbury 13 mi – Dover 12 mi
Guildhall ✆ (01304) 613565, info@ticsandwich.wanadoo.co.uk
Town★

The Bell at Sandwich rm,
The Quay ✉ CT13 9EF – ✆ (01304) 613 388 – www.bellhotelsandwich.co.uk
37 rm – †£ 95/110 ††£ 110/225
Rest *The Old Dining Room* – ✆ (01304) 626 992 – Menu £ 15 (lunch) – Carte £ 23/33
◆ Situated by River Stour with original Victorian fittings in situ. Refurbishment has resulted in stunning transformation of bedrooms: now cool, elegant, stylish and welcoming. Pleasant brasserie with strong seafood base.

SANDYPARK – Devon – **503** I31 – see Chagford

SAPPERTON – Glos. – see Cirencester

SARK – C.I. – **503** P33 – see Channel Islands

SAWDON – N. Yorks. – see Scarborough

SCARBOROUGH – North Yorkshire – 502 S21 – pop. 38 364 23 D1

Great Britain

- London 253 mi – Kingston-upon-Hull 47 mi – Leeds 67 mi – Middlesbrough 52 mi
- Brunswick, Westborough - Harbourside, Sandside ✆ (01723) 383636, tourismbureau@scarborough.gov.uk
- Scarborough North Cliff North Cliff Ave, Burniston Rd, NW : 2 mi. by A 165, ✆ (01723) 355 397
- Scarborough South Cliff Deepdale Ave, S : 1 mi. by A 165, off Filey Rd, ✆ (01723) 374 737
- Robin Hood's Bay★, N : 16 mi on A 171 and minor rd to the right (signposted) – Whitby Abbey★, N : 21 mi on A 171 – Sledmere House★, S : 21 mi on A 645, B 1249 and B 1253 (right)

ENGLAND

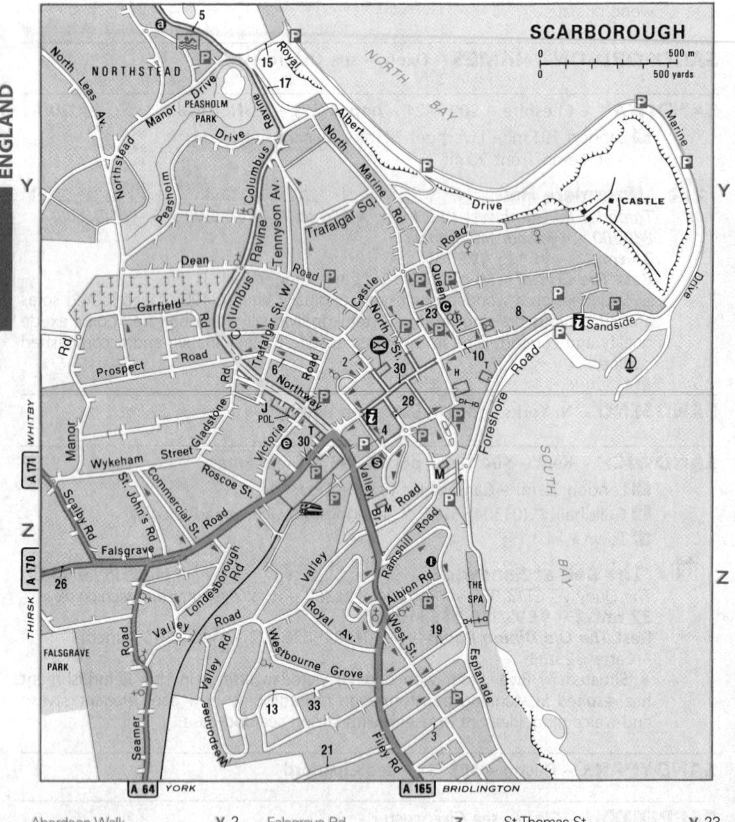

Aberdeen Walk . . . . . Y 2
Avenue Victoria . . . . . Z 3
Brunswick Pavillon Shopping Centre . . . . . Z 4
Burniston Rd . . . . . Y 5
Cambridge St . . . . . Y 6
Eastborough . . . . . Y 8
Falsgrave Rd . . . . . Z
Newborough . . . . . Y 10
Oriel Crescent . . . . . Z 13
Peasholm Gap . . . . . Y 15
Peasholm Rd . . . . . Y 17
Prince of Wales Terrace . . . . . Z 19
Queen Margaret's Rd . . . . . Z 21
St Thomas St . . . . . Y 23
Stepney Rd . . . . . Z 26
Vernon Rd . . . . . Z 28
Victoria Rd . . . . . YZ
Westborough . . . . . YZ 30
Westbourne Rd . . . . . Z 33

Crown Spa rm, rest, VISA AE

8-10 Esplanade ✉ YO11 2AG – ☎ (01723) 357 400 – www.crownspahotel.com
114 rm – **†£ 134/234 ††£ 248 – 1 suite** Zi
Rest *Taste* – ☎ (01723) 357 439 – Menu £ 30 **s** – Carte £ 27/36 **s**
◆ Refurbished 19C landmark hotel, in a prime position on the headland. Contemporary guest areas and good leisure facilities. Smart bedrooms with bespoke furnishings and latest mod cons. Four-roomed restaurant: 2 in bistro style, 2 more informal with a TV and bar.

Beiderbecke's rest, VISA AE

1-3 The Cres. ✉ YO11 2PW – ☎ (01723) 365 766 – www.beiderbeckes.com
26 rm – **†£ 85/90 ††£ 120/130 – 1 suite** Zs
Rest *Marmalade's* – Menu £ 22 (dinner) – Carte £ 27/35
◆ Named after the jazz musician. Although housed in a restored Georgian building, the rooms' décor is balanced between period style and contemporary feel with bright colours. Colourful, contemporary brasserie.

Ox Pasture Hall VISA AE

Lady Edith's Dr., Raincliffe Woods, West : 3.25 mi by A 171 following signs for Raincliffe Woods ✉ YO12 5TD – ☎ (01723) 365 295 – www.oxpasturehall.com
20 rm – **†£ 75/195 ††£ 250/395**
Rest *Courtyard* – *(closed Monday and Tuesday)* Carte approx. £ 29 **s**
Rest *Brasserie* – Menu £ 17/25 **s** – Carte £ 29/36 **s**
◆ Charming, creeper-clad part-17C farmhouse, in 17 acres of landscaped gardens and grounds. Stylish, contemporary guest areas. Characterful bedrooms in main house; smarter rooms in rear courtyard. Linen-laid restaurant offers concise, modern à la carte. Brasserie serves simpler menu.

Alexander VISA

33 Burniston Rd ✉ YO12 6PG – ☎ (01723) 363 178
– www.alexanderhotelscarborough.co.uk – April-October Ya
8 rm – **†£ 55/64 ††£ 70/82**
Rest – *(closed Sunday) (dinner only)* Menu £ 19 **s**
◆ 1930s red-brick house at the popular North Beach end of town. Well-kept, classically styled lounge. Contemporary bedrooms with flat-screen TVs, good comforts and clean, uncluttered style; some boast feature walls. Traditional cocktail bar and linen-laid dining room offering 3 choice set menu; local seafood a feature.

Lanterna VISA

33 Queen St ✉ YO11 1HQ – ☎ (01723) 363 616 – www.lanterna-ristorante.co.uk
– Closed mid-October-mid-November, 25-26 December and Monday in winter
Rest – Italian – *(dinner only)* Carte £ 30/90 Yc
◆ Scarborough's best known restaurant: a landmark for decades. Endearing trattoria style "clutter". Classic Italian menu, plus a renowned selection of truffle dishes.

Green Room VISA

138 Victoria Rd ✉ YO11 1SL – ☎ (01723) 501 801
– www.thegreenroomrestaurant.com – closed Sunday and Monday
Rest – *(dinner only)* Menu £ 18 – Carte £ 32/41 Ze
◆ Pleasant family run bistro; son cooks and mum is out front serving. Great care is taken to use only locally sourced produce and ingredients. Cooking is modern and imaginative.

at Sawdon **Southwest : 9.75 mi by A 170 - Z - ✉ Scarborough**

Anvil Inn VISA

Main St ✉ YO13 9DY – ☎ (01723) 859 896 – www.theanvilinnsawdon.co.uk
– Closed 25-26 December, 1 January, Monday and Tuesday
Rest – Carte £ 18/28
◆ Formerly a smithy, with bellows, tools, forge and anvil still in situ. Classical cooking features locally sourced produce and the odd international influence. Intimate restaurant.

SCAWTON – **N. Yorks.** – **502** Q21 – **see Helmsley**

ENGLAND

SCILLY (Isles of) – Cornwall – 503 A/B34 — 1 A3

London 295 mi – Camborne 23 mi – Saint Austell 52 mi – Falmouth 36 mi

Access Helicopter service from St Mary's and Tresco to Penzance : (01736) 363871

St Mary's Airport : (01720) 422677, E : 1.5 mi from Hugh Town

from Hugh Town to Penzance (Isles of Scilly Steamship Co. Ltd) (summer only) (2 h 40 mn)

Hugh Street, St Mary's (01720) 424031, tic@scilly.gov.uk

Islands★ - The Archipelago (≤★★★)

St Agnes : Horsepoint★

BRYHER – Cornwall – pop. 78 – ✉ — 1 A3

Watch Hill (≤★) – Hell Bay★

Hell Bay

✉ *TR23 0PR – (01720) 422 947 – www.hellbay.co.uk – 7 March-October*
11 rm (dinner included) – ♦£ 169/375 ♦♦£ 169/375 – 14 suites – ♦♦£ 270/600
Rest – *(booking essential for non-residents)* Menu £ 35 (dinner) – Carte £ 32/40
♦ Several charming New England style buildings set around a central courtyard. Fabulous coastal location with far-reaching views. Contemporary inner has nautical edge and impressive modern art collection. Immaculately kept bedrooms come with good extras. Informal lunches in bar/courtyard/terrace; elaborate daily dinners.

Bank Cottage without rest

✉ *TR23 0PR – (01720) 422 612 – www.bank-cottage.com – May-October*
4 rm – ♦£ 50/54 ♦♦£ 108
♦ Friendly guesthouse with bright sub-tropical garden, koi carp pond and rowing boat. Breakfast room, lounge and honesty bar; free use of kitchen. Simple, compact bedrooms; one with roof terrace.

TRESCO – Cornwall – pop. 167 – ✉ — 1 A3

Island★ - Abbey Gardens★★ **AC** (Lighthouse Way ≤★★)

New Inn

New Grimsby ✉ *TR24 0QQ – (01720) 423 006 – www.tresco.co.uk*
16 rm – ♦£ 70/150 ♦♦£ 140/230
Rest – *(booking essential for non-residents)* Carte £ 21/37
♦ Stone-built inn boasting a large terrace, an appealing outdoor pool and pleasant coastal views. Bedrooms are bright, fresh and very comfy. Regular live music events attract guests from near and far. Hugely characterful bar and restaurant offer accessible menu.

ST MARTIN'S – Cornwall – pop. 113 — 1 A3

St Martin's Head (≤★★)

St Martin's on the Isle

✉ *TR25 0QW – (01720) 422 092 – www.stmartinshotel.co.uk – 4 April-September*
27 rm (dinner included) – ♦£ 140/205 ♦♦£ 280/370 – 3 suites
Rest *Teän* – see restaurant listing
Rest *Bistro* – *(closed November-March and Monday)* Carte £ 25/35 **s**
♦ Contemporary hotel in stunning location, with unrivalled views of white beaches and blue sea. Comfortable bedrooms: most overlook the water; some look onto the garden. The best is 'Volunteer'; a large first floor suite with views to the lighthouse. Lively ground floor bistro with terrace; simple dishes, ideal for lunch.

Teän – St Martin's on the Isle

✉ *TR25 0QW – (01720) 422 092 – www.stmartinshotel.co.uk – 4 April-September*
Rest – *(dinner only) (booking essential)* Menu £ 40 **s**
♦ First floor restaurant with fantastic views. Short menu of classically based dishes; cooking is precise, with hearty portions making the best of local produce. Professional service.

ST MARY'S – **Cornwall** – **pop. 1 607** **1** A3

Carn Morval, ✆(01720) 422 692

Gig racing★★ - Garrison Walk★ (←★★) – Peninnis Head★ – Hugh Town - Museum★

Star Castle

The Garrison ✉ TR21 0JA – ✆(01720) 422 317 – www.star-castle.co.uk – Closed 3 January-6 February and 1-22 December
34 rm (dinner included) – †£ 98/250 ††£ 262/380 – 4 suites
Rest *Castle Dining Room* – *(dinner only)* Carte £ 29/35
Rest *Conservatory* – Seafood – *(dinner only)* Carte £ 29/35
♦ Elizabethan castle in the shape of an 8-pointed star. Well-appointed, classical bedrooms; brighter garden suites – some harbour/island views. 17C staircase leads from stone ramparts to charming Dungeon bar. Fabulous fireplace and kitchen garden produce in dining room. Seafood menus in Conservatory.

Atlantic

Hugh St, Hugh Town ✉ TR21 0PL – ✆(01720) 422 417 – www.atlantichotelscilly.co.uk – 8 February–November
25 rm (dinner included) – †£ 120/150 ††£ 180/270
Rest – *(bar lunch)* Menu £ 20 (dinner) – Carte £ 20/30
♦ Former Customs Office in a charming bay setting, affording lovely views across the harbour. Bedrooms – accessed through twisty passages – are well-equipped; many share the view. Comfortable lounge and small bar. Wicker-furnished restaurant offers accessible menu.

Evergreen Cottage without rest

Parade, Hugh Town ✉ TR21 0LP – ✆(01720) 422 711 – www.evergreencottageguesthouse.co.uk – Closed 1 week February, 30 October-8 November and 21 December-3 January
5 rm – †£ 30/60 ††£ 60/80
♦ 300 year old captain's cottage in the heart of town. Welcoming window boxes. Cosy inner with small, low-ceilinged lounge and breakfast room. Compact, spotlessly kept, pine-furnished bedrooms.

ENGLAND

SCUNTHORPE – **North Lincolnshire** – **502** S23 – **pop. 72 669** **23** C3

London 167 mi – Leeds 54 mi – Lincoln 30 mi – Sheffield 45 mi

Humberside Airport : ✆ (01652) 688456, E : 15 mi by A 18

Ashby Decoy Burringham Rd, ✆(01724) 842 913

Kingsway, ✆(01724) 840 945

Grange Park Messingham Butterwick Rd, ✆(01724) 762 945

San Pietro

11 High St. East ✉ DN15 6UH – ✆(01724) 277 774 – www.sanpietro.uk.com – Closed Monday lunch and Sunday
Rest – Menu £ 16/20 (weekday dinner) – Carte £ 27/45
♦ Characterful former pub with private dining room, housed in 19C listed windmill. Seasonal menus offer skilfully cooked Mediterranean dishes. Professional service from smartly attired staff.

SEAHAM – **Durham** – **501** P/Q19 – **pop. 21 153** **24** B2

London 284 mi – Carlisle 77 mi – Leeds 84 mi – Middlesbrough 24 mi

Seaham Hall

Lord Byron's Walk, North : 1.25 mi by B 1287 ✉ SR7 7AG – ✆(0191) 516 1400 – www.seaham-hall.co.uk
17 rm – †£ 200/300 ††£ 285/350 – 2 suites
Rest *White Room* – *(dinner only and Sunday lunch) (booking essential for non-residents)* Menu £ 50 **s**
Rest *Ozone* – *(closed 25 December and Sunday dinner)* Menu £ 20 **s**
♦ Impressive extended coastal mansion with portico entrance, modern styling, spacious sitting room and superb oriental spa. Large bedrooms boast luxury bathrooms and impressive technology. Well-presented, modern dishes in the White Room. A blend of Asian and European food in Ozone.

SEAHOUSES – Northumberland – 501 P17 Great Britain — 24 B1

London 328 mi – Edinburgh 80 mi – Newcastle upon Tyne 46 mi

Car Park, Seafield Rd ✆ (01665) 720884,(April- Oct) seahouses.tic@northumberland.gov.uk

Beadnell Rd, ✆ (01665) 720 794

Farne Islands★ (by boat from harbour)

Olde Ship

9 Main St ✉ NE68 7RD – ✆ (01665) 720 200 – www.seahouses.co.uk – February-November

13 rm – †£ 50/116 ††£ 100/116 – 5 suites

Rest – *(bar lunch Monday-Saturday)* Carte £ 17/30

◆ Cosy, part-18C family-run inn, close to thriving harbour – with old ships' decking floors, nautical bric-a-brac and great harbour views from wardroom. Comfy, individually designed bedrooms. Characterful bar and classical dining room.

SEASALTER – Kent – 504 X29 – see Whitstable

SEAVIEW – I.O.W. – 503 Q31 – see Wight (Isle of)

SEER GREEN – Buckinghamshire – see Beaconsfield

SETTLE – North Yorkshire – 502 N21 – pop. 3 621 — 22 A2

ENGLAND

London 238 mi – Bradford 34 mi – Kendal 30 mi – Leeds 41 mi

Town Hall, Cheapside ✆ (01729) 825192, settle@ytbtic.co.uk

Giggleswick, ✆ (01729) 825 288

Little House

17 Duke St ✉ BD24 9DJ – ✆ (01729) 823 963 – www.littlehouserestaurant.co.uk – closed 2 weeks January, 1 week September and Sunday-Tuesday

Rest – *(dinner only) (booking essential)* Carte £ 22/30

◆ Former 19C gate house, a 'little house' of stone that was once a cobblers. Well-kept, rustic style within a compact space. Traditional and classic styles of cooking prevail.

SHAFTESBURY – Dorset – 503 N30 – pop. 6 665 — 4 C3

London 115 mi – Bournemouth 31 mi – Bristol 47 mi – Dorchester 29 mi

8 Bell St ✆ (01747) 853514, tourism@shaftesburydorset.com

Gold Hill★ (≤★) – Local History Museum★ **AC**

Wardour Castle★ **AC**, NE : 5 m

Hotel Grosvenor

The Commons ✉ SP7 8JA – ✆ (01747) 850 580 – www.hotelgrosvenor.com

16 rm – †£ 85/99 ††£ 125/250

Rest *Greenhouse* – see restaurant listing

◆ Stylish former coaching inn with Georgian-style façade and spacious, trendy bar. Bedrooms feature stark décor and modern facilities including flat screen TVs and espresso machines.

Fleur de Lys

Bleke St ✉ SP7 8AW – ✆ (01747) 853 717 – www.lafleurdelys.co.uk – Closed 2 weeks January

7 rm – †£ 75/100 ††£ 100/175

Rest – *(closed lunch Monday-Tuesday and Sunday dinner)* Menu £ 30 (dinner) – Carte £ 32/44

◆ Keenly run, ivy-clad stone house in lovely market town. Comfortable, well-kept bedrooms named after grape varieties; each comes with its own laptop. Cosy lounge with mahogany bar. Dine from traditional menus in L-shaped restaurant or on wood-furnished terrace.

Retreat without rest

47 Bell St ✉ SP7 8AE – ☎ (01747) 850 372 – www.the-retreat.co.uk – closed January

10 rm – †£ 50/70 ††£ 85/90

◆ Pretty Georgian house on narrow street in delightful market town – once a school for poor boys. Wood-furnished breakfast room; immaculately kept bedrooms with good facilities. Charming owner.

Greenhouse – at Hotel Grosvenor

The Commons ✉ SP7 8JA – ☎ (01747) 850 580 – www.hotelgrosvenor.com

Rest – Menu £ 25 (dinner) – Carte £ 22/33

◆ Ground floor restaurant enlivened by boldly coloured abstract art. Enjoy aperitifs in the enclosed courtyard. Refined brasserie cooking; good value set menus. Excellent service.

SHALDON – Devon – 503 J32 – pop. 1 628 — 2 D2

London 188 mi – Exeter 16 mi – Torquay 7 mi – Paignton 13 mi

ODE

21 Fore St ✉ TQ14 0DE – ☎ (01626) 873 977 – www.odetruefood.co.uk – Closed October, 25 December, Sunday, Monday and bank holidays

Rest – Organic – *(dinner only and lunch Thursday-Friday) (booking essential)*
Menu £ 22/25 (weekday dinner) – Carte dinner £ 28/40

◆ Intimate neighbourhood restaurant in glass-fronted Georgian house – leave time to park. Cooking has a strong seafaring base and often involves water baths. Produce is local and 100% organic.

SHANKLIN – I.O.W. – 503 Q32 – see Wight (Isle of)

SHAPWICK – Dorset – see Blandford Forum

SHEDFIELD – Hampshire – 503 Q31 – pop. 3 558 – ✉ Southampton — 6 B2

London 75 mi – Portsmouth 13 mi – Southampton 10 mi

Meon Valley Shedfield Sandy Lane, off A 334, ☎ (01329) 833 455

Vatika

Botley Rd, Wickham Vineyard, on A334 ✉ SO32 2HL – ☎ (01329) 830 405 – www.vatikarestaurant.co.uk – Closed 24 December-26 January and Sunday dinner

Rest – *(dinner only and lunch Friday-Sunday) (booking advisable at dinner)*
Menu £ 35/40 **s** – Carte £ 40/79 **s**

◆ Sleek, contemporary restaurant overlooking delightful vineyard. Refined fusion cooking uses modern techniques to create unusual, highly artistic British and Indian combinations.

SHEFFIELD – South Yorkshire – 502 P23 – pop. 439 866 Great Britain — 22 B3

London 174 mi – Leeds 36 mi – Liverpool 80 mi – Manchester 41 mi

14 Norfolk Row ☎ (0114) 221 1900, visitor@yorkshiresouth.com

Tinsley Park Darnall High Hazel Park, ☎ (0114) 203 7435

Beauchief Abbey Lane, ☎ (0114) 236 7274

Birley Wood Birley Lane, ☎ (0114) 264 7262

Concord Park Shiregreen Lane, ☎ (0114) 257 7378

Abbeydale Dore Twentywell Lane, ☎ (0114) 236 0763

Lees Hall Norton Hemsworth Rd, ☎ (0114) 255 4402

Cutlers' Hall★ CZ **A** – Cathedral Church of SS. Peter and Paul CZ **B** : Shrewsbury Chapel (Tomb★)

Magna★ **AC**, NE : 3 mi by A 6178 - BY - and Bessemer Way

Plans pages 586, 587

SHEFFIELD

Barrow Rd . . . . BY 4	Holywell Rd. . . . . BY 29	Newhall Rd . . . . BY 36
Bawtry Rd . . . . BY 5	Main Rd . . . . BZ 32	Westbourne Rd . . . . AZ 47
Bradfield Rd . . . . AY 7	Meadowhall Shopping Centre . . . . BY	Western Bank. . . . . AZ 48
Brocco Bank . . . . AZ 8	Meadow Hall Rd . . . . BY 33	Whitham Rd . . . . AZ 49
Broughton Lane . . . . BY 10	Middlewood Rd . . . . AY 34	Woodbourn Rd. . . . . BYZ 50
Burngreave Rd . . . . AY 12		Woodhouse Rd. . . . . BZ 51
Handsworth Rd . . . . BZ 24		

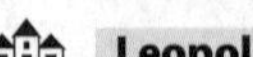

Leopold

Leopold Sq ✉ S1 1GZ – ✆ (0114) 252 40 00 – www.leopoldhotels.com – Closed 24 December-3 January CZ**a**

76 rm – †£ 90/169 ††£ 90/169, ☕ £ 10.50 – 14 suites

Rest – *(bar meals)* Carte £ 28/45

◆ Former Boys Grammar School, now an elegant boutique townhouse with stylish, contemporary bedrooms, state-of-the-art facilities and old school photos on the walls. Light meals served in the bar.

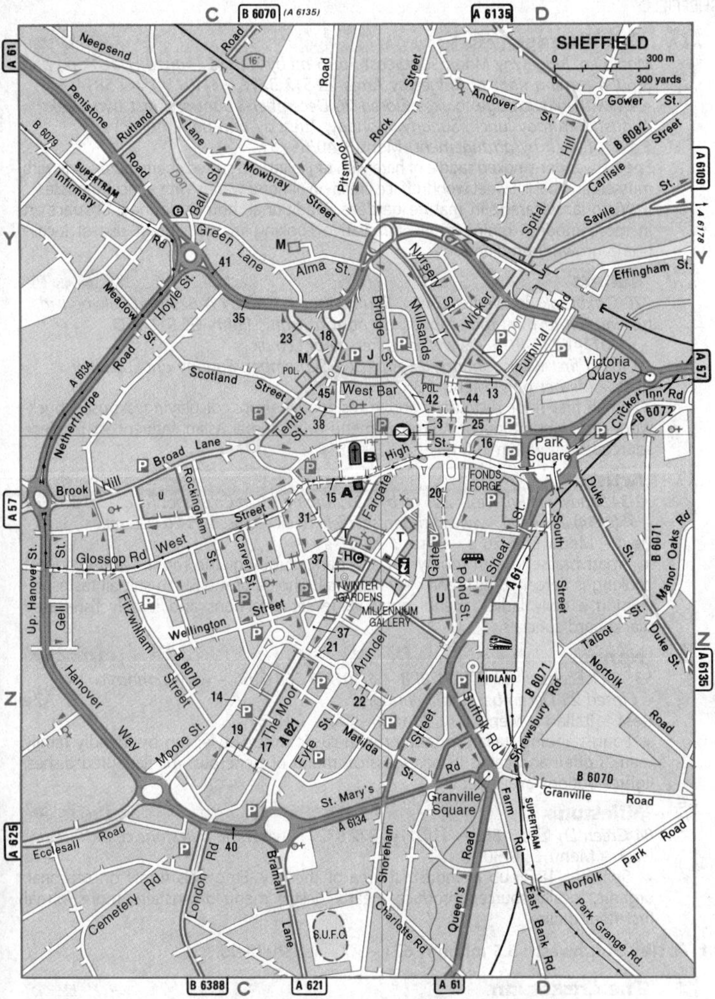

SHEFFIELD

0 300 m
0 300 yards

Street	Grid	No.
Angel St	DY	3
Blonk St	DY	6
Castle Gate	DY	13
Charter Row	CZ	14
Church St	CZ	15
Commercial St	DZ	16
Corporation St	CY	18
Cumberland St	CZ	17
Fargate	CZ	
Fitzwilliam Gate	CZ	19
Flat St	DZ	20
Furnival Gate	CZ	21
Furnival St	CZ	22
Gibraltar St	CY	23
Haymarket	DY	25
High St	DZ	
Leopold St	CZ	31
Moorfields	CY	35
Pinstone St	CZ	37
Queen St	CY	38
St Mary's Gate	CZ	40
Shalesmoor	CY	41
Snig Hill	DY	42
Waingate	DY	44
West Bar Green	CY	45
West St	CZ	

Westbourne House without rest

25 Westbourne Rd ✉ S10 2QQ – ✆ (0114) 266 0109
– www.westbournehousehotel.com – Closed Christmas AZ**c**

8 rm ☕ – 🚹£ 52/62 🚹🚹£ 75/85

◆ Red brick Victorian house in residential area; lovely breakfast room and rear bedrooms overlook mature gardens. Individually styled bedrooms boast original features and good facilities.

Old Vicarage (Tessa Bramley)

Marsh Ln, Ridgeway Moor, Southeast : 6.75 mi by A 6135 (signed Hyde Park) and B 6054 turning right at Ridgeway Arms ✉ S12 3XW – ✆ (0114) 247 5814 – www.theoldvicarage.co.uk – Closed 26 December-8 January, first two weeks August, Saturday lunch, Sunday, Monday, Tuesday and bank holidays

Rest – *(lunch by arrangement)* Menu £ 40/65

Spec. Lavender-smoked saddle of hare with tagliolini and spiced cherry purée. Brill with mussels and basil. Sweet woodruff ice cream in almond wafers with apricot mousse.

◆ Victorian vicarage in mature gardens. Traditional, homely lounge; abstract art in more modern dining room. Innovative cooking makes vibrant use of local/-home grown ingredients.

Rafters

220 Oakbrook Rd, Nether Green, Southwest : 2.5 mi by A 625 and Fulwood rd, turning left at mini roundabout, on right at traffic lights ✉ S11 7ED – ✆ (0114) 230 4819 – www.raftersrestaurant.co.uk – Closed first week January, 22 August-2 September, Sunday and Tuesday

Rest – *(dinner only)* Menu £ 36

◆ Small first floor restaurant above residential shops, displaying exposed brick-work and vibrant decor. Classical menu with some Asian influences; produce sourced from within 100 miles.

Artisan

32-34 Sandygate Rd, West : 2.25 mi by A 57, turning left at Crosspool Tavern ✉ S10 5RY – ✆ (0114) 266 6096 – www.artisanofsheffield.co.uk – Closed 25-26 December

Rest – Menu £ 16/26 **s** – Carte £ 22/37 **s**

◆ Smart brasserie with roomy bar and dark, clubby dining room. Careful, honest cooking is fiercely British and very seasonal. Choice of menus to suit all tastes, including a daily ladies' menu, good value set selections and largely fish-based blackboard specials.

Nonnas

535-541 Ecclesall Rd ✉ S11 8PR – ✆ (0114) 268 6166 – www.nonnas.co.uk – Closed 25 December and 1 January AZ**e**

Rest – Italian – Menu £ 12 (lunch) – Carte £ 18/31

◆ Long-standing Italian restaurant with rustic, bistro-style; run by friendly family team. Coffee and cakes in bar. Classical menu of generous, full-flavoured dishes; lighter options available.

Milestone

84 Green Ln ✉ S3 8SE – ✆ (0114) 272 8327 – www.the-milestone.co.uk

Rest – Menu £ 20/30 CY**e**

◆ Spacious 18C pub in industrial area of the city. Emphasis firmly on seasonal, organic, locally sourced produce. Hearty gastro menu downstairs; more formal first floor dining.

at Totley Southwest : 5.5 mi on A 621 - AZ – ✉ Sheffield

The Cricket Inn

Penny Ln ✉ S17 3AZ – ✆ (0114) 236 5256 – www.relaxeatanddrink.co.uk

Rest – Menu £ 15 – Carte £ 18/25

◆ Hidden away next to cricket pitch, with open fires and rustic wood floors. Wide-ranging, Yorkshire-based menu offers bar snacks through to grills and roasts. Hearty, wholesome cooking.

SHEFFORD – Bedfordshire – 504 S27 – pop. 3 319 **12** A1

London 48 mi – Bedford 10 mi – Luton 16 mi – Northampton 37 mi

The Black Horse with rm

Ireland, Northwest : 1.5 mi by Northbridge St and B 658 on Ireland rd ✉ SG17 5QL – ✆ (01462) 811 398 – www.blackhorseireland.com – Closed 25-26 December, 1 January and Sunday dinner

2 rm – †£ 55 ††£ 55 **Rest** – Carte £ 23/29

◆ Traditional façade masks an ultra-modern interior with marble floors, granite bar and hi-tech fittings. Eclectic menu ranges from pizza and pies to confit of duck and sea bass. Delightfully cosy bedrooms.

SHELLEY – W. Yorks. – **502** O23 – see Huddersfield

SHERBORNE – Dorset – **503** M31 – pop. 9 350 **4** C3

London 128 mi – Bournemouth 39 mi – Dorchester 19 mi – Salisbury 36 mi

3 Tilton Court, Digby Rd (01935) 815341, sherborne.tic@westdorset-dc.gov.uk

Higher Clatcombe, (01935) 812 274

Town★ - Abbey★★ - Castle★ **AC**

Sandford Orcas Manor House★ **AC**, NW : 4 mi by B 3148 – Purse Caundle Manor★ **AC**, NE : 5 mi by A 30. Cadbury Castle (<★★) N : 8 mi by A 30 – Parish Church★, Crewkerne, W : 14 mi on A 30

at Oborne Northeast : 2 mi by A 30 – ✉ Sherborne

Grange

✉ *DT9 4LA – (01935) 813 463 – www.thegrangeatoborne.co.uk*
18 rm – †£ 87/130 ††£ 101/160 **Rest** – Menu £ 25/35

♦ Family-run, stone-built country house in pretty village; dating back 200 years. Comfy guest areas overlook attractive mature gardens. Spacious bedrooms boast good facilities; some have balconies or patios. Menus showcase the latest local, seasonal ingredients.

SHERE – Surrey – **504** S30 – see Guildford

SHERINGHAM – Norfolk – **504** X25 – pop. 7 143 **15** C1

London 136 mi – Cromer 5 mi – Norwich 27 mi

Ashbourne House without rest

1 Nelson Rd ✉ NR26 8BT – (01263) 821 555 – www.ashbournehousesheringham.co.uk
3 rm – †£ 50 ††£ 75

♦ Well-appointed guesthouse in elevated position, with large, landscaped garden. Comfortable bedrooms: two with coastal views. Impressive fireplace in wood-panelled breakfast room.

SHERWOOD BUSINESS PARK – Nottingham – see Nottingham

SHILTON – W. Mids. – **503** P26 – see Coventry

SHINFIELD – Reading – **504** R29 – see Reading

SHIPLAKE ROW – Oxfordshire – - see Henley-on-Thames

SHIPLEY – West Yorkshire – **502** O22 – pop. 28 162 **22** B2

London 216 mi – Bradford 4 mi – Leeds 12 mi

Northcliffe High Bank Lane, (01274) 584 085

Bingley Beckfoot Lane, Cottingley Bridge, (01274) 568 652

Zaara's

34-38 Bradford Rd ✉ BD18 3NT – (01274) 588 114 – www.zaaras.com
Rest – Indian – *(dinner only)* Carte £ 10/18 AT**a**

♦ Funky, modern restaurant with bright décor and lots of neon. Tasty, authentic Indian cooking, with an emphasis on Punjabi dishes. Efficient service from smartly dressed team.

SHIPSTON-ON-STOUR – Warwickshire – **503** P27 – pop. 4 456 **19** C3

London 85 mi – Oxford 30 mi – Stratford-upon-Avon 12 mi

at Long Compton South : 5 mi on A 3400 – pop. 1 994 – ✉ Shipston-On-Stour

The Red Lion with rm

on A 3400 ✉ CV36 5JS – (01608) 684 221 – www.redlion-longcompton.co.uk
5 rm – †£ 55 ††£ 80/100
Rest – Menu £ 15 (lunch and early dinner) – Carte £ 23/35

♦ 18C former coaching inn with flag floors, log fires and a warm, modern feel. Seasonal menu of tasty, home-cooked pub classics, with more adventurous daily specials. Stylish, contemporary bedrooms.

SHOCKLACH – Cheshire 20 A3

London 193 mi – Liverpool 42 mi – Stoke-on-Trent 37 mi – Saint Helens 45 mi

The Bull

Worthenbury Rd ✉ SY14 7BL – ✆ (01829) 250 239 – www.thebullshocklach.com – Closed 25 December

Rest – Carte £ 22/30

◆ Small village pub that's really part of the community. Beams and hand-painted quarry tiles are offset by contemporary colours and eclectic artwork. Cooking is refined, flavoursome and generous.

SHOTTLE – Derbs. – see Belper

SHREWSBURY – Shropshire – 502 L25 – pop. 67 126 Great Britain 18 B2

London 164 mi – Birmingham 48 mi – Chester 43 mi – Derby 67 mi

Rowley's House, Barker St ✆ (01743) 281200, visitorinfo@shropshire.gov.uk

Condover, ✆ (01743) 872 977

Meole Brace, ✆ (01743) 364 050

Abbey★ **D**

Ironbridge Gorge Museum★★ **AC** (The Iron Bridge★★ - Coalport China Museum★★ - Blists Hill Open Air Museum★★ – Museum of the Gorge and Visitor Centre★) SE : 12 mi by A 5 and B 4380

Pinewood House without rest

Shelton Park, The Mount, Northwest : 1.5 mi on A 458 ✉ SY3 8BL – ✆ (01743) 364 200 – Closed 4 days Christmas

3 rm – †£ 45/48 ††£ 62/68

◆ Lovely Edwardian property on the edge of town, converted from three coach houses. Fresh, uncluttered feel throughout, with large, light-filled drawing room and flowers all around. One split-level bedroom with bathroom in the old dove-cote. Communal breakfasts.

Mad Jack's with rm

15 St. Mary's St. ✉ SY1 1EQ – ✆ (01743) 358 870 – www.madjacks.uk.com – Closed 25 December **a**

4 rm – †£ 70/100 ††£ 105/145 **Rest** – Carte £ 19/29

◆ Centrally located in the heart of a busy market town. Spacious main dining area, snug and hidden courtyard, with plain décor and marble tables. Good service, slightly eclectic menu. Modern, comfy bedrooms.

at Grinshill North : 7.5 mi by A 49 – ✉ Shrewsbury

Inn at Grinshill with rm

The High St. ✉ SY4 3BL – ✆ (01939) 220 410 – www.theinnatgrinshill.co.uk – Closed Sunday dinner, Monday, and dinner bank holidays

7 rm – †£ 80/90 ††£ 100/120 **Rest** – Carte £ 19/29

◆ 18C former stable block in small village. Rustic bar and light, airy restaurant boasting an open kitchen, grand piano and wine bar. À la carte offers mix of old classics and more modern tasting boards; simpler bar menu. Up-to-date bedrooms provide good comforts.

at Atcham Southeast : 3 mi by A 5064 on B 4380

Mytton and Mermaid

✉ SY5 6QG – ✆ (01743) 761 220 – www.myttonandmermaid.co.uk – Closed 25 December

16 rm – †£ 90/95 ††£ 190

Rest ***Restaurant*** – see restaurant listing

◆ Impressive Georgian riverside house with neat lawned gardens. Characterful, traditionally styled bedrooms in main house, some with views; smaller, more contemporary rooms in old stables.

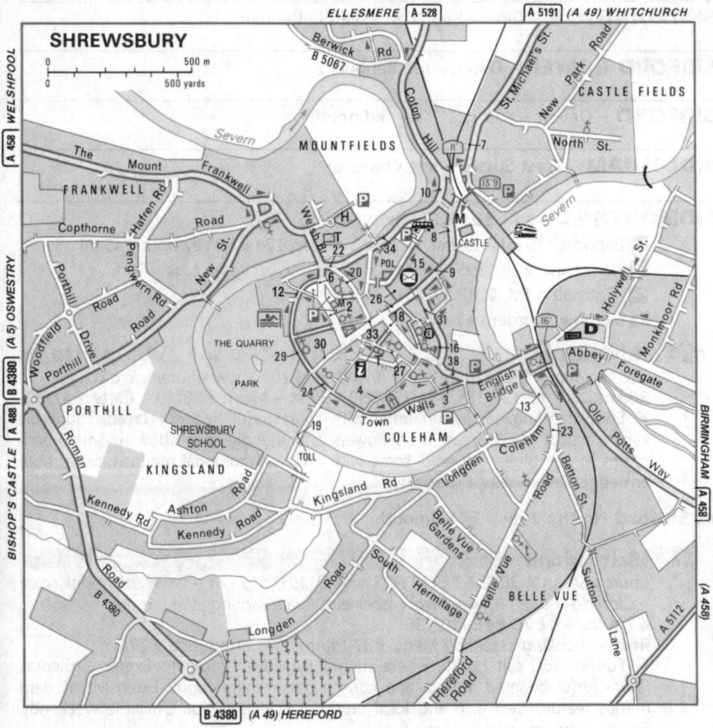

Barker St.	2	Coleham Head	13	Pride Hill	26
Beeches Lane	3	Darwin Centre	15	Princess St	27
Belmont	4	Dogpole	16	St Chad's Terrace	29
Bridge St.	6	High St	18	St John's Hill	30
Castle Foregate	7	Kingsland Bridge	19	St Mary's St	31
Castle Gates	8	Mardol	20	Shoplatch	33
Castle St	9	Mardol Quay	22	Smithfield Rd	34
Chester St	10	Moreton Crescent	23	Wyle Cop	38
Claremont Bank	12	Murivance	24		

Restaurant – at The Mytton and Mermaid Hotel

⊠ *SY5 6QG* – *✆ (01743) 761 220* – *www.myttonandmermaid.co.uk*
– *Closed 25 December*

Rest – Carte £ 21/34

◆ Choice of three dining areas: casual bar, more formal dining room or pleasant outside terraces. Same menu served throughout, offering tasty classically based dishes and daily specials.

SHREWTON – Wiltshire – **503** O30 – **pop. 1 648** **4** D2

London 91 mi – Bristol 53 mi – Southampton 52 mi – Reading 69 mi

The Manor 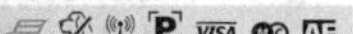

Southeast : 0.5 mi on A 360 ⊠ *SP3 4HF* – *✆ (01980) 620 216*
– *www.rollestonemanor.com*

7 rm – †£ 65/95 ††£ 90/110

Rest – *(dinner only and Sunday lunch)* Menu £ 10 – Carte £ 10/26

◆ Grade II listed former farmhouse set on main road, just out of the village. Good-sized, antique-furnished bedrooms offer modern facilities. Traditional lounge. Two-roomed restaurant for classic dishes at linen-laid tables.

SHURDINGTON – Glos. – 503 N28 – see Cheltenham

SIBFORD GOWER – Oxon. – see Banbury

SIDFORD – Devon – 503 K31 – see Sidmouth

SIDLESHAM – West Sussex – see Chicester

SIDMOUTH – Devon – 503 K31 – pop. 12 066 — 2 D2

London 176 mi – Exeter 14 mi – Taunton 27 mi – Weymouth 45 mi
Ham Lane ✆ (01395) 516441, sidmouthtic@eclipse.co.uk
Cotmaton Rd, ✆ (01395) 513 451
Bicton★ (Gardens★) **AC**, SW : 5 m

Riviera — rest, VISA MC AE

The Esplanade ✉ EX10 8AY – ✆ (01395) 515 201 – www.hotelriviera.co.uk
26 rm – £ 125/185 £ 250/350 **Rest** – Menu £ 28/40 – Carte £ 42/50
♦ Long-standing, family-run hotel with characterful Regency façade. Superbly kept classical guest areas; fresh flowers and friendly staff abound. Smart bedrooms in rich blues and gold, some with a view. Traditional menus have a modern edge. Cream teas a speciality.

ENGLAND

at Sidford North : 2 mi – ✉ Sidmouth

XX **Salty Monk** with rm — VISA MC

Church St, on A 3052 ✉ EX10 9QP – ✆ (01395) 513 174 – www.saltymonk.co.uk – Closed January, 2 weeks November and lunch Monday-Wednesday
6 rm – £ 70 £ 110/136
Rest – *(booking essential)* Menu £ 37 (dinner) – Carte lunch £ 27/33
♦ Former 16C salt house, where monks stayed en route to Exeter Cathedral. Characterful beamed lounge and conservatory dining room. Extensive modern menus feature fresh fish and local produce; tasting option available weekends. Smart bedrooms and mini spa facility.

at Newton Poppleford Northwest : 4 mi by B 3176 on A 3052 – ✉ Sidmouth

XX **Moores'** — VISA MC AE

6 Greenbank, High St ✉ EX10 0EB – ✆ (01395) 568 100 – www.mooresrestaurant.co.uk – Closed 3-22 January, Sunday dinner and Monday
Rest – Menu £ 20/28
♦ Two pretty 18C cottages set back from the main road are the setting for this busy, personally run restaurant with conservatory extension. Modern, locally sourced dishes.

SINNINGTON – N. Yorks. – 502 R21 – see Pickering

SISSINGHURST – Kent – 504 V30 – see Cranbrook

SITTINGBOURNE – Kent – 504 W29 – pop. 39 974 — 9 C1

London 44 mi – Canterbury 18 mi – Maidstone 15 mi – Sheerness 9 mi

Hempstead House — rm, VISA MC AE

London Rd, Bapchild, East : 2 mi on A 2 ✉ ME9 9PP – ✆ (01795) 428 020 – www.hempsteadhouse.co.uk
27 rm – £ 85 £ 160
Rest *Lakes* – *(residents only Sunday dinner)* Menu £ 18/25 – Carte £ 25/37
♦ Privately run, part-Victorian, red-brick house in landscaped gardens. Cosy, wood-panelled lounges. Classical bedrooms in main house; more contemporary rooms above impressive spa. Formal conservatory restaurant features Georgian columns and classically based menu.

at Milstead South : 3 mi by Highsted rd

Red Lion

Rawling St ✉ ME9 0RT – ☎ (01795) 830 279 – www.theredlionmilstead.co.uk – Closed Sunday and Monday

Rest – *(booking advisable at weekends)* Carte £ 20/26

◆ Simple, cosy country pub, personally run by an experienced couple. Ever-changing blackboard menu offers French-influenced country cooking. Dishes are honest, wholesome and richly flavoured.

SIZERGH – Cumbria – see Kendal

SKIPTON – North Yorkshire – **502** N22 – **pop. 14 313** Great Britain **22** A2

London 217 mi – Kendal 45 mi – Leeds 26 mi – Preston 36 mi

35 Coach St ☎ (01756) 792809, skipton@ytbtic.co.uk

Short Lee Lane, off NW Bypass, ☎ (01756) 793 922

Castle★ **AC**

The Bull

West : 3 mi on A 59 ✉ BD23 3AE – ☎ (01756) 792 065 – www.thebullatbroughton.co.uk – Closed 25 December

Rest – Carte £ 17/28

◆ Part of Ribble Valley Inns, a burgeoning pub company which proudly promotes local and very British ingredients and dishes. This solid, sizeable pub boasts log fires, beams and stone floors.

at Hetton North : 5.75 mi by B 6265 – ✉ Skipton

Angel Inn and Barn Lodgings with rm

✉ BD23 6LT – ☎ (01756) 730 263 – www.angelhetton.co.uk – Closed 25-26 December and 1 January

5 rm – †£ 150 ††£ 165/190

Rest – *(booking essential)* Menu £ 15 – Carte £ 19/30

◆ Well regarded restaurant with stone walls, beams and roaring log fire. Fine quality, locally sourced produce. Bedrooms with antique furniture and modern appointments.

Angel Inn

✉ BD23 6LT – ☎ (01756) 730 263 – www.angelhetton.co.uk – Closed 10 days January, 25 December and dinner 26 and 31 December

Rest – *(booking essential)* Carte £ 22/30

◆ Remotely set 18C stone inn that's become a Yorkshire institution: the wine cave is worth a visit. Menus offer something for everyone, featuring local produce in tasty, satisfying dishes.

SLALEY – Northd. – see Hexham

SLAPTON – Devon – **503** J33 **2** C3

London 223 mi – Dartmouth 7 mi – Plymouth 29 mi

Dartmouth★★, N : 7 mi by A 379 – Kingsbridge★, W : 7 mi by A 379

The Tower Inn with rm

Church Rd ✉ TQ7 2PN – ☎ (01548) 580 216 – www.thetowerinn.com – Closed Monday in winter

3 rm – †£ 65 ††£ 85 **Rest** – Carte £ 20/30

◆ Charming pub overlooked by the ruins of a chantry tower. Menus differ between services and offer pub food with a twist: maybe venison sausages with sauerkraut of fish and chips in vodka batter. Simple bedrooms await.

SNAINTON – North Yorkshire – 502 S21 — 23 C2

London 241 mi – Pickering 8 mi – Scarborough 10 mi

Coachman Inn with rm

Pickering Rd west, West : 0.5 mi by A 170 on B 1258 ✉ YO13 9PL – ✆ (01723) 859 231 – www.coachmaninn.co.uk

3 rm – †£ 70 ††£ 85 **Rest** – Carte £ 15/30

♦ Grade II listed coaching inn with a rustic bar and spacious linen-laid restaurant – which is run with some formality. Cooking is classical but presentation is modern and refined. Simpler pub favourites offered at lunch. Bedrooms are smart and spacious.

SNAPE – Suffolk – 504 Y27 – pop. 1 509 — 15 D3

London 113 mi – Ipswich 19 mi – Norwich 50 mi

Crown Inn

Bridge Rd ✉ IP17 1SL – ✆ (01728) 688 324 – www.snape-crown.co.uk

Rest – Carte £ 20/30

♦ Charming 15C former smugglers' inn on village outskirts. Constantly evolving menu offers highly seasonal dishes, light bites and appealing specials. Produce is local, home-grown or home-reared.

SNETTISHAM – Norfolk – 504 V25 – pop. 2 145 — 14 B1

London 113 mi – King's Lynn 13 mi – Norwich 44 mi

The Rose and Crown with rm

Old Church Rd ✉ PE31 7LX – ✆ (01485) 541 382 – www.roseandcrownsnettisham.co.uk

16 rm – †£ 75/105 ††£ 95/130 **Rest** – Carte £ 20/30

♦ A warren of rooms with uneven floors and low beamed ceilings. Gutsy cooking uses locally sourced produce, with globally influenced dishes alongside trusty pub classics. Modern bedrooms are decorated in sunny colours, with a good level of facilities.

ENGLAND

SOAR MILL COVE – Devon – 503 I33 – see Salcombe

SOLIHULL – West Midlands – 503 O26 – pop. 94 753 — 19 C2

London 109 mi – Birmingham 7 mi – Coventry 13 mi – Warwick 13 mi

Central Library, Homer Rd ✆ (0121) 704 6130, artsbook@solihull.gov.uk

Town House

727 Warwick Rd ✉ B91 3DA – ✆ (0121) 704 1567 – www.thetown-house.com – Closed 1 January

Rest – Menu £ 13/16 (weekdays) – Carte £ 28/37

♦ Smart, keenly run eatery with bright interior and spacious bar-lounge for cocktails. Keenly priced, international menu ranges from small plates and mini desserts to a 5 course tasting selection.

at Olton Northwest : 2.5 mi on A 41 – ✉ Solihull

Rajnagar

256 Lyndon Rd, Northeast : 1 mi by Richmond rd. ✉ B92 7QW – ✆ (0121) 742 8140 – www.rajnagar.com

Rest – Indian – *(dinner only)* Menu £ 15 – Carte £ 21/32

♦ A busy, modern neighbourhood favourite, privately owned, offering authentic, regional specialities of Indian cuisine. Service is flexible and friendly.

SOMERTON – Somerset – 503 L30 – pop. 4 133 — 3 B2

London 138 mi – Bristol 32 mi – Taunton 17 mi

Town★ - Market Place★ (cross★) – St Michael's Church★

Long Sutton★ (Church★★) SW : 2.5 mi by B 3165 – Huish Episcopi (St Mary's Church Tower★★) SW : 4.5 mi by B 3153 – Lytes Cary★, SE : 3.5 mi by B 3151 – Street - The Shoe Museum★, N : 5 mi by B 3151. Muchelney★★ (Parish Church★★) SW : 6.5 mi by B 3153 and A 372 – High Ham (≤★★, St Andrew's Church★), NW : 9 mi by B 3153, A 372 and minor rd – Midelney Manor★ **AC**, SW : 9 mi by B 3153 and A 378

Lynch Country House without rest

4 Behind Berry ✉ TA11 7PD – ✆ (01458) 272 316 – www.thelynchcountryhouse.co.uk

9 rm ☕ – 🚹£ 70 🚹🚹£ 100

◆ Stands on a crest overlooking the Cary Valley. The grounds of this Regency house are equally rich with unusual shrubs, trees and lake. Coach house rooms more modern.

SONNING-ON-THAMES – Wokingham – 504 R29 – see Reading

SOUTHAMPTON – Southampton – 503 P31 – pop. 234 224 6 B2

Great Britain

London 87 mi – Bristol 79 mi – Plymouth 161 mi

Access Itchen Bridge (toll) AZ

Southampton/Eastleigh Airport : ✆ (0844) 481 7777, N : 4 mi BY

to Hythe (White Horse Ferries Ltd) frequent services daily (12 mn) – to the Isle of Wight (Cowes) (Red Funnel Ferries) frequent services daily (approx. 22 mn)

to the Isle of Wight (East Cowes) (Red Funnel Ferries) frequent services daily (55 mn)

9 Civic Centre Rd ✆ (023) 8083 3333, tourist.information@southampton.gov.uk

Southampton Municipal Bassett Golf Course Rd, ✆ (023) 8076 0546

Stoneham Bassett Monks Wood Close, ✆ (023) 8076 9272

Chilworth Main Rd, ✆ (023) 8074 0544

Old Southampton AZ : Bargate★ **B** - Tudor House Museum★ **M1**

ENGLAND

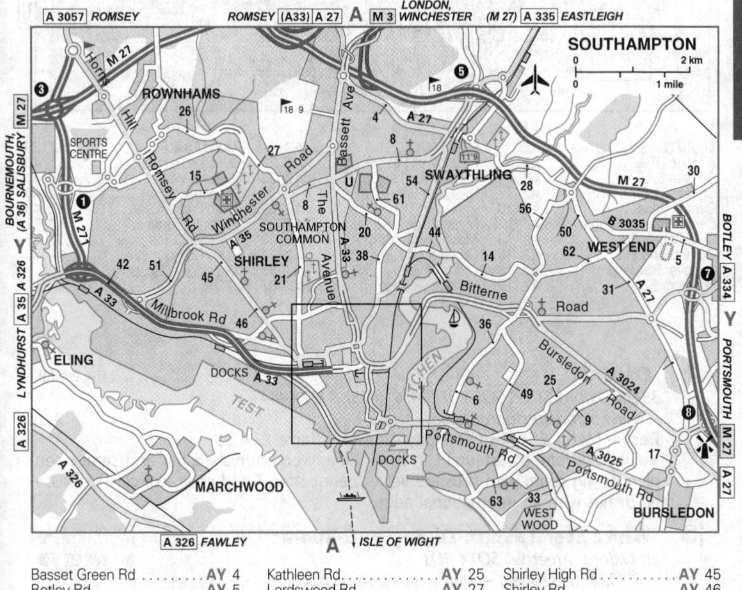

Basset Green Rd . . . . AY 4
Botley Rd. . . . . AY 5
Bridge Rd . . . . AY 6
Burgess Rd . . . . AY 8
Butts Rd . . . . AY 9
Cobden Ave . . . . AY 14
Coxford Rd . . . . AY 15
Hamble Lane . . . . AY 17
Highfield Lane. . . . . AY 20
Hill Lane. . . . . AY 21
Kane's Hill . . . . AY 24
Kathleen Rd. . . . . AY 25
Lordswood Rd . . . . AY 27
Lords Hill Way. . . . . AY 26
Mansbridge Rd . . . . AY 28
Moorgreen Rd . . . . AY 30
Moor Hill . . . . AY 31
Newtown Rd . . . . AY 33
Peartree Ave . . . . AY 36
Portswood Rd. . . . . AY 38
Redbridge Rd . . . . AY 42
St Denys Rd . . . . AY 44
Shirley High Rd . . . . AY 45
Shirley Rd . . . . AY 46
Spring Rd. . . . . AY 49
Swaything Rd . . . . AY 50
Tebourba Way. . . . . AY 51
Thomas Lewis Way . . . . AY 54
Townhill Way. . . . . AY 56
Welbeck Ave. . . . . AY 61
Westend Rd . . . . AY 62
Weston Lane . . . . AY 63

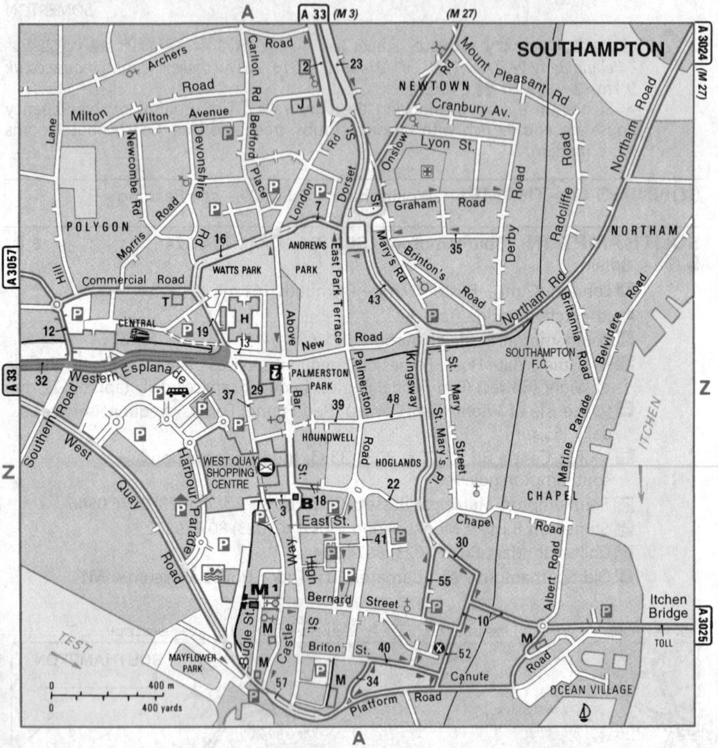

SOUTHAMPTON

Above Bar St . . . . AZ
Avenue (The) . . . . AZ 2
Bargate St . . . . AZ 3
Brunswick Pl. . . . . AZ 7
Central Bridge . . . . AZ 10
Central Station Bridge . . . . . AZ 12
Civic Centre Rd . . . . AZ 13
Cumberland Pl. . . . . AZ 16
Hanover Buildings . . . . AZ 18
Havelock Rd . . . . AZ 19
High St . . . . AZ
Houndwell Pl. . . . . AZ 22
Inner Ave . . . . AZ 23
Marlands Shopping Centre . . . . AZ 29
Marsh Lane . . . . AZ 30
Mountbatten Way . . . . AZ 32
Orchard Pl. . . . . AZ 34
Oxford Ave . . . . AZ 35
Portland Terrace . . . . AZ 37
Pound Tree Rd . . . . AZ 39
Queen's Terrace . . . . AZ 40
Queen's Way . . . . AZ 41
St Andrew's Rd . . . . AZ 43
South Front . . . . AZ 48
Terminus Terrace . . . . AZ 52
Threefield Lane . . . . AZ 55
Town Quay . . . . AZ 57
West Quay Shopping Centre . . . . AZ

Oxfords

35-36 Oxford St ✉ SO14 3DS – ☎ (023) 8022 4444 – www.oxfordsrestaurant.com AZ**x**

Rest – Menu £ 16/18 (weekday dinner) – Carte £ 24/29

◆ Double-fronted restaurant in lively area. Wood-furnished bar and semi open-plan dining room with brushed velvet banquettes. Good choice of classic brasserie dishes with an international edge.

White Star Tavern, Dining and Rooms with rm

rest,

28 Oxford Street ✉ SO14 3DJ – ☎ (023) 8082 1990 – www.whitestartavern.co.uk – Closed 25-26 December AZ**x**

13 rm – †£ 89/109 ††£ 99/119, ☕ £ 3.50

Rest – Carte £ 20/28

◆ Eye-catching black pub with vast windows and smart pavement terrace, set in the lively maritime district. Choice of all day tapas-style small plates or modern British à la carte of meaty dishes. Smart, modern bedrooms boast good facilities and extra touches.

at Hamble-le-Rice Southeast : 5 mi by A 3025 - A - on B 3397 – ✉ Southampton

The Bugle
High St ✉ SO31 4HA – ✆ (023) 8045 3000 – www.buglehamble.co.uk – Closed 25 December
Rest – *(booking essential)* Carte £ 17/28 **s**
◆ Attractive pub down a cobbled street, its terrace overlooking the marina. Bar menu offers sandwiches, small plates and pub classics. More ambitious à la carte available in the dining room.

at Netley Marsh West : 6.5 mi by A 33 off A 336

Hotel TerraVina
174 Woodlands Rd ✉ SO40 7GL – ✆ (023) 8029 3784 – www.hotelterravina.co.uk
11 rm – †£ 145 ††£ 250, ☕ £ 12.95
Rest – Menu £ 29 (lunch) – Carte dinner £ 31/56
◆ Neat Victorian red-brick house with wood-clad extensions, set in a peaceful New Forest location. Comfy lounge and good-sized bar. Brown and orange hues create a relaxed Mediterranean atmosphere. Bedrooms boast good facilities and extras; some have roof terraces. Menus mix modern British and Mediterranean influences.

SOUTH BRENT – 503 I32 – pop. 2 136 – ✉ Devon 2 C2

London 201 – Plymouth 17 – Torbay 15 – Exeter 29

The Royal Oak with rm
Station Rd ✉ TQ10 9BE – ✆ (01364) 72 133 – www.oakonline.net – Closed dinner 25 December
5 rm ☕ – †£ 60/80 ††£ 70/90 **Rest** – Carte £ 18/26
◆ This pub boasts a traditional bar and a more modern restaurant with an attractive courtyard. Lunch offers a simple bar menu and a fish and a dish 'of the day', while dinner is more complex. The cheesecakes are worth saving room for. Modern, spacious bedrooms.

SOUTH DALTON – East Riding – see Beverley

SOUTHEND-ON-SEA – Southend-on-Sea – 504 W29 – pop. 160 257 13 C3

London 39 mi – Cambridge 69 mi – Croydon 46 mi – Dover 85 mi
Southend-on-Sea Airport : ✆ (01702) 608100, N : 2 m
Western Esplanade ✆ (01702) 215120, vic@southend.gov.uk
18 Belfairs Leigh-on-Sea Eastwood Road North, ✆ (01702) 525 345
18 Ballards Gore G. & C.C. Gore Rd, Canewdon, ✆ (01702) 258 917
27 Garon Park Golf Complex Garon Park, Eastern Ave, ✆ (01702) 601 701

Beaches without rest
192 Eastern Esplanade, Thorpe Bay ✉ SS1 3AA – ✆ (01702) 586 124 – www.beachesguesthouse.co.uk
7 rm – †£ 40/70 ††£ 80
◆ A sunny guesthouse on Thorpe Bay with panorama of Thames Estuary. Continental buffet breakfast. Individually styled rooms: four have sea views; two have balconies.

Pebbles without rest
190 Eastern Esplanade, Thorpe Bay ✉ SS1 3AA – ✆ (01702) 582 329
7 rm ☕ – †£ 45/65 ††£ 65/70
◆ Friendly guesthouse on the Esplanade overlooking estuary; away from bustle of town but within easy walking distance. Rooftop garden and sea views from most bedrooms.

Pier View without rest
5 Royal Terr. ✉ SS1 1DY – ✆ (01702) 437 900 – www.pierviewguesthouse.co.uk – Closed 22 December-6 January
9 rm – †£ 55/85 ††£ 75/95
◆ Set in Georgian terrace close to centre of town, with superb views of cliffs, pier and estuary. Bedrooms decorated in pastel shades, with flat screen TVs and Egyptian bedding.

SOUTH LEIGH - Oxon. - **503** P28 - see Witney

SOUTH MOLTON - Devon - **503** I30 - pop. 4 093 **2** C1

London 197 mi - Barnstaple 11 mi - Bristol 81 mi

at Knowstone Southeast : 9.5 mi by A 361 - ✉ South Molton

The Masons Arms (Mark Dodson)

✉ EX36 4RY - ✆ (01398) 341 231 - www.masonsarmsdevon.co.uk - Closed first 2 weeks January, 1 week August, Sunday dinner and Monday

Rest - *(booking essential)* Carte £ 34/45

Spec. Seared peppered tuna with oriental salad. Best end of lamb with aubergine and courgette, toasted cumin seed jus. Rhubarb crumble tart with clotted cream ice cream

◆ Pretty 13C thatched inn set in Exmoor's foothills, with cosy bar and bright dining room featuring celestial ceiling mural. Sophisticated cooking of French and British classics using local produce. Pronounced, assured flavours.

SOUTHPORT - Merseyside - **502** K23 - pop. 91 404 **20** A2

London 221 mi - Liverpool 25 mi - Manchester 38 mi - Preston 19 mi

112 Lord St ✆ (01704) 533333, info@visitsouthport.com

Southport Golf Links Park Road West, ✆ (01704) 535 286

Vincent

98 Lord St. ✉ PR8 1JR - ✆ (01704) 883 800 - www.thevincenthotel.com

59 rm - †£ 150 ††£ 150 - 3 suites

Rest *V-Cafe* - Carte £ 18/37

◆ Striking glass, steel and stone hotel, beside the gardens and bandstand. Stylish, boutique interior with chic bar, fitness room and spa. Sleek, modern bedrooms, in dark colours, with Nespresso machines and Japanese soaking tubs. Informal café boasts a sushi bar.

Bistrot Vérité

7 Liverpool Rd, Birkdale, South : 1.5 mi by A 565 ✉ PR8 4AR - ✆ (01704) 564 199 - Closed 1 week winter, 1 week summer, 25-26 December, 1 January, Sunday and Monday

Rest - French - *(booking essential)* Carte £ 21/31

◆ Simple bistro with tiled floor and panelled walls; sit on the red banquette which runs down one side. Rustic, hearty French cooking; desserts a speciality. Friendly, efficient service.

SOUTH RAUCEBY - Lincolnshire - **502** S24/2 - pop. 335 **17** C2

London 131 - Sheffield 68 - Leicester 54 - Kingston upon Hull 69

The Bustard Inn

44 Main St ✉ NG34 8QG - ✆ (01529) 488 250 - www.thebustardinn.co.uk - Closed 1 January, Sunday dinner and Monday

Rest - Carte £ 24/40

◆ Grade II listed inn set in a peaceful hamlet. Traditional pub favourites served in flag-floored bar. Modern-style English dishes and old-fashioned puddings in the spacious beamed restaurant.

SOUTHROP - Glos. - **503** O28 - see Lechlade

SOUTHWOLD - Suffolk - **504** Z27 - pop. 3 858 **15** D2

London 108 mi - Great Yarmouth 24 mi - Ipswich 35 mi - Norwich 34 mi

69 High St ✆ (01502) 724729, southwold.tic@waveney.gov.uk

The Common, ✆ (01502) 723 234

Swan

Market Pl. ✉ IP18 6EG - ✆ (01502) 722 186 - www.adnams.co.uk

40 rm - †£ 95/175 ††£ 210/250 - 2 suites

Rest - Menu £ 25/35 - Carte £ 25/36

◆ Attractive 18C coaching inn set in the town centre. Subtle modernisations and stylish touches in cosy lounge and bar. Mix of bedrooms: some traditional, some boldly coloured, some charming. Grand dining room with portraits and chandeliers; modern European menu.

The Crown with rm

90 High St ✉ IP18 6DP – ✆ (01502) 722 275 – www.adnams.co.uk

14 rm – £ 95/115 £ 145/165 – 1 suite **Rest** – Carte £ 25/30

◆ 17C Georgian-fronted former coaching inn with appealing, relaxed style, buzzing atmosphere and nautically themed locals bar. Modern, seasonal menu served in all areas. Contemporary, individually styled bedrooms; those at the rear are the quietest.

SOWERBY BRIDGE – West Yorkshire – 502 O22 – pop. 9 901 22 A2 – ✉ Halifax

London 211 mi – Bradford 10 mi – Burnley 35 mi – Manchester 32 mi

El Gato Negro

Oldham Rd ✉ HX6 4DN – ✆ (01422) 823 070 – www.elgatonegrotapas.co.uk – Closed 2 weeks summer, 24 December-7 January, Sunday dinner, Monday, Tuesday and bank holidays

Rest – Spanish – *(dinner only and lunch Friday-Sunday) (booking advisable)* Carte approx. £ 35

◆ Fun, relaxed former pub with solid stone walls and open fires, serving tasty, authentic tapas. Menus printed on placemats: choose 5 or 6 dishes between 2 people. Staff give sound advice.

The Millbank

Mill Bank, Southwest : 2.25 mi by A 58 ✉ HX6 3DY – ✆ (01422) 825 588 – www.themillbank.com – Closed 1 January and Monday

Rest – *(booking essential)* Menu £ 16 (lunch and early dinner Friday and Saturday) – Carte £ 22/32

◆ Modern dining pub set on a steep hill in a remote Yorkshire village, with great views over the Ryburn Valley. Extensive à la carte offers a diverse range of dishes. Regular food-themed events.

at Rishworth Southwest : 4 mi by A 58 on A 672 – ✉ Sowerby Bridge

The Old Bore

Oldham Rd, South : 0.5 mi on A 672 ✉ HX6 4QU – ✆ (01422) 822 291 – www.oldbore.co.uk

Rest – Carte £ 24/30

◆ 19C stone coaching inn hidden away in a charming rural area. Cosy, characterful interior crammed with knick-knacks and memorabilia. Appealingly robust cooking often features local game.

SPARSHOLT – Hants. – 503 P30 – see Winchester

SPEEN – Buckinghamshire – 504 R28 – ✉ Princes Risborough 11 C2

London 41 mi – Aylesbury 15 mi – Oxford 33 mi – Reading 25 mi

Old Plow (Restaurant)

Flowers Bottom, West : 0.5 mi by Chapel Hill and Highwood Bottom ✉ HP27 0PZ – ✆ (01494) 488 300 – www.yeoldplough.co.uk – Closed August, 1 week late May, Christmas-New Year, Sunday and Monday

Rest – Menu £ 30/34

◆ Characterful 17C building with oak beams and log fires, set in peaceful Chiltern Hills hamlet. Extensive 2/3 course set menus feature traditional French dishes, classical sauces and fish specials.

Old Plow (Bistro)

Flowers Bottom, West : 0.5 mi by Chapel Hill and Highwood Bottom ✉ HP27 0PZ – ✆ (01494) 488 300 – www.yeoldplough.co.uk – Closed August, 1 week late May, Christmas-New Year, Sunday and Monday

Rest – *(booking essential)* Menu £ 15 (lunch and weekday dinner) – Carte £ 24/42

◆ Cosy low-ceilinged bistro with lovely views from garden. Flexible blackboard menu features quality meats and fresh Brixham fish. Choice of à la carte or set menu; and tapas Saturday lunchtime.

SPELDHURST - Kent - 504 U30 - see Royal Tunbridge Wells

SPRIGG'S ALLEY - Oxon. - see Chinnor

STADDLEBRIDGE - N. Yorks. - see Northallerton

STADHAMPTON - Oxfordshire - 503 Q28 - pop. 718 — 10 B2

London 53 mi - Aylesbury 18 mi - Oxford 10 mi

Crazy Bear with rm

Bear Ln., off Wallingford rd ✉ OX44 7UR - ✆ (01865) 890 714 - www.crazybeargroup.co.uk

17 rm - †£ 130 ††£ 400, ☕ £ 15

Rest - Menu £ 20 (lunch) - Carte £ 28/37

Rest *Thai Thai* - Thai - *(booking essential)* Carte £ 24/34

◆ Wacky eatery with red London bus reception, smart glasshouse and huge toy bear in trendy bar. Flamboyant English restaurant serves British and French brasserie dishes. More intimate room offers authentic Thai cuisine. Glamorous, individually styled bedrooms boast chic designer furnishings; some have infinity baths.

STAFFORD - Staffordshire - 502 N25 - pop. 63 681 — 19 C1

London 142 mi - Birmingham 26 mi - Derby 32 mi - Shrewsbury 31 mi

Eastgate St ✆ (0871) 7161932, tic@staffordbc.gov.uk

Stafford Castle Newport Rd, ✆ (01785) 223 821

Moat House

rm, rest,

Lower Penkridge Rd, Acton Trussell, South : 3.75 mi by A 449 ✉ ST17 0RJ - ✆ (01785) 712 217 - www.moathouse.co.uk - Closed 25 December

40 rm ☕ - †£ 135 ††£ 155 - 1 suite

Rest *The Conservatory* - Menu £ 20 (lunch) - Carte £ 33/42

◆ Timbered 15C moated manor house with modern extensions and lawned gardens, within sight of the M6. Characterful rustic bar. Colourful rooms with individual style. Bright, airy conservatory restaurant overlooks canal.

STAINES - Middx. - 504 S29 - pop. 50 538 — 7 C1

London 26 mi - Reading 25 mi

The Three Horseshoes

25 Shepperton Rd, South : 2 mi on B 376 ✉ TW18 1SE - ✆ (01784) 469 606 - www.3horseshoeslaleham.co.uk

Rest - Carte £ 20/35

◆ A sturdy 17C inn which has had a sympathetic makeover. Pretty enclosed garden and inviting interior divided into three dining areas with charm and character. Traditional food, done well.

STAMFORD - Lincolnshire - 502 S26 - pop. 19 525 Great Britain — 17 C2

London 92 mi - Leicester 31 mi - Lincoln 50 mi - Nottingham 45 mi

The Arts Centre, 27 St Mary's St ✆ (01780) 755611, stamfordtic@southkesteven.gov.uk

Town★★ - St Martin's Church★ - Lord Burghley's Hospital★ - Browne's Hospital★ **AC**

Burghley House★★ **AC**, SE : 1.5 mi by B 1443

The George of Stamford

71 St Martin's ✉ PE9 2LB - ✆ (01780) 750 750 - www.georgehotelofstamford.com

46 rm ☕ - †£ 98 ††£ 110 - 1 suite

Rest - Carte £ 40/65

Rest *Garden Room* - Carte £ 29/63

◆ Historic inn, over 900 years old. Crusading knights stayed here en route to Jerusalem. Walled garden and courtyard with 17C mulberry tree. Original bedrooms; designer décor. Oak panelled dining room exudes elegance. Garden Room boasts leafy courtyard.

Crown rest,
All Saints Pl. ✉ PE9 2AG – ✆ (01780) 763 136 – www.thecrownhotelstamford.co.uk
31 rm – †£ 120/165 ††£ 130/180
Rest – Menu £ 12 (lunch) – Carte dinner £ 24/35
♦ Former coaching inn set in historic market town. Main house bedrooms have a funky, boutique style; those in the Town House are larger with a more classical feel. Dine in the modern cocktail bar, in one of the cosy lounges or in the quieter rear dining room.

Jim's Yard
3 Ironmonger St, off Broad St ✉ PE9 1PL – ✆ (01780) 756 080 – www.jimsyard.biz – Closed last week July-second week August, 2 weeks Christmas, Sunday and Monday
Rest – Menu £ 17 (lunch) – Carte £ 22/31
♦ Two 18C houses in a courtyard: conservatory or first-floor dining options. Smart tableware enhances enjoyment of great value menus employing well-executed, classic cooking.

at Collyweston **Southwest : 3.5 mi on A 43 – ✉ Stamford**

The Collyweston Slater with rm
87-89 Main Rd ✉ PE9 3PQ – ✆ (01780) 444 288 – www.collywestonslater.co.uk
5 rm – †£ 75 ††£ 120
Rest – Carte £ 22/34
♦ 17C coaching inn offering a choice: comforting classics like ploughman's or pies in the bar or refined, modern dishes in the more formal dining room. Friendly service. Clean, comfortable bedrooms with contemporary furnishings; Ortega and Bacchus are the largest.

at Clipsham **Northwest : 9.5 mi by B 1081 off A 1 – ✉ Stamford**

The Olive Branch & Beech House (Sean Hope) with rm rm,
Main St ✉ LE15 7SH – ✆ (01780) 410 355 – www.theolivebranchpub.com
6 rm – †£ 95/110 ††£ 170/190
Rest – *(booking essential)* Menu £ 21/28 – Carte £ 25/45
Spec. Tapas board. Chargrilled pork chop, pease pudding and apple fondant. Blackcurrant treacle tart.
♦ Characterful, rustic pub with charming garden, which really captures the heart of the local community. Well-prepared, classically based dishes are flavoursome and robust, and display plenty of respect for fresh, local ingredients. Stylish bedrooms include a host of extras and the homemade breakfasts are a delight.

ENGLAND

STANDISH – **Greater Manchester** – **502** M23 – **pop. 14 350** – **✉ Wigan** **20** A2
London 210 mi – Liverpool 25 mi – Manchester 21 mi – Preston 15 mi

at Wrightington Bar **Northwest : 3.5 mi by A 5209 on B 5250 – ✉ Wigan**

The Mulberry Tree
9 Wood Ln ✉ WN6 9SE – ✆ (01257) 451 400 – www.themulberrytree.info
Rest – Carte £ 21/35
♦ Spacious 19C pub with laid-back bar and more formal, linen-laid dining room. Wide-ranging menus of good value, generously proportioned dishes, with plenty of pub favourites.

STANSTED MOUNTFITCHET – **Essex** – **504** U28 – **see Bishop's Stortford (Herts.)**

STANTON – Suffolk – 504 W27 – pop. 2 073 15 C2

London 88 mi – Cambridge 38 mi – Ipswich 40 mi – King's Lynn 38 mi

Leaping Hare

Wyken Vineyards, South : 1.25 mi by Wyken Rd ✉ IP31 2DW – ☎ (01359) 250 287 – www.wykenvineyards.co.uk – Closed 25 December-5 January
Rest – *(lunch only and dinner Friday-Saturday) (booking essential)*
Menu £ 19/25 – Carte £ 26/33

♦ Beautiful 17C barn with lovely terrace; at the centre of a vineyard. Interesting all-day light bites or accomplished weekly menu. Well-sourced, seasonal ingredients; many from their own farm. Carefully judged cooking relies on quality produce and natural flavours.

STANTON ST QUINTIN – Wilts. – 503 N29 – see Chippenham

STANWICK – Northamptonshire – pop. 1 924 17 C3

London 83 mi – Northampton 18 mi – Milton Keynes 36 mi – Peterborough 27 mi

Courtyard Luxury Lodge

West St ✉ NN9 6QY – ☎ (01933) 622 233 – www.thecourtyardluxury.co.uk
20 rm – †£ 70 ††£ 85
Rest – Menu £ 13/17 – Carte £ 13/39

♦ Traditional whitewashed house and annexe set in pretty gardens. Comfy, well-kept bedrooms boast good facilities: country house style rooms in main house; more contemporary feel in former stables. Airy modern restaurant with bar, lounge and international menus.

STAPLEFORD – Nottinghamshire – 504 Q25 – see Nottingham

STATHERN – Leics. – see Melton Mowbray

STAVERTON – Devon – 503 I32 – pop. 682 – ✉ Totnes 2 C2

London 220 mi – Exeter 20 mi – Torquay 33 mi

Kingston House

Northwest : 1 mi on Kingston rd ✉ TQ9 6AR – ☎ (01803) 762 235 – www.kingston-estate.com – Closed Christmas-New Year
3 rm – †£ 110/120 ††£ 180/200
Rest – *(dinner only) (residents only, set menu only)* Menu £ 38 **s**

♦ Attractive Georgian mansion in a stunning location. Original features and antiques abound. Spacious bedrooms boast feature beds and good views over the parterre garden; some have original baths. Vaulted basement dining room serves classical, home-cooked dishes.

STAVERTON – Northants. – 504 Q27 – see Daventry

STILTON – Cambridgeshire – 504 T26 – pop. 2 500 – ✉ Peterborough 14 A2

London 76 mi – Cambridge 30 mi – Northampton 43 mi – Peterborough 6 mi

Bell Inn

Great North Rd ✉ PE7 3RA – ☎ (01733) 241 066 – www.thebellstilton.co.uk – Closed 25 December
22 rm – †£ 73/83 ††£ 110
Rest *Village Bar* – see restaurant listing
Rest *Galleried Restaurant* – *(dinner only and Sunday lunch)* Menu £ 30 – Carte £ 17/30

♦ Historic coaching inn with hospitable, hands-on owner. Comfortable bedrooms have traditional feel: some have four-posters; the three newest are in the former smithy, overlooking the garden. First floor restaurant offers seasonal menu with strong classical base.

ENGLAND

Village Bar – at Bell Inn
Great North Rd ✉ PE7 3RA – ✆ (01733) 241 066 – www.thebellstilton.co.uk – Closed 25 December
Rest – Carte £ 20/34 **s**
♦ 17C coaching inn where Stilton cheese was born. Choose from a characterful bar or more modern bistro area. Served throughout, the classical menu is a step above your usual pub fare.

STOCKBRIDGE – Hampshire – 503 P30 – pop. 570 — 6 B2

London 75 mi – Salisbury 14 mi – Southampton 19 mi – Winchester 9 mi

The Greyhound with rm
31 High St ✉ SO20 6EY – ✆ (01264) 810 833 – www.thegreyhound.info – Closed 3 days Christmas, 31 December-1 January and Sunday dinner
8 rm – †£ 70 ††£ 95/125
Rest – Carte £ 25/40
♦ Unassuming pub with low-beamed bar and comfy lounge. Lunch mainly aimed at one course; concise evening à la carte features pub dishes with restaurant-style touches and refined presentation. Picnic by the river in the garden. Spacious bedrooms with huge showers.

at Longstock North : 1.5 mi on A 3057 – ✉ Stockbridge

The Peat Spade Inn with rm
Village St ✉ SO20 6DR – ✆ (01264) 810 612 – www.peatspadeinn.co.uk – Closed 25 December
6 rm – †£ 130 ††£ 130 **Rest** – *(booking essential)* Carte £ 24/34
♦ Charming 19C inn with country pursuits theme, period furnishings and welcoming candlelight. Menus offer classically based dishes that have been brought up-to-date. Stylish bedrooms are split between the inn and annexe. Shooting/-fishing trips can be arranged.

STOCKPORT – Greater Manchester – 502 N23 – pop. 136 082 — 20 B3

London 201 mi – Liverpool 42 mi – Leeds 50 mi – Sheffield 52 mi

Damson
113 Heaton Moor Rd, Northwest : 2.25 mi by A 6, Heaton Rd, A 5145 and Bank Hall Rd ✉ SK4 4HY – ✆ (0161) 432 46 66 – www.damsonrestaurant.co.uk – Closed 25-26 December and 1 January
Rest – Menu £ 15 (lunch) – Carte £ 26/42
♦ Smart, modern, glass-fronted restaurant with damson walls, velvet chairs and rustic tables. Appealing menu of traditional dishes with modern touches. Attentive, formal service.

STOKE BY NAYLAND – Suffolk – 504 W28 — 15 C3

London 70 mi – Bury St Edmunds 24 mi – Cambridge 54 mi – Colchester 11 mi

The Crown with rm
✉ CO6 4SE – ✆ (01206) 262 001 – www.crowninn.net – Closed 25-26 December
11 rm – †£ 75 ††£ 200
Rest – Carte £ 20/33
♦ Spacious 16C pub with smart wood-furnished patio; set in a hillside village overlooking the valley. Menus feature locally sourced, seasonal produce, a daily catch and seafood specials. Spacious bedrooms boast country views; some have French windows and a terrace.

STOKE HOLY CROSS – Norfolk – 504 X26 – see Norwich

STOKENCHURCH – Buckinghamshire – **504** R29 – pop. 3 949 **11** C2

London 42 mi – High Wycombe 10 mi – Oxford 18 mi

at Radnage Northeast : 1.75 mi by A 40 – ✉ Stokenchurch

The Three Horseshoes Inn with rm
Bennett End, North : 1.25 mi by Town End rd. ✉ HP14 4EB – ✆ (01494) 483 273 – www.thethreehorseshoes.net – Closed Sunday dinner and Monday lunch
6 rm – ♦£ 75/95 ♦♦£ 85/145
Rest – Menu £ 18 (lunch) – Carte £ 19/36
◆ Attractive pub with lovely terrace, set in a fantastic hillside location. Classically prepared dishes display French touches. Lighter offerings at lunch; à la carte or tapas at dinner. Sunday lunch is a veritable feast. Comfortable yet minimalistic bedrooms have character beds and modern bathrooms. Molières is best.

STOKE-ON-TRENT – Stoke-on-Trent – **502** N24 – pop. 259 252 **19** C1

Great Britain

ENGLAND

London 162 mi – Birmingham 46 mi – Leicester 59 mi – Liverpool 58 mi

Victoria Hall, The Cultural Quarter, City Centre ✆ (01782) 236000, stoke.tic@stoke.gov.uk

Greenway Hall Stockton Brook, ✆ (01782) 503 158

Parkhall Weston Coyney Hulme Rd, ✆ (01782) 599 584

The Potteries Museum and Art Gallery★ Y **M** – Gladstone Pottery Museum★ **AC** V

The Wedgwood Story★ **AC**, S : 7 mi on A 500, A 34 and minor rd V. Little Moreton Hall★★ **AC**, N : 10 mi by A 500 on A 34 U – Biddulph Grange Garden★, N : 7 mi by A 52, A 50 and A 527 U

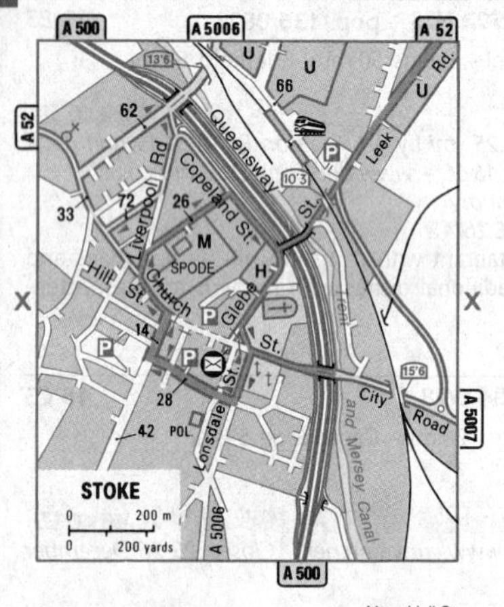

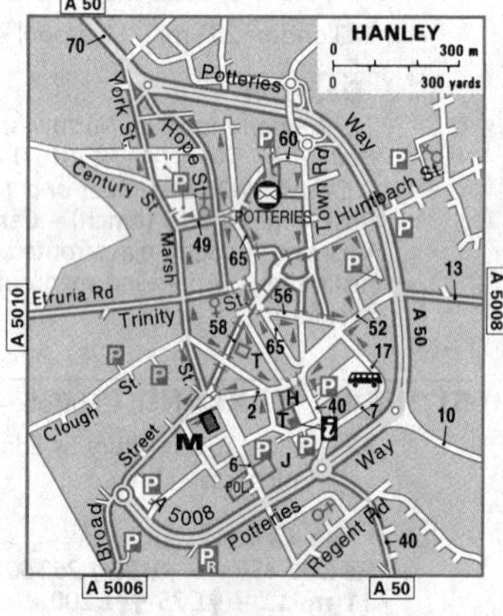

HANLEY

Albion St . . . Y 2
Bethesda St . . . Y 6
Birch Terrace . . . Y 7
Botteslow St . . . Y 10
Bucknall New Rd . . . Y 13
Charles St . . . Y 17
Lichfield St . . . Y 40
New Hall St . . . Y 49
Old Hall St . . . Y 52
Parliament Row . . . Y 55
Percy St . . . Y 56
Piccadilly . . . Y 58
Potteries Shopping Centre . . . Y
Quadrant Rd . . . Y 60
Stafford St . . . Y 65
Vale Pl. . . . Y 70

STOKE-ON-TRENT

Campbell Pl. . . . X 14
Church St . . . X
Elenora St . . . X 26
Fleming Rd . . . X 28
Hartshill Rd . . . X 33
London Rd . . . X 42
Shelton Old Rd . . . X 62
Station Rd . . . X 66
Vale St . . . X 72

STOKE-ON-TRENT NEWCASTLE-UNDER-LYME

Street	Grid	No.
Alexandra Rd	U	3
Bedford Rd	U	4
Brownhills Rd	U	12
Church Lane	U	19
Cobridge Rd	U	21
Davenport St.	U	23
Elder Rd	U	24
Etruria Vale Rd	U	27
Grove Rd.	V	30
Hanley Rd.	U	31
Heron St	V	34
Higherland.	V	37
High St	U	35
Manor St	V	44
Mayne St	V	45
Moorland Rd.	U	48
Porthill Rd	U	59
Snow Hill	U	63
Stoke Rd.	U	68
Strand (The)	V	69
Victoria Park Rd	U	75
Victoria Pl. Link	V	76
Watlands View	U	77
Williamson St	U	78
Wolstanton Link Rd	U	80

The Manor at Hanchurch

Newcastle Rd, Hanchurch, Southwest : 3.5 mi by A 500 and A 519 ✉ *ST4 8SD – ✆ (01782) 643 030 – www.hanchurchmanor.co.uk* V**x**

6 rm ☕ – 🚹£ 100 🚹🚹£ 150

Rest *Maldini's* – Italian – *(Closed Sunday dinner)* Carte approx. £ 30

◆ 17C neo-Tudor house and outbuildings, set within their own parkland. Smart bedrooms boast quality furnishings, heavy fabrics and modern bathrooms; some have spa baths. Contemporary bar for cocktails. Two-roomed restaurant offers traditional Italian cooking.

STOKE POGES – Buckinghamshire – 504 S29 – pop. 4 112 **11** D3

London 30 mi – Aylesbury 28 mi – Oxford 44 mi

Stoke Park Park Rd, ✆ (01753) 717 171

 **Stoke Park**

Park Rd ✉ SL2 4PG – ✆ (01753) 717 171 – www.stokepark.com – Closed 25-26 December and first week January
49 rm – †£ 545 ††£ 545, ☐ £ 22
Rest *The Dining Room* – Menu £ 25/45
♦ Grand, palatial hotel in huge grounds, with golf course, extensive sporting activities and impressive spa. Choice of smart classical or stunning contemporary bedrooms. Lounge offers all day brasserie menu. Stylish restaurant displays classical à la carte.

Stoke Place rm,

Stoke Green, South : 0.5 mi by B 416 ✉ SL2 4HT – ✆ (01753) 534 790 – www.stokeplace.co.uk
29 rm ☐ – †£ 110/185 ††£ 110/185
Rest *The Garden Room* – *(closed Sunday dinner) (dinner only and lunch Saturday-Sunday)* Carte £ 30/36
♦ 17C Queen Anne mansion, by a lake, in 22 acres of grounds. Chic, quirky guest areas display bold print wallpapers and original furnishings; sleek, modern bedrooms boast clean lines and stylish beds. Contemporary menu served in both the Garden and Vyse Rooms.

STOKESLEY – North Yorkshire – 502 Q20 – pop. 4 725 23 C1

– ✉ Middlesbrough Great Britain

London 239 mi – Leeds 59 mi – Middlesbrough 8 mi – Newcastle upon Tyne 49 mi

Great Ayton (Captain Cook Birthplace Museum★ **AC**), NE : 2.5 mi on A 173

Chapter's with rm rest,

27 High St ✉ TS9 5AD – ✆ (01642) 711 888 – www.chaptershotel.co.uk – Closed 25-26 December, 1 January and Sunday dinner
13 rm ☐ – †£ 66/74 ††£ 99 **Rest** – Menu £ 10 (lunch) – Carte £ 24/40
♦ Solid, mellow brick Victorian house with colour washed rooms. Bistro style dining with strong Mediterranean colour scheme. Eclectic menu: classics and more modern dishes.

STON EASTON – Somerset – 503 M30 – pop. 579 4 C2

– ✉ Bath (Bath & North East Somerset)

London 131 mi – Bath 12 mi – Bristol 11 mi – Wells 7 mi

Ston Easton Park

✉ BA3 4DF – ✆ (01761) 241 631 – www.stoneaston.co.uk
20 rm ☐ – †£ 125/510 ††£ 160/545 – 2 suites
Rest *The Sorrel* – *(booking essential for non-residents)* Menu £ 23 (lunch) – Carte £ 45/53
♦ Aristocratic Palladian mansion; grounds designed by Humphrey Repton, given subtle contemporary styling. Lavish rooms: Grand Saloon with Kentian plasterwork. Formal restaurant served by a Victorian kitchen garden.

STONEHALL COMMON – Worcestershire – see Worcester

STORRINGTON – West Sussex – 504 S31 – pop. 7 727 7 C2

London 54 mi – Brighton 20 mi – Portsmouth 36 mi

Old Forge

6 Church St ✉ RH20 4LA – ✆ (01903) 743 402 – www.oldforge.co.uk – Closed 2 weeks spring, 1 week autumn, Saturday lunch and dinner Sunday-Wednesday
Rest – Menu £ 15/34 – Carte £ 26/34
♦ Appealing whitewashed and brick cottages with three dining rooms bearing all hallmarks of flavoursome traditional cuisine. Array of cheeses; fine wine from small producers.

STOWMARKET – Suffolk – 504 W27 – pop. 15 059 — 15 C3

London 95 mi – Ipswich 14 mi – Colchester 35 mi – Clacton-on-Sea 40 mi

at Buxhall West : 3.75 mi by B 115 – ✉ Stowmarket

The Buxhall Crown
Mill Rd ✉ IP14 3DW – ☎ (01449) 736 521 – www.thebuxhallcrown.co.uk – Closed 25-26 December, Sunday dinner and Monday
Rest – Menu £ 16 (lunch) – Carte £ 20/35
◆ Part-16C country pub set off the beaten track, with bright dining room and cosy, low-beamed bar. Classic dishes offered on seasonal menu. Good value set 2 course menu and fun retro puds.

STOW-ON-THE-WOLD – Gloucestershire – 503 O28 – pop. 2 074 — 4 D1

Great Britain

London 86 mi – Birmingham 44 mi – Gloucester 27 mi – Oxford 30 mi
Chastleton House★★, NE : 6.5 mi by A 436 and A 44

Grapevine
Sheep St ✉ GL54 1AU – ☎ (01451) 830 344 – www.thegrapevinehotel.com
22 rm – †£ 72/88 ††£ 113/164
Rest *The Conservatory* – Menu £ 35
Rest *Lavigna* – Carte £ 18/23
◆ Among the antique shops, two extended 17C houses. Rooms in bright, modern décor with a nod to tradition, half with beams and bare stone. Timbered bar; sepia photos of Stow. In Conservatory black grapes hang from spreading vine. Easy-going, informal Lavigna.

The Royalist
Digbeth St ✉ GL56 1BN – ☎ (01451) 830 670 – www.theroyalisthotel.com
14 rm – †£ 68/120 ††£ 103/185
Rest *Eagle & Child* – Carte £ 19/25
Rest *947 AD* – Menu £ 37 (dinner) – Carte lunch £ 24/29
◆ Historic high street inn - reputedly England's oldest. Comfortable, stylish rooms, individual in shape and décor and quieter at the rear. Two-room bar in exposed stone. Robust cooking in the attached stone pub. Fine dining in the intimate, beamed restaurant with ingelnook fireplace.

Fosse Manor
Fosse Way, South : 1.25 mi on A 429 ✉ GL54 1JX – ☎ (01451) 830 354 – www.fossemanor.co.uk
19 rm – †£ 54/99 ††£ 90/135 **Rest** – Carte £ 22/36
◆ Former coaching inn on the main road. Contemporary public areas with informal feel. Up-to-date bedrooms, some of which are set in the coach house. Classically proportioned dining room with menu of Mediterranean favourites.

Number Nine without rest
9 Park St ✉ GL54 1AQ – ☎ (01451) 870 333 – www.number-nine.info
3 rm – †£ 45/55 ††£ 65/75
◆ Ivy-clad 18C Cotswold stone house run by friendly owners on the high street. Winding staircase leads to the large bedrooms which occupy each floor.

Old Butchers
Park St ✉ GL54 1AQ – ☎ (01451) 831 700 – www.theoldbutchers.com – Closed 1 week May and 1 week October
Rest – Menu £ 16 (lunch) – Carte £ 25/32
◆ Former butcher's shop of Cotswold stone: closely set tables in a very busy, modern restaurant. Daily changing, affordable, modish menus feature prominent use of local produce.

at Upper Oddington East : 2 mi by A 436 – ✉ Stow-on-the-Wold

Horse & Groom Village Inn with rm
✉ GL56 0XH – ☎ (01451) 830 584 – www.horseandgroom.uk.com
7 rm – †£ 79/95 ††£ 99/110 **Rest** – Carte £ 20/30
◆ Part-16C mellow-stone inn in a village designated an AONB. Seasonal menus feature strictly homemade and local produce, with consideration given to ethical production and sustainable sourcing. Cosy bedrooms; serious breakfasts include local eggs and sausages.

ENGLAND

at Lower Oddington East : 3 mi by A 436 – ✉ Stow-on-the-Wold

The Fox Inn with rm

✉ *GL56 0UR* – ☎ *(01451) 870 555* – *www.foxinn.net* – *Closed 25 December*
3 rm – †£ 75/95 ††£ 75/95 **Rest** – *(booking essential)* Carte £ 20/35
♦ Quintessentially English, creeper-clad inn with cosy, characterful bar, charming garden and heated terrace. Cooking is hearty and satisfying; produce is sourced from local markets. Uniquely designed bedrooms display lovely antiques; some boast feature beds.

at Daylesford East : 3.5 mi by A 436 – ✉ Stow-on-the-Wold

Cafe at Daylesford Organic

✉ *GL56 0YG* – ☎ *(01608) 731 700* – *www.daylesfordorganic.com*
– *Closed 25-26 December and 1 January*
Rest – Organic – *(lunch only) (bookings not accepted)* Carte £ 22/30
♦ Stylish café attached to the rear of a farm shop, its rustic interior boasting an open charcoal grill and wood-fired oven. Menus showcase an interesting array of home-cooked dishes. Everything is organic, with much of the produce coming from the farm itself.

at Bledington Southeast : 4 mi by A 436 on B 4450 – ✉ Kingham

The Kings Head Inn with rm

The Green ✉ *OX7 6XQ* – ☎ *(01608) 658 365* – *www.kingsheadinn.net* – *Closed 25-26 December*
12 rm – †£ 65/75 ††£ 125 **Rest** – Carte £ 20/35
♦ 15C stone inn with low-ceilinged, beamed bar and comfortable dining room. Traditional dishes with odd international influence; robust, rustic cooking. Smart bedrooms; those in pub more characterful; those in annex more stylish.

ENGLAND

at Lower Swell West : 1.25 mi on B 4068 – ✉ Stow-on-the-Wold

Rectory Farmhouse without rest

by Rectory Barns Rd ✉ *GL54 1LH* – ☎ *(01451) 832 351* – *Closed Christmas-New Year*
3 rm – †£ 65/70 ††£ 95/100
♦ 17C former farmhouse of Cotswold stone. Bedrooms are very comfortable and decorated in distinctive cottage style. Breakfast in kitchen, conservatory or, in summer, on the terrace.

STRATFORD-UPON-AVON – Warwickshire – 503 P27 — 19 C3

– pop. 22 187 Great Britain

London 96 mi – Birmingham 23 mi – Coventry 18 mi – Leicester 44 mi
Bridgefoot ☎ (0870) 160 7930, info@shakespeare-country.co.uk
Tiddington Rd, ☎ (01789) 205 749
Menzies Welcombe Hotel & GC Warwick Rd, ☎ (01789) 413 800
Stratford Oaks Snitterfield Bearley Rd, ☎ (01789) 731 980
Town★★ - Shakespeare's Birthplace★ **AC**, AB
Mary Arden's House★ **AC**, NW : 4 mi by A 3400 A. Ragley Hall★ **AC**, W : 9 mi by A 422 A

Welcombe H. Spa and Golf Club

Warwick Rd, Northeast : 1.5 mi on A 439
✉ *CV37 0NR* – ☎ *(01789) 295 252* – *www.menzieshotels.co.uk*
73 rm – †£ 99/180 ††£ 109/200 – 5 suites
Rest *Trevelyan* – *(closed Saturday lunch)* Menu £ 25/35 – Carte £ 30/60
♦ Imposing Jacobean-style house built in 1866, with attractive grounds, superb spa/leisure club and classical guest areas. Choose from corporate, or traditional, antique-filled bedrooms. Formal dining room overlooks the gardens and water features.

STRATFORD-UPON-AVON

Banbury Rd . . . . B 2
Bell Court Shopping Centre . . . . A 39
Benson Rd. . . . . B 3
Bridge Foot . . . . B 6
Bridge St . . . . B 8
Chapel Lane . . . . A 13
Chapel St. . . . . A 14
Church St . . . . A 16
Clopton Bridge . . . . B 18
College Lane . . . . A 19
Ely St . . . . A 22
Evesham Pl. . . . . A 24
Great William St . . . . . . A 25
Greenhill St . . . . A 27
Guild St . . . . A 28
Henley St. . . . . A 29
High St . . . . A 31
Rother St . . . . A 32
Scholars Lane . . . . A 33
Sheep St . . . . AB 35
Tiddington Rd . . . . B 38
Trinity St. . . . . A 40
Warwick Rd. . . . . B 42
Waterside . . . . B 43
Windsor St . . . . A 45
Wood St . . . . A 47

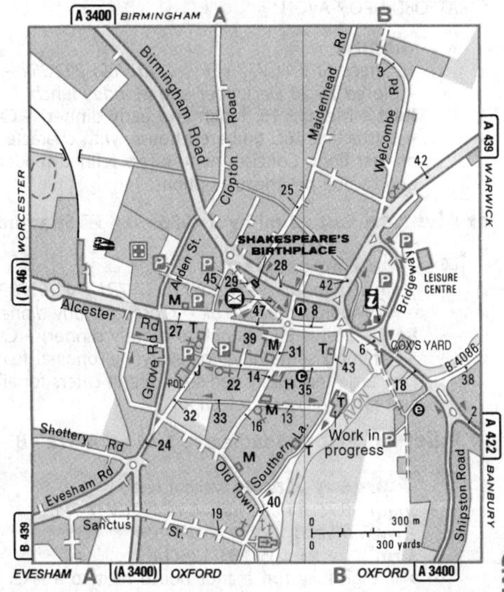

ENGLAND

Ettington Park

Alderminster, Southeast : 6.25 mi on A 3400 ✉ *CV37 8BU*
– ✆ (0845) 072 7454 – www.handpicked.co.uk
43 rm – 🛉£ 105/205 🛉🛉£ 145/225 – 5 suites
Rest – Menu £ 35 **s** – Carte £ 33/39 **s**

◆ Impressive Gothic mansion surrounded by lovely gardens and wooded grounds. Large, characterful guest areas boast impressive ornate ceilings. Smart, stylish bedrooms have modern facilities. Formal restaurant offers classical British menus.

Cherry Trees without rest

Swan's Nest Ln. ✉ *CV37 7LS* – ✆ *(01789) 292 989*
– *www.cherrytrees-stratford.co.uk* **B**e
3 rm – 🛉£ 65/75 🛉🛉£ 95/115

◆ Smart, proudly run guest house in peaceful location. Spacious bedrooms boast quality furnishings, state-of-the-art showers, conservatory seating areas and thoughtful extras. Cake served on arrival.

White Sails without rest

85 Evesham Rd, Southwest : 1 mi on B 439 ✉ *CV37 9BE* – ✆ *(01789) 264 326*
– *www.white-sails.co.uk*
4 rm – 🛉£ 97 🛉🛉£ 122

◆ Friendly guest house boasting excellent bedrooms; all individually furnished and with a high level of facilities, including superb bathrooms. Leather furnished lounge with local info.

Malbec Petit Bistro

6 Union St ✉ *CV37 6QT* – ✆ *(01789) 269 106*
– *www.malbecrestaurant.co.uk*
– *Closed 1 week Christmas, Sunday and Monday* **A**n
Rest – Menu £ 15 (lunch) – Carte £ 28/33

◆ Smart restaurant with intimate, barrel-ceilinged, basement bistro and excellent service. Concise, constantly evolving menus offer rustic, flavoursome dishes with a refined edge; set lunch option provides the best value.

Lambs

12 Sheep St ✉ CV37 6EF – ☎ (01789) 292 554 – www.lambsrestaurant.co.uk – Closed 25-26 December and Monday lunch **Bc**

Rest – Menu £ 15 (lunch and early dinner) – Carte £ 24/31

♦ Attractive 16C timbered house, with characterful beams and original features on first floor. Concise menu offers refined modern dishes and fish specials, with good value pre-theatre options.

at Alveston East : 2 mi by B 4086 - B – ✉ Stratford-upon-Avon

The Baraset Barn

1 Pimlico Ln, on B 4086 ✉ CV37 7RJ – ☎ (01789) 295 510 – www.barasetbarn.co.uk – Closed Sunday dinner

Rest – Menu £ 15 (lunch and early dinner) – Carte £ 20/30

♦ Offering something for everyone: original features, contemporary furnishings and large terraces. Good-sized menu caters for all and includes daily fish specials and tasty rotisserie selection.

at Pillerton Priors Southeast : 7 mi on A 422 - B – ✉ Stratford-upon-Avon

Fulready Manor without rest

South : 0.75 mi on Halford rd ✉ CV37 7PE – ☎ (01789) 740 152 – www.fulreadymanor.co.uk

3 rm – †£ 105 ††£ 125/140

♦ Delightfully run manor house next to a lake, in 125 acres of peaceful arable farmland. Spacious lounge. Elegant bedrooms with feature beds, smart bathrooms and extras. Excellent views.

ENGLAND

STRETE – **Devon** – see Dartmouth

STRETTON – **Staffs.** – **502** P25 – see Burton-upon-Trent

STROUD – **Gloucestershire** – **503** N28 – **pop. 32 052** **4** C1

London 113 mi – Bristol 30 mi – Gloucester 9 mi

Subscription Rooms, George St ☎ (01453) 760960, tic@stroud.gov.uk

Minchinhampton, ☎ (01453) 833 840

Painswick Golf Course Rd, ☎ (01452) 812 180

at Brimscombe Southeast : 2.25 mi on A 419 – ✉ Stroud

Burleigh Court

Burleigh Ln, South : 0.5 mi by Burleigh rd via The Roundabouts ✉ GL5 2PF – ☎ (01453) 883 804 – www.burleighcourthotel.co.uk – Closed 25-26 December

18 rm – †£ 90 ††£ 195 **Rest** – Menu £ 25 (lunch) – Carte dinner £ 33/40

♦ Regency house with mature garden, on edge of a steep hill overlooking Golden Valley. Swimming pool and terrace at the rear a real suntrap. Smart bedrooms with views. Comfortable dining room overlooks the gardens.

STUCKTON – **Hants.** – see Fordingbridge

STUDLAND – **Dorset** – **503** O32 – **pop. 471** **4** C3

London 135 mi – Bournemouth 25 mi – Southampton 53 mi – Weymouth 29 mi

Shell Bay

Ferry Rd, North : 3 mi or via car ferry from Sandbanks ✉ BH19 3BA – ☎ (01929) 450 363 – www.shellbay.net – March-October

Rest – Seafood – *(booking essential)* Carte £ 26/34

♦ Airy, simply furnished seafood restaurant with decked terrace; superbly set on the waterfront and boasting views over the harbour to Brownsea Island – all tables have a view. Choose between an informal lunch/early evening menu or classically based daily menu.

SUMMERCOURT – Cornwall – 503 F32 – ✉ Newquay **1** B2

London 263 mi – Newquay 9 mi – Plymouth 45 mi

Viners

Carvynick, 1.5 mi Northwest off the junction of A 30 and A 3058. ✉ TR8 5AF – ✆ (01872) 510 544 – www.vinersrestaurant.co.uk – Closed 2 weeks January, Sunday dinner, Monday and lunch midweek out of season

Rest – Menu £ 19 (weekday lunch) – Carte £ 35/41

♦ Rustic, stone-built former farmhouse. Snacks available amongst roaring log fires and low slung beams in the bar. Relaxed first floor restaurant offers seasonal menu of old classics, a few more ambitious dishes and tasty daily specials. Keen, friendly service.

SUNBURY ON THAMES – Surrey – 504 S29 – pop. 27 415 **7** C1

London 16 mi – Croydon 38 mi – Barnet 44 mi – Ealing 10 mi

Indian Zest

21 Thames St ✉ TW16 5QF – ✆ (01932) 765 000 – www.indianzest.co.uk

Rest – Indian – Carte £ 22/27

♦ Original in its decoration and food. 450 year old building; a series of small rooms set around a bar; subtle colonial feel. Interesting mix of modern Indian and traditional regional cuisine.

SUNNINGDALE – Windsor and Maidenhead – 504 S29 **11** D3

London 33 mi – Croydon 39 mi – Barnet 46 mi – Ealing 22 mi

Bluebells

Shrubbs Hill, London Rd, Northeast : 0.75 mi on A 30 ✉ SL5 0LE – ✆ (01344) 622 722 – www.bluebells-restaurant.com – Closed 1-12 January, 25-26 December, Sunday dinner and Monday

Rest – Menu £ 16 (lunch) – Carte dinner £ 34/52

♦ Smart, well-manicured façade matched by sophisticated interior of deep green. Large rear terrace, deck and garden. Modern British cooking with original starting point.

SUNNISIDE – Tyne and Wear **24** B2

London 283 mi – Newcastle upon Tyne 6 mi – Sunderland 16 mi – Middlesbrough 41 mi

Hedley Hall without rest

Hedley Lane, South : 2 m by A 6076 ✉ NE16 5EH – ✆ (01207) 231 835 – www.hedleyhall.com

4 rm – †£ 52/60 ††£ 85

♦ Pleasant former farmhouse in quiet rural location close to Beamish, with spacious conservatory and sitting room. Rooms are large, with good levels of comfort and country views.

SUTTON COLDFIELD – West Midlands – 503 O26 – pop. 105 452 **19** C2

London 124 mi – Birmingham 8 mi – Coventry 29 mi – Nottingham 47 mi

18 Pype Hayes Walmley Eachelhurst Rd, ✆ (0121) 351 1014

18 Boldmere Monmouth Dr., ✆ (0121) 354 3379

18 110 Thornhill Rd, ✆ (0121) 580 7878

36 The Belfry Wishaw Lichfield Rd, ✆ (01675) 470 301

Plan : see Birmingham pp. 2 and 3

Mint

52 Thornhill Rd, Little Aston, Northwest : 3.5 mi by A 5127, A 454 and B 4151 on B 4138. ✉ B74 3EN – ✆ (0121) 353 0488 – www.mint-restaurant.com – Closed first week January, last week August, first week September, Easter, Monday and Tuesday

Rest – Menu £ 18/35

♦ Bright, modern, brasserie-style restaurant set in a smart residential area. Short menu of flavoursome, visually appealing British dishes. Good value lunch menu. Hands-on owner.

SUTTON COURTENAY – Oxfordshire – pop. 2 413 **10** B2

London 72 mi – Bristol 77 mi – Coventry 70 mi

The Fish

4 Appleford Rd ✉ OX14 4NQ – ✆ (01235) 848 242 – www.thefishatsuttoncourtenay.co.uk – Closed January, Sunday dinner and Monday

Rest – Menu £ 16 (Tuesday-Saturday lunch) – Carte £ 23/30

◆ Robust, seasonal country cooking: escargots and crème brûlée meet steak and kidney pie and profiteroles on Franco-Anglo menu. Neat garden and bright conservatory. Charming service.

Guesthouses don't provide the same level of service as hotels. They are often characterised by a warm welcome and a décor which reflects the owner's personality. Those shown in red are particularly pleasant.

SUTTON GAULT – Cambs. – **504** U26 – see Ely

SUTTON-ON-THE-FOREST – North Yorkshire – **502** P21 – pop. 281 **23** C2

London 230 mi – Kingston-upon-Hull 50 mi – Leeds 52 mi – Scarborough 40 mi

Rose & Crown

Main St ✉ YO61 1DP – ✆ (01347) 811 333 – www.rosecrown.co.uk – Closed Sunday dinner and Monday

Rest – *(booking essential)* Menu £ 20 – Carte £ 22/28

◆ Always a welcoming atmosphere at this village pub, with its cosy bar and busy dining room. Variety of menus ensures something for everyone; good food and local specialities. Large terrace and gazebo.

The Blackwell Ox Inn with rm

Huby Rd ✉ YO61 1DT – ✆ (01347) 810 328 – www.blackwelloxinn.co.uk – Closed 25 December, 1 January and Sunday dinner

7 rm – †£ 65 ††£ 110

Rest – Menu £ 14 **s** – Carte £ 15/30 **s**

◆ Smart, contemporary inn with homely bar/lounge and formal, linen-clad dining room. Blackboard snacks and daily changing à la carte; dishes range from the down-to-earth to more ambitious. Spacious, stylish bedrooms; some boast four-posters and Room 2 has a roll-top bath.

SWAY – Hants. – **503** P31 – see Brockenhurst

SWINBROOK – Oxon. – **503** P28 – see Burford

SWINDON – Swindon – **503** O29 – pop. 155 432 **4** D2

London 83 mi – Bournemouth 69 mi – Bristol 40 mi – Coventry 66 mi

37 Regent St ✆ (01793) 530328, infocentre@swindon.gov.uk

Broome Manor Pipers Way, ✆ (01793) 532 403

Shrivenham Park Shrivenham Penny Hooks, ✆ (01793) 783 853

The Wiltshire G & CC Wootton Bassett Vastern, ✆ (01793) 849 999

Wrag Barn G & C.C. Highworth Shrivenham Rd, ✆ (01793) 861 327

Great Western Railway Museum★ **AC** – Railway Village Museum★ **AC** Y **M**

Lydiard Park (St Mary's★) W : 4 mi U. Ridgeway Path★★, S : 8.5 mi by A 4361 – Whitehorse (≤★)E : 7.5 mi by A 4312, A 420 and B 400 off B 4057

Plans pages 613, 614

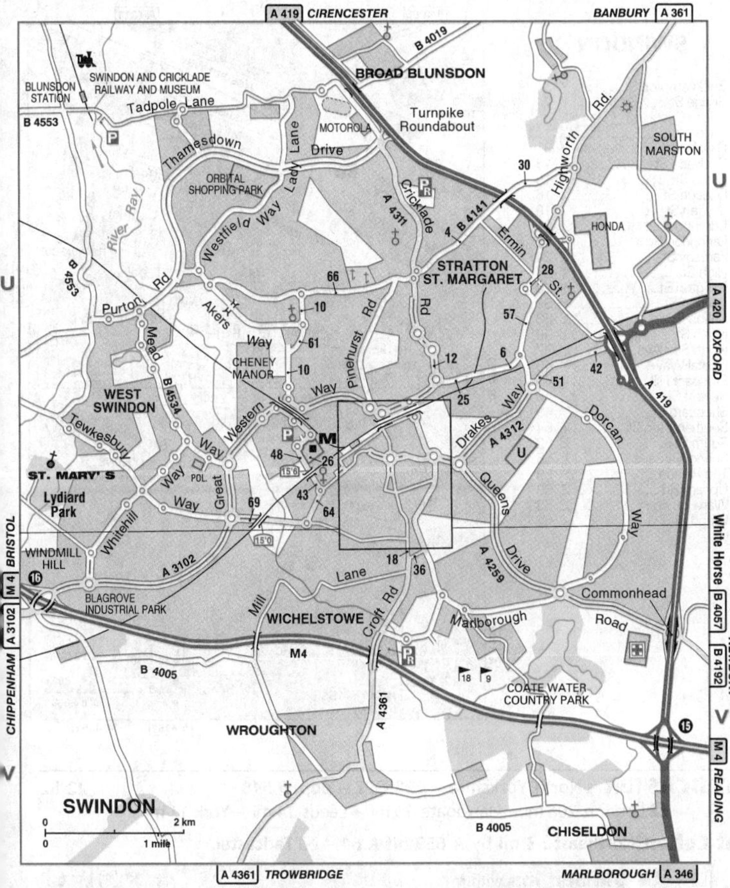

Beechcroft Rd	U 4	Great Western Retail Outlet	U 26	Rodbourne Rd	U 48
Bridge End Rd	U 6	Hobley Drive	U 28	Slade Drive	U 51
Cheney Manor Rd.	U 10	Kingsdown Rd	U 30	Swindon Rd	U 57
Cirencester Way	U 12	Newport St	V 36	Vicarage Rd	U 61
Devises Rd	V 18	Oxford Rd	U 42	Westcott Pl.	U 64
Gipsy Lane	U 25	Park Lane	U 43	Whitworth Rd	U 66
				Wootton Basset Rd	U 69

at Bishopstone East : 5.5 mi by A 4312 off A 420

The Royal Oak

Cues Ln ✉ *SN6 8PP – ✆ (01793) 790 481*
– www.royaloakbishopstone.co.uk

Rest – Carte £ 22/32

◆ Relaxing country pub with open fires and rustic décor. Menu changes according to what's fresh, local and seasonal, with much of the produce coming from the owner's organic farm.

Don't confuse the couvert rating with the stars ✿! Couverts defines comfort and service, while stars are awarded for the best cuisine across all categories of comfort.

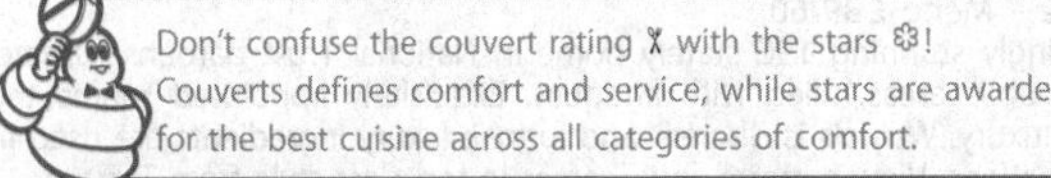

SWINDON

Beckhampton St . . . . Y 3
Bridge St . . . . Y 7
Brunel Shopping Centre . . . . YZ
Canal Walk . . . . Y 9
Cricklade St . . . . Z 13
Cross St . . . . Z 15
Deacon St . . . . Z 16
Dryden St . . . . Z 19
Edmund St . . . . Z 21
Faringdon Rd . . . . Y 22
Farnsby St . . . . YZ 24
High St . . . . Z 27
Islington St . . . . Y 29
London St . . . . Y 31
Milton Rd . . . . YZ 33
North St . . . . Z 39
North Star Ave . . . . Y 37
Ocotal Way . . . . Y 40
Prospect Hill . . . . Z 45
Regent St . . . . YZ 46
Sheppard St . . . . Y 49
Southampton St . . . . Y 54
South St . . . . Z 52
Spring Gardens . . . . Y 55
The Parade . . . . Y 58
Upham Rd . . . . Z 60
Warwick Rd . . . . Z 63
Wood St . . . . Z 67

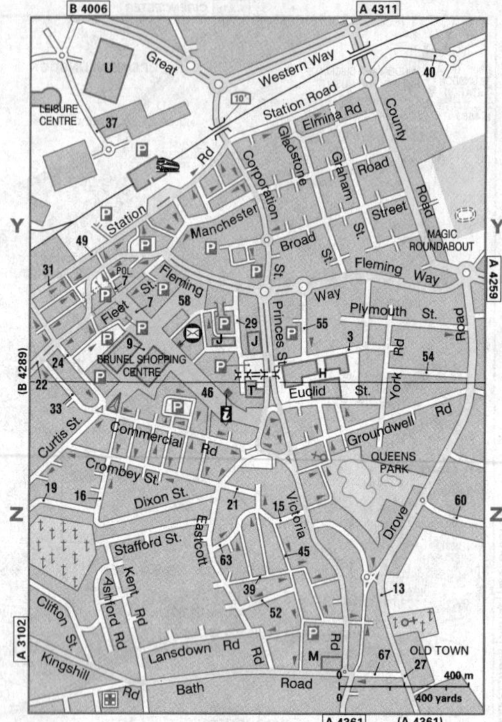

TADCASTER – North Yorkshire – **502** Q22 – **pop. 6 548** **22** B2

London 206 mi – Harrogate 16 mi – Leeds 14 mi – York 11 mi

at Colton Northeast : 3 mi by A 659 off A 64 – ✉ Tadcaster

Ye Old Sun Inn with rm

Main St ✉ LS24 8EP – ✆ (01904) 744 261 – www.yeoldsuninn.co.uk – Closed Monday lunch

3 rm – £ 75 £ 90/120 **Rest** – Menu £ 18 (lunch) – Carte £ 25/35

◆ Rustic, family-run pub with warming open fires and a small deli. Owners are great ambassadors of local suppliers and seasonal produce, and give regular cookery demonstrations. Smart bedrooms are located in the house next door.

TANGMERE – W. Sussex – **504** R31 – see Chichester

TANWORTH-IN-ARDEN – Warks. – **503** O26 – see Henley-in-Arden

TAPLOW – Buckinghamshire – **504** R29 **11** C3

London 33 mi – Maidenhead 2 mi – Oxford 36 mi – Reading 12 mi

Cliveden

North : 2 mi by Berry Hill ✉ SL6 0JF – ✆ (01628) 668 561 – www.clivedenhouse.co.uk

31 rm – £ 210/590 £ 210/590 – 8 suites

Rest *Waldo's* – *(dinner only) (booking essential)* Menu £ 68

Rest *Terrace* – Menu £ 39/60

◆ Breathtakingly stunning 19C stately home in National Trust gardens. Ornate, sumptuous public areas, filled with antiques. Exquisitely appointed rooms the last word in luxury. Waldo's is discreet and formal; luxury ingredients are used in ambitious creations. View parterre and Thames in top class style from Terrace.

TARPORLEY - Cheshire - 502 L/M24 - pop. 2 634 — 20 A3

London 186 mi – Chester 11 mi – Liverpool 27 mi – Shrewsbury 36 mi

Portal G & C.C. Cobblers Cross Lane, (01829) 733 933

Portal Premier Forest Rd, (01829) 733 884

at Little Budworth Northeast : 3.5 mi on A 49 – Tarporley

Cabbage Hall

Forest Rd. CW6 9ES – (01829) 760 292 – www.cabbagehallrestaurant.com – Closed 3-13 January, 24-25 December and Sunday dinner

Rest – Carte £ 31/39

◆ Unassuming former pub in 11 acres; run by experienced chef. Bold, modern inner with comfy lounge, laminated tables and low-backed dining chairs. Several classical menus from which to choose.

TARR STEPS - Somerset - 503 J30 — 3 A2

London 191 mi – Taunton 31 mi – Tiverton 20 mi

Tarr Steps★★ (Clapper Bridge★★)

Tarr Farm Inn with rm

TA22 9PY – (01643) 851 507 – www.tarrfarm.co.uk – Closed 1-12 February

9 rm – †£ 75 ††£ 150 **Rest** – Menu £ 15/20 – Carte £ 22/28

◆ Beside a river, in idyllic countryside, this is a true destination pub. Food ranges from cream teas and sandwiches to three courses at lunch, with more ambitious dishes at dinner. Bedrooms are elegant, luxurious and extremely well-equipped.

TATTENHALL - Cheshire - 502 L24 - pop. 1 860 — 20 A3

London 200 mi – Birmingham 71 mi – Chester 10 mi – Liverpool 29 mi

Higher Huxley Hall without rest

North : 2.25 mi on Huxley rd CH3 9BZ – (01829) 781 484 – www.huxleyhall.co.uk – Closed 25 December

4 rm – †£ 50/75 ††£ 90/95

◆ Attractive part-13C farmhouse boasting field and castle views. Classical, open-fired lounge and linen-laid breakfast room. Original Elizabethan staircase. Homely bedrooms have good facilities.

at Higher Burwardsley Southeast : 1 mi – Tattenhall

The Pheasant Inn with rm

CH3 9PF – (01829) 770 434 – www.thepheasantinn.co.uk – Closed 25 December

12 rm – †£ 70/90 ††£ 90/145 **Rest** – Carte £ 21/33

◆ Characterful stone pub boasting reclaimed beams, stone columns and great views over the Cheshire Plains. Extensive daily menus offer refined pub dishes and Mediterranean influences. Bedrooms are compact, stylish and comfortable; most have views.

TAUNTON - Somerset - 503 K30 - pop. 58 241 — 3 B3

London 168 mi – Bournemouth 69 mi – Bristol 50 mi – Exeter 37 mi

The Library, Paul St (01823) 336344, tauntontic@tauntondeane.gov.uk

Taunton Vale Creech Heathfield, (01823) 412 220

Vivary Vivary Park, (01823) 289 274

Taunton and Pickeridge Corfe, (01823) 421 537

Town★ - St Mary Magdalene★ V – Somerset County Museum★ **AC** V **M** – St James'★ U – Hammett St★ V **25** – The Crescent★ V – Bath Place★ V **3**

Trull (Church★), S : 2.5 mi by A 38 – Hestercombe Gardens★, N : 5 mi by A 3259 BY and minor roads to Cheddon Fitzpaine. Bishops Lydeard★ (Church★), NW : 6 mi – Wellington : Church★, Wellington Monument (≤★★), SW : 7.5 mi by A 38 – Combe Florey★, NW : 8 mi – Gaulden Manor★ **AC**, NW : 10 mi by A 358 and B 3227

Plan on next page

ENGLAND

ENGLAND

TAUNTON

Street	Grid	No.
Bath Pl.	V	3
Billetfield	V	6
Billet St.	V	4
Birch Grove	U	7
Bishop's Hull Rd	AZ	9
Bridge St	U	12
Bridge (The)	U	10
Burton Pl.	V	13
Cann St	V	15
Chritchard Parkway	BYZ	45
Cleveland St	U	16
Comeytrowe Lane	AZ	18
Corporation St	V	19
County Walk Shopping Centre	V	
Duke St	V	21
East St	V	
Fore St	V	22
Hamilton Rd	BZ	24
Hammet St	V	25
High St	V	
Hurdle Way	V	27
Ilminster Rd	BZ	28
Magdalene St	V	30
Middleway	AZ	31
North St	V	33
Obridge Viaduct	BY	34
Old Market Shopping Centre	V	
Portland St	U	36
Priory Ave	U	37
Shoreditch Rd	BZ	39
Shuttern	V	40
Silver St South	V, Z	42
Upper High St	V	43
Upper Wood St	U	44
Wellington New Rd	AZ	46
Wilton St	V	48
Winchester St	U	49
Wood St	U	51

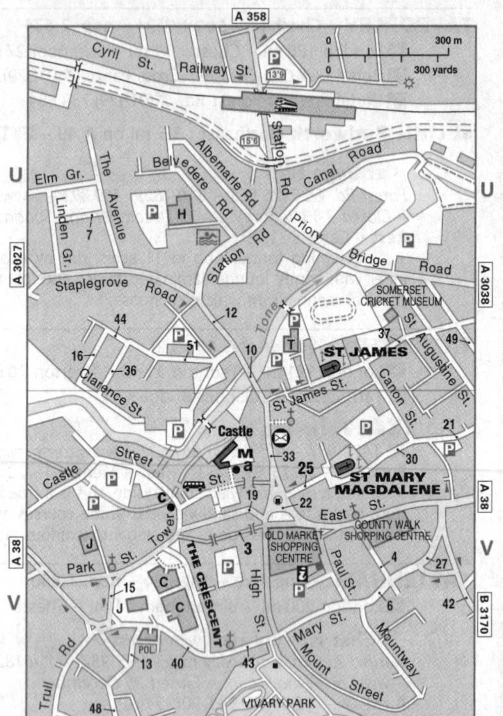

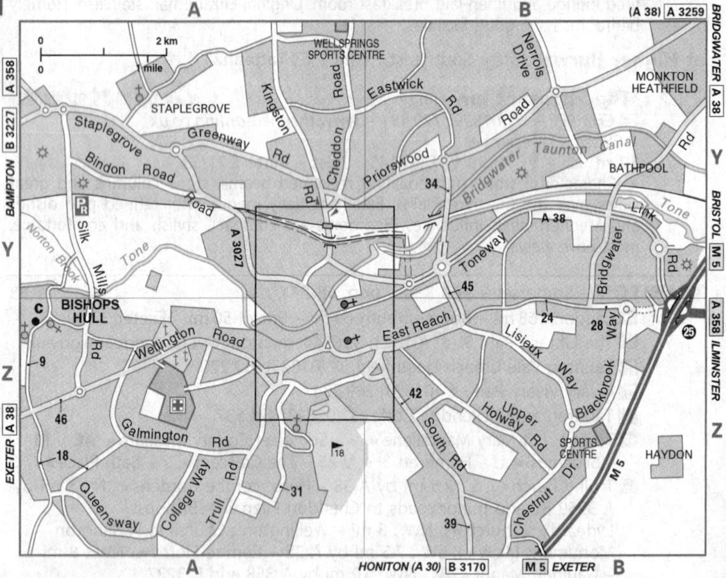

(A 38) A 3259
BRIDGWATER A 38
MINEHEAD A 358
BAMPTON B 3227
BRISTOL M 5
A 358 ILMINSTER
EXETER A 38
HONITON (A 30) B 3170
M 5 EXETER
2 km
1 mile
WELLSPRINGS SPORTS CENTRE
STAPLEGROVE
MONKTON HEATHFIELD
BATHPOOL
Staplegrove Road
Greenway
Kingston Rd
Cheddon Road
Eastwick Rd
Nerrols Drive
Road
Priorswood Rd
Bindon Road
Bridgwater Taunton Canal
Tone
Norton Brook
Silk Mills Road
A 3027
A 38
Toneway
Link Rd
Bridgwater Way
BISHOPS HULL
Wellington Road
East Reach
Lisieux Way
Galmington Rd
Blackbrook
Upper Holway Rd
South Rd
SPORTS CENTRE
HAYDON
Queensway
College Way
Trull Rd
Chestnut Dr.
M 5

Castle

Castle Green ✉ *TA1 1NF* – ✆ *(01823) 272 671* – *www.the-castle-hotel.com* Va

44 rm – †£ 140/170 ††£ 230/335, ☕ £ 15.50

Rest – *(closed Sunday and Monday)* Menu £ 23 – Carte £ 33/48

♦ Wisteria-clad, 12C Norman castle with pleasant gardens; run since 1950 by 3 generations of the same family. Individually decorated bedrooms; great views from the penthouse suite. Smart bar with modern edge. Traditional, formal dining room with menu to match.

Meryan House

Bishop's Hull Rd, West : 0.75 mi by A 38 ✉ *TA1 5EG* – ✆ *(01823) 337 445* – *www.meryanhouse.co.uk* AZc

12 rm ☕ – †£ 70/75 ††£ 90

Rest – *(dinner only) (booking essential for non-residents)* Menu £ 24 – Carte £ 16/30

♦ Spacious house; well-run run by charming owner. Open sitting room features fantastic juke box. Highly individual bedrooms boast quality wallpapers and beautiful feature beds – many are antiques. Cosy bar. Traditional, open-fired dining room with classical menu.

Willow Tree

3 Tower Ln ✉ *TA1 4AR* – ✆ *(01823) 352 835* – *www.willowtreerestaurant.co.uk* – *Closed January, August, Sunday, Monday and Thursday* Vc

Rest – *(dinner only)* Menu £ 28/34

♦ Converted 17C townhouse with intimate dining rooms, exposed beams and large inglenook. Bi-monthly menu blends a classical base with artful, innovative ideas. Friendly, efficient service.

at Henlade East : 3.5 mi on A 358 - BZ – ✉ Taunton

Mount Somerset

Lower Henlade, South : 0.5 mi by Stoke Rd ✉ *TA3 5NB* – ✆ *(01823) 442 500* – *www.mountsomersethotel.co.uk*

19 rm ☕ – †£ 145/245 ††£ 205/350

Rest – *(booking advisable)* Menu £ 20/50 – Carte £ 25/55 **s**

♦ Fine Regency country house with formal gardens, set in four acres. Elegant bedrooms, excellent bathrooms and spacious, modern sitting rooms. Capacious dining room with immaculately set tables. Menus offer a mix of traditional and modern dishes.

at Hatch Beauchamp Southeast : 6 mi by A 358 - BZ – ✉ Taunton

Farthings

Village Rd ✉ *TA3 6SG* – ✆ *(01823) 480 664* – *www.farthingshotel.co.uk*

12 rm ☕ – †£ 80/120 ††£ 90/195

Rest – Menu £ 29/34 **s** – Carte £ 30/40 **s**

♦ Fine Georgian house in mature, well-tended gardens. Small bar and open lounge; many original features remain. Immaculately kept, antique-filled bedrooms – master rooms are particularly comfortable. Two-roomed restaurant offers constantly evolving, seasonal menu.

at West Bagborough Northwest : 10.5 mi by A 358 - AY – ✉ Taunton

Rising Sun Inn with rm

✉ *TA4 3EF* – ✆ *(01823) 432 575* – *www.risingsuninn.info* – *Closed Sunday dinner and Monday September-March*

2 rm – †£ 55 ††£ 75/85 **Rest** – Carte £ 20/30

♦ Warm, intimate inn with a lovely 'village pub' atmosphere. Locally sourced ingredients contribute to a well-balanced mix of modern and traditional dishes – with plenty of care taken in the kitchen. Two very comfortable bedrooms; one boasts a four-poster.

ENGLAND

at Triscombe Northwest : 11 mi by A 358 - AY – ✉ Taunton

Blue Ball Inn with rm

✉ TA4 3HE – ✆ (01984) 618 242 – www.theblueballinn.com – Closed 1 week spring, 1 week autumn, 25 December, Monday and dinner Sunday except August

3 rm – £ 45 £ 90 **Rest** – Carte £ 24/33

◆ Thatched, picture postcard pub in delightful rural location; relaxing, rustic inner – the former stables – features open fires, exposed beams and hunting theme. Pleasant terraced gardens. Weekly changing menu of tasty, hearty dishes makes good use of local produce. Original pub now houses three plush, stylish bedrooms.

TAVISTOCK – Devon – **503** H32 – **pop. 11 018** **2** C2

London 239 mi – Exeter 38 mi – Plymouth 16 mi

Town Hall, Bedford Sq ✆ (01822) 612938, tavistocktic@westdevon.gov.uk

Down Rd, ✆ (01822) 612 344

Hurdwick Tavistock Hamlets, ✆ (01822) 612 746

Morwellham★ **AC**, SW : 4.5 m. E : Dartmoor National Park★★ – Buckland Abbey★★ **AC**, S : 7 mi by A 386 – Lydford★★, N : 8.5 mi by A 386

Browns

80 West St ✉ PL19 8AQ – ✆ (01822) 618 686 – www.brownsdevon.co.uk

20 rm – £ 69/109 £ 119/209, £ 7

Rest – Menu £ 24/40 **s** – Carte £ 36/55 **s**

◆ Smart hotel in former coaching inn – the oldest licensed premises in town. Bedrooms take on a modern style while still retaining original features; those in the old coach house are best. Open-plan bar and lounge. Simple, all-day brasserie offering modern menu.

at Gulworthy West : 3 mi on A 390 – ✉ Tavistock

The Horn of Plenty with rm rest,

Gulworthy, West : 4 mi by A 390 off Chipshop rd ✉ PL19 8JD – ✆ (01822) 832 528 – www.thehornofplenty.co.uk

10 rm – £ 190 £ 200 **Rest** – Menu £ 27/47

◆ Stylish, contemporary restaurant featuring local artwork, in enchanting, creeper-clad country house. Classic cooking uses local ingredients. Polite service. Modern country house style bedrooms; those in annex have terrace.

at Milton Abbot Northwest : 6 mi on B 3362 – ✉ Tavistock

Hotel Endsleigh

Southwest : 1 mi ✉ PL19 0PQ – ✆ (01822) 870 000 – www.hotelendsleigh.com – Closed last 2 weeks January

14 rm – £ 187/221 £ 220/260 – 2 suites **Rest** – Menu £ 30/40

◆ Painstakingly restored Regency lodge in magnificent Devonian gardens and grounds. Stylish lounge and refined bedrooms are imbued with an engaging, understated elegance. Interesting, classically based dishes served in two minimalist dining rooms.

at Chillaton Northwest : 6.25 mi by Chillaton rd – ✉ Tavistock

Tor Cottage without rest

Southwest : 0.75 mi by Tavistock rd, turning right at bridle path sign, down unmarked track for 0.5 mi ✉ PL16 0JE – ✆ (01822) 860 248 – www.torcottage.co.uk – Closed mid-December-1 February

5 rm – £ 98 £ 140

◆ Remotely set cottage set in 28 hillside acres, with peaceful gardens and lovely outdoor pool. Bedrooms, most in converted outhouses, boast small kitchenettes and wood burning stoves. Breakfast is taken on the terrace or in the conservatory. Charming owner.

TEFFONT – Wilts. – see Salisbury

ENGLAND

TEIGNMOUTH – Devon – 503 J32 – pop. 14 799 2 D2

London 216 mi – Exeter 16 mi – Torquay 8 mi

The Den, Sea Front ✆ (01626) 215666, teigntic@teignbridge.gov.uk

Thomas Luny House without rest

Teign St, follow signs for the Quays, off the A 381 ✉ TQ14 8EG – ✆ (01626) 772 976 – www.thomas-luny-house.co.uk – Closed January-mid-February

4 rm – †£ 68/75 ††£ 88/102

♦ Georgian merchant's house with attractive walled garden. Classical lounge and antique-filled breakfast room; tea and cake on arrival. One bedroom with hand-painted oriental furniture, another with a four-poster. Quality breakfasts and home-grown figs in season.

TEMPLE SOWERBY – Cumbria – 502 M20 – see Penrith

TENTERDEN – Kent – 504 W30 – pop. 6 977 9 C2

London 57 mi – Folkestone 26 mi – Hastings 21 mi – Maidstone 19 mi

Town Hall, High St ✆ (01580) 763572, tentic@ashford.gov.uk

Richard Phillips at Chapel Down

Tenterden Vineyard, Small Hythe, South: 2.5 mi on B 2082 ✉ TN30 7NG – ✆ (01580) 761 616 – www.richardphillipsatchapeldown.co.uk – Closed 27 December and Monday

Rest – *(lunch only and dinner Thursday-Saturday)* Menu £ 15 (lunch) Carte £ 27/36

♦ Spacious modern restaurant and casual bar on 1st floor of a barn conversion; terrace has countryside views. Good value lunch menu and more elaborate à la carte showcase seasonal produce.

TETBURY – Gloucestershire – 503 N29 – pop. 5 250 Great Britain 4 C1

London 113 mi – Bristol 27 mi – Gloucester 19 mi – Swindon 24 mi

33 Church St ✆ (01666) 503552, tourism@tetbury.org

Westonbirt, ✆ (01666) 880 242

Westonbirt Arboretum★ **AC**, SW : 2.5 mi by A 433

Calcot Manor

Calcot, West : 3.5 mi on A 4135 ✉ GL8 8YJ – ✆ (01666) 890 391 – www.calcotmanor.co.uk

34 rm – †£ 234 ††£ 260 – 1 suite

Rest *The Gumstool Inn* – see restaurant listing

Rest *Conservatory* – *(booking essential)* Menu £ 24 (lunch) **s** – Carte £ 34/50 **s**

♦ Impressive Cotswold farmhouse, gardens and meadows with converted ancient barns and stables. Superb spa. Variety of luxuriously appointed rooms with contemporary flourishes. Stylish Conservatory serves interesting modern dishes.

The Chef's Table

49 Long St ✉ GL8 8AA – ✆ (01666) 504 466 – www.thechefstable.co.uk – Closed 25-26 December, Sunday and dinner Monday and Tuesday

Rest – Carte £ 28/35

♦ Glass-fronted deli shop with busy, informal restaurant to the rear; mix of tables and high stools. Daily blackboard menu displays rustic, generous dishes of local, organic produce.

The Gumstool Inn – at Calcot Manor Hotel

West : 3.5 mi on A 4135 ✉ GL8 8YJ – ✆ (01666) 890 391 – www.calcotmanor.co.uk

Rest – *(booking essential)* Carte £ 25/33

♦ Converted farm out-building on the Calcot Estate, which dates back to the 14C. Cooking is seasonal, rustic and hearty, with a wide-ranging menu and extensive daily specials.

The Trouble House

Cirencester Rd, Northeast : 2 mi on A 433 ✉ GL8 8SG – ✆ (01666) 502 206 – www.troublehousetetbury.co.uk – Closed Sunday dinner and Monday

Rest – Carte £ 22/32

♦ Unassuming roadside pub with a homely style, where you'll discover a warm welcome and tasty food. Dishes range from sardines on toast to rib of beef for two. Specials usually feature fish.

TEWKESBURY – Gloucestershire – 503 N28 – pop. 9 978 Great Britain 4 C1

London 108 mi – Birmingham 39 mi – Gloucester 11 mi
100 Church St ✆ (01684) 855040, outofthehat@tewkesbury.gov.uk
Tewkesbury Park Hotel Lincoln Green Lane, ✆ (01684) 295 405
Town★ – Abbey★★ (Nave★★, vault★)
St Mary's, Deerhurst★, SW : 4 mi by A 38 and B 4213

at Corse Lawn Southwest : 6 mi by A 38 and A 438 on B 4211 – ✉ Gloucester

Corse Lawn House
✉ GL19 4LZ – ✆ (01452) 780 771 – www.corselawn.com
15 rm – 🚹£ 90 🚹🚹£ 160 – 3 suites
Rest *The Restaurant* – Menu £ 26/33 – Carte £ 26/33
Rest *Bistro* – Carte £ 22/37 **s**
♦ Elegant Queen Anne Grade II listed house, set back from village green and fronted by former 'coach wash'. Two comfortable lounges and classic country house style rooms. Formal restaurant, nicely set overlooking rear garden. Classic style of dishes; quality wine list. Informal Bistro.

at Eldersfield Southwest : 8.5 mi by A 38 and A 438 off B 4211

The Butchers Arms
Lime St, Southeast : 1 mi ✉ GL19 4NX – ✆ (01452) 840 381 – www.thebutchersarms.net – Closed 1 week early January, 1 week late August, Monday, dinner Sunday and lunch Tuesday
Rest – *(booking essential)* Carte £ 30/37
♦ Traditional pub run by a husband and wife team. Concise regularly-changing menu features local or homemade produce and refined cooking, but hurry, only 25 diners can be accommodated.

ENGLAND

THAXTED – Essex – 504 V28 – pop. 2 066 13 C2

London 44 mi – Cambridge 24 mi – Colchester 31 mi – Chelmsford 20 mi

Crossways without rest
32 Town St ✉ CM6 2LA – ✆ (01371) 830 348 – www.crosswaysthaxted.co.uk
3 rm – 🚹£ 45/50 🚹🚹£ 65/70
♦ Passionately run 16C house in picturesque market town, with pleasant breakfast room and small open-fired lounge. Spotless bedrooms furnished in period style. Good, old-fashioned hospitality.

THIRSK – North Yorkshire – 502 P21 – pop. 9 099 22 B1

London 227 mi – Leeds 37 mi – Middlesbrough 24 mi – York 24 mi
49 Market Pl ✆ (01845) 522755, thirsktic@hambleton.gov.uk
Thirsk & Northallerton Thornton-Le-Street, ✆ (01845) 525 115

at Asenby Southwest : 5.25 mi by A 168 – ✉ Thirsk

Crab Manor
Dishforth Rd ✉ YO7 3QL – ✆ (01845) 577 286 – www.crabandlobster.co.uk
14 rm – 🚹£ 90/120 🚹🚹£ 230
Rest *Crab and Lobster* – see restaurant listing
♦ Split between an 18C Georgian Manor and individual Scandinavian log cabins, the stylish bedrooms are themed around famous hotels of the world. All have sharing or private hot tubs.

Crab and Lobster – at Crab Manor Hotel
Dishforth Rd ✉ YO7 3QL – ✆ (01845) 577 286 – www.crabandlobster.com
Rest – Seafood – Menu £ 15/35 – Carte £ 30/53
♦ Charming thatched pub with characterful, quirky interior. Extensive menu features plenty of seafood – from fish soup to whole lobster – as well as traditional British dishes.

THORNBURY – South Gloucestershire – 503 M29 – pop. 11 969 4 C1
– ✉ Bristol

London 128 mi – Bristol 12 mi – Gloucester 23 mi – Swindon 43 mi

Thornbury Castle
Castle St ✉ *BS35 1HH* – ✆ *(01454) 281 182* – *www.thornburycastle.co.uk*
24 rm – †£ 115/160 ††£ 135/295 – 3 suites **Rest** – Menu £ 26/45
♦ 16C castle built by Henry VIII with gardens and vineyard. Two lounges boast plenty of antiques. Rooms of stately comfort; several bathrooms resplendent in marble. Restaurant exudes formal aura.

THORNHAM MAGNA – **Suffolk** – **504** X27 – ✉ **Eye** **15** C2
London 96 mi – Cambridge 47 mi – Ipswich 20 mi – Norwich 30 mi

at Yaxley **Northeast : 2.25 mi by Eye rd on A 140 – ✉ Eye**

Bull Auberge
Ipswich Rd, on A140 ✉ *IP23 8BZ* – ✆ *(01379) 783 604* – *www.the-auberge.co.uk*
11 rm – †£ 60/80 ††£ 100/120
Rest – *(closed Saturday lunch, Sunday and Monday)* Menu £ 25 (dinner) – Carte £ 19/33
♦ 15C inn by busy road; rustic origins enhanced by brick walls, beams and open fire. Original, well presented, modern menus prepared with care. Stylish, well appointed rooms.

THORNTON – **Lancs.** – **502** K22 – **see Blackpool**

THORPE LANGTON – **Leics.** – **see Market Harborough**

THUNDER BRIDGE – **W. Yorks.** – **see Huddersfield**

THUNDERSLEY – **Essex** – **504** V29 – **see Rayleigh**

THURSFORD GREEN – **Norfolk** **15** C1
London 120 mi – Fakenham 7 mi – Norwich 29 mi

Holly Lodge
The Street ✉ *NR21 0AS* – ✆ *(01328) 878 465* – *www.hollylodgeguesthouse.co.uk*
3 rm – †£ 90 ††£ 120 **Rest** – Menu £ 20
♦ Remotely set 18C house with delightful gardens and nice pond. Individually themed bedrooms are located in the old stable block and boast exposed beams, feature beds and numerous extra touches. Communal breakfasts, in smart conservatory, use local and homemade produce. Home-cooked dinners from daily changing set menu.

TICKTON – **East Riding of Yorkshire** – **502** S22 – **see Beverley**

TILSTON – **Cheshire** – **502** L24 – **see Malpas**

TINTINHULL – **Somerset** – **503** L31 – **pop. 956**
London 131 mi – Bristol 39 mi – Cardiff 97 mi – Southampton 92 mi

The Crown and Victoria Inn with rm
14 Farm St ✉ *BA22 8PZ* – ✆ *(01935) 823 341* – *www.thecrownandvictoria.co.uk* – *Closed Sunday dinner*
5 rm – †£ 75 ††£ 95 **Rest** – Carte £ 20/30
♦ Enthusiastically run, solid stone pub boasting mature grounds – set next to award winning National Trust gardens. Flavoursome cooking has an honest, homemade, classical base and produce is local, organic and ethically sourced. Bedrooms are cosy and welcoming.

TITCHWELL – **Norfolk** – **504** V25 – **pop. 99** **15** C1
London 128 mi – King's Lynn 25 mi – Boston 56 mi – Wisbech 36 mi

Titchwell Manor rm,
✉ *PE31 8BB* – ✆ *(01485) 210 221* – *www.titchwellmanor.com*
27 rm – †£ 65/95 ††£ 110/250 **Rest** – Menu £ 40 (dinner) – Carte £ 23/35
♦ Attractive red-brick former farmhouse. Stylish inner with bare floorboards, leather sofas and seaside photos. Classical bedrooms in main house; stylish rooms in grounds. Informal bar and terrace. Smart, conservatory restaurant with modern 7 course tasting menu.

ENGLAND

TITLEY – Herefordshire – 503 L27 – see Kington

TOLLARD ROYAL – Wiltshire 4 C3

London 118 mi – Bristol 63 mi – Southampton 40 mi – Portsmouth 59 mi

King John Inn with rm

SP5 5PS – (01725) 516 207 – www.kingjohninn.co.uk

8 rm – £ 100 £ 150 **Rest** – Carte £ 20/40

◆ Red-brick Victorian pub in pretty village; smart, spacious and open-plan. Daily changing, classically based menus, with game a speciality. Comfortable, contemporary bedrooms mix modern facilities with antique furniture; some are in the coach house opposite.

TOOT BALDON – Oxon. – see Oxford

TOPSHAM – Devon – 503 J31 – pop. 3 545 – Exeter 2 D2

London 175 mi – Torbay 26 mi – Exeter 4 mi – Torquay 24 mi

La Petite Maison

35 Fore St EX3 OHR – (01392) 873 660 – www.lapetitemaison.co.uk – Closed 2 weeks autumn, Christmas, Sunday and Monday

Rest – *(booking essential at lunch)* Menu £ 36

◆ Cosy two-roomed restaurant in charming village by River Clyst. Flavourful, classic dishes are presented in a modern style and come in generous portions. Friendly, welcoming owners.

ENGLAND

TORQUAY – Torbay – 503 J32 – pop. 62 968 2 C-D2

London 223 mi – Exeter 23 mi – Plymouth 32 mi

5 Vaughan Parade (01803) 211211, torquay.tic@torbay.gov.uk

St Marychurch Petitor Rd, (01803) 327 471

Torbay★ – Kent's Cavern★ **AC** CX **A**

Paignton Zoo★★ **AC**, SE : 3 mi by A 3022 - Cockington★, W : 1 mi AX

Plans on following pages

The Osborne

Hesketh Cres, Meadfoot TQ1 2LL – (01803) 213 311 – www.osborne-torquay.co.uk CX**n**

32 rm – £ 50/105 £ 100/230

Rest *Langtry's* – *(dinner only and Sunday lunch October-May)* Menu £ 28 **s**

Rest *Brasserie* – Carte £ 19/30 **s**

◆ Smart hotel in stunning Regency crescent, with lovely gardens and Torbay views. Modern lounge. Stylish bedrooms with light wood furniture, dark leather chairs and good mod cons; some have balconies. Traditional Langtry's offers British classics. Informal dining in split-level Brasserie.

Marstan without rest

Meadfoot Sea Rd TQ1 2LQ – (01803) 292 837 – www.marstanhotel.co.uk – Closed 2 January-12 February CX**a**

9 rm – £ 55/65 £ 79/142

◆ Substantial 19C house in quiet area; given a 21C edge with hot tub, sun deck and pool. Opulent interior with gold coloured furniture and antiques. Room décor of high standard.

The Somerville without rest

515 Babbacombe Rd. TQ1 1HJ – (01803) 294 755 – www.somervillehotel.co.uk – Closed 25-26 December CX**u**

9 rm – £ 80/120 £ 100/180

◆ Comfortable hotel, an easy walk down the hill into town. Modern, opulently decorated bedrooms boast all mod cons. One has a small private courtyard; Room 4 is the largest.

Colindale
20 Rathmore Rd, Chelston ✉ TQ2 6NY – ☎ (01803) 293 947 – www.colindalehotel.co.uk BZ**a**
6 rm – £ 45/50 £ 65/80 **Rest** – Menu £ 20
◆ Yellow hued 19C terraced house with pretty front garden. Particularly attractive sitting room with deep sofas and books. Welsh dresser in breakfast room. Immaculate bedrooms. Homecooked dishes have a French accent.

Kingston House without rest
75 Avenue Rd ✉ TQ2 5LL – ☎ (01803) 212 760 – www.kingstonhousehotel.co.uk
5 rm – £ 72/86 £ 80/95 BY**n**
◆ Sunny yellow Victorian house enhanced by vivid summer floral displays; run by friendly husband and wife. Convivial sitting room; bedrooms of individual character.

Room in the Elephant (Simon Hulstone)
3-4 Beacon Terr, (1st Floor) ✉ TQ1 2BH – ☎ (01803) 200 044 – www.elephantrestaurant.co.uk – Closed October-Easter, Sunday and Monday
Rest – *(dinner only)* Menu £ 45 CZ**e**
Spec. Scallops with a lemon and cabbage risotto, mussel foam. Breast of Crediton duckling with beetroot and spiced honey. Chocolate, peanut, banana and salted butter.
◆ First floor restaurant in elegant Georgian terrace overlooking Torbay and the marina. Modern cocktail bar and simply decorated dining room. Concise à la carte and tasting menu offer appealing, flavoursome, classical combinations with no unnecessary elaboration.

Brasserie
3-4 Beacon Terr, (Ground Floor) ✉ TQ1 2BH – ☎ (01803) 200 044 – www.elephantrestaurant.co.uk – Closed 2 weeks January, Sunday and Monday
Rest – Menu £ 20/30 CZ**e**
◆ Light, airy brasserie run by pleasant team. Appealing, set price menus revolve around the seasons; cooking is fresh and simple. Good value wine selection – or visit the upstairs cocktail bar.

Number 7
Beacon Terr. ✉ TQ1 2BH – ☎ (01803) 295 055 – www.no7-fish.com – Closed 2 weeks February, 1 week November, Christmas-New Year, Monday in winter and Sunday except dinner July-September CZ**e**
Rest – Seafood – *(dinner only and lunch Wednesday-Saturday) (booking advisable)* Carte £ 30/36
◆ On harbour front in centre of town: modest, friendly, family run restaurant specialising in simply prepared fresh fish, mostly from Brixham. Fishing themes enhance ambience.

The Orange Tree
14-16 Parkhill Rd ✉ TQ1 2AL – ☎ (01803) 213 936 – www.orangetreerestaurant.co.uk – Closed 2 weeks November, 1 week January, 26-31 December, Sunday and bank holiday Mondays CZ**u**
Rest – *(dinner only) (booking essential)* Carte £ 26/40
◆ Intimate neighbourhood eatery hidden away from the town, with homely décor and a modern, comfortable feel. Classical cooking displays a French base and uses local, seasonal produce.

at Babbacombe Northeast : 2 mi on A 379

The Cary Arms with rm
Babbacombe Beach, East : 0.25 mi by Beach Rd. ✉ TQ1 3LX – ☎ (01803) 327 110 – www.caryarms.co.uk CX**i**
8 rm – £ 100/145 £ 200/250 **Rest** – Carte £ 22/34 **s**
◆ Idyllic location built into the rocks, with terraces down to the shore. Stone/-slate-floored bar serving traditional pub dishes. Nautically styled residents lounge and modern, boutique-chic bedrooms in New England style, with roll-top baths looking out to sea.

ENGLAND

TORBAY
TORQUAY-PAIGNTON

Street	Grid	No.
Abbey Pl.	CZ	2
Castle Circus	CY	4
Chestnut Ave	BY	6
East St	BY	13
Fleet St	CYZ	
Goshen Rd	BY	14
Grange Rd	AZ	15
Hatfield Rd	CY	16
Lucius St	BY	20
Manor Rd	BX	22
Market St	CY	
Pimlico	CY	23
Reddenhill Rd	CX	24
Shedden Hill Rd	CYZ	26
South St	BY	28
Stentiford Hill Rd	CY	32
Strand	CZ	33
Temperance St	CY	34
Tor Church Rd	BCY	36
Tor Hill Rd	CY	37
Trematon Ave	CY	38
Union Square Shopping Centre	CY	
Union St	CY	
Vaughan Parade	CZ	39
Victoria Parade	CZ	41

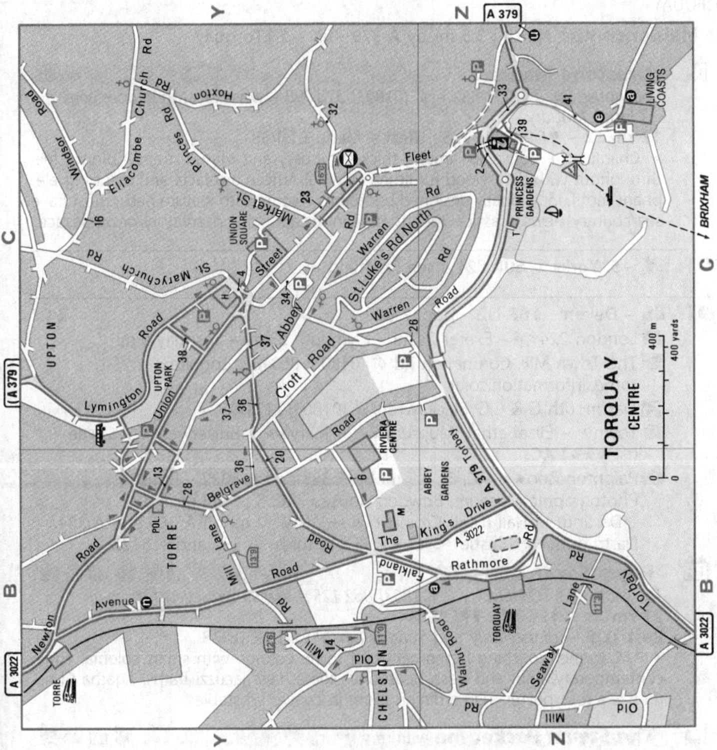

TORQUAY
CENTRE

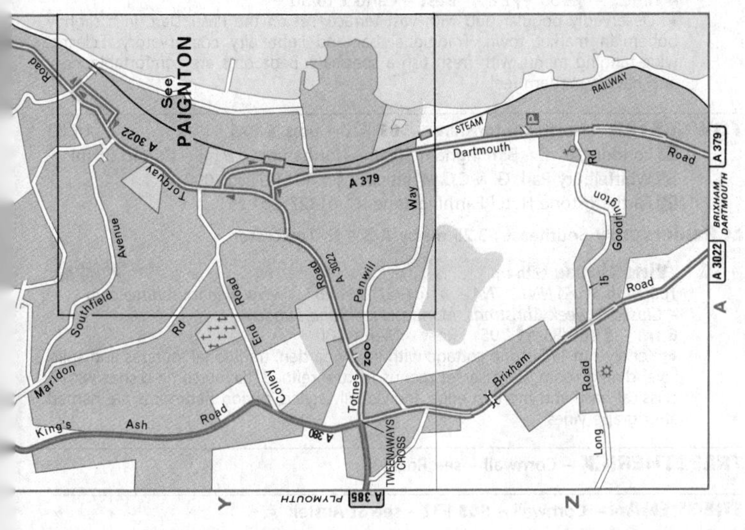

ENGLAND

at Maidencombe North : 3.5 mi by A 379 - BX – ✉ Torquay

Orestone Manor
Rockhouse Ln. ✉ TQ1 4SX – ✆ (01803) 328 098 – www.orestonemanor.com – Closed January
12 rm – ♦£ 99 ♦♦£ 225 **Rest** – Menu £ 20/38
◆ Characterful house set among thick shrubbery and mature trees. Colonial feel throughout with dark wood furniture, Oriental/African artefacts and recurring elephant motif. Individually designed bedrooms – some with feature beds; most have sea/country views. Classical menus; dine in restaurant, conservatory or on terrace.

TOTLEY – S. Yorks. – 502 P24 – see Sheffield

TOTNES – Devon – 503 I32 – pop. 7 929 2 C2

London 224 mi – Exeter 24 mi – Plymouth 23 mi – Torquay 9 mi
The Town Mill, Coronation Rd ✆ (01803) 863168, enquire@totnesinformation.co.uk
Dartmouth G & C.C. Blackawton, ✆ (01803) 712 686
Town★ – Elizabethan Museum★ - St Mary's★ – Butterwalk★ – Castle (≤★★★) AC
Paignton Zoo★★ **AC**, E : 4.5 mi by A 385 and A 3022 – British Photographic Museum, Bowden House★ **AC**, S : 1 mi by A 381 – Dartington Hall (High Cross House★), NW : 2 mi on A 385 and A 384. Dartmouth★★ (Castle ≤★★★), SE : 12 mi by A 381 and A 3122

Royal Seven Stars
The Plains ✉ TQ9 5DD – ✆ (01803) 862 125 – www.royalsevenstars.co.uk
21 rm – ♦£ 50/79 ♦♦£ 109
Rest ***TQ9*** – *(dinner only and Sunday lunch)* Carte £ 18/28
◆ 17C former coaching inn in centre of town. Lounge with smart colonial edge, contemporary, light and fresh bedrooms; some have jacuzzi baths, Agatha Christie has a four poster. TQ9 a dining room in converted stables.

The Steam Packet Inn with rm
St Peter's Quay ✉ TQ9 5EW – ✆ (01803) 863 880 – www.steampacketinn.co.uk
4 rm – ♦£ 60 ♦♦£ 80 **Rest** – Carte £ 16/30
◆ Deservedly popular pub with vast terrace; set on the River Dart, in a slightly bohemian market town. Traditional bar and light, airy conservatory. Eclectic, wide-ranging menu, with fresh fish a speciality. Bedrooms are comfortable, cosy and have a modern feel.

TOWCESTER – Northamptonshire – 503 R27 – pop. 8 073 16 B3

London 70 mi – Birmingham 50 mi – Northampton 9 mi – Oxford 36 mi
Whittelbury Park G. & C.C. Whittlebury, ✆ (01327) 850 000
Farthingstone Hotel Farthingstone, ✆ (01327) 361 291

at Paulerspury Southeast : 3.25 mi by A 5 – ✉ Towcester

XX **Vine House** with rm
100 High St ✉ NN12 7NA – ✆ (01327) 811 267 – www.vinehousehotel.com – Closed 1 week Christmas, Monday lunch and Sunday
6 rm – ♦£ 69/85 ♦♦£ 95 **Rest** – Menu £ 30
◆ Keenly run 17C stone cottage with lovely garden, traditional lounges and split-level dining room. Concise set menus feature refined, flavoursome dishes with a classical base and modern edge. Individually styled, period bedrooms are named after grape vines.

TREBETHERICK – Cornwall – see Rock

TREGREHAN – Cornwall – 503 F32 – see St Austell

TRELOWARREN – Cornwall – see Helston

ENGLAND

TRESCO – Cornwall – **503** B34 – see Scilly (Isles of)

TRISCOMBE – Somerset – **503** K30 – see Taunton

TROTTON – West Sussex – see Midhurst

TROUTBECK – Cumbria – **502** L20 – see Windermere

TROWBRIDGE – Wiltshire – 503 N30 – pop. 34 401 — 4 C2

London 115 mi – Bristol 27 mi – Southampton 55 mi – Swindon 32 mi

St Stephen's Pl ✆ (01225) 710535, tic@trowbridge.gov.uk

Westwood Manor★, NW : 3 mi by A 363 – Farleigh Hungerford★ (St Leonard's Chapel★) **AC**, W : 4 m. Longleat House★★★ **AC**, SW : 12 mi by A 363, A 350 and A 362 - Bratton Castle (≤★★) SE : 7.5 mi by A 363 and B 3098 – Steeple Ashton★ (The Green★) E : 6 mi – Edington (St Mary, St Katherine and All Saints★) SE : 7.5 m

Old Manor

Trowle, Northwest : 1 mi on A 363 ✉ BA14 9BL – ✆ (01225) 777 393 – www.oldmanorhotel.com

21 rm (dinner included) – †£ 65/95 ††£ 150/190

Rest – *(dinner only)* Menu £ 27 **s** – Carte £ 24/28 **s**

◆ Attractive Grade II listed Queen Anne house with 15C origins. Lovely gardens and pleasant lounges: wealth of beams adds to charm. Most bedrooms - some four poster - in annex. Spacious restaurant with welcoming ambience.

Red or White

Evolution House, 46 Castle St ✉ BA14 8AY – ✆ (01225) 781 666 – www.redorwhite.biz – Closed 21-31 August, 25-26 December, 1 January, Sunday and bank holidays

Rest – Italian – Menu £ 14/23 – Carte £ 24/29

◆ Spacious restaurant whose names indicates its owners' passion for wine. Frequently changing Sicilian-based menu and regular theme nights. Impressive coloured-glass dome and small food shop.

TRUMPET – Herefordshire – see Ledbury

TRURO – Cornwall – 503 E33 – pop. 20 920 — 1 B3

London 295 mi – Exeter 87 mi – Penzance 26 mi – Plymouth 52 mi

Municipal Buildings, Boscawen St ✆ (01872) 274555, tic@truro.gov.uk

Treliske, ✆ (01872) 272 640

Killiow Kea Killiow, ✆ (01872) 270 246

Royal Cornwall Museum★★ **AC**

Trelissick Garden★★ (≤★★) **AC**, S : 4 mi by A 39 – Feock (Church★) S : 5 mi by A 39 and B 3289. Trewithen★★★, NE : 7.5 mi by A 39 and A 390 – Probus★ (tower★ - garden★) NE : 9 mi by A 39 and A 390

Mannings

Lemon St ✉ TR1 2QB – ✆ (01872) 270 345 – www.manningshotels.co.uk

34 rm – †£ 79/99 ††£ 99/129

Rest *Mannings* – ✆ (01872) 247 900 *(closed Sunday lunch)* Carte £ 21/35

◆ Imposing city centre hotel close to the cathedral, with bright, modern, stylish bedrooms. Spacious, apartment-style rooms in the next door mews boast oversized beds and galley kitchens. Chic cocktail bar and trendy restaurant which offers extensive seasonal menu.

Tabb's

85 Kenwyn St ✉ TR1 3BZ – ✆ (01872) 262 110 – www.tabbs.co.uk – Closed Sunday and Monday

Rest – *(dinner only)* Carte £ 30/36

◆ Series of pleasant slate-floored rooms in small cottage conversion. Chef is a passionate chocolatier. Appealing menu of refined dishes, where quality produce shines through. Duck a speciality.

Saffron

5 Quay St ✉ TR1 2HB – ✆ (01872) 263 771 – www.saffronrestauranttruro.co.uk – Closed 25-26 December, Sunday, Monday dinner January-May and bank holiday Mondays
Rest – Menu £ 20 (dinner) – Carte £ 28/34
♦ Keenly run restaurant in the heart of town, close to the cathedral. Simply appointed, rustic inner with hearty, flavoursome cooking to match. Extensive menus showcase seasonal Cornish produce.

TUNBRIDGE WELLS – Kent – 504 U30 – see Royal Tunbridge Wells

TURNERS HILL – West Sussex – 504 T30 – pop. 1 534 7 D2

London 33 mi – Brighton 24 mi – Crawley 7 mi

Alexander House

East St, East : 1 mi on B 2110 ✉ RH10 4QD – ✆ (01342) 714 914 – www.alexanderhouse.co.uk
36 rm – †£ 185/225 ††£ 325 – 2 suites
Rest *Reflections Brasserie* – Carte £ 36/46
Rest *AG's Grill Room* – *(closed Monday and Tuesday) (booking essential)* Menu £ 20 (lunch) – Carte £ 38/63
♦ Stunning country house in extensive grounds; once owned by Percy Shelley's family. Comfy guest areas; superb spa with 25 treatment rooms. Spacious, well-equipped bedrooms – some with four-posters, claw-foot baths or double showers. Light, seasonal dishes in brasserie. Grill menu in AG's.

TURVILLE – Buckinghamshire – ✉ Henley-On-Thames 11 C2

London 45 mi – Oxford 22 mi – Reading 17 mi

The Bull & Butcher

✉ RG9 6QU – ✆ (01491) 638 283 – www.thebullandbutcher.com
Rest – *(booking advisable)* Carte £ 20/32
♦ Characterful 16C pub boasting pleasant country views, located in a tranquil village that's been the setting for many TV shows. Cooking is generous and robust; regular theme nights feature.

TWO BRIDGES – Devon – 503 I32 – ✉ Yelverton 2 C2

London 226 mi – Exeter 25 mi – Plymouth 17 mi
Dartmoor National Park★★

Prince Hall

East : 1 mi on B 3357 ✉ PL20 6SA – ✆ (01822) 890 403 – www.princehall.co.uk
8 rm – †£ 70/150 ††£ 140/170
Rest – *(booking essential for non-residents)* Menu £ 21/40
♦ Remotely set hotel with welcoming interior. Cosy lounges boast real fires and eclectic art. Comfy, homely bedrooms display subtle modern touches and smart bathrooms; some overlook the moor. Small bar. Bright restaurant with wood burning stove and classical menus.

TYNEMOUTH – Tyne and Wear – 501 P18 – pop. 17 056 24 B2

London 290 mi – Newcastle upon Tyne 8 mi – Sunderland 7 mi

Grand

Grand Par ✉ NE30 4ER – ✆ (0191) 293 6666 – www.grandhotel-uk.com
45 rm – †£ 95/105 ††£ 165/175
Rest *Victoria* – *(closed Sunday dinner)* Menu £ 13/24
♦ Impressive Victorian hotel built as home for Duchess of Northumberland. Commanding views over coastline. Atmospheric lounges and bars. Well-equipped rooms with fine views. Classical dining room with imposing drapes, floral displays and ceiling cornices.

Martineau Guest House without rest
57 Front St ✉ NE30 4BX – ☎ (0191) 257 9038 – www.martineau-house.co.uk
4 rm – †£ 58/75 ††£ 85/90
♦ 18C Georgian stone terraced house in main street, named after Harriet Martineau. Breakfast in open plan kitchen. Homely spacious individually styled rooms, two with view.

UCKFIELD – East Sussex – **504** U31 – **pop. 15 374** **8** A2
London 45 mi – Brighton 17 mi – Eastbourne 20 mi – Maidstone 34 mi

Horsted Place
Little Horsted, South : 2.5 mi by B 2102 and A 22 on A 26 ✉ TN22 5TS – ☎ (01825) 750 581 – www.horstedplace.co.uk – Closed first week January
15 rm – †£ 140/175 ††£ 140/175 – 3 suites
Rest – *(closed Saturday lunch)* Menu £ 21 (lunch) – Carte approx. £ 40
♦ Imposing country house from the height of the Victorian Gothic revival; handsome Pugin-inspired drawing rooms and luxurious bedrooms overlook formal gardens and parkland. Pristine restaurant with tall 19C archways and windows.

ULLSWATER – Cumbria – **502** L20 – **pop. 1 199** – ✉ **Penrith** **21** B2
London 296 mi – Carlisle 25 mi – Kendal 31 mi – Penrith 6 mi
Beckside Car Park, Glenridding, Penrith ☎ (017684) 82414, ullswatertic@lake-district.gov.uk

at Pooley Bridge on B 5320 – ✉ Penrith

Sharrow Bay Country House rest,
South : 2 mi on Howtown rd ✉ CA10 2LZ – ☎ (017684) 86 301 – www.sharrowbay.co.uk
21 rm (dinner included) – †£ 120/290 ††£ 460/500 – 3 suites
Rest – *(booking essential)* Menu £ 43/70 – Carte
Spec. Suissesse soufflé of spinach and stilton. Tournedos of beef, Sarladaise potato and roasted shallots. Francis Coulson's icky sticky toffee sponge with cream.
♦ Long-standing Victorian villa in mature gardens, beautifully located on the shores of Ullswater. Guest areas made up of various drawing rooms/lounges; traditional country house style throughout. Bedrooms have a cottagey feel. Two dining rooms; one with lake views. Classical cooking served in generous portions.

at Watermillock on A 592 – ✉ Penrith

Rampsbeck Country House
✉ CA11 0LP – ☎ (017684) 86 442 – www.rampsbeck.co.uk – Closed January
18 rm – †£ 99/225 ††£ 140/295 – 1 suite
Rest *Restaurant* – see restaurant listing
♦ Immaculately whitewashed country house in mature grounds, affording lovely views over Ullswater and the fells. Spacious guest areas boast heavy fabrics and antique furniture. Contemporary country house bedrooms display up-to-date facilities and marble bathrooms.

Restaurant – at Rampsbeck Country House Hotel
✉ CA11 0LP – ☎ (017684) 86 442 – www.rampsbeck.co.uk – Closed January
Rest – *(booking essential) (lunch by arrangement)* Menu £ 32/49 **s**
♦ Elegant restaurant with good-sized tables, high-backed chairs and beautiful lake/fell views. Oft-changing set menu of well-prepared, refined, classical dishes. Canapés and coffee in the lounge.

ULVERSTON – Cumbria – **502** K21 – **pop. 11 210** **21** A3
London 278 mi – Kendal 25 mi – Lancaster 36 mi
Coronation Hall, County Sq ☎ (01229) 587140, ulverstontic@southlakeland.gov.uk

ENGLAND

Eden Lodge

Coast Rd, Bardsea, South : 2 mi on A 5087. ✉ LA12 9QZ – ✆ (01229) 587 067 – www.eden-lodge.com

10 rm – 🚹£ 79/85 🚹🚹£ 99/135 **Rest** – Menu £ 30 (lunch) **s** Carte £ 25/30 **s**

◆ Large, bay-windowed Victorian house with pleasant gardens. Variously sized, modern bedrooms boast excellent bathrooms; superior rooms are larger, with a view out to Morecambe Bay. Therapies and treatments available. Good value weekend rates. Traditional menus.

UPPER ODDINGTON – Glos. – **503** O28 – see Stow-on-the-Wold

UPPER SLAUGHTER – Glos. – **503** O28 – see Bourton-on-the-Water

---

UPPER WOODFORD – Wiltshire – **503** O30 – see Salisbury

UPPINGHAM – Rutland – 504 R26 – pop. 3 947 — 17 C2

London 101 mi – Leicester 19 mi – Northampton 28 mi – Nottingham 35 mi

XX **Lake Isle** with rm — rest,

16 High St East ✉ LE15 9PZ – ✆ (01572) 822 951 – www.lakeisle.co.uk – Closed 27 December-4 January, Sunday dinner and Monday lunch

12 rm – 🚹£ 55/83 🚹🚹£ 100 **Rest** – *(light lunch)* Carte £ 23/34

◆ Pleasant town centre property, accessed via narrow passageway. Heavy wood-furnished dining room; concise, classically based menu of quality produce displaying unfussy modern touches. Bedrooms boast good facilities/extras: superior are largest, with whirlpool baths.

ENGLAND

at Lyddington South : 2 mi by A 6003 – ✉ Uppingham

Old White Hart with rm

51 Main St ✉ LE15 9LR – ✆ (01572) 821 703 – www.oldwhitehart.co.uk – Closed Sunday dinner in winter

10 rm – 🚹£ 70 🚹🚹£ 95 **Rest** – Menu £ 14 – Carte £ 18/28

◆ Traditional coaching inn with neat garden and canopy covered terrace. Monthly changing menus display simple, unfussy pub classics. Regular petanque evenings offer game play and dinner. Stylish, modern bedrooms boast smart bathrooms.

UPTON SCUDAMORE – Wilts. – **503** N30 – see Warminster

URMSTON – Greater Manchester – 502 M23 – pop. 40 964 — 20 B2

London 204 mi – Manchester 9 mi – Sale 4 mi

X **Isinglass**

46 Flixton Rd ✉ M41 5AB – ✆ (0161) 749 8400 – www.isinglassrestaurant.com – Closed lunch Saturday and Sunday

Rest – English – Carte £ 23/38

◆ Rustic neighbourhood eatery with simple, almost bohemian atmosphere. Hearty, flavourful cooking features generously proportioned, homemade British dishes. Only seasonal English produce used.

UTTOXETER – Staffordshire – 503 O25 – pop. 12 023 — 19 C1

London 150 mi – Birmingham 41 mi – Stafford 16 mi

at Beamhurst Northwest : 3 mi on A 522 – ✉ Uttoxeter

XX **Gilmore at Strine's Farm**

✉ ST14 5DZ – ✆ (01889) 507 100 – www.restaurantgilmore.com – Closed 1 week January, 1 week Easter, 1 week July-August, 1 week October-November, Monday, Tuesday, Sunday dinner and lunch Saturday and Wednesday

Rest – *(booking essential)* Menu £ 29/42

◆ Personally run converted farmhouse in classic rural setting. Three separate, beamed, cottage style dining rooms. New approach to classic dishes: fine local ingredients used.

VENTNOR – I.O.W. – **503** Q32 – see Wight (Isle of)

VERYAN – Cornwall – **503** F33 – **pop. 877** – ✉ **Truro** **1** B3

London 291 mi – St Austell 13 mi – Truro 13 mi

Village★

Nare rest, VISA AE

Carne Beach, Southwest : 1.25 mi ✉ TR2 5PF – ✆ (01872) 501 111 – www.narehotel.co.uk

30 rm – †£ 130/286 ††£ 378/466 – 8 suites

Rest *The Dining Room* – *(dinner only and Sunday lunch) (booking essential to non-residents)* Menu £ 45

Rest *Quarterdeck* – ✆ (01872) 500 000 *(booking essential to non-residents)* Carte £ 22/29

◆ Personally run country house hotel. Take afternoon tea in the drawing room overlooking the bay; canapés in the bar in the evening. Classical bedrooms: some with patios/balconies; most with a view. Dining Room offers stunning views and classical daily menu. Nautical Quarterdeck serves lighter options and sharing plates.

VIRGINSTOW – Devon – **503** H31 **2** C2

London 227 mi – Bideford 25 mi – Exeter 41 mi – Launceston 11 mi

Percy's VISA

Coombeshead Estate, Southwest : 1.25 mi on Tower Hill rd ✉ EX21 5EA – ✆ (01409) 211 236 – www.percys.co.uk

7 rm – †£ 110/150 ††£ 195

Rest – *(dinner only) (booking essential for non residents) (set menu only)* Menu £ 40

◆ Stone hotel in 130 acres of fields and woodland; where the owners grow veg, rear pigs/sheep, breed racehorses and sell wool, skins and produce. Spacious, comfy bedrooms in former barn; one has a jacuzzi bath. Set 3 course menu uses ingredients from the estate.

WADDESDON – Buckinghamshire – **504** R28 – **pop. 1 865** – ✉ **Aylesbury** **11** C2

London 51 mi – Aylesbury 5 mi – Northampton 32 mi – Oxford 31 mi

Chiltern Hills★

Waddesdon Manor★★, S : 0.5 mi by a 41 and minor rd – Claydon House★, N : by minor rd

XX **Five Arrows** with rm VISA AE

High St ✉ HP18 0JE – ✆ (01296) 651 727 – www.thefivearrows.com

10 rm – †£ 70/95 ††£ 125/175 – 1 suite

Rest – Menu £ 13 (lunch) – Carte £ 25/41

◆ Beautiful 19C inn on Rothschild estate, an influence apparent in pub crest and wine cellar. Striking architecture, stylish dining, relaxed ambience, Anglo-Mediterranean menu. Individually decorated bedrooms - some four posters - divided between main house and courtyard, the latter being smaller but quieter.

WADEBRIDGE – Cornwall – **503** F32 – **pop. 6 222** **1** B2

London 245 mi – Plymouth 41 mi – Torbay 68 mi – Torquay 88 mi

at St Kew **Northeast : 4.5 mi by A 39**

St Kew Inn VISA

✉ PL30 3HB – ✆ (01208) 841 259 – www.stkewinn.co.uk – Closed 25 December

Rest – Menu £ 20 (weekday lunch)/40 – Carte £ 20/32

◆ Characterful country pub in quintessentially English location. Wide-ranging menu of fresh, tasty dishes and St Austell beer in wooden casks. Attractive garden with picnic tables and heaters.

WALBERSWICK – Suffolk – **504** Y27 – **pop. 1 648** **15** D2

London 115 mi – Norwich 31 mi – Ipswich 31 mi – Lowestoft 16 mi

The Anchor with rm VISA AE

Main St ✉ IP18 6UA – ✆ (01502) 722 112 – www.anchoratwalberswick.com – Closed 25 December

8 rm – †£ 85/110 ††£ 85/110 **Rest** – Carte £ 23/35

◆ An Arts and Crafts building with a sizeable garden and seaward views. Global flavours alongside British classics on interesting menu; careful cooking uses local, seasonal produce. Excellent beers and wines. Simple chalet bedrooms; impressive breakfasts.

ENGLAND

WALFORD – County of Herefordshire – see Ross-on-Wye

WALLINGFORD – Oxfordshire – 503 Q29 – pop. 8 019 Great Britain 10 B3

London 54 mi – Oxford 12 mi – Reading 16 mi

Town Hall, Market Pl ✆ (01491) 826972, ticwallingford@freenet.co.uk

Ridgeway Path★★

North Moreton House without rest

North Moreton, West : 4 mi by A 4130 ✉ OX11 9AT – ✆ (01235) 813 283 – www.northmoretonhouse.co.uk

3 rm – ♦£ 48/50 ♦♦£ 75/80

♦ Grade II listed house in mature lawned gardens with fine 17C barn. Spacious, individually decorated bedrooms. Breakfast on local organic produce at vast antique table.

The Partridge

32 St Mary's St ✉ OX10 0ET – ✆ (01491) 825 005 – www.partridge-inn.com – Closed Sunday dinner

Rest – Menu £ 16/18 **s** – Carte £ 29/41 **s**

♦ Former pub, now a stylish, contemporary restaurant, with separate lounge, garden and raised rear terrace. Well-priced market menu offered alongside interesting à la carte of European dishes: cooking is flavourful, confident and accomplished. Efficient service.

WANTAGE – Oxfordshire – 504 P29 – pop. 9 452 10 B3

London 71 mi – Oxford 16 mi – Reading 24 mi – Swindon 21 mi

Vale and Downland Museum, 19 Church St ✆ (01235) 760176, tourism@wantage.com

The Boar's Head with rm

Church St, Ardington, East : 2.5 mi by A 417 ✉ OX12 8QA – ✆ (01235) 833 254 – www.boarsheadardington.co.uk

3 rm – ♦£ 80 ♦♦£ 95/140 **Rest** – Menu £ 18 (lunch) – Carte £ 25/38

♦ Attractive 18C part-timbered pub set in a picture perfect Victorian model village. Wide-ranging menus offer something for everyone, from a 'Rapide' lunch to a gourmet tasting menu. Bedrooms are modern, stylish and spacious.

WAREHAM – Dorset – 503 N31 – pop. 2 568 4 C3

London 123 mi – Bournemouth 13 mi – Weymouth 19 mi

Holy Trinity Church, South St ✆ (01929) 552740, tic@purbeck-dc.gov.uk

Town★ – St Martin's★★

Blue Pool★ **AC**, S : 3.5 mi by A 351 – Bovington Tank Museum★ **AC**, Woolbridge Manor★, W : 5 mi by A 352. Moreton Church★★, W : 9.5 mi by A 352 – Corfe Castle★ (≤★★) **AC**, SE : 6 mi by A 351 – Lulworth Cove★, SW : 10 mi by A 352 and B 3070 – Bere Regis★ (St John the Baptist Church★), NW : 6.5 mi by minor rd

Priory

Church Grn. ✉ BH20 4ND – ✆ (01929) 551 666 – www.theprioryhotel.co.uk

16 rm – ♦£ 188 ♦♦£ 285 – 2 suites

Rest – Menu £ 43 (dinner) – Carte lunch £ 31/39

♦ Charming, privately run part 16C priory, friendly and discreetly cosy. Well-equipped rooms. Manicured four-acre gardens lead down to River Frome: luxury suites in boathouse. Charming restaurant beneath stone vaults of undercroft.

Gold Court House without rest

St John's Hill ✉ BH20 4LZ – ✆ (01929) 553 320 – www.goldcourthouse.co.uk – Closed 25 December to 1 January

3 rm – ♦£ 50 ♦♦£ 75

♦ Affable hosts are justly proud of this pretty 1760s house on a quiet square. Classically charming sitting room and bedrooms; well-chosen books and antiques.

WAREN MILL – Northd. – 501 O17 – see Bamburgh

ENGLAND

WARKWORTH – Northumberland – **502** P17 **24** B2

London 316 mi – Alnwick 7 mi – Morpeth 24 mi

Roxbro House without rest
5 Castle Terr. ✉ *NE65 0UP* – ☎ *(01665) 711 416* – *www.roxbrohouse.co.uk*
– Closed 24-27 December
3 rm – †£ 50/100 ††£ 100/150
◆ A discreet style enhances this 19C stone house in the shadow of Warkworth castle. Stylish lounge in harmony with very smart boutique bedrooms, two of which face the castle.

WARMINSTER – Wiltshire – **503** N30 – **pop. 17 486** **4** C2

London 111 mi – Bristol 29 mi – Exeter 74 mi – Southampton 47 mi
Central Car Park ☎ (01985) 218548, visitwarminster@btconnect.com
Longleat House★★★ **AC**, SW : 3 m. Stonehenge★★★ **AC**, E : 18 mi by A 36 and A 303 – Bratton Castle (≤★★) NE : 6 mi by A 350 and B 3098

at Upton Scudamore North : 2.5 mi by A 350 – ✉ Warminster

The Angel Inn with rm
✉ *BA12 0AG* – ☎ *(01985) 213 225* – *www.theangelinn.co.uk*
10 rm – †£ 80 ††£ 85 **Rest** – Carte £ 15/30
◆ Dependable village local with cottagey dining room and lovely terrace. Menus are fairly formal and classical, offering the likes of home-cured gravadlax, roast duck, venison steak and old-fashioned puddings. Individually themed bedrooms are cosy and well-kept.

at Heytesbury Southeast : 3.75 mi by B 3414 – ✉ Warminster

Resting Post without rest
67 High St ✉ *BA12 0ED* – ☎ *(01985) 840 204* – *www.therestingpost.co.uk*
3 rm – †£ 50/60 ††£ 70/75
◆ Immaculately kept Grade II listed building dating back to 17C – originally a post office and general store run by the same couple. Individually styled bedrooms, one with a 6ft bed.

ENGLAND

The Angel Inn
High St ✉ *BA12 0ED* – ☎ *(01985) 840 330* – *www.theangelheytesbury.co.uk*
– Closed Sunday dinner
Rest – Carte £ 16/30
◆ Pretty 16C pub with open fires and wooden beams; boasts a typically English feel emphasized by the locals and their dogs. Dishes make good use of fresh, local produce; steaks are a speciality.

at Crockerton South : 2 mi by A 350

Bath Arms with rm
Clay St, on Shear Water rd ✉ *BA12 8AJ* – ☎ *(01985) 212 262*
– www.batharmscrockerton.co.uk
2 rm – †£ 80/95 ††£ 80/95 **Rest** – Carte £ 17/26
◆ Down-to-earth pub with big ambitions, situated on Longleat Estate. Daily changing menu features classic pub dishes, snacks and grills alongside more modern fare. Two ultra-spacious, contemporary bedrooms.

at Horningsham Southwest : 5 mi by A 362 – ✉ Wiltshire

The Bath Arms with rm
Longleat ✉ *BA12 7LY* – ☎ *(01985) 844 308* – *www.batharms.co.uk*
15 rm – †£ 85/140 ††£ 95/150
Rest – Menu £ 15/30 – Carte approx. £ 30
◆ Charming pub within the Longleat estate, with open fire in bar, grand dining room and delightful terrace. Appealing menus offer something for everyone; produce is locally sourced, much of it from the estate. Quirky, comfortable, individually themed bedrooms.

WARTLING – E. Sussex – **504** V31 – see Herstmonceux

WARWICK – Warwickshire – **503** P27 – **pop. 23 350** Great Britain **19** C3

London 96 mi – Birmingham 20 mi – Coventry 11 mi – Leicester 34 mi

The Court House, Jury St ✆ (01926) 492212, touristinfo@warwick-uk.co.uk

Warwick Racecourse, ✆ (01926) 494 316

Town★ - Castle★★ **AC** Y – Leycester Hospital★ **AC** Y **B** – Collegiate Church of St Mary★ (Tomb★) Y **A**

Charter House without rest

87 West St ✉ CV34 6AH – ✆ (01926) 496 965

– Closed 1 January and 24-26 & 31 December Y**c**

3 rm – †£ 65 ††£ 85

◆ Timbered 15C house not far from the castle. Comfortable, delicately ordered rooms with a personal touch: pretty counterpanes and posies of dried flowers. Tasty breakfasts.

WARWICK-ROYAL LEAMINGTON SPA

Birmingham Rd	Z	7
Bowling Green St	Y	9
Brook St	Y	12
Butts (The)	Y	13
Castle Hill	Y	15
Church St	Y	17
High St	Y	23
Jury St	Y	
Lakin Rd	Y	25
Linen St	Y	26
Market Pl.	Y	29
Old Square	Y	35
Old Warwick Rd	Z	36
Radford Rd	Z	39
Rock (The)	Y	32
St John's Rd	Y	42
St Nicholas Church St	Y	43
Shires Retail Park	Z	
Smith St	Y	
Swan St	Y	46
Theatre St	Y	48
West St	Y	50

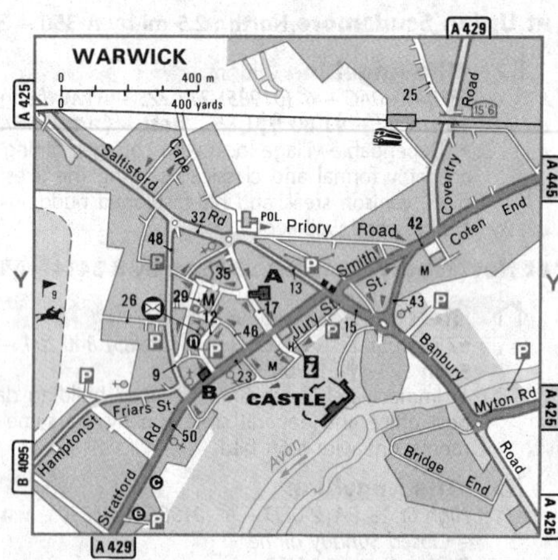

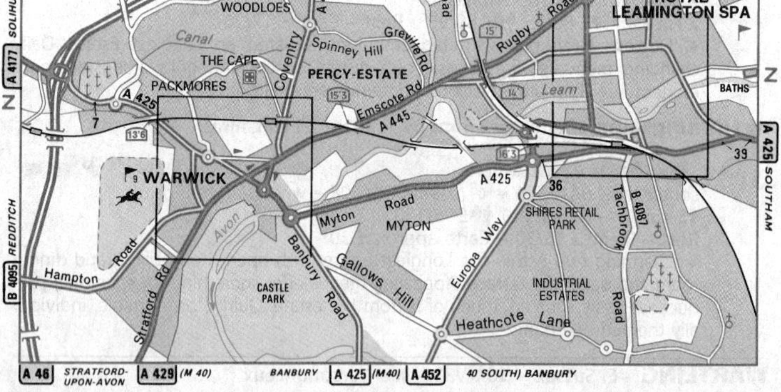

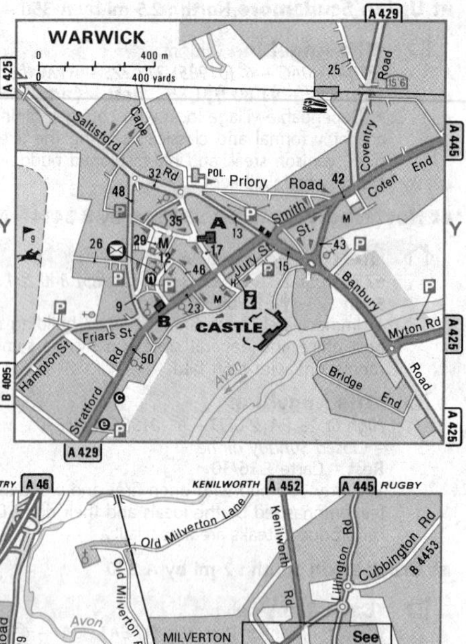

WARWICK
0 400 m
0 400 yards
A 429
A 425
A 445
A 4095
Saltisford
Cape
Rd
POL.
Priory Road
Coventry Road
Coten End
Smith St.
Jury St.
Banbury
Myton Rd
Bridge End
Road
Friars St.
Hampton St
Stratford Rd
Avon
CASTLE
A
B
Y

BUILT UP AREA
0 1 km
0 1/2 mile
COVENTRY A 46
KENILWORTH A 452
A 445 RUGBY
Old Milverton Lane
Kenilworth Rd
Lillington Rd
Cubbington Rd
B 4453
Old Milverton Road
Avon
A 46
Road A 429
WOODLOES
MILVERTON
See ROYAL LEAMINGTON SPA
Rugby Road
Canal
Coventry
Spinney Hill
Greville Rd
THE CAPE
PERCY-ESTATE
PACKMORES
Emscote Rd
A 445
Leam
BATHS
A 425
WARWICK
Myton Road
MYTON
SHIRES RETAIL PARK
Tachbrook
B 4087
Europa Way
Hampton Road
Stratford Rd
Banbury Road
Gallows Hill
CASTLE PARK
INDUSTRIAL ESTATES
Heathcote Lane
Road
SOLIHULL A 4177
REDDITCH B 4095
A 425 SOUTHAM
A 46 STRATFORD-UPON-AVON
A 429 (M 40)
BANBURY A 425 (M40)
A 452 (M 40 SOUTH) BANBURY
N Z

Park Cottage without rest

113 West St ✉ CV34 6AH – ✆ (01926) 410 319 – www.parkcottagewarwick.co.uk

7 rm – ♦£ 50/65 ♦♦£ 70/80 Ye

♦ Between the shops and restaurants of West Street and the River Avon, a listed part Tudor house offering a homely lounge and sizeable, traditionally appointed bedrooms.

XX **Saffron Gold**

Unit 1, Westgate House, Market St ✉ CV34 4DE – ✆ (01926) 402 061 – www.saffronwarwick.co.uk – Closed 25 December Yn

Rest – Indian – *(dinner only)* Menu £ 20 – Carte £ 17/32

♦ Split-level dining room hung with sitars and prints from the subcontinent. Piquant seafood and Goan dishes are the specialities of a freshly prepared Indian repertoire.

WATERGATE BAY – Cornwall – 503 E32 – see Newquay

WATERMILLOCK – Cumbria – 502 L20 – see Ullswater

WATFORD – Hertfordshire – 504 S29 – pop. 120 960 12 A2

London 21 mi – Aylesbury 23 mi

18 West Herts. Cassiobury Park, ✆ (01923) 236 484

9 Oxhey Park South Oxhey Prestwick Rd, ✆ (01923) 248 213

Plan : see Greater London (North-West) 2

Grove rm,

Chandler's Cross, Northwest : 2 mi on A 411 ✉ WD3 4TG – ✆ (01923) 807 807 – www.thegrove.co.uk

215 rm – ♦£ 305 ♦♦£ 305, £ 23 – 12 suites

Rest *Colette's* – ✆ (01923) 296 010 *(dinner only)* Menu 62

Rest *Stables* – ✆ (01923) 296 015 – Carte £ 29/47

Rest *Glasshouse* – *(buffet)* Menu £ 30/40

♦ Impressive Grade II listed country house in 300 acres of gardens/woodland. Mix of period and contemporary bedrooms and suites. Leisure facilities include tennis, croquet, golf and volleyball; as well as a spa, outdoor pool and urban beach. Formal menu in Colette's. Casual dining in Stables. Buffet meals in Glasshouse.

XX **Clarendon**

Red Hall Ln., West : 5 mi by A 412, Baldwins Lane and Sarratt Rd ✉ WD3 4LU – ✆ (01923) 270 009 – www.theclarendon.co.uk – Closed 25 December

Rest – Menu £ 19 (lunch) – Carte £ 24/40

♦ Former pub deep in country lanes; now a vibrantly decorated, modern restaurant with bar and open kitchen. Tasty British classics and good old-fashioned puds. Attentive service.

WATTON – Norfolk – 504 W26 – pop. 7 435 15 C2

London 95 mi – Norwich 22 mi – Swaffham 10 mi

XX **Café at Brovey Lair** with rm rest,

Carbrooke Rd., Ovington, Northeast : 1.75 mi by A 1075 ✉ IP25 6SD – ✆ (01953) 882 706 – www.broveylair.com

2 rm – ♦£ 130 ♦♦£ 145

Rest – Seafood – *(booking essential 2 days in advance) (set menu only)* Menu £ 53

♦ Keenly run restaurant with integral kitchen. Unique dinner party style dining from single-choice seafood menu, where ambitious dishes display largely Asian and Mediterranean influences. Well-appointed bedrooms sit beside a pool and terrace in lovely gardens.

ENGLAND

WELFORD-ON-AVON – Warwickshire 19 C3

London 109 mi – Alcester 9 mi – Stratford-upon-Avon 4 mi

Bell Inn

Binton Rd ✉ CV37 8EB – ✆ (01789) 750 353 – www.thebellwelford.co.uk
Rest – Menu £ 16 (lunch) – Carte £ 20/27
◆ 17C red-brick inn with attractive terrace, boasting various beamed snugs and a glass-roofed dining room. Extensive menus use local produce and display a real mix of dishes. Good veggie choices.

WELLINGHAM – Norfolk – 504 W25 15 C1

London 120 mi – King's Lynn 29 mi – Norwich 28 mi

Manor House Farm without rest

✉ PE32 2TH – ✆ (01328) 838 227 – www.manor-house-farm.co.uk
3 rm – †£ 60/70 ††£ 90/100
◆ Attractive, wisteria-clad farmhouse with large gardens, set by a church in a beautifully peaceful spot. Spacious, airy bedrooms in former stables. Home-grown/home-reared produce at breakfast.

WELLINGTON – County of Herefordshire – 503 L27 18 B3

London 161 mi – Gloucester 38 mi – Worcester 31 mi – Hereford 6 mi

The Wellington

✉ HR4 8AT – ✆ (01432) 830 367 – www.wellingtonpub.co.uk – Closed 25-26 December, Sunday dinner and Monday lunch
Rest – Carte £ 24/30
◆ Bright and airy neighbourhood pub where locals gather fireside in the spacious bar. Enjoy flavourful dishes from the daily changing menu in the more formal conservatory dining room.

WELLS – Somerset – 503 M30 – pop. 10 406 4 C2

London 132 mi – Bristol 20 mi – Southampton 68 mi – Taunton 28 mi
Town Hall, Market Pl ✆ (01749) 672552, touristinfo@wells.gov.uk
East Horrington Rd, ✆ (01749) 675 005
City★★ – Cathedral★★★ – Bishop's Palace★ (≤★★) **AC** – St Cuthbert★
Glastonbury★★ - Abbey★★ (Abbot's Kitchen★) **AC**, St John the Baptist★★, Somerset Rural Life Museum★ **AC**, Glastonbury Tor★ (≤★★★), SW : 5.5 mi by A 39 – Wookey Hole★ (Caves★ **AC**, Papermill★), NW : 2 m. Cheddar Gorge★★ (Gorge★★, Caves★, Jacob's Ladder ✳★) - St Andrew's Church★, NW : 7 mi by A 371 – Axbridge★★ (King John's Hunting Lodge★, St John the Baptist Church★), NW : 8.5 mi by A 371

Swan

rm,

11 Sadler St ✉ BA5 2RX – ✆ (01749) 836 300 – www.swanhotelwells.co.uk
48 rm – †£ 94/104 ††£ 116/176 – 1 suite
Rest – Carte £ 17/33
◆ Refurbished to a very good standard, this friendly former posting inn faces the Cathedral's west front. Two firelit lounges; stylish, individually decorated rooms. Stunning Cathedral suite. Restaurant boasts framed antique clothing and oak panelling.

Beryl without rest

East : 1.25 mi by B 3139 off Hawkers Lane ✉ BA5 3JP – ✆ (01749) 678 738 – www.beryl-wells.co.uk – Closed 24-26 December
10 rm – †£ 70/90 ††£ 100/140
◆ Neo-gothic former hunting lodge in formal gardens run in idiosyncratic style. Impeccable antique-filled drawing room. Traditional rooms, larger on first floor. Charming hosts.

Old Spot

12 Sadler St ✉ BA5 2SE – ✆ (01749) 689 099 – www.theoldspot.co.uk – *Closed 1 week Christmas, Monday, Sunday dinner and Tuesday lunch*
Rest – Menu £ 15/28
♦ Simple, understated, city centre restaurant run by a husband and wife team; its plain walls hung with framed menus and opening out onto the cathedral at the rear. Well-executed, classical dishes rely on flavoursome English produce. Preparation is kept simple.

at Wookey Hole Northwest : 1.75 mi by A 371 – ✉ Wells

Miller's at Glencot House

Glencot Ln ✉ *BA5 1BH* – ✆ *(01749) 677 160* – *www.glencothouse.co.uk*
15 rm – †£ 165 ††£ 295, ☕ £ 9.95
Rest – *(booking essential for non-residents)* Carte £ 30/34
♦ 19C mansion in Jacobean style, bursting with personality and now owned by Martin Miller who has filled the house with antiques. Rooms all refurbished; relaxed atmosphere throughout. French inspired menu with good local produce.

at Easton Northwest : 3 mi on A 371 – ✉ Wells

Beaconsfield Farm without rest

on A 371 ✉ *BA5 1DU* – ✆ *(01749) 870 308* – *www.beaconsfieldfarm.co.uk* – *Closed 23 December-2 January*
3 rm ☕ – †£ 65/75 ††£ 70/90
♦ In the foothills of the Mendips, a renovated farmhouse offering well-fitted, cottage-style rooms. Generous breakfasts in the parlour overlooking the four-acre grounds.

A red **Rest** mention denotes an establishment with an award for culinary excellence, ✿ (star) or ☺ (Bib Gourmand).

ENGLAND

WELLS-NEXT-THE-SEA – Norfolk – 504 W25 – pop. 2 451 15 C1

London 122 mi – Cromer 22 mi – Norwich 38 mi

Crown

The Buttlands ✉ *NR23 1EX* – ✆ *(01328) 710 209* – *www.flyingkiwisiinns.co.uk*
12 rm ☕ – †£ 70/140 ††£ 90/160
Rest *Crown* – Menu £ 13 – Carte £ 21/39
♦ Characterful 16C former coaching inn located in the centre of town, overlooking the green. Individually styled bedrooms blend classical furniture with more modern décor and facilities. Dine from an accessible menu in the charming bar, orangery or dining room.

Machrimore without rest

Burnt St., on A 149 ✉ *NR23 1HS* – ✆ *(01328) 711 653* – *www.machrimore.co.uk*
4 rm ☕ – †£ 60 ††£ 80
♦ Converted farm buildings with delightful gardens and illuminated water features. Accessed via the garden, bedrooms have quality furniture, good facilities, their own patio and seating.

at Wighton Southeast : 2.5 mi by A149

Meadowview without rest

53 High St ✉ *NR23 1PF* – ✆ *(01328) 821 527* – *www.meadow-view.net*
5 rm ☕ – †£ 60 ††£ 90
♦ Set in peaceful village, with neat garden, hot tub, comfy furniture and gazebo overlooking meadow. Smart, modern interior with comfy furnishings; good facilities. Breakfast cooked on Aga.

WELWYN – Hertfordshire – **504** T28 – pop. 10 512 — **12** B2

London 31 mi – Bedford 31 mi – Cambridge 31 mi

Tewin Bury Farm

Southeast : 3.5 mi by A 1000 on B 1000 ✉ AL6 0JB – ✆ (01438) 717 793 – www.tewinbury.co.uk

29 rm – †£ 143 ††£ 158 **Rest** – Carte £ 26/33

◆ Consisting of a range of converted farm buildings on 400-acre working farm. 17C tythe barn used as function room located next to river. Individual rooms have beamed ceilings. Restaurant located in timbered farm building.

WELWYN GARDEN CITY – Hertfordshire – **504** T28 – pop. 43 512 — **12** B2

London 22 mi – Luton 21 mi

Panshanger Golf Complex Old Herns Lane, ✆ (01707) 333 312

Auberge du Lac

Brocket Hall, West : 3 mi by A 6129 on B 653 ✉ AL8 7XG – ✆ (01707) 368 888 – www.brocket-hall.co.uk – Closed 27 December-14 January, Sunday and Monday

Rest – Menu £ 33/55

Spec. Caramelised foie gras, pain d'épices, vanilla yoghurt and pickled peach. Turbot with cannelloni of smoked eel and golden raisins. Wild strawberry and vanilla cheesecake, strawberry sorbet and shortbread.

◆ You get buzzed in at the gates to reach this part 18C former hunting lodge in the grounds of Brocket Hall; a charming setting with its lakeside terrace. The cooking is technically adept and the focus is on flavours; excellent cheeseboard.

ENGLAND

WENTBRIDGE – West Yorkshire – **502** Q23 – ✉ Pontefract — **22** B3

London 183 mi – Leeds 19 mi – Nottingham 55 mi – Sheffield 28 mi

Wentbridge House

Old Great North Rd ✉ WF8 3JJ – ✆ (01977) 620 444 – www.wentbridgehouse.co.uk

41 rm – †£ 105 ††£ 170/220

Rest *Fleur de Lys* – *(closed Sunday dinner) (dinner only and Sunday lunch)* Carte £ 34/53

Rest *Wentbridge Brasserie* – Carte £ 23/43

◆ Personally run, part-18C bay-windowed house, surrounded by 20 acres of immaculately kept gardens. Bedrooms are a mix of characterful, period styles and spacious, modern designs. Modern dining room with Italian chandeliers. Smart brasserie offers a huge choice.

WEST BAGBOROUGH – Somerset – **503** K30 – see Taunton

WEST DIDSBURY – Gtr Manchester – see Manchester

WEST END – Surrey – **504** S29 – pop. 4 135 – ✉ Guildford — **7** C1

London 37 mi – Bracknell 7 mi – Camberley 5 mi – Guildford 8 mi

The Inn @ West End

42 Guildford Rd, on A 322 ✉ GU24 9PW – ✆ (01276) 858 652 – www.the-inn.co.uk

Rest – Carte £ 26/37

◆ A snug and friendly village pub with a roaring fire and a country feel. An array of menus offer something for everyone. Interesting selection of wines and a pleasant garden/terrace.

WESTFIELD – East Sussex – **504** V31 – pop. 1 509 — **8** B3

London 66 mi – Brighton 38 mi – Folkestone 45 mi – Maidstone 30 mi

Wild Mushroom

Woodgate House, Westfield Ln., Southwest : 0.5 mi on A 28 ✉ TN35 4SB – ✆ (01424) 751 137 – www.webbesrestaurants.co.uk – Closed Sunday dinner and Monday

Rest – *(booking essential)* Menu £ 20 (lunch) – Carte dinner £ 24/32

◆ Rural roadside house with classical dining room and intimate conservatory bar. Good value French/European menus feature well-presented, tried-and-tested combinations. Tasting menu available.

WEST HOATHLY – West Sussex – pop. 2 121 – ✉ RH19 **7** D2

London 36 mi – Croydon 26 mi – Barnet 78 mi – Ealing 60 mi

The Cat Inn with rm

Queen's Sq ✉ RH19 4PP – ✆ (01342) 810 369 – www.catinn.co.uk – Closed Sunday dinner

4 rm – £ 80 £ 140

Rest – Carte £ 20/31

♦ Charming 17C pub in a pleasant hamlet, run by experienced owners and a bubbly team. A myriad of rooms range from rustic and intimate, to larger and more formally laid. Menus feature satisfying country classics. Bedrooms are modern and extremely comfortable.

WEST KIRBY – Merseyside – 502 K23 Great Britain **20** A3

London 219 mi – Chester 19 mi – Liverpool 12 mi

Liverpool★ - Cathedrals★★, The Walker★★, Merseyside Maritime Museum★ and Albert Dock★, E : 13.5 mi by A 553

Peel Hey without rest

Frankby Rd, Frankby, East : 2.25 mi by A 540 on B 5139 ✉ CH48 1PP – ✆ (0151) 677 9077 – www.peelhey.com

9 rm – £ 65/75 £ 85/95

♦ Personally run, 19C house with attractive bedrooms; those to the rear are quieter, with countryside views. Comfortable conservatory and pleasant lawned garden. Pubs for dinner close by.

WESTLETON – Suffolk – 504 Y27 – ✉ Saxmundham **15** D2

London 97 mi – Cambridge 72 mi – Ipswich 28 mi – Norwich 31 mi

The Westleton Crown with rm

The Street ✉ IP17 3AD – ✆ (01728) 648 777 – www.westletoncrown.co.uk

34 rm – £ 95 £ 120/165

Rest – Carte £ 23/36

♦ Good-looking red-brick 17C former coaching inn, in a pretty little village. Welcoming bar but venture further in for the modern conservatory. Same appealing menu served throughout. Uncluttered bedrooms with smart bathrooms.

WEST MALLING – Kent – 504 V30 – pop. 2 144 **8** B1

London 35 mi – Maidstone 7 mi – Royal Tunbridge Wells 14 mi

Addington Maidstone, ✆ (01732) 844 785

Swan

35 Swan St ✉ ME19 6JU – ✆ (01732) 521 910 – www.theswanwestmalling.co.uk

Rest – *(booking essential)* Menu £ 21 (weekday dinner) – Carte £ 25/45

♦ Informal 15C former coaching inn where original beams blend with stylish, contemporary furnishings. Nicely appointed bar and comfy lounge are located upstairs. Modern European menus offer cleanly presented, flavoursome combinations; side dishes are required.

WEST MEON – Hampshire – 504 Q30 **6** B2

London 74 mi – Southampton 27 mi – Portsmouth 21 mi – Basingstoke 32 mi

The Thomas Lord

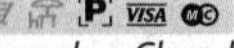

High St ✉ GU32 1LN – ✆ (01730) 829 244 – www.thethomaslord.co.uk – Closed Monday

Rest – Carte £ 22/29

♦ Named after the founder of Lord's Cricket Ground; memorabilia abounds among the shabby-chic styling. Locally sourced produce informs oft-changing menu of tasty British dishes.

WESTON-SUPER-MARE – North Somerset – 503 K29 – 3 B2 – pop. 78 044

- London 147 mi – Bristol 24 mi – Taunton 32 mi
- Beach Lawns ☎ (01934) 888800, westontouristinfo@n-somerset.gov.uk
- 18 Worlebury Monks Hill, ☎ (01934) 625 789
- Seafront (< ★★) BZ
- Axbridge★★ (King John's Hunting Lodge★, St John the Baptist Church★) SE : 9 mi by A 371 - BY - and A 38 – Cheddar Gorge★★ (Gorge★★, Caves★, Jacob's Ladder ✻★) – Clevedon★ (< ★★, Clevedon Court★), NE : 10 mi by A 370 and M 5 – St Andrew's Church★, SE : 10.5 mi by A 371

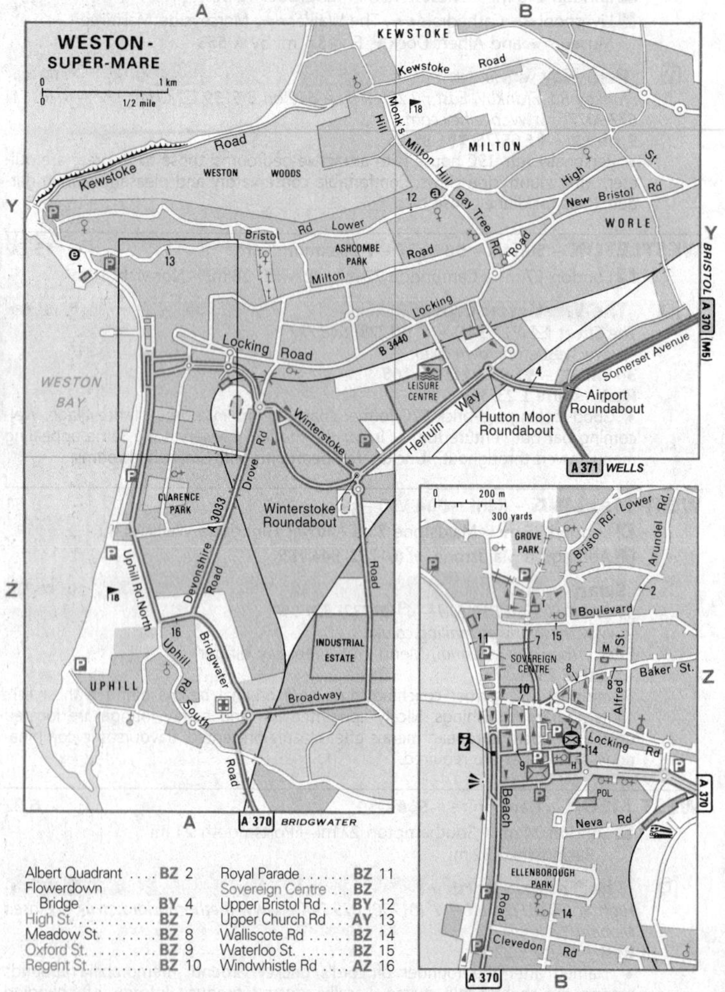

Albert Quadrant	BZ	2
Flowerdown Bridge	BY	4
High St.	BZ	7
Meadow St.	BZ	8
Oxford St.	BZ	9
Regent St.	BZ	10
Royal Parade	BZ	11
Sovereign Centre	BZ	
Upper Bristol Rd	BY	12
Upper Church Rd	AY	13
Walliscote Rd	BZ	14
Waterloo St.	BZ	15
Windwhistle Rd	AZ	16

Duets

103 Upper Bristol Rd. ✉ BS22 8ND – ✆ (01934) 413 428 – www.duets.co.uk – Closed Sunday dinner, Monday and Tuesday BY**a**

Rest – Menu £ 20/30 – Carte £ 31/35

♦ Diligent and unfussy service sets the tone in this traditionally styled restaurant, deservedly a neighbourhood favourite. Ably judged cooking on a tasty classical base.

Cove

Birnbeck Rd ✉ BS23 2BX – ✆ (01934) 418 217 – www.the-cove.co.uk – Closed weekdays January-February, Sunday dinner and Monday AY**e**

Rest – Menu £ 15 (lunch) – Carte £ 20/32

♦ Seafront eatery with striking lines, contemporary styling and bay views. Modern, seasonal menu displays European flair and seafood slant; most produce from within 20 miles. Tapas 3-9pm.

WESTON UNDER WETHERLEY – Warks. – 503 P27 – see Royal Leamington Spa

WEST TANFIELD – North Yorkshire – 502 P21 – pop. 551 – ✉ Ripon 22 B2

London 237 mi – Darlington 29 mi – Leeds 32 mi – Middlesbrough 39 mi

Old Coach House without rest

2 Stable Cottage, Southeast : 1 mi on A 6108 ✉ HG4 3HT – ✆ (01765) 634 900 – www.oldcoachhouse.info – Closed 2 January-10 February

8 rm – †£ 55/69 ††£ 95

♦ Smart 18C former coach house, nestled between the dales and moors. Bedrooms – in two main buildings – differ in size, but all have a bright, modern style and are furnished by local craftsmen. Breakfast room overlooks the pleasant courtyard garden and fountain.

WEST WITTON – N. Yorks. – 502 O21 – ✉ Leyburn 22 B1

London 241 mi – Kendal 39 mi – Leeds 60 mi – Newcastle upon Tyne 65 mi

Wensleydale Heifer

✉ DL8 4LS – ✆ (01969) 622 322 – www.wensleydaleheifer.co.uk

13 rm – †£ 90 ††£ 170

Rest – Seafood – Menu £ 19 (lunch) – Carte £ 29/43

♦ Pretty whitewashed former pub on main street of village. Quirky, themed bedrooms boast quality linen and all mod cons. Characterful lounge with roaring fire. Dine in the fish bar or at clothed tables in the beamed restaurant; cooking has strong seafood base.

WEYBRIDGE – Surrey – 504 S29 – pop. 52 890 7 C1

London 23 mi – Crawley 27 mi – Guildford 17 mi – Reading 33 mi

Brooklands

Brooklands Dr., Southwest : 1.5 mi by B 374 and A 318 ✉ KT13 OSL – ✆ (01937) 355 700 – www.brooklandshotelsurrey.com

105 rm – †£ 275 ††£ 275, £ 15.95 – 15 suites

Rest ***Brasserie*** – see restaurant listing

♦ Contemporary hotel with art deco feel, situated next to Mercedes Benz World on what was Brooklands racetrack. Buzzy bar; great spa. Stylish, comfortable, good-sized bedrooms.

Brasserie – at Brooklands Hotel

Brooklands Dr, Southwest : 1.5 mi by B 374 and A 318 ✉ KT13 OSL – ✆ (01932) 355 700 – www.brooklandshotelsurrey.com

Rest – Italian influences – Menu £ 32 **s** – Carte approx. £ 31 **s**

♦ Bright, modern dining room, with black décor and a funky feel. Choose a traditional 3 course meal or a number of tasting plates. Tasty, authentic Italian cooking; effective service.

WEYMOUTH – Dorset – **503** M32 – **pop. 48 279** **4** C3

London 142 mi – Bournemouth 35 mi – Bristol 68 mi – Exeter 59 mi

to Guernsey (St Peter Port) and Jersey (St Helier) (Condor Ferries Ltd)

The King's Statue, The Esplanade ✆ (01305) 785747, tic@weymouth.gov.uk

Links Rd, ✆ (0844) 980 9909

Town★ – Timewalk★ **AC** – Nothe Fort (≤★) **AC** – Boat Trip★ (Weymouth Bay and Portland Harbour) **AC**

Chesil Beach★★ – Portland★ - Portland Bill (✳★★) S : 2.5 mi by A 354. Maiden Castle★★ (≤★) N : 6.5 mi by A 354 – Sub-Tropical Gardens★ **AC**, St Catherine's Chapel★) NW : 9 mi by B 3157

Chandlers without rest

4 Westerhall Rd ✉ DT4 7SZ – ✆ (01305) 771 341 – www.chandlershotel.com – Closed Christmas, New Year and restricted opening December-January

10 rm – £ 60/130 £ 155

◆ Substantial Victorian house near the promenade, run by friendly owners. Stylish, modern interior with comfy lounge and airy breakfast room. Bedrooms have plain walls and colour-themed fabrics.

WHALLEY – Lancashire – **502** M22 – **pop. 3 230** – ✉ **Blackburn** **20** B2

London 233 mi – Blackpool 32 mi – Burnley 12 mi – Manchester 28 mi

Long Leese Barn Clerkhill, ✆ (01254) 822 236

Food by Breda Murphy

Abbots Ct, 41 Station Rd ✉ BB7 9RH – ✆ (01254) 823 446 – www.foodbybredamurphy.com – Closed 24 December-4 January, Sunday and Monday

Rest – *(lunch only)* Carte £ 22/43

◆ Bright, modern restaurant with popular deli. Extensive menu of tasty, traditional, home-cooked dishes – from salads and sandwiches to the full three courses. Charming service.

at Mitton Northwest : 2.5 mi on B 6246 – ✉ Whalley

The Three Fishes

Mitton Rd ✉ BB7 9PQ – ✆ (01254) 826 888 – www.thethreefishes.com – Closed 25 December

Rest – *(bookings not accepted)* Carte £ 19/30

◆ Spacious, modern country inn offering extensive, seasonally changing menu which celebrates Lancastrian produce. Family-friendly, with a children's menu and popular Sunday roast.

WHEPSTEAD – Suffolk – **504** W27 – see Bury St Edmunds

WHITBY – North Yorkshire – **502** S20 – **pop. 13 594** Great Britain **23** C1

London 257 mi – Middlesbrough 31 mi – Scarborough 21 mi – York 45 mi

Langborne Rd ✆ (01723) 383637, tourismbureau@scarborough.gov.uk

Low Straggleton Sandsend Rd, ✆ (01947) 600 660

Abbey★

Bagdale Hall

1 Bagdale ✉ YO21 1QL – ✆ (01947) 602 958 – www.bagdale.co.uk

14 rm – £ 60/90 £ 90/180 **Rest** – *(dinner only)* Carte £ 19/33

◆ Tudor manor with fine fireplaces in carved wood and 19C Delft tiles; panelled rooms with mullioned windows; four-posters in period style bedrooms. Annexe for more modern rooms. Dining room boasts timbered ceiling and massive wooden fireplace.

Green's

13 Bridge St ✉ YO22 4BG – ✆ (01947) 600 284 – www.greensofwhitby.com – Closed 25-26 December and 1 January

Rest – Seafood – *(booking essential)* Menu £ 43 (dinner) – Carte £ 27/45

◆ Established eatery near the quay. Formal dining room offers 3 course menu. Lively bistro serves concise à la carte and daily specials – mainly market fish. Influences range from Italian to Thai.

Red Chard Lounge and Grill

22-23 Flowergate ✉ YO21 3BA – ☎ (01947) 606 660 – www.redchard.com – Closed first week January, 25 December, Monday and lunch Saturday-Tuesday

Rest – Beef specialities – Carte £ 26/40

♦ Modern town centre bar/lounge/dining room in one; funky and relaxing, with art-covered walls. Wide ranging menu with local produce to the fore; quality 21 day hung beef.

at Briggswath Southwest : 3.5 mi by A 171 (Teesdale Rd), A 169 on B 1410 – ✉ Whitby

Lawns without rest

73 Carr Hill Ln. ✉ YO21 1RS – ☎ (01947) 810 310 – www.thelawnsbedandbreakfastwhitby.co.uk – Closed Christmas and New Year

3 rm – †£ 74 ††£ 74

♦ Sizeable, converted house above a south-facing garden and verge of evergreens. Stripped wooden floors, understated décor. Spotless rooms. Fine views of moors and Esk valley.

at Sandsend Northwest : 3 mi on A 174 – ✉ Whitby

Estbek House with rm

East Row ✉ YO21 3SY – ☎ (01947) 893 424 – www.estbekhouse.co.uk – Closed 2 January-10 February

4 rm – †£ 80/100 ††£ 150/190

Rest – Seafood – *(dinner only)* Carte £ 35/51

♦ This personally run Regency house, adjacent to beach, boasts delightful terrace, basement bar, smart restaurant serving local, wild seafood, and utterly charming rooms.

at Goldsborough Northwest : 6 mi by A 174

Fox & Hounds

✉ YO21 3RX – ☎ (01947) 893 372 – www.foxandhoundsgoldsborough.co.uk – Closed 2 weeks January, Christmas, and Sunday-Tuesday

Rest – *(dinner only)* Carte £ 29/39

♦ Former village pub with homely, cottagey style, set in tiny coastal hamlet. Constantly evolving menu features local produce and unfussy cooking, with emphasis on fresh fish and seafood.

WHITEHAVEN – Cumbria – 502 J20 – pop. 24 978 — 21 A2

London 332 mi – Carlisle 39 mi – Keswick 28 mi – Penrith 47 mi

Zest

Low Rd, South : 0.5 mi on B 5345 (St Bees) ✉ CA28 9HS – ☎ (01946) 692 848 – www.zestwhitehaven.com – Closed 25-31 December and Sunday-Tuesday

Rest – *(dinner only)* Carte £ 22/35

♦ Unassuming exterior conceals stylish, red-hued room with brushed velvet chairs and leather banquettes. Large, modern menu with Asian edge and blackboard specials. Unfussy, flavoursome cooking.

WHITEWELL – Lancashire – 502 M22 – pop. 5 617 – ✉ Clitheroe — 20 B2

London 281 mi – Lancaster 31 mi – Leeds 55 mi – Manchester 41 mi

The Inn at Whitewell with rm

Forest of Bowland ✉ BB7 3AT – ☎ (01200) 448 222 – www.innatwhitewell.com

23 rm – †£ 83/109 ††£ 162/189 – 1 suite

Rest – Carte £ 25/40

♦ 14C creeper-clad inn, high on the banks of the River Hodder, with panoramic valley views. Atmospheric bar and more formal restaurant. Classic menus of regionally inspired dishes. Spacious bedrooms; some traditional in style, with four-posters and antique baths.

WHITSTABLE – Kent – 504 X29 – pop. 30 195 — 9 C1

London 68 mi – Dover 24 mi – Maidstone 37 mi – Margate 12 mi

7 Oxford St ☎ (0871) 7162449, whitstableinformation@canterbury.gov.uk

ENGLAND

Whitstable Oyster Fishery Co.

Royal Native Oyster Stores, The Horsebridge ✉ CT5 1BU – ✆ (01227) 276 856 – www.oysterfishery.co.uk – Closed 25-26 December and Monday dinner
Rest – Seafood – *(booking essential)* Carte £ 30/47
♦ Former oyster warehouse right by the sea. Large, rough, wood-furnished interior with great informal atmosphere. Blackboard displays simply prepared seafood dishes. Fresh oysters at the counter.

at Seasalter Southwest : 2 mi by B 2205 – ✉ Whitstable

The Sportsman (Steve Harris)

Faversham Rd, Southwest : 2 mi following coast rd ✉ CT5 4BP – ✆ (01227) 273 370 – www.thesportsmanseasalter.co.uk – Closed 24 dinner to 26 December, Sunday dinner and Monday
Rest – *(booking advisable)* Carte £ 30/40
Spec. Crab risotto. Brill braised in vin jaune with smoked pork. Lemon tart & meringue ice cream
♦ Unassuming pub set by the sea wall, with a modest, open-plan interior. Concise daily blackboard menu offers simple-sounding dishes, which are rarely as straightforward as they seem. Preparation is precise; flavours, well-judged; and presentation, original.

WHORLTON – Durham – see Barnard Castle

WICKFORD – Essex – 504 V29 – see Basildon

WIGHT (Isle of) – Isle of Wight – 503 P/Q31 – pop. 138 500 6 A/B 3

Great Britain

from Ryde to Portsmouth (Hovertravel Ltd) frequent services daily (10 mn) – from Ryde to Portsmouth (Wightlink Ltd) frequent services daily (15 mn) – from East Cowes to Southampton (Red Funnel Ferries) frequent services daily (22 mn)

from East Cowes to Southampton (Red Funnel Ferries) frequent services daily (1 h)
– from Yarmouth to Lymington (Wightlink Ltd) frequent services daily (30 mn)
– from Fishbourne to Portsmouth (Wightlink Ltd) frequent services daily (35 mn)

Island★★

Osborne House, East Cowes★★ **AC** – Carisbrooke Castle, Newport★★ **AC** (Keep ≤★) – Brading★ (Roman Villa★ **AC**, St Mary's Church★, Nunwell House★ **AC**) – Shorwell : St Peter's Church★ (wall paintings★)

BONCHURCH – Isle of Wight 6 B3

Pond Café

✉ PO38 1RG – ✆ (01983) 855 666 – www.pondcafe.com – Closed January, 1 week April, 2 weeks November, Tuesday and Wednesday
Rest – Carte £ 22/30
♦ Intimate neighbourhood restaurant with candlelit, bistro-style interior. Attractive terrace with fairy lights overlooks duck pond. Generously proportioned, flavoursome dishes use island produce.

GODSHILL – Isle of Wight 6 B3

The Taverners

High Street ✉ PO38 3HZ – ✆ (01983) 840 707 – www.thetavernersgodshill.co.uk – Closed 3 weeks early January, Sunday dinner except bank holiday weekends and school holidays
Rest – Carte £ 18/25
♦ Whitewashed pub with cosy bar and two large dining rooms. Cooking is fresh and tasty, mixing traditional pub classics with more ambitious daily specials. Local island produce is a feature.

NITON – Isle of Wight 6 B3

The Hermitage

North : 3 m by Newport rd (A3020) ✉ PO38 2PD – ✆ (01983) 730 010 – www.hermitage-iow.co.uk

10 rm – †£ 45/90 ††£ 45/95

Rest – *(dinner only)* Menu £ 18

♦ Large 19C country house with 12 acres of gardens/woodland; set in pleasant rural location. Traditionally styled drawing room and peaceful lounge. Individually designed, well-equipped bedrooms. Elegant dining room displays a contemporary edge; classical menus.

SEAVIEW – Isle of Wight – pop. 2 286 6 B3

Priory Bay

Priory Dr., Southeast : 1.5 mi by B 3330 ✉ PO34 5BU – ✆ (01983) 613 146 – www.priorybay.co.uk

18 rm – †£ 105/225 ††£ 250/300 – 2 suites

Rest *The Restaurant* – Menu £ 25/35 – Carte £ 28/53

♦ Peaceful medieval priory with romantic shabby-chic interior, spacious guest areas and relaxed vibe. Bedrooms boast good facilities, modern bathrooms, and range from classic to nautical styles. Formal dining room displays impressive island murals dating from 1810.

Seaview

High St ✉ PO34 5EX – ✆ (01983) 612 711 – www.seaviewhotel.co.uk – Closed 1 week Christmas

25 rm – †£ 115/160 ††£ 135/160 – 3 suites

Rest *The Restaurant and Sunshine Room* – *(dinner only and lunch during summer) (booking essential)* Carte £ 20/33

♦ Long-standing, bay-windowed hotel covered in foliage. Interesting nautical-themed décor with paintings/model ships throughout. Smart, modern bedrooms in various styles; some in outbuildings. One bright and one more intimate room in restaurant; classical cooking.

ENGLAND

SHANKLIN – Isle of Wight – pop. 8 055 6 B3

Newport 9 mi

67 High St ✆ (01983) 813813, info@islandbreaks.co.uk

The Fairway Lake Sandown, ✆ (01983) 403 217

Rylstone Manor

Rylstone Gdns ✉ PO37 6RG – ✆ (01983) 862 806 – www.rylstone-manor.co.uk – Closed 28 December-31 January

9 rm – †£ 65/120 ††£ 130/160

Rest – *(dinner only)* Menu £ 30 **s**

♦ Originally a gift from the Queen to one of her physicians: an attractive part-Victorian house close to the historic gardens. Classical interior boasts heavy fabrics and warm, cosy feel. Bedrooms combine antique furniture and modern facilities. Formal dining room.

Foxhills without rest

30 Victoria Ave ✉ PO37 6LS – ✆ (01983) 862 329 – www.foxhillsofshanklin.co.uk – March-October

8 rm – †£ 65/75 ††£ 72/102

♦ Large, stone-built house in leafy residential avenue. Spacious, Victorian-styled lounge and modern breakfast room; comfy bedrooms in pastel hues. Jacuzzi, spa and beauty treatments available.

A red **Rest** mention denotes an establishment with an award for culinary excellence, ✿ (star) or ☺ (Bib Gourmand).

VENTNOR – **Isle of Wight** – **pop. 6 257** **6** B3

Newport 10 mi

Steephill Down Rd, (01983) 853 326

Royal

Belgrave Rd ✉ PO38 1JJ – (01983) 852 186 – www.royalhoteliow.co.uk – Closed 3-17 January

54 rm – £ 120/185 £ 260/280

Rest – *(dinner only and Sunday lunch October-June)* Menu £ 40

◆ Large Victorian building with mature lawned gardens and heated outdoor pool. Modern touches in lounge and bar. Traditionally styled bedrooms with good facilities: premier rooms are larger; some have lovely sea views. Classical menu served in formal dining room.

Hambrough with rm

rest, VISA

Hambrough Rd ✉ PO38 1SQ – (01983) 856 333 – www.thehambrough.com – Closed January, 1 week May and 2 weeks November

7 rm – £ 210 £ 300

Rest – *(closed Sunday and Monday) (booking essential)* Menu £ 26/55

Spec. Smoked eel with foie gras, pork belly and apple. Pigeon with oak smoked gnocchi, broad beans, peas and wild mushrooms. Rum baba with poached peach, lemon thyme and vanilla ice cream.

◆ Eye-catching clifftop villa with leather-furnished lounge and two warm, stylish dining rooms boasting excellent sea views. Skilful, confident chef uses top quality ingredients to create refined, modern dishes. Service is polite and knowledgeable. Smart, comfortable bedrooms feature quality linens and espresso machines.

ENGLAND

WOOTTON BRIDGE **6** B3

Lakeside Park

High St. ✉ PO33 4LJ – (01983) 882 266 – www.lakesideparkhotel.com

44 rm – £ 135/180 £ 135/280

Rest *Oyster Room* – *(closed Sunday dinner, Monday and Tuesday) (booking essential)* Menu £ 25 (lunch) – Carte dinner £ 44/49

Rest *Brasserie* – Carte £ 18/34

◆ Purpose-built hotel with lawned gardens. Stylish, comfortable, modern bedrooms offer a high level of facilities. Smart, fine dining restaurant with lounge and private terrace. Open-plan split-level bar, lounge and brassiere with large decked terrace and view over lake.

YARMOUTH – **Isle of Wight** – **pop. 855** **6** A3

Newport 10 mi

The Quay, PO41 OPQ (01983) 813 813

George

Quay St ✉ PO41 0PE – (01983) 760 331 – www.thegeorge.co.uk

19 rm – £ 120/150 £ 190/210

Rest *Brasserie* – Carte £ 34/55

◆ 17C townhouse on the waterfront; a former governor's house. Flag-floored reception with traditional panelled lounge and bar. Bedrooms feature wood-clad walls and smart, co-ordinating fabrics. Bright, modern brasserie with terrace offers seasonal European menus.

WIGHTON – **Norfolk** – **504** W25 – **see Wells-Next-The-Sea**

WILLIAN – **Herts.** – **504** T28 – **see Letchworth**

WILMINGTON – **Kent** – **504** V29 – **see Dartford**

WIMBORNE MINSTER – **Dorset** – **503** O31 – **pop. 14 844** **4** C3

London 112 mi – Bournemouth 10 mi – Dorchester 23 mi – Salisbury 27 mi

29 High St (01202) 886116, wimbornetic@eastdorset.gov.uk

Town★ - Minster★ – Priest's House Museum★ **AC**

Kingston Lacy★★ **AC**, NW : 3 mi by B 3082

XXX **Les Bouviers** with rm

Arrowsmith Rd, Canford Magna, Southeast : 2.25 mi by A 349 on A 341
✉ *BH21 3BD – ✆ (01202) 889 555 – www.lesbouviers.co.uk*
6 rm – †£ 165/182 ††£ 215/225
Rest – *(Closed Sunday dinner)* Menu £ 20 (lunch)/32 (weekday dinner) Carte £ 44/60
◆ Formerly a private residence, now a two-roomed restaurant overlooking a terrace and large lawned grounds. Small leather-furnished lounge; large rear function room. Formal team serve complex dishes from traditional menus. Smart, comfy, slightly kitsch bedrooms.

WIMBORNE ST GILES – Dorset – 504 O31 — 4 C3

London 107 mi – Bristol 72 mi – Southampton 32 mi – Reading 75 mi

The Bull Inn with rm

Coach Rd ✉ BH21 5NF – ✆ (01725) 517 300 – www.bullwsg.com
5 rm – †£ 45 ††£ 110/120 **Rest** – Carte £ 17/28
◆ Smart, modern, olive green pub with neutrally hued interior. Menus change daily and sometimes between services. Produce is sourced from their farm and within the county. Refined dishes use interesting ingredients and unusual cuts. Smart, stylish bedrooms.

WINCHCOMBE – Gloucestershire – 503 O28 – pop. 3 682 — 4 D1

London 100 mi – Birmingham 43 mi – Gloucester 26 mi – Oxford 43 mi
Town Hall, High St ✆ (01242) 602925, winchcombetic@tewkesbury.gov.uk

Westward without rest

Sudeley Lodge, East : 1.5 mi by Castle St on Sudeley Lodge/Parks/Farm rd
✉ *GL54 5JB – ✆ (01242) 604 372 – www.westward-sudeley.co.uk*
– April-November
3 rm – †£ 65/95 ††£ 100
◆ Secluded, personally run 18C farmhouse: elegant, wood-floored drawing room and charming sitting room, bedrooms share fine views of 550-acre estate and mature gardens.

XX **5 North St** (Marcus Ashenford)

5 North St ✉ GL54 5LH – ✆ (01242) 604 566 – Closed 2 weeks January, 1 week August, Monday, Tuesday lunch and Sunday dinner
Rest – Menu £ 26 (lunch) – Carte (dinner) £ 36/46
Spec. Chicken, Morteau and parsley sausage with brown sauce. Old Spot pork belly, mushy peas and pickled apples. White chocolate and cherries.
◆ Long-standing neighbourhood restaurant that's very personally run by a husband and wife team. Characterful low-beamed ceilings and burgundy walls create an intimate feel. Menus change with the seasons and feature British ingredients in tried-and-tested combinations. Dishes are precise, well-crafted and full of flavour.

XX **Wesley House** with rm

High St ✉ GL54 5LJ – ✆ (01242) 602 366 – www.wesleyhouse.co.uk
5 rm – †£ 65 ††£ 90/110
Rest – *(Closed Sunday dinner)* Menu £ 16/25 – Carte £ 20/39
◆ Hugely characterful part 15C house: dine amongst the beams or in the stylish glass-roofed extension. Tasty modern British cooking with original twists. Smilingly quaint rooms.

WINCHELSEA – East Sussex – 504 W31 Great Britain — 9 C3

London 64 mi – Brighton 46 mi – Folkestone 30 mi
Town★ – St Thomas Church (effigies★)

Strand House

Tanyard's Ln., East : 0.25 mi on A 259 ✉ TN36 4JT – ✆ (01797) 226 276 – www.thestrandhouse.co.uk
10 rm – †£ 85/125 ††£ 100/140
Rest – *(Closed Monday-Wednesday)* Menu £ 35 **s**
◆ 14C and 15C half-timbered house of low beams and inglenook fireplaces: carefully tended rear garden shaded by tall trees, snug lounge; well-kept rooms in traditional style. Simple homecooking.

ENGLAND

WINCHESTER – Hampshire – 503 P30 – pop. 41 420 Great Britain **6** B2

London 72 mi – Bristol 76 mi – Oxford 52 mi – Southampton 12 mi

Guildhall, High Street ✆ (01962) 840500, tourism@winchester.gov.uk

City★★ - Cathedral★★★ **AC** B – Winchester College★ **AC** B **B** – Castle Great Hall★ B **D** – God Begot House★ B **A**

St Cross Hospital★★ **AC** A

Hotel du Vin

rm, VISA AE

14 Southgate St ✉ SO23 9EF – ✆ (01962) 841 414 – www.hotelduvin.com

24 rm – †£ 140/165 ††£ 185/210, ☕ £ 13.95 B**i**

Rest ***Bistro*** – *(booking essential)* Carte £ 33/41

◆ Attractive red-brick Georgian house on the main road into town; the original Hotel du Vin. Shabby-chic lounge and characterful champagne bar. Stylish, minimalist bedrooms with good facilities and wine-themed art. Characterful bistro with wine-related memorabilia.

Giffard House without rest

VISA AE

50 Christchurch Rd ✉ SO23 9SU – ✆ (01962) 852 628 – www.giffardhotel.co.uk – Closed 24 December-2 January B**s**

12 rm ☕ – †£ 69/119 ††£ 89/135

◆ Imposing red-brick house. Spacious, classically styled guest areas with comfy drawing room and formal breakfast room. Individually styled bedrooms boast quality furnishings and good facilities.

29 Christchurch Road without rest

29 Christchurch Rd. ✉ SO23 9SU – ✆ (01962) 868 661 – www.fetherstondilke.com

3 rm ☕ – †£ 50/75 ††£ 75/90 B**v**

◆ Modern, Regency style guesthouse in attractive residential area close to town. Comfortable lounge and communal, linen-laid breakfast room. Simple bedrooms with plain walls and floral drapes.

Chesil Rectory

VISA AE

Chesil St. ✉ SO23 0HU – ✆ (01962) 851 555 – www.chesilrectory.co.uk – Closed 25 December and bank holidays B**r**

Rest – Menu £ 20 (lunch and early dinner Monday-Saturday) – Carte £ 23/32

◆ Timbered 15C house on edge of the town centre; its characterful interior taking in beamed ceilings and a large inglenook fireplace. Appealing menu of classically based dishes.

Brasserie Blanc

VISA AE

19-20 Jewry St ✉ SO23 8RZ – ✆ (01962) 810 870 – www.brasserieblanc.com – Closed 25 December B**x**

Rest – French – *(booking advisable)* Menu £ 15/19 – Carte £ 23/44

◆ Bustling informal brasserie in city centre. Spacious, split-level dining with 2 small terraces; open-plan kitchen on first-floor. Extensive menus of classical French dishes and local specials.

The Black Rat

VISA AE

88 Chesil St. ✉ SO23 0HX – ✆ (01962) 844 465 – www.theblackrat.co.uk – Closed 10 days spring, 10 days October and 2 weeks December-January B**a**

Rest – British – *(dinner only and lunch Saturday-Sunday)* Carte £ 32/37 **s**

Spec. Suckling pig terrine with cured foie gras and pancetta. Plaice, scallops, Salardaise potatoes and fennel. Strawberry bavarois, peppered strawberries and doughnuts.

◆ Unassuming exterior conceals quirky, bohemian-style inner with small bar, lounge and two-roomed restaurant. Refined, classically based cooking with Mediterranean influences and modern twists; local, seasonal produce. Four wicker-roofed booths on rear terrace.

The Wykeham Arms with rm

VISA AE

75 Kingsgate St ✉ SO23 9PE – ✆ (01962) 853 834 – www.fullers.co.uk

14 rm ☕ – †£ 70 ††£ 119 B**u**

Rest – *(booking essential)* Carte £ 25/35

◆ Appealingly shabby, 18C red-brick inn tucked away on a cobbled street and packed with memorabilia. Dishes range from simple soups, pies and pastas to more elaborate lobster. Bedrooms have good facilities: those upstairs are characterful; those opposite, quieter.

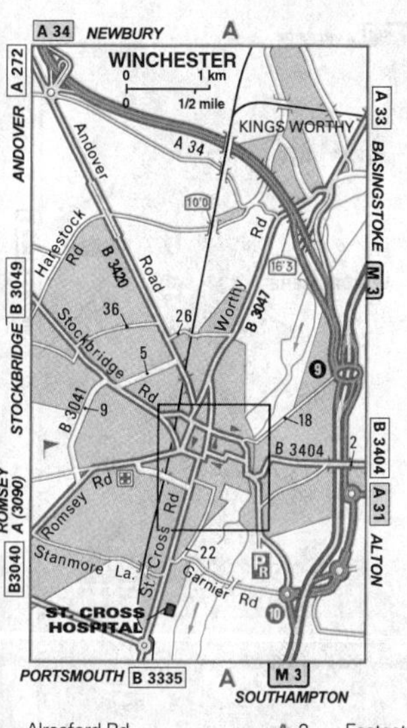

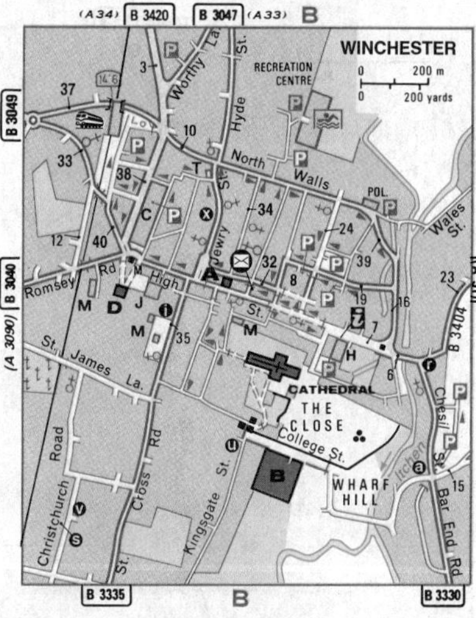

Alresford Rd	A 2	Eastgate St	B 16	St George's St	B 32
Andover Rd	B 3	Easton Lane	A 18	St Paul's Hill	B 33
Bereweeke Rd	A 5	East Hill	B 15	St Peter's St	B 34
Bridge St	B 6	Friarsgate	B 19	Southgate St	B 35
Broadway (The)	B 7	High St	B	Stockbridge Rd	B 37
Brooks Shopping Centre	B 8	Kingsgate Rd	A 22	Stoney Lane	A 36
Chilbolton Ave	A 9	Magdalen Hill	B 23	Sussex St	B 38
City Rd	B 10	Middle Brook St	B 24	Union St	B 39
Clifton Terrace	B 12	Park Rd	A 26	Upper High St	B 40

at Sparsholt Northwest : 3.5 mi by B 3049 - A – ✉ Winchester

Lainston House

Woodman Lane ✉ SO21 2LT – ✆ (01962) 776 088 – www.exclusivehotels.co.uk

49 rm – †£ 245 ††£ 245, ☕ £ 20 – 1 suite

Rest *Avenue* – Menu £ 32/45 – Carte approx. £ 51

◆ Impressive 17C manor house in mature grounds. Guest areas include a clubby, wood-panelled drawing room, more up-to-date country house lounge and small gym. Spacious bedrooms vary from classical to contemporary styles; all boast good facilities. One traditional and one modern dining room overlook an avenue of lime trees.

WINDERMERE – Cumbria – 502 L20 – pop. 7 941 Great Britain 21 A2

London 274 mi – Blackpool 55 mi – Carlisle 46 mi – Kendal 10 mi

Victoria St ✆ (015394) 46499, windermeretic@southlakeland.gov.uk

Lake Windermere★★ – Brockhole National Park Centre★ **AC**, NW : 2 mi by A 591

Plan on next page

Holbeck Ghyll

Holbeck Ln., Northwest : 3.25 mi by A 591 ✉ LA23 1LU – ✆ (015394) 32 375 – www.holbeckghyll.com – Closed 2-19 January

20 rm (dinner included) ☕ – †£ 225/250 ††£ 320/390 – 3 suites

Rest – *(booking advisable at lunch)* Menu £ 32/59

Spec. Honey glazed pork belly with spiced carrot. Label Anglaise chicken with creamed leeks, truffle risotto and cep purée. Chocolate soufflé with orange sorbet.

◆ Victorian hunting lodge in mature grounds, boasting excellent lake/country views. Traditional guest areas display antiques and heavy fabrics. Similarly styled bedrooms, some in annexes, have good facilities. Two-roomed restaurant; one with a view. Precise, confident, classical cooking employs quality local produce.

ENGLAND

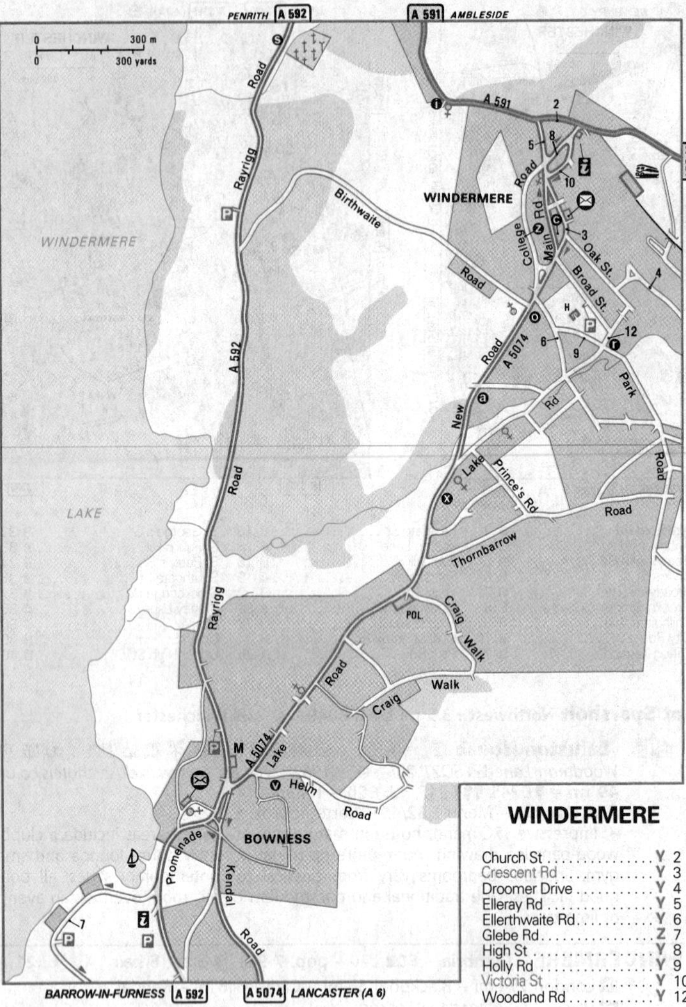

PENRITH A 592
A 591 AMBLESIDE
A 591 KENDAL
BARROW-IN-FURNESS A 592
A 5074 LANCASTER (A 6)

WINDERMERE

Miller Howe

Rayrigg Rd ✉ *LA23 1EY* – *✆ (015394) 42 536*
– *www.millerhowe.com*
– *Closed 2 weeks January* Ys

13 rm (dinner included) – ♦£ 120/180 ♦♦£ 260/290
– 2 suites

Rest – *(booking essential)* Menu £ 24 (lunch)/40 – Carte £ 33/42

♦ Superbly situated Victorian villa in mature gardens, looking down the lake to the mountains. Spacious, comfortable bedrooms display a classical style and contemporary edge. Fabulous views from conservatory. Split-level dining room offers traditional cooking.

The Windermere Suites without rest
New Rd ✉ LA23 2LA – ✆ (01539) 444 739 – www.windermeresuites.co.uk
7 rm ☕ – 🚹£ 135/195 🚹🚹£ 180/260 – 1 suite Yo
♦ Spacious Victorian house with seductive interior. Luxurious bedrooms boast bold modern décor, designer furniture and walk-in wardrobes. Huge bathrooms feature TVs and colour-changing lights. Breakfast served in your room.

Cedar Manor
Ambleside Rd ✉ LA23 1AX – ✆ (015394) 43 192 – www.cedarmanor.co.uk – Closed 3-27 January and 10-27 December Yi
10 rm ☕ – 🚹£ 75/100 🚹🚹£ 140/160 – 1 suite
Rest – *(dinner only)* Menu £ 38 – Carte £ 32/42
♦ Attractive slate house complete with cedar tree. Modern guest areas boast smart furnishings. Contemporary country house bedrooms display locally made furniture, feature walls and up-to-date facilities; some have lovely views. Appealing menus of local produce.

The Howbeck without rest
New Rd ✉ LA23 2LA – ✆ (015394) 44 739 – www.howbeck.co.uk Yo
11 rm ☕ – 🚹£ 70/90 🚹🚹£ 100/134
♦ Smart slate house 5min from town. Comfy leather-furnished lounge with honesty bar; black-themed breakfast room with interesting menu. Plain, modern décor in bedrooms; some feature four-posters.

Newstead without rest
New Rd ✉ LA23 2EE – ✆ (015394) 44 485 – www.newstead-guesthouse.co.uk – Closed 10 December-1 February Ya
9 rm ☕ – 🚹£ 50/80 🚹🚹£ 70/110
♦ Imposing Victorian house with spacious, classical interior; original features include servants' bells and ornate coving. Traditional bedrooms have sinks in the rooms; some boast four-posters.

Fir Trees without rest
Lake Rd ✉ LA23 2EQ – ✆ (015394) 42 272 – www.fir-trees.co.uk Zx
9 rm ☕ – 🚹£ 52/62 🚹🚹£ 64/72
♦ Welcoming guesthouse boasting original Victorian staircase and lovely tile-floored hallway. Surprisingly spacious interior includes simple, comfy bedrooms and wood-furnished breakfast room.

1 Park Rd
1 Park Rd ✉ LA23 2AN – ✆ (015394) 42 107 – www.1parkroad.com – Closed 25-26 December Yr
6 rm ☕ – 🚹£ 60/70 🚹🚹£ 100/104
Rest – *(residents only Saturday and Sunday)* Menu £ 23
♦ Larger corner property in residential part of town; run by friendly owners. Comfy lounge complete with piano. Good-sized, homely bedrooms with modern facilities and locally made toiletries. Simple, linen-laid dining room serving home-cooked meals by arrangement.

Jerichos with rm
College Rd ✉ LA23 1BX – ✆ (015394) 42 522 – www.jerichos.co.uk – Closed 3 weeks January, 3 weeks November, 24-26 December, and Thursday
10 rm ☕ – 🚹£ 40/85 🚹🚹£ 95/125 **Rest** – *(dinner only)* Yz
Carte £ 29/41
♦ Traditional Victorian house in town centre. Two-roomed restaurant with modern, understated styling. Concise, constantly evolving menus of ambitious dishes crafted from quality produce. Smart, contemporary bedrooms boast bold feature walls and good facilities.

Francine's
27 Main Rd ✉ LA23 1DX – www.francinesrestaurantwindermere.co.uk – ✆ (015394) 44 088 – Closed 1 January, 2 weeks end January, 2 weeks November-December, 25-26 December, Monday and dinner Sunday and Tuesday
Rest – *(booking essential at dinner)* Menu £ 13/18 – Carte £ 20/31 Yc
♦ Intimate neighbourhood restaurant decorated in red and cream. Simple, homely feel and friendly service. Straightforward classical cooking has French influences; chef is passionate about game.

ENGLAND

at Bowness-on-Windermere South : 1 mi - Z - ✉ Windermere

Gilpin Lodge

Crook Rd, Southeast : 2.5 mi by A 5074 on B 5284 ✉ LA23 3NE – ✆ (015394) 88 818 – www.gilpinlodge.co.uk
20 rm (dinner included) – £ 180 ££ 270/380
Rest – *(booking essential for non-residents)* Menu £ 28/53
◆ Family-run, country house hotel in appealing rural location, with comfy lounge, retro bar and landscaped terrace. Individually themed bedrooms, most in contemporary styles; vast garden suites boast their own hot tubs. Slick service. Four differently styled dining rooms, where classical cooking displays modern touches.

Linthwaite House

Crook Rd, South : 0.75 mi by A 5074 on B 5284 ✉ LA23 3JA – ✆ (015394) 88 600 – www.linthwaite.com
31 rm (dinner included) – £ 155/204 ££ 252/472
Rest – Menu £ 20 (lunch)/49 **s**
◆ Traditional country house in peaceful setting, overlooking the lake/fells. Stylish, modern lounges; funky bar with fish tank in wall. Smart bedrooms boast feature walls, mood lighting, double showers and views from the front. Contemporary, three-roomed restaurant.

Lindeth Howe

Lindeth Dr, Longtail Hill, South : 1.25 mi by A 5074 on B 5284 ✉ LA23 3JF – ✆ (015394) 45 759 – www.lindeth-howe.co.uk – Closed 3-14 January
34 rm – £ 95 ££ 280 – 1 suite
Rest *The Dining Room* – Menu £ 18/43 – Carte dinner £ 29/42
◆ Attractive country house once owned by Beatrix Potter. Homely, clubby bar and lounge; pleasant views from drawing room. Traditional bedrooms – top floor boasts the best views; suites are more contemporary. Large, classically styled restaurant has menus to match.

Storrs Hall

✉ LA23 3LG – ✆ (015394) 47 111 – www.elh.co.uk
29 rm – £ 122 ££ 328 – 1 suite
Rest *The Terrace* – Menu £ 20/44 **s** – Carte £ 41/52 **s**
◆ Part-Georgian mansion in 17 acres, with gardens leading to the lakeside. Variety of spacious, country house guest areas. Comfy, well-equipped bedrooms range from classical to bold, modern styles; some have lake views. Formal restaurant offers traditional menus.

Fayrer Garden House

Lyth Valley Rd, South : 1 mi on A 5074 ✉ LA23 3JP – ✆ (015394) 88 195 – www.fayrergarden.com
28 rm (dinner included) – £ 57/120 ££ 260/280
Rest *The Terrace* – *(dinner only) (booking essential for non-residents)* Menu £ 40 **s**
◆ Edwardian slate house on the hillside, affording lovely views over the lake and mountains. Comfy lounges with quality, cottagey furniture. Cosy, classical bedrooms with floral themes; some have whirlpool baths. Two-roomed restaurant offers traditional menus.

Gilpin Lake House without rest

Crook, Southeast : 3.75 mi by A 5074 and B 5284, turning right at Wild Boar Hotel ✉ LA8 8LN – ✆ (015394) 88 818 – www.gilpinlodge.co.uk
6 rm – £ 180 ££ 270/380
◆ Classic stone-built Lakeland house in magical location. Homely, comfortable lounge. Spacious bedrooms boast a modern country house style and either lake or countryside views. Set in 100 acres; lawned garden with hot tub. Dinner can be taken at Gilpin Lodge.

Angel Inn

Helm Rd ✉ LA23 3BU – ✆ (015394) 44 080 – www.the-angelinn.com – Closed 24-25 December Zv
13 rm – £ 75/90 ££ 170/180 **Rest** – Carte £ 21/33
◆ Cream-washed pub off the main street, boasting smart, contemporary bedrooms with iPod docks, flat screen TVs and modern bathrooms; the largest in an annexed 18C cottage. Large, semi-open-plan bar and wood-furnished, terraced garden offer classic pub-style dishes.

ENGLAND

Fair Rigg without rest
Ferry View, South : 0.5 mi on A 5074 ✉ LA23 3JB – ✆ (015394) 43 941 – www.fairrigg.co.uk – Closed 4 January -1 April and 21-29 December
6 rm – †£ 45/55 ††£ 78/90
◆ Late 19C detached house affording distant lake and hill views; run by friendly owners. Neat, linen-laid breakfast room. Immaculately kept bedrooms with quality furniture and good facilities.

at Troutbeck North : 4 mi by A 592 - Y – ✉ Windermere

The Queen's Head with rm
North : 0.75 mi on A 592 ✉ LA23 1PW – ✆ (01539) 432 174 – www.queensheadtroutbeck.co.uk – Closed dinner 25 December
15 rm – †£ 80 ††£ 150 **Rest** – Carte £ 23/40
◆ Amazingly characterful, memorabilia-filled pub in delightful Lakeland setting, with several interlinking rooms and unique four-poster bar counter. Extensive menu offers something for everyone. Smart bedrooms have strong comforts; 10 and 11 have the best views.

at Winster South : 4 mi on A 5074 – ✉ Windermere

Brown Horse Inn with rm
on A 5074 ✉ LA23 3NR – ✆ (01539) 443 443 – www.thebrownhorseinn.co.uk
9 rm – †£ 50/70 ††£ 90/100
Rest – Carte £ 19/30
◆ Shabby-chic coaching inn with lovely split-level terrace. Seasonal menus feature unfussy, generous dishes and more adventurous specials. Much of the produce is from their fields out the back. Bedrooms are a mix of classic and boutique styles; some have terraces.

ENGLAND

WINDLESHAM – Surrey – 504 S29 – pop. 4 103 — 7 C1

London 40 mi – Reading 18 mi – Southampton 53 mi

The Bee
School Rd ✉ GU20 6PD – ✆ (01276) 479 244 – www.thebeepub.co.uk – Closed Sunday dinner
Rest – Menu £ 16 (lunch) – Carte £ 22/35
◆ Stylish, modern pub with buzzing atmosphere. Daily changing menus showcase seasonal, local produce in precisely cooked dishes. Good value two course lunch. Summer barbecues.

The Brickmakers
Chertsey Rd, East : 1 mi on B 386 ✉ GU20 6HT – ✆ (01276) 472 267 – www.thebrickmakerswindlesham.co.uk
Rest – Menu £ 20 (Sunday) – Carte £ 20/30
◆ Red-brick pub in pretty location; its immaculately kept garden is quite a feature in summer. Simple bar menu and more interesting à la carte; dishes are good value and full of flavour.

WINDSOR – Windsor and Maidenhead – 504 S29 – pop. 30 568 — 11 D3

Great Britain

London 28 mi – Reading 19 mi – Southampton 59 mi

to Marlow, Maidenhead and Cookham (Salter Bros. Ltd) (summer only)

The Old Booking Hall, Central Station, Thames St ✆ (01753) 743900, windsor.tic@rbwm.gov.uk

Town★ – Castle★★★ : St George's Chapel★★★ **AC** (stalls★★★), State Apartments★★ **AC**, North Terrace (€★★) Z – Eton College★★ **AC** (College Chapel★★, Wall paintings★) Z

Windsor Park★ **AC** Y

Plan on next page

WINDSOR

Bexley St . . . . Z 2
Bolton Rd . . . . Y 3
Castle Hill . . . . Z 4
Charles St . . . . Z 5
Claremont Rd . . . . Z 6
Clarence Crescent . . . . Z 7
Clewer Crescent Rd . . . . Z 8
Datchet Rd . . . . Z 9
Goswell Rd . . . . Z 10
Grove Rd . . . . Z 12
High St . . . . Z 13
High St DATCHET . . . . Y 14
Horton Rd . . . . Y 16
Keats Lane . . . . Z 17
King Edward Court Centre . . . . . . Z
Peascod St . . . . Z 19
Ragstone Rd . . . . Y 20
River St . . . . Z 21
Sheet St Rd . . . . Y 22
Stovell Rd . . . . Z 23
Thames Ave . . . . Z 24
Thames St . . . . Z 25
Trinity Pl . . . . Z 27
Windsor Bridge . . . . Z 28
Windsor Rd . . . . Y 29

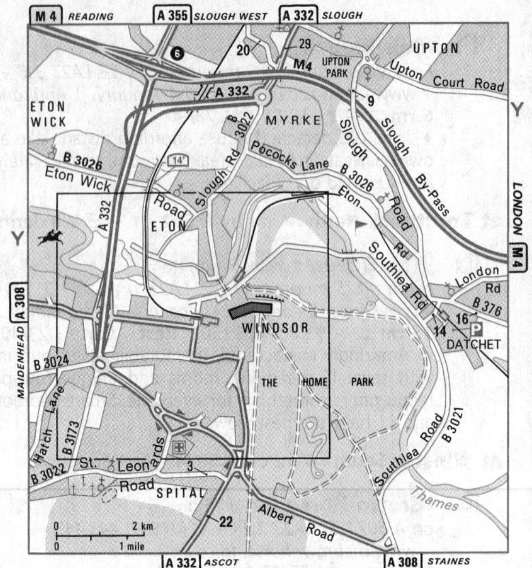

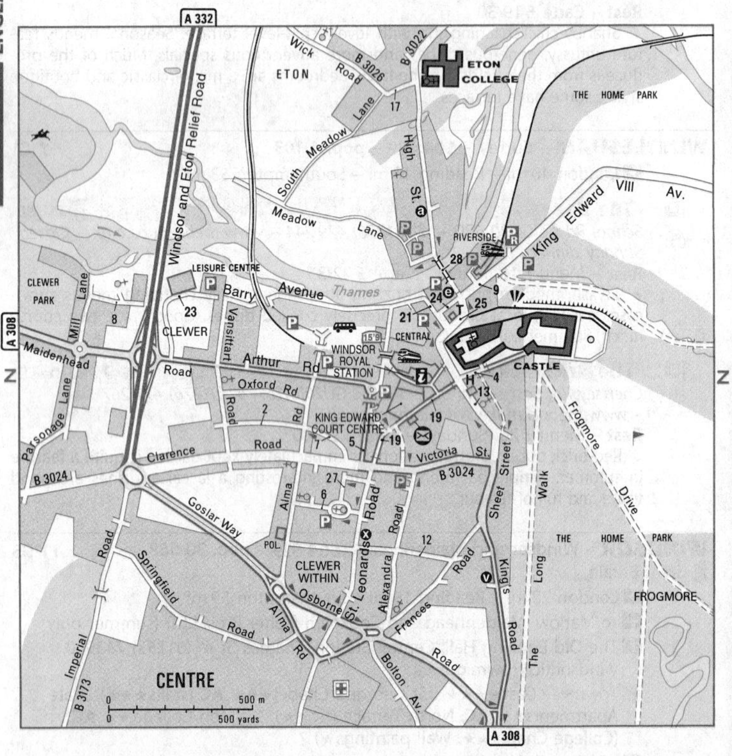

A 332
ETON
ETON COLLEGE
THE HOME PARK
Windsor and Eton Relief Road
South Meadow Lane
Meadow Lane
High St.
King Edward VIII Av.
RIVERSIDE
LEISURE CENTRE
Barry Avenue
Thames
CLEWER PARK
Mill Lane
CLEWER
Vansittart Road
WINDSOR ROYAL STATION
CENTRAL
CASTLE
A 308
Maidenhead Road
Arthur Rd
Oxford Rd
KING EDWARD COURT CENTRE
Victoria St.
B 3024
Clarence Road
Parsonage Lane
Goslar Way
Alma Rd
St. Leonards Road
Alexandra Road
Sheet Street
Frogmore Drive
The Long Walk
THE HOME PARK
FROGMORE
POL.
CLEWER WITHIN
Osborne Rd
Frances Road
Kings Road
Springfield Road
Imperial Road
Bolton Av.
B 3173
CENTRE
0 500 m
0 500 yards
A 308

ENGLAND

Sir Christopher Wren's House
Thames St ✉ SL4 1PX – ☎ (01753) 861 354
– www.sirchristopherwren.co.uk Ze
93 rm – †£ 80/230 ††£ 85/230, ☕ £ 11.50 – 2 suites
Rest *Strok's* – Menu £ 29 (lunch) **s** – Carte £ 39/53 **s**
♦ Built by Wren as his family home in 1676, he supposedly haunts his old rooms. On banks of Thames close to station and Windsor Castle. Antique furnished in original building. Restaurant has views of Thames and elegant dining terrace.

Royal Adelaide
46 Kings Rd ✉ SL4 2AG – ☎ (01753) 863 916 – www.theroyaladelaide.com
42 rm ☕ – †£ 69/140 ††£ 99/170 **Rest** – Carte £ 26/50 Z**v**
♦ Three adjoining Georgian houses with light blue painted façade. Just outside town centre. Rooms vary in shapes and sizes, all in individual traditional style. Dining room offers daily changing, international menus.

Christopher
110 High St, Eton ✉ SL4 6AN – ☎ (01753) 852 359 – www.thechristopher.co.uk
33 rm – †£ 99/155 ††£ 144/174, ☕ £ 12 **Rest** – Carte £ 26/32 Z**a**
♦ Refurbished 17C former coaching inn close to Eton College and perfect for walking to the castle. Contemporary bedrooms split between main building and mews annex. Simple homecooking.

Windsor Grill
65 St Leonards Rd ✉ SL4 3BX – ☎ (01753) 859 658 – www.awtrestaurants.com
– Closed 25-26 December and Monday lunch Z**x**
Rest – Beef specialities – Menu £ 15 (lunch) – Carte £ 27/42
♦ Rustic Victorian property owned by Antony Worrall Thompson. Wide menu displays classic comfort dishes, including well flavoured hung beef and pork/chicken from his farm.

The Greene Oak
Oakley Grn, West : 3 mi by A 308 on B 3024 ✉ SL4 5UW – ☎ (01753) 864 294
www.thegreeneoak.co.uk – Closed 25 December, Sunday and dinner bank holiday
Rest – *(booking advisable)* Menu £ 15 (lunch except Friday and Sunday) Carte £ 22/39
♦ Set on the west side of Windsor, with appealing green-hued décor and contemporary soft furnishings. Seasonal menu of tasty European dishes. Popular terrace for alfresco dining.

WINEHAM – W. Sussex – **504** T31 – see Henfield

WINFORTON – County of Herefordshire – **503** L27 – see Hereford

---

WINSFORD – Somerset – 503 J30 – pop. 270 – ✉ Minehead 3 A2

London 194 mi – Exeter 31 mi – Minehead 10 mi – Taunton 32 mi
Village ★
Exmoor National Park ★★

Royal Oak Inn with rm
Exmoor National Park ✉ TA24 7JE – ☎ (01643) 851 455
– www.royaloakexmoor.co.uk
8 rm ☕ – †£ 70 ††£ 150 **Rest** – Menu £ 25 (dinner) – Carte £ 18/28
♦ Delightful 12C thatched pub set by a ford in a picturesque Exmoor village. Arriving exactly as described, British dishes use homemade, local and seasonal produce. Smart, individually styled bedrooms; private in-room therapy treatments available.

WINSTER – Cumbria – **502** L20 – see Windermere

WINTERBOURNE STEEPLETON – Dorset – **503** M31 – see Dorchester

---

WINTERINGHAM – North Lincolnshire – 502 S22 – pop. 4 714 23 C3
– ✉ Scunthorpe

London 176 mi – Kingston-upon-Hull 16 mi – Sheffield 67 mi

XXXX **Winteringham Fields** with rm

1 Silver St ✉ DN15 9ND – ✆ (01724) 733 096 – www.winteringhamfields.com
8 rm – †£ 140/180 ††£ 180/220, ☕ £ 20 – 2 suites
Rest – *(closed Sunday-Monday) (booking essential for non-residents)* Menu £ 40 – Carte approx. £ 75

◆ Characterful 16C house with pleasant garden, elegant dining room and several antique-filled private rooms. Self-taught chef adopts a complex, modern approach to cooking, offering a concise à la carte and daily 6 course 'Menu Surprise'. Comfortable, antique-furnished bedrooms, with breakfast in spacious rear dining room.

WISWELL – 502 M22 – see Clitheroe

WITHERSLACK – Cumbria – 502 L21 — 21 A3

London 266 mi – Liverpool 83 mi – Manchester 78 mi – Bradford 65 mi

The Derby Arms with rm

✉ LA11 6RH – ✆ (015395) 52 207 – www.thederbyarms.co.uk
6 rm ☕ – †£ 65 ††£ 85 **Rest** – Carte £ 17/25

◆ Substantial 19C coaching inn with characterful shabby-chic interior, beams, open fires and a small community shop. Cooking is rustic yet refined and puddings are suitably old-fashioned. Classical bedrooms display antiques; some boast views or roll-top baths.

WITNEY – Oxfordshire – 503 P28 – pop. 22 765 — 10 B2

London 69 mi – Gloucester 39 mi – Oxford 13 mi

Town Centre Shop, 3 Welch Way ✆ (01993) 775802, witney.vic@westoxon.gov.uk

The Fleece with rm

11 Church Grn. ✉ OX28 4AZ – ✆ (01993) 892 270 – www.fleecewitney.co.uk
10 rm ☕ – †£ 80 ††£ 90 **Rest** – Carte £ 19/30

◆ Smart Georgian pub with worthy values, set overlooking the green. Using local, seasonal, free range produce, menus offer a choice of dish size and appealing 'create your own' deli boards. Bedrooms are bright, modern and spacious.

at North Leigh Northeast : 3 mi by A 4095 – ✉ Oxfordshire

Gorselands Hall without rest

Boddington Ln. , North : 0.75 mi by A 4095 on East End Rd ✉ OX29 6PU – ✆ (01993) 882 292 – www.gorselandshall.com – Closed 1 January, 1 week March, 1 week June, 2 weeks October, 24-26 December
6 rm ☕ – †£ 42/56 ††£ 68/70

◆ Spacious house in countryside setting, halfway between Woodstock and Witney. Sitting room with French windows, snooker table, books and games. Neat bedrooms in uniform style.

at South Leigh Southeast : 3 mi by A 40 – ✉ Witney

XX **Mason Arms**

✉ OX29 6XN – ✆ (01993) 702 485 – Closed August, 25 December, Sunday dinner and Monday
Rest – Carte £ 37/75

◆ Privately owned 15C thatched inn with unique style and much individuality. Dimly lit, with intimate atmosphere. French influenced traditional cooking and extensive wine list.

WIVETON – Norfolk – see Blakeney

WOBURN – Bedfordshire – 504 S28 – pop. 1 534 – ✉ Milton Keynes — 12 A2

Great Britain

London 49 mi – Bedford 13 mi – Luton 13 mi – Northampton 24 mi

Woburn Abbey★★

Inn at Woburn

George St ✉ *MK17 9PX – ☎ (01525) 290 441 – www.woburn.co.uk*
50 rm – †£ 80/145 ††£ 135/165, ☕ £ 11.95 – 5 suites
Rest *Olivier's* – Menu £ 14 (lunch) – Carte dinner £ 25/35
◆ 18C coaching inn, part of Woburn Estate with its abbey and 3000 acre park. Pleasant modern furnishings and interior décor. Tastefully decorated rooms: book a Cottage suite. Classic dishes in contemporary Olivier's.

Paris House

Woburn Park, Southeast : 2.25 mi on A 4012 ✉ *MK17 9QP – ☎ (01525) 290 692 – www.parishouse.co.uk – Closed dinner 24 December-8 January, Sunday dinner, Tuesday lunch and Monday*
Rest – *(booking essential)* Menu £ 29/59
Spec. Scallops and globe artichokes with lemon and cockle dressing. Rib of beef with snail and bone marrow fricassee, béarnaise sauce. Rhubarb and custard pain perdu with vanilla mousse.
◆ Striking black and white timbered house, originally built in Paris and reassembled in this charming location, where deer wander freely. Classic dishes are given an imaginative modern makeover, with confident flavours and artistic presentation. Polished, unobtrusive service.

The Birch

20 Newport Rd., North : 0.5 mi on A 5130 ✉ *MK17 9HX – ☎ (01525) 290 295 – www.birchwoburn.com – Closed 25-26 December, 1 January and Sunday dinner*
Rest – *(booking essential)* Carte £ 18/39
◆ Smart, well run pub whose traditional façade masks a bright, modern interior with contemporary furnishings. Menu offers old favourites, daily specials and grills by the ounce.

WOKING – Surrey – 504 S30 — 7 C1

London 34 mi – Farnborough 14 mi – Guildford 7 mi

Red Lion

High St, Horsell, Northwest : 1.5 mi by A 324 ✉ *GU21 4SS – ☎ (01483) 768 497 – www.redlionhorsell.co.uk*
Rest – *(booking advisable)* Carte £ 15/25
◆ A modern take on the traditional pub, with all-day dining, plenty of outside seating and occasional live music. Traditional pub food, with sharing plates and fish dishes the highlights.

WOLD NEWTON – East Riding of Yorkshire — 23 D2

London 229 mi – Bridlington 25 mi – Scarborough 13 mi

Wold Cottage

South : 0.5 mi on Thwing rd ✉ *YO25 3HL – ☎ (01262) 470 696 – www.woldcottage.com*
5 rm ☕ – †£ 60/75 ††£ 110/150 **Rest** – Menu 25
◆ Georgian former farmhouse set in many rural acres; a country house style prevails with antique furniture in all areas. Spacious, individually named rooms: two in barn annex.

WOLSINGHAM – Durham – 502 O19 – pop. 2 020 — 24 A3

London 269 mi – Newcastle upon Tyne 38 mi – Sunderland 30 mi – Middlesbrough 34 mi

The Mill Race

✉ *DL13 3AP – ☎ (01388) 526 551 – www.themillracehotel.co.uk – Closed 26 December, 1 January, Monday and Sunday dinner*
Rest – *(dinner only and lunch Friday and Sunday)* Menu £ 16 (dinner) – Carte £ 20/35
◆ Situated in centre of picturesque town; the gateway to Weardale. Well-presented, flavourful restaurant-style dishes. Good value fixed price menu midweek and early Saturday evenings.

WOLVERCOTE – Oxfordshire – 504 Q28 – see Oxford

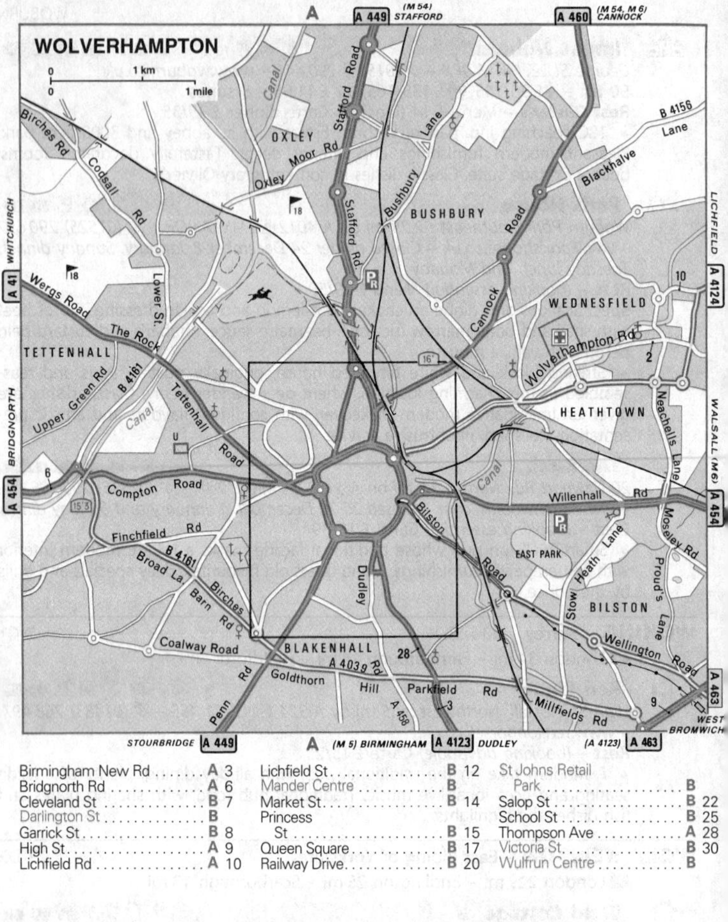

WOLVERHAMPTON

Birmingham New Rd	A 3	Lichfield St	B 12	St Johns Retail Park	B
Bridgnorth Rd	A 6	Mander Centre	B	Salop St	B 22
Cleveland St	B 7	Market St	B 14	School St	B 25
Darlington St	B	Princess St	B 15	Thompson Ave	A 28
Garrick St	B 8	Queen Square	B 17	Victoria St	B 30
High St	A 9	Railway Drive	B 20	Wulfrun Centre	B
Lichfield Rd	A 10				

WOLVERHAMPTON – West Midlands – 502 N26 – pop. 251 462   19 C2

London 132 mi – Birmingham 15 mi – Liverpool 89 mi – Shrewsbury 30 mi

18 Queen Sq ✆ (01902) 312051, visitorinfo@wolverhampton.gov.uk

Plan of Enlarged Area : see Birmingham pp. 4 and 5

XX Bilash

No 2 Cheapside ✉ WV1 1TU
– ✆ (01902) 427 762
– www.thebilash@co.uk
– Closed 1 January, 25-26 December and Sunday   B**c**

Rest – Indian – Menu £ 12/19 – Carte £ 29/48

♦ Long-standing, personally-run restaurant with several family generations involved. Appealing menu of freshly cooked Indian dishes and tempting specials. Strictly local and homemade produce.

When you make a booking, check the price and category of the room.

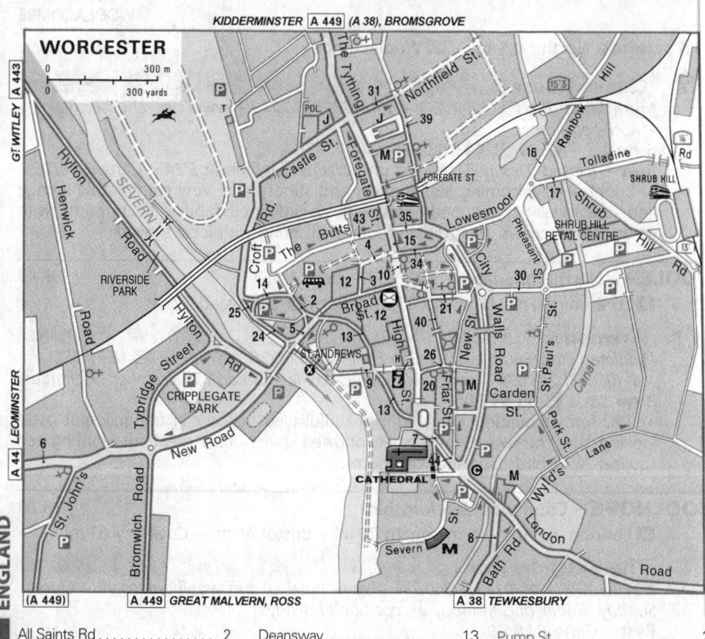

at Stonehall Common Southeast : 5.75 mi by A 38 and Norton rd.

The Inn at Stonehall

✉ WR5 3QG – ✆ (01905) 820 462 – www.theinnatstonehall.com – *Closed first week January, Sunday dinner and Monday*
Rest – Menu £ 15 (lunch) – Carte £ 25/27
◆ Smart, modern dining pub in a peaceful hamlet, with comfy lounge, airy dinin room and lovely views. Concise menus feature well-prepared, flavoursome, sea sonal dishes; desserts a speciality.

WORFIELD – Shrops. – see Bridgnorth

WORKSOP – Nottinghamshire – **502** Q24 – pop. 39 072 **16** B

London 160 mi – Sheffield 20 mi – Nottingham 37 mi – Rotherham 17 mi

Browns without rest

The Old Orchard Cottage, Holbeck Ln. , Southwest : 4.5 mi by A 60 ✉ *S80 3NF* – ✆ *(01909) 720 659 – www.brownsholbeck.co.uk – Closed 25 December*
3 rm – †£ 57 ††£ 85
◆ Cosy, comfortable, individually-decorated bedrooms in cottage dating fron 1730 and named after the owners. Mature orchard and tranquil garden. Compre hensive breakfast.

WORTH – Kent – **504** Y30 – see Deal

WOOBURN COMMON – Bucks. – **504** S29 – see Beaconsfield

WOODBRIDGE – Suffolk – **504** X27 – pop. 10 956 **15** D3

London 81 mi – Great Yarmouth 45 mi – Ipswich 8 mi – Norwich 47 mi
Cretingham Grove Farm, ✆ (01728) 685 275
Seckford Great Bealings Seckford Hall Rd, ✆ (01394) 388 000

Seckford Hall

rm, rest,

Southwest : 1.25 mi by A 12 ✉ *IP13 6NU* – ✆ *(01394) 385 678 – www.seckford.co.uk – Closed 25 December*
25 rm – †£ 85/150 ††£ 150/220, £ 13.95 – 7 suites
Rest – *(Closed Monday lunch)* Menu £ 17 (weekday lunch)/33 (dinner) **s**
◆ Reputedly once visited by Elizabeth I, a part Tudor country house set in attractive gardens. Charming traditionally panelled public areas. Comfortable bedrooms. Local lobster proudly served in smart dining room.

Riverside

Quayside ✉ IP12 1BH – ✆ (01394) 382 587 – www.theriverside.co.uk – Closed 25-26 December, 1 January and Sunday dinner

Rest – *(booking essential)* Menu £ 30 (weekday dinner) – Carte £ 17/41

◆ Not just a restaurant, but a cinema too! Floor to ceiling windows and busy terrace. Appealing menus offer modern, well-presented cooking. Set menu includes ticket for film.

Crown with rm

Thoroughfare ✉ IP12 1AD – ✆ (01394) 384 242 – www.thecrownatwoodbridge.co.uk – Closed dinner 25 December

10 rm – †£ 95 ††£ 180 **Rest** – Carte £ 22/35

◆ Modern dining pub in town centre, with smart granite-floored bar and four different dining areas. Extensive menu makes good use of local produce. Well presented, rustic cooking and polite, friendly service. Stylish, contemporary bedrooms boast good facilities.

WOODHOUSE EAVES – Leics. – 503 Q25 – see Loughborough

WOODSTOCK – Oxfordshire – 503 P28 – pop. 2 389 Great Britain 10 B2

London 65 mi – Gloucester 47 mi – Oxford 8 mi

Oxfordshire Museum, Park St ✆ (01993) 813276, woodstock.vic@westoxon.gov.uk

Blenheim Palace★★★ (Park★★★) **AC**

Bear

Park St ✉ OX20 1SZ – ✆ (0844) 879 9143 – www.macdonald-hotels.co.uk/bear

47 rm – †£ 120 ††£ 120/250 – 7 suites **Rest** – Menu £ 32

◆ Characterful part 16C inn. Original personality and charm; oak beams, open fires and stone walls. Particularly comfortable contemporarily furnished rooms. Dining room exudes an elegant air.

Feathers

Market St ✉ OX20 1SX – ✆ (01993) 812 291 – www.feathers.co.uk

16 rm – †£ 125/195 ††£ 195/225 – 4 suites

Rest – *(Closed Sunday dinner and Monday lunch) (booking essential)* Menu £ 45 – Carte £ 45/58

◆ Stylish 17C house boasting individually styled bedrooms with boutique twists: some have feature walls; others, modern art and bold fabrics. Bar-lounge and terrace offer casual menu. Formal dining room serves classically based dishes with a creative, original edge.

The Kings Arms

19 Market St ✉ OX20 1SU – ✆ (01993) 813 636 – www.kings-hotel-woodstock.co.uk

15 rm – †£ 75 ††£ 140 **Rest** – Carte £ 21/40

◆ Keenly run contemporary hotel in heart of busy market town. Immaculately kept, with sleek, spacious bedrooms – named after Kings – displaying golden wood, starched linen and plump cushions. Informal bar-restaurant offers local, seasonal British dishes.

WOOFFERTON – Shrops. – 503 L26 – see Ludlow

WOOKEY HOLE – Somerset – 503 L30 – see Wells

WOOLACOMBE – Devon – 503 H30 2 C1

London 237 mi – Barnstaple 15 mi – Exeter 55 mi

The Esplanade ✆ (01271) 870553, info@woolacombetourism.co.uk

Exmoor National Park★★ - Mortehoe★★ (St Mary's Church★, Morte Point - vantage point★) N : 0.5 mi – Ilfracombe : Hillsborough (<★★) **AC**, Capstone Hill★ (<★), St Nicholas' Chapel (<★) **AC**, NE : 5.5 mi by B 3343 and A 361. Braunton★ (St Brannock's Church★, Braunton Burrows★), S : 8 mi by B 3343 and A 361

at Mortehoe North : 0.5 mi – ✉ Woolacombe

Cleeve House

North Morte Rd. ✉ EX34 7ED – ✆ (01271) 870 719 – www.cleevehouse.co.uk – April-September

6 rm – †£ 59/61 ††£ 88/92

Rest – *(closed 21 July-31 August and Wednesday)* Menu £ 24 – Carte £ 28/35

◆ Bright and welcoming feel in décor and atmosphere. Very comfortable lounge and individually styled bedrooms with co-ordinated fabrics. Rear rooms with great country views. Neat dining room; walls hung with local artwork.

WOOLER – Northumberland – 502 N17 – pop. 1 857 24 A1

London 330 mi – Alnwick 17 mi – Berwick-on-Tweed 17 mi

Firwood without rest

Middleton Hall, South : 1.75 mi by Earle rd on Middleton Hall rd ✉ NE71 6RD – ✆ (01668) 283 699 – www.firwoodhouse.co.uk – Closed 23 December -31 January

3 rm – †£ 60 ††£ 85

◆ 19C former hunting lodge with beautiful tiled hall, set in tranquil spot overlooking the Cheviots. Comfy bay-windowed guest areas great for sighting red squirrels/wild birds. Spacious bedrooms.

WOOLHOPE – County of Herefordshire 18 B3

London 138 mi – Birmingham 70 mi – Bristol 66 mi – Coventry 81 mi

The Butchers Arms

✉ HR1 4RF – ✆ (01432) 860 281 – www.butchersarmswoolhope.co.uk – Closed Sunday dinner and Monday except bank holidays

Rest – Carte £ 19/29

◆ Stephen Bull's third pub is an attractive, half-timbered 16C inn, with a pretty garden by a babbling brook and charming bars with low-slung beams and open fires. Daily changing menu of honest, well-priced, regional dishes; local lamb and cheese the highlights.

WOOLSTHORPE-BY-BELVOIR – Lincs. – 502 R25 – see Grantham

WOOTTON BRIDGE – 503 P31 – see WIGHT (Isle of)

WORCESTER – Worcestershire – 503 N27 – pop. 94 029 Great Britain 18 B3

London 124 mi – Birmingham 26 mi – Bristol 61 mi – Cardiff 74 mi

The Guildhall, High St ✆ (01905) 726311, touristinfo@cityofworcester.gov.uk

Perdiswell Park Bilford Rd, ✆ (01905) 754 668

City★ – Cathedral★★ – Royal Worcester Porcelain Works★ (Museum of Worcester Porcelain★) **M**

The Elgar Trail★

Plan on next page

Glasshouse

Sidbury ✉ WR1 2HU – ✆ (01905) 611 120 – www.theglasshouse.co.uk – Closed Sunday and bank holidays **c**

Rest – Menu £ 17 – Carte £ 26/44

◆ Leather furnished lounge. Stylish chocolate and blue hued dining areas; the first floor has glass wall and views of city. Brasserie style menu offers modern British dishes.

Brown's

24 Quay St ✉ WR1 2JJ – ✆ (01905) 26 263 – www.brownsrestaurant.co.uk – Closed Monday and dinner Sunday **x**

Rest – Menu £ 15 (lunch) – Carte £ 27/46

◆ Converted riverside corn mill. Spacious, open interior as befits the building's origins. Impressive collection of modern artwork. Mainly British dishes are renowned locally.

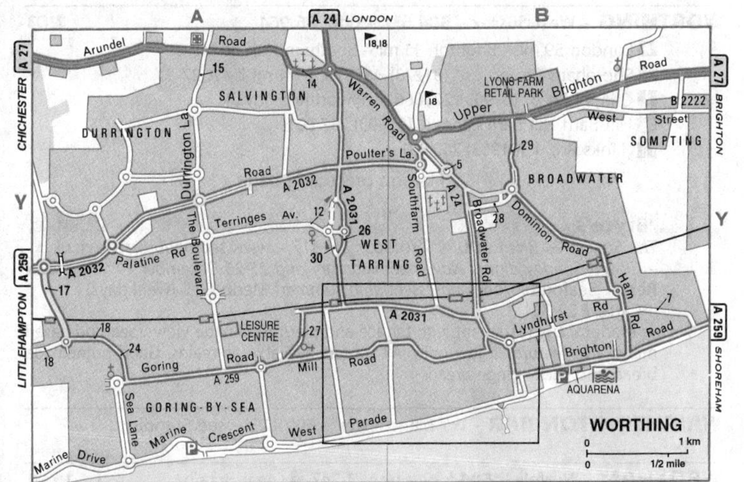

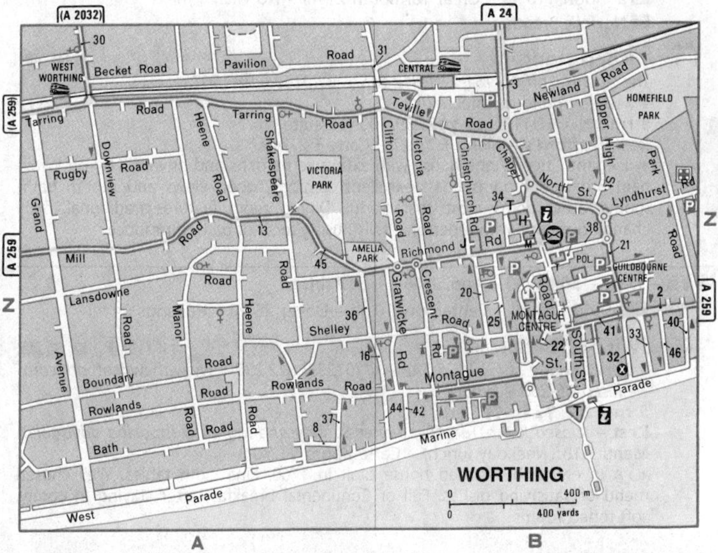

A
B
A 24 LONDON
A 27 CHICHESTER
A 27 BRIGHTON
A 259 LITTLEHAMPTON
A 259 SHOREHAM
Y
Arundel Road
Upper Brighton Road
LYONS FARM RETAIL PARK
B 2222
West Street
SOMPTING
SALVINGTON
DURRINGTON
BROADWATER
Durrington La.
Warren Road
Poulter's La.
A 2032
Road
Terringes Av.
The Boulevard
A 2031
WEST TARRING
Southfarm Road
Broadwater Rd
Dominion Road
Ham Rd
Palatine Rd
A 2032
LEISURE CENTRE
A 2031
Lyndhurst Rd
Road
Brighton
Goring Road
Mill Road
A 259
Sea Lane
GORING-BY-SEA
AQUARENA
Marine Crescent
West Parade
Marine Drive
WORTHING
0 1 km
0 1/2 mile

(A 2032)
A 24
(A 259)
A 259
A 259
N
WEST WORTHING
Becket Road
Pavilion Road
CENTRAL
Tarring Road
Tarring Road
Teville Road
Newland Road
HOMEFIELD PARK
Heene Road
Shakespeare Road
Downview Road
VICTORIA PARK
Clifton Road
Victoria Road
Christchurch Rd
Chapel Rd
Upper High St
Park Rd
North St.
Lyndhurst Rd
Rugby Road
Grand Avenue
Mill Road
AMELIA PARK
Richmond Rd
POL.
GUILDBOURNE CENTRE
Lansdowne Road
Manor Road
Heene Road
Gratwicke Rd
Crescent Road
MONTAGUE CENTRE
South St.
Shelley Road
Montague St.
Boundary Road
Rowlands Road
Rowlands Road
Road
Road
Bath Road
Marine Parade
West Parade
WORTHING
0 400 m
0 400 yards
A
B

WORTHING – West Sussex – 504 S31 – pop. 96 964 7 D3

London 59 mi – Brighton 11 mi – Southampton 50 mi

Shoreham Airport : ✆ (01273) 467373, E : 4 mi by A 27 BY

Chapel Rd ✆ (01903) 221066, tic@worthing.gov.uk

Hill Barn Hill Barn Lane, ✆ (01903) 237 301

Links Rd, ✆ (01903) 260 801

Plan on preceding page

Bryce's

The Steyne ✉ BN11 3DU – ✆ (01903) 214 317 – www.seafoodbrasserie.co.uk – Closed Sunday dinner November-February and 25-26 December BZx

Rest – Seafood – *(booking essential in summer)* Menu £ 15 (weekdays) – Carte £ 22/30

◆ Modern, airy restaurant with terrace and pier/promenade views. Seafood based menu also features a few grills. All starters available as mains. Good homemade bread and sticky gingerbread.

WRIGHTINGTON BAR – Gtr Manchester – 502 L23 – see Standish

WROXHAM – Norfolk – 504 Y25 – pop. 3 247 Great Britain 15 D1

London 118 mi – Great Yarmouth 21 mi – Norwich 7 mi

Norfolk Broads★

ENGLAND

Broad House

The Avenue, off A 1151 ✉ NR12 8TS – ✆ (01603) 783 567 – www.broadhousehotel.co.uk

8 rm – †£ 110/180 ††£ 239/300 – 1 suite

Rest *Trafford's* – Menu £ 23/27 – Carte £ 27/49

◆ Elegant Queen Anne house with extensive gardens and private jetty on Wroxham Broad. Bedrooms boast excellent comforts, good views and superb bathrooms; attic rooms most characterful. Dining room features traditional, daily changing menus with a personal twist, using local or garden produce.

WYE – Kent – 504 W30 – pop. 2 066 – ✉ Ashford 9 C2

London 60 mi – Canterbury 10 mi – Dover 28 mi – Hastings 34 mi

Wife of Bath with rm

4 Upper Bridge St ✉ TN25 5AF – ✆ (01233) 812 232 – www.thewifeofbath.com – Closed 25-26 December

5 rm – †£ 75 ††£ 115

Rest – *(closed lunch Tuesday, dinner Sunday and Monday) (booking advisable)* Menu £ 18 (weekday lunch) – Carte approx. £ 30

◆ A lovely timber-framed house built in 1760. Fine cloth tables. Well chosen menu of satisfying dishes. Full or Continental breakfast after staying in comfy, soft-toned rooms.

YARM – Stockton-on-Tees – 502 P20 – pop. 8 929 24 B3

London 242 mi – Middlesbrough 8 mi – Newcastle upon Tyne 47 mi

Judges Country House

Kirklevington Hall, Kirklevington, South : 1.5 mi on A 67 ✉ TS15 9LW – ✆ (01642) 789 000 – www.judgeshotel.co.uk

21 rm – †£ 85/175 ††£ 135/205, £ 14.50

Rest – Menu £ 24 (lunch) – Carte £ 47/66

◆ Former Victorian judge's residence surrounded by gardens. Welcoming panelled bar and spacious lounge filled with antiques and curios. Attractive rooms with a host of extras. Conservatory dining room overlooks the gardens.

YARMOUTH – I.O.W. – 503 P31 – see Wight (Isle of)

YATTENDON – West Berkshire – 503 Q29 – pop. 288 – ✉ Newbury 10 B3

London 61 mi – Oxford 23 mi – Reading 12 mi

The Royal Oak with rm

The Square ✉ RG18 0UF – ✆ (01635) 201 325 – www.royaloakyattendon.com
5 rm – ♦£ 85 ♦♦£ 85
Rest – *(booking advisable)* Menu £ 15 (weekday lunch) – Carte £ 20/30
♦ Pretty redbrick pub with attractive gardens, in picture postcard village just off the M4; a beamed bar with roaring fire at its hub. Honest British dishes and traditional puddings; Sunday roast of 28-day aged rib of beef. Comfy bedrooms in country house style.

at Frilsham South : 1 mi by Frilsham rd on Bucklebury rd – ✉ Yattendon

The Pot Kiln

✉ RG18 0XX – ✆ (01635) 201 366 – www.potkiln.org – Closed 25 December and Tuesday
Rest – Menu £ 20 (weekday lunch) – Carte £ 26/30
♦ Pleasant pub in prime game country. Flavoursome British dishes arrive in unashamedly gutsy portions. Chef-owner stalks or gathers much of the produce himself. Fish is from Looe or local rivers.

YAXLEY – Suffolk – see Thornham Magna

YEOVIL – Somerset – 503 M31 – pop. 41 871 3 B3

London 136 mi – Exeter 48 mi – Southampton 72 mi – Taunton 26 mi

Hendford ✆ (01935) 845946, yeoviltic@southsomerset.gov.uk Cart Gate Picnic Site, stoke sub-hamdon ✆ (01935) 829333 (seasonal opening), cartgate.tic@southsomerset.gov.uk

Sherborne Rd, ✆ (01935) 422 965

St John the Baptist★

Monacute House★★ **AC**, W : 4 mi on A 3088 – Fleet Air Arm Museum, Yeovilton★★ **AC**, NW : 5 mi by A 37 – Tintinhull House Garden★ **AC**, NW: 5.5 mi – Ham Hill (≤★★) W : 5.5 mi by A 3088 – Stoke sub Hamdon (parish church★) W : 5.25 mi by A 3088. Muchelney★★ (parish church★★) NW : 14 mi by A 3088, A 303 and B 3165 – Lytes Cary★, N : 7.5 mi by A 37, B 3151 and A 372 – Sandford Orcas Manor House★, NW : 8 mi by A 359 – Cadbury Castle (≤★★) NE : 10.5 mi by A 359 – East Lambrook Manor★ **AC**, W : 12 mi by A 3088 and A 303

Lanes

rm,

West Coker, Southwest : 3 mi on A 30 ✉ BA22 9AJ – ✆ (01935) 862 555 – www.laneshotel.net
29 rm – ♦£ 90 ♦♦£ 130
Rest – *(closed Saturday lunch)* Menu £ 17 (lunch) – Carte £ 19/28
♦ 18C former rectory in pleasant walled grounds. Airy interior boasts modern meeting rooms, laid-back lounge and large bar. Relax in smart leisure suite or on croquet lawn. Stylish bedrooms with up-to-date bathrooms. Modern bistro dishes in striking dining room.

at Barwick South : 2 mi by A 30 off A 37 – ✉ Yeovil

Little Barwick House with rm

rest,

✉ BA22 9TD – ✆ (01935) 423 902 – www.littlebarwickhouse.co.uk – Closed 26 December-8 January
6 rm – ♦£ 80/100 ♦♦£ 138/154
Rest – *(closed Monday, Tuesday lunch and Sunday dinner) (booking essential)* Menu £ 26/40
♦ Charming Georgian dower house in a secluded spot, run by a delightful and hospitable couple. The cooking is robust, gutsy and visually bold but without gimmicks. Comfortable, stylish and immaculately kept bedrooms.

YORK – York – **502** Q22 – **pop. 198 900** Great Britain **23** C2

London 203 mi – Kingston-upon-Hull 38 mi – Leeds 26 mi – Middlesbrough 51 mi

Museum St ✆ (01904) 550099, info@visityork.org.

Strensall Lords Moor Lane, ✆ (01904) 491 840

Heworth Muncastergate Muncaster House, ✆ (01904) 424 618

City★★★ – Minster★★★ (Stained Glass★★★, Chapter House★★, Choir Screen★★) CDY – National Railway Museum★★★ CY – The Walls★★ CDXYZ – Castle Museum★ **AC** DZ **M2** – Jorvik Viking Centre★ **AC** DY **M1** – Fairfax House★ **AC** DY **A** – The Shambles★ DY **54**

Cedar Court Grand H. & Spa

rm,

Station Rise ✉ YO1 6HT – ✆ (01904) 380 038 – www.cedarcourtgrand.co.uk CY**v**

94 rm – ♦£ 149/179 ♦♦£ 169/199 – 13 suites

Rest *HQ* – ✆ (01904) 655 554 – Menu £ 20 (lunch) – Carte £ 30/44

♦ Early 20C building – former HQ of the North Eastern Railway Co. – where original features blend with contemporary décor. Impressive spa and leisure facilities in cellar. Spacious bedrooms. Modern menu served in HQ, with views of the castle walls.

Middlethorpe Hall

rm,

Bishopthorpe Rd, South : 1.75 mi ✉ YO23 2GB – ✆ (01904) 641 241 – www.middlethorpe.com

20 rm – ♦£ 129/159 ♦♦£ 199/269, £ 6.95 – 9 suites

Rest – *(booking essential for non-residents)* Menu £ 25 (lunch) **s** – Carte dinner £ 34/59 **s**

♦ Impressive William and Mary country house dating from 1699. Elegantly and carefully restored; abundantly furnished with antiques. Most characterful rooms in main house. Wood-panelled, three-roomed restaurant with period feel.

Grange

1 Clifton ✉ YO30 6AA – ✆ (01904) 644 744 – www.grangehotel.co.uk CX**u**

35 rm – ♦£ 123/198 ♦♦£ 168/235 – 1 suite

Rest *Ivy Brasserie* – *(closed Sunday) (dinner only)* Carte £ 27/32

Rest *New York Grill* – Menu £ 13 (lunch) – Carte £ 27/32

♦ Well-maintained hotel with traditional feel: floral decorations and horse racing memorabilia abound. Choose between classical four-poster bedrooms and newer rooms with well-appointed bathrooms. Contemporary brasserie serves modern menu. New York Grill offers informal à la carte.

Hotel du Vin

89 The Mount ✉ YO24 1AX – ✆ (01904) 557 350 – www.hotelduvin.com CZ**a**

44 rm – ♦£ 210 ♦♦£ 210, £ 14.50

Rest *Bistro* – see restaurant listing

♦ Georgian house close to Knavesmire racecourse and just outside of city centre. As part of a 'wine-orientated' group, the contemporary bedrooms boast smart, wine-coloured themes.

York Pavilion

rm,

45 Main St, Fulford, South : 1.5 mi on A 19 ✉ YO10 4PJ – ✆ (01904) 622 099 – www.yorkpavilionhotel.com

63 rm – ♦£ 79/99 ♦♦£ 89/130

Rest *Langtons Brasserie* – Carte £ 26/31

♦ Georgian house on main road in suburbs. Wood panelled reception and period-style lounge. Older, more individual rooms in main house and uniform, chintzy style in extension. Informal dining.

YORK

Street	Grid	No.
Bishopgate St.	CZ	3
Bishophill Senior	CZ	4
Blake St	CY	5
Campleshon Rd	AZ	7
Church St	DY	8
Clifford St	DY	10
Colliergate	DY	12
Coney St	CY	13
Cromwell Rd	CZ	15
Davygate	CY	16
Deangate	DY	18
Duncombe Pl.	CY	20
Fawcett St	DZ	21
Fetter Lane	CY	22
Goodramgate	DY	25
High Ousegate	DY	26
High Petergate	CY	28
Knavesmire Rd	AZ	29
Leeman Rd.	AY, CY	30
Lendal	CY	32
Lord Mayor's Walk	DX	33
Low Petergate	DY	35
Melrosegate	BY	36
Museum St	CY	39
Parliament St	DY	42
Pavement	DY	43
Peasholme Green	DY	45
Penley's Grove St	DX	46
Queen St	CZ	49
St Helen's Rd	AZ	50
St Leonard's Pl.	CY	52
St Maurice's Rd	DXY	53
Shambles (The)	DY	54
Station Rd.	CY	55
Stonebow (The)	DY	56
Stonegate	CY	58
Tower St.	DZ	59
University Rd	BZ	60

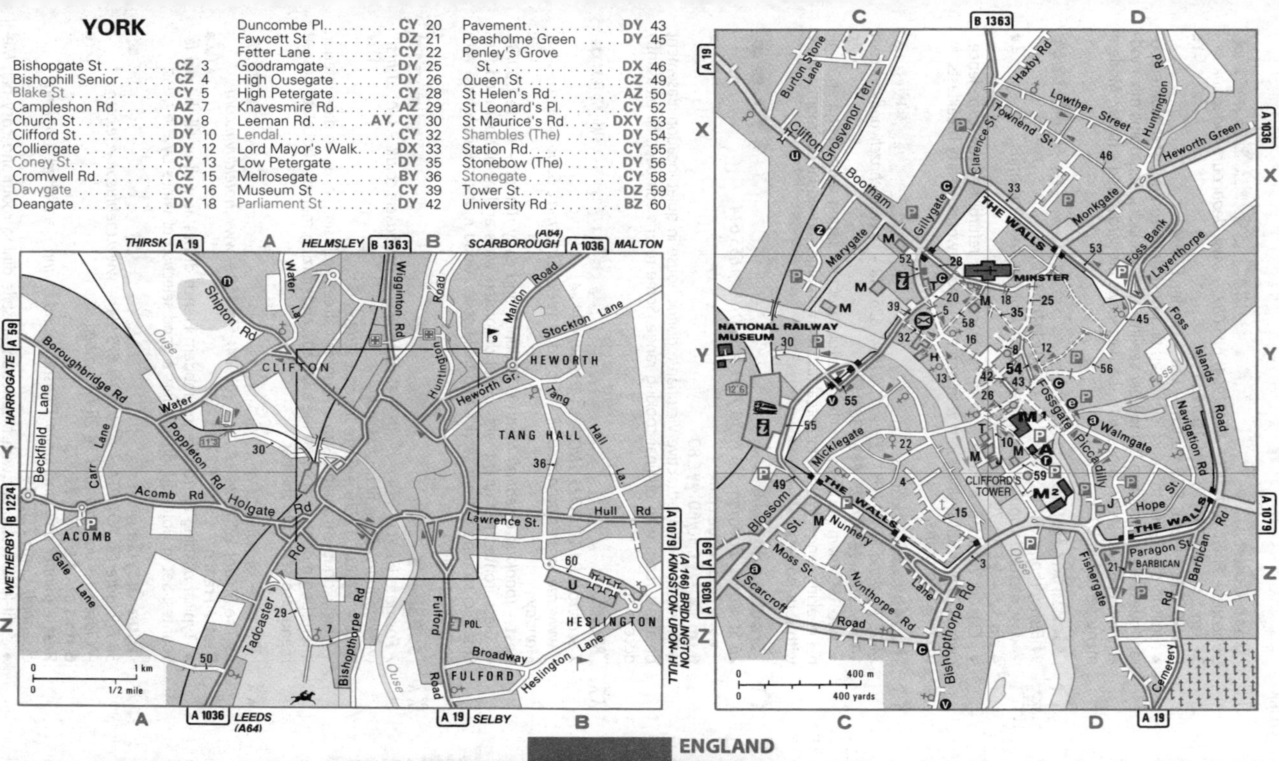

Dean Court rest,
Duncombe Pl ✉ YO1 7EF – ☎ (01904) 625 082 – www.deancourt-york.co.uk
37 rm – £ 75/170 £ 100/235 CY**c**
Rest *D.C.H* – Menu £ 19 (lunch) – Carte dinner £ 29/44
♦ Built in the 1950s to house clerics visiting next door York Minster. Contemporary guest areas include a lounge-bar serving all day snacks. Bedrooms mix modern and classical styles; those with the best views are larger and smarter. Modern menu served in D.C.H.

Alexander House without rest
94 Bishopthorpe Rd ✉ Y023 1JS – ☎ (01904) 625 016 – www.alexanderhouseyork.co.uk – Closed January and Christmas CZ**v**
4 rm – £ 59/79 £ 69/85
♦ Classic Victorian terraced house, immaculately refurbished by experienced owners. Delightful sitting room with porcelain and artworks. Hearty breakfasts. Attractive bedrooms.

Hazelwood without rest
24-25 Portland St ✉ Y031 7EH – ☎ (01904) 626 548 – www.thehazelwoodyork.com
14 rm – £ 60/125 £ 130/150 CX**c**
♦ Two 19C town houses with characterful basement sitting room featuring original cooking range. Welcoming breakfast room in blue. Individual bedrooms, some with four posters.

Crook Lodge without rest
26 St Mary's, Bootham ✉ YO30 7DD – ☎ (01904) 655 614 – www.crooklodge.co.uk CX**z**
6 rm – £ 50/60 £ 80
♦ Privately owned, attractive Victorian redbrick house in quiet location. Basement breakfast room with original cooking range. Some rooms compact, all pleasantly decorated.

ENGLAND

Melton's
7 Scarcroft Rd ✉ YO23 1ND – ☎ (01904) 634 341 – www.meltonsrestaurant.co.uk – Closed 3 weeks Christmas, Sunday and Monday CZ**c**
Rest – *(booking essential)* Menu £ 23 (lunch and early dinner) – Carte £ 30/36
♦ Glass fronted restaurant with mural decorated walls and neighbourhood feel. Smart, crisp tone in both service and table cover. Good modern British food with some originality.

J. Baker's
7 Fossgate ✉ YO1 9TA – ☎ (01904) 622 688 – www.jbakers.co.uk – Closed first week January, Sunday and Monday DY**c**
Rest – Menu £ 12/30 – Carte lunch £ 20/26
♦ Lively, double-fronted bistro on cobbled street, with simple, up-to-date interior. Interesting modern dishes on the à la carte and grazing menus. Chocolate dessert menu also served in the bar.

Bistro – at Hotel du Vin
89 The Mount ✉ YO24 1AX – ☎ (01904) 567 350 – www.hotelduvin.com
Rest – French – Carte £ 27/45 CZ**a**
♦ Typical bustling Bistro offering modern French dishes as well as all the old favourites. Set in Hotel du Vin, it offers a good selection of wines by the glass.

Blue Bicycle with rm
34 Fossgate ✉ YO1 9TA – ☎ (01904) 673 990 – www.thebluebicycle.com – Closed 1-9 January and 24-28 December DY**e**
6 rm – £ 175 £ 175
Rest – *(dinner only and lunch Thursday-Sunday and December) (booking essential)* Carte £ 33/49
♦ Split-level restaurant with Mediterranean-style dining room and cosy bar. Menus offer modern classics: some simple, some more elaborate in style. Smart, studio style bedrooms in rear mews, each with a kitchen; create your own breakfast from ingredients provided.

31 Castlegate

31 Castlegate ✉ YO1 9RN – ☎ (01904) 621 404 – www.31castlegate.co.uk – Closed 25-26 December, 1 January and Monday DY**r**

Rest – Menu £ 15 (lunch and early dinner) – Carte £ 25/34

◆ Former Georgian architect's house boasting original fireplaces and plasterwork. Café atmosphere by day; more intimate restaurant by night. Classical cooking is presented in a modern manner.

Melton's Too

25 Walmgate ✉ YO1 9TX – ☎ (01904) 629 222 – www.meltonstoo.co.uk – Closed dinner 24 December, 25-26 December, dinner 31 December and 1 January DY**a**

Rest – Carte £ 20/24

◆ Café-bistro 'descendant' of Melton's restaurant. Located in former saddlers shop with oak beams and exposed brick walls. Good value eclectic dishes, with tapas a speciality.

at Newton-on-Ouse **Northwest : 8 mi by A 19**

Dawnay Arms

✉ YO30 2BR – ☎ (01347) 848 345 – www.thedawnayatnewton.co.uk

Rest – Menu £ 13 – Carte £ 16/28

◆ Spacious 18C inn boasting handsome rustic style, with beamed ceilings and roaring fires. Tasty, good value dishes on seasonal menus. Dining room looks out over River Ouse.

ZENNOR – Cornwall – 503 D33 1 A3

London 305 mi – Penzance 11 mi – St Ives 5 mi

The Gurnard's Head with rm

Treen, West : 1.5 mi on B 3306 ✉ TR26 3DE – ☎ (01736) 796 928 – www.gurnardshead.co.uk – Closed 4 days January and 24-25 December

7 rm – †£ 60/75 ††£ 90 **Rest** – Carte £ 19/28

◆ Remotely located and dog-friendly, with stone floors, shabby-chic décor, blazing fires and a relaxed, cosy feel. Simple menu relies on regional produce. Traditional puddings; interesting wine list. Comfy beds feature good quality linen; communal breakfasts.

O. Forir/MICHELIN

ABERDEEN – Aberdeen City – 501 [illegible] – pop. 184 788 [illegible] 28 D1

Edinburgh [illegible] – Dundee 67 mi

Aberdeen Airport, Dyce : [illegible] NW : 7 mi by A 96 X

[illegible] Shetland Islands (Lerwick) and via Orkney Islands (Stromness) [illegible] (Scottish Ferries) [illegible] daily [illegible]

23 Union St [illegible] aberdeen@visitscotland.com

[illegible]

[illegible] Aberdeen, Golden of Don Links [illegible]

[illegible]

[illegible] Links Golf [illegible]

[illegible]

[illegible] Links Bridge of Don, [illegible]

[illegible] Bonnyview Rd. [illegible]

City ★★ – Old Aberdeen ★★ [illegible] – St Machar's Cathedral ★★ (West Front ★★★, Heraldic Ceiling ★★★) [illegible] – Art Gallery ★★ (Macdonald Collection ★★) [illegible] – Mercat Cross ★★ [illegible] – King's College Chapel ★ (Crown Spire ★★★, medieval fittings ★★) [illegible] – Provost Skene's House ★ (painted ceilings ★★) [illegible] – Maritime Museum ★ [illegible] – Marischal College ★ [illegible] – [illegible] – Duthie Park [illegible] – Winter Gardens [illegible]

[illegible] Castle ★★ (Gardens ★★★) [illegible] – Dunnottar Castle ★★ [illegible] – Haddo House ★ [illegible] – Pitmedden Garden ★★ [illegible] – Castle Fraser ★ (exterior ★★) [illegible] – Fyvie Castle ★ [illegible]

Plans pages [illegible]

[illegible]

[illegible] www.marcliffe.com

[illegible] 2 suites

Conservatory – see restaurant listing

[illegible] country house, popular with business [illegible] acres of [illegible] grounds. Individually decorated rooms, with [illegible]

The Malmaison

[illegible] www.malmaison.com

79 rm – [illegible] 160/195 [illegible]

Rest Brasserie [illegible] – Carte £ 28/45

[illegible] building with modern facilities outer city centre. Cosy, very comfortable well furnished bedrooms [illegible] suites have their own [illegible] longe with two private dining rooms in the superb Brasserie, [illegible] cooking has [illegible] Scottish base.

The Hotel Aberdeen

[illegible] www.thecitykindhotels.co.uk

[illegible]

Modern hotel just off the main high street. In functional, minimalist style in keeping with [illegible] school of design. [illegible] bedrooms have a [illegible]

[illegible]

[illegible] Gate [illegible] www.[illegible]aberdeen.com

– [illegible]

24 rm [illegible] – **Rest** – Carte [illegible]

[illegible] hotel set in leafy suburbs; well run by friendly staff. Traditional lounge bar, well priced up-to-date rooms. A useful address for visitors to the city, dining room specialises in traditional and tasted Scottish [illegible].

[illegible]

[illegible] www.[illegible]cliffe.com

Rest – [illegible] £ 32 (Sunday lunch) [illegible]

[illegible] conservatory [illegible] with [illegible] hearty tasty dishes including [illegible] favourite [illegible] service and [illegible] atmosphere.

ABERDEEN – Aberdeen City – 501 N12 – pop. 184 788 Scotland **28** D1

Edinburgh 130 mi – Dundee 67 mi

Aberdeen Airport, Dyce : (0844) 481 6666, NW : 7 mi by A 96 X

to Shetland Islands (Lerwick) and via Orkney Islands (Stromness) (P and O Scottish Ferries) 1-2 daily

23 Union St (01224) 288828, aberdeen@visitscotland.com

Hazelhead Hazelhead Park, (01224) 321 830

Royal Aberdeen Bridge of Don Links Rd, (01224) 702 571

Balnagask St Fitticks Rd, (01224) 871 286

King's Links Golf Rd, (01224) 632 269

Portlethen Badentoy Rd, (01224) 781 090

Murcar Links Bridge of Don, (01224) 704 354

Auchmill West Heatheryfold Bonnyview Rd, (01224) 715 214

City★★ - Old Aberdeen★★ X – St Machar's Cathedral★★ (West Front★★★, Heraldic Ceiling★★★) X **A** – Art Gallery★★ (Macdonald Collection★★) Y **M** – Mercat Cross★★ Y **B** – King's College Chapel★ (Crown Spire★★★, medieval fittings★★★) X **D** – Provost Skene's House★(painted ceilings★★) Y **E** – Maritime Museum★ Z **M1** – Marischal College★ Y **U**

Brig o' Balgownie★, by Don St X. SW : Deeside★★ - Crathes Castle★★ (Gardens★★★) **AC**, SW : 16 mi by A 93 X – Dunnottar Castle★★ **AC** (site★★★), S : 18 mi by A 90 X – Pitmedden Garden★★, N : 14 mi by A 90 on B 999 X – Castle Fraser★ (exterior★★) **AC**, W : 16 mi by A 944 X - Fyvie Castle★, NW : 26.5 mi on A 947

Plans pages 673, 674

SCOTLAND

Marcliffe H. and Spa

North Deeside Rd AB15 9YA – (01224) 861 000 – www.marcliffe.com

40 rm – †£ 165/229 ††£ 185/249 – 2 suites Xr

Rest *Conservatory* – see restaurant listing

◆ Spacious, professionally run modern country house, popular with business travellers. Eight acres of pleasant grounds. Individually decorated rooms with antique furniture. Large spa.

Malmaison

49-53 Queens Rd AB15 4YP – (01224) 327 370 – www.malmaison.com

79 rm – †£ 160/195 ††£ 160/195, £ 13.95 Xv

Rest *Brasserie* – Menu £ 18 (early dinner) – Carte £ 26/45

◆ Period building with modern facilities, out of city centre. Cosy, very comfortable, well-furnished bedrooms; the sexy suites have their own balconies. A huge inner and two private dining rooms in the superb Brasserie, where cooking has fiercely Scottish base.

bauhaus without rest

52-60 Langstone Pl. AB11 6EN – (01224) 212 122 – www.thebauhaus.co.uk

40 rm – †£ 80/105 ††£ 110 Zr

◆ Modern hotel just off the main high street; its functional, minimalist style in keeping with the Bauhaus school of design. Colour-coded bedrooms have a clean, uncluttered feel.

Atholl

54 King's Gate AB15 4YN – (01224) 323 505 – www.atholl-aberdeen.com – Closed 1 January Xs

34 rm – †£ 95/125 ††£ 145 **Rest** – Carte £ 17/36

◆ Baronial style hotel set in leafy suburbs; well run by friendly staff. Traditional lounge bar; well-priced, up-to-date rooms. A useful address for visitors to the city. Dining room specialises in tried-and-tested Scottish cooking.

Conservatory – at The Marcliffe H. and Spa

North Deeside Rd AB15 9YA – (01224) 861 000 – www.marcliffe.com

Rest – Menu £ 33 (Sunday lunch) **s** – Carte £ 32/48 **s** Xr

◆ Spacious conservatory dining room with large open kitchen. Fiercely Scottish menu; hearty tasty dishes, including superbly flavourful steaks. Warm service and a relaxing atmosphere.

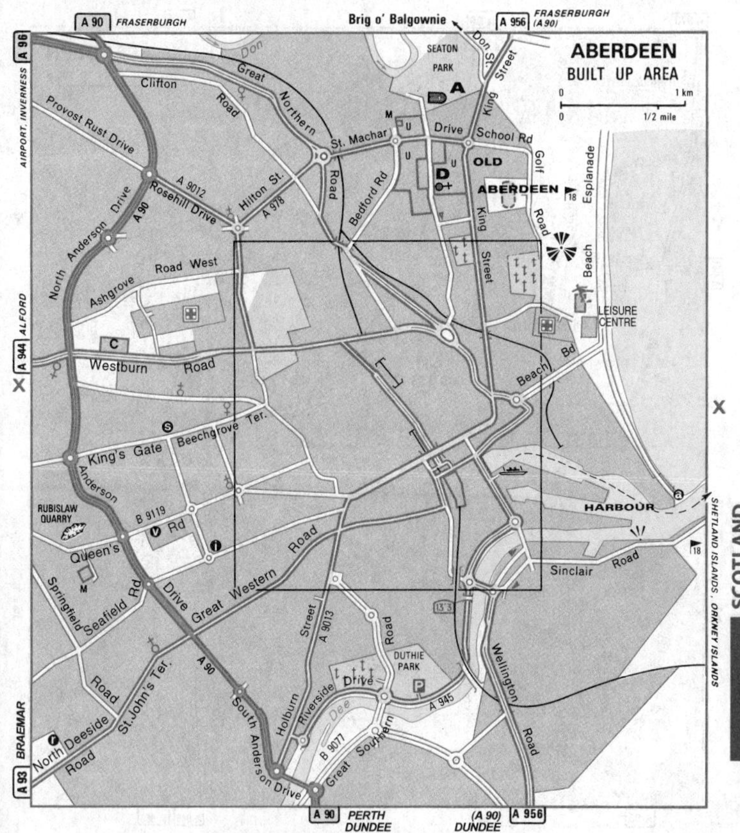

XX La Stella

28 Adelphi ✉ AB11 5BL – ✆ (01224) 211 414 – www.lastella.co.uk
– *Closed Sunday* **Zs**

Rest – Menu £ 13 (lunch)/34

◆ Snug bistro hidden away down a side street, with simple, bright décor and a neighbourhood feel. Seasonally changing menus focus on quality ingredients, with fish a speciality.

XX Silver Darling

Pocra Quay, North Pier ✉ *AB11 5DQ* – ✆ *(01224) 576 229*
– *www.thesilverdarlingrestaurant.co.uk – Closed 2 weeks Christmas-New Year, Saturday lunch and Sunday* **Xa**

Rest – Seafood – Menu £ 20 (lunch) – Carte dinner £ 36/52

◆ Former customs house attractively set at port entrance; panoramic views across harbour and coastline. Attentive service of superb quality seafood prepared in imaginative ways.

XX Nargile

77-79 Skene St ✉ *AB10 1QD* – ✆ *(01224) 636 093*
– *www.rendezvousatnargile.co.uk – closed 25 December and 1 January*

Rest – Turkish – *(dinner only)* Carte £ 19/31 **Ya**

◆ Traditionally decorated Turkish restaurant with subdued lighting from Turkish lamps. Open-plan kitchen allows the diner to watch the chefs prepare the authentic dishes.

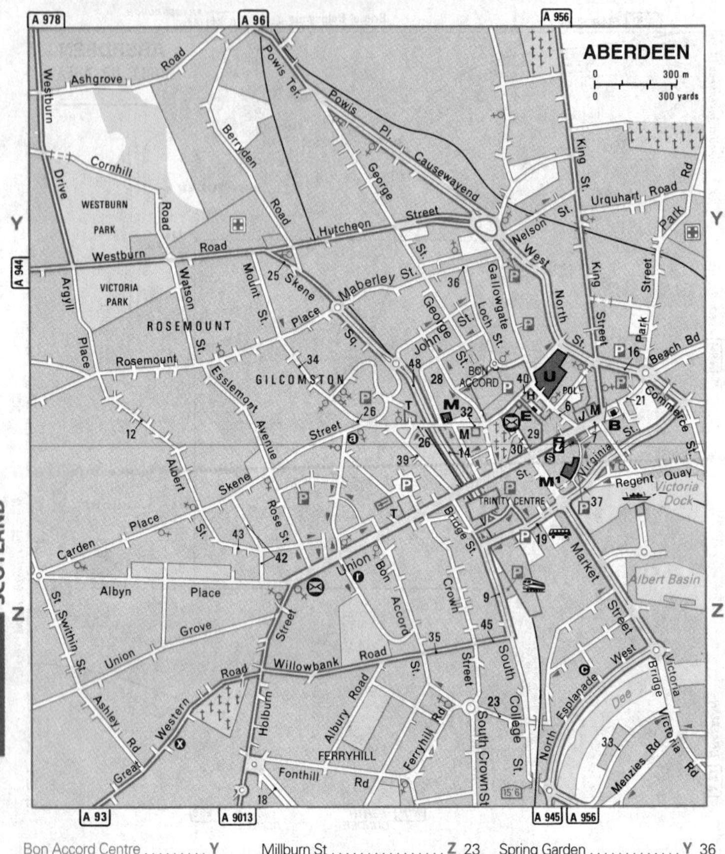

Yatai

VISA MC

75 Skene St. ✉ AB10 1QD – ✆ (01224) 635 480 – www.yatai.co.uk – Closed 25 December-2 January and Monday Y**a**

Rest – Japanese – *(dinner only)* Carte £ 30/50

◆ Minimalist Japanese restaurant; its formally structured menu offering fresh, tasty, authentic dishes but no sushi. The chef, who spent time in Kyoto, makes good use of Scottish produce.

Rendezvous at Nargile

AC VISA MC AE

106-108 Forest Ave ✉ AB15 4UP – ✆ (01224) 323 700 – www.rendezvousatnargile.co.uk – Closed 1-2 January and 25-26 December

Rest – Turkish – Menu £ 19 – Carte £ 19/33 X**i**

◆ Bright, refreshing neighbourhood restaurant set opposite the Rendezvous Gallery. All day menus offer plenty of choice, with cooking influenced by the Mediterranean, and in particular, Turkey.

ABERFELDY – Perth and Kinross – 501 I14 – pop. 1 895 — 28 C2

Edinburgh 75 mi – Dunkeld 17 mi – Pitlochry 14 mi

at Fortingall West : 8 mi by B 846 on Fortingall rd

Fortingall

PH15 2NQ – (01887) 830 367 – *www.fortingallhotel.com*

10 rm – £ 90/110 £ 120/160 **Rest** – *(set menu only)* Menu £ 45

• Arts and Crafts style house on tranquil private estate, boasting lovely country views. Stylish interior with contemporary country fabrics. Modern bedrooms remain in keeping with the building's age. Light snacks in cosy bar; contemporary cooking in restaurant.

ABERLOUR – Moray – 501 K11 – pop. 785 Scotland — 28 C1

Edinburgh 192 mi – Aberdeen 60 mi – Elgin 15 mi – Inverness 55 mi

Rothes Blackhall, (01340) 831 443

Dufftown (Glenfiddich Distillery★), SE : 6 mi by A 95 and A 941

Dowans

Southwest : 0.75 mi by A 95 AB38 9LS – (01340) 871 488 – *www.dowanshotel.com – Closed 23-26 December*

19 rm – £ 68/85 £ 150 **Rest** – Carte £ 20/42

• Welcoming baronial-style hotel in 3 acres of informal gardens overlooking the town and river – a favourite with fishermen. Comfy, well-equipped bedrooms. Cosy bar offering a good selection of whiskies. Traditional two-roomed restaurant serves classical menu.

ABOYNE – Aberdeenshire – 501 L12 – pop. 2 202 Scotland — 28 D1

Edinburgh 131 mi – Aberdeen 30 mi – Dundee 68 mi

Formanston Park, (013398) 86 328

Craigievar Castle★ **AC**, NE : 12 mi by B 9094, B 9119 and A 980

Struan Hall without rest

Ballater Rd AB34 5HY – (013398) 87 241 – *www.struanhall.co.uk*

3 rm – £ 40/55 £ 70/80

• An agreeable and welcoming guesthouse with attractive garden. Well kept throughout. Large sitting room and antique breakfast table. Simple, comfy bedrooms.

ABRIACHAN – Highland – 501 G11 – pop. 120 — 30 C2

London 573 mi – Edinburgh 168 mi – Inverness 11 mi – Elgin 50 mi

Loch Ness Lodge

Brachla, on A 82 IV3 8LA – (01456) 459 469 – *www.loch-ness-lodge.com – Closed January*

7 rm – £ 185/335 £ 245/395

Rest – *(dinner only) (booking essential to non residents)* Carte approx. £ 50

• Comfortable, modern country house overlooking Loch Ness; warmly decorated, spacious bedrooms boast a high level of facilities. Sauna and hot tub for guests. Daily changing 5 course menu uses Scottish produce; cooking is flavourful and classically based. Linen laid dining room with excellent views; attentive service.

ACHILTIBUIE – Highland – 501 D9 — 30 C1

Edinburgh 243 mi – Inverness 84 mi – Ullapool 25 mi

Summer Isles

IV26 2YG – (01854) 622 282 – *www.summerisleshotel.com – April to October*

10 rm – £ 115 £ 210 – 3 suites

Rest *Summer Isles Bar* – see restaurant listing

Rest – *(booking essential) (set menu only at dinner, light seafood lunch)* Menu £ 56

• Remotely located hotel, with magnificent views over the eponymous islands. Individually styled, comfortable bedrooms split between main house and various converted outbuildings. Pleasant restaurant, with polished, well-set tables. Daily set menu of traditional dishes, with emphasis on seafood.

SCOTLAND

Summer Isles (Bar) – at Summer Isles Hotel
✉ *IV26 2YG – ✆ (01854) 622 282 – www.summerisleshotel.com – April-October*
Rest – Seafood – *(bookings not accepted)* Carte £ 20/30
♦ 19C former crofters' bar boasting two snug rooms, a large garden and a small terrace with glorious views. Daily changing menus feature local ingredients and have a strong seafood base.

ALYTH – Perth and Kinross – 501 J14 – pop. 2 301 — 28 C2

Edinburgh 63 mi – Aberdeen 69 mi – Dundee 16 mi – Perth 21 mi

Pitcrocknie, ✆ (01828) 632 268

Tigh Na Leigh
22-24 Airlie St ✉ PH11 8AJ – ✆ (01828) 632 372 – www.tighnaleigh.co.uk – Closed 2 January to 1 February, 25-26 and 31 December
5 rm – †£ 42/74 ††£ 88/102
Rest – *(dinner only) (residents only)* Menu £ 25
♦ Extremely spacious, modern bedrooms in this comfortable and contemporary conversion, which retains many original features. Look out for Tom and Eddie, the cats. Dining room overlooks kitchen garden, church and carp pond. Daily-changing dinner menu and small wine list.

ANNBANK – South Ayrshire – 501 G17 – pop. 854 — 25 B2

Edinburgh 84 mi – Ayr 6 mi – Dumfries 54 mi – Dumfries 38 mi

Enterkine
Southeast : 0.5 mi on B 742 (Coylton rd) ✉ KA6 5AL – ✆ (01292) 520 580 – www.enterkine.com
13 rm (dinner included) – †£ 90 ††£ 250/400 – 1 suite
Rest – *(booking essential)* Menu £ 19 (lunch) – Carte £ 24/42
♦ 1930s country house surrounded by extensive gardens and woodlands. Spacious, comfortable lounges. Luxurious bedrooms; one with large roof terrace. Charming library. Formal restaurant with views over River Ayr serves modern cooking; popular with non-residents.

ANSTRUTHER – Fife – 501 L15 – pop. 3 442 Scotland — 28 D2

Edinburgh 46 mi – Dundee 23 mi – Dunfermline 34 mi

Scottish Fisheries Museum, Harbourhead ✆ (01333) 311073 (April-October), anstruther@visitscotland.com

Marsfield Shore Rd, ✆ (01333) 310 956

Scottish Fisheries Museum★★ **AC**

The East Neuk★★ – Crail★★ (Old Centre★★, Upper Crail★) NE : 4 mi by A 917. Kellie Castle★ **AC**, NW : 7 mi by B 9171, B 942 and A 917

The Spindrift
Pittenweem Rd ✉ KY10 3DT – ✆ (01333) 310 573 – www.thespindrift.co.uk – Closed January and 24-26 December
8 rm – †£ 45/60 ††£ 64/80 **Rest** – Menu £ 22
♦ Detached Victorian house on the edge of the village, originally owned by a tea clipper captain. Comfortable lounge with honesty bar. Cosy, individually furnished bedrooms, some with distant sea views – opt for the top floor Captain's Cabin. Homely cooking relies on local produce, with seafood from East Neuk to the fore.

Cellar
24 East Green ✉ KY10 3AA – ✆ (01333) 310 378 – www.cellaranstruther.co.uk – Closed 24-26 December, Monday in winter and Sunday
Rest – Seafood – *(booking essential)* Menu £ 25/40
♦ Long-standing restaurant hidden behind the Fisheries Museum. Atmospheric beamed room with flickering candlelight and open fire. Simply prepared, fresh, quality seafood from the local coast.

SCOTLAND

APPLECROSS – Highland – 501 C11 29 B2

London 639 mi – Edinburgh 234 mi – Gairloch 56 mi – Portree 76 mi

The Potting Shed

Applecross Walled Garden, Northeast : 0.5 mi ✉ IV54 8ND – ☎ (01520) 744 440 – www.applecrossgarden.co.uk – March-October

Rest – Carte £ 16/24

◆ Lovely 17C walled kitchen garden whose restaurant has grown from a tea-room. Its simple structure belies its tasty dishes, fresh from owner's fishing boat or the garden itself.

Applecross Inn with rm

Shore St ✉ IV54 8LR – ☎ (01520) 744 262 – www.applecross.uk.com – Closed 25 December and 1 January

7 rm – †£ 50/70 ††£ 90/100 **Rest** – *(booking essential)* Carte £ 25/40

◆ Charming Highland inn set in an extremely remote location, boasting stunning water and hill views. Menus feature local, seasonal produce from the nearby estate and bay; seafood a speciality. Set in old fishermen's cottages, smart, comfy bedrooms boast sea views.

ARBROATH – Angus – 501 M14 – pop. 22 785 28 D2

Edinburgh 72 mi – Dundee 17 mi – Montrose 12 mi

The Old Vicarage without rest

2 Seaton Rd, Northeast : 0.75 mi by A 92 and Hayshead Rd ✉ DD11 5DX – ☎ (01241) 430 475 – www.theoldvicaragebandb.co.uk

3 rm – †£ 55/60 ††£ 80/90

◆ Detached 19C house, of large proportions, clothed in Victorian style throughout. Antique furnished bedrooms: ask for view of Arbroath Abbey.

ARCHIESTOWN – Moray – 501 K11 – ✉ Aberlour (Aberdeenshire) 28 C1

Edinburgh 194 mi – Aberdeen 62 mi – Inverness 49 mi

Archiestown

The Square ✉ AB38 7QL – ☎ (01340) 810 218 – www.archiestownhotel.co.uk – Closed 2 January-11 February and 21-29 December

11 rm – †£ 60/90 ††£ 120/140

Rest *Bistro* – Menu £ 15/25

◆ Welcoming hotel hidden away in a small hamlet; ideally located for shooters/-fishermen. Spacious, comfy sitting rooms with warming open fires. Cosy bedrooms, many boasting country views. Daily changing dishes in laid-back bistro.

ARDEONAIG – Perth and Kinross – 501 H14 – see Killin (Stirling)

ARDHASAIG – Western Isles Outer Hebrides – 501 Z10 – see Lewis and Harris (Isle of)

ARDUAINE – Argyll and Bute – 501 D15 – ✉ Oban Scotland 27 B2

Edinburgh 142 mi – Oban 20 mi

Loch Awe★★, E : 12 mi by A 816 and B 840

Loch Melfort

✉ PA34 4XG – ☎ (01852) 200 233 – www.lochmelfort.co.uk – Closed 2 weeks January

25 rm (dinner included) – †£ 94 ††£ 190

Rest *Arduaine* – Seafood – *(dinner only)* Menu £ 39

Rest *Chartroom Two* – Carte approx. £ 19

◆ Next to the beautiful Arduaine gardens and boasting amazing views over the Sound of Jura. Modern lounges with tartan/nautical touches. Largest bedrooms in main house; lovely outlook from terraces of wing rooms. Refined, seasonal dishes in Arduaine. Simple, seafood-based menus in Chartroom Two.

ARRAN (Isle of) – North Ayrshire – 501 E17 – pop. 5 058 Scotland 25 A2

London 449 mi – Edinburgh 95 mi – Glasgow 45 mi – Paisley 31 mi

from Brodick to Ardrossan (Caledonian MacBrayne Ltd) 4-6 daily (55 mn)
– from Lochranza to Kintyre Peninsula (Claonaig) (Caledonian MacBrayne Ltd) frequent services daily (30 mn)
– from Brodick to Isle of Bute (Rothesay) (Caledonian MacBrayne Ltd) 3 weekly (2 h 5 mn)

Island★★ - Brodick Castle★★ **AC**

BRODICK – North Ayrshire – pop. 621 25 A2

The Pier ✆ (01770) 303776, brodick@visitscotland.com

Brodick, ✆ (01770) 302 349

Machrie Bay, ✆ (01770) 850 232

Kilmichael Country House

Glen Cloy, West : 1 mi by Shore Rd, taking left turn opposite Golf Club
✉ KA27 8BY – ✆ (01770) 302 219 – www.kilmichael.com – Easter-October
5 rm – †£ 75/95 ††£ 120/160 – 3 suites
Rest – *(Closed Monday and Tuesday) (dinner only) (booking essential)* Menu £ 45
◆ Reputedly the oldest house on the Isle of Arran, in peaceful location with immaculate lawned grounds. Comfortable country house style and individually decorated bedrooms. Welcoming owners. Restaurant housed in extension. Daily-changing menus.

Alltan without rest

Knowe Rd, West : 0.5 mi by Shore Rd taking left at Golf Club ✉ KA27 8BY – ✆ (01770) 302 937 – www.alltanarran.co.uk – March-October
3 rm – †£ 38/42 ††£ 38/42
◆ Friendly, modern guest house outside village. Comfortable rear lounge with woodburning stove overlooks garden and river. Raised decked balcony with wrought iron furniture.

LOCHRANZA

Apple Lodge

✉ KA27 8HJ – ✆ (01770) 830 229 – Closed 15 December-15 January, minimum 3 night stay in high season
4 rm – †£ 55 ††£ 84 **Rest** – Menu £ 26
◆ Extended period house with small garden and pleasing views, in centre of quiet village. Homely cottage-style decor with antique furniture and a welcoming atmosphere. Food is home-cooked and uses island and home produce in good, hearty, varied dishes.

ASCOG – Argyll and Bute – 501 E16 – see Bute (Isle of)

AUCHENCAIRN – Dumfries and Galloway – 501 I19 – ✉ Castle Douglas 25 B3

Edinburgh 94 mi – Dumfries 21 mi – Stranraer 60 mi

Balcary Mews without rest

Balcary Bay, Southeast : 2 mi on Balcary rd ✉ DG7 1QZ – ✆ (01556) 640 270 – www.balcarymews.co.uk – February-November
3 rm – †£ 55 ††£ 80
◆ Former mews for the neighbouring country house, boasting superb views over Balcary Bay and the Solway Firth. Lovely garden with a gate down to the shore. Neat sun lounge and traditional bedrooms; all have views. Homemade bread and jam feature at breakfast.

AUCHTERARDER – Perth and Kinross – 501 I15 – pop. 3 945 28 C2
Scotland

Edinburgh 55 mi – Glasgow 45 mi – Perth 14 mi

Ochil Rd, ✆ (01764) 662 804

Dunning Rollo Park, ✆ (01764) 684 747

Tullibardine Chapel★, NW : 2 m

SCOTLAND

Gleneagles

Southwest : 2 mi by A 824 on A 823 ✉ *PH3 1NF* – ✆ *(01764) 662 231* – *www.gleneagles.com*

216 rm – ††£ 425/525 – 16 suites

Rest ***Andrew Fairlie at Gleneagles*** – see restaurant listing

Rest ***Strathearn*** – ✆ (01764) 694 270 *(dinner only and Sunday lunch)* Menu £ 42/68 **s**

Rest ***Deseo*** – ✆ (01764) 694 270 – Carte £ 34/51 **s**

◆ World famous for its championship golf courses and extensive leisure facilities. Graceful art deco and constant reinvestment ensure the impressive grandeur of this early 20C mansion remains. Strathearn is elegant art deco dining room. Deseo offers Mediterranean dishes in informal atmosphere.

Andrew Fairlie at Gleneagles

Southwest : 2 mi by A 824 on A 823 ✉ *PH3 1NF* – ✆ *(01764) 694 267* – *www.andrewfairlie.co.uk* – *Closed 3 weeks January, 24-25 December and Sunday*

Rest – *(dinner only)* Menu £ 75/85

Spec. Home-smoked lobster, lime and herb butter. Loin, shoulder and sweetbreads of Perthshire lamb. Textures of chocolate.

◆ Elegant, understated restaurant where reserved yet passionate chef creates precise, balanced, flavourful dishes with a refined French style and Scottish edge. Concise à la carte includes signature smoked lobster. Dégustation menu showcases dishes 'en miniature'. Menu du Marché offers latest seasonal produce.

AULTBEA – Highland – 501 D10 — 29 B2

London 636 mi – Edinburgh 231 mi – Gairloch 13 mi – Ullapool 45 mi

Mellondale without rest

47 Mellon Charles, Northwest : 3 mi on Mellon Charles rd ✉ *IV22 2JL* – ✆ *(01445) 731 326* – *www.mellondale.co.uk* – *March-October*

4 rm – †£ 40/45 ††£ 60/70

◆ Remotely located whitewashed house with neat garden. Immaculately kept dining room and homely lounge look to Loch Ewe. Smart, modern bedrooms with bright décor, two with views.

AVIEMORE – Highland – 501 I12 – pop. 2 397 Scotland — 30 D3

Edinburgh 129 mi – Inverness 29 mi – Perth 85 mi

Unit 7, Grampian Rd ✆ (08452) 255121, aviemore@visitscotland.com

Town★

The Cairngorms★★ (<★★★) - ✵★★★ from Cairn Gorm, SE : 11 mi by B 970 – Landmark Visitor Centre (The Highlander★) **AC**, N : 7 mi by A 9 – Highland Wildlife Park★ **AC**, SW : 7 mi by A 9

The Old Minister's Guest House without rest

Rothiemurchus, Southeast : 1 mi on B 970 ✉ *PH22 1QH* – ✆ *(01479) 812 181* – *www.theoldministershouse.co.uk*

4 rm – †£ 50/65 ††£ 84/96

◆ Early 20C house on outskirts of town, with a river at the bottom of its pretty garden. Nicely-laid breakfast room. Spacious bedrooms, finished to high standard.

AYR – South Ayrshire – 501 G17 – pop. 46 431 Scotland — 25 A2

Edinburgh 81 mi – Glasgow 35 mi

22 Sandgate ✆ (01292) 290300, ayr@visitscotland.com

Seafield Doonfoot Rd, Belleisle Park, ✆ (01292) 441 258

Dalmilling Westwood Ave, ✆ (01292) 263 893

Doon Valley Patna Hillside, ✆ (01292) 531 607

Alloway★ (Burns Cottage and Museum★ **AC**) S : 3 mi by B 7024 BZ. Culzean Castle★ **AC** (setting★★★, Oval Staircase★★) SW : 13 mi by A 719 BZ

Plan on next page

SCOTLAND

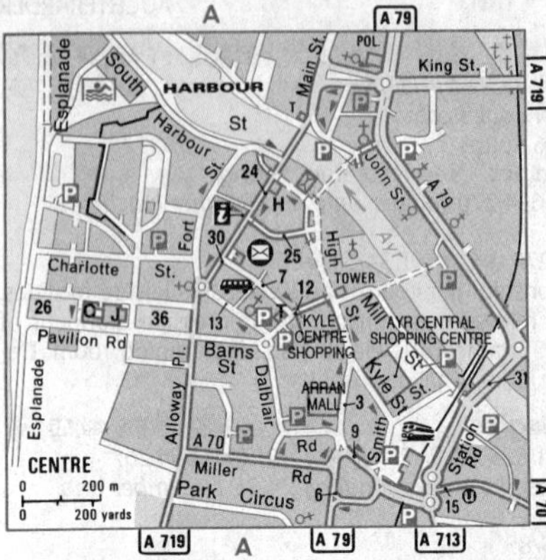

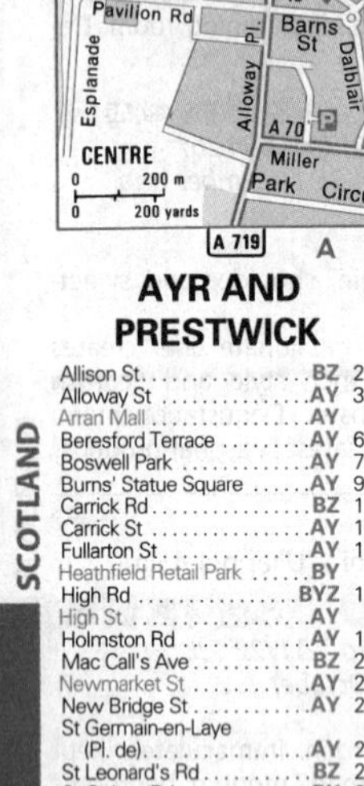

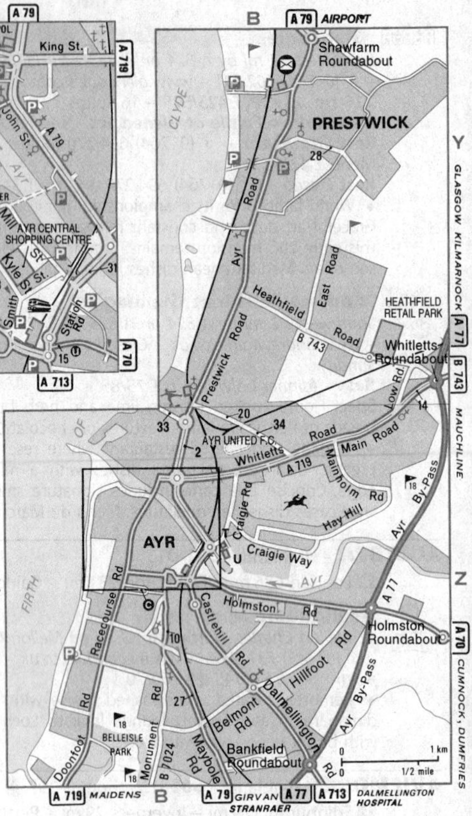

AYR AND PRESTWICK

Allison St. . . . . BZ 2
Alloway St . . . . AY 3
Arran Mall . . . . AY
Beresford Terrace . . . . AY 6
Boswell Park . . . . AY 7
Burns' Statue Square . . . . . . AY 9
Carrick Rd . . . . BZ 10
Carrick St . . . . AY 12
Fullarton St . . . . AY 13
Heathfield Retail Park . . . . . . BY
High Rd . . . . BYZ 14
High St . . . . AY
Holmston Rd . . . . AY 15
Mac Call's Ave . . . . BZ 20
Newmarket St . . . . AY 25
New Bridge St . . . . AY 24
St Germain-en-Laye (Pl. de). . . . . AY 26
St Leonard's Rd . . . . BZ 27
St Quivox Rd . . . . BY 28
Sandgate . . . . AY 30
Victoria Bridge . . . . AY 31
Waggon Rd . . . . BZ 33
Walker Rd. . . . . BZ 34
Wellington Square . . . . AY 36

SCOTLAND

No.26 The Crescent without rest

26 Bellevue Cres ✉ KA7 2DR – ✆ (01292) 287 329
– www.26crescent.co.uk
– Closed 1 January and 25 December BZ**c**

5 rm – ♦£ 50/70 ♦♦£ 70

♦ Superior, well-priced guest house with mix of traditional and modern décor. Comfortable and well-run, with individually-furnished bedrooms – best one at front has four poster.

Coila without rest

10 Holmston Rd ✉ KA7 3BB – ✆ (01292) 262 642
– www.coila.co.uk AY**u**

4 rm – ♦£ 35/50 ♦♦£ 70/80

♦ Spotlessly-kept house proudly decorated with owners' personal ornaments and family photos. Warm, homely lounge. Good-sized bedrooms with king-size beds and modern facilities.

BALLACHULISH – Highland – 501 E13 – pop. 615 Scotland 30 C3

Edinburgh 117 mi – Inverness 80 mi – Kyle of Lochalsh 90 mi – Oban 38 mi

Loan sern ✆ (01855) 811866, info@glencoetourism.co.uk

Glen Coe★★, E : 6 mi by A 82

Ardno House without rest
Lettermore, Glencoe, West : 3.5 mi by A 82 on A 828 ✉ PH49 4JD – ✆ (01855) 811 830 – www.ardnohouse.co.uk – April-October
3 rm – †£ 55/70 ††£ 70/75
♦ Purpose-built guesthouse with fine view of Loch Linnhe and the Morven Hills. Personally run and providing good value, comfortable accommodation. Spacious bedrooms.

BALLANTRAE – South Ayrshire – **501** E18 – **pop. 672** – ✉ **Girvan** **25** A2
Edinburgh 115 mi – Ayr 33 mi – Stranraer 18 mi

Glenapp Castle
South : 1 mi by A 77 taking first right turn after bridge ✉ KA26 0NZ – ✆ (01465) 831 212 – www.glenappcastle.com – Closed 2 January - late March and Christmas
14 rm (dinner included) – †£ 265/285 ††£ 415/455 – 3 suites
Rest – *(booking essential for non-residents) (set menu only at dinner)* Menu £ 38 (lunch)/60
♦ Long wooded drive leads to beautifully manicured gardens and stunning baronial castle. Grand, antique-filled interior boasts oak-panelled hallways, impressively proportioned lounges and Ailsa Craig views. Handsomely appointed bedrooms benefit from tall Victorian windows. Complex, ambitious dishes served in dining room.

Cosses Country House
East : 2.25 mi by A 77 (South) taking first turn left after bridge ✉ KA26 0LR ✆ (01465) 831 363 – www.cossescountryhouse.com – Closed 22 December-1 March
3 rm – †£ 75 ††£ 90 **Rest** – Menu £ 35
♦ 17C shooting lodge with lovely gardens, in idyllic rural location. Immaculately kept bedrooms – some in the old stables and byre – boast iPod docks, fresh flowers and underfloor heated bathrooms. Homemade cake on arrival in the kitchen, dining room or garden. 4 course, single-choice set dinner uses local/garden produce.

SCOTLAND

BALLATER – Aberdeenshire – **501** K12 – **pop. 1 446** **28** C1
Edinburgh 111 mi – Aberdeen 41 mi – Inverness 70 mi – Perth 67 mi
Old Royal Station, Station Square ✆ (013397) 55306, ballater@visitscotland.com
Victoria Rd, ✆ (013397) 55 567

Darroch Learg
Braemar Rd ✉ AB35 5UX – ✆ (013397) 55 443 – www.darrochlearg.co.uk – Closed last 3 weeks January and Christmas
12 rm (dinner included) – †£ 125/145 ††£ 260/320
Rest *The Conservatory* – see restaurant listing
♦ Country house hotel: enjoy superb views from its elevated position. Plush lounges with soft suites, open fires and antiques. Enticing bedrooms: upper floors have best outlook.

The Auld Kirk
Braemar Rd ✉ AB35 5RQ – ✆ (013397) 55 762 – www.theauldkirk.com – Closed 25-26 December
6 rm – †£ 70/75 ††£ 100/115
Rest – *(Closed Sunday and Sunday-Monday in winter) (dinner only)* Menu £ 35
♦ Hotel in former church with bar, lounge and breakfast room refurbished in contemporary style. Well equipped bedrooms currently being redecorated to similar standard. Restaurant in former side chapel has vaulted ceiling and chandeliers and serves traditional menu.

Moorside House without rest
26 Braemar Rd ✉ AB35 5RL – ✆ (013397) 55 492 – www.moorsidehouse.co.uk – April-October
9 rm – †£ 45 ††£ 65
♦ Detached Victorian pink stone guesthouse on main road just outside town centre. Neat garden. Vividly coloured breakfast room. Sizeable, well-furnished rooms.

XX **The Conservatory** – at Darroch Learg Hotel
Braemar Rd ✉ AB35 5UX – ✆ (013397) 55 443 – www.darrochlearg.co.uk – Closed Christmas and last 3 weeks January
Rest – *(dinner only and Sunday lunch)* Menu £ 24 (lunch)/45
◆ Attractive conservatory restaurant with a fine view from its garden location: comfortable dining enhanced by attentive service. Notably impressive wine list.

XX **Green Inn** with rm
9 Victoria Rd ✉ AB35 5QQ – ✆ (013397) 55 701 – www.green-inn.com – Closed January and November
3 rm – †£ 58 ††£ 76, ☕ £ 12.50
Rest – *(Closed Sunday-Monday) (dinner only)* Menu £ 41
◆ Former temperance hall, opposite the green, boasting comfy lounges and pleasant conservatory. Interesting, well sourced and accomplished modern British cooking. Cosy rooms.

BALLOCH – West Dunbartonshire – 501 G15 – ✉ Alexandria ▌Scotland 25 B1

Edinburgh 72 mi – Glasgow 20 mi – Stirling 30 mi
The Old Station Building, Balloch Rd ✆ (08707) 200607, info@balloch.visitscotland.com
N : Loch Lomond★★

Cameron House
Loch Lomond, Northwest : 1.5 mi by A 811 on A 82 ✉ G83 8QZ – ✆ (01389) 755 565 – www.devere.co.uk
128 rm ☕ – †£ 139/329 ††£ 159/349 – 12 suites
Rest *Martin Wishart at Loch Lomond* – see restaurant listing
Rest *Camerons Grill* – *(dinner only)* Carte £ 32/53
◆ Extensive Victorian house superbly situated on shores of Loch Lomond. Impressive leisure facilities. Luxurious rooms with four posters and panoramic views. Camerons Grill has a contemporary feel.

XXX **Martin Wishart at Loch Lomond** – at Cameron House Hotel
Loch Lomond, Northwest : 1.5 mi by A 811 on A 82 ✉ G83 8QZ – ✆ (01389) 722 504 – www.martinwishartlochlomond.co.uk – Closed 1-19 January, Monday and Tuesday
Rest – *(dinner only and Saturday-Sunday lunch)* Carte approx. £ 60
◆ Intimate restaurant with views of the mountains and loch; plush, contemporary styling, comfy central banquettes, formal service and well-presented, modern cooking.

BALLYGRANT – Argyll and Bute – 501 B16 – see Islay (Isle of)

BALMACARA – ✉ Highland 29 B2

London 582 mi – Edinburgh 198 mi – Inverness 75 mi

Balmacara Mains without rest
Glaick, West : 0.75 mi by A 87 ✉ IV40 8DN – ✆ (01599) 566 240 – www.ontheloch.com
8 rm ☕ – †£ 105/120 ††£ 105/120
◆ Superb lochside location, between Eilean Donan Castle and Skye Bridge. Stylish bedrooms vary in size, some cosy, some huge; most have loch views. Large lounge with open fire.

BALMEDIE – Aberdeenshire – 501 N12 – pop. 1 653 28 D1

Edinburgh 137 mi – Aberdeen 7 mi – Peterhead 24 mi

Cock and Bull
Ellon Rd, Blairton, North : 1 mi on A 90 ✉ AB23 8XY – ✆ (01358) 743 249 – www.thecockandbull.co.uk
Rest – Menu £ 22 (Sunday) – Carte £ 22/30
◆ Quirky pub with a profusion of knick-knacks; dine in cosy lounge, formal dining room or airy conservatory. Big, hearty portions of honest, manly food, with nothing too fancy or fiddly.

BALQUHIDDER – Stirling – 501 G14 – see Lochearnhead

BALTASOUND – Shetland Islands – **501** R1 – see Shetland Islands (Island of Unst)

BANCHORY – Aberdeenshire – **501** M12 – pop. 6 034 Scotland **28** D2

Edinburgh 118 mi – Aberdeen 17 mi – Dundee 55 mi – Inverness 94 mi

Bridge St ✆ (01330) 822000 (Easter-October), banchory@visitscotland.com

Kinneskie Kinneskie Rd, ✆ (01330) 822 365

Torphins Bog Rd, ✆ (013398) 82 115

Crathes Castle★★ (Gardens★★★) **AC**, E : 3 mi by A 93 – Cairn o'Mount Road★ (≤★★), S : by B 974. Dunnottar Castle★★ (site★★★) **AC**, SW : 15.5 mi by A 93 and A 957 – Aberdeen★★, NE : 17 mi by A 93

Banchory Lodge

Dee St ✉ AB31 5HS – ✆ (01330) 822 625 – www.banchorylodge.co.uk

22 rm – †£ 75/95 ††£ 150/170

Rest – Menu £ 21 (lunch)/25 – Carte £ 14/35

◆ Part 16C former coaching inn delightfully situated on River Dee. Country house style accentuated by antiques and china. Individually decorated bedrooms. Dee views and floral displays enhance the attraction of the dining room.

BARRA – Western Isles – **501** X12/1 – ✉ **Castlebay** **29** A3

London 506 mi – Edinburgh 132 mi

CASTLEBAY – Western Isles **29** A3

Castlebay

✉ HS9 5XD – ✆ (01871) 810 223 – www.castlebayhotel.com – Closed 22 December-31 January

15 rm – †£ 49/85 ††£ 120/150 **Rest** – *(bar lunch)* Carte £ 17/33

◆ Homely hotel boasting excellent castle and island views – the hub of the island community. Bedrooms mix styles: newer rooms feature subtle tartan fabrics; MacNeil has harbour views. Cosy lounge and busy locals bar. Linen-clad dining room serves seafood specials.

Grianamul without rest

✉ HS9 5XD – ✆ (01871) 810 416 – www.isleofbarraaccommodation.com – April-October

3 rm – †£ 40 ††£ 60

◆ Set at the heart of a small hamlet; a homely guesthouse run by caring owners. Bright, clean, spacious bedrooms. Comfortable lounge and sunny breakfast room, where huge breakfasts are served.

NORTH BAY – Western Isles **29** A3

Heathbank

✉ HS9 5YQ – ✆ (01871) 890 266 – www.barrahotel.co.uk – April- October

5 rm – †£ 60/80 ††£ 90 **Rest** – *(bar lunch) (booking essential)* Carte £ 16/26

◆ Former Presbyterian Church, now a smart, modern hotel that's popular with locals and visitors alike. Fresh, up-to-date bedrooms. Bright, airy bar that forms the hotel's hub and, along with the dining room, serves straightforward, local seafood orientated menus.

BENDERLOCH – Argyll and Bute – **501** D14 – see Connel

BERNISDALE – Highland – **501** A/B11 – see Skye (Isle of)

BISHOPTON – Renfrewshire – **501** G16 **25** B1

Edinburgh 59 mi – Dumbarton 9 mi – Glasgow 13 mi

Mar Hall

Earl of Mar Estate, Northeast : 1 mi on B 815 ✉ PA7 5NW – ✆ (0141) 812 9999 – www.marhall.com

50 rm – †£ 120/205 ††£ 140/205 – 3 suites

Rest *Cristal* – Menu £ 40 – Carte £ 29/44

◆ Stunning Gothic mansion with period charm, boasting well-equipped gym, impressive spa, and championship golf course. Stylish interior; chic, superior bedrooms. 250 acres of parkland stretch to the Clyde. High-ceilinged Cristal offers classical fine dining and unusual combinations.

SCOTLAND

BLAIRGOWRIE – Perth and Kinross – **501** J14 – **pop. 7 965** Scotland **28** C2

Edinburgh 60 mi – Dundee 19 mi – Perth 16 mi

26 Wellmeadow ✆ (01250) 872960, blairgowrie@visitscotland.com

Scone Palace★★ **AC**, S : 12 mi by A 93

Kinloch House

West : 3 mi on A 923 ✉ PH10 6SG – ✆ (01250) 884 237 – www.kinlochhouse.com – Closed 14-29 December

17 rm – †£ 100/225 ††£ 220/320 – 1 suite

Rest – Menu £ 32 (Sunday lunch)/52 (dinner)

◆ Wonderfully tranquil, ivy-clad 19C country house set in its own grounds. Appealingly traditional lounges. Conservatory and leisure centre. Large, smart, well-furnished rooms. Restaurant with bright yellow décor and Scottish influenced cooking.

Heathpark House without rest

Coupar Angus Rd, Rosemount, Southeast : 0.75 mi on A 923 ✉ PH10 6JT – ✆ (01250) 870 700 – www.heathparkhouse.com – Closed 24-26 December

3 rm – †£ 45 ††£ 75

◆ Substantial Victorian guesthouse in a quiet residential spot with mature gardens. Spacious lounge; breakfasts taken in welcoming dining room. Large, individually styled rooms.

Gilmore House without rest

Perth Rd, Southwest : 0.5 mi on A 93 ✉ PH10 6EJ – ✆ (01250) 872 791 – www.gilmorehouse.co.uk – Closed November and December

3 rm – †£ 65/80 ††£ 65/80

◆ Traditional stone-built guesthouse only a few minutes' walk from town, well run by owners. Comfortable front lounge and breakfast room. Cosy and keenly priced accommodation.

SCOTLAND

BONNYRIGG – Midlothian – **501** K16 – **pop. 14 457** **26** C1

Edinburgh 8 mi – Galashiels 27 mi – Glasgow 50 mi

Dalhousie Castle

Southeast : 1.25 mi on B 704 ✉ EH19 3JB – ✆ (01875) 820 153 – www.dalhousiecastle.co.uk

36 rm – ††£ 125/340 – 2 suites

Rest *Dungeon* – *(dinner only) (booking essential for non-residents)* Menu £ 50

Rest *The Orangery* – Menu £ 20 – Carte £ 30/42

◆ Stunning 13C castle on the riverbank, with falconry centre in its grounds. Medieval-styled interior with several drawing rooms and libraries. Bedrooms range from 'budget' to 'feature'; the best boast four-poster or canopied beds. Atmospheric Dungeon restaurant with barrel-vaulted ceiling. Good outlook from The Orangery.

BOWMORE – Argyll and Bute – **501** B16 – **see Islay (Isle of)**

BRAEMAR – Aberdeenshire – **501** J12 – **pop. 500** Scotland **28** C2

Edinburgh 85 mi – Aberdeen 58 mi – Dundee 51 mi – Perth 51 mi

The Mews, Mar Rd ✆ (013397) 41600, braemar@visitscotland.com

Cluniebank Rd, ✆ (013397) 41 618

Lin O'Dee★, W : 5 m

Callater Lodge without rest

9 Glenshee Rd ✉ AB35 5YQ – ✆ (013397) 41 275 – www.hotel-braemar.co.uk – closed 22-28 December

6 rm – †£ 40/75 ††£ 60/80

◆ Stone house in large garden on the road to Glenshee. Lounge with leather chairs and library with inglenook. Pleasant spacious bedrooms, some with view across the valley.

BREASCLETE – Western Isles Outer Hebrides – **501** Z9 – **see Lewis and Harris (Isle of)**

BROADFORD – Highland – **501** C12 – **see Skye (Isle of)**

BRODICK – North Ayrshire – **501** E17 – **see Arran (Isle of)**

BRORA – Highland – **501** I9 – **pop. 1 140** **30** D2

Edinburgh 234 mi – Inverness 78 mi – Wick 49 mi

Golf Rd, (01408) 621 417

Royal Marine

Golf Rd KW9 6QS – (01408) 621 252 – www.royalmarinebrora.com

21 rm – £ 95/119 £ 134/200 **Rest** – Carte £ 20/41

♦ Cream-washed former laird's house set next to a top golf course. Leather-furnished lounges and wood-floored bar. Smart, modern, country house bedrooms with warm fabrics and good level of facilities. Formal linen-laid restaurant offers traditional Scottish menus.

BROUGHTY FERRY – Dundee – **501** L14 – see Dundee

BUNCHREW – Highland – see Inverness

BURRAY – Orkney Islands – **501** L7 – see Orkney Islands

BUTE (Isle of) – Argyll and Bute – **501** E16 – **pop. 7 354** **27** B3

from Rothesay to Wemyss Bay (Mainland) (Caledonian MacBrayne Ltd) frequent services daily (35 mn) – from Rhubodach to Colintraive (Mainland) (Caledonian MacBrayne Ltd) frequent services daily (5 mn)

Ascog – Argyll and Bute **27** B3

Balmory Hall without rest

Balmory Rd PA20 9LL – (01700) 500 669 – www.balmoryhall.com – Closed Christmas and New Year

4 rm – £ 155 £ 170

♦ 19C Italianate mansion with boules pitch and croquet lawn. Impressive original features include ornate plaster ceilings, gilt cornicing, Doric columns and a grand cantilevered staircase. Dramatic photos and family artwork abound. Homemade bread/jam at breakfast.

CADBOLL – Highland – see Tain

CALLANDER – Stirling – **501** H15 – **pop. 2 754** Scotland **28** C2

Edinburgh 52 mi – Glasgow 43 mi – Oban 71 mi – Perth 41 mi

Rob Roy and Trossachs Visitor Centre, Ancaster Sq (08707) 200628, callander@visitscotland.com

Aveland Rd, (01877) 330 090

Town★

The Trossachs★★★ (Loch Katrine★★) – Hilltop Viewpoint★★★ (✻★★★) W : 10 mi by A 821

Roman Camp

Main St FK17 8BG – (01877) 330 003 – www.romancamphotel.co.uk

11 rm – £ 95/145 £ 185/195 – 3 suites

Rest ***The Restaurant*** – see restaurant listing

♦ Attractive 17C former hunting lodge by Roman settlement. Characterful interior with beautiful drawing room, antique-filled library and chapel. Classical bedrooms boast bold floral designs.

Lubnaig without rest

Leny Feus FK17 8AS – (01877) 330 376 – www.lubnaighouse.co.uk – Open May to October

8 rm – £ 45/55 £ 74/84

♦ Built in 1864, a characterful Victorian house on the outskirts of town. Well-kept mature gardens visible from communal rooms. Homely bedrooms, two in converted stables.

XXX **The Restaurant** – at Roman Camp Hotel

Main St ✉ FK17 8BG – ✆ (01877) 330 003 – www.romancamphotel.co.uk

Rest – Menu £ 27 (lunch)/49 – Carte dinner £ 44/68

◆ Spacious country house restaurant with unique ceiling and impressive flower displays. Daily changing set menu and concise à la carte offer ambitious modern dishes of local, seasonal produce.

X **Mhor Fish**

75-77 Main St ✉ FK17 8DX – ✆ (01877) 330 213 – www.mhor.net – Closed 25-26 December, 1 January and Monday

Rest – Seafood – Carte £ 18/30

◆ Simple, busy, well-run eatery on main street; popular with locals. Great variety of fish, homemade pies and chips cooked in beef dripping. A touch more serious in the evening.

CARINISH – Western Isles – 501 Y11 – see Uist (Isles of)

CARNOUSTIE – Angus – 501 L14 – pop. 10 561 — 28 D2

Edinburgh 68 mi – Aberdeen 59 mi – Dundee 12 mi

Carnoustie Library, 21 High St ✆ (01241) 859620, carnoustie.library@angus.gov.uk

Monifieth Golf Links Princes St, Medal Starter's Box, ✆ (01382) 532 767

Burnside Links Par, ✆ (01241) 802 290

Panmure Barry, ✆ (01241) 855 120

Buddon Links Links Par, ✆ (01241) 802 280

The Old Manor without rest

Panbride, Northeast : 1.25 mi by A 930 on Panbride Rd ✉ DD7 6JP – ✆ (01241) 854 804 – www.oldmanorcarnoustie.com – Closed Christmas and New Year

5 rm – †£ 60 ††£ 80

◆ Substantial 18C house five minutes' drive from championship golf course. Good views of Tay Estuary. Hearty Scottish breakfast guaranteed. Smart rooms, some with brass beds.

CARRADALE – Argyll and Bute – 501 D17 – see Kintyre (Peninsula)

CASTLEBAY – Western Isles – 501 X12/1 – see Barra (Isle of)

CASTLE DOUGLAS – Dumfries and Galloway – 501 I19 – pop. 3 671 — 25 B3

Scotland

Edinburgh 98 mi – Ayr 49 mi – Dumfries 18 mi – Stranraer 57 mi

Market Hill ✆ (01556) 502611 (Easter-October), castledouglastic@visitscotland.com

Abercromby Rd, ✆ (01556) 502 801

Threave Garden★★ **AC**, SW : 2.5 mi by A 75 – Threave Castle★ **AC**, W : 1 m

Douglas House without rest

63 Queen St ✉ DG7 1HS – ✆ (01556) 503 262 – www.douglas-house.com – Closed January and Christmas

4 rm – †£ 37/65 ††£ 70/85

◆ Attractive 19C stone-built house, set close to the high street. Open-plan lounge and breakfast room. Comfy, individually decorated bedrooms with contemporary feel. Extensive breakfast menu.

CAWDOR – Highland – 501 I11 – pop. 812 – ✉ Inverness — 30 D2

Edinburgh 170 mi – Aberdeen 100 mi – Inverness 14 mi

Cawdor Tavern

The Lane ✉ IV12 5XP – ✆ (01667) 404 777 – www.cawdortavern.co.uk – Closed 2 weeks January, 25 December and 1 January

Rest – *(booking essential)* Carte £ 16/26

◆ Charming, personally run whitewashed pub – formerly the joiners' workshop of Cawdor Castle. Wide-ranging menu offers a good selection of frequently changing, classically based dishes.

SCOTLAND

CHIRNSIDE – Scottish Borders – 501 N16 – pop. 1 204 – ✉ Duns 26 D1

Edinburgh 52 mi – Berwick-upon-Tweed 8 mi – Glasgow 95 mi – Newcastle upon Tyne 70 mi

Chirnside Hall

East : 1.75 mi on A 6105 ✉ TD11 3LD – ✆ (01890) 818 219 – www.chirnsidehallhotel.com – Closed March

10 rm – †£ 95/165 ††£ 165/180

Rest – *(dinner only) (booking essential for non-residents)* Menu £ 30

♦ Sizeable 1834 country house with lovely revolving door; boasting beautiful views over the Cheviots. Grand lounges with original cornicing and huge fireplaces. Cosy, classical bedrooms, some have four-posters. Local, seasonal dishes in traditional dining room.

CLEAT – Orkney Islands – 501 K/L6 – see Orkney Islands (Island of Westray) – ✉ Orkney Islands

COLONSAY (Isle of) – Argyll and Bute – 501 B15 – pop. 106 27 A2

London 502 mi – Edinburgh 129 mi – Greenock 98 mi

from Scalasaig to Oban (Caledonian MacBrayne Ltd) 3 weekly (2 h) – from Scalasaig to Kintyre Peninsula (Kennacraig) via Isle of Islay (Port Askaig) (Caledonian MacBrayne Ltd) weekly

Colonsay, ✆ (01951) 200 290

SCALASAIG – Argyll and Bute – ✉ Colonsay 27 A2

The Colonsay

✉ PA61 7YP – ✆ (01951) 200 316 – www.colonsayestate.co.uk – March-October, Christmas and New Year

9 rm – †£ 65/110 ††£ 90/110, £ 6.50

Rest – *(bar lunch)* Carte £ 21/29

♦ Listed building from mid-18C; a thoroughly rural, remote setting. Public areas include excellent photos of local scenes and the only bar on the island. Bright, modern rooms. Welcoming, informal dining room.

COMRIE – Perth and Kinross – 501 I14 – pop. 1 926 28 C2

Edinburgh 66 mi – Glasgow 56 mi – Oban 70 mi – Perth 24 mi

Comrie Laggan Braes, ✆ (01764) 670 055

Royal

Melville Sq ✉ PH6 2DN – ✆ (01764) 679 200 – www.royalhotel.co.uk – Closed 25-26 December

11 rm – †£ 85 ††£ 140

Rest *Royal* – Menu £ 29 (dinner) – Carte £ 21/30

♦ 18C coaching inn in centre of town: Queen Victoria once stayed here. Stylish, contemporary feel, especially individually decorated bedrooms, with four posters and antiques. Restaurant with two rooms: conservatory brasserie or intimate dining room.

CONNEL – Argyll and Bute – 501 D14 – ✉ Oban 27 B2

Edinburgh 118 mi – Glasgow 88 mi – Inverness 113 mi – Oban 5 mi

Ards House without rest

on A 85 ✉ PA37 1PT – ✆ (01631) 710 255 – www.ardshouse.com – Closed Christmas and New Year

4 rm – †£ 50/60 ††£ 90/94

♦ Attractive house with equally welcoming, hospitable owner. Large, homely, open-fired lounge packed with books and antiques. Cosy, personally decorated bedrooms show good attention to detail; small bathrooms boast locally made toiletries. Excellent breakfasts.

Oyster Inn with rm
✉ *PA37 1PJ – ✆ (01631) 710 666 – www.oysterinn.co.uk – Closed 26 December*
11 rm ☕ – †£ 55/71 ††£ 95/125 **Rest** – Seafood – Carte £ 15/55
◆ Cosy 18C pub looking over the Falls or Lora and the bay. Rustic bar serves pub classics. Smarter, nautically themed restaurant offers a regularly changing seafood menu and views of the sunset. Bedrooms are modern and colourful; budget bunk rooms are available.

at Benderloch North : 2.5 mi by A 828 – ✉ Connel

Dun Na Mara without rest
✉ *PA37 1RT – ✆ (01631) 720 233 – www.dunnamara.com – Closed December and January*
7 rm ☕ – †£ 50/65 ††£ 95/120
◆ Whitewashed Edwardian house affording excellent bay/Isle of Mull views; its name meaning 'Hill Foot by the Sea'. Charming interior with minimalist, Scandinavian feel; bedrooms boast original fireplaces and modern bathrooms. Lovely gardens lead to a private beach.

CRAIGNURE – Argyll and Bute – **501** C14 – see Mull (Isle of)

CRIEFF – Perth and Kinross – **501** I14 – pop. 6 579 Scotland **28** C2

Edinburgh 60 mi – Glasgow 50 mi – Oban 76 mi – Perth 18 mi
Town Hall, High St ✆ (01764) 652578, criefftic@visitscotland.com
27 Perth Rd, ✆ (01764) 652 909
9 Muthill Peat Rd, ✆ (01764) 681 523
Town★
Drummond Castle Gardens★ **AC**, S : 2 mi by A 822. Scone Palace★★ **AC**, E : 16 mi by A 85 and A 93

Merlindale
Perth Rd, on A 85 ✉ PH7 3EQ – ✆ (01764) 655 205 – www.merlindale.co.uk – Mid-January to mid-December
3 rm ☕ – †£ 60/65 ††£ 80/90 **Rest** – Menu £ 30
◆ Spacious manor house with comfy lounge, well-stocked library and dark wood furnished dining room with long communal table. Large, immaculately kept bedrooms have classical furnishings and heavy floral drapes. Sizeable bathrooms boast roll-top or jacuzzi baths. Family style breakfasts. Home-cooked, set 3 course dinners.

Yann's at Glenearn House with rm
Perth Rd, on A 85 ✉ PH7 3EQ – ✆ (01764) 650 111 – www.yannsatglenearnhouse.com – Closed 2 weeks spring, 2 weeks October
5 rm ☕ – †£ 55/60 ††£ 80/85
Rest – French – *(Closed 25-26 December, Monday-Tuesday, and Wednesday-Friday lunch)* Carte £ 20/29
◆ Busy, keenly run, bistro-style restaurant with informal lounge. Well-priced, French cooking makes good use of Scottish produce; Savoyard sharing dishes a speciality. Polite, swift service. Comfortable bedrooms with good facilities and a relaxed, bohemian style.

at Muthill South 3mi by A 822

Barley Bree with rm
6 Willoughby St ✉ PH5 2AB – ✆ (01764) 681 451 – www.barleybree.com – Closed 2 weeks January, 2 weeks October, Monday and Tuesday
6 rm ☕ – †£ 60 ††£ 100/130 **Rest** – *(booking advisable)* Carte £ 16/32 **s**
◆ Converted coaching inn in centre of busy village; spacious, fire-lit sitting room and dining room hung with farming implements. Generous portions of classical rustic cooking utilise local ingredients. Cloth-clad tables and friendly service. Comfortable bedrooms.

CRINAN – Argyll and Bute – **501** D15 – ✉ **Lochgilphead** Scotland **27** B2

Edinburgh 137 mi – Glasgow 91 mi – Oban 36 mi

Hamlet★

Kilmory Knap (Macmillan's Cross★) SW : 14 m

Crinan

✉ PA31 8SR – ☎ (01546) 830 261 – www.crinanhotel.com – Closed 4-31 January and 22-28 December

20 rm (dinner included) – †£ 120/145 ††£ 200/320

Rest *Westward* – *(dinner only)* Menu £ 40

Rest *Mainbrace* – Carte £ 18/34

◆ Superbly located, well-run hotel with commanding views of Loch Crinan and Sound of Jura. Simply furnished bedrooms set over 3 floors; best on 3rd floor are spacious with large windows. Emphasis on fresh seafood in Westward Restaurant. Interesting bar menu in The Mainbrace.

CULLODEN – Highland – **501** H11 – see Inverness

CUPAR – Fife – **501** K15 – **pop. 8 506** **28** C2

Edinburgh 45 mi – Dundee 15 mi – Perth 23 mi

Ostler's Close

25 Bonnygate ✉ KY15 4BU – ☎ (01334) 655 574 – www.ostlerclose.co.uk – Closed 1-2 January, 25-26 December, Sunday and Monday

Rest – *(dinner only and Saturday lunch)* Carte £ 25/42

◆ Personally run, welcoming restaurant with snug cottage feel and characterful low ceilings; hidden away down an alley. Particular attention given to prime Scottish meat and local fish.

CURRIE – City of Edinburgh – **501** K16 – See Edinburgh

DALRY – North Ayrshire – **501** F16 **25** A1

Edinburgh 70 mi – Ayr 21 mi – Glasgow 25 mi

Lochwood Farm Steading without rest

Southwest : 5 mi by A 737 and Saltcoats rd ✉ KA21 6NG – ☎ (01294) 552 529 – www.lochwoodfarm.co.uk – February-November

3 rm – ††£ 130

◆ Remotely located farmhouse on 100 acre working dairy farm. 3 substantial outbuildings house luxuriously appointed suites boasting fine linens, Isle of Arran toiletries and outdoor hot tubs.

Braidwoods (Keith Braidwood)

Drumastle Mill Cottage, Southwest : 1.5 mi by A 737 on Saltcoats rd ✉ KA24 4LN – ☎ (01294) 833 544 – www.braidwoods.co.uk – Closed 25 December for 3 weeks, 2 weeks September, Sunday dinner, Monday, Tuesday lunch and Sunday from May-September

Rest – *(booking essential)* Menu £ 25/40

Spec. Seared scallops on tomato and coriander dhal. Best end of Ayrshire lamb with Savoy cabbage parcel. Iced honeycomb parfait with a tayberry coulis.

◆ Well-established crofter's cottage in remote location; very personally run by husband and wife team. Two-part dining room with homely feel. Seasonal, regional produce is the cornerstone of the flavoursome classical dishes. Smooth service.

DINGWALL – Highland – **501** G11 – **pop. 5 026** **30** C2

Edinburgh 172 mi – Inverness 14 mi

Cafe India Brasserie

Lockhart House, Tulloch St ✉ IV15 9JZ – ☎ (01349) 862 552 – www.cafeindiadingwall.co.uk – closed 25 December

Rest – Indian – Menu £ 9 (lunch)/39 – Carte £ 22/33

◆ Bustling, locally regarded Indian restaurant, handily located in town centre. Updated décor is fresh and modern. Authentically prepared, tasty regional Indian food.

DORNOCH – Highland – **501** H10 – **pop. 1 206** Scotland **30** D2

Edinburgh 219 mi – Inverness 63 mi – Wick 65 mi

Sheriff Court House, Castle St (08452) 255121, dornoch@visitscotland.com

Royal Dornoch Golf Rd, (01862) 810 219

Town★

Highfield House without rest

Evelix Rd IV25 3HR – (01862) 810 909 – www.highfieldhouse.co.uk – Closed Christmas and New Year

4 rm – †£ 55 ††£ 75/90

◆ Welcoming guesthouse with immaculately kept gardens and pleasant summer house. Spacious interior boasts conservatory style lounge and smart breakfast room. Comfy bedrooms have good facilities.

DOUNBY – Orkney Islands – **501** K6 – see Orkney Islands

DRUMBEG – Highland – **501** E9 – Highland **30** C1

Edinburgh 262 mi – Inverness 105 mi – Ullapool 48 mi

Blar na Leisg at Drumbeg House

take first right on entering village from Kylesku direction IV27 4NW – (01571) 833 325 – www.drumbeghouse.co.uk

4 rm (dinner included) – †£ 125 ††£ 250

Rest – Menu £ 45

◆ Remotely set Edwardian house, affording lovely loch views. Large, open-fired sitting room filled with a vast array of books; spacious, luxuriously appointed bedrooms. Impressive modern art collection includes lots of Bauhaus works. Smart, contemporary dining room; fresh, local fish and shellfish are a speciality.

DRUMNADROCHIT – Highland – **501** G11 – **pop. 813** – Milton **30** C2
Scotland

Edinburgh 172 mi – Inverness 16 mi – Kyle of Lochalsh 66 mi

Loch Ness★★ – Loch Ness Monster Exhibition★ **AC** – The Great Glen★

Drumbuie Farm without rest

Drumbuie, East : 0.75 mi by A 82 IV63 6XP – (01456) 450 634 – www.loch-ness-farm.co.uk – Closed Christmas

3 rm – †£ 40/45 ††£ 65/70

◆ Immaculate purpose-built guesthouse on working farm with Highland cattle. Pleasant breakfast room has Loch Ness views. Good collection of malt whiskies. Spacious bedrooms.

DUISDALEMORE – Highland – see Skye (Isle of)

DUMFRIES – Dumfries and Galloway – **501** J18 – **pop. 31 146** **26** C3
Scotland

Edinburgh 80 mi – Ayr 59 mi – Carlisle 34 mi – Glasgow 79 mi

64 Whitesands (01387) 253862, dumfriestic@visitscotland.com A

Dumfries & Galloway Maxwelltown 2 Laurieston Ave, (01387) 253 582

Dumfries & County Edinburgh Rd, Nunfield, (01387) 253 585

Crichton Bankend Rd, (01387) 247 894

Town★ – Midsteeple★ A **A**

Lincluden College (Tomb★) **AC**, N : 1.5 mi by College St A. Drumlanrig Castle★★ (cabinets★) **AC**, NW : 16.5 mi by A 76 A – Shambellie House Museum of Costume (Costume Collection★) S : 7.25 mi by A 710 A - Sweetheart Abbey★ **AC**, S : 8 mi by A 710 A – Caerlaverock Castle★ (Renaissance fa 0.5ade★★) **AC**, SE : 9 mi by B 725 B – Glenkiln (Sculptures★) W : 9 mi by A 780 - A - and A 75

SCOTLAND

DUMFRIES

Street	Grid	No.
Aldermanhill Rd	B	2
Bank St	A	3
Buccleuch St	A	4
Cardoness St	B	5
Cassalands	A	6
Castle Douglas Rd	A	8
Castle St	A	7
Catherine St	B	9
Corberry Ave	A	10
Cornwall Mount Rd	B	12
Cuckoo Bridge Retail Park	A	
Friars Vennel	A	13
Galloway St	A	14
Glebe St	B	15
Great King St	A	16
Hermitage Drive	A	17
High St	A	18
Loreburn Centre	A	20
Loreburn St	A	21
Nith St	AB	22
Queensberry St	A	24
Queen St	B	23
Rae St	B	26
St Mary's St	B	27
St Michael St	B	28
St Michael's Bridge Rd	A	30
Shakespeare St	B	31
Union St	A	32
Whitesands	A	34

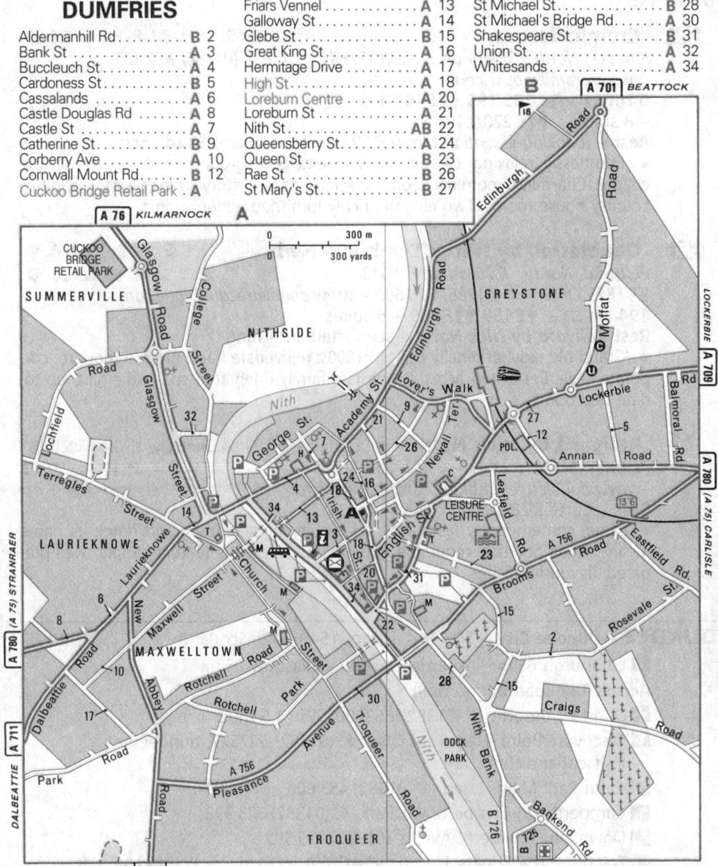

Hazeldean House without rest
4 Moffat Rd ✉ DG1 1NJ – ✆ (01387) 266 178 – www.hazeldeanhouse.com
6 rm ☐ – 🛉£ 35/45 🛉🛉£ 60 **Bu**
◆ Victorian villa built in 1898. Lovely garden; curio-filled lounge and conservatory breakfast room. Victorian-themed bedrooms, 3 with four-posters; basement room has a nautical cabin style.

Hamilton House without rest
12 Moffat Rd ✉ DG1 1NJ – ✆ (01387) 266 606
– www.hamiltonhousedumfries.co.uk – Closed Christmas and New Year
7 rm ☐ – 🛉£ 40/45 🛉🛉£ 58/60 **Bc**
◆ Converted Victorian townhouse next to the bowls club. Large conservatory lounge; neat breakfast tables overlook the tennis courts. Large bedrooms combine the classical and the contemporary.

DUNBLANE – Stirling – **501** I15 – **pop. 7 911** Scotland **28** C2

Edinburgh 42 mi – Glasgow 33 mi – Perth 29 mi

Town★ – Cathedral★★ (west front★★)

Doune★ (castle★ **AC**) W : 4.5 mi by A 820

Cromlix House
Kinbuck, North : 3.5 mi on B 8033 ✉ *FK15 9JT* – ✆ *(01786) 822 125*
– *www.cromlixhouse.com*
6 rm – £ 105/195 £ 105/195
– 8 suites – £ 220/295
Rest – *(booking essential)* Menu £ 22 (weekday lunch)/50 (dinner)
◆ Effortlessly relaxing 19C mansion in extensive grounds with ornate private chapel. Charming morning room; spacious conservatory with plants. Definitive country house rooms. Two elegant, richly furnished dining rooms.

Doubletree by Hilton Dunblane Hydro
Perth Rd, North : .0.75 mi on B 8033
✉ *FK15 OHG* – ✆ *(01786) 826 600* – *www.doubletreedunblane.com*
194 rm – £ 159 £ 169 – 6 suites
Rest *Kailyard by Nick Nairn* – see restaurant listing
◆ 'Grand old lady' originally built in 1800s; rejuvenated and given a modern, corporate style. Set in ten acres, it boasts a family orientated spa and smart, up-to-date bedrooms.

Kailyard by Nick Nairn – at Doubletree by Hilton Dunblane Hydro Hotel
Perth Rd ✉ *FK15 OHG* – ✆ *(01786) 822 551*
– *www.doubletreedunblane.com/the_kailyard*
Rest – Carte £ 28/33
◆ Large, contemporary restaurant set within characterful, grand hotel; its name means 'small Scottish vegetable garden'. Rustic menus feature simple, well-prepared, flavourful dishes.

SCOTLAND

DUNDEE – Dundee City – 501 L14 – pop. 154 674 Scotland 28 C2

Edinburgh 63 mi – Aberdeen 67 mi – Glasgow 83 mi
Access Tay Road Bridge (toll) Y
Dundee Airport : ✆ (01382) 662200, SW : 1.5 mi Z
Discovery Point, Discovery Quay ✆ (01382) 527527, dundee@visitscotland.com
Caird Park Mains Loan, ✆ (01382) 453 606
Camperdown Camperdown Park, ✆ (01382) 623 398
Downfield Turnberry Ave, ✆ (01382) 825 595
Town★ - The Frigate Unicorn★ **AC** Y **A** – Discovery Point★ **AC** Y **B** – Verdant Works★ Z **D** – McManus Galleries★ Y **M**

Apex City Quay
1 West Victoria Dock Rd ✉ *DD1 3JP* – ✆ *(01382) 202 404*
– *www.apexhotels.co.uk* Y**a**
150 rm – £ 80/230 £ 80/230, £ 13.50 – 2 suites
Rest *Metro Brasserie* – Menu £ 14/22 – Carte £ 24/35
◆ Modern hotel on the waterfront. Business and leisure facilities to the fore, the smart spa offering plenty of treatments. Vast bar and lounge. Airy, up-to-date rooms all with views. Comfy banquette booths and modern menu in informal Metro Brasserie.

at Broughty Ferry East : 4.5 mi by A 930 - Z – ✉ Dundee

Broughty Ferry
16 West Queen St ✉ *DD5 1AR* – ✆ *(01382) 480 027*
– *www.hotelbroughtyferry.co.uk*
16 rm – £ 68/80 £ 88
Rest *Bombay Brasserie* – Indian – Carte £ 16/26 **s**
◆ Family owned and friendly modern hotel beside the main road. The spacious, individually decorated bedrooms are furnished to a high standard. Brasserie serves elaborate, authentic Indian and European-influenced menus.

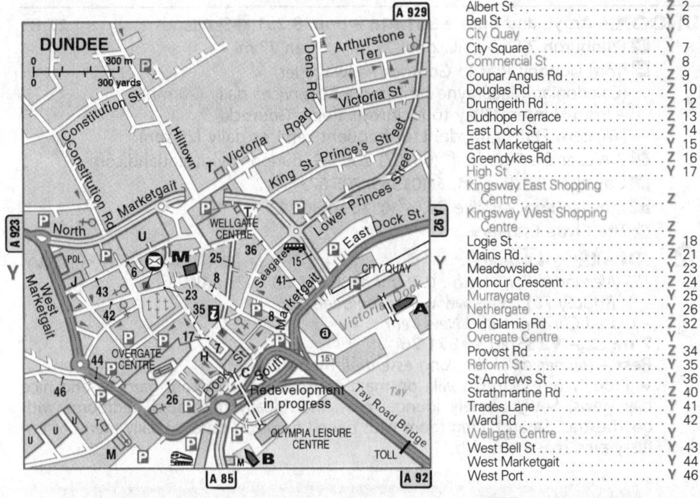

Albert St	Z	2
Bell St	Y	6
City Quay	Y	
City Square	Y	7
Commercial St	Y	8
Coupar Angus Rd	Z	9
Douglas Rd	Z	10
Drumgeith Rd	Z	12
Dudhope Terrace	Z	13
East Dock St	Z	14
East Marketgait	Y	15
Greendykes Rd	Z	16
High St	Y	17
Kingsway East Shopping Centre	Z	
Kingsway West Shopping Centre	Z	
Logie St	Z	18
Mains Rd	Z	21
Meadowside	Y	23
Moncur Crescent	Z	24
Murraygate	Y	25
Nethergate	Y	26
Old Glamis Rd	Z	32
Overgate Centre	Y	
Provost Rd	Z	34
Reform St	Y	35
St Andrews St	Y	36
Strathmartine Rd	Z	40
Trades Lane	Y	41
Ward Rd	Y	42
Wellgate Centre	Y	
West Bell St	Y	43
West Marketgait	Y	44
West Port	Y	46

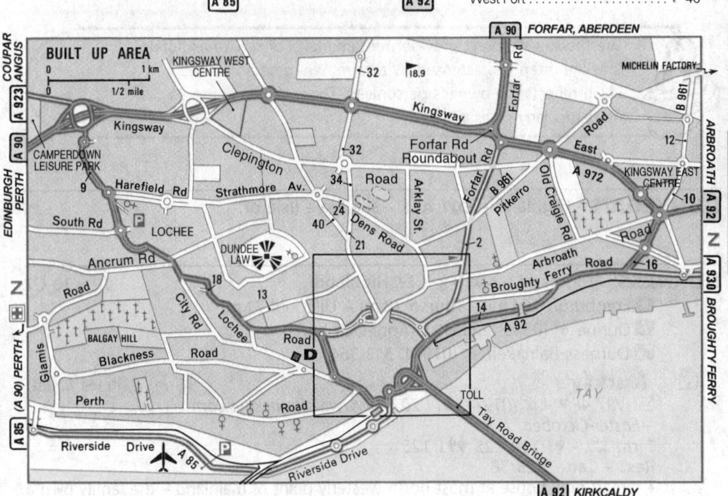

SCOTLAND

DUNKELD – Perth and Kinross – 501 J14 – pop. 1 005 Scotland 28 C2

Edinburgh 58 mi – Aberdeen 88 mi – Inverness 98 mi – Perth 14 mi

The Cross ✆ (01350) 727688 (April-October), dunkeld@visitscotland.com

Dunkeld & Birnam Fungarth, ✆ (01350) 727 524

Village★ - Cathedral Street★

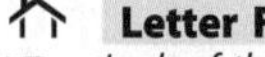

Letter Farm without rest

Loch of the Lowes, Northeast : 3 mi by A 923 on Loch of Lowes rd ✉ PH8 0HH – ✆ (01350) 724 254 – www.letterfarm.co.uk – May-November

3 rm – †£ 45 ††£ 76

◆ Attractive, traditional farm house close to the Loch of Lowes Nature Reserve. Welcoming, homely atmosphere and comfortable bedrooms.

DUNOON – Argyll and Bute – 501 F16 – pop. 8 251 Scotland 27 B3

Edinburgh 73 mi – Glasgow 27 mi – Oban 77 mi

from Dunoon Pier to Gourock Railway Pier
(Caledonian MacBrayne Ltd) frequent services daily (20 mn)
– from Hunters Quay to McInroy's Point, Gourock
(Western Ferries (Clyde) Ltd) frequent services daily (20 mn)

7 Alexandra Parade (08707) 200629, dunoon@visitscotland.com

Cowal Ardenslate Rd, (01369) 705 673

Innellan Knockamillie Rd, (01369) 830 242

The Clyde Estuary★

Dhailling Lodge

rm, VISA

155 Alexandra Par, North : 0.75 mi on A 815 PA23 8AW
– (01369) 701 253 – www.dhaillinglodge.com
– Closed Christmas and New Year

7 rm – £ 35/40 £ 71/76

Rest – *(dinner only) (booking essential)* Menu £ 20

◆ Proudly run Victorian villa on main seafront, with pleasant gardens and nice bay views. Snug, homely lounge; cosy, individually decorated bedrooms with good extras. Smart dining room with period fireplace; classical daily menu of unfussy pies, roasts and fish.

Guesthouses don't provide the same level of service as hotels. They are often characterised by a warm welcome and a décor which reflects the owner's personality. Those shown in red are particularly pleasant.

SCOTLAND

DUNVEGAN – Highland – 501 A11 – see Skye (Isle of)

DURNESS – Highland – 501 F8 – Highland 30 C1

Edinburgh 266 mi – Thurso 78 mi – Ullapool 71 mi

Durine (0845) 2255121 (April-October)

Durness Balnakeil, (01971) 511 364

Mackay's

rm, VISA AE

IV27 4PN – (01971) 511 202 – www.visitmackays.com
– Easter-October

7 rm – £ 110/125 £ 125

Rest – Carte £ 23/38

◆ Smart grey house at most north westerly point of mainland – the family own a number of places in the village. Two nicely furnished, oak-clad lounges. Lovely bedrooms with exposed wood floors, plasma screens and iPod docks. Formal dining room offers ambitious menu.

DUROR – Highland – 501 E14 29 B3

Edinburgh 131 mi – Ballachulish 7 mi – Oban 26 mi

Bealach House

VISA AE

Salachan Glen, Southeast : 4.5 mi by A 828 PA38 4BW
– (01631) 740 298 – www.bealach-house.co.uk
– Mid-February to early November

3 rm – £ 70 £ 100

Rest – Menu £ 30

◆ Superbly set, former crofter's house with impressive 1.5 mile driveway lined with mature, deer-filled forest: the scenery is breathtaking. Snug conservatory and cosy bedrooms; homely guest areas are hung with Lowry tapestries. Classical, daily changing menu.

DYKE – Moray – **501** J11 – see Forres

EDDLESTON – Scottish Borders – **501** K16 – see Peebles

EDINBANE – Highland – **501** A11 – see Skye (Isle of)

M.-P. Renier/MICHELIN

EDINBURGH

County: City of Edinburgh
Michelin regional map: **501** K16
Glasgow 46 mi
– Newcastle upon Tyne 105 mi

Population: 430 082
Scotland
Map reference: **26** C1

PRACTICAL INFORMATION

Tourist Information

Edinburgh & Scotland Information Centre, 3 Princes St (08452) 255 121, info@visitscotland.com

Edinburgh International Airport, (0870) 040 0007, edinburgh.airport@visitscotland.com

Airport

Edinburgh Airport : (0844) 481 8989, W : 6 mi by A 8 AV

Golf Courses

36 Braid Hills Braid Hills Rd, (0131) 447 6666

18 Carrick Knowe Glendevon Park, (0131) 337 10 96

18 Duddingston Duddingston Road West, (0131) 661 7688

18 Silverknowes Parkway, (0131) 336 3843

18 Liberton 297 Gilmerton Rd, Kingston Grange, (0131) 664 3009

36 Marriott Dalmahoy Hotel & C.C. Kriknewton, (0131) 335 80 10

9 Portobello Stanley St, (0131) 669 4361

SIGHTS

In town

City★★★ - Edinburgh International Festival★★★ (August) - Royal Museum of Scotland★★★ EZ **M2** – National Gallery of Scotland★★ DY **M4** - Royal Botanic Garden★★★ AV – The Castle★★ **AC** DYZ : Site★★★ - Palace Block (Honours of Scotland★★★) - St Margaret's Chapel (✻★★★) - Great Hall (Hammerbeam Roof★★) – ⋞★★ from Argyle and Mill's Mount DZ - Abbey and Palace of Holyroodhouse★★ **AC** (Plasterwork Ceilings★★★, ✻★★ from Arthur's Seat) BV – Royal Mile★★ : St Giles' Cathedral★★ (Crown Spire★★★) EYZ - Gladstone's Land★ **AC** EYZ **A** - Canongate Talbooth★ EY **B** – New Town★★ (Charlotte Square★★★ CY **14** - The Georgian House★ **AC** CY **D** – Scottish National Portrait Gallery★ EY **M6** - Dundas House★ EY **E**) – Scottish National Gallery of Modern Art★ AV **M1** - Victoria Street★ EZ **84** – Scott Monument★ (⋞★) **AC** EY **F** - Craigmillar Castle★ **AC**, SE : 3 mi by A 7 BX – - Calton Hill (✻★★★ **AC** from Nelson's Monument) EY – Dean Gallery★ AV opposite **M1** - Royal Yacht Britannia★ BV

On the outskirts

Edinburgh Zoo★★ **AC** AV – Hill End Ski Centre (✻★★) **AC**, S : 5.5 mi by A 702 BX – The Royal Observatory (West Tower ⋞★) **AC** BX – Ingleston, Scottish Agricultural Museum★, W : 6.5 mi by A 8 AV

In the surrounding area

Rosslyn Chapel★★ **AC** (Apprentice Pillar★★★) S : 7.5 mi by A 701 - BX - and B 7006 – Forth Bridges★★, NW : 9.5 mi by A 90 AV – Hopetoun House★★ **AC**, NW : 11.5 mi by A 90 - AV - and A 904 – Dalmeny★ - Dalmeny House★ **AC**, St Cuthbert's Church★ (Norman South Doorway★★) NW : 7 mi by A 90 AV – Crichton Castle (Italianate courtyard range★) **AC**, SE : 10 mi by A 7 - X - and B 6372

EDINBURGH

Street	Grid	No.
Bernard Terrace	EZ	3
Bread St	DZ	6
Bristo Pl.	EZ	7
Candlemaker Row	EZ	9
Castlehill	DZ	10
Castle St	DY	
Chambers St	EZ	12
Chapel St	EZ	13
Charlotte Square	CY	14
Deanhaugh St	CY	23
Douglas Gardens	CY	25
Drummond St	EZ	27
Forrest Rd	EZ	31
Frederick St	DY	
Gardner's Crescent	CZ	32
George IV Bridge	EZ	33
George St	DY	
Grassmarket	DZ	35
Hanover St	DY	
High St	EYZ	37
Home St	DZ	38
Hope St	CY	39
Johnston Terrace	DZ	42
King's Bridge	DZ	44
King's Stables Rd	DZ	45
Lawnmarket	EYZ	46
Leith St	EY	47
Leven St	DZ	48
Lothian St	EZ	51
Mound (The)	DY	55
North Bridge	EY	61
North St Andrew St	EY	66
Princes St	DY	
Raeburn Pl.	CY	69
Randolph Crescent	CY	71
St Andrew Square	EY	73
St James Centre	EY	
St Mary's St	EY	75
Shandwick Pl.	CYZ	77
South Charlotte St	DY	78
South St David St	DEY	79
Spittal St	DZ	83
Victoria St	EZ	84
Waterloo Pl.	EY	87
Waverley Bridge	EY	89
Waverley Market	EY	
West Maitland St	CZ	92

Traffic subject to disruption due to tram construction

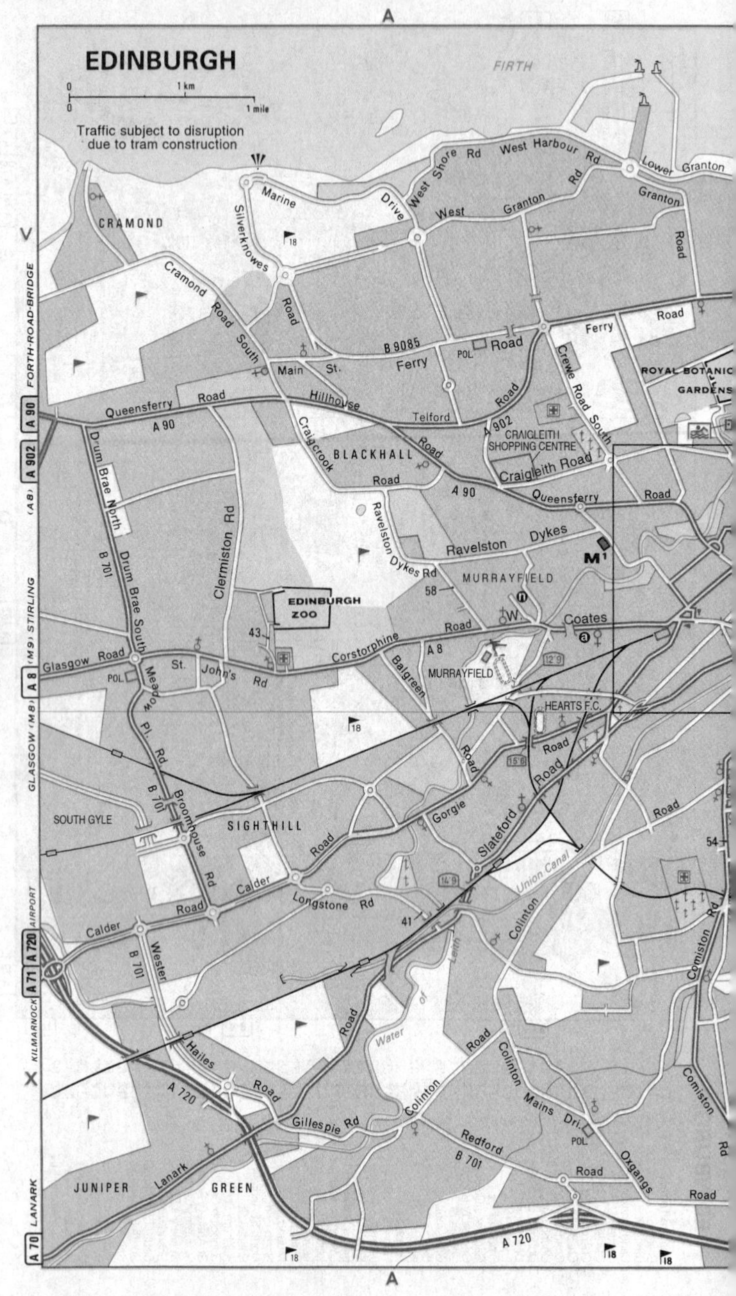
EDINBURGH
0 1 km
0 1 mile
Traffic subject to disruption due to tram construction
FIRTH
CRAMOND
Marine Drive
Silverknowes Road
West Shore Rd
West Harbour Rd
Lower Granton
West Granton Rd
Granton Road
Cramond Road South
Main St.
B 9085 Ferry Road
POL.
Ferry Road
Crewe Road South
ROYAL BOTANIC GARDENS
Queensferry Road
A 90
Hillhouse Road
Telford Road
A 902
CRAIGLEITH SHOPPING CENTRE
Craigleith Road
Craigcrook Road
BLACKHALL
Drum Brae North
Queensferry Road
Ravelston Dykes
Ravelston Dykes Rd
M1
MURRAYFIELD
Clermiston Rd
EDINBURGH ZOO
B 701
Drum Brae South
Coates
Corstorphine Road
A 8
Glasgow Road
St. John's Rd
Meadow Pl. Rd
Balgreen Road
MURRAYFIELD
HEARTS F.C.
Gorgie Road
Slateford Road
Union Canal
SOUTH GYLE
SIGHTHILL
Broomhouse Rd
Calder Road
Longstone Rd
Colinton Road
Comiston Rd
Calder Road
Wester Hailes Road
Water of Leith
Colinton Road
Colinton Mains Dri.
Comiston Rd
A 720
Gillespie Rd
Redford Road
B 701
Oxgangs Road
JUNIPER GREEN
Lanark
A 720
A
V
X
FORTH-ROAD-BRIDGE A 90
(A8) A 902
GLASGOW (M8) (M9) STIRLING A 8
AIRPORT A 720
KILMARNOCK A 71
LANARK A 70
SCOTLAND

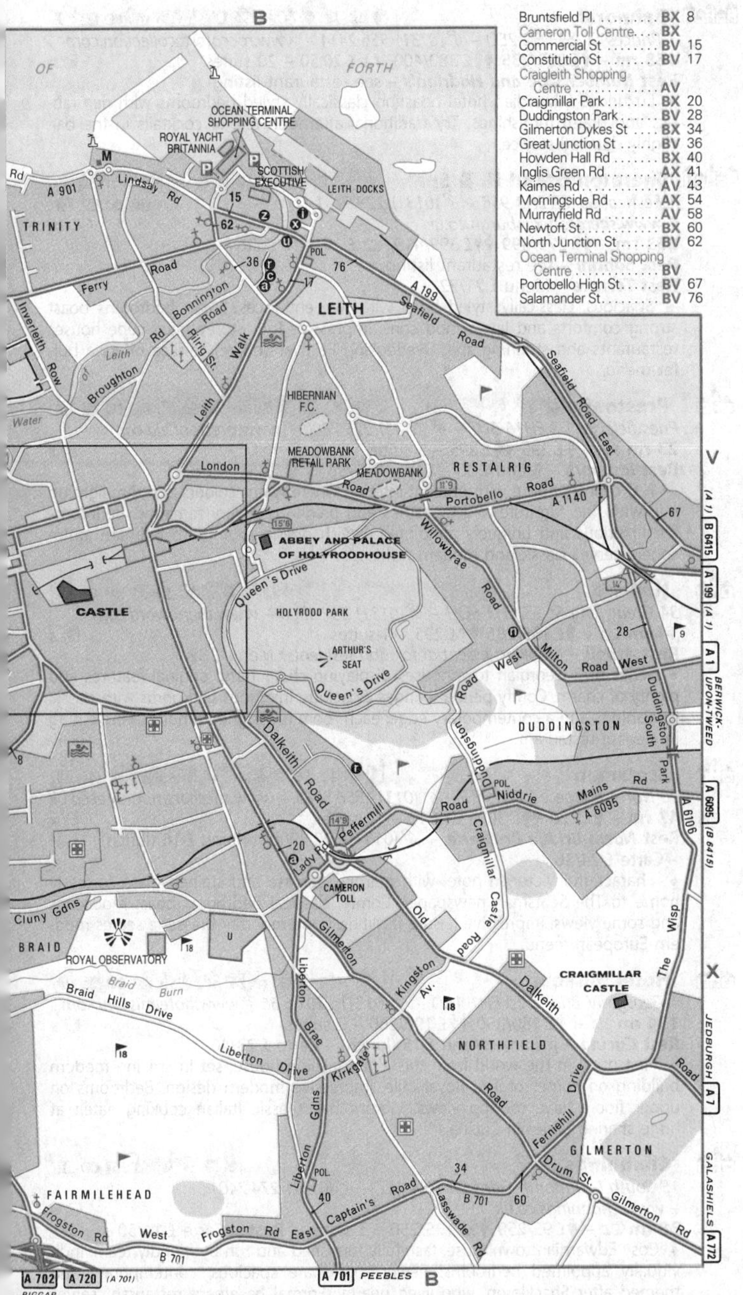
Bruntsfield Pl. . . . . BX 8
Cameron Toll Centre. . . . BX
Commercial St . . . . BV 15
Constitution St . . . . BV 17
Craigleith Shopping Centre . . . . AV
Craigmillar Park . . . . . . BX 20
Duddingston Park . . . . . . BV 28
Gilmerton Dykes St . . . . BX 34
Great Junction St . . . . . . BV 36
Howden Hall Rd . . . . BX 40
Inglis Green Rd . . . . AX 41
Kaimes Rd . . . . AV 43
Morningside Rd . . . . AX 54
Murrayfield Rd . . . . AV 58
Newtoft St . . . . BX 60
North Junction St . . . . . . BV 62
Ocean Terminal Shopping Centre . . . . BV
Portobello High St. . . . . . BV 67
Salamander St. . . . . BV 76
B
OF
FORTH
OCEAN TERMINAL SHOPPING CENTRE
ROYAL YACHT BRITANNIA
SCOTTISH EXECUTIVE
LEITH DOCKS
M
Rd
A 901
Lindsay Rd
TRINITY
15
62
76
36
17
POL.
Ferry
Road
Bonnington
Road
Inverleith
Row
Leith
Rd
Pilrig St.
Walk
Broughton
Water
Leith
LEITH
A 199
Seafield
Road
Seafield
Road
East
HIBERNIAN F.C.
MEADOWBANK RETAIL PARK
MEADOWBANK
London
Road
RESTALRIG
Portobello
Road
A 1140
67
V
ABBEY AND PALACE OF HOLYROODHOUSE
CASTLE
Queen's Drive
HOLYROOD PARK
ARTHUR'S SEAT
Queen's Drive
Willowbrae
Road
West
Road
Milton
Road
West
28
9
Duddingston
South
Duddingston
Park
DUDDINGSTON
(A 1) B 6415
A 199 (A 1)
A 1
BERWICK-UPON-TWEED
Dalkeith
Road
POL.
Niddrie
Mains
Rd
Road
A 6095
A 6095 (B 6415)
A 6106
Peffermill
Lady Rd
20
8
Craigmillar
Castle
Road
CAMERON TOLL
Old
Dalkeith
Cluny Gdns
BRAID
U
18
ROYAL OBSERVATORY
Braid
Burn
Braid Hills Drive
Gilmerton
Liberton
Brae
Kingston
Av.
18
The Wisp
X
CRAIGMILLAR CASTLE
JEDBURGH
Road
A 7
NORTHFIELD
Liberton Drive
Kirkgate
18
Gdns
Liberton
Road
Drive
Ferniehill
GILMERTON
GALASHIELS
POL.
40
Captain's
Road
34
Lasswade
Rd
B 701
60
Drum St.
Gilmerton
Rd
A 772
FAIRMILEHEAD
Frogston Rd West
Frogston Rd East
B 701
A 702 A 720 (A 701)
BIGGAR
A 701 PEEBLES
B
SCOTLAND

Balmoral
1 Princes St ✉ *EH2 2EQ – ✆ (0131) 556 2414 – www.roccofortecollection.com*
168 rm – †£ 320/335 ††£ 380/400, ☕ £ 20.50 – 20 suites EY**n**
Rest ***Number One and Hadrian's*** – see restaurant listing
♦ Luxurious Edwardian hotel boasting classically styled bedrooms with rich fabrics and grand furnishings. Try traditional afternoon tea, or cocktails in the bar. Highly detailed service.

Sheraton Grand H. & Spa
1 Festival Sq ✉ *EH3 9SR – ✆ (0131) 229 9131*
– www.sheratonedinburgh.co.uk CDZ**v**
253 rm – †£ 379/399 ††£ 399/419, ☕ £ 19 – 16 suites
Rest ***Santini*** – see restaurant listing
Rest ***Terrace*** – Menu £ 21/22
♦ Spacious, classically styled hotel with two entrances. Smart bedrooms boast strong comforts and latest mod cons. Impressive four storey glass cube houses restaurants and stunning spa. Overlooking Festival Square, Terrace offers a buffet menu.

Prestonfield
Priestfield Rd ✉ *EH16 5UT – ✆ (0131) 225 7800 – www.prestonfield.com*
23 rm ☕ – †£ 295 ††£ 295 – 5 suites BX**r**
Rest ***Rhubarb*** – Menu £ 30 – Carte £ 35/56
♦ 17C country house with opulent interior, where warm colours and dim lighting mix with fine furniture, old tapestries and paintings – very romantic. Bedrooms are luxurious and uniquely appointed. Lavish dining room with intimate atmosphere serves classic and modern dishes.

SCOTLAND

Howard
34 Great King St ✉ *EH3 6QH – ✆ (0131) 557 3500 – www.thehoward.com*
14 rm ☕ – †£ 155/285 ††£ 295 – 4 suites DY**s**
Rest ***Atholl*** – *(booking essential for non-residents)* Menu £ 32
♦ Series of 3 Georgian townhouses displaying characterful original features and plenty of charm. Comfy period lounges. Spacious, luxurious bedrooms with classic furnishings and a contemporary edge; each room is assigned a butler. Fine dining in elegant restaurant.

Scotsman
20 North Bridge ✉ *EH1 1TR – ✆ (0131) 556 5565 – www.thescotsmanhotel.co.uk*
47 rm – †£ 120 ††£ 300, ☕ £ 15 – 12 suites EY**x**
Rest ***North Bridge Brasserie*** – ✆ (0131) 622 2900 – Menu £ 16 (lunch) – Carte £ 24/36
♦ Characterful Victorian hotel with marble staircase and stained glass; formerly home to The Scotsman newspaper. Comfy, classical bedrooms boast mod cons and some views. Impressive leisure facilities. Contemporary brasserie serves modern European menu.

Hotel Missoni
1 George IV Bridge ✉ *EH1 1AD – ✆ (0131) 220 66 66 – www.hotelmissoni.com*
134 rm ☕ – †£ 180/250 ††£ 190/260 – 2 suites EZ**v**
Rest ***Cucina*** – Italian – Menu £ 15 (lunch) – Carte £ 23/40
♦ First hotel in the world from this Milan fashion house; set in striking modern building on corner of The Royal Mile. Impressive modern design. Bedrooms on upper floors have rooftop views. Vibrant bar. Classic Italian cooking eaten at huge sharing tables in Cucina.

Channings
15 South Learmonth Gdns ✉ *EH4 1EZ – ✆ (0131) 274 7401*
– www.channings.co.uk CY**e**
38 rm ☕ – †£ 95/250 ††£ 125/250 – 3 suites **Rest** – Carte £ 14/30 **s**
♦ Cosy Edwardian townhouse, tastefully furnished and run by friendly team. Individually appointed bedrooms: newer rooms are spacious, contemporary and themed after Shackleton, who lived nearby. Formal basement restaurant serves Gallic dishes.

Hotel du Vin

11 Bristo Pl ✉ EH1 1EZ – ☎ (0131) 247 49 00 – www.hotelduvin.com/edinburgh EZ**n**
47 rm – †£ 115/250 ††£ 115/250, ☕ £ 14.50
Rest *Bistro* – Carte £ 22/36
♦ Boutique hotel located in city's former asylum, with contemporary, wine-themed bedrooms. Search out the murals featuring a caricature of Burke and Hare, and the whisky snug with its 300 spirits. Bistro offers superb wine list and a classic European menu.

Tigerlily

125 George St ✉ EH2 4JN – ☎ (0131) 225 5005 – www.tigerlilyedinburgh.co.uk – Closed 25 December DY**a**
33 rm ☕ – †£ 195/225 ††£ 195/225
Rest – Menu £ 23/33 – Carte £ 27/41
♦ Classic Georgian townhouse concealing a funky, boutique interior. Large, individually designed bedrooms are luxurious, boasting seductive lighting, quality furnishings and superb wet rooms. Busy open-plan bar and dining room have similarly stylish, modern décor.

The Glasshouse without rest

2 Greenside Pl ✉ EH1 3AA – ☎ (0131) 525 8200 – www.theetoncollection.com – Closed 23-26 December EY**o**
65 rm – †£ 295 ††£ 295/450, ☕ £ 16.50
♦ Contemporary glass hotel with 150 year old church façade. Stylish bedrooms have floor to ceiling windows and some balconies. Impressive two acre roof garden; honesty bar and 3 course room service.

SCOTLAND

Number Ten

6-10 Gloucester Pl. ✉ EH3 6EF – ☎ (0131) 225 2720 – www.numbertenhotel.com DY**u**
30 rm ☕ – †£ 128/168 ††£ 148/198
Rest – *(closed Sunday) (dinner only)* Carte £ 22/40
♦ Luxurious adjoining townhouses with romantic interiors and stunning restored staircases. Decorated in gold, black and silver colour schemes, bedrooms boast top class furnishings and jacuzzis. Characterful dining room located in original house.

Rutland

1-3 Rutland St. ✉ EH1 2AE – ☎ (0131) 229 34 02 – www.therutland.com – Closed 25 December CZ**a**
12 rm – †£ 250/350 ††£ 250/350, ☕ £ 8
Rest – Menu £ 14 (lunch) – Carte £ 25/44
♦ Boutique hotel with commanding position at top of Princes Street. Stylish, modern bedrooms have bold décor, flat screen TVs and large, slate-floored shower rooms. Intimate basement lounge. Contemporary restaurant uses plenty of Scottish produce in its classic dishes.

Kildonan Lodge

27 Craigmillar Park ✉ EH16 5PE – ☎ (0131) 667 2793 – www.kildonanlodgehotel.co.uk BX**a**
12 rm ☕ – †£ 65/118 ††£ 98/159
Rest *Mathew's* – *(dinner only, booking essential)* Menu £ 19 – Carte £ 25/34
♦ Well-managed detached Victorian house on main road into city. Spacious and traditionally furnished, with cosy fire-lit drawing room and comfy bedrooms; some with four-posters and jacuzzis. Mathew's offers classical dining and plenty of Scottish produce.

Davenport House without rest

58 Great King St ✉ EH3 6QY – ☎ (0131) 558 8495 – www.davenport-house.com – Closed 1 week Christmas DY**v**
6 rm ☕ – †£ 65/110 ††£ 75/110
♦ Luxurious Georgian townhouse restored to its former glory. Cosy sitting room and spacious breakfast room. Bedrooms are at the top of the house and are decorated to a very high standard, with bathrooms to match.

Kew House without rest
1 Kew Terrace, Murrayfield ✉ EH12 5JE – ☎ (0131) 313 0700 – www.kewhouse.com – Closed 4-31 January AV**a**
7 rm – †£ 78/145 ††£ 90/170
◆ Personally run stone-built terraced house; larger than it looks from outside. Bedrooms are immaculately kept and up-to-date. Comfortable sitting room with free use of computer.

Elmview without rest
✉ EH3 9LN – ☎ (0131) 228 1973 – www.elmview.co.uk – April-November
5 rm – †£ 90/110 ††£ 100/130 DZ**e**
◆ Occupies the basement of a Victorian house in pretty terrace overlooking The Meadows. Bedrooms are spotlessly kept and are very large, with modern bathrooms. Owners are very welcoming.

Beverley without rest
40 Murrayfield Ave ✉ EH12 6AY – ☎ (0131) 337 1128 – www.thebeverley.com – Closed 23-26 December AV**n**
8 rm – †£ 45/85 ††£ 70/100
◆ Family-run, bay-windowed Victorian house in a peaceful tree-lined avenue, close to town. Elegant, individually furnished bedrooms display a classical style, boasting co-ordinating fabrics and matching bathrooms. Choice of cooked or continental buffet breakfast.

SCOTLAND

Number One – at The Balmoral Hotel
1 Princes St ✉ EH2 2EQ – ☎ (0131) 557 6727 – www.restaurantnumberone.com
Rest – Modern – *(dinner only)* Menu £ 59 EY**n**
Spec. Scallops with sweetcorn purée, pak choi, peanut and lime juice. Rump of lamb with aubergine purée and smoked tomato pepper stew. Peach and strawberry beignet with lemon verbena parfait.
◆ Stylish restaurant in a grand hotel, displaying bold red walls hung with fine art, well-spaced tables and deep corner banquettes. Ambitious cooking uses quality Scottish produce to create elaborate, precisely executed dishes. Assured, attentive service.

21212 (Paul Kitching) with rm
3 Royal Ter ✉ EH7 5AB – ☎ (0845) 222 12 12 – www.21212restaurant.co.uk – Closed 10 days January and 10 days July EY**c**
4 rm – †£ 325 ††£ 325
Rest – Inventive – *(closed Sunday and Monday)* Menu £ 35 (lunch)/65 (5 course dinner)
Spec. Fillet of Cumbrian Old Spot pork with an assiette of Cumberland sausage, ham and black pudding. Pink trout fillet with globe artichokes, confit of leeks, crumpets and ginger butter sauce. Summer trifle with milk and white chocolate custard, vanilla cinnamon and apple
◆ Smart Georgian townhouse with high-ceilinged dining room, contemporary décor and an open kitchen. The restaurant's name reflects the number of dishes per course; skilful and innovative cooking offers some quirky combinations. Opulent 1st floor sitting room and luxurious bedrooms.

Castle Terrace
33-35 Castle Ter. ✉ EH1 2EL – ☎ (0131) 229 1222 – www.castleterracerestaurant.com – Closed 1-24 January, Sunday and Monday
Rest – Modern European – Menu £ 20 (lunch) – Carte £ 37/51 DZ**a**
◆ Set in the shadows of the castle, an understatedly elegant restaurant with gilded ceiling and lovely bar. Refined cooking showcases seasonal, local produce in an assured, unfussy manner, following a 'nature to plate' philosophy.

Oloroso
33 Castle St ✉ EH2 3DN – ☎ (0131) 226 7614 – www.oloroso.co.uk – Closed 25-26 December DY**o**
Rest – Innovative – Menu £ 25/40 **s** – Carte £ 30/52 **s**
◆ Contemporary rooftop restaurant with buzzy atmosphere and good service. Huge glass windows and superb terrace boast city, river and castle views. Bar and grill menus display modern cooking.

XXX **Hadrian's** – at Balmoral Hotel

2 North Bridge ✉ EH1 1TR – ✆ (0131) 557 5000 – www.roccofortecollection.com

Rest – Brasserie – Menu £ 23/25 **s** – Carte £ 28/41 **s** EY**n**

◆ Delightful restaurant where lime green colour scheme offsets dark floors and brown leather chairs. Brasserie classics display plenty of Scottish produce; excellent value 3 course set menu.

XX **Atrium**

10 Cambridge St ✉ EH1 2ED – ✆ (0131) 228 8882 – www.atriumrestaurant.co.uk – Closed 1 January, 24-26 December, Saturday lunch and Sunday except August DZ**c**

Rest – Modern European – Menu £ 20/25 – Carte £ 28/42

◆ Seductively lit restaurant with tables made out of old railway sleepers. Great value set selection, interesting à la carte and more ambitious tasting menu. Modern cooking uses local ingredients.

XX **Ondine**

2 George IV Bridge (first floor) ✉ EH1 1AD – ✆ (0131) 226 1888 – www.ondinerestaurant.co.uk – Closed 2-10 January and Christmas EZ**s**

Rest – Seafood – Menu £ 18 (lunch and early dinner) – Carte £ 27/42

◆ Smart, lively restaurant dominated by granite-topped bar and crustacean counter. Classic menus showcase prime Scottish seafood. Straightforward, tasty cooking. Well-structured service.

XX **Dining Room**

The Scotch Malt Whisky Society, 28 Queen St ✉ EH2 1JX – ✆ (0131) 220 20 44 – www.thediningroomedinburgh.co.uk – Closed Sunday and dinner Monday

Rest – Modern European – *(booking essential)* Menu £ 19 (lunch) – Carte £ 20/41 DY**w**

◆ Set in fine Georgian building. Informal bistro by day, offering classic menu; linen and lights by night, with accomplished, modern dishes. Unsurprisingly superb range of whiskies.

SCOTLAND

XX **Forth Floor - Restaurant (at Harvey Nichols)**

30-34 St Andrew Sq ✉ EH2 2AD – ✆ (0131) 524 8350 – www.harveynichols.com – Closed 1 January, 25 December, dinner Sunday and Monday EY**z**

Rest – Modern European – Menu £ 25 (weekdays)/34 (weekend lunch) – Carte dinner Friday and Saturday approx. £ 40

◆ Wonderful skyline views from huge room-length window; great sunsets. Bar divides it into formal area with pricier modern European menu, and more causal brasserie; good Scottish ingredients.

XX **Santini** – at Sheraton Grand H. & Spa.

8 Conference Sq ✉ EH3 8AN – ✆ (0131) 221 7788 – www.santiniedinburgh.co.uk – Closed 1 January, Saturday lunch and Sunday CDZ**v**

Rest – Italian – Menu 19 – Carte £ 21/45

◆ Smart restaurant in huge glass cube. Dining room split in two: the right side more relaxed with piazza views and pleasant terrace. Wide-ranging menu of Italian classics; good value set selection.

X **Wedgwood**

267 Canongate ✉ EH8 8BQ – ✆ (0131) 558 87 37 – www.wedgwoodtherestaurant.co.uk – Closed 3-21 January and 25-26 December

Rest – Modern European – Menu £ 14 (lunch) – Carte £ 30/41 EY**a**

◆ Neat restaurant with bold white and crimson décor, hidden away at bottom of Royal Mile. Personally run, with friendly staff. Well presented, seasonal dishes; generous portions.

X **Dogs**

110 Hanover St. ✉ EH2 1DR – ✆ (0131) 220 1208 – www.thedogsonline.co.uk

Rest – British – Carte £ 15/22 DY**c**

◆ Set on the first floor of a classic Georgian mid-terrace; impressive staircase, simple décor, high-ceilings. Robust, good value comfort food crafted from local, seasonal produce.

Blue

10 Cambridge St ✉ EH1 2ED – ☎ (0131) 221 1222 – www.bluescotland.co.uk – Closed 1 January, 24-26 December and Sunday except during Edinburgh festival DZc

Rest – Modern European – Menu £ 20 – Carte £ 19/33

◆ Strikes a modern note with bright, curving walls, glass and simple settings. A café-bar with a light, concise and affordable menu drawing a young clientele. Bustling feel.

Zucca

15-17 Grindlay St ✉ EH3 9AX – ☎ (0131) 221 93 23 – www.zuccarestaurant.co.uk DZs

Rest – Italian – *(booking essential)* Menu £ 11/19 – Carte £ 22/36

◆ Friendly, well-run restaurant adjacent to Lyceum Theatre. Head upstairs for classic Italian dishes and all-Italian wine list, with great value pre-theatre menus. Book or come after 8pm.

Amore Dogs

104 Hanover St ✉ EH2 1DR – ☎ (0131) 220 51 55 – www.amoredogs.co.uk – Closed 25 December DYc

Rest – Italian – Carte £ 17/21

◆ Sister to 'The Dogs' next door, with similar canine-themed décor. Simple, spacious and open-plan, with a buzzy atmosphere and friendly service. Good value, rustic Italian dishes.

SCOTLAND

L'Escargot Bleu

56-56a Broughton St ✉ EH1 3SA – ☎ (0131) 557 1600 – www.lescargotbleu.co.uk – Closed Christmas EYu

Rest – French – Carte £ 24/33

◆ Authentic French bistro with basement épicerie; sit in the front room, with its large windows, gingham tablecloths and buzzy atmosphere. Keenly priced menus offer classic French dishes.

Le Café Saint-Honoré

34 North West Thistle Street Ln. ✉ EH2 1EA – ☎ (0131) 226 2211 – www.cafesthonore.com – Closed 1 January and 25-26 December DYr

Rest – French – *(booking essential)* Menu £ 23 – Carte £ 27/43

◆ Long-standing classical French bistro, hidden away down a side street. Simple interior crammed full of mirrors and bric-a-brac. Affordable daily menu with Gallic touch. Friendly service.

Seadogs

43 Rose St ✉ EH2 2NH – ☎ (0131) 225 8028 – www.seadogsonline.co.uk – Closed 1 January and 25 December DYe

Rest – Seafood – *(booking advisable)* Carte £ 16/20

◆ Lively seafood restaurant with canine motif, funky wallpaper and fast, friendly service. Well-priced menus offer sustainable fish and chips, plus a choice of tasty lighter dishes.

at Leith

Malmaison

rm,

1 Tower Pl ✉ EH6 7DB – ☎ (0131) 468 5000 – www.malmaison-edinburgh.com BVi

100 rm – †£ 99/205 ††£ 99/205, ☕ £ 14.95

Rest *Brasserie* – Menu £ 16 (lunch) – Carte £ 28/50

◆ Elegantly styled converted sailors' mission, located on the quayside. Comfortable, well-equipped bedrooms; superiors/suites are stylish, luxurious and boast attractive harbour views. Large, bustling bar. Busy brasserie offering menu of classically based dishes.

XXX **Martin Wishart** VISA MC AE

54 The Shore ✉ EH6 6RA – ✆ (0131) 553 3557 – www.martin-wishart.co.uk – Closed 25-26 and 31 December, 1-15 January, Sunday and Monday BVu

Rest – Innovative – *(booking essential)* Menu £ 25 (weekday lunch)/60

Spec. Roasted Kilbrannan scallops with Bellotta ham and parmesan velouté. Loin of Borders roe deer with goat's cheese gnocchi. Jivara milk chocolate mousse with Earl Grey ice cream.

♦ Discrete façade leads to tastefully decorated room with bold, modern designs. Underpinned by a classical base, well presented dishes display carefully judged modern touches and excellent ingredients. Two tasting menus available.

XX **Kitchin** (Tom Kitchin) A/C VISA MC AE

78 Commercial Quay ✉ EH6 6LX – ✆ (0131) 555 1755 – www.thekitchin.com – Closed 1-14 January, Sunday and Monday BVz

Rest – French – Menu £ 25 (lunch) – Carte £ 55/61

Spec. Razor clams with chorizo and lemon confit. Lobster thermidor with buttered samphire, sea spinach and sautéed squid. Gooseberry panna cotta with a chilled gooseberry consommé and crème fraîche ice cream.

♦ Converted dockside warehouse overlooking the quay. Expect refreshingly honest, very flavoursome and unfussy cooking from menus offering considerable choice. Seasonality, freshness and provenance are at the heart of the chef's philosophy.

XX **Plumed Horse** (Tony Borthwick) VISA MC AE

50-54 Henderson St ✉ EH6 6DE – ✆ (0131) 554 5556 – www.plumedhorse.co.uk – Closed 2 weeks July, 1 week November, Christmas, 1-2 January, Sunday and Monday BVa

Rest – Modern – Menu £ 26/48 **s**

Spec. Millefeuille of crab and langoustines, passion fruit mayonnaise, sweet and sour pineapple. Fillets of sea bream and red mullet with fennel gnocchi. Peach and raspberry baked Alaska with candied pistachios.

♦ Personally run restaurant with ornate ceiling, vivid paintings, an intimate feel and formal service. Well-crafted, classical cooking with strong, bold flavours and good use of Scottish ingredients.

XX **Vintners Rooms** VISA MC AE

The Vaults, 87 Giles St ✉ EH6 6BZ – ✆ (0131) 554 6767 – www.vintersrooms.com – Closed 23 December-7 January, Sunday and Monday

Rest – Mediterranean – Menu £ 23 (lunch) – Carte £ 40/48 BVr

♦ Hugely atmospheric: one characterful, flag-floored room and another more intimate, candlelit room with superb 1739 stucco ceiling. Wide-ranging Mediterranean menu. Over 1,200 single malts.

X **Cafe Fish** VISA MC AE

60 Henderson St ✉ EH6 6DE – ✆ (0131) 538 6131 – www.cafefish.net – Closed 3 weeks January, 25-26 December, Sunday dinner and Monday BVc

Rest – Seafood – Menu £ 14/24 – Carte approx. £ 26

♦ Light, modern, quasi-industrial style, with brushed aluminium bar and open-plan kitchen. Short menus of simply cooked seafood; good value fresh fish from sustainable Scottish sources.

The Ship on the Shore VISA MC AE

24-26 The Shore ✉ EH6 6QN – ✆ (0131) 555 0409 – www.theshipontheshore.co.uk BVx

Rest – Seafood – Menu £ 15 – Carte £ 30/45

♦ Smart period building on the quayside, modelled on the Royal Yacht Britannia and filled with nautical memorabilia. Seafood menu offers fresh, simply prepared, classical dishes.

The Kings Wark VISA MC

36 The Shore ✉ EH6 6QU – ✆ (0131) 554 9260 – www.kingswark.com – Closed 25-26 December BVu

Rest – Traditional – Carte £ 13/30

♦ Brightly coloured pub with old-fashioned interior, set on the quayside. Handwritten menus offer hearty, classical dishes; blackboard displays freshly prepared, locally sourced specials.

at Currie Southwest : 5 m on A 70

Violet Bank House without rest
167 Lanark Road West ✉ EH14 5NZ – ☎ (0131) 451 51 03
– www.violetbankhouse.co.uk
3 rm – †£ 70/90 ††£ 120/130
◆ Comfortable, well-run cottage with charming, individually decorated bedrooms and attractive garden running down to river. Impressive Scottish breakfast features lots of choice.

at Kirknewton Southwest : 7 mi on A 71 - AX – ✉ Edinburgh

Dalmahoy H. & Country Club
✉ EH27 8EB – ☎ (0131) rm, rest,
333 1845 – www.marriottdalmahoy.co.uk
212 rm – †£ 120/180 ††£ 120/180 – 3 suites
Rest *Pentland* – *(dinner only)* Carte £ 28/42
Rest *The Long Weekend* – Carte £ 17/41
◆ Extended Georgian mansion boasting 2 championship golf courses and extensive leisure facilities. Country house style guest areas; classically styled bedrooms. Fine dining and good views over the 1,000 acre grounds in Pentland. Laid-back dining in The Long Weekend.

at Ingliston West : 7 mi on A 8 – ✉ EH28 8

Norton House rm, rest,
West : 6 mi on A 89 ✉ EH28 8LX – ☎ (0131) 333 12 75
– www.handpicked.co.uk/nortonhouse
79 rm – †£ 110/170 ††£ 120/180 – 4 suites
Rest *Ushers* – *(closed Sunday and Monday) (dinner only)* Menu £ 30 – Carte £ 30/50
Rest *Brasserie* – Carte £ 23/37
◆ 19C country house in mature grounds, with impressive oak staircase and superb spa. Classic bedrooms in original house. Large, luxurious junior suites in extension; most have balconies. Classic cooking with seasonal Scottish produce in intimate Ushers. Stylish, modern Brasserie.

SCOTLAND

EDNAM – Borders – see Kelso

ELGIN – Moray – 501 K11 – pop. 20 829 Scotland 28 C1

Edinburgh 198 mi – Aberdeen 68 mi – Fraserburgh 61 mi – Inverness 39 mi

Elgin Library, Cooper Park ☎ (01343) 562 608, elgin@visitscotland.com

Moray Lossiemouth Stotfield Rd, ☎ (01343) 812 018

Hardhillock Birnie Rd, ☎ (01343) 542 338

Hopeman Moray, ☎ (01343) 830 578

Town★ - Cathedral★ (Chapter house★★)**AC**

Glenfiddich Distillery★, SE : 10 mi by A 941

Mansion House
The Haugh, via Haugh Rd ✉ IV30 1AW – ☎ (01343) 548 811
– www.mansionhousehotel.co.uk – Closed 25 December
23 rm – †£ 99/116 ††£ 187 **Rest** – Menu £ 23 (lunch) – Carte £ 19/35
◆ Substantial 19C baronial mansion in attractive grounds, boasting a delightful lounge, snooker room and small leisure club. Elegant bedrooms; some with sleigh beds, four-posters or river views. Relaxed bistro. Formal dining room relies on fresh, local produce.

Pines without rest
East Rd, East : 0.5 mi on A 96 ✉ IV30 1XG – ☎ (01343) 552 495
– www.thepinesguesthouse.com
5 rm – †£ 45/55 ††£ 66/70
◆ Substantial Victorian house with charming interior; run by keen owners. Homely lounge. Comfy bedrooms; one with an antique four-poster. Home-baked bread and Highland products at breakfast.

at Urquhart East : 5 mi by A 96 – ✉ Elgin

Parrandier

The Old Church of Urquhart, Meft Rd, Northwest : 0.25 mi by Main St off Meft Rd ✉ IV30 8NH – ✆ (01343) 843 063 – www.oldchurch.eu
3 rm – †£ 41 ††£ 62 **Rest** – Menu £ 14
◆ Converted church set in peaceful gardens; some original features remain. Warm, welcoming owners will show you round and explain the history. Open-plan lounge and split-level dining area; compact bedrooms with no TVs. Fresh, home-cooked meals at communal table.

ELIE – Fife – **501** L15 – **pop. 942** **28** D2
Edinburgh 44 mi – Dundee 24 mi – St Andrews 13 mi

Sangster's (Bruce Sangster)

51 High St ✉ KY9 1BZ – ✆ (01333) 331 001 – www.sangsters.co.uk – Closed January, 1 week November, 25-26 December, Sunday dinner, Monday, and Tuesday November-March
Rest – *(dinner only and Sunday lunch) (booking essential)* Carte £ 38/44
Spec. Roulade of smoked salmon, lemon sole and lobster, cucumber and dill dressing. Roast quail breast, confit legs, creamed cabbage and seared foie gras. Drambuie panna cotta with raspberry and yoghurt ice cream.
◆ This sweet little restaurant is run by a husband and wife team. The understated decoration includes a collection of local artwork on the walls. The cooking is detailed, finely tuned and informed by the seasons.

ERISKA (Isle of) – Argyll and Bute – **501** D14 – ✉ **Oban** **27** B2
Edinburgh 127 mi – Glasgow 104 mi – Oban 12 mi

Isle of Eriska

rm, rest,

Benderloch ✉ PA37 1SD – ✆ (01631) 720 371 – www.eriska-hotel.co.uk – February-December
23 rm – †£ 170/250 ††£ 330/400 – 7 suites
Rest – *(light lunch residents only) (booking essential)* Menu £ 44 (dinner)
◆ 19C baronial mansion on private island, boasting fantastic views over Lismore and the mountains. Classically styled, open-fired guest areas display modern touches. Comfy bedrooms feature bright fabrics and hi-tech equipment. Superb spa and leisure facilities. Contemporary dining room offers daily menu of local produce.

EUROCENTRAL – Glasgow – see Glasgow

FAIRLIE – North Ayrshire – **501** F16 – **pop. 1 510** **25** A1
Edinburgh 75 mi – Ayr 50 mi – Glasgow 36 mi

Fins

Fencebay Fisheries, Fencefoot Farm, South : 1.5 mi on A 78 ✉ KA29 0EG – ✆ (01475) 568 989 – www.fencebay.co.uk – Closed 1-2 January, 25-26 December, Monday and Sunday dinner
Rest – Seafood – *(booking essential)* Carte £ 23/35
◆ Converted farm buildings house a simple, flag-floored restaurant, craft shops and a traditional beech smokery. Friendly service and fresh seasonal seafood.

FIONNPHORT – **501** A15 – see MULL (Isle of)

FLODIGARRY – Highland – **501** B11 – see Skye (Isle of)

FORGANDENNY – Perth. and Kinross – **501** J14 – see Perth

FORRES – Moray – **501** J11 – **pop. 8 967** Scotland **28** C1
Edinburgh 165 mi – Aberdeen 80 mi – Inverness 27 mi
116 High St ✆ (01309) 672938 (Easter-October), forres@visitscotland.com
Muiryshade, ✆ (01309) 672 949
Sueno's Stone★★, N : 0.5 mi by A 940 on A 96 – Brodie Castle★ **AC**, W : 3 mi by A 96. Elgin★ (Cathedral★, chapter house★★ **AC**), E : 10.25 mi by A 96

SCOTLAND

Knockomie

Grantown Rd, South : 1.5 mi on A 940 ✉ IV36 2SG – ☎ (01309) 673 146 – www.knockomie.co.uk – Closed 23-28 December

15 rm – †£ 145 ††£ 180

Rest *The Grill Room* – Carte £ 30/37

◆ Extended Arts and Crafts house in comfortable seclusion off a rural road. Country house atmosphere. Bedrooms in main house older and more characterful. Contemporary restaurant offers seasonally changing menu of local, seasonal produce.

Ramnee

Victoria Rd ✉ IV36 3BN – ☎ (01309) 672 410 – www.ramneehotel.com – Closed 1-3 January and 25-26 December

19 rm – †£ 85/130 ††£ 110/160 – 1 suite

Rest *Hamlyns* – Carte £ 17/32 **s**

◆ Family owned Edwardian building in town centre with extensive lawned grounds. Welcoming public areas include panelled reception and pubby bar. Warmly traditional bedrooms. Formal dining room in traditional style.

at Dyke West : 3.75 mi by A 96 – ✉ Forres

Old Kirk without rest

Northeast : 0.5 mi ✉ IV36 2TL – ☎ (01309) 641 414 – www.oldkirk.co.uk

3 rm – †£ 55 ††£ 80

◆ Former 19C church in country location. Stained glass window in first floor lounge; wood furnished breakfast room. Pleasantly furnished bedrooms with original stonework.

SCOTLAND

FORT AUGUSTUS – Highland – ✉ PH32 **30** C3

London 543 mi – Edinburgh 159 mi – Inverness 34 mi – Fort William 32 mi

Lovat

✉ PH32 4DU – ☎ (01456) 459 250 – www.thelovat.com

28 rm – †£ 95/165 ††£ 150/265

Rest – Menu £ 35 (dinner) – Carte £ 20/41

◆ Professionally run Victorian house with traditional lounge and lawned gardens, set in pleasant village at southern end of Loch Ness. Variously sized bedrooms have a contemporary feel and good facilities. Smart, modern brasserie offers classic cooking.

FORTINGALL – Perth and Kinross – 501 H14 – see Aberfeldy

FORTROSE – Highland – 501 H11 – pop. 1 174 **30** C2

London 574 mi – Edinburgh 168 mi – Inverness 14 mi – Nairn 27 mi

Water's Edge without rest

Canonbury Ter, on A 832 ✉ IV10 8TT – ☎ (01381) 621 202 – www.watersedge.uk.com – restricted opening in winter

3 rm – †£ 80 ††£ 125

◆ Personally run guest house with attractive gardens and superb views over the Moray Firth. Immaculately kept guest areas. Three 1st floor rooms have French windows onto terrace.

FORT WILLIAM – Highland – 501 E13 – pop. 9 908 Scotland **30** C3

Edinburgh 133 mi – Glasgow 104 mi – Inverness 68 mi – Oban 50 mi

15 High St ☎ (0845) 2255121, info@visitscotland.com

North Rd, ☎ (01397) 704 464

Town★

The Road to the Isles★★ (Neptune's Staircase (≤★★), Glenfinnan★ ≤★, Arisaig★, Silver Sands of Morar★, Mallaig★), NW : 46 mi by A 830 – Ardnamurchan Peninsula★★ - Ardnamurchan Point (≤★★), NW : 65 mi by A 830, A 861 and B 8007 - SE : Ben Nevis★★ (≤★★) - Glen Nevis★

Inverlochy Castle
Torlundy, Northeast : 3 mi on A 82 ✉ PH33 6SN – ☎ (01397) 702 177 – www.inverlochycastlehotel.com
17 rm – †£ 260/515 ††£ 410/515 – 1 suite
Rest – *(booking essential for non-residents)* Menu £ 38/65
Spec. Roasted sea bass, curried Loch Linnhe prawns and a golden raisin jus. Slow cooked pork cheeks with caramelised scallops, petits pois and apple. Lime parfait with apple and coriander sorbet.
◆ Striking castellated house in beautiful grounds, boasting stunning loch/mountain views. Classical country house interior with sumptuous open-fired lounges. Elegant bedrooms offer the height of luxury Choice of smart dining rooms serving traditional dishes executed with care and precision. Top quality Scottish produce.

Distillery House without rest
Nevis Bridge, North Rd ✉ PH33 6LR – ☎ (01397) 700 103 – www.stayinfortwilliam.co.uk – Closed 2 weeks Christmas
10 rm – †£ 55/84 ††£ 84/104
◆ Smart hotel – formerly 3 distillery workers' cottages – at the foot of Ben Nevis. Comfy lounge with shortbread, whisky and books about the area. Landscaped gardens; terrace boasts lovely views.

Grange without rest
Grange Rd, South : 0.75 m by A 82 and Ashburn Lane ✉ PH33 6JF – ☎ (01397) 705 516 – www.thegrange-scotland.co.uk – April-October
3 rm – †£ 110/120 ††£ 120/130
◆ Delightful Victorian house with attractive garden and immaculate interior, set in a quiet residential area. Beautiful lounge displays fine fabrics; lovely breakfast room boasts Queen Anne style chairs. Bedrooms are extremely well appointed.

SCOTLAND

Ashburn House without rest
18 Achintore Rd, South : 0.5 mi on A 82 ✉ PH33 6RQ – ☎ (01397) 706 000 – www.highland5star.co.uk – Closed Christmas
7 rm – †£ 55 ††£ 110
◆ Attractive Victorian house with comfy lounge and conservatory breakfast room. Bright, modern pine-furnished bedrooms; Room 2 is largest and has the best view. Homemade shortbread on arrival.

Gantocks without rest
Achintore Rd, South : 1 mi on A 82 ✉ PE33 6RN – ☎ (01397) 702 050 – www.fortwilliam5star.co.uk – March-October
3 rm – †£ 70/90 ††£ 90/110
◆ Whitewashed bungalow with loch views; run by experienced owners. Spacious, modern bedrooms boast king-sized beds, large baths and nice toiletries. Unusual offerings and water views at breakfast.

Crannog
Town Pier ✉ PH33 6DB – ☎ (01397) 705 589 – www.crannog.net
Rest – Seafood – *(booking essential)* Menu £ 16 – Carte £ 29/37
◆ Brightly painted eatery set on the pier over Loch Eil. Good value set lunch. À la carte and daily blackboard menu of local fish and shellfish; try the mussels. Owners also have a seafood shop.

GALSON – **Western Isles Outer Hebrides – 501** A8 – **see Lewis and Harris (Isle of)**

GATTONSIDE – **Borders – see Melrose**

O. Forir/MICHELIN

GLASGOW

County: Glasgow City
Michelin regional map: **501** H16
▶ Edinburgh 46 mi
– Manchester 221 mi

Population: 629 501
Scotland
Map reference: **25** B1

PRACTICAL INFORMATION

Tourist Information

11 George Sq ✆ (0141) 204 4400, glasgow@visitscotland.com

Glasgow Airport, Tourist Information Desk ✆ (0141) 848 4440, glasgowairport@visitscotland.com

Airports

Glasgow Airport : ✆ (0844) 481 5555, W : 8 mi by M 8, AV

Access to Oban by helicopter

Golf courses

Littlehill Auchinairn Rd, ✆ (0141) 276 07 04

Rouken Glen Thornlibank Stewarton Rd, ✆ (0141) 638 7044

Linn Park Simshill Rd, ✆ (0141) 633 0377

Lethamhill Cumbernauld Rd, ✆ (0141) 770 6220

Alexandra Park Dennistoun, ✆ (0141) 276 0600

King's Park Croftfoot 150a Croftpark Ave, ✆ (0141) 630 1597

Knightswood Lincoln Ave, ✆ (0141) 959 6358

SIGHTS

In town

City★★★ – Cathedral★★★ (≤★) DZ - The Burrell Collection★★★ AX M1 – Hunterian Art Gallery★★ (Whistler Collection★★★ - Mackintosh Wing★★★) AC CY M4 – Museum of Transport★★ (Scottish Built Cars★★★, The Clyde Room of Ship Models★★★) AV M6 – Art Gallery and Museum Kelvingrove★★ CY – Pollok House★ (The Paintings★★) AX D – Tolbooth Steeple★ DZ - Hunterian Museum (Coin and Medal Collection★) CY M5 – City Chambers★ DZ C – Glasgow School of Art★ AC CY M3 – Necropolis (≤★ of Cathedral) DYZ – Gallery of Modern Art★ – Glasgow (National) Science Centre★, Pacific Quay AV

On the outskirts

Paisley Museum and Art Gallery (Paisley Shawl Section★), W : 4 mi by M 8 AV

In the surrounding area

The Trossachs★★★, N : 31 mi by A 879 - BV -, A 81 and A 821 – Loch Lomond★★, NW : 19 mi by A 82 AV – New Lanark★★, SE : 20 mi by M 74 and A 72 BX

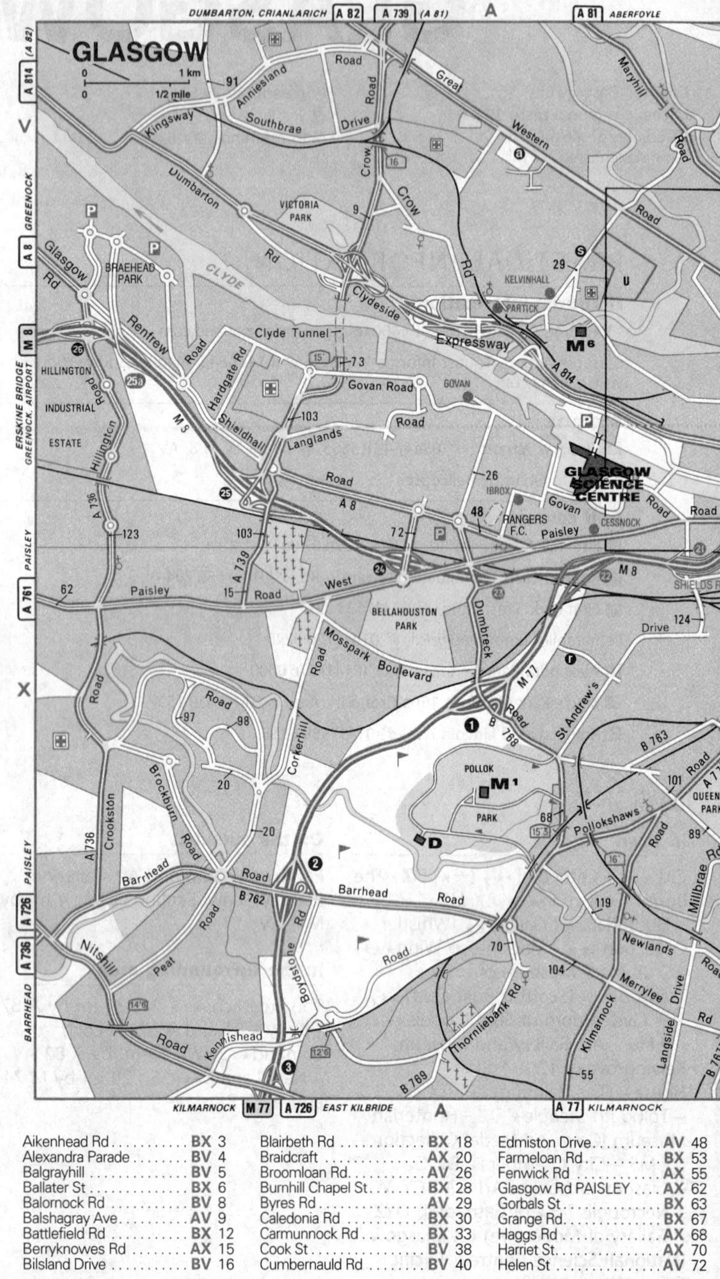

DUMBARTON, CRIANLARICH
A 82
A 739
(A 81)
A
A 81
ABERFOYLE
GLASGOW
0 1 km
0 1/2 mile
Anniesland
Road
Southbrae
Drive
Kingsway
Great
Western
Road
Maryhill
Road
Crow
Crow
Rd
Dumbarton
Rd
VICTORIA PARK
CLYDE
Glasgow
Rd
BRAEHEAD PARK
Renfrew
Road
Clydeside
Expressway
Clyde Tunnel
KELVINHALL
PARTICK
U
A 814
Hardgate Rd
Govan Road
GOVAN
Road
Shieldhall
Langlands
Road
A 8
HILLINGTON
INDUSTRIAL
ESTATE
Hillington
Road
A 736
M 8
GLASGOW SCIENCE CENTRE
IBROX
RANGERS F.C.
Govan
Road
Paisley
Road
CESSNOCK
M 8
SHIELDS RD
Paisley
Road
West
A 739
BELLAHOUSTON PARK
Mosspark
Boulevard
Dumbreck
Road
M 77
B 768
St Andrew's
Drive
B 763
Road
A 77
QUEEN'S PARK
POLLOK
M 1
PARK
D
Pollokshaws
Road
Millbrae Rd
Road
Road
Brockburn
Road
Corkerhill
Road
Crookston
A 736
Barrhead
Road
B 762
Barrhead
Road
Boydstone
Rd
Road
Peat
Road
Nitshill
Road
Kennishead
Thornliebank Rd
B 769
Kilmarnock
Newlands
Road
Merrylee
Drive
Langside
Rd
B 767
V
X
A 814
(A 82)
GREENOCK
A 8
M 8
ERSKINE BRIDGE
GREENOCK, AIRPORT
PAISLEY
A 761
PAISLEY
A 726
A 736
BARRHEAD
KILMARNOCK
M 77
A 726
EAST KILBRIDE
A
A 77
KILMARNOCK
SCOTLAND

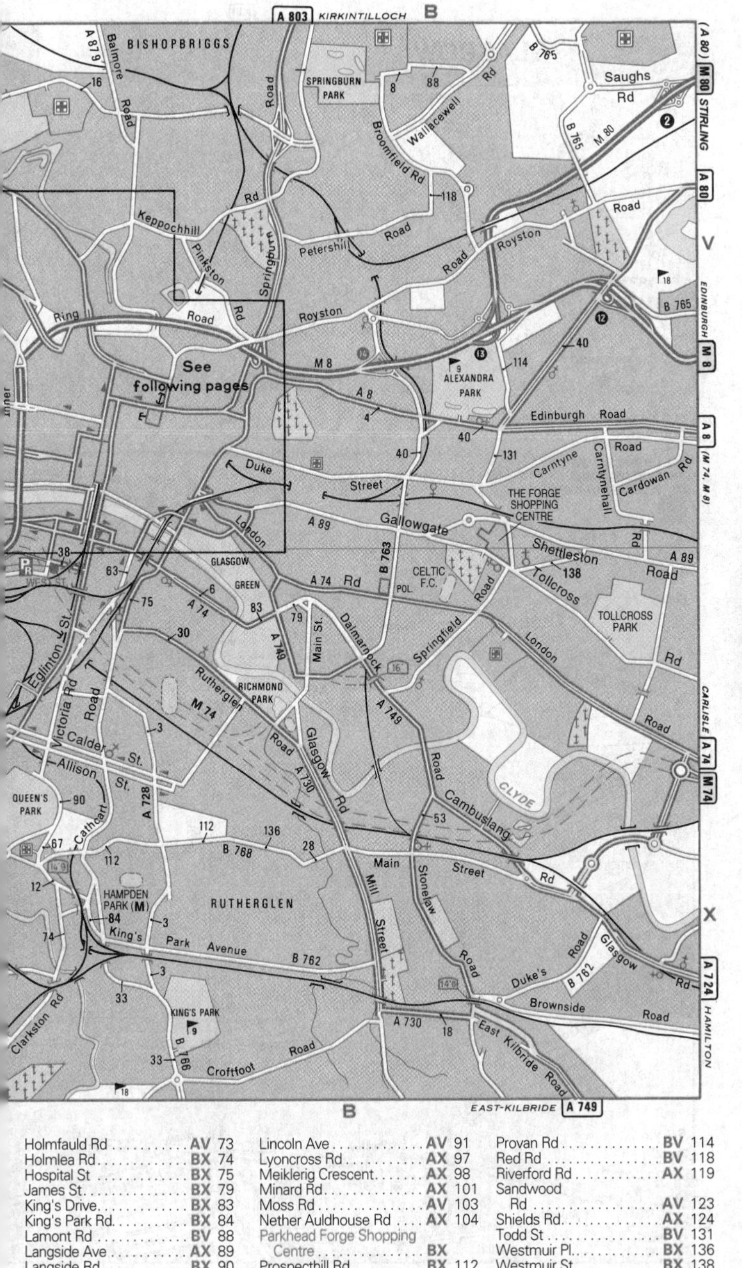
A 803 KIRKINTILLOCH
B
BISHOPBRIGGS
SPRINGBURN PARK
Saughs Rd
M 80 STIRLING
A 80
V
EDINBURGH M 8
ALEXANDRA PARK
See following pages
Edinburgh Road
A 8 (M 74, M 8)
THE FORGE SHOPPING CENTRE
Gallowgate
Shettleston
Tollcross
TOLLCROSS PARK
GLASGOW GREEN
CELTIC F.C.
RICHMOND PARK
QUEEN'S PARK
HAMPDEN PARK (M)
RUTHERGLEN
CLYDE
CARLISLE A 74 M 74
X
A 724 HAMILTON
KING'S PARK
Croftfoot Road
East Kilbride Road
EAST-KILBRIDE A 749
SCOTLAND

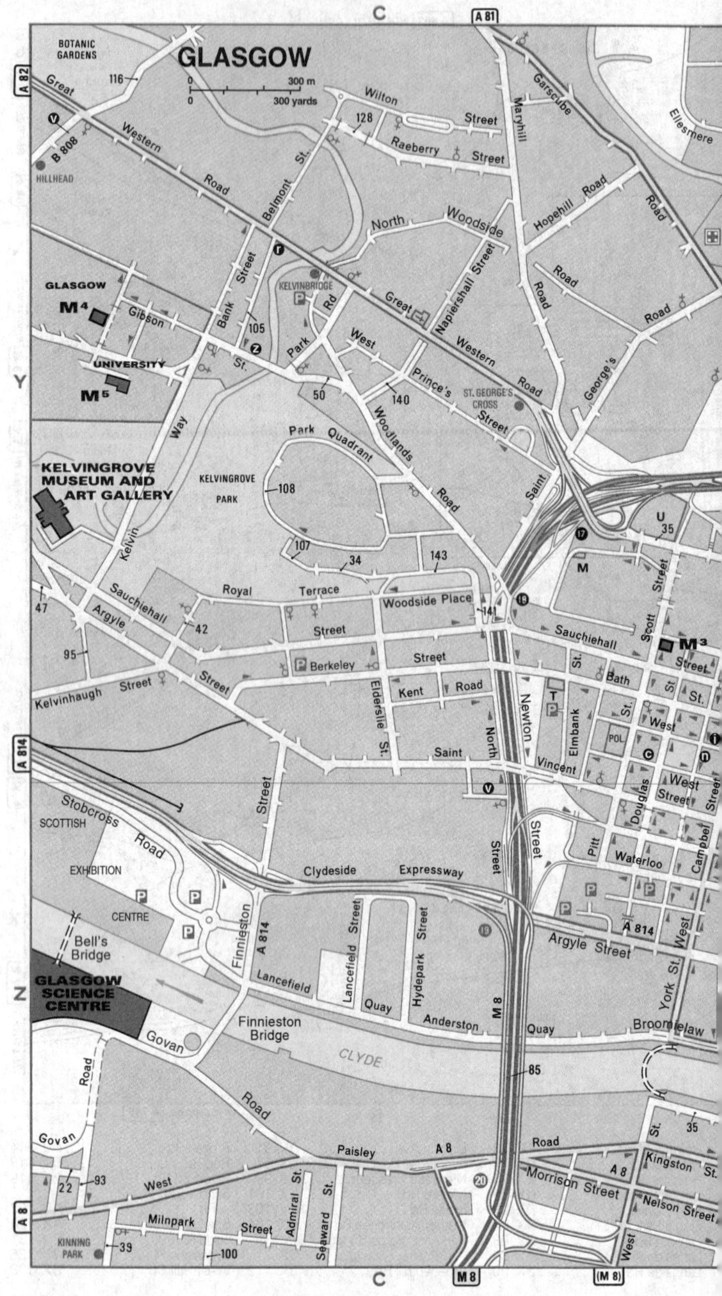
GLASGOW
BOTANIC GARDENS
Great Western Road
HILLHEAD
Belmont St.
Wilton Street
Raeberry Street
Maryhill Road
Garscube Road
Ellesmere
North Woodside Road
Hopehill Road
Napiershall Street
KELVINBRIDGE
Park Rd
Bank Street
Gibson St.
GLASGOW UNIVERSITY
West Prince's Street
ST. GEORGE'S CROSS
St George's Road
Park Quadrant
Woodlands Road
KELVINGROVE MUSEUM AND ART GALLERY
KELVINGROVE PARK
Kelvin Way
Saint
Royal Terrace
Woodside Place
Sauchiehall Street
Argyle Street
Berkeley Street
Kelvinhaugh Street
Kent Road
Elderslie St.
Newton Street
North Street
Saint Vincent Street
Scott Street
Bath St.
Elmbank St.
West Regent St.
Douglas St.
Pitt Street
Waterloo Street
Campbell Street
West Street
Stobcross Road
SCOTTISH EXHIBITION CENTRE
Bell's Bridge
GLASGOW SCIENCE CENTRE
Clydeside Expressway
Finnieston Street
Lancefield Street
Lancefield Quay
Hydepark Street
Anderston Quay
Argyle Street
York St.
Broomielaw
Finnieston Bridge
Govan Road
CLYDE
Paisley Road West
Kingston St.
Morrison Street
Nelson Street
Milnpark Street
Admiral St.
Seaward St.
KINNING PARK
M 8
A 8
A 814
A 81
A 82
B 808
300 m
300 yards

SCOTLAND

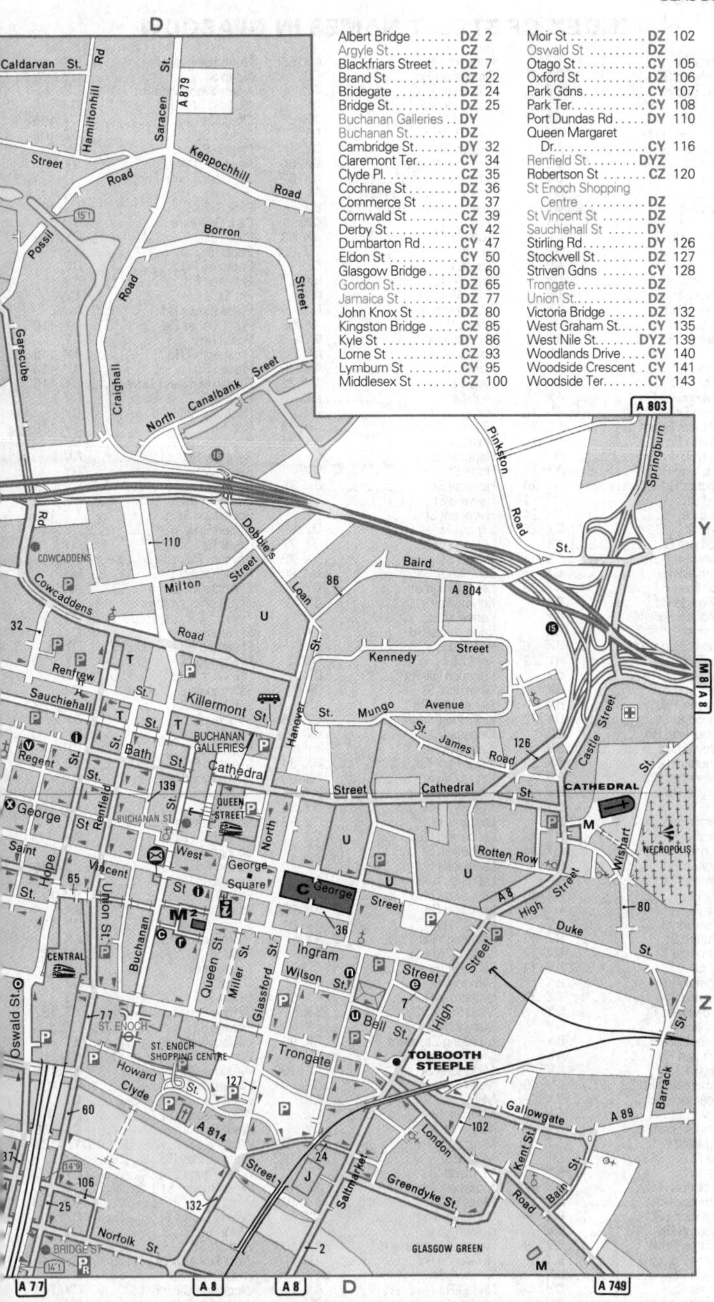

Albert Bridge DZ 2
Argyle St CZ
Blackfriars Street DZ 7
Brand St CZ 22
Bridegate DZ 24
Bridge St. DZ 25
Buchanan Galleries DY
Buchanan St. DZ
Cambridge St. DY 32
Claremont Ter. CY 34
Clyde Pl. CZ 35
Cochrane St DZ 36
Commerce St DZ 37
Cornwald St CZ 39
Derby St CY 42
Dumbarton Rd CY 47
Eldon St CY 50
Glasgow Bridge DZ 60
Gordon St DZ 65
Jamaica St DZ 77
John Knox St DZ 80
Kingston Bridge CZ 85
Kyle St DY 86
Lorne St CZ 93
Lymburn St CY 95
Middlesex St CZ 100
Moir St DZ 102
Oswald St DZ
Otago St CY 105
Oxford St DZ 106
Park Gdns CY 107
Park Ter. CY 108
Port Dundas Rd DY 110
Queen Margaret Dr. CY 116
Renfield St DYZ
Robertson St CZ 120
St Enoch Shopping Centre DZ
St Vincent St DZ
Sauchiehall St DY
Stirling Rd DY 126
Stockwell St DZ 127
Striven Gdns CY 128
Trongate DZ
Union St DZ
Victoria Bridge DZ 132
West Graham St CY 135
West Nile St DYZ 139
Woodlands Drive CY 140
Woodside Crescent CY 141
Woodside Ter. CY 143
D
Y
Z
SCOTLAND
CATHEDRAL
NECROPOLIS
TOLBOOTH STEEPLE
GLASGOW GREEN
BUCHANAN GALLERIES
QUEEN STREET
CENTRAL
ST. ENOCH
ST. ENOCH SHOPPING CENTRE
BUCHANAN ST.
COWCADDENS
BRIDGE ST.
George Square
A 803
A 804
A 8
M 8
A 77
A 749
A 814
A 89
A 879

INDEX OF STREET NAMES IN GLASGOW

Blythswood Square
✉ G2 4AD – ✆ (0141) 248 8888 – *www.blythswoodsquare.com* CYn
99 rm ☕ – 🚹£ 195 🚹🚹£ 285 – 1 suite
Rest ***Restaurant*** – see restaurant listing
♦ Stunning property – former home of the Scottish RAC – set on delightful Georgian square; original features include beautifully ornate tiled entrance. Good-sized, modern bedrooms.

Hotel du Vin at One Devonshire Gardens
1 Devonshire Gardens ✉ *G12 OUX* – ✆ *(0141) 339 2001* – *www.hotelduvin.com* AVa
45 rm – 🚹£ 150 🚹🚹£ 325, ☕ £ 17 – 4 suites
Rest ***Bistro*** – *(Closed Saturday lunch and dinner 25 December)* Menu £ 18 (weekday lunch) – Carte dinner £ 31/51
♦ Collection of adjoining 19C houses in terrace, refurbished with attention to detail. Warm, intimate and comfortable bedrooms are named after wines. High levels of service. Smart Bistro offers classic grill menu as well as more innovative carte.

Radisson Blu Glasgow
301 Argyle St ✉ *G2 8DL* – ✆ *(0141) 204 3333* DZo
246 rm – 🚹£ 135 🚹🚹£ 145, ☕ £ 16 – 1 suite
Rest ***Collage*** – Mediterranean – Menu £ 20 – Carte £ 20/35
♦ Stylish modern commercial hotel with impressive open-plan interior; set in central location close to the station. Three styles of bedroom – all offering good levels of comfort. Spacious dining room with central buffet area and all-encompassing menu.

Malmaison
278 West George St ✉ *G2 4LL* – ✆ *(0141) 572 1000* – *www.malmaison.com* CYc
68 rm – 🚹£ 150 🚹🚹£ 150, ☕ £ 13.95 – 4 suites
Rest ***The Brasserie*** – Menu £ 16 – Carte £ 29/41
♦ Visually arresting former Masonic chapel. Comfortable, well-proportioned rooms seem effortlessly stylish with bold patterns and colours and thoughtful extra attentions. Informal Brasserie with French themed menu and Champagne bar.

Abode Glasgow
129 Bath St ✉ *G2 2SZ* – ✆ *(0141) 221 6789* – *www.abodehotels.co.uk* DYv
59 rm – 🚹£ 130/175 🚹🚹£ 130/175, ☕ £ 13.50
Rest ***Michael Caines*** – see restaurant listing
Rest ***Bar MC & Grill*** – *(Closed Sunday and Monday)* Menu £ 13 (lunch) – Carte £ 37/44
♦ Near Mackintosh's School of Art, an early 20C building decorated with a daring modern palette: striking colour schemes and lighting in the spacious, elegantly fitted rooms. All-day dining in stylish bar and grill.

Sherbrooke Castle
11 Sherbrooke Ave, Pollokshields ✉ *G41 4PG* – ✆ *(0141) 427 4227* – *www.sherbrooke.co.uk* AXr
16 rm ☕ – 🚹£ 75/105 🚹🚹£ 75/175 – 1 suite
Rest ***Morrisons*** – Menu £ 14 (lunch) – Carte dinner £ 26/38
♦ Late 19C baronial Romanticism given free rein inside and out. The hall is richly furnished and imposing; rooms in the old castle have a comfortable country house refinement. Panelled Victorian dining room with open fire.

Brian Maule at Chardon d'Or
176 West Regent St ✉ *G2 4RL* – ✆ *(0141) 248 3801* – *www.brianmaule.com* – *Closed Sunday* CYi
Rest – Modern – Menu £ 20 – Carte £ 34/52
♦ Sizeable Georgian house in suburbs, boasting original pillars, ornate carved ceiling and modern art. Well-spaced linen-clad tables; formal service from well-versed team. Classic Scottish cooking.

SCOTLAND

XXX **Rogano**

11 Exchange Pl ✉ G1 3AN – ✆ (0141) 248 4055 – www.roganoglasgow.com – Closed 1 January DZ**c**

Rest – Seafood – Menu £ 22 (lunch and early dinner) – Carte £ 35/57

◆ Long-standing Glasgow institution; art deco, with original panelling, stained glass windows and etched mirrors. Classic menus lean towards local seafood. The langoustines are a must.

XXX **Two Fat Ladies at The Buttery**

652 Argyle St ✉ G3 8UF – ✆ (0141) 221 8188 – www.twofatladiesrestaurant.com – Closed 26 December and 1-2 January CZ**v**

Rest – British – Menu £ 19 (lunch) – Carte £ 31/45

◆ Wood-panelled restaurant with banquette seating and tartan furnishings; an old classic revived. Tasty, seasonal cooking; charming, attentive service and a great range of whiskies.

XX **Restaurant** – at Blythswood Square Hotel

11 Blythswood Sq ✉ G2 4AD – ✆ (0141) 248 8888 – www.blythswoodsquare.com CY**n**

Rest – Modern – Carte £ 33/54

◆ Spacious, stylish salon with large bar and booths. Eclectic menu offers choice between classic and contemporary European dishes, with separate grill section. Smooth, friendly service.

XX **Michael Caines** – at Abode Glasgow Hotel

129 Bath St ✉ G2 2SZ – ✆ (0141) 221 6789 – www.michaelcaines.co.uk – Closed first 2 weeks January and 2 weeks July DY**v**

Rest – Modern – *(Closed Sunday and Monday)* Menu £ 16 (lunch)/19 (dinner) – Carte £ 38/47

◆ Smart, stylish restaurant in boutique hotel, a mirrored wall creating impression of size. Quality décor matched by clean, unfussy cooking prepared with finesse and skill.

XX **La Vallée Blanche**

360 Byres Rd ✉ G12 8AY – ✆ (0141) 334 3333 – www.lavalleeblanche.com – Closed 25 December, 1 January and Monday CY**v**

Rest – French – Menu £ 17 (lunch) – Carte £ 21/39

◆ First floor restaurant-cum-ski-lodge, with wood-clad walls, stag antler lights and myriad candles. Classical cooking with a seasonal French base. Formal service from a jolly team.

XX **Grill Room at The Square**

Second Floor, 29 Royal Exchange Sq ✉ G1 3AJ – ✆ (0141) 225 5615 – www.grillroomglasgow.com – Closed 1 January DZ**r**

Rest – Steakhouse – *(booking advisable)* Menu £ 20 (lunch) – Carte £ 30/58

◆ Second floor of impressive Georgian building on Royal Exchange Square. Appealing menu focuses on seafood and 28-day hung Scottish steak, with choice of sauce and chunky chips.

XX **Urban**

23-25 St Vincent Pl ✉ G1 2DT – ✆ (0141) 248 5636 – www.urbanbrasserie.co.uk – Closed 1-2 January and 25-26 December DZ**i**

Rest – Modern – Menu £ 20 – Carte £ 24/45

◆ Imposing 19C building in heart of city centre. Stylish, modern interior with individual booths and illuminated glass ceiling. Modern English cooking. Live piano at weekends.

XX **Dining Room**

104 Bath St ✉ G2 2EN – ✆ (0141) 332 6678 – www.diningroomglasgow.co.uk – Closed 25-26 December, 1-2 January and Sunday DY**i**

Rest – Mediterranean – Menu £ 18 – Carte £ 29/38

◆ Parrot motifs recur everywhere, even on the door handles. Well-spaced tables and mirrored walls add a sense of space to the basement. A free-ranging fusion style prevails.

SCOTLAND

XX **Gamba**

225a West George St ✉ G2 2ND – ✆ (0141) 572 0899 – www.gamba.co.uk – Closed 1-2 January, 25-26 December and Sunday lunch DZ**x**

Rest – Seafood – Menu £ 20 (lunch)/25 – Carte £ 35/48

◆ Extensive and appealing seafood menu; simple and effective cooking from chef-owner, with lemon sole a speciality. Comfortable dining room with good service from well-versed team.

XX **La Parmigiana**

447 Great Western Rd, Kelvinbridge ✉ G12 8HH – ✆ (0141) 334 0686 – www.laparmigiana.co.uk – Closed 1 January, 25 December and Sunday dinner CY**r**

Rest – Italian – *(booking essential)* Menu £ 17 (lunch)/19 (early dinner) – Carte £ 27/40

◆ Compact, pleasantly decorated traditional eatery with a lively atmosphere and good local reputation. Obliging, professional service and a sound, authentic Italian repertoire.

X **Dhabba**

44 Candleriggs ✉ G1 1LE – ✆ (0141) 553 1249 – www.thedhabba.com – Closed 1 January DZ**u**

Rest – Indian – Menu £ 10 (lunch) – Carte £ 22/43

◆ In the heart of the Merchant City, this large, modern restaurant boasts bold colours and huge wall photos. Concentrates on authentic, accomplished North Indian cooking.

X **Stravaigin**

28 Gibson St, (basement) ✉ G12 8NX – ✆ (0141) 334 2665 – www.stravaigin.com – Closed 25 December and 1 January CY**z**

Rest – Modern – *(dinner only and lunch Saturday-Sunday)* Carte £ 24/32

◆ Well-run, long-standing eatery with relaxed, informal feel. Bustling bar and welcoming basement dining room with soft, low lighting. Interesting modern menus display worldwide influences.

X **Stravaigin 2**

8 Ruthven Lane, off Byres Rd ✉ G12 9BG – ✆ (0141) 334 7165 – www.stravaigin.com – Closed 1 January, lunch 2 January and 25-26 December AV**s**

Rest – Modern – Menu £ 13 (lunch)/15 (early dinner) – Carte £ 18/30

◆ Lilac painted cottage tucked away in an alley off Byres Road. Simple, unfussy, modern bistro-style interior, spread over two floors. Eclectic menu offers something for everyone.

X **Dakhin**

First Floor, 89 Candleriggs ✉ G1 1NP – ✆ (0141) 553 2585 – www.dakhin.com – Closed 1 January DZ**n**

Rest – South Indian – Menu £ 10 (lunch) – Carte £ 22/43

◆ Large open-plan first floor restaurant in redeveloped area of city, serving authentic, flavoursome south Indian cooking. Friendly, informal atmosphere; knowledgeable service.

X **Shandon Belles**

652 Argyle St ✉ G3 8UF – ✆ (0141) 221 8188 – www.twofatladiesrestaurant.com – Closed 1-2 January, 26 December and Sunday CZ**v**

Rest – Scottish – *(booking advisable)* Menu £ 16 (lunch and early dinner) – Carte £ 18/23

◆ Rustic restaurant in the basement of The Buttery, with exposed brick walls, church pews and simply laid tables. Tasty, unfussy dishes with a hearty base. Friendly service.

Babbity Bowster

16-18 Blackfriars St ✉ G1 1PE – ✆ (0141) 552 5055 – Closed 25 December and 1 January DZ**e**

Rest – Traditional – Carte £ 15/21

◆ Double-fronted Georgian pub with fiercely Scottish interior; close to the Merchant City. Honest, seasonal cooking features traditional Scottish favourites; restaurant menu is more elaborate.

SCOTLAND

at Eurocentral East : 12 mi by M 8 off A 8 – ✉ Glasgow

Dakota

✉ *ML1 4WJ – ℘ (01698) 835 444 – www.dakotahotels.co.uk – Closed 2-7 January*

90 rm – †£ 98 ††£ 199, ☕ £ 11.95

Rest ***Grill*** – Menu £ 30 – Carte £ 21/48

◆ Stylish, modern hotel with sleek, masculine feel. Well-thought out bedrooms have king-sized beds and plasma TVs. Comfortable lounge popular for afternoon tea. Open plan bar and grill offers good selection of modern cooking.

GLENDEVON – Perth and Kinross – 501 I/J15 — 28 C2

Edinburgh 37 mi – Perth 26 mi – Stirling 19 mi

Tormaukin Inn with rm

✉ *FK14 7JY – ℘ (01259) 781 252 – www.tormaukinhotel.co.uk*

13 rm ☕ – †£ 85 ††£ 100 **Rest** – Menu £ 13/20 – Carte £ 20/30

◆ Simple whitewashed roadside inn set in picturesque glen, with huge granite fireplace, cosy beamed bar and spacious, traditional dining room. Fresh, carefully executed, classically based cooking displays modern touches. Friendly, personable service. Immaculately kept bedrooms; breakfast served in the conservatory.

GLENKINDIE – Aberdeenshire – 501 L12 — 28 D1

London 537 mi – Edinburgh 125 mi – Aberdeen 41 mi – Dundee 85 mi

Glenkindie Arms with rm

✉ *AB33 8SX – ℘ (01975) 641 288 – www.theglenkindiearms.co.uk – Closed November-April, Monday and Tuesday*

3 rm ☕ – †£ 35/40 ††£ 50/70 **Rest** – *(booking essential)* Carte £ 20/25

◆ Remotely set, 400 year old, rustic Highland inn. Charming bar with an open fire and a huge collection of malt whiskies. Concise, daily changing blackboard menu of unfussy, seasonal dishes crafted from local produce. Simple bedrooms complete the picture.

GLENROTHES – Fife – 501 K15 – pop. 38 679 Scotland — 28 C2

Edinburgh 33 mi – Dundee 25 mi – Stirling 36 mi

Thornton Station Rd, ℘ (01592) 771 173

Golf Course Rd, ℘ (01592) 758 686

Balbirnie Park Markinch, ℘ (01592) 612 095

Auchterderran Cardenden Woodend Rd, ℘ (01592) 721 579

Leslie Balsillie Laws, ℘ (01592) 620 040

Falkland★ (Palace of Falkland★ **AC**, Gardens★ **AC**) N : 5.5 mi by A 92 and A 912

Balbirnie House

Balbirnie Park, Markinch, Northeast : 1.75 mi by A 911 and A 92 on B 9130

✉ *KY7 6NE – ℘ (01592) 610 066 – www.balbirnie.co.uk*

30 rm ☕ – †£ 95/125 ††£ 210

Rest ***Orangery*** – *(closed Monday and Tuesday)* Menu £ 18 (lunch)/35 – Carte lunch £ 26/32

Rest ***Bistro*** – Menu £ 13 – Carte £ 17/31

◆ Stunning Palladian mansion with formal gardens and extensive parkland. Large, well-furnished drawing rooms in country house style; period features abound. Mix of spacious, luxurious bedrooms and smaller, standard rooms. Elegant glass-roofed Orangery serves classics with a twist. Basement Bistro offers French favourites.

GRANTOWN-ON-SPEY – Highland – 501 J12 – pop. 2 166 — 30 D2

Edinburgh 143 mi – Inverness 34 mi – Perth 99 mi

54 High St ℘ (01479) 872773 (Seasonal), grantown@host.co.uk

Golf Course Rd, ℘ (01479) 872 079

Abernethy Nethy Bridge, ℘ (01479) 821 305

SCOTLAND

Culdearn House
Woodlands Terrace ✉ PH26 3JU – ✆ (01479) 872 106 – www.culdearn.com
6 rm (dinner included) – †£ 90/100 ††£ 195/220
Rest – *(dinner only) (booking essential for non-residents)* Menu £ 35 **s**
◆ Personally run Victorian granite stone hotel offering a high degree of luxury, including beautifully furnished drawing room and very tastefully furnished bedrooms. Formally attired dining room; good Scottish home cooking.

Dulaig without rest
Seafield Ave ✉ PH26 3JF – ✆ (01479) 872 065 – www.thedulaig.com – Closed Christmas and New Year
3 rm – †£ 90/100 ††£ 130/140
◆ Small, detached, personally run guest house, built in 1910 and tastefully furnished with original Arts and Crafts pieces. Modern fabrics and uncluttered feel in comfortable bedrooms. Tea on arrival. Communal breakfast includes homemade muffins and bread.

The Pines
Woodside Ave ✉ PH26 3JR – ✆ (01479) 872 092 – www.thepinesgrantown.co.uk – March-October
3 rm – †£ 75 ††£ 130 **Rest** – *(dinner only)* Menu £ 38
◆ Top level hospitality in an attractive 19C house with lovely rear garden leading onto woods and Spey. Elegant lounges display fine collection of artwork. Bedrooms are individually appointed. Candlelit dinners, full of Scottish flavours, are a special event.

Glass House
Grant Rd ✉ PH26 3LD – ✆ (01479) 872 980 – www.theglasshouse.grantown.co.uk – Closed 1-2 January, 2 weeks November, 25-26 December, Monday, Sunday dinner and Tuesday lunch
Rest – Menu £ 21 (lunch) – Carte dinner £ 34/41
◆ Conservatory style dining in a house extension near the high street. Light-filled interior overlooks the garden. Amiable owner serves tasty, seasonal modern British dishes.

SCOTLAND

GRULINE – **Argyll and Bute** – **see Mull (Isle of)**

GUILDTOWN – **Perth and Kinross** – **501** J14 – **see Perth**

GULLANE – **East Lothian** – **501** L15 – **pop. 2 172** Scotland **26** C1
Edinburgh 19 mi – North Berwick 5 mi
Dirleton★ (Castle★) NE : 2 mi by A 198

Greywalls
Duncur Rd, Muirfield ✉ EH31 2EG – ✆ (01620) 842 144 – www.greywalls.co.uk
23 rm – †£ 80/300 ††£ 260/320
Rest *Chez Roux* – see restaurant listing
◆ Classic Edwardian country house by Lutyens, in superb location adjoining the famous Muirfield golf course. Spacious, antique-furnished bedrooms. Delightful formal gardens by Jekyll.

Chez Roux – at Greywalls Hotel
Duncur Rd, Muirfield ✉ EH31 2EG – ✆ (01620) 842 144 – www.greywalls.co.uk
Rest – French – *(booking essential for non-residents)* Menu £ 23/25 Carte £ 27/36
◆ Country house style dining room with a modern edge; sit on high-backed chairs at well-spaced tables, overlooking the golf course. Classical French menus with a Roux signature style.

La Potinière
Main St ✉ EH31 2AA – ✆ (01620) 843 214 – www.la-potiniere.co.uk – Closed 3 weeks January, 25-26 December, Sunday dinner October-April, Monday and Tuesday
Rest – *(booking essential)* Menu £ 23/40
◆ Sweet restaurant dressed in pink and white, serving fresh, seasonal cooking. Regularly changing menus of traditional dishes, with ingredients from local suppliers. Good value lunch.

HARRAY – Orkney Islands – **501** K6 – see Orkney Islands (Mainland)

HARRIS (Isle of) – Western Isles Outer Hebrides – **501** Z10 – see Lewis and Harris (Isle of)

INGLISTON – City of Edinburgh – **501** J16 – see Edinburgh

INNERLEITHEN – Borders – **501** – pop. 2 586 – ✉ Peebles **26** C2

Edinburgh 31 mi – Dumfries 57 mi – Glasgow 60 mi

Caddon View

14 Pirn Rd. ✉ EH44 6HH – ✆ (01896) 830 208 – www.caddonview.co.uk

8 rm – †£ 55/75 ††£ 94/115

Rest – *(Closed Sunday and Monday dinner)* Carte £ 17/24

◆ Substantial Victorian house run by hospitable couple. Individually decorated bedrooms with modern touches; spacious Yarrow, and Moorfoot with its view, are the best. Bright, airy dining room; regularly changing menu of local produce from the Tweed Valley.

INVERGARRY – Highland – **501** F12 – ✉ **Inverness** Scotland **30** C3

Edinburgh 159 mi – Fort William 25 mi – Inverness 43 mi – Kyle of Lochalsh 50 mi

The Great Glen★

Glengarry Castle

on A 82 ✉ PH35 4HW – ✆ (01809) 501 254 – www.glengarry.net – 26 March- 6 November

26 rm – †£ 65/95 ††£ 156/176

Rest – *(light lunch Monday-Saturday)* Menu £ 29 **s**

◆ Family-run Victorian house, named after the ruined castle in its 60 acre grounds. 2 large, open-fired sitting rooms; stuffed wild animals abound. Classical, individually styled bedrooms, some with original art deco baths. Formal dining from 4 course Scottish menu.

Invergarry

on A 87 – ✆ (01809) 501 206 – www.invergarryhotel.co.uk – Closed 2 January-10 February and 25 December

13 rm – †£ 55/94 ††£ 89/119 **Rest** – Carte £ 25/35

◆ Welcoming hotel in the style of a traditional inn. Smaller, quirky bedrooms in the eaves; first floor superior rooms offer more space and luxury. Comfy lounge featuring shotguns, open fires and tartan carpets. Simple cooking focuses on fresh Highland produce.

INVERKEILOR – Angus – **501** M14 – pop. 902 – ✉ Arbroath **28** D2

Edinburgh 85 mi – Aberdeen 32 mi – Dundee 22 mi

XX **Gordon's** with rm

32 Main St ✉ DD11 5RN – ✆ (01241) 830 364 – www.gordonsrestaurant.co.uk – Closed 2 weeks January

5 rm – †£ 75 ††£ 125 **Rest** – *(Closed Monday, Tuesday lunch and Sunday dinner to non residents, except May-October) (booking essential)* Menu £ 28/45 **s**

◆ Family owned restaurant in small village. Welcoming atmosphere, beams, open fires and rugs on the wood floors. Good cooking with some innovative touches. Well-kept bedrooms.

INVERMORISTON – Highland – **501** G12 **30** C2

London 550 mi – Edinburgh 166 mi – Inverness 28 mi – Dingwall 42 mi

Tigh na Bruach without rest

Southwest : 0.5 mi on A 82 ✉ IV63 7YE – ✆ (01320) 351 349 – www.tighnabruach.com – March to mid-December

3 rm – †£ 78/87 ††£ 104/116

◆ Name means 'house on the bank'. Located by Loch Ness, it boasts splendid loch/mountain views and beautiful gardens. Very comfy bedrooms have pleasant terraces which overlook the lake.

SCOTLAND

INVERNESS – Highland – **501** H11 – **pop. 40 949** Scotland **30** C2

Edinburgh 156 mi – Aberdeen 107 mi – Dundee 134 mi
Inverness Airport, Dalcross : ✆ (01667) 464000, NE : 8 mi by A 96 Y
Castle Wynd ✆ (01463) 234353 Y, invernesstic@host.co.uk
Culcabock Rd, ✆ (01463) 239 882
Torvean Glenurquhart Rd, ✆ (01463) 225 651
Town★ – Museum and Art Gallery★ Y **M**
Loch Ness★★, SW : by A 82 Z – Clava Cairns★, E : 9 mi by Culcabock Rd, B 9006 and B 851 Z – Cawdor Castle★ **AC**, NE : 14 mi by A 96 and B 9090 Y

Rocpool Reserve

Culduthel Rd ✉ IV2 4AG – ✆ (01463) 240 089 – www.rocpool.com
11 rm ☕ – **♂£** 150/175 **♂♂£** 320/395 — Z**r**
Rest ***Chez Roux*** – see restaurant listing
◆ Ultra-stylish boutique hotel with elegant, modern furnishings and sexy bar. Chic, comfortable bedrooms; some with their own terrace and hot tub. Attentive, professional service.

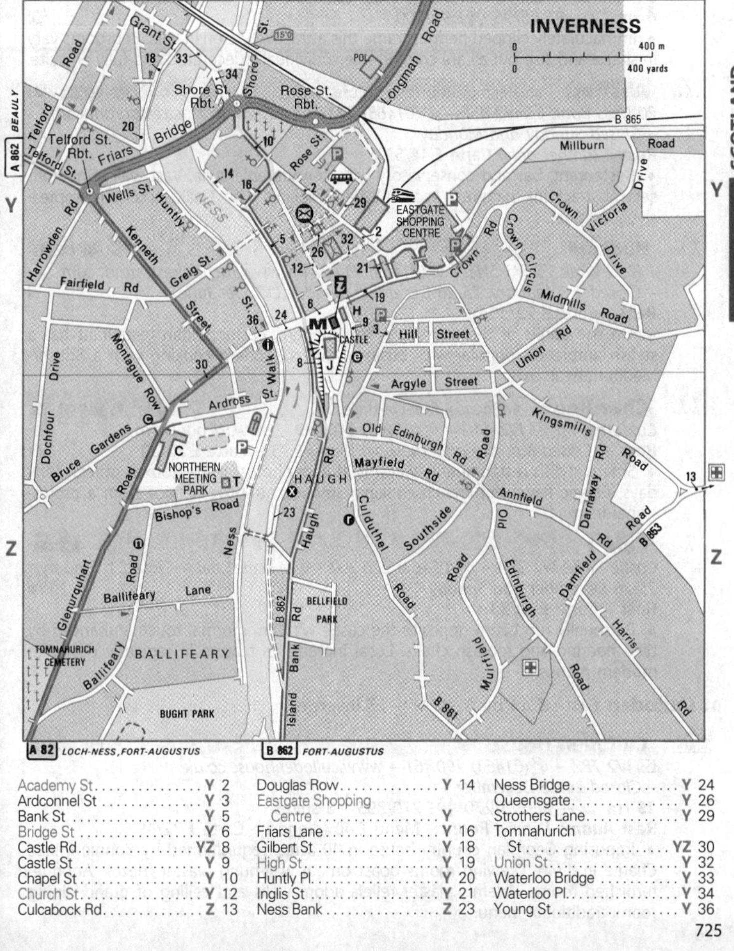

SCOTLAND

Glenmoriston Town House

20 Ness Bank ✉ *IV2 4SF* – ✆ *(01463) 223 777*
– www.glenmoristontownhouse.com Z**x**
30 rm – ♦£ 95/130 ♦♦£ 130/160
Rest *Abstract* – see restaurant listing
Rest *Contrast* – Carte £ 19/44
◆ Chic, stylish town house. Modern cocktail bar a trendy meeting point. Bedrooms are individualistic, those on the front enjoying river views; those at the rear are quieter. Locally sourced cooking at Contrast.

Ballifeary House without rest

10 Ballifeary Rd ✉ *IV3 5PJ* – ✆ *(01463) 235 572*
– www.ballifearyguesthouse.co.uk – Closed 24-28 December Z**n**
7 rm – ♦£ 35/70 ♦♦£ 76/80
◆ Pleasant house set away from town centre, with homely sitting room and comfortable, immaculately kept bedrooms. Smart breakfast room with crisp linen and polished glassware.

Moyness House without rest

6 Bruce Gdns ✉ *IV3 5EN* – ✆ *(01463) 233 836 – www.moyness.co.uk*
6 rm – ♦£ 65/95 ♦♦£ 94/100 Z**c**
◆ Immaculately clipped hedges frame this attractive Victorian villa. Bedrooms vary in shape and size but all are comfortable, individually decorated and fully en suite.

Abstract – at Glenmoriston Town House Hotel

20 Ness Bank ✉ *IV2 4SF* – ✆ *(01463) 223 777 – www.abstractrestaurant.com*
– Closed Sunday and Monday Z**x**
Rest – *(dinner only)* Carte £ 44/53
◆ Restaurant, bar and conservatory with considerable style. Vast wall mirror offsets abstract ink pictures. Accomplished cooking with Gallic accent is impressively original.

Rocpool

1 Ness Walk ✉ *IV3 5NE* – ✆ *(01463) 717 274 – www.rocpoolrestaurant.com*
– Closed 1-3 January, 25-26 December, Sunday October-June Y**i**
Rest – Carte £ 22/36
◆ On the banks of the river Ness, this modern, cosmopolitan restaurant has a stylish ambience, popular with business diners. Modern cooking with a British/-Mediterranean axis.

Chez Roux – at Rocpool Reserve Hotel

Culduthel Rd ✉ *IV2 4AG* – ✆ *(01463) 240 089 – www.rocpool.com*
Rest – *(Closed Monday and Tuesday)* Menu £ 23 – Carte £ 20/28 Z**r**
◆ Smart, stylish restaurant; its walls filled with photos of the Roux brothers' early days. Classic flavourful French cooking; smooth, attentive service from a professional team.

Café 1

Castle St ✉ *IV2 3EA* – ✆ *(01463) 226 200 – www.cafe1.net – Closed 1 January, 25-26 December and Sunday* Y**e**
Rest – Carte £ 20/33 **s**
◆ Personally run bistro opposite the castle with an informal touch, enhanced by tiled flooring and modish chairs. Local ingredients feature in regularly changing modern menus.

at Culloden East : 3 mi by A 96 - Y – ✉ Inverness

Culloden House

✉ *IV2 7BZ* – ✆ *(01463) 790 461 – www.cullodenhouse.co.uk*
– Closed 24-26 December
25 rm – ♦£ 175/270 ♦♦£ 270/395 – 3 suites
Rest *Adams Dining Room* – Menu £ 40 (dinner) – Carte £ 32/49
◆ Imposing Georgian country house in 40 acres, requisitioned by Bonnie Prince Charlie in 1746. Drawing rooms boast ornate wall-hung plaster friezes. Antique-furnished rooms. Adam's plaster reliefs adorn walls and ceiling of grand dining room; traditional menu.

at Bunchrew West : 3 mi on A 862 - Y – ✉ Inverness

Bunchrew House
✉ *IV3 8TA – ✆ (01463) 234 917 – www.bunchrewhousehotel.com – Closed 23-27 December*
16 rm – ♦£ 115/185 ♦♦£ 170/270 **Rest** – Menu £ 24 (lunch)/40
◆ Unhurried relaxation is assured at this 17C Scottish mansion nestling in a tranquil spot on the shores of Bealy Firth. Drawing room is wood panelled; bedrooms restful. Gardens seen through the windows provide a pleasant backdrop to spacious dining room.

ISLAY (Isle of) – Argyll and Bute – 501 B16 — 27 A3

Port Ellen Airport : ✆ (01496) 302361

from Port Askaig to Isle of Jura (Feolin) (Caledonian MacBrayne Ltd) frequent services daily (approx. 4 mn) – from Port Ellen or Port Askaig to Kintyre Peninsula (Kennacraig) (Caledonian MacBrayne Ltd) 1-2 daily – from Port Askaig to Oban via Isle of Colonsay (Scalasaig) (Caledonian MacBrayne Ltd) weekly – from Port Askaig to Isle of Colonsay (Scalasaig) and Kintyre Peninsula (Kennacraig) (Caledonian MacBrayne Ltd) weekly

The Square, Main St, Bowmore ✆ (01496) 810254, bowmore@visitscotland.com

Port Ellen 25 Charlotte St, ✆ (01496) 300 094

BALLYGRANT – Argyll and Bute — 27 A3

Kilmeny
Southwest : 0.5 m on A 846 ✉ PA45 7QW – ✆ (01496) 840 668 – www.kilmeny.co.uk – Closed Christmas and New Year
5 rm – ♦£ 95 ♦♦£ 128/148 **Rest** – Menu £ 38
◆ Delightful house in over 350 acres of working farmland. Large lounge with mock open fire and fine array of books about Islay. Superb bedrooms with beautiful feature beds, lovely tartans/tweeds/woollens woven on the island and thoughtful extras. Spacious dining room serves garden/island produce. Truly welcoming owner.

BOWMORE – Argyll and Bute — 27 A3

Harbour Inn with rm
The Square ✉ PA43 7JR – ✆ (01496) 810 330 – www.harbour-inn.com
11 rm – ♦£ 99/190 ♦♦£ 130/150 **Rest** – Carte £ 22/44
◆ Traditional restaurant with pleasant bar and chunky wooden tea tables covered in deep blue cloths. Classical cooking uses fresh local seafood and island meats. Bedrooms are brightly decorated. Two cosy residents' lounges afford fantastic bay and island views.

PORT CHARLOTTE – Argyll and Bute — 27 A3

Port Charlotte
Main St ✉ PA48 7TU – ✆ (01496) 850 360 – www.portcharlotte.co.uk – Closed 24-26 December
10 rm – ♦£ 95 ♦♦£ 170 **Rest** – *(bar lunch)* Carte £ 18/33
◆ Waterside hotel packed full of modern art. Large lounge with wood burning stove; cosy bar hung with old island photos. Bedrooms display traditional furniture and modern colour schemes; most have a sea view. Good mix of meat and fish dishes in the restaurant.

PORT ELLEN – Argyll and Bute — 27 A3

Glenegedale House
Northwest : 4.75 mi on A 846 ✉ PA42 7AS – ✆ (01496) 300 400 – www.glenegedalehouse.co.uk
8 rm – ♦£ 90 ♦♦£ 110 **Rest** – *(by arrangement)* Menu £ 35
◆ Well-run hotel opposite the airport. Immaculately kept bedrooms feature designer fabrics. Choice of two sitting rooms, both displaying leather sofas, coffee tables and an array of curios. Traditional menu of island produce served in smartly laid dining rooms.

SCOTLAND

Glenmachrie Farmhouse without rest

Northwest : 4.5 mi on A 846 ✉ PA42 7AQ – ✆ (01496) 302 560 – www.glenmachrie.com

5 rm – 🚹£ 75 🚹🚹£ 90

◆ Homely tartan-themed guesthouse where antiques and curious abound. Exclusive access to private loch; catch a fish and they will prepare and even smoke it for you. Breakfast at Glenegedale House.

JEDBURGH – Scottish Borders – **501** M17 – **pop. 4 090** Scotland **26** D2

Edinburgh 48 mi – Carlisle 54 mi – Newcastle upon Tyne 57 mi

Murray's Green ✆ (01835) 863170, jedburgh@visitscotland.com

Jedburgh Dunion Rd, ✆ (01835) 863 587

Town★ - Abbey★★ **AC** – Mary Queen of Scots House Visitor Centre★ **AC** – The Canongate Bridge★

Waterloo Monument (※★★) N : 4 mi by A 68 and B 6400

Willow Court without rest

The Friars ✉ TD8 6BN – ✆ (01835) 863 702 – www.willowcourtjedburgh.co.uk

3 rm – 🚹£ 65/70 🚹🚹£ 80

◆ A contemporary guesthouse; comfortable ground floor bedrooms offer a light, stylish space, with flat screens, iPod docks and DVD players. Communal breakfasts, with eggs from their own hens.

SCOTLAND

KELSO – Scottish Borders – **501** M17 – **pop. 5 116** Scotland **26** D2

Edinburgh 44 mi – Hawick 21 mi – Newcastle upon Tyne 68 mi

Town House, The Square ✆ (01835) 863170 (mornings only in winter), bordersinfo@visitscotland.com

Golf Course Rd, ✆ (01573) 223 009

Town★ - The Square★★ – ≤★ from Kelso Bridge

Tweed Valley★★ - Floors Castle★ **AC**, NW : 1.5 mi by A 6089. Mellerstain★★ (Ceilings★★★, Library★★★) **AC**, NW : 6 mi by A 6089 – Waterloo Monument (※★★), SW : 7 mi by A 698 and B 6400 – Jedburgh Abbey★★ **AC**, SW : 8.5 mi by A 698 - Dryburgh Abbey★★ **AC** (setting★★★), SW : 10.5 mi by A 6089, B 6397 and B 6404 – Scott's View★★, W : 11 mi by A 6089, B 6397, B 6404 and B 6356 – Smailholm Tower★ (※★★), NW : 6 mi by A 6089 and B 6397 - Lady Kirk (Kirk o'Steil★), NE : 16 mi by A 698, A 697, A 6112 and B 6437

Roxburghe

Heiton, Southwest : 3.5 mi by A 698 ✉ TD5 8JZ – ✆ (01573) 450 331 – www.roxburghe-hotel.com

20 rm – 🚹£ 99/190 🚹🚹£ 99/190 – 2 suites

Rest – Menu £ 35 (dinner) **s** – Carte £ 32/49 **s**

◆ Characterful Jacobean style mansion in extensive parkland, owned by the Duke of Roxburghe. Plush lounge and cosy library bar boating antiques/heirlooms. Feature bedrooms the most luxurious; courtyard rooms, more modern. Formal dining – local produce to the fore.

Ednam House

Bridge St. ✉ TD5 7HT – ✆ (01573) 224 168 – www.ednamhouse.com – Closed 20 December-7 January

32 rm – 🚹£ 71/133 🚹🚹£ 111/161 **Rest** – Menu £ 15/30

◆ Longstanding sports hotel on the Tweed; in the family since 1928. Original features, grand drawing rooms and classically styled bedrooms boasting a timeless elegance. Fishing-themed bar displays mural of the Tweed. 4 course classical dinner overlooking the river.

at Ednam North : 2.25 mi on B 6461 – ✉ Kelso

Edenwater House
off Stichill rd ✉ TD5 7QL – ✆ (01573) 224 070 – www.edenwaterhouse.co.uk – February-October
5 rm – †£ 50/75 ††£ 95/110
Rest – *(Closed Sunday except Bank Holidays) (dinner only)* Menu £ 38
◆ Delightful house run by charming couple, boasting a lovely garden and stream. Antique-filled lounges and comfy, classical bedrooms with tasteful décor and antique furniture. Pleasant dining room overlooks a meadow and offers a traditional, daily changing set menu.

KENMORE – **Perth and Kinross** – **501** I14 – **pop. 596** Scotland **28** C2

Edinburgh 82 mi – Dundee 60 mi – Oban 71 mi – Perth 38 mi
18 Taymouth Castle Aberfeldy, ✆ (01887) 830 228
27 Mains of Taymouth, ✆ (01887) 830 226
Village★
Loch Tay★★. Ben Lawers★★, SW : 8 mi by A 827

Kenmore rest,
The Square ✉ PH15 2NU – ✆ (01887) 830 205 – www.kenmorehotel.com
40 rm – †£ 95/105 ††£ 159/179
Rest *Taymouth* – Carte £ 20/34
◆ Scotland's oldest inn. Standing on the Tay, it is now a smart, white-fronted hotel with Poet's Parlour featuring original pencilled verse by Burns. Cosy, well-kept rooms. Restaurant with panoramic river views.

KILBERRY – **Argyll and Bute** – **501** D16 – **see Kintyre (Peninsula)**

KILCHRENAN – **Argyll and Bute** – **501** E14 – ✉ **Taynuilt** Scotland **27** B2

Edinburgh 117 mi – Glasgow 87 mi – Oban 18 mi
Loch Awe★★, E : 1.25 m

Ardanaiseig
Northeast : 4 mi ✉ PA35 1HE – ✆ (01866) 833 333 – www.ardanaiseig.com – Closed January
17 rm – †£ 69/142 ††£ 218/370 – 1 suite
Rest – *(booking essential for non-residents)* Menu £ 25 (lunch)/50
◆ Stunningly located, laid-back country house boasting a vast azalea-filled estate and lovely views down the loch. Large sitting room with impressive columns; bedrooms mix styles – the Lake Suite is best. Elegant formal dining room; daily set menu of local produce.

Roineabhal rm,
✉ PA35 1HD – ✆ (01866) 833 207 – www.roineabhal.com – Easter-November
3 rm – †£ 70 ††£ 100 **Rest** – Menu £ 45
◆ Purpose-built log cabin style guesthouse; jolly owner serves tea and home-made biscuits on arrival. Cosy bedrooms reached via spiral staircase: all have showers; roll-top bath is shared. Bluebell-lined walk in garden. Tasty home cooking of local/garden produce.

KILDRUMMY – **Aberdeenshire** – **501** L12 – ✉ **Alford** Scotland **28** D1

Edinburgh 137 mi – Aberdeen 35 mi
Castle★ **AC**
Huntly Castle (Heraldic carvings★★★) N : 15 mi by A 97 – Craigievar Castle★, SE : 13 mi by A 97, A 944 and A 980

Kildrummy Castle
South : 1.25 mi on A 97 ✉ AB33 8RA – ✆ (019755) 71 288 – www.kildrummycastlehotel.co.uk – Closed 3 January-10 February
16 rm – †£ 98/130 ††£ 217
Rest *Dining Room* – *(closed lunch Monday and Tuesday)* Menu £ 20/37
◆ Imposing, stone built 19C mansion in superb grounds with fine view of original 13C castle. Baronial, country house style abounds: lounges flaunt antiques. Variable rooms. Delightfully wood-panelled dining room; homely Scottish cooking.

KILLIECRANKIE – Perth and Kinross – 501 I13 – see Pitlochry

KILLIN – Stirling – 501 H14 – pop. 666 Scotland 27 B2

Edinburgh 72 mi – Dundee 65 mi – Oban 54 mi – Perth 43 mi

The Old Mill, Falls of Dochart ✆ (08707) 200627, (April- Oct) killin.sdtourism@btconnect.com

Killin, ✆ (01567) 820 312

Loch Tay★★, Ben Lawers★★, NE : 8 mi by A 827

at Ardeonaig Northeast : 6.75 mi – ✉ **Killin (Stirling)**

Ardeonaig

rm, VISA

South Road Loch Tay ✉ *FK21 8SU* – ✆ *(01567) 820 400 – www.ardeonaighotel.co.uk*

26 rm (dinner included) – £ 100/125 £ 220/240

Rest ***Restaurant*** – *(dinner only)* Menu £ 35

◆ Wonderful setting beside Loch Tay. Enthusiastic owner has stamped his own style and service is professional yet unobtrusive. Cosy bar, chic sitting room and charming library. Deluxe rooms in extension. Kitchen merges South African influences with local ingredients.

KINCLAVEN – Perth and Kinross – 501 J14 – pop. 394 – ✉ Stanley 28 C2

SCOTLAND

Edinburgh 56 mi – Perth 12 mi

Ballathie House

rm, VISA AE

Stanley ✉ *PH1 4QN* – ✆ *(01250) 883 268 – www.ballathiehousehotel.com*

39 rm – £ 60/130 £ 120/210 – 3 suites **Rest** – Menu £ 25/45 **s**

◆ Imposing mid 19C former shooting lodge on banks of Tay, imbued with tranquil, charming atmosphere. Elegant, individually furnished bedrooms with a floral theme. Richly alluring restaurant overlooking river.

KINGAIRLOCH – 501 D14 29 B3

London 521 mi – Edinburgh 147 mi – Greenock 116 mi

Boathouse and Steadings with rm

rm, VISA AE

Ardgour ✉ *PH33 7AE* – ✆ *(01967) 411 232 – www.kingairloch.co.uk – March-October*

5 rm – £ 45 £ 80

Rest – *(closed Monday -Wednesday and Sunday dinner) (booking advisable)* Carte £ 17/31

◆ A converted Victorian boathouse on the shore of Loch a'Choire in the heart of the Kingairloch Estate. Appealing dishes use estate produce, including full-flavoured venison, and seasonal herbs and vegetables from the kitchen garden. Spacious, immaculately maintained bedrooms in The Steadings. Dramatic mountain views.

KINGUSSIE – Highland – 501 H12 – pop. 1 410 Scotland 30 C3

Edinburgh 117 mi – Inverness 41 mi – Perth 73 mi

Gynack Rd, ✆ (01540) 661 600

Highland Wildlife Park★ **AC**, NE : 4 mi by A 9. Aviemore★, NE : 11 mi by A 9 – The Cairngorms★★ (★★★) - ★★★ from Cairn Gorm, NE : 18 mi by B 970

Hermitage

VISA

Spey St ✉ *PH21 1HN* – ✆ *(01540) 662 137 – www.thehermitage-scotland.com – Closed Christmas-New Year*

5 rm – £ 45/65 £ 64/100 **Rest** – Menu £ 22 **s**

◆ Pleasant Victorian detached house with views of Cairngorms. Attractive lawned garden. Homely, welcoming lounge with log fire. Colourful, floral rooms. Garden views from conservatory style dining room.

Cross at Kingussie with rm
Tweed Mill Brae, Ardbroilach Rd ✉ PH21 1LB – ✆ (01540) 661 166 – www.thecross.co.uk – Closed 4 weeks winter, 1 week autumn, 25 December, Sunday and Monday
8 rm (dinner included) – £ 145/185 ££ 250/280
Rest – *(dinner only) (booking essential)* Menu £ 50 **s**
◆ Personally run converted tweed mill restaurant in four acres of waterside grounds with beamed ceilings and modern artwork. Modish Scottish cuisine. Comfortable rooms.

KINROSS – Perth and Kinross – 501 J15 – pop. 4 681 — 28 C2

Edinburgh 28 mi – Dunfermline 13 mi – Perth 18 mi – Stirling 25 mi
Kinross Information Centre, Loch Leven Nature Reserve ✆ (01577) 863680 (closed weekends October-April), kinrosstic@perthshire.co.uk
Green Hotel 2 The Muirs, ✆ (01577) 863 407
Milnathort South St, ✆ (01577) 864 069
Bishopshire Kinnesswood Woodmarch

Green
2 Muirs ✉ KY13 8AS – ✆ (01577) 863 467 – www.green-hotel.com
46 rm – £ 62 ££ 72
Rest ***Basil's*** – Carte £ 17/29
◆ 18C former coaching inn in neat grounds off village high street. Spacious, welcoming lounge. Try your hand at curling. Comfortable, modern rooms. Bright, airy modern restaurant with modish menus to match.

SCOTLAND

KINTYRE (Peninsula) – Argyll and Bute – 501 D16 Scotland — 27 B3

Campbeltown Airport : ✆ (01586) 553797
from Claonaig to Isle of Arran (Lochranza) (Caledonian MacBrayne Ltd) frequent services daily (30 mn)
– from Kennacraig to Isle of Islay (Port Ellen or Port Askaig) (Caledonian MacBrayne Ltd) 1-3 daily
– from Kennacraig to Oban via Isle of Colonsay (Scalasaig) and Isle of Islay (Port Askaig) 3 weekly
Machrihanish Campbeltown, ✆ (01586) 810 213
Dunaverty Campbeltown Southend, ✆ (01586) 830 677
Gigha Isle of Gigha, ✆ (01583) 505 242
Carradale★ – Saddell (Collection of grave slabs★)

CARRADALE – Argyll and Bute — 27 B3

Dunvalanree
Port Righ Bay ✉ PA28 6SE – ✆ (01583) 431 226 – www.dunvalanree.com – Closed Christmas
5 rm (dinner included) – £ 100 ££ 190 **Rest** – *(dinner only)* Menu £ 28
◆ 1930s house in its own bay, with gardens and terrace overlooking the beach and Sound. Charming interior with many original Arts and Crafts features. Individually furnished bedrooms – one in Mackintosh style; some with views. Homely cooking with a seafood base.

KILBERRY – Argyll and Bute — 27 A3

Kilberry Inn with rm
✉ PA29 6YD – ✆ (01880) 770 223 – www.kilberryinn.com – Closed January-February and Monday
5 rm (dinner included) – £ 100 ££ 195
Rest – *(booking essential at dinner)* Carte £ 24/36 **s**
◆ Remotely set, rustic country inn with wooden beams, stone walls, open fires and mix of bare and linen-laid tables. Classical dishes are crafted from carefully sourced local produce; meat and fish are smoked in-house. Well-stocked bar. Comfy, modern bedrooms are named after nearby islands; one has an outdoor hot tub.

KIRKBEAN – Dumfries and Galloway – 501 J19 Scotland **26** C3

Edinburgh 92 mi – Dumfries 13 mi – Kirkcudbright 29 mi

Sweetheart Abbey★, N : 5 mi by A 710. Threave Garden★★ and Threave Castle★, W : 20 mi by A 710 and A 745

Cavens

DG2 8AA – (01387) 880 234 – www.cavens.com – Closed January-February
8 rm – £ 80/130 £ 180/200 **Rest** – *(dinner only)* Menu £ 30

◆ Attractive 18C country house in mature grounds. Elegant drawing room with grand piano and cosy, book-filled 'Green Room'. Luxurious 'Estate' bedrooms boast views over the Solway Firth; comfy 'Country' rooms are simpler. Linen-clad dining room offers unfussy 3 course menu of local produce. Complimentary afternoon tea.

KIRKCUDBRIGHT – Dumfries and Galloway – 501 H19 – pop. 3 447 **25** B3
Scotland

Edinburgh 108 mi – Dumfries 28 mi – Stranraer 50 mi

Harbour Sq (01557) 330494 (Easter-October), kirkcudbright@visitscotland.com

Stirling Crescent, (01557) 330 314

Town★

Dundrennan Abbey★ **AC**, SE : 5 mi by A 711

Selkirk Arms

High St DG6 4JG – (01557) 330 402 – www.selkirkarmshotel.co.uk
17 rm – £ 55/105 £ 66/116 – 2 suites
Rest *Selkirk Arms* – Menu £ 28 (dinner) – Carte £ 23/32

◆ Well-run 18C former coaching inn where Robert Burns reputedly wrote the Selkirk Grace. Spacious, comfortable bedrooms and cosy sports bar. Light meals in bistro; wide choice of classical dishes in the restaurant. Galloway Beef and Kirkcudbright scallops feature.

Fludha

Tongland Rd., North : 0.75 mi on A 711 DG6 4UU – (01557) 331 443 – www.fludha.com
6 rm – £ 75 £ 95/100 **Rest** – Menu £ 28 **s**

◆ 19C stone-built house affording fine views of the River Dee. Bedrooms individually furnished to a high standard. Those at the front benefit from the view; those to the rear offer more luxurious bathrooms. Regularly changing menu features local ingredients.

Gladstone House

48 High St DG6 4JX – (01557) 331 734 – www.kirkcudbrightgladstone.com
3 rm – £ 55 £ 72 **Rest** – Menu £ 25

◆ Attractive 18C former merchant's house with friendly owners. Comfy, antique-furnished lounge. Simple, pastel-hued bedrooms with seating areas by the windows and views over the rooftops. 3 course dinner of local produce, tailored around guests' preferences.

KIRKMICHAEL – Perth and Kinross – 501 J13 **28** C2

Edinburgh 73 mi – Aberdeen 85 mi – Inverness 102 mi – Perth 29 mi

The Strathardle Inn with rm

on A 924 PH10 7NS – (01250) 881 224 – www.strathardleinn.co.uk – Closed Monday lunch and Tuesday-Friday lunch November-March
8 rm – £ 40/50 £ 70/80
Rest – Carte (dinner only and lunch Saturday-Sunday) £ 18/30

◆ 18C drover's inn serving robust cooking with a Scottish twist. Concise lunch menu of pub favourites. Dinner menu might feature smoked salmon or local venison. Simple, modern bedrooms.

KIRKNEWTON – Edinburgh – 501 J16 – see Edinburgh

KIRKWALL – Orkney Islands – 501 L7 – see Orkney Islands

KIRK YETHOLM - Scottish Borders 26 D2

London 346 mi - Edinburgh 57 mi - Hawick 26 mi - Galashiels 27 mi

Mill House without rest

Main St ✉ TD5 8PE - ✆ (01573) 420 604 - www.millhouseyetholm.co.uk

3 rm - £ 50/60 £ 90

◆ Charming former grain mill set on the edge of the village, looking down the valley. Spacious interior with vast lounge and equally large dining room. Comfy bedrooms are simply furnished, with modern bathrooms. Indoor hot tub. Extensive offerings at breakfast.

KIRRIEMUIR - Angus - 501 K13 - pop. 5 963 28 C2

Edinburgh 65 mi - Aberdeen 50 mi - Dundee 16 mi - Perth 30 mi

Purgavie Farm

Lintrathen, West : 5.5 mi on B 951 ✉ DD8 5HZ - ✆ (01575) 560 213 - www.purgavie.co.uk

3 rm - £ 40/45 £ 60/70 **Rest** - Menu £ 15

◆ Farmhouse on working farm at foot of Glen Isla, part of lovely Glens of Angus. Homely lounge with open fire. Large, comfortable rooms with panoramic views. Meals are taken communally in the comfortable dining room.

KYLESKU - Highland - 501 E9 Scotland 30 C1

Edinburgh 256 mi - Inverness 100 mi - Ullapool 34 mi

Loch Assynt★★, S : 6 mi by A 894

Kylesku

✉ IV27 4HW - ✆ (01971) 502 231 - www.kyleskuhotel.co.uk - March-October

8 rm - £ 68 £ 102

Rest *Kylesku (Bar)* - see restaurant listing

Rest - *(dinner only)* Carte £ 21/28

◆ Delightfully located 17C coaching inn, set beside 2 sea-lochs in a peaceful village. Spectacular panoramic views from cosy lounge, restaurant and most of the homely bedrooms. Cooking centres around fresh Highland game and locally landed seafood.

Kylesku (Bar) - at Kylesku Hotel

✉ IV27 4HW - ✆ (01971) 502 231 - www.kyleskuhotel.co.uk - March-October

Rest - Menu £ 29 (dinner) - Carte £ 20/31

◆ Friendly staff and relaxed atmopshere, with breathtaking views of Loch Glendhu and the spectacular surrounding scenery. Menu focuses on fresh seafood landed daily in front of the inn.

LAIRG - Highland - 501 G9 - pop. 857 30 C2

Edinburgh 218 mi - Inverness 61 mi - Wick 72 mi

Ferrycroft Countryside Centre, Sutherland ✆ (01549) 402160 (April-October), ferrycroft@croftersrestaurant.fsnet.co.uk

Park House

✉ IV27 4AU - ✆ (01549) 402 208 - www.parkhousesporting.com - Closed 2 weeks Christmas

4 rm - £ 50/60 £ 80/90 **Rest** - Menu £ 25

◆ Victorian sporting lodge offering fishing and field sports, its walls fittingly hung with rods and hunting prints. Cosy, open-fired sitting room and good-sized, homely bedrooms. Dining room offers loch views and a classical menu. Game and seafood feature highly.

LANGASS - Western Isles - see Uist (Isles of)

LEITH - Edinburgh - 501 K16 - see Edinburgh

LERWICK - Shetland Islands - 501 Q3 - see Shetland Islands (Mainland)

SCOTLAND

LEWIS and HARRIS (Isle of) – 501 A9 Scotland

from Stornoway to Ullapool (Mainland) (Caledonian MacBrayne Ltd) 2/3 daily (2 h 40 mn) – from Kyles Scalpay to the Isle of Scalpay (Caledonian MacBrayne Ltd) (10 mn) – from Tarbert to Isle of Skye (Uig) (Caledonian MacBrayne Ltd) 1-2 daily (1 h 45 mn) – from Tarbert to Portavadie (Caledonian MacBrayne Ltd) (summer only) frequent services daily (25 mn) – from Leverburgh to North Uist (Otternish) (Caledonian MacBrayne Ltd) (3-4 daily) (1 h 10 mn)

Callanish Standing Stones★★ – Carloway Broch★ – St Clement's Church, Rodel (tomb★)

LEWIS – Western Isles 29 A1

London 618 mi – Edinburgh 212 mi

BREASCLETE – Western Isles 29 B1

Eshcol rm,

21 Breasclete ✉ HS2 9ED – ✆ (01851) 621 357 – www.eshcol.com – March-October

3 rm – †£ 40/60 ††£ 80/90 **Rest** – Menu £ 25

◆ Immaculately kept guesthouse set on a small croft, in a former weaving village. Lovely loch and island views from the lounge and conservatory. Simple, homely bedrooms also share the view. Breakfast and dinner served in next door sister guesthouse 'Loch Roag'.

Loch Roag

22A Breasclete ✉ HS2 9EF – ✆ (01851) 621 357 – www.lochroag.com

4 rm – †£ 40/70 ††£ 80/90 **Rest** – *(by arrangement)* Menu £ 22

◆ Run in conjunction with sister guesthouse 'Eshcol'. Simple, well-maintained bedrooms are a little larger than next door. Comfy lounge and dining room; big windows take in the view. Local specialities to start the day – home-cooked regional produce to finish it.

GALSON – Western Isles 29 B1

Galson Farm

South Galson ✉ HS2 0SH – ✆ (01851) 850 492 – www.galsonfarm.co.uk

4 rm – †£ 46/48 ††£ 94 **Rest** – Menu £ 25

◆ Welcoming guesthouse in a wonderfully remote location, boasting views out across the Atlantic. Traditional, homely guest areas and cosy bedrooms. The owner also operates the village post office from just inside the porch. Freshly prepared, home-cooked meals.

STORNOWAY – Western Isles 29 B1

26 Cromwell St ✆ (01851) 703088, stornaway@visitscotland.com

Lady Lever Park, ✆ (01851) 702 240

Braighe House without rest

20 Braighe Rd, Southeast : 3 mi on A 866 ✉ HS2 0BQ – ✆ (01851) 705 287 – www.braighehouse.co.uk

5 rm – †£ 75/125 ††£ 115/145

◆ Smart dormer bungalow with relaxed, modern interior. Deluxe rooms have sleigh beds and sea outlooks. Complimentary port and use of fishing rods. Car/-golf club hire arranged. Diverse breakfasts.

HARRIS – Western Isles 29 A1

London 638 mi – Edinburgh 254 mi

ARDHASAIG – Western Isles 29 A1

XX **Ardhasaig House** with rm

✉ HS3 3AJ – ✆ (01859) 502 500 – www.ardhasaig.co.uk

6 rm – †£ 50/120 ††£ 80/160

Rest – *(dinner only) (booking essential for non-residents)* Menu £ 38

◆ Purpose-built house that's been in the family for over 100 years. Modern, airy bar-lounge; flag-floored dining room with antique tables and dramatic bay/mountain views. Set menu offers local meats and seafood. Cosy bedrooms; the one in the stone lodge is the best.

SCALPAY - Western Isles 29 B2

Hirta House without rest

✉ HS4 3XZ – ☎ (01859) 540 394 – www.hirtahouse.co.uk
3 rm ☕ – †£ 40/50 ††£ 60/70
◆ Simple, characterful guesthouse in a small fishing village. Harbour views from lounge and conservatory. One traditional four-poster bedroom; two more modern rooms, one with a queen-sized bed.

SCARISTA - Western Isles 29 A2

Scarista House

✉ HS3 3HX – ☎ (01859) 550 238 – www.scaristahouse.com – *March-16 December*
5 rm ☕ – †£ 125/140 ††£ 190/220
Rest – *(dinner only) (booking essential for non-residents) (set menu only)*
Menu £ 45
◆ Simple whitewashed house boasting amazing bay and mountain views. Caring owners; cosy, homely interior with open-fired library and drawing room. Traditional bedrooms, those at the rear are best. Set dinners use garden produce and offer the choice of meat or fish.

TARBERT - Western Isles - pop. 1 338 - ✉ Harris 29 A2

Hotel Hebrides

Pier Rd ✉ *HS3 3DG* – ☎ *(01859) 502 364* – *www.hotel-hebrides.com*
21 rm ☕ – †£ 65/75 ††£ 130/250
Rest ***Pier House*** – Menu £ 15 (lunch) **s** – Carte £ 28/45 **s**
◆ Keenly run, boutique-style hotel situated next to the ferry terminal on the harbour. Cosy, stylish, well thought out bedrooms; smart, friendly bar and good service. Modern menu showcases the island's superb produce in Pier House; dishes are packed with flavour.

Ceol na Mara without rest

7 Direcleit, South : 1 mi by A859 ✉ *HS3 3DP* – ☎ *(01859) 502 464* – *www.ceolnamara.com*
4 rm ☕ – †£ 70 ††£ 90
◆ Former crofter's cottage – one of only three on the island with three storeys. Spacious, homely interior. Various well-kept lounges and good-sized, comfy bedrooms. Stunning lochside location.

LEWISTON - Highland - 501 G12 Scotland 30 C2

Edinburgh 173 mi – Inverness 17 mi
Loch Ness★★ – The Great Glen★

Woodlands without rest

East Lewiston ✉ *IV63 6UJ* – ☎ *(01456) 450 356* – *www.woodlands-lochness.co.uk* – *March-October*
3 rm ☕ – †£ 40/65 ††£ 65/75
◆ Spacious, purpose-built guesthouse with large garden and decked terrace; situated just away from the village centre. Bedrooms are airy, comfortable and immaculately kept.

Loch Ness Inn with rm

✉ *IV63 6UW* – ☎ *(01456) 450 991* – *www.staylochness.co.uk*
12 rm ☕ – †£ 57/89 ††£ 75/99
Rest – Carte £ 17/30
◆ Honest local pub with traditional bar, contemporary dining room and smart wood-furnished rear terrace. Pub classics on the blackboard at lunch, more restaurant-style dishes at dinner. Individually styled bedrooms have a country feel.

SCOTLAND

LINLITHGOW - West Lothian - 501 J16 - pop. 13 370 Scotland 26 C1

Edinburgh 19 mi - Falkirk 9 mi - Glasgow 35 mi

County Buildings, High St ✆ (01506) 775320 (April-October), linlithgow@visitscotland.com

Braehead, ✆ (01506) 842 585

West Lothian Airngath Hill, ✆ (01506) 826 030

Town★★ - Palace★★ **AC** : Courtyard (fountain★★), Great Hall (Hooded Fireplace★★), Gateway★ - Old Town★ - St Michaels★

Cairnpapple Hill★ **AC**, SW : 5 mi by A 706 - House of the Binns (plasterwork ceilings★) **AC**, NE : 4.5 mi by A 803 and A 904. Hopetoun House★★ **AC**, E : 7 mi by A 706 and A 904 - Abercorn Parish Church (Hopetoun Loft★★) NE : 7 mi by A 803 and A 904

Arden House without rest

Belsyde, Southwest : 2.25 mi on A 706 ✉ EH49 6QE - ✆ (01506) 670 172 - www.ardencountryhouse.com - Closed 25-26 December

3 rm - †£ 56/90 ††£ 90/110

◆ Purpose built guesthouse set in 105 acres of sheep farming land. Spacious, tastefully styled bedrooms boast modern, slate-floored bathrooms and plenty of extras. Tasty, wide-ranging breakfasts are a highlight. Welcoming owner pays great attention to detail.

Champany Inn with rm

Northeast : 2 mi on A 803 at junction with A 904 ✉ EH49 7LU - ✆ (01506) 834 532 - www.champany.com - Closed 1-2 January, 25-26 December, Saturday lunch and Sunday

16 rm - †£ 115 ††£ 135

Rest *Chop and Ale House* - see restaurant listing

Rest - Beef specialities - Menu £ 28/40 - Carte £ 51/75

Spec. Hot smoked salmon with sherry hollandaise. Rib-eye of Aberdeen Angus beef. Cheesecake with seasonal berries.

◆ Collection of buildings that create a 'mini-village'. Polished tables, smart silverware and formal service in restaurant. Classically based dishes, with superb quality 21-day aged Aberdeen Angus beef their speciality. Excellent wine list with extensive South African selection. Smart, spacious, tartan-themed bedrooms.

Livingston's

52 High St ✉ EH49 7AE - ✆ (01506) 846 565 - www.livingstons-restaurant.co.uk - Closed 2 weeks January, 1 week June, 1 week October, Sunday and Monday

Rest - Menu £ 15/38 - Carte £ 31/45

◆ Long-standing, family-run restaurant. Conservatory-like dining room with large garden and terrace; friendly, efficient service. Set menus feature Scottish produce and Mediterranean touches.

Chop and Ale House - at Champany Inn

Champany, Northeast : 2 mi on A 803 at junction with A 904 ✉ EH49 6QE ✆ (01506) 834 532 - www.champany.com - closed 1 January and 25-26 December

Rest - Carte £ 24/38

◆ Cosy restaurant with stone walls and beamed ceilings hung with animal traps and hunting prints. Menu offers quality steaks, speciality burgers, South African Boerewors and seafood classics.

LOANS - South Ayrshire - 501 G17 - see Troon

LOCHALINE - Highland - 501 C14 29 B3

Edinburgh 162 mi - Craignure 6 mi - Oban 7 mi

Whitehouse

✉ PA34 5XT - ✆ (01967) 421 777 - www.thewhitehouserestaurant.co.uk - Closed November-Easter, Monday and Sunday dinner

Rest - Carte £ 21/29

◆ Understated, wood-panelled restaurant in remote headland village. Constantly evolving blackboard menu of local seafood, game and garden produce. Unfussy, flavoursome cooking. Hands-on owners.

SCOTLAND

LOCHEARNHEAD – Stirling – **501** H14 Scotland **28** C2

Edinburgh 65 mi – Glasgow 56 mi – Oban 57 mi – Perth 36 mi

at Balquhidder Southwest : 5 mi by A84 – ✉ Stirling

Monachyle Mhor

West : 4 mi ✉ FK19 8PQ – ✆ (01877) 384 622 – www.mhor.net – Closed 3-31 January

14 rm (dinner included) – †£ 238 ††£ 292

Rest – *(booking essential for non residents)* Menu £ 25 (weekday lunch)/46 (dinner) – Carte £ 29/35

◆ Passionately run, remote hotel with its own working farm. Bedrooms in direct contrast to the farmhouse feel as they are modern and stylish; bathrooms are particularly smart. Owner-chef uses much of the farm's produce in his modern dishes.

LOCHINVER – Highland – **501** E9 – **pop. 470** – ✉ Lairg Scotland **30** C1

Edinburgh 251 mi – Inverness 95 mi – Wick 105 mi

Assynt Visitor Centre, Kirk Lane ✆ (01506) 832 222 (April-October), lochinver@visitscotland.com

Village★

Loch Assynt★★, E : 6 mi by A 837

Inver Lodge

Iolaire Rd ✉ IV27 4LU – ✆ (01571) 844 496 – www.inverlodge.com – April-October

20 rm – †£ 115 ††£ 215

Rest ***Chez Roux*** – see restaurant listing

◆ Well-run hotel on the hillside, overlooking a quiet fishing village. Spacious open-fired lounge, elegant bar and billiard room. Smart bedrooms with good mod cons and great bay/island views.

Ruddyglow Park Country House

Loch Assynt, Northeast : 6.75 mi on A 837 ✉ IV27 4HB – ✆ (01571) 822 216 – www.ruddyglowpark.com

3 rm – †£ 80/130 ††£ 100/200 **Rest** – Menu £ 45 **s**

◆ Yellow-washed house in superb location, boasting fantastic loch and mountain views. Spacious guest areas filled with antiques, paintings and silverware. High level of facilities and extras in classically styled bedrooms; modern log cabin room offers extra privacy. Communal, home dining; local seafood and game feature.

Albannach (Colin Craig and Lesley Crosfield) with rm

Baddidarroch, West : 1 mi by Baddidarroch rd ✉ IV27 4LP – ✆ (01571) 844 407 – www.thealbannach.co.uk – Closed 3 January-18 March

5 rm (dinner included) – †£ 200 ††£ 240/355

Rest – *(Closed Monday (except to residents) and Tuesday-Wednesday November-March (except in the festive season)) (dinner only) (booking essential for non-residents) (set menu only)* Menu £ 55

Spec. Wood pigeon with wild mushroom ravioli and chocolate sauce. Wild turbot with braised fennel, black potatoes, asparagus and red wine sauce. Rhubarb and vanilla parfait with Muscat poached rhubarb.

◆ Substantial 19C Scottish house in remote location, boasting exceptional bay/-mountain views from the conservatory, terrace and garden. Strong focus on the food. Traditional daily 5 course set menu of local, seasonal produce. Well-appointed bedrooms are spread about the building; one boasts a private terrace and hot tub.

Chez Roux – at Inver Lodge Hotel

Iolaire Rd ✉ IV27 4LU – ✆ (01571) 844 496 – www.inverlodge.com – April-October

Rest – Menu £ 16/42 – Carte £ 32/41

◆ Romantic restaurant hung with photos of the eponymous brothers and boasting well-spaced tables that take in fantastic bay and mountain views. Regularly changing, classical French menus.

LOCHMADDY – Western Isles Outer Hebrides – **501** Y11 – see Uist (Isles of)

LOCHRANZA – North Ayrshire – **501** E16 – see Arran (Isle of)

MELROSE – Scottish Borders – 501 L17 – pop. 1 656 Scotland 26 D2

Edinburgh 38 mi – Hawick 19 mi – Newcastle upon Tyne 70 mi

Abbey House, Abbey St ✆ (01835) 863170, melrose@visitscotland.com

Melrose Dingleton Dingleton Rd, ✆ (01896) 822 855

Town★ - Abbey★★ (decorative sculpture★★★) **AC**

Eildon Hills (✳★★★) – Scott's View★★ – Abbotsford★★ **AC**, W : 4.5 mi by A 6091 and B 6360 – Dryburgh Abbey★★ **AC** (setting★★★), SE : 4 mi by A 6091 – Tweed Valley★★. Bowhill★★ **AC**, SW : 11.5 mi by A 6091, A 7 and A 708 – Thirlestane Castle (plasterwork ceilings★★) **AC**, NE : 21 mi by A 6091 and A 68

Burts

Market Sq. ✉ TD6 9PL – ✆ (01896) 822 285 – www.burtshotel.co.uk – Closed 4-9 January and 25-26 December

20 rm – †£ 70/105 ††£ 110/140 **Rest** – Carte £ 27/35

◆ Characterful coaching inn on the main square; run by the same family for two generations. Appealing bedrooms blend contemporary furnishings with original features. Cosy bar serves old classics; formal dining room offers a mix of modern and traditional dishes.

Townhouse

Market Sq. ✉ TD6 9PQ – ✆ (01896) 822 645 – www.thetownhousemelrose.co.uk – Closed 3-10 January and 24-26 December

11 rm – †£ 70/105 ††£ 100/150

Rest – Menu £ 33 (dinner) – Carte £ 23/34

◆ Former home of Catherine Spence and contemporary sister to nearby Burts. Stylish bedrooms are decorated in black and purple and display bold feature walls; standards are shower only. Trendy all day café-cum-bar; dining room offers the best Border ingredients.

SCOTLAND

at Gattonside North : 2 mi by B 6374 on B 6360 – ✉ Melrose

Fauhope House without rest

East : 0.25 mi by B 6360 taking unmarked lane to the right of Monkswood Rd at edge of village ✉ TD6 9LU – ✆ (01896) 823 184 – www.fauhopehouse.com

3 rm – †£ 70 ††£ 90/110

◆ Charming 19C house by the Tweed, overlooking Melrose. Quirky interior displays an eclectic mix of art and antiques. Bedrooms are all very different; some boast stylish bold colour schemes.

MEMUS – Angus 28 D2

London 497 mi – Edinburgh 86 mi – Aberdeen 52 mi – Dundee 25 mi

Drovers

✉ DD8 3TY – ✆ (01307) 860 322 – www.the-drovers.com

Rest – Carte £ 24/38

◆ Remote Highland inn with cosy bar, set on the fringes of a peaceful hamlet. Cooking is hearty and warming, offering plenty of comfort food. Set restaurant menu is more elaborate.

MOFFAT – Dumfries and Galloway – 501 J17 – pop. 2 135 Scotland 26 C2

Edinburgh 61 mi – Carlisle 43 mi – Dumfries 22 mi – Glasgow 60 mi

Churchgate ✆ (01683) 220620 (Easter-October), moffat@visitscotland.com

Coatshill, ✆ (01683) 220 020

Grey Mare's Tail★★, NE : 9 mi by A 708

Hartfell House

Hartfell Cres. ✉ DG10 9AL – ✆ (01683) 220 153 – www.hartfellhouse.co.uk – Closed Christmas-New Year

7 rm – †£ 40/50 ††£ 70

Rest *Lime Tree* – see restaurant listing

◆ Keenly run Victorian house in quiet crescent. Original features include parquet floors and ornate cornicing. Comfy lounge boasts nice southerly aspect. Large, traditionally decorated bedrooms.

Bridge House

Well Rd., East : 0.75 mi by Selkirk rd. (A 708) taking left hand turn before bridge ✉ DG10 9JT – ✆ (01683) 220 558 – www.bridgehousemoffat.co.uk

7 rm – †£ 55 ††£ 75/105

Rest – Menu £ 28

♦ Large Victorian house on quiet residential road, run by experienced owners. Comfy lounge with deep sofas. Individually decorated bedrooms – those to the front are biggest. Beautiful valley views. Lovely cornicing in dining room; extensive menu has Asian twists.

Well View

rest, VISA MC AE

Ballplay Rd., East : 0.75 mi by Selkirk rd (A 708) ✉ DG10 9JU – ✆ (01683) 220 184 – www.wellview.co.uk

3 rm – †£ 75 ††£ 110 **Rest** – Menu £ 35 **s**

♦ Substantial 19C house located in a peaceful suburb, boasting spacious, traditionally styled bedrooms and good comforts. Formerly a restaurant, dinner is still a key focus here. The daily changing 4 course set menu is taken at a communal table; wine is included.

Lime Tree – at Hartfell House Hotel

Hartfell Cres. ✉ DG10 9AL – ✆ (01683) 220 153 – www.hartfellhouse.co.uk – Closed Christmas-New Year

Rest – *(closed Sunday dinner and Monday) (dinner only and Sunday lunch) (booking essential)* Menu £ 28

♦ Small hotel restaurant with smartly laid tables, open fire and attractive marquetry. Large bay window looks down the valley. Good value weekly menu features tasty, well-presented classics.

SCOTLAND

MONTROSE – Angus – 501 M13 – pop. 10 845 Scotland 28 D2

Edinburgh 92 mi – Aberdeen 39 mi – Dundee 29 mi

Montrose Museum, Panmure Place ✆ (01674) 673232 (Seasonal), montrose.museum@angus.gov.uk

36 Traill Drive, ✆ (01674) 672 932

Edzell Castle★ (The Pleasance★★★) **AC**, NW : 17 mi by A 935 and B 966 – Cairn O'Mount Road★ (★★) N : 17 mi by B 966 and B 974 – Brechin (Round Tower★) W : 7 mi by A 935 – Aberlemno (Aberlemno Stones★, Pictish sculptured stones★) W : 13 mi by A 935 and B 9134

36 The Mall without rest

VISA MC AE

36 The Mall, North : 0.5 mi by A 92 at junction with North Esk Road ✉ DD10 8SS – ✆ (01674) 673 646 – www.36themall.co.uk

3 rm – †£ 48/60 ††£ 58/80

♦ Bay windowed 19C former manse with pleasant conservatory lounge. Impressive plate collection the talking point of communal breakfast room. Well-kept rooms with high ceilings.

MUIR OF ORD – Highland – 501 G11 – pop. 1 812 30 C2

Edinburgh 173 mi – Inverness 10 mi – Wick 121 mi

18 Great North Rd, ✆ (01463) 870 825

Dower House

rest, VISA MC

Highfield, North : 1 mi on A 862 ✉ IV6 7XN – ✆ (01463) 870 090 – www.thedowerhouse.co.uk – Closed 2 weeks November and 25 December

4 rm – †£ 75/95 ††£ 135/150

Rest – *(dinner only) (set menu only)* Menu £ 42

♦ Personally run, part 17C house in mature garden. Stacked bookshelves, soft fireside armchairs, cosy bedrooms and fresh flowers: a relaxed but well-ordered country home. Dining room offers careful cooking of fine fresh ingredients.

MULL (Isle of) – Argyll and Bute – 501 B/C14 – pop. 1 841 Scotland 27 A2

from Fionnphort to Isle of Iona (Caledonian MacBrayne Ltd) frequent services daily (10 mn) – from Pierowall to Papa Westray (Orkney Ferries Ltd) (summer only) (25 mn)

from Craignure to Oban (Caledonian MacBrayne Ltd) frequent services daily (45 mn)
– from Fishnish to Lochaline (Mainland) (Caledonian MacBrayne Ltd) frequent services daily (15 mn)
– from Tobermory to Isle of Tiree (Scarinish) via Isle of Coll (Arinagour) (Caledonian MacBrayne Ltd) 3 weekly (2 h 30 mn)
– from Tobermory to Kilchoan (Caledonian MacBrayne Ltd) 4 daily (summer only) (35 mn)

The Pier, Craignure ☎ (08707) 200610, mull@visitscotland.com
- Main Street, Tobermory ☎ (01688) 302182 (April-October), tobermory@visitscotland.com

Craignure Scallastle, ☎ (01688) 302 517

Island★ - Calgary Bay★★ – Torosay Castle **AC** (Gardens★ ≤★)

Isle of Iona★ (Maclean's Cross★, St Oran's Chapel★, St Martin's High Cross★, Infirmary Museum★ **AC** (Cross of St John★))

CRAIGNURE – Argyll and Bute 27 B2

Birchgrove without rest

Lochdon, Southeast : 3 mi on A 849 ✉ PA64 6AP – ☎ (01680) 812 364 – www.birchgrovebandb.co.uk – April-22 October

3 rm – †£ 36/40 ††£ 55/65

◆ Simple, uncluttered guesthouse built by the owners themselves; she loves art and makes birds and puffins out of rocks. Peaceful pine-furnished bedrooms with large showers. Small breakfast room.

FIONNPHORT – Argyll and Bute

XX **Ninth Wave**

Bruach Mhor, East 0.75 mi by A 849 ✉ PA66 6BL – ☎ (01681) 700 757 – www.ninthwaverestaurant.co.uk – Closed Monday April-October, restricted opening in winter

Rest – Seafood – *(dinner only) (booking essential)* Menu £ 38

◆ Converted farm building featuring stylish, modern décor, with trinkets from the owner's travels. Daily changing menu focuses on local seafood, with strong Asian flavours. Try the lobster.

GRULINE – Argyll and Bute 27 A2

Gruline Home Farm

✉ PA71 6HR – ☎ (01680) 300 581 – www.gruline.com – Closed Christmas-New Year

3 rm (dinner included) – †£ 148 ††£ 200 **Rest** – Menu £ 40

◆ Very rurally set, in 3 acres of land, with colourful gardens and lovely mountain views. Relax in the large lounges or spot sea eagles from the telescope in the spacious conservatory. Good-sized, antique-furnished bedrooms. Mousey Thompson pieces in the traditionally styled dining room. Classical, daily changing menu.

TIRORAN – Argyll and Bute 27 A2

Tiroran House

✉ PA69 6ES – ☎ (01681) 705 232 – www.tiroran.com – Easter-October

7 rm – †£ 100 ††£ 190 **Rest** – *(dinner only)* Menu £ 45 **s**

◆ Stunning 19C whitewashed house, set in 17 acres of parkland that run down to the water's edge. Charming, antique-filled interior with two open-fired lounges and immaculate, highly individual bedrooms. Welcoming owner. Dining room split into conservatory area and darker, more clubby area. Concise, daily changing menus.

TOBERMORY – Argyll and Bute – pop. 980 **27** A2

Erray Rd, ✆ (01688) 302 387

Tobermory

53 Main St ✉ PA75 6NT – ✆ (01688) 302 091 – www.thetobermoryhotel.com – Closed 7 January-3 February and 21-28 December
16 rm – ♦£ 38/64 ♦♦£ 93/125
Rest *Waters Edge* – *(dinner only)* Menu £ 32
♦ Converted fishermen's cottages right on the quayside, close to the local distillery. Bedrooms vary in size but most have a pleasant harbour view. Small lounge; popular dining room with seafaring feel. Concise, classical menu of island produce. Plenty of seafood.

Sonas House without rest

The Fairways, North : 0.5 mi by Black Brae and Erray Rd following signs for the golf club ✉ PA75 6PS – ✆ (01688) 302 304 – www.sonashouse.co.uk – Closed Christmas
3 rm – ♦£ 60/80 ♦♦£ 100/125
♦ In elevated position above Tobermory, with views over the Sound of Mull. Choose a room in the house or the annexe studio; all come with a host of extras and superb views. Luxury swimming pool.

Brockville without rest

Raeric Rd, by Back Brae ✉ PA75 6RS – ✆ (01688) 302 741 – www.brockville-tobermory.co.uk
3 rm – ♦£ 40/60 ♦♦£ 60/80
♦ Welcoming guesthouse with warm, homely feel. Good-sized bedrooms offer everything you could want. Communal breakfast room boasts nice sea views. Friendly owner has plenty of local knowledge.

Highland Cottage with rm

Breadalbane St, via B 8073 ✉ PA75 6PD – ✆ (01688) 302 030 – www.highlandcottage.co.uk – March-October
6 rm – ♦£ 125/155 ♦♦£ 140/190
Rest – *(dinner only) (booking essential for non-residents)* Menu £ 50
♦ Long-standing, personally run restaurant in intimate cottage; family antiques and knick-knacks abound. Classical linen-laid dining room and homely lounge. Traditional daily menu with a seafood base and plenty of local produce. Snug, individually styled bedrooms.

MUTHILL – **501** I15 – see Crieff

NAIRN – Highland – **501** I11 – pop. 8 418 Scotland **30** D2

Edinburgh 172 mi – Aberdeen 91 mi – Inverness 16 mi

Seabank Rd, ✆ (01667) 453 208

Nairn Dunbar Lochloy Rd, ✆ (01667) 452 741

Forres (Sueno's Stone★★) E : 11 mi by A 96 and B 9011 - Cawdor Castle★ **AC**, S : 5.5 mi by B 9090 – Brodie Castle★ **AC**, E : 6 mi by A 96. Fort George★, W : 8 mi by A 96, B 9092 and B 9006

Golf View rest,

The Seafront ✉ IV12 4HD – ✆ (01667) 452 301 – www.golfviewhotel.com
41 rm – ♦£ 85/170 ♦♦£ 120/220 – 1 suite
Rest *Restaurant* – *(dinner only and Sunday lunch)* Menu £ 30 – Carte £ 32/42
Rest *Conservatory* – Carte £ 32/42
♦ Non-golfers may prefer the vista of the Moray Firth from one of the sea-view rooms or a poolside lounger. Smart, traditional accommodation, up-to-date gym and beauty salon. Half-panelled dining room. Stylish, spacious conservatory restaurant.

SCOTLAND

Boath House rm,

Auldearn, East : 2 mi on A 96 ✉ IV12 5TE – ✆ (01667) 454 896 – www.boath-house.com

8 rm – ♦£ 160 ♦♦£ 320 **Rest** – *(booking essential)* Menu £ 30/70 **s**

Spec. Scallops with leek, truffle and egg cream. Roe deer with ceps and peas. Pineapple with pistachio cake and rum jelly.

♦ 1820s neo-classical mansion, owned by a charming couple, hosts modern Highland art collections. Intimate, elegant bedrooms; some have half-tester beds/views of the trout lake. Smart, contemporary bathrooms. Formally laid dining room has garden views; accomplished cooking, with vivid presentation and subtle flavours.

Bracadale House without rest

Albert St ✉ IV12 4HF – ✆ (01667) 452 547 – www.bracadalehouse.com – Closed Christmas-New Year

3 rm – ♦£ 40/50 ♦♦£ 60

♦ This elegant Victorian house, near the beach, is enthusiastically run by a friendly owner. There's an attractive first floor lounge and rooms finished with a tasteful palette.

Cawdor House

7 Cawdor St ✉ IV12 4QD – ✆ (01667) 455 855 – www.cawdorhousenairn.co.uk – Closed Christmas-New Year

5 rm – ♦£ 45/70 ♦♦£ 65/80 **Rest** – Menu £ 25

♦ Comfortable house whose original features blend with contemporary styling; friendly owners are a font of local knowledge. Variously sized bedrooms are clean and uncluttered. Cosy lounge with log fire. Simple dining room; set menu dinner by arrangement.

SCOTLAND

NEWTON STEWART – **Dumfries and Galloway** – **501** G19 – **pop. 3 573** Scotland **25** B3

Edinburgh 131 mi – Dumfries 51 mi – Glasgow 87 mi – Stranraer 24 mi

Dashwood Sq ✆ (01671) 402431 (June- Sept), newtonstewarttic@visitscotland.com

Minnigaff Kirroughtree Ave, ✆ (01671) 402 172

Wigtownshire County Glenluce Mains of Park, ✆ (01581) 300 420

Galloway Forest Park★, Queen's Way★ (Newton Stewart to New Galloway) N : 19 mi by A 712

Kirroughtree House

Northeast : 1.5 mi by A 75 on A 712 ✉ DG8 6AN – ✆ (01671) 402 141 – www.kirroughtreehouse.co.uk – Closed 2 January-mid February

15 rm – ♦£ 105/140 ♦♦£ 210/230 – 2 suites

Rest – *(booking essential for non-residents)* Menu £ 35 (dinner) **s** – Carte lunch Monday-Saturday £ 21/32 **s**

♦ Impressive 1719 mansion in landscaped gardens, overlooking the woods and bay. Grand interior with vast open-fired hall and impressive staircase. Traditionally styled bedrooms with plenty of extras. Concise 4 course menu of quality produce in classic combinations.

NIGG – **501** H10 – **see Tain**

NORTH BAY – **Western Isles** – **see Barra (Isle of)**

NORTH BERWICK – **East Lothian** – **501** L15 – **pop. 6 223** Scotland **26** D1

Edinburgh 24 mi – Newcastle upon Tyne 102 mi

1 Quality St ✆ (01620) 892197

North Berwick Beach Rd, West Links, ✆ (01620) 890 312

Glen East Links, Tantallon Terrace, ✆ (01620) 892 726

North Berwick Law (✻★★★) S : 1 mi - Tantallon Castle★★ (clifftop site★★★) **AC**, E : 3.5 mi by A 198 – Dirleton★ (Castle★ **AC**) SW : 2.5 mi by A 198. Museum of Flight★, S : 6 mi by B 1347 – Preston Mill★, S : 8.5 mi by A 198 and B 1047 – Tyninghame★, S : 7 mi by A 198 – Coastal road from North Berwick to Portseton★, SW : 13 mi by A 198 and B 1348

Glebe House without rest
Law Rd ✉ EH39 4PL – ✆ (01620) 892 608 – www.glebehouse-nb.co.uk
– Closed Christmas
3 rm – 🕴£ 75 🕴🕴£ 100
◆ Spacious Georgian house with walled gardens and views over the town and sea. Classical, country house drawing room and antique breakfast table. Well-furnished bedrooms boast modern bathrooms.

NORTH QUEENSFERRY – Fife – 501 J15 – pop. 1 102 — 28 C3

Edinburgh 13 mi – Dunfermline 6 mi – Glasgow 45 mi

Wee Restaurant
17 Main St ✉ KY11 1JT – ✆ (01383) 616 263 – www.theweerestaurant.co.uk
– Closed 25-26 December
Rest – Menu £ 19/30 **s**
◆ Wee by name, wee by nature. Simple quarry-floored restaurant consisting of just 7 tables. Fresh Scottish ingredients are served in neatly presented, classical combinations. Concise lunch menu.

NORTH UIST – Western Isles Outer Hebrides – 501 X/Y10 – see Uist (Isles of)

Don't confuse the couvert rating with the stars !
Couverts defines comfort and service, while stars are awarded
for the best cuisine across all categories of comfort.

SCOTLAND

OBAN – Argyll and Bute – 501 D14 – pop. 8 120 Scotland — 27 B2

Edinburgh 123 mi – Dundee 116 mi – Glasgow 93 mi – Inverness 118 mi
Access Access to Glasgow by helicopter
to Isle of Mull (Craignure) (Caledonian MacBrayne Ltd) (45 mn)
– to Isle of Tiree (Scarinish) via Isle of Mull (Tobermory) and Isle of Coll (Arinagour) (Caledonian MacBrayne Ltd)
– to Isle of Islay (Port Askaig) and Kintyre Peninsula (Kennacraig) via Isle of Colonsay (Scalasaig) (Caledonian MacBrayne Ltd) (summer only)
– to Isle of Lismore (Achnacroish) (Caledonian MacBrayne Ltd) 2-3 daily (except Sunday) (55 mn)
– to Isle of Colonsay (Scalasaig) (Caledonian MacBrayne Ltd) 3 weekly (2 h)
Church Building, Argyll Sq ✆ (08707) 200630, oban@visitscotland.com
Glencruitten Glencruitten Rd, ✆ (01631) 562 868
Loch Awe★★, SE : 17 mi by A 85 – Bonawe Furnace★, E : 12 mi by A 85 – Cruachan Power Station★ **AC**, E : 16 mi by A 85 – Seal and Marine Centre★ **AC**, N : 14 mi by A 828

Manor House
Gallanach Rd ✉ PA34 4LS – ✆ (01631) 562 087 – www.manorhouseoban.com
– Closed 25-26 December
11 rm – 🕴£ 99/199 🕴🕴£ 120/210
Rest – *(lunch by arrangement)* Menu £ 24/36
◆ 18C dower house, formerly part of the Argyll Estate. Country house style interior offers traditional comforts; spacious lounge and rustic bar boast delightful bay and harbour views. Individually styled bedrooms. Classical daily menu served in formal dining room.

Glenburnie House without rest
Corran Esplanade ✉ PA34 5AQ – ✆ (01631) 562 089 – www.glenburnie.co.uk
– March-November
12 rm – 🕴£ 45/80 🕴🕴£ 80/100
◆ Bay-windowed house on main esplanade, affording great bay and island views. Period features include a delightful staircase and etched glass widows; antiques abound. Comfy, good-sized bedrooms.

Alltavona without rest
Corran Esplanade ✉ PA34 5AQ – ✆ (01631) 565 067 – www.alltavona.co.uk – Closed December
10 rm – †£ 40/90 ††£ 60/90
◆ Commanding bay and island views from this charming 19C villa on the main esplanade. Fresh, tasty breakfasts in stylish black, white and red room. Striking modern bedrooms boast feature beds.

Coast
104 George St ✉ PA34 5NT – ✆ (01631) 569 900 – www.coastoban.com – Closed 2 weeks in January, 25-26 December, Sunday dinner October-March and Sunday lunch
Rest – Menu £ 15 (lunch) – Carte £ 24/39
◆ Busy high street restaurant with wooden floor and khaki fabric strips on the walls. Unfussy, modern cooking with good seasoning; local produce is key. Plenty of shellfish and steaks on offer.

Waterfront
No 1, The Pier ✉ PA34 4LW – ✆ (01631) 563 110 – www.waterfrontoban.co.uk – Closed 25 December
Rest – Seafood – Carte £ 19/31
◆ Former seaman's mission boasting harbour/bay views. Extensive menu features local produce and mixes modern and classical cooking. Lots of daily specials; fish a strength. Relaxed bistro feel.

SCOTLAND

Ee-usk
The North Pier ✉ PA34 5QD – ✆ (01631) 565 666 – www.eeusk.com – Closed 25-26 December, 1 January and restricted opening in January
Rest – Seafood – Carte £ 20/35
◆ Long-standing local seafood restaurant on the harbour, run by experienced owners. Stylish modern building with brasserie feel and great bay views. Large, in-depth menu with good value specials.

OLDMELDRUM – Aberdeenshire – 501 N11 – pop. 2 003 Scotland 28 D1

Edinburgh 140 mi – Aberdeen 17 mi – Inverness 87 mi
Oldmeldrum Kirkbrae, ✆ (01651) 872 648
Haddo House★, NE : 9 mi by B 9170 on B 9005

Cromlet Hill without rest

South Rd ✉ AB51 0AB – ✆ (01651) 872 315 – www.cromlethill.co.uk – Closed Christmas
3 rm – †£ 45 ††£ 70
◆ Half Georgian, half Victorian house with attractive front garden. Characterful sitting room; smart, airy, well-equipped rooms. Communal breakfast at antique dining table.

ONICH – Highland – 501 E13 – ✉ Fort William 29 B3

Edinburgh 123 mi – Glasgow 93 mi – Inverness 79 mi – Oban 39 mi

Lochleven Seafood Café

Lockleven, Southeast : 6.5 mi by A 82 on B 863 ✉ PH33 6SA – ✆ (01855) 821 048 – www.lochlevenseafoodcafe.co.uk – Restricted opening November-February
Rest – Seafood – *(booking advisable at dinner)* Carte £ 23/33 **s**
◆ Stunning Lochside location looking toward Glencoe Mountains. Extremely fresh, simply prepared seafood; shellfish platter and razor clams a speciality. Themed evenings in winter.

ORKNEY ISLANDS – 501 K/L7 – pop. 19 800 Scotland

see Kirkwall

from Burwick (South Ronaldsay) to John O'Groats (John O'Groats Ferries) 2-4 daily (40 mn) (summer only)

service between Isle of Hoy (Longhope), Isle of Hoy (Lyness), Isle of Flotta and Houton (Orkney Ferries Ltd) – from Stromness to Scrabster (P & O Scottish Ferries) (1-3 daily) (2 h) – from Stromness to Shetland Islands (Lerwick) and Aberdeen (Northlink Ferries) 1-2 daily – from Kirkwall to Westray, Stronsay via Eday and Sanday (Orkney Ferries Ltd) – from Tingwall to Wyre via Egilsay and Rousay (Orkney Ferries Ltd) – from Kirkwall to Shapinsay (Orkney Ferries Ltd) (25 mn) – from Stromness to Isle of Hoy (Moness) and Graemsay (Orkney Ferries Ltd) – from Kirkwall to North Ronaldsay (Orkney Ferries Ltd) weekly (2 h 40 mn) - from Kirkwall to Invergordon (Orcargo Ltd) daily (8 h 30 mn) – from Houton to Isle of Hoy (Lyness), Flotta and Longhope (Orkney Ferries Ltd)

Old Man of Hoy★★★ – Islands★★ – Maes Howe★★ **AC** – Skara Brae★★ **AC** – Kirkbuster Museum and Corrigal Farm Museum★ **AC** – Brough of Birsay★ **AC** – Birsay (<★) – Ring of Brodgar★ – Unstan Cairn★

MAINLAND – Orkney Islands — 31 A3

London 683 mi – Edinburgh 278 mi

BURRAY – Orkney Islands — 31 A3

Sands

✉ KW17 2SS – ✆ (01856) 731 298 – www.thesandshotel.co.uk – Closed 1-3 January and 25-26 December

8 rm – ♦£ 60/80 ♦♦£ 90/100 – 2 suites **Rest** – Carte £ 14/26

♦ Converted 19C herring packing store in small hamlet overlooking Scapa Flow. Pleasant bedrooms boast smart bathrooms. Bar with pool table and dartboard offers traditional menu. Dining room serves more refined dishes, featuring island produce and lots of shellfish.

DOUNBY – Orkney Islands — 31 A3

Ashleigh without rest

Howaback Rd, South : 0.75 mi by A986 ✉ KW17 2JA – ✆ (01856) 771 378 – www.ashleigh-orkney.com – Closed 20 December-9 January

4 rm – ♦£ 35/42 ♦♦£ 70/72

♦ Purpose-built house in the heart of the island's countryside, boasting loch/-mountain views. Large breakfast room and lounge filled with guidebooks. Good-sized bedrooms with modern facilities.

HARRAY – Orkney Islands — 31 A3

Merkister

off A 986 ✉ KW17 2LF – ✆ (01856) 771 366 – www.merkister.com – Closed 23 December-4 January

16 rm – ♦£ 45/95 ♦♦£ 70/175

Rest – *(dinner only) (booking essential)* Menu £ 24 **s** – Carte £ 25/41 **s**

♦ Family-run, lochside hotel affording wonderful water and mountain views. Comfortable, well-kept bedrooms; those outside have their own terraces and gardens. Snug, open-fired bar serves snacks. Dining room offers strictly Orkney-based produce and a scenic backdrop.

Holland House without rest

on St Michael's Church rd ✉ KW17 2LQ – ✆ (01856) 771 400 – www.hollandhouseorkney.co.uk – Closed 5-10 January

3 rm – ♦£ 48/60 ♦♦£ 96

♦ Converted manse run by a welcoming owner, with commanding views throughout. Open-fired lounge – packed with local art and handmade furniture – stone-floored breakfast room and conservatory. Spotless bedrooms with a host of extras and great attention to detail.

KIRKWALL – Orkney Islands Scotland **31** A3

Kirkwall Airport : ✆ (01856) 886210, S : 3.5 mi
West Castle St ✆ (01856) 872856, info@visitorkney.com
Grainbank, ✆ (01856) 872 457
Kirkwall★★ - St Magnus Cathedral★★ – Western Mainland★★, Eastern Mainland (Italian Chapel★) - Earl's Palace★ **AC** – Tankerness House Museum★ **AC** – Orkney Farm and Folk Museum★

Ayre
Ayre Rd ✉ KW15 1QX – ✆ (01856) 873 001 – www.ayrehotel.co.uk – Closed 24-26 December, 1-2 January
51 rm – †£ 75/95 ††£ 100/130 **Rest** – Carte £ 17/33
♦ Well-run hotel close to the harbour. Formerly 3 Victorian houses, now a traditionally styled hotel with comfortable bedrooms – the newer extension rooms are biggest and best. Spacious bar filled with locals. Dining room offers sizeable menu of Orcadian produce.

Lynnfield
Holm Rd ✉ KW15 1SU – ✆ (01856) 872 505 – www.lynnfieldhotel.com – Closed 1-10 January and 25-26 December
7 rm – †£ 70/90 ††£ 100/135 – 3 suites **Rest** – Carte £ 20/36
♦ Spacious hotel with cosy sitting rooms, Orcadian furniture and a fine range of Scotch whiskies. Supremely comfortable bedrooms; two with four-posters. Formal dining room with large conservatory affording great views of the countryside. Seasonal menus.

SCOTLAND

Avalon House without rest
Carness Rd, Northeast : 1.5 mi by Shore St. ✉ KW15 1UE – ✆ (01856) 876 665 – www.avalon-house.co.uk – Closed 2 weeks Christmas
5 rm – †£ 40/50 ††£ 70/75
♦ Modern, purpose-built guesthouse in a pleasant residential area. Lounge filled with maps and books about the islands. Good-sized bedrooms with simple, homely feel. Nice coastal outlook.

Foveran with rm
St Ola, Southwest : 3 mi on A 964 ✉ KW15 1SF – ✆ (01856) 872 389 – www.foveranhotel.co.uk – restricted opening October-April
8 rm – †£ 75/93 ††£ 113 **Rest** – *(dinner only)* Carte £ 25/35
♦ Spacious restaurant boasting superb panoramic views over Scapa Flow and the south islands. Traditional menu features local, seasonal produce, including Orcadian lamb/beef and plenty of fresh seafood. Homely, well-kept bedrooms display simple colour schemes.

ST MARGARET'S HOPE – Orkney Islands **31** A3

Creel with rm
Front Rd ✉ KW17 2SL – ✆ (01856) 831 311 – www.thecreel.co.uk – April-October
3 rm – †£ 70/80 ††£ 95/110
Rest – Seafood – *(closed Monday and Tuesday) (dinner only)* Menu £ 38
♦ Long-standing, family-run restaurant in seafront village. Spacious dining room is hung with local oils and prints. Daily changing menu displays a fresh, traditional seafood base. Comfortable, cosy bedrooms boast modern, co-ordinated furnishings and bay views.

STROMNESS – Orkney Islands Scotland **31** A3

Town★ - Pier Gallery (collection of abstract art★)

Hamnavoe
35 Graham Pl, off Victoria St ✉ KW16 3BY – ✆ (01856) 850 606 – restricted opening in winter
Rest – *(Closed Monday) (dinner only)* Carte £ 29/35
♦ Homely restaurant in a sleepy harbourside town. Plain walls are dotted with local oils and open fires. Unfussy home cooking uses fresh market produce; local, where possible. Booking essential.

ISLE OF WESTRAY - Orkney Islands 31 A2

London 696 mi - Edinburgh 290 mi

CLEAT - Orkney Islands 31 A2

Cleaton House

KW17 2DB - (01857) 677 508 - www.cleatonhouse.com
6 rm - £ 65 £ 95
Rest - *(bar lunch) (booking essential for non-residents)* Menu £ 35
◆ Victorian former laird's mansion, set on a peninsula and boasting panoramic views over the bay and Papa Westray. Original tiled floors, antique-filled lounge and rear bar. Spacious, classically styled bedrooms. Formal set menu relies on local island produce.

PIEROWALL - Orkney Islands 31 A2

No 1 Broughton

KW17 2DA - (01857) 677 726 - www.no1broughton.co.uk - Closed Christmas and New Year
3 rm - £ 35/60 £ 60 **Rest** - Menu £ 18
◆ 19C pink-washed house boasting views over Pierowall Bay and out to Papa Westray. Comfy lounge and conservatory. Simple, homely bedrooms with modern bathrooms. Sauna on request. Home-cooked meals showcase local meats/seafood; homemade bread and shortcake feature.

PEAT INN - Fife 28 D2

London 462 mi - Edinburgh 45 mi - Dundee 17 mi - Kirkcaldy 19 mi

Peat Inn (Geoffrey Smeddle) with rm

KY15 5LH - (01334) 840 206 - www.thepeatinn.co.uk - Closed 2 weeks January, third week November, Sunday and Monday
8 rm - £ 115/145 £ 175/195
Rest - *(booking essential)* Menu £ 16/34 - Carte £ 27/49
Spec. Feuilleté of scallops, smoked haddock and langoustines with hollandaise sauce. Roast rump and confit of lamb, artichokes and tarragon jus. Elderflower and blackcurrant pavlova with elderflower curd.
◆ Passionately run, former inn found in the heart of the Fife countryside. Roaring fire in the lounge; three cosy dining rooms with beams. The accomplished, classically based cooking, with just a hint of the modern, uses fine Scottish produce. Comfortable annexed bedrooms overlook the lovely back garden.

PEEBLES - Scottish Borders - 501 K17 - pop. 8 065 Scotland 26 C2

Edinburgh 24 mi - Glasgow 53 mi - Hawick 31 mi
High St (01835) 863170, bordersinfo@visitscotland.com
Kirkland St, (01721) 720 197
Tweed Valley★★. Traquair House★★ **AC**, SE : 7 mi by B 7062 - Rosslyn Chapel★★ **AC**, N : 16.5 mi by A 703, A 6094, B 7026 and B 7003

Cringletie House

Edinburgh Rd., North : 3 mi on A 703 EH45 8PL - (01721) 725 750 - www.cringletie.com - Closed January
12 rm - £ 160/215 - 1 suite
Rest *Sutherland Room* - *(dinner only)* Menu £ 25/30
◆ Handsome Victorian house boasting far-reaching Tweed Valley views. Luxurious interior with library, drawing room and cosy bar. Tastefully furnished bedrooms have subtle contemporary style. Formal restaurant offers elaborate dining beneath stunning 1902 mural.

Rowanbrae without rest

103 Northgate EH45 8BU - (01721) 721 630 - February-November
3 rm - £ 45 £ 60
◆ Tiny cottage close to the town, with pretty front terrace and surprisingly spacious interior. Long-standing owners provide a warm welcome and a cosy, homely atmosphere reigns. Pleasant, well-kept bedrooms have a modern edge, courtesy of their soft furnishings.

SCOTLAND

XX **Osso** VISA AE

Innerleithen Rd ✉ EH45 8BA – ✆ (01721) 724 477 – www.ossorestaurant.com – Closed 1-2 January, 25 December, dinner Sunday and Monday, and restricted dinner opening in winter

Rest – Menu £ 22 (dinner) – Carte £ 19/31

◆ Coffee shop by day, serving light lunches. By night, a sophisticated restaurant offering a regularly changing, great value menu of tasty, well-presented dishes, with the occasional Asian influence. Friendly, attentive service.

at Eddleston North : 4.5 mi on A 703

XX **Horseshoe Inn** with rm rm, P VISA

Edinburgh Rd. ✉ EH45 8QP – ✆ (01721) 730 225 – www.horseshoeinn.co.uk – Closed 2 weeks January, 1 week November and 25 December

8 rm – †£ 70 ††£ 150

Rest – Menu £ 20 (lunch) – Carte dinner £ 36/59

Rest *Bistro* – Carte £ 20/32

◆ Former roadside inn; now a smart, columned restaurant with elegant tableware and formal, white-gloved service. Sophisticated à la carte and tasting menu offer ambitious, well-presented, European-influenced dishes. Old classics served in the bistro. Chic, modern bedrooms are in the annexe.

SCOTLAND

PERTH – Perth and Kinross – 501 J14 – pop. 43 450 Scotland **28** C2

Edinburgh 44 mi – Aberdeen 86 mi – Dundee 22 mi – Dunfermline 29 mi

Lower City Mills, West Mill St ✆ (01738) 450600, perth@visitscotland.com

Craigie Hill Cherrybank, ✆ (01738) 620 829

King James VI Moncreiffe Island, ✆ (01738) 625 170

Murrayshall New Scone, ✆ (01738) 554 804

North Inch, c/o Perth & Kinross Council 35 Kinncoll St, ✆ (01738) 636 481

City★ – Black Watch Regimental Museum★ Y **M1** – Georgian Terraces★ Y – Museum and Art Gallery★ Y **M2**

Scone Palace★★ **AC**, N : 2 mi by A 93 Y – Branklyn Garden★ **AC**, SE : 1 mi by A 85 Z – Kinnoull Hill (≤★) SE : 1.25 mi by A 85 Z – Huntingtower Castle★ **AC**, NW : 3 mi by A 85 Y – Elcho Castle★ **AC**, SE : 4 mi by A 912 - Z - and Rhynd rd. Abernethy (11C Round Tower★), SE : 8 mi by A 912 - Z - and A 913

Parklands P VISA

2 St Leonard's Bank ✉ PH2 8EB – ✆ (01738) 622 451 – www.theparklandshotel.com Z**n**

15 rm – †£ 83/153 ††£ 113/183

Rest *No.1 The Bank* – see restaurant listing

◆ Modern hotel set opposite the railway station. Contemporary bedrooms – some overlooking the garden – boast spacious bathrooms and good facilities; great for business travellers.

Taythorpe without rest P

Isla Rd, North : 1 mi on A 93 ✉ PH2 7HQ – ✆ (01738) 447 994 – www.taythorpe.co.uk Y**a**

3 rm – †£ 35/45 ††£ 70/80

◆ Immaculately kept, modern guesthouse close to Scone Palace. Good value accommodation. Welcoming, homely lounge. Cosy, communal breakfasts. Warmly inviting, well-kept bedrooms.

XX **63 Tay Street** VISA

63 Tay St ✉ PH2 8NN – ✆ (01738) 441 451 – www.63taystreet.co.uk – Closed 10 days Christmas, Sunday and Monday Z**r**

Rest – Carte £ 25/33

◆ Contemporary style restaurant close to the riverside. Subtle décor with bright sea-blue chairs. Well-priced modern cuisine with penchant for seasonal ingredients.

XX **No.1 The Bank** – at Parklands Hotel

2 St Leonard's Bank ✉ PH2 8EB
– ✆ (01738) 622 451
– www.theparklandshotel.com **Zn**

Rest – Carte £ 24/31

◆ Set close to the station within a contemporary hotel. Cooking combines the best local and seasonal produce with modern techniques and artistic flair. Confident flavours.

XX **Deans @ Let's Eat**

77-79 Kinnoull St ✉ PH1 5EZ
– ✆ (01738) 643 377
– www.letseatperth.co.uk
– Closed 2 weeks January, Sunday and Monday **Yc**

Rest – Menu £ 16 (lunch)/24 (weekday dinner)
– Carte £ 24/36

◆ Loyal local following for this husband and wife run restaurant. Warm and chatty service and a relaxed, comfortable setting. Cooking is mostly traditional but also displays ambition.

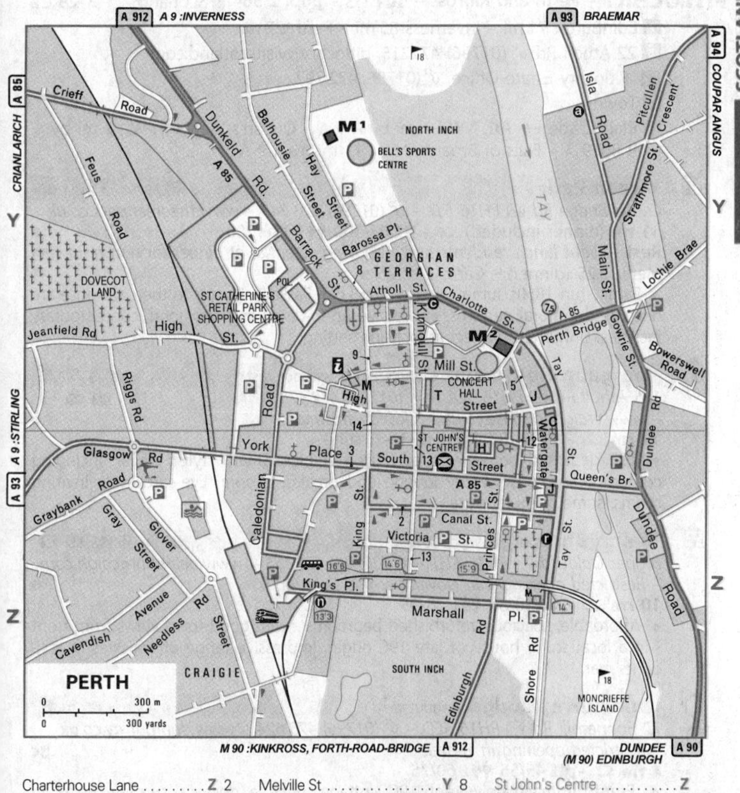

Charterhouse Lane . . . . Z 2
County Pl. . . . . Z 3
George St . . . . Y 5
High St. . . . . Y
Melville St . . . . Y 8
North Methven St. . . . . Y 9
St Catherine's Retail Park . . . . Y
St John St . . . . Z 12
St John's Centre . . . . Z
Scott St . . . . Z 13
South Methven St. . . . . Y 14
South St. . . . . Z

at Guildtown North : 5 mi on A 93 - Y – ✉ Perth

The Anglers Inn with rm

Main Rd ✉ PH2 6BS – ✆ (01821) 640 329 – www.theanglersinn.co.uk – Closed Monday
5 rm – †£ 50 ††£ 100 **Rest** – Menu £ 15 (lunch) – Carte £ 21/31
◆ Whitewashed roadside inn in a tiny hamlet, with plain décor and restaurant styling. Good value à la carte menu with a classical French base uses careful cooking and fresh ingredients. Clean simple rooms.

at Forgandenny Southwest : 6.5 mi by A 912 - Z - on B 935 – ✉ Perth

Battledown without rest

by Station Rd on Church and School rd ✉ PH2 9EL – ✆ (01738) 812 471 – www.accommodationperthshire.com
3 rm – †£ 35/40 ††£ 65/70
◆ Immaculately whitewashed, part 18C cottage in quiet village. Lovely garden; owner's paintings on show. Cosy, pine-furnished breakfast room. Neat, tidy rooms, all on ground level.

PIEROWALL – Orkney Islands – **501** K6 – see Orkney Islands (Isle of Westray)

PITLOCHRY – Perth and Kinross – **501** I13 – pop. 2 564 Scotland **28** C2

Edinburgh 71 mi – Inverness 85 mi – Perth 27 mi
22 Atholl Rd ✆ (01796) 472215, pitlochry@visitscotland.com
Pitlochry Estate Office, ✆ (01796) 472 792
Town★
Blair Castle★★ **AC**, NW : 7 mi by A 9 A – Queen's View★★, W : 7 mi by B 8019 A – Falls of Bruar★, NW : 11 mi by A 9 A

Green Park

Clunie Bridge Rd ✉ PH16 5JY – ✆ (01796) 473 248 – www.thegreenpark.co.uk
51 rm (dinner included) – †£ 68/100 ††£ 136/200 **Aa**
Rest – *(light lunch residents only) (booking essential at dinner for non-residents)* Menu £ 25 (dinner) – Carte £ 17/25 **s**
◆ Family run 1860s summer retreat on Loch Faskally. Rooms in the old house are decorated in floral patterns; impressive up-to-date wing has good, contemporary facilities. Unhurried dinners at lochside setting.

Craigatin House and Courtyard without rest

165 Atholl Rd ✉ PH16 5QL – ✆ (01796) 472 478 – www.craigatinhouse.co.uk – Closed Christmas **Ae**
12 rm – †£ 63/83 ††£ 73/93 – 1 suite
◆ 19C detached house with converted stables. Smart, stylish décor, including contemporary conservatory lounge and breakfast room. Eye-catchingly inviting rooms, some in the annexe.

Beinn Bhracaigh without rest

Higher Oakfield ✉ PH16 5HT – ✆ (01796) 470 355 – www.beinnbhracaigh.com – Restricted opening mid November-mid February **Bn**
10 rm – †£ 50/80 ††£ 75/95
◆ Affordable, spacious, refurbished bedrooms - with good town views from front - in a local stone house of late 19C origin. Impressive range of whiskies in residents' bar.

Dunmurray Lodge without rest

72 Bonnethill Rd ✉ PH16 5ED – ✆ (01796) 473 624 – www.dunmurray.co.uk – Restricted opening in winter. **Bc**
4 rm – †£ 45/55 ††£ 60/75
◆ Pretty, immaculately kept 19C cottage, once a doctor's surgery. Relax in homely sitting room's squashy sofas. Bedrooms are small and cosy with soothing cream colour scheme.

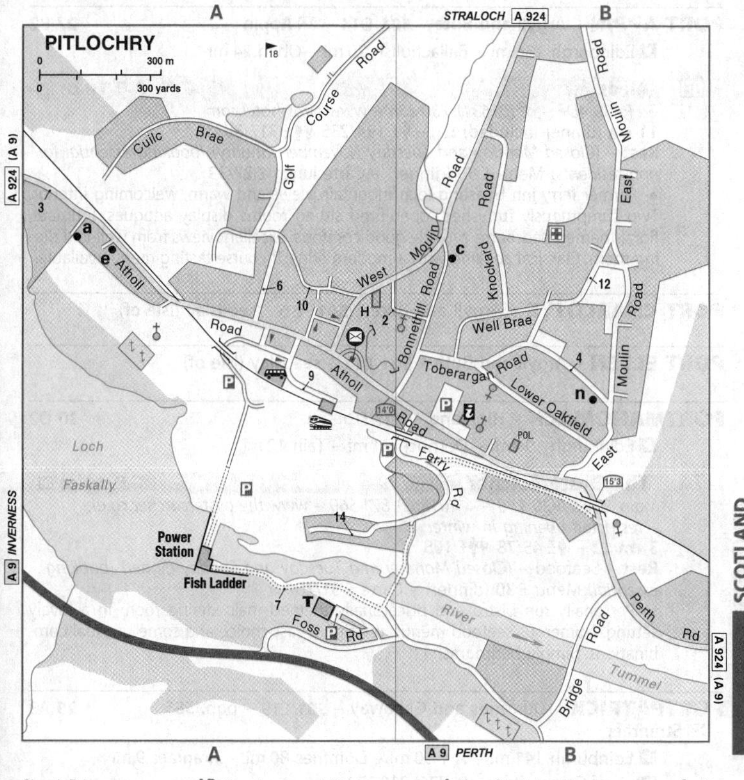

Church Rd . . . . AB 2	Larchwood Rd. . . . . A 6	Strathview Terrace . . . . A 10
Clunie Bridge Rd . . . . A 3	Port Na Craig Rd . . . . A 7	Tom Na Moan Rd . . . . B 12
Higher Oakfield . . . . B 4	Station Rd . . . . A 9	Tummel Crescent . . . . A 14

at Killiecrankie **Northwest : 4 mi by A 924 - A - and B 8019 on B 8079 – ✉ Pitlochry**

Killiecrankie House
✉ *PH16 5LG – ✆ (01796) 473 220 – www.killiecrankiehotel.co.uk*
– Closed 3 January - 11 March
9 rm (dinner included) – †£ 105/155 ††£ 230/250 – 1 suite
Rest – *(bar lunch)* Menu £ 35
♦ Quiet and privately run, a converted 1840 vicarage with a distinct rural feel. The sizeable bedrooms come in co-ordinated patterns and overlook pleasant countryside. Warm, red dining room; garden produce prominent on menus.

PLOCKTON – Highland – 501 D11 Scotland **29** B2

Edinburgh 210 mi – Inverness 88 mi
Village★
Wester Ross★★★

Plockton Hotel with rm
41 Harbour St ✉ IV52 8TN – ✆ (01599) 544 274 – www.plocktonhotel.co.uk
15 rm – †£ 55/85 ††£ 120 **Rest** – Carte £ 15/35
♦ Formerly two cottages on the lochside, now a family-run pub with small terrace and restaurant. Cooking uses local Highland or Scottish produce, with fresh seafood dishes a speciality. Bedrooms, in the pub and annexe, boast bay views to the front.

PORT APPIN – Argyll and Bute – 501 D14 – ✉ Appin 27 B2

Edinburgh 136 mi – Ballachulish 20 mi – Oban 24 mi

Airds

✉ PA38 4DF – ☎ (01631) 730 236 – www.airds-hotel.com

11 rm (dinner included) – †£ 194/235 ††£ 317/383

Rest – *(Closed Monday and Tuesday November-January) (booking essential for non-residents)* Menu £ 53 (dinner) – Carte lunch £ 27/33

◆ Former ferry inn boasting loch/mountain views and warm, welcoming interior. Two sumptuously furnished, open-fired sitting rooms display antiques. Intimate, floral-themed bedrooms provide good comforts. Excellent views from well-laid dining room. Classical cooking with a modern edge; 7 course tasting menu available.

PORT CHARLOTTE – Argyll and Bute – 501 A16 – see Islay (Isle of)

PORT ELLEN – Argyll and Bute – 501 B17 – see Islay (Isle of)

PORTMAHOMACK – Highland – 501 I10 30 D2

Edinburgh 194 mi – Dornoch 21 mi – Tain 12 mi

The Oystercatcher with rm

Main St ✉ IV20 1YB – ☎ (01862) 871 560 – www.the-oystercatcher.co.uk – restricted opening in winter

3 rm – †£ 45/78 ††£ 105

Rest – Seafood – *(Closed Monday and Tuesday and Sunday dinner) (booking essential)* Menu £ 30 (dinner) – Carte £ 31/70

◆ Personally run bistro and piscatorially themed main dining room in a lovely setting. Numerous seafood menus, offering a vast choice and some unusual combinations. Simple bedrooms.

PORTPATRICK – Dumfries and Galloway – 501 E19 – pop. 585 – ✉ Stranraer 25 A3

Edinburgh 141 mi – Ayr 60 mi – Dumfries 80 mi – Stranraer 9 mi

Golf Course Rd, ☎ (01776) 810 273

Knockinaam Lodge

Southeast : 5 mi by A 77 off B 7042 ✉ DG9 9AD – ☎ (01776) 810 471 – www.knockinaamlodge.com

10 rm (dinner included) – †£ 155/205 ††£ 260/420

Rest – *(booking essential for non-residents) (set menu only)* Menu £ 40/55

Spec. Salad of Drummore lobster with avocado and watermelon. Lamb with black pudding and herb crust, shallot purée. Hot vanilla rice pudding soufflé with mango sorbet.

◆ Charming country house in a private cove. Classical guest areas include open-fired sitting rooms and a wood-panelled bar; a relaxed atmosphere pervades. Traditionally furnished bedrooms boast antiques. Gold-hued dining room offers sea views and a carefully judged, 5 course daily menu of top quality, seasonal produce.

RANNOCH STATION – Perth and Kinross – 501 G13 27 B2

Edinburgh 108 mi – Kinloch Rannoch 17 mi – Pitlochry 36 mi

Moor of Rannoch

✉ PH17 2QA – ☎ (01882) 633 238 – www.moorofrannoch.co.uk – *14 February-October*

5 rm – †£ 60/98 ††£ 98

Rest – *(dinner only)* Carte £ 28/30 **s**

◆ Immaculately whitewashed 19C property "in the middle of nowhere", next to railway station with link to London! Comfy, sofa-strewn lounges. Rustic rooms with antiques. Home-cooked menus in characterful dining room with conservatory.

RATAGAN - Highland **29** B2

London 572 mi – Edinburgh 187 mi – Inverness 65 mi

Grants at Craigellachie

IV40 8HP – (01599) 511 331 – www.housebytheloch.co.uk – Mid February-mid December

4 rm (dinner included) – ♦£ 93/100 ♦♦£ 155/240 **Rest** – *(Closed Sunday) (dinner only) (booking essential for non residents)* Carte £ 28/35

♦ Set in an idyllic spot beside Loch Duich; compact modern bedrooms are divided between the main house and a building in the rear garden. Local produce and Mediterranean influences inform the menu. Interesting wine list and a good selection of malt whiskies.

ST ANDREWS - Fife - **501** L14 - **pop. 14 209** Scotland **28** D2

Edinburgh 51 mi – Dundee 14 mi – Stirling 51 mi

70 Market St (01334) 472021, standrews@visitscotland.com

Duke's Craigtoun Park, (01334) 474 371

City★★ - Cathedral★ (✳★★) **AC** B – West Port★ A

Leuchars (parish church★), NW : 6 mi by A 91 and A 919. The East Neuk★★, SE : 9 mi by A 917 and B 9131 B – Crail★★ (Old Centre★★, Upper Crail★) SE : 9 mi by A 917 B – Kellie Castle★ **AC**, S : 9 mi by B 9131 and B 9171 B – Ceres★, SW : 9 mi by B 939 - E : Inland Fife★ A

Old Course H. Golf Resort and Spa

rm, Ab

Old Station Rd KY16 9SP – (01334) 474 371 – www.oldcoursehotel.co.uk

116 rm – ♦£ 205/360 ♦♦£ 235/390 – 21 suites

Rest *Road Hole* – *(closed Sunday and Monday) (dinner only)* Menu £ 46

Rest *Sands Grill* – Carte £ 26/58

♦ Famed for its golf course and its unrivalled views of the bay. Relax into richly furnished formal interiors and enjoy luxurious pampering in the impressive spa. Bedrooms are a mix of the modern and classic. Road Hole has a fine view of the 17th hole. Sands Grill has a classic brasserie menu.

ST ANDREWS

Street	Grid	No.
Abbey St	B	2
Abbey Walk	B	3
Alexandra Pl.	A	5
Alfred Pl.	A	6
Bridge St.	A	7
Butts Wynd	B	9
Castle St	B	10
Church St	AB	13
Ellice Pl.	A	15
Gibson Pl.	A	17
Gillespie Terrace	A	18
Greenside Pl.	B	20
Gregory Lane	B	21
Gregory Pl.	B	22
Greyfriars Garden	A	24
Hepburn Gardens	A	25
Link Crescent	A	27
Murray Park	A	28
Murray Pl.	A	29
Pilmour Links	A	31
Pilmour Pl.	A	32
Playfair Terrace	A	34
Queen's Gardens	A	35
Queen's Terrace	B	36
St Mary's Pl.	A	37
Union St	B	38

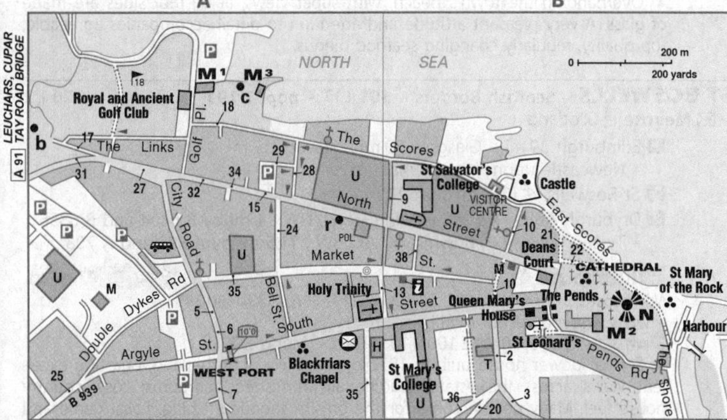

Fairmont St Andrews
Southeast : 3 mi on A 917 ✉ KY16 8PN – ✆ (01334) 837 000 – www.fairmont.com/standrews
192 rm – †£ 219/299 ††£ 219/299 – 6 suites
Rest *The Squire* – ✆ (01334) 837 441 *(dinner only)* Menu £ 33 (dinner)
Rest *Esperante* – ✆ (01334) 837 271 *(closed Monday-Tuesday) (dinner only)* Menu £ 43
♦ Considerable refurbishment at this large, golf oriented, purpose-built resort hotel. Wonderful Tayside views and pristine fairways. Impressive spa. Spacious, comfortable and well-equipped bedrooms. Informal Squire popular with golfers. Mediterranean influenced Esperante.

Rufflets Country House
Strathkinness Low Rd, West : 1.5 mi on B 939 ✉ KY16 9TX – ✆ (01334) 472 594 – www.rufflets.co.uk
22 rm – †£ 140/235 ††£ 200/260 – 2 suites
Rest *Terrace* – *(Closed Sunday lunch)* Carte approx. £ 16
Rest *Library* – *(dinner only and Sunday lunch)* Carte £ 28/54
♦ Handsome 1920s house set in ornamental gardens. Traditional drawing room with cosy fireside sofas. Thoughtfully appointed bedrooms that mix classic and contemporary styles. Terrace restaurant offers fine vantage point to view the lawns. Informal lunches in Library, with its mock bookshelf wallpaper.

SCOTLAND

18 Queens Terrace without rest
18 Queens Terr, by Queens Gardens ✉ KY16 9QF – ✆ (01334) 478 849 – www.18queensterrace.com – Closed Christmas and New Year
4 rm – †£ 65/75 ††£ 90/95
♦ Victorian townhouse, retaining much of its original character, with attractive drawing room and spacious, tastefully decorated bedrooms. Pleasantly located, with a secluded cottage garden.

Aslar House without rest
120 North St ✉ KY16 9AF – ✆ (01334) 473 460 – www.aslar.com – Closed 4-20 January and 20-28 December A**r**
6 rm – †£ 45/80 ††£ 90/96
♦ Victorian house, privately run in a welcoming spirit. Homely, pine furnished rooms, all en suite, are larger on the top floor; most overlook a quiet rear garden. Good value.

The Seafood
The Scores ✉ KY16 9AB – ✆ (01334) 479 475 – www.theseafoodrestaurant.com – Closed 1 January and 25-26 December A**c**
Rest – Seafood – *(booking essential)* Menu £ 26 (lunch)/45
♦ Overhanging the town's beach, with super views, as all four sides are made of glass. A very pleasant attitude and attention to detail accompanies agreeable, top quality, regularly changing seafood menus.

ST BOSWELLS – Scottish Borders – 501 L17 – pop. 1 199 — 26 D2
– ✉ Melrose Scotland

Edinburgh 39 mi – Glasgow 79 mi – Hawick 17 mi – Newcastle upon Tyne 66 mi

St Boswells, ✆ (01835) 823 527

Dryburgh Abbey★★ **AC** (setting★★★), NW : 4 mi by B 6404 and B 6356 – Tweed Valley★★. Bowhill★★ **AC**, SW : 11.5 mi by A 699 and A 708

Whitehouse
Northeast : 3 mi on B 6404 ✉ TD6 0ED – ✆ (01573) 460 343 – www.whitehousecountryhouse.com
3 rm – †£ 75/80 ††£ 100/110 **Rest** – Menu £ 29
♦ Former dower house built in 1872 by the Duke of Sutherland, boasting excellent views across the estate. Traditionally furnished bedrooms; cosy, country house feel. Many people come for the on-site shooting/fishing. Local game and wild salmon feature at dinner.

Clint Lodge

North : 2.25 mi by B 6404 on B 6356 ✉ TD6 0DZ – ✆ (01835) 822 027 – www.clintlodge.co.uk

5 rm – †£ 50/80 ††£ 110 **Rest** – Menu £ 33

♦ Former shooting lodge with superb river and hill views. Characterful interior boasts antiques and fishing memorabilia. Traditionally decorated bedrooms; luxurious No. 4 and south facing rooms are the best. Daily changing 5 course dinner served at beautiful table.

ST FILLANS – Perth and Kinross – 501 H14 28 C2

Edinburgh 65 mi – Lochearnhead 8 mi – Perth 29 mi

Achray House

✉ *PH6 2NF – ✆ (01764) 685 231 – www.achray-house.com – Closed January and February*

8 rm – †£ 75/80 ††£ 90/120 **Rest** – Menu £ 13 (lunch) – Carte £ 21/30

♦ Well run, former Edwardian villa with a stunning Loch Earn view. A homely warmth pervades all areas. Bedrooms are clean and simple; some are suitable for families. Freshly prepared seafood a feature of dining room menus.

Four Seasons

Lochside ✉ PH6 2NF – ✆ (01764) 685 333 – www.thefourseasonshotel.co.uk – Closed 3 January-4 March, and Tuesday-Wednesday March, November and December

12 rm – †£ 55/80 ††£ 150 **Rest** – Menu £ 13 (lunch)/35 – Carte £ 19/31

♦ Small hotel in enviable location beside Loch Earn, with welcoming atmosphere, neat bedrooms and slightly retro edge; front facing rooms have Loch views. Cosy bar and lounge. Bistro open for lunch, restaurant for 4 course dinner.

SCOTLAND

ST MARGARET'S HOPE – Orkney Islands – 501 L7 – see Orkney Islands

ST MONANS – Fife – 501 L15 – pop. 3 965 28 D2

Edinburgh 47 mi – Dundee 26 mi – Perth 40 mi – Stirling 56 mi

Seafood

16 West End ✉ KY10 2BX – ✆ (01333) 730 327 – www.theseafoodrestaurant.com – Closed 1 week January, 25-26 December and Monday and Tuesday September-May

Rest – Seafood – *(booking essential)* Menu £ 26 (lunch)/40

♦ Former pub with nautical memorabilia in a delightful spot overlooking the harbour. Comfortable lounge leads into neatly set restaurant. Local fish prepared with care and precision.

SANQUHAR – Dumfries and Galloway – 501 I17 – pop. 2 028 25 B2

London 368 mi – Edinburgh 58 mi – East Kilbride 51 mi – Hamilton 43 mi

Blackaddie House with rm

Blackaddie Rd ✉ DG4 6JJ – ✆ (01659) 50 270 – www.blackaddiehotel.co.uk

9 rm – †£ 60/85 ††£ 100/120 **Rest** – Menu £ 27 (lunch) – Carte £ 38/49

♦ 16C stone house by the river. Lunch offers good value classics. Dinner is more elaborate and features complex, original cooking. Ingredients are luxurious and dishes, well presented. Simpler bar menu also available. Bedrooms are named after whisky distilleries.

SCALASAIG – Argyll and Bute – 501 B15 – see Colonsay (Isle of)

SCALPAY – Western Isles – 501 A10 – see Lewis and Harris (Isle of)

SCARISTA – Western Isles Outer Hebrides – 501 Y10 – see Lewis and Harris (Isle of)

SCOURIE – Highland – 501 E8 – ✉ Lairg Scotland 30 C1

Edinburgh 263 mi – Inverness 107 mi

Cape Wrath★★★ (≤★★) **AC**, N : 31 mi (including ferry crossing) by A 894 and A 838 – Loch Assynt★★, S : 17 mi by A 894

Eddrachilles

Badcall Bay, South : 2.5 mi on A 894 ✉ IV27 4TH – ☎ (01971) 502 080 – www.eddrachilles.com – April-September

11 rm – **♦£ 73/76 ♦♦£ 100/106** **Rest** – *(bar lunch)* Menu £ 30

◆ Remotely set, converted 18C manse with views of the countryside, Badcall Bay and its islands. Cosy, well-kept bedrooms. Snug bar and flag-floored dining room; delightful outlook from conservatory lounge. Daily menu with strong French slant. Meats cured on-site.

SCRABSTER – **Highland** – **501** J8 – **see Thurso**

SHETLAND ISLANDS – 501 P/Q3 – pop. 21 988 Scotland

Sumburgh Airport : ☎ (01950) 460905, S : 25 mi of Lerwick by A 970 - Tingwall Airport: 01595) 840246, NW: 6m. of Lerwick by A971

from Foula to Walls (Shetland Islands Council) 1-2 weekly (2 h 30 mn) – from Fair Isle to Sumburgh (Shetland Islands Council) 1-2 weekly (2 h 40 mn)

from Lerwick (Mainland) to Aberdeen and via Orkney Islands (Stromness) (P and O Scottish Ferries) – from Vidlin to Skerries (Shetland Islands Council) booking essential 3-4 weekly (1 h 30 mn) – from Lerwick (Mainland) to Skerries (Shetland Islands Council) 2 weekly (booking essential) (2 h 30 mn) – from Lerwick (Mainland) to Bressay (Shetland Islands Council) frequent services daily (7 mn) – from Laxo (Mainland) to Isle of Whalsay (Symbister) (Shetland Islands Council) frequent services daily (30 mn) – from Toft (Mainland) to Isle of Yell (Ulsta) (Shetland Islands Council) frequent services daily (20 mn) – from Isle of Yell (Gutcher) to Isle of Fetlar (Oddsta) and via Isle of Unst (Belmont) (Shetland Islands Council) – from Fair Isle to Sumburgh (Mainland) (Shetland Islands Council) 3 weekly (2 h 40 mn)

Islands★ - Up Helly Aa (last Tuesday in January) – Mousa Broch★★★ **AC** (Mousa Island) – Jarlshof★★ - Lerwick to Jarlshof★ (<★) – Shetland Croft House Museum★ **AC**

MAINLAND – **Shetland Islands** **31** B2

London 559 mi – Edinburgh 148 mi

Lerwick – **Shetland Islands** – **pop. 6 830** Scotland **31** B2

The Market Cross, Lerwick ☎ (08452) 255 121, info@visitshetland.com

Shetland Gott Dale, ☎ (01595) 840 369

Clickhimin Broch★

Gulber Wick (<★), S : 2 mi by A 970

Kveldsro House

Greenfield Pl ✉ ZE1 0AQ – ☎ (01595) 692 195 – www.shetlandhotels.com – Closed 1-2 January and 25-26 December

17 rm – **♦£ 105 ♦♦£ 130**

Rest – *(bar lunch Monday-Saturday, carvery lunch Sunday)* Carte £ 21/34 **s**

◆ Spacious Georgian house hidden in the town centre; its name means 'evening peace'. Cosy sitting room with original ceiling mouldings, comfy bar with views of the islands and traditionally styled bedrooms. Menus offer mainly island produce; portions are hearty.

Glen Orchy House rm,

20 Knab Rd ✉ ZE1 0AX – ☎ (01595) 692 031 – www.guesthouselerwick.com

24 rm – **♦£ 65/90 ♦♦£ 90**

Rest – Thai – *(booking essential) (residents only)* Carte £ 11/17

◆ Family-run hotel set in a 1904 former convent. Neat, well-kept guest areas include an honesty bar and spacious, comfortable lounge. Simple, cosy bedrooms – those in the wing boast underfloor heating. Homely dining room; unusually, cooking is totally Thai-based.

VEENSGARTH – **Shetland Islands** **31** B2

Herrislea House

✉ *ZE2 9SB – ✆ (01595) 840 208 – www.herrisleahouse.co.uk – Restricted opening in winter*

13 rm – †£ 70/100 ††£ 100/130

Rest – *(dinner only) (booking essential for non-residents)* Carte £ 19/30

♦ Large, family-run hotel set just out of town. Unusual African hunting theme with mounted antlers, animal heads and skins on display. Cosy, individually designed bedrooms; some with valley views. Fresh cooking uses local produce and meats from the family crofts.

SHIELDAIG – **Highland** – **501** D11 – ✉ **Strathcarron** Scotland **29** B2

Edinburgh 226 mi – Inverness 70 mi – Kyle of Lochalsh 36 mi

Wester Ross★★★

Tigh An Eilean

✉ *IV54 8XN – ✆ (01520) 755 251 – www.tighaneilean.co.uk – Closed January, restricted opening in winter*

11 rm – †£ 60/120 ††£ 120/170

Rest – *(booking essential for non-residents) (bar lunch)* Menu £ 45 (dinner)

♦ In a sleepy lochside village, an attractive, personally run 19C inn with fine views of the Shieldaig Islands. Cosy, well-kept bedrooms and a comfy lounge with a homely feel. Linen-clad dining room showing eclectic variety of art; Scottish produce to the fore.

SKIRLING – **Scottish Borders** – **501** J17 – ✉ **Biggar** Scotland **26** C2

Edinburgh 29 mi – Glasgow 45 mi – Peebles 16 mi

Biggar★ - Gladstone Court Museum★, Greenhill Covenanting Museum★, S : 3 mi by A 72 and A 702. New Lanark★★, NW : 16 mi by A 72 and A 73

Skirling House

✉ *ML12 6HD – ✆ (01899) 860 274 – www.skirlinghouse.com – Closed January, February and 1 week November*

5 rm – †£ 90 ††£ 130 **Rest** – Menu £ 35

♦ On the green in an attractive hamlet; a personally run, Scots Pine, Arts and Crafts house. Beautiful Florentine carved ceiling and eclectic range of memorabilia in drawing room. Simple, characterful bedrooms with extras. Accomplished cooking uses home-grown produce; daily 4 course menu can be taken in the conservatory.

SKYE (Isle of) – **Highland** – **501** B11 – **pop. 9 232** Scotland **29** B2

from Mallaig to Isles of Eigg, Muck, Rhum and Canna (Caledonian MacBrayne Ltd) (summer only) – from Mallaig to Armadale (Caledonian MacBrayne Ltd) (summer only) 1-2 weekly (30 mn)

from Mallaig to Armadale (Caledonian MacBrayne Ltd) 1-5 daily (30 mn) – from Uig to North Uist (Lochmaddy) or Isle of Harris (Tarbert) (Caledonian MacBrayne Ltd) 1-3 daily (1 h 50 mn) – from Sconser to Isle of Raasay (Caledonian MacBrayne Ltd) 9-10 daily (except Sunday) (15 mn)

Island★★ - The Cuillins★★★ – Skye Museum of Island Life★ **AC**

N : Trotternish Peninsula★★ – W : Duirinish Peninsula★ – Portree★

BERNISDALE – **Highland**

Spoons without rest

75 Aird Bernisdale ✉ IV51 9NU – ✆ (01470) 532 217 – www.thespoonsonskye.com – Closed 22 December-29 January

3 rm – †£ 105/120 ††£ 135/150

♦ Luxurious, purpose-built guest house in unspoilt hamlet, with airy, wood-floored lounge and Scandinavian-style breakfast room. Bedrooms are individually decorated in a crisp, modern style. 3 course breakfasts, with eggs from the charming owners' chickens.

BROADFORD – Highland **29** B2

Tigh an Dochais rm,

13 Harrapool, on A 87 ✉ IV49 9AQ – ✆ (01471) 820 022 – www.skyebedbreakfast.co.uk – mid-March to mid-December

3 rm – £ 75 £ 84 **Rest** – Menu £ 25

♦ Striking house with award-winning architecture, overlooking Broadford Bay and the Applecross Peninsula. Comfortable lounge has well-stocked bookshelves. Modern, minimalist bedrooms boast superb views and good facilities, including underfloor heating and plenty of extras. Communal, home-cooked meals by arrangement.

DUISDALEMORE – Highland **29** B2

Duisdale House rm,

Sleat, on A 851. ✉ IV43 8QW – ✆ (01471) 833 202 – www.duisdale.com

18 rm – £ 75/150 £ 130/202 – 1 suite

Rest – Menu £ 42 (dinner) – Carte £ 19/46

♦ Stylish, up-to-date hotel with lawned gardens, hot tub and coastal views. Comfortable bedrooms boast bold décor, excellent bathrooms and a pleasing blend of contemporary and antique furniture. Modern cooking makes good use of local produce. Smart uniformed staff.

DUNVEGAN – Highland **29** B2

Roskhill House without rest

Roskhill, Southeast : 2.5 mi by A 863 ✉ IV55 8ZD – ✆ (01470) 521 317 – www.roskhillhouse.co.uk – Closed January and December

5 rm – £ 45/57 £ 70/80

♦ Welcoming 19C croft house with small garden, set in peaceful location close to the water. Formerly the old post office, the lounge boasts exposed stone, wooden beams and an open fire. Fresh, bright bedrooms have a contemporary edge and smart, modern bathrooms.

SCOTLAND

The Three Chimneys & The House Over-By with rm

✉ IV55 8ZT – ✆ (01470) 511 258 – www.threechimneys.co.uk – Closed 3 weeks January

6 rm – £ 285 £ 285

Rest – Seafood – *(booking essential)* Menu £ 35/60

♦ Immaculately kept crofter's cottage in stunning lochside setting. Three characterful low-beamed dining rooms display modern artwork. Choose from accomplished, classical seafood-orientated dishes or 7 course tasting menu. Split-level bedrooms are spacious and stylishly understated; great outlook from residents' lounge.

EDINBANE – Highland **29** B2

Greshornish House

North : 3.75 mi by A 850 in direction of Dunvegan ✉ IV51 9PN – ✆ (01470) 582 266 – www.greshornishhouse.com – Restricted opening in winter

6 rm – £ 95/130 £ 150/185

Rest – *(Closed Monday and Tuesday in winter) (booking essential)* Menu £ 20 (lunch)/40

♦ Early 18C lochside house in 10 acres. Comfy panelled drawing room; billiard room with snooker table, piano, books and games. Country house style bedrooms; some four-posters/loch views. Breakfast in conservatory; seasonal, island dinners in candlelit dining room.

FLODIGARRY – Highland – ✉ Staffin **29** B2

Flodigarry Country House

✉ IV51 9HZ – ✆ (01470) 552 203 – www.flodigarry.co.uk – Closed 3 January to 10 February and 7 November to 22 December

18 rm – £ 65/115 £ 160/210

Rest – *(dinner only and Sunday lunch bar lunch Monday-Saturday)* Carte £ 33/57 **s**

♦ Victorian house and cottage annexe which was once Flora MacDonald's home. Comfy, antique-filled interior with excellent island views over gardens that run down to the coast. Cosy, homely bedrooms. Characterful bar and part-panelled dining room; classical menu.

PORTREE - Highland - pop. 1 917 — 29 B2

Bayfield House, Bayfield Rd ✆ (08452) 255121

Cuillin Hills

Northeast : 0.75 mi by A 855 ✉ IV51 9QU – ✆ (01478) 612 003 – www.cuillinhills-hotel-skye.co.uk

26 rm – †£ 190/260 ††£ 210/260

Rest – *(bar lunch Monday-Saturday, buffet lunch Sunday)* Carte £ 22/44 **s**

• Yellow-washed 19C hunting lodge in 15 acres of gardens and grounds; overlooking the bay and hills. Comfy lounge and stylish open-plan bar. Bedrooms offer good facilities; the best are to the front. Bright dining room offers good outlook and traditional menus.

Bosville

Bosville Ter ✉ IV51 9DG – ✆ (01478) 612 846 – www.macleodhotels.co.uk/bosville

19 rm – †£ 69/120 ††£ 88/150

Rest *Chandlery* – see restaurant listing

Rest *Bistro* – Carte £ 16/31

• Boldly painted, purpose-built hotel in town centre. Wood-furnished bar – formerly the village bank – and small, traditionally decorated, first floor lounge. Modern bedrooms with co-ordinating fabrics and good facilities. Accessible menu served in popular bistro.

Almondbank without rest

Viewfield Rd, Southwest : 0.75 mi on A 87 ✉ IV51 9EU – ✆ (01478) 612 696

4 rm – †£ 55/65 ††£ 70/80

• Friendly guesthouse with large lawned gardens, set on a sloping bank and boasting lovely views across the bay. Spacious lounge and linen-laid breakfast room. Immaculately kept bedrooms.

Chandlery – at Bosville Hotel

Bosville Ter ✉ IV51 9DG – ✆ (01478) 612 846 – www.macleodhotels.co.uk

Rest – Carte £ 16/31

• Hotel restaurant displaying deep red walls, linen-laid tables and high-backed chairs. Concise 3 course set menu offers classically based meat and seafood dishes. Friendly service.

SLEAT - Highland — 30 C1

Kinloch Lodge

✉ IV43 8QY – ✆ (01471) 833 214 – www.kinloch-lodge.co.uk – Closed 25 December

14 rm (dinner included) – †£ 169/240 ††£ 218/340 – 1 suite

Rest – *(booking essential for non-residents)* Menu £ 30/60 **s**

Spec. Crab mousse with Drumfearn mussels. Pigeon breast wrapped in Parma ham, beetroot and lentils. Vanilla and Achmore crème fraîche panna cotta, Caipirinha sorbet.

• 17C lochside hunting lodge surrounded by heather-strewn moorland. Antique-filled country house interior with comfy lounges. Individually styled bedrooms boast good facilities/extras. Menus offer 2 choices per course and showcase local island produce. Classical cooking displays some clever modern touches. Good service.

STRUAN - Highland — 29 B2

Ullinish Country Lodge

West : 1.5 mi by A 863 ✉ IV56 8FD – ✆ (01470) 572 214 – www.theisleofskye.co.uk – Closed January, 1 week November and 25 December

6 rm – †£ 120 ††£ 160 **Rest** – *(dinner only)* Menu £ 43

• Personally run, 17C whitewashed house in windswept location, affording lovely loch/hill views. Comfy lounge filled with ornaments and books about the area. Warmly decorated bedrooms boast good facilities and extras. Formal dining room offers complex 5 course menu.

SCOTLAND

Teangue

Toravaig House

Knock Bay, on A 851 ✉ IV44 8RE – ✆ (01471) 820 200 – www.skyehotel.co.uk
9 rm – †£ 70/150 ††£ 120/198
Rest – *(booking essential for non-residents)* Menu £ 22 (lunch)/44 – Carte £ 23/46
◆ Stylish whitewashed house with neat gardens, set on the road to the Mallaig ferry. Cosy, open-fired lounge with baby grand piano and heavy fabrics. Individually designed bedrooms boast quality materials and furnishings. Good service with extras. Two-roomed restaurant offers concise, classical menu of island produce.

WATERNISH – Highland 29 A2

Loch Bay Seafood

1 MacLeod Terr, Stein ✉ IV55 8GA – ✆ (01470) 592 235 – www.lochbay-seafood-restaurant.co.uk – 18 March-mid-October
Rest – Seafood – *(closed Saturday-Monday) (booking essential)* Carte £ 23/37
◆ Whitewashed cottage in a tiny hamlet overlooking the loch. Small room with low-backed chairs and benches. Concise menu of simply prepared seafood and blackboard specials. Friendly service.

Stein Inn with rm

MacLeod Ter, Stein ✉ IV55 8GA – ✆ (01470) 592 362 – www.stein-inn.co.uk
5 rm – †£ 40 ††£ 100
Rest – Seafood – *(residents only Monday dinner except Bank Holidays)* Carte £ 15/40
◆ Set in a tiny fishing village, this characterful inn is the oldest on Skye. Menus are formed around the latest local produce available, with lighter toasties and salads on offer at lunchtime. Bedrooms are simple, well-kept and boast lovely bay outlooks.

SLEAT – Highland – see Skye (Isle of)

SORN – East Ayrshire – 501 H17 25 B2

Edinburgh 67 mi – Ayr 15 mi – Glasgow 35 mi

The Sorn Inn with rm

35 Main St ✉ KA5 6HU – ✆ (01290) 551 305 – www.sorninn.com – Closed 2 weeks January and Monday
4 rm – †£ 40 ††£ 70 **Rest** – Menu £ 19/24 – Carte £ 19/29
◆ Simple whitewashed inn; very much a family affair. Robust cooking offered in the snug bar and more refined, knowledgeably executed dishes with a Mediterranean edge in the dining room. Neat, simple bedrooms are good value.

SPEAN BRIDGE – Highland – 501 F13 30 C3

Edinburgh 143 mi – Fort William 10 mi – Glasgow 94 mi – Inverness 58 mi
The Kingdom of Scotland, by Fort William, Inverness-shire v (0845) 2255121 (April-October), info@visitscotland.com
Spean Bridge GC Station Rd, ✆ 077 471 47 090

Corriegour Lodge

Loch Lochy, North : 8.75 mi on A 82 ✉ PH34 4EA – ✆ (01397) 712 685 – www.corriegour-lodge-hotel.com – Closed 2 January-1 March and 1 November-28 December
12 rm (dinner included) – †£ 110/260 ††£ 220/260
Rest – *(dinner only)* Menu £ 49
◆ 19C hunting lodge with pretty gardens, in great lochside location; owner's father is the local gamekeeper. Homely, curio-filled sitting room; high quality beds, linens and fabrics. Every dining table has a loch view; classical 4 course menu features local meats.

Distant Hills without rest

Roy Bridge Rd, East : 0.5 mi on A86 ✉ PH34 4EU – ✆ (01397) 712 452 – www.distanthills.com – March-October
7 rm – †£ 42/72 ††£ 71/84
◆ Welcoming guesthouse with friendly owners, who suggest walks and provide packed lunches. French windows in large lounge lead to stream-side seating. Modern bedrooms. Wide-ranging breakfasts.

Corriechoille Lodge

East : 2.75 mi on Corriechoille rd ✉ PH34 4EY – ✆ (01397) 712 002 – www.corriechoille.com – Closed November-March, Sunday and Monday

4 rm – £ 48 £ 76 **Rest** – Menu £ 28

◆ Charming, part-18C house in remote location, boasting large gardens and views over the Grey Corries and Aonach Mor. Comfy lounge and spacious, pine-furnished bedrooms; two wooden bothy lodges provide more intimacy. Homely cooking; the fish is smoked on site.

Russell's at Smiddy House with rm

Roybridge Rd ✉ PH34 4EU – ✆ (01397) 712 335 – www.smiddyhouse.co.uk – Closed 2 weeks November and Monday-Tuesday during winter

4 rm – £ 65/80 £ 75/90

Rest – *(dinner only) (booking essential)* Menu £ 35 **s**

◆ Passionately run restaurant in an appealing Highland village. Snug lounge and two intimate, candlelit dining rooms. Classical menus of tried-and-tested combinations which rely on natural flavours. Cosy, well-equipped bedrooms boast comfy beds and fine linens.

Old Pines with rm

Northwest : 1.5 mi by A 82 on B 8004 ✉ PH34 4EG – ✆ (01397) 712 324 – www.oldpines.co.uk – 16 February-October

7 rm – £ 60/75 £ 90/120

Rest – *(booking essential for non-residents)* Carte £ 27/35

◆ Log cabin style building that blends well with the Highland scenery. Comfy lounge; simple dining room with tables arranged around the windows. Classical menus offer lots of local seafood and beef. Up-to-date, pine-furnished bedrooms feature traditional quilts.

SCOTLAND

SPITTAL OF GLENSHEE – Perth and Kinross – 501 J13 28 C2

– ✉ Blairgowrie Scotland

Edinburgh 69 mi – Aberdeen 74 mi – Dundee 35 mi

Glenshee (★★) (chairlift **AC**)

Dalmunzie Castle

✉ PH10 7QG – ✆ (01250) 885 224 – www.dalmunzie.com – Closed December

17 rm (dinner included) – £ 95/170 £ 170/285

Rest – *(bar lunch)* Menu £ 45

◆ Edwardian hunting lodge in a magnificent spot, encircled by mountains. Traditional rooms mix antique and pine furniture. Bar with cosy panelled alcove and leather chairs. Modern dining room with views down the valley.

STEVENSTON – North Ayrshire – 501 F17 – pop. 9 129 25 A2

Edinburgh 82 mi – Ayr 19 mi – Glasgow 36 mi

Ardeer Farm Steading without rest

Ardeer Mains Farm, East : 0.75 mi by A 738 and B 752, on no through rd ✉ KA20 3DD – ✆ (01294) 465 438 – www.ardeersteading.co.uk

6 rm – £ 35 £ 48/50

◆ Comfortable family-owned guest house has contemporary furnishings, with bright cushions and bed throws. Pleasant breakfast room and modern lounge with cream leather sofas.

STIRLING – Stirling – 501 I15 – pop. 32 673 Scotland 28 C2

Edinburgh 37 mi – Dunfermline 23 mi – Falkirk 14 mi – Glasgow 28 mi

41 Dumbarton Rd ✆ (08707) 200620, stirling@visitscotland.com- Pirnhall, Motorway Service Area, junction 9, M 9/ M80 ✆ (01786) 814111 (April-October), info@pirnhall.visitscotland.com

Town★★ – Castle★★ **AC** (Site★★★, external elevations★★★, Stirling Heads★★, Argyll and Sutherland Highlanders Regimental Museum★) B – Argyll's Lodging★ (Renaissance decoration★) B **A** – Church of the Holy Rude★ B **B**

Wallace Monument (★★) NE : 2.5 mi by A 9 - A - and B 998. Dunblane★ (Cathedral★★, West Front★★), N : 6.5 mi by A 9 A

Plan on next page

Park Lodge

32 Park Ter ✉ *FK8 2JS – ✆ (01786) 474 862 – www.parklodge.net – Closed Christmas and New Year* **Ba**

9 rm ☕ – †£ 65/85 ††£ 85/110

Rest – *(Closed Sunday)* Menu £ 15 (lunch)/25 **s**

◆ Creeper-clad Georgian and Victorian house, still in private hands and furnished with an enviable collection of antiques. Compact but well-equipped rooms with a stylish feel. Intimate dining room overlooking a pretty garden.

Number 10 without rest

Gladstone Pl ✉ *FK8 2NN – ✆ (01786) 472 681 – www.cameron-10.co.uk* **Bv**

3 rm ☕ – †£ 45/60 ††£ 60

◆ Surprisingly spacious 19C terrace house in a pleasant suburb. Pine furnished en suite bedrooms are characteristically well kept and comfortable. Friendly owner.

West Plean House without rest

South : 3.5 mi on A 872 (Denny rd) ✉ *FK7 8HA – ✆ (01786) 812 208 – www.westpleanhouse.com – Closed 15 December-15 January*

3 rm ☕ – †£ 45/60 ††£ 80

◆ Attractive country house dating from 1801; the estate includes a working farm. Drawing rooms filled with antiques and family heirlooms. Individually decorated bedrooms are warm and traditional.

SCOTLAND

STIRLING

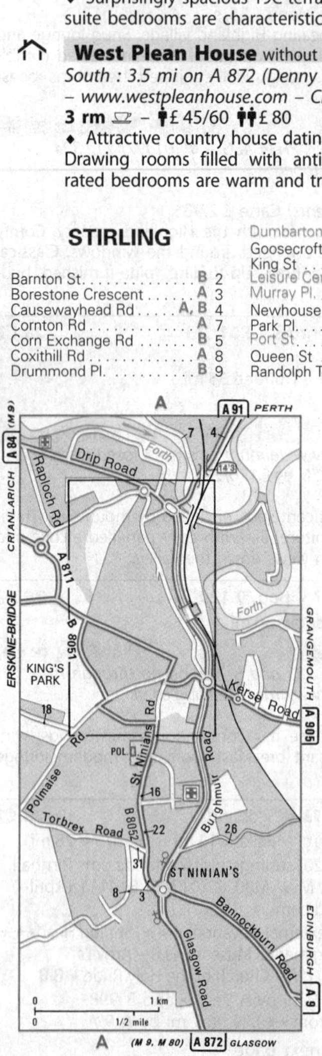

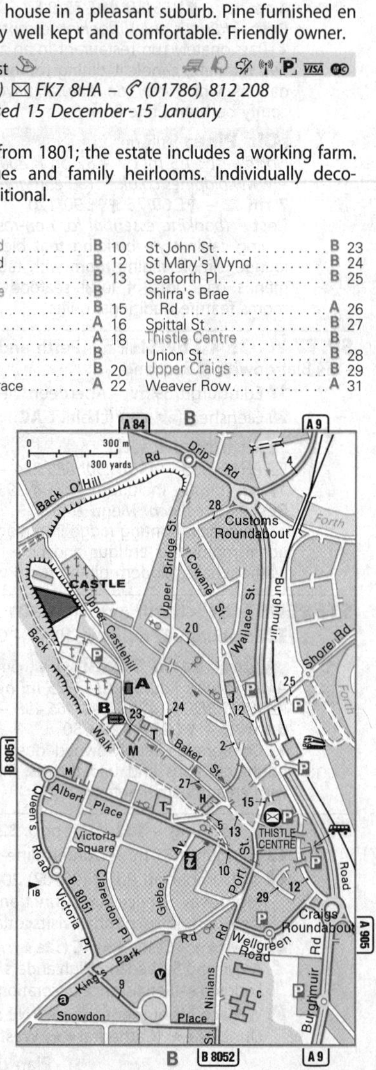

STONEHAVEN – Aberdeenshire – 501 N13 – pop. 9 577 Scotland 28 D2

Edinburgh 109 mi – Aberdeen 16 mi – Montrose 22 mi

Dunnottar Castle★★, S : 1.5 mi by A 92

Tolbooth

Old Pier, Harbour ✉ AB39 2JU – ✆ (01569) 762 287 – www.tolbooth-restaurant.co.uk – Closed 25-26 December, January, Sunday October-April and Monday

Rest – Seafood – Menu £ 22 (lunch) – Carte £ 31/42

♦ Stonehaven's oldest building, delightfully located by the harbour. Rustic interior with lovely picture window table. Various menus available, with the emphasis on local seafood.

Carron

20 Cameron St ✉ AB39 2HS – ✆ (01569) 760 460 – www.carron-restaurant.co.uk – Closed 24 December-11 January, Sunday and Monday

Rest – Carte £ 19/35

♦ 1930s Art Deco elegance fully restored to its original splendour. Panelled walls with old mono photos. Sunny front terrace. Popular menus highlighted by daily lobster dishes.

STORNOWAY – Western Isles Outer Hebrides – 501 A9 – see Lewis and Harris (Isle of)

STRACHUR – Argyll and Bute – 501 E15 – pop. 628 27 B2

Edinburgh 112 mi – Glasgow 66 mi – Inverness 162 mi – Perth 101 mi

Creggans Inn

✉ PA27 8BX – ✆ (01369) 860 279 – www.creggans-inn.co.uk

13 rm – †£ 80/100 ††£ 100/150 – 1 suite

Rest *Loch Fyne Dining Room* – Menu £ 26 (dinner) – Carte £ 21/35

Rest *Mac Phunn's Bar* – Carte £ 23/31

♦ Long-standing inn on the shores of Loch Fyne. Traditional décor respects the building's age. Pleasant, well-kept bedrooms are spacious and comfortable. Conservatory popular for afternoon teas. Delightful dining room offers great views and a formal 4 course daily menu. Bar, with pool tables, offers more pub-style dishes.

Inver Cottage

Strathlaclan, Southwest : 6.5 mi by A 886 on B 8000 ✉ PA27 8BU – ✆ (01369) 860 537 – www.invercottage.com – Closed Monday and Tuesday except July-August

Rest – Carte £ 21/34

♦ Lochside former crofter's cottage boasting water/mountain views. Small bar and casual tables for drinks/afternoon tea; simple, airy restaurant. Constantly evolving menu uses only local produce.

STRATHPEFFER – Highland – 501 G11 – pop. 918 30 C2

Edinburgh 174 mi – Inverness 18 mi

Pump Room Museum ✆ (01997) 421415, (June- Sept), info@visitscotland.com

Strathpeffer Spa Golf Course Rd, ✆ (01997) 421 219

Craigvar without rest

The Square ✉ IV14 9DL – ✆ (01997) 421 622 – www.craigvar.com – Closed 20 December-11 January and 7-22 October

3 rm – †£ 40/60 ††£ 72/84

♦ Georgian house overlooking the main square of pleasant former spa town. Charming owner guarantees an agreeable stay. Bedrooms are crammed with antiques and original fittings.

STRATHYRE – Stirling – 501 H15 – ✉ Callander Scotland 27 B2

Edinburgh 62 mi – Glasgow 53 mi – Perth 42 mi

The Trossachs★★★ (Loch Katrine★★) SW : 14 mi by A 84 and A 821 – Hilltop viewpoint★★★ (✻★★★) SW : 16.5 mi by A 84 and A 821

Creagan House with rm
on A 84 ✉ FK18 8ND – ✆ (01877) 384 638 – www.creaganhouse.co.uk – Closed 19 January-10 March, 9-24 November and 24-26 December
5 rm – †£ 73 ††£ 125
Rest – *(Closed Wednesday and Thursday) (dinner only)* Menu £ 32
♦ Personally run baronial dining room in 17C former farmhouse. Concise fixed price menu of fine seasonal Scottish produce; classical dishes prepared with care. 'Smokie and a Pokie,' a speciality. Watch red squirrels in the garden from the cosy bedrooms.

STROMNESS – **Orkney Islands** – **501** K7 – **see Orkney Islands**

STRONTIAN – **Highland** – **501** D13 **29** B3
Edinburgh 139 mi – Fort William 23 mi – Oban 66 mi
Acharacle ✆ (08452) 255121 (April-October), strontian@visitscotland.com

Kilcamb Lodge
✉ PH36 4HY – ✆ (01967) 402 257 – www.kilcamblodge.co.uk – Closed 3 January-1 February
10 rm (dinner included) – †£ 155/203 ††£ 296/307
Rest – Menu £ 18 (lunch)/50
♦ Charming lochside hunting lodge, with 19 acres of gardens and woodland running down to a private shore. Traditional interior boasts rich fabrics, log fires and up-to-date bedrooms. Formal restaurant offers a traditional menu; seafood and game feature highly.

STRUAN – **Highland** – **see Skye (Isle of)**

SWINTON – **Scottish Borders** – **501** N16 – **pop. 472** – ✉ **Duns** **26** D2
Edinburgh 49 mi – Berwick-upon-Tweed 13 mi – Glasgow 93 mi – Newcastle upon Tyne 66 mi

The Wheatsheaf with rm
Main St ✉ TD11 3JJ – ✆ (01890) 860 257 – www.wheatsheaf-swinton.co.uk – Closed lunch Monday-Tuesday
10 rm – †£ 75 ††£ 112/138 **Rest** – Menu £ 32 (dinner) – Carte £ 19/35
♦ Substantial stone inn overlooking the village green. Lunch menu offers pub classics; concise evening à la carte is more adventurous. Both feature local produce, including meat from nearby farms and fish from Eyemouth. Bedrooms are spacious, cosy and well-equipped.

TAIN – **Highland** – **501** H10 – **pop. 4 540** **30** D2
Edinburgh 191 mi – Inverness 35 mi – Wick 91 mi
Tain Chapel Rd, ✆ (01862) 892 314
Tarbat Portmahomack, ✆ (01862) 871 278

Golf View House without rest
13 Knockbreck Rd ✉ IV19 1BN – ✆ (01862) 892 856 – www.tainbedandbreakfast.co.uk – March-October
5 rm – †£ 45/52 ††£ 65/72
♦ 19C former manse near the golf course. Neat lawned garden with comfy seating in wooden bothy hut. Leather-furnished lounge and bright, modern bedrooms; front rooms have water/mountain views.

at Nigg **Southeast: 7 mi by A9, B 9175 and Pitcalnie Rd.**

Wemyss House
Bayfield, South : 1 mi past church ✉ IV19 1QW – ✆ (01862) 851 212 – www.wemysshouse.com
3 rm – †£ 90 ††£ 90 **Rest** – Menu £ 35 (dinner)
♦ Remote, rurally set guesthouse with charming owners, well-maintained gardens and pleasant views. Cosy sitting room with grand piano. Spacious, immaculately kept bedrooms. Freshly prepared dishes use local ingredients. Excellent quality breakfasts.

at Cadboll Southeast : 8.5 mi by A 9 and B 9165 (Portmahomack rd) off Hilton rd – ✉ Tain

Glenmorangie House
Fearn ✉ IV20 1XP – ✆ (01862) 871 671 – www.theglenmorangiehouse.com
9 rm (dinner included) – †£ 250 ††£ 400 – 3 suites **Rest** – Menu £ 50
◆ Charming 17C house owned by the famous distillery. Antiques, hand-crafted local furnishings and open peat fires feature; there's even a small whisky tasting room. Luxuriously appointed bedrooms show good attention to detail; those in the courtyard cottages are suites. Communal dining from classical Scottish-based menu.

TALMINE – Highland – **501** G8 – ✉ **Lairg** **30** C1

Edinburgh 245 mi – Inverness 86 mi – Thurso 48 mi

Cloisters without rest
Church Holme ✉ IV27 4YP – ✆ (01847) 601 286 – www.cloistertal.demon.co.uk
3 rm – †£ 33 ††£ 55
◆ Converted church boasting great views over Tongue Bay and the Rabbit Islands. Homely interior packed with memorabilia. Leather-furnished lounge, snug breakfast area and simple, well-kept bedrooms.

TARBERT – Western Isles Outer Hebrides – **501** Z10 – see Lewis and Harris (Isle of)

TARBET – Argyll and Bute – **501** F15 – ✉ **Arrochar** **27** B2

Edinburgh 88 mi – Glasgow 42 mi – Inverness 138 mi – Perth 78 mi

Lomond View Country House without rest
on A 82 ✉ G83 7DG – ✆ (01301) 702 477 – www.lomondview.co.uk
3 rm – †£ 55/70 ††£ 75/80
◆ Purpose-built guesthouse which lives up to its name: there are stunning loch views. Spacious sitting room. Light and airy breakfast room. Sizeable, modern bedrooms.

TAYVALLICH – Argyll and Bute – **501** D15 – ✉ **Lochgilphead** **27** B2

Edinburgh 148 mi – Glasgow 103 mi – Inverness 157 mi

Tayvallich Inn
✉ PA31 8PL – ✆ (01546) 870 282 – www.tayvallichinn.co.uk – Closed Monday November-March
Rest – Carte £ 16/26
◆ Dine in bar, more formal dining room or on decked terrace, with views over the bay. Menu focuses on locally caught fish and shellfish, but also lists classic pub dishes like steak and chips.

TEANGUE – Highland – see Skye (Isle of)

THORNHILL – Dumfries and Galloway – **501** I18 – **pop. 1 633** Scotland **25** B2

Edinburgh 64 mi – Ayr 44 mi – Dumfries 15 mi – Glasgow 63 mi

Drumlanrig Castle★★ (cabinets★) **AC**, NW : 4 mi by A 76

Gillbank House without rest
8 East Morton St ✉ DG3 5LZ – ✆ (01848) 330 597 – www.gillbank.co.uk
6 rm – †£ 50 ††£ 70
◆ Red stone house built in 1895; originally the Jenner family holiday home. Lovely stained glass front door, spacious, light-filled interior and airy breakfast room with distant hill views. Large, simply furnished bedrooms: two with feature beds; all with wet rooms.

THURSO – Highland – **501** J8 – **pop. 7 737** Scotland **30** D1

Edinburgh 289 mi – Inverness 133 mi – Wick 21 mi

from Scrabster to Stromness (Orkney Islands) (P and O Scottish Ferries) (2 h)

Riverside ✆ (0845) 2255121 (April-October), thurso@visitscotland.com

Newlands of Geise, ✆ (01847) 893 807

Strathy Point★ (<★★★) W : 22 mi by A 836

Forss House

Forss, West : 5.5 mi on A 836 ✉ *KW14 7XY – ☏ (01847) 861 201 – www.forsshousehotel.co.uk – Closed 24 December-2 January*
14 rm ☕ – 🚹£ 110 🚹🚹£ 160 **Rest** – *(dinner only)* Carte £ 32/39
◆ Traditional Scottish hotel centred around fishing and offering timeshares on the river. Rods and mounted fish sit beside deer heads and open fires. Good-sized bedrooms – annexe rooms are most modern. Elegant dining room serves classic menu; seafood a speciality.

Murray House

1 Campbell St ✉ *KW14 7HD – ☏ (01847) 895 759 – www.murrayhousebb.com – Closed 24 December-7 January*
5 rm ☕ – 🚹£ 30/60 🚹🚹£ 50/70 **Rest** – *(by arrangement)* Menu £ 15
◆ A centrally located and family owned Victorian town house. Pine furnished bedrooms are colourfully decorated and carefully maintained. Modern dining room with home-cooked evening meals.

at Scrabster **Northwest : 2.25 mi on A 9**

Captain's Galley

The Harbour ✉ *KW14 7UJ – ☏ (01847) 894 999 – www.captainsgalley.co.uk – Closed 1-2 January, 25-26 and 31 December, Sunday and Monday*
Rest – Seafood – *(dinner only) (booking essential)* Carte approx. £ 46
◆ Rustic seafood restaurant on the pier, with vaulted stone dining room, cosy lounge and old chimney from its former smokery days. Owner was once a fisherman, so has excellent local contacts; he keeps some produce in creels in the harbour. Classical daily menu.

SCOTLAND

TIGHNABRUAICH – Argyll and Bute – 501 E16 27 B3

Edinburgh 113 mi – Glasgow 63 mi – Oban 66 mi

The Royal An Lochan

✉ *PA21 2BE – ☏ (01700) 811 239 – www.anlochan.co.uk – Closed 2 weeks Christmas*
11 rm ☕ – 🚹£ 110/190 🚹🚹£ 110/190 **Rest** – Carte £ 23/40 **s**
◆ Spacious 19C hotel located in a peaceful village, overlooking the Kyles of Bute. Comfortable bedrooms; some with excellent outlooks. Charming bar with nautical theme serves snack menu. Formal conservatory restaurant offers water views and mainly seafood dishes.

TIRORAN – Argyll and Bute – 501 B14 – see Mull (Isle of)

TOBERMORY – Argyll and Bute – 501 B14 – see Mull (Isle of)

TONGUE – Highland – 501 G8 – pop. 552 – ✉ Lairg Scotland 30 C1

Edinburgh 257 mi – Inverness 101 mi – Thurso 43 mi

Cape Wrath★★★ (≤★★) W : 44 mi (including ferry crossing) by A 838 – Ben Loyal★★, S : 8 mi by A 836 – Ben Hope★ (≤★★★) SW : 15 mi by A 838 – Strathy Point★ (≤★★★) E : 22 mi by A 836 – Torrisdale Bay★ (≤★★) NE : 8 mi by A 836

Tongue

Main St ✉ *IV27 4XD – ☏ (01847) 611 206 – www.tonguehotel.co.uk – Closed 24 December-14 March*
18 rm ☕ – 🚹£ 65/70 🚹🚹£ 110/130
Rest – *(bar lunch)* Menu £ 30 (dinner) – Carte £ 23/34
◆ Fiercely Scottish former hunting lodge overlooking the Kyle of Tongue; Highland shooting and fishing memorabilia abounds. Snug, open-fired lounge and contemporary bedrooms. Snacks served in linen-laid bars; classical menus of local ingredients in dining room.

TORRIDON – Highland – 501 D11 – ✉ Achnasheen Scotland 29 B2

Edinburgh 234 mi – Inverness 62 mi – Kyle of Lochalsh 44 mi

Wester Ross★★★

The Torridon
South : 1.5 mi on A 896 ✉ IV22 2EY – ☎ (01445) 791 242 – www.thetorridon.com – Closed January
18 rm (dinner included) – †£ 153/295 ††£ 430/505 – 1 suite
Rest – *(bar lunch) (booking essential)* Menu £ 45 – Carte lunch £ 20/28
◆ Family-owned and run former hunting lodge; remotely set, with wonderful views of Loch Torridon and mountains. Ornate ceilings, peat fires and Highland curios. Some very contemporary bedrooms; others more classic in style. Traditional wood-panelled restaurant uses fine local produce, some from the grounds.

Torridon Inn
South : 1.5 mi on A 896 ✉ IV22 2EY – ☎ (01445) 791 242 – www.thetorridon.com – Closed January
12 rm – †£ 87 ††£ 87, £ 6.50 **Rest** – Carte £ 23/27
◆ Peaceful, rural location in grounds of Torridon House. Spacious, functional bedrooms in annexe; the larger ones ideal for families. Characterful, rustic restaurant serving classic pub dishes.

TROON – South Ayrshire – 501 G17 – pop. 14 766 — 25 A2

Edinburgh 77 mi – Ayr 7 mi – Glasgow 31 mi
to Northern Ireland (Larne) (P and O Irish Sea) 2 daily
Troon Municipal Harling Drive, ☎ (01292) 312 464

Lochgreen House
Monktonhill Rd, Southwood, Southeast : 2 mi on B 749 ✉ KA10 7EN – ☎ (01292) 313 343 – www.costley-hotels.co.uk
37 rm – †£ 145/160 ††£ 190/205 – 1 suite
Rest *Tapestry* – see restaurant listing
◆ Attractive, coastal Edwardian house in mature grounds. Lounges exude luxurious country house feel. Large rooms, modern or traditional, have a good eye for welcoming detail.

Tapestry – at Lochgreen House Hotel
Monktonhill Rd, Southwood, Southeast : 2 mi on B 749 ✉ KA10 7EN – ☎ (01292) 313 343
Rest – Menu £ 23/35 – Carte £ 35/50
◆ Spacious dining room with baronial feel. Elegant chandeliers; large pottery cockerels. Classical, modern cooking, with a strong Scottish base.

at Loans East : 2 mi on A 759 – ✉ Troon

Highgrove House
Old Loans Rd, East : 0.25 mi on Dundonald rd ✉ KA10 7HL – ☎ (01292) 312 511 – www.costleyhotels.co.uk
9 rm – †£ 69 ††£ 110 **Rest** – Carte £ 20/36
◆ Immaculate whitewashed hotel in elevated position, offering superb coastal panorama. Comfy floral bedrooms; 1 and 2 have the best views. Tartan carpets remind you where you are. Large restaurant with floor to ceiling windows and granite columns.

TURNBERRY – South Ayrshire – 501 F18 – ✉ Girvan Scotland — 25 A2

Edinburgh 97 mi – Ayr 15 mi – Glasgow 51 mi – Stranraer 36 mi
Culzean Castle★ **AC** (setting★★★, Oval Staircase★★) NE : 5 mi by A 719

Turnberry rm, rest,
on A 719 ✉ KA26 9LT – ☎ (01655) 331 000 – www.luxurycollection.com/turnberry
207 rm – †£ 395 ††£ 415 – 4 suites
Rest *1906* – *(dinner only)* Carte £ 39/47
Rest *Tappie Toorie* – *(lunch only)* Carte £ 24/31
Rest *Ailsa Bar and Lounge* – Carte £ 23/29
◆ This celebrated Edwardian hotel with panoramic views of the coast and world famous golf courses was fully refurbished in 2009. Extensive spa facilities; luxuriously appointed bedrooms. Classic brasserie in 1906. Informal Tappie Toorie Grill for golfers. All-day dining in Ailsa.

SCOTLAND

UDNY GREEN - Aberdeenshire **28** D1

London - 554 mi – Edinburgh 143 mi – Aberdeen 15 mi – Arbroath 67 mi

Eat on the Green

AB41 7RS – (01651) 842 337 – www.eatonthegreen.co.uk – Closed Monday, Tuesday and Saturday lunch

Rest – Menu £ 24 (lunch)/49 (Saturday dinner) – Carte dinner £ 32/43

◆ Converted pub by the village green, with snug seating area and two smart dining rooms. Accomplished, flavourful dishes make good use of seasonal, local produce. Polished service.

UIST (Isles of) - 501 X/Y11 - pop. 3 510

from Lochmaddy to Isle of Skye (Uig) (Caledonian MacBrayne Ltd) 1-3 daily (1 h 50 mn) – from Otternish to Isle of Harris (Leverburgh) (Caledonian MacBrayne Ltd) (1 h 10 mn)

NORTH UIST - Western Isles **29** A2

London 639 mi – Edinburgh 254 mi

CARINISH - Western Isles **29** A2

Temple View

HS6 5EJ – (01876) 580 676 – www.templeviewhotel.co.uk

10 rm – £ 55/75 £ 105

Rest – *(bar lunch)* Menu £ 23 (dinner) **s** – Carte £ 16/26 **s**

◆ Victorian house with uncluttered interior and modern yet homely style. Small bar, sitting room and sun lounge. Simple, comfortable bedrooms with moor views to rear and sea/13C ruins of Trinity Temple to front. Cosy dining room offers popular seafood specials.

LANGASS - Western Isles

Langass Lodge

rm,

HS6 5HA – (01876) 580 285 – www.langasslodge.co.uk – Closed 1 January, February and 25 December

12 rm – £ 65 £ 110 **Rest** – *(dinner only)* Menu £ 35

◆ Former Victorian shooting lodge nestled in heather-strewn hills and boasting distant loch views. Characterful bedrooms in main house; more modern, spacious rooms with good views in wing. Eat in comfy bar or linen-clad dining room from simple, seafood based menu.

LOCHMADDY - Western Isles **29** A2

Tigh Dearg

rm,

HS6 5AE – (01876) 500 700 – www.tighdearghotel.co.uk – Closed 24 December-10 January

9 rm – £ 79/109 £ 89/149

Rest – *(closed lunch September-April)* Carte £ 17/35

◆ Stylish hotel with sleek, boutique style. Well-equipped gym, sauna and steam room. Chic, modern bedrooms offer good facilities. Forward-thinking owner continually reinvests. Smart bar and dining room; menus display plenty of seafood. Bikes available for hire.

ULLAPOOL - Highland - 501 E10 - pop. 1 308 Scotland **30** C2

Edinburgh 215 mi – Inverness 59 mi

to Isle of Lewis (Stornoway) (Caledonian MacBrayne Ltd) (2 h 40 mn)

20 Argyle St (0845) 2255121, ullapool@visitscotland.com

Town★

Wester Ross★★★ - Loch Broom★★. Falls of Measach★★, S : 11 mi by A 835 and A 832 - Corrieshalloch Gorge★, SE : 10 mi by A 835 – Northwards to Lochinver★★, Morefield (★★ of Ullapool), ★ Loch Broom

Point Cottage without rest 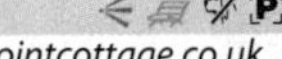
22 West Shore St ✉ IV26 2UR – ☎ (01854) 612 494 – www.pointcottage.co.uk – March-October
3 rm ☕ – 🚹£ 40/70 🚹🚹£ 60/80
◆ 18C converted fisherman's cottage on the shores on Loch Broom, not far from the ferry terminal. Simple, homely interior; cosy, floral bedrooms boast lovely views. Snug sitting room is filled with oil paintings, locals maps and guides. Friendly, chatty owner.

 **Ardvreck** without rest 
Morefield Brae, Northwest : 2 mi by A 835 ✉ IV26 2TH – ☎ (01854) 612 028 – www.smoothhound.co.uk/hotels/ardvreck – March -November
10 rm ☕ – 🚹£ 35/70 🚹🚹£ 72/80
◆ Modern house set away from the town centre, affording amazing views over the loch and mountains. Bedrooms are fresh and up-to-date; local watercolours feature. Friendly, accommodating owner.

UNST (Isle of) – **Shetland Islands** – **501** R1 – **see Shetland Islands**

URQUHART – **Moray** – **see Elgin**

VEENSGARTH – **Shetland Islands** – **see Shetland Islands (Mainland)**

WALKERBURN – **Scottish Borders** – **pop. 647** **26** C2

▶ Edinburgh 30 mi – Galashiels 23 mi – Peebles 8 mi

Windlestraw Lodge
on A 72 ✉ EH43 6AA – ☎ (01896) 870 636 – www.windlestraw.co.uk – Closed 1 week June, Christmas-New Year
6 rm ☕ – 🚹£ 99 🚹🚹£ 176 **Rest** – *(dinner only)* Menu £ 46
◆ Attractive Arts and Crafts property built in 1906, boasting original fireplaces, old plaster ceilings and great valley views. Stylish, tastefully modernised bedrooms. Comfy bar, plush lounge and attractive, wood-panelled dining room offering daily changing menu.

WATERNISH – **Highland** – **501** A11 – **see Skye (Isle of)**

WESTRAY (Isle of) – **Orkney Islands** – **501** K/L6 – **see Orkney Islands**

WICK – **Highland** – **501** K8 – **pop. 9 713** Scotland **30** D1

▶ Edinburgh 282 mi – Inverness 126 mi

✈ Wick Airport : ☎ (01955) 602215, N : 1 m

ℹ Whitechapel Rd ☎ (0845) 2255121, info@visitscotland.com

⛳18 Reiss, ☎ (01955) 602 726

Duncansby Head★ (Stacks of Duncansby★★) N : 14 mi by A 9 – Grey Cairns of Camster★ (Long Cairn★★) S : 17 mi by A 9 – The Hill O'Many Stanes★, S : 10 mi by A 9

 **Clachan** without rest
13 Randolph Pl, South Rd, South : 0.75 mi on A 99 ✉ KW1 5NJ – ☎ (01955) 605 384 – www.theclachan.co.uk – Closed Christmas-New Year
3 rm ☕ – 🚹£ 45/55 🚹🚹£ 60/65
◆ Detached house on edge of town, in an area formerly housing herring workers during the 1930s. Rebuilt and having undergone a contemporary makeover, it now boasts stylish, modern bedrooms and a smart breakfast room hung with period photos. Accommodating owner.

 **Bord De L'Eau** VISA
2 Market St (Riverside) ✉ KW1 4AR – ☎ (01955) 604 400 – Closed first 2 weeks January, 25-26 December, Sunday lunch and Monday
Rest – French – Carte £ 22/36
◆ Long-standing riverside bistro with simple dining room and conservatory. Framed Eiffel Tower prints and French posters on the walls. Authentic, classic Gallic dishes; plenty of local seafood.

Y. Duhamel/MICHELIN

ABERAERON (Aber Aeron) – Ceredigion – 503 H27 – pop. 1 520 — 33 B3

Cardiff 90 mi – Aberystwyth 16 mi – Fishguard 41 mi

Ty Mawr Mansion Country House

Cilcennin, East : 4.5 mi by A 482 ✉ SA48 8DB – ☎ (01570) 470 033 – www.tymawrmansion.co.uk – Closed 1-17 January

8 rm – †£ 110/180 ††£ 160/220 – 1 suite

Rest – *(Closed Sunday) (dinner only)* Menu £ 25 – Carte £ 35/44

◆ Grade II listed Georgian stone mansion in 12 acres of grounds. Three sumptuous reception rooms matched by luxurious bedrooms, which are oversized and full of top facilities. Chefs rear pigs for locally renowned restaurant boasting bold edge to cooking.

Llys Aeron without rest

Lampeter Rd, on A 482 ✉ SA46 0ED – ☎ (01545) 570 276 – www.llysaeron.co.uk

3 rm – †£ 45/70 ††£ 75/105

◆ Imposing Georgian house on main road. Hearty Aga cooked breakfasts overlooking well-established, rear-walled garden. Comfy lounge and light, airy bedrooms in clean pastel shades.

3 Pen Cei without rest

3 Quay Par ✉ SA46 0BT – ☎ (01545) 571 147 – www.pencei.co.uk – Closed 25-26 December

5 rm – †£ 80/85 ††£ 95/140

◆ Brightly painted, modern-style guest house on harbourfront, featuring spacious bedrooms named after nearby rivers. Aeron has bathroom with free-standing bath and large walk-in shower.

Harbourmaster with rm

Quay Par ✉ SA46 0BA – ☎ (01545) 570 755 – www.harbour-master.com – Closed 25 December

13 rm – †£ 60 ††£ 230/250

Rest – Carte £ 19/38

◆ Vibrant blue pub with modern bar-lounge, traditional dining room and lovely harbour views. Choice of bar snacks, set price lunch or more substantial evening à la carte and daily specials. Comfy, brightly decorated bedrooms; some boast huge windows or terraces.

ABERDOVEY (Aberdyfi) – Gwynedd – 503 H26 – pop. 869 — 32 B2

London 230 mi – Dolgellau 25 mi – Shrewsbury 66 mi

Snowdonia National Park★★★

Llety Bodfor without rest

Bodfor Ter ✉ LL35 0EA – ☎ (01654) 767 475 – www.lletybodfor.co.uk – Closed December

9 rm – †£ 50/140 ††£ 135/160

◆ Two 19C seafront houses, now a guest house with a difference: a relaxed atmosphere prevails but the design is stylish and contemporary. Spacious New England themed bedrooms boast bay views.

at Pennal Northeast : 6.5 mi on A 493 – ✉ Aberdovey

Penmaendyfi without rest

Cwrt, Southwest : 1.25 mi by A 493 ✉ SY20 9LD – ☎ (01654) 791 246 – www.penmaendyfi.co.uk – March-September

6 rm – †£ 60/80 ††£ 80/100

◆ Attractive 18C country house in quiet rural location, with distant estuary views, beautiful wooden veranda and comfy lounge. Spacious bedrooms boast sleigh beds and smart modern bathrooms.

ABERGAVENNY (Y-Fenni) – Monmouthshire – 503 L28 — 33 C4
– pop. 14 055

London 163 mi – Cardiff 31 mi – Gloucester 43 mi – Newport 19 mi

Swan Meadow, Monmouth Rd ☎ (01873) 853254, abergavennyic@breconbeacons.org

Monmouthshire Llanfoist, ☎ (01873) 852 606

Town★ - St Mary's Church★ (Monuments★★)

Brecon Beacons National Park★★ – Blaenavon Ironworks★, SW : 5 mi by A 465 and B 4246. Raglan Castle★ **AC**, SE : 9 mi by A 40

Llansantffraed Court

Llanvihangel Gobion, Southeast : 6.5 mi by A 40 and B 4598 off old Raglan rd
✉ NP7 9BA – ☎ (01873) 840 678 – www.llch.co.uk
21 rm – †£ 90/120 ††£ 120/175
Rest – Menu £ 15/30 – Carte £ 30/37

♦ Historic country house beside ornamental pond and fountain, in 19 acres of grounds. Large lounges and bar. Dark-hued bedrooms with smart bathrooms: room 19 has double aspect mountain/valley views. Classical menus showcase local ingredients.

Angel

15 Cross St ✉ NP7 5EN – ☎ (01873) 857 121
– www.angelhotelabergavenny.com – Closed 25 December
32 rm – †£ 74/80 ††£ 96/190
Rest – Carte £ 22/37 **s**

♦ Georgian former coaching inn run by friendly, attentive team. Smart exterior and very modern guest areas: traditionally styled bedrooms undergoing refurbishment. Contemporary bar and restaurant with courtyard offer extensive bistro menu and popular afternoon teas.

The Hardwick with rm

Old Raglan Rd, Southeast : 2 mi by A 40 on B 4598 ✉ NP7 9AA – ☎ (01873) 854 220 – www.thehardwick.co.uk
8 rm – †£ 95 ††£ 160
Rest – *(booking essential)* Menu £ 24 (lunch) – Carte £ 27/40

♦ Unassuming whitewashed pub overlooking the mountains. Extensive menus, with dishes ranging from 21-day dry aged steak to 'a taste of local beef' for two. Simplicity is key and the use of seasonal, local produce is paramount. Contemporary bedrooms boast king-sized beds, DVD players and iPod docks.

at Llanddewi Skirrid Northeast : 3.25 mi on B 4521

The Walnut Tree (Shaun Hill)

✉ NP7 8AW – ☎ (01873) 852 797 – www.thewalnuttreeinn.com – Closed 1 week Christmas, Sunday and Monday
Rest – *(booking essential)* Menu £ 25 (lunch) – Carte £ 35/42
Spec. Scallops with lentil and coriander sauce. Turbot braised with clams. Chilled cherry soup with roast hazelnuts.

♦ A reinvigorated, long-standing Welsh institution set in a valley. Welcoming staff and always bustling with regulars. It takes skill to make cooking look this simple; it's seasonal and each dish bursts with flavour.

at Cross Ash Northeast : 8.25 mi on B 4521

1861

✉ NP7 8PB – ☎ (0845) 388 1861 – www.18-61.co.uk – Closed first 2 weeks January, Sunday dinner and Monday
Rest – Menu £ 24/32 – Carte £ 24/45

♦ Former pub; now a cosy restaurant, with contemporary furnishings and exposed brick fireplace. Classically based menus make use of good quality local produce. Personable service.

at Nant-Y-Derry Southeast : 6.5 mi by A 40 off A 4042 – ✉ Abergavenny

The Foxhunter

Nant-y-Derry ✉ NP7 9DD – ✆ (01873) 881 101 – www.thefoxhunter.com – Closed Sunday dinner and Monday
Rest – Menu £ 24 – Carte £ 28/35
♦ Former station master's house with fresh, bright feel, flagstone floors and wood burning stoves. Dishes range in style from classic British to fusion and come in large, hearty portions.

at Llanover South : 5.5 mi by A 40 off A 4042

Llansabbath Country House without rest

✉ NP7 9BY – ✆ (01873) 840 068 – www.llansabbathcountryhouse.co.uk
5 rm – †£ 55 ††£ 85/110
♦ Former farmhouse renovated in a modern style. Large lounge with wood burning stove; conservatory breakfast with eggs from hens who roam the garden. Comfortable bedrooms have all mod cons.

ABERGELE – Conwy – 503 J24 – pop. 17 574 — 32 C1

London 229 mi – Cardiff 182 mi – Liverpool 51 mi – Manchester 75 mi

at Betws-yn-Rhos Southwest : 4.25 mi by A 548 on B 5381

Ffarm Country House

✉ LL22 8AR – ✆ (01492) 680 448 – www.ffarmcountryhouse.co.uk – Closed 1 week Christmas
8 rm – †£ 69/87 ††£ 79/135
Rest – *(dinner only Friday and Saturday)* Menu £ 28
♦ Gothic-style country house; stylish, comfortable and personally run. Beautiful tiled hall with vaulted wood ceiling. Tastefully furnished bedrooms named after wine regions. Seasonal menus make the most of local produce; open to non-residents as well as guests.

ABERSOCH – Gwynedd – 502 G25 – pop. 805 – ✉ Pwllheli — 32 B2

London 265 mi – Caernarfon 28 mi – Shrewsbury 101 mi
Golf Rd, ✆ (01758) 712 636
Lleyn Peninsula★★ – Plas-yn-Rhiw★ AC, W : 6 mi by minor roads. Bardsey Island★, SW : 15 mi by A 499 and B 4413 – Mynydd Mawr★, SW : 17 mi by A 499, B 4413 and minor roads

Venetia with rm

Lon Sarn Bach ✉ LL53 7EB – ✆ (01758) 713 354 – www.venetiawales.com – Closed 1 January-10 February and 25-26 December
5 rm – †£ 103/133 ††£ 118/148
Rest – Italian – *(dinner only)* Carte £ 25/35
♦ Smart, modernised detached house boasts minimalist bar/lounge and stark white dining room. Classic Italian dishes, well presented in a distinctly modern style, with fish a speciality. Friendly, efficient service. Comfortable, well-equipped bedrooms.

at Bwlchtocyn South : 2 mi – ✉ Pwllheli

Porth Tocyn

✉ LL53 7BU – ✆ (01758) 713 303 – www.porth-tocyn-hotel.co.uk – April-October
17 rm – †£ 70/170 ††£ 95/170, £ 6.50
Rest – *(bar lunch Monday-Saturday, buffet lunch Sunday)* Menu £ 40
♦ Set high on the headland overlooking Cardigan Bay, a traditional hotel in the family for three generations. Comfy lounges. Mix of classic and more modern bedrooms; some with balconies/sea views. Modern menus display interesting, soundly executed dishes.

WALES

ABERYSTWYTH (Aberestuuth) – **Ceredigion** – **503** H26 **32** B2 – **pop. 15 935**

London 238 mi – Chester 98 mi – Fishguard 58 mi – Shrewsbury 74 mi

Terrace Rd (01970) 612125, aberystwythtic@ceredigion.gov.uk

Bryn-y-Mor, (01970) 615 104

Town★★ - The Seafront★ – National Library of Wales (Permanent Exhibition★)

Vale of Rheidol★★ (Railway★★ **AC**) - St Padarn's Church★, SE : 1 mi by A 44. Devil's Bridge (Pontarfynach)★, E : 12 mi by A 4120 – Strata Florida Abbey★ **AC** (West Door★), SE : 15 mi by B 4340 and minor rd

Gwesty Cymru

19 Marine Ter ✉ SY23 2AZ – (01970) 612 252 – www.gwestycymru.com – Closed 23-28 December

8 rm – †£ 65/155 ††£ 87/155

Rest – Carte £ 24/36

♦ Georgian Grade II listed building on promenade, with front terrace and sea views. Thoughtfully designed bedrooms are colour-themed in décor and furnishings; impressive bathrooms. Small dining room serves traditional dishes made from local produce.

ANGLESEY (Isle of) (Sir Ynys Môn) – **Isle of Anglesey** – **503** G/H24 **32** B1 – **pop. 68 900**

London 270 mi – Cardiff 205 mi – Liverpool 92 mi – Birkenhead 86 mi

Beaumaris – **Isle of Anglesey** – ✉ **Isle Of Anglesey** **32** B1

London 253 mi – Birkenhead 74 mi – Holyhead 25 mi

Baron Hill, (01248) 810 231

Town★★ - Castle★ **AC**

Anglesey★★ – Penmon Priory★, NE : 4 mi by B 5109 and minor roads. Plas Newydd★ **AC**, SW : 7 mi by A 545 and A 4080

Ye Olde Bull's Head Inn

Castle St ✉ LL58 8AP – (01248) 810 329 – www.bullsheadinn.co.uk – Closed 24-25 December

13 rm – †£ 85/90 ††£ 110/115

Rest *Loft* – see restaurant listing

Rest *Brasserie* – *(bookings not accepted)* Carte £ 17/28

♦ Welcoming 17C coaching inn; its characterful, beamed bar a marked contrast to the chic, stylish lounge. Bedrooms, named after Dickens' characters, also mix the traditional with the contemporary. The Brasserie offers a wide-ranging menu with a Mediterranean slant.

Townhouse without rest

10 Castle St ✉ LL58 8AP – (01248) 810 329 – www.townhousewales.co.uk – Closed 24-25 December

13 rm – †£ 80/90 ††£ 110/115

♦ Stylish 16C townhouse, with striking bedrooms boasting an extensive range of modern facilities, including media hubs. Comprehensive continental breakfast served in your room.

Cleifiog without rest

Townsend ✉ LL58 8BH – (01248) 811 507 – www.cleifiogbandb.co.uk – Closed Christmas-New Year

3 rm – †£ 65 ††£ 100

♦ Attractively furnished 16C seafront townhouse, with neat garden and lovely outlook. Owner's art and needlework feature throughout, along with antique tapestries. Great levels of comfort.

XX **Loft** – at Ye Olde Bull's Head Inn
Castle St ✉ LL58 8AP – ✆ (01248) 810 329 – www.bullsheadinn.co.uk – Closed 25 December and 1 January
Rest – *(closed Sunday and Monday) (dinner only)* Menu £ 40
◆ Stylish, contemporary restaurant with exposed beams, bold crimson end walls and linen-clad tables. Well-presented, ambitious cooking uses many local ingredients. Efficient service.

BENLLECH – Isle of Anglesey – ✉ Isle Of Anglesey 32 B1

Hafod without rest
Amlwch Rd ✉ LL74 8SR – ✆ (01248) 853 092 – Closed 25 December
4 rm – †£ 50 ††£ 66
◆ Sensitively renovated 19C house with pleasant lawned garden and views of the sea and local bays. Comfortably finished bedrooms are well-maintained by the charming owner.

CEMAES (Cemais) – Isle of Anglesey – ✉ Isle Of Anglesey 32 B1

Hafod Country House without rest
South : 0.5 mi on Llanfechell rd ✉ LL67 ODS – ✆ (01407) 711 645 – www.anglesey-countryhouse.co.uk – April-September
3 rm – †£ 45 ††£ 75
◆ Pleasant Edwardian guesthouse with very welcoming owner, set on the outskirts of a picturesque fishing village. Comfortable sitting room. Neat, tidy bedrooms that are immaculately kept.

WALES

LLANERCHYMEDD – Isle of Anglesey – ✉ Isle Of Anglesey 32 B1

Llwydiarth Fawr without rest
North : 1 mi on B 5111 ✉ LL71 8DF – ✆ (01248) 470 321 – www.llwydiarthfawr.com
4 rm – †£ 45/65 ††£ 85/100
◆ Sizeable Georgian house in 1,000 acres of farmland. Country house feel with impressive hallway/landing, plush drawing room and fine views. Individually decorated bedrooms boast extras.

MENAI BRIDGE (Porthaethwy) – Isle of Anglesey – ✉ Isle Of Anglesey 32 B1

Neuadd Lwyd
Penmynydd, Northwest : 4.75 mi by B 5420 on Eglwys St Gredifael Church rd ✉ LL61 5BX – ✆ (01248) 715 005 – www.neuaddlwyd.co.uk – Closed 28 November-20 January
4 rm (dinner included) – †£ 145/205 ††£ 195/255 **Rest** – Menu £ 42
◆ This fine 19C rectory, set in a beautiful rural location, has had a sleek and stylish refit, lending it a luxurious air. Elegant interiors are matched by stunning bedrooms. Freshest Welsh ingredients incorporated into tasty evening meals.

RHOSCOLYN – Isle of Anglesey – ✉ Isle Of Anglesey

The White Eagle
✉ LL65 2NJ – ✆ (01407) 860 267 – www.white-eagle.co.uk
Rest – Carte £ 20/37
◆ Spacious pub with cosy bar, modern dining room, decked terrace and sea views. Monthly menu offers everything from sandwiches and salads, to pub classics and more sophisticated fare.

VALLEY – Isle of Anglesey – ✉ Isle Of Anglesey

Cleifiog Uchaf
off Spencer Rd ✉ LL65 3AB – ✆ (01407) 741 888 – www.cleifioguchaf.co.uk
6 rm – †£ 69/79 ††£ 95/145 – 2 suites
Rest – *(Closed Sunday and Monday) (dinner only)* Carte £ 23/45
◆ Restored 16C longhouse, simply and stylishly furnished. Bedrooms boast character beds and every mod con including flat screens, DVDs and Roberts radios. Slate-floored, bistro-style dining room for classical combinations of locally sourced, seasonal ingredients.

BALA – Gwynedd – pop. 1 980 – ✉ Gwynedd 32 B2

London - 213 mi – Cardiff 160 mi – Liverpool 75 mi – Stoke-on-Trent 84 mi

Abercelyn Country House without rest

Llanycil, Southwest : 1 mi on A 494 ✉ LL23 7YF – ☎ (01678) 521 109 – www.abercelyn.co.uk – February-October

3 rm – 🛉£ 60 🛉🛉£ 90

◆ Attractive former rectory, with pleasant garden and brook. Warmly decorated bedrooms, named after surrounding mountains. Eggs from owners' hens, plus homemade jams and breads.

BARMOUTH (Abermaw) – Gwynedd – 502 H25 – pop. 2 306 32 B2

London 231 mi – Chester 74 mi – Dolgellau 10 mi – Shrewsbury 67 mi

The Station, Station Rd ☎ (01341) 280787, (summer only) barmouth.tic@gwynedd.gov.uk

Town★ - Bridge★ **AC**

Snowdonia National Park★★★

Llwyndu Farmhouse

Northwest : 2.25 mi on A 496 ✉ LL42 1RR – ☎ (01341) 280 144 – www.llwyndu-farmhouse.co.uk – Closed 24-26 December

7 rm – 🛉£ 65 🛉🛉£ 94/110

Rest – Menu £ 29

◆ Grade II listed 16C farmhouse below the Rhinog Mountains, overlooking Cardigan Bay. Traditional beams, inglenooks and quirky, characterful features abound. Using quality Welsh produce, candlelit dinners combine the traditional with the modern.

BEAUMARIS – Isle of Anglesey – 504 H24 – see Anglesey (Isle of)

BEDDGELERT (Bedkelerd) – Gwynedd – 502 H24 – pop. 535 32 B1

London 249 mi – Caernarfon 13 mi – Chester 73 mi

Snowdonia National Park★★★ - Aberglaslyn Pass★, S : 1.5 mi on A 498

Sygun Fawr Country House

Northeast : 0.75 mi by A 498 ✉ LL55 4NE – ☎ (01766) 890 258 – www.sygunfawr.co.uk – Closed 2 January - 11 February

12 rm – 🛉£ 40/60 🛉🛉£ 105

Rest – *(closed Monday) (dinner only) (booking essential)* Carte £ 19/25

◆ Part-16C stone-built house in Gwynant Valley. Superbly located, an elevated spot which affords exceptional views of Snowdon, particularly from double deluxe rooms. Dine in conservatory extension or traditional room in house.

BENLLECH – Isle of Anglesey – 502 H24 – see Anglesey (Isle of)

BETWS GARMON – Gwynedd 32 B1

Cardiff 194 mi – Betws-y-Coed 25 mi – Caernarfon 5 mi

Betws Inn

Northwest : 1 mi on A 4085 ✉ LL54 7YY – ☎ (01286) 650 324 – www.betws-inn.co.uk

3 rm – 🛉£ 60/80 🛉🛉£ 70/85

Rest – Menu £ 25

◆ Former village coaching inn with characterful beamed lounge. After a day's trekking, sleep in well-priced, good-sized rooms with quality wood furniture and smart fabrics. Home-cooked local produce proudly served in rustic dining room.

BETWS-Y-COED – Conwy – 502 I24 – pop. 848 32 B1

London 226 mi – Holyhead 44 mi – Shrewsbury 62 mi

Royal Oak Stables ✆ (01690) 710426, tic.byc@eryri-npa.gov.uk

Clubhouse, ✆ (01690) 710 556

Town★

Snowdonia National Park★★★. Blaenau Ffestiniog★ (Llechwedd Slate Caverns★ **AC**), SW : 10.5 mi by A 470 – The Glyders and Nant Ffrancon (Cwm Idwal★), W : 14 mi by A 5

Tan-y-Foel Country House

East : 2.5 mi by A 5, A 470 and Capel Garmon rd on Llanwrst rd ✉ LL26 ORE – ✆ (01690) 710 507 – www.tyfhotel.co.uk – restricted opening mid-December-January

6 rm – †£ 95/140 ††£ 155/195 **Rest** – *(dinner only)* Carte approx. £ 48

◆ Personally run, part-16C country house, stylishly decorated in modern vein. Stunning views of Vale of Conwy and Snowdonia. Lovely rooms revel in the quality and elegance of the establishment. Contemporary rear room makes up the restaurant.

Bryn Bella without rest

Lôn Muriau, Llanrwst Rd, Northeast : 1 mi by A 5 on A 470 ✉ LL24 0HD – ✆ (01690) 710 627 – www.bryn-bella.co.uk

5 rm – †£ 75 ††£ 80

◆ Comfy, well-kept guesthouse with pleasant garden, valley views and every conceivable extra in the bedrooms. Keen owners provide reliable local info. Fresh, tasty eggs from their rescued hens.

Pengwern without rest

Allt Dinas, Southeast : 1.5 mi on A 5 ✉ LL24 0HF – ✆ (01690) 710 480 – www.snowdoniaaccommodation.co.uk – Closed 1 week Christmas

3 rm – †£ 60/70 ††£ 72/82

◆ Former Victorian artist 'colony' with a comfy, homely and stylish lounge, warmly decorated breakfast room and individually appointed bedrooms, two with superb valley vistas.

at Penmachno Southwest : 4.75 mi by A 5 on B 4406 – ✉ Betws-Y-Coed

Penmachno Hall

on Ty Mawr rd ✉ LL24 0PU – ✆ (01690) 760 410 – www.penmachnohall.co.uk – Closed Christmas-New Year

3 rm – †£ 85/95 ††£ 95 **Rest** – *(set menu only)* Menu £ 35

◆ Former rectory built in 1862 with neat garden; super country setting. Sunny morning room where breakfast is served. Modern, bright bedrooms personally styled by the owners. Tasty home-cooking in deep burgundy communal dining room.

BETWS-YN-RHOS – Conwy – 502 J24 – see Abergele

BODUAN – Gwynedd – see Pwllheli

BONVILSTON (Tresimwn) – The Vale of Glamorgan – 503 J29 33 C4

London 164 mi – Cardiff 9 mi – Swansea 25 mi

Great Barn without rest

Lillypot, Northwest : 1 mi by A 48 off Tre-Dodridge rd ✉ CF5 6TR – ✆ (01446) 781 010 – www.greatbarn.com

6 rm – †£ 38/42 ††£ 70/75

◆ Converted corn barn, personally run in simple country home style. Pleasant antiques, pine and white furniture in rooms. Great traditional breakfasts; relax in conservatory.

BRECON – Powys – **503** J28 – **pop. 7 901** **33** C3

London 171 mi – Cardiff 40 mi – Carmarthen 31 mi – Gloucester 65 mi

Cattle Market Car Park ✆ (01874) 622485, brectic@powys.gov.uk

Cradoc, Penoyre Park, ✆ (01874) 623 658

Newton Park Llanfaes, ✆ (01874) 622 004

Town★ - Cathedral★ **AC** – Penyclawdd Court★

Brecon Beacons National Park★★. Llanthony Priory★★, S : 8 mi of Hay-on-Wye by B 4423 - Dan-yr-Ogof Showcaves★ **AC**, SW : 20 mi by A 40 and A 4067 – Pen-y-Fan★★, SW : by A 470

Canal Bank without rest

Southeast : 0.5 mi by B 4601 turning right over bridge onto unmarked road after petrol station ✉ LD3 7HG – ✆ (01874) 623 464 – www.accommodation-breconbeacons.co.uk

3 rm – ♦£ 50/90 ♦♦£ 95

♦ Delightfully stylish and peaceful 18C canalside cottage. Charming garden with pergola and access to River Usk. Organic breakfasts. Immaculate rooms with extra attention to detail.

Cantre Selyf without rest

5 Lion St ✉ LD3 7AU – ✆ (01874) 622 904 – www.cantreselyf.co.uk – Closed Christmas and New Year

3 rm – ♦£ 60 ♦♦£ 85

♦ Charming, centrally located 17C townhouse with peaceful garden, period bedrooms and modern shower rooms. Contemporary colours blend with original Georgian features and antiques throughout.

Felin Glais

Aberyscir, West : 4 mi by Upper Chapel rd off Cradoc Golf Course rd turning right immediately after bridge ✉ LD3 9NP – ✆ (01874) 623 107 – www.felinglais.co.uk

4 rm – ♦£ 80 ♦♦£ 90

Rest – Menu £ 38

♦ 17C house and barn in tranquil hamlet. Spacious interior with pleasant 'lived in' feel; rooms filled with books and knick-knacks. Homely bedrooms; good toiletries; towels/bedding from Harrods. Lengthy menu of modern classics: order dinner two days ahead.

The Felin Fach Griffin with rm

Felin Fach, Northeast : 4.75 mi by B 4602 off A 470 ✉ LD3 0UB – ✆ (01874) 620 111 – www.felinfachgriffin.co.uk – Closed 24-25 December

7 rm – ♦£ 75/85 ♦♦£ 100/120

Rest – Menu £ 19/27 – Carte £ 22/35

♦ Rather unique pub with extremely laid back atmosphere. Following the motto "simple things, done well", dishes are straightforward, tasty and arrive in refined, well presented portions. Bedrooms boast super-comfy beds and excellent bedding.

BRIDGEND (Pen-y-Bont) – Bridgend – **503** J29 – **pop. 39 429** **33** B4

London 177 mi – Cardiff 20 mi – Swansea 23 mi

Bridgend Designer Outlet Village, The Derwen, junction 36, M 4 ✆ (01656) 654906, bridgendtic@bridgend.gov.uk

at Laleston West : 2 mi on A 473 – ✉ **Bridgend**

Great House

High St, on A 473 ✉ CF32 0HP – ✆ (01656) 657 644 – www.great-house-laleston.co.uk

12 rm – ♦£ 85/95 ♦♦£ 150

Rest *Leicester's* – *(Closed Sunday dinner and bank holiday Mondays)*
Menu £ 13 (lunch)/20 – Carte £ 29/46

♦ 15C Grade II listed building, believed to have been a gift from Elizabeth I to the Earl of Leicester. Personally run – attention to detail particularly evident in the bedrooms. Comfortable dining; imaginative, seasonal menus use fine local produce.

BWLCHTOCYN – Gwynedd – 502 G25 – see Abersoch

CAERNARFON – Gwynedd – 502 H24 – pop. 9 726 **32** B1

London 249 mi – Birkenhead 76 mi – Chester 68 mi – Holyhead 30 mi
Oriel Pendeitsh, Castle St. ✆ (01286) 672232, caernarfon.tic@gwynedd.gov.uk
Aberforeshore Llanfaglan, ✆ (01286) 673 783
Town★★ - Castle★★★ **AC**
Snowdonia National Park★★★

Plas Dinas

South : 2 mi on A 487 ✉ LL54 7YF – ✆ (01286) 830 214 – www.plasdinas.co.uk – Closed Christmas and New Year
10 rm – †£ 89/119 ††£ 169/179
Rest – *(Closed Sunday and Monday) (dinner only) (residents only)* Menu £ 30
♦ Personally run country house: the family home of Lord Snowdon; antiques and portraits abound. Bedrooms range from the simply furnished to a four-poster suite; some are more contemporary, with striking feature walls. Small, regularly changing menu of home-cooked dishes.

at Seion **Northeast : 5.5 mi by A 4086 and B 4366 on Seion rd – ✉ Gwynedd**

Ty'n Rhos Country House with rm

Southwest : 0.25 mi ✉ LL55 3AE – ✆ (01248) 670 489 – www.tynrhos.co.uk
14 rm – †£ 65/120 ††£ 90/150
Rest – *(booking essential at lunch)* Menu £ 23/38 – Carte £ 25/38
♦ Formal restaurant with contemporary furnishings, French windows and views over Anglesey. Classic country house cooking uses local, seasonal produce to create hearty old favourites. Modern bedrooms, some with views/terraces.

at Groeslon **South : 3 mi by A 487**

Y Goeden Eirin

Dolydd, North : 0.5 mi ✉ LL54 7EF – ✆ (01286) 830 942 – www.ygoedeneirin.co.uk – Closed Christmas to New Year
3 rm – †£ 60 ††£ 90 **Rest** – Menu £ 28
♦ Attractive stone house between mountains and sea. Picture windows in lounge; interesting artwork and furniture. Charming bedrooms – those in annexe have stable doors and slate-floored bathrooms. Dining room boasts original oils, grand piano and fresh, seasonal dishes.

at Llandwrog **South : 4.25 mi by A 487 on A 499**

Rhiwafallen with rm

AC rest,

North : 1 mi on A 499 ✉ LL54 5SW – ✆ (01286) 830 172 – www.rhiwafallen.co.uk
5 rm – †£ 80/120 ††£ 120
Rest – *(Closed Sunday dinner and Monday) (dinner only and Sunday lunch)* Menu £ 20 (lunch)/35 – Carte approx. £ 35
♦ 19C farmhouse run by enthusiastic young couple; dine in slate-floored conservatory with pleasant view. Seasonal, monthly changing menu; well presented, modern-style dishes based on classic combinations. Stylish, contemporary bedrooms, with bathrooms to match.

The symbol guarantees a good night's sleep. In red ? The very essence of peace: only the sound of birdsong in the early morning...

CAERSWS - Powys - 502 J26 32 C2

London 194 mi - Aberystwyth 39 mi - Chester 63 mi - Shrewsbury 42 mi

at Pontdolgoch Northwest : 1.5 mi on A 470 - ✉ Newtown

The Talkhouse with rm

Newtown ✉ SY17 5JE - ✆ (01686) 688 919 - www.talkhouse.co.uk - Closed Sunday dinner and Monday

3 rm - †£ 70 ††£ 125

Rest - *(dinner only and Sunday lunch) (booking essential)* Carte £ 22/32

♦ 17C coaching inn with comfy lounge and cosy bar; dining room overlooks garden. Daily changing menu offers hearty portions and bold flavours. Cottage-style bedrooms with antique furniture; Myfanwy is the best.

Y. Duhamel/MICHELIN

CARDIFF

County: Cardiff
Michelin regional map: **503** K29
London 155 mi
– Birmingham 110 mi
– Bristol 46 mi – Coventry 124 mi

Population: 292 150
Wales
Map reference: **33** C4

PRACTICAL INFORMATION

Tourist Information

The Old Library, The Hayes, Working St ✆(0870) 1211258, visitor@cardiff.gov.uk

Airport

Cardiff (Wales) Airport : ✆ (01446) 711111, SW : 8 mi by A 48 AX

Golf Courses

Dinas Powis Old Highwalls, ✆(029) 2051 2727

SIGHTS

In town

City★★★ - National Museum and Gallery★★★ **AC** (Evolution of Wales★★, Picture galleries★★) BY – Castle★ **AC** BZ – Llandaff Cathedral★ AV **B** – Cardiff Bay★ (Techniquest★ **AC**) AX

On the outskirts

Museum of Welsh Life★★ **AC**, St Fagan's, W : 5 mi by A 4161 AV – Castell Coch★★ **AC**, NW : 5 mi by A 470 AV

In the surrounding area

Caerphilly Castle★★ **AC**, N : 7 mi by A 469 AV – Dyffryn Gardens★ **AC**, W : 8 mi by A 48 AX

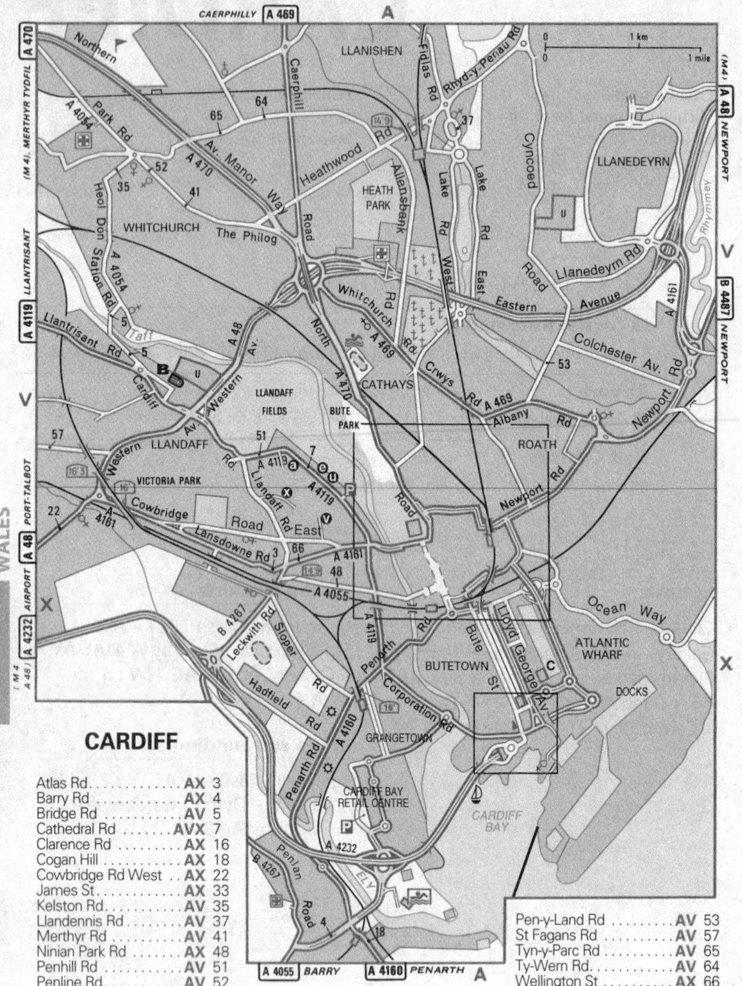

CARDIFF

The St David's H. & Spa rm, VISA AE

Havannah St, Cardiff Bay ✉ *CF10 5SD*
– ✆ *(029) 2045 4045*
– *www.principal-hayley.com/thestdavids* CUa

120 rm – 🛉£ 99/329 🛉🛉£ 109/329, ☕ £ 18.95
– 12 suites

Rest *Tides Grill* – Menu £ 20 – Carte £ 31/48

◆ Striking modern hotel with panoramic views across waterfront. Hi-tech meeting rooms and fitness club. Well-proportioned bedrooms, all with balconies, in minimalist style. Informal Tides Grill.

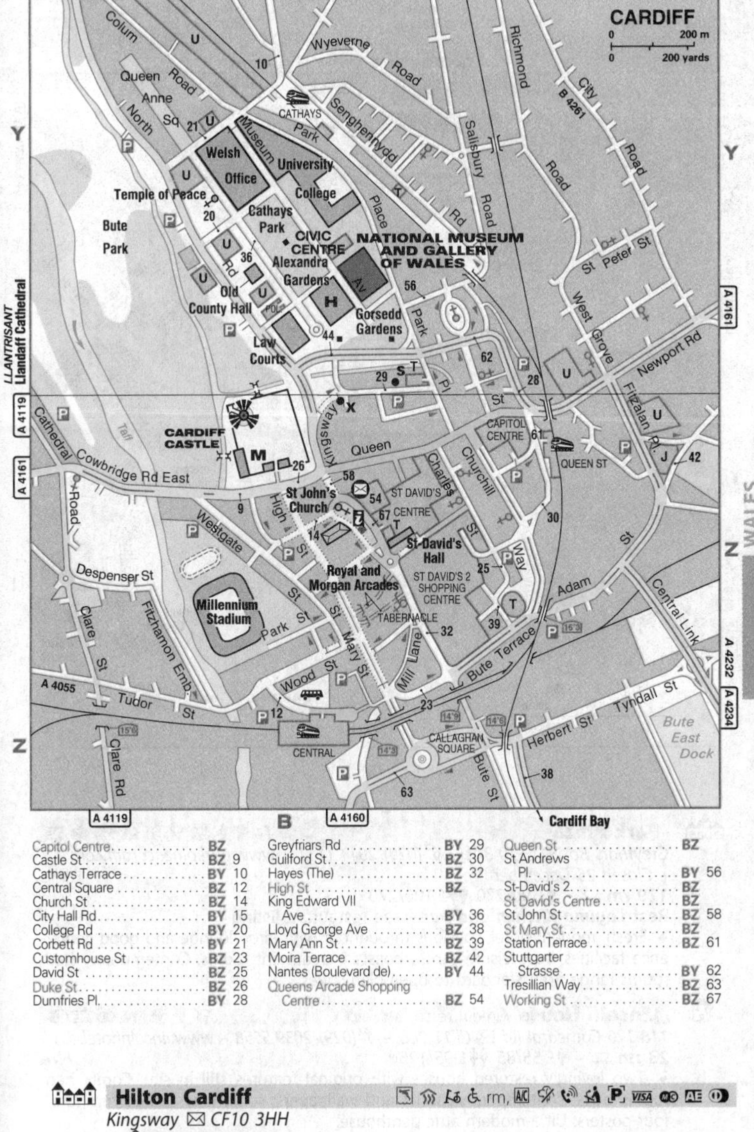

Capitol Centre	BZ		Greyfriars Rd	BY	29	Queen St	BZ	
Castle St	BZ	9	Guilford St	BZ	30	St Andrews Pl.	BY	56
Cathays Terrace	BY	10	Hayes (The)	BZ	32	St-David's 2	BZ	
Central Square	BZ	12	High St	BZ		St David's Centre	BZ	
Church St	BZ	14	King Edward VII Ave	BY	36	St John St	BZ	58
City Hall Rd	BY	15	Lloyd George Ave	BZ	38	St Mary St	BZ	
College Rd	BY	20	Mary Ann St	BZ	39	Station Terrace	BZ	61
Corbett Rd	BY	21	Moira Terrace	BZ	42	Stuttgarter Strasse	BY	62
Customhouse St	BZ	23	Nantes (Boulevard de)	BY	44	Tresillian Way	BZ	63
David St	BZ	25	Queens Arcade Shopping Centre	BZ	54	Working St	BZ	67
Duke St	BZ	26						
Dumfries Pl.	BY	28						

Hilton Cardiff

rm,

Kingsway ✉ *CF10 3HH*
– ✆ *(029) 2064 6300*
– *www.hilton.co.uk/cardiff*

BZx

193 rm – £ 99/170 £ 120/170
– 4 suites

Rest ***Razzi*** – Menu £ 19/28

◆ State-of-the-art meeting rooms and leisure facilities feature in this imposingly modern corporate hotel. Spacious, comfy bedrooms boast fine views of castle or City Hall. Popular menu in conservatory-style restaurant.

CARDIFF BAY

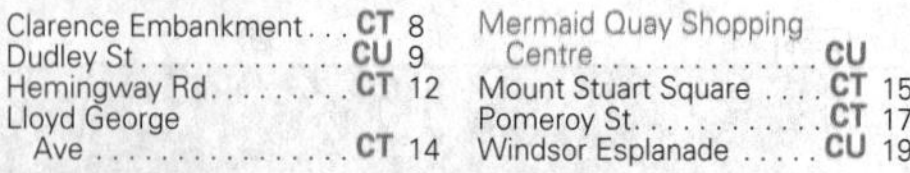

Britannia Quay . . . . CU 2
Bute Crescent . . . . CT 4
Clarence Embankment . . . CT 8
Dudley St . . . . CU 9
Hemingway Rd . . . . CT 12
Lloyd George Ave . . . . CT 14
Mermaid Quay Shopping Centre . . . . CU
Mount Stuart Square . . . . CT 15
Pomeroy St. . . . . CT 17
Windsor Esplanade . . . . . CU 19

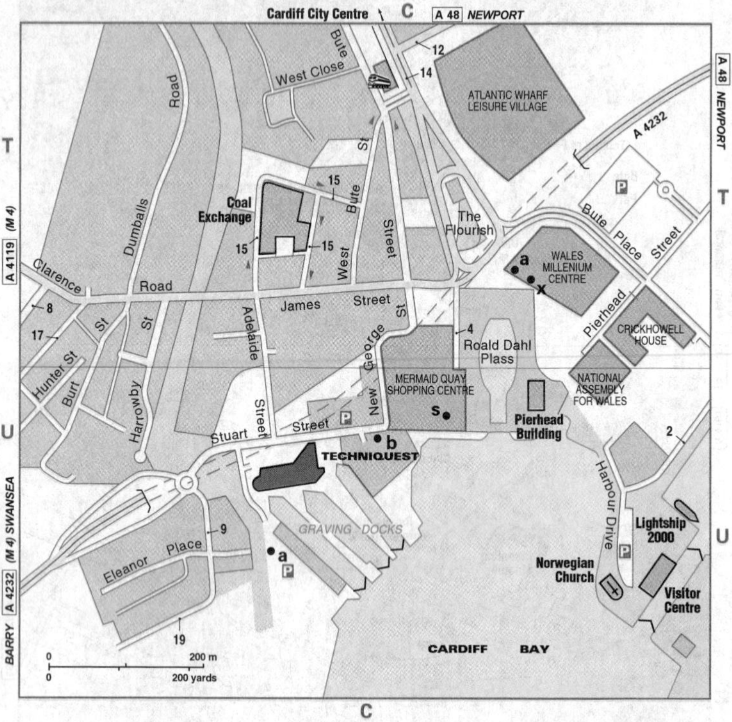

Park Plaza

Greyfriars Rd ✉ *CF10 3AL –* ✆ *(029) 2011 1111 – www.parkplazacardiff.com – Closed 25 December* BY **s**

129 rm – †£ 90/270 ††£ 100/270

Rest ***Laguna Kitchen and Bar*** – see restaurant listing

♦ Fresh, modern hotel: spacious throughout with large lounge and good conference facilities. Vast leisure centre boasts 8 treatment rooms. Contemporary bedrooms range from standard to open-plan suites.

Lincoln House without rest

118-120 Cathedral Rd ✉ *CF11 9LQ –* ✆ *(029) 2039 5558 – www.lincolnhotel.co.uk* AV **e**

23 rm – †£ 55/85 ††£ 95/125

♦ Two lovingly restored houses with original features still in situ. Comfy bedrooms boast contemporary fabrics and wallpapers; some have period furniture/-four-posters. Ultra-modern attic penthouse.

Town House without rest

70 Cathedral Rd ✉ *CF11 9LL –* ✆ *(029) 2023 9399 – www.thetownhousecardiff.co.uk* AV **u**

8 rm – †£ 50/65 ††£ 70/90

♦ Carefully restored Victorian house, hospitably run by owners. Light and airy bedrooms have some thoughtful touches and are well-appointed: ones at front are the most spacious.

XX **Le Gallois**

⊠ *CF11 9NR – ✆ (029) 2034 1264 – www.legallois.co.uk – Closed 24 December-5 January, Sunday and Monday* AX**x**

Rest – Menu £ 25 (lunch)/35 – Carte £ 25/40

◆ Bright and relaxed restaurant where keen owners provide both the friendly service and the assured modern European cooking. Gallic and Welsh combinations with inventive edge.

XX **Laguna Kitchen and Bar** – at Park Plaza Hotel

Greyfriars Rd. ⊠ *CF10 3AL – ✆ (029) 2011 1103 – www.lagunakitchenandbar.com – Closed 25 December* BY**s**

Rest – Menu £ 17 (lunch) – Carte £ 17/32

◆ On ground floor of hotel, this smart, modern restaurant serves an intriguing mix of local and international dishes.There's a bar, too, with an area of booths for casual dining.

X **Woods Brasserie**

The Pilotage Building, Stuart St, Cardiff Bay ⊠ *CF10 5BW – ✆ (029) 2049 2400 – www.woods-brasserie.com – Closed Sunday dinner from October-June*

Rest – *(booking essential at dinner)* Menu £ 18/20 – Carte £ 27/33 CU**b**

◆ Modern brasserie dishes and European influences from an open kitchen. Bay view from the first floor terrace. Popular for business lunches and bay visitors in the evening.

X **Garçon**

9 Upper Mermaid Quay ⊠ *CF10 5BZ – ✆ (029) 2049 0990 – www.garcon-resto.co.uk – Closed first week January, 24-26 December, Sunday dinner and Monday October-February* CU**s**

Rest – Menu £ 16 (weekday lunch) – Carte £ 23/41

◆ Classic brasserie style, with leather banquettes, mirrors and a large bar counter. Extensive menus offer filling and flavourful French classics. Friendly, efficient service.

X **Patagonia**

11 Kings Rd ⊠ *CF11 9BZ – ✆ (029) 2019 0265 – www.patagonia-restaurant.co.uk – Closed 24 December-24 January, Sunday and Monday* AX**v**

Rest – *(dinner only)* Menu £ 29

◆ Friendly neighbourhood restaurant set over two floors, with brightly coloured walls and eclectic artwork. Short menu offers wholesome and tasty modern European cooking.

The New Conway

53 Conway Rd ⊠ *CF11 9NW – ✆ (029) 2022 4373 – www.theconway.co.uk – Closed 25 December* AV**a**

Rest – Carte £ 24/35

◆ Neighbourhood pub with pleasingly simple approach to food which sees fresh, seasonal, local produce used to create tasty pub classics like toad in the hole or apple and raisin crumble.

at Penarth South : 3 mi by A 4160 - AX – ⊠ Cardiff

Holm House

Marine Par ⊠ *CF64 3BG – ✆ (029) 2070 1572 – www.holmhouse.com*

12 rm (dinner included) – †£ 145/225 ††£ 225/450

Rest *Neale's* – *(dinner only and lunch Friday-Sunday)* Menu £ 20/30 **s**

◆ Built in 1920s for son of local shipbuilder. Part art deco, part modern styling, displaying flock wallpapers and bold colours; some bedrooms boast feature baths and oversized windows. Restaurant with views to distant Holm Islands; weekly menus of simple, wholesome combinations.

XX **The Olive Tree**

21 Glebe St ⊠ *CF64 1EE – ✆ (029) 2070 7077 – www.the-olive-tree.net – Closed 25-26 December, Sunday dinner and Monday*

Rest – *(dinner only and Sunday lunch)* Menu £ 19 – Carte £ 26/40

◆ Rewarding discovery tucked away in the centre of town. Relaxing feel augmented by vivid artwork. Warm, friendly service of good value, seasonal, frequently changing dishes.

WALES

CARMARTHEN – Carmarthenshire – 503 H28 – pop. 14 648 33 B3

London 219 mi – Fishguard 47 mi – Haverfordwest 32 mi – Swansea 27 mi
113 Lammas St ✆ (01267) 231557, carmarthentic@carmarthenshire.gov.uk
Kidwelly Castle★ – National Botanic Garden★

at Felingwm Uchaf Northeast : 8 mi by A 40 on B 4310 – ✉ Carmarthen

Allt y Golau Uchaf without rest
North : 0.5 mi on B 4310 ✉ SA32 7BB – ✆ (01267) 290 455 – www.alltygolau.com – Closed Christmas and New Year
3 rm – £ 45 £ 68
◆ Georgian farmhouse in uplifting elevated position, perfect for walkers. Tranquil garden bursts to life in spring. Home-baked breakfasts of repute. Neat, pretty, compact rooms.

at Nantgaredig East : 5 mi on A 40 – ✉ Carmarthen

Y Polyn
South : 1 mi by B 4310 on B 4300 ✉ SA32 7LH – ✆ (01267) 290 000 www.ypolynrestaurant.co.uk – Closed 25-26 December, Sunday dinner and Monday
Rest – Menu £ 15/30 – Carte £ 20/35
◆ Welcoming dining pub in a great rural location by a stream. Cooking is classically based but with modern touches. Hearty and wholesome dishes, with a greater choice at dinner.

CEMAES – Isle of Anglesey – 502 G23 – see Anglesey (Isle of)

COLWYN BAY (Bae Colwyn) – Conwy – 502 I24 – pop. 30 269 32 B1

London 237 mi – Birkenhead 50 mi – Chester 42 mi – Holyhead 41 mi
Information Point, Cayley Promenade, Rhos-on-Sea ✆ (01492) 548778
Abergele Tan-y-Goppa Rd, ✆ (01745) 824 034
Old Colwyn Woodland Ave, ✆ (01492) 515 581
Welsh Mountain Zoo★ **AC** (≤★)
Bodnant Garden★★ **AC**, SW : 6 mi by A 55 and A 470

Rathlin Country House without rest
48 Kings Rd, Southwest : 0.25 mi on B 5113 ✉ LL29 7YH – ✆ (01492) 532 173 – www.rathlincountryhouse.co.uk – Closed 24-25 December
3 rm – £ 65/85 £ 85
◆ Large Arts and Crafts house in mature gardens, boasting ornate ceilings, leaded windows and parquet floors. Individually furnished bedrooms; one with steam shower. Good breakfasts.

Pen-y-Bryn
Pen-y-Bryn Rd, Upper Colwyn Bay, Southwest : 1 mi by B 5113 ✉ LL29 6DD – ✆ (01492) 533 360 – www.penybryn-colwynbay.co.uk – Closed 25 December
Rest – Carte £ 20/30
◆ Modern, laid-back pub set on a residential street; its unassuming façade concealing impressive bay views. Extensive daily menu ranges from pub classics to more adventurous fare.

at Rhos-on-Sea Northwest : 1 mi – ✉ Colwyn Bay

Plas Rhos without rest
Cayley Promenade ✉ LL28 4EP – ✆ (01492) 543 698 – www.plasrhos.co.uk – February to November
7 rm – £ 50/70 £ 90/100
◆ 19C house on first promenade from Colwyn Bay. Homely front lounge with bay view. Breakfasts feature local butcher's produce. Immaculately kept rooms: superior ones to front.

CONWY – Conwy – 502 I24 – pop. 3 847 32 B1

London 241 mi – Caernarfon 22 mi – Chester 46 mi – Holyhead 37 mi
Conwy Castle Visitor Centre ✆ (01492) 592248, conwytic@conwy.gov.uk
Penmaenmawr Conway Old Rd, ✆ (01492) 623 330
Town★★ - Castle★★ **AC** – Town Walls★★ - Plas Mawr★★
Snowdonia National Park★★★ – Bodnant Garden★★ **AC**, S : 8 mi by A 55 and A 470 – Conwy Crossing (suspension bridge★)

Castle
High St ✉ *LL32 8DB* – ✆ *(01492) 582 800* – *www.castlewales.co.uk*
27 rm – †£ 79/164 ††£ 160/170 – 1 suite
Rest *Dawson's* – Carte £ 29/37
◆ Adjoining brick and flint coaching inns within walled town, on site of former Cistercian abbey. Comfy firelit country house sitting room; mix of classic/modern bedrooms. Some castle views. Contemporary dining room offers extensive menu of brasserie classics.

The Groes Inn with rm
South : 3 mi on B 5106 ✉ *LL32 8TN* – ✆ *(01492) 650 545* – *www.groesinn.com* – *Closed 25 December*
14 rm – †£ 85 ††£ 105/125 **Rest** – Carte £ 23/40
◆ Characterful inn, beautifully set overlooking the estuary, in the foothills of Snowdonia. Local Welsh and British dishes arrive in neat, generous portions; more adventurous restaurant menu. Tastefully styled bedrooms boasts views; some have terraces and balconies.

at Llansanffraid Glan Conwy **Southeast : 2.5 mi by A 547 on A 470 – ✉ Conwy**

Old Rectory Country House without rest
Llanrwst Rd, on A 470 ✉ *LL28 5LF* – ✆ *(01492) 580 611* – *www.oldrectorycountryhouse.co.uk* – *Restricted opening in winter*
6 rm – †£ 99/119 ††£ 99/159
◆ Personally run country house with attractive gardens and estuary views. Beautifully furnished Georgian-style sitting room displays china and antiques. Bedrooms, split between the house and annexe, boast comfy feature beds and luxury bathrooms. Good breakfasts.

at Rowen **South : 3.5 mi by B 5106**

Tir Y Coed
✉ *LL32 8TP* – ✆ *(01492) 650 219* – *www.tirycoed.com*
7 rm – †£ 104 ††£ 165 **Rest** – *(dinner only)* Menu £ 35
◆ In secluded valley at foothills of Snowdonia, with balcony terrace overlooking mature garden. Tastefully furnished bedrooms. Intimate, candlelit dining room features fine collection of Victorian lithographs. Daily changing menu reflects the best of local produce.

COWBRIDGE (Y Bont Faen) – The Vale of Glamorgan – 503 J29 – pop. 3 616 — 33 B4

London 170 mi – Cardiff 15 mi – Swansea 30 mi

Huddarts
69 High St ✉ *CF71 7AF* – ✆ *(01446) 774 645* – *www.huddartsrestaurant.co.uk* – *Closed 26 December-11 January, Sunday dinner and Monday*
Rest – Menu £ 20 (Sunday lunch)/26 (dinner weekdays) – Carte £ 22/32
◆ Intimate, family-run restaurant located on high street of this ancient market town. Welsh tapestries on wall. Skilfully executed traditional dishes with modern influences.

CRICCIETH – Gwynedd – 502 H25 – pop. 1 826 — 32 B2

London 249 mi – Caernarfon 17 mi – Shrewsbury 85 mi
18 Ednyfed Hill, ✆ (01766) 522 154
Lleyn Peninsula★★ – Ffestiniog Railway★★

Mynydd Ednyfed Country House
Caernarfon Rd, Northwest : 0.75 mi on B 4411 ✉ *LL52 0PH* – ✆ *(01766) 523 269* – *www.criccieth.net* – *Closed 23 December-4 January*
8 rm – †£ 78 ††£ 115 **Rest** – *(dinner only)* Carte £ 22/28
◆ Cosy, personally run 17C country house in eight acres of gardens and woodland. Traditional bedrooms – some with four-posters and fine bay views; all with stylish modern bathrooms. Dinner served in conservatory, which also boasts great outlook.

WALES

CRICKHOWELL (Crucywel) – Powys – 503 K28 – pop. 2 166 **33** C4

London 169 mi – Abergavenny 6 mi – Brecon 14 mi – Cardiff 40 mi

Resource and Information Centre, Beaufort St ✆ (01873) 811970, tic@crickhowellinfo.org.uk

Brecon Beacons National Park★★. Llanthony Priory★★, NE : 10 mi by minor roads

Gliffaes Country House

West : 3.75 mi by A 40 ✉ NP8 1RH – ✆ (01874) 730 371 – www.gliffaeshotel.com – closed 3-27 January

23 rm – †£ 92/122 ††£ 245

Rest – *(light lunch Monday-Saturday)* Menu £ 38 **s**

◆ 19C country house and gardens on banks of the River Usk, offering great tranquillity. Welcoming bar, lounge and conservatory. Popular for outdoor pursuits. Luxuriously individual rooms. Bold, country house dining room has pleasant garden views.

Bear

High St ✉ NP8 1BW – ✆ (01873) 810 408 – www.bearhotel.co.uk

34 rm – †£ 70/153 ††£ 153 – 1 suite

Rest *Bear* – see restaurant listing

◆ Well-maintained 15C coaching inn full of nooks and crannies. Stylish bedrooms, some with jacuzzis; most characterful are in main house and feature beams, four-posters and fireplaces.

Glangrwyney Court

South : 2 mi on A 40 ✉ NP8 1ES – ✆ (01873) 811 288 – www.glancourt.co.uk

8 rm – †£ 77/98 ††£ 95/135 **Rest** – Carte £ 29/38

◆ Passionately run guest house with large lounge and high-ceilinged breakfast room. Fresh flowers and objets d'art cover every surface. Bedrooms boasts rich fabrics, good facilities and country views. Dinner by arrangement or transport provided to the local pub.

Ty Gwyn without rest

Brecon Rd ✉ NP8 1DG – ✆ (01873) 811 625 – www.tygwyn.com – Closed December

3 rm – †£ 40/50 ††£ 75

◆ A homely place boasting spotlessly kept, simply furnished bedrooms, with comfort and character. Well-tended garden with stream. Enthusiastic owner has vast local knowledge.

Bear

High St ✉ NP8 1BW – ✆ (01873) 810 408 – www.bearhotel.co.uk

Rest – Carte £ 21/32

◆ Keenly run coaching inn serving classical, tried-and-tested menu available both in characterful bar and more formal restaurant. Swift, assured service from young, cheery team.

Nantyffin Cider Mill Inn

Brecon Rd, West : 1 mi on A 40 ✉ NP8 1SG – ✆ (01873) 810 775 – www.cidermill.co.uk – Closed 25-26 December, Monday except bank holidays and Sunday dinner from October-March

Rest – Carte £ 20/28

◆ Converted 16C cider mill featuring original cider press. Predominantly Mediterranean dishes; blackboard of fish specials and set menu of old favourites. Cider and real ales on tap.

CROSS ASH – Monmouthshire – see Abergavenny

CROSSGATES – Powys – 503 J27 – see Llandrindod Wells

DEGANWY – Conwy – 502 I24 – see Llandudno

DOLFOR – Powys – 503 K26 — 32 C2

London 199 – Cardiff 93 – Oswestry 34 – Ludlow 39

Old Vicarage

North : 1.5 mi by A 483 ✉ SY16 4BN – ✆ (01686) 629 051 – www.theoldvicaragedolfor.co.uk

5 rm – ♦£ 65 ♦♦£ 110 **Rest** – Menu £ 30

♦ Characterful 19C detached house with large gardens; formerly a vicarage. Cosy bedrooms, named after nearby rivers, mix period furniture with modern colours. Concise menu of home-cooked dishes features local produce and veg from garden. Preserves/chutneys for sale.

DOLGELLAU – Gwynedd – 502 I25 – pop. 2 407 — 32 B2

London 221 mi – Birkenhead 72 mi – Chester 64 mi – Shrewsbury 57 mi

Ty Meirion, Eldon Sq ✆ (01341) 422888, tic.dolgellau@eryri-npa.gov.uk

Hengwrt Estate Pencefn Rd, ✆ (01341) 422 603

Town★

Snowdonia National Park★★★ - Cadair Idris★★★ - Precipice Walk★, NE : 3 mi on minor roads

Penmaenuchaf Hall

Penmaenpool, West : 1.75 mi on A 493 (Tywyn Rd) ✉ LL40 1YB – ✆ (01341) 422 129 – www.penhall.co.uk

14 rm – ♦£ 95/151 ♦♦£ 240/250 **Rest** – Menu £ 18/40 – Carte £ 40/45

♦ Personally run Victorian house with wood panelling, ornate ceilings, friendly staff and family feel. Country house style bedrooms; some with balconies. Beautiful grounds and superb mountain and estuary views. Formal conservatory dining room with garden outlook.

Ffynnon without rest

Love Ln, (off Cader Rd) ✉ LL40 1RR – ✆ (01341) 421 774 – www.ffynnontownhouse.com

5 rm – ♦£ 130 ♦♦£ 175/195

♦ A haven of luxury; lovingly restored and modernised, yet retaining many original features. Stylish sitting room and spacious, tastefully decorated suites, boasting every mod con.

Tyddyn Mawr without rest

Islawdref, Cader Rd, Southwest : 2.5 mi by Tywyn rd on Cader Idris rd ✉ LL40 1TL – ✆ (01341) 422 331 – www.wales-guesthouse.co.uk – February-November

3 rm – ♦£ 55 ♦♦£ 70

♦ Set on secluded working sheep farm, stunningly situated beneath Cader Idris mountain. Immaculate bedrooms boast superb views and plenty of extras; one has a balcony, another, a terrace. Five course breakfast taken beside impressive inglenook. Great hospitality.

at Llanelltyd Northwest : 2.25 mi by A 470 on A 496

Mawddach

✉ LL40 2TA – ✆ (01341) 424 020 – www.mawddach.com – Closed 1 week spring, 2 weeks autumn, 1 week winter, Sunday dinner, Monday and Tuesday

Rest – Menu £ 17 (Sunday lunch) – Carte £ 26/30

♦ Stylish modern barn conversion on family farm; first floor dining room dominated by glass wall with superb view. Well-priced, straightforward cooking; more adventurous dinner menu.

EAST ABERTHAW (Aberddawan) – The Vale of Glamorgan – 503 J29 – ✉ Barry — 33 B-C4

London 180 mi – Cardiff 20 mi – Swansea 33 mi

The Blue Anchor Inn

✉ CF62 3DD – ✆ (01446) 750 329 – www.blueanchoraberthaw.com – Closed Sunday dinner

Rest – Carte £ 15/26

♦ Thatched stone-built pub dating back to 1380, with characterful bar and vast upstairs restaurant. Traditional, wholesome dishes boast straightforward presentation and plenty of flavour.

FELINGWM UCHAF – Carmarthenshire – see Carmarthen

FISHGUARD – Pembrokeshire – 503 F28 – pop. 3 193 33 A3

London 265 mi – Cardiff 114 mi – Gloucester 176 mi – Holyhead 169 mi

to Republic of Ireland (Rosslare) (Stena Line) 2-4 daily (1 h 50 mn/3 h 30 mn)

Town Hall, The Square ✆ (01437) 776636, fishguard.tic@pembrokeshire.gov.uk - Ocean Lab, The Parrog, Goodwick ✆ (01348) 872037, fishguardharbour.tic@pembrokeshire.gov.uk

Pembrokeshire Coast National Park★★

Manor Town House without rest VISA

11 Main St ✉ SA65 9HG – ✆ (01348) 873 260 – www.manortownhouse.com – Closed 1 week Christmas

6 rm – ♦£ 55/65 ♦♦£ 75/105

♦ Georgian Grade II listed house. Bedrooms are individually styled and furnished with antiques, choose from Victorian and art deco; some with harbour and sea views.

at Welsh Hook Southwest : 7.5 mi by A 40 – ✉ Haverfordwest

XX **Stone Hall** with rm P VISA AE

✉ SA62 5NS – ✆ (01348) 840 212 – www.stonehall-mansion.co.uk – Closed 25-26 December, Sunday and Monday

4 rm – ♦£ 85 ♦♦£ 110

Rest – *(dinner only) (booking essential)* Menu £ 30 – Carte £ 30/39

♦ Charming, part-14C manor house with 17C additions. Tranquil setting and personal hospitality. Home-cooked, French-style dishes using prime seasonal produce. Comfy bedrooms.

GRESFORD = Groes-ffordd – Wrexham – 502 L24 – see Wrexham

GROESLON – Gwynedd – see Caernarfon

HARLECH – Gwynedd – 502 H25 – pop. 1 233 32 B2

London 241 mi – Chester 72 mi – Dolgellau 21 mi

High St ✆ (01766) 780658, tic.harlech@aryri-npa.gov.uk

Royal St David's, ✆ (01766) 780 203

Castle★★ AC

Snowdonia National Park★★★

XX **Castle Cottage** with rm VISA

Pen Llech, by B 4573 ✉ LL46 2YL – ✆ (01766) 780 479 – www.castlecottageharlech.co.uk – Closed 2 weeks November and Christmas

7 rm – ♦£ 85 ♦♦£ 170

Rest – *(dinner only) (booking essential)* Menu £ 38

♦ Attractive cottage behind Harlech Castle, with cosy yet surprisingly contemporary interior. Classical, daily changing menus display passionately sourced local produce and modern touches. Bedrooms are spacious and comfy; some have stunning castle/mountain views.

HAVERFORDWEST (Hwlffordd) – Pembrokeshire – 503 F28 – pop. 13 367 33 A3

London 250 mi – Fishguard 15 mi – Swansea 57 mi

Old Bridge ✆ (01437) 763110, haverfordwest.tic@pembrokeshire.gov.uk

Arnolds Down, ✆ (01437) 763 565

Scolton Museum and Country Park★

Pembrokeshire Coast National Park★★. Skomer Island and Skokholm Island★, SW : 14 mi by B 4327 and minor roads

Lower Haythog Farm
Spittal, Northeast : 5 mi on B 4329 ✉ SA62 5QL – ✆ (01437) 731 279 – www.lowerhaythogfarm.co.uk
5 rm – †£ 40/60 ††£ 75/85 **Rest** – Menu £ 25
◆ Friendly atmosphere, traditional comforts and a warm welcome at this 250 acre working dairy farm with accessible woodland walks. Well-kept and comfortable throughout. Dining room in homely, country style reflected in hearty, home-cooked food.

Paddock
✉ SA62 5QL – ✆ (01437) 731 531 – www.thepaddockwales.co.uk
3 rm – †£ 55/70 ††£ 75/90 **Rest** – Carte £ 23/28
◆ Very modern new build guesthouse set on working farm; minimalist ground floor bedrooms feature chunky furniture and Egyptian cotton bedding. Comfy lounge with books, magazines and board games. Set 2 or 3 course dinner makes good use of local produce.

HAWARDEN (Penarlâg) – Flintshire – 502 K24 – pop. 1 858 — 32 C1

London 205 mi – Chester 9 mi – Liverpool 17 mi – Shrewsbury 45 mi

Hawarden Brasserie
68 The Highway ✉ CH5 3DH – ✆ (01244) 536 353 – www.thehawardenbrasserie.com – Closed Saturday lunch
Rest – *(booking advisable)* Carte £ 18/28
◆ Long-standing neighbourhood restaurant run by experienced owners and popular with the locals. Light lunch; bistro classics at dinner. Dishes are good value, tasty and neatly presented.

HAY-ON-WYE (Y Gelli) – Powys – 503 K27 – pop. 1 846 — 33 C3

London 154 mi – Brecon 16 mi – Cardiff 59 mi – Hereford 21 mi
Craft Centre, Oxford Rd ✆ (01497) 820144, post@hay-on-wye.co.uk
Rhosgoch Builth Wells, ✆ (01497) 851 251
Town★
Brecon Beacons National Park★★. Llanthony Priory★★, SE : 12 mi by minor roads

Old Black Lion with rm
26 Lion St ✉ HR3 5AD – ✆ (01497) 820 841 – www.oldblacklion.co.uk – Closed 24-26 December
10 rm – †£ 35/53 ††£ 95/115 **Rest** – Carte £ 22/31
◆ Characterful part-13C inn with lots of old world charm. Traditional menu offers tasty, honest dishes, hearty portions and plenty of choice, with more favourites on the board. Bedrooms boast either antique furnishings or rich colours and modern bathrooms.

Three Tuns
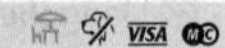
4 Broad St ✉ HR3 5DB – ✆ (01497) 821 855 – www.three-tuns.com – Closed Monday, Tuesday and Sunday dinner
Rest – Carte £ 22/28
◆ Grade II listed 16C pub, reputedly the oldest building in the town. Bar and terrace offer blackboard classics; formal upstairs dining room displays more Italian influences.

HOWEY – Powys – see Llandrindod Wells

KNIGHTON (Trefyclawdd) – Powys – 503 K26 – pop. 2 851 — 33 C3

London 162 mi – Birmingham 59 mi – Hereford 31 mi – Shrewsbury 35 mi
Offa's Dyke Centre, West St ✆ (01547) 528753, oda@offasdyke.demon.co.uk
Ffrydd Wood, ✆ (01547) 528 646
Town★
Offa's Dyke★, NW : 9.5 m

Milebrook House

Ludlow Rd, Milebrook, East : 2 mi on A 4113 ✉ LD7 1LT – ✆ (01547) 528 632 – www.milebrookhouse.co.uk
10 rm – †£ 77 ††£ 122
Rest – *(closed Monday lunch)* Menu £ 16/33 – Carte lunch £ 20/31
♦ Located in the Teme Valley; good for exploring the Welsh Marches. Possesses a fine, formal garden well-stocked with exotic plants. Rooms are large and pleasingly decorated. The kitchen garden provides most of the vegetables which appear in the restaurant.

LAKE VYRNWY – Powys – 502 J25 – ✉ Llanwddyn 32 C2

London 204 mi – Chester 52 mi – Llanfyllin 10 mi – Shrewsbury 40 mi
The Shop in the Corner, Vyrnwy Craft Workshops ✆ (01691) 870346
Lake★

Lake Vyrnwy

rm,

✉ *SY10 0LY – ✆ (01691) 870 692 – www.lakevyrnwyhotel.co.uk*
51 rm – †£ 105/114 ††£ 225/237 – 1 suite **Rest** – Menu £ 21/43
♦ Victorian country house built from locally quarried stone overlooking the lake; an RSPB sanctuary and sporting estate, ideal for game enthusiasts. Rooms have timeless chic. Spectacular lakeside views from the restaurant are matched by accomplished cooking.

LALESTON – Bridgend – 503 J29 – see Bridgend

LAMPHEY = Llandyfai – Pembrokeshire – 503 F28 – see Pembroke

LAUGHARNE – Carmarthenshire – 503 G28 33 B4

London 230 mi – Cardiff 80 mi – Carmarthen 13 mi

Hurst House

rest,

East Marsh, South : 3 mi by A 4066 taking left turn on unmarked road opposite Hill Crest house ✉ SA33 4RS – ✆ (01994) 427 417 – www.hurst-house.co.uk
18 rm – †£ 100 ††£ 220/350
Rest – *(booking advisable for non-residents)* Menu £ 31 – Carte £ 28/49
♦ Former farmhouse set by the marshes in Dylan Thomas country; a restful hotel to suit the modern young traveller. State-of-the-art rooms boast natural materials and thoughtful extras. Small spa. Keenly priced, traditional menus in restaurant overlooking terrace and gardens.

LLANARMON DYFFRYN CEIRIOG – Wrexham – 502 K25 32 C2
– ✉ Llangollen (Denbighshire)

London 196 mi – Chester 33 mi – Shrewsbury 32 mi

The Hand at Llanarmon with rm

rm,

✉ *LL20 7LD – ✆ (01691) 600 666 – www.thehandhotel.co.uk*
13 rm – †£ 50/70 ††£ 90/125 **Rest** – Carte £ 18/32
♦ Rustic, personally run inn providing a warm welcome and wholesome meals to travellers through the lush Ceiriog Valley. Generous portions of fresh, flavoursome cooking. Cosy bedrooms with hill views and modernised bathrooms.

LLANDDEWI SKIRRID – Monmouthshire – see Abergavenny

LLANDEILO – Carmarthenshire – 503 I28 – pop. 1 731 33 B3

London 218 mi – Brecon 34 mi – Carmarthen 15 mi – Swansea 25 mi
Town★ - Dinefwr Park★ **AC**
Brecon Beacons National Park★★ – Black Mountain★, SE : by minor roads – Carreg Cennen Castle★ **AC**, SE : 4 mi by A 483 and minor roads

Plough Inn rm, rest,
Rhosmaen, North : 1 mi on A 40 ✉ SA19 6NP – ✆ (01558) 823 431 – www.ploughrhosmaen.com – Closed 26 December
20 rm – 🛉£ 70 🛉🛉£ 95
Rest – Menu £ 14/17 – Carte £ 20/29
◆ Powder blue building boasting contemporary interior and pleasant country views to the rear. Modern bedrooms are spacious, comfy and well-equipped: 305 has a whirlpool bath. Snacks, light lunches and more substantial dinners served in large vaulted restaurant.

at Salem North : 3 mi by A 40 off Pen-y-banc rd – ✉ Llandeilo

The Angel
✉ SA197LY – ✆ (01558) 823 394 – www.angelsalem.co.uk – Closed Sunday dinner, Monday and Tuesday
Rest – Carte £ 25/30
◆ Village pub with inviting bar lounge and formal, Edwardian style dining room. Traditional cooking, enlivened by Asian and Italian influences and some interesting combinations.

LLANDENNY – Monmouthshire – 503 L28 – see Usk

LLANDOVERY – Carmarthenshire – 503 I28 – pop. 2 235 33 B3

London 207 mi – Cardiff 61 mi – Swansea 37 mi – Merthyr Tydfil 34 mi

New White Lion rm,
43 Stone St ✉ SA20 0BZ – ✆ (01550) 720 685 – www.newwhitelion.co.uk – Closed 25-26 December
6 rm – 🛉£ 80/85 🛉🛉£ 135/145
Rest – *(dinner only) (booking essential residents only)* Menu £ 25
◆ Stylish Grade II listed hotel with individually designed bedrooms named after characters from local folklore, and cool sitting room with honesty bar. Cosy dining room; homemade dishes make good use made of local, seasonal produce.

LLANDRILLO – Denbighshire – 502 J25 – pop. 1 048 – ✉ Corwen 32 C2

London 210 mi – Chester 40 mi – Dolgellau 26 mi – Shrewsbury 46 mi

Tyddyn Llan (Bryan Webb) with rm rm,
✉ LL21 0ST – ✆ (01490) 440 264 – www.tyddynllan.co.uk – Closed last 2 weeks January and midweek 10 January-10 February
13 rm (dinner included) – 🛉£ 135 🛉🛉£ 145/300
Rest – *(dinner only and lunch Friday-Sunday) (booking essential)*
Menu £ 32/49
Spec. Dressed crab with fennel and pea shoot salad. Madgett's Farm duck breast, cider and apples. Whimberry crème brûlée
◆ Personally run country house with pretty gardens. Dine in one of two spacious rooms. Menu offers considerable choice; cooking is classical in style and dishes are expertly balanced, using sensible combinations. Tidy, well-equipped bedrooms.

LLANDRINDOD WELLS – Powys – 503 J27 – pop. 5 024 33 C3

London 204 mi – Brecon 29 mi – Carmarthen 60 mi – Shrewsbury 58 mi
Old Town Hall, Memorial Gardens ✆ (01597) 822600, llandrindodtic@btconnect.com
Llandrindod Wells The Clubhouse, ✆ (01597) 823 873
Elan Valley★★ (Dol-y-Mynach and Claerwen Dam and Reservoir★★, Caban Coch Dam and Reservoir★, Garreg-ddu Viaduct★, Pen-y-Garreg Reservoir and Dam★, Craig Goch Dam and Reservoir★), NW : 12 mi by A 4081, A 470 and B 4518

Metropole rm, rest,

Temple St ✉ *LD1 5DY* – ✆ *(01597) 823 700* – *www.metropole.co.uk*

112 rm – ♦£ 94 ♦♦£ 120/140 – 2 suites

Rest *Radnor* – *(dinner only)* Carte £ 23/30 **s**

Rest *Spencer's* – Carte £ 20/27 **s**

♦ Brightly painted hotel run for many years by Baird-Murray family. Some modern bedrooms; others more traditional. Pool in Victorian-style conservatory. Menu in formal Radnor showcases local produce. All day menu in Spencer's; a contemporary bar and brasserie.

at Crossgates **Northeast : 3.5 mi on A 483 – ✉ Llandrindod Wells**

Guidfa House

✉ *LD1 6RF* – ✆ *(01597) 851 241* – *www.guidfahouse.co.uk*

6 rm – ♦£ 70/80 ♦♦£ 80/110 **Rest** – *(Closed Sunday-Tuesday)* Menu £ 29

♦ Georgian house with white painted façade and pleasant garden to relax in. Indoors, find spacious, bright bedrooms. A friendly welcome is given with tips on local activities. Seasonally changing menu of zesty home cooking in traditionally decorated dining room.

at Howey **South : 1.5 mi by A 483 – ✉ Llandrindod Wells**

Acorn Court Country House without rest

Chapel Rd, Northeast : 0.5 mi ✉ *LD1 5PB* – ✆ *(01597) 823 543* – *www.acorncourt.co.uk* – *Closed 25-26 December*

4 rm – ♦£ 36/52 ♦♦£ 70/76

♦ Chalet-style house in lovely countryside; guests can fish in the lake. Bedrooms are large with many extra touches: hairdryers, stationery, soft toys – homely and welcoming.

WALES

LLANDUDNO – Conwy – 502 I24 – pop. 14 872 **32** B1

London 243 mi – Birkenhead 55 mi – Chester 47 mi – Holyhead 43 mi

Library Building, Mostyn St ✆ (01492) 577577, llandudnotic@conwy.gov.uk

Rhos-on-Sea Penrhyn Bay, ✆ (01492) 549 641

72 Bryniau Rd West Shore, ✆ (01492) 875 325

Hospital Rd, ✆ (01492) 876 450

Town★ - Pier★ B – The Great Orme★ (panorama★★, Tramway★, Ancient Copper Mines★ **AC**) AB

Bodnant Garden★★ **AC**, S : 7 mi by A 470 B

Bodysgallen Hall rm,

Southeast : 2 mi on A 470 ✉ *LL30 1RS* – ✆ *(01492) 584 466* – *www.bodysgallen.com*

18 rm – ♦£ 145 ♦♦£ 415, £ 7.50 – 18 suites – ♦♦£ 215/415

Rest *The Dining Room* – *(Closed Sunday dinner and Monday) (booking essential)* Menu £ 23 (lunch)/46 **s**

Rest *1620* – *(Closed Sunday lunch)* Carte £ 26/32 **s**

♦ Beautiful country house with 13C tower, stunning gardens and tasteful spa. Characterful wood panelled main lounge with inglenook. Antique-furnished bedrooms, some with splendid views towards Snowdon. Formal Dining Room overlooks gardens. 1620 serves brasserie classics.

Empire rm,

73 Church Walks ✉ *LL30 2HE* – ✆ *(01492) 860 555* – *www.empirehotel.co.uk* – *Closed 18-29 December* A**e**

46 rm – ♦£ 65/95 ♦♦£ 98/118 – 1 suite

Rest *Watkins and Co.* – *(dinner only and Sunday lunch)* Menu £ 15 (lunch)/22

♦ Grand columned façade leads to Victorian interior hung with chandeliers and Russell Flint prints. Bedrooms feature brass/cast iron beds, antiques and contrasting hi-tech mod cons. Set on site of former wine merchants, Watkins and Co. offers fine dining.

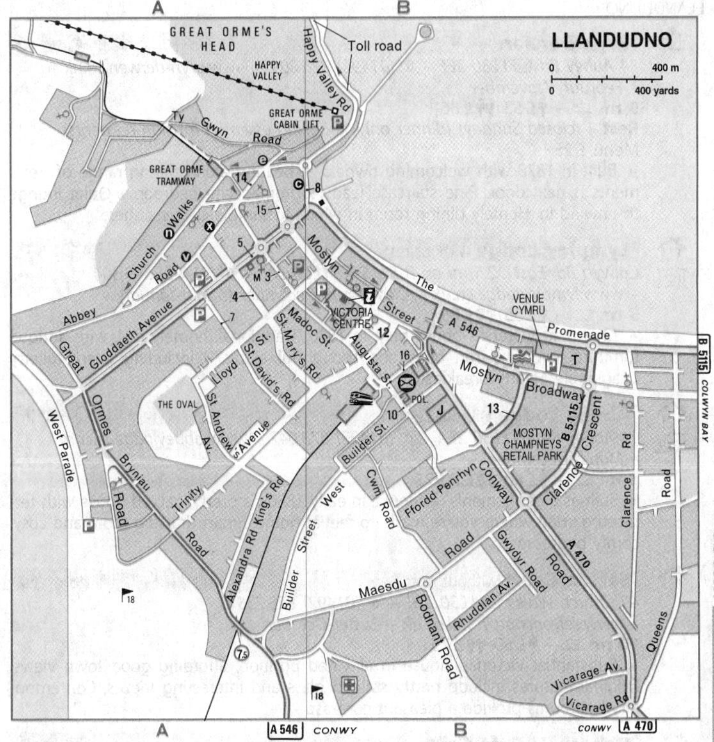

Chapel St . . . . A 3	Mostyn St . . . . B	Tudor Crescent . . . . B 13
Deganwy Ave . . . . A 4	North Parade . . . . AB 8	Upper Mostyn St . . . . A 15
Gloddaeth St . . . . A 5	Oxford Rd . . . . B 10	Vaughan St . . . . B 16
Maelgwyn Rd . . . . A 7	Trinity Square . . . . B 12	Victoria Centre . . . . B
Mostyn Champneys Retail Park . . . . B	Tudno St . . . . A 14	

Osborne House

17 North Par ✉ *LL30 2LP – ✆ (01492) 860 330 – www.osbornehouse.co.uk – Closed 18-29 December* **Ac**

7 rm – †£ 130/170 ††£ 145/210

Rest ***Osborne's Cafe Grill*** – see restaurant listing

♦ Sumptuous interior: huge rooms extend length of house; bedrooms epitomise Victorian luxury – original wood flooring, elaborate silk drapes, fine antiques. Richly hued lounge.

St Tudno

North Par ✉ *LL30 2LP – ✆ (01492) 874 411 – www.st-tudno.co.uk* **Ac**

17 rm – †£ 75/95 ††£ 100/105 – 1 suite

Rest ***Terrace*** – Menu £ 20 **s** – Carte dinner £ 27/36 **s**

♦ Personally run seaside hotel opposite pier. Classical in style, from comfy guest areas to individually designed bedrooms with thoughtful extras. High levels of service from established team. Formal dining room offers ambitious, intricate modern cooking.

Escape Boutique B&B without rest

48 Church Walks ✉ *LL30 2HL – ✆ (01492) 877 776 – www.escapebandb.co.uk – Closed 1 week Christmas* **An**

9 rm – †£ 70/120 ††£ 135

♦ Attractive Arts and Crafts house with stained glass windows, parquet floors and a chic, modern interior that sets it apart. Bedrooms are spacious and contemporary; the lounge is suitably stylish.

Bryn Derwen
34 Abbey Rd ✉ LL30 2EE – ✆ (01492) 876 804 – www.bryn-derwen.co.uk – February-November Av
9 rm – †£ 53 ††£ 86
Rest – *(closed Sunday) (dinner only) (booking essential for non-residents)* Menu £ 25
◆ Built in 1878 with welcoming owners. A beauty salon offering range of treatments is next door. Pine staircase leads to immaculate bedrooms. Quiet lounge to unwind in. Homely dining room in which to sample classic dishes.

Lympley Lodge without rest
Colwyn Rd, East : 2.5 mi on B 5115 ✉ LL30 3AL – ✆ (01492) 549 304 – www.lympleylodge.co.uk – Closed mid-December to mid-January
3 rm – †£ 55 ††£ 85
◆ Charming Victorian house built in 1870. Traditional, homely feel, with antique furniture, wrought iron beds and thoughtful extras – including every toiletry imaginable. Hearty breakfast.

Abbey Lodge without rest
14 Abbey Rd ✉ LL30 2EA – ✆ (01492) 878 042 – www.abbeylodgeuk.com – March-December Ax
4 rm – †£ 40 ††£ 70/75
◆ Built as a gentlemen's residence in early 1850s; a pretty, gabled house with terraced garden where you're made to feel at home. Smart drawing room and cosy, comfy bedrooms.

WALES

Sefton Court without rest
49 Church Walks ✉ LL30 2HL – ✆ (01492) 875 235 – www.seftoncourt-hotel.co.uk – Easter-October An
10 rm – †£ 50 ††£ 75
◆ Substantial Victorian house in elevated position, affording good town views. Original features include pretty stained glass and interesting friezes. Contemporary bedrooms provide a pleasant contrast.

Osborne's Cafe Grill – at Osborne House Hotel
17 North Par ✉ LL30 2LP – ✆ (01492) 860 330 – www.osbornehouse.co.uk – Closed 18-29 December Ac
Rest – Menu £ 19 – Carte £ 18/34
◆ Quirky hotel restaurant that exudes impressive Victorian opulence yet has a buzzy, informal feel. Classical brasserie menus offer something for everyone. Service is fittingly enthusiastic.

at Deganwy South : 2.75 mi on A 546 - A – ✉ Llandudno

Quay H. & Spa
Deganwy Quay ✉ LL31 9DJ – ✆ (01492) 564 100 – www.quayhotel.co.uk
55 rm – †£ 95/120 ††£ 105/155 – 19 suites
Rest *Grill Room* – Menu £ 25 (Sunday lunch) – Carte £ 34/47
◆ Stylish hotel on Conwy estuary, boasting superb harbour/castle views, large guest areas, extensive facilities and excellent spa. Spacious, contemporary bedrooms include 3 private towers. Nautically-themed first floor restaurant offers modern cuisine and stunning outlook.

Nikki Ip's
57 Station Rd ✉ LL31 9DF – ✆ (01492) 596 611 – www.nikkiips.com – Closed 1 January and 25-26 December
Rest – Chinese – *(booking essential)* Menu £ 12/29 – Carte £ 20/38
◆ Choice of casual eatery/bar or friendly restaurant with estuary views. Dim sum and concise set menu at lunch; extensive à la carte and specials at dinner. Fresh, tasty ingredients; good flavours.

LLANDWROG – Gwynedd – **503** H24 – see Caernarfon

LLANDYRNOG - Denbighshire - **503** J/K24 **32** C1

Cardiff 158 mi - Denbigh 7 mi - Ruthin 6 mi

Pentre Mawr

North : 1.25 mi by B 5429 taking left hand fork after 0.75 mi ✉ LL16 4LA – ✆ (01824) 790 732 – www.pentremawrcountryhouse.co.uk – Closed 25 December

7 rm – †£ 100/170 ††£ 120/130 **Rest** – Menu £ 33

◆ Set in 200 acres. Choice of 17C farmhouse with cosy open-fired lounges, country house atmosphere and antique-furnished bedrooms; or luxury African-themed canvas lodges with private terraces and hot tubs. Dinner served in wood-floored conservatory; local ingredients a feature.

LLANELLTYD - Gwynedd - **503** I25 - see Dolgellau

LLANERCHYMEDD - Isle of Anglesey - **502** G24 - see Anglesey (Isle of)

LLAN FFESTINIOG - Gwynedd **32** B2

London 234 mi - Bangor 35 mi - Wrexham 52 mi

Llechwedd Slate Caverns★ **AC** N : 4 mi by A 470

Cae'r Blaidd Country House

North : 0.75 mi by A 470 on Blaenau Rd ✉ LL41 4PH – ✆ (01766) 762 765 – www.caerblaidd.fsnet.co.uk – February-December

3 rm – †£ 49 ††£ 79 **Rest** – Menu £ 20

◆ Sizeable Victorian house in remote setting, boasting panoramic mountain views. Spacious guest areas; light, airy bedrooms – two with superb outlooks. Welcoming owners are mountain guides. Daily changing dishes of local produce served at large communal table.

LLANFIHANGEL - Powys - **502** J25 - see Llanfyllin

LLANFYLLIN - Powys - **502** K25 - pop. 1 267 **32** C2

London 188 mi - Chester 42 mi - Shrewsbury 24 mi - Welshpool 11 mi

Pistyll Rhaeadr★, NW : 8 mi by A 490, B 4391, B 4580 and minor roads

Seeds

5 Penybryn Cottages, High St ✉ SY22 5AP – ✆ (01691) 648 604 – Closed 2 weeks Easter, 23-28 December, Sunday-Tuesday and lunch Wednesday

Rest – *(restricted opening in winter)* Menu £ 26 (Saturday dinner) – Carte £ 21/33

◆ Converted 16C red-brick cottages in sleepy town, run by hands-on husband and wife team. Simple, rustic interior featuring old kitchen range; matched by unfussy, flavoursome, classical dishes.

at Llanfihangel Southwest : 5 mi by A 490 and B 4393 on B 4382 – ✉ Llanfyllin

Cyfie Farm

South : 1.5 mi by B 4382 ✉ SY22 5JE – ✆ (01691) 648 451 – www.cyfiefarm.co.uk – March-October

4 rm – †£ 60/65 ††£ 100/130 **Rest** – Menu £ 28

◆ 17C longhouse, now a sheep farm, with super views of Meifod Valley. One room has distinctly quaint feel. Luxurious new cottages: outdoor hot tub affords great vistas. Cordon Bleu trained owners serve at communal table.

LLANGAMMARCH WELLS - Powys - **503** J27 **33** B3

London 200 mi - Brecon 17 mi - Builth Wells 8 mi - Cardiff 58 mi

Lake Country House and Spa

East : 0.75 mi ✉ LD4 4BS – ✆ (01591) 620 202 – www.lakecountryhouse.co.uk

rm,

22 rm – †£ 135 ††£ 205 – 8 suites

Rest – *(booking essential)* Menu £ 20/39 – Carte £ 18/25

◆ 19C country house in mature grounds. Welsh teas a speciality. Rooms in house or lodge full of antiques, flowers and extravagant fabrics. Tranquil spa adds to the experience. Candlelit dining; super wine list.

WALES

LLANGOLLEN – Denbighshire – 502 K25 – pop. 2 930 — 32 C2

London 194 mi – Chester 23 mi – Holyhead 76 mi – Shrewsbury 30 mi

Y Chapel, Castle St ☎ (01978) 860828, llangollen@nwtic.com

Vale of Llangollen Holyhead Rd, ☎ (01978) 860 906

Town★ - Railway★ **AC** - Plas Newydd★ **AC**

Pontcysyllte Aqueduct★★, E : 4 mi by A 539 - Castell Dinas Bran★, N : by footpath – Valle Crucis Abbey★ **AC**, N : 2 mi by A 542. Chirk Castle★★ **AC** (wrought iron gates★), SE : 7.5 mi by A 5 – Rug Chapel★ **AC**, W : 11 mi by A 5 and A 494

Gales

18 Bridge St ✉ LL20 8PF – ☎ (01978) 860 089 – www.galesofllangollen.co.uk – Closed 24 December-2 January

13 rm – †£ 55 ††£ 70, ☕ £ 5 – 2 suites

Rest – *(Closed Sunday dinner)* Carte £ 17/28

◆ Pair of family-run, brick-built townhouses with characterful wine theme throughout. Spacious beamed bedrooms boast modern bathrooms and complimentary port. Below are a wine/kitchenware shop and atmospheric wood-panelled wine bar with wide-ranging blackboard menu.

LLANGRANNOG – Ceredigion – 503 G27 — 33 B3

London 241 mi – Caerdydd / Cardiff 96 mi – Aberystwyth / Aberyswyth 30 mi – Caerfyrddin / Carmarthen 28 mi

The Grange without rest

Pentregat, Southeast : 3 mi by B 4321 on A 487 ✉ SA44 6HW – ☎ (01239) 654 121 – www.grangecountryhouse.co.uk – Closed 24-31 December

4 rm ☕ – †£ 45/55 ††£ 75/85

◆ Originally the manor house of the adjacent estate. Traditionally furnished guest areas; afternoon tea from real silver teapot on arrival. Well-maintained bedrooms boast roll-top baths.

LLANIGON – Powys – 503 K27 – see Hay-on-Wye

LLANOVER – Monmouthshire – see Abergavenny

LLANRHIDIAN – Swansea – 503 H29 – see Swansea

LLANSANFFRAID GLAN CONWY – Conwy – 502 I24 – see Conwy

LLANTWIT MAJOR (Llanilltud Fawr) – The Vale of Glamorgan — 33 B4 – 503 J29 – pop. 13 366

London 175 mi – Cardiff 18 mi – Swansea 33 mi

West House

West St ✉ CF61 1SP – ☎ (01446) 792 406 – www.westhouse-hotel.co.uk

20 rm ☕ – †£ 59/75 ††£ 90/120

Rest – *(Closed 24-25 December) (dinner only and lunch Friday-Sunday)* Menu £ 18 (Sunday lunch) – Carte £ 18/36 **s**

◆ 16C building with pleasant walled garden, set in old part of town. Cosy lounge with wood burning stove. Bedrooms in contemporary style; period furniture. Dining room showcases local, seasonal produce.

LLANUWCHLLYN – Gwynedd – 503 I/J25 — 32 B2

Cardiff 147 mi – Dolgellau 13 mi – Llangollen 27 mi

Eifionydd without rest

✉ LL23 7UB – ☎ (01678) 540 622 – www.visitbala.com – March-October

3 rm ☕ – †£ 40/70 ††£ 70/120

◆ Comfy guest house in small hamlet, boasting beautiful rear views across a stream to the mountains beyond. Pleasant sun lounge, conservatory and breakfast room. Immaculately kept, individually decorated bedrooms with compact modern bathrooms.

LLANWRTYD WELLS – Powys – 503 J27 – pop. 649 33 B3

London 214 mi – Brecon 32 mi – Cardiff 68 mi – Carmarthen 39 mi

Ty Barcud, The Square ✆ (01591) 610666, enquiries@llanwrtyd.com

Abergwesyn-Tregaron Mountain Road★, NW : 19 mi on minor roads

Lasswade Country House

Station Rd ✉ LD5 4RW – ✆ (01591) 610 515 – www.lasswadehotel.co.uk – Closed 25 December, January, February, Sunday and Monday

8 rm – †£ 55/75 ††£ 75/115

Rest – *(dinner only)* Menu £ 38

◆ Keenly run detached house close to town, with book-filled lounge and conservatory breakfast room. Traditional décor has been replaced by more modern styles; light hues in bedrooms. Concise menu features their own hot-smoked salmon and other local produce.

Carlton Riverside with rm

Irfon Cres ✉ LD5 4SP – ✆ (01591) 610 248 – www.carltonriverside.co.uk

5 rm – †£ 50/60 ††£ 100

Rest – *(Closed Sunday dinner) (dinner only and Sunday lunch)* Menu £ 25 (dinner) – Carte approx. £ 40

◆ 400 yards from its original premises, overlooking the River Irfon. Skilled cooking based on traditional combinations uses quality ingredients. Two comfy lounges and courteous host. Simple, well-priced bedrooms.

LLYSWEN – Powys – 503 K27 – ✉ Brecon 33 C3

London 188 mi – Brecon 8 mi – Cardiff 48 mi – Worcester 53 mi

Brecon Beacons National Park★★

Llangoed Hall

Northwest : 1.25 mi on A 470 ✉ LD3 0YP – ✆ (01874) 754 525 – www.llangoedhall.com

23 rm – †£ 175/190 ††£ 325/350

Rest – *(booking essential for non-residents)* Menu £ 25/45

◆ Homely country house by river, built by Williams-Ellis and owned by family of late Bernard and Laura Ashley. Spacious rooms mix period and modern furnishings. Impressive art collection includes Whistler. Restaurant serves classical dishes with a modern edge.

MACHYNLLETH – Powys – 503 I26 – pop. 2 147 32 B2

London 220 mi – Shrewsbury 56 mi – Welshpool 37 mi

Royal House, Penrallt St ✆ (01654) 702401, mactic@powys.gov.uk

Felingerrig, ✆ (01654) 702 000

Town★ - Celtica★ AC

Snowdonia National Park★★★ - Centre for Alternative Technology★★ AC, N : 3 mi by A 487

Ynyshir Hall

Eglwysfach, Southwest : 6 mi on A 487 ✉ SY20 8TA – ✆ (01654) 781 209 – www.ynyshir-hall.co.uk

6 rm – †£ 225/320 ††£ 300/325 – 3 suites

Rest – *(dinner only and Sunday lunch) (booking essential)* Menu £ 70

Spec. Poached and roasted quail, ravioli of quail egg. Assiette of Welsh Black beef with asian spices. Treacle tart, walnuts and banana.

◆ Part-Georgian house set within 1,000 acre RSPB reserve. Bright, individually appointed bedrooms, cosy drawing room with art, antiques and Welsh pottery. Charming and very attentive service. Adroit cooking skilfully blends the classic with the modern.

MENAI BRIDGE – Isle of Anglesey – 502 H24 – see Anglesey (Isle of)

MOLD (Yr Wyddgrug) – Flintshire – 502 K24 – pop. 9 568 **32** C1

London 211 mi – Chester 12 mi – Liverpool 22 mi – Shrewsbury 45 mi
Library and Museum , Earl Rd ✆ (01352) 759331, mold@nwtic.com
Pantmywyn Clicain Rd, ✆ (01352) 740 318
Old Padeswood Station Rd, Old Padeswood, ✆ (01244) 547 701
Padeswood & Buckley Station Lane, The Caia, ✆ (01244) 550 537
Caerwys, ✆ (01352) 721 222
St Mary's Church★

Tower without rest

Nercwys, South : 1 mi by B 5444, Nercwys rd on Treuddyn rd ✉ CH7 4EW – ✆ (01352) 700 220 – www.towerwales.co.uk – Closed 17 December-2 January
3 rm – †£ 65 ††£ 105
◆ Impressive fortified house with pond and extensive grounds, dating from 1465 and in family almost as long. Huge high-ceilinged bedrooms boast character beds, antiques and vast modern showers.

Glasfryn

Raikes Ln, Sychdyn, North : 1 mi by A 5119 on Civic Centre rd (Theatr Clwyd) ✉ CH7 6LR – ✆ (01352) 750 500 – www.glasfryn-mold.co.uk – Closed 25 December
Rest – Carte £ 21/30
◆ Sizeable red-brick pub with Arts and Crafts styling and pleasant town outlook. Menu offers plenty of choice from pub to culinary classics. Portions are generous and service is swift.

MONMOUTH (Trefynwy) – Monmouthshire – 503 L28 – pop. 8 547 **33** C4

London 135 mi – Abergavenny 19 mi – Cardiff 40 mi
Town★

at Whitebrook South : 8.25 mi by A 466 – ✉ Monmouth

Crown at Whitebrook with rm

✉ NP25 4TX – ✆ (01600) 860 254 – www.crownatwhitebrook.co.uk – Closed 2 weeks Christmas
8 rm – †£ 110 ††£ 150
Rest – *(closed Sunday dinner) (booking essential)* Menu £ 28/48 – Carte £ 48/70
Spec. Lobster with ham hock, parsnip and coffee. Lamb with celeriac, tomato and Madeira. Poached rhubarb, strawberry, rosewater and lemon.
◆ Attentively run by smart, personable staff. Lounge bar with deep leather sofas and immaculately laid dining room. The kitchen effectively employs modern techniques to produce original, flavoursome dishes. Smart bedrooms in contemporary colours.

at Rockfield Northwest : 2.5 mi on B 4233 – ✉ Monmouth

Stonemill

West : 1 mi on B 4233 ✉ NP25 5SW – ✆ (01600) 716 273 – www.thestonemill.co.uk – Closed 25-26 December, 2 weeks January, Sunday dinner and Monday
Rest – Menu £ 15/19 – Carte £ 29/34
◆ Converted 16C stone cider mill with exposed timbers, and leather sofa in sitting area/bar. Attentive service. Well-sourced modern seasonal dishes feature produce from small local suppliers.

MONTGOMERY (Trefaldwyn) – Powys – 503 K26 – pop. 1 059 **32** C2

London 194 mi – Birmingham 71 mi – Chester 53 mi – Shrewsbury 30 mi
Town★

Little Brompton Farm without rest

Southeast : 2 mi on B 4385 ✉ SY15 6HY – ✆ (01686) 668 371 – www.littlebromptonfarm.co.uk
3 rm – †£ 36 ††£ 62
◆ Part-17C cottage on working farm, run by friendly couple: husband's lived here all his life. Cosy beamed lounge and inglenook. Hearty breakfast. Traditionally appointed rooms.

NANTGAREDIG - Carmarthenshire - **503** H28 - see Carmarthen

NANT-Y-DERRY - Monmouthshire - see Abergavenny

NARBERTH - Pembrokeshire - **503** F28 - pop. 1 869 **33** A4

London 234 mi - Caerdydd / Cardiff 88 mi - Abertawe / Swansea 51 mi - Rhondda 79 mi

Grove

Molleston, South : 2 mi by A 478 on Herons Brook rd ✉ SA67 8BX - ✆ (01834) 860 915 - www.thegrove-narberth.co.uk

12 rm - †£ 120/140 ††£ 210/260

Rest - *(booking essential at lunch)* Menu £ 23 (lunch) **s** - Carte £ 30/40 **s**

◆ Part-Georgian, part-Victorian house in charming rural location. Bedrooms blend bold walls and fabrics with traditional furnishings; spacious bathrooms boast every modern amenity. Monthly changing menus offer traditional dishes with a few Italian influences.

NEWPORT - Newport - **503** L29 - pop. 116 143 **33** C4

London 145 mi - Bristol 31 mi - Cardiff 12 mi - Gloucester 48 mi

Museum and Art Gallery, John Frost Sq ✆ (01633) 842962, newport.tic@newport.gov.uk

Caerleon Broadway, ✆ (01633) 420 342

Parc Coedkernew Church Lane, ✆ (01633) 680 933

Museum and Art Gallery★ AX **M** - Transporter Bridge★ **AC** AY - Civic Centre (murals★) AX

Caerleon Roman Fortress★★ **AC** (Fortress Baths★ - Legionary Museum★ - Amphitheatre★), NE : 2.5 mi by B 4596 AX - Tredegar House★★ (Grounds★ - Stables★), SW : 2.5 mi by A 48 AY. Penhow Castle★, E : 8 mi by A 48 AX

Celtic Manor Resort

Coldra Woods, East : 3 mi on A 48 ✉ NP18 1HQ - ✆ (01633) 413 000 - www.celtic-manor.com

298 rm - †£ 150/258 ††£ 258 - 32 suites

Rest *Crown at Celtic Manor* - *(closed Sunday and Monday)* Menu £ 20/50 - Carte £ 50/70

Rest *Rafters* - Menu £ 22 (dinner) - Carte £ 26/55

Rest *Olive Tree* - *(dinner only and Sunday lunch)* Menu £ 30

◆ Modern resort-style hotel in 1,400 acres. Large conference rooms, 3 golf courses, extensive leisure facilities and small shopping mall. Classical bedrooms; impressive presidential suites. Modern fine dining in The Crown. Favourites and grills in informal Rafters. Buffet and carvery in Olive Tree.

NEWPORT (Trefdraeth) - Pembrokeshire - **503** F27 - pop. 1 162 **33** A3

London 258 mi - Fishguard 7 mi

Bank Cottages, Long St ✆ (01239) 820912 (summer only), newporttic@pembrokeshirecoast.org.uk

Newport Links, ✆ (01239) 820 244

Pembrokeshire Coast National Park★★

Cnapan

East St, on A 487 ✉ SA42 0SY - ✆ (01239) 820 575 - www.cnapan.co.uk - Closed 25-26 December and 5 January-mid-March

5 rm - †£ 54 ††£ 88

Rest - *(closed Tuesday) (dinner only) (booking essential)* Menu £ 30

◆ Keenly run, well-maintained house with traditionally furnished lounge and bar. Fresh, compact bedrooms with white walls, coloured throws and slightly old-fashioned feel. Candlelit restaurant opens onto spacious garden and offers extensive home-cooked menu.

WALES

XX **Llysmeddyg** with rm

East St ✉ SA42 0SY – ✆ (01239) 820 008 – www.llysmeddyg.com – Restricted opening first 2 weeks January

8 rm – ♦£ 70/85 ♦♦£ 150

Rest – *(Closed Sunday and Monday in winter) (booking essential at lunch)* Carte £ 30/43

♦ Earnestly laid-back style; lunch offered in the cellar bar. Dinner, with fine art surroundings, has more of a modern edge. Bright bedrooms with good bathrooms.

NEWTOWN – Powys – pop. 10 358 – ✉ Blaenau Gwent 32 C2

London 194 mi – Cardiff 98 mi – Birmingham 81 mi – Wolverhampton 69 mi

Highgate without rest

Bettws Cedewain, Northeast : 2.5 mi by B 4568 on Llanfair Rd. ✉ SY16 3LF – ✆ (01686) 623 763 – www.highgatebandb.co.uk. – Closed 25-26 December

4 rm – ♦£ 45/65 ♦♦£ 85/105

♦ Built in 1631, with colourful gardens, stables for your horse and superb views across rolling fields. Tastefully furnished, it boasts good-sized bedrooms and a warm, welcoming feel.

PEMBROKE (Penfro) – Pembrokeshire – 503 F28 – pop. 7 214 33 A4

London 252 mi – Carmarthen 32 mi – Fishguard 26 mi

Access Cleddau Bridge (toll)

to Republic of Ireland (Rosslare) (Irish Ferries) 2 daily (4 h) – to Republic of Ireland (Cork) (Swansea Cork Ferries) daily (8 h 30 mn)

Pembroke Visitor Centre, Commons Rd ✆ (01646) 622388 (summer only), pembroke.tic@pembrokeshire.gov.uk

18 Pembroke Dock Military Rd, ✆ (01646) 621 453

Town★★ - Castle★★ **AC**

Pembrokeshire Coast National Park★★ - Carew Castle★ **AC**, NE : 4 mi by A 4075. Bosherston (St Govan's Chapel★), S : 7 mi by B 4319 and minor roads – Stack Rocks★, SW : 9 mi by B 4319 and minor roads

at Lamphey East : 1.75 mi on A 4139 – ✉ Pembroke

Lamphey Court

✉ SA71 5NT – ✆ (01646) 672 273 – www.lampheycourt.co.uk

39 rm – ♦£ 104 ♦♦£ 124/164 **Rest** – Carte £ 28/33

♦ Large Georgian mansion surrounded by parkland, built by Charles Mathias in an idyllic location. Well-furnished throughout with fine mahogany in the coordinated bedrooms. Formal restaurant with a good country house style menu.

PENARTH – Cardiff – 503 K29 – see Cardiff

PENMACHNO – Conwy – 502 I24 – see Betws-y-Coed

PENNAL – Gwnyedd – 503 I26 – see Aberdovey

PONTDOLGOCH – Powys – see Caersws

PORTHCAWL – Bridgend – 503 I29 – pop. 15 640 33 B4

London 183 mi – Cardiff 28 mi – Swansea 18 mi

The Old Police Station, John St ✆ (01656) 786639, porthcawltic@bridgend.gov.uk

Glamorgan Heritage Coast★

Foam Edge without rest

9 West Dr ✉ CF36 3LS – ✆ (01656) 782 866 – www.foam-edge.co.uk – Closed Christmas

3 rm – ♦£ 50/65 ♦♦£ 75/90

♦ Unassuming house by the promenade masks stylish, modern interior with superb Bristol Channel views. A family home in essence, with comfy lounge and communal breakfast. Bedrooms in pastel hues.

WALES

PORTHGAIN – Pembrokeshire – see St Davids

PORTMEIRION – Gwynedd – **502** H25 **32** B2

London 245 mi – Caernarfon 23 mi – Colwyn Bay 40 mi – Dolgellau 24 mi

Village★★★ **AC**

Snowdonia National Park★★★ - Lleyn Peninsula★★ – Ffestiniog Railway★★ **AC**

Portmeirion

LL48 6ET – (01766) 770 000 – www.portmerion-village.com

28 rm – £ 140/210 £ 170/240 – 14 suites

Rest – *(booking essential for non-residents)* Menu £ 24/38

♦ Set in a very unique, private Italianate village, designed by Williams-Ellis, this hotel has an appealing 1930s style and boasts fabulous estuary views. Individually designed bedrooms are spread about the gardens/woodland. Beautiful parquet-floored restaurant.

Castell Deudraeth rest,

LL48 6EN – (01766) 772 400 – www.portmeirion-village.com

9 rm – £ 180/250 £ 215/285 – 2 suites

Rest ***Grill*** – Carte £ 27/58

♦ Impressive crenellated manor house displaying original stone fireplace. Relaxed, informal atmosphere; fine Snowdonia views. Huge bedrooms boast chic, contemporary décor and kitchen areas. Choose from brasserie classics in conservatory or pleasant walled garden.

PWLLHELI – Gwynedd – **502** G25 – **pop. 3 861** **32** B2

London 261 mi – Aberystwyth 73 mi – Caernarfon 21 mi

Min Y Don, Station Sq (01758) 613000, pwllheli.tic@gwynedd.gov.uk

Golf Rd, (01758) 701 644

Lleyn Peninsula★★

XX **Plas Bodegroes** with rm

Northwest : 1.75 mi on A 497 LL53 5TH – (01758) 612 363 – www.bodegroes.co.uk – 13 February-29 November

10 rm – £ 50/90 £ 180

Rest – *(closed Sunday dinner and Monday) (dinner only and Sunday lunch) (booking essential)* Menu £ 20/44

♦ Delightful Grade II listed Georgian house in secluded gardens. Local art decorates the pale green dining room. Classically based cooking, using good quality local ingredients. Contemporary, Scandinavian-style bedrooms.

at Boduan Northwest : 3.75 mi on A 497 – Pwllheli

The Old Rectory without rest

LL53 6DT – (01758) 721 519 – www.theoldrectory.net – Closed 1 week Christmas

3 rm – £ 60/95 £ 75/95

♦ Lovely part-Georgian family home with paddock, run by charming owner. Comfy lounge with carved wooden fireplace; cakes on arrival. Tasteful bedrooms boast period furnishings and garden views.

RHOSCOLYN – Isle of Anglesey – **503** G24 – see Anglesey (Isle of)

RHOS-ON-SEA = Llandrillo-yn-Rhos – Conwy – **502** I24 – see Colwyn Bay

The symbol guarantees a good night's sleep. In red ? The very essence of peace: only the sound of birdsong in the early morning...

RHYL – Denbighshire – 502 J24 – pop. 24 889 — 32 C1

Cardiff 182 mi – Chester 34 mi – Llandudno 18 mi

Rhuddlan Castle★★, S : 3 mi by A 525 – Bodelwyddan★★, S : 5 mi by A 525 and minor rd – St Asaph Cathedral★, S : 5 mi by A 525. Llandudno★, W : 16 mi by A 548, A 55 and B 5115

Barratt's at Ty'n Rhyl with rm

167 Vale Rd., South : 0.5 mi on A 525 ✉ LL18 2PH – ✆ (01745) 344 138 – www.barrattsoftynrhyl.co.uk

3 rm – ♦£ 69 ♦♦£ 90

Rest – *(dinner only and Sunday lunch) (booking essential)* Carte approx. £ 38

◆ Rhyl's oldest house boasts comfortable lounges with rich oak panelling. Dine in either the conservatory or original house. Ambitious cooking displays a classic base. Bedrooms are individually designed.

ROCKFIELD – Monmouthshire – 503 L28 – see Monmouth

ROWEN – Conwy – see Conwy

RUTHIN (Rhuthun) – Denbighshire – 502 K24 – pop. 5 218 — 32 C1

London 210 mi – Birkenhead 31 mi – Chester 23 mi – Liverpool 34 mi

Ruthin-Pwllglas, ✆ (01824) 702 296

Llandyrnog (St Dyfnog's Church★), Llanrhaeder-yng-Nghinmeirch (Jesse Window★★), N : 5.5 mi by A 494 and B 5429. Denbigh★, NW : 7 mi on A 525

Firgrove

Llanfwrog, West : 1.25 mi by A 494 on B 5105 ✉ LL15 2LL – ✆ (01824) 702 677 – www.firgrovecountryhouse.co.uk – March-October

3 rm – ♦£ 60 ♦♦£ 90/120 **Rest** – Menu £ 35

◆ Attractive stone-built house in pleasant gardens. Sit by cosy inglenook in winter or in delightful glasshouse in summer. Comfy four-poster bedrooms and self-contained cottage offer valley views. Communal dinners feature locally sourced farm produce.

Eyarth Station without rest

Llanfair Dyffryn Clwyd, South : 1.75 mi by A 525 ✉ LL15 2EE – ✆ (01824) 703 643 – www.eyarthstation.co.uk

6 rm – ♦£ 50/75 ♦♦£ 75

◆ Former railway station: platform at heart of house, tracks under conservatory. Simple pine-furnished bedrooms feature railway memorabilia. Panoramic windows in lounge afford great rural views.

Manorhaus with rm

Well St ✉ LL15 1AH – ✆ (01824) 704 830 – www.manorhaus.com – Closed 1 week Christmas

8 rm – ♦£ 60/110 ♦♦£ 90/130 **Rest** – *(dinner only)* Menu £ 33

◆ Classical Georgian property with conservatory extension; weekly changing menu features locally sourced ingredients. Each bedroom individually styled to correspond to the work of one of the contemporary Welsh artists exhibited here. Small gym and mini-cinema.

ST ASAPH – Denbighshire – 503 J24 – pop. 3 491 — 32 C1

London 223 mi – Cardiff 176 mi – Liverpool 46 mi – Manchester 69 mi

Tan-yr-Onnen without rest

Waen, East : 1.5 mi by A 55 and B 5429 on Tremeirchion rd ✉ LL17 0DU – ✆ (01745) 583 821 – www.northwalesbreaks.co.uk – Closed 25-26 December

6 rm – ♦£ 69/109 ♦♦£ 89/125

◆ Just off the A55, this spacious house offers stylish, up-to-date bedrooms, well-equipped with silent fridges, DVD players and digital TVs. Large conservatory and lounge; full Welsh breakfast.

ST CLEARS – Carmarthenshire – **503** G28 – **pop. 1 587** **33** B3

London 221 mi – Caerdydd / Cardiff 76 mi – Abertawe / Swansea 37 mi – Llanelli 33 mi

Coedllys Country House without rest

Llangynin, Northwest : 3.5 mi by A 40 turning first left after 30 mph sign on entering village. ✉ *SA33 4JY* – ✆ *(01994) 231 455 – www.coedllyscountryhouse.co.uk – Closed 23-27 December*

3 rm – †£ 58/62 ††£ 90/100

◆ Idyllic country house and animal sanctuary with picture perfect façade. Delightful owner keeps everything immaculate. Superb breakfasts. Bedrooms with an unerring eye for detail.

ST DAVIDS (Tyddewi) – Pembrokeshire – **503** E28 – **pop. 1 959** **33** A3 – ✉ Haverfordwest

London 266 mi – Carmarthen 46 mi – Fishguard 16 mi

Oriel Y Parc ✆ (01437) 720392, orielyparc@pembrokeshirecoast.org.uk

St Davids City Whitesands Bay, ✆ (01437) 721 751

Town★ – Cathedral★★ - Bishop's Palace★ **AC**

Pembrokeshire Coast National Park★★

Warpool Court

Southwest : 0.5 mi by Porth Clais rd ✉ *SA62 6BN* – ✆ *(01437) 720 300 – www.warpoolcourthotel.com – Closed November and first 2 weeks December*

22 rm (dinner included) – †£ 235 ††£ 285/300

Rest – *(light lunch/dinner)* Menu £ 45 **s**

◆ Over 3,000 hand-painted tiles of Celtic or heraldic design decorate the interior of this 19C house. Modern bedrooms, some with views over neat lawned gardens to the sea. Daily changing classic menus accompanied by fine views.

Ramsey House

Lower Moor, Southwest : 0.5 mi on Porth Clais Rd ✉ *SA62 6RP* – ✆ *(01437) 720 321 – www.ramseyhouse.co.uk – February-November*

6 rm – †£ 60/110 ††£ 90/110 **Rest** – Menu £ 30

◆ Unassuming bungalow hiding stylish, contemporary interior with superb comforts, small lounge and bar. Bedrooms display modern colour schemes and state-of-the-art shower rooms. Traditional menus offer tasty three course dinners.

The Waterings without rest

Anchor Drive, High St, East : 0.25 mi on A 487 ✉ *SA62 6QH* – ✆ *(01437) 720 876 – www.waterings.co.uk*

5 rm – †£ 50/85 ††£ 75/85

◆ Located in peaceful landscaped gardens and named after a sheltered cove on Ramsey Island. Spacious bedrooms furnished in solid pine and set around a central courtyard. Likeable hosts.

Cwtch

22 High St ✉ *SA62 6SD* – ✆ *(01437) 720 491 – www.cwtchrestaurant.co.uk – Closed Sunday and Monday November-March*

Rest – *(dinner only) (booking advisable)* Menu £ 29

◆ Simple, friendly restaurant. Daily menu features hearty portions of honest British classics, crafted from local produce and arriving with large side of veg; old school desserts.

at Porthgain Northeast : 7.75 mi by A 487 – ✉ St Davids

The Shed

The Quay ✉ *SA62 5BN* – ✆ *(01348) 831 518 – www.theshedporthgain.co.uk – Restricted opening in winter*

Rest – Seafood – *(booking essential)* Carte £ 32/39

◆ At the tip of the harbour in a charming spot, this locally renowned rustic eatery started life as a lobster pot store and now serves simply prepared, tasty seafood dishes.

SALEM – Carmarthenshire – see Llandeilo

SAUNDERSFOOT – Pembrokeshire – 503 F28 – pop. 2 946 — 33 A4

London 241 mi – Cardiff 90 mi – Pembroke 12 mi

St Brides Spa

St Brides Hill ✉ SA69 9NH – ✆ (01834) 812 304 – www.stbridesspahotel.com

46 rm – †£ 125/190 ††£ 150/280

Rest ***Cliff*** – Carte £ 32/44 **s**

◆ Occupying a great position over Carmarthen Bay, with breathtaking spa equipped to the highest spec. Fabulous terraces and outdoor infinity pool. Superbly designed bedrooms. Modern European cooking in fine dining restaurant with informal style.

SEION – Gwynedd – see Caernarfon

SKENFRITH – Monmouthshire — 33 C4

London 135 mi – Hereford 16 mi – Ross-on-Wye 11 mi

The Bell at Skenfrith with rm

✉ NP7 8UH – ✆ (01600) 750 235 – www.skenfrith.co.uk – Closed last week January, first week February and Tuesday November-Easter

11 rm – †£ 75/120 ††£ 220

Rest – *(booking essential)* Menu £ 24 (Sunday lunch) – Carte £ 20/35

◆ Well-run pub in verdant valley offering clean, fresh cooking of classic dishes with an innovative twist. Excellent choice of champagnes; warm and unobtrusive service. Understated elegance in super-comfy bedrooms.

SWANSEA – Swansea – 503 I29 – pop. 169 880 — 33 B4

London 191 mi – Birmingham 136 mi – Bristol 82 mi – Cardiff 40 mi

Plymouth St ✆ (01792) 468321, tourism@swansea.gov.uk

Morriston 160 Clasemont Rd, ✆ (01792) 796 528

Clyne Mayals 120 Owls Lodge Lane, ✆ (01792) 401 989

Langland Bay, ✆ (01792) 361 721

Fairwood Park Fairwood Blackhills Lane, ✆ (01792) 297 849

Inco Clydach, ✆ (01792) 841 257

Allt-y-Graban Pontllin Allt-y-Graban Rd, ✆ (01792) 885 757

Palleg Swansea Valley Lower Cwmtwrch, ✆ (01639) 842 193

Town★ - Maritime Quarter★ B – Maritime and Industrial Museum★ B – Glynn Vivian Art Gallery★ B – Guildhall (British Empire Panels★ A **H**)

Gower Peninsula★★ (Rhossili★★), W : by A 4067 A. The Wildfowl and Wetlands Trust★, Llanelli, NW : 6.5 mi by A 483 and A 484 A

Plans on following pages

Morgans

Somerset Pl ✉ SA1 1RR – ✆ (01792) 484 848 – www.morganshotel.co.uk — B**b**

41 rm – †£ 125 ††£ 250 **Rest** – Carte £ 17/35

◆ Converted hotel near docks. Contemporary feel: neutral colours, leather sofas. Splendid original features include soaring cupola. Very stylish rooms. Modish cooking in sleek surroundings.

Didier & Stephanie's

56 St Helens Rd ✉ SA1 4BE – ✆ (01792) 655 603 – Closed Sunday and Monday — A**a**

Rest – French – *(booking essential)* Menu £ 15 (lunch) – Carte (dinner) £ 27/31

◆ Cosy, neighbourhood-styled restaurant with a strong Gallic influence. Welcoming owners provide tasty, good value, seasonally changing menus with lots of French ingredients.

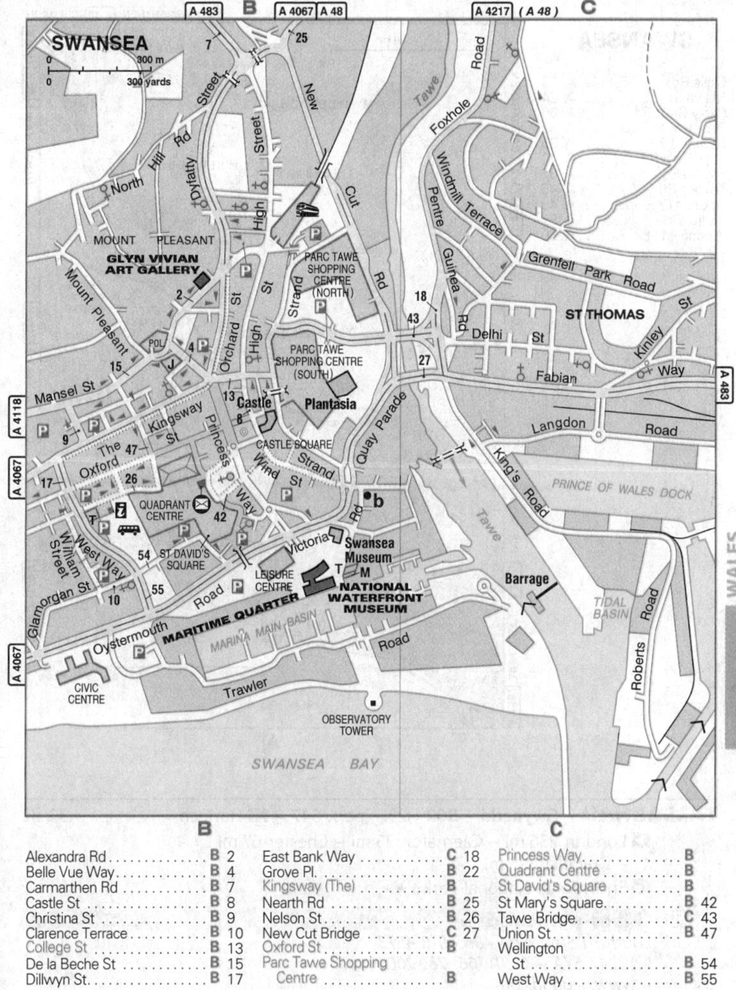

B C

Alexandra Rd . . . . B 2
Belle Vue Way. . . . . B 4
Carmarthen Rd . . . . B 7
Castle St . . . . B 8
Christina St . . . . B 9
Clarence Terrace . . . . B 10
College St . . . . B 13
De la Beche St . . . . B 15
Dillwyn St. . . . . B 17
East Bank Way . . . . C 18
Grove Pl. . . . . B 22
Kingsway (The) . . . . B
Nearth Rd . . . . B 25
Nelson St. . . . . B 26
New Cut Bridge . . . . C 27
Oxford St . . . . B
Parc Tawe Shopping Centre . . . . B
Princess Way. . . . . B
Quadrant Centre . . . . B
St David's Square . . . . B
St Mary's Square. . . . . B 42
Tawe Bridge. . . . . C 43
Union St. . . . . B 47
Wellington St . . . . B 54
West Way . . . . B 55

at Llanrhidian West : 10.5 mi by A 4118 - A - on B 4271 – ✉ Reynoldston

Fairyhill

Reynoldston, West : 2.5 mi by Llangennith Rd ✉ SA3 1BS – ☎ (01792) 390 139 – www.fairyhill.net – Closed 1-27 January and 26 December

8 rm ☕ – 🚹£ 155 🚹🚹£ 275

Rest – Menu £ 20 (weekday lunch)/45 – Carte lunch £ 22/41

◆ Georgian country house in extensive parkland and gardens. Mix includes sleek lounge, eclectic bedrooms, treatment and meeting rooms, all set within general modish ambience. Gower produce dominates seasonal menus.

Welcome To Town

✉ SA3 1EH – ☎ (01792) 390 015 – www.thewelcometotown.co.uk – *Closed 2 weeks November, 25-26 December, Sunday dinner and Monday*

Rest – *(booking essential)* Menu £ 20/32 **s**

◆ Converted pub set on picturesque peninsula. Cosy, traditional interior with good service of seasonal dishes cooked with real quality from wide choice menu.

SWANSEA

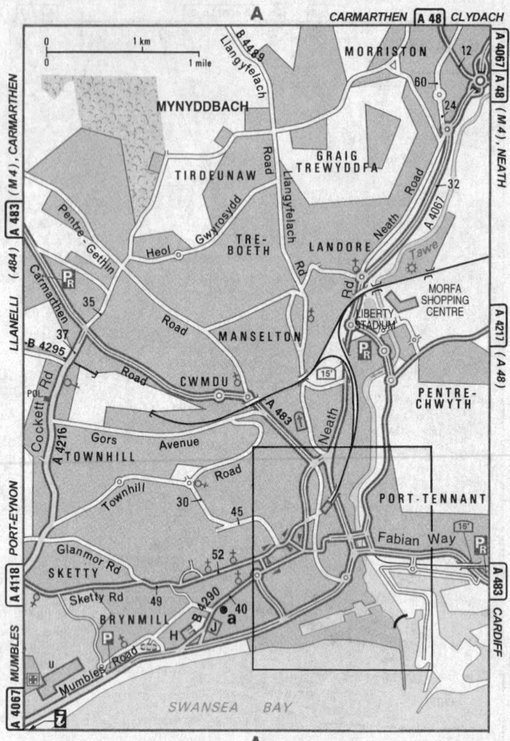

TALSARNAU – Gwynedd – **502** H25 – **pop. 647** – ✉ **Harlech** **32** B2

London 236 mi – Caernafon 33 mi – Chester 67 mi – Dolgellau 25 mi

Snowdonia National Park★★★

Maes-y-Neuadd

South : 1.5 mi by A 496 off B 4573
✉ LL47 6YA – ☎ (01766) 780 200
– www.neuadd.com
14 rm – £ 114/119 ££ 270/285 – 1 suite
Rest – Menu £ 35 (dinner) – Carte lunch £ 18/29
♦ Part-14C country house with pleasant gardens in delightful rural seclusion. Furnished throughout with antiques and curios. Charming service. Individually styled bedrooms. Traditional dining room with linen-clad tables.

TREMEIRCHION – Denbighshire – **502** J24 – ✉ **St Asaph** **32** C1

London 225 mi – Chester 29 mi – Shrewsbury 59 mi

Bach-Y-Graig without rest

Southwest : 2 mi by B 5429 off Denbigh rd
✉ LL17 0UH – ☎ (01745) 730 627
– www.bachygraig.co.uk
3 rm – £ 50/55 ££ 75/80
♦ Attractive brick-built farmhouse dating from the 16C, set on a working farm, in a quiet spot, with woodland trails nearby. Large open fires and wood-furnished bedrooms with cast iron beds.

USK – Monmouthshire – 503 L28 – pop. 2 318 33 C4

London 144 mi – Bristol 30 mi – Cardiff 26 mi – Gloucester 39 mi

Alice Springs Usk Kemeys Commander, (01873) 880 708

Raglan Castle★ **AC**, NE : 7 mi by A 472, A 449 and A 40

Glen-Yr-Afon House

rm, rest,

Pontypool Rd NP15 1SY – (01291) 672 302 – www.glen-yr-afon.co.uk

27 rm – £ 94 £ 136

Rest *Clarkes* – Carte £ 19/33

◆ Just across a bridge from town, is this warmly run 19C villa with relaxing country house ambience. Several welcoming lounges and comfy, well-kept bedrooms. Friendly welcome. Stylish restaurant.

at Llandenny Northeast : 4.25 mi by A 472 off B 4235 – Usk

Raglan Arms

NP15 1DL – (01291) 690 800 – www.raglanarms.com – Closed Sunday dinner and Monday

Rest – Menu £ 22 (Sunday lunch) – Carte £ 19/35

◆ Cosy village pub with fireside sofas and simply laid tables. Local produce employed in a range of cooking styles; lunchtime main courses offer particularly good value.

VALLEY – Isle of Anglesey – 503 G24 – see Anglesey (Isle of)

WELSH HOOK – Pembrokeshire – 503 F28 – see Fishguard

WHITEBROOK – Monmouthshire – see Monmouth

WOLF'S CASTLE (Cas-Blaidd) – Pembrokeshire – 503 F28 – pop. 616 33 A3 – Haverfordwest

London 258 mi – Fishguard 7 mi – Haverfordwest 8 mi

Pembrokeshire Coast National Park★★

Wolfscastle Country H.

rest,

SA62 5LZ – (01437) 741 225 – www.wolfscastle.com – Closed 24-26 December

20 rm – £ 75 £ 95/135 **Rest** – Menu £ 14 (lunch) – Carte £ 21/32

◆ Former manor house that's been greatly expanded over the years and is popular for weddings/conferences. Tidy, well-equipped bedrooms – some with four-posters; modern bathrooms. Traditional bar. Contemporary restaurant offers everything from snacks to 3 courses.

WREXHAM (Wrecsam) – Wrexham – 502 L24 – pop. 42 576 32 C1

London 192 mi – Chester 12 mi – Liverpool 35 mi – Shrewsbury 28 mi

Lambpit St (01978) 292015, tic@wrexham.gov.uk

Chirk, (01691) 774 407

Clays Golf Centre Bryn Estyn Rd, (01978) 661 406

Moss Valley Moss Rd, (01978) 720 518

Pen-y-Cae Ruabon Rd, (01978) 810 108

Plassey Oaks Golf Complex Eyton, (01978) 780 020

St Giles Church★

Erddig★★ **AC** (Gardens★★), SW : 2 m – Gresford (All Saints Church★), N : 4 mi by A 5152 and B 5445

at Gresford Northeast : 3 mi by A 483 on B 5445

Pant-yr-Ochain

Old Wrexham Rd, South : 1 mi LL12 8TY – (01978) 853 525 – www.pantyrochain-gresford.co.uk

Rest – Carte £ 20/35

◆ Classic country manor house with mature, manicured gardens and a lake. Daily changing menu offers hearty, wholesome dishes ranging from pub classics to more modern fare. Over 12s only.

WALES

USK – Monmouthshire – 503 L 28 – pop. 2 318 32 C1

London 144 mi – Bristol 30 mi – Cardiff 26 mi – Gloucester 39 mi

Twyn Square, Usk [illegible]

[illegible]

Glen-yr-Afon [illegible]

Pontypool Rd, NP15 1SY – ℰ (01291) 672 302 – www.glen-yr-afon.co.uk

27 rm – [illegible]

Rest [illegible] – Carte £ 19/33

• [illegible] across a bridge from town, is this warmly run 19C villa with relaxing country house ambience. Several welcoming lounges and comfy, well-kept bedrooms. Friendly welcome. Stylish restaurant.

at Llangybi South : 2¾ mi on [illegible] – ⊠ Usk

Cwrt Bleddyn [illegible]

[illegible] – ℰ (01291) 672 790 – [illegible] – Closed Sunday

[illegible]

Rest – [illegible] (Sunday) [illegible] – Carte [illegible]

• [illegible] with fireside sofas [illegible] tables. Local produce [illegible] range of cooking styles [illegible] courses [illegible]

VALLEY – Isle of Anglesey – 502 G 24 – see Anglesey (Isle of)

VELFREY – Pembrokeshire – 503 F 28 – see Whitland

WHITEBROOK – Monmouthshire – see Monmouth

WOLF'S CASTLE (Cas-Blaidd) – Pembrokeshire – 503 F 28 – pop. 616 33 A3

Haverfordwest

London [illegible] – Haverfordwest 8 mi

Pembrokeshire [illegible]

Wolfscastle Country H. [illegible]

[illegible] – [illegible] .co.uk

– Closed 24-26 December

20 rm [illegible] – Rest – [illegible] (lunch) – Carte £ 20/32

• Former [illegible] house that's been [illegible] over the years and is popular for weddings [illegible] conferences. [illegible] bedrooms, some with four-posters, modern bathrooms. Traditional [illegible] contemporary restaurant offers everything from snacks to [illegible] courses.

WREXHAM (Wrecsam) – Wrexham – 502 L 24 – pop. 42 576 32 C1

London 192 mi – Chester 12 mi – Liverpool 35 mi – Shrewsbury 28 mi

[illegible] – ℰ (01978) 292 015, [illegible]

[illegible] ℰ (01691) 77 [illegible]

[illegible] Centre [illegible] Rd [illegible]

[illegible] Gresford Rd, ℰ (01978) 261 [illegible]

[illegible]

[illegible] ℰ (01978) 780 020

[illegible] Church

[illegible] (Gardens [illegible]) SW : 2 mi – Gresford (All Saints Church) [illegible] by A 483 and B 5445

at Gresford Northeast : 3 mi by A 483 on B 5445

Pant-yr-Ochain

Old Wrexham Rd, South : 1 mi ⊠ LL12 8TY – ℰ (01978) 853 525 – www.pantyrochain-gresford.co.uk

Rest – Carte £ 20/35

• Classic country manor house with mature manicured gardens and a lake. Daily changing menu offers hearty, wholesome dishes, ranging from pub classics to more modern fare. Over 12s only.

Ireland

O. Forir/MICHELIN

ANNAHILT = Eanach Eilte – Down – 712 N/O4 – see Hillsborough

BALLINTOY – Moyle – 712 M2

Belfast 59 mi – Ballycastle 6 mi – Londonderry 45 mi – Larne ... mi

Whitepark House without rest
150 Whitepark Rd, Whitepark Bay, West: 1.5 mi on A 2 – ☎ (028) 2073 1482
– www.whiteparkhouse.com
3 rms
• Charming 18C house with personable owner. Comfy open fired lounge and individually decorated bedrooms filled with antiques, plants, books and art. Breakfast and communal table.

BALLYCLARE (Bealach Cláir) – Newtownabbey – 712 N3

Belfast 14 mi – Newtownabbey 9 mi – Lisburn 25 mi

Oregano
29 Ballyrobert Rd, Ballyclare, 1.25 mi ... A 57 on B 56 ... ☎ (028) 9084 0099 – www.oreganorestaurant.co.uk
... Sunday dinner ...
... Carte £ 24/29
• Stylish... restaurant ... furnished lounge. ... Italian cooking ... local produce ...

BALLYMENA (An Baile Meánach) – Ballymena – 712 N3
– pop. ...

Belfast 27 mi – Dundalk 78 mi – Larne 21 mi – Londonderry 51 mi
1-29 Bridge St ☎ (028) 2563 5900, tourist.information@ballymena.gov.uk
128 Raceview Rd ☎ (028) 2586 1207
Antrim Glens ... Glenariff Forest Park ... Antrim Round Tower ...
... by A 26

at Galgorm West: 1 mi on A 42

Galgorm Resort & Spa
136 Fenaghy Rd, West: 1.5 mi on Cullybackey rd
... ☎ (028) 2588 1001 – www.galgorm.com
75 rm
River Room – (Tuesday-Saturday dinner and Sunday lunch) Carte £ 32/45
Gillies – Carte £ 20/40
• Victorian manor house in smart grounds ... bedrooms with excellent facilities ...

BANGOR (Beannchar) – North Down – 712 O4 – pop. 58 388 28 C1

Belfast 15 mi – Newtownards 5 mi
... Quay St ☎ (028) 9127 0069 ...
... Tower ...
Ulster Folk and Transport Museum ... Mount Stewart ... Newtownards ...
... Grey Abbey ...

ANNAHILT = Eanach Eilte – Down – 712 N/O4 – see Hillsborough

BALLINTOY – Moyle – 712 M2 — 35 C1

Belfast 59 mi – Ballycastle 8 mi – Londonderry 48 mi – Lisburn 67 mi

Whitepark House without rest

150 Whitepark Rd, West : 1.5 mi on A 2 ✉ BT54 6NH – ✆ (028) 2073 1482 – www.whiteparkhouse.com

3 rm – †£ 75 ††£ 100

◆ Charming 18C house with personable owner. Comfy, open-fired lounge and individually decorated bedrooms filled with antiques, plants, books and art. Breakfast around communal table.

BALLYCLARE (Bealach Cláir) – Newtownabbey – 712 N/O3 – pop. 8 770 — 35 D2

Belfast 14 mi – Newtownabbey 6 mi – Lisburn 23 mi

Oregano

29 Ballyrobert Rd, South : 3.25 mi by A 57 on B 56 ✉ BT39 9RY – ✆ (028) 9084 0099 – www.oreganorestaurant.co.uk – Closed 1 January, 12-13 July, 24-26 December, Saturday lunch, Sunday dinner and Monday

Rest – Menu £ 15 (lunch)/18 – Carte £ 24/39

◆ Whitewashed Victorian house hides stylish restaurant with leather-furnished bar/lounge. Good value modern British cooking uses local produce. European influences; clean, unfussy flavours.

NORTHERN IRELAND

BALLYMENA (An Baile Meánach) – Ballymena – 712 N3 – pop. 28 717 Ireland — 35 C2

Belfast 27 mi – Dundalk 78 mi – Larne 21 mi – Londonderry 51 mi

1-29 Bridge St ✆ (028) 2563 5900, tourist.information@ballymena.gov.uk

128 Raceview Rd, ✆ (028) 2586 1207

Antrim Glens★★★ - Murlough Bay★★★ (Fair Head ≤★★★), NE : 32 mi by A 26, A 44, A 2 and minor road - Glengariff Forest Park★★ **AC** (Waterfall★★), NW : 13 mi by A 43 – Glengariff★, NE : 18 mi by A 43 - Glendun★, NE : 19 mi by A 43, B 14 and A2 – Antrim (Round Tower★) S : 9.5 mi by A 26

at Galgorm West : 3 mi on A 42

Galgorm Resort and Spa rest,

136 Fenaghy Rd, West : 1.5 mi on Cullybacky rd ✉ BT42 1EA – ✆ (028) 2588 1001 – www.galgorm.com

75 rm – †£ 145 ††£ 145/295

Rest *River Room* – *(Thursday-Saturday dinner and Sunday lunch)* Carte £ 32/45

Rest *Gillies* – Carte £ 20/46

◆ Victorian manor house in smart grounds. Stylish lounges, huge function rooms, superb spa/leisure club. Modern bedrooms with excellent facilities in annexes; more traditional rooms in main house. Classical fine dining in River Room. Informal and al fresco dining in Gillies steak house.

BANGOR (Beannchar) – North Down – 712 O/P4 – pop. 58 388 Ireland — 35 D2

Belfast 15 mi – Newtownards 5 mi

34 Quay St ✆ (028) 9127 0069, tic@northdown.gov.uk

North Down Heritage Centre★

Ulster Folk and Transport Museum★★ **AC**, W : 8 mi by A 2. Newtownards : Movilla Priory (Cross Slabs★) S : 4 mi by A 21 - Mount Stewart★★★ **AC**, SE : 90 mi by A 21 and A 20 – Scrabo Tower (≤★★) S : 6.5 mi by A 21 – Ballycopeland Windmill★, SE : 10 mi by B 21 and A 2, turning right at Millisle – Strangford Lough★ (Castle Espie Centre★ **AC** - Nendrum Monastery★) - Grey Abbey★ **AC**, SE : 20 mi by A 2, A 21 and A 20

Clandeboye Lodge

10 Estate Rd, Clandeboye, Southwest : 3 mi by A 2 and Dundonald rd following signs for Blackwood Golf Centre ✉ BT19 1UR – ✆ (028) 9185 2500 – www.clandeboyelodge.com – Closed 24-26 December
43 rm – †£ 75/105 ††£ 85/175
Rest *Clanbrasserie* – *(bar lunch Monday-Saturday)* Carte £ 19/34 **s**
♦ On site of former estate school house, surrounded by 4 acres of woodland. Well placed for country and coast. Meetings and weddings in separate extension. Contemporary bedrooms. Restaurant boasts minimal, stylish décor. Modish menus.

Cairn Bay Lodge without rest

278 Seacliffe Rd, East : 1.25 mi by Quay St ✉ BT20 5HS – ✆ (028) 9146 7636 – www.cairnbaylodge.com – closed 3 weeks January
5 rm – †£ 50/70 ††£ 75/80
♦ Large, whitewashed Edwardian house overlooking the bay. Comfy guest areas feature unusual objets d'art and ornaments; spacious, individually styled bedrooms boast plenty of extras. Friendly owners leave homemade cake on the landing. Small beauty/therapy facility.

Shelleven House without rest

59-61 Princetown Rd ✉ BT20 3TA – ✆ (028) 9127 1777 – www.shellevenhouse.com
11 rm – †£ 35/55 ††£ 75/80
♦ Personally run, end of terrace, double front Victorian house; short stroll to marina. Large, uniformly appointed rooms: ask for a large one at the front. Homely, good value.

The Boat House

Seacliff Rd ✉ BT20 5HA – ✆ (028) 9146 9253 – www.theboathouseni.co.uk – Closed 2 weeks February, 2 weeks October, Monday and Tuesday
Rest – Menu £ 22 (lunch) – Carte £ 28/41
♦ Harbourfront former lifeboat station housing intimate, linen-laid restaurant run by two brothers. Classically based cooking with some French/Italian influences. Good use of local produce.

Jeffers by the Marina

7 Grays Hill ✉ BT20 3BB – ✆ (028) 9185 9555 – www.jeffersbythemarina.com – Closed 12-13 July, 25-26 December and Monday except bank holidays
Rest – Carte £ 25/33
♦ Narrow, glass-fronted restaurant opposite marina, with mirrored wall and black, granite-topped tables. Modern cooking makes good use of indigenous produce. Polite, friendly service.

Coyle's

44 High St ✉ BT20 5AZ – ✆ (028) 9127 0362 – www.coylesbistro.co.uk – Closed 25 December
Rest – Carte £ 22/25
♦ Friendly, laid-back, typically Irish pub; a great place for a quiet drink and a good meal. Bar menu offers classics and some international influences; bistro menu steps things up a gear.

O. Forir/MICHELIN

BELFAST (Béal Feirste)

County: Belfast
Michelin regional map: 712 O4
Dublin 103 mi – Londonderry 70 mi
Population: 276 459

Ireland
Map reference: 35 D2

PRACTICAL INFORMATION

Tourist Information

47 Donegal Pl ✆ (028) 9024 6609, info@belfastvisitor.com

Belfast International Airport, Information desk ✆ (028) 9448 4677

George Best Belfast City Airport, Sydenham Bypass ✆ (028) 9093 5372

Airports

Belfast International Airport, Aldergrove : ✆ (028) 9448 4848, W : 15.5 mi by A 52 AY

George Best Belfast City Airport : ✆ (028) 9093 9093

Ferries and Shipping Lines

to Isle of Man (Douglas) (Isle of Man Steam Packet Co. Ltd) (summer only) (2 h 45 mn)
– to Stranraer (Stena Line) 4-5 daily (1 h 30 mn/3 h 15 mn), (Seacat Scotland) March-January (90 mn)
– to Liverpool (Norfolkline Irish Sea) daily (8 h 30 mn)

Golf Courses

18 Balmoral 518 Lisburn Rd, ✆(028) 9038 1514

18 Belvoir Park Newtonbreda 73 Church Rd, ✆(028) 9049 1693

18 Fortwilliam Downview Ave, ✆(028) 9037 0770

18 The Nock Club Dundonald Summerfield, ✆(028) 9048 2249

18 Shandon Park 73 Shandon Park, ✆(028) 9080 5030

9 Cliftonville Westland Rd, ✆(028) 9022 8585

9 Ormeau 50 Park Road, ✆(028) 9064 1069

SIGHTS

In the suurounding area

Carrickfergus (Castle★★ **AC**, St Nicholas' Church★) NE : 9.5 mi by A 2 – Talnotry Cottage Bird Garden, Crumlin★ **AC**, W : 13.5 mi by A 52

In town

City★ - Ulster Museum★★ (Spanish Armada Treasure★★, Shrine of St Patrick's Hand★) AZ **M1** – City Hall★ BY – Donegall Square★ BY **20** – Botanic Gardens (Palm House★) AZ – St Anne's Cathedral★ BX – Crown Liquor Saloon★ BY – Sinclair Seamen's Church★ BX – St Malachy's Church★ BY

On the outskirts

Belfast Zoological Gardens★★ **AC**, N : 5 mi by A 6 AY

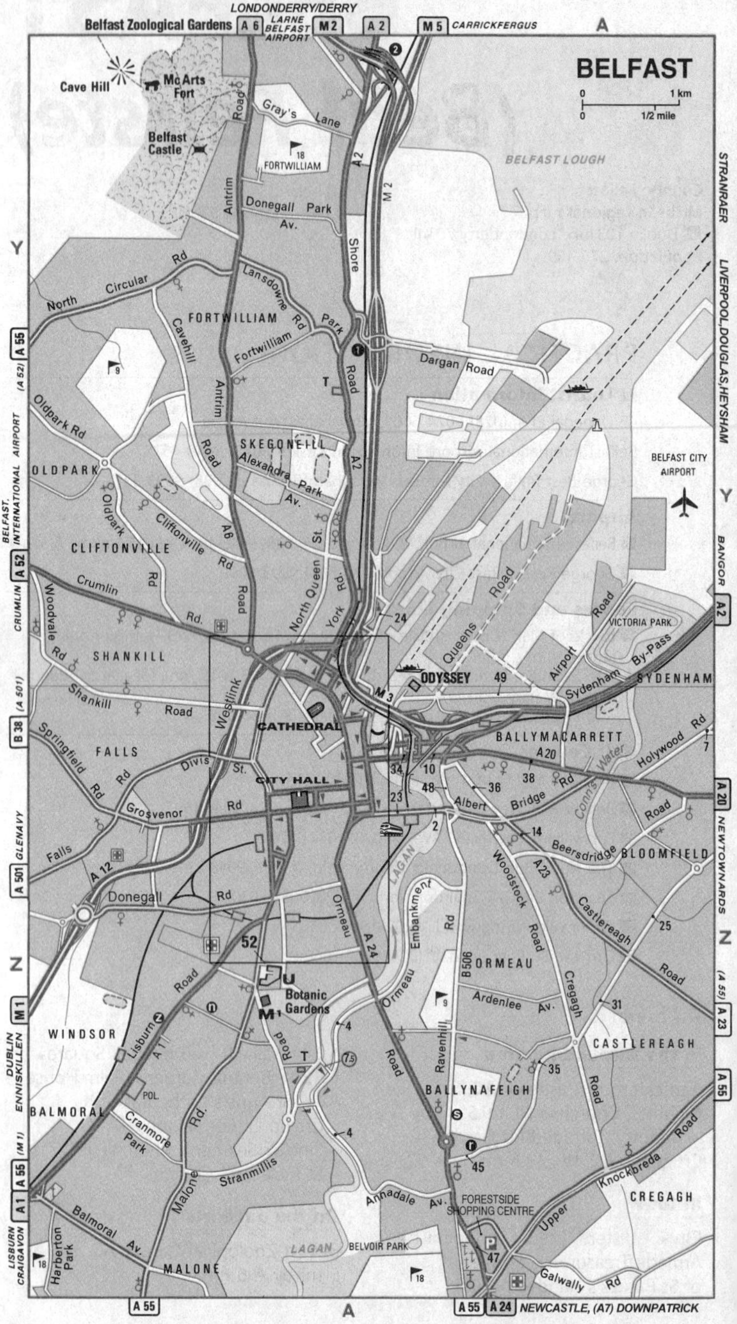

BELFAST

0 1 km
0 1/2 mile

LONDONDERRY/DERRY
Belfast Zoological Gardens A 6
LARNE BELFAST AIRPORT M 2
A 2
M 5 CARRICKFERGUS

Cave Hill
McArts Fort
Belfast Castle
Gray's Lane
FORTWILLIAM
Antrim Road
Donegall Park Av.
Shore
A2
M 2
BELFAST LOUGH
STRANRAER
LIVERPOOL,DOUGLAS,HEYSHAM
North Circular Rd
Lansdowne Rd
Park
FORTWILLIAM
Fortwilliam
Cavehill
Dargan Road
A 55
(A 52) BELFAST. INTERNATIONAL AIRPORT
NORTHERN IRELAND
Oldpark Rd
OLDPARK
Oldpark
SKEGONEILL
Alexandra Park Av.
BELFAST CITY AIRPORT
CLIFTONVILLE
Cliftonville Rd
North Queen St.
York Rd.
A6
BANGOR
A 52 CRUMLIN
Crumlin Rd.
Woodvale Rd
SHANKILL
Queens Road
Airport Road
VICTORIA PARK
Sydenham By-Pass
SYDENHAM
A2
ODYSSEY
M 3
49
(A 501)
Shankill Road
Westlink
CATHEDRAL
BALLYMACARRETT
B 38
Springfield Rd
FALLS
Divis St.
Holywood Rd
7
A20
Connswater
CITY HALL
34
10
38
Rd
48
36
Albert Bridge
A 20
Grosvenor Rd
23
2
Road
NEWTOWNARDS
14
Beersbridge
BLOOMFIELD
A 501 GLENAVY
Falls
A 12
Donegall Rd
LAGAN
Woodstock Road
A23
Castlereagh Road
25
Ormeau
A 24
Embankment
Rd
52
N
Z
B 506
ORMEAU
Cregagh Road
U
M1
Botanic Gardens
(A 55)
A 23
Ardenlee Av.
31
M1 DUBLIN ENNISKILLEN
WINDSOR
Lisburn Road
A 1
4
Ormeau Road
Ravenhill
CASTLEREAGH
Road
T
75
35
A 55
POL.
BALMORAL
Cranmore Park
Malone Rd.
BALLYNAFEIGH
Road
4
Stranmillis
Knockbreda Road
45
(M1) A 55
A 1
Annadale Av.
FORESTSIDE SHOPPING CENTRE
Upper
CREGAGH
LISBURN CRAIGAVON
Balmoral Av.
Harberton Park
LAGAN
BELVOIR PARK
P
47
Galwally Rd
MALONE
A 55
A 55 A 24 NEWCASTLE, (A7) DOWNPATRICK

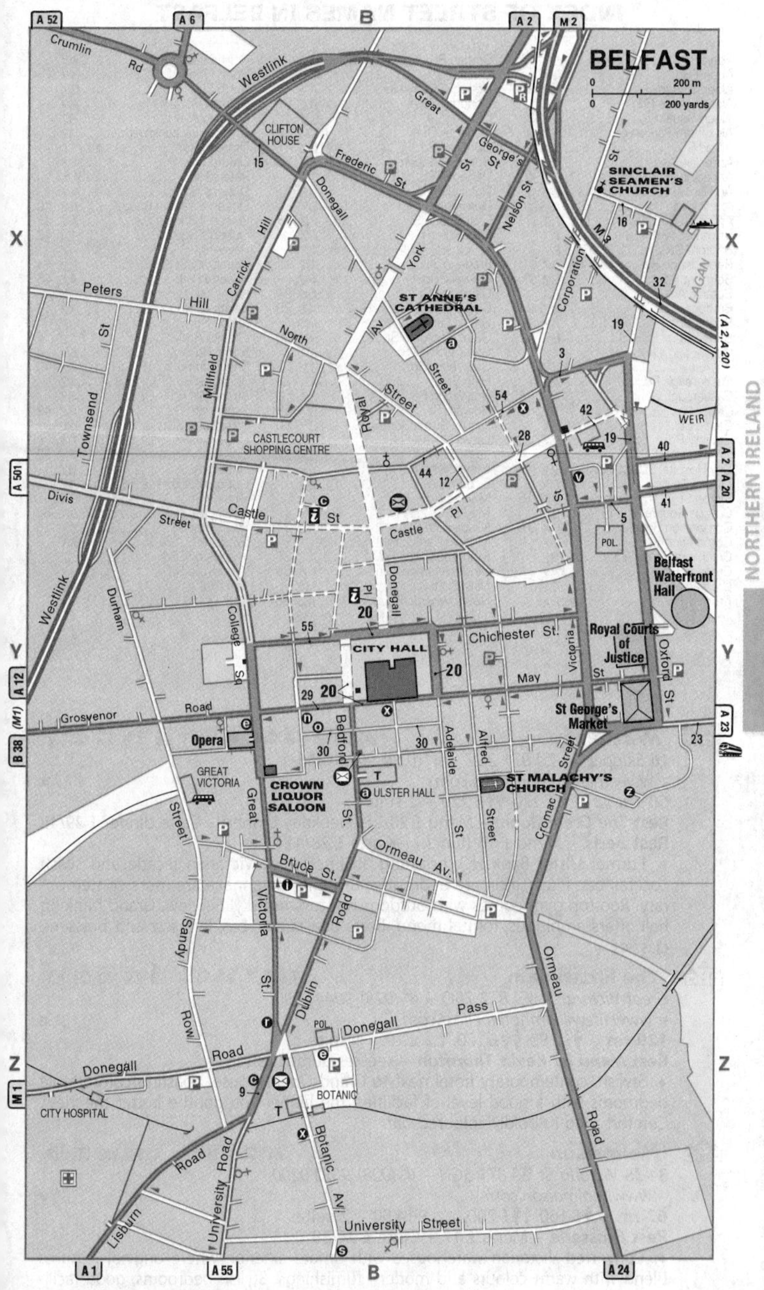
BELFAST
0 200 m
0 200 yards
A 52
A 6
B
A 2
M 2
Crumlin Rd
Westlink
Great George's St
CLIFTON HOUSE
Frederic St
Donegall St
York St
Nelson St
SINCLAIR SEAMEN'S CHURCH
M 3
LAGAN
Corporation St
ST ANNE'S CATHEDRAL
Carrick Hill
Peters Hill
North Street
Royal Av
Millfield
Townsend St
CASTLECOURT SHOPPING CENTRE
WEIR
Divis Street
Castle St
Castle Pl
Victoria St
POL.
Belfast Waterfront Hall
Durham St
College Sq
Donegall Pl
CITY HALL
Chichester St.
Royal Courts of Justice
Oxford St
May St
Grosvenor Road
St George's Market
Opera
Bedford St.
Adelaide St
Alfred Street
GREAT VICTORIA
CROWN LIQUOR SALOON
ULSTER HALL
ST MALACHY'S CHURCH
Cromac Street
Great Victoria St.
Ormeau Av.
Bruce St.
Dublin Road
Sandy Row
Ormeau Road
Donegall Pass
POL
Donegall Road
CITY HOSPITAL
BOTANIC
Lisburn Road
University Road
Botanic Av.
University Street
X
Y
Z
A 501
A 12
(M1)
B 38
M 1
A 1
A 55
A 24
A 23
(A 2, A 20)
A 2
A 20
15
16
32
19
3
54
42
28
44
12
40
41
5
55
20
29
30
23
9

INDEX OF STREET NAMES IN BELFAST

Merchant

16 Skipper St. ✉ *BT1 2DZ* – ✆ *(028) 9023 4888*
– *www.themerchanthotel.com* **BXx**

60 rm – £ 220 £ 220 – 2 suites

Rest *The Great Room* – Menu £ 20/25 (weekday dinner) – Carte dinner £ 29/48

Rest *Berts* – Menu £ 16 (lunch) – Carte £ 28/41

◆ Former Ulster Bank HQ, boasting an impressive Victorian façade and swish cocktail bar. Plush, intimate bedrooms; those in the annexe are more contemporary. Rooftop gym comes with outdoor hot tub and skyline view. Grand banking hall offers ambitious, formal menu. Berts boasts zinc bar, live jazz and brasserie classics.

The Fitzwilliam

Great Victoria St ✉ *BT2 7BQ* – ✆ *(028) 9044 2080*
– *www.fitzwilliamhotelbelfast.com* **BYe**

129 rm – £ 180 £ 180, £ 19 – 1 suite

Rest *Menu by Kevin Thornton* – see restaurant listing

◆ Stylish, contemporary hotel next to Grand Opera House, boasting comfortable bedrooms with a good level of facilities; the higher you go, the better the view. Comfort food in boldly coloured bar.

Malmaison

rest,

34-38 Victoria St ✉ *BT1 3GH* – ✆ *(028) 9022 0200*
– *www.malmaison.com* **BYv**

62 rm – £ 160 £ 200, £ 14.50 – 2 suites

Rest *Brasserie* – Menu £ 17 – Carte £ 27/38

◆ Converted Victorian warehouses with ornate exterior, where original features blend with warm colours and modern furnishings. Stylish bedrooms, good facilities and extras. Small fitness/meeting rooms; stylish bar. Pleasant French brasserie serving classical fare.

Radisson Blu
3 Cromac Pl, Cromac Wood ✉ BT7 2JB – ☎ (028) 9043 4065 – www.radissonblu.co.uk/belfast BYz
119 rm – †£ 83/160 ††£ 83/160, ☕ £ 15.95 – 1 suite
Rest *Filini* – Italian influences – *(closed Sunday)* Carte £ 32/42
♦ Stylish, modern hotel on the site of former gasworks. Smart, up-to-date facilities. Two room styles - Urban or Nordic; both boast fine views over city and waterfront. Restaurant/bar with floor-to-ceiling windows and part-open kitchen.

Ten Square
10 Donegall Sq South ✉ BT1 5JD – ☎ (028) 9024 1001 – www.tensquare.co.uk – Closed 25 December BYx
23 rm ☕ – †£ 149/170 ††£ 149/170
Rest *Grill Room* – Carte £ 18/36
♦ Large Victorian building in central location behind city hall, with busy conference facility. Stylish bedrooms display contemporary feature walls, good facilities and smart bathrooms. Spacious informal bar/restaurant offers accessible menu.

Malone Lodge
60 Eglantine Ave ✉ BT9 6DY – ☎ (028) 9038 8000 – www.malonelodgehotelbelfast.com AZn
58 rm ☕ – †£ 160 ††£ 160 – 35 suites – ††£ 99/200
Rest *The Green Door* – *(closed Sunday dinner)* Carte £ 18/22
♦ Well-run, privately owned hotel in peaceful 19C terrace. Bedrooms display good facilities, with smart corporate bedrooms in main house and executive rooms/apartments in various annexes. Wood-furnished bar; simple restaurant offering classical menus.

Crescent Townhouse
13 Lower Cres ✉ BT7 1NR – ☎ (028) 9032 3349 – www.crescenttownhouse.com – Closed 1 January ,12-13 July, and 24-26 December BZx
17 rm ☕ – †£ 75 ††£ 85/100
Rest *Metro Brasserie* – *(dinner only) (bar lunch)* Carte £ 22/32
♦ Centrally located Regency-style townhouse on corner site, where original features blend well with modern facilities. Spacious bedrooms boast quality décor/-furnishings and smart bathrooms. Dark wood bar; informal brasserie offering popular menus.

Benedicts
7-21 Bradbury Pl, Shaftesbury Sq ✉ BT7 1RQ – ☎ (028) 9059 1999 – www.benedictshotel.co.uk – Closed 24-25 December and 11-12 July
32 rm ☕ – †£ 70 ††£ 85 BZc
Rest – Menu £ 20 (dinner) **s** – Carte £ 15/26 **s**
♦ A lively, strikingly designed bar with nightly entertainment can be found at the heart of this busy commercial hotel. Well-appointed bedrooms above offer modern facilities. Relaxed, popular restaurant.

Ravenhill House without rest

690 Ravenhill Rd ✉ BT6 0BZ – ☎ (028) 9020 7444 – www.ravenhillhouse.com – Closed 1-6 January and 23-31 December AZs
5 rm ☕ – †£ 45/55 ††£ 75
♦ Personally run detached 19C house, attractively furnished in keeping with its age. The largely organic breakfast is a highlight. Good-sized rooms with bold shades predominant.

Roseleigh House without rest
19 Rosetta Park, South : 1.5 mi by A 24 (Ormeau Rd) ✉ BT6 0DL – ☎ (028) 9064 4414 – www.roseleighhouse.co.uk – Closed Christmas-New Year
6 rm ☕ – †£ 45/50 ††£ 70 AZr
♦ Imposing Victorian house close to the Belvoir Park golf course and in a fairly quiet residential suburb. Brightly decorated and well-kept bedrooms with modern amenities.

XX **Deanes**

36 Howard St. ✉ BT1 6PF – ✆ (028) 9033 1134
– www.michaeldeane.co.uk
– Closed 25-26 December, 11-16 July, Sunday and May bank holidays
Rest – Menu £ 23 (lunch and early dinner) – Carte £ 25/44 BY**n**

♦ Three places in one. Stylish brasserie offers interesting, classically based dishes with original modern style. Smaller eatery offers more casual seafood dining. Limited opening in upstairs restaurant, which serves elaborate, inventive, 5/7 course tasting menus.

XX **James Street South**

21 James St South ✉ BT2 7GA – ✆ (028) 9043 4310
– www.jamesstreetsouth.co.uk – Closed 1 January, Easter Sunday, 12 July, 25-26 December, Monday and Sunday lunch BY**o**
Rest – Menu £ 17/19 – Carte £ 25/37

♦ Smart backstreet restaurant with Victorian façade, slate-floored bar and bright, modern dining room. Good-sized menus offer tasty dishes of simply cooked local produce. Efficient service.

XX **Menu by Kevin Thornton** – at The Fitzwilliam Hotel

Great Victoria St ✉ BT27BQ – ✆ (028) 9044 2080
– www.fitzwilliamhotelbelfast.com BY**r**
Rest – Menu £ 13 (lunch) – Carte £ 23/48

♦ Three-roomed restaurant on 1st floor of stylish hotel; large centre table seats one large party or several smaller; if you're a couple, choose a booth. Classic dishes cooked in modern Irish style.

NORTHERN IRELAND

XX **Cayenne**

7 Ascot House, Shaftesbury Sq ✉ BT2 7DB
– ✆ (028) 9033 1532 – www.cayenne-restaurant.co.uk
– Closed 1 January, 12-13 July and 25-26 December BZ**r**
Rest – Asian influences – *(dinner only and lunch Thursday, Friday and Sunday) (booking essential)* Menu £ 16 (lunch)/27 – Carte £ 27/41

♦ Striking modern artwork and a lively atmosphere feature in this busy, relaxed and stylish restaurant. Carefully prepared selection of creative Asian-influenced dishes.

XX **Shu**

253 Lisburn Rd ✉ BT9 7EN
– ✆ (028) 9038 1655 – www.shu-restaurant.com
– Closed 1 January, 12-13 July, 24-26 December and Sunday AZ**z**
Rest – Menu £ 16/27 – Carte £ 25/38

♦ Modern L-shaped restaurant in affluent residential district, with cream/dark wood décor and lively atmosphere. Modern British cooking is guided by seasonality and availability of local produce.

X **No 27**

27 Talbot St ✉ BT1 2LD – ✆ (028) 9031 2884 – www.no27.co.uk
– Closed 12-13 July, 25-26 December and Sunday BX**a**
Rest – Menu £ 23 (weekday dinner) – Carte £ 29/40

♦ Bustling restaurant opposite cathedral; sleekly styled with wooden floor, modern lighting and open kitchen. Simple lunch choices; daily changing dinner menu of modern British cooking.

X **Deanes Deli**

42-44 Bedford St ✉ BT2 7FF
– ✆ (028) 9024 8800 – www.michaeldeane.co.uk
– Closed 1 January, Easter, 1 week July, 25-26 December and Sunday
Rest – Menu £ 25 – Carte £ 25/33 BY**a**

♦ Spacious, glass-fronted city centre restaurant serving a mix of comfort food and globally influenced dishes, with a good choice of daily specials. Bustling, chatty atmosphere.

X **Ginger Bistro**

7-8 Hope St ✉ BT12 5EE – ✆ (028) 9024 4421 – www.gingerbistro.com – Closed Christmas, 11-12 July, Sunday and lunch Monday BYZi

Rest – Carte £ 18/30

◆ Keenly run neighbourhood eatery with modern artwork for sale and bespoke fish-themed paintings. Eclectic menus display Irish produce and worldwide influences; good value lunch/pre-theatre.

X **The Ginger Tree**

23 Donegall Pass ✉ BT7 1DQ – ✆ (028) 9032 7151 – www.ni.gingertree.co.uk – Closed 24-26 December, 12-13 July and Sunday lunch BZe

Rest – Japanese – Menu £ 10/28 – Carte £ 16/29

◆ Simple glass fronted restaurant with black-clothed tables, framed Japanese clothing on walls and Asian-themed fittings. Extensive menus include various set options and à la carte; authentic cooking.

X **Molly's Yard**

1 College Green Mews, Botanic Ave ✉ BT7 1LW – ✆ (028) 9032 2600 – www.mollysyard.co.uk – Closed 24-26 December, 1 January, 12 July and Sunday

Rest – *(booking essential)* Carte £ 20/33 BZs

◆ Friendly split-level bistro in former coach house/stables. Cosier downstairs, with exposed brickwork and courtyard. Menus display fresh, unfussy, modern bistro fare; simpler dishes at lunch.

X **Mourne Seafood Bar**

34-36 Bank St ✉ BT1 1HL – ✆ (028) 9024 8544 – www.mourneseafood.com – Closed 1 January, 17 March, 12-13 July, 25-26 December and dinner Sunday-Monday

Rest – Seafood – *(booking essential at dinner) (lunch bookings not accepted)* Carte £ 18/27 BYc

◆ Classic seafood menu supplemented by daily specials; mussels are a speciality, served in black enamel pots. Gets very busy, so arrive early, or be prepared to wait.

BUSHMILLS (Muileann na Buaise) – Moyle – 712 M2 – pop. 1 319 35 C1

– ✉ Bushmills ▮ Ireland

Belfast 57 mi – Ballycastle 12 mi – Coleraine 10 mi

Bushfoot Portballintrae 50 Bushfoot Rd, ✆ (028) 2073 1317

Giant's Causeway★★★ (Hamilton's Seat ≤★★) N : 2 mi by A 2 and minor road - Dunluce Castle★★ **AC** W : 3 mi by A 2 – Carrick-a-rede Rope Bridge★★★ **AC**, E : 8 mi by A 2 – Magilligan Strand★★, W : 18 mi by A 2, A 29 and A 2 - Gortmore Viewpoint★★, SW : 23 mi by A 2, A 29, A 23 and minor road from Downhill – Downhill★ (Mussenden Temple★), W : 15 mi by A 2, A 29 and A 2

Bushmills Inn

9 Dunluce Rd ✉ BT57 8QG – ✆ (028) 2073 3000 – www.bushmillsinn.com

32 rm – †£ 118/168 ††£ 178/298

Rest *The Restaurant* – *(carvery lunch Sunday)* Carte £ 24/38

◆ Part-17C whitewashed inn. Original building features traditionally styled bedrooms, a circular library, turf fires and oil lamps. Extensions play host to more modern bedrooms and seating areas. Extensive classical menu served in cosy restaurant and on terrace.

COLERAINE (Cúil Raithin) – Coleraine – 712 L2 – pop. 24 089 ▮ Ireland 35 C1

Belfast 53 mi – Ballymena 25 mi – Londonderry 31 mi – Omagh 65 mi

Railway Rd ✆ (028) 7034 4723, info@northcoastni.com

Castlerock 65 Circular Rd, ✆ (028) 7084 8314

Brown Trout 209 Agivey Rd, Aghadowey, ✆ (028) 7086 8209

Giant's Causeway★★★ (Hamilton's Seat ≤★★), NE : 14 mi by A 29 and A2 - Dunluce Castle★★ **AC**, NE : 8 mi by A 29 and A 2 – Carrick-a-rede-Rope Bridge★★★ **AC**, NE : 18 mi by A 29 and A2 – Benvarden★ **AC** E : 5 mi by B 67 – Magilligan Strand★★, NW : 8 mi by A 2 - Gortmore Viewpoint★★, NW : 12 mi by A 2 and minor road from Downhill - Downhill★**AC** (Mussenden Temple★), NE : 7 mi by A 2

Greenhill House without rest
24 Greenhill Rd, Aghadowey, South : 9 mi by A 29 on B 66 ✉ BT51 4EU – ☎ (028) 7086 8241 – www.greenhill-house.co.uk – Open March-October
6 rm – †£ 45 ††£ 70
◆ An agreeably clean-lined Georgian house with large windows overlooking fields. Game and course fishing available locally. Neat bedrooms replete with extra touches.

COMBER (An Comar) – Ards – 712 O4 – pop. 8 933 — 35 D2

Belfast 10 mi – Newtownards 5 mi – Lisburn 17 mi

Anna's House without rest
Tullynagee, 35 Lisbarnett Rd, Southeast : 3.5 mi by A 22 ✉ BT23 6AW – ☎ (028) 9754 1566 – www.annashouse.com – Closed Christmas-New Year
4 rm – †£ 70 ††£ 100
◆ Farmhouse with cosy lounge and comfy bedrooms with lovely vistas. Glass-walled extension has geo-thermal heating and lake views. Organic breakfasts utilise produce from garden.

CRUMLIN (Cromghlinn) – Antrim – 712 N4 – pop. 4 259 — 35 C2

Belfast 14 mi – Ballymena 20 mi

Caldhame Lodge without rest
102 Moira Rd, Nutts Corner, Southeast : 1.25 mi on A 26 ✉ BT29 4HG – ☎ (028) 9442 3099 – www.caldhamelodge.co.uk
8 rm – †£ 40/48 ††£ 55/75
◆ Spic and span, with thoroughly polished, wood-furnished hall, complete with grandfather clock. Immaculate, coordinated, individualistic rooms; bridal suite boasts whirlpool bath.

DERRY/LONDONDERRY = Doire – Londonderry – 712 K2/3 – see Londonderry

DONAGHADEE (Domhnach Daoi) – Ards – 712 P4 – pop. 6 470 — 35 D2

Ireland

Belfast 18 mi – Ballymena 44 mi
Warren Rd, ☎ (028) 9188 3624
Ballycopeland Windmill★ **AC** S : 4 mi by A 2 and B 172. Mount Stewart★★★ **AC**, SW : 10 mi by A 2 and minor road SW – Movilla (cross slabs★), Newtownards, SW : 7 mi by B 172

Grace Neill's
33 High St ✉ BT21 0AH – ☎ (028) 9188 4595 – www.graceneills.com
Rest – Carte £ 13/30
◆ Characterful beamed pub – the oldest in Ireland – decorated with antiques and old pictures. Extensive, largely classical menu, with express lunches and daily fish and seafood specials.

Pier 36 with rm
36 The Parade ✉ BT21 0HE – ☎ (028) 9188 4466 – www.pier36.co.uk – Closed 25 December
7 rm – †£ 50 ††£ 90 **Rest** – Menu £ 20 (Sunday lunch) – Carte £ 20/35
◆ Spacious harbourside pub, set opposite a lighthouse. Extensive menus feature a mix of classic, modern and international influences, and plenty of fresh, local seafood. Good weekday deals. Simple, comfy bedrooms boast sea views.

DOWNPATRICK (Dún Pádraig) – Down – 712 O4/5 – pop. 10 316 — 35 D3

Ireland

Belfast 23 mi – Newry 31 mi – Newtownards 22 mi
Cathedral★ **AC** - Down County Museum★ **AC**
Struell Wells★ **AC**, SE : 2 mi by B 1 - Ardglass★ (Jordan's Castle**AC**), SE : 7 mi by B 1 – Inch Abbey★ **AC**, NW : 2 mi by A 7 – Quoile Countryside Centre★ **AC**, E : 2 mi by A 25 – Castle Ward★★ **AC** (Audley's Castle★), E : 8 mi by A 25

Pheasants' Hill Farm without rest
37 Killyleagh Rd, North : 3 mi on A 22 ✉ BT30 9BL – ✆ (028) 4461 7246 – www.pheasantshill.com – Closed 16 December-4 January
3 rm – £ 45/55 £ 60/85
◆ Purpose-built house surrounded by an organic smallholding with livestock which provides many ingredients for hearty breakfasts. Homely, pine-furnished bedrooms.

DUNDRUM (Dún Droma) – Down – 712 O5 – pop. 1 065 Ireland 35 D3

Belfast 29 mi – Downpatrick 9 mi – Newcastle 4 mi
Castle★ AC
Castlewellan Forest Park★★ **AC**, W : 4 mi by B 180 and A 50 - Tollymore Forest Park★ **AC**, W : 3 mi by B 180 - Drumena Cashel and Souterrain★, W : 4 mi by B 180

The Carriage House without rest
71 Main St ✉ BT33 0LU – ✆ (028) 4375 1635 – www.carriagehousedundrum.com
3 rm – £ 45 £ 80
◆ Welcoming, lilac-washed terraced house with colourful window boxes and attractive rear garden. Comfy, traditionally styled guest areas. Simple bedrooms with plain décor and antique furniture.

Buck's Head Inn
77-79 Main St ✉ BT33 0LU – ✆ (028) 4375 1868 – www.bucksheadrestaurant.com – Closed 24-25 December and Monday October-Easter
Rest – Seafood – Menu £ 29 (dinner) – Carte £ 19/29
◆ Informal restaurant with attractive terrace and garden. Lounge for pre-meal drinks; choice of dining rooms. Good-sized menus of unfussy, traditional cooking with a local seafood base.

Mourne Seafood Bar
10 Main St ✉ BT33 0LU – ✆ (028) 4375 1377 – www.mourneseafood.com – Closed Tuesday and Wednesday (October to April)
Rest – Seafood – *(booking essential in summer)* Menu £ 27 (Saturday dinner) – Carte £ 25/29
◆ Informal, rustic restaurant, set on main street; wood-furnished interior with coastal oil paintings. Classical seafood cooking, with oysters and mussels from owners' beds a speciality.

DUNGANNON (Dún Geanainn) – Dungannon – 712 L4 35 C2 – pop. 11 139 Ireland

Belfast 42 mi – Ballymena 37 mi – Dundalk 47 mi – Londonderry 60 mi
The Argory★, S : 5 mi by A 29 and east by minor rd. Ardboe Cross★, NW : 17 mi by A 45, B 161 and B 73 – Springhill★ **AC**, NE : 24 mi by A 29 – Sperrin Mountains★ : Wellbrook Beetling Mill★ **AC**, NW : 22 mi by A 29 and A 505 - Beaghmore Stone Circles★, NW : 24 mi by A 29 and A 505

Grange Lodge
7 Grange Rd, Moy, Southeast : 3.5 mi by A 29 ✉ BT71 7EJ – ✆ (028) 8778 4212 – www.grangelodgecountryhouse.com – Closed 20 December-1 February
5 rm – £ 65/75 £ 85/89
Rest – Menu £ 36
◆ Attractive Georgian country house surrounded by well-kept mature gardens with a peaceful ambience. Fine hospitality and period furnishings. Tastefully decorated bedrooms. Large dining room furnished with elegant antiques and fine tableware.

ENNISKILLEN (Inis Ceithleann) – Fermanagh – 712 J4 – pop. 13 599 34 A2
Ireland

Belfast 87 mi – Londonderry 59 mi

Wellington Rd ✆ (028) 6632 3110, tic@fermanagh.gov.uk

Castlecoole, ✆ (028) 6632 5250

Castle Coole★★★ **AC**, SE : 1 m – Florence Court★★ **AC**, SW : 8 mi by A 4 and A 32 – Marble Arch Caves and Forest Nature Reserve★ **AC**, SW : 10 mi by A 4 and A 32. NW by A 26 : Lough Erne★★ : Cliffs of Magho Viewpoint★★★ **AC**- Tully Castle★ **AC** – N by A 32, B 72, A 35 and A 47 : Devenish Island★ **AC** - Castle Archdale Forest Park★ **AC** - White Island★ - Janus Figure★

Lough Erne Golf Resort

Belleek Rd, Northwest : 4 mi on A 46 ✉ BT93 7ED – ✆ (028) 6632 3230 – www.lochernegolfresort.com

89 rm – †£ 90/170 ††£ 160/220 – 31 suites – ††£ 280/340

Rest *Catalina* – *(dinner only and Sunday lunch)* Menu £ 40

Rest *Lochside Clubhouse Bar* – *(dinner only)* Carte £ 20/37

◆ Busy hotel in golf resort on peninsula between Castle Hume Lough and Lough Erne: a spacious, modern building boasting heritage style, with features such as wood panelling and antique furniture. Fine dining with lough views in Catalina. Informal brasserie in the Clubhouse.

Manor House

Killadeas, North : 7.5 mi by A 32 on B 82 ✉ BT94 1NY – ✆ (028) 6862 2200 – www.manorhouseresorthotel.com

81 rm – †£ 67/130 ††£ 75/130 – 2 suites **Rest** – Menu £ 18/28

◆ Impressive manor house overlooking Lough Erne. Characterful guest areas; well-equipped leisure and meeting facilities. Traditional bedrooms in main house, more modern rooms in extensions. Formal dining room boasts ornate plasterwork and offers classical menus.

Cedars

301 Killadeas Rd, Irvinestown, North : 10 mi by A 32 on B 82 ✉ BT94 1PG – ✆ (028) 6862 1493 – www.cedarsguesthouse.com – Closed 1 week Christmas

10 rm – †£ 40/50 ††£ 100/110

Rest *Rectory Bistro* – *(closed Monday-Tuesday in winter) (dinner only and Sunday lunch)* Carte £ 24/31

◆ Good value, converted 19C former rectory with pleasant gardens. Exudes impression of spaciousness; country-style décor. Individually designed bedrooms: ask for numbers 2 or 5. Rustic bistro serves hearty cuisine.

GALGORM Antrim – Ballymena – 712 N3 – see Ballymena

HILLSBOROUGH (Cromghlinn) – Lisburn – 712 N4 – pop. 3 400 35 C2
Ireland

Belfast 12 mi

The Courthouse, The Square ✆ (028) 9268 9717, tic.hillsborough@lisburn.gov.uk

Town★ – Fort★

Rowallane Gardens★ **AC**, Saintfield, E : 10 mi by B 178 and B 6. The Argory★, W : 25 mi by A 1 and M 1

The Plough Inn

3 The Square ✉ BT26 6AG – ✆ (028) 9268 2985 – www.bar-retro.com

Rest – *(Sunday)* Menu £ 17/25 – Carte £ 20/35

◆ Family-run 18C coaching inn that's three establishments in one: a bar with adjoining dining room, café and bistro. Dishes range from light snacks and pub classics to modern, international fare.

at Annahilt Southeast : 4 mi on B 177 – ✉ Hillsborough

Fortwilliam without rest

210 Ballynahinch Rd, Northwest : 0.25 mi on B 177 ✉ BT26 6BH – ☎ (028) 9268 2255 – www.fortwilliamcountryhouse.com

4 rm – †£ 50 ††£ 70

◆ Attractive bay-windowed farmhouse with neat gardens – keenly run and comfortable throughout. Individually designed bedrooms boast pleasant outlooks and extras; two have private bathrooms.

The Pheasant

410 Upper Ballynahinch Rd, North : 1 mi on Lisburn rd ✉ BT26 6NR – ☎ (028) 9263 8056 – www.thepheasantrestaurant.co.uk – Closed 25-26 December

Rest – Menu £ 20 (lunch) £ 24 (dinner) – Carte £ 20/35

◆ Sizeable yellow-washed pub with gothic styling and typical Irish feel. Menus offer local, seasonal produce, with seafood a speciality in summer and game featuring highly in the winter.

HOLYWOOD (Ard Mhic Nasca) – North Down – 712 O4 – pop. 12 037 Ireland

35 D2

Belfast 7 mi – Bangor 6 mi

Holywood Demesne Rd, Nuns Walk, ☎ (028) 9042 2138

Cultra : Ulster Folk and Transport Museum★★ AC, NE : 1 mi by A 2

Culloden

rest,

142 Bangor Rd, East : 1.5 mi on A 2 ✉ BT18 0EX – ☎ (028) 9042 1066 – www.hastingshotels.com

102 rm – †£ 190 ††£ 240 – 3 suites

Rest *Mitre* – *(dinner only and Sunday lunch)* Menu £ 30 (Sunday lunch)/45 (Saturday) – Carte £ 32/42

Rest *Cultra Inn* – ☎ (028) 9042 5840 – Carte £ 20/28

◆ Gothic mansion overlooking Belfast Lough. Spacious guest areas boast open fires and antiques. Bedrooms range from characterful to stylish and contemporary. Smart spa/leisure facilities. Mitre offers classical menus and good views. Informal Cultra Inn offers simpler fare.

Rayanne House

60 Demesne Rd, by My Lady's Mile Rd ✉ BT18 9EX – ☎ (028) 9042 5859 – www.rayannehouse.com

11 rm – †£ 65/90 ††£ 110/140

Rest – *(dinner only) (residents only)* Carte £ 30/45

◆ Victorian red-brick house in peaceful residential area. Homely, antique-filled guest areas. Stylish, contemporary bedrooms with country house feel, good facilities, smart bathrooms and extras. Formal dining room with seasonal menu; interesting breakfasts.

Beech Hill without rest

23 Ballymoney Rd, Craigantlet, Southeast : 4.5 mi by A 2 on Craigantlet rd ✉ BT23 4TG – ☎ (028) 9042 5892 – www.beech-hill.net

3 rm – †£ 55/60 ††£ 90/100

◆ Country house in rural location. Pleasant clutter of trinkets and antiques in guest areas which include a conservatory. Neat, traditionally styled bedrooms: a very fine home.

Fontana

61A High St ✉ BT18 9AE – ☎ (028) 9080 9908 – Closed 1 January, 25-27 December, Saturday lunch, Sunday dinner and Monday

Rest – Menu £ 15/20 – Carte £ 23/35

◆ Smart, first floor restaurant in town centre, accessed via narrow passageway. Modern British cooking displays some Mediterranean influences. Good value set lunch and midweek dinner.

KILLINCHY – Ards – **712** O4 **35** D2

Belfast 16 mi – Newtownards 11 mi – Lisburn 17 mi – Bangor 16 mi

Balloo House - Restaurant

1 Comber Rd.,(1st floor), West : 0.75 mi on A 22 ✉ BT23 6PA – ✆ (028) 9754 1210 – www.balloohouse.com – Closed Sunday and Monday

Rest – *(dinner only) (booking essential)* Menu £ 27 – Carte £ 32/38

◆ Intimate, first floor restaurant with high beamed ceilings and linen-laid tables. Flavourful classic cooking has modern touches; hearty yet refined dishes feature local produce.

LARNE (Latharna) – Larne – **712** O3 – pop. 18 228 Ireland **35** D2

Belfast 23 mi – Ballymena 20 mi

to Fleetwood (Stena Line) daily (8 h) – to Cairnryan (P & O Irish Sea) 3-5 daily (1 h/2 h 15 mn)

Narrow Gauge Rd ✆ (028) 2826 0088, larnetourism@btconnect.com

Cairndhu Ballygally 192 Coast Rd, ✆ (028) 2858 3954

SE : Island Magee (Ballylumford Dolmen★), by ferry and 2 mi by B 90 or 18 mi by A 2 and B 90. NW : Antrim Glens★★★ - Murlough Bay★★★ (Fair Head ≤★★★), N : 46 m by A 2 and minor road – Glenariff Forest Park★★ **AC** (Waterfall★★), N : 30 mi by A 2 and A 43 - Glenariff★, N : 25 mi by A 2 - Glendun★, N : 30 mi by A 2 – Carrickfergus (Castle★★ - St Nicholas' Church★), SW : 15 mi by A 2

Manor House without rest

23 Olderfleet Rd, Harbour Highway ✉ BT40 1AS – ✆ (028) 2827 3305 – www.themanorguesthouse.com – Closed 25-26 December

8 rm – †£ 30/35 ††£ 55/58

◆ Spacious Victorian terraced house, two minutes from ferry terminal. Well-furnished lounge with beautifully varnished wood floors. Small breakfast room. Cosy, homely bedrooms.

LIMAVADY (Léim an Mhadaidh) – Limavady – **712** L2 – pop. 12 135 **34** B1

Ireland

Belfast 62 mi – Ballymena 39 mi – Coleraine 13 mi – Londonderry 17 mi

Council Offices, 7 Connell St ✆ (028) 7776 0307, tourism@limavady.gov.uk

Benone Par Three Benone 53 Benone Ave, ✆ (028) 7775 0555

Sperrin Mountains★ : Roe Valley Country Park★ **AC**, S : 2 mi by B 68 - Glenshane Pass★, S : 15 mi by B 68 and A 6

Lime Tree

60 Catherine St ✉ BT49 9DB – ✆ (028) 7776 4300 – www.limetreerest.com – Closed 1 week spring, 1 week July, 25-26 December, Sunday and Monday

Rest – *(dinner only)* Menu £ 18 (early dinner mid week) – Carte £ 27/37

◆ Keenly run neighbourhood restaurant, where a traditional exterior hides smart modern hues. Good-sized menus of unfussy classical dishes, with seafood a speciality. Friendly, detailed service.

LONDONDERRY/DERRY (Doire) – Derry – **712** K2/3 – pop. 83 699 **34** B1

Ireland

Belfast 70 mi – Dublin 146 mi

City of Derry Airport : ✆ (028) 7181 0784, E : 6 mi by A 2

44 Foyle St ✆ (028) 7126 7284, info@derryvisitor.com

City of Derry 49 Victoria Rd, ✆ (028) 7134 6369

Town★ - City Walls and Gates★★ – Guildhall★ **AC** – Long Tower Church★ – St Columb's Cathedral★ **AC** – Tower Museum★ **AC**

Grianan of Aileach★★ (≤★★) (Republic of Ireland) NW : 5 mi by A 2 and N 13. Ulster-American Folk Park★★, S : 33 mi by A 5 - Ulster History Park★ **AC**, S : 32 mi by A 5 and minor road – Sperrin Mountains★ : Glenshane Pass★ (≤★★), SE : 24 mi by A 6 - Sawel Mountain Drive★ (≤★★), S : 22 mi by A 5 and minor roads via Park – Roe Valley Country Park★ **AC**, E : 15 mi by A 2 and B 68 – Beaghmore Stone Circles★, S : 52 mi by A 5, A 505 and minor road

City

Queens Quay ✉ BT48 7AS – ✆ (028) 7136 5800 – www.cityhotelderry.com – Closed 24-26 December

145 rm – †£ 79/149 ††£ 86/156 – 1 suite

Rest *Thompson's on the River* – *(bar lunch Monday-Saturday)* Menu £ 22 **s** – Carte dinner £ 25/33 **s**

♦ Hotel in purpose-built modern style. Well-located, close to the city centre and the quay. Smart rooms ordered for the business traveller. Useful conference facilities. Modern restaurant overlooks water.

Beech Hill Country House

32 Ardmore Rd, Southeast : 3.5 mi by A 6 ✉ BT47 3QP – ✆ (028) 7134 9279 – www.beech-hill.com – Closed 24- 25 December

25 rm – †£ 95/105 ††£ 115/135 – 2 suites

Rest *The Ardmore* – Menu £ 22/32 **s** – Carte dinner £ 33/44 **s**

♦ 18C country house, now personally run but once a US marine camp; one lounge is filled with memorabilia. Accommodation varies from vast rooms to more traditional, rural ones. Restaurant housed within conservatory and old billiard room. Fine garden.

Ramada H. Da Vinci's

15 Culmore Rd, North : 1 mi following signs for Foyle Bridge ✉ BT48 8JB – ✆ (028) 7127 9111 – www.davincishotel.com – Closed 24-25 December

70 rm – †£ 50/90 ††£ 50/90, £ 8.95

Rest *The Grill Room* – *(dinner only and Sunday lunch)* Carte £ 17/25

♦ Set beside a characterful Irish pub – now the trendy hotel bar – at the northern edge of the city. Photos of stars who've stayed here fill one wall. Well-equipped, uniform bedrooms improve with grade. Charming brasserie displays rustic beams and exposed brickwork.

Don't confuse the couvert rating with the stars !
Couverts defines comfort and service, while stars are awarded for the best cuisine across all categories of comfort.

NORTHERN IRELAND

MAGHERA (Machaire Rátha) – Magherafelt – 712 L3 – pop. 3 711 — 35 C2

Belfast 40 mi – Ballymena 19 mi – Coleraine 21 mi – Londonderry 32 mi

Ardtara Country House

8 Gorteade Rd, Upperlands, North : 3.25 mi by A 29 off B 75 ✉ BT46 5SA – ✆ (028) 7964 4490 – www.ardtara.com

9 rm – †£ 65/75 ††£ 120/130

Rest – *(booking essential for non-residents)* Carte £ 20/32

♦ 19C house with a charming atmosphere. The interior features 'objets trouvés' collected from owner's travels; original fireplaces set off the individually styled bedrooms. Restaurant set in former billiard room with hunting mural and panelled walls.

NEWCASTLE (An Caisleán Nua) – Down – 712 O5 – pop. 7 444 — 35 D3

Ireland

Belfast 32 mi – Londonderry 101 mi

10-14 Central Promenade ✆ (028) 4372 2222, newcastle.tic@downdc.gov.uk

Castlewellan Forest Park★★ **AC**, NW : 4 mi by A 50 – Tolymore Forest Park★ **AC**, W : 3 mi by B 180 – Dundrum Castle★ **AC**, NE : 4 mi by A 2. Silent Valley Reservoir★ (≤★) - Spelga Pass and Dam★ - Kilbroney ForestPark (viewpoint★) – Annalong Marine Park and Cornmill★ **AC**, S : 8 mi by A 2 – Downpatrick : Cathedral★ **AC**, Down Country Museum★ **AC**, NE : 20 mi by A 2 and A 25

Slieve Donard
Downs Rd ✉ BT33 0AH – ☏ (028) 4372 1066 – www.hastingshotels.com
178 rm – †£ 110/165 ††£ 150/200
Rest *Oak* – *(dinner only and lunch July-August)* Menu £ 30/38
Rest *Percy French* – Carte £ 30/40
♦ Grand railway hotel boasting marble-floored lobby, interesting museum, superb leisure facilities and excellent sea/mountain views. Spacious bedrooms in classic or contemporary styles; good mod cons. Formal Oak offers classical menu. More accessible fare in casual bar-restaurant Percy French.

Burrendale H. & Country Club rest,
51 Castlewellan Rd, North : 1 mi on A 50
✉ BT33 0JY – ☏ (028) 4372 2599 – www.burrendale.com
67 rm – †£ 80 ††£ 140 – 1 suite
Rest *Vine* – *(dinner only and Sunday lunch)* Carte £ 24/29 **s**
Rest *Cottage Kitchen* – Carte £ 18/25 **s**
♦ Set between the Mourne Mountains and Irish Sea, with the Royal County Down Golf Course nearby. Leisure oriented. Range of rooms from small to very spacious. Linen-clad Vine for traditional dining. Homely cooking to the fore at Cottage Kitchen.

NEWTOWNARDS (Baile Nua na hArda) – Ards – 712 O4 – pop. 27 821 — 35 D2

Belfast 10 mi – Bangor 144 mi – Downpatrick 22 mi

Edenvale House without rest
130 Portaferry Rd, Southeast : 2.75 mi on A 20 ✉ BT22 2AH – ☏ (028) 9181 4881 – www.edenvalehouse.com – Closed 1 week Christmas
3 rm – †£ 50 ††£ 100
♦ Attractive Georgian farmhouse with pleasant mountain views. Traditionally decorated, with comfy drawing room and wicker-furnished sun room. Spacious, homely bedrooms boast good facilities.

PORTRUSH (Port Rois) – Coleraine – 712 L2 – pop. 6 372 Ireland — 35 C1

Belfast 58 mi – Coleraine 4 mi – Londonderry 35 mi

Sandhill Drive ☏ (028) 7082 3333 (March-October), portrushtic@btconnect.com

Royal Portrush Dunluce Rd, ☏ (028) 7082 2311

Giant's Causeway★★★ (Hamilton's Seat ★★, E: 9 m by A 2) - Carrick-a-rede Rope Bridge★★★, E: 14 mi by A 2 and B 15 - Dunluce Castle★★ **AC**, E: 3 mi by A 2 – Gortmore Viewpoint★★, E: 14 mi by A 29, A 2 and minor road - Magilligan Strand★★, E: 13 mi by A 29 and A 2 – Downhill★ (Mussenden Temple★), E: 12 mi by A 29 and A 2

Beulah without rest
16 Causeway St ✉ BT56 8AB – ☏ (028) 7082 2413 – www.beulahguesthouse.com – February-November
11 rm – †£ 30/55 ††£ 60/70
♦ Terraced Victorian house in perfect central location. Sound Irish breakfasts. Homely guest lounge. Colourful, co-ordinated and immaculately kept modern bedrooms.

PORTSTEWART (Port Stióbhaird) – Coleraine – 712 L2 — 35 C1

Belfast 60 mi – Ballymena 32 mi – Coleraine 6 mi

York
2 Station Rd, on A2 ✉ BT55 7DA – ☏ (028) 7083 3594 – www.theyorkportstewart.co.uk
8 rm – †£ 59/89 ††£ 120/140 **Rest** – Menu £ 8 (lunch) – Carte £ 17/28 **s**
♦ Smart, contemporary hotel overlooking the North Coast. Stylish bedrooms offer all mod cons; the two front rooms are the largest, with terraces and excellent views. Trendy, marble-floored bar. Ground floor restaurant with extensive menus and a large terrace.

WARRENPOINT (An Pointe) – **Newry and Mourne** – **712** N5 **35** C3 – **pop. 7 000**

Belfast 44 mi – Newry 7 mi – Lisburn 37 mi

XX **Restaurant 23**

Balmoral Hotel (1st floor), 13 Seaview ✉ BT34 3NJ – ☎ (028) 4175 3222 – www.restaurant23.com – Closed dinner 24-26 December, Tuesday and Monday except bank holidays

Rest – Menu £ 15 (weekday dinner)/26 **s** – Carte £ 27/39 **s**

◆ Long-standing restaurant that's moved from the high street to a seafront hotel. Trendy bar and lounge. Dining room with boldly patterned wallpapers, red banquettes and fantastic lough views. Neatly presented, unfussy classics at lunch; enticing modern dishes in the evening.

O. Forir/MICHELIN

ACHILL ISLAND (Acaill) – Mayo – 712 B6 Ireland

Dublin 288 km – Castlebar 54 km [illegible]

Achill Sound [illegible] tourist office [illegible]

[illegible]

Doogort – Mayo – ⊠ Achill Island

[illegible]

• [illegible] row of [illegible] washed cottages with a homely atmosphere [illegible] and simple but spotless bedrooms [illegible] walks.

Keel – Mayo – ⊠ Achill Island

[illegible]

[illegible] Walking [illegible] Keel beach [illegible] with [illegible] views.

ADARE (Áth Dara) – Limerick – 712 F10 – pop. 982 Ireland

Dublin 210 km – Killarney 95 km – Limerick 16 km

Heritage Centre [illegible] tourist office [illegible]

[illegible]

[illegible] Adare Parish Church [illegible]

[illegible]

[illegible] Adare Manor [illegible]

[illegible] closed [illegible] December

[illegible]

Rest The Oakroom [illegible] dinner only [illegible]

Rest The Carriage House [illegible]

• [illegible] Gothic mansion on banks of River Maigue in extensive park and impressively elaborate interiors [illegible]. Most distinctive rooms in the oldest part. Oak-panelled dining room [illegible] Carriage house.

[illegible] Dunraven Arms

[illegible] www.dunravenhotel.com

[illegible]

Rest Maigue Restaurant [illegible] dinner only and Sunday lunch [illegible]

• [illegible] opposite [illegible] thatched [illegible] Understated country house style [illegible] Maigue [illegible]

The Wild Geese

[illegible] Carriage [illegible] closed [illegible] January and Monday

[illegible] Sunday [illegible]

[illegible]

• Traditional [illegible] cottage on main street [illegible] welcoming [illegible] with classic and international [illegible]

ACHILL ISLAND (Acaill) – Mayo – 712 B5/6 Ireland — 36 A2

Dublin 288 km – Castlebar 54 km – Galway 144 km

Achill Sound ✆ (098) 45384, (July- Sept) achill.touristoffice@failteireland.ie

Achill Island Keel, ✆ (098) 43 456

Island★

DOOGORT (Dumha Goirt) – Mayo – ✉ Achill Island

Gray's

– *✆ (098) 43 244 – 17 March-September*

14 rm – €40/55 €80/110 **Rest** – *(dinner only)* Menu €26/32

◆ A row of tranquil whitewashed cottages with a homely atmosphere; popular with artists. Cosy sitting rooms with fireplaces and simple but spotless bedrooms. Local scene paintings adorn dining room walls.

KEEL – Mayo – ✉ Achill Island

Achill Cliff House

– *✆ (098) 43 400 – www.achillcliff.com*

10 rm – €50/80 €70/110

Rest – *(dinner only and Sunday lunch)* Menu €19/27 – Carte €29/41

◆ Whitewashed modern building against a backdrop of countryside and ocean. Within walking distance of Keel beach. Well-kept, spacious bedrooms with modern furnishings. Spacious restaurant with sea views.

ADARE (Áth Dara) – Limerick – 712 F10 – pop. 982 Ireland — 38 B2

Dublin 210 km – Killarney 95 km – Limerick 16 km

Heritage Centre, Mains St ✆ (061) 396255, touristofficeadare@shannondevelopment.ie

Town★ – Adare Friary★ - Adare Parish Church★

Rathkeale (Castle Matrix★ **AC** - Irish Palatine Heritage Centre★) W : 12 km by N 21 – Newcastle West★, W : 26 km by N 21 – Glin Castle★ **AC**, W : 46.5 km by N 21, R 518 and N 69

Adare Manor H. and Golf Resort

– *✆ (061) 396 566 – www.adaremanor.com*

– closed 24-26 December

62 rm – €290/493 €290/493

Rest *The Oakroom* – *(dinner only)* Carte €53/63 **s**

Rest *The Carraigehouse* – Carte €30/50 **s**

◆ Part 19C Gothic mansion on banks of River Maigue in extensive parkland. Impressively elaborate interiors and capacious lounges. Most distinctive rooms in the oldest parts. Oak-panelled dining room overlooks river. Informal Carraigehouse.

Dunraven Arms

Main St – ✆ (061) 605 900 – www.dunravenhotel.com

86 rm – €130/180 €155/195, €17

Rest *Maigue Restaurant* – ✆ (061) 396 633 *(dinner only and Sunday lunch)* Carte €24/35

◆ Considerably extended 18C building opposite charming thatched cottages. Understated country house style. Comfortable bedrooms in bright magnolia. Antique chairs and historical paintings in formal restaurant. Menus offer some eclectic choices on an Irish backbone.

The Wild Geese

Rose Cottage – ✆ (061) 396 451 – www.thewild-geese.com – closed 3-20 January and Monday

Rest – *(dinner only and Sunday lunch) (booking essential)* Menu €25 (lunch)/35 (early dinner) – Carte €36/52

◆ Traditional 18C cottage on main street. Friendly service and cosy welcoming atmosphere. Varied menu with classic and international influences uses much fresh local produce.

White Sage

Main Street – (061) 396 004 – www.whitesagerestaurant.com – closed last 2 weeks January, 24-26 December and Monday

Rest – *(dinner only) (booking advisable)* Menu € 30 – Carte € 35/46

◆ Set in a row of thatched cottages, with a spacious, candlelit inner and small rear terrace. Experienced chef creates tasty European dishes using regional produce. Charming service.

ARAN ISLANDS (Oileáin Árann) – Galway – 712 C/D8 – pop. 1 280 — 38 B1

Ireland

Dublin 260 km – Galway 43 km – Limerick 145 km – Ennis 111 km

Access Access by boat or aeroplane from Galway city or by boat from Kilkieran, Rossaveel or Fisherstreet (Clare) and by aeroplane from Inverin

Cill Ronain, Inis Mor (099) 61263, aran@failteireland.ie

Islands★ – Inishmore (Dún Aonghasa★★★)

INISHMORE – Galway

Óstán Árann

Kilronan – (099) 61 104 – www.aranislandshotel.com

22 rm – € 69/89 € 98/138

Rest – *(bar lunch)* Menu € 20 **s** – Carte € 24/43 **s**

◆ Comfortable, family-owned hotel with great view of harbour. Bustling bar with live music most nights in the season. Spacious, up-to-date bedrooms decorated in bright colours. Traditional dishes served in wood-floored restaurant.

Pier House

Kilronan – (099) 61 417 – www.pierhousearan.com – mid March-October

12 rm – € 50/65 € 80/110

Rest *The Restaurant* – see restaurant listing

◆ Purpose-built hotel, perfectly located at the end of the pier with an attractive outlook from residents lounge. Cosy bedrooms furnished in a comfortable, modern style. Some family rooms.

Ard Einne Guesthouse

Killeany – (099) 61 126 – www.ardeinne.com – February-November

8 rm – € 90 € 90/120 **Rest** – Menu € 27

◆ Purpose-built chalet-style establishment in isolated spot with superb views of Killeany Bay. Homely atmosphere amidst traditional appointments. Simple, comfortable bedrooms. Spacious dining room provides home-cooked meals.

The Restaurant – at Pier House Hotel

Kilronan – (099) 61 417 – www.pierhouserestaurant.com – March-October

Rest – *(light lunch)* Menu € 30 – Carte € 30/44

◆ Well-regarded restaurant with cosy ambience. Light lunches replaced by more serious dinner menus, with a strong selection of local seafood. Tasty, homely cooking with the odd Asian influence.

INISHMAAN – Galway

Inis Meáin Restaurant & Suites with rm

– (086) 826 60 26 – www.inismeain.com – March-September, 2 night minimum stay

3 rm – € 185 € 250

Rest – *(closed Sunday and Monday) (dinner only) (booking essential)* Carte € 29/55

◆ Striking stone building in futuristic design owned and run by charming native of this unspoilt island. Unpretentious modern cooking exploits finest local ingredients, including seafood caught in currachs and delicious home-grown potatoes. Minimalist bedrooms feature natural furnishings. Breakfast delivered to room.

ARDMORE (Aird Mhór) – Waterford – 712 I12 – pop. 412 39 C3

Dublin 240 km – Waterford 71 km – Cork 60 km – Kilkenny 123 km

Cliff House

– ✆ (024) 87 800 – *www.thecliffhousehotel.com* – *restricted opening January and December*

36 rm – **††** € 200/225 – 3 suites

Rest *House* – see restaurant listing

Rest *Bar* – Menu € 29 (Sunday lunch in winter)/33 – Carte € 33/49

◆ Stylish hotel on the cliffside, overlooking the bay. Slate walls, Irish fabrics and bold colours feature throughout; lower floor houses a relaxing spa. Modern bedrooms boast backlit glass artwork: some have balconies; all have smart bathrooms and a view. Comfy bar and slate-floored terrace offer an extensive menu.

House – at Cliff House Hotel

– ✆ (024) 87 800 – *www.thecliffhousehotel.com* – *Closed Monday and restricted opening January and December*

Rest – *(dinner only)* Carte approx. € 65

Spec. Organic Bantry Bay salmon with herb cream. Skeaghanore duck with cappoquin cherries. Dark chocolate tart.with olive oil crumbs.

◆ Smart hotel restaurant, where full length windows provide every table with an impressive coastal view. Irish/garden produce features in concise menus; cooking is technically strong and complex. Creative, original dishes combine good flavours and textures.

ARTHURSTOWN (Colmán) – Wexford – 712 L11 – pop. 159 39 D2

Dublin 166 km – Cork 159 km – Limerick 162 km – Waterford 42 km

Dunbrody Country House

– ✆ (051) 389 600 – *www.dunbrodyhouse.com* – *Closed Christmas and Sunday-Monday 10 September-15 July*

16 rm – **†** € 123/165 **††** € 325/390 – 6 suites

Rest – *(dinner only and Sunday lunch bar lunch Monday-Saturday) (booking essential for non-residents) (residents only Sunday dinner)* Menu € 35/55 – Carte € 55/75

◆ Fine country house hotel with a pristine, elegant style, set within a part-Georgian former hunting lodge affording much peace. Smart, comfortable bedrooms. Elegant dining room serving modern-style menu, with Mediterranean and Asian influences. Bar lunch starts at 2pm.

ASHBOURNE (Cill Dhéagláin) – Meath – 712 M7 – pop. 8 528 37 D3

Dublin 21 km – Drogheda 26 km – Navan 27 km

Broadmeadow Country House without rest

Bullstown, Southeast : 4 km by R 135 on R 125 (Swords rd) – ✆ (01) 835 2823 – *www.irishcountryhouse.com* – *closed 23 December-2 January*

8 rm – **†** € 50/60 **††** € 90/120

◆ Substantial creeper-clad guesthouse and equestrian centre in rural area yet close to airport. Light and airy breakfast room overlooks garden. Spacious rooms have country views.

ASHFORD (Áth na Fuinseog) – Wicklow – 712 N8 – pop. 1 349 39 D2

Dublin 43 km – Rathdrum 17 km – Wicklow 6 km

Ballyknocken House

Glenealy, South : 4.75 km on L 1096 – ✆ (0404) 44 627 – *www.ballyknocken.com* – *closed mid December- mid January*

7 rm – **†** € 69/75 **††** € 110/118

Rest – *(dinner only Friday-Saturday)* Menu € 45

◆ Part-Victorian guesthouse on a working farm, with adjoining cookery school. Comfy bedrooms are furnished with antiques, and some have claw-foot baths. Light, airy dining room. Set daily changing menu of traditional Irish cooking.

ATHLONE (Baile Átha Luain) – Westmeath – 712 I7 – pop. 17 544 37 C3

Ireland

Dublin 120 km – Galway 92 km – Limerick 120 km – Roscommon 32 km

Athlone Castle, St Peter's Sq ☎ (090) 647 2107 (April-October), athlone@failteireland.ie

Hodson Bay, ☎ (090) 649 20 73

Clonmacnois★★★ (Grave Slabs★, Cross of the Scriptures★) S : 21 km by N 6 and N 62 – N : Lough Ree (Ballykeeran Viewpoint★)

Sheraton Athlone

Gleeson St – ☎ (090) 645 1000 – www.sheratonathlone.com – Closed 25 December

164 rm – 🚹 € 85/105 🚹🚹 € 118/150 – 1 suite **Rest** – Carte € 29/40

◆ 12 storey glass tower beside the shopping centre. Bedroom grades increase with floor number: all have excellent mod cons; some boast super lough and river views. Very smart leisure, spa and aquatics area. Eat in laid-back café, chic bar or elegant restaurant.

Shelmalier House without rest

Retreat Rd., Cartrontroy, East : 2.5 km by Dublin rd (N 6) – ☎ (090) 647 22 45 – www.shelmalierhouse.com – March-October

7 rm – 🚹 € 45 🚹🚹 € 70

◆ Well-run guesthouse with friendly owners, sauna and hot tub. Clean, comfortable bedrooms, most with polished wood floors – Room 3 is best. Extensive breakfast menu includes a daily special.

Left Bank Bistro

Fry Pl – ☎ (090) 649 44 46 – www.leftbankbistro.com – Closed 1 week Christmas, Sunday and Monday

Rest – Menu € 25 (dinner) – Carte € 20/46

◆ Keenly run bistro with airy interior, rough floorboards, brick walls and open-plan kitchen. Extensive menus offer an eclectic mix, from Irish beef and local fish specials through to Asian fare.

Kin Khao

Abbey Lane – ☎ (090) 649 88 05 – www.kinkhaothai.ie – Closed 24 April and 24-26 December

Rest – Thai – *(dinner only lunch Wednesday-Friday and Sunday)* Menu € 20 – Carte € 29/38

◆ Vivid yellow building with red window frames. Small downstairs bar; tapestries hang in main room. Good choice of authentic Thai dishes and daily specials – try the owner's recommendations.

at Glassan Northeast : 8 km on N 55 – ✉ Athlone

Wineport Lodge

Southwest : 1.5 km – ☎ (090) 643 90 10 – www.wineport.ie – Closed 24-26 December

28 rm – 🚹 € 95/150 🚹🚹 € 170/225 – 1 suite

Rest – *(dinner only and Sunday lunch)* Carte € 37/61

◆ Superbly set, with the bedroom wing following the line of the lough shore and each room boasting a waterside terrace or balcony. Rooms range in size but all are luxurious. 2 treatment rooms and a rooftop hot tub for relaxation. Extensive menus of seasonal produce.

Glasson Golf H. & Country Club

West : 2.75 km – ☎ (090) 648 51 20 – www.glassongolfhotel.ie

rm,

65 rm – 🚹 € 75/125 🚹🚹 € 90/210

Rest – *(bar lunch)* Menu € 27/38 **s** – Carte € 27/47 **s**

◆ Greatly extended period house in an elevated position, with views over the golf course and Lough Ree. Many visitors are golfers and golfing memorabilia fills the walls. Spacious, modern bedrooms; some with huge balconies. Classical menu served in dining room.

Glasson Stone Lodge without rest
– ☎ *(090) 648 50 04 – www.glassonstonelodge.com – May-October*
6 rm – € 50 € 76
♦ Smart guesthouse built from Irish limestone. Pine features strongly; bedrooms boast thoughtful extras and locally made furniture. Breakfast includes homemade bread and fruit from the garden.

Fatted Calf
– ☎ *(09064) 85 208 – www.thefattedcalf.ie – Closed 25 December, Good Friday and Monday in winter*
Rest – Menu € 22 (dinner) – Carte € 22/41
♦ Popular locals pub with rustic, wood-panelled bar. Wide range of dishes include plenty of pub favourites and a daily changing roast of the day. Friendly, attentive service.

AUGHRIM (Eachroim) – Wicklow – 712 N9 – pop. 1 145 — 39 D2

Dublin 74 km – Waterford 124 km – Wexford 96 km
The Battle of Aughrim Visitors Centre, Ballinasloe ☎ (090) 9763939 (summer only)

Brooklodge H & Wells Spa
Macreddin Village, North : 3.25 km – ☎ (0402) 36 444 – www.brooklodge.com
89 rm – € 135/150 € 135/150 – 1 suite
Rest *Strawberry Tree* – *(dinner only)* Menu € 65
Rest *Armento* – *(closed Sunday and Monday) (dinner only)* Menu € 30
Rest *Orchard Cafe* – *(closed March-October and Monday-Thursday)* Carte € 18/20
♦ 180 acre estate in secluded Wicklow valley featuring well-appointed, contemporary bedrooms with spacious bathrooms, a state-of-the-art spa and restaurants serving solely organic food. Ornate, linen-clad Strawberry Tree offers a traditional menu. Italian dishes in Armento. Orchard Café for a light lunch.

AVOCA (Abhóca) – Wicklow – 712 N9 – pop. 734 Ireland — 39 D2

Dublin 75 km – Waterford 116 km – Wexford 88 km
Avondale★, N : by R 752 – Meeting of the Waters★, N : by R 752

Keppel's Farmhouse without rest
Ballanagh, South : 3.25 km by unmarked rd – ☎ (0402) 35 168 – www.keppelsfarmhouse.ie – May-October
5 rm – € 50/55 € 70/80
♦ Small farmhouse with colourful garden and friendly owners. Neat, brightly painted bedrooms with compact shower rooms and lovely views over the vale. Large home-cooked and buffet breakfasts.

BAGENALSTOWN (Muine Bheag) – Carlow – 712 L9 – pop. 2 532 — 39 D2

Dublin 101 km – Carlow 16 km – Kilkenny 21 km – Wexford 59 km

Kilgraney Country House
South : 6.5 km by R 705 (Borris Rd) – ☎ (059) 977 52 83 – www.kilgraneyhouse.com – closed January, February, December and Monday-Wednesday March-November
8 rm – € 120 € 280 – 2 suites
Rest – *(dinner only) (booking essential)* Menu € 52
♦ Georgian country house adopting a truly holistic approach. Period features blend with modern, minimalist furnishings; the mood is calm and peaceful. Small tea room, craft gallery and spa with relaxation room; pleasant herb, veg, zodiac and monastic gardens. Modern menus of clean, fresh cooking; some Asian influences.

BALLINA (Béal an Átha) – **Mayo** – **712** E5 – **pop. 10 490** Ireland **36** B2

Dublin 241 km – Galway 117 km – Roscommon 103 km – Sligo 59 km

Cathedral Rd ✆ (096) 70848 (April-October), ballina.touristoffice@failteireland.ie

Mossgrove Shanaghy, ✆ (096) 21 050

Rosserk Abbey★, N : 6.5 km by R 314. Moyne Abbey★, N : 11.25 km by R 314 - Pontoon Bridge View (★), S : 19.25 km by N 26 and R 310 – Downpatrick Head★, N : 32 km by R 314

Ice House

The Quay Village, Northeast : 2.5 km by N 59 – ✆ (096) 23 500 – www.theicehouse.ie – closed 24-26 December

32 rm – € 125/150 € 160/200 – 6 suites

Rest – *(dinner only and Sunday lunch)* Menu € 39 – Carte € 33/80

◆ A former ice vault for local fishermen with two modern extensions. Terrific river views. The bedrooms a quirky mix of the old and the new; some with full-length windows. Modern menus in restaurant.

Crockets on the Quay with rm

The Quay, Northeast : 2.5 km by N 59 – ✆ (096) 75 930 – www.crocketsonthequay.ie – Closed 25 December, lunch Monday-Friday and Good Friday

8 rm – € 40 € 70 **Rest** – Menu € 20 (lunch Sunday) – Carte € 25/50

◆ Vibrant orange pub with a lively atmosphere, which hosts regular poker, quiz and music nights. Tasty, generously proportioned dishes include local Irish steaks. Serves dinner only. Modest, well-kept bedrooms; those over the restaurant are the quietest.

BALLINADEE = Baile na Daidhche – **Cork** – **712** G12 – **see Kinsale**

BALLINASLOE (Béal Átha na Sluaighe) – **Galway** – **712** H8 **36** B3 – **pop. 6 303** Ireland

Dublin 146 km – Galway 66 km – Limerick 106 km – Roscommon 58 km

Bridge St, (0909) 642604 (July-Oct), ballinasloe@failteireland.ie

Rossgloss, ✆ (0905) 42 126

Mountbellew, ✆ (090) 967 92 59

Clonfert Cathedral★ (west doorway★★), SW : by R 355 and minor roads. Turoe Stone, Bullaun★, SW : 29 km by R 348 and R 350 – Loughrea (St Brendan's Cathedral★), SW : 29 km by N 6 – Clonmacnoise★★★ (grave slabs★, Cross of the Scriptures★) E : 21 km by R 357 and R 444

Moycarn Lodge rm,

Shannonbridge Rd, Southeast : 2.5 km by N 6 off R 357 – ✆ (090) 964 5050 – www.moycarnlodge.ie – Closed 25-26 December

15 rm – € 39/69 € 78/99 **Rest** – Carte € 19/33

◆ Pleasant rural spot next to River Suck, with berthing available for boats and family cruisers for hire. Light, simply furnished bedrooms; some with river view. Hospitable owners. Rustically-styled restaurant.

BALLINCOLLIG (Baile an Chollaigh) Cork – **Cork** – **712** D12 **38** B3 – **pop. 16 339**

Dublin 168 km – Cork 6 km – Carrigaline 17 km – Cobh 20 km

Oriel House

West : 1 km on A 608 – ✆ (021) 420 84 00 – www.corkluxuryhotels.com – closed 25-26 December

76 rm – € 110 € 140 – 2 suites

Rest – *(bar lunch Monday-Saturday)* Menu € 25 **s** – Carte € 36/46 **s**

◆ Former manor house with modern extensions boasts smart spa, conference suite and contemporary bar. Most bedrooms are in the new wings; those at the rear are quieter. Simple menu served in smart, airy restaurant.

BALLINGARRY (Baile an Gharraí) – Limerick – 712 F10 – pop. 441 **38** B2

Ireland

Dublin 227 km – Killarney 90 km – Limerick 29 km

Kilmallock★ (Kilmallock Abbey★, Collegiate Church★), SE : 24 km by R 518 – Lough Gur Interpretive Centre★ **AC**, NE : 29 km by R 519, minor road to Croom, R 516 and R 512 – Monasteranenagh Abbey★, NE : 24 km by R 519 and minor road to Croom

Mustard Seed at Echo Lodge

– *(069) 68 508 – www.mustardseed.ie – Closed 9 January-10 February and 24-26 December*

14 rm – € 95/130 € 260 – 2 suites

Rest – *(dinner only)* Menu € 63 (dinner) – Carte € 35/54

◆ Converted convent with very neat gardens and peaceful appeal. Cosy lounge with fireplace and beautiful fresh flowers. Individually furnished rooms with mix of antiques. Meals enlivened by home-grown herbs and organic farm produce.

BALLINROBE (Baile an Róba) – Mayo – 712 E7 – pop. 2 098 **36** B3

Dublin 163 km – Castlebar 18 km – Galway 31 km – Westport 20 km

JJ Gannons with rm

Main St – (094) 954 1008 – www.jjgannons.com – Closed 25 December and Good Friday

10 rm – € 65/70 € 120/150

Rest – Menu € 25 (dinner) – Carte € 25/40

◆ Run by the third generation of the Gannon family, with an atmospheric front bar and a smart, spacious restaurant. Satisfyingly traditional dishes, fish specials and eager service. Spacious, comfortable bedrooms have a bright, minimalist style.

BALLSBRIDGE = Droichead na Dothra – Dublin – 712 N8 – see Dublin

BALLYBOFEY (Bealach Féich) – Donegal – 712 I3 – pop. 4 176 **37** C1

Dublin 238 km – Londonderry 48 km – Sligo 93 km

Ballybofey & Stranorlar The Glebe, (074) 31 093

Kee's

Main St, Stranorlar, Northeast : 0.75 km on N 15 – (074) 913 10 18 – www.keeshotel.ie

53 rm – € 96/106 € 158/178 **Rest** – Carte € 25/50 **s**

◆ Long-standing, family-run hotel in town centre. Bedrooms in newer building are more spacious and modern. Atmospheric bar and raised lounge area. Popular favourites served in informal, wood-furnished restaurant.

BALLYBUNION (Baile an Bhuinneánaigh) – Kerry – 712 D10 **38** A2 – pop. 1 365

Ireland

Dublin 283 km – Limerick 90 km – Tralee 42 km

Ballybunnion Sandhill Rd, (068) 27 146

Rattoo Round Tower★, S : 10 km by R 551. Ardfert★, S : 29 km by R 551, R 556 and minor road W – Banna Strand★, S : 28 km by R 551 – Carrigafoyle Castle★, NE : 21 km by R 551 – Glin Castle★ **AC**, E : 30.5 km by R 551 and N 69

Teach de Broc Country House

Link Rd, South : 2.5 km on Golf Club rd – (068) 27 581 – www.ballybuniongolf.com – closed November, restricted opening in winter

14 rm – € 80/120 € 130/170

Rest – *(closed Monday) (light lunch)* Menu € 25 (lunch and early dinner) – Carte € 25/40

◆ Stylish house by the Ballybunion golf course. Spacious, modern interior boasts a nicely furnished bar-lounge with outdoor seating. Bedrooms are extremely comfortable and have smart bathrooms. Elegant dining room with smartly laid tables offers wide-ranging menu.

The 19th Lodge without rest
Golf Links Rd, South : 2.75 km by Golf Club rd – ✆ (068) 27 592 – www.19thlodge-ballybunion.com – February-November
14 rm – € 70/120 € 100/180
◆ Orange washed house aimed at golfers playing at adjacent course. First floor lounge with honesty bar and comfy sofas. Linen-clad breakfast room. Luxurious rooms.

BALLYCASTLE (Baile an Chaisil) – Mayo – 712 D5 – pop. 215 — 36 B2

Ireland

Dublin 267 km – Galway 140 km – Sligo 88 km
Cáide Fields★, **AC**, NE : 8 km by R 314

Stella Maris
Northwest : 3 km by R 314 – ✆ (096) 43 322 – www.stellamarisireland.com – April-September
12 rm – € 170 € 250
Rest – *(dinner only) (booking essential)* Carte € 35/55
◆ Former coastguard station and fort in a great spot overlooking the bay. Public areas include a long conservatory. Attractive rooms with antique and contemporary furnishings. Modern menus in stylish dining room.

BALLYCONNELL (Báal Atha Conaill) – Cavan – 712 J5 – pop. 747 — 37 C2

Dublin 143 km – Drogheda 122 km – Enniskillen 37 km
Slieve Russell, ✆ (049) 952 6458

Slieve Russell
Southeast : 2.75 km on N 87 – ✆ (049) 952 6444 – www.quinnhotels.com
220 rm – € 109 € 158 – 2 suites
Rest *Conall Cearnach* – ✆ (049) 952 5016 *(dinner only and Sunday lunch)* Menu € 50 **s** – Carte € 35/45 **s**
Rest *Setanta* – ✆ (049) 952 5014 – Menu € 19 (lunch) **s** – Carte dinner € 29/45 **s**
◆ Impressive façade in mock-Georgian style, with neo-classical lobby. Bedrooms overlooking grounds are large and luxurious with every modern convenience. Restaurants named after Irish folk heroes. Classical dishes in formal Conall Cearnach. Relaxed, stylish Setanta offers eclectic Mediterranean menu.

BALLYCOTTON (Baile Choitín) – Cork – 712 H12 – pop. 412 — 39 C3

Ireland

Dublin 265 km – Cork 43 km – Waterford 106 km
Cloyne Cathedral★, NW : by R 629

Bayview
– ✆ (021) 464 67 46 – www.thebayviewhotel.com – May-October
33 rm – € 85/120 € 175 – 2 suites
Rest – *(bar lunch Monday-Saturday)* Menu € 28/45 – Carte € 45/50
◆ A series of cottages in an elevated position with fine views of bay, harbour and island. Bar and lounge in library style with sofas. Spacious, comfy rooms with ocean views. Warm, inviting dining room.

BALLYDAVID (Baile na nGall) – Kerry – 712 A11 – ✉ Dingle — 38 A2

Dublin 362 km – Dingle 11 km – Tralee 58 km

Old Pier
An Fheothanach, North : 3 km on Feomanagh rd – ✆ (066) 915 52 42 – www.oldpier.com
5 rm – € 40/50 € 70/80 **Rest** – *(March-October)* Carte € 25/51
◆ Modern, purpose-built guesthouse with great views over the headland, harbour and Three Sisters. Simple, pine-furnished bedrooms boast orthopaedic beds and are hung with silk paintings of local sights. Menus offer something for everyone; local seafood is a feature.

REPUBLIC OF IRELAND

BALLYFARNAN (Béal Átha Fearnáin) – Roscommon – 712 H5 – pop. 182 — 37 C2

Dublin 111 km – Roscommon 42 km – Sligo 21 km – Longford 38 km

Kilronan Castle

South East : 3.5 km on Keadew rd – ✆ (071) 961 80 00 – www.kilronancastle.ie

84 rm – † € 150/195 †† € 300/390

Rest ***Douglas Hyde*** – *(dinner only and Sunday lunch)* Menu € 30 (lunch) – Carte € 25/70

◆ Imposing restored castle, with wood panelling, antiques, portraits and a suit of armour. Opulent red and gold bedrooms offer a high level of comfort. Impressive hydrotherapy centre. Grand dining room; traditional menu uses local produce.

BALLYLICKEY (Béal Átha Leice) – Cork – 712 D12 – ✉ Bantry Ireland — 38 A3

Dublin 347 km – Cork 88 km – Killarney 72 km

Bantry Bay Donemark, ✆ (027) 50 579

Bantry Bay★ - Bantry House★ **AC**, S : 5 km by R 584. Glengarriff★ (Ilnacullin★★, access by boat) NW : 13 km by N 71 - Healy Pass★★ (<★★) W : 37 km by N 71, R 572 and R 574 – Slieve Miskish Mountains (<★★) W : 46.75 km by N 71 and R 572 – Lauragh (Derreen Gardens★ **AC**) NW : 44 km by N 71, R 572 and R 574 – Allihies (copper mines★) W : 66.75 km by N 71, R 572 and R 575 – Garnish Island (<★) W : 70.75 km by N 71 and R 572

Seaview House

rm,

– ✆ (027) 50 462 – www.seaviewhousehotel.com – Mid March-mid November

25 rm – † € 60/80 †† € 120/185

Rest – *(dinner only and Sunday lunch)* Menu € 20/45 **s**

◆ Tall, well-run, whitewashed Victorian house set amidst lush gardens which tumble down to Bantry Bay. Traditional lounges with bar and spacious, individually designed rooms. Warmly decorated dining room.

Ballylickey House without rest

– ✆ (027) 50 071 – www.ballylickeymanorhouse.com – May-August

6 rm – † € 65/75 †† € 80/110

◆ Impressive hotel with attractive gardens set amongst Bantry Bay's ragged inlets. Spacious, cosy bedrooms, named after flowers and birds. Breakfast room with fireside armchairs.

BALLYLIFFIN (Baile Lifín) – Donegal – 712 J2 – pop. 357 — 37 C1

Dublin 174 km – Lifford 46 km – Letterkenny 39 km

Ballyliffin Lodge

rest,

Shore Rd – ✆ (074) 937 82 00 – www.ballyliffinlodge.com – Closed 25 December, restricted opening in winter

40 rm – † € 90/124 †† € 130/198

Rest – *(bar lunch Monday-Saturday)* Menu € 20 (dinner) – Carte € 26/38

◆ Modern, purpose-built hotel with rural/beach views. Comfortable lounges and good quality spa. Well-appointed bedrooms; the front-facing ones are larger and look towards Malin Head. Small, formal restaurant offers traditional menus.

BALLYMACARBRY (Baile Mhac Cairbre) – Waterford – 712 I11 – pop. 436 – ✉ Clonmel Ireland — 39 C2

Dublin 190 km – Cork 79 km – Waterford 63 km

Clonmel★ (St Mary's Church★, County Museum★ **AC**), N : 16 km by R 671 – Lismore★ (Castle Gardens★ **AC**, St Carthage's Cathedral★), SW : 26 km by R 671and N 72 – W : Nier Valley Scenic Route★★

Hanora's Cottage
Nire Valley, East : 6.5 km by Nire Drive rd on Nire Valley Lakes rd – ✆ (052) 613 61 34 – www.hanorascottage.com – closed 1 week Christmas
10 rm – € 75 € 150
Rest – *(dinner only and Sunday lunch) (booking essential for non-residents)* Menu € 45
♦ Pleasant 19C farmhouse with purpose-built extensions in quiet location at foot of mountains. Very extensive and impressive breakfast buffet. Stylish rooms, all with jacuzzis. Locally renowned menus, brimming with fresh produce.

Glasha Farmhouse
Northwest : 4 km by R 671 – ✆ (052) 613 61 08 – www.glashafarmhouse.com – January-November
6 rm – € 50/60 € 90/100 **Rest** – ✆ (052) 636 108 – Menu € 40
♦ Large farmhouse set between the Knockmealdown and Comeragh Mountains. Guest areas include a spacious lounge, airy conservatory and patio. Comfy bedrooms; some with jacuzzis. Welcoming owners have good local knowledge. Home-cooked meals; picnic lunches available.

BALLYMORE EUSTACE (An Baile Mór) – Kildare – pop. 725 — 39 D1

Dublin 48 km – Naas 12 km – Drogheda 99 km

Ballymore Inn
– ✆ (045) 864 585 – www.ballymoreinn.com
Rest – Menu € 22/35 – Carte € 35/42
♦ Remote village pub with spacious bar and Parisian brasserie-style dining area. Generous portions include tasty homemade bread, pizzas, tarts and pastries. Small artisan producers favoured.

BALLYNAHINCH (Baile na hInse) – Galway – 712 C7 – ✉ Recess — 36 A3

Ireland

Dublin 225 km – Galway 66 km – Westport 79 km

Connemara★★★ – Roundstone★, S : by R 341 – Cashel★, SE : by R 341 and R 340

Ballynahinch Castle
– ✆ (095) 31 006 – www.ballynahinch-castle.com – Closed 30 January-24 February and 18-27 December
37 rm – € 220/290 € 300/380 – 3 suites
Rest – *(dinner only) (booking essential for non-residents)* Menu € 60 **s**
♦ Grey stone, part 17C castle in magnificent grounds with fine river views. Two large sitting rooms, characterful bar frequented by fishermen. Spacious rooms with antiques. Inviting dining room with stunning river views.

BALLYVAUGHAN (Baile Uí Bheacháin) – Clare – 712 E8 – pop. 224 — 38 B1

Ireland

Dublin 240 km – Ennis 55 km – Galway 46 km

The Burren★★ (Scenic Route★★, Aillwee Cave★ **AC** (Waterfall★★), Corcomroe Abbey★, Poulnabrone Portal Tomb★) – Kilfenora (Crosses★, Burren Centre★ **AC**), S : 25 km N 67 and R 476. Cliffs of Moher★★★, S : 32 km by N 67 and R 478

Gregans Castle
Southwest : 6 km on N 67 – ✆ (065) 707 7005 – www.gregans.ie – 11 February-27 November
16 rm – € 152/192 € 195/235 – 4 suites
Rest – *(closed Sunday dinner) (bar lunch)* Menu € 65 **s**
♦ Idyllically positioned, family owned hotel with fine views to The Burren and Galway Bay. Relaxing sitting room, cosy bar lounge, country house-style bedrooms. Sizeable conservatory dining room specialising in seasonal, regional dishes.

REPUBLIC OF IRELAND

Drumcreehy House without rest

Northeast : 2 km on N 67 – ✆ (065) 707 73 77 – www.drumcreehyhouse.com – March-October

12 rm – € 50/100 € 84/100

◆ Efficiently run, pristine house overlooking Galway Bay. Stylish lounge with honesty bar. Bedrooms, named after flowers, are excellent value: spacious, comfortable and furnished in German stripped oak. Great choice at breakfast.

Ballyvaughan Lodge without rest

– ✆ (065) 707 72 92 – www.ballyvaughanlodge.com – Closed 25-26 December

11 rm – € 45/50 € 80/90

◆ Welcoming guesthouse with colourful flower display and decking. Comfy, light-filled lounge. Bedrooms boast co-ordinating fabrics and furnishings. Quality farmers' market produce at breakfast.

Cappabhaile House without rest

Southwest : 1.5 km on N 67 – ✆ (065) 707 72 60 – www.cappabhaile.com – March-October

10 rm – € 53/75 € 86/96

◆ Proudly run, grey-stone house with nice gardens, offering great views over The Burren. Spacious lounge-cum-breakfast room; comfy, good-sized bedrooms. Pool table and regular live music sessions.

BALTIMORE (Dún na Séad) – Cork – 712 D13 – pop. 377 Ireland 38 A3

Dublin 344 km – Cork 95 km – Killarney 124 km

Sherkin Island★ (by ferry) – Castletownshend★, E : 20 km by R 595 and R 596 – Glandore★, E : 26 km by R 595, N 71 and R 597

Casey's of Baltimore

East : 0.75 km on R 595 – ✆ (028) 20 197 – www.caseysofbaltimore.com – Closed 20-27 December

14 rm – € 99/115 € 154/182 **Rest** – Menu € 24 – Carte € 31/49 **s**

◆ Popular hotel near sea-shore. Cosy bar with open fires and traditional music at weekends, with beer garden overlooking bay. Large, well-decorated rooms with pine furniture. Great sea views from dining room.

Baltimore Townhouse without rest

– ✆ (028) 20 197 – www.baltimoretownhouse.com – Closed 20-27 December

6 rm – € 120/160 € 120/160

◆ Six open plan suites comprising bedroom, living area, small kitchen and bathroom. Check in at Casey's on your way into the village; breakfast is also served here.

Slipway without rest

The Cove, East : 0.75 km – ✆ (028) 20 134 – www.theslipway.com – May-September

4 rm – € 60/70 € 72/80

◆ Relaxed, informal guesthouse with yellow façade and lovely views of local harbour, particularly from veranda outside breakfast room. Simple, individualistic, well-kept rooms.

BANDON (Droichead na Bandan) – Cork – 712 F12 – pop. 5 822 38 B3

Dublin 181 km – Cork 20 km – Carrigaline 28 km – Cobh 33 km

Poacher's Inn

Clonakilty Rd, Southwest : 1.5 km on N 71 – ✆ (023) 884 1159 – www.poachersinnbandon.com – Closed 25 December

Rest – Carte € 18/36

◆ Cosy neighbourhood pub that's popular with the locals. Light snack menu in the bar and snug; hearty, classical seafood dishes in the upstairs restaurant, which opens later in the week.

BANSHA - 712 H10 39 C2

Dublin 121 km - Clonmel 21 km - Cork 59 km - Limerick 31 km

Rathellen House

Southeast : 3.5 km. by N 24 on Coopers Cottage rd - (062) 54 376 - www.rathellenhouse.com

6 rm - € 60/65 € 90/110

Rest - *(dinner only) (residents only set menu)* Menu € 40/55

♦ Very comfortable, Georgian-style house with classic country house feel, set in peaceful location. Variously-sized bedrooms feature antique furniture and pleasant countryside/mountain outlooks; bathrooms boast heated flooring. Formal dining room with antique tables; home-cooked meals utilise local, often organic produce.

BANTRY (Beanntraí) Cork - Cork - 712 D12 38 A3

Dublin 215 km - Cork 53 km - Killarney 49 km - Macroom 34 km

O'Connor's

The Square - (035327) 50 221 - www.oconnorseafood.com - Restricted opening in winter

Rest - Seafood - *(booking essential)* Menu € 30 (early dinner) - Carte € 31/45

♦ Popular seafood restaurant on edge of the harbour, with rustic stone floor, granite-topped tables and maritime décor. Tasty, classically cooked local seafood. Pleasant service.

BARNA (Bearna) - Galway - 712 E8 - pop. 12 795 36 B3

Dublin 227 km - Galway 9 km

The Twelve

Barna Crossroads - (091) 597 000 - www.thetwelvehotel.ie

38 rm - € 89/139 € 99/150 - 10 suites

Rest *West* - *(closed Monday) (dinner only)* Menu € 25 **s** - Carte € 36/43 **s**

Rest *The Pins* - Menu € 25 - Carte € 25/39 **s**

♦ Boutique hotel whose bedrooms are stylish and modern with quality furniture, up-to-date technology and designer toiletries. Original menu offered in elegant West restaurant. The Pins offers an interesting menu of European dishes in an informal atmosphere.

O'Grady's on the Pier

- (091) 592 223 - www.ogradysonthepier.com - Closed 24-27 December

Rest - Seafood - *(booking essential)* Carte € 32/48

♦ Converted quayside pub on two floors with great views of Galway Bay. Cheerful, attentive staff and daily menus of simple, flavourful seafood have earned good local reputation.

BARRELLS CROSS - Cork - 712 G12 - see Kinsale

BEAUFORT = Lios an Phúca - Kerry - 712 D11 - see Killarney

BIRR (Biorra) - Offaly - 712 I8 - pop. 5 081 Ireland 39 C1

Dublin 140 km - Athlone 45 km - Kilkenny 79 km - Limerick 79 km

The Civic Office, Wilmer Rd (057) 912 0923

The Glenns, (057) 912 00 82

Town★ - Birr Castle Demesne★★ **AC** (Telescope★★)

Clonfert Cathedral★ (West doorway★★), NW : 24 km by R 439, R 356 and minor roads - Portumna★ (Castle★ **AC**), W : 24 km by R 489 - Roscrea★ (Damer House★ **AC**) S : 19.25 km by N 62 - Slieve Bloom Mountinas★, E : 21 km by R 440

Maltings without rest

Castle St - (057) 91 21 345

10 rm - € 50/55 € 80/90

♦ Characterful 19C hotel on riverside near Birr Castle, originally built to store malt for Guinness. Cosy bar and lounge. Bedrooms enriched by flowery fabrics and drapes.

BLACKLION (An Blaic) – Cavan – 712 I5 – pop. 174 — 34 A3

Dublin 194 km – Drogheda 170 km – Enniskillen 19 km
Blacklion Toam, ✆ (071) 985 30 24

XXX **MacNean House** with rm — rest, VISA

Main St – ✆ (071) 985 30 22 – www.macneanrestaurant.com – closed 25 December and January
19 rm – € 90 € 140
Rest – *(closed Monday, Tuesday and Sunday dinner) (dinner only and Sunday lunch) (booking essential)* Menu € 39 (lunch) – Carte approx. € 70
◆ Stylish, modern restaurant in smart townhouse, with plush seating, linen-clad tables and subtle cream décor. Refined, complex dishes use good quality seasonal and local ingredients. Keenly run, with friendly local staff. Comfortable, contemporary bedrooms.

BLARNEY (An Bhlarna) – Cork – 712 G12 – pop. 2 400 – ✉ Cork — 38 B3

Ireland

Dublin 268 km – Cork 9 km
Town Centre (021) 4381624, (May- Sept) blarneytio@failteireland.ie
Blarney Castle★★ AC – Blarney Castle House★ AC

Killarney House without rest

Station Rd, Northeast : 1.5 km – ✆ (021) 438 18 41 – www.killarneyhouseblarney.com
6 rm – € 45/50 € 60/70
◆ Spacious, modern guesthouse set above attractive village. Very comfortable lounge. Breakfast room equipped to high standard. Sizeable, immaculately kept rooms.

at Tower West : 3.25 km on R 617 – ✉ Cork

Ashlee Lodge — VISA AE

– ✆ (021) 438 53 46 – www.ashleelodge.com – closed 20 December-20 January
10 rm – € 65/95 € 140/180 **Rest** – *(dinner only)* Carte approx. € 38 **s**
◆ Smart hotel with open-fired lounge complete with board games and honesty bar. Comfy bedrooms offer all you could want; some have whirlpool baths. Outdoor Canadian hot tub, sauna and in-room treatments. Dining room offers freshly prepared, home-cooked dishes.

BORRIS – Carlow – 712 L10 – pop. 582 — 39 D2

Dublin 121 km – Carlow 36 km – Waterford 66 km

Step House — VISA

– ✆ (059) 977 3209 – www.stephousehotel.ie – Closed 25 December
19 rm – € 65/85 € 150 – 1 suite
Rest *Cellar* – *(dinner only Friday, Saturday and Sunday lunch)* Carte € 35/46
◆ Extended Georgian townhouse offers spacious, modern bedrooms decorated in cool pastel shades. All have freestanding roll-top baths; the penthouse has floor to ceiling windows and a terrace overlooking the mountains. Traditional cooking served in Cellar.

BOYLE (Mainistir na Búille) – Roscommon – 712 H6 – pop. 2 522 — 36 B2

Ireland

Dublin 175 km – Longford 53 km – Sligo 45 km
King House (071) 966 2145, (May- Sept) boyle.touristoffice@failteireland.ie
King House★ AC
Boyle Abbey★ AC, E : 2 km by N 4 – Lough Key Forest Park★ AC, E : 3.25 km by N 4. Arigna Scenic Drive★ (≤★), NE : 20 km by N 4, R 280 and R 207 – Curlew Mountains (≤★), NW : 3.5 km by N 4

Rosdarrig House without rest — VISA

Carrick Rd, (East : 1.5 km) – ✆ (071) 966 20 40 – www.rosdarrig.com – April-October
5 rm – € 45/50 € 70/75
◆ Neat house on the edge of town, close to the abbey, where friendly owners offer genuine Irish hospitality. Comfy lounge and linen-laid breakfast room. Pleasant bedrooms overlook the garden.

REPUBLIC OF IRELAND

BUNDORAN (Bun Dobhráin) – Donegal – 712 H4 – pop. 1 964 — 37 C2
Ireland

Dublin 259 km – Donegal 27 km – Sligo 37 km

The Bridge, Main St ✆ (071) 9842539 (April-October)

Creevykeel Court Cairn★, S : 5 km by N 15 – Rossnowlagh Strand★★, N : 8.5 km by N 15 and R 231

Fitzgerald's

– *✆ (071) 984 13 36 – www.fitzgeraldshotel.com – Closed 1 January-10 February and 28 November-31 December*

16 rm – € 55/84 € 90/147

Rest *The Bistro* – *(closed Monday-Tuesday) (dinner only)* Menu € 30 **s** – Carte € 28/34 **s**

◆ Family owned hotel in centre of popular seaside town overlooking Donegal Bay. Reception rooms warmed by wood-burning stove. Sumptuous sofas abound. Sea-facing front bedrooms. Linen-clad, informal Bistro with carefully compiled menu.

BUNRATTY (Bun Raite) – Clare – 712 F9 Ireland — 38 B2

Dublin 207 km – Ennis 24 km – Limerick 13 km

Town★★ – Bunratty Castle★★

Bunratty Manor

– *✆ (061) 707 984 – www.bunrattymanor.net – Closed 1 week Christmas*

20 rm – € 79/99 € 99/120

Rest – *(closed Monday) (dinner only and Sunday lunch)* Carte € 30/45

◆ Smart hotel not far from the castle and folk park, in a busy tourist town. Good-sized, brightly decorated bedrooms display colourful fabrics; most bathrooms have showers only. Comfy lounge. Traditional bar with courtyard offers both pub and restaurant-style menus.

Bunratty Grove without rest

Castle Rd., North : 3 km on Buratty Castle rd – ✆ (061) 369 579 – www.bunrattygrove.com

6 rm – € 35/50 € 50/60

◆ Purpose-built guesthouse with mature gardens, set in a peaceful area out of town. Tidy, well-kept lounge and pine-furnished breakfast room. Good-sized bedrooms with polished wood floors.

CAHERDANIEL (Cathair Dónall) – Kerry – 712 B12 – pop. 352 — 38 A3
– ✉ Killarney Ireland

Dublin 383 km – Killarney 77 km

Ring of Kerry★★ – Derrynane National Historic Park★★ – Skellig Islands★★ **AC**, by boat – Sneem★, E : 19 km by N 70 – Staigue Fort★, E : 8 km by N 70 and minor road

Iskeroon without rest

West : 8 mi by N 70 and Bunavalla Pier rd taking left turn at junction then turning left onto track immediately before pier – ✆ (066) 947 51 19 – www.iskeroon.com – May-October , minimum stay 2 nights

3 rm – € 115/120

◆ A "design icon", this low-lying house looking out to Derrynane Harbour was built in 1930s by the Earl of Dunraven. Lush gardens; boldly designed, vividly coloured bedrooms.

CAHERLISTRANE (Cathair Loistreáin) – Galway – 712 E7 — 36 B3

Dublin 256 km – Ballina 74 km – Galway 42 km

Lisdonagh House

Northwest : 4 km by R 333 off Shrule rd – ✆ (093) 31 163 – www.lisdonagh.com – May-October

10 rm – € 89/150 € 140/180 **Rest** – *(dinner only)* Menu € 45

◆ Ivy-clad Georgian house with lough views. Traditional country house interior boasts eye-catching mural and open-fired lounges. Antique-furnished bedrooms have marble bathrooms; first floor rooms are larger and brighter. Formal dining room offers home-cooked meals.

CAHERSIVEEN (Cathair Saidhbhín) – Kerry – 712 B12 – pop. 1 294 38 A2
Ireland

Dublin 355 km – Killarney 64 km

Ring of Kerry★★

O'Neill's (The Point) Seafood Bar

Renard Point, Southwest : 2.75 km by N 70 – (066) 947 2165 – Closed November-February

Rest – *(bookings not accepted)* Carte € 28/38

◆ Striking blue pub beside the Valentia Island ferry terminal; run by the O'Neill family for over 150 years. Traditional Irish cooking; generous dishes with a strong seafood base. Unusually, no chips or desserts and no credit card payments.

CAMPILE (Ceann Poill) – Wexford – 712 L11 – pop. 347 Ireland 39 D2

Dublin 154 km – Waterford 35 km – Wexford 37 km

Dunbrody Abbey★, S : 3.25 km by R 733 – J F Kennedy Arboretum★, N : 3.25 km by R 733. Tintern Abbey★, SE : 12.75 km by R 733 – Duncannon Fort★, S : 12.75 km by R 733

Kilmokea Country Manor

rm, VISA

West : 8 km by R 733 and Great Island rd – (051) 388 109 – www.kilmokea.com – February-4 November

6 rm – € 75/120 € 180/300

Rest – *(booking essential for non-residents)* Menu € 50 (dinner) – Carte lunch approx. € 30

◆ Former Georgian rectory in large public gardens. Elegantly furnished. Games room, tennis and fishing. Comfortable bedrooms in house and converted stable block. Formal dining room with polished tables and period style; breakfast in conservatory.

REPUBLIC OF IRELAND

CAPPOQUIN (Ceapach Choinn) – Waterford – 712 I11 – pop. 740 39 C2
Ireland

Dublin 219 km – Cork 56 km – Waterford 64 km

Lismore★ (Lismore Castle Gardens★ **AC**, St Carthage's Cathedral★), W : 6.5 km by N 72. The Gap★ (≤★) NW : 14.5 km by R 669

Richmond House with rm

VISA

Southeast : 0.75 km on N 72 – (058) 54 278 – www.richmondhouse.net – Closed 23 December-15 January, Sunday and Monday

9 rm – € 70/100 € 130/190 **Rest** – *(dinner only)* Carte € 35/55

◆ Built for Earl of Cork and Burlington in 1704; retains Georgian style with stately, cove-ceilinged dining room: local produce to the fore. Individually decorated period rooms.

at Millstreet East : 11.25 km by N 72 on R 671 – ✉ Cappoquin

Castle Country House without rest

VISA

– (058) 68 049 – www.castlecountryhouse.com – April-October

5 rm – € 50/65 € 80/100

◆ Extended farmhouse on working dairy and beef farm with 15C origins. Rural location and lovely gardens. Individual bedrooms with cottage style decor.

CARAGH LAKE (Loch Cárthaí) – Kerry – 712 C11 Ireland 38 A2

Dublin 341 km – Killarney 35 km – Tralee 40 km

18 Dooks Glenbeigh, (066) 976 82 05

Lough Caragh★

Iveragh Peninsula★★ (Ring of Kerry★★)

Ard-Na-Sidhe

VISA AE

– (066) 976 91 05 – www.ardnasidhe.com – May-October

18 rm – € 160/270 € 170/300

Rest – *(dinner only) (booking essential for non-residents)* Carte € 35/56

◆ Built 1880 by an English Lady who called it "House of Fairies". Elizabethan in style; gardens lead down to lake. Possesses atmosphere of private home. Antique filled rooms. Tasteful dining room with intimate feel.

Carrig Country House

– ✆ (066) 976 91 00 – www.carrighouse.com – March-November
17 rm – € 125/140 € 150/250
Rest – *(dinner only) (booking essential for non-residents)* Carte € 37/52
♦ Down a wooded drive, the yellow ochre façade of the house immediately strikes you. Its loughside setting assures good views. Ground floor rooms have their own private patio. Caragh Lough outlook from dining room windows.

CARLINGFORD (Cairlinn) – Louth – 712 N5 – pop. 623 Ireland — 37 D2

Dublin 106 km – Dundalk 21 km
Town★
Windy Gap★, NW : 12.75 km by R 173 – Proleek Dolmen★, SW : 14.5 km by R 173

Four Seasons

– ✆ (042) 937 35 30 – www.4seasonshotelcarlingford.ie
59 rm – € 65/125 € 99/210
Rest – *(bar lunch Monday-Saturday)* Menu € 30 – Carte € 21/41
♦ Purpose-built hotel on outskirts of scenic market town. Extensive conference facilities; smart leisure centre. Spacious and well-equipped bedrooms. Popular bar leading to intimate dining room with Irish menus.

Beaufort House without rest

– ✆ (042) 937 38 79 – www.beauforthouse.net – Closed 25 December
5 rm – € 65/85 € 120
♦ Modern house on the shores of the lough; run by welcoming owners. Spacious lounge displays local art and old maritime charts. Large, comfortable bedrooms boast water or mountain views.

CARLOW (Ceatharlach) – Carlow – 712 L9 – pop. 20 724 — 39 D2

Dublin 80 km – Kilkenny 37 km – Wexford 75 km
College St ✆ (059) 9131554, carlowtouristoffice@failteireland.ie
Carlow Dublin Rd, Deer Park, ✆ (059) 913 16 95

Seven Oaks

Athy Rd – ✆ (059) 913 13 08 – www.sevenoakshotel.com – closed 24-26 December
89 rm – € 65/85 € 110/140
Rest – *(closed Saturday lunch)* Menu € 25 (lunch)/38 – Carte € 24/37
♦ Close to the sights of the River Barrow walk, this neat hotel in a residential area makes a good resting place. Well-kept rooms: ask for those in the new wing. Intimate booths in tranquil dining room.

Barrowville Town House without rest

Kilkenny Rd, South : 0.75 km on N 9 – ✆ (059) 914 33 24 – www.barrowville.com – Closed 25 December
7 rm – € 50/80 € 100/120
♦ Delightful Georgian property filled with beautiful furniture, including a grand piano in the drawing room. Conservatory breakfast room looks out over the garden. Spacious, homely bedrooms.

CARNAROSS (Carn na Ros) – Meath – 712 L6 – ✉ Kells — 37 D3

Dublin 69 km – Cavan 43 km – Drogheda 48 km

Forge

Pottlereagh, Northwest : 5.5 km by N 3 on Oldcastle rd – ✆ (046) 924 50 03 – www.theforgerestaurant.ie – Closed 24-26 and 31 December, 1 January, 2 weeks August, Sunday dinner, Monday and Tuesday
Rest – *(dinner only and Sunday lunch)* Menu € 30/50 – Carte € 46/57
♦ Former forge tucked away in rural isolation. Family run, traditionally styled restaurant serving tried-and-tested dishes with modern twist: ample, good value choice.

REPUBLIC OF IRELAND

CARNE – Wexford – **712** M11 **39** D3

Dublin 169 km – Waterford 82 km – Wexford 21 km

The Lobster Pot

Ballyfane – (053) 913 1110 – Closed January-mid February, 25-26 December, Good Friday and Monday except bank holidays

Rest – Seafood – Carte € 35/55

◆ Popular pub full of nautical memorabilia. Large menus feature tasty, home-style cooking. Fresh seafood dishes are a must try, with oysters and lobster the specialities. No children after 5pm.

CARRICKMACROSS (Carraig Mhachaire Rois) – Monaghan – **712** L6 – pop. 4 387 Ireland **37** D2

Dublin 92 km – Dundalk 22 km

Nuremore Hotel & CC, (042) 966 14 38

Dún a' Rí Forest Park★, SW : 8 km by R 179 – St Mochta's House★, E : 7 km by R 178 and minor road S

Nuremore

South : 1.5 km on N 2 – (042) 966 14 38 – www.nuremore.com

72 rm – € 135/160 € 180/295

Rest *The Restaurant* – see restaurant listing

◆ Much extended Victorian house in attractive grounds; a rural retreat in which to swim, ride or practice golf. Comfortable rooms, most with views over countryside.

The Restaurant – at Nuremore Hotel

South : 1.5 km on N 2 – (042) 966 14 38 – www.nuremore.com

Rest – *(dinner only and Sunday lunch)* Carte € 40/52

◆ Spacious, classical, split-level dining room. Tables feature crisp linen; service is attentive. Cooking uses luxurious, seasonal ingredients; dishes are original and stylishly presented.

Courthouse

1 Monaghan St – (042) 969 28 48 – Closed one week January, Monday (except bank holidays) and Tuesday

Rest – Carte € 21/42

◆ Relaxed, rustic restaurant featuring wooden floors, exposed ceiling rafters and bare brick. Carefully prepared, flavourful dishes; good value midweek menu. Friendly efficient service.

CARRICK-ON-SHANNON (Cora Droma Rúisc) – Leitrim – **712** H6 – pop. 3 163 Ireland **37** C2

Dublin 156 km – Ballina 80 km – Galway 119 km – Roscommon 42 km

Old Barrel Store, The Marina (0719) 620170 (April-October), leitrim@failteireland.ie

Carrick-on-Shannon Woodbrook, (071) 966 7015

Town★

Lough Rynn Demesne★

The Landmark

rm, rest,

on N 4 – (071) 962 22 22 – www.thelandmarkhotel.com – Closed 25 December

60 rm – € 79/125 € 130/198

Rest *Boardwalk* – Carte € 23/30

◆ Next to the Shannon, with a water feature in reception and water-themed pictures throughout. Traditional style bedrooms; some overlooking the river. Stylish cocktail lounges with stunning modern design. Boardwalk boasts pleasant river views.

Hollywell without rest

Liberty Hill, off N 4, taking first left over bridge – (071) 962 11 24 – March-October

4 rm – € 65/75 € 110/120

◆ A charming part 18C house in a peaceful spot by the river. Read up on area in a well-appointed lounge, take breakfast in dining room run by hospitable owner. Neat rooms.

Oarsman

Bridge St. – ✆ (071) 962 1733 – www.theoarsman.com – Closed Sunday and Monday

Rest – Menu € 30/35 – Carte € 20/40

◆ Traditional, brightly coloured, family-run pub filled with pottery, bygone artefacts and fishing tackle. Cooking is simple and produce, local. Comfy restaurant area opens later in the week.

CARRIGALINE (Carraig Uí Leighin) – Cork – 712 G12 – pop. 12 835 — 38 B3

Dublin 262 km – Cork 14 km

Fernhill, ✆ (021) 437 2226

Carrigaline Court

rm, rest,

Cork Rd – ✆ (021) 485 21 00 – www.carrigcourt.com – closed 23-27 December

89 rm – € 80/140 € 140/220 – 2 suites

Rest – *(dinner only) (meals served in bar Sunday-Thursday)* Carte € 30/50 **s**

◆ Modern hotel with airy interiors; rooms are spacious, with all mod cons, whilst leisure centre boasts a 20m pool, steam room, sauna. Corporate friendly with large ballroom. Local products to the fore in stylish restaurant.

Raffeen Lodge without rest

Ringaskiddy Rd, Monkstown, Northeast : 4 km by R 611 and N 28 off R 610 – ✆ (021) 437 16 32 – www.raffeenlodge.com – closed 20 December-6 January

6 rm – € 40/45 € 70

◆ A short drive from the fishing village of Ringaskiddy and Cork airport. A neat and tidy, good value house; rooms are uniformly decorated in pastel shades, simple in style.

CARRIGANS (An Carraigain) – Donegal – 712 J3 – pop. 191 — 37 C1

Dublin 225 km – Donegal 66 km – Letterkenny 230 km – Sligo 124 km

Mount Royd without rest

– ✆ (074) 914 01 63 – www.mountroyd.com – Restricted opening in winter

4 rm – € 40/45 € 65/75

◆ Genuinely hospitable owners keep this creeper-clad period house in excellent order. En suite rooms are cosy and individually styled. Traditional, pleasantly cluttered lounge.

CASHEL (An Caiseal) – Galway – 712 C7 Ireland — 36 A3

Dublin 278 km – Galway 66 km

Town★

Connemara★★★

Cashel House

– ✆ (095) 31 001 – www.cashel-house-hotel.com – Restricted opening in winter

30 rm – € 125/320 € 250/340

Rest – *(bar lunch Monday-Saturday) (booking essential for non-residents)* Carte € 32/60

◆ Built 1840; a very comfortable and restful country house, warmly decorated with delightful gardens. General de Gaulle stayed in one of the luxurious country house rooms. Dining room, with Queen Anne style chairs, opens into elegant conservatory.

CASHEL (Caiseal) – Tipperary – 712 I10 – pop. 2 936 Ireland — 39 C2

Dublin 162 km – Cork 96 km – Kilkenny 55 km – Limerick 58 km

Heritage Centre, Town Hall, Main St ✆ (062) 62511, cashelhc@iol.ie

Town★★★ – Rock of Cashel★★★ **AC** – Cormac's Chapel★★ – Round Tower★ – Museum★ – Cashel Palace Gardens★ – GPA Bolton Library★ **AC**

Holy Cross Abbey★★, N : 14.5 km by R 660 – Athassel Priory★, W : 8 km by N 74. Caher (Castle★★, Swiss Cottage★), S : 18 km by N 8 – Glen of Aherlow★, W : 21 km by N 74 and R 664

Cashel Palace
Main St – ✆ (062) 62 707 – www.cashel-palace.ie – Closed 24-27 December
19 rm – €95/130 €130/238
Rest – *(carvery lunch Monday-Saturday)* Menu €49 – Carte €25/45
◆ A stately Queen Anne house, once home to an Archbishop, in walled gardens with path leading up to Cashel Rock. Inside, an extensive, pillared lounge and capacious rooms. Harmonious dining room: vaulted ceilings, open fire and light, bright colours.

Baileys of Cashel
Main St – ✆ (062) 61 937 – www.baileyshotelcashel.com – Closed 23 December-2 January
20 rm – €85/95 €110/130 **Rest** – Carte €23/37
◆ Extended Georgian townhouse, used as grain store during Irish famine. Contemporary bedrooms are furnished to a high standard. Small lounge with library; bar area in basement. Restaurant with open plan kitchen serves modern European cooking.

Aulber House without rest
Deerpark, Golden Rd, West : 0.75 km on N 74 – ✆ (062) 63 713 – www.aulberhouse.com – March-November
12 rm – €50/70 €80/100
◆ Modern house in Georgian style with lawned gardens; five minutes from town centre. Comfy, leather furnished lounge. Smart, individually styled rooms.

Chez Hans
Rockside, Moor Lane St – ✆ (062) 61 177 – www.chezhans.net – Closed 2 weeks January, 2 weeks September, 25 December, Sunday and Monday
Rest – *(dinner only) (booking essential)* Menu €29/35 (early weekday dinner) – Carte €35/60
◆ A converted synod hall with stained glass windows, near Cashel Rock: an unusual setting for a restaurant. Carefully prepared and cooked meals, using local ingredients.

Cafe Hans
Rockside, Moore Lane St. – ✆ (062) 63 660 – Closed 2 weeks January, 1 week October, Sunday and Monday
Rest – *(lunch only) (bookings not accepted)* Carte €20/34
◆ Next door to Chez Hans; white emulsioned walls, open kitchen and glass roof. Simple, tasty dishes are prepared with good, local ingredients. Come early as you can't book.

CASTLEBALDWIN (Béal Átha na gCarraigíní) – Sligo – 712 G5 36 B2
– ✉ Boyle (roscommon) Ireland

Dublin 190 km – Longford 67 km – Sligo 24 km

Carrowkeel Megalithic Cemetery (<★★), S : 4.75 km. Arigna Scenic Drive★, N : 3.25 km by N 4 - Lough Key Forest Park★ **AC**, SE : 16 km by N 4 – View of Lough Allen★, N : 14.5 km by N 4 on R 280 – Mountain Drive★, N : 9.5 km on N 4 – Boyle Abbey★ **AC**, SE : 12.75 km by N 4 - King House★, SE : 12.75 km by N 4

Cromleach Lodge
Ballindoon, Southeast : 5.5 km – ✆ (071) 916 51 55 – www.cromleach.com – Closed Christmas
57 rm – €135/160 €210/260
Rest *Moira's* – see restaurant listing
◆ Remotely located hotel in fine position overlooking Lough Arrow. Large, luxurious bedrooms; some modern, some classic; deluxe rooms with views and either balcony or terrace are well worth the extra.

Moira's – at Cromleach Lodge Hotel
Ballindoon, Southeast : 5.5 km – ✆ (071) 916 51 55 – www.cromleach.com – Closed Christmas
Rest – Menu €35 (lunch)/56 – Carte approx. €60
◆ Spacious, contemporary restaurant with views to Lough Arrow. Rear booths ideal for large groups. Fixed price menu of modern Irish cooking, with local produce to the fore.

CASTLEGREGORY (Caisleán Ghriaire) – Kerry – 712 B11 – pop. 205 — 38 A2

Dublin 330 km – Dingle 24 km – Killarney 54 km

Shores Country House without rest

Conor Pass Rd, Kilcummin, Southwest : 6 km on Brandon rd – (066) 713 91 95 – www.shorescountryhouse.com – Closed 2 December-10 January

6 rm – € 50/90 € 70/90

◆ Between Stradbally Mountain and a long sandy beach, a modern guest house run by a friendly longstanding owner. Immaculate, comfortable rooms, some with antique beds.

CASTLELYONS (Caisleán Ó Liatháin) – Cork – 712 H11 – pop. 203 — 38 B2

Dublin 219 km – Cork 30 km – Killarney 104 km – Limerick 64 km

Ballyvolane House

Southeast : 5.5 km by Midleton rd on Britway rd – (025) 36 349 – www.ballyvolanehouse.ie – Closed Christmas and New Year

6 rm – € 120/125 € 170/198 **Rest** – *(dinner only)* Menu € 49

◆ Stately 18C Italianate mansion mentioned in local legend, with lakes in parkland. Name means "place of springing heifers". Antique-filled rooms, some with Victorian baths. Dining room with silver candlesticks and balanced dishes.

CASTLEMARTYR (Baile na Martra) Cork – Cork – 712 H12 – pop. 978 — 39 C3

Dublin 174 km – Cork 20 km – Ballincollig 25 km – Carrigaline 24 km

Castlemartyr

– (021) 464 4050 – www.castlemartyrresort.com – Closed Monday-Thursday November to March

83 rm – € 195/290 € 195/459 – 26 suites

Rest *Bell Tower* – *(dinner only)* Menu € 65 **s** – Carte approx. € 54 **s**

◆ Grand 17C manor house in 220 acres, with river, castle ruins, golf course and spa. Maximum luxury; from the meeting room and lounge to the contemporary bedrooms and suites. Traditional fine dining in the Bell Tower.

CASTLEPOLLARD (Baile na gCros) – Westmeath – 712 K6 – pop. 1 004 — 37 C3

Dublin 63 km – Mullingar 13 km – Tullamore 37 km – Édenderry 36 km

Lough Bishop House

Derrynagarra, Collinstown, South : 6 km by R 394 taking L 5738 opposite church and school after 4 km – (044) 966 13 13 – www.loughbishophouse.com – Closed Christmas-New Year

3 rm – € 55/70 € 110 **Rest** – Menu € 30

◆ Charming 18C farmhouse on tranquil, south-facing hillside. Hospitable owners and their dogs greet you; tea and cake are served on arrival. Simple bedrooms with neat shower rooms; no TVs. Communal dining: home-cooked dishes include meats and eggs from their farm.

CASTLETOWNBERE (Baile Chaisleáin Bhéarra) – Cork – 712 C13 – pop. 868 Ireland — 38 A3

Dublin 360 km – Cork 130 km – Killarney 93 km

Berehaven Millcove, (027) 70 700

Ring of Beara★, W : by R 572 (Allihies, mines★ - Garnish Bay ★) – Slieve Miskish Mountains (★)

Rodeen without rest

East : 3.25 km by R 572 – (027) 70 158 – www.rodeencountryhouse.com – April-October

6 rm – € 40/50 € 70

◆ Owner used to run a horticulture business and this is evident in the variety of shrubs in the garden. Rooms are compact but nicely decorated; some look out to Bantry Bay.

CASTLETOWNSHEND (Baile an Chaisleáin) – Cork – 712 E13 38 B3 – pop. 188 Ireland

Dublin 346 km – Cork 95 km – Killarney 116 km

Glandore★, NE : 10 km R 596 – Sherkin Island★ **AC**, W : 15 km by R 596 and R 595 and ferry

Mary Ann's

Main St – (028) 36 146 – www.westcorkweek.com/maryanns/ – Closed 24-26 December, 3 weeks in January and Monday and lunch Tuesday October-April

Rest – *(bookings not accepted)* Menu € 28 (dinner) – Carte € 23/45

◆ Bold red pub set up a steep street in a sleepy village. Simple rustic interior and a lovely garden with enclosed dining area. All-encompassing menus display a seafood base and Asian influences.

CAVAN (An Cabhán) – Cavan – 712 J6 – pop. 7 883 Ireland 37 C2

Dublin 114 km – Drogheda 93 km – Enniskillen 64 km

Central Library, 1st Floor, Farnham St (049) 4331942 (April-September), cavan@failteireland.ie

Killykeen Forest Park★, W : 9.5 km by R 198

Radisson Blu Farnham Estate

Farnham Estate, Northwest : 3.75 km on R 198 – (049) 437 77 00 – www.farnhamestatecom

rest,

154 rm – € 215 € 240 – 4 suites

Rest *Botanica* – *(dinner only and Sunday lunch)* Carte € 32/50 **s**

◆ Set in extensive parkland, boasting every conceivable outdoor activity and an impressive spa. Original Georgian features are combined with contemporary furnishings. Luxury bedrooms offer superb views. Local, seasonal produce served in botanically-themed restaurant.

Cavan Crystal

Dublin Rd, East : 1.5 km on N 3 – (049) 436 0600 – www.cavancrystalhotel.com – Closed 24-27 December

85 rm – € 70/120 € 130/190

Rest *Opus One* – see restaurant listing

◆ Modern hotel next to – and owned by – the Cavan Crystal factory. Impressive atrium and spacious, stylish lounge-bar. Good meeting and leisure facilities. Up-to-date bedrooms in uniform designs.

Opus One – at Cavan Crystal Hotel

Dublin Rd, East : 1.5 km on N 3 – (049) 436 0600 – www.cavancrystalhotel.com – Closed 24-27 December

Rest – *(light lunch)* Carte € 33/40

◆ Contemporary first floor restaurant. Fresh, unfussy dishes at lunch; sophisticated, modern dishes with unusual combinations and textures in evening. Quality ingredients and well-judged cooking.

at Cloverhill North : 12 km by N 3 on N 54 – Belturbet

The Olde Post Inn with rm

rest, rm,

– (047) 55 555 – www.theoldepostinn.com – Closed 24-27 December, 3-19 January and Monday (including bank holidays)

6 rm – € 60/65 € 100/110

Rest – *(dinner only and Sunday lunch)* Menu € 35 (lunch)/56 – Carte € 42/54

◆ Keenly run former village post office; now a characterful restaurant with large rafters and exposed stone and brick. Attractive wooden conservatory. Seasonally changing menu of well presented, modern Irish cooking. Stylish, modern bedrooms.

CELBRIDGE – Kildare – pop. 17 262 712 M 7

Dublin 13 km – Naas 16 km – City Centre 14 km – Rathmines 17 km

La Serre

The Village at Lyons, South : 4.5 km. by Ardclough rd. – (01) 630 3500 – www.villageatlyons.com – Closed Monday and Tuesday

Rest – Menu € 30 (lunch)/45 – Carte € 34/56

♦ Charming restaurant in The Village at Lyons. Dine in ornate 17C conservatory, rustic courtyard or private baronial-style hall. Modern menus let quality ingredients speak for themselves and include amuse bouches, pre-desserts and petit fours. Good value set lunch.

CLAREMORRIS (Clár Chlainne Mhuiris) – Mayo – 712 E/F6 – pop. 2 595 36 B2

Dublin 149 km – Castlebar 18 km – Galway 39 km – Newbridge 41 km

McWilliam Park

rm, rest,

Knock Rd, East : 2 km on N 60 – (094) 937 8000 – www.mcwilliampark.ie

101 rm – € 110/130 € 130/170 – 2 suites

Rest – *(carvery lunch Monday-Saturday)* Menu € 38 **s** – Carte € 28/41 **s**

♦ Named after a local 18C landowner, this busy, purpose built hotel is located on the outskirts of town, convenient for the N17, Knock and the airport. Modern bedrooms. Stylish restaurant offers dishes made using local produce.

CLIFDEN (An Clochán) – Galway – 712 B7 – pop. 1 497 Ireland 36 A3

Dublin 291 km – Ballina 124 km – Galway 79 km

Galway Rd (095) 21163 (March-October), clifdentouristoffice@failteireland.ie

Connemara★★★, NE : by N 59 – Sky Road★★ (≤★★), NE : by N 59 – Connemara National Park★, NE : 1.5 km by N 59 – Killary Harbour★, NE : 35 km by N 59 – Kylemore Abbey★ **AC**, N : 18 km by N 59

Clifden Station House

rm,

– (095) 21 699 – www.clifdenstationhouse.com

78 rm – € 88/140 € 100/240

Rest – *(closed weekdays November-February) (bar lunch)* Menu € 30 – Carte € 30/45

♦ Purpose-built hotel on site of the old Galway-Clifden railway line, in a modern complex. Residents only kids club, leisure and wellness centre. Uniform bedrooms with good facilities. Local seafood orientated menus in restaurant. BBQs on the platform in summer.

Ardagh

Ballyconneely Rd, South : 3 km. on R 341 – (095) 21 384 – www.ardaghhotel.com – Easter-October

21 rm – € 49/109 € 99/199

Rest – *(dinner only)* Menu € 49 – Carte € 41/71

♦ Neat hotel with modern interior, overlooking a small bay. Three lounges. Pleasant bedrooms – many with bold fabrics and colourful headboards designed by the owner; some with window seats and views. Bright restaurant affords excellent outlook; seafood a speciality.

Dolphin Beach Country House

Lower Sky Rd, West : 5.5 km. by Sky Rd – (095) 21 204 – www.dolphinbeachhouse.com – mid February-October

9 rm – € 65/100 € 140/160

Rest – *(dinner only) (residents only)* Menu € 40 **s**

♦ Terracotta-coloured former farmhouse in peaceful hillside location. Mediterranean villa style interior with bright décor and red stone tiles. Good-sized bedrooms with artwork by friendly owner. Traditional home-cooked meals; wonderful bay views from dining room.

Quay House without rest

Beach Rd – ✆ (095) 21 369 – www.thequayhouse.com – mid-March-November

14 rm – € 75/95 € 130/150

◆ Cream-washed former harbourmaster's house and monastery, overlooking the bay. Relaxed, bohemian interior with antiques and wild animal memorabilia. Comfy, spacious bedrooms; those in the wing have kitchenettes. Homemade bread and local cheese feature at breakfast.

Sea Mist House without rest

– ✆ (095) 21 441 – www.seamisthouse.com – Closed Christmas and restricted opening in winter

6 rm – € 50/70 € 90/100

◆ Centrally located stone-built house with traditional lounge and pleasant gardens. Simple, modern bedrooms boast colourful fabrics and co-ordinating drapes; no TVs. Conservatory breakfast area.

Buttermilk Lodge without rest

Westport Rd – ✆ (095) 21 951 – www.buttermilklodge.com – Closed 25 December and January

11 rm – € 50/75 € 80/100

◆ Immaculately kept guesthouse. Lounge has games, hot drinks and a real turf fire; a cow theme predominates. Homely, colour co-ordinated bedrooms. Friendly owners offer local info/packed lunches.

Tower View without rest

Lower Sky Rd, West : 4 km by Sky Rd – ✆ (095) 21 965 – April-September

3 rm – € 30/65 € 30/65

◆ Yellow-painted house overlooking Clifden Bay. Well-priced, cosy bedrooms are spotlessly kept, with plain décor, bright fabrics and fully tiled bathrooms. All have views but no TVs.

REPUBLIC OF IRELAND

CLOGHEEN (An Chloichín) – Tipperary – 712 I11 – pop. 509 — 39 C2

Dublin 122 km – Tipperary 23 km – Clonmel 21 km – Dungarvan 28 km

Old Convent with rm

Mount Anglesby, Southeast : 0.5 km on R 668 (Lismore rd) – ✆ (052) 746 55 65 – www.theoldconvent.ie – Closed 23 December-7 February and Sunday-Wednesday

6 rm – € 120/150 € 170

Rest – *(dinner only) (booking essential) (set menu only)* Menu € 65

◆ Home to the Sisters of Mercy for over 100 years, this converted convent retains a serene feel. Dine in the candlelit former chapel on seasonal 8 course tasting menu. Comfortable bedrooms, decorated in calming colours.

CLONAKILTY (Cloich na Coillte) – Cork – 712 F13 – pop. 4 154 — 38 B3

Ireland

Dublin 310 km – Cork 51 km

25 Ashe St ✆ (023) 8833226, clonakiltytio@failteireland.ie

Dunmore Muckross, ✆ (023) 34 644

West Cork Regional Museum★ AC

Courtmacsherry★, E : 12 km by R 600 and R 601 – Timoleague Friary★, E : 8 km by R 600. Carbery Coast★ (Drombeg Stone Circle★, Glandore★, Castletownshend★) by N 71 and R 597

Inchydoney Island Lodge & Spa

South : 5.25 km by N 71 following signs for Inchydoney Beach – ✆ (023) 883 31 43 – www.inchydoneyisland.com – Closed 23-26 December

rest,

63 rm – € 145/170 € 190/250 – 4 suites

Rest *The Gulfstream* – ✆ (023) 882 11 19 *(dinner only)* Menu € 65 **s** – Carte approx. € 56 **s**

Rest *Dunes Bistro* – ✆ (023) 882 11 16 – Carte € 23/47 **s**

◆ Set on a headland looking out to sea. Range of leisure facilities; treatments - aquamarine spa, underwater massages - are especially good. Big, bright bedrooms with extras. The Gulfstream has fine sea views. The Dunes Bistro has a hearty, nautical theme.

An Súgan with rm

41 Wolfe Tone St – (023) 883 3719 – www.ansugan.com – Closed 25-26 December and Good Friday

7 rm – € 30 € 70 **Rest** – Menu € 30 (dinner) – Carte € 30/40

◆ Charming, personally run, salmon-pink pub with characterful dining rooms. Menus are based around daily arrivals of fresh local fish/seafood; some meat dishes also feature. Bedrooms, in the old harbourmaster's house, boast bold feature walls and flat screen TVs.

CLONEGALL (Cluain na nGall) – Carlow – 712 M9 – pop. 231 — 39 D2

Dublin 73 km – Carlow 20 km – Kilkenny 39 km – Wexford 30 km

Sha Roe Bistro

Main St – (053) 937 56 36 – Closed January, 1 week April, 1 week October, Sunday dinner, Monday and Tuesday

Rest – *(dinner only and Sunday lunch) (booking essential)* Menu € 34 (lunch) – Carte € 32/43

◆ Spacious sitting room, comfy sofas, rustic artwork and candles help create relaxing feel. Simple dining room with inglenook fireplace; seasonal cooking uses local ingredients.

CLONTARF = Cluain Tarbh – Dublin – 712 N7 – see Dublin

CLOVERHILL = Droim Caiside – Cavan – 712 J5 – see Cavan

COBH (An Cóbh) – Cork – 712 H12 – pop. 11 303 Ireland — 38 B3

Dublin 264 km – Cork 24 km – Waterford 104 km

Ballywilliam, (021) 812 399

Town★ – St Colman's Cathedral★ – Lusitania Memorial★

Fota Island★ (Fota House★★ **AC**, Fota Wildlife Park★ **AC**), N : 6.5 km by R 624 – Cloyne Cathedral★, SE : 24 km by R 624/5, N 25, R 630 and R 629

Knockeven House without rest

Rushbrooke, West : 2 km by R 624 – (021) 481 17 78 – www.knockevenhouse.com

4 rm – € 65/75 € 75/100

◆ Spacious, yellow-painted Victorian house with comfortable lounge and communal breakfast room. Traditional bedrooms feature antique furniture; flat screen TVs provide a modern touch.

CONG (Conga) – Mayo – 712 E7 – pop. 150 Ireland — 36 A3

Dublin 257 km – Ballina 79 km – Galway 45 km

Old Courthouse (094) 9546542 (March-October), congtouristoffice@failteireland.ie

Town★

Lough Corrib★★. Ross Errilly Abbey★ (Tower ★) – Joyce Country★★ (Lough Nafooey★) W : by R 345

Ashford Castle

– (094) 954 60 03 – www.ashford.ie

78 rm – € 155/435 € 375/750 – 5 suites

Rest *George V Room* – *(dinner only and Sunday lunch) (residents only)* Menu € 68

Rest *Cullen's at the Cottage* – *(closed October-April and Wednesday-Thursday)* Carte € 24/48 **s**

◆ Hugely imposing restored castle in formal grounds on Lough Corrib. Suits of armour and period antiques in a clubby lounge. Handsomely furnished country house rooms. George V imbued with air of genteel formality. Cullens serves bistro-style menu in informal atmosphere.

Lisloughrey Lodge
The Quay, Southeast : 2.25 km by R 345 off R 346 – (094) 954 54 00 – www.lisloughrey.ie – Closed 23-26 December
41 rm – € 120/150 € 150/200 – 9 suites
Rest *Salt* – Menu € 55 (dinner) – Carte € 45/65
◆ Georgian house in 10 acres of gardens. Guest areas boast contemporary feature walls and brushed velvet sofas. Bright, modern bedrooms have smart bathrooms and bold colour schemes; most are located in the courtyard. Three-roomed restaurant serves a modern menu.

Michaeleen's Manor without rest
Quay Rd, Southeast : 1.5 km by R 346 – (094) 954 60 89 – www.quietman-cong.com
12 rm – € 50/75 € 75/80
◆ Named after the lead character in the film 'The Quiet Man', filmed in the village; comfortable, brightly decorated bedrooms follow suit. Homely lounges; airy breakfast room.

Ballywarren House
East : 3.5 km on R 346 – (094) 954 69 89 – www.ballywarrenhouse.com
3 rm – € 124/136 € 136/148 **Rest** – Menu € 45 **s**
◆ Passionately run by a charming couple who ensure each guest's stay is special. Open fires, galleried landing and oak staircase. Bedrooms boast luxurious linen and lovely views. Aga-cooked breakfast and tasty homemade dinners.

REPUBLIC OF IRELAND

CORK (Corcaigh) – **Cork** – **712** G12 – **pop. 119 418** Ireland **38** B3

Dublin 248 km
Cork Airport : (021) 4313131, S : 6.5 km by L 42 X
to France (Roscoff) (Brittany Ferries) weekly (14 h/16 h) – to Pembroke (Swansea Cork Ferries) 2-6 weekly (8 h 30 mn)
Cork City, Grand Parade (021) 4255100, corktio@failteireland.ie
Douglas, (021) 489 10 86
Mahon Blackrock Cloverhill, (021) 429 25 43
Monkstown Parkgarriffe, (021) 484 13 76
Little Island, (021) 435 34 51
City★★ – Shandon Bells★★ Y, St Fin Barre's Cathedral★★ **AC** Z, Cork Public Museum★ X **M** – Grand Parade★ Z, South Mall★ Z, St Patrick Street★ Z, Crawford Art Gallery★ Y – Elizabethan Fort★ Z
Dunkathel House★ **AC**, E : 9.25 km by N 8 and N 25 X. Fota Island★ (Fota House★★ **AC**, Fota Wildlife Park★ **AC**), E : 13 km by N 8 and N 25 X – Cobh★ (St Colman's Cathedral★, Lusitania Memorial★) SE : 24 km by N 8, N 25 and R 624 X

Plans pages 861, 862

Hayfield Manor
Perrott Ave, College Rd – (021) 484 59 00 – www.hayfieldmanor.ie
84 rm – € 380 € 380 – 4 suites X**z**
Rest *Orchids* – *(closed Sunday and Tuesday) (dinner only) (booking essential)*
Menu € 39/65 – Carte € 45/62
Rest *Perrotts* – Menu € 32 (lunch) **s** – Carte € 34/53 **s**
◆ Purpose-built yet Georgian in character. Stately interiors and harmoniously styled bedrooms with marble bathrooms and quality furniture - armchairs, coffee tables and desks. Twin dining options to suit all tastes.

Lancaster Lodge without rest
Lancaster Quay, Western Rd – (021) 425 11 25 – www.lancasterlodge.com – Closed 23-28 December Z**i**
48 rm – € 89/119 € 99/139
◆ Purpose-built hotel with crisp, modern interior. Bedrooms are chintz-free, pleasingly and sparingly decorated. Largest rooms on the fourth floor; rear rooms are quieter.

Baker's Rd . . . . . X 4	Great William O'Brien St . . . . X 22	Thomas Davis St. . . . . X 49
Commons Rd . . . . . X 12	Horgan Quay . . . . . X 23	Victoria Cross Rd. . . . . X 50
Curragh Rd . . . . . X 14	Lower Mayfield Rd . . . . . X 31	Western Rd. . . . . X 53
Gardiner's Hill . . . . . X 20	Middle Glanmire Rd . . . . . X 33	Wilton Rd. . . . . X 55

Crawford House without rest

Western Rd – (021) 427 90 00 – www.crawfordguesthouse.com
– Closed mid-December to mid-January Xx

12 rm – € 55/85 € 80/100

◆ Victorian-style building offering bright, airy and comfortable guesthouse accommodation. Modern interiors with a choice of wood floors or carpeting in guest rooms.

Garnish House without rest

Western Rd – (021) 427 51 11 – www.garnish.ie Xr

26 rm – € 59/89 € 79/99

◆ Justifiably proud of gourmet breakfast: 30 options include pancakes and porridge. Guests are welcomed with home-made scones in cosy rooms; those at the rear have quiet aspect.

Augustine's

Clarion Hotel, Lapps Quay – (021) 427 9375 – www.augustines.ie
– Closed Sunday and Monday Zu

Rest – *(dinner only)* Carte € 34/52

◆ Smart, spacious ground floor restaurant set in corporate hotel. Modern, carefully crafted dishes made with quality seasonal produce. Formal but friendly service from uniformed staff.

Flemings with rm

Silver Grange House, Tivoli, East : 4.5 km on N 8
– (021) 482 16 21 – www.flemingsrestaurant.ie
– Closed 24-26 December Xu

3 rm – € 90/110 € 95/110

Rest – *(closed Sunday dinner)* Menu € 35 (lunch) – Carte € 42/60

◆ Classical cuisine, French bias; uses local produce, organically home-grown vegetables, herbs. Two dining rooms in keeping with Georgian character of house. Period furnished bedrooms.

Jacques

Phoenix St – (021) 427 73 87 – www.jacquesrestaurant.ie
– Closed 25-28 December, Sunday and bank holidays Zc

Rest – *(dinner only)* Menu € 25/35 – Carte € 37/45

◆ A long, warmly decorated room with modern tables on which old Irish classics are delivered. Farm ducks, wild game, fresh fish and organic vegetables are used in the cooking.

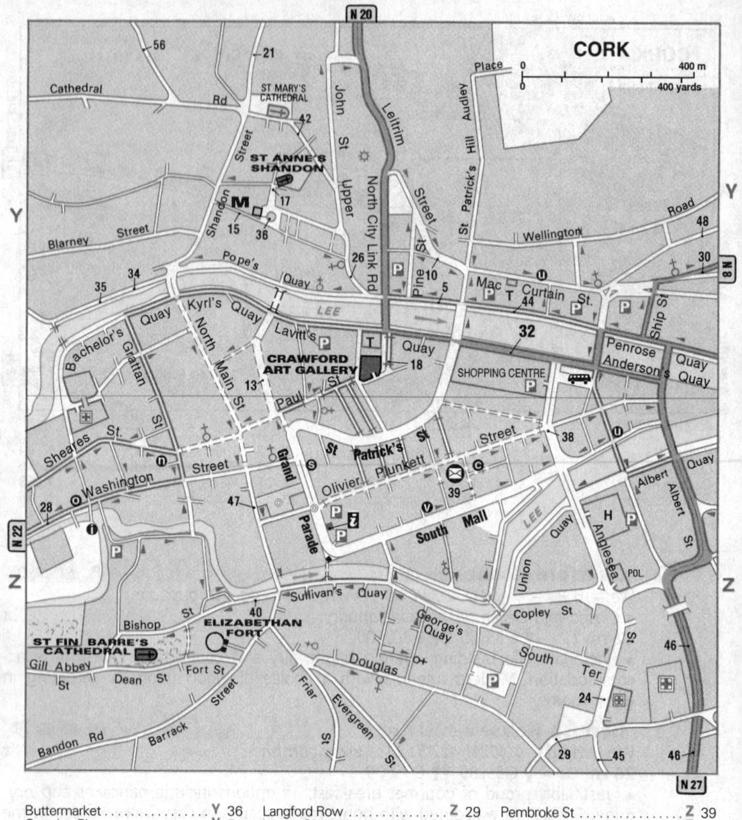

- Buttermarket . . . . . Y 36
- Camden Pl. . . . . . Y 5
- Coburg St. . . . . . Y 10
- Corn Market St . . . . . Y 13
- Dominic St . . . . . Y 15
- Eason Hill . . . . . Y 17
- Emmet Pl. . . . . . Y 18
- Gerald Griffin St . . . . . Y 21
- Infirmary Rd . . . . . Z 24
- John Redmond St . . . . . Y 26
- Lancaster Quay . . . . . Z 28
- Langford Row . . . . . Z 29
- Lower Glanmire Rd . . . . . Y 30
- Merchant Quay Shopping Centre . . . . . Y
- Merchant's Quay . . . . . Y 32
- Newsom's Quay . . . . . Y 34
- North Main Street . . . . . YZ
- North Mall . . . . . Y 35
- Olivier Plunkett St . . . . . Z
- Parnell Pl. . . . . . Z 38
- Pembroke St . . . . . Z 39
- Proby's Quay . . . . . Z 40
- Roman St . . . . . Y 42
- St Patrick's Quay . . . . . Y 44
- St Patrick's St . . . . . Z
- Southern Rd . . . . . Z 45
- South City Link Rd . . . . . Z 46
- South Main St . . . . . Z 47
- Summer Hill . . . . . Y 48
- Wolfe Tone St . . . . . Y 56

XX Gourmandises

VISA MC AE D

17 Cook St – ✆ (021) 425 19 59 – www.lesgourmandises.ie
– Closed 1 week March, 1 week August, Sunday dinner and Monday
Rest – French – *(dinner only and Sunday lunch) (booking essential)* Z**v**
Menu €42

◆ Relaxed city centre restaurant boasting stained glass door, skylight and comfy lounge bar with red banquettes and modern art. Irish produce employed on classic French menus.

X Isaacs Restaurant

VISA MC AE D

48 MacCurtain St – ✆ (021) 450 38 05
– Closed 25-27 December and Sunday lunch Y**u**
Rest – *(booking essential)* Carte €25/34 **s**

◆ Tall brick arches and modern art in converted warehouse: buzzy, friendly and informal. Modern and traditional brasserie dishes plus home-made desserts and blackboard specials.

X **Cafe Paradiso** with rm

16 Lancaster Quay, Western Rd – ✆ (021) 427 79 39 – www.cafeparadiso.ie – Closed 3 days at Christmas Zo

3 rm ☕ – 🚹 € 160 🚹🚹 € 160

Rest – Vegetarian – *(closed Sunday and Monday) (dinner only and lunch Friday and Saturday) (booking essential)* Carte € 29/47

♦ A growing following means booking is essential at this relaxed vegetarian restaurant. Colourful and inventive international combinations; blackboard list of organic wines. Spacious bedrooms in bright colours; the back one is the quietest.

X **Fenn's Quay**

5 Sheares St – ✆ (021) 427 95 27 – www.fennsquay.ie – Closed 25-26 December, Sunday and Bank Holidays Zn

Rest – Menu € 28 **s** – Carte € 27/46

♦ In a renovated 18C terrace in historic part of the city, this informal café-restaurant boasts modern art on display. Popular for mid-morning coffees and, light lunches.

X **Farmgate Cafe**

English Market (1st floor), Princes St – ✆ (021) 427 81 34 – Closed 24 December-4 January, Sunday and Bank Holidays Zs

Rest – *(lunch only)* Menu € 16 (lunch) – Carte € 22/28

♦ Long-standing café on 1st floor of the English Market. Small daily changing menu of food from the stalls below or from the counties of Munster; all simple, homemade and fresh.

at Cork Airport South : 6.5 km by N 27 - X – ✉ Cork

International Airport

Gate 2 – ✆ (021) 454 9800 – www.corkinternationalairporthotel.com – Closed 24-26 December

145 rm – 🚹 € 200 🚹🚹 € 200, ☕ €15

Rest – *(closed dinner Sunday -Tuesday) (carvery lunch)* Menu € 35 (dinner) – Carte € 35/48

♦ Quirky hotel with aviation theme and various eateries. Decent-sized bedrooms come in Deluxe and Executive versions. The superb Pullman lounge resembles the cabin of a plane. Modern restaurant has interesting smoking terrace.

CORK AIRPORT = Aerfort Chorcaí Cork – Cork – 712 G12 – see Cork

CORROFIN (Cora Finne) – Clare – 712 E9 – pop. 485 38 B1

▶ Dublin 228 km – Gort 24 km – Limerick 51 km

Fergus View without rest

Kilnaboy, North : 3.25 km on R 476 – ✆ (065) 683 76 06 – www.fergusview.com – March-November

6 rm ☕ – 🚹 € 45/53 🚹🚹 € 78

♦ Charming bay-windowed house with open-fired lounge, cosy breakfast room and country views. Bright, immaculately kept bedrooms: tiny bathrooms; no TVs. Delightful owners offer superb hospitality.

CROOKHAVEN (An Cruachán) – Cork – 712 C13 – pop. 1 669 38 A3

▶ Dublin 373 km – Bantry 40 km – Cork 120 km

Galley Cove House without rest

West : 0.75 km on R 591 – ✆ (028) 35 137 – www.galleycovehouse.com – March-October

4 rm ☕ – 🚹 € 50/60 🚹🚹 € 75/90

♦ Perched overlooking eponymous bay and its pleasant harbour. Conservatory breakfast room has bamboo seating. Rooms are neat and tidy, and enhanced by colourful fabrics.

CROSSMOLINA (Crois Mhaoilíona) – Mayo – 712 E5 – pop. 930 — 36 B2

Ireland

Dublin 252 km – Ballina 10 km

Errew Abbey★, SE : 9.5 km by R 315. Cáide Fields★ **AC**, N : 24 km by R 315 and R 314 W – Killala★, NE : 16 km by R 315 and minor road – Moyne Abbey★, NE : 18 km by R 115, minor road to Killala, R 314 and minor road – Rosserk Abbey★, NE : 18 km by R 115, minor road to Killala, R 314 and minor road

Enniscoe House

Castlehill, South : 3.25 km on R 315 – (096) 31 112 – www.enniscoe.com – Closed 7 January-31 March and 1 November-27 December

6 rm – € 130/150 € 220/260

Rest – *(dinner only) (booking essential for non-residents)* Menu € 48/56 **s**

◆ Georgian manor, overlooking Lough Conn, on Enniscoe estate with walled garden and heritage centre. Hallway boasts original family tree; antique beds in flower-filled rooms. Home cooked country dishes served in the dining room.

DALKEY (Deilginis) – Dún Laoghaire-Rathdown – 712 N8 – pop. 8 076 — 39 D1

Ireland

Dublin 13 km – Bray 9 km

Killiney Bay (★★), S : by coast road

Jaipur

21 Castle St – (01) 285 0552 – www.jaipur.ie – closed 25 December

Rest – Indian – *(dinner only and lunch Thursday-Saturday)* Menu € 16 (lunch)/22 (early dinner) – Carte € 28/44

◆ Central location and smart, lively, brightly coloured, modern décor. Well-spaced, linen-clad tables. Warm, friendly ambience. Contemporary Indian dishes.

DINGLE (An Daingean) – Kerry – 712 B11 – pop. 1 772 Ireland — 38 A2

Dublin 347 km – Killarney 82 km – Limerick 153 km

The Quay (066) 9151188, dingletio@failteireland.ie

Town★ – St Mary's Church★ – Diseart (stained glass★ **AC**)

Gallarus Oratory★★, NW : 8 km by R 559 – NE : Connor Pass★★ – Kilmalkedar★, NW : 9 km by R 559. Dingle Peninsula★★ – Connor Pass★★, NE : 8 km by minor road – Stradbally Strand★★, NE : 17 km via Connor Pass – Corca Dhuibhne Regional Museum★ **AC**, NW : 13 km by R 559 – Blasket Islands★, W : 21 km by R 559 and ferry from Dunquin

Emlagh Country House without rest

– (066) 915 23 45 – www.emlaghhouse.com – 16 March-October — Yd

10 rm – € 90/125 € 160/220

◆ Modern hotel in Georgian style. Inviting lounge with a log fire and well-fitted, antique furnished bedrooms: the colours and artwork of each are inspired by a local flower.

Heatons without rest

The Wood, West : 0.75 km on R 559 – (066) 915 22 88 – www.heatonsdingle.com — Yc

16 rm – € 49/110 € 98/170

◆ Carefully planned and recently built house with a spacious, modern look: comfortably furnished lounge area and bedrooms take up the contemporary style.

Castlewood House without rest

The Wood – (066) 915 2788 – www.castlewooddingle.com – Closed 9 January-10 February and 9-27 December — Yw

12 rm – € 90/115 € 150/180

◆ Well run, spacious and comfortable house. Individually decorated bedrooms; some with antique brass beds, others more contemporary. All have jacuzzi bath; most have view.

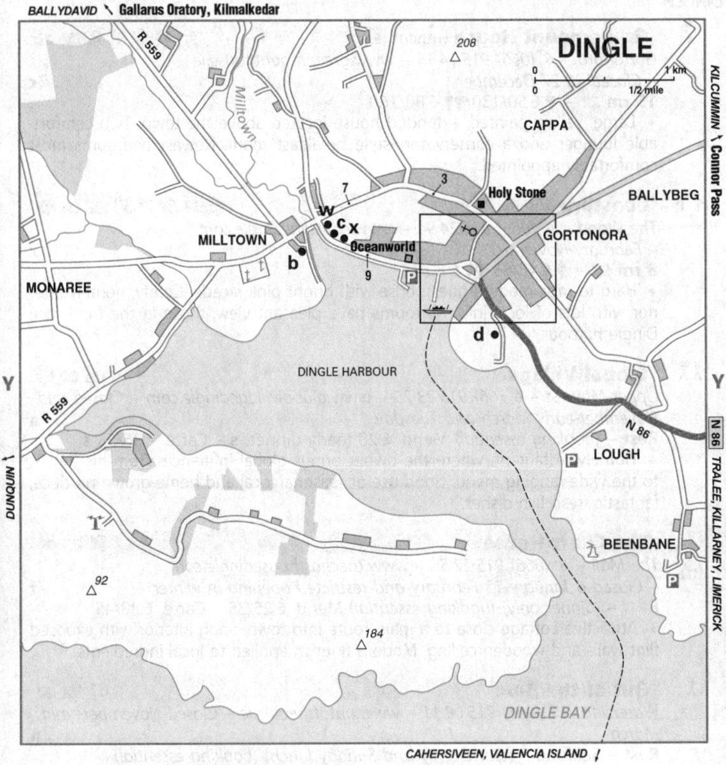

BALLYDAVID
Gallarus Oratory, Kilmalkedar
DINGLE
0 1 km
0 1/2 mile
KILCUMMIN
Connor Pass
R 559
Milltown
208
CAPPA
3
7
Holy Stone
BALLYBEG
W
C
X
MILLTOWN
Oceanworld
GORTONORA
b
9
MONAREE
d
DINGLE HARBOUR
Y
Y
R 559
N 86
N 86
LOUGH
DUNQUIN
TRALEE, KILLARNEY, LIMERICK
BEENBANE
92
184
DINGLE BAY
CAHERSIVEEN, VALENCIA ISLAND

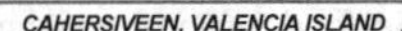

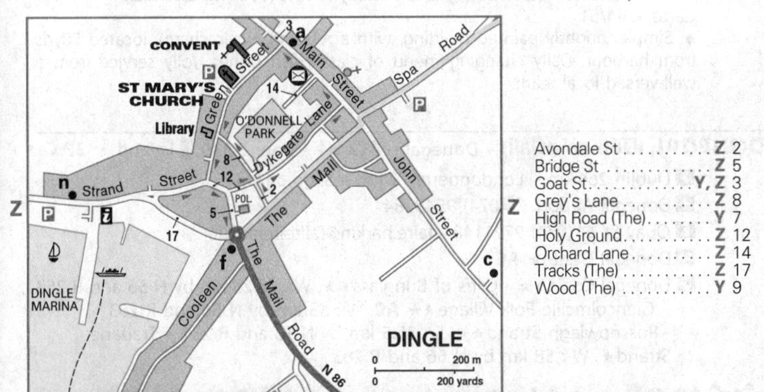

REPUBLIC OF IRELAND

3
a
CONVENT
Main
Street
Spa
Road
ST MARY'S
CHURCH
Green
Street
14
Library
O'DONNELL
PARK
Dykegate
Lane
The
Mall
John
Street
8
12
2
n
Strand
Street
POL
Z
Z
5
17
The
f
c
The
Mall
DINGLE
MARINA
Cooleen
Road
N 86
DINGLE
0 200 m
0 200 yards

Avondale St	Z 2
Bridge St	Z 5
Goat St	Y, Z 3
Grey's Lane	Z 8
High Road (The)	Y 7
Holy Ground	Z 12
Orchard Lane	Z 14
Tracks (The)	Z 17
Wood (The)	Y 9

Milltown House without rest

– ✆ (066) 915 13 72 – *www.milltownhousedingle.com*
– *12 May-24 October* **Yb**
10 rm ☕ – 🚹 € 85/135 🚹🚹 € 170

◆ Warm, welcoming establishment in a good location outside Dingle. Conservatory breakfast room and personally furnished and comfortable bedrooms, all with seating area.

Greenmount House without rest
Gortonora – ✆ (066) 915 14 14 – www.greenmounthouse.ie – Closed 20-27 December Zc
15 rm – € 50/130 € 80/160
◆ Large, yellow painted, extended house located above the town. Two comfortable lounges and a conservatory-style breakfast room. Newest bedrooms most comfortably appointed.

Coastline without rest
The Wood – ✆ (066) 915 24 94 – www.coastlinedingle.com – February-November Yx
8 rm – € 48/65 € 80/95
◆ Hard to miss modern guesthouse with bright pink façade. Comfy, homely interior with lots of local info. All rooms have pleasant view; those at the front face Dingle harbour.

Global Village
Upper Main St – ✆ (66) 915 23 25 – www.globalvillagedingle.com – Closed mid November-early March and Tuesday Za
Rest – *(booking essential)* Menu € 28 (early dinner) **s** – Carte € 36/53 **s**
◆ Homely restaurant, where the owner brings global influences from his travels to the wide-ranging menu. Good use of seasonal local and home-grown produce; fantastic fresh fish dishes.

The Chart House
The Mall – ✆ (066) 915 22 55 – www.thecharthousedingle.com – Closed 6 January-13 February and restricted opening in winter Zf
Rest – *(dinner only) (booking essential)* Menu € 25/35 – Carte € 38/45
◆ Attractive cottage close to a main route into town. Snug interior with exposed flint walls and wooden ceiling. Modern flourish applied to local ingredients.

Out of the Blue
Waterside – ✆ (066) 915 08 11 – www.outoftheblue.ie – Closed November- mid March Zn
Rest – Seafood – *(dinner only and Sunday lunch) (booking essential)* Carte € 44/51
◆ Simple, brightly painted building, with a relaxing, rustic charm, located 50yds from harbour. Daily changing menu of classic fish dishes. Jolly service from a well-versed local team.

DONEGAL (Dún na nGall) – Donegal – 712 H4 – pop. 2 339 Ireland 37 C1

Dublin 264 km – Londonderry 77 km – Sligo 64 km

Donegal Airport ✆ (074) 9548284

Quay St ✆ (074) 9721148, claire.harkin@failteireland.ie

Donegal Castle★ **AC**

Donegal Coast★★ - Cliffs of Bunglass★★, W : 48.25 km by N 56 and R 263 – Glencolmcille Folk Village★★ **AC**, W : 53 km by N 56 and R 263 - Rossnowlagh Strand★★, S : 35.5 km by N 15 and R 231 – Trabane Strand★, W : 58 km by N 56 and R 263

Solis Lough Eske Castle rest,
Northeast : 6.5 km by N15 (Killybegs rd) – ✆ (074) 9725 100 – www.solisloughheskecastle.com – Closed Sunday-Wednesday 3 January-31 March and 1 November-16 December
95 rm – € 285/410 € 300/425 – 1 suite
Rest *Cedars* – Menu € 55 (dinner) **s** – Carte lunch € 35/61 **s**
◆ Rebuilt 17C castle with a driveway that skirts the lough. The many extensions detract somewhat from the character but the bedrooms are comfortable and contemporary in style. Superb wellness centre. Bright, modern and stylish restaurant; traditional menu.

Harvey's Point

Lough Eske, Northeast : 7.25 km by T 27 (Killybegs rd) – (074) 972 22 08 – www.harveyspoint.com – Restricted opening in winter

67 rm – € 175 € 320 – 4 suites

Rest *The Restaurant* – see restaurant listing

◆ Sprawling, classical hotel in restful loughside setting, with wood-panelled rooms and leather-furnished lounge. Bedrooms in wing have high level of facilities; more traditional courtyard rooms.

Ardeevin without rest

Lough Eske, Barnesmore, Northeast : 9 km by N 15 following signs for Lough Eske Drive – (074) 972 17 90 – www.members.tripod.com/ardeevin – March-November

6 rm – € 45/50 € 65/70

◆ Inviting, individual rooms, almost all with superb views of Lough Eske and the quiet countryside. Hearty Irish breakfasts with fresh bread baked by the long-standing owners.

The Restaurant – at Harvey's Point Hotel

Lough Eske, Northeast : 7.25 km by T 27 (Killybegs rd) – (074) 972 22 08 – www.harveyspoint.com – Restricted opening in winter

Rest – *(dinner only and bar lunch)* Menu € 59 **s**

◆ Large restaurant with semicircular glass side providing lovely lough views. Traditional cooking, local ingredients and a few international touches. Attentive, formal service.

DONNYBROOK = Domhnach Broc – Dublin – 712 N8 – see Dublin

DOOGORT = Dumha Goirt – Mayo – 712 B5/6 – see Achill Island

DOOLIN (Dúlainm) – Clare – 712 D8 Ireland — 38 B1

Dublin 275 km – Galway 69 km – Limerick 80 km

The Burren★★ (Cliffs of Moher★★★, Scenic Route★★, Aillwee Cave★ **AC** (Waterfall★★), Poulnabrone Portal Tomb★, Corcomroe Abbey★, Kilfenora Crosses★, Burren Centre★ **AC**)

Tír Gan Éan House

– (065) 707 57 26 – www.tirganean.ie – Restricted opening in winter

12 rm – € 50/120 € 110/180

Rest – *(Closed Monday and Tuesday) (dinner only and Sunday lunch bar lunch Monday-Saturday)* Carte € 20/27

◆ Stylish hotel on main road into the village; part of a small holiday cottage complex. Open-plan guest areas include a comfy lounge and bar. Modern bedrooms are decorated in browns/creams and have a high level of facilities. Accessible menus feature local produce.

Ballyvara House without rest

Southeast : 1 km on Cliffs of Moher rd. – (065) 707 44 67 – www.ballyvarahouse.ie – May-August

9 rm – € 50/130 € 120/150 – 2 suites

◆ Extended farmhouse in pleasant grounds, close to busy village. Spacious guest areas include a comfy lounge with corner bar and decked terrace. Bedrooms boast good facilities and jacuzzi baths.

Cullinan's with rm

– (065) 707 41 83 – www.cullinansdoolin.com – Closed 1 December-10 February,

8 rm – € 40/70 € 70/100

Rest – *(Closed 25 October-22 April, Sunday and Wednesday) (dinner only) (booking essential)* Menu € 30 (early dinner) – Carte € 34/45

◆ Orange building in the middle of the Burren; run by a keen husband and wife team. Two walls of full length windows offer excellent views. Classical cooking uses Irish produce and portions are generous. Comfy, pine-furnished bedrooms; some overlook a small river.

REPUBLIC OF IRELAND

DROGHEDA (Droichead Átha) – Louth – **712** M6 – pop. 35 090 **37** D3

Ireland

Dublin 46 km – Dundalk 35 km

Mayoralty St ✆ (041) 9837070, tourism@drogheda.ie

Seapoint Termonfeckin, ✆ (041) 982 23 33

Towneley Hall Tullyallen, ✆ (041) 984 2229

Town★ – Drogheda Museum★ – St Laurence Gate★

Monasterboice★★, N : 10.5 km by N 1 – Boyne Valley★★, on N 51 – Termonfeckin★, NE : 8 km by R 166. Newgrange★★★, W : 5 km by N 51 on N 2 – Mellifont Old Abbey★ **AC** - Knowth★

The D

rest, VISA AE

Scotch Hall, Marsh Rd – ✆ (041) 987 77 00 – www.thed.com – Closed 23-30 December

104 rm – € 99/169 € 99/169 **Rest** – Menu € 25 **s** – Carte € 20/35 **s**

◆ Stylish hotel adjacent to shopping centre on banks of the Boyne. Modish, minimalistic interiors include two comfy bars and spacious bedrooms with a cool, clinical appeal. Popular menus in the airy dining room.

Scholars Townhouse

VISA AE

King St, by West St and Lawrence St turning left at Lawrence's Gate – ✆ (041) 983 54 10 – www.scholarshotel.com – Closed 25-26 December

18 rm – € 89/99 € 109/129 **Rest** – Menu € 28 – Carte € 26/92

◆ Well-run, privately owned hotel; formerly a 19C priest's house. Appealing bar and cosy lounge; smart wood panelling and ornate coving feature throughout. Comfy, well-kept bedrooms. Dine on classically based dishes under impressive mural of the Battle of Boyne.

REPUBLIC OF IRELAND

O. Forir/MICHELIN

DUBLIN
(Baile Átha Cliath)

County: Dublin
Michelin regional map: 712 N7
Belfast 166 km – Cork 248 km – Londonderry 235 km

Population: 1 045 769
Ireland
Map reference: 39 D1

PRACTICAL INFORMATION

Tourist Information

Suffolk St, (01) 605 7700, information@dublintourism.ie

Airport

Dublin Airport : (01) 814 1111, N : 9 km by N 1 BS

Ferries

to Holyhead (Irish Ferries) 4 daily (3 h 15 mn) – to Holyhead (Stena Line) 1-2 daily (3 h 45 mn) – to the Isle of Man (Douglas) (Isle of Man Steam Packet Co. Ltd) (2 h 45 mn/4 h 45 mn) – to Liverpool (P & O Irish Sea) (8 h)

Golf Courses

- Elm Park Donnybrook, Nutley House, (01) 269 3438
- Milltown Lower Churchtown Rd, (01) 497 6090
- Royal Dublin Dollymount North Bull Island, (01) 833 6346
- Forrest Little Cloghran, (01) 840 17 63
- Lucan Celbridge Rd, (01) 628 2106
- Edmondstown, (01) 493 24 61
- Coldwinters St Margaret's, Newtown house, (01) 864 0324

SIGHTS

In town

Suffolk St - Arrivals Hall, Dublin Airport - The Square Shopping Centre, TallaghtCity★★★ - Trinity College★★ JY - Old Library★★★ (Treasury★★★, Long Room★★) – Dublin Castle★★ (Chester Beatty Library★★★) HY - Christ Church Cathedral★★ HY - St Patrick's Cathedral★★ HZ - Marsh's Library★★ HZ – National Museum★★ (The Treasury★★) KZ - National Gallery★★ KZ - Newman House★★ JZ - Bank of Ireland★★ JY – Custom House★★ KX - Kilmainham Gaol Museum★★ AT **M6** - Kilmainham Hospital★★ AT – Phoenix Park★★ AS - National Botanic Gardens★★ BS - Marino Casino★★ CS – Tailors' Hall★ HY - City Hall★ HY - Temple Bar★ HJY - Liffey Bridge★ JY – Merrion Square★ KZ - Number Twenty-Nine★ KZ **D** - Grafton Street★ JYZ - Powerscourt Centre★ JY – Rotunda Hospital Chapel★ JX - O'Connell Street★ (GPO Building★) JX - Hugh Lane Municipal Gallery of Modern Art★ JX **M4** – Pro-Cathedral★ JX - Bluecoat School★ BS **F** - Guinness Museum★ BT **M7** - Rathfarnham Castle★ AT – Zoological Gardens★ AS – Ceol★ BS **n**

On the outskirts

The Ben of Howth★ (≤★), NE : 9.5 km by R 105 CS

In the surrounding area

Powerscourt★★ (Waterfall★★ **AC**), S : 22.5 km by N 11 and R 117 EV – Russborough House★★★, SW : 35.5 km by N 81 BT

DUBLIN

Street	Grid	No.
Adelaïde Rd	BT	3
Alfie Byrne Rd	CS	5
Bath Ave	CT	9
Benburb St	BS	15
Berkeley Rd	BS	16
Botanic Rd	BS	19
Canal Rd	BT	30
Clanbrassil St	BT	40
Conyngham Rd	AS	48
Denmark St	BS	52
Donnybrook Rd	CT	54
Dorset St	BS	55
Drimnagh Rd	AT	57
Eglinton Rd	CT	63
Grand Parade	BT	72
Inchicore Rd	AT	79
Infirmary Rd	AS	81
James St	BT	84
Leeson St Upper	BT	94
Macken St	BST	99
Morehampton Rd	BT	108
Mount St Upper	BT	112
Palmerston Park	BT	123
Phibsborough Rd	BS	132
Rathmines Rd Upper	BT	135
Ringsend Rd	CT	139
St Agnes Rd	AT	141
St Alphonsus Rd	BS	144
St John's Rd West	AS	147
Sandford Rd	BT	151
Shelbourne Rd	CT	157
Shrewsbury Rd	CT	159
South Circular Rd	AS	162
Suir Rd	AT	168
Terenure Rd East	BT	172
Thomas St West	BT	174
Victoria Quay	BS	178
Western Way	BS	184
Wolfe Tone Quay	BS	195

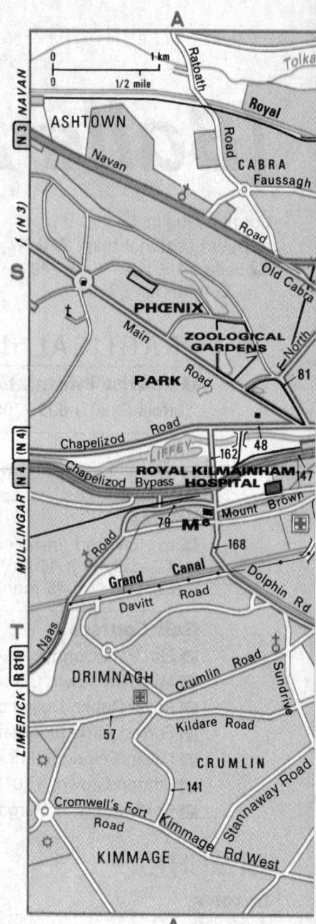

Shelbourne

27 St Stephen's Green ✉ *D2* – ✆ *(01) 663 4500* – *www.theshelbourne.ie* JZc

243 rm – 🚹 € 450 🚹🚹 € 450, ☕ €29 – 19 suites

Rest *Saddle Room* – see restaurant listing

♦ Landmark Georgian hotel with elegant guest areas, contemporary furnishings and state-of-the-art facilities. Bedrooms in original house are most characterful. High level of services and extras.

Merrion

Upper Merrion St ✉ *D2* – ✆ *(01) 603 0600* – *www.merrionhotel.com* KZe

133 rm – 🚹 € 460 🚹🚹 € 480, ☕ €29 – 10 suites

Rest *Cellar* – see restaurant listing

Rest *Cellar Bar* – *(closed Sunday)* Carte € 26/34

♦ Elegant hotel boasting opulent lounges and stylish cocktail bar. Spacious bedrooms – some with original features, some more corporate in style – boast smart marble bathrooms and good facilities. Characterful barrel-ceilinged bar offers concise carvery menu.

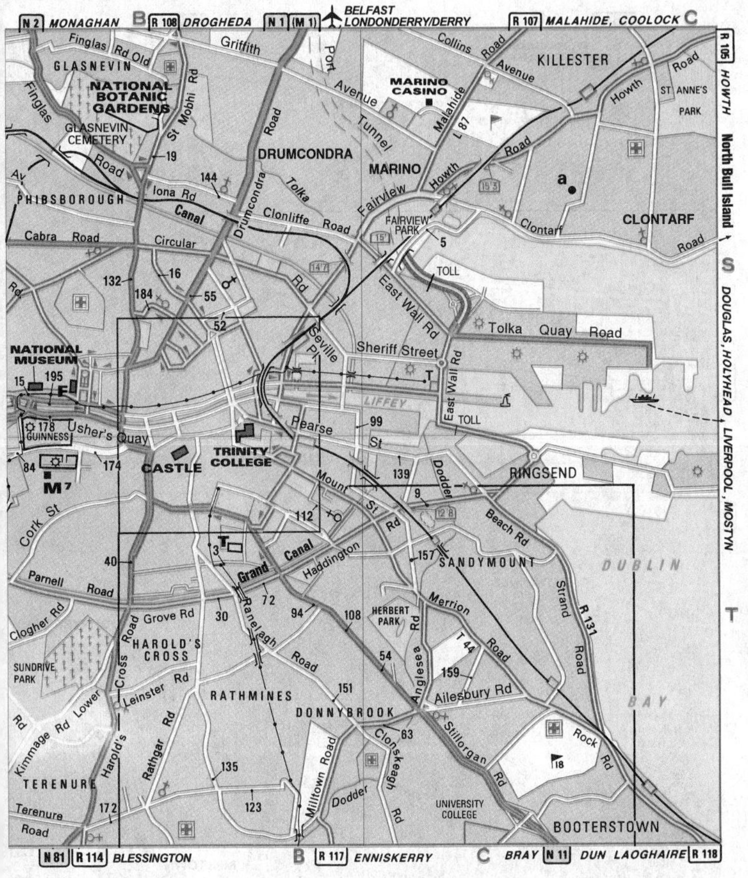

Westin

Westmoreland St ✉ D2 – ✆ *(01) 645 1000 – www.thewestindublin.com*
153 rm – 🚹 € 474 🚹🚹 € 474, ☕ €19.95 – 10 suites JY**n**
Rest *Exchange* – *(closed Sunday and Monday) (dinner only and Sunday lunch)*
Menu € 25 (early dinner) – Carte € 32/43
Rest *Mint* – *(dinner only)* Carte € 30/40

◆ Once a bank; now a smart hotel set over 6 period buildings, with comfy lounges, impressive conference rooms and good facilities. Georgian-style bedrooms boast heavy fabrics and marble bathrooms. Modern European cooking in semi-formal Exchange. Classic pub dishes in The Mint (formerly the bank's vaults).

Dylan

Eastmoreland Pl ✉ D2 – ✆ *(01) 660 3000 – www.dylan.ie – Closed 24-26 December* EU**a**
44 rm – 🚹 € 175/395 🚹🚹 € 175/395, ☕ €27
Rest – Menu € 22/40 – Carte € 36/54

◆ Modern boutique hotel with vibrant use of colour. Supremely comfortable, individually decorated bedrooms boast an opulent feel and a host of unexpected extras. French-influenced menus served in warm, stylish dining room.

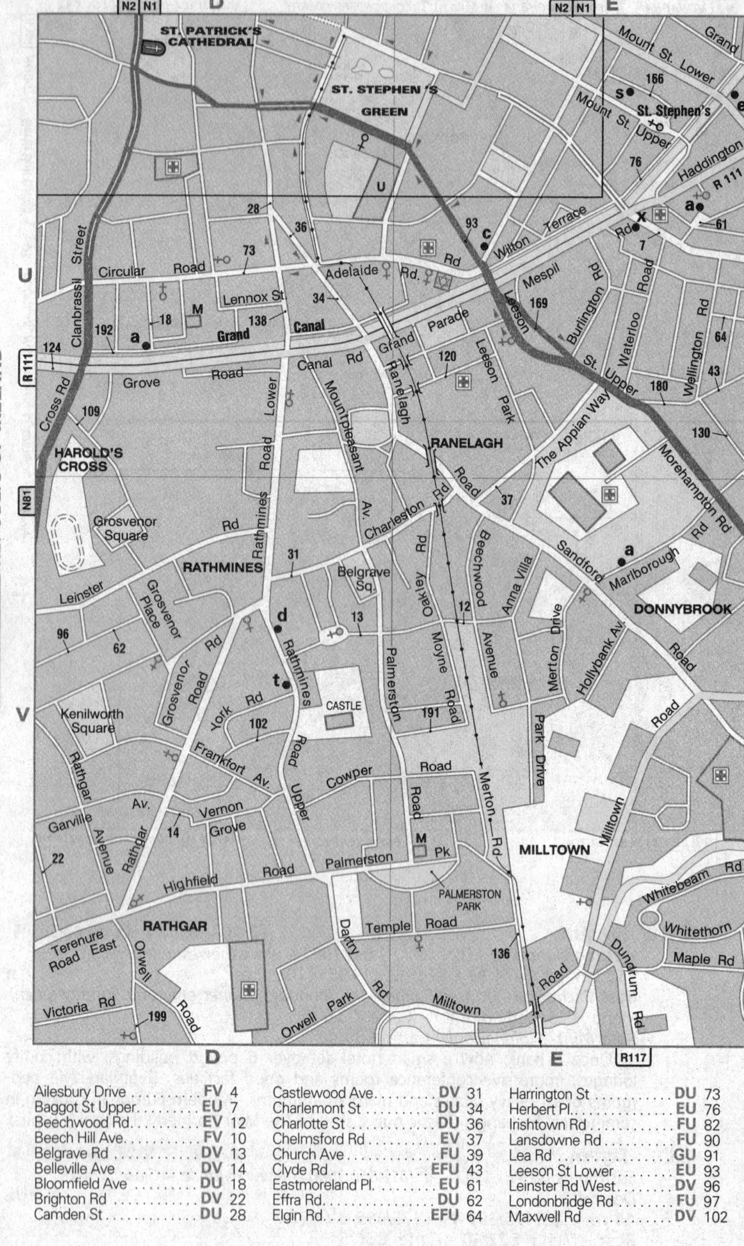

Ailesbury Drive . . . . FV 4	Castlewood Ave. . . . . DV 31	Harrington St . . . . DU 73
Baggot St Upper. . . . . EU 7	Charlemont St . . . . DU 34	Herbert Pl. . . . . EU 76
Beechwood Rd. . . . . EV 12	Charlotte St . . . . DU 36	Irishtown Rd . . . . FU 82
Beech Hill Ave. . . . . FV 10	Chelmsford Rd . . . . EV 37	Lansdowne Rd . . . . FU 90
Belgrave Rd . . . . DV 13	Church Ave . . . . FU 39	Lea Rd . . . . GU 91
Belleville Ave . . . . DV 14	Clyde Rd. . . . . EFU 43	Leeson St Lower . . . . EU 93
Bloomfield Ave . . . . DU 18	Eastmoreland Pl. . . . . EU 61	Leinster Rd West. . . . . DV 96
Brighton Rd . . . . DV 22	Effra Rd. . . . . DU 62	Londonbridge Rd . . . . FU 97
Camden St. . . . . DU 28	Elgin Rd. . . . . EFU 64	Maxwell Rd . . . . DV 102

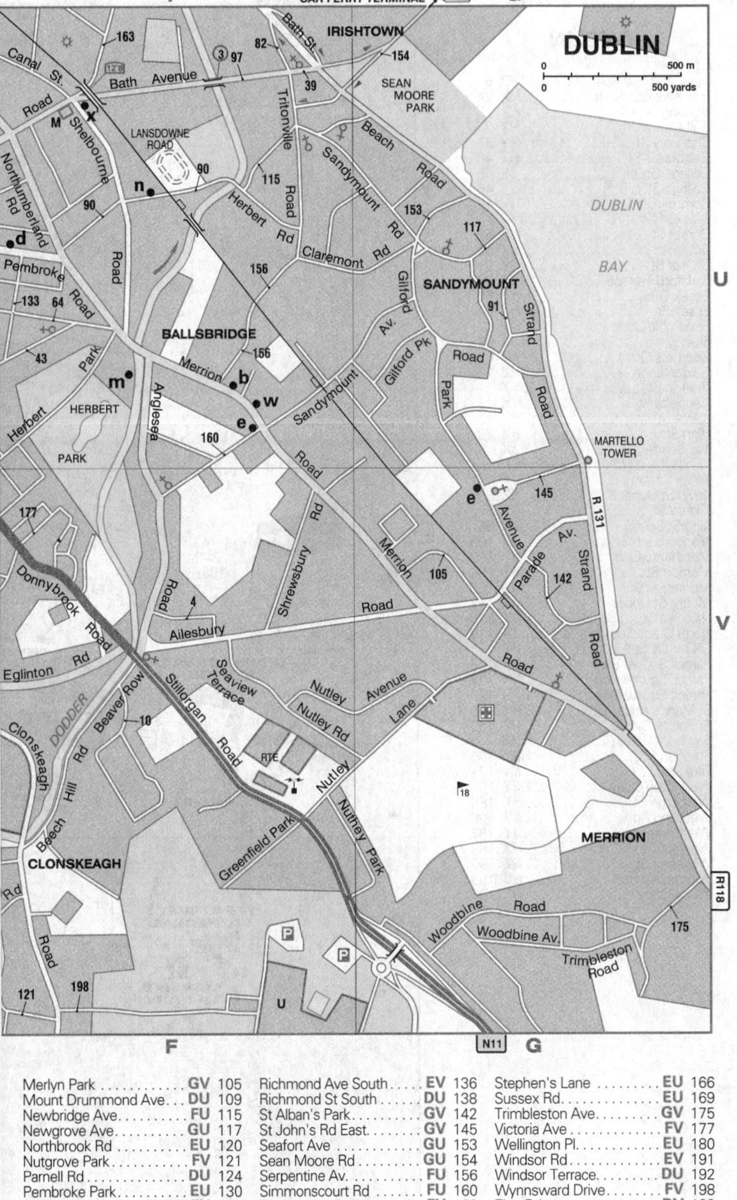

Merlyn Park	GV 105	Richmond Ave South	EV 136	Stephen's Lane	EU 166
Mount Drummond Ave	DU 109	Richmond St South	DU 138	Sussex Rd	EU 169
Newbridge Ave	FU 115	St Alban's Park	GV 142	Trimbleston Ave	GV 175
Newgrove Ave	GU 117	St John's Rd East	GV 145	Victoria Ave	FV 177
Northbrook Rd	EU 120	Seafort Ave	GU 153	Wellington Pl	EU 180
Nutgrove Park	FV 121	Sean Moore Rd	GU 154	Windsor Rd	EV 191
Parnell Rd	DU 124	Serpentine Av.	FU 156	Windsor Terrace	DU 192
Pembroke Park	EU 130	Simmonscourt Rd	FU 160	Wynnsward Drive	FV 198
Raglan Rd	FU 133	South Lotts Rd	FU 163	Zion Rd	DV 199

DUBLIN

Street	Grid	No.
Anne St South	JYZ	6
Brunswick St North	HX	24
Buckingham St	KX	25
Bull Alley	HZ	27
Chancery St	HY	33
Clanbrassil St	HZ	40
College Green	JY	45
College St	JY	46
Cornmarket	HY	49
Dawson St	JYZ	
Dorset St	HX	55
Duke St	JY	58
D'Olier St	JY	51
Earlsford Terrace	JZ	60
Essex Quay	HY	65
Essex St	HY	66
Fishamble St	HY	67
Fleet St	JY	68
George's Quay	KY	69
Golden Lane	HZ	70
Grafton St	JYZ	
Henrietta St	HX	75
Henry St	JX	
High St	HY	78
Ilac Centre	HJX	
Irish Life Mall Centre	JKX	
Jervis Centre	HJX	
Kevin St Upper	HZ	85
Kildare St	JKZ	87
King St South	JZ	88
Marlborough St	JX	100
Merchants Quay	HY	103
Merrion St	KZ	104
Montague St	JZ	106
Mount St Upper	KZ	112
Nicholas St	HY	118
North Great George's St	JX	119
O'Connell St	JX	
Parnell Square East	JX	126
Parnell Square North	JX	127
Parnell Square West	HJX	129
St Mary's Abbey St	HY	148
St Patrick Close	HZ	150
Stephens Green	JZ	
Stephen St	HJY	165
Tara St	KY	171
Wellington Quay	HJY	181
Werburgh St	HY	183
Westland Row	KY	186
Westmoreland St	JY	187
Wexford St	HZ	189
Whitefriar St	HZ	190
Winetavern St	HY	193
Wood Quay	HY	196

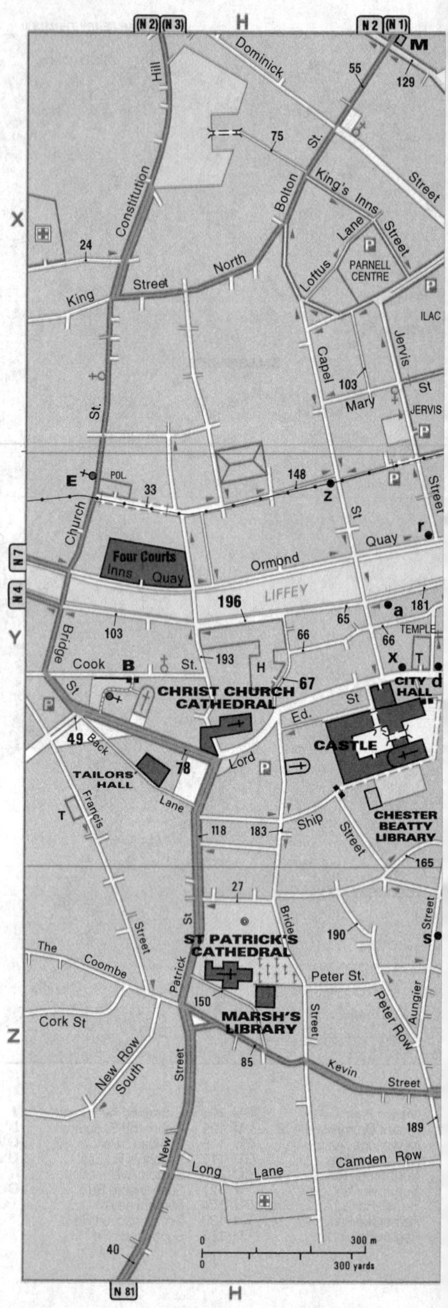

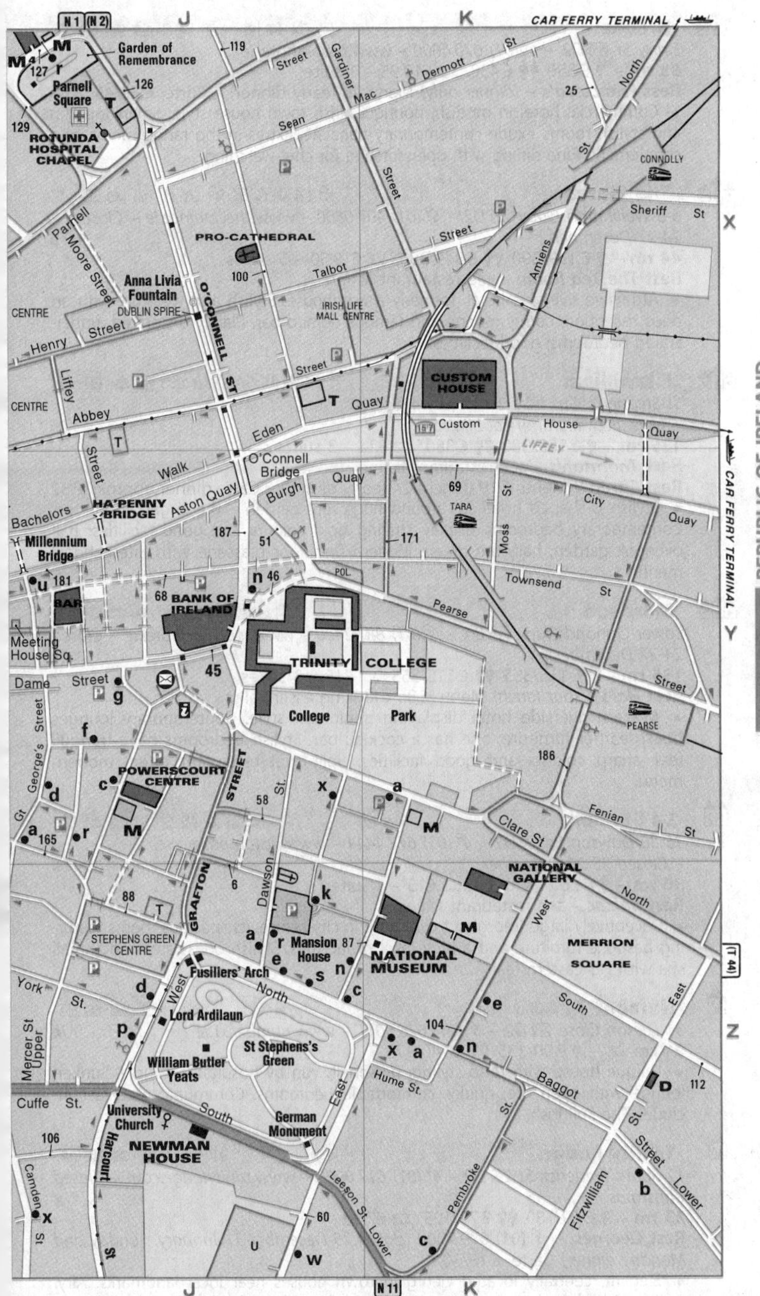
Garden of Remembrance
Parnell Square
ROTUNDA HOSPITAL CHAPEL
PRO-CATHEDRAL
Anna Livia Fountain
DUBLIN SPIRE
O'CONNELL ST
IRISH LIFE MALL CENTRE
CUSTOM HOUSE
CONNOLLY
CAR FERRY TERMINAL
O'Connell Bridge
HA'PENNY BRIDGE
Millennium Bridge
BANK OF IRELAND
TRINITY COLLEGE
College Park
TARA
PEARSE
Meeting House Sq.
POWERSCOURT CENTRE
GRAFTON STREET
NATIONAL GALLERY
MERRION SQUARE
Mansion House
NATIONAL MUSEUM
STEPHENS GREEN CENTRE
Fusiliers' Arch
Lord Ardilaun
St Stephens's Green
William Butler Yeats
University Church
NEWMAN HOUSE
German Monument
REPUBLIC OF IRELAND

Brooks
Drury St ✉ *D2* – ✆ *(01) 670 4000* – *www.brookshotel.ie* JY**r**
98 rm – † € 350 †† € 430, ☕ €19.95 – 1 suite
Rest *Francesca's* – *(dinner only)* Menu 26 (early dinner) – Carte € 29/45
♦ Commercial hotel in modish, boutique, Irish town house style. Smart lounges and stylish rooms exude contemporary panache. Extras in top range rooms, at a supplement. Fine dining with open kitchen for chef-watching.

The Clarence
6-8 Wellington Quay ✉ *D2* – ✆ *(01) 407 0800* – *www.theclarence.ie* – *Closed 24-27 December* HY**a**
44 rm – † € 139/390 †† € 349/390, ☕ €19.50 – 5 suites
Rest *The Tea Room* – see restaurant listing
♦ Attractive riverside hotel, formerly a warehouse. Stylish and well-run, with art deco reception, comfy lounge and famous domed bar. Plainly decorated, understated bedrooms; good facilities.

Fitzwilliam
St Stephen's Grn ✉ *D2* – ✆ *(01) 478 7000* – *www.fitzwilliamhoteldublin.com* JZ**d**
135 rm – † € 169/380 †† € 380, ☕ €24 – 3 suites
Rest *Thornton's* – see restaurant listing
Rest *Citron* – Menu € 19 (lunch)/24 (early dinner) – Carte dinner approx. € 32
♦ Stylish U-shaped hotel set around huge roof garden – the largest in Europe. Contemporary bedrooms display striking bold colours and good facilities; half overlook garden; half, the green. Modern first floor brasserie with international menu.

Morrison
Lower Ormond Quay ✉ *D1* – ✆ *(01) 887 2400* – *www.morrisonhotel.ie* – *Closed 24-27 December* HY**r**
135 rm – † € 115/355 †† € 115/355, ☕ €15 – 3 suites
Rest *Halo* – *(bar lunch)* Menu € 35 (booking essential) **s**
♦ Modern riverside hotel displaying minimalist style. Contemporary lounges boast leather furniture: one has a cocktail bar. Stylish bedrooms have tranquil feel, sharp colours and good facilities. Split-level restaurant offers modern menu.

La Stampa
35-36 Dawson St ✉ *D2* – ✆ *(01) 677 4444* – *www.lastampa.ie* – *Closed 25-26 December* JZ**a**
36 rm – † € 260 †† € 260, ☕ €15 – 1 suite
Rest *Balzac* – see restaurant listing
♦ Deceptively large Georgian townhouse in city centre, its spacious rooms featuring bespoke furniture and a high level of facilities. Stylish guest areas and small spa with Far Eastern feel.

Number 31 without rest
31 Leeson Close ✉ *D2* – ✆ *(01) 676 5011* – *www.number31.ie* EU**c**
21 rm ☕ – † € 90/135 †† € 140/175
♦ Unique house with retro styling, personally run by hospitable couple. Sunken lounge with open fire; quirky, comfortable bedrooms. Communal breakfast includes The Full Irish.

Trinity Lodge
12 South Frederick St ✉ *D2* – ✆ *(01) 617 0900* – *www.trinitylodge.com* – *Closed Christmas* JY**x**
23 rm – † € 69/180 †† € 79/195, ☕ €7.50
Rest *Georges* – ✆ *(01) 679 7000 (closed 25 December-31 January, Sunday and Monday dinner)* Carte € 18/30 **s**
♦ Elegant, centrally located Georgian town houses near local landmarks. Airy, well-furnished bedrooms with good level of comfort: the larger deluxe rooms are worth asking for. Modern restaurant and popular wine bar.

REPUBLIC OF IRELAND

Eliza Lodge

23-24 Wellington Quay ✉ D2
– ✆ (01) 671 8044 – www.elizalodge.com
– Closed 20-29 December **JYu**
18 rm ☕ – 🚹 € 50/90 🚹🚹 € 69/130
Rest *Italian Corner* – Italian – ✆ (01) 671 9114 – Carte € 30/40
◆ Friendly, family-owned hotel ideally situated for lively Temple Bar area. Uniform bedrooms; those at the top have the best outlook over the city and river; two have balconies. Bright restaurant serves popular Italian menus overlooking the Liffey.

XXXX ✿✿ Patrick Guilbaud (Guillaume Lebrun)

21 Upper Merrion St ✉ D2 – ✆ (01) 676 4192
– www.restaurantpatrickguilbaud.ie
– Closed 25-26 December, 17 March, 22 April, Sunday and Monday
Rest – French – Menu € 50 (lunch) **s** – Carte € 93/149 **s** **KZe**
Spec. Lobster ravioli, pasta and toasted almonds. Caramelised veal sweetbreads with Cevenne onions. Warm Criollo chocolate biscuit with stout ice cream
◆ Smart, stylish and personally run restaurant within a restored and sympathetically extended Georgian house; decorated with contemporary Irish art. Accomplished and harmonious cooking, with cleverly complementing flavours and textures.

XXXX Shanahan's on the Green

119 St Stephen's Grn ✉ D2 – ✆ (01) 407 0939 – www.shanahans.ie
– Closed 25-26 December and Sunday **JZp**
Rest – Beef specialities – *(dinner only and lunch Friday) (booking essential)*
Menu € 45 (early dinner weekdays) – Carte € 59/81
◆ Sumptuous Georgian town house; upper floor window tables survey the Green. Supreme comfort enhances your enjoyment of strong seafood dishes and choice cuts of Irish beef.

XXXX ✿ Thornton's – at The Fitzwilliam Hotel

128 St Stephen's Grn. ✉ D2
– ✆ (01) 478 7008 – www.thorntonsrestaurant.com
– Closed 25 December-5 January, Sunday, Monday, lunch Tuesday and Wednesday **JZd**
Rest – Modern – Menu € 49 (lunch)/79 **s**
– Carte € 79/125 **s**
Spec. Dublin bay prawns with prawn bisque. Mallard duck glazed with honey and pistachio. Prune and Armagnac soufflé, pear sorbet.
◆ Elegant hotel restaurant where smart glass panels divide the room; eye-catching food photos adorn the walls. Choice of classical à la carte, or modern tasting menu displaying innovative texture and flavour combinations. Knowledgeable service.

XXX ✿ L'Ecrivain (Derry Clarke)

109A Lower Baggot St ✉ D2
– ✆ (01) 661 1919 – www.lecrivain.com
– Closed 24-27 December, lunch 28-30 December, 31 December-9 January, lunch 10 January, Sunday, lunch Tuesday and Wednesday, and bank holidays
Rest – Contemporary – *(booking essential)* Menu € 25/65 **KZb**
– Carte € 72/81
Spec. Duck liver with pain d'épices, hazelnuts and pea purée. Halibut with herb gnocchi, baby leek, braised shin and parsley purée. Marshmallow and pineapple Chiboust with caramel spiced pineapple and coconut sorbet.
◆ Three-floored, former warehouse with piano bar, whiskey-themed private dining room, mezzanine and attractive terrace. Refined cooking arrives with modern touches and contemporary presentation. Service is formal but comes with personality.

A red **Rest** mention denotes an establishment with an award for culinary excellence, ✿ (star) or ☺ (Bib Gourmand).

REPUBLIC OF IRELAND

Chapter One (Ross Lewis)

The Dublin Writers Museum, 18-19 Parnell Sq ✉ D1 – ☎ (01) 873 2266 – www.chapteronerestaurant.com – Closed 2 weeks August, 2 weeks Christmas, Sunday and Monday JXr

Rest – Modern – *(booking essential)* Menu € 38 (lunch) **s** – Carte dinner € 60/68 **s**

Spec. Terrine of foie gras with cherries and fig vinegar gel. Halibut with Dublin Bay brown shrimp and black sesame oil. Chocolate macaroon with raspberries and chocolate ganache.

◆ Long-established, popular restaurant in basement of historic building; contemporary lounge/bar and two smart dining rooms. Seasonal, classically-based cooking demonstrates skill and understanding. Attentive, formal service.

Forty One

41 St. Stephen's Green ✉ D2 – ☎ (01) 662 00 00 – www.fortyone.ie – Closed dinner 24-dinner 31 December, Sunday and Monday KZx

Rest – Modern European – *(booking advisable)* Menu € 25 (lunch) – Carte € 54/71

◆ Richly furnished, intimate restaurant set in an attractive, creeper-clad 18C townhouse, tucked away in a corner of St Stephen's Green. Accomplished, classical cooking uses luxurious ingredients.

Cliff Townhouse with rm

22 St. Stephen's Green ✉ D2 – ☎ (01) 638 39 39 – www.thecliftownhouse.com – Closed 25-27 December JZs

9 rm – † € 125/145 †† € 145/185

Rest – Modern European – *(booking advisable)* Menu € 25/45

◆ Impressive Georgian townhouse overlooking the green. Large dining room with marble-topped bar and blue leather seating. Good value fixed price menus offer straightforward, classical combinations. Bedrooms display contemporary colour schemes and good comforts.

Saddle Room – at Shelbourne Hotel

27 St Stephen's Green ✉ D2 – ☎ (01) 663 4500 – www.theshelbourne.ie

Rest – Grills – Menu € 24/40 – Carte dinner € 45/62 JZc

◆ Smart restaurant with well-spaced, linen-laid tables: some are set by the window; some are in in booths; and some, in glass-walled private rooms. Open kitchen specialises in seafood and steaks.

One Pico

5-6 Molesworth Pl ✉ D2 – ☎ (01) 676 0300 – www.onepico.com – Closed 24-25 December and Bank Holidays JZk

Rest – Modern – Menu € 25/39 – Carte € 49/69

◆ Wide-ranging cuisine, classic and traditional by turns, always with an original, eclectic edge. Décor and service share a pleasant formality, crisp, modern and stylish.

Salon des Saveurs

16 Aungier St ✉ D2 – ☎ (01) 475 88 40 – www.salondessaveurs.com – Closed Sunday, and Monday (except December) HZs

Rest – Modern European – Menu € 22 (lunch)/56 – Carte € 26/76

◆ Dark, smoky, retro-chic style restaurant with mirrors and high-backed leather chairs. Set tasting menus showcase elaborate cooking, with wine pairings available. Attentive service.

Pearl Brasserie

20 Merrion St Upper ✉ D2 – ☎ (01) 661 3572 – www.pearl-brasserie.com – Closed 25 December-5 January and Sunday KZn

Rest – French – Carte € 31/59

◆ A metal staircase leads down to this intimate, newly refurbished, vaulted brasserie where Franco-Irish dishes are served at smart, linen-laid tables. Amiable, helpful service.

REPUBLIC OF IRELAND

Locks Brasserie

1 Windsor Terr. ✉ D8 – ✆ (01) 420 05 55 – www.locksbrasserie.com – Closed 25 December-7 January and bank holidays DU**a**

Rest – Modern European – *(dinner only and lunch Thursday-Sunday)* Menu € 27 (lunch and early dinner) – Carte € 29/50

◆ Attractive, well-lit restaurant with a relaxed atmosphere and professional, engaging staff. Dining is split over two floors, with comfy banquette seating and a cocktail bar. Menu of modern European classics; well-presented dishes make use of fine ingredients.

Pichet

14-15 Trinity St ✉ D2 – ✆ (01) 677 10 60 – www.pichetrestaurant.com – Closed 1-10 January JY**g**

Rest – Modern European – *(booking advisable)* Menu € 25 (lunch and early dinner) – Carte € 31/47

◆ Popular brasserie with buzzy atmosphere; its long narrow room dominated by an open-plan kitchen counter. Front bar/café and heated terrace. Neat, flavoursome modern European cooking, with good value, daily changing menus.

Dax

23 Pembroke Street Upper ✉ D2 – ✆ (01) 676 1494 – www.dax.ie – Closed Christmas and New Year, Sunday and Monday KZ**c**

Rest – French – *(booking essential)* Menu € 29 (lunch)/39 (dinner Tuesday-Thursday) – Carte € 44/58

◆ Hidden away in basement of Georgian terrace, with rustic inner, immaculately laid tables, wine cellar and bar serving tapas. Knowledgable staff serve French influenced menus.

Dobbin's

15 Stephen's Lane, (off Stephen's Place) off Lower Mount St ✉ D2 – ✆ (01) 661 9536 – www.dobbins.ie – Closed 24 December-2 January, Saturday lunch, Sunday dinner and bank holidays EU**s**

Rest – Traditional – *(booking essential)* Menu € 24 (lunch)/38 – Carte € 46/54

◆ Smart, well-established restaurant in residential area. Small bar with booths leads to spacious, neatly laid dining room with warm, modern décor. Large menu displays international influences.

Cellar – at Merrion Hotel

Upper Merrion St ✉ D2 – ✆ (01) 603 0630 – www.merrionhotel.com KZ**e**

Rest – Modern – *(Closed Saturday lunch)* Menu € 20/30 **s** – Carte € 36/67 **s**

◆ Set in hotel cellars, a formal restaurant with linen-laid tables, high-backed chairs and characterful curved ceiling. Good-sized menus of modern Irish cooking feature local, regional produce.

The Tea Room – at The Clarence Hotel

6-8 Wellington Quay ✉ D2 – ✆ (01) 407 0813 – Closed 24-27 December HY**a**

Rest – Modern – *(booking essential)* Menu € 24 (dinner) – Carte € 36/54

◆ Spacious hotel restaurant, where small mezzanine level overlooks larger main room with central banquette island. Ambitious cooking displays Gallic influences. Polite, formal service.

Les Frères Jacques

74 Dame St ✉ D2 – ✆ (01) 679 4555 – www.lesfreresjacques.com – Closed 25 December-2 January, Saturday lunch, Sunday and bank holiday Mondays HY**x**

Rest – French – Menu € 23 (lunch)/38 – Carte € 48/65

◆ Long-standing restaurant on narrow cobbled alley, with typical French styling and team. Classical Gallic cooking with seafood a speciality: daily fresh fish and lobster tank on display.

XX **Peploe's**

16 St Stephen's Green ✉ D2 – ☎ (01) 676 3144 – www.peploes.com – Closed 25-29 December and 22 April JZ**e**

Rest – Mediterranean – *(booking essential)* Menu € 25 (lunch and early dinner) – Carte € 36/47

◆ Well-run, atmospheric brasserie named after Scottish artist and set in former bank vault. Small bar; main room with smart mural and linen-laid tables. Extensive menu with influences from the Med.

XX **Bleu**

Joshua House, Dawson St. ✉ D2 – ☎ (01) 676 7015 – www.bleu.ie – Closed 25-26 December JZ**r**

Rest – Modern European – Menu € 22 (lunch)/26 (early dinner) – Carte € 25/40

◆ Stylish, modern eatery on a bustling street. Smart and contemporary interior, with framed mirrors a feature. The appealing, varied menu keeps its influences within Europe.

XX **Town Bar and Grill**

21 Kildare St ✉ D2 – ☎ (01) 662 4800 – www.townbarandgrill.com – Closed 25-27 December and bank holidays JZ**n**

Rest – Italian influences – *(booking essential)* Menu € 25 (lunch) – Carte dinner € 38/62

◆ Located in wine merchant's old cellars: brick pillars divide a large space; fresh flowers and candles add a personal touch. Italian flair in bold cooking with innovative edge.

XX **Fallon & Byrne**

First Floor, 11-17 Exchequer St ✉ D2 – ☎ (01) 472 1000 – www.fallonandbyrne.com – Closed 25 December, 1 January and Sunday dinner JY**f**

Rest – Bistro – Menu € 30 (weeekday and early Saturday dinner) – Carte € 24/39

◆ Food emporium boasting vast basement wine cellar, ground floor full of fresh quality produce, and first floor French style bistro with banquettes, mirrors and tasty bistro food.

XX **Balzac** – at La Stampa Hotel

35-36 Dawson St ✉ D2 – ☎ (01) 677 8611 – www.lastampa.ie – Closed Sunday JZ**a**

Rest – French – *(dinner only)* Menu € 25 – Carte € 22/50

◆ Spacious restaurant in former dance hall, with high glass ceiling, linen-laid tables and banquette seating. Comfy lounge bar and appealing French themed menus.

XX **Bang**

11 Merrion Row ✉ D2 – ☎ (01) 400 4229 – www.bang-restaurant.com – Closed 25 December-1 January, first week January, and Saturday-Sunday lunch KZ**a**

Rest – Modern – *(booking essential)* Menu € 25 (lunch)/27 (early dinner) – Carte dinner € 34/46

◆ Stylish three floor restaurant displaying impressive modern art by leading Irish/international artists. Good value lunch/early evening menus; more luxurious, modern dishes on the à la carte.

XX **Jaipur**

41 South Great George's St ✉ D2 – ☎ (01) 677 0999 – www.jaipur.ie – Closed 25-26 December JY**a**

Rest – Indian – *(dinner only and lunch Thursday-Sunday)* Menu € 20 (weekday dinner) – Carte € 30/46

◆ Long-standing restaurant set over two floors, with orange and red hues, stainless steel staircase and full length windows. Extensive menu displays interesting flavours from all over India.

Camden Kitchen

3a Camden Mkt, Grantham St ✉ D8 – ✆ (01) 476 01 25 – www.camdenkitchen.ie – Closed 25 December-7 January

Rest – Modern – *(closed Sunday dinner and Monday)* Carte € 28/41

◆ Appealing bistro with canopied façade and rustic inner, set over two floors. Open kitchen serving gutsy menu of robust, modern dishes. Relaxed, friendly service from a young team.

Pig's Ear

4 Nassau St ✉ D2 – ✆ (01) 670 38 65 – www.thepigsear.ie – Closed 3-13 January, Sunday and bank holiday Mondays KY**a**

Rest – Modern European – Menu € 20 (lunch)/22 (early dinner) – Carte € 32/42

◆ Bistro-style restaurant set in Georgian city centre house with striking pink door. Well-priced, refined bistro cooking with French influences and Irish produce. Service with personality.

La Maison

15 Castlemarket ✉ D2 – ✆ (01) 672 7258 – www.lamaisonrestaurant.ie – Closed 25-26 and 31 December and 1 January JY**c**

Rest – French – *(bookings not accepted)* Menu € 23 (lunch and early dinner) – Carte € 32/48

◆ A simple and appealing French bistro, decorated with original posters. Personable service and a menu of carefully prepared and seasonal Gallic classics at a good price.

Mermaid Café

69-70 Dame St ✉ D2 – ✆ (01) 670 8236 – www.mermaid.ie – Closed 1 January, Good Friday, 25 and 26 December HY**d**

Rest – Modern – *(Sunday brunch) (booking essential)* Menu € 21 – Carte € 28/36

◆ This informal restaurant with unfussy décor and bustling atmosphere offers an interesting and well cooked selection of robust modern dishes. Efficient service.

L'Gueuleton

1 Fade St ✉ D2 – ✆ (01) 675 3708 – www.lgueuleton.com – Closed dinner 24-28 and 31 December-2 January JY**d**

Rest – French – *(bookings not accepted)* Carte € 24/45

◆ Rustic restaurant with beamed ceilings, Gallic furnishings and rear terrace. Interesting French menus use local, seasonal produce. Flavoursome country cooking; friendly, efficient service.

at Ballsbridge

Four Seasons

Simmonscourt Rd ✉ D4 – ✆ (01) 665 4000 – www.fourseasons.com/dublin FU**e**

157 rm – † € 245/305 †† € 245/305, ☕ €29 – 40 suites – †† € 390/2600

Rest *Seasons* – Menu € 35 – Carte € 35/74

◆ Set in grounds of the RDS arena. Elegant guest areas, state-of-the-art meeting rooms and impressive ballrooms boast ornate décor, antiques and Irish art. Spacious bedrooms; plenty of extras. Fine dining with fountain/garden views in Seasons.

Herbert Park

✉ D4 – ✆ (01) 667 2200 – www.herbertparkhotel.ie FU**m**

151 rm – † € 250/360 †† € 385, ☕ €19.50 – 2 suites

Rest *The Pavilion* – Carte € 30/45

◆ Contemporary hotel overlooking suburban park, with smart marble-floored reception, stylish seating areas and chic bar. Modern bedrooms display quality furnishings and marble bathrooms. Sizeable, formal restaurant offers interesting menu.

Merrion Hall without rest
54-56 Merrion Rd ✉ D4 – ✆ (01) 668 1426 – www.halpinsprivatehotels.com
34 rm – € 169/189 € 199/229 **FUb**
◆ Red-brick Victorian house boasts spacious, antique-furnished guest areas with a Georgian feel. Comfortable, stylish bedrooms have a traditional edge; those to rear are quieter.

Ariel House without rest
50-54 Lansdowne Rd ✉ D4 – ✆ (01) 668 5512 – www.ariel-house.net – Closed 22-28 December **FUn**
37 rm – € 110/150 € 160/250
◆ Personally run Victorian townhouse with comfy, traditionally styled guest areas and antique furnishings. Warmly decorated bedrooms have modern facilities and smart bathrooms; some four-posters.

Aberdeen Lodge without rest
53-55 Park Ave ✉ D4 – ✆ (01) 283 8155 – www.halpinsprivatehotels.com
17 rm – € 169/189 € 199/229 **GVe**
◆ Two Victorian townhouses in smart suburban setting, knocked through into one impressive hotel. Comfy lounge, warm homely atmosphere and well-equipped bedrooms – some with garden views.

Pembroke Townhouse without rest
90 Pembroke Rd ✉ D4 – ✆ (01) 660 0277 – www.pembroketownhouse.ie – Closed 18 December-5 January **FUd**
48 rm – € 199 € 310, € 15
◆ Formerly three Georgian houses, now a friendly hotel with traditional styling, comfy lounge and sunny breakfast room. Bedrooms vary in shape and size: duplex rooms are the cosiest.

Glenogra House without rest
64 Merrion Rd ✉ D4 – ✆ (01) 668 3661 – www.glenogra.com – Closed 23-27 December **FUw**
13 rm – € 59/119 € 79/139
◆ Personally run red-brick Victorian house with informal reception, comfy lounge and homely furnishings. Simply decorated bedrooms vary in shape and size; all boast modern facilities.

Bloom Brasserie
11 Upper Baggot St ✉ D4 – ✆ (01) 668 7170 – www.bloombrasserie.ie – Closed 25 December **EUx**
Rest – Modern European – Carte € 29/48
◆ Sizeable basement brasserie with cool, contemporary styling, vibrant art and garden terrace. Menus offer a mix of traditional and more modern dishes; excellent value set 2 course lunch.

Chop House
2 Shelbourne Rd ✉ D4 – ✆ (1) 660 23 90 – www.thechophouse.ie – Closed lunch Saturday and Sunday **FUx**
Rest – Modern European – Carte € 23/47
◆ Whitewashed pub in prominent position; sit in the brighter, conservatory-style area rather than the bar. Informal lunches and more elaborate dinner menu of carefully prepared, tasty dishes.

at Donnybrook

Marble Hall without rest
81 Marlborough Rd ✉ D4 – ✆ (01) 497 7350 – www.marblehall.net – February-November **EVa**
3 rm – € 55 € 80/90
◆ Georgian townhouse with effusive welcome guaranteed. Individually styled throughout, with plenty of antiques and quality soft furnishings. Stylish, warmly decorated bedrooms.

REPUBLIC OF IRELAND

at Rathmines

XX **Zen**

89 Upper Rathmines Rd ✉ D6 – ☎ (01) 497 94 28 – ww.zenrestaurant.ie – Closed 25-27 December **DVt**

Rest – Chinese – *(dinner only and Friday lunch)* Menu €20 – Carte €18/31

♦ Renowned family run Chinese restaurant in the unusual setting of an old church hall. Imaginative, authentic oriental cuisine with particular emphasis on spicy Szechuan dishes.

at Dublin Airport North : 10.5 km by N 1 - BS - and M 1 – ✉ Dublin

Carlton H. Dublin Airport

Old Airport Rd, Cloughran, on R 132 Santry rd – ☎ (01) 866 7500 – www.carlton.ie/dublinairport – Closed 24-26 December

117 rm – 🛉€89/129 🛉🛉€89/129, ☕ €13.50 – 1 suite

Rest *Kittyhawks* – Carte €29/46

♦ Modern commercial hotel with spacious marbled reception and comfy guest areas. Uniform bedrooms display good facilities and smart bathrooms. Some rooms overlook airfield; some have balconies. Informal all-day brasserie offers popular menu.

Bewleys

Baskin Lane, East : 1.5 km on A 32 – ☎ (01) 871 1000 – www.bewleyshotels.com – Closed 25 December

466 rm – 🛉€89/199 🛉🛉€89/199, ☕ €12

Rest *The Brasserie* – Menu €20 (lunch)/25 (early dinner) – Carte dinner €25/60

♦ Immense eight floor hotel, ten minutes from the airport, with selection of small meeting rooms. Immaculately kept bedrooms; good value for money. Wide-ranging menu served in The Brasserie.

at Clontarf Northeast : 5.5 km by R 105 – ✉ Dublin

Clontarf Castle

Castle Ave ✉ D3 – ☎ (01) 833 2321 – www.clontarfcastle.ie **CSa**

108 rm ☕ – 🛉€365 🛉🛉€365 – 3 suites

Rest *Fahrenheit Grill* – *(dinner only)* Menu €25 – Carte €40/46

♦ Set in an historic castle, partly dating back to 1172. Striking medieval style entrance lobby. Modern rooms and characterful luxury suites, all with cutting edge facilities. Restaurant boasts grand medieval style décor reminiscent of a knights' banqueting hall; fresh local meats and seafood feature.

at Sandyford Southeast : 12 km by N 11 and R 112 off R 133 - CT – ✉ Dublin

The Beacon rest,

Beacon Court, Sandyford Business Region ✉ D18 – ☎ (01) 291 5000 – www.thebeacon.com – Closed 24-25 December

87 rm ☕ – 🛉€110/150 🛉🛉€120/160 – 1 suite

Rest *My Thai* – Thai – Menu €25/45 **s** – Carte €29/40 **s**

♦ Ultra-stylish hotel with uniquely quirky entrance lobby featuring a chandelier on the floor and bed with central seating! Modish bar, low-key meeting rooms, sleek bedrooms. Funky, relaxed restaurant serving authentic Asian dishes.

at Foxrock Southeast : 13 km by N 11 - CT – ✉ Dublin

XX **Bistro One**

3 Brighton Rd ✉ D18 – ☎ (01) 289 7711 – www.bistro-one.ie – Closed 25 December-4 January, Sunday and Monday

Rest – *(booking essential)* Menu €24 (lunch) – Carte €27/35

♦ Long-standing neighbourhood restaurant; popular with the locals. Daily lunch and monthly dinner menus display a mix of Irish and Mediterranean influences. Good use of local produce.

at Dundrum Southeast : 8 km by N 11 - CT – ✉ Dublin

XXX **Harvey Nichols First Floor Restaurant**

Harvey Nichols, Town Square, Sandyford Rd ✉ D16 – ☎ (01) 291 0488 – www.harveynichols.com – Closed 25 December, Sunday dinner and Monday
Rest – Menu €25/30 – Carte €32/41
◆ Up the lift to ultra-stylish bar and plush, designer-led restaurant. Attentive, professional service. Dishes are modern, seasonal and confident with a fine dining feel.

XX **Ananda**

Town Square ✉ D14 – ☎ (01) 296 00 99 – www.anandarestarant.ie – Closed 25-26 December, lunch Monday-Wednesday
Rest – Indian – Menu €16 – Carte €30/56 **s**
◆ Meaning 'bliss' in ancient Sanskrit. Stylish restaurant located in city centre arcade. Beautiful décor, attractive fretwork and gorgeous lighting. Flavourful modern Indian cuisine.

DUBLIN AIRPORT = Aerfort Bhaile Átha Cliath – **Dublin** – **712** N7 – **see Dublin**

DUNBOYNE (Dún Búinne) – **Meath** – **712** M7 – **pop. 5 713** **37** D3

Dublin 17 km – Drogheda 45 km – Newbridge 54 km

Dunboyne Castle

– ☎ (01) 801 35 00 – www.dunboynecastlehotel.com
141 rm – 🛉€125/180 🛉🛉€150/220 – 4 suites
Rest – *(dinner only and Sunday lunch)* Menu €25 (early dinner) – Carte €29/50
◆ Georgian house with vast, modern extensions, set in 26 acres. Ornate ceilings typify style in original house; now used for conferences. Some bedrooms have balconies; most overlook grounds. Discreet, stylish spa. Large, formal restaurant serves classic Irish dishes.

DUNCANNON (Dún Canann) – **Wexford** – **712** L11 – **pop. 291** **39** D2
Ireland

Dublin 167 km – New Ross 26 km – Waterford 48 km
Fort★ **AC**
Dunbrody Abbey★ **AC**, N : 9 km by R 733 – Kilmokea Gardens★ **AC**, N : 11 km by R 733 – Tintern Abbey★ **AC**, E : 8 km by R 737 and R 733. Kennedy Arboretum★ **AC**, N : 21 km by R 733

XX **Aldridge Lodge** with rm

South : 1 km by Hook Head Rd – ☎ (051) 389 116 – www.aldridgelodge.com – Closed 3 weeks January, 25-26 December, Monday and Tuesday
3 rm – 🛉€55 🛉🛉€100
Rest – *(dinner only) (booking essential)* Menu €39 **s**
◆ Close to the beach, a smart, cheery restaurant with gardens serving good value, quality local menus: lobster a speciality as owner's dad's a lobster fisherman! Cosy rooms.

X **Sqigl**

Quay Rd – ☎ (051) 389 700 – www.sqiglrestaurant.com – Closed 9 January-17 March
Rest – *(dinner only) (booking essential)* Menu €25 – Carte €31/39
◆ Stone-built restaurant; a converted barn standing adjacent to a popular bar in this coastal village. Faux leopard skin banquettes. Modern European cuisine with amiable service.

DUNDALK (Dún Dealgan) – **Louth** – **712** M5/6 – **pop. 35 085** **37** D2
Ireland

Dublin 82 km – Drogheda 35 km
Killinbeg Killin Park, ☎ (042) 933 93 03
Dún a' Rí Forest Park★, W : 34 km by R 178 and R 179 – Proleek Dolmen★, N : 8 km by N 1 R 173

Crowne Plaza
Green Park, South : 2.5 km on N 52 – ℰ (042) 939 49 00 – www.cpdundalk.ie – Closed 25 December
128 rm – 🛉 € 55/99 🛉🛉 € 69/109, ☕ €15 – 1 suite
Rest – *(bar lunch Monday-Saturday)* Menu € 35 **s** – Carte € 30/45 **s**
◆ Modern 14 storey hotel tower block with stylish ground floor bar/lounge and good conference facilities. Uniform bedrooms boast views of surrounding countryside. Top floor restaurant offers seasonally changing menu of classic dishes and has superb 360° vista.

Rosemount without rest
Dublin Rd, South : 2.5 km on R 132 – ℰ (042) 933 58 78 – www.rosemountireland.com
6 rm ☕ – 🛉 € 40/45 🛉🛉 € 70
◆ Attractive guesthouse with flower-filled gardens; run by welcoming couple. Laura Ashley and Brown Thomas fabrics/furnishings feature throughout. Individually styled bedrooms; some with sofas and flat screen TVs. Freshly cooked breakfasts; tea and cake on arrival.

Rosso
5 Roden Pl – ℰ (042) 935 6502 – www.rossorestaurant.com – Closed 25-26 December, Saturday lunch and Monday
Rest – Menu € 26 (dinner) – Carte € 30/46
◆ Unassuming grey townhouse that blends original features with stylish modern furnishings. Light lunches; à la carte, daily specials or express menu in the evening. Interesting, original dishes demonstrate a good understanding of flavours. Presentation is careful.

at Jenkinstown **Northeast : 9 km by N 52 on R 173**

Fitzpatricks
Rockmarshall, Southeast : 1 km – ℰ (042) 937 61 93 – www.fitzpatricks-restaurant.com – Closed 24-27 December, September-May and Good Friday
Rest – Menu € 25 (dinner) – Carte € 50/60
◆ Hugely characterful pub with beautiful flower displays and intriguing memorabilia. Extensive menu of hearty, flavoursome dishes and plenty of classics; local seafood and steaks a speciality.

DUNDRUM = Dún Droma – Dublin – 712 N8 – see Dublin

DUNFANAGHY (Dún Fionnachaidh) – Donegal – 712 I2 – pop. 316 37 C1

– ✉ Letterkenny ▮ Ireland

Dublin 277 km – Donegal 87 km – Londonderry 69 km
Dunfanaghy Letterkenny, ℰ (074) 913 6335
Horn Head Scenic Route★, N : 4 km. Doe Castle★, SE : 11.25 km by N 56 – The Rosses★, SW : 40.25 km by N 56 and R 259

Arnolds
Main St – ℰ (074) 913 62 08 – www.arnoldshotel.com – May-October
30 rm ☕ – 🛉 € 65/115 🛉🛉 € 130/170
Rest ***Sea Scapes*** – *(bar lunch)* Menu € 35 – Carte € 30/40
◆ Pleasant traditional coaching inn with a variety of extensions. Spacious lounge area and a charming bar with open fires. Family run with traditional bedrooms. Informal Sea Scapes serves wide-ranging menus.

The Mill with rm
Southwest : 0.75 km on N 56 – ℰ (074) 913 69 85 – www.themillrestaurant.com – Closed January-February, midweek March, November and December, and Monday-Wednesday October.
6 rm ☕ – 🛉 € 75 🛉🛉 € 110 **Rest** – *(Closed Monday) (dinner only)* Menu € 45
◆ Former flax mill on New Lake with Mount Muckish view. Locally renowned and warmly run; enhanced by personally decorated ambience. Traditional cooking served in split-level, linen-laid dining room. Unfussy bedrooms with simple facilities.

REPUBLIC OF IRELAND

DUNGARVAN (Dún Garbhán) – Waterford – 712 J11 – pop. 8 362 39 C3

Ireland

Dublin 190 km – Cork 71 km – Waterford 48 km

The Courthouse (058) 41741, info@dungarvantourism.com

Knocknagrannagh, (058) 41 605

Gold Coast Ballinacourty, (058) 42 249

East Bank (Augustinian priory, ★)

Ringville (★), S : 13 km by N 25 and R 674 – Helvick Head★ (★), SE : 13 km by N 25 and R 674

Gortnadiha Lodge without rest

South : 6.5 km by N 25 off R 674 – (058) 46 142 – www.gortnadihalodge.com

3 rm – € 50 € 90

◆ Friendly guesthouse set in its own glen with fine bay views, a first floor terrace for afternoon tea, homemade jams and breads for breakfast, and antique furnished bedrooms.

Tannery with rm rest,

10 Quay St, via Parnell St – (058) 45 420 – www.tannery.ie – Closed 2 weeks January, 25-26 December, Good Friday, and Sunday except July and August

14 rm – € 60/70 € 100/120

Rest – *(dinner only and lunch Friday and Sunday)* Menu € 29 (weekdays) – Carte € 45/55

◆ Characterful 19C former tannery; high-ceilinged dining room with informal ambience. Imaginative modern menus centre round produce from kitchen garden. Super cooking school. Stylish, comfortable bedrooms in adjacent townhouse.

DUNKINEELY (Dún Cionnaola) – Donegal – 712 G4 – pop. 363 37 C1

Dublin 156 km – Lifford 42 km – Sligo 53 km – Ballybofey 28 km

Castle Murray House with rm

St John's Point, Southwest : 1.5 km by N 56 on St John's Point rd – (074) 973 70 22 – www.castlemurray.com – Closed mid January-mid February, Monday and Tuesday September-June and 24-25 December

10 rm – € 50/60 € 80/100

Rest – *(dinner only and Sunday lunch, light lunch in summer)* Menu € 31/45

◆ In delightful, picturesque position with view of sea and sunsets from the lounges and the pleasant dining room. Good local seafood. Comfortable and contemporary styled bedrooms.

DUN LAOGHAIRE (Dún Laoghaire) – Dún Laoghaire-Rathdown – 712 N8 – pop. 23 857 Ireland 39 D1

Dublin 14 km

to Holyhead (Stena Line) 4-5 daily (1 h 40 mn)

v (01) 6057 700, info@dlrtourism.com

Dun Laoghaire Eglinton Park, (01) 280 3916

★★ of Killiney Bay from coast road south of Sorrento Point

Rasam

1st Floor (above Eagle House pub), 18-19 Glasthule Rd – (01) 230 0600 – www.rasam.ie – Closed 25-26 December and Good Friday **e**

Rest – Indian – *(dinner only)* Carte € 42/53

◆ Located above Eagle House pub, this airy, modern, stylish restaurant shimmers with silky green wallpaper. Interesting, authentic dishes covering all regions of India.

Cavistons

58-59 Glasthule Rd – (01) 280 9245 – www.cavistons.com – Closed 23-26 December, Sunday and Monday **a**

Rest – Seafood – *(lunch only and dinner Friday and Saturday) (booking essential)* Carte € 28/48

◆ Simple, informal restaurant attached to the well-established seafood shop which specialises in finest piscine produce. Mermaid friezes and quality crustacean cuisine.

Tribes

57a Glasthule Rd – ☎ (01) 236 5971 – www.tribes.ie – Closed 25-26 December and Good Friday x

Rest – *(dinner only and Sunday lunch)* Menu € 26 – Carte € 34/42

◆ Personally run neighbourhood restaurant next to Cavistons. Smart, original interior harmonises seamlessly with creative modern European menus that evolve slowly over time.

DUNLAVIN (Dún Luáin) – Wicklow – 712 L8 – pop. 849 — 39 D2

Dublin 50 km – Kilkenny 71 km – Wexford 98 km

Rathsallagh, ☎ (045) 403 316

Rathsallagh House

Southwest : 3.25 km on Grangecon Rd – ☎ (045) 403 112 – www.rathsallagh.com

28 rm – † € 150/185 †† € 220/250 – 1 suite

Rest – *(bar lunch Monday-Saturday)* Menu € 65 (dinner Friday-Saturday) – Carte dinner midweek € 50/65

◆ 18C converted stables set in extensive grounds and golf course. Picturesque walled garden. Characterful, country house-style public areas and cosy, individual bedrooms. Kitchen garden provides ingredients for welcoming dining room.

DUNMORE EAST (Dún Mór) – Waterford – 712 L11 – pop. 1 547 39 C2
– ✉ Waterford ▮ Ireland

▶ Dublin 174 km – Waterford 19 km

Dunmore East, ✆(051) 383 151

Village★

The Beach without rest

1 Lower Village – ✆(051) 383 316 – www.dunmorebeachguesthouse.com – March-October

7 rm – € 50/60 € 80/90

◆ Modern house close to the beach. Wonderful views from conservatory breakfast/lounge area. Very spacious bedrooms with pine furniture and modern facilities; some with balcony.

DURRUS (Dúras) – Cork – 712 D13 – pop. 313 38 A3

▶ Dublin 338 km – Cork 90 km – Killarney 85 km

Blairs Cove with rm

Southwest : 1.5 km on R 591 – ✆(027) 62 913 – www.blairscove.ie – Closed January and February

4 rm – € 105/140 € 150/260

Rest – *(closed Sunday dinner and Monday) (dinner only and Sunday lunch) (booking essential)* Menu € 35 (lunch)/58 **s**

◆ Charming 18C house with large gardens, cobbled paths, a courtyard and lily pond; run by one family since 1972. Chic bar and elegant beamed restaurant in old stables; buffet starters, followed by meats cooked over an open wood grill. Modern, well-equipped bedrooms.

Good Things Cafe

Ahakista Rd, West : 0.75 km on Ahakista rd – ✆(027) 61 426 – www.thegoodthingscafe.com – Easter-August

Rest – *(closed Tuesday and Wednesday)* Carte € 29/43

◆ Simple and unpretentious. Walls filled with shelves full of books and foods of all kinds for sale. Open-plan kitchen serves accomplished dishes full of quality local produce.

ENNISCORTHY (Inis Córthaidh) – Wexford – 712 M10 – pop. 9 538 39 D2
▮ Ireland

▶ Dublin 122 km – Kilkenny 74 km – Waterford 54 km – Wexford 24 km

1798 Rebellion Centre, Millpark Rd ✆ (0539) 234699, info@1798centre.ie

Knockmarshal, ✆(053) 923 31 91

Enniscorthy Castle★ (County Museum★)

Ferns★, NE : 13 km by N 11 – Mount Leinster★, N : 27.25 km by N 11

Monart

rest,

The Still, Northwest : 3 km by N 11 (Dublin rd) – ✆(053) 923 8999 – www.monart.ie – Closed 18-27 December

68 rm – € 135/295 € 190/510 – 2 suites

Rest *Garden Lounge* – Carte approx. € 33

Rest *The Restaurant* – *(dinner only and Sunday lunch)* Menu € 25 (lunch) – Carte € 32/63

◆ Spa resort in 100 acres; enter via the elegant Georgian house and experience various therapies in state-of-the-art treatment rooms. Bedrooms all have views; many have balconies. Enjoy lighter dishes in the Garden Lounge or out on the terrace. Formal dining in The Restaurant.

Ballinkeele House

Ballymurn, Southeast : 10.5 km by unmarked road on Curracloe rd – ✆(053) 91 38 105 – www.ballinkeele.com – February-November

5 rm – € 90/105 € 150/170 **Rest** – Menu € 48 **s**

◆ High ceilinged, firelit lounge plus sizeable rooms with period-style furniture and countryside views add to the charm of a quiet 1840 manor, well run by experienced owners. Dining room enriched by candlelight and period oils.

ENNISKERRY (Áth an Sceire) – Wicklow – 712 N8 – pop. 1 881 — 39 D1

Ireland

Dublin 25 km – Wicklow 32 km

Powerscourt Powerscourt Estate, ☎ (01) 204 6033

Powerscourt★★ **AC** (Waterfall★★, **AC**)

Ritz Carlton

West : 2 km. by Powerscourt rd – ☎ (01) 274 8888 – www.ritzcarlton.com

76 rm – † € 255 †† € 315, ☐ €29 – 124 suites – †† € 305/365

Rest *Gordon Ramsay at Powerscourt* – ☎ (01) 274 9377 *(dinner only and lunch Saturday and Sunday)* Menu € 40 (lunch)/80 – Carte € 73/80

Rest *The Sugar Loaf* – Carte € 43/50

◆ Opened in 2008 within the Powerscourt House Estate, a vast and impressive structure with lots of leisure activities. Many rooms are suites; bathrooms are luxurious. Formal restaurant with mountain views and mix of Gordon Ramsay dishes and reinterpreted Irish classics. Relaxed Sugar Loaf.

FETHARD (Fiodh Ard) – Tipperary – 712 I10 – pop. 1 374 Ireland — 39 C2

Dublin 161 km – Cashel 16 km – Clonmel 13 km

Cashel★★★ : Rock of Cashel★★★ **AC** (Cormac's Chapel★★, Round Tower★), Museum★ **AC**, Cashel Palace Gardens★, GPA Bolton Library★ **AC**, NW : 15 km by R 692 – Clonmel★ : County Museum★ **AC**, St Mary's Church★, S : 13 km by R 689

Mobarnane House

North : 8 km by Cashel rd on Ballinure rd – ☎ (052) 613 19 62 – www.mobarnanehouse.com – Restricted opening in winter

4 rm ☐ – † € 105 †† € 150

Rest – *(dinner only)* Menu € 45

◆ Very personally run classic Georgian house with mature gardens in quiet rural setting, tastefully restored to reflect its age. Ask for a bedroom with its own sitting room. Beautiful dining room for menus agreed in advance.

FOTA ISLAND (Oileán Fhóta) – Cork – 712 H12 — 38 B3

Dublin 263 km – Cork 17 km – Limerick 118 km – Waterford 110 km

Fota Island

– ☎ (021) 488 3700 – www.fotaisland.ie – closed 24-26 December

123 rm ☐ – † € 300 †† € 330 – 8 suites

Rest *Fota* – *(dinner only)* Carte € 36/56

◆ All-encompassing resort location within Ireland's only wildlife park boasting Wellness Centre with 'walking river' and 18 hole golf course. Stylish rooms from the top drawer. Fota's appealing menus suit all tastes.

FOXROCK = Carraig an tSionnaigh – Dublin – 712 N7 – see Dublin

FURBOGH/FURBO (Na Forbacha) – Galway – 712 E8 – pop. 1 236 — 36 A3

Dublin 228 km – Galway 11 km

Connemara Coast

– ☎ (091) 592 108 – www.sinnotthotels.com – Closed 23-27 December

141 rm ☐ – † € 130/200 †† € 178/350 – 1 suite

Rest *The Gallery* – *(bar lunch)* Menu € 40 **s** – Carte € 40/50 **s**

◆ Sprawling hotel geared to families, with super views of Galway Bay, The Burren and Aran from the spacious bedrooms. Comprehensive leisure facilities. Club for kids. Two dining options; The Gallery for adults only.

GALWAY (Gaillimh) – Galway – 712 E8 – pop. 72 414 Ireland — 36 B3

Dublin 217 km – Limerick 103 km – Sligo 145 km

Carnmore Airport : (091) 755569, NE : 6.5 km

Discover Ireland Centre, Aras Failte, Forster St (091) 537700, irelandwestinfo@failteireland.ie Salthill Promenade (091) 520500 (May-August)

Galway Salthill Blackrock, (091) 522 033

City★★ – St Nicholas' Church★ BY - Roman Catholic Cathedral★ AY – Eyre Square : Bank of Ireland Building (sword and mace★) BY

NW : Lough Corrib★★. W : by boat, Aran Islands (Inishmore - Dun Aenghus★★★) BZ - Thoor Ballylee★, SE : 33.75 km by N 6 and N 18 D – Dunguaire Castle, Kinvarra★ **AC**, S : 25.75 km by N 6, N 18 and N 67 D – Aughnanure Castle★, NW : 25.75 km by N 59 - Oughterard★ (<★★), NW : 29 km by N 59 - Knockmoy Abbey★, NE : 30.5 km by N 17 and N 63 D – Coole Park (Autograph Tree★), SE : 33.75 km by N 6 and N 18 D - St Mary's Cathedral, Tuam★, NE : 33.75 km by N 17 D – Loughrea (St Brendan's Cathedral★), SE : 35.5 km by N 6 D - Turoe Stone★, SE : 35.5 km by N 6 and north by R 350

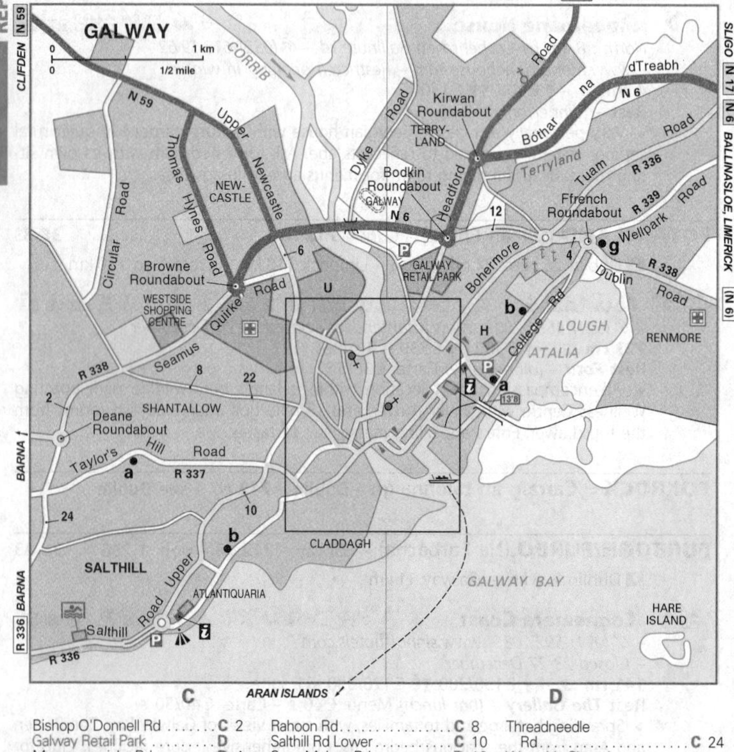

Bishop O'Donnell Rd . . . . . . C 2	Rahoon Rd . . . . C 8	Threadneedle Rd . . . . C 24
Galway Retail Park . . . . D	Salthill Rd Lower . . . . C 10	Westside Shopping Centre C
Moneenageisha Rd . . . . D 4	Sean Mulvoy Rd . . . . D 12	
Newcastle Rd Lower . . . . . . C 6	Shantalla Rd . . . . C 22	

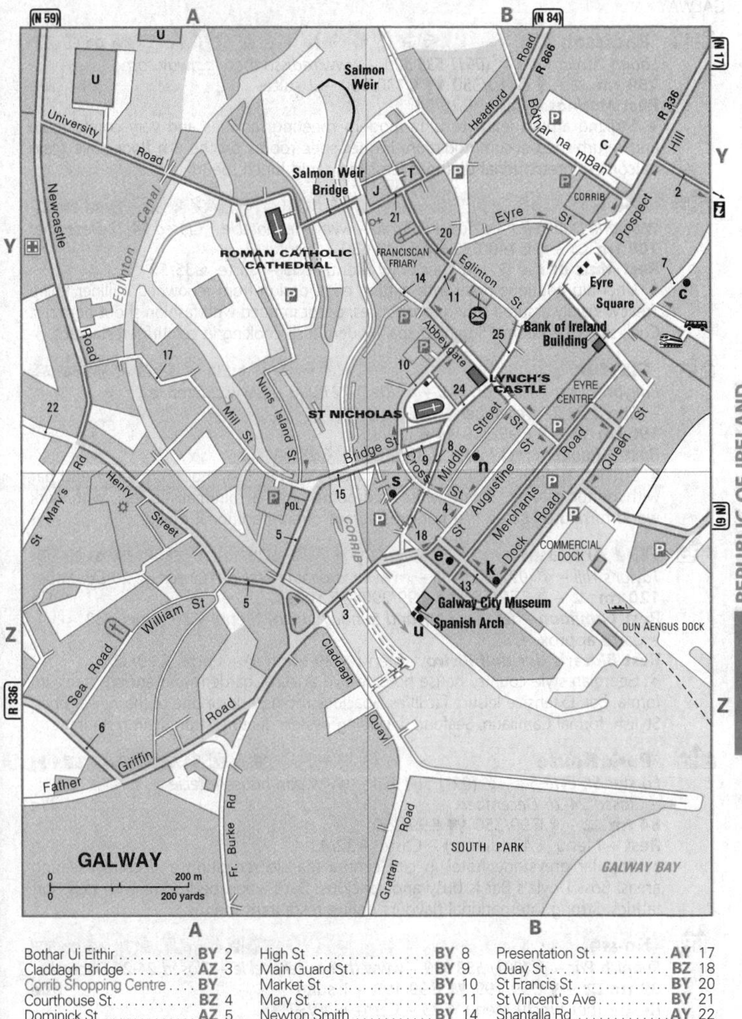

Bothar Ui Eithir	BY	2	High St	BY	8	Presentation St	AY	17
Claddagh Bridge	AZ	3	Main Guard St	BY	9	Quay St	BZ	18
Corrib Shopping Centre	BY		Market St	BY	10	St Francis St	BY	20
Courthouse St	BZ	4	Mary St	BY	11	St Vincent's Ave	BY	21
Dominick St	AZ	5	Newton Smith	BY	14	Shantalla Rd	AY	22
Father Griffin Ave	AZ	6	New Dock St	BZ	13	Shop St	BY	24
Forster St	BY	7	O'Brien Bridge	AY	15	William St	BY	25

Glenlo Abbey rm,

Bushypark, Northwest : 5.25 km on N 59 – ✆ (091) 526 666 – www.glenlo.com – Closed 23-27 December

42 rm – † € 189/315 †† € 250/400, ☕ €22 – 4 suites

Rest *River Room* – *(dinner only Thursday-Sunday)* Menu € 35 – Carte € 36/54

Rest *Pullman* – *(dinner only Monday-Saturday)* Carte € 37/52

♦ Imposing 18C grey stone country house with impressive grounds and church/-bay views. Very comfortable lounge, leading into chapel. Spacious, traditional rooms. Formal River Room boasts golf course views. Pullman, a converted railway carriage, offers modern dishes with an Asian base.

Radisson Blu
Lough Atalia Rd – ☎ (091) 538 300 – www.radissonhotelgalway.com
259 rm – † € 110/350 †† € 130/350 – 2 suites Da
Rest *Marinas* – Carte € 25/54
♦ Striking atrium leads to ultra-modern meeting facilities and very comfortable and refurbished accommodation. Higher spec rooms on the 5th floor have glass balconies. International dining; accessible, rapid lunch menu.

The G rm,
Wellpark, Dublin Rd – ☎ (091) 865 200 – www.theghotel.ie – Closed 24-27 December
100 rm – † € 140/630 †† € 140/630 – 1 suite Dg
Rest *Matz at the G* – *(dinner only)* Menu € 55 – Carte € 35/52
♦ Uber-hip boutique hotel with cutting edge design from renowned milliner Philip Treacy. Vividly assured sitting room styles; décor imbued with fashion shoot portraits. Cool, slinky bedrooms. Stunning spa. Modern Irish cooking in colourful restaurant.

Clayton rm,
Ballybrit, East : 4 km on N 6 – ☎ (091) 721 900 – www.clayton.ie – Closed 23-27 December
196 rm – † € 99/350 †† € 120/350
Rest – *(dinner only)* Menu € 35 – Carte € 28/34
♦ Striking angular building on edge of city, with stylish, modern interior and bar with buffet carvery. Smart white bedrooms have a minimalistic feel, with dark wood furniture. Large first floor restaurant offers traditional menu.

The Ardilaun rest,
Taylor's Hill – ☎ (091) 521 433 – www.theardilaunhotel.ie – Closed 22-26 December
120 rm – † € 79/150 †† € 99/290 – 5 suites Ca
Rest *Camilaun* – *(dinner only and Sunday lunch)* Menu € 20 (lunch)/32 – Carte approx. € 32
Rest *Blazer's Bar and Bistro* – Menu € 29 (dinner) – Carte € 20/33
♦ Georgian style country house hotel in five acres of gardens and ancient trees. Informal bar. Extensive leisure facilities. Spacious rooms; ask for one of the newer ones. Stylish, formal Camilaun. Seafood, including oysters, feature strongly in restaurant.

Park House
Forster St, Eyre Sq – ☎ (091) 564 924 – www.parkhousehotel.ie – Closed 24-26 December BYc
84 rm – † € 99/350 †† € 99/350
Rest – Menu € 42 (dinner) – Carte € 32/42
♦ Popular greystone hotel in city centre. Marble reception and comfy seating areas. Boss Doyle's Bar is busy and spacious. Dark wood bedrooms with rich, soft fabrics. Strong international flavours define restaurant menus.

House rm,
Spanish Par – ☎ (091) 538 900 – www.thehousehotel.ie – Closed 24-26 December
39 rm – † € 99/199 †† € 99/199 – 1 suite BZe
Rest – *(bar lunch)* Menu € 23 – Carte € 20/37
♦ Luxury boutique hotel, blending contemporary design with a cosy, relaxed style. Bedrooms are divided between cosy, classy and swanky. Modern menus take on a global reach; try to get a seat on the outdoor deck.

Ardawn House without rest
College Rd – ☎ (091) 568 833 – www.ardawnhouse.com – Closed 22-26 December
8 rm – † € 60/120 †† € 110/160 Db
♦ Sample Irish hospitality at this family-run guest house. Individually decorated bedrooms and comfy lounge. Extensive breakfast menu served at linen-clad tables.

XX **Kirwan's Lane**
Kirwan's Lane – ☎ (091) 568 266 – Closed 25 December, Sunday dinner in winter and Sunday lunch BZs
Rest – Menu € 30 (weekday dinner) – Carte € 34/48
♦ Modern restaurant in warm, autumnal shades. Adventurous menus. Welcoming atmosphere and a genuine neighbourhood feel.

REPUBLIC OF IRELAND

XX **Vina Mara**

19 Middle St – ☎ (091) 561 610 – www.vinamara.com – Closed 24-26 December
Rest – Menu € 20 (lunch)/28 – Carte € 24/40 BY**n**

◆ Spacious restaurant in warm welcoming colours - smart yet informal; attentive service. Mediterranean style dishes with Irish and other touches. Affordable but limited lunch choice.

X **Ard Bia at Nimmos**

Spanish Arch – ☎ (091) 561 114 – www.ardbia.com – Closed 25-26 December and Monday lunch BZ**u**
Rest – *(light lunch) (booking essential at dinner)* Carte € 30/43

◆ Simple restaurant in two-storey building with buzzy, bohemain feel. Generous, full-flavoured dishes have Mediterranean and Irish influences. Lighter lunches; upstairs used at weekends.

Sheridan's on the Docks

3 Dock St (1st floor) – ☎ (091) 564 905 – www.sheridansonthedocks.com – Closed Sunday and Monday BZ**k**
Rest – *(Booking advisable for dinner)* Carte approx.

◆ Head for candlelit upstairs dining room for flavourful, seasonal food; passionately and respectfully prepared, with some ingredients foraged for by the chef. Atmospheric ground floor pub.

GARRYKENNEDY – Tipperary – 712 G9 — 39 C2

Dublin 176 km – Killaloe 14 km – Youghal 2 km

Larkins

– ☎ (067) 23 232 – www.larkinspub.com – Closed 25 December, Good Friday and Monday-Friday lunch (November-April)
Rest – Carte € 30/36

◆ Thatched, whitewashed pub in a charming loughside location. Traditional interior plays host to folk music sessions and Irish dancers. Simple, unfussy bar menu; more ambitious à la carte.

GARRYVOE (Garraí Uí Bhuaigh) – Cork – 712 H12 – pop. 560 — 39 C3

– ✉ Castlemartyr

Dublin 259 km – Cork 37 km – Waterford 100 km

Garryvoe

– ☎ (021) 464 67 18 – www.garryvoehotel.com – Closed 24-25 December
65 rm – † € 85/120 †† € 175 – 1 suite
Rest – *(Closed Monday and Tuesday in winter) (dinner only and Sunday lunch bar lunch Monday-Saturday)* Menu € 28 (lunch)/45 – Carte € 45/50

◆ Traditionally styled hotel adjacent to the beach with good sea views, to be enjoyed in characterful locals bar. A purpose-built, up-to-date wing features smart, modern rooms. Bright, colourful, contemporary restaurant.

GLASLOUGH = Glasloch – Monaghan – 712 L5 – see Monaghan

GLASSAN = Glasán – Westmeath – 712 I7 – see Athlone

GOLEEN (An Góilín) – Cork – 712 C13 — 38 A3

Dublin 230 km – Cork 74 km – Killarney 67 km

The Heron's Cove

The Harbour – ☎ (028) 35 225 – www.heronscove.com – Closed Christmas, restricted opening in winter
5 rm – † € 60/70 †† € 70/90
Rest – *(April-October) (dinner only)* Menu € 30 – Carte € 32/46

◆ Hidden away in pretty location on the waterfront, with simple, comfortable bedrooms and harbour views. Open dining room has pleasant vista. Local seafood menu of flavourful, seasonal dishes.

GOREY (Guaire) – Wexford – 712 N9 – pop. 7 193 Ireland 39 D2

Dublin 93 km – Waterford 88 km – Wexford 61 km

Main St ✆ (055) 942 1248, info@northwexford.com

Courtown Kiltennel, ✆ (055) 25 166

Ferns★, SW : 17.75 km by N 11

Marlfield House

Courtown Rd, Southeast : 1.5 km on R 742 – ✆ (053) 942 11 24 – www.marlfieldhouse.com – Closed 2 January-4 March and restricted opening in November

19 rm – € 100/145 € 200/250

Rest – *(dinner only and Sunday lunch) (booking essential for non-residents)* Menu € 42/64

◆ Luxuriously comfortable Regency mansion, with extensive gardens and woods. Utterly charming public areas with fine antiques and splendid fabrics. Thoughtfully furnished rooms. Very comfortable conservatory restaurant utilising produce from the garden.

Kin Khao

3 Main St – ✆ (053) 943 0677 – www.kinkhaothai.ie – Closed 24 April and 24-26 December

Rest – Thai – *(dinner only and lunch Wednesday-Friday and Sunday)* Menu € 20 (dinner) – Carte € 29/38

◆ No-frills restaurant above shops serving elaborate, well presented cooking. Extensive menu, with some daily specials; cheery service and a good wine list. Choose a table at the front.

REPUBLIC OF IRELAND

GRAIGUENAMANAGH (Gráig na Manach) – Kilkenny – 712 L10 – pop. 1 376 Ireland 39 D2

Dublin 125 km – Kilkenny 34 km – Waterford 42 km – Wexford 26 km

Duiske Abbey★★ **AC**

Jerpoint Abbey★★ **AC**, W : 15 km by R 703 and N 9 – Inistioge★, SW : 8 km by minor road – Kilfane Glen and Waterfall★ **AC**, SW : 17 km by R 703 and N 9

Waterside with rm

The Quay – ✆ (059) 972 42 46 – www.watersideguesthouse.com – Closed January and 24-26 December

10 rm – € 55/75 € 90/110

Rest – *(Closed Monday-Tuesday and Wednesday-Thursday in winter) (dinner only and Sunday lunch)* Menu € 23 (lunch) – Carte € 25/36 **s**

◆ Converted 19C cornstore on banks of river Barrow, at foot of Brandon Hill. Base for hillwalkers. Modern cooking with Mediterranean flourishes. Beamed rooms with river views.

GREYSTONES (Na Clocha Liatha) – Wicklow – 712 N8 – pop. 14 569 Ireland 39 D1

Dublin 35 km

Greystones, ✆ (01) 287 4136

Killruddery House and Gardens★ **AC**, N : 5 km by R 761 – Powerscourt★★ (Waterfall★★) **AC**, NW : 10 km by R 761, minor road, M 11 and minor road via Enniskerry. Wicklow Mountains★★

Chakra by Jaipur

Meridan Point Centre (1st floor), Church Rd – ✆ (01) 201 7222 – Closed 25 December

Rest – Indian – *(dinner only and Sunday lunch)* Menu € 22 (early dinner) – Carte € 28/44

◆ Red and ochre restaurant overlooked by elephant god, Ganesh, on 1st floor of modern shopping centre. Vibrant Indian cooking represents all regions; a blend of old and new.

GWEEDORE (Gaoth Dobhair) – **Donegal** – **712** H2 **37** C1

Dublin 278 km – Donegal 72 km – Letterkenny 43 km – Sligo 135 km

Gweedore Court

on N 56 – (074) 953 2900 – www.gweedorecourthotel.ie – Closed 24-26 December

66 rm – € 69/100 € 170/190

Rest – *(dinner only and Sunday lunch) (bar lunch Monday-Saturday)* Menu € 22/35 – Carte € 20/39

◆ Rebuilt 19C house sharing grounds with a Gaelic craft centre. Spacious accommodation in classic patterns; east-facing rooms enjoy superb views of Glenreagh National Park. Classic menu matched by traditional surroundings and period-inspired décor.

HORSE AND JOCKEY (An Marcach) – **Tipperary** – **712** I10 **39** C2

Dublin 146 km – Cashel 14 km – Thurles 9 km

Horse and Jockey rm,

– (0504) 44 192 – www.horseandjockeyhotel.com – Closed 25 December

65 rm – € 95 € 180 – 1 suite **Rest** – Carte € 27/42 **s**

◆ Much extended hotel with stylish, state-of-the-art meeting rooms, superb spa and great gift shop. Bar full of horse racing pictures on walls. Spacious, contemporary bedrooms. Easy going dining room with traditional menus.

HOWTH (Binn Éadair) – **Fingal** – **712** N7 – **pop. 8 186** – **Dublin** **39** D1

Ireland

Dublin 16 km

Deer Park Hotel Howth Castle, (01) 832 6039

The Cliffs★ (★)

Aqua

1 West Pier – (01) 832 0690 – www.aqua.ie – Closed 22 April, 25-26 December and Monday

Rest – Seafood – Menu € 30 (lunch) – Carte € 44/75

◆ Glass sided, first floor restaurant in former yacht club, with super bay views. Intimate bar filled with local photos, whetting the appetite for accomplished dishes of fresh seafood. Chefs on view.

King Sitric with rm rest,

East Pier – (01) 832 5235 – www.kingsitric.ie – Closed Christmas

8 rm – € 145 € 205

Rest – Seafood – *(closed Tuesday, Monday in winter and bank holidays) (dinner only and Sunday lunch)* Menu € 35 – Carte € 35/55

◆ Established in 1971 and one of Ireland's original seafood restaurants. Enjoy locally caught produce in first floor dining room with bay views. Modern, comfy bedrooms.

INISHMAAN = Inis Meáin – **Galway** – **712** D8 – **see Aran Islands**

INISHMORE = Árainn – **Galway** – **712** C/D8 – **see Aran Islands**

INISTIOGE (Inis Tíog) – **Kilkenny** – **712** K10 – **pop. 263** **39** C2

Dublin 82 km – Kilkenny 16 km – Waterford 19 km – Wexford 33 km

Bassetts at Woodstock

Woodstock Gdns, Northwest : 3 km – (056) 775 8820 – www.bassetts.ie – Closed 15 January-1 April, Monday, Tuesday and Sunday dinner

Rest – Carte € 30/43 **s**

◆ Personally run restaurant at entrance to Woodstock gardens. Homely inner with delightful terrace. Food is ethical, seasonal and traceable, and the owner rears his own pigs.

JENKINSTOWN = Baile Sheinicín – **Louth** – **see Dundalk**

KANTURK (Ceann Toirc) – **Cork** – **712** F11 – **pop. 1 915** Ireland **38** B2

Dublin 259 km – Cork 53 km – Killarney 50 km – Limerick 71 km

Fairy Hill, ✆ (029) 50 534

Town★ - Castle★

Glenlohane without rest

East : 4 km by R 576 and Charlville rd on Cecilstown rd – ✆ (029) 50 014 – www.glenlohane.com

3 rm – € 75 € 150

◆ In the family for over 250 years, a Georgian country house at the centre of wooded parkland and a working farm. Library and cosy, en suite rooms overlooking the fields.

KEEL = An Caol – **Mayo** – **712** B5/6 – **see Achill Island**

KENMARE (Neidín) – **Kerry** – **712** D12 – **pop. 1 701** Ireland **38** A3

Dublin 338 km – Cork 93 km – Killarney 32 km

Heritage Centre ✆ (064) 664 1233 (April-Oct.), kenmaretio@failteireland.ie AY

Kenmare, ✆ (064) 41 291

Town★

Ring of Kerry★★ - Healy Pass★★ (≤★★), SW : 30.5 km by R 571 and R 574 AY – Mountain Road to Glengarriff (≤★★) S : by N 71 AY - Slieve Miskish Mountains (≤★★), SW : 48.25 km by R 571 AY – Gougane Barra Forest Park★★, SE : 16 km AY - Lauragh (Derreen Gardens★ **AC**), SW : 23.5 km by R 571 AY – Allihies (Copper Mines★), SW : 57 km by R 571 and R 575 AY – Garnish Island (≤★), SW : 68.5 km by R 571, R 575 and R 572 AY

Park

– ✆ (064) 664 12 00 – www.parkkenmare.com

– May-September and 23 December-2 January BY**k**

46 rm – € 220/520 € 440/550

Rest – *(dinner only)* Menu €68 – Carte €56/68

◆ Privately run country house boasts many paintings and antiques. Superb spa facilities. Inviting, classically tastefully rooms; many offer superb views of Kenmare Bay and hills. Grand, bay-windowed dining room; local produce to fore.

KENMARE

Back Lane	BY	2
Cromwell's Bridge	AY	
Davitt's Place	AY	
Downing's Row	BY	5
East Park St	AY	7
Finnihy Bridge	AY	
Henry St	AY	
Henry's Lane	ABY	8
Killarney Rd	AY	
Main St	BY	
Market St	AY	
New St	AY	
Old Bridge St	AY	12
Railway Rd	BY	
Rock St	BY	14
Shelborne St	BY	
The Square	AY	

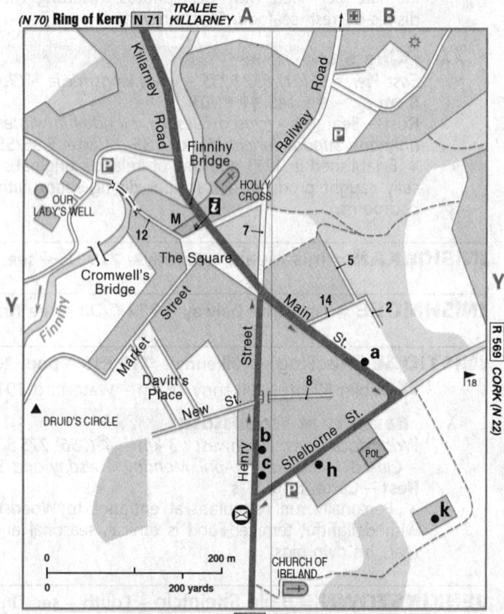

Sheen Falls Lodge
Southeast : 2 km by N 71 – ℰ (064) 664 16 00 – www.sheenfallslodge.ie – Closed 1 January-4 February, and Sunday-Thursday February-March and November-December
57 rm – † € 310/455 †† € 310/455, ☕ €24 – 9 suites – †† € 465/1870
Rest *La Cascade* – Carte € 60/68 **s**
◆ Modern, purpose-built hotel in idyllic location, with superb views of the famous falls. Spacious bedrooms have everything you could want. Extensive spa, gym and stables. Floodlit river views at La Cascade. Attentive, formal service.

Brook Lane
rm,
Gortamullen, North : 1 km by N 71 on N 70 – ℰ (064) 664 2077 – www.brooklanehotel.com
20 rm ☕ – † € 65/110 †† € 120/160
Rest *Casey's Bistro* – Menu € 25 (dinner) – Carte € 24/44
◆ Homely charms with a contemporary, designer edge, within easy walking distance of the town centre. The main strength here are the airy bedrooms, which are delightfully comfy with a host of extras. Spacious, formal dining room; menu offers something for everyone.

Shelburne Lodge without rest
East : 0.75 km on R 569 (Cork Rd) – ℰ (064) 664 10 13 – www.shelburnelodge.com – mid-March-mid-November
9 rm ☕ – † € 75/110 †† € 140/160
◆ Georgian farmhouse with pleasant lawns and herb garden. Antiques stylishly combined with contemporary colours and modern art. Firelit lounge and cosy rooms. Affable hosts.

Sallyport House without rest
South : 0.5 km on N 71 – ℰ (064) 664 20 66 – www.sallyporthouse.com – April-October
5 rm ☕ – † € 70/90 †† € 100/130
◆ 1930s house in garden and orchard. Wood floored hall, full of books and local information, leads to pristine, antique furnished bedrooms and a pretty front sitting room.

Lime Tree
Shelbourne St – ℰ (064) 664 12 25 – www.limetreerestaurant.com – Easter-October and weekends only in winter BY**h**
Rest – *(dinner only)* Carte € 35/42
◆ Tasty, unelaborate modern Irish cooking in a 19C former schoolhouse: stone walls, modern art on walls and in first-floor gallery. Busy, affordable and unfailingly friendly.

Mulcahys
36 Henry St – ℰ (064) 66 42 383 – Closed 22-27 December and Tuesday
Rest – *(dinner only)* Menu € 30 – Carte € 26/46 AY**c**
◆ Stylish wine racks, high-backed chairs, polished tables and friendly, attentive service set the tone here. Modern dishes appeal to the eye and palate alike.

35 Restaurant
35 Main St – ℰ (064) 664 15 59 – www.no35kenmare.com BY**a**
Rest – *(dinner only) (booking essential)* Menu € 25 – Carte € 21/42
◆ Long-standing restaurant in the heart of town, with simple, rustic, split-level interior. Good value menus, with lighter snacks available at lunch and seasonal classics offered in the evening.

Packies
Henry St – ℰ (064) 664 15 08 – www.kenmarerestaurants.com – Closed February and Monday AY**b**
Rest – *(dinner only) (booking essential)* Carte € 27/49
◆ Locally popular, personally run little place with understated rustic feel. Handwritten menu of fresh, modern Irish dishes prepared with care and super local seafood. Friendly staff.

REPUBLIC OF IRELAND

KILBRITTAIN (Cill Briotáin) – Cork – 712 F12 – pop. 185 — 38 B3

Dublin 289 km – Cork 38 km – Killarney 96 km

The Glen without rest

Southwest : 6.5 km by unmarked rd off R 600 – (023) 884 98 62 – www.glencountryhouse.com – May-October

5 rm – € 55/65 € 120/130

◆ Early Georgian house in 300 acres of mature parkland; the family have farmed the land for over 350 years. Comfy lounge and antique-filled breakfast room. Smart bedrooms with distant sea views.

Casino House

Coolmain Bay, Southeast : 3.5 km by unmarked rd on R 600 – (023) 88 49 944 – www.casinohouse.ie – Closed January-17 March and Wednesdays

Rest – *(dinner only and Sunday lunch)* Carte € 36/51 **s**

◆ Whitewashed former farmhouse in a charming wooded vale. Bright, modern interior boasts quarry tiled floors and a conservatory extension affording partial coastal views. Concise menus feature local, organic produce in classically based dishes. Efficient service.

KILCOLGAN (Cill Cholgáin) – Galway – 712 F8 – ✉ Oranmore — 36 B3

Dublin 220 km – Galway 17 km

Moran's Oyster Cottage

The Weir, Northwest : 2 km by N 18 – (091) 796 113 – www.moransoystercottage.com

Rest – Seafood – Carte € 34/64

◆ Attractive whitewashed pub with golden thatch, hidden away in a tiny hamlet – a very popular place in summer. Largely cold seafood dishes, with oysters a speciality and tasty homemade bread.

KILKENNY (Cill Chainnigh) – Kilkenny – 712 K10 – pop. 22 179 — 39 C2

Ireland

Dublin 114 km – Cork 138 km – Killarney 185 km – Limerick 111 km

Shee Alms House (056) 7751500, kevin.dowling@failteireland.ie

18 Glendine, (056) 776 5400

18 Callan Geraldine, (056) 772 5136

9 Castlecomer Drumgoole, (056) 444 1139

Town★★ – St Canice's Cathedral★★ – Kilkenny Castle and Park★★ **AC** – Black Abbey★ – Rothe House★

Jerpoint Abbey★★ **AC**, S : 19.25 km by R 700 and N 9 – Kilfane Glen and Waterfall★ **AC**, S : 21 km by R 700 and N 9 – Kells Priory★, S : 12.5 km by R 697 – Dunmore Cave★ **AC**, N: 11.25 km by N 77 and N 78

Kilkenny rm, rest,

College Rd, Southwest : 1.25 km at junction with N 76 – (056) 776 20 00 – www.hotelkilkenny.ie

138 rm – € 70/100 € 120/180

Rest *Taste* – Menu € 25 – Carte € 20/36

◆ Unremarkable exterior contrasts with the thoughtfully designed and contemporary interior. Bedrooms are brightly decorated. Well-equipped leisure centre and large meeting rooms available. Italian menu served in split level dining room.

Butler House without rest

15-16 Patrick St – (056) 776 57 07 – www.butler.ie – Closed 23-29 December

12 rm – € 70/140 € 130/180 – 1 suite

◆ Substantial part Georgian house. Spacious accommodation with 1970s-style furnishings - superior bow-fronted bedrooms to the rear overlook neat, geometric lawned gardens.

Blanchville House without rest

Dunbell, Maddoxtown, Southeast : 10.5 km by N 10 turning right 0.75 km after the Pike Inn – (056) 772 71 97 – www.blanchville.ie – March-October

6 rm – € 65 € 120/130

◆ Antique-furnished former manor house with Peel Tower in garden and large, firelit drawing room. Spacious bedrooms, with homemade tea and cakes on arrival.

Fanad House without rest
Castle Rd, South : 0.75 km on R 700 – (056) 776 41 26 – www.fanadhouse.com
12 rm – € 45/70 € 100/120
◆ Modern, purpose-built, green painted house looking out towards the castle. A warm welcome and bright, well-appointed bedrooms await the visitor.

Campagne
5 The Arches – (056) 777 2858 – www.campagne.ie – Closed 2 weeks January, Sunday dinner and Monday
Rest – *(dinner only and lunch Friday, Saturday and Sunday) (booking advisable)* Menu € 29 **s** – Carte € 34/51 **s**
◆ Hidden close to the railway arches, away from the city centre. Crescent shaped dining room with bright contemporary art. Modern French and Irish cooking; tasty, unfussy dishes.

Zuni with rm
26 Patrick St – (056) 772 39 99 – www.zuni.ie – Closed 25-26 December
13 rm – € 90/100 € 130
Rest – Menu € 23 (lunch)/29 (early dinner) – Carte € 36/46
◆ Chic modern design in leather and dark wood draws the smart set to this former theatre. Friendly service; bold, generous and eclectic cooking. Stylish, good-value rooms.

Ristorante Rinuccini
1 The Parade – (056) 776 15 75 – www.rinuccini.com – Closed 25-26 December
Rest – Italian – Carte € 20/52
◆ This family owned restaurant is bigger than it looks and has long been a local favourite. They come for the classic Italian cooking and thoughtful service. It's named after the 17C papal nuncio.

KILLALOE (Cill Dalua) – Clare – 712 G9 – pop. 1 035 Ireland 38 B2

Dublin 175 km – Ennis 51 km – Limerick 21 km – Tullamore 93 km
The Bridge (061) 376866, (May- Sept) tourisminfo@shannon-dev.ie
Town★ – St Flannan's Cathedral★
Graves of the Leinstermen (★), N : 7.25 km by R 494 – Castleconnell★, S : 16 km by R 494 and R 466 – Clare Glens★, S : 24 km by R 494, R 504 and R 503. Nenagh (Castle★), NE : 19.25 km by R 496 and N 7 – Holy Island★ **AC**, N : 25.75 km by R 463 and boat from Tuamgraney

Cherry Tree
Lakeside, Ballina, following signs for Lakeside H. – (061) 375 688 – www.cherrytreerestaurant.ie – Closed 1-10 January, 25-26 December, Sunday dinner, and Sunday lunch October-May
Rest – *(dinner only and Sunday lunch)* Menu € 29 (Sunday lunch)/39 (dinner) – Carte € 40/45
◆ Contemporary, relaxing interior, polite staff and a wide range of original, well-sourced modern Irish dishes on offer from an open kitchen. Seasonal produce of the essence.

KILLARNEY (Cill Airne) – Kerry – 712 D11 – pop. 14 603 Ireland 38 A2

Dublin 304 km – Cork 87 km – Limerick 111 km – Waterford 180 km
Kerry (Farranfore) Airport : (066) 976 4644, N : 15.25 km by N 22
Beech Rd (064) 663 1633, killarneytio@failteireland.ie
Mahoney's Point, (064) 31 034
Town★★ – St Mary's Cathedral★ CX
Killarney National Park★★★ (Muckross Friary★, Muckross House and Farms★) AZ - Gap of Dunloe★★, SW : 9.5 km by R 562 AZ – Ross Castle★ **AC**, S : 1.5 km by N 71 and minor rd – Torc Waterfall★, S : 8 km by N 71 BZ. Ring of Kerry★★ – Ladies View★★, SW : 19.25 km by N 71 BZ – Moll's Gap★, SW : 25 km by N 71 BZ

Plans pages 902, 903

REPUBLIC OF IRELAND

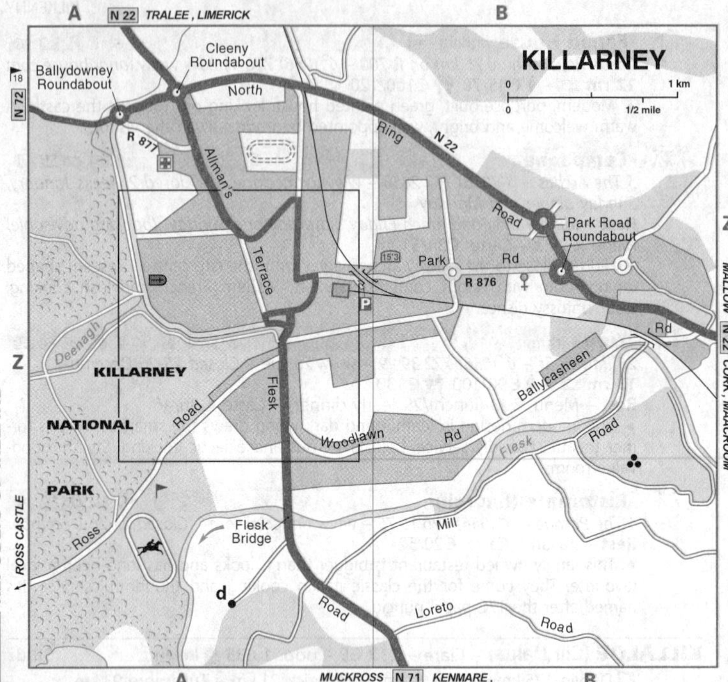

REPUBLIC OF IRELAND

Killarney Park

– ✆ (064) 663 55 55 – www.killarneyparkhotel.ie
– *Closed 24-26 December* **DXk**
65 rm – € 250/350 € 250/350 – 3 suites
Rest *Park* – *(dinner only bar lunch)* Menu € 55 – Carte € 43/56
◆ Smart modern hotel. Firelit library, panelled billiard room and the bedrooms' décor and fine details balance old-world styling and contemporary convenience. Armchair dining beneath sparkling chandeliers and Corinthian capitals.

Aghadoe Heights H. and Spa

Northwest : 4.5 km by N 22 – ✆ (064) 663 17 66
– www.aghadoeheights.com – restricted opening in winter
72 rm – € 300/420 € 250/370 – 2 suites
Rest *Lake Room* – see restaurant listing
◆ Striking glass-fronted hotel: stylish bar, modern health and fitness centre and contemporary rooms, many with sumptuous sofas. Balconied front rooms offer views of the lough.

Europe

Fossa, West : 4.75 km by R 562 on N 72 – ✆ (064) 667 13 00
– www.theeurope.com – 18 March-October
138 rm – € 190/275 € 220/290 – 49 suites – € 460/1500
Rest *Panorama* – *(Closed Sunday)* Carte € 41/59
Rest *Brasserie* – Carte € 30/51
◆ An immense hotel boasting opulently furnished public areas, state-of-the-art meeting facilities and a sublime spa over 3 floors. Traditional décor in bedrooms. Superb views over Lough Leane and Macgillycuddy's Reeks. Refined cooking with a view in Panorama. Lighter dishes in The Brasserie.

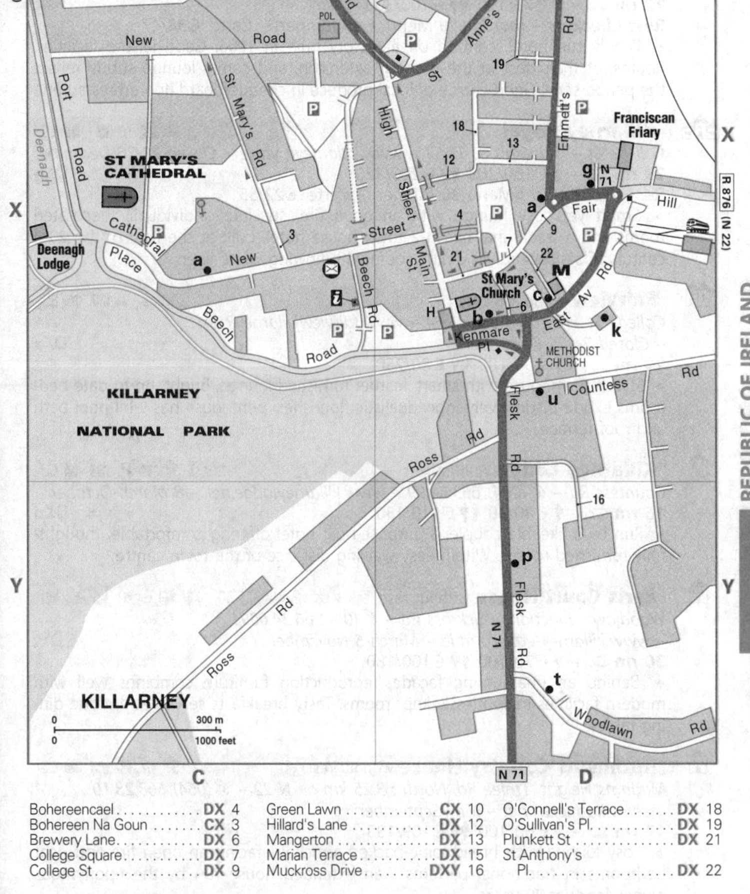

Ross

– ✆ (064) 663 18 55 – www.theross.ie – Closed 24-27 December DX**b**

29 rm – † € 160/220 †† € 160/220

Rest – *(dinner only bar lunch)* Menu € 45 – Carte € 30/50

◆ Boutique hotel boasting extreme comfort and style, with trendy pink bar, friendly staff and quality bedrooms with enormous beds; the best at the front overlooking the street. Ultra modern pink and lime green restaurant - accessed down winding metal staircase - serves modern international food to match.

Cahernane House

Muckross Rd – ✆ *(064) 663 18 95* – *www.cahernane.com* – *Closed December-16 March*

37 rm – † € 95/145 †† € 150 – 1 suite AZ**d**

Rest *The Herbert Room* – *(closed Sunday) (bar lunch)* Menu € 15 (lunch)/37 – Carte € 38/49

◆ Peacefully located 19C house with pleasant mountain outlook. Array of lounges in sympathetic style. Rooms in main house or modern wing: all are large, comfy and well equipped. Restaurant offers formal dining with inspiring views.

Randles Court rest,

Muckross Rd – (064) 663 53 33 – www.randlescourt.com – Closed 3 days Christmas DYp

72 rm – € 79/190 € 100/300

Rest *Checkers* – *(bar lunch)* Menu € 45 (dinner) – Carte € 38/47

◆ Family run hotel, centred on a rectory built in 1906. Good leisure facilities. Rooms, at their best in the modern extension, and comfy lounge subtly reflect the period style. Good choice of local produce in chequerboard floored restaurant.

Killarney Royal

College St – (064) 663 18 53 – www.killarneyroyal.ie – Closed 25-26 December

29 rm – € 160/205 € 240/320 DXg

Rest – *(bar lunch)* Menu 30 (dinner) – Carte € 22/35

◆ Smart yet cosy lounge with an open fire, spacious, individually decorated rooms and a traditional bar in a town house hotel, built at the turn of the 20th century. Classic, candlelit dining room with flowing white linen.

Fairview without rest

College St – (064) 663 41 64 – www.fairviewkillarney.com – Closed 24-25 December DXa

29 rm – € 55/180 € 80/250

◆ Stylish townhouse with smart, leather furnished lounge. Bright, up-to-date bedrooms exude distinctively individualistic flourishes; penthouse has whirlpool bath and roof terrace.

Killarney Lodge without rest

Countess Rd – (064) 663 64 99 – www.killarneylodge.net – 8 March-October

16 rm – € 80/90 € 110/130 DXu

◆ Run by a likeable couple, a purpose-built hotel offering comfortable, thoughtfully furnished rooms. Within easy walking distance of the town centre.

Earls Court House without rest

Woodlawn Junction, Muckross Rd – (064) 66 34 009 – www.killarney-earlscourt.ie – March-6 November DYt

30 rm – € 70/100 € 100/180

◆ Behind an unassuming façade, reproduction furniture combines well with modern facilities in spotlessly kept rooms. Tasty breakfasts served at antique dining tables.

Kathleens Country House without rest

Madams Height, Tralee Rd, North : 3.25 km on N 22 – (064) 663 28 10 – www.kathleens.net – May-September

17 rm – € 60/100 € 109/135

◆ Cosy lounge with broad, pine-backed armchairs facing an open fire and neat bedrooms in traditional patterns - an extended house run by the eponymous owner for over 20 years.

XXX **Lake Room** – Aghadoe Heights H. and Spa

Northwest : 4.5 km by N 22 – (064) 663 17 66 – www.aghadoeheights.com – restricted opening in winter

Rest – *(bar lunch Monday-Saturday)* Menu € 45 – Carte € 35/57

◆ Luxurious dining room with commanding countryside views. Classic, technically skilled cooking makes good use of seasonal, regional ingredients. Effective, professional service.

XX **Chapter Forty**

40 New St – (064) 66 71 833 – www.chapter40.ie – Closed Sunday and Monday CXa

Rest – *(dinner only)* Menu € 35 – Carte € 34/49

◆ Smart restaurant in contemporary browns and creams with small bar area and window looking into kitchen. Large menu includes some eclectic combinations. Great soda bread.

REPUBLIC OF IRELAND

XX **Cucina Italiana**

17 St Anthonys Pl – ✆ (064) 662 65 75 – Closed 7 January-7 February, and Tuesday in winter DXc

Rest – Italian – *(dinner only)* Menu € 29 (early dinner) – Carte € 42/57

◆ Stylish, modern restaurant set over three floors, in centre of town. Fresh, authentic Italian cooking; hearty, with a strong Neapolitan feel. Effective service from smart Italian staff.

at Beaufort **West : 9.75 km by R 562 - AZ - off N 72 – ✉ Killarney**

Dunloe Castle

Southeast : 1.5 km on Dunloe Golf Course rd – ✆ (064) 664 41 11 – www.thedunloe.com – April-October

100 rm – 🛉 € 170/250 🛉🛉 € 210/290 – 2 suites

Rest – *(light lunch)* Carte € 26/61 **s**

◆ Creeper-clad modern hotel offers sizeable, well-equipped rooms and smart conference suites, not forgetting an impressive view of the Gap of Dunloe and Macgilllicuddy's Reeks. Restaurant serves Irish classic dishes.

KILLENARD – Laois 39 C-D1

Dublin 48 km – Portlaoise 19 km – Naas 25 km – Carlow 36 km

Heritage

– ✆ (057) 864 55 00 – www.theheritage.com – Closed 24-27 December

94 rm – 🛉 € 160/325 🛉🛉 € 160/325 – 25 suites

Rest *Arlington* – *(closed December) (dinner only)* Menu € 40 – Carte € 36/47 **s**

Rest *Greens* – Carte € 21/33 **s**

Rest *Sol Oriens* – *(closed Monday-Tuesday) (dinner only)* Carte € 22/30 **s**

◆ Stunning hotel surrounded by extensive gardens and golf course. State-of-the-art meeting facilities and superb spa. Capacious, elegant bedrooms offer supreme comforts. Formal dining in The Arlington. More of a brasserie feel to Greens, in the leisure centre. Pizza, pasta, salad and steaks in informal Sol Oriens.

KILLORGLIN (Cill Orglan) – Kerry – 712 C11 – pop. 1 627 Ireland 38 A2

Dublin 333 km – Killarney 19 km – Tralee 26 km

Killorglin Stealroe, ✆ (669) 761 979

Lough Caragh★, SW : 9 km by N 70 and minor road S. Ring of Kerry★★

Grove Lodge without rest

Killarney Rd, East : 0.75 km on N 72 – ✆ (066) 976 11 57 – www.grovelodge.com – Closed 20-31 December

10 rm – 🛉 € 50/80 🛉🛉 € 90/110

◆ Comfortable, well-fitted rooms - one with four-poster bed and private patio - in a smoothly run riverside house. Try smoked salmon and eggs or a full Irish breakfast.

KILMALLOCK (Cill Mocheallóg) – Limerick – 712 G10 – pop. 1 443 38 B2

Ireland

Dublin 212 km – Limerick 34 km – Tipperary 32 km

Abbey★ - Collegiate Church★

Lough Gur Interpretive Centre★ **AC**, N : 16 km by R 512 and minor road – Monasteranenagh Abbey★, N : 24 km by R 512 to Holycross and minor road W

Flemingstown House

Southeast : 4 km on R 512 – ✆ (063) 98 093 – www.flemingstown.com – March-October

5 rm – 🛉 € 60 🛉🛉 € 100/120 **Rest** – Carte € 30/45

◆ Creeper clad, extended 19C house in centre of 200 acre working farm. The attractively decorated bedrooms boast countryside vistas and pieces of antique furniture. Satisfying homemade fare served in comfy dining room.

REPUBLIC OF IRELAND

KINLOUGH (Cionn Locha) – Leitrim – 712 H4 – pop. 690 37 C2

Dublin 220 km – Ballyshannon 11 km – Sligo 34 km

Courthouse with rm

Main St. – (071) 984 23 91 – www.thecourthouserest.com – Closed 1 week spring, 1 week autumn, Tuesday, 3 days Christmas and Monday-Wednesday October-February

4 rm – € 35/45 € 70/75

Rest – Italian – *(dinner only and Sunday lunch)* Menu € 28 – Carte € 28/43

◆ Former courthouse with stained glass entrance. Sardinian chef-owner creates extensive, seasonally changing classical menu of honest, authentic Italian dishes – including local fish/shellfish. Informal atmosphere; friendly service. Simple, good value bedrooms.

KINSALE (Cionne tSáile) – Cork – 712 G12 – pop. 4 099 Ireland 38 B3

Dublin 286 km – Cork 27 km

Pier Rd (021) 4772234, kinsaletio@eircom.net

Town★★ – St Multose Church★ Y – Kinsale Regional Museum★ **AC** Y **M1**

Kinsale Harbour★ (<★ from St Catherine's Anglican Church, Charles Fort★). Carbery Coast★, W : 61 km by R 600

Perryville House without rest

Long Quay – (021) 477 27 31 – www.perryvillehouse.com – 16 April-October

18 rm – € 99/140 € 200/300 Y**f**

◆ Delightful Georgian house on the shores of the bay. Antiques, open fires and period charm throughout; lovely sitting room. Bedrooms are spacious and stylish. Service is keen and friendly.

Blue Haven

AC rest,

3 Pearse St – (021) 477 22 09 – www.bluehavencollection.com Y**c**

17 rm – € 65/140 € 110/160

Rest *Blu* – Menu € 28 (lunch)/40 – Carte € 25/47

Rest *Blue Haven* – *(carvery)* Carte € 19/33

◆ Well established hotel in centre of town boasts refurbished public areas and floral bedrooms of varying size, named after wine estates; the largest at the front. Blu serves a traditional British menu. Wood panelled Blue Haven looks like the interior of a yacht, and has small terrace.

Old Bank House without rest

11 Pearse St – (021) 477 40 75 – www.oldbankhousekinsale.com – Closed 24-25 December Y**d**

17 rm – € 65/110 € 80/195

◆ Personally and enthusiastically run town house: cosy lounge and comfortable, neatly kept accommodation - bedrooms above the post office are slightly larger.

The Old Presbytery without rest

43 Cork St – (021) 477 20 27 – www.oldpres.com – mid February-mid November Y**a**

9 rm – € 90/170 € 130/180

◆ Tucked away down a side street, a Georgian house run by a husband and wife team. Comfortable, thoughtfully furnished bedrooms in old Irish pine.

Desmond House without rest

42 Cork St – (021) 477 35 35 – www.desmondhousekinsale.com – May-October

4 rm – € 70/110 € 100/140 Y**x**

◆ Small guest house with comfortable lounge and breakfast room. Traditional bedrooms have period furniture and jacuzzi baths and are named after castles. Friendly owners.

Max's

AC

48 Main St – (021) 477 24 43 – www.kinsalerestaurants.com – Closed mid December-March, restricted opening in winter Z**m**

Rest – Carte € 32/54

◆ Unadorned yet intimate restaurant: try light lunches, early evening menu or full à la carte menu. Keenly devised wine list. Friendly service.

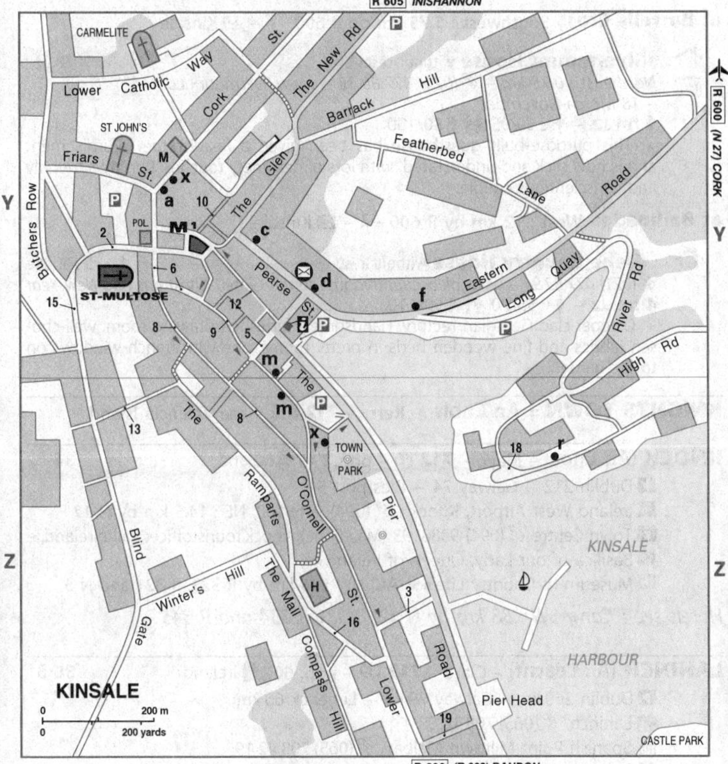

Church St. . . . . **Y** 2
Denis Quay . . . . **Z** 3
Emmet St . . . . **Y** 5
Guardwell . . . . **Y** 6
Higher O'Connel St . . . . **YZ** 8
Main St . . . . **Y** 9
Market Pl. . . . . **Y** 10
Market Quay . . . . **Y** 12
Ramparts Lane . . . . **Z** 13
Rose Abbey . . . . **Y** 15
St John's Hill . . . . **Z** 16
Seilly Walk . . . . **Z** 18
World's End . . . . **Z** 19

Fishy Fishy Cafe

Pier Rd – (021) 470 04 15 – www.fishyfishy.ie – Closed dinner Sunday-Thursday in winter and Sunday dinner Z**x**

Rest – Seafood – *(bookings not accepted)* Carte € 32/43

◆ Friendly, informal and busy: arrive early, be prepared to queue (or the original little 'Fishy' is a 5 minute walk). Good-value seafood, with daily catch on view in display fridges.

Thai Cottage

6 Main Street – (021) 477 7775 – www.thaicottage.ie – Closed mid January-March and Tuesday Y**m**

Rest – Carte approx. € 30

◆ Simply decorated restaurant with ornately stencilled dark wood and many a carved Buddha. Smartly attired, graceful staff. Very tasty, authentic Thai food; fresh, with vibrant flavours.

Bulman

Summercove, East : 2 km by R 600 – (021) 477 21 31 – www.thebulman.com – Closed 25 December, Monday and Good Friday

Rest – Carte € 22/29 **s**

◆ Rustic pub with nautical theme and view of Kinsale and the bay. Daily changing menu focuses on local seafood; lunch served in the bar, dinner in the more formal first floor restaurant.

at Barrells Cross Southwest : 5.75 km on R 600 - Z – ✉ Kinsale

Rivermount House without rest

Northeast : 0.75 km – ✆ (021) 477 80 33 – www.rivermount.com – 18 March-November

6 rm – € 50/95 € 80/100

◆ This purpose-built guesthouse has been given a head-to-toe refurbishment and is now slick and understated, with lots of designery touches. Run by a friendly and conscientious couple.

at Ballinadee West : 12 km by R 600 - Z – ✉ Kinsale

Glebe Country House without rest

✆ (021) 477 82 94 – www.glebecountryhouse.com – Closed Christmas and New Year

4 rm – € 55/70 € 90/110

◆ Creeper-clad Georgian rectory. Handsomely furnished drawing room; well-chosen fabrics and fine wooden beds in pretty rooms, one with french windows on to the garden.

KNIGHTS TOWN = An Chois – Kerry – 712 B12 – see Valencia Island

KNOCK (An Cnoc) – Mayo – 712 F6 – pop. 745 Ireland 36 B2

Dublin 212 – Galway 74 – Westport 51

Ireland West Airport, Knock : ✆ (094) 9368100, NE : 14.5 km by N 17

Town Centre ✆ (094) 9388193 (May-Sept.), knock.touristoffice@failteireland.ie

Basilica of our Lady, Queen of Ireland★

Museum of Country Life★★ **AC**, NW : 26 km by R 323, R 321 and N 5

*Hotels see : **Cong** SW : 58 km by N 17, R 331 R 334 and R 345*

LAHINCH (An Leacht) – Clare – 712 D9 – pop. 607 Ireland 38 B1

Dublin 260 km – Galway 79 km – Limerick 66 km

Lahinch, ✆ (065) 708 10 03

Spanish Point Miltown Malbay, ✆ (065) 708 42 19

Cliffs of Moher★★★ – Kilfenora (Burren Centre★ **AC**, High Crosses★), NE : 11 km by N 85 and R 481

Vaughan Lodge

Ennistymon Rd – ✆ (065) 708 11 11 – www.vaughanlodge.ie – Open April to October

22 rm – € 120/160 € 140/220

Rest – *(closed Sunday and Monday) (dinner only)* Carte € 41/64

◆ Stylish roadside hotel. Bright, modern interior boasts a leather-furnished lounge with flat screen TV and plenty of malts behind the bar. Smart, spacious bedrooms – in browns and creams – offer good facilities. Linen-laid dining room serves seafood-based menus.

Moy House

Southwest : 3 km on N 67 (Milltown Malbay rd) – ✆ (065) 708 28 00 – www.moyhouse.com – Closed January- mid February

8 rm – € 145/255 € 240/280, 1 suite **Rest** – *(dinner only)* Menu € 55

◆ Italian-style clifftop villa, overlooking the bay. Traditional interior with a comfy drawing room, honesty bar and small library; antiques, oil paintings and heavy fabrics/drapes feature. Individually designed, classically styled bedrooms boast good extras; most have views. Friendly, attentive service. Formal dining.

LEENANE (An Líonán) – Galway – 712 C7 – ✉ Clifden Ireland 36 A3

Dublin 278 km – Ballina 90 km – Galway 66 km

Killary Harbour★

Joyce Country★★ – Lough Nafooey★, SE : 10.5 km by R 336 – Aasleagh Falls★, NE : 4 km. Connemara★★★ – Lough Corrib★★, SE : 16 km by R 336 and R 345 – Doo Lough Pass★, NW : 14.5 km by N 59 and R 335

Delphi Lodge

Northwest : 13.25 km by N 59 on Louisburgh rd – (095) 42 222 – www.delphilodge.ie – Closed mid October-mid March
12 rm – € 132 € 198 **Rest** – Menu € 20 (lunch)/49
◆ Georgian sporting lodge in a stunning loughside setting with extensive gardens and grounds. Haven for fishermen. Country house feel and simple bedrooms. Communal dining table: fisherman with the day's best catch sits at its head.

LEIGHLINBRIDGE (Leithghlinn an Droichid) Carlow – Carlow – 712 L9 – pop. 674 39 D2

Dublin 63 km – Carlow 8 km – Kilkenny 16 km – Athy 22 km

Lord Bagenal

Main St – (059) 977 40 00 – www.lordbagenal.com – Closed 25-26 December
39 rm – € 75/85 € 110/130 **Rest** – *(carving lunch)* Menu € 35
◆ Impressive hotel on banks of River Barrow; originally a coaching inn, now with vast new extension. Characterful bar with excellent collection of Irish art. Spacious bedrooms. Traditional menus in Lord Bagenal bar and restaurant.

LETTERFRACK (Leitir Fraic) – Galway – 712 C7 Ireland 36 A3

Dublin 304 km – Ballina 111 km – Galway 91 km
Connemara★★★ - Sky Road★★ (≤★★) – Connemara National Park★ – Kylemore Abbey★, E : 4.75 km by N 59

Rosleague Manor

West : 2.5 km. on N 59 – (095) 41 101 – www.rosleague.com – mid March-mid November
20 rm – € 85/130 € 160/210
Rest – *(dinner only)* Menu € 40 (dinner) **s** – Carte € 32/40 **s**
◆ Foliage-clad country house in mature grounds, boasting excellent bay and mountain views. Spacious, antique-filled drawing rooms and wicker-furnished conservatory. Large, classically styled bedrooms with flat screen TVs. Formal dining room overlooks the gardens.

LETTERKENNY (Leitir Ceanainn) – Donegal – 712 I3 – pop. 17 586 37 C1

Dublin 241 km – Londonderry 34 km – Sligo 116 km
Neil T Blaney Rd (074) 9121160, letterkenny@failteireland.ie
Dunfanaghy, (074) 913 6335
Glenveagh National Park★★ (Gardens★★), NW : 19.25 km by R 250, R 251 and R 254 – Grianan of Aileach★★ (≤★★) NE : 28 km by N 13 – Church Hill (Glebe House and Gallery★ **AC**) NW : 16 km by R 250

Radisson Blu

rest,
Paddy Harte Rd – (074) 919 44 44 – www.radissonblu.ie/letterkenny
114 rm – € 90/135 € 115/253
Rest – *(early dinner and Sunday lunch)* Menu € 20 **s** – Carte € 25/36 **s**
◆ Corporate accommodation on edge of town. Bar serves a daily changing menu; rooms are identically appointed: all are clean, modern and spacious. Business Class has extras. Dinner in restaurant offers modern international choice.

LIMERICK (Luimneach) – Limerick – 712 G9 – pop. 90 757 Ireland 38 B2

Dublin 193 km – Cork 93 km
Shannon Airport : (061) 712000, W : 25.75 km by N 18 Z
Arthur's Quay (061) 317522 Y, limericktouristoffice@shannondev.ie
City★★ - St Mary's Cathedral★ Y – Hunt Museum★★ **AC** Y - Georgian House★ **AC** Z – King John's Castle★ **AC** Y - Limerick Museum★ Z **M2** – John Square★ Z **20** – St John's Cathedral★ Z
Bunratty Castle★★ **AC**, W : 12 km by N 18 – Cratloe Wood (≤★) NW : 8 km by N 18 Z. Castleconnell★, E : 11.25 km by N 7 - Lough Gur Interpretive Centre★ **AC**, S : 17.75 km by R 512 and R 514 Z – Clare Glens★, E : 21 km by N 7 and R 503 Y – Monasteranenagh Abbey★, S : 21 km by N 20 Z

Plan on next page

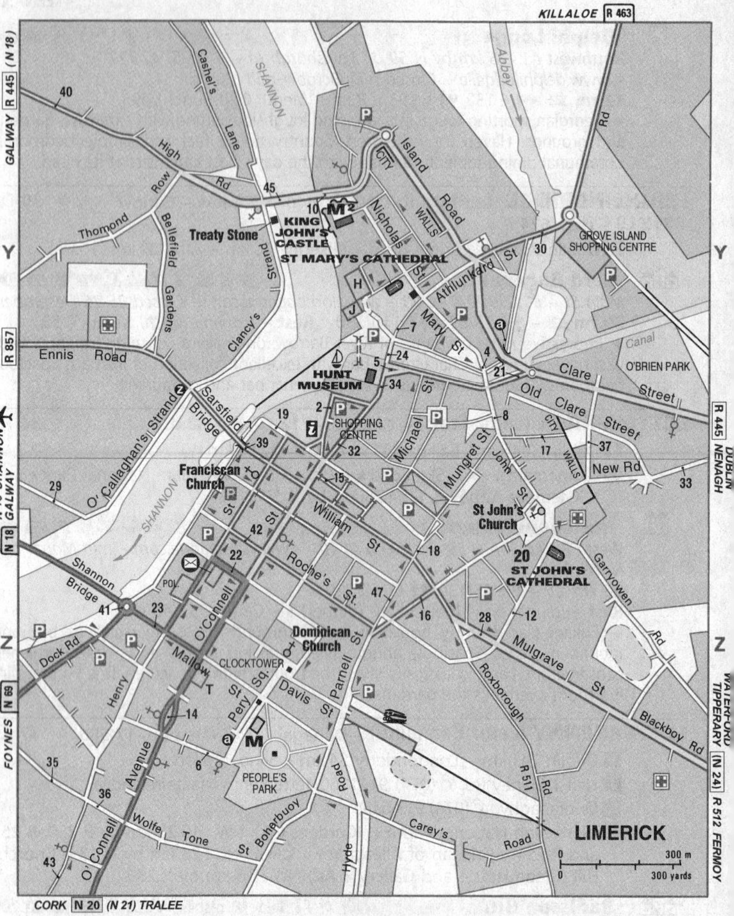

Arthur Quay . . . . Y 2
Arthur Quay Shopping Centre . . . . Y
Baal's Bridge . . . . Y 4
Bank Pl. . . . . Y 5
Barrington St . . . . Z 6
Bridge St . . . . Y 7
Broad St. . . . . Y 8
Castle St . . . . Y 10
Cathedral Pl. . . . . Z 12
Charlotte's Quay . . . . Y 13
Cruises St. . . . . Z 15
Gerald Griffen St . . . . Z 16
Grattan St. . . . . Y 17
Grove Island Shopping Centre . . . . Y
High St . . . . Z 18
Honan's Quay . . . . Y 19
John Square. . . . . Z 20
Lock Quay . . . . Y 21
Lower Cecil St . . . . Z 22
Lower Mallow St. . . . . Z 23
Mathew Bridge . . . . Y 24
Newtown Mahon . . . . Z 28
North Circular Rd . . . . Z 29
O'Connell St . . . . Z
O'Dwyer Bridge . . . . Y 30
Patrick St . . . . YZ 32
Penniwell Rd . . . . Z 33
Roches St . . . . Z
Rutland St . . . . Y 34
St Alphonsus St. . . . . Z 35
St Gerard St . . . . Z 36
St Lelia St . . . . YZ 37
Sarfield St . . . . Y 39
Sexton St North. . . . . Y 40
Shannonside Roundabout . . . . Z 41
Shannon St . . . . Z 42
South Circular Rd. . . . . Z 43
The Crescent. . . . . Z 14
Thomond Bridge . . . . Y 45
Wickham St . . . . Z 47
William St. . . . . Z

Limerick Strand

Ennis Rd. – ✆ (061) 421 800 – www.strandlimerick.ie – Closed 25 December
184 rm – 🚹 € 189 🚹🚹 € 189/229, ☕ €10 Yz
Rest *River Restaurant* – *(bar lunch)* Menu € 27 **s**

◆ Extensive function and leisure facilities. Modern bedrooms come in dark wood and autumnal browns and oranges; Junior suites have balconies. Terrace bar overlooks River Shannon. River Restaurant serves mix of traditional and more modern dishes.

Absolute H. & Spa

Sir Harry's Mall – (061) 463 600 – www.absolutehotel.com Ya

99 rm – € 149/199 € 159/209

Rest – Menu € 25 (dinner) – Carte € 23/40

♦ Stylish, modern hotel and spa on outskirts of city centre; designed like an old mill to reflect the area's industrial heritage. Clever use of space in light-coloured bedrooms. Restaurant serves traditional menu and overlooks river.

Radisson Blu H. & Spa rest,

Ennis Rd, Northwest : 6.5 km on N 18 – (061) 456 200 – www.radissonblu.ie/hotel-limerick

152 rm – € 109/159 € 109/159 – 2 suites

Rest ***Porters*** – (061) 456 524 – Menu € 21 (lunch)/35 **s** – Carte € 27/44 **s**

♦ Modern hotel with tastefully used chrome and wood interiors. Well-equipped conference rooms and a leisure centre which includes tennis court. Smart, state-of-the-art bedrooms. Informal Porters restaurant with traditional menus.

No 1 Pery Square

Pery Sq – (061) 402 402 – www.oneperysquare.com – Closed dinner 24 December and 25-28 December Za

19 rm – € 109/135 € 145/165 – 1 suite

Rest ***Brasserie One*** – see restaurant listing

♦ Charming, personally run house in the historic Georgian quarter of the city. Beautiful spa facility and wine shop in cellar. Well-proportioned, luxuriously appointed bedrooms.

Brasserie One – at No 1 Pery Square Hotel

Pery Sq – (061) 402 402 – www.oneperysquare.com – Closed dinner 24 December and 25-27 December Za

Rest – *(Closed Monday)* Menu € 25 (lunch)/30 (weekday dinner) – Carte € 25/48

♦ Set on first floor of hotel, with well-spaced tables, Georgian-style furniture and semi-open kitchen. Tasty bistro dishes with a modern slant. Good service from a well-versed team.

LISCANNOR (Lios Ceannúir) – Clare – 712 D9 – pop. 71 Ireland 38 B1

Dublin 272 km – Ennistimmon 9 km – Limerick 72 km

Cliffs of Moher★★★, NW : 8 km by R 478 – Kilfenora (Burren Centre★ **AC**, High Crosses★), NE : 18 km by R 478, N 67 and R 481

Vaughan's Anchor Inn with rm

Main St – (065) 708 1548 – www.vaughans.ie – Closed 24-25 December

7 rm – € 50 € 70 **Rest** – Seafood – Carte € 25/40

♦ Lively, family-run pub in a picturesque fishing village near the Cliffs of Moher. Old favourites at lunch and more elaborate meals in the evening, with the emphasis firmly on seafood. Bedrooms boast bright local artwork, colourful throws and modern bathrooms.

LISDOONVARNA (Lios Dúin Bhearna) – Clare – 712 E8 – pop. 767 38 B1

Ireland

Dublin 268 km – Galway 63 km – Limerick 75 km

The Burren★★ (Cliffs of Moher★★★, Scenic Route★★, Aillwee Cave★ **AC** (Waterfall★★), Corcomroe Abbey★, Kilfenora Crosses★)

Sheedy's Country House rm,

– (065) 707 40 26 – www.sheedys.com – Easter-October

11 rm – € 85/110 € 130/190

Rest – *(dinner only) (booking essential for non-residents)* Menu € 28 (dinner) – Carte approx. € 50

♦ Mustard-yellow house in village centre, with kitchen garden in front. Comfy library, wicker-furnished sun lounge and traditional bar. Bedrooms display plain décor with flowery fabrics and good facilities. Classical menu offered in dining room; exacting service.

REPUBLIC OF IRELAND

Wild Honey Inn with rm

South : 0.5 km on Ennistimon rd – ✆ (065) 707 43 00 – www.wildhoneyinn.com – Closed January-12 February and restricted opening November, December, late February and March

14 rm – **†** € 55/65 **††** € 80/90

Rest – *(bookings not accepted)* Carte € 24/38

♦ Characterful inn close to The Burren and the Cliffs of Moher. Short, simple lunch menu; wider selection of classics at dinner. Specials best display the chef's talent and are truly satisfying. Neatly kept, simply furnished bedrooms and comfy residents' lounge.

LISMORE (Lios Mór) – **Waterford** – **712** I11 – **pop. 1 240** **39** C2

Dublin 227 km – Cork 56 km – Fermoy 26 km

Lismore House rm,

Main St – ✆ (058) 72 966 – www.lismorehousehotel.com – Closed 3 January to 9 February

29 rm – **†** € 59/84 **††** € 99

Rest – *(bar lunch)* Menu € 25/29 – Carte € 24/37

♦ Georgian house with purpose built rear. Bedrooms boast up-to-date facilities including plasmas and playstations; several overlook the Millennium Gardens. Intimate dining room.

O'Brien Chop House

Main St – ✆ (058) 53 810 – www.obrienchophouse.ie – Closed Monday,Tuesday, and Wednesday October-March, Sunday dinner except bank holidays

Rest – Menu € 28 (lunch) – Carte € 26/40

♦ Timeless Victorian bar leads through to rustic restaurant, with bare wooden floorboards and whitewashed walls. Very appealing, value-for-money menu of wholesome Irish dishes which make excellent use of locally sourced produce. Polite, friendly service.

LISTOWEL (Lios Tuathail) – **Kerry** – **712** D10 – **pop. 4 338** Ireland **38** B2

Dublin 270 km – Killarney 54 km – Limerick 75 km – Tralee 27 km

St John's Church ✆ (068) 22590 (June-September), listoweltio@failteireland.ie

Ardfert★ **AC**, SW : 32 km by N 69 and minor roads via Abbeydorney – Banna Strand★, SW : 35 km by N 69 and minor roads via Abbeydorney – Carrigafoyle Castle★, N : 17 km by R 552 and minor road – Glin Castle★ **AC**, N : 24 km by N 69 – Rattoo Round Tower★, W : 19 km by R 553, R 554 and R 551

Allo's Bar with rm

41 Church St – ✆ (068) 22 880 – Closed 1 January, Sunday, Monday and bank holidays

3 rm – **†** € 60/80 **††** € 80/100 **Rest** – *(booking essential)* Carte € 25/50

♦ Colourful pub in the heart of town, with characterful old-world décor and laid-back feel. Locals gather in the bar; smarter dining room next door. Rustic home cooking with tasty puddings. Each bedroom has its own floor and boasts a four-poster or sleigh bed.

LONGFORD (An Longfort) – **Longford** – **712** I6 – **pop. 8 836** **37** C3

Dublin 124 km – Drogheda 120 km – Galway 112 km – Limerick 175 km

Market Square ✆ (043) 42577, info@longfordtourism.com

Viewmount House

Dublin Rd, Southeast : 1.5 km by R 393 – ✆ (043) 334 19 19 – www.viewmounthouse.com

15 rm – **†** € 50/70 **††** € 100/140 – 5 suites

Rest *VM* – *(Closed 25 December, 22 April, Monday, Tuesday and Sunday dinner) (dinner only and Sunday lunch)* Menu € 31 (lunch)/53

♦ Impressive Georgian house in four acres; breakfast room has ornate vaulted ceiling, lounge is reached by fine staircase. Rooms boast antique beds and period furniture. Formal VM restaurant in converted stable block offers à la carte menu of modern dishes.

REPUBLIC OF IRELAND

MALAHIDE (Mullach Íde) – Fingal – 712 N7 – pop. 14 937 Ireland 39 D1

Dublin 14 km – Drogheda 38 km

Beechwood The Grange, ✆ (01) 846 1611

Castle★★

Newbridge House★ AC, N : 8 km by R 106, M1 and minor road

XXX Bon Appétit (Oliver Dunne)

✿ *9 St James Terr, (1st floor) – ✆ (01) 845 0314 – www.bonappetit.ie – Closed first 2 weeks January, first 2 weeks August, Sunday and Monday*

Rest – French – *(dinner only and Friday lunch) (booking essential)* Menu € 60

Spec. Seared foie gras with caramelised pineapple, pickled artichoke and feta cheese sorbet. Fillet of skate, brandade bonbons, fresh peas and caviar velouté. Gariguette strawberries, mint panna cotta and mint chocolate madeleine.

◆ Set in delightful converted Georgian terrace. Sumptuous, subtly lit bar; elegant, formally set dining room with fine china and linen. Cooking uses classic combinations and has a French accent. Formal service, with good attention to detail.

XX Jaipur

5 St James Terr – ✆ (01) 845 5455 – www.jaipur.ie – Closed 25-26 December

Rest – Indian – *(dinner only)* Menu € 18 (early dinner) – Carte € 27/52

◆ Basement restaurant in terraced Georgian parade. Tasty, contemporary Indian cooking with Tandoori Jhinga (large prawns marinated in Indian spices) a speciality. Friendly, efficient service.

XX Brasserie at Bon Appétit

9 St James Terr., (basement) – ✆ (01) 845 0314 – www.bonappetit.ie – Closed Monday

Rest – *(dinner only and Sunday lunch) (booking essential)* Menu € 30 – Carte € 33/47

◆ In basement of Georgian terraced house – a popular alternative to the more formal 'Bon Appétit' upstairs – serving classical brasserie dishes such as moules or steak frites.

REPUBLIC OF IRELAND

MALLOW (Mala) – Cork – 712 F11 – pop. 10 241 Ireland 38 B2

Dublin 240 km – Cork 34 km – Killarney 64 km – Limerick 66 km

Ballyellis, ✆ (022) 21 145

Town★ – St James' Church★

Annes Grove Gardens★, E : 17.75 km by N 72 and minor rd – Buttevant Friary★, N : 11.25 km by N 20 – Doneraile Wildlife Park★ AC, NE : 9.5 km by N 20 and R 581 – Kanturk★ (Castle★), W : 16 km by N 72 and R 576

Longueville House

West : 5.5 km by N 72 – ✆ (022) 47 156 – www.longuevillehouse.ie

20 rm – € 75/140 € 160/180

Rest *Presidents* – *(closed Monday and Tuesday) (dinner only and Sunday lunch) (booking essential)* Menu € 45 – Carte € 44/51

◆ Part Georgian manor; exudes history from oak trees planted in formation of battle lines at Waterloo and views of Dromineen Castle to richly ornate, antique-filled bedrooms. Restaurant offers gourmet cuisine.

MIDLETON (Mainistir na Corann) – Cork – 712 H12 – pop. 3 266 39 C3

Dublin 259 km – Cork 19 km – Waterford 98 km

Jameson Heritage Centre ✆ (021) 4613702

East Cork Gortacrue, ✆ (021) 463 16 87

Cloyne Cathedral★ AC, S : 8 km by R 630 and R 629

X Farmgate Restaurant and Country Store

Midleton – ✆ (021) 463 2771 – www.farmgate.ie – Closed 24 December-3 January, Sunday and bank holidays

Rest – Carte € 29/51

◆ Busy and appealingly rustic, with entrance through shop and local art on display. Market-bought produce, simply cooked; perhaps an Irish stew, some tasty squid or a freshly baked tart.

MILLSTREET = Sráid an Mhuilinn – Waterford – 712 I11 – see Cappoquin

MOHILL (Maothail) – Leitrim – 712 I6 – pop. 931 37 C2

Dublin 98 km – Carrick-on-Shannon 11 km – Cavan 41 km – Castlerea 44 km

Lough Rynn Castle

East : 4 km by R 201 off Drumlish rd – ☎ (071) 963 27 00 – www.loughrynn.ie
42 rm – € 99/175 € 125/195
Rest *Sandstone* – Menu € 27/40 – Carte € 40/61
◆ 18C country house in 60 acres. Impressive interior with numerous lounges. Original features include a grand fireplace and parquet floor in the Baronial Hall. Large, well-appointed bedrooms in the house/stables. Formal dining room offers ambitious French cuisine.

MONAGHAN (Muineachán) – Monaghan – 712 L5 – pop. 6 710 37 D2

Dublin 133 km – Belfast 69 km – Drogheda 87 km – Dundalk 35 km
Clones Rd ☎ (047) 81122 (June-September), northwestinfo@failteireland.ie

at Glaslough Northeast : 9.5 km by N 12 on R 185 – ✉ Monaghan

Castle Leslie

Castle Leslie Estate – ☎ (047) 88 100 – www.castleleslie.com – Closed 21 December-5 January
20 rm – € 150/200 € 250/320 **Rest** – *(dinner only)* Menu € 65
◆ Impressive castle set in large grounds: home to 4th generation of the Leslie family. Ornate, comfortable, antique-furnished guest areas and individually styled bedrooms. Intimate, linen-laid dining room overlooking the lough; classically based menus.

The Lodge at Castle Leslie Estate

– ☎ (047) 88 100 – www.castleleslie.com – Closed 21 December-5 January
29 rm – € 150/200 € 250/320 – 1 suite
Rest *Snaffles* – *(dinner only)* Menu € 65
◆ Victorian former hunting lodge in 1000 acres with equestrian centre. Plenty of antiques and equine-themed pictures; relaxed and informal atmosphere. Stylish and contemporary bedrooms, some with balconies. Snaffles mezzanine brasserie has open kitchen and serves Mediterranean meets Irish cooking.

MULLINGAR (An Muileann gCearr) – Westmeath – 712 J/K7 – pop. 18 416 Ireland 37 C3

Dublin 79 km – Drogheda 58 km
Market Sq. ☎ (0449) 348650, eastandmidlandsinfo@failteireland.ie
Belvedere House and Gardens★ **AC**, S : 5.5 km by N 52. Fore Abbey★, NE : 27.25 km by R 394 – Multyfarnhan Franciscan Friary★, N : 12.75 km by N 4 – Tullynally★ **AC**, N : 21 km by N 4 and R 394

Mullingar Park

Dublin Rd, East : 2.5 km on Dublin Rd (N 4) – ☎ (044) 933 7500 – www.mullingarparkhotel.com – Closed 25-26 December
94 rm – € 100/160 € 150/250 – 1 suite
Rest – Menu € 24/30 **s** – Carte dinner € 33/47 **s**
◆ Large, contemporary hotel set on a business park, close to the main road to Dublin. Well-equipped, modern bedrooms in uniform style. Comprehensive leisure and spa facilities. Horseshoe bar-lounge and spacious formal dining room offering classical Irish cooking.

Marlinstown Court without rest

Dublin Rd, East : 2.5 km on Dublin Rd (N 4) – ☎ (044) 934 00 53 – www.marlinstowncourt.com – Closed 23-27 December
5 rm – € 40/45 € 70/75
◆ Clean, tidy guesthouse close to junction with N4. Modern rear extension. Light and airy pine-floored lounge and breakfast room overlooking garden. Brightly furnished bedrooms.

MULRANNY (An Mhala Raithní) – Mayo – 712 C6 36 A2

Dublin 270 km – Castlebar 35 km – Westport 29 km

Mulranny Park

on N 59 – (098) 36 000 – www.mulrannyparkhotel.ie – Closed 2 January-4 February and 6 November-31 December

40 rm – € 75/145 € 150/240 – 21 suites

Rest *Nephin* – see restaurant listing

Rest *Waterfront Bistro* – Carte € 24/35 **s**

♦ Purpose-built business oriented hotel behind 19C façade: lovely Clew Bay views. Impressive leisure and conference facilities. Airy rooms with slightly minimalist interiors. Waterfront Bistro has informal, relaxing ambience.

Nephin – at Mulranny Park Hotel

on N 59 – (098) 36 000 – www.mulrannyparkhotel.ie – Closed 2 January-4 February and 6 November-31 December

Rest – *(dinner only)* Menu € 39 **s** – Carte € 48/63 **s**

♦ Large, lively restaurant with fine southerly views. Modern, intricately presented cooking offers interesting combinations based around well sourced, quality ingredients.

NAAS (An Nás) – Kildare – 712 L/M8 – pop. 20 044 Ireland 39 D1

Dublin 30 km – Kilkenny 83 km – Tullamore 85 km

Kerdiffstown Naas, (045) 874 644

Russborough★★★ **AC**, S : 16 km by R 410 and minor road – Castletown House★★ **AC**, NE : 24 km by R 407 and R 403

Killashee House H. & Villa Spa

South : 1.5 km on R 448 (Kilcullen Rd) – (045) 879 277 – www.killasheehouse.com – Closed 24-26 December

129 rm – € 140 € 275 – 12 suites

Rest *Turners* – *(dinner only Friday-Saturday)* Menu € 35/45

Rest *Jack's* – Carte € 22/32

♦ Imposing part 1860s hunting lodge in acres of parkland. Rooms in the original house are most characterful: French antique furniture, original panelling and fireplaces. Elegant Turners overlooking garden. Informal Jack's.

Vie de Châteaux

The Harbour – (045) 888 478 – www.viedechateaux.ie – Closed 25 December-7 January, lunch Saturday and Sunday and bank holidays

Rest – *(booking essential)* Menu € 25/29 – Carte € 32/46

♦ Stylish, popular restaurant with open-plan kitchen and a brasserie feel. Concise, keenly priced menu moves with the seasons; mainly French dishes but with some Mediterranean influences.

NAVAN (An Uaimh) – Meath – 712 L7 – pop. 24 851 Ireland 37 D3

Dublin 48 km – Drogheda 26 km – Dundalk 51 km

Moor Park Mooretown, (046) 27 661

Royal Tara Bellinter, (046) 902 5244

Brú na Bóinne : Newgrange★★★ **AC**, Knowth★, E : 16 km by minor road to Donore – Bective Abbey★, S : 6.5 km by R 161 – Tara★ **AC**, S : 8 km by N 3. Kells★ (Round Tower and High Crosses★★, St Columba's House★), NW : by N 3 – Trim★ (castle★★), SW : 12.75 km by R 161

Ma Dwyers without rest

Dublin Rd, South : 1.25 km on N 3 – (046) 907 79 92

26 rm – € 40/50 € 75

♦ Surprisingly spacious detached house on the main road into town. Comfortable lounge and large breakfast room. Bright, up-to-date bedrooms, in uniform style, provide good value. Showers only.

REPUBLIC OF IRELAND

NEWMARKET-ON-FERGUS (Cora Chaitlín) – Clare – 712 F7 – pop. 1 542 Ireland 38 B2

Dublin 219 km – Ennis 13 km – Limerick 24 km

Dromoland Castle, (061) 368 444

Bunratty Castle★★ **AC**, S : 10 km by N 18 – Craggaunowen Centre★ **AC**, NE : 15 km by minor road towards Moymore – Knappogue Castle★ **AC**, NE : 12 km N 18 and minor roads via Quin – Quin Friary★ **AC**, N : 10 km by N 18 and minor road to Quin

Dromoland Castle

rm,

Northwest : 2.5 km on R 458 – (061) 368 144 – www.dromoland.ie – Closed 24-25 December

94 rm – € 238/442 € 499/878, €25 – 5 suites

Rest *Earl of Thomond* – *(dinner only)* Menu € 68

Rest *Fig Tree* – *(bar lunch)* Carte € 30/50

◆ Impressive 16C castle in 375 acres. Various antique-filled, country house lounges; comfy, classical bedrooms with heavy fabrics, iPod docks and flat screen TVs. Popular golf/leisure/wellness facilities. Formal fine dining in the restaurant. More casual meals in Fig Tree.

REPUBLIC OF IRELAND

NEWPORT (Baile Uí Fhiacháin) – Mayo – 712 D6 – pop. 590 Ireland 36 A2

Dublin 264 km – Ballina 59 km – Galway 96 km

James St, Westport (098) 25711, westport@failteireland.ie

Burrishoole Abbey★, NW : 3.25 km by N 59 – Furnace Lough★, NW : 4.75 km by N 59. Achill Island★, W : 35 km by N 59 and R 319

Newport House

– (098) 41 222 – www.newporthouse.ie – 19 March-October

16 rm – € 140/190 € 228/328

Rest – *(dinner only)* Carte € 48/58 **s**

◆ Mellow ivy-clad Georgian mansion; grand staircase up to gallery and drawing room. Bedrooms in main house or courtyard; some in self-contained units ideal for families and those with dogs. Enjoy the fresh Newport estate produce used in the dishes served in the elegant dining room.

OUGHTERARD (Uachtar Ard) – Galway – 712 E7 – pop. 1 305 Ireland 36 A3

Dublin 240 km – Galway 27 km

Main Street (091) 552808, oughterardoffice@eircom.net

Gortreevagh, (091) 552 131

Town★

Lough Corrib★★ (Shore road - NW - ★★) – Aughnanure Castle★ **AC**, SE : 3.25 km by N 59

Currarevagh House

Northwest : 6.5 km on Glann rd – (091) 552 312 – www.currarevagh.com – mid-March-mid-October

12 rm – € 70/120 € 135/170

Rest – *(dinner only) (set menu only)* Menu € 45

◆ Victorian manor on Lough Corrib, set in 180 acres. Period décor throughout plus much fishing memorabilia. Two lovely sitting rooms. Comfortable, well-kept rooms. Four course dinner menu makes good use of garden produce.

Ross Lake House

Rosscahill, Southeast : 7.25 km by N 59 – (091) 550 109 – www.rosslakehotel.com – 16 March-October

12 rm – € 105/115 € 150/170 – 1 suite

Rest – *(dinner only)* Menu € 50

◆ Personally run Georgian country house with attractive gardens, set in a wooded estate. Traditionally styled bedrooms; Strefens suite and Killaguile are the best. Begin the evening in the cocktail bar before dining by candlelight at smartly set, cloth-clad tables.

Railway Lodge without rest

West : 0.75 km by Costello rd taking first right onto unmarked road – (091) 552 945 – www.railwaylodge.net

4 rm – € 60/80 € 100/110

◆ Elegantly furnished modern guest house in remote farm location. Plenty of choice at breakfast. Open fires, books and magazines; TV only in lounge. Beautifully kept bedrooms.

Waterfall Lodge without rest

West : 0.75 km on N 59 – (091) 552 168 – www.waterfalllodge.net

6 rm – € 50 € 80

◆ Two minutes from the centre, a well-priced guesthouse rebuilt with gleaming wood and original Victorian fittings. A good fishing river flows through the charming gardens.

PARKNASILLA (Páirc na Saileach) – Kerry – 712 C12 Ireland 38 A3

Dublin 360 km – Cork 116 km – Killarney 55 km

Sneem★, NW : 4 km by N 70. Ring of Kerry★★ : Derrynane National Historic Park★★, W : 25.75 km by N 70 – Staigue Fort★, W : 21 km by N 70

Parknasilla rest,

– (064) 667 56 00 – www.parknasillahotel.ie – mid April-early January

83 rm – € 99/159 € 129/220 – 8 suites

Rest *Pigmaylion* – *(064) 45 122 (dinner only) (booking essential for non residents)* Carte € 40/50

◆ Set in 500 acres and built by the railway. Huge sums have been spent, with state-of-the-art spa and leisure facilities. Bedrooms kept fairly light; bigger ones in main house. Traditionally formal restaurant; lighter lunches in bar.

PORTLAOISE (Port Laoise) – Laois – 712 K8 – pop. 14 613 39 C2

Dublin 88 km – Carlow 40 km – Waterford 101 km

Ivyleigh House without rest

Bank Pl, Church St – (057) 862 20 81 – www.ivyleigh.com

6 rm – € 50/85 € 80/160

◆ Attractive Georgian listed house with gardens. Breakfast a feature: owner makes it all herself from fresh produce. Charming period drawing room. Airy bedrooms with antiques.

PORTMAGEE (An Caladh) – Kerry – 712 A12 – pop. 375 Ireland 38 A2

Dublin 365 km – Killarney 72 km – Tralee 82 km

Ring of Kerry★★

Moorings rest,

– (066) 947 71 08 – www.moorings.ie – Closed 24-25 December

16 rm – € 60/100 € 90/100

Rest – *(closed November-mid March and Monday except bank bolidays) (bar lunch)* Carte € 30/60

◆ Pub-style hotel in the high street of this attractive village. Spacious, nautical themed bar and trim upstairs lounge. Bedrooms with views over harbour and its fishing boats. Stone-walled, candlelit dining room with seafaring curios.

PORTMARNOCK (Port Mearnóg) – Fingal – 712 N7 – pop. 8 979 39 D1 Ireland

Dublin 8 km – Drogheda 45 km

Malahide Castle★★ **AC**, N : 4 km by R 124 – Ben of Howth★, S : 8 km by R 124 – Newbridge House★ **AC**, N : 16 km by R 124, M 1 and minor road east

REPUBLIC OF IRELAND

Portmarnock H. and Golf Links rest, rm,
Strand Rd – (01) 846 0611 – www.portmarnock.com – Closed 24-26 December
138 rm – € 79/169 € 89/179 – 3 suites
Rest *The Osborne* – *(closed Sunday and Monday) (dinner only)*
Menu € 25/38 **s** – Carte dinner € 38/43 **s**
♦ Large golf-oriented hotel with challenging 18-hole course. Original fittings embellish characterful, semi-panelled Jamesons Bar. Very comfortable, individually styled rooms. Smart brasserie with traditional menus.

RATHDRUM – Wicklow – 712 N9 – pop. 2 235 — 39 D2

Dublin 60 km – Wicklow 17 km – Drogheda 127 km

Bates
3 Market St – (0404) 29 988 – www.batesrestaurant.ie – Closed 25 December, 1 January, and Monday
Rest – *(dinner only)* Menu € 26 (weekdays) – Carte € 27/45
♦ Champions local produce, with counter selling local cheese, home-cured meats and Italian staples. Various menus offer mostly Italian dishes, with bold flavours and hearty portions.

RATHMELTON (Ráth Mealtain) – Donegal – 712 J2 – pop. 2 119 — 37 C1

Ireland

Dublin 248 km – Donegal 59 km – Londonderry 43 km – Sligo 122 km

Town★

Ardeen without rest
turning by the Town Hall – (074) 915 12 43 – www.ardeenhouse.com – Easter-September
5 rm – € 45/55 € 90
♦ Simple Victorian house, with very welcoming owner, on edge of village. Homely ambience in lounge and breakfast room. Immaculately kept bedrooms.

RATHMINES = Ráth Maonais – Dublin – 712 N8 – see Dublin

RATHMULLAN (Ráth Maoláin) – Donegal – 712 J2 – pop. 469 — 37 C1

– ✉ Letterkenny Ireland

Dublin 265 km – Londonderry 58 km – Sligo 140 km

Otway Saltpans, (074) 915 1665

Knockalla Viewpoint★, N : 12.75 km by R 247 – Rathmelton★, SW : 11.25 km by R 247

Rathmullan House
North : 0.5 mi on R 247 – (074) 915 81 88 – www.rathmullanhouse.com – Closed 6 January-10 February and 23-27 December
34 rm – € 80/175 € 160/260
Rest *Rathmullan House* – *(bar lunch)* Menu € 55
♦ Part 19C country house with fine gardens in secluded site on Lough Swilly. Choose a lounge as pleasant spot for lunch. Stylish, individualistic rooms: newer ones very comfy. Restaurant boasts serious dinner menus at linen-clad tables.

RATHNEW = Ráth Naoi – Wicklow – 712 N8 – see Wicklow

RIVERSTOWN (Baile idir Dhá Abhainn) – Sligo – 712 G5 – pop. 310 — 36 B2

Dublin 198 km – Sligo 21 km

Coopershill
– (071) 916 51 08 – www.coopershill.com – April-October
8 rm – € 144/157 € 218/244
Rest – *(dinner only) (booking essential for non-residents)* Menu € 45
♦ Magnificent Georgian country house set within 500 acre estate. Home to six generations of one family. Antique furnished communal areas and rooms exude charm and character. Family portraits, antique silver adorn dining room.

REPUBLIC OF IRELAND

ROSCOMMON (Ros Comáin) – Roscommon – 712 H7 – pop. 5 017 — 36 B3

Ireland

Dublin 151 km – Galway 92 km – Limerick 151 km

Harrison Hall ✆ (090) 6626342 (June-August), roscommon.touristoffice@failteireland.ie

Moate Park, ✆ (09066) 26 382

Castle★

Castlestrange Stone★, SW : 11.25 km by N 63 and R 362 – Strokestown★ (Famine Museum★ **AC**, Strokestown Park House★ **AC**), N : 19.25 km by N 61 and R 368 – Castlerea : Clonalis House★ **AC**, NW : 30.5 km by N 60

Abbey

rm,

on N 63 (Galway rd) – ✆ (090) 662 62 40 – www.abbeyhotel.ie – Closed 24-26 December

50 rm – € 160/180 € 280/300 **Rest** – Menu € 50 (dinner) Carte € 29/41

♦ Part-18C, family-run manor house with impressive castellated façade; overlooking ruins of 13C Abbey. Most characterful bedrooms in original house; some boast feature beds and roll-top baths. Good function and leisure facilities. Large bar and formal restaurant.

ROSSLARE (Ros Láir) – Wexford – 712 M11 – pop. 1 359 Ireland — 39 D2

Dublin 167 km – Waterford 80 km – Wexford 19 km

Kilrane ✆ (053) 33232 (April-September)

Rosslare Strand, ✆ (053) 913 2203

Irish Agricultural Museum, Johnstowon Castle★★ **AC**, NW : 12 km by R 740, N 25 and minor road. Kilmore Quay★, SW : 24 km by R 736 and R 739 – Saltee Islands★, SW : 24 km by R 736, R 739 and ferry

Kelly's Resort

rest,

– ✆ (053) 91 32 114 – www.kellys.ie – Closed 3 weeks January, 1 week autumn, 24-26 December, Sunday and Monday

121 rm – € 154 € 154/210

Rest *Beaches* – Menu € 25/45

Rest *La Marine* – Carte € 34/37

♦ Large, purpose-built hotel on the beachfront of this popular holiday town. Good range of leisure facilities; well-appointed rooms. Beaches dining room offers a classic popular menu. La Marine is a French inspired, bistro-style restaurant.

ROSSLARE HARBOUR (Calafort Ros Láir) – Wexford – 712 N11 – pop. 1 041 — 39 D2

Dublin 169 km – Waterford 82 km – Wexford 21 km

to France (Cherbourg and Roscoff) (Irish Ferries) (17 h/15 h)
– to Fishguard (Stena Line) 1-4 daily (1 h 40 mn/3 h 30 mn)
– to Pembroke (Irish Ferries) 2 daily (3 h 45 mn)

Kilrane ✆ (053) 33232 (April-October)

at Tagoat West : 4 km on N 25 – ✉ Rosslare

Churchtown House without rest

North : 0.75 km on Rosslare rd – ✆ (053) 913 2555 – www.churchtownhouse.com – April-October

6 rm – € 85/110 € 140

♦ Part-18C house with extension, set in a spacious, well-kept garden. Traditional country house style lounge and wood furnished breakfast room. Individually decorated bedrooms.

ROUNDSTONE (Cloch na Rón) – Galway – 712 C7 – pop. 207 Ireland — 36 A3

Dublin 293 km – Galway 76 km – Ennis 144 km

Town★

Connemara★★★: Sky Road, Clifden★★, W : 24 km by R 341 and minor road – Cashel★, E : 15 km by R 341 – Connemara National Park★ **AC**, N : 40 km by R 341 and N 59 – Kylemore Abbey★ **AC**, N : 44 km by R 341 and N 59

O'Dowds
(095) 35 809 – www.odowdsbar.com
– Closed 25 December and Good Friday
Rest – Seafood – *(booking advisable)* Carte € 20/35
◆ Busy pub in pretty harbourside town; popular with tourists and locals alike. Owned by the O'Dowd family for over 100 years, it specialises in fresh, simply cooked seafood.

SANDYFORD = Áth an Ghainimh – Dublin – 712 N8 – see Dublin

SHANAGARRY (An Seangharraí) – Cork – 712 H12 – pop. 297 39 C3
– Midleton Ireland

Dublin 262 km – Cork 40 km – Waterford 103 km
Cloyne Cathedral★, NW : 6.5 km by R 629

Ballymaloe House
Northwest : 2.75 km on L 35 – (021) 465 25 31 – www.ballymaloe.ie
– Closed 2 weeks January and 24-26 December
30 rm – € 110/130 € 220/250
Rest – *(booking essential)* Menu € 40/75
◆ Part-16C, part-Georgian house surrounded by 400 acres of farmland. Warm, laid-back atmosphere and period furnishings. Individually styled bedrooms filled with Irish art and textiles. Menus feature local, seasonal produce. This is where Irish cookery really started.

SKERRIES (Na Sceirí) – Fingal – 712 N7 – pop. 9 535 Ireland 39 D1

Dublin 30 km – Drogheda 24 km
Skerries Mills (01) 849 5208, skerriesmills@indigo.ie
Skerries Hacketstown, (01) 849 1567
Malahide Castle★★ **AC**, S : 23 km by R 127, M 1 and R 106 – Ben of Howth (≤★), S : 23 km by R 127, M 1 and R 106 – Newbridge House★ **AC**, S : 16 km by R 217 and minor road

Redbank House with rm
5-7 Church St – (01) 849 1005 – www.redbank.ie
18 rm – € 75 € 110/140
Rest – Seafood – *(Closed Sunday dinner) (dinner only and Sunday lunch)*
Menu € 29 (lunch)/25 (early dinner) – Carte € 47/59
◆ One of Ireland's most well-renowned and long-standing restaurants. Fresh seafood from Skerries harbour is served simply or in more elaborate fashion. Smart, comfy bedrooms.

SKIBBEREEN – Cork – 712 E13 – pop. 2 000 Ireland 38 B3

Dublin 338 km – Cork 85 km – Killarney 104 km
Town Hall (028) 21766
Castletownshend★, SE : 9 km by R 596. Sherkin Island★, SW : 35 km by R 595 and ferry from Baltimore – Skull★, W : 24 km by N 71 and R 592 – Mount Gabriel (≤★), W : 29 km by N 71, R 592 and minor road N

Over the Moon
46 Bridge St – (028) 22 100 – www.overthemoonskibbereen.com
– Closed Sunday and Monday September-June and restricted opening in November and January
Rest – *(booking essential)* Carte € 19/40
◆ Unpretentious restaurant with quarry tiled flooring and a Mediterranean feel. Fresh, flavoursome, well-presented cooking proves good value for money. Polite, friendly service.

SLANE – Meath – 712 M6 – pop. 823 37 B3

Dublin 34 km – Navan 8 km – City Centre 35 km – Craigavon 69 km

Tankardstown

Northwest : 6 km by N 51off R 163 – (041) 982 46 21 – www.tankardstown.ie – Closed 25-26 December

7 rm – € 145 € 315 – 3 suites

Rest *Brabazon* – see restaurant listing

Rest *Bistro* – *(closed Monday-Tuesday) (lunch only and Saturday dinner)*

Carte € 31/45 **s**

◆ Fine Georgian manor house on mature country estate; extensively restored to a luxurious level. Large, antique-furnished bedrooms in the house; some with silk-lined walls. Rooms in courtyard boast kitchens. Vaulted ceilings and relaxed all-day dining in Bistro.

Brabazon – at Tankardstown Hotel

Northwest : 6 km by N 51 off R 163 – (041) 982 46 21 – www.tankardstown.ie – Closed 25-26 December

Rest – *(closed Monday-Tuesday) (dinner only and Sunday lunch)*

Carte € 31/41 **s**

◆ Relaxed, rustic restaurant set in former piggery of the manor house, with pleasant terrace overlooking landscaped courtyard. Contemporary cooking makes use of good quality ingredients.

SLIGO (Sligeach) – Sligo – 712 G5 – pop. 19 402 Ireland 36 B2

Dublin 214 km – Belfast 203 km – Dundalk 170 km – Londonderry 138 km

Sligo Airport, Strandhill : (071) 9168280

Aras Reddan, Temple St (071) 9161201, northwestinfo@failteireland.ie

Rosses Point, (071) 917 7134

Town★★ – Abbey★ **AC** – Model Arts and the Niland Gallery★ **AC**

SE : Lough Gill★★ – Carrowmore Megalithic Cemetery★ **AC**, SW : 4.75 km – Knocknarea★ (≤★★) SW : 9.5 km by R 292. Drumcliff★, N : by N 15 - Parke's Castle★ **AC**, E : 14.5 km by R 286 – Glencar Waterfall★, NE : 14.5 km by N 16 – Creevykeel Court Cairn★, N : 25.75 km by N 15

Clarion

rm, rest,

Clarion Rd, Northeast : 3 km by N 16 – (071) 911 90 00 – www.clarionhotelsligo.com – Closed 20 December-4 January

163 rm – € 69/129 € 119/169

Rest *Kudos* – Carte € 20/28 **s**

Rest *Sinergie* – Menu € 23 (dinner) – Carte € 20/28 **s**

◆ Extensive Victorian building with granite façade: now the height of modernity with excellent leisure club and impressive, spacious bedrooms; large choice of smart suites. Informal Asian inspired Kudos. Modern European menus at Sinergie.

Tree Tops without rest

Cleveragh Rd, South : 1.25 km by Dublin rd – (071) 916 01 60 – www.sligobandb.com – Closed Christmas-New Year

5 rm – € 48/50 € 70/74

◆ Pleasant guesthouse in residential area. Stunning collection of Irish art. Cosy public areas include small lounge and simple breakfast room. Neat, comfortable rooms.

Montmartre

Market Yard – (071) 916 99 01 – www.montmartrerestaurant.ie – Closed 3 weeks January, 1 week autumn, 24-26 December, Sunday and Monday

Rest – *(dinner only)* Menu € 37 – Carte € 28/47 **s**

◆ Smart, modern restaurant near cathedral with small bar at entrance and plenty of light from windows. Efficient, formal staff serve broadly influenced classic French food.

SPANISH POINT (Rinn na Spáinneach) – **Clare** – **712** D9 **38** B2
– ✉ Milltown Malbay

Dublin 275 km – Galway 104 km – Limerick 83 km

Red Cliff Lodge without rest
– ☎ *(065) 708 57 56 – www.redclifflodge.ie*
– *Easter-October*
6 rm – † € 100 †† € 150
♦ Thatched cottage with spacious courtyard bedrooms. Comfortable, modern lounges boast bold feature walls and antique furniture. Breakfast comes in a wicker basket delivered to your room.

STRAFFAN (Teach Srafáin) – **Kildare** – **712** M8 – **pop. 439** Ireland **39** D1

Dublin 24 km – Mullingar 75 km
Naas Kerdiffstown, ☎ (045) 874 644
Castletown House, Celbridge★ **AC**, NW : 7 km by R 406 and R 403

K Club
– ☎ *(01) 601 7200 – www.kclub.ie – Closed January*
60 rm – † € 325 †† € 395 – 9 suites
Rest *Byerley Turk* – ☎ (01) 601 7221 *(closed Sunday-Thursday) (dinner only) (booking essential for non-residents)* Menu € 69/99
Rest *Legends* – *(closed Sunday-Tuesday)* Menu € 45 – Carte € 37/84
Rest *River Room* – ☎ (01) 601 7250 *(dinner only and Sunday lunch)* Menu € 45/55 – Carte € 37/79
♦ Part early 19C country house overlooking River Liffey, with gardens, arboretum and championship golf course. Huge leisure centre. Exquisitely sumptuous rooms. Opulent food in the formal Byerley Turk. Informal Legends has views of the golf course. Accessible menu offered in The River Room.

Barberstown Castle rm,
North : 0.75 km – ☎ (01) 628 8157 – www.barberstowncastle.ie – Closed January, Easter and 24-26 December
58 rm – † € 120/200 †† € 195/280
Rest – *(dinner only) (booking essential) (residents only Sunday-Thursday)* Menu € 55
♦ Whitewashed Elizabethan and Victorian house with 13C castle keep and gardens. Country house style lounges exude style. Individually decorated, very comfortable bedrooms. Dine in characterful, stone-clad keep.

TAGOAT = Teach Gót – **Wexford** – **712** M11 – **see Rosslare Harbour**

TAHILLA (Tathuile) – **Kerry** – **712** C12 – **pop. 193** Ireland **38** A3

Dublin 357 km – Cork 112 km – Killarney 51 km
Ring of Kerry★★ – Sneem★, NW : 6.5 km by N 70

Tahilla Cove without rest 
– ☎ *(064) 66 45 204 – www.tahillacove.com*
– *April-September*
9 rm – † € 105 †† € 150
♦ Two houses surrounded by oak forest, with Caha Mountains as a backdrop and garden sweeping down to Coongar harbour. Some bedrooms have balconies from which to savour views.

Don't confuse the couvert rating ✗ with the stars ✿!
Couverts defines comfort and service, while stars are awarded for the best cuisine across all categories of comfort.

REPUBLIC OF IRELAND

TERMONBARRY – Roscommon – 712 I6 – pop. 518 Ireland 37 C3

Dublin 130 km – Galway 137 km – Roscommon 35 km – Sligo 100 km

Strokestown★ (Famine Museum★ **AC**, Strokestown Park House★ **AC**), NW : by N 5

Keenan's

– *(043) 332 6052 – www.keenans.ie – Closed 25-26 December*
12 rm – € 60/75 € 89/99
Rest – *(Closed Sunday dinner and bank holiday dinner)* Menu € 25/35 – Carte € 25/38

◆ Modern hotel on the banks of the Shannon, with cosy residents lounge. Stylish bedrooms have flat screens and showers; some have river views; some also have balconies. Large contemporary restaurant offers à la carte menu; characterful bar serves pub classics.

THOMASTOWN (Baile Mhic Andáin) – Kilkenny – 712 K10 – pop. 1 837 – ✉ Kilkenny Ireland 39 C2

Dublin 124 km – Kilkenny 17 km – Waterford 48 km – Wexford 61 km

Jerpoint Abbey★★, SW : 3 km by N9 – Graiguenamanagh★ (Duiske Abbey★★ **AC**), E : 16 km by R 703 – Inistioge★, SE : 8 km by R 700 – Kilfane Glen and Waterfall★ **AC**, SE : 5 km by N 9

Abbey House without rest

Jerpoint Abbey, Southwest : 2 km on N 9 – (056) 772 41 66 – www.abbeyhousejerpoint.com – Closed 23-30 December
6 rm – € 50/65 € 80/85

◆ Neat inside and out, this whitewashed house in well-kept gardens offers simple but spacious rooms and pretty wood furnished breakfast room. Read up on area in lounge.

THURLES (Durlas) – Tipperary – 712 I9 – pop. 7 682 Ireland 39 C2

Dublin 148 km – Cork 114 km – Kilkenny 48 km – Limerick 75 km

18 Turtulla, (0504) 21 983

Holy Cross Abbey★★ **AC**, SW : 8 km by R 660

Inch House

rest,

(0504) 51 348 – www.inchhouse.ie – Closed 2 weeks Christmas and 1 week Easter
5 rm – € 55/65 € 110/130
Rest – *(closed Sunday-Monday) (dinner only) (booking essential for non-residents)* Menu € 55 – Carte € 45/60

◆ 1720s country house on a working farm; lovely rural views. Handsomely restored with a fine eye for decorative period detail. Individually styled en suite bedrooms. Classically proportioned yet intimate dining room.

TOORMORE (An Tuar Mór) – Cork – 712 D13 – pop. 207 – ✉ Goleen 38 A3

Dublin 355 km – Cork 109 km – Killarney 104 km

Fortview House without rest

Gurtyowen, Northeast : 2.5 km on Durrus rd (R 591) – (028) 35 324 – www.fortviewhousegoleen.com – April-September
5 rm – € 50 € 100

◆ Stone built farmhouse; antique country pine furniture in coir carpeted rooms and brass, iron bedsteads. Fresh vegetable juice, home-made muesli, potato cake for breakfast.

Rock Cottage

Barnatonicane, Northeast : 3.25 km on Durrus rd (R 591) – (028) 35 538 – www.rockcottage.ie
3 rm – € 100 € 140 **Rest** – Menu € 50

◆ Charming Georgian house, formerly a hunting lodge, set in 17 acres of parkland. Attractive open-fired sitting room; local art and lithographs hang on the walls. Cosy, country-style bedrooms. Traditional home-cooked meals served in high-ceilinged dining room.

TOWER – Cork – **712** G12 – see Blarney

TRALEE (Trá Lí) – Kerry – **712** C11 – **pop. 22 744** Ireland **38** A2

Dublin 297 km – Killarney 32 km – Limerick 103 km

Ashe Memorial Hall, Denny St (066) 7121288, traleetouristoffice@failteireland.ie

Kerry - The Kingdom★ **AC**

Blennerville Windmill★ **AC**, SW : 3.25 km by N 86 – Ardfert★, NW : 8 km by R 551. Banna Strand★, NW : 12.75 km by R 551 - Crag Cave★ **AC**, W : 21 km by N 21 – Rattoo Round Tower★, N : 19.25 km by R 556

 **Carlton H. Tralee**

Dan Springs Rd, East : 2 km on N 70 – (066) 719 9100 – www.carlton.ie/tralee – Closed 23-28 December

165 rm – € 110/160 € 160/200

Rest ***Morels*** – Menu € 17 (lunch) – Carte € 24/30

◆ Corporate hotel on outskirts of city centre with contemporary style throughout. Bedrooms come in three grades; all are a good size, Executive come with a balcony and view. Traditional dishes served in Morels restaurant.

 **Meadowlands**

Oakpark, Northeast : 1.25 km on N 69 – (066) 718 04 44 – www.meadowlandshotel.com – Closed 24-26 December

56 rm – € 90/120 € 150/200 – 2 suites

Rest – *(closed Sunday) (bar lunch)* Menu € 30 – Carte € 32/47

◆ Smart, terracotta hotel, a good base for exploring area. Inside are warmly decorated, air conditioned rooms and mellow library lounge with open fire and grandfather clock. Proprietor owns fishing boats, so seafood takes centre stage in dining room.

Grand rest,

Denny St – (066) 712 14 99 – www.grandhoteltralee.com – Closed 25 December

44 rm – € 70/115 € 109/169

Rest – Menu € 25 (dinner) **s** – Carte € 20/40 **s**

◆ Established 1928; enjoys a central position in town. Rooms are decorated with mahogany furniture whilst the popular bar, once a post office, bears hallmarks of bygone era. Appetising dinners in restaurant with historic ambience.

Brook Manor Lodge without rest

Fenit Rd, Spa, Northwest : 3.5 km by R 551 on R 558 – (066) 712 04 06 – www.brookmanorlodge.com – Closed 21-31 December

8 rm – € 55/90 € 90/120

◆ Modern purpose-built manor in meadowland looking across to the Slieve Mish mountains: good for walks and angling. Breakfast in conservatory. Immaculate bedrooms.

TRAMORE (Trá Mhór) – Waterford – **712** K11 – **pop. 9 634** Ireland **39** C2

Dublin 170 km – Waterford 9 km

(051) 381572 (June-August)

Dunmore East★, E : 18 km by R 675, R 685 and R 684

Glenorney without rest

Newtown, Southwest : 1.5 km by R 675 – (051) 381 056 – www.glenorney.com – March-November

6 rm – € 50/80 € 80/90

◆ On a hill overlooking Tramore Bay. Inside are personally decorated rooms: family photographs and curios; sun lounge with plenty of books. Rear rooms have lovely bay views.

REPUBLIC OF IRELAND

TRIM (Baile Átha Troim) - Meath - 712 L7 - pop. 6 870 Ireland — 37 D3

Dublin 43 km - Drogheda 42 km - Tullamore 69 km

Old Town Hall, Castle St ✆ (046) 9437227, trimvisitorcentre@eircom.net

County Meath Newtownmoynagh, ✆ (046) 943 1463

Trim Castle★★ - Town★

Bective Abbey★, NE : 6.5 km by R 161

Trim Castle

rm, rest,

Castle St. - ✆ (046) 948 3000 - www.trimcastlehotel.com
- Closed 25 December
68 rm - € 170 € 270
Rest *Jules* - *(closed Monday-Thursday)* Menu € 25 (dinner)

♦ Modern hotel boasting excellent castle views from its guest areas. Good-sized bedrooms in contemporary beige/chocolate hues; front rooms have the view. Discounted use of local leisure facilities. Food served in the café and bar. Restaurant opens Fri/Sat evening.

Highfield House without rest

Maudlins Rd. - ✆ (046) 943 63 86 - www.highfieldguesthouse.com
- closed 23 December-10 January
9 rm - € 55 € 80

♦ Substantial 18C stone house close to the river and castle. Well-appointed lounge and breakfast room, delightful terraced courtyard and boldly coloured bedrooms. Breakfast is comprehensive.

REPUBLIC OF IRELAND

VALENCIA ISLAND (Dairbhre) - Kerry - 712 A/B12 - pop. 650 — 38 A2

Dublin 381 km - Killarney 88 km - Tralee 92 km

KNIGHTS TOWN - Kerry — 38 A2

Glanleam House

rm,

Glanleam, West : 2 km taking right fork at top of Market St
- ✆ (066) 947 61 76 - www.glanleam.com
- Mid-March to October
5 rm - € 60/130 € 140/260 - 1 suite
Rest - *(dinner only) (booking essential for non-residents) (communal dining)* Menu € 50

♦ Part 17C and 18C country house in extensive sub-tropical gardens, superbly located off West Kerry coast. Art Deco interiors. Spacious drawing room. Individually styled rooms. Communal dining; produce grown in hotel's 19C walled gardens.

WATERFORD (Port Láirge) - Waterford - 712 K11 - pop. 49 213 — 39 C2
Ireland

Dublin 154 km - Cork 117 km - Limerick 124 km

Waterford Airport, Killowen : ✆ (051) 846600

The Granary, The Quay ✆ (051) 875823 Y, southeastinfo@failteireland.ie
Crystal Visitor Centre, Cork Rd ✆ (051) 358397 (seasonal), WaterfordCrystal@failteireland.ie

Newrath, ✆ (051) 876 748

Town★ - City Walls★ - Waterford Treasures★ **AC** Y

Waterford Crystal★, SW : 2.5 km by N 25 Y. Duncannon★, E : 19.25 km by R 683, ferry from Passage East and R 374 (south) Z - Dunmore East★, SE : 19.25 km by R 684 Z - Tintern Abbey★, E : 21 km by R 683, ferry from Passage East, R 733 and R 734 (south) Z

Plan on next page

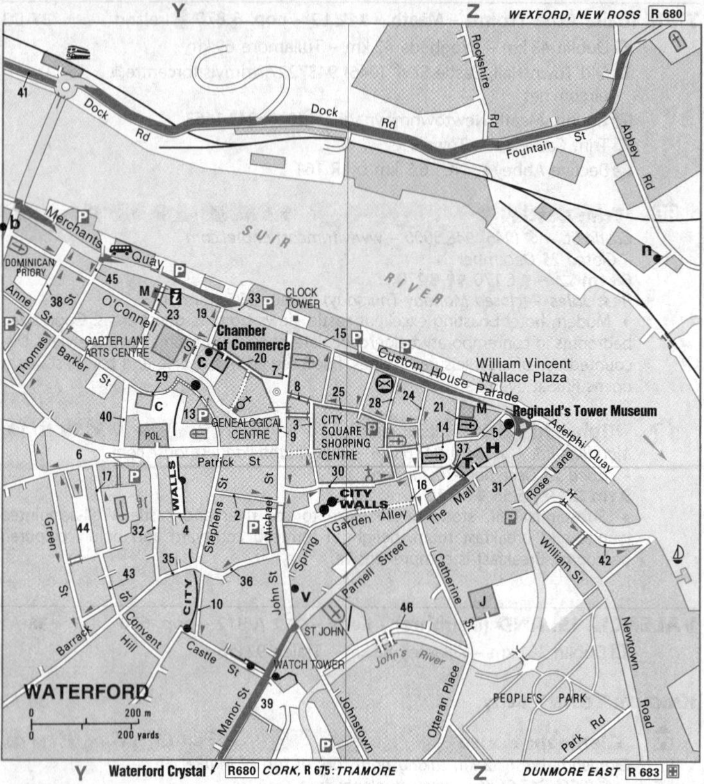

Y Z WEXFORD, NEW ROSS R 680

LIMERICK, KILKENNY, DUBLIN N 9

WATERFORD

0 200 m
0 200 yards

Waterford Crystal / R680 CORK, R 675: TRAMORE DUNMORE EAST R 683

Alexander St . . . . . . Y 2
Arundel Square . . . . . . Y 3
Bachelors Walk . . . . . . Y 4
Bailey's New St . . . . . . Z 5
Ballybricken Green . . . . . . Y 6
Barronstrand St . . . . . . Y 7
Blackfriars St . . . . . . Y 8
Broad St . . . . . . Y 9
Brown's Lane . . . . . . Y 10
Carrigeen Park . . . . . . Y 13
Cathedral Square . . . . . . Z 14
City Square Shopping Centre . . . . . . YZ
Coal Quay . . . . . . Y 15
Colbeck St . . . . . . Z 16
Five Alley Lane . . . . . . Y 17
George St . . . . . . Y 20
Gladstone St . . . . . . Y 19
Greyfriar's St . . . . . . Z 21
Hanover St . . . . . . Y 23
Henrietta St . . . . . . Z 24
High St . . . . . . YZ 25
Jenkin's Lane . . . . . . Y 27
Keiser St . . . . . . Z 28
King's Terrace . . . . . . Y 29
Lady Lane . . . . . . YZ 30
Lombard St . . . . . . Z 31
Mayors Walk . . . . . . Y 32
Meagher's Quay . . . . . . Y 33
Newgate St . . . . . . Y 35
New St . . . . . . Y 36
Palace Lane . . . . . . Z 37
Penrose Lane . . . . . . Y 38
Railway Square . . . . . . Y 39
St Patrick Terrace . . . . . . Y 40
Sally Park . . . . . . Y 41
Scotch Quay . . . . . . Z 42
Shortcourse . . . . . . Y 43
Trinity Square . . . . . . Y 44
Vulcan St . . . . . . Y 45
Water Side . . . . . . Z 46

Waterford Castle H. and Golf Club

The Island, Ballinakill, East : 4 km by R 683, Ballinakill Rd and private ferry – ✆ (051) 878 203 – www.waterfordcastle.com – closed 24-26 December

14 rm – 🚹 € 95/180 🚹🚹 € 190/640 – 5 suites

Rest *Munster Dining Room* – *(bar lunch Monday-Saturday)* Menu € 65 (dinner) – Carte lunch € 31/45

♦ Part 15C and 19C castle in charmingly secluded, historic river island setting. Classic country house ambience amid antiques and period features. Comfortable, elegant rooms. Oak panelled dining room with ornate ceilings and evening pianist.

Athenaeum House rest,
Christendom, Ferrybank, Northeast : 1.5 km by N 25 – (051) 833 999 – www.athenaeumhousehotel.com – Closed Christmas and January Zn
29 rm – € 99/100 € 145/150, € 12
Rest *Zak's* – Menu € 29 (dinner) – Carte lunch € 18/36
◆ In a quiet residential area, this extended Georgian house has retained some original features; elsewhere distinctly modern and stylish. Well equipped rooms exude modish charm. Eclectic mix of dishes in restaurant overlooking garden.

Fitzwilton rm,
Bridge St – (051) 846 900 – www.fitzwiltonhotel.ie – Closed 23-26 December Yb
91 rm – € 69/139 € 125/155
Rest – Menu € 25 (lunch) – Carte dinner € 31/43
◆ Central hotel featuring glass façade and trendy bar. Bedrooms are modern, with a good finish: some are more spacious than others; those at the back are much quieter. Contemporary restaurant offers international dishes made with Irish ingredients.

Foxmount Country House without rest
Passage East Rd, Southeast : 7.25 km by R 683, off Cheekpoint rd – (051) 874 308 – www.foxmountcountryhouse.com – mid March-mid October
4 rm – € 65 € 110/130
◆ Ivy-clad house, dating from the 17C, on a working farm. Wonderfully secluded and quiet yet within striking distance of Waterford. Neat, cottage-style bedrooms.

La Bohème
2 George's St – (051) 875 645 – www.labohemerestaurant.ie – closed 25-27 December, Sunday, Monday and bank holidays Yc
Rest – French – *(dinner only) (booking essential)* Menu 29 (weekday early dinner) – Carte € 40/54
◆ Careful restoration of this historic building has created an atmospheric, candlelit dining room. Classic French cooking, traditionally prepared, includes daily market specials.

Bodéga
54 John St – (051) 844 177 – www.bodegawaterford.com – Closed 1 January, 22nd April, 25-26 December, Saturday lunch, Sunday and bank holidays Yv
Rest – Carte € 28/47
◆ Tucked away in the heart of the city. Purple exterior; orange interior, augmented by mosaics and wall murals. Classic rustic French menus or warming lunchtime dishes.

WATERVILLE (An Coireán) – Kerry – 712 B12 – pop. 546 Ireland 38 A3

Dublin 383 km – Killarney 77 km
Main St. (066) 9474646 (June-September)
Ring of Kerry Golf Links Rd, (066) 947 41 02
Ring of Kerry★★ – Skellig Islands★★, W: 12.75 km by N 70, R 567 and ferry from Ballinskelligs – Derrynane National Historic Park★★ **AC**, S: 14.5 km by N70 – Leacanabuaile Fort (<★★), N: 21 km by N 70

Brookhaven House without rest
New Line Rd, North : 1.25 km on N 70 – (066) 947 44 31 – www.brookhavenhouse.com – February-14 November
6 rm – € 55/90 € 90/110
◆ Spacious modern guesthouse overlooking Waterville golf course; large and neat, with restful lounge and cottage style bedrooms. Proud of its home-baked breakfasts.

REPUBLIC OF IRELAND

Dublin 262 km – Galway 80 km – Sligo 104 km

James St ✆ (098) 25711, westport@failteireland.ie

Town★★ (Centre★) – Westport House★★ **AC**

Ballintubber Abbey★, SE : 21 km by R 330. SW : Murrisk Peninsula★★ – Croagh Patrick★, W : 9.5 km by R 335 – Bunlahinch Clapper Bridge★, W : 25.75 km by R 335 - Doo Lough Pass★, W : 38.5 km by R 335 – Aasleagh Falls★, S : 35.5 km by N 59

Ardmore Country House

The Quay, West : 2.5 km on R 335 – ✆ (098) 25 994 – www.ardmorecountryhouse.com – 18 March-October
13 rm – ♦ € 100/130 ♦♦ € 100/180
Rest – *(dinner only) (booking essential residents only on Sunday)* Menu € 40 – Carte € 30/49
◆ Attractive, personally run hotel in commanding setting with views across gardens and Clew Bay. Neat, comfortable bedrooms have a sumptuous yet homely feel. Passionate chef-owner produces traditional dishes using local ingredients.

Westport Country Lodge

rm,

Aghagower, Southeast : 4 km by R 330 – ✆ (098) 56 030 – www.westportlodge.ie
21 rm – ♦ € 59/129 ♦♦ € 59/169, €10
Rest – Menu € 20 (dinner) – Carte € 19/31
◆ Hotel set in 36 acres, with 9 hole pitch and putt. Rooms have big beds, flat screens and mod cons; many also have countryside views out towards Croagh Patrick. Contemporary bar and dining room. Unpretentious homemade food, with classics given a modern touch.

Augusta Lodge without rest

Golf Links Rd, North : 0.75 km by N 59 – ✆ (098) 28 900 – www.augustalodge.ie – closed 23-26 December
10 rm – ♦ € 45/70 ♦♦ € 70/90
◆ Family run, purpose-built guesthouse, convenient for Westport Golf Club; play the piano in the lounge while admiring the golfing memorabilia. Homely, simple bedrooms.

Quay West without rest

Quay Rd, West : 0.75 km – ✆ (098) 27 863 – www.quaywestport.com
6 rm – ♦ € 35/50 ♦♦ € 60/70
◆ Purpose-built guesthouse located within walking distance of the town centre. Simply appointed throughout providing sensibly priced, well kept rooms.

Sheebeen

Rosbeg, West : 3 km on R 335 – ✆ (098) 26 528 – www.croninssheebeen.com – Closed lunch weekdays November-mid March
Rest – Carte € 25/40
◆ Thatched roadside pub to west of town. Cosy front bar has some tables but main dining is upstairs. Fresh, accurate cooking; go for the fresh local fish and seafood specials.

Prices quoted after the symbol ♦ refer to the lowest rate in low season followed by the highest rate in high season, for a single room. The same principle applies to the symbol ♦♦ for a double room.

REPUBLIC OF IRELAND

WEXFORD (Loch Garman) – Wexford – 712 M10 – pop. 18 163 39 D2

Ireland

Dublin 141 km – Kilkenny 79 km – Waterford 61 km

Crescent Quay ✆ (053) 23111

Mulgannon, ✆ (053) 42 238

Town★ - Main Street★ YZ - Franciscan Friary★ Z – St Iberius' Church★ Y **D** - Twin Churches★ Z

Irish Agricultural Museum, Johnstown Castle★★ **AC**, SW : 7.25 km X – Irish National Heritage Park, Ferrycarrig★ **AC**, NW : 4 km by N 11 V – Curracloe★, NE : 8 km by R 741 and R 743 V. Kilmore Quay★, SW : 24 km by N 25 and R 739 (Saltee Islands★ - access by boat) X – Enniscorthy Castle★ (County Museum★ **AC**) N : 24 km by N 11 V

Whites

rm, rm, VISA AE

Abbey St – *✆ (053) 912 2311* – *www.whitesofwexford.ie*
– *Closed 24-26 December* Y**a**

152 rm – € 65/85 € 130/190

Rest *Whites* – *(dinner only)* Menu 25 – Carte € 26/42

♦ Smart new hotel built around a paved central courtyard. Spacious and modern, with a busy bar, popular meeting rooms, superb leisure facilities and very comfortable bedrooms. Traditional menu served in contemporary dining room.

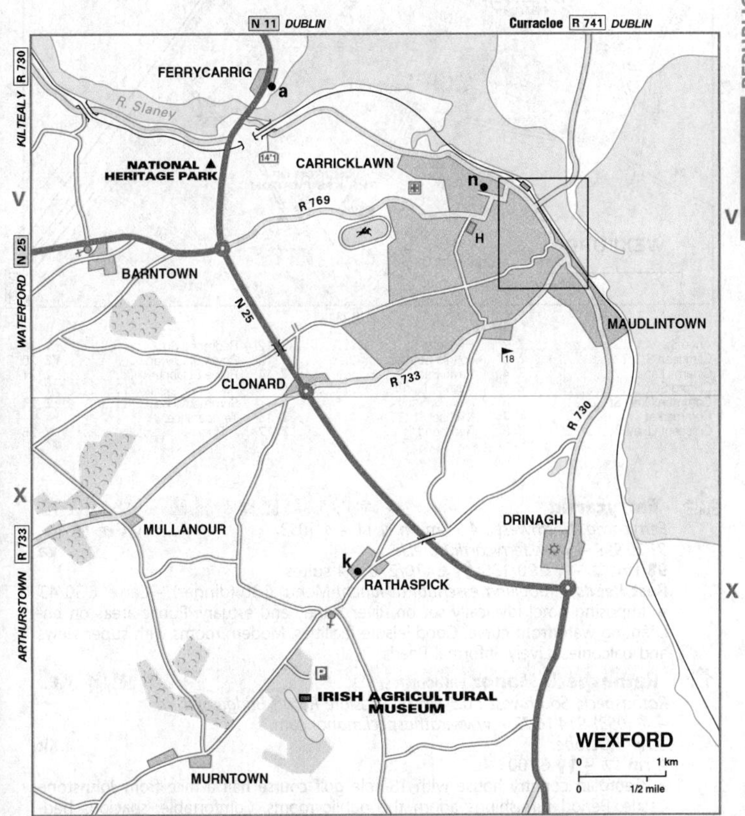

REPUBLIC OF IRELAND

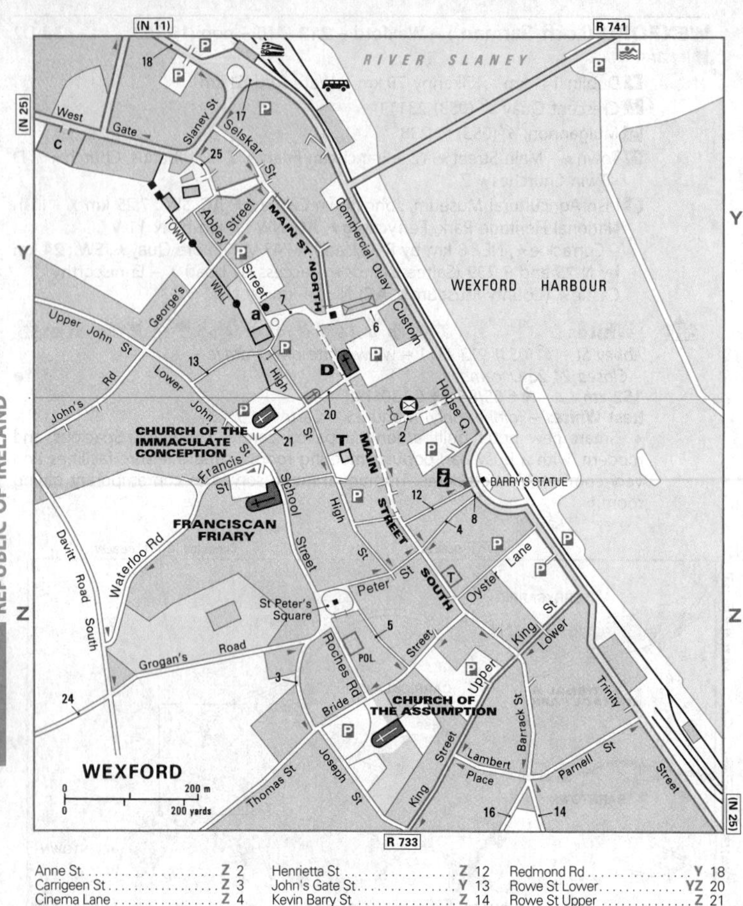

Anne St. . . . . Z 2	Henrietta St . . . . Z 12	Redmond Rd . . . . Y 18
Carrigeen St . . . . Z 3	John's Gate St . . . . Y 13	Rowe St Lower . . . . YZ 20
Cinema Lane . . . . Z 4	Kevin Barry St . . . . Z 14	Rowe St Upper . . . . Z 21
Clifford St . . . . Z 5	Main St North . . . . Y	Selskar St . . . . Y
Common Quay St . . . . Y 6	Main St South . . . . Z	Summerhill Rd . . . . Z 24
Cornmarket . . . . Y 7	Michael St . . . . Z 16	Temperance Row . . . . Y 25
Crescent Quay . . . . Z 8	Redmond Pl. . . . . Y 17	

Ferrycarrig

Ferrycarrig, Northwest : 4.5 km on N 11 – ✆ (053) 91 20 999 – www.ferrycarrighotel.ie

rm, rest, VISA MC AE

Va

98 rm – € 90/135 € 170/270 – 4 suites

Rest *Reeds* – *(booking essential at lunch)* Menu € 30 (dinner) – Carte € 30/43

♦ Imposing hotel idyllically set on River Slaney and estuary. Public areas on enchanting waterfront curve. Good leisure facilities. Modern rooms with super views and balconies. Lively, informal Reeds.

Rathaspeck Manor without rest

Rathaspeck, Southwest : 6.5 km by Rosslare Rd off Bridgetown rd – ✆ (053) 914 16 72 – www.rathaspeckmanor.com – April-October

Xk

4 rm – € 100

♦ Georgian country house with 18-hole golf course half a mile from Johnstone Castle. Period furnishings adorn the public rooms. Comfortable, spacious bedrooms.

McMenamin's Townouse without rest

6 Glena Ter. – (053) 914 6442
– March-November Xn
4 rm – € 50/60 € 90/110
◆ Homely Victorian townhouse retaining many original features. Friendly, hands-on owners. Legendary breakfasts include homemade breads, preserves, omelettes and drop scones.

WICKLOW (Cill Mhantáin) – Wicklow – 712 N9 – pop. 10 071 39 D2

Ireland

Dublin 53 km – Waterford 135 km – Wexford 108 km
Fitzwilliam Sq (0404) 69117, wicklow@failteireland.ie
Mount Usher Gardens, Ashford★ AC, NW : 6.5 km by R 750 and N 11 – Devil's Glen★, NW : 12.75 km by R 750 and N 11. Glendalough★★★ (Lower Lake★★★, Upper Lake★★, Cathedral★★, Round Tower★★, St Kevin's Church★★, St Saviour's Priory★) – W : 22.5 km by R 750, N 11, R 763, R 755 and R 756 – Wicklow Mountains★★ (Wicklow Gap★★, Sally Gap★★, Avondale★, Meeting of the Waters★, Glenmacnass Waterfall★, Glenmalur★, – Loughs Tay and Dan★)

at Rathnew Northwest : 3.25 km on R 750 – ✉ Wicklow

Tinakilly House rm, rest,

on R 750 – (0404) 69 274 – www.tinakilly.ie
50 rm – € 150/200 € 200/250 – 1 suite
Rest ***The Brunel*** – *(dinner only and Sunday lunch)* Menu € 65 – Carte € 45/50
◆ Part Victorian country house with views of sea and mountains. Grand entrance hall hung with paintings. Mix of comfortable room styles, those in main house most characterful. Large dining room with rich drapes, formal service.

Hunter's

Newrath Bridge, North : 1.25 km by N 11 on R 761 – (0404) 40 106 – www.hunters.ie – Closed 24-26 and 31 December
16 rm – € 65/110 € 130/190 **Rest** – Menu € 25/45 – Carte € 35/40
◆ Converted 18C coaching inn set in 2 acres of attractive gardens. Characterful, antique furnished accommodation. Elegant, traditionally appointed communal areas. Dining room in hotel's welcoming country style.

YOUGHAL (Eochaill) – Cork – 712 I12 – pop. 6 785 Ireland 39 C3

Dublin 235 km – Cork 48 km – Waterford 75 km
Market House, Market Sq (024) 20170, info@youghalchamber.ie
Knockaverry, (024) 92 787
Town★ – St Mary's Collegiate Church★★ – Town Walls★ - Clock Gate★
Helvick Head★ (≤★), NE : 35.5 km by N 25 and R 674 – Ringville (≤★), NE : 32.25 km by N 25 and R 674 – Ardmore★ - Round Tower★ - Cathedral★ (arcade★), N : 16 km by N 25 and R 674 – Whiting Bay★, SE : 19.25 km by N 25, R 673 and the coast road

XX **Aherne's** with rm rm,

163 North Main St – (024) 92 424 – www.ahernes.com
– Closed 24-27 December
12 rm – € 125/130 € 170/210
Rest – Seafood – *(bar lunch)* Menu € 45 – Carte € 27/52
◆ A sitting room fireplace greets you at this family-run restaurant. Choose between a formal dining room or cosy bar. It's all about the seafood which is all the better for being simply prepared.

REPUBLIC OF IRELAND

International Dialling Codes

Note: When making an international call, do not dial the first (0) of the city code (except for calls to Italy).

from \ to	A	B	CH	CZ	D	DK	E	FIN	F	GB	GR
A Austria		0032	0041	00420	0049	0045	0034	00358	0033	0044	0030
B Belgium	0043		0041	00420	0049	0045	0034	00358	0033	0044	0030
CH Switzerland	0043	0032		00420	0049	0045	0034	00358	0033	0044	0030
CZ Czech Republic	0043	0032	0041		0049	0045	0034	00358	0033	0044	0030
D Germany	0043	0032	0041	00420		0045	0034	00358	0033	0044	0030
DK Denmark	0043	0032	0041	00420	0049		0034	00358	0033	0044	0030
E Spain	0043	0032	0041	00420	0049	0045		00358	0033	0044	0030
FIN Finland	0043	0032	0041	00420	0049	0045	0034		0033	0044	0030
F France	0043	0032	0041	00420	0049	0045	0034	00358		0044	0030
GB United Kingdom	0043	0032	0041	00420	0049	0045	0034	00358	0033		0030
GR Greece	0043	0032	0041	00420	0049	0045	0034	00358	0033	0044	
H Hungary	0043	0032	0041	00420	0049	0045	0034	00358	0033	0044	0030
I Italy	0043	0032	0041	00420	0049	0045	0034	00358	0033	0044	0030
IRL Ireland	0043	0032	0041	00420	0049	0045	0034	00358	0033	0044	0030
J Japan	00143	00132	00141	001420	00149	00145	00134	001358	00133	00144	00130
L Luxembourg	0043	0032	0041	00420	0049	0045	0034	00358	0033	0044	0030
N Norway	0043	0032	0041	00420	0049	0045	0034	00358	0033	0044	0030
NL Netherlands	0043	0032	0041	00420	0049	0045	0034	00358	0033	0044	0030
PL Poland	0043	0032	0041	00420	0049	0045	0034	00358	0033	0044	0030
P Portugal	0043	0032	0041	00420	0049	0045	0034	00358	0033	0044	0030
RUS Russia	81043	81032	81041	6420	81049	81045	*	810358	81033	81044	*
S Sweden	0043	0032	0041	00420	0049	0045	0034	00358	0033	0044	0030
USA	01143	01132	01141	001420	01149	01145	01134	01358	01133	01144	01130

** Direct dialling not possible*

(H)	(I)	(IRL)	(J)	(L)	(N)	(NL)	(PL)	(P)	(RUS)	(S)	(USA)	
0036	0039	00353	0081	00352	0047	0031	0048	00351	007	0046	001	**A Austria**
0036	0039	00353	0081	00352	0047	0031	0048	00351	007	0046	001	**B Belgium**
0036	0039	00353	0081	00352	0047	0031	0048	00351	007	0046	001	**CH Switzerland**
0036	0039	00353	0081	00352	0047	0031	0048	00351	007	0046	001	**CZ Czech Republic**
0036	0039	00353	0081	00352	0047	0031	0048	00351	007	0046	001	**D Germany**
0036	0039	00353	0081	00352	0047	0031	0048	00351	007	0046	001	**DK Denmark**
0036	0039	00353	0081	00352	0047	0031	0048	00351	007	0046	001	**E Spain**
0036	0039	00353	0081	00352	0047	0031	0048	00351	007	0046	001	**FIN Finland**
0036	0039	00353	0081	00352	0047	0031	0048	00351	007	0046	001	**F France**
0036	0039	00353	0081	00352	0047	0031	0048	00351	007	0046	001	**GB United Kingdom**
0036	0039	00353	0081	00352	0047	0031	0048	00351	007	0046	001	**GR Greece**
	0039	00353	0081	00352	0047	0031	0048	00351	007	0046	001	**H Hungary**
0036		00353	0081	00352	0047	0031	0048	00351	*	0046	001	**I Italy**
0036	0039		0081	00352	0047	0031	0048	00351	007	0046	001	**IRL Ireland**
00136	00139	001353		001352	00147	00131	00148	001351	*	001146	0011	**J Japan**
0036	0039	00353	0081		0047	0031	0048	00351	007	0046	001	**L Luxembourg**
0036	0039	00353	0081	00352		0031	0048	00351	007	0046	001	**N Norway**
0036	0039	00353	0081	00352	0047		0048	00351	007	0046	001	**NL Netherlands**
0036	0039	00353	0081	00352	0047	0031		00351	007	0046	001	**PL Poland**
0036	0039	00353	0081	00352	0047	0031	048		007	0046	001	**P Portugal**
81036	*	*	*	*	*	81031	1048	*		*	*	**RUS Russia**
0036	0039	00353	0081	00352	0047	0031	0048	00351	007		001	**S Sweden**
01136	01139	011353	01181	011352	01147	01131	01148	011351	*	011146		**USA**

Index of towns

O. Forir/MICHELIN

A

B

C

D

E

F

G

H

I

J

K

P

Q

R

S

T

U

V

W

Y

Z

Major hotel groups

Central reservation telephone numbers

ACCOR HOTELS (NOVOTEL)	0871 6630624
DE VERE HOTELS PLC	0845 3752808
DOYLE COLLECTION	0870 9072222
HILTON HOTELS	08705 515151
HOLIDAY INN & CROWNE PLAZA WORLDWIDE	0800 897121 *(Freephone)*
HYATT HOTELS WORLDWIDE	0845 8881234
INTERCONTINENTAL HOTELS	0800 0289387 *(Freephone)*
MACDONALD HOTELS PLC	08457 585593
MARRIOTT HOTELS	0800 2289290 *(Freephone)*
MILLENNIUM & COPTHORNE HOTELS PLC	0845 3020001
RADISSON HOTELS WORLDWIDE	0800 374411 *(Freephone)*
SHERATON HOTELS & RESORTS WORLDWIDE	0800 353535 *(Freephone)*

Maps

Regional maps of listed towns

Places with at least one

- hotel or restaurant
- starred establishment
-  « Bib Gourmand » restaurant
-  « Bib Hotel »
- particularly pleasant restaurant
- particulary pleasant pub
- particularly pleasant hotel
- particularly pleasant guesthouse
- particularly quiet hotel

Distances in miles

(except for the Republic of Ireland: km). The distance is given from each town to other nearby towns and to the capital of each region as grouped in the guide. To avoid excessive repetition some distances have only been quoted once – you may therefore have to look under both town headings.
The distances quoted are not necessarily the shortest but have been based on the roads which afford the best driving conditions and are therefore the most practical.

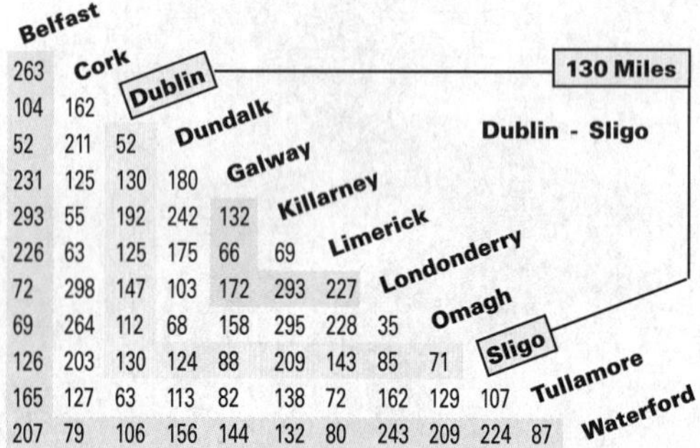

	Belfast	Cork	Dublin	Dundalk	Galway	Killarney	Limerick	Londonderry	Omagh	Sligo	Tullamore
Cork	263										
Dublin	104	162									
Dundalk	52	211	52								
Galway	231	125	130	180							
Killarney	293	55	192	242	132						
Limerick	226	63	125	175	66	69					
Londonderry	72	298	147	103	172	293	227				
Omagh	69	264	112	68	158	295	228	35			
Sligo	126	203	130	124	88	209	143	85	71		
Tullamore	165	127	63	113	82	138	72	162	129	107	
Waterford	207	79	106	156	144	132	80	243	209	224	87

Distances between major towns

Edinburgh - Southampton

433 Miles

	Aberdeen	Ayr	Birmingham	Blackpool	Brighton	Bristol	Cambridge	Cardiff	Carlisle	Coventry	Dover	Dumfries	Dundee	Edinburgh	Glasgow	Inverness	Ipswich	Kingston-upon-Hull	Leeds	Leicester	Liverpool	London	Manchester	Middlesbrough	Newcastle	Norwich	Nottingham	Oban	Oxford	Plymouth	Portsmouth	Sheffield	Southampton	Stoke-on-Trent	Swansea
Ayr	182																																		
Birmingham	424	328																																	
Blackpool	329	233	127																																
Brighton	597	501	178	300																															
Bristol	505	409	98	208	158																														
Cambridge	488	392	100	222	122	175																													
Cardiff	526	430	118	229	192	45	206																												
Carlisle	230	134	196	101	369	277	261	298																											
Coventry	442	346	23	145	159	94	87	124	214																										
Dover	605	509	202	324	105	203	123	236	376	181																									
Dumfries	210	59	229	134	402	311	294	331	35	249	410																								
Dundee	66	125	359	265	532	441	414	461	165	379	530	146																							
Edinburgh	127	87	292	198	467	374	354	394	98	312	470	79	56																						
Glasgow	147	38	291	197	464	373	356	393	97	311	472	78	88	47																					
Inverness	105	208	449	354	622	531	514	551	255	469	630	235	142	157	171																				
Ipswich	539	443	151	273	127	208	55	241	310	137	128	343	464	404	406	564																			
Kingston-upon-Hull	399	303	138	139	277	227	144	248	171	142	260	203	324	264	266	424	195																		
Leeds	360	264	119	86	258	208	150	228	132	123	267	164	285	225	227	385	201	61																	
Leicester	444	348	45	147	166	119	72	152	216	31	187	248	368	308	311	469	123	118	99																
Liverpool	355	259	98	58	271	180	194	200	127	117	295	159	290	224	222	380	245	127	73	119															
London	538	442	119	241	53	119	63	152	310	98	77	343	473	405	405	563	84	216	196	104	213														
Manchester	350	254	96	53	269	178	171	198	122	116	293	154	285	219	217	375	222	98	44	117	35	210													
Middlesbrough	290	227	175	132	314	264	201	284	95	179	317	127	219	158	190	320	252	112	66	155	142	251	113												
Newcastle	253	193	207	151	346	296	233	317	60	211	349	93	182	121	156	284	284	144	99	188	175	284	146	43											
Norwich	537	441	163	284	178	243	66	269	308	149	179	341	462	401	403	562	45	158	198	134	257	119	219	248	281										
Nottingham	416	320	52	137	191	141	90	161	188	55	211	221	342	281	283	442	141	92	73	29	110	128	82	128	161	139									
Oban	182	126	388	293	561	469	453	490	194	408	569	174	121	124	98	110	503	363	318	408	319	501	315	287	253	501	380								
Oxford	498	402	79	201	107	86	102	119	270	60	144	302	433	366	365	523	139	190	171	79	173	59	170	227	259	164	104	462							
Plymouth	619	524	212	322	219	132	285	153	391	208	287	424	554	488	486	645	306	342	322	232	295	217	291	378	410	341	255	584	206						
Portsmouth	580	484	161	283	53	123	152	156	352	142	140	384	515	449	447	605	161	272	253	161	255	84	252	309	341	209	186	544	84	172					
Sheffield	390	294	91	103	230	180	133	200	162	94	250	195	316	255	257	416	184	66	41	71	90	167	50	102	135	181	44	354	142	293	224				
Southampton	565	469	146	267	66	107	151	140	336	126	152	369	500	433	432	590	172	257	238	145	240	82	236	293	326	207	170	529	69	153	19	210			
Stoke-on-Trent	382	286	45	85	218	127	141	147	154	65	242	186	317	250	249	407	192	128	92	63	57	159	54	161	193	203	54	346	119	240	201	81	186		
Swansea	561	465	154	264	227	80	241	42	333	156	263	366	496	430	428	586	277	283	264	186	184	187	233	320	352	303	197	525	154	187	190	237	175	183	
Wick	205	308	549	454	722	631	614	651	355	569	730	336	242	258	271	104	665	525	479	570	480	663	476	421	384	662	541	213	623	744	705	516	690	507	687

For distances refer to the colour key in the table

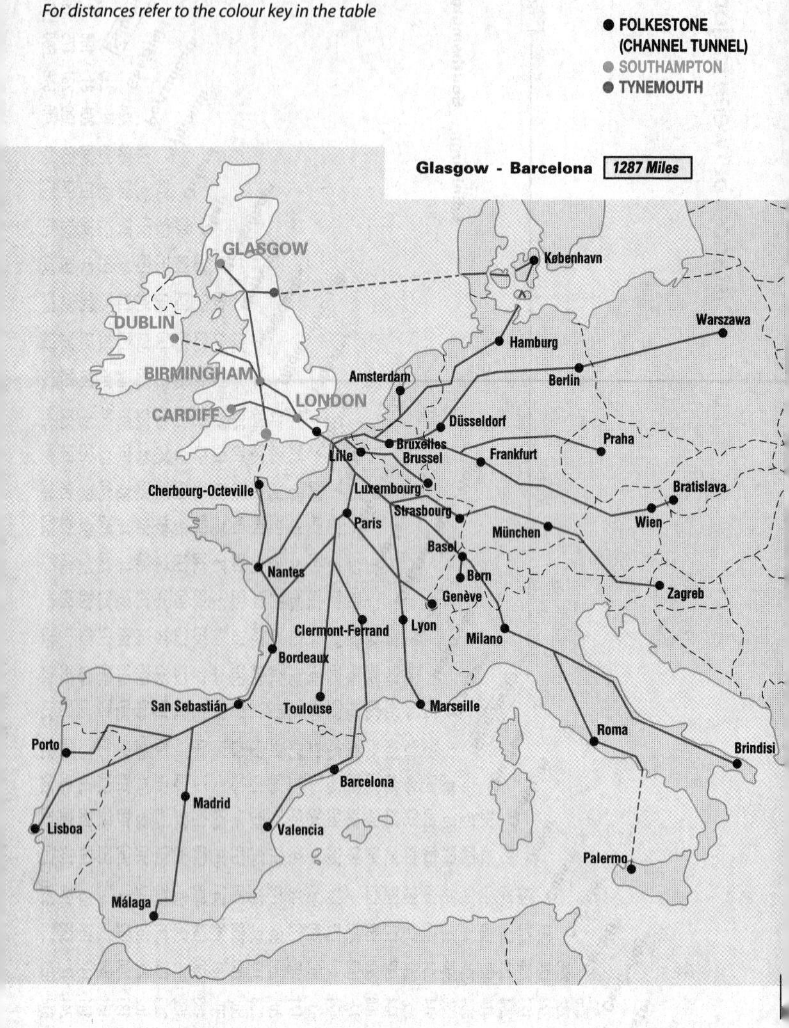

● FOLKESTONE (CHANNEL TUNNEL)
● SOUTHAMPTON
● TYNEMOUTH

Glasgow - Barcelona | *1287 Miles*

GLASGOW
København
DUBLIN
Warszawa
Hamburg
BIRMINGHAM
Berlin
Amsterdam
LONDON
CARDIFF
Düsseldorf
Praha
Bruxelles
Brussel
Lille
Frankfurt
Luxembourg
Bratislava
Cherbourg-Octeville
Strasbourg
Wien
Paris
München
Basel
Bern
Nantes
Genève
Zagreb
Clermont-Ferrand
Lyon
Milano
Bordeaux
San Sebastián
Toulouse
Marseille
Roma
Porto
Brindisi
Barcelona
Madrid
Lisboa
Valencia
Palermo
Málaga

Birmingham	Cardiff	Dublin	Glasgow	London	
231	455	399	336	304	**Amsterdam**
1017	1043	1184	1287	891	**Barcelona**
665	690	832	935	539	**Basel**
773	799	941	724	648	**Berlin**
725	750	892	995	599	**Bern**
735	760	902	1005	609	**Bordeaux**
1059	1085	1227	1330	934	**Bratislava**
1492	1518	1660	1763	1367	**Brindisi**
319	345	486	590	194	**Bruxelles-Brussel**
161	156	329	448	86	**Cherbourg**
637	663	804	907	511	**Clermont-Ferrand**
440	466	608	711	315	**Düsseldorf**
566	591	733	836	440	**Frankfurt am Main**
703	729	870	974	578	**Genève**
509	691	677	605	540	**Hamburg**
701	883	868	796	731	**København**
264	290	431	535	139	**Lille**
1455	1481	1623	1726	1330	**Lisboa**
452	478	619	722	326	**Luxembourg**
667	693	834	937	541	**Lyon**
1165	1191	1333	1436	1040	**Madrid**
1495	1521	1663	1766	1370	**Málaga**
861	887	1028	1132	736	**Marseille**
874	900	1042	1145	749	**Milano**
798	824	965	1069	673	**München**
563	589	731	834	274	**Nantes**
1787	1813	1955	2058	1662	**Palermo**
369	395	536	640	244	**Paris**
1360	1386	1527	1631	1234	**Porto**
879	905	1047	1150	754	**Praha**
1240	1266	1407	1510	1114	**Roma**
879	905	1046	1149	753	**San Sebastián**
580	605	747	850	454	**Strasbourg**
794	820	962	1065	669	**Toulouse**
1229	1255	1397	1500	1104	**Valencia**
1119	1144	1286	1070	993	**Warszawa**
1006	1032	1174	1277	881	**Wien**
1117	1143	1285	1388	992	**Zagreb**

Great Britain & Ireland in 39 maps

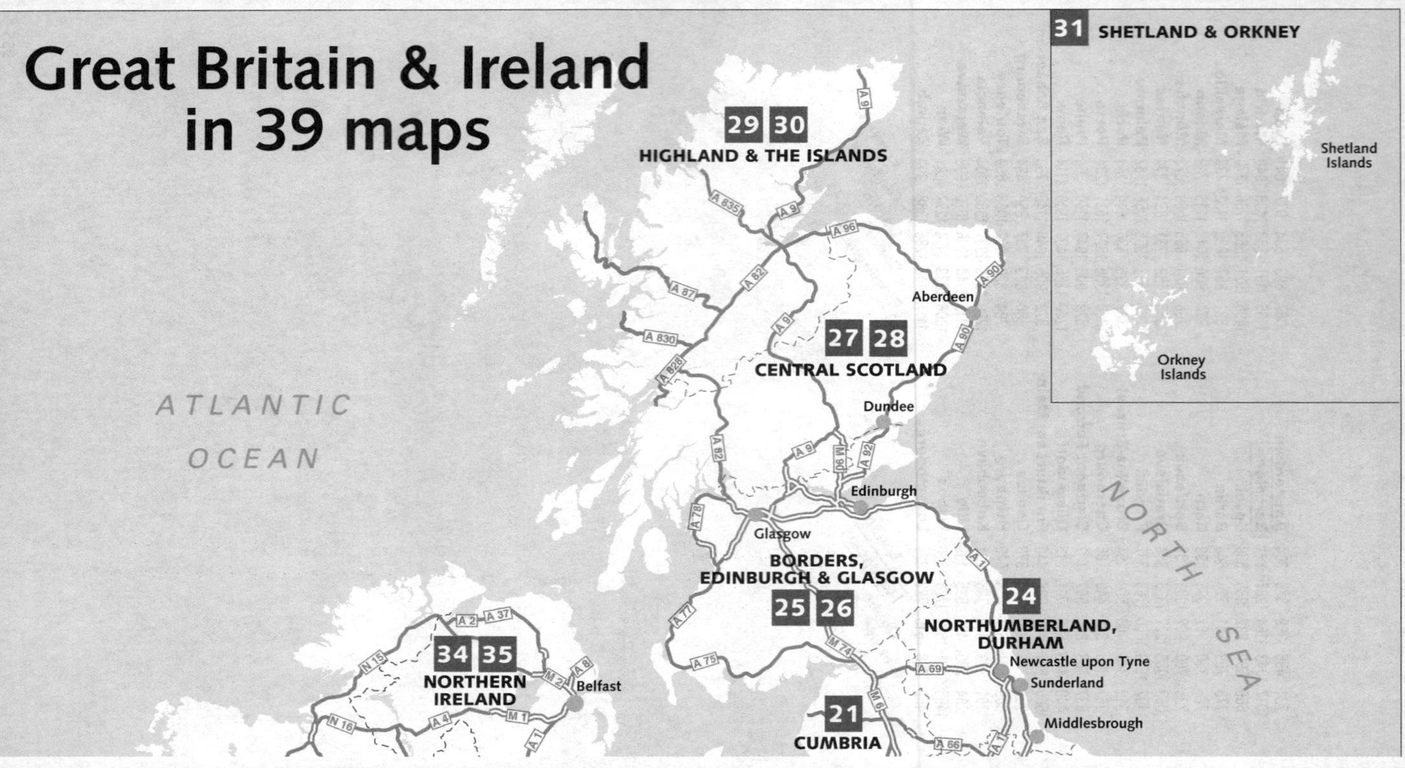

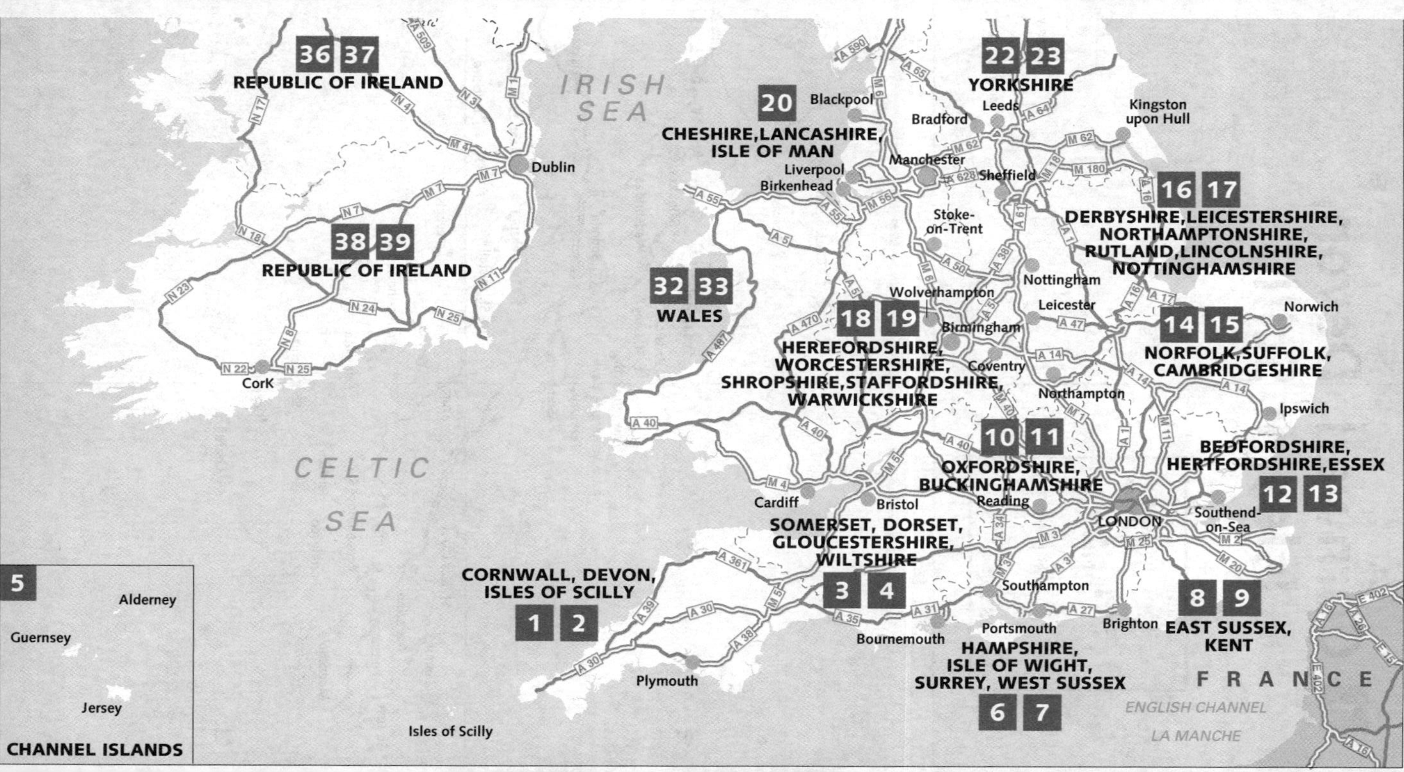

36 37
REPUBLIC OF IRELAND
38 39
REPUBLIC OF IRELAND
Dublin
Cork
IRISH SEA
CELTIC SEA
20
CHESHIRE, LANCASHIRE, ISLE OF MAN
22 23
YORKSHIRE
16 17
DERBYSHIRE, LEICESTERSHIRE, NORTHAMPTONSHIRE, RUTLAND, LINCOLNSHIRE, NOTTINGHAMSHIRE
32 33
WALES
18 19
HEREFORDSHIRE, WORCESTERSHIRE, SHROPSHIRE, STAFFORDSHIRE, WARWICKSHIRE
14 15
NORFOLK, SUFFOLK, CAMBRIDGESHIRE
10 11
OXFORDSHIRE, BUCKINGHAMSHIRE
BEDFORDSHIRE, HERTFORDSHIRE, ESSEX
12 13
SOMERSET, DORSET, GLOUCESTERSHIRE, WILTSHIRE
3 4
CORNWALL, DEVON, ISLES OF SCILLY
1 2
8 9
EAST SUSSEX, KENT
HAMPSHIRE, ISLE OF WIGHT, SURREY, WEST SUSSEX
6 7
Blackpool
Leeds
Bradford
Kingston upon Hull
Manchester
Liverpool
Birkenhead
Sheffield
Stoke-on-Trent
Nottingham
Wolverhampton
Leicester
Birmingham
Norwich
Coventry
Northampton
Ipswich
Cardiff
Bristol
Reading
LONDON
Southend-on-Sea
Southampton
Portsmouth
Brighton
Bournemouth
Plymouth
Isles of Scilly
FRANCE
ENGLISH CHANNEL
LA MANCHE
5
CHANNEL ISLANDS
Alderney
Guernsey
Jersey

1 Cornwall, Devon, Isles of Scilly

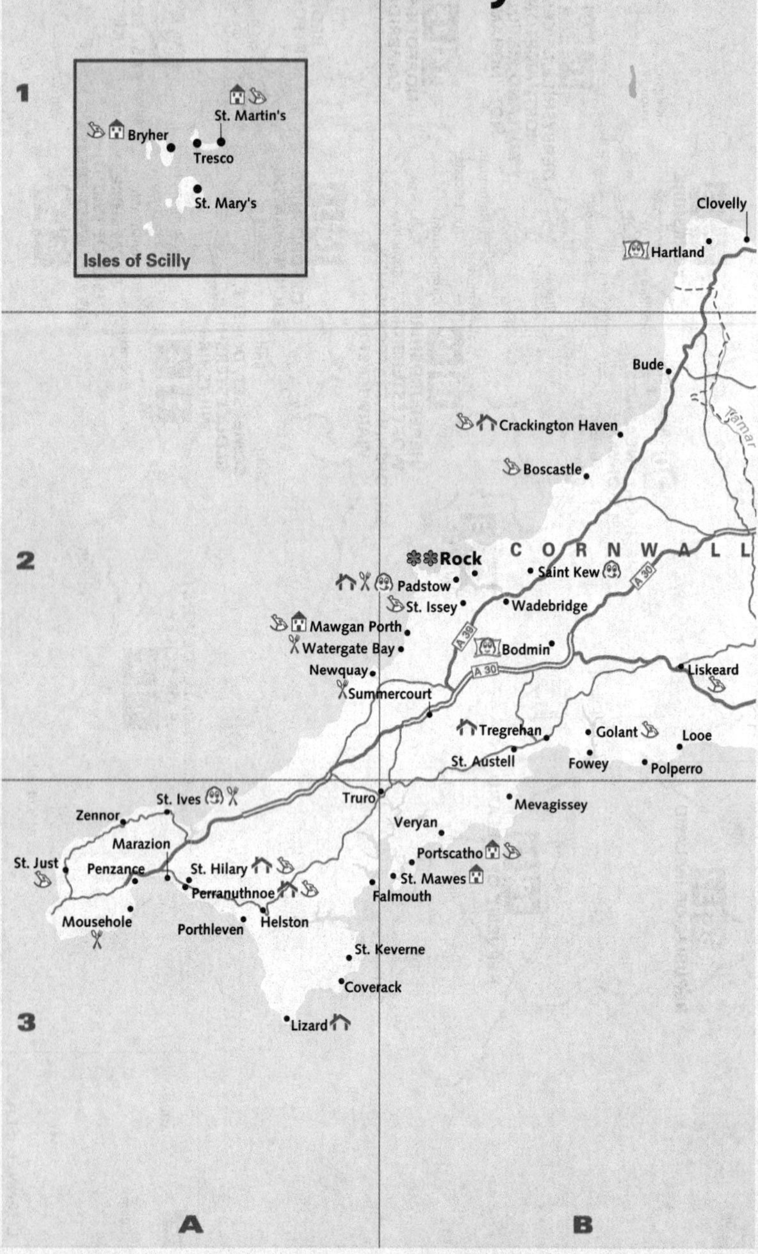

A B

BRIS

1

Isles of Scilly

St. Martin's

Bryher

Tresco

St. Mary's

Clovelly

Hartland

Bude

Tamar

Crackington Haven

Boscastle

2

CORNWALL

Rock

Saint Kew

Padstow

St. Issey

Wadebridge

A 30

A 39

Mawgan Porth

Watergate Bay

Bodmin

Newquay

A 30

Liskeard

Summercourt

Tregrehan

Golant

Looe

St. Austell

Fowey

Polperro

St. Ives

Truro

Mevagissey

Zennor

Veryan

Marazion

Portscatho

St. Just

Penzance

St. Hilary

St. Mawes

Perranuthnoe

Falmouth

Mousehole

Porthleven

Helston

St. Keverne

Coverack

3

Lizard

A B

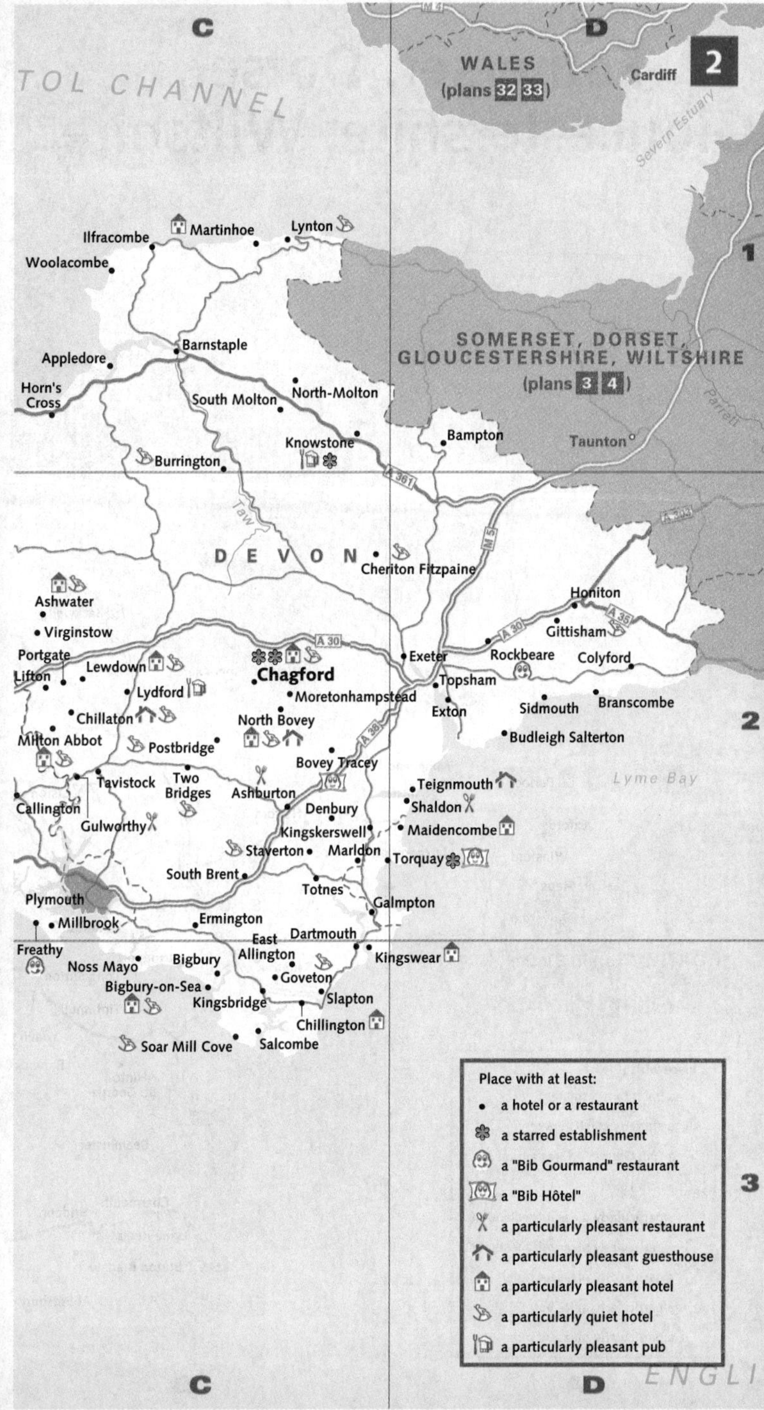
C
D
2
TOL CHANNEL
WALES
(plans 32 33)
Cardiff
Severn Estuary
Martinhoe
Lynton
Ilfracombe
Woolacombe
1
SOMERSET, DORSET, GLOUCESTERSHIRE, WILTSHIRE
(plans 3 4)
Barnstaple
Appledore
Horn's Cross
South Molton
North-Molton
Knowstone
Bampton
Taunton
Parrett
Burrington
A 361
Taw
M 5
DEVON
Cheriton Fitzpaine
A 303
Honiton
Ashwater
Virginstow
A 30
A 35
Gittisham
Portgate
Lifton
Lewdown
Chagford
Exeter
Rockbeare
Colyford
Lydford
Moretonhampstead
Topsham
Chillaton
North Bovey
Exton
Sidmouth
Branscombe
2
Milton Abbot
Postbridge
A 38
Budleigh Salterton
Bovey Tracey
Tavistock
Two Bridges
Ashburton
Teignmouth
Lyme Bay
Callington
Shaldon
Gulworthy
Denbury
Kingskerswell
Maidencombe
Staverton
Marldon
Torquay
South Brent
Totnes
Plymouth
Galmpton
Millbrook
Ermington
Dartmouth
Freathy
East Allington
Kingswear
Noss Mayo
Bigbury
Goveton
Bigbury-on-Sea
Kingsbridge
Slapton
Chillington
Soar Mill Cove
Salcombe
Place with at least:
a hotel or a restaurant
a starred establishment
a "Bib Gourmand" restaurant
a "Bib Hôtel"
a particularly pleasant restaurant
a particularly pleasant guesthouse
a particularly pleasant hotel
a particularly quiet hotel
a particularly pleasant pub
3
C
D
ENGLI

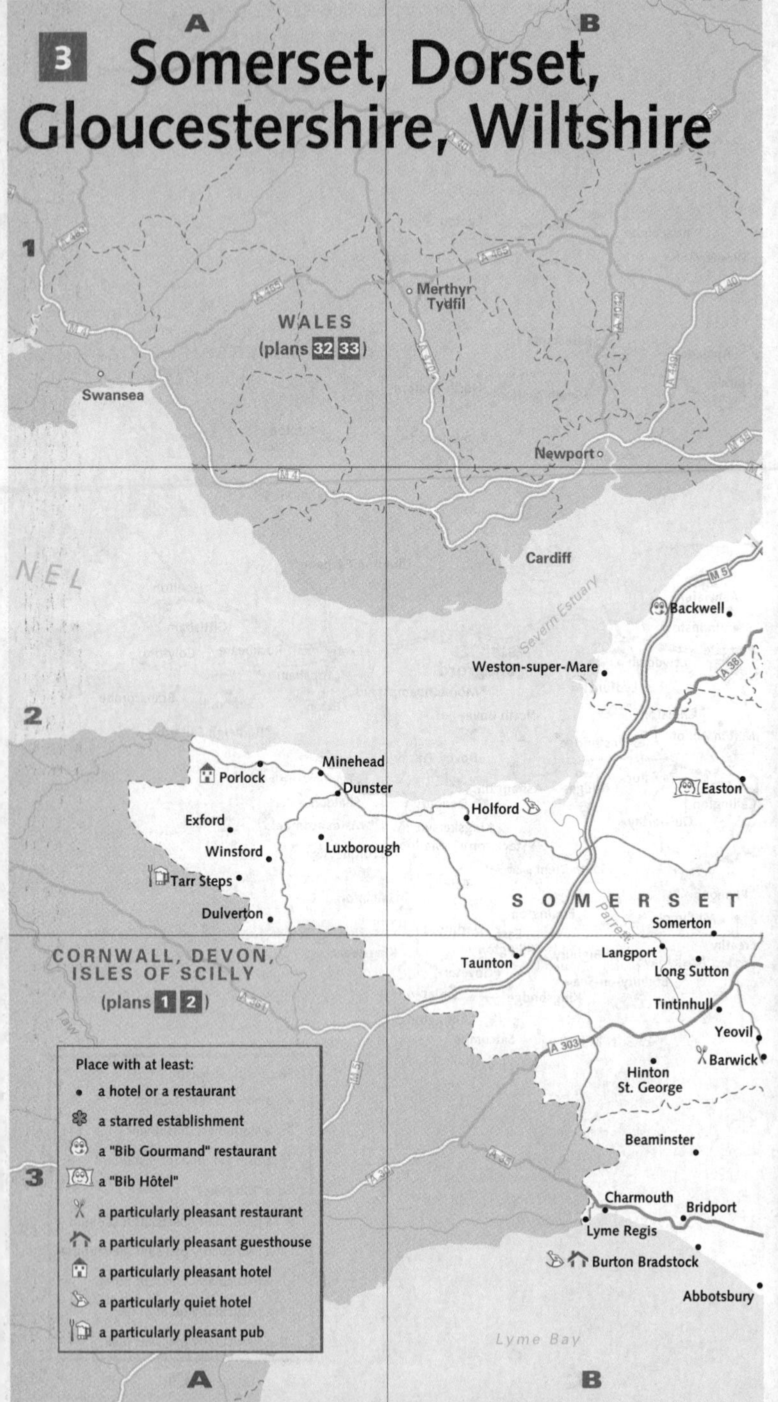
3
Somerset, Dorset, Gloucestershire, Wiltshire
A
B
1
2
3
WALES
(plans 32 33)
Merthyr Tydfil
Swansea
Newport
Cardiff
Severn Estuary
Backwell
Weston-super-Mare
Minehead
Porlock
Dunster
Holford
Exford
Luxborough
Winsford
Tarr Steps
Dulverton
Easton
SOMERSET
Parrett
Somerton
Langport
Long Sutton
Taunton
Tintinhull
Yeovil
Barwick
Hinton St. George
Beaminster
Charmouth
Bridport
Lyme Regis
Burton Bradstock
Abbotsbury
Lyme Bay
CORNWALL, DEVON, ISLES OF SCILLY
(plans 1 2)
Taw
M 4
M 5
A 38
A 303
A 35
A 30
A 361
A 40
A 465
A 483
A 470
A 4042
A 449
Place with at least:
a hotel or a restaurant
a starred establishment
a "Bib Gourmand" restaurant
a "Bib Hôtel"
a particularly pleasant restaurant
a particularly pleasant guesthouse
a particularly pleasant hotel
a particularly quiet hotel
a particularly pleasant pub

4
HEREFORDSHIRE, WORCESTERSHIRE, SHROPSHIRE, STAFFORDSHIRE, WARWICKSHIRE
(plans 18 19)
GLOUCESTERSHIRE
OXFORDSHIRE, BUCKINGHAMSHIRE
(plans 10 11)
WILTSHIRE
HAMPSHIRE, ISLE OF WIGHT, SURREY, WEST SUSSEX
(plans 6 7)
DORSET
Chipping Campden
Broad Campden
Blockley
Tewkesbury
Moreton-in-Marsh
Winchcombe
Lower Swell
Stow-on-the-Wold
Cheltenham
Daylesford
Upper Slaughter
Lower Slaughter
Bourton-on-the-Water
Cowley
Cockleford
Arlingham
Northleach
Clearwell
Painswick
Barnsley
Bibury
Stroud
Sapperton
Coln St. Aldwyns
Fairford
Nailsworth
Cirencester
Marston Meysey
Tetbury
Thornbury
Oaksey
Cricklade
Malmesbury
Purton
Swindon
Bristol
Castle Combe
Colerne
Chippenham
Corsham
Calne
Chew Magna
Bath
Box
Lacock
Marlborough
Monkton Combe
Bradford-on-Avon
Devizes
Little Bedwyn
Newbury
Combe Hay
Potterne
Trowbridge
Ston Easton
Midsomer Norton
Norton St. Philip
East Chisenbury
Wells
Lower Vobster
Frome
Warminster
Shrewton
Maiden Bradley
Ditcheat
Bruton
Little Langford
Castle Cary
Hindon
Teffont
Wincanton
Salisbury
Buckhorn Weston
Gillingham
Corton Denham
Shaftesbury
Donhead-St-Andrew
Sherborne
Tollard Royal
Nomansland
Farnham
Wimborne St. Giles
Evershot
Blandford Forum
Southampton
Buckland Newton
Cerne Abbas
Piddletrenthide
Wimborne Minster
Bournemouth
Dorchester
Poole
Highcliffe
Christchurch
Wareham
Studland
Isle of Wight
Weymouth
Corfe Castle
R. Wye
Thames
Avon
A 40
M 5
A 417
A 48
M 4
A 36
A 303
A 31
A 35
M 27
A 34
M 50
A 49
C
D
1
2
3

The MICHELIN Guide

A collection to savour!

Belgique & Luxembourg
Deutschland
España & Portugal
France
Great Britain & Ireland
Italia
Nederland
Portugal
Suisse-Schweiz-Svizzera
Main Cities of Europe

Also:

Hong Kong Macau
Kyoto Osaka Kobe
London
New York City
Paris
San Francisco
Tokyo Kamakura Yokohama

Channel Islands 5

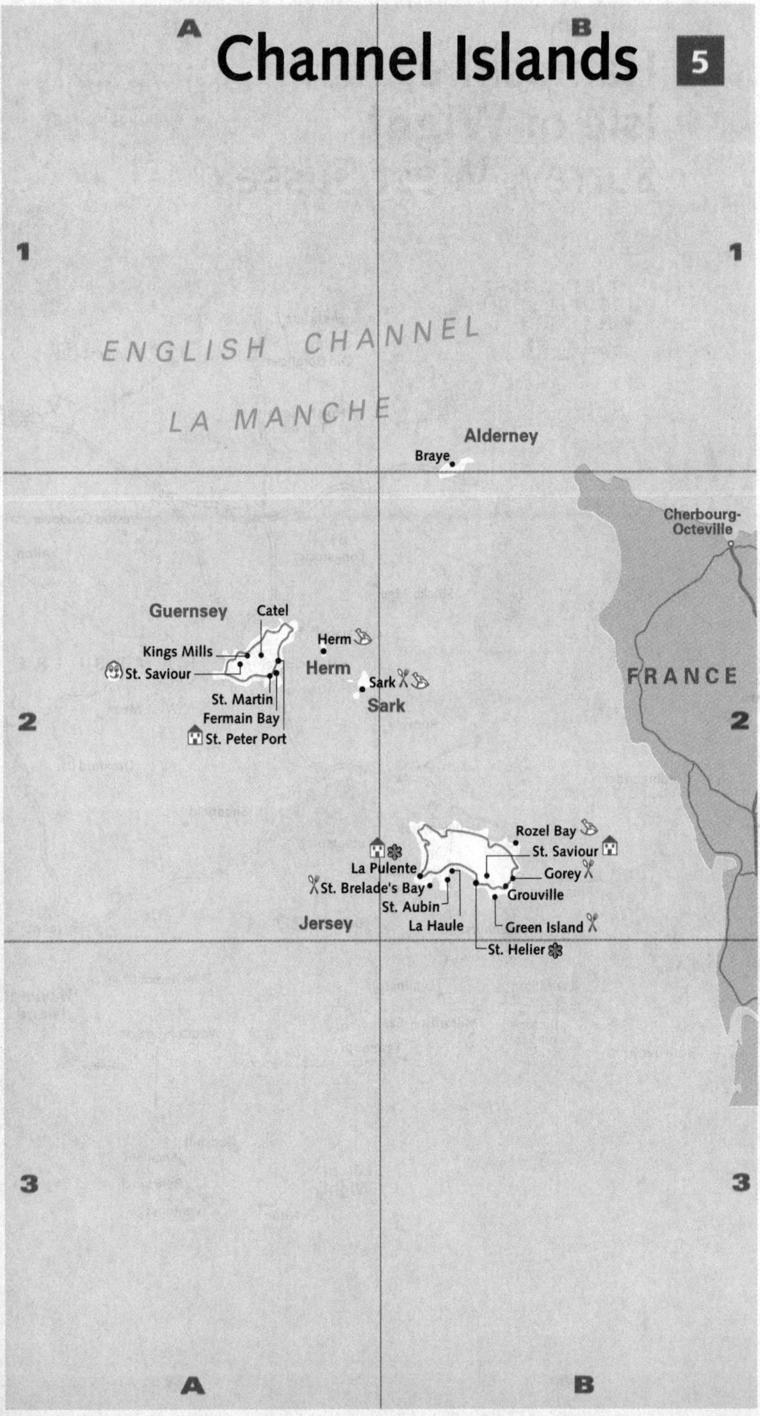

A B

1 1

ENGLISH CHANNEL

LA MANCHE

Alderney

Braye

Cherbourg-Octeville

Guernsey

Catel

Kings Mills

St. Saviour

St. Martin

Fermain Bay

St. Peter Port

Herm

Herm

Sark

Sark

FRANCE

2 2

Rozel Bay

St. Saviour

La Pulente

Gorey

St. Brelade's Bay

Grouville

St. Aubin

Jersey

La Haule

Green Island

St. Helier

3 3

A B

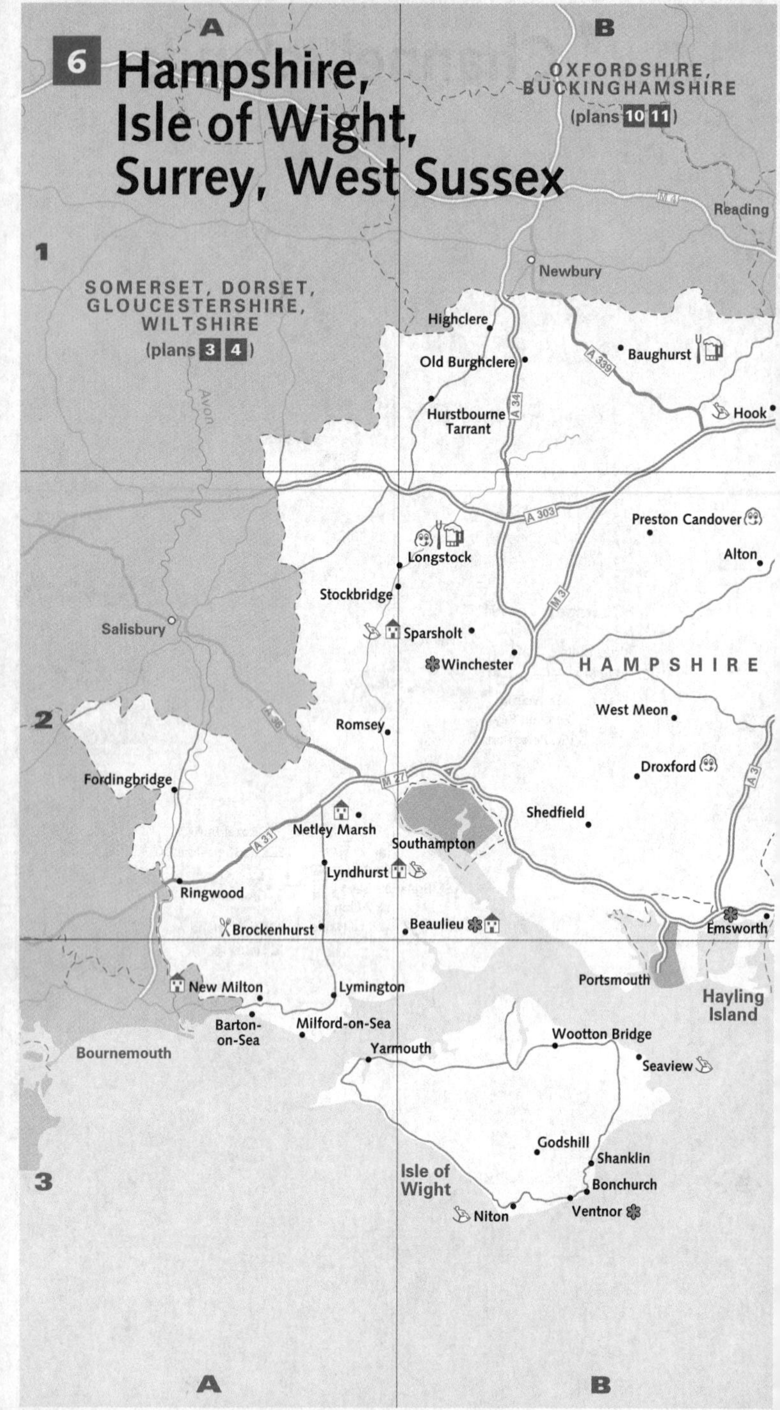
6
Hampshire, Isle of Wight, Surrey, West Sussex
A
B
OXFORDSHIRE, BUCKINGHAMSHIRE
(plans 10 11)
M 4
Reading
1
Newbury
SOMERSET, DORSET, GLOUCESTERSHIRE, WILTSHIRE
(plans 3 4)
Highclere
Old Burghclere
A 339
Baughurst
Avon
A 34
Hurstbourne Tarrant
Hook
A 303
Preston Candover
Longstock
Alton
M 3
Stockbridge
Salisbury
Sparsholt
Winchester
HAMPSHIRE
2
A 36
West Meon
Romsey
Droxford
Fordingbridge
M 27
A 3
Netley Marsh
Shedfield
A 31
Southampton
Lyndhurst
Ringwood
Brockenhurst
Beaulieu
Emsworth
Portsmouth
New Milton
Lymington
Hayling Island
Barton-on-Sea
Milford-on-Sea
Wootton Bridge
Bournemouth
Yarmouth
Seaview
Godshill
Shanklin
3
Isle of Wight
Bonchurch
Niton
Ventnor
A
B

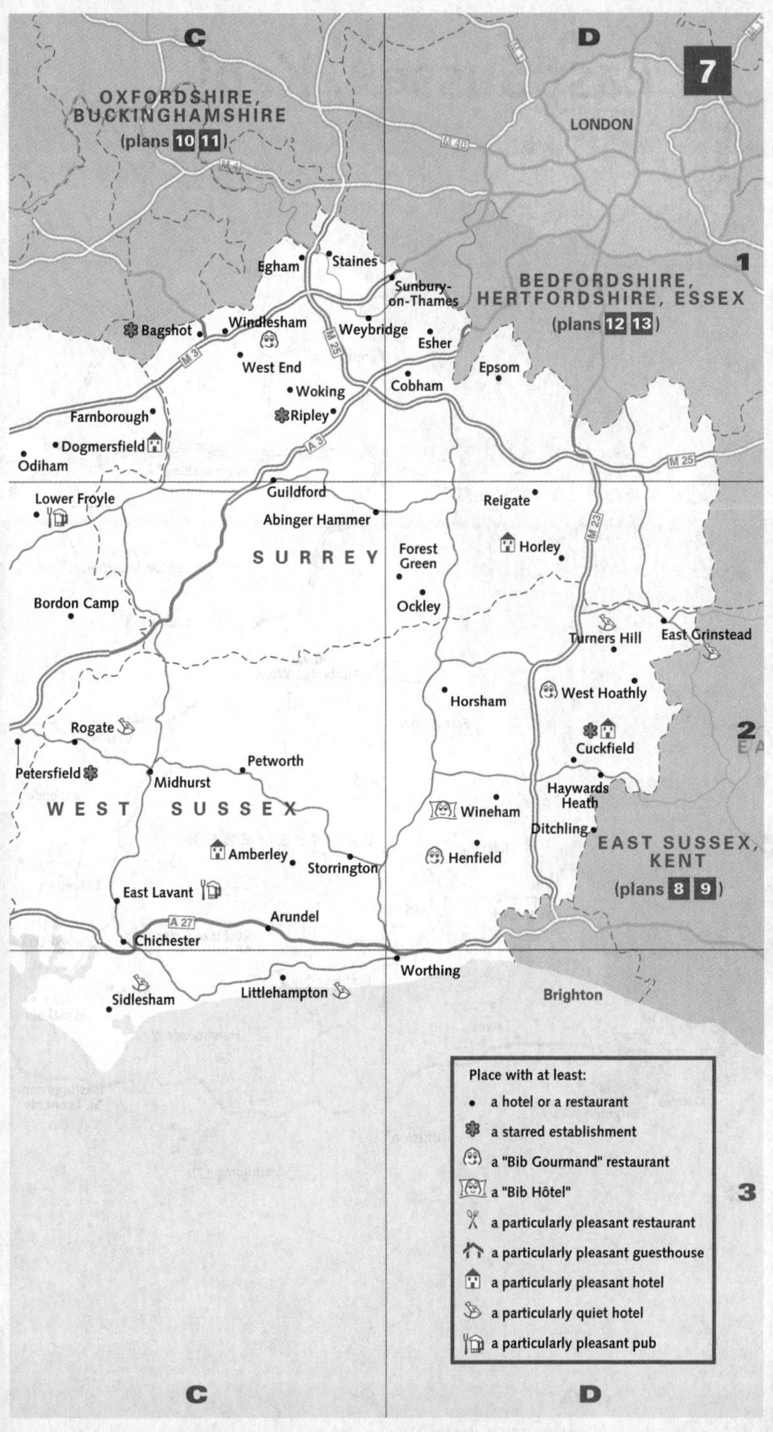
C
D
7
OXFORDSHIRE, BUCKINGHAMSHIRE
(plans 10 11)
LONDON
M 40
M 4
Egham
Staines
Sunbury-on-Thames
BEDFORDSHIRE, HERTFORDSHIRE, ESSEX
(plans 12 13)
1
Bagshot
Windlesham
Weybridge
Esher
M 3
M 25
West End
Epsom
Cobham
Woking
Farnborough
Ripley
Dogmersfield
A 3
M 25
Odiham
Lower Froyle
Guildford
Reigate
Abinger Hammer
M 23
SURREY
Forest Green
Horley
Ockley
Bordon Camp
Turners Hill
East Grinstead
Horsham
West Hoathly
Rogate
2
Cuckfield
Petworth
Petersfield
Midhurst
Haywards Heath
WEST SUSSEX
Wineham
Ditchling
EAST SUSSEX, KENT
Amberley
Henfield
Storrington
(plans 8 9)
East Lavant
A 27
Arundel
Chichester
Worthing
Littlehampton
Brighton
Sidlesham
Place with at least:
a hotel or a restaurant
a starred establishment
a "Bib Gourmand" restaurant
a "Bib Hôtel"
a particularly pleasant restaurant
a particularly pleasant guesthouse
a particularly pleasant hotel
a particularly quiet hotel
a particularly pleasant pub
3
C
D

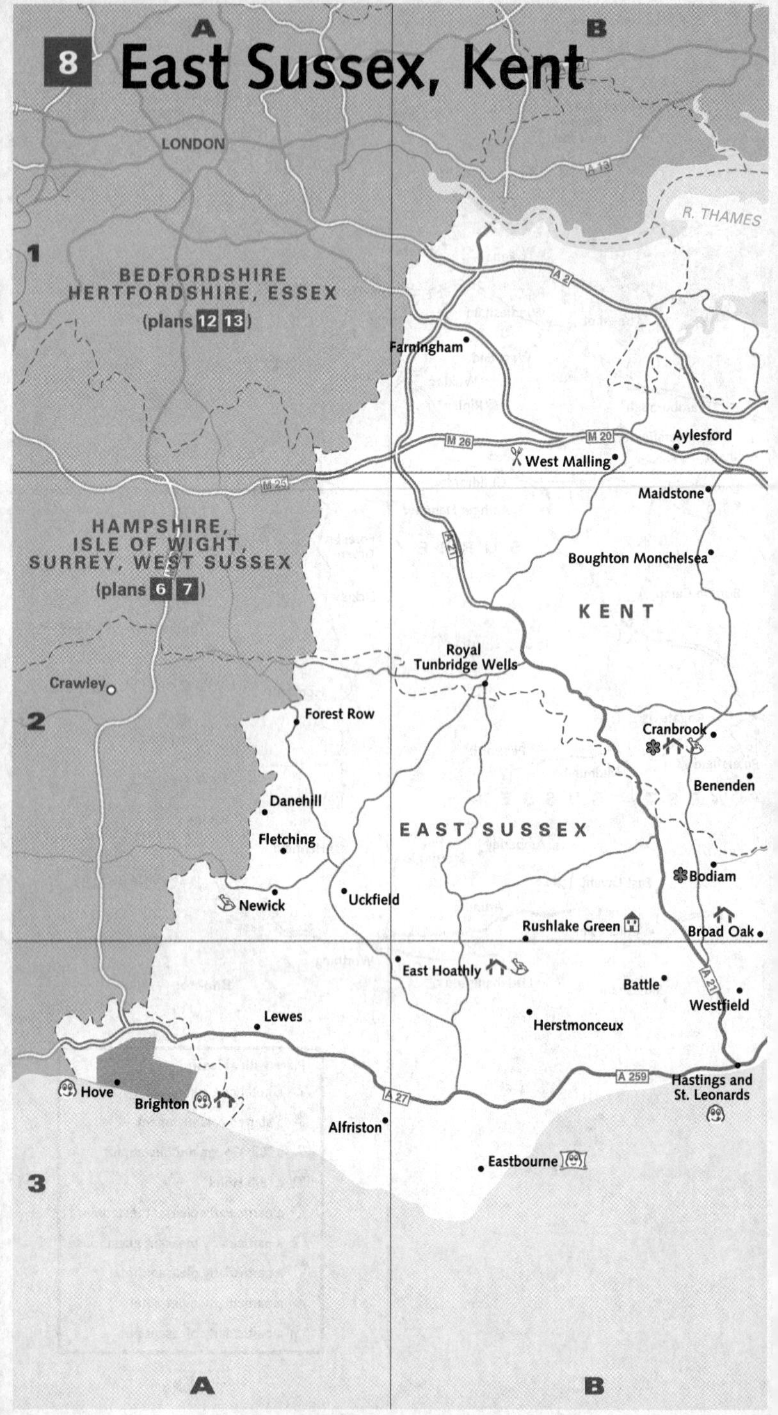
8
East Sussex, Kent
A
B
LONDON
A 13
R. THAMES
1
BEDFORDSHIRE
HERTFORDSHIRE, ESSEX
(plans 12 13)
A 2
Farningham
M 26
M 20
Aylesford
West Malling
M 25
Maidstone
HAMPSHIRE,
ISLE OF WIGHT,
SURREY, WEST SUSSEX
(plans 6 7)
A 21
Boughton Monchelsea
KENT
Royal
Tunbridge Wells
Crawley
2
Forest Row
Cranbrook
Benenden
Danehill
EAST SUSSEX
Fletching
Bodiam
Newick
Uckfield
Rushlake Green
Broad Oak
East Hoathly
Battle
A 21
Westfield
Lewes
Herstmonceux
A 259
Hastings and
St. Leonards
Hove
Brighton
A 27
Alfriston
Eastbourne
3
A
B

C
D
9
BEDFORDSHIRE
HERTFORDSHIRE, ESSEX
(plans 12 13)
Southend-
on-Sea
1
Margate
Rainham
Whitstable
A 299
Broadstairs
Seasalter
Sittingbourne
Ramsgate
Faversham
M 2
Doddington
Ash
Sandwich
Canterbury
Goodnestone
KENT
A 2
Deal
Wye
Alkham
Ashford
Biddenden
M 20
Dover
2
Folkestone
Tenterden
A 259
Ivychurch
New Romney
Rye
Winchelsea
Icklesham
Place with at least:
a hotel or a restaurant
a starred establishment
a "Bib Gourmand" restaurant
a "Bib Hôtel"
a particularly pleasant restaurant
a particularly pleasant guesthouse
a particularly pleasant hotel
a particularly quiet hotel
a particularly pleasant pub
3
DOVER
C
D

10 Oxfordshire, Buckinghamshire
A
B
HEREFORDSHIRE, WORCESTERSHIRE SHROPSHIRE, STAFFORDSHIRE, WARWICKSHIRE
(plans 18 19)
1
SOMERSET, DORSET, GLOUCESTERSHIRE, WILTSHIRE
(plans 3 4)
Banbury
Deddington
Chipping Norton
Church Enstone
Churchill
Kingham
Bicester
Kirtlington
Ascott-under-Wychwood
Woodstock
Murcott
Burford
Witney
A 34
A 40
M 40
A 46
OXFORDSHIRE
Oxford
2
Clanfield
Thames
Lechlade
Buckland Marsh
Toot Baldon
Abingdon
Stadhampton
Sutton Courtenay
Wantage
Harwell
Wallingford
Swindon
M 4
Aston Tirrold
Moulsford
Lambourn
Goring
Pangbourne
Chieveley
Yattendon
3
Hungerford
Newbury
HAMPSHIRE, ISLE OF WIGHT, SURREY, WEST SUSSEX
(plans 6 7)
A 339
Place with at least:
a hotel or a restaurant
a starred establishment
a "Bib Gourmand" restaurant
a "Bib Hôtel"
a particularly pleasant restaurant
a particularly pleasant guesthouse
a particularly pleasant hotel
a particularly quiet hotel
a particularly pleasant pub

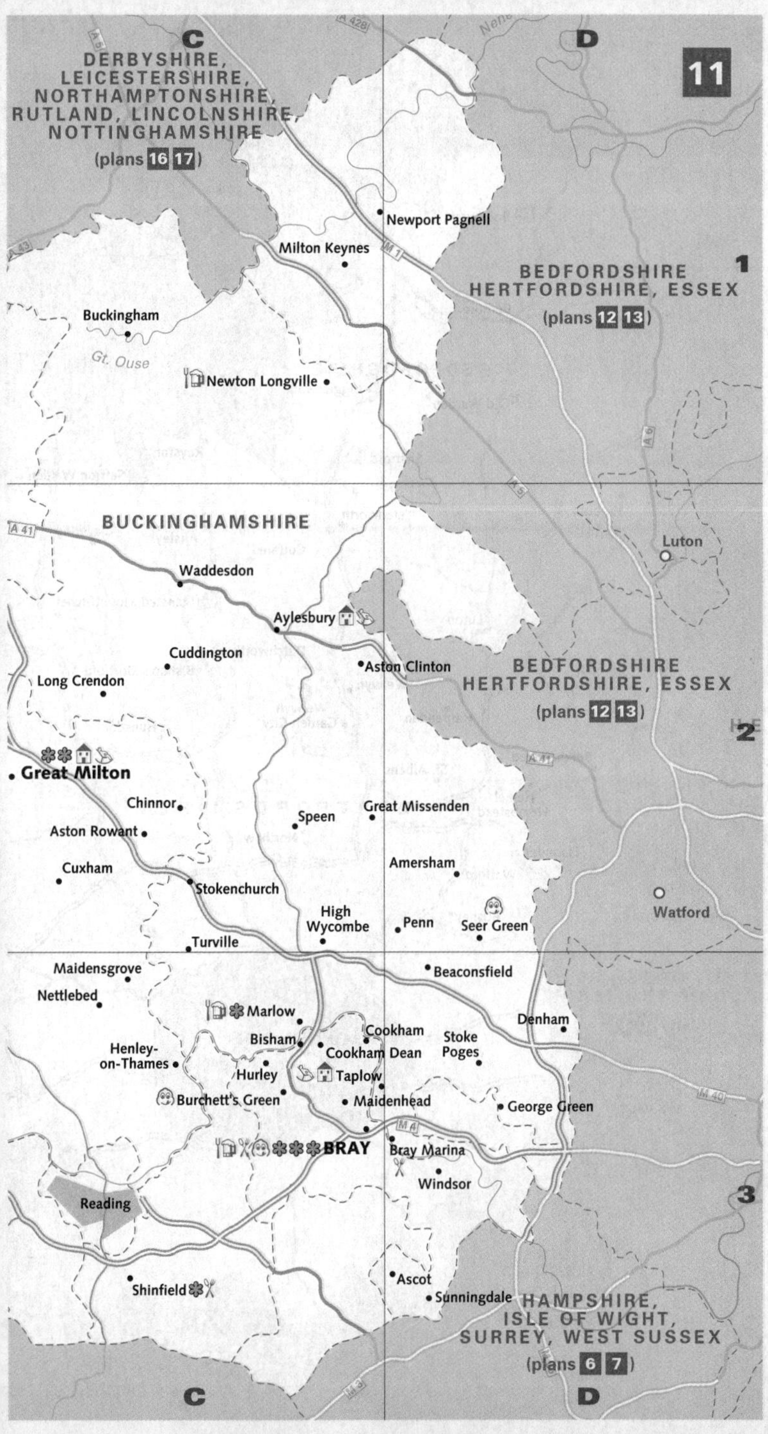
C
D
11
DERBYSHIRE, LEICESTERSHIRE, NORTHAMPTONSHIRE, RUTLAND, LINCOLNSHIRE, NOTTINGHAMSHIRE
(plans 16 17)
Newport Pagnell
Milton Keynes
BEDFORDSHIRE HERTFORDSHIRE, ESSEX
(plans 12 13)
1
Buckingham
Gt. Ouse
Newton Longville
BUCKINGHAMSHIRE
Luton
Waddesdon
Aylesbury
Cuddington
Aston Clinton
Long Crendon
BEDFORDSHIRE HERTFORDSHIRE, ESSEX
(plans 12 13)
2
Great Milton
Chinnor
Speen
Great Missenden
Aston Rowant
Amersham
Cuxham
Stokenchurch
Watford
High Wycombe
Penn
Seer Green
Turville
Maidensgrove
Beaconsfield
Nettlebed
Marlow
Denham
Cookham
Bisham
Stoke Poges
Cookham Dean
Henley-on-Thames
Hurley
Taplow
Burchett's Green
Maidenhead
George Green
BRAY
Bray Marina
Windsor
3
Reading
Ascot
Shinfield
Sunningdale
HAMPSHIRE, ISLE OF WIGHT, SURREY, WEST SUSSEX
(plans 6 7)
C
D

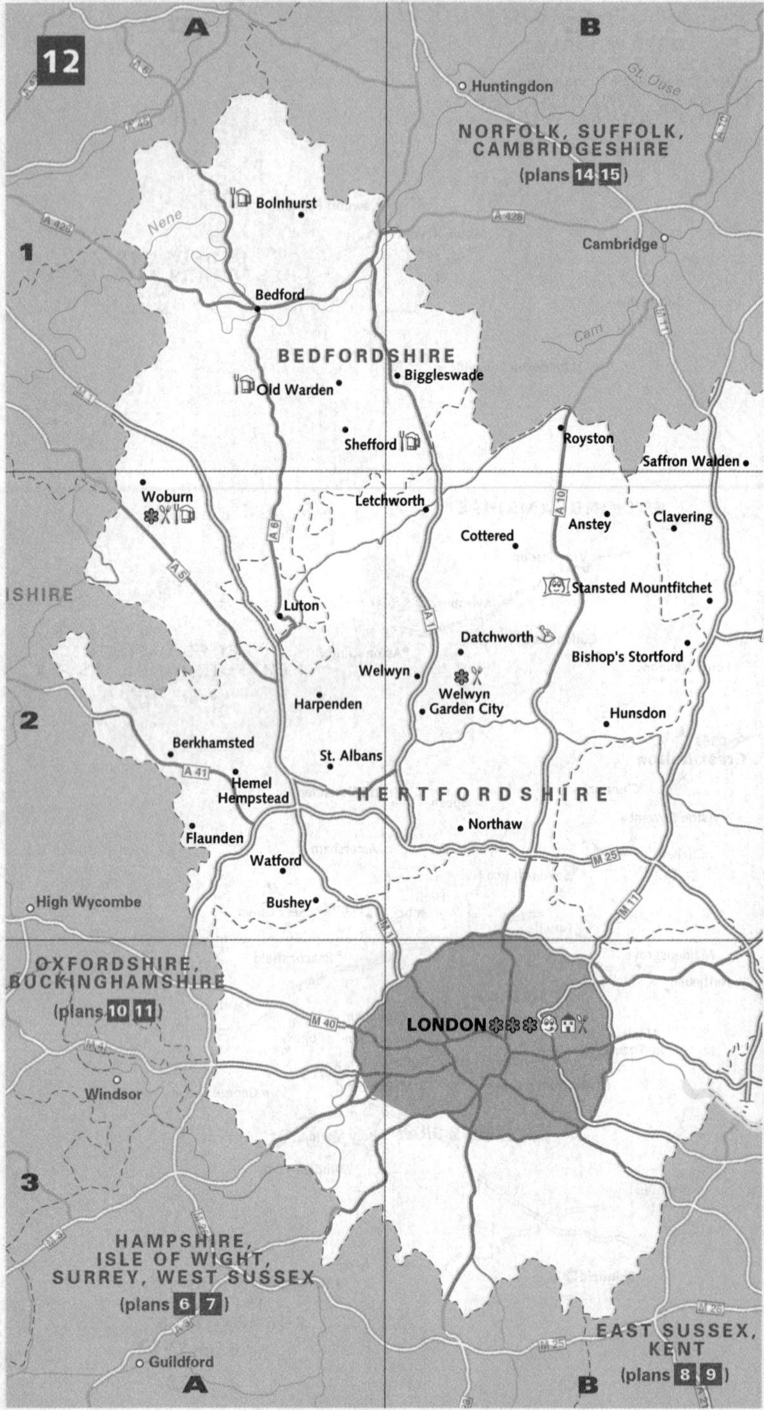
12
A
B
Huntingdon
Gt. Ouse
NORFOLK, SUFFOLK, CAMBRIDGESHIRE
(plans 14 15)
Bolnhurst
Nene
A 428
Cambridge
1
Bedford
Cam
BEDFORDSHIRE
Biggleswade
Old Warden
M 1
Shefford
Royston
Saffron Walden
Woburn
Letchworth
A 6
A 10
Anstey
Clavering
Cottered
A 5
SHIRE
Stansted Mountfitchet
Luton
A 1
Datchworth
Bishop's Stortford
Welwyn
Welwyn Garden City
Harpenden
Hunsdon
2
Berkhamsted
St. Albans
A 41
Hemel Hempstead
HERTFORDSHIRE
Flaunden
Northaw
M 25
Watford
High Wycombe
Bushey
M 11
OXFORDSHIRE, BUCKINGHAMSHIRE
(plans 10 11)
M 40
LONDON
M 4
Windsor
3
M 3
HAMPSHIRE, ISLE OF WIGHT, SURREY, WEST SUSSEX
(plans 6 7)
EAST SUSSEX, KENT
(plans 8 9)
Guildford

Bedfordshire, Hertfordshire, Essex

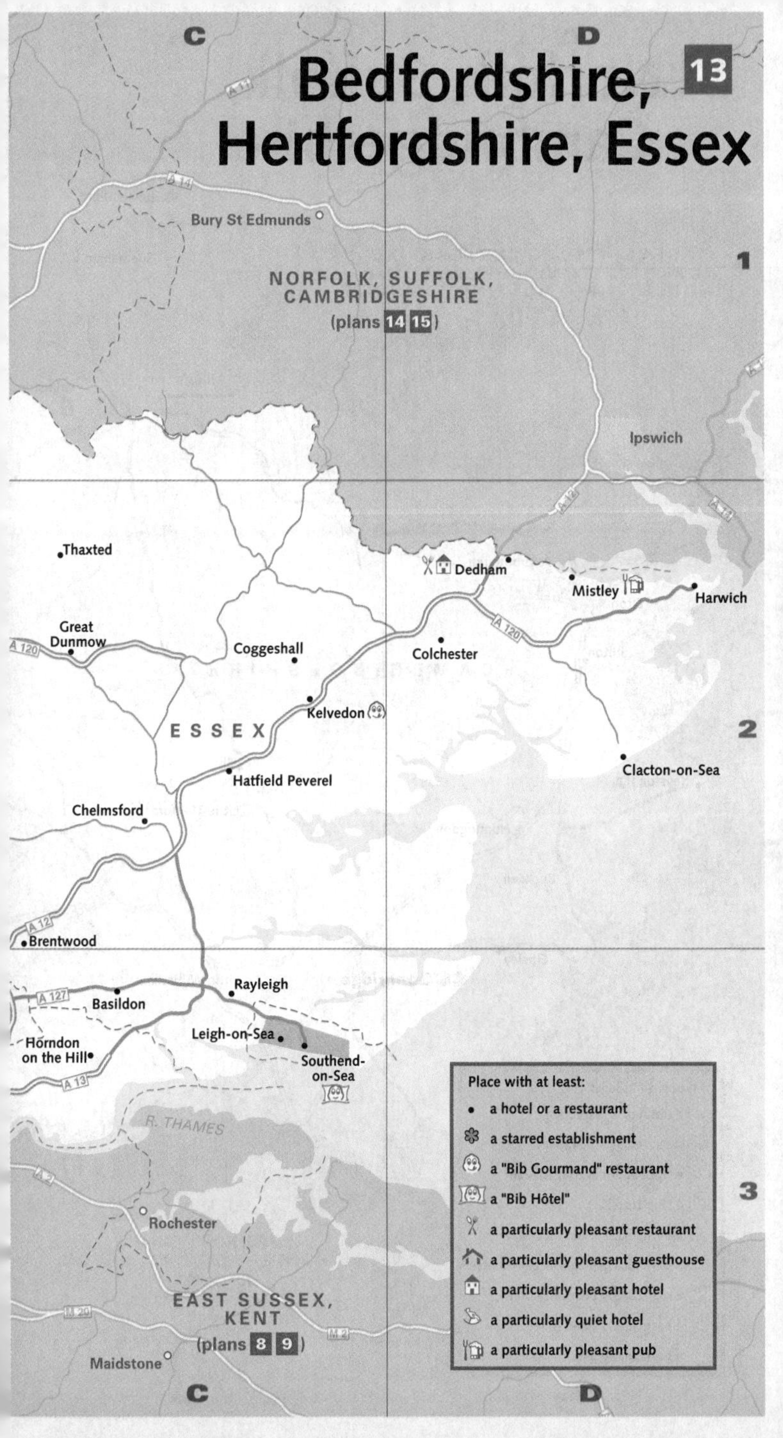

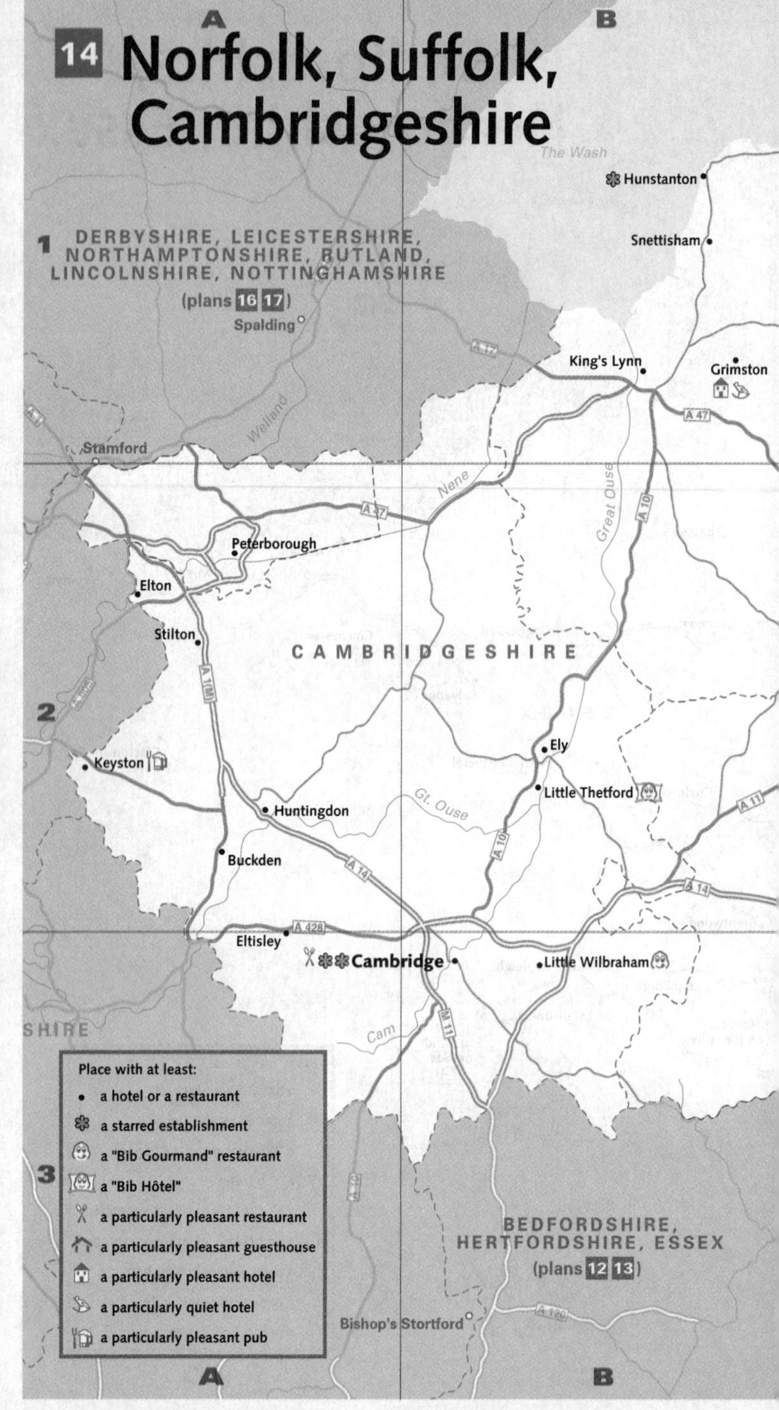
14
Norfolk, Suffolk, Cambridgeshire
A
B
1
2
3
The Wash
Hunstanton
Snettisham
DERBYSHIRE, LEICESTERSHIRE, NORTHAMPTONSHIRE, RUTLAND, LINCOLNSHIRE, NOTTINGHAMSHIRE
(plans 16 17)
Spalding
A 17
King's Lynn
Grimston
A 47
Welland
Stamford
Nene
Great Ouse
A 10
A 47
Peterborough
Elton
Stilton
CAMBRIDGESHIRE
A 1(M)
Ely
Keyston
Little Thetford
Gt. Ouse
A 11
Huntingdon
Buckden
A 14
A 14
A 428
Eltisley
Cambridge
Little Wilbraham
SHIRE
Cam
M 11
Place with at least:
a hotel or a restaurant
a starred establishment
a "Bib Gourmand" restaurant
a "Bib Hôtel"
a particularly pleasant restaurant
a particularly pleasant guesthouse
a particularly pleasant hotel
a particularly quiet hotel
a particularly pleasant pub
BEDFORDSHIRE, HERTFORDSHIRE, ESSEX
(plans 12 13)
A 120
Bishop's Stortford
A
B

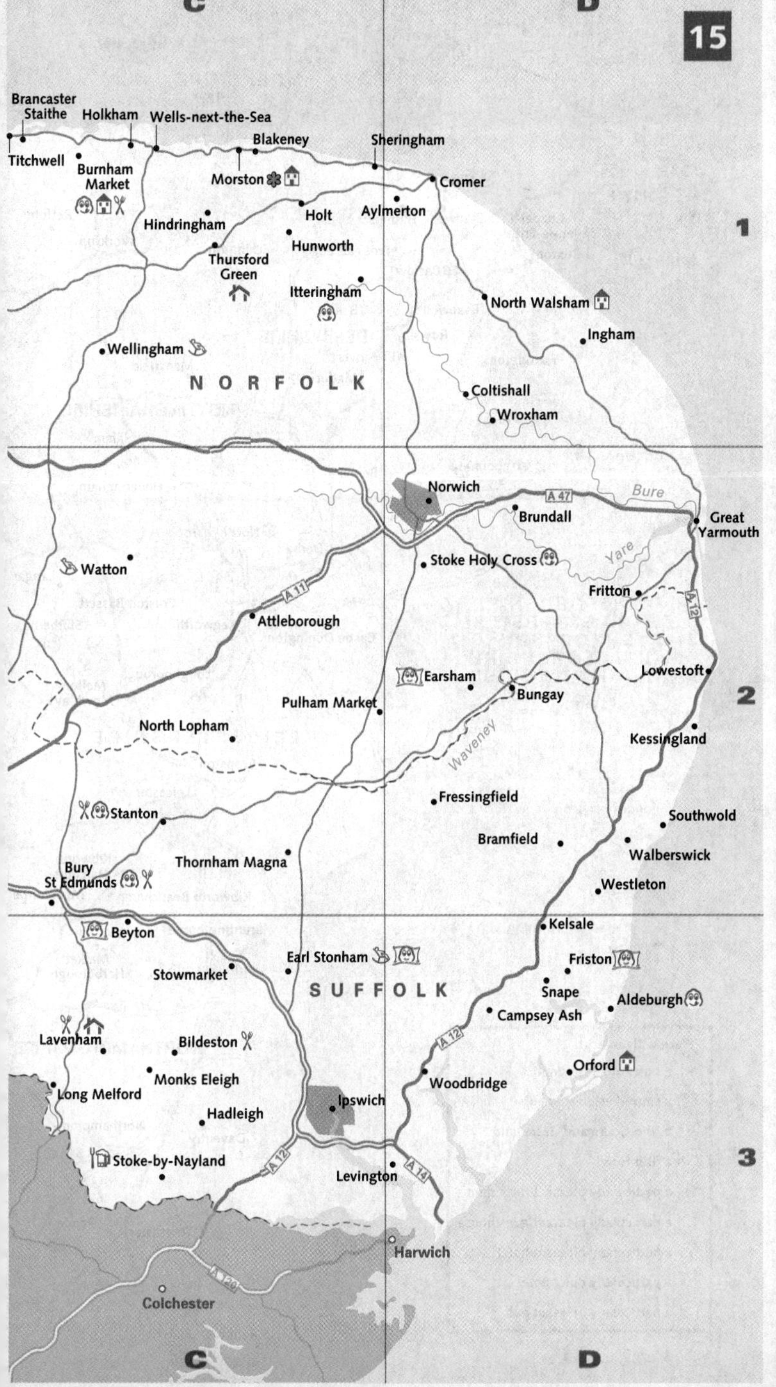
C
D
Brancaster Staithe
Holkham
Wells-next-the-Sea
Titchwell
Burnham Market
Blakeney
Sheringham
Morston
Cromer
Holt
Aylmerton
Hindringham
Hunworth
Thursford Green
Itteringham
North Walsham
Ingham
Wellingham
NORFOLK
Coltishall
Wroxham
Norwich
A 47
Bure
Brundall
Great Yarmouth
Watton
Stoke Holy Cross
Yare
A 11
Fritton
A 12
Attleborough
Earsham
Lowestoft
Bungay
Pulham Market
North Lopham
Kessingland
Waveney
Fressingfield
Stanton
Southwold
Bramfield
Walberswick
Thornham Magna
Bury St Edmunds
Westleton
Kelsale
Beyton
Earl Stonham
Friston
Stowmarket
SUFFOLK
Snape
Aldeburgh
Campsey Ash
Lavenham
Bildeston
Monks Eleigh
Orford
Woodbridge
Long Melford
Ipswich
Hadleigh
Stoke-by-Nayland
Levington
A 14
Harwich
Colchester
1
2
3

16
A
B
Manchester
Barnsley
Doncaster
YORKSHIRE
(plans 22 23)
Rotherham
Sheffield
Derwent
CHESHIRE,
LANCASHIRE,
ISLE OF MAN
(plan 20)
1
Hope
Bradwell
Hathersage
Chapel-en-le-Frith
Buxton
Froggatt Edge
Baslow
Eckington
Worksop
Retford
Bakewell
Beeley
Rowsley
DERBYSHIRE
Hartington
Birchover
Matlock
Mansfield
NOTTINGHAMSHIRE
Halam
Stoke-on-Trent
Ashbourne
Belper
Hoveringham
R. Trent
Nottingham
Derby
Langar
Colston Bassett
Stathern
HEREFORDSHIRE,
WORCESTERSHIRE,
SHROPSHIRE,
STAFFORDSHIRE,
WARWICKSHIRE
(plans 18 19)
Castle Donington
Kegworth
Loughborough
Melton
Mowbray
2
LEICESTERSHIRE
Cropston
Leicester
Wolverhampton
Kibworth
Harcourt
Kibworth Beauchamp
Medbourne
Birmingham
Bruntingthorpe
North Kilworth
Market
Harborough
Coventry
NORTHAMPTONSHIRE
Daventry
Northampton
3
Towcester
Roade
Aynho
Gt. Ouse
CESTERSHIRE
Place with at least:
a hotel or a restaurant
a starred establishment
a "Bib Gourmand" restaurant
a "Bib Hôtel"
a particularly pleasant restaurant
a particularly pleasant guesthouse
a particularly pleasant hotel
a particularly quiet hotel
a particularly pleasant pub

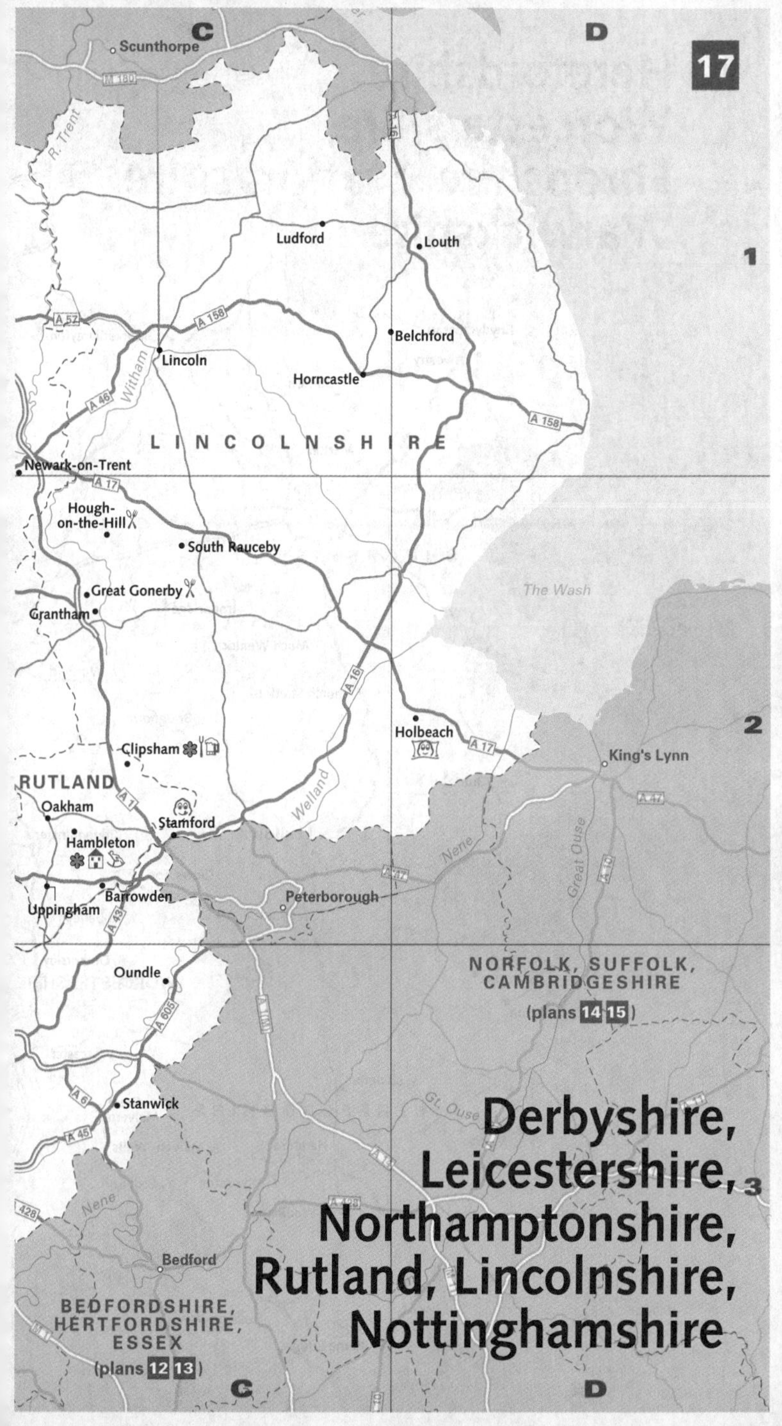

17
C
D
Scunthorpe
M 180
R. Trent
Ludford
Louth
1
A 57
A 158
Belchford
Lincoln
Witham
Horncastle
A 46
A 158
LINCOLNSHIRE
Newark-on-Trent
A 17
Hough-on-the-Hill
South Rauceby
Great Gonerby
The Wash
Grantham
A 16
Holbeach
2
Clipsham
A 17
King's Lynn
RUTLAND
A 1
Welland
A 47
Oakham
Stamford
Hambleton
Nene
Great Ouse
A 47
A 10
Barrowden
Peterborough
Uppingham
A 43
NORFOLK, SUFFOLK, CAMBRIDGESHIRE
(plans 14 15)
Oundle
A 605
Stanwick
A 6
Gt. Ouse
A 45
Derbyshire, Leicestershire, Northamptonshire, Rutland, Lincolnshire, Nottinghamshire
3
Nene
A 428
Bedford
BEDFORDSHIRE, HERTFORDSHIRE, ESSEX
(plans 12 13)
C
D

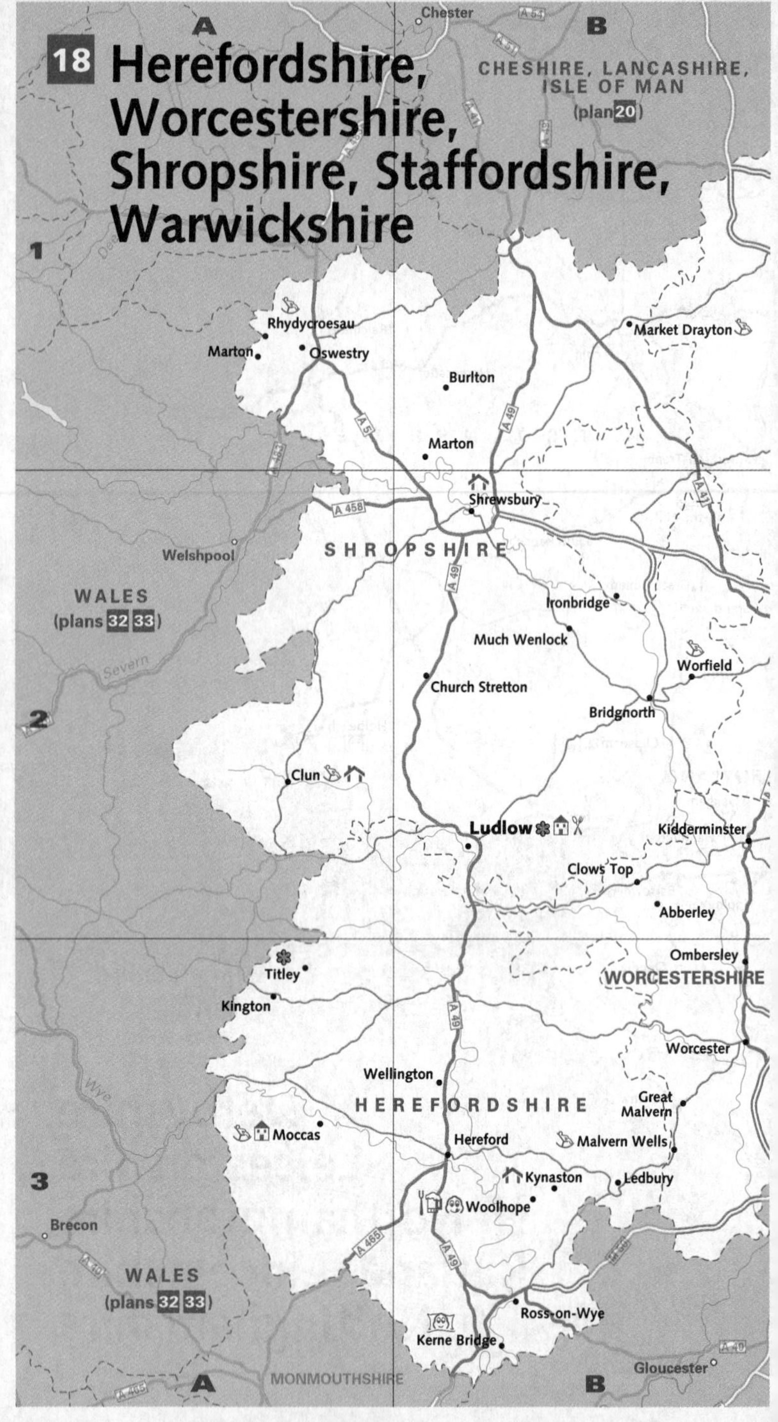

18
Herefordshire, Worcestershire, Shropshire, Staffordshire, Warwickshire
A
B
Chester
CHESHIRE, LANCASHIRE, ISLE OF MAN
(plan 20)
1
2
3
Rhydycroesau
Marton
Oswestry
Market Drayton
Burlton
Marton
Shrewsbury
A 458
A 5
A 49
A 41
Welshpool
SHROPSHIRE
WALES
(plans 32 33)
Severn
Ironbridge
Much Wenlock
Worfield
Church Stretton
Bridgnorth
Clun
Ludlow
Kidderminster
Clows Top
Abberley
Ombersley
WORCESTERSHIRE
Titley
Kington
Worcester
Wellington
Wye
HEREFORDSHIRE
Great Malvern
Moccas
Hereford
Malvern Wells
Kynaston
Ledbury
Woolhope
Brecon
A 465
WALES
(plans 32 33)
Ross-on-Wye
Kerne Bridge
A 40
Gloucester
MONMOUTHSHIRE

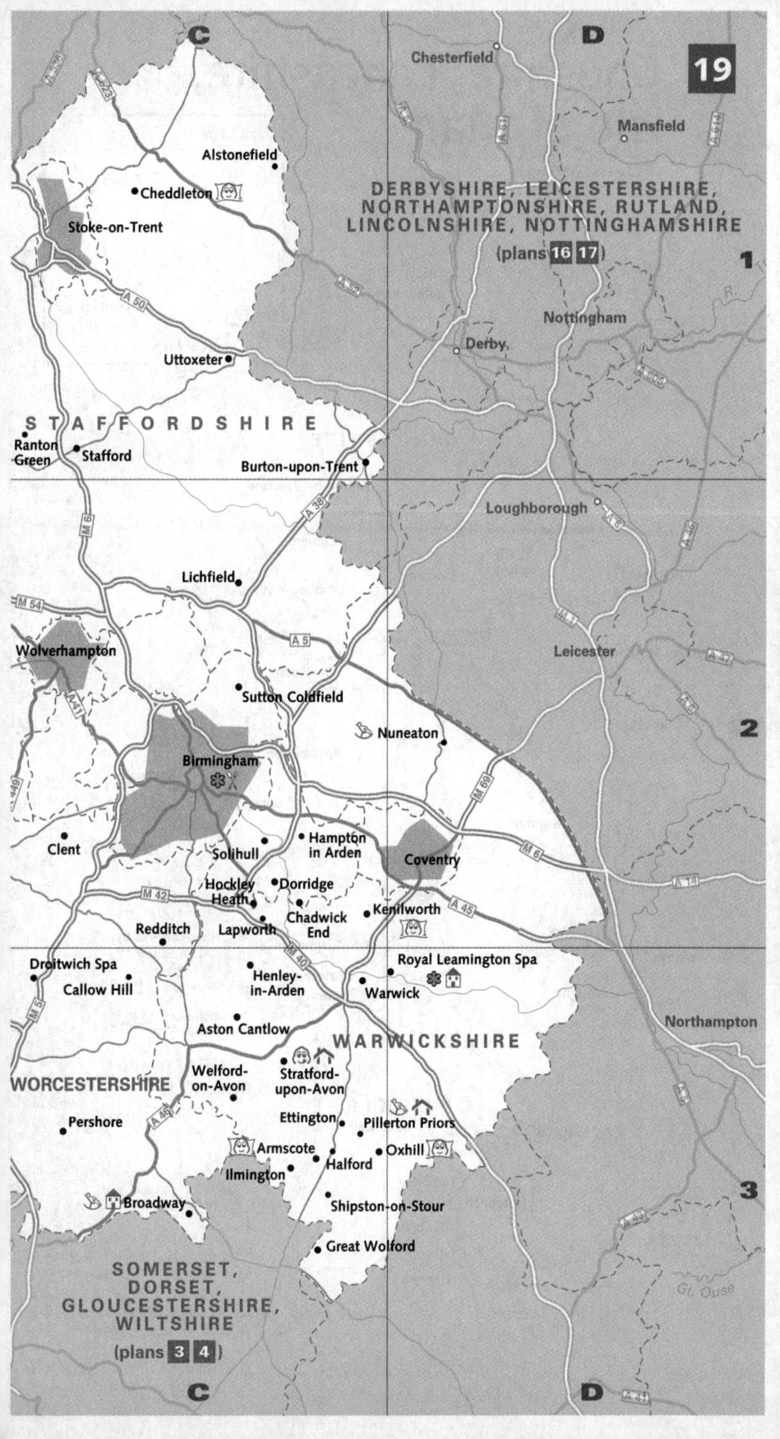

19
C
D
Chesterfield
Mansfield
Alstonefield
Cheddleton
Stoke-on-Trent
DERBYSHIRE, LEICESTERSHIRE, NORTHAMPTONSHIRE, RUTLAND, LINCOLNSHIRE, NOTTINGHAMSHIRE
(plans 16 17)
1
Nottingham
Derby
Uttoxeter
STAFFORDSHIRE
Ranton Green
Stafford
Burton-upon-Trent
Loughborough
Lichfield
Wolverhampton
Leicester
Sutton Coldfield
Nuneaton
2
Birmingham
Clent
Solihull
Hampton in Arden
Coventry
Hockley Heath
Dorridge
Chadwick End
Kenilworth
Redditch
Lapworth
Droitwich Spa
Callow Hill
Henley-in-Arden
Royal Leamington Spa
Warwick
Aston Cantlow
WARWICKSHIRE
Northampton
WORCESTERSHIRE
Welford-on-Avon
Stratford-upon-Avon
Pershore
Ettington
Pillerton Priors
Armscote
Oxhill
Halford
Ilmington
Broadway
Shipston-on-Stour
3
Great Wolford
SOMERSET, DORSET, GLOUCESTERSHIRE, WILTSHIRE
(plans 3 4)
Gt. Ouse
A 50
A 38
M 6
M 54
A 5
A 41
M 69
A 45
M 42
M 40
M 5
A 46
A 14
A 47
M 1
A 6
A 61
A 614
A 52
A 606
A 43
A 449

20 Cheshire, Lancashire, Isle of Man

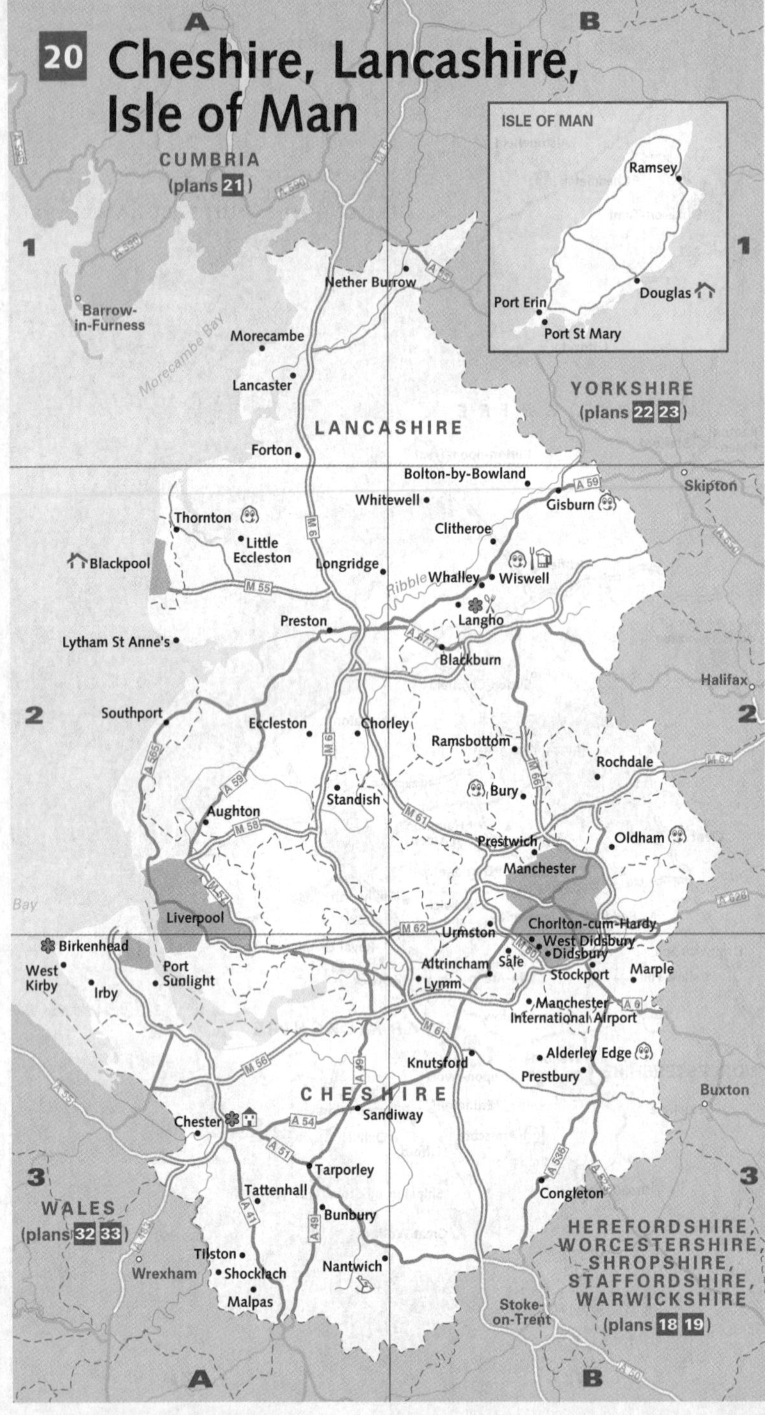

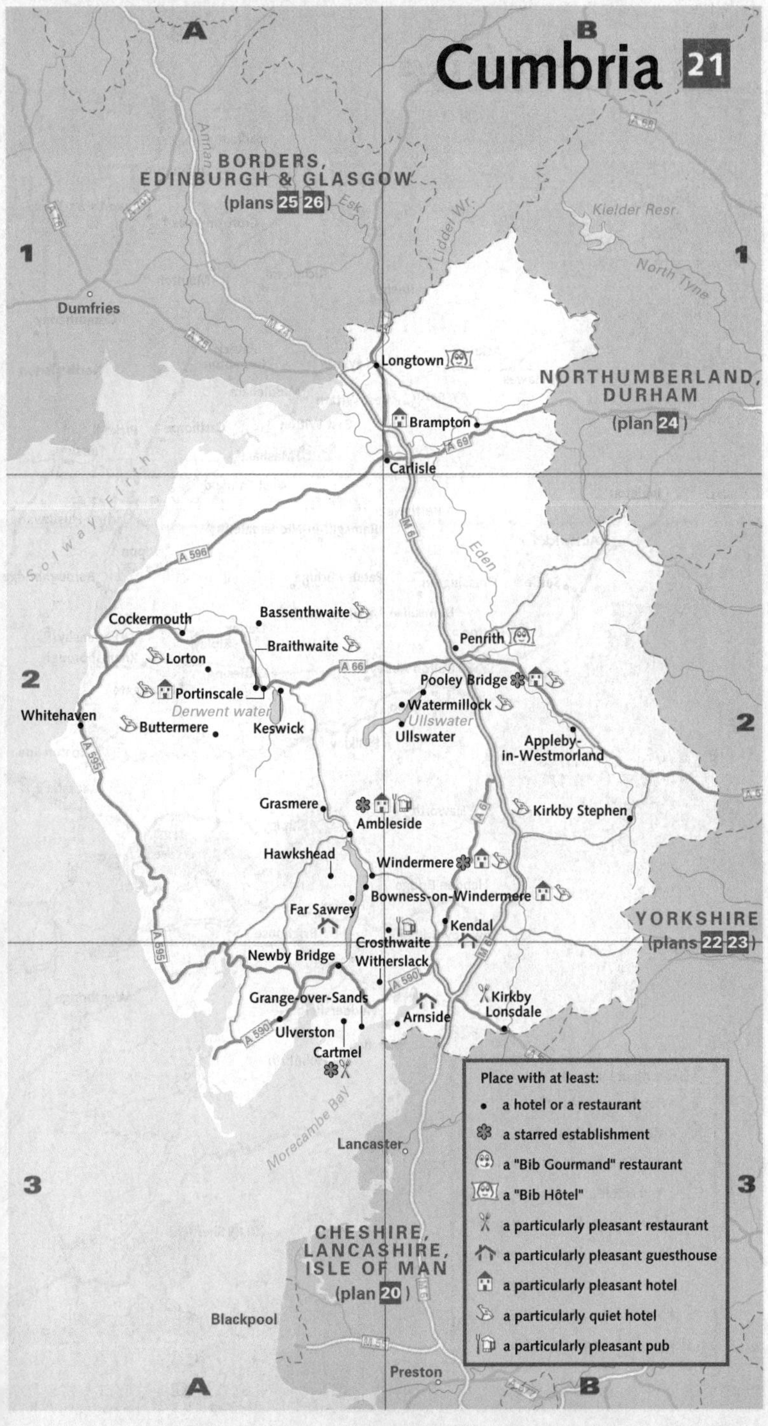

Cumbria
21
A
B
1
2
3
BORDERS,
EDINBURGH & GLASGOW
(plans 25 26)
Esk
Liddel Wr.
Kielder Resr
North Tyne
Dumfries
Longtown
NORTHUMBERLAND,
DURHAM
(plan 24)
Brampton
A 69
Carlisle
Solway Firth
A 596
M 6
Eden
Bassenthwaite
Cockermouth
Braithwaite
Lorton
A 66
Penrith
Pooley Bridge
Portinscale
Derwent water
Watermillock
Ullswater
Whitehaven
Buttermere
Keswick
Ullswater
Appleby-in-Westmorland
A 595
Grasmere
Ambleside
A 6
Kirkby Stephen
Hawkshead
Windermere
Bowness-on-Windermere
Far Sawrey
Kendal
YORKSHIRE
(plans 22 23)
Crosthwaite
Newby Bridge
Witherslack
A 590
Grange-over-Sands
Kirkby Lonsdale
Arnside
Ulverston
Cartmel
Morecambe Bay
Lancaster
CHESHIRE,
LANCASHIRE,
ISLE OF MAN
(plan 20)
Blackpool
Preston
Place with at least:
a hotel or a restaurant
a starred establishment
a "Bib Gourmand" restaurant
a "Bib Hôtel"
a particularly pleasant restaurant
a particularly pleasant guesthouse
a particularly pleasant hotel
a particularly quiet hotel
a particularly pleasant pub

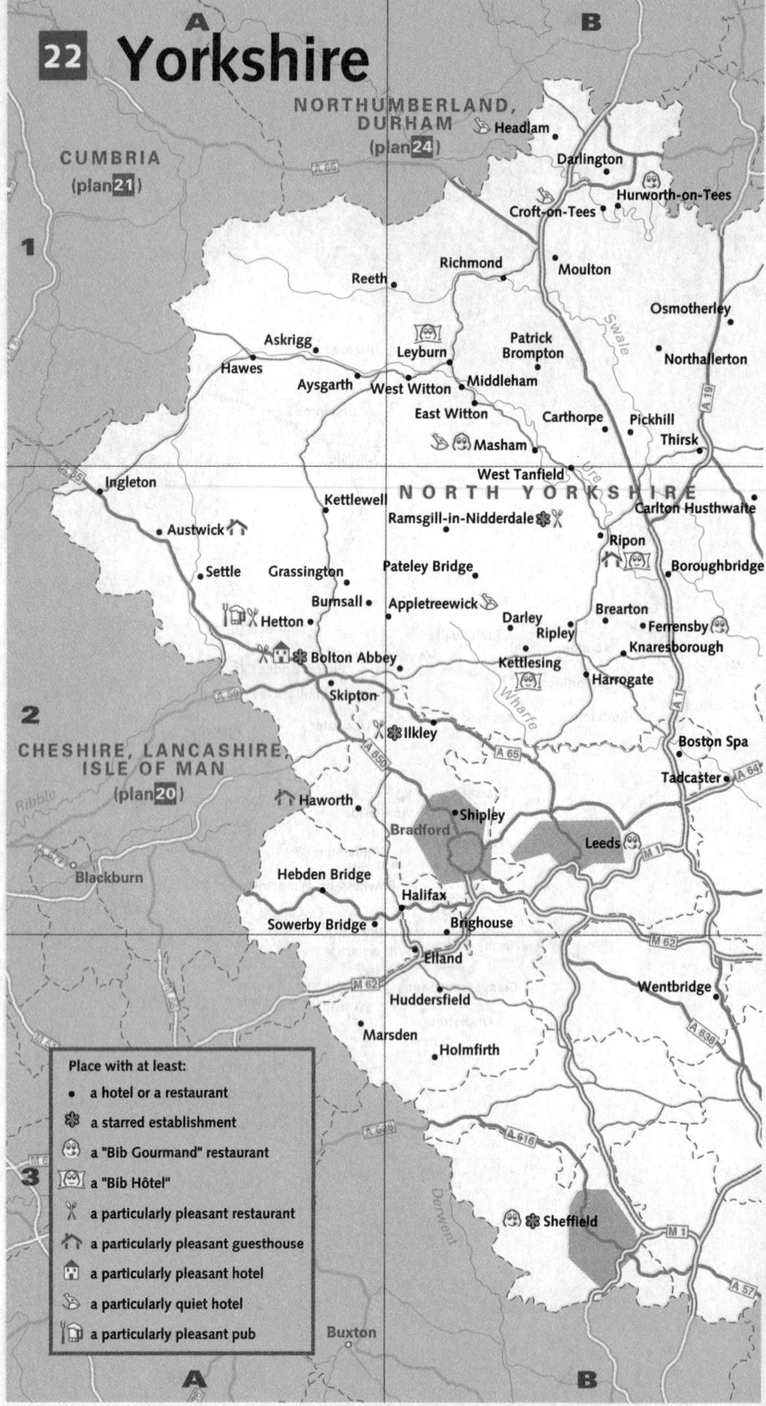
22 Yorkshire
A
B
NORTHUMBERLAND, DURHAM (plan 24)
CUMBRIA (plan 21)
CHESHIRE, LANCASHIRE, ISLE OF MAN (plan 20)
NORTH YORKSHIRE
1
2
3
Headlam
Darlington
Hurworth-on-Tees
Croft-on-Tees
Richmond
Moulton
Reeth
Osmotherley
Askrigg
Leyburn
Patrick Brompton
Northallerton
Hawes
Aysgarth
West Witton
Middleham
East Witton
Carthorpe
Pickhill
Thirsk
Masham
West Tanfield
Ingleton
Kettlewell
Carlton Husthwaite
Ramsgill-in-Nidderdale
Austwick
Ripon
Settle
Grassington
Pateley Bridge
Boroughbridge
Burnsall
Appletreewick
Brearton
Hetton
Darley
Ripley
Ferrensby
Knaresborough
Bolton Abbey
Kettlesing
Harrogate
Skipton
Ilkley
Boston Spa
Tadcaster
Haworth
Shipley
Bradford
Leeds
Blackburn
Hebden Bridge
Halifax
Sowerby Bridge
Brighouse
Elland
Wentbridge
Huddersfield
Marsden
Holmfirth
Sheffield
Buxton
Swale
Ure
Wharfe
Ribble
Derwent
A 65
A 19
A 1
A 59
A 650
A 64
M 1
M 62
A 638
A 616
A 628
A 57
Place with at least:
a hotel or a restaurant
a starred establishment
a "Bib Gourmand" restaurant
a "Bib Hôtel"
a particularly pleasant restaurant
a particularly pleasant guesthouse
a particularly pleasant hotel
a particularly quiet hotel
a particularly pleasant pub

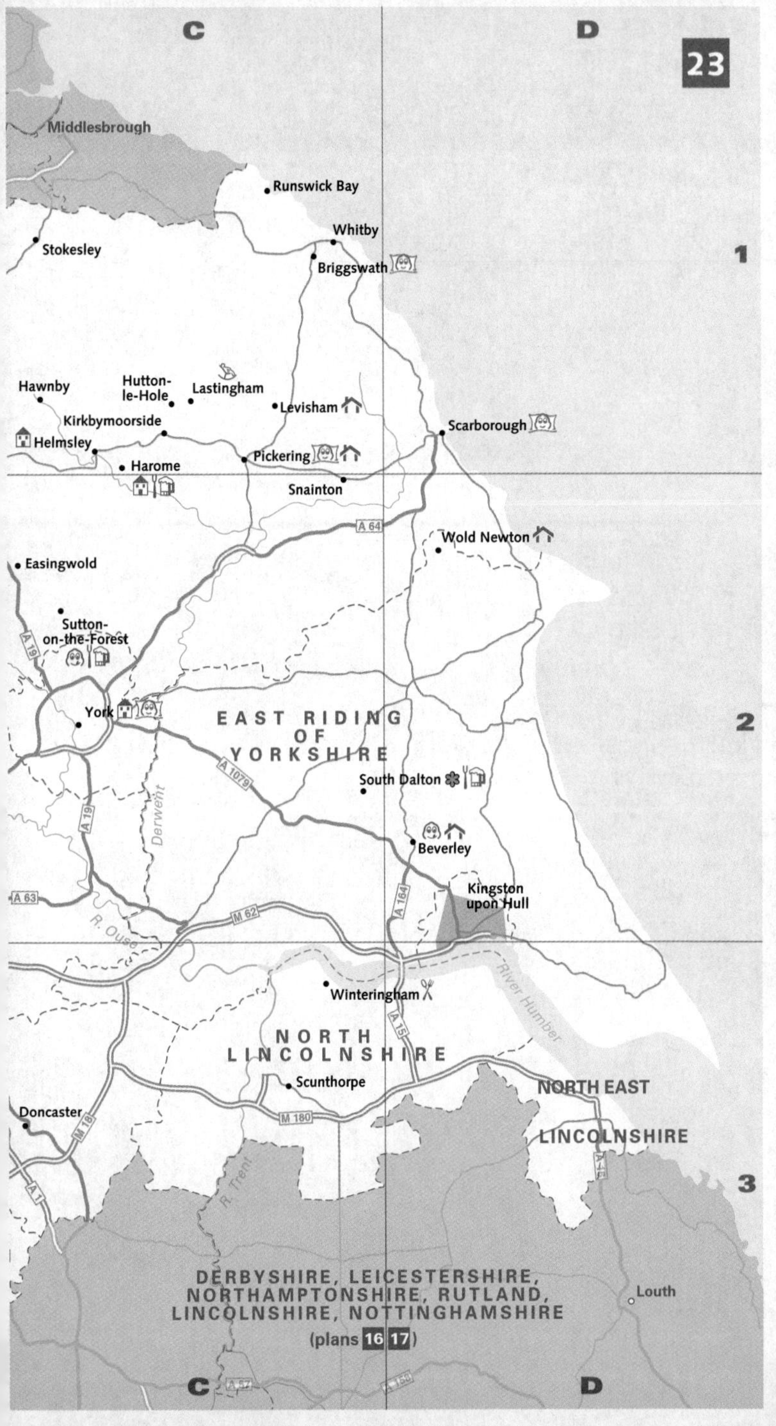
C
D
23
Middlesbrough
Runswick Bay
Whitby
Stokesley
Briggswath
1
Hawnby
Hutton-le-Hole
Lastingham
Levisham
Kirkbymoorside
Scarborough
Helmsley
Pickering
Harome
Snainton
A 64
Wold Newton
Easingwold
Sutton-on-the-Forest
A 19
York
EAST RIDING OF YORKSHIRE
2
A 1079
South Dalton
A 19
Derwent
Beverley
Kingston upon Hull
A 63
A 164
M 62
R. Ouse
River Humber
Winteringham
A 15
NORTH LINCOLNSHIRE
Scunthorpe
NORTH EAST LINCOLNSHIRE
Doncaster
M 18
M 180
R. Trent
A 1
3
DERBYSHIRE, LEICESTERSHIRE, NORTHAMPTONSHIRE, RUTLAND, LINCOLNSHIRE, NOTTINGHAMSHIRE
(plans 16 17)
Louth
A 57
A 158
C
D

Northumberland, Durham

24

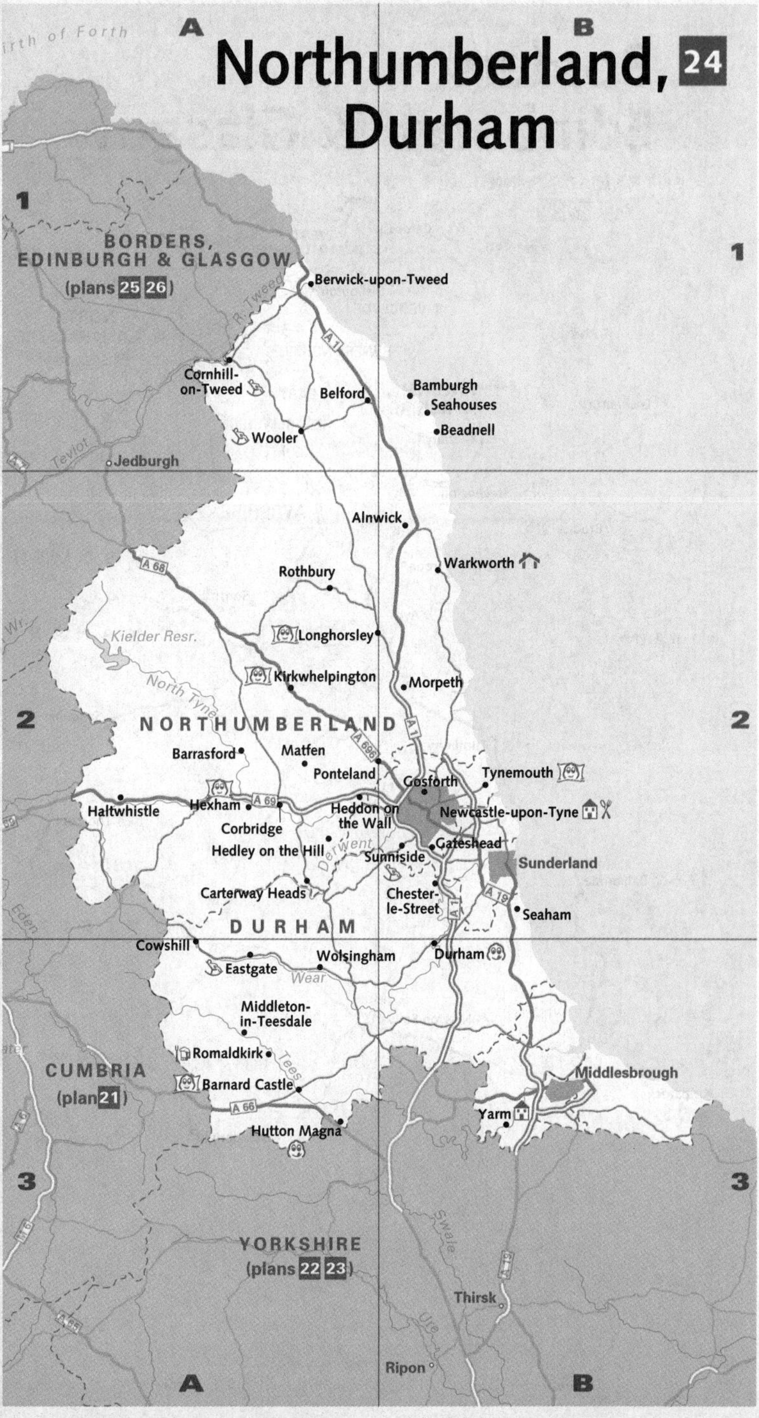

A B

1

BORDERS, EDINBURGH & GLASGOW (plans 25 26)

Firth of Forth

R. Tweed

Berwick-upon-Tweed

A 1

Cornhill-on-Tweed

Belford

Bamburgh

Seahouses

Beadnell

Wooler

Teviot

Jedburgh

Alnwick

A 68

Warkworth

Rothbury

Longhorsley

Kielder Resr.

Kirkwhelpington

Morpeth

North Tyne

2

NORTHUMBERLAND

A 696

Barrasford

Matfen

Ponteland

Tynemouth

Gosforth

Haltwhistle

Hexham

A 69

Heddon on the Wall

Newcastle-upon-Tyne

Corbridge

Hedley on the Hill

Derwent

Sunniside

Gateshead

Sunderland

Carterway Heads

Chester-le-Street

A 19

Seaham

Eden

DURHAM

Cowshill

Eastgate

Wolsingham

Durham

Wear

Middleton-in-Teesdale

Romaldkirk

Tees

CUMBRIA (plan 21)

Barnard Castle

Middlesbrough

A 66

Yarm

Hutton Magna

3

YORKSHIRE (plans 22 23)

Swale

A 19

Thirsk

Ure

A 65

Ripon

A B

25 Borders, Edinburgh & Glasgow

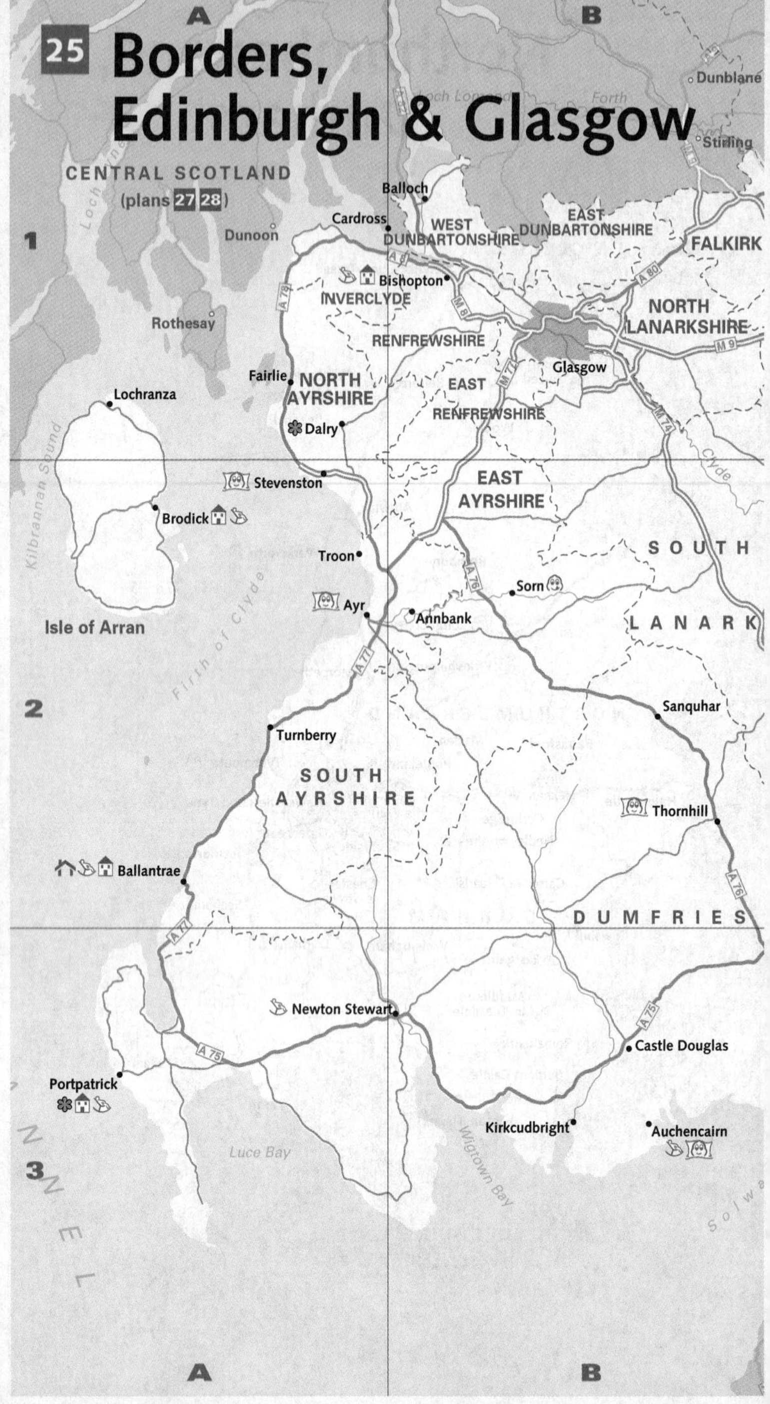

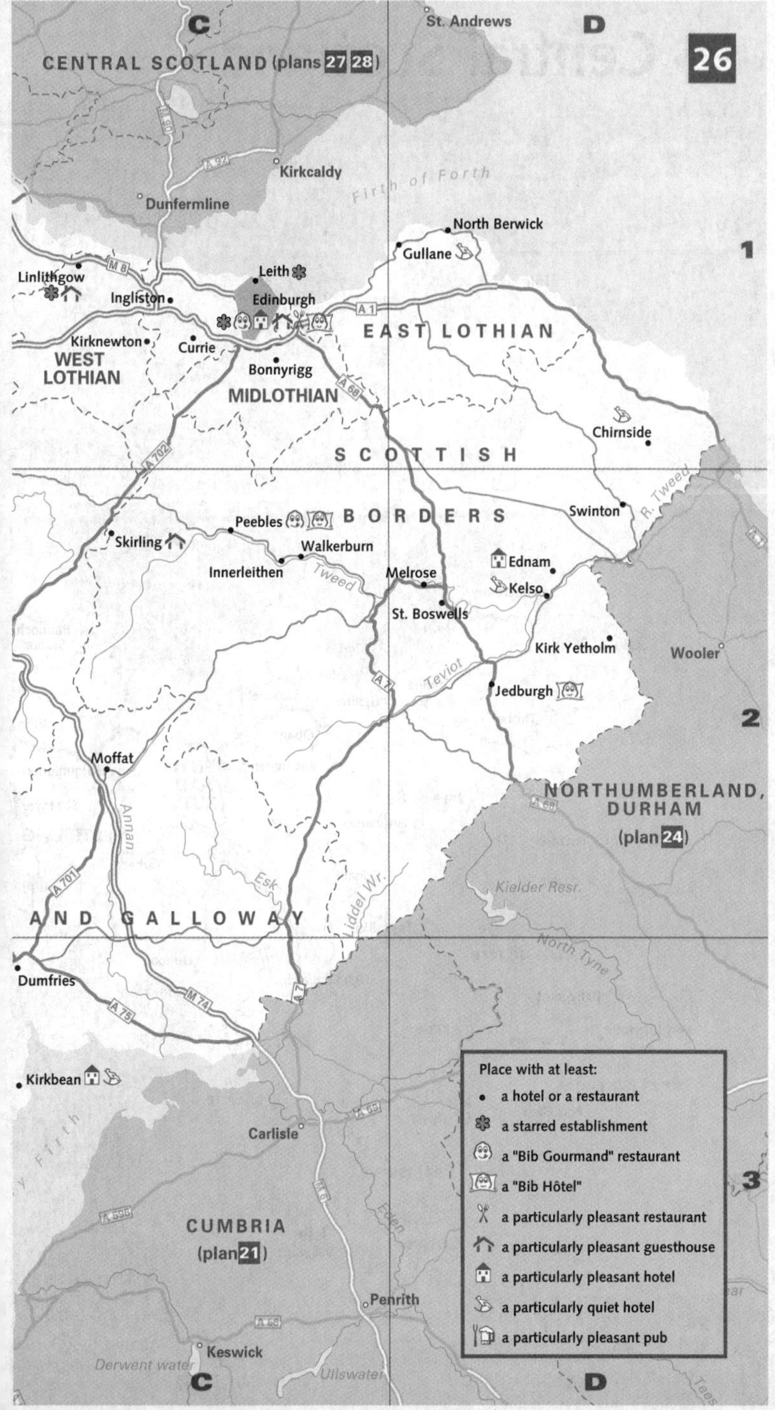

C
D
26
CENTRAL SCOTLAND (plans 27 28)
St. Andrews
Kirkcaldy
Firth of Forth
Dunfermline
North Berwick
Gullane
1
Linlithgow
Leith
Ingliston
Edinburgh
A 1
Kirknewton
Currie
EAST LOTHIAN
WEST LOTHIAN
Bonnyrigg
MIDLOTHIAN
Chirnside
SCOTTISH
R. Tweed
Swinton
Peebles
BORDERS
Skirling
Walkerburn
Ednam
Innerleithen
Tweed
Melrose
Kelso
St. Boswells
Kirk Yetholm
Wooler
Teviot
Jedburgh
2
Moffat
NORTHUMBERLAND, DURHAM
(plan 24)
Annan
Kielder Resr.
Esk
Liddel Wr.
AND GALLOWAY
North Tyne
Dumfries
Kirkbean
Carlisle
CUMBRIA
(plan 21)
Eden
Penrith
Keswick
Derwent water
Ullswater
3
C
D
Place with at least:
a hotel or a restaurant
a starred establishment
a "Bib Gourmand" restaurant
a "Bib Hôtel"
a particularly pleasant restaurant
a particularly pleasant guesthouse
a particularly pleasant hotel
a particularly quiet hotel
a particularly pleasant pub

27 Central Scotland

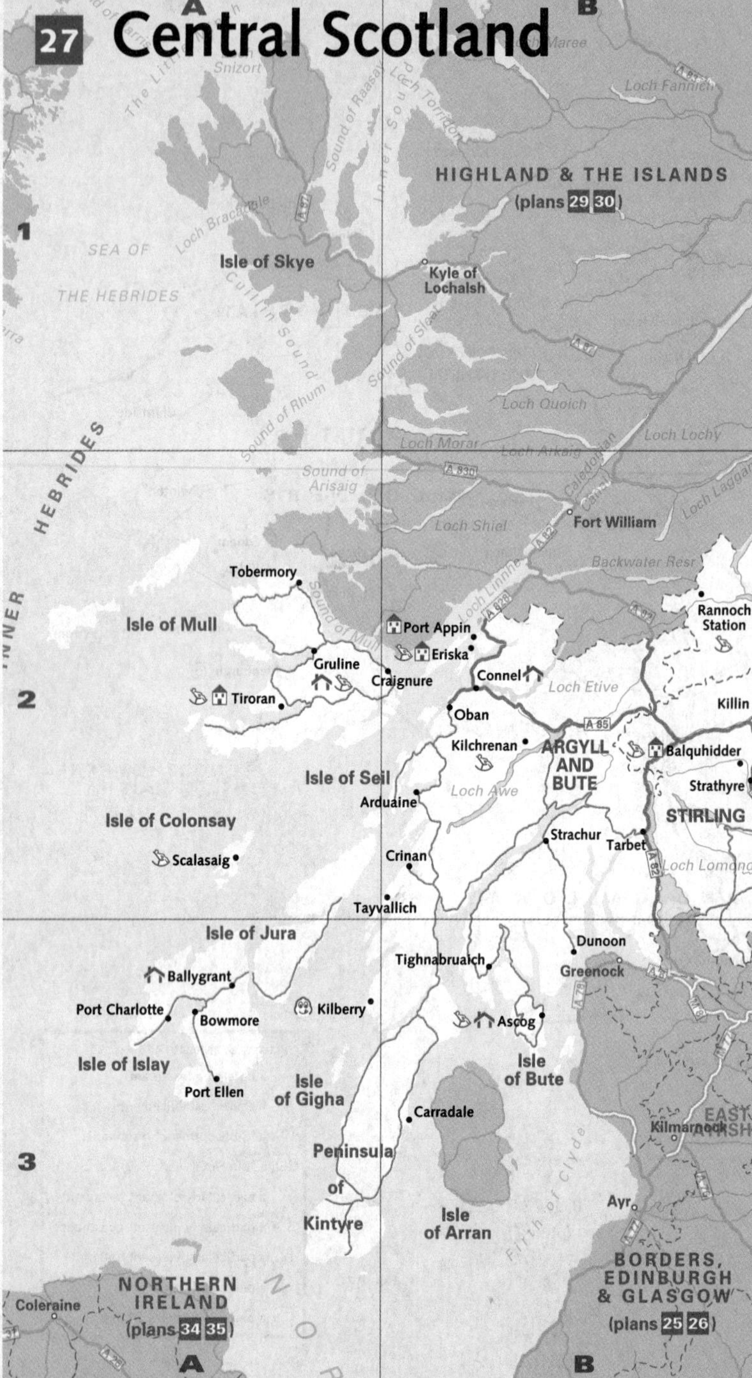

C
D
28
Moray Firth
Elgin
Urquhart
Dyke
Forres
Archiestown
Aberlour
Deveron
1
Loch Ness
HIGHLAND
& THE ISLANDS
(plans 29 30)
MORAY
Oldmeldrum
Udny Green
Kildrummy
Balmedie
Glenkindie
Don
ABERDEENSHIRE
Aberdeen
Aboyne
Ballater
Dee
Braemar
Banchory
Stonehaven
N. Esk
PERTH AND KINROSS
Spittal of Glenshee
ANGUS
Loch Rannoch
Kirkmichael
Pitlochry
Memus
Kirriemuir
Aberfeldy
Montrose
Kenmore
Alyth
Blairgowrie
Inverkeilor
Dunkeld
Loch Tay
Kinclaven
Ardeonaig
Arbroath
2
Dundee
Lochearnhead
Carnoustie
St. Fillans
Comrie
Crieff
Perth
Auchterarder
St. Andrews
Callander
Cupar
Peat Inn
Glendevon
FIFE
Largoward
Dunblane
Kinross
Anstruther
Forth
Glenrothes
St. Monans
Elie
Stirling
Firth of Forth
North Berwick
North Queensferry
Edinburgh
Glasgow
Clyde
Peebles
3
Tweed
BORDERS,
EDINBURGH
& GLASGOW
(plans 25 26)
Teviot
Annan
Esk
Kielder Resr.
C
D
Place with at least:
a hotel or a restaurant
a starred establishment
a "Bib Gourmand" restaurant
a "Bib Hôtel"
a particularly pleasant restaurant
a particularly pleasant guesthouse
a particularly pleasant hotel
a particularly quiet hotel
a particularly pleasant pub

29 Highland & The Islands

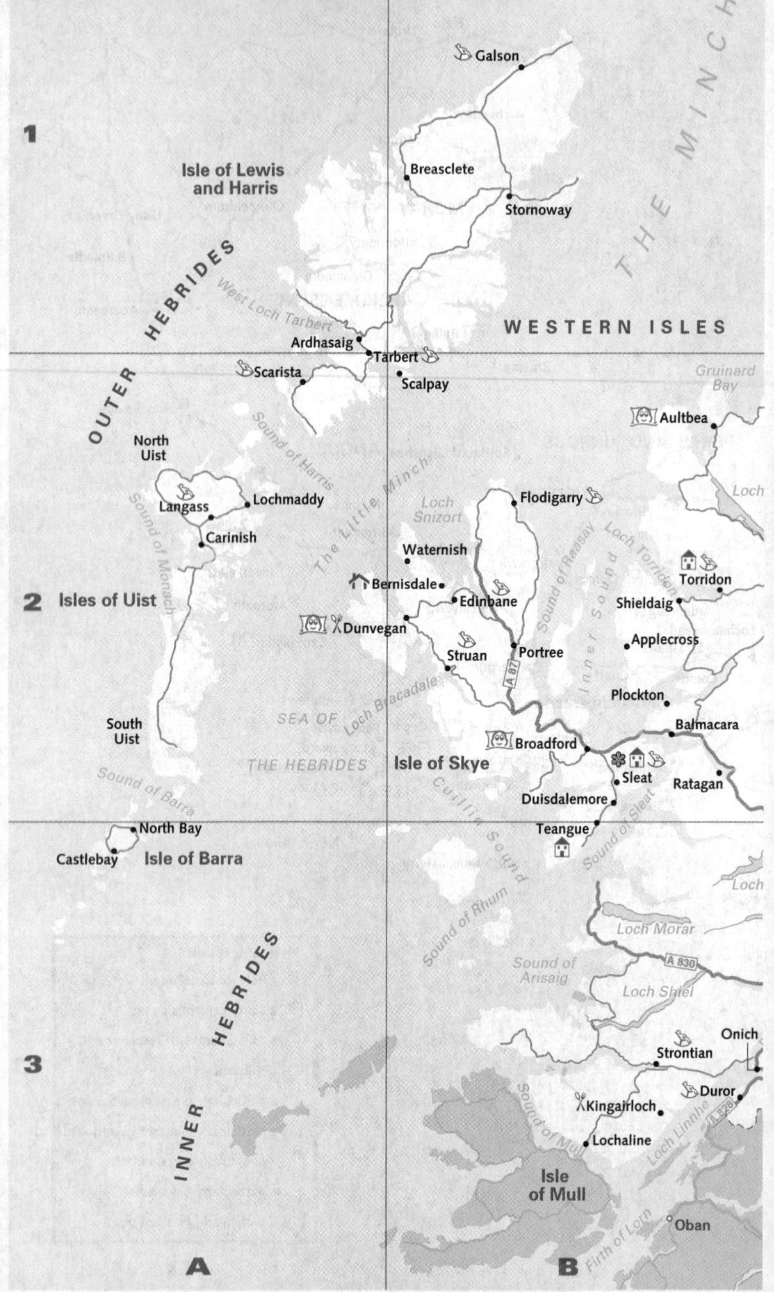

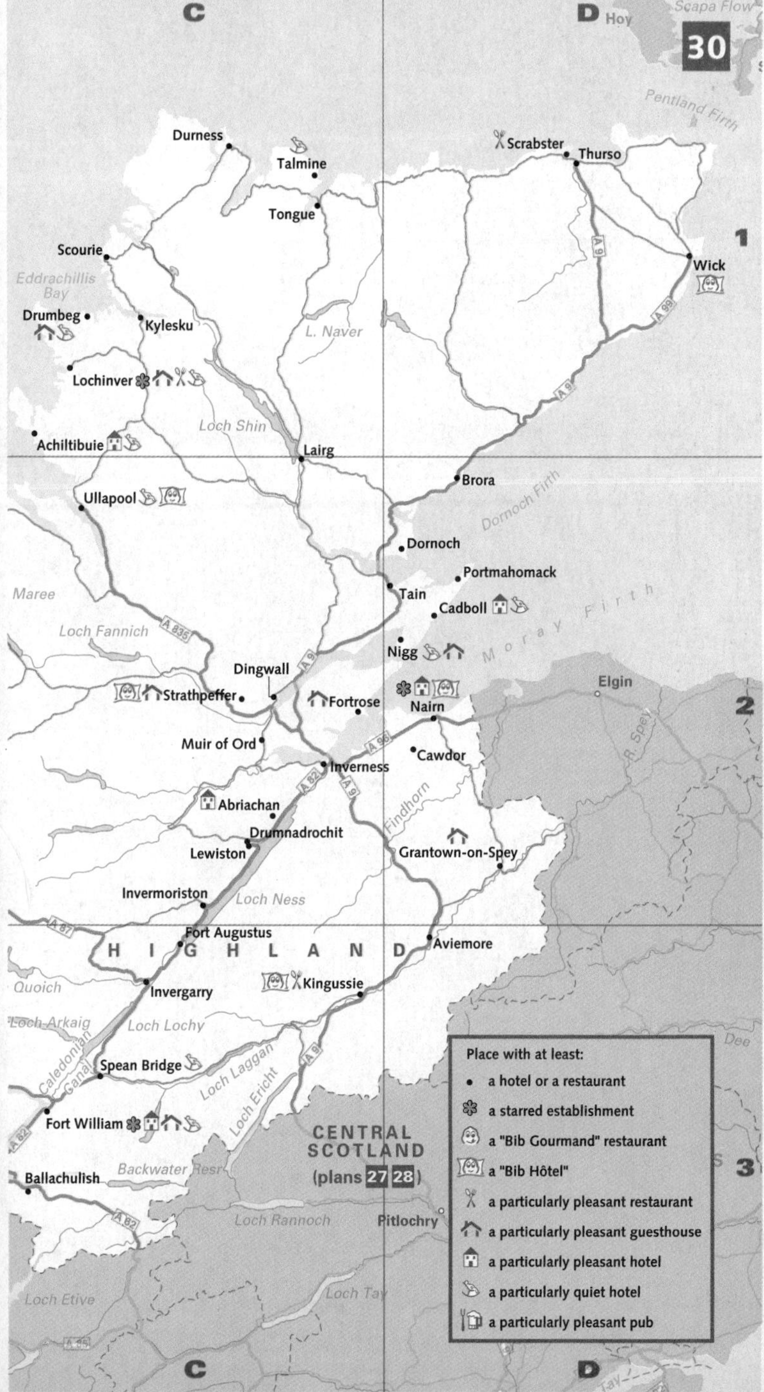
30
C
D
Hoy
Scapa Flow
Pentland Firth
1
2
3
Durness
Talmine
Tongue
Scrabster
Thurso
Wick
Scourie
Eddrachillis Bay
Drumbeg
Kylesku
L. Naver
Lochinver
Loch Shin
Achiltibuie
Lairg
Brora
Dornoch Firth
Ullapool
Dornoch
Portmahomack
Tain
Cadboll
Maree
Moray Firth
Loch Fannich
Nigg
Dingwall
Strathpeffer
Fortrose
Nairn
Elgin
R. Spey
Muir of Ord
Cawdor
Inverness
Findhorn
Abriachan
Drumnadrochit
Lewiston
Grantown-on-Spey
Invermoriston
Loch Ness
Fort Augustus
HIGHLAND
Aviemore
Quoich
Invergarry
Kingussie
Loch Arkaig
Loch Lochy
Dee
Caledonian Canal
Spean Bridge
Loch Laggan
Loch Ericht
Fort William
CENTRAL SCOTLAND
(plans 27 28)
Backwater Resr
Ballachulish
Loch Rannoch
Pitlochry
Loch Etive
Loch Tay
Tay
A 9
A 99
A 835
A 96
A 82
A 87
A 85
Place with at least:
a hotel or a restaurant
a starred establishment
a "Bib Gourmand" restaurant
a "Bib Hôtel"
a particularly pleasant restaurant
a particularly pleasant guesthouse
a particularly pleasant hotel
a particularly quiet hotel
a particularly pleasant pub

Shetland & Orkney

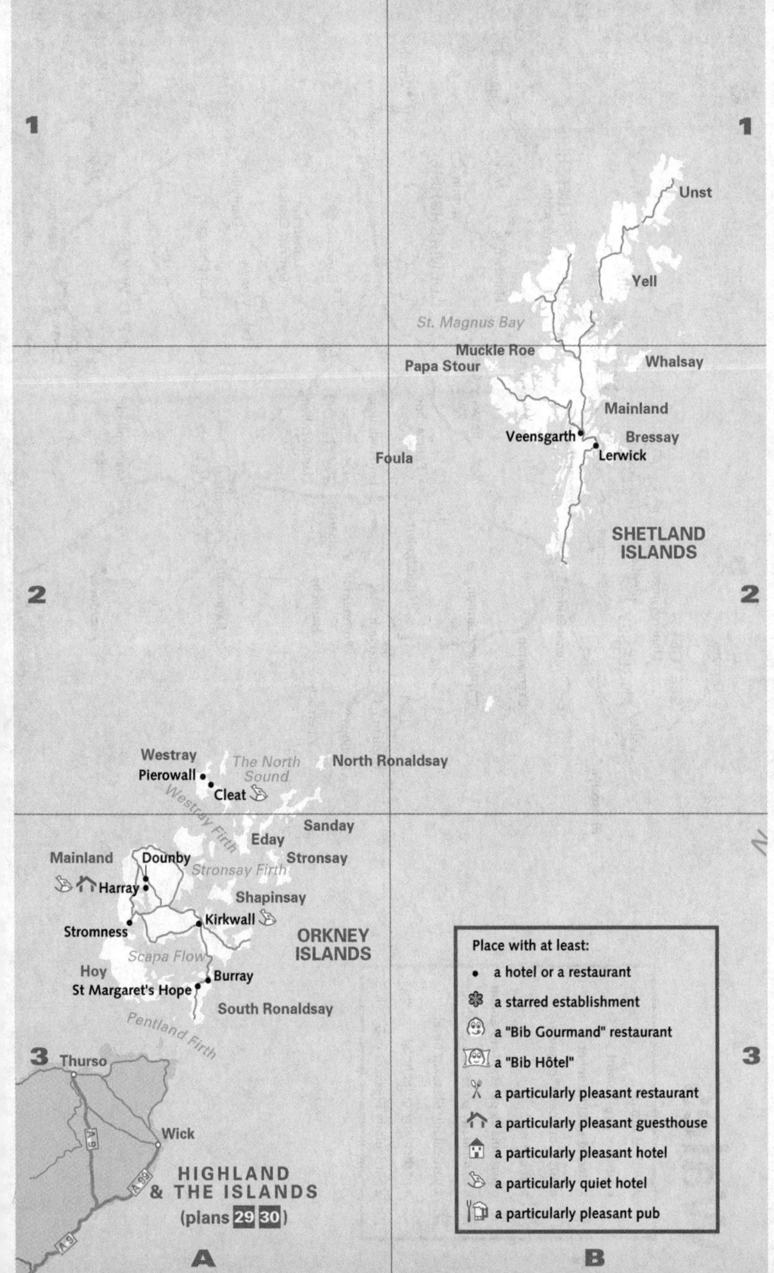

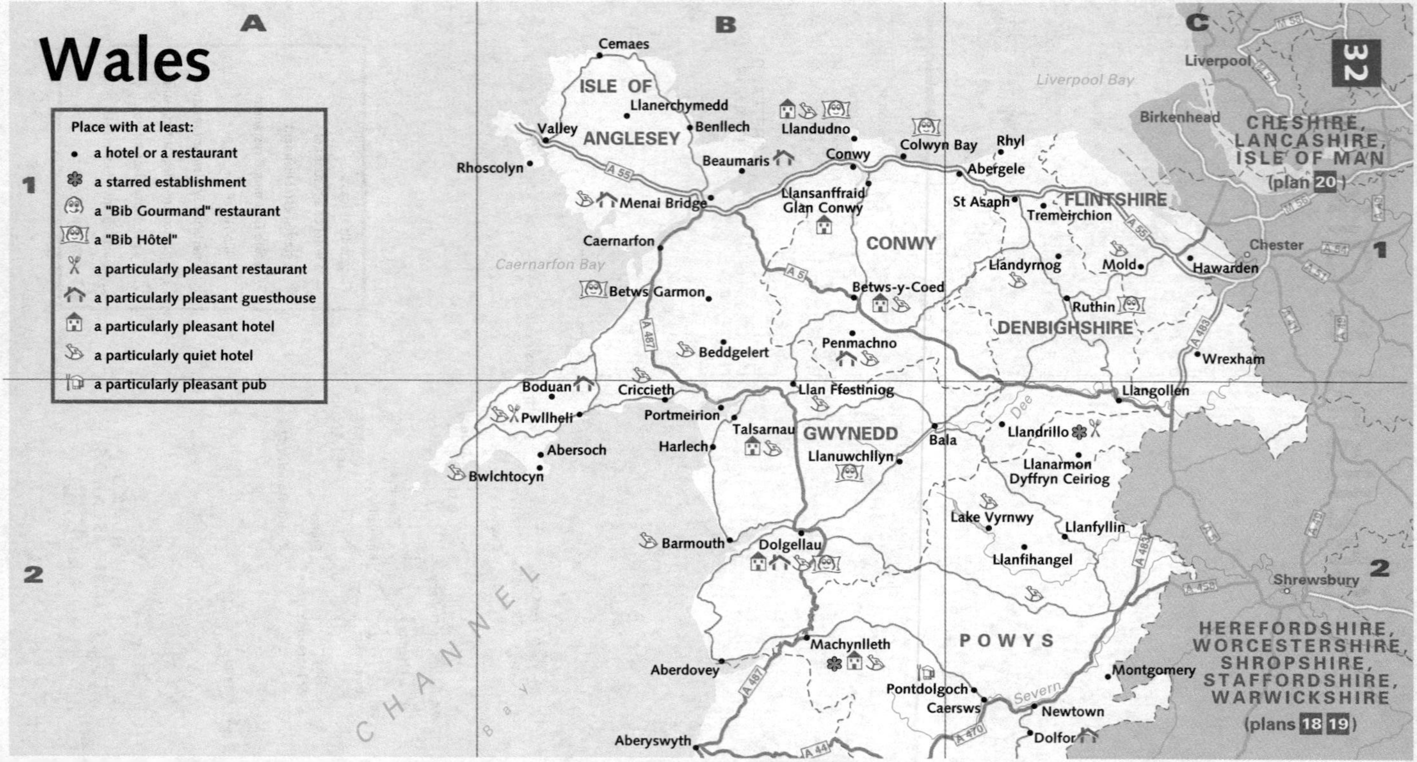

Wales

Place with at least:

- a hotel or a restaurant
- a starred establishment
- a "Bib Gourmand" restaurant
- a "Bib Hôtel"
- a particularly pleasant restaurant
- a particularly pleasant guesthouse
- a particularly pleasant hotel
- a particularly quiet hotel
- a particularly pleasant pub

A
B
C
1
2

Liverpool Bay
Caernarfon Bay
CHANNEL
Bay

ISLE OF ANGLESEY
CONWY
FLINTSHIRE
DENBIGHSHIRE
GWYNEDD
POWYS

CHESHIRE, LANCASHIRE, ISLE OF MAN (plan 20)

HEREFORDSHIRE, WORCESTERSHIRE, SHROPSHIRE, STAFFORDSHIRE, WARWICKSHIRE (plans 18 19)

Cemaes
Llanerchymedd
Valley
Benllech
Rhoscolyn
Beaumaris
Menai Bridge
Llandudno
Conwy
Colwyn Bay
Rhyl
Abergele
St Asaph
Tremeirchion
Llansanffraid Glan Conwy
Caernarfon
Betws Garmon
Betws-y-Coed
Llandyrnog
Mold
Hawarden
Chester
Liverpool
Birkenhead
Ruthin
Wrexham
Penmachno
Beddgelert
Boduan
Criccieth
Llan Ffestiniog
Llangollen
Pwllheli
Portmeirion
Talsarnau
Harlech
Abersoch
Bwlchtocyn
Llanuwchllyn
Bala
Llandrillo
Llanarmon Dyffryn Ceiriog
Dee
Lake Vyrnwy
Llanfyllin
Llanfihangel
Barmouth
Dolgellau
Machynlleth
Aberdovey
Pontdolgoch
Caersws
Severn
Newtown
Dolfor
Montgomery
Shrewsbury
Aberyswyth

A 55
A 5
A 487
A 483
A 470
A 44
A 458
A 49
A 41
A 51
A 54
M 56
M 53
M 57

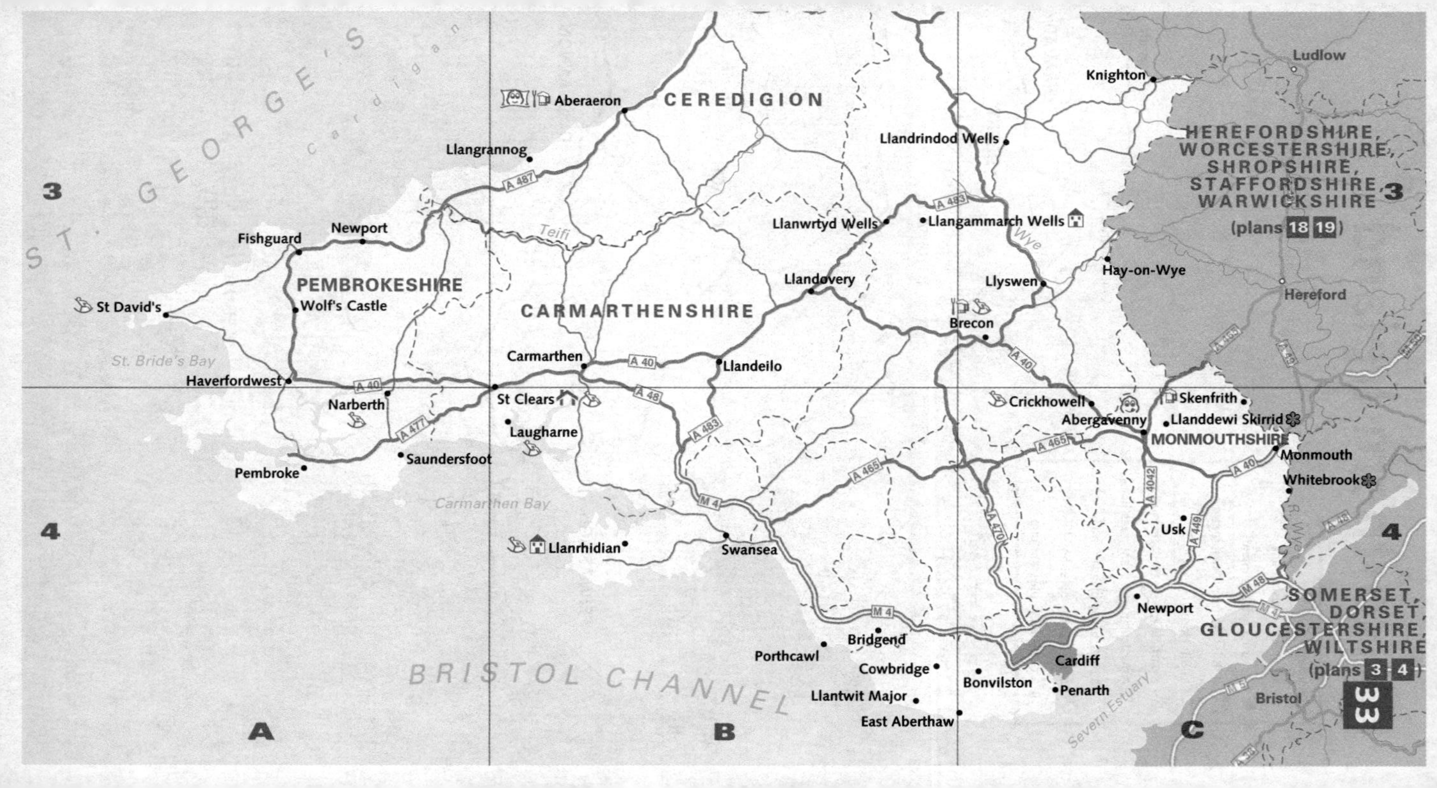
ST. GEORGE'S
Cardigan
CEREDIGION
PEMBROKESHIRE
CARMARTHENSHIRE
MONMOUTHSHIRE
HEREFORDSHIRE, WORCESTERSHIRE, SHROPSHIRE, STAFFORDSHIRE, WARWICKSHIRE
(plans 18 19)
SOMERSET, DORSET, GLOUCESTERSHIRE, WILTSHIRE
(plans 3 4)
33
Aberaeron
Llangrannog
Fishguard
Newport
Wolf's Castle
St David's
St. Bride's Bay
Haverfordwest
Narberth
Pembroke
Saundersfoot
Carmarthen
St Clears
Laugharne
Carmarthen Bay
Llanrhidian
Swansea
Llandeilo
Llandovery
Llanwrtyd Wells
Llangammarch Wells
Llandrindod Wells
Knighton
Ludlow
Hay-on-Wye
Hereford
Llyswen
Brecon
Crickhowell
Abergavenny
Skenfrith
Llanddewi Skirrid
Monmouth
Whitebrook
Usk
Newport
Cardiff
Penarth
Bonvilston
East Aberthaw
Llantwit Major
Cowbridge
Bridgend
Porthcawl
Bristol
BRISTOL CHANNEL
Severn Estuary
Teifi
Wye
R. Wye
A 487
A 40
A 477
A 48
A 483
A 465
A 470
A 4042
A 449
M 4
M 48
M 5
3
4
A
B
C

34 Northern Ireland

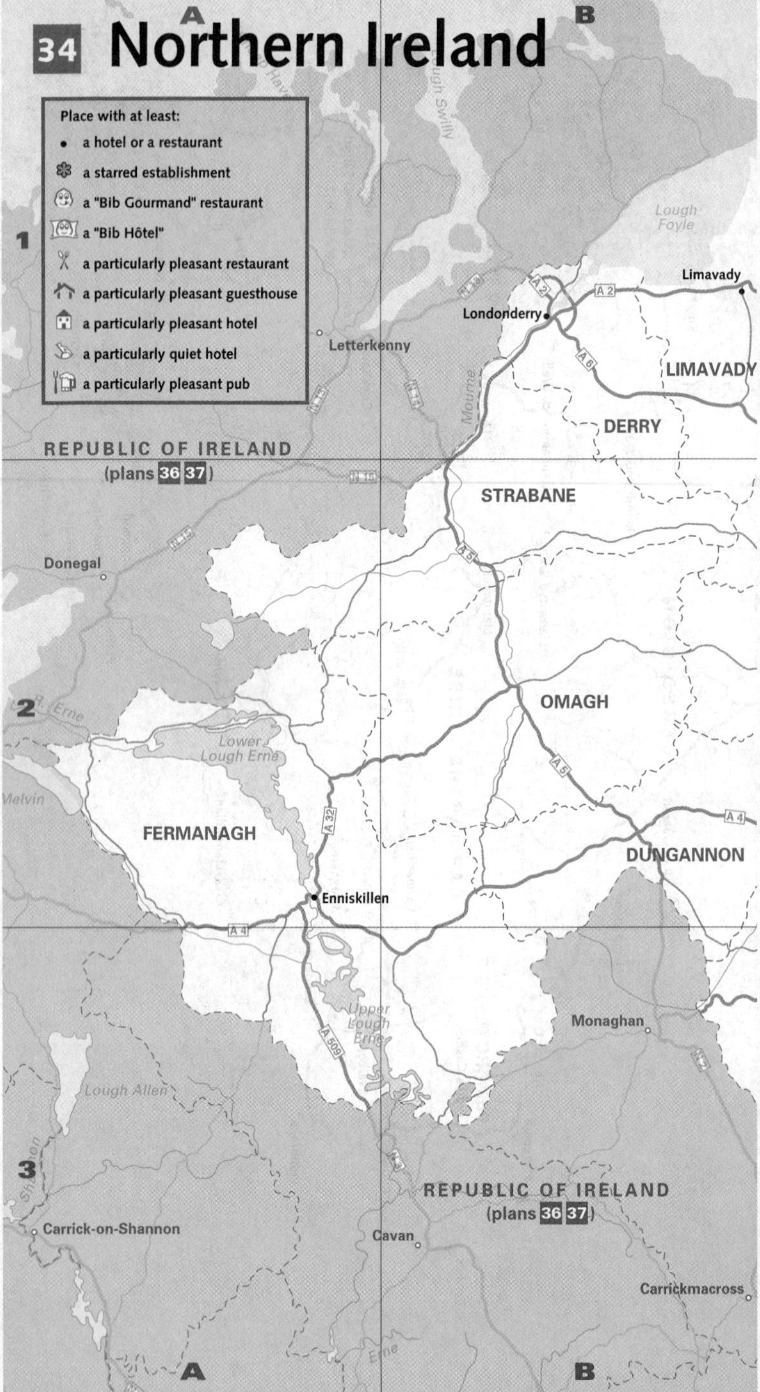

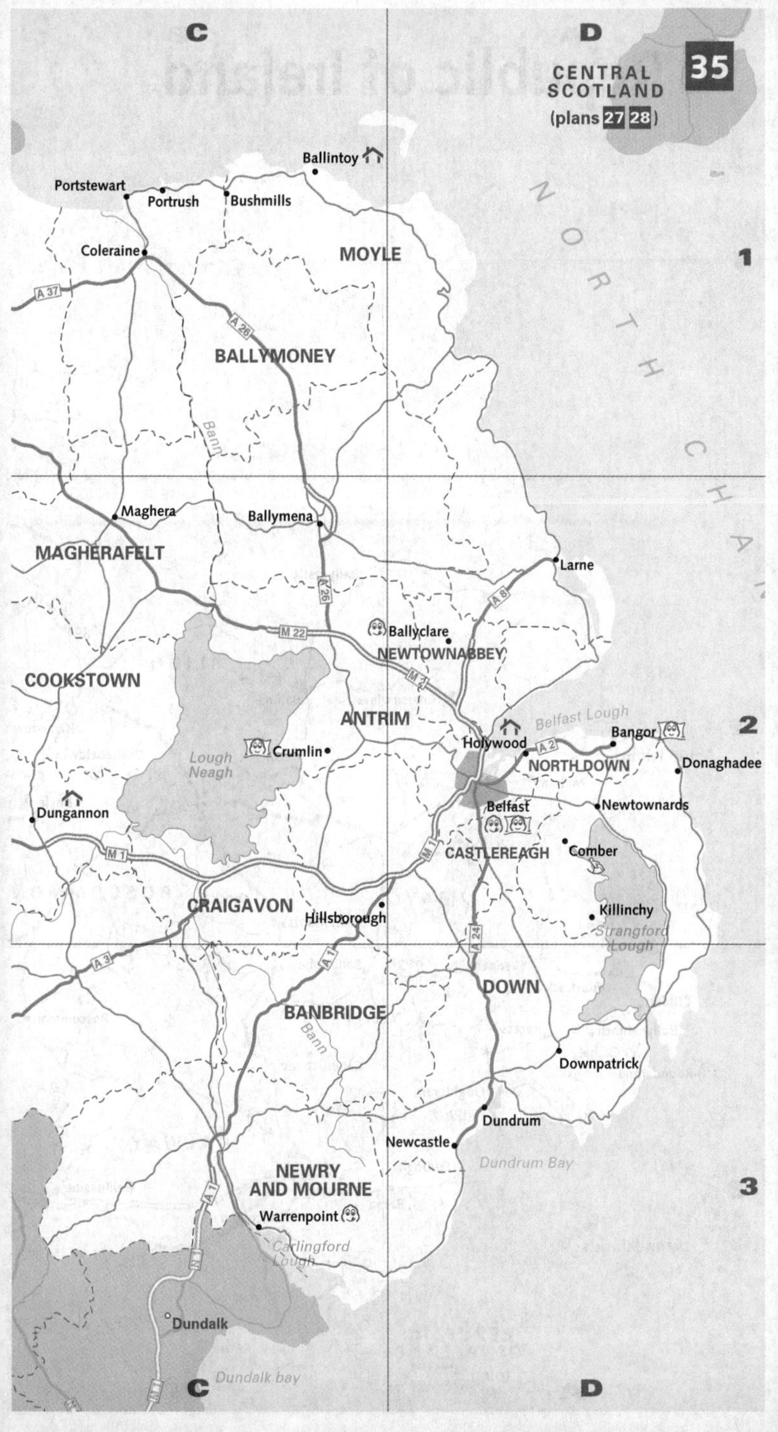

C
D
CENTRAL SCOTLAND
(plans 27 28)
35
NORTH CHANNEL
1
2
3
Ballintoy
Portstewart
Portrush
Bushmills
Coleraine
MOYLE
A 37
A 26
BALLYMONEY
Bann
Maghera
Ballymena
MAGHERAFELT
Larne
A 26
A 8
M 22
Ballyclare
NEWTOWNABBEY
COOKSTOWN
M 2
ANTRIM
Belfast Lough
Holywood
Bangor
A 2
Crumlin
Lough Neagh
NORTH DOWN
Donaghadee
Dungannon
Belfast
Newtownards
M 1
M 1
CASTLEREAGH
Comber
CRAIGAVON
Hillsborough
Killinchy
A 24
Strangford Lough
A 3
A 1
DOWN
BANBRIDGE
Bann
Downpatrick
Dundrum
Newcastle
Dundrum Bay
NEWRY AND MOURNE
A 1
Warrenpoint
Carlingford Lough
Dundalk
Dundalk bay
C
D

36 Republic of Ireland

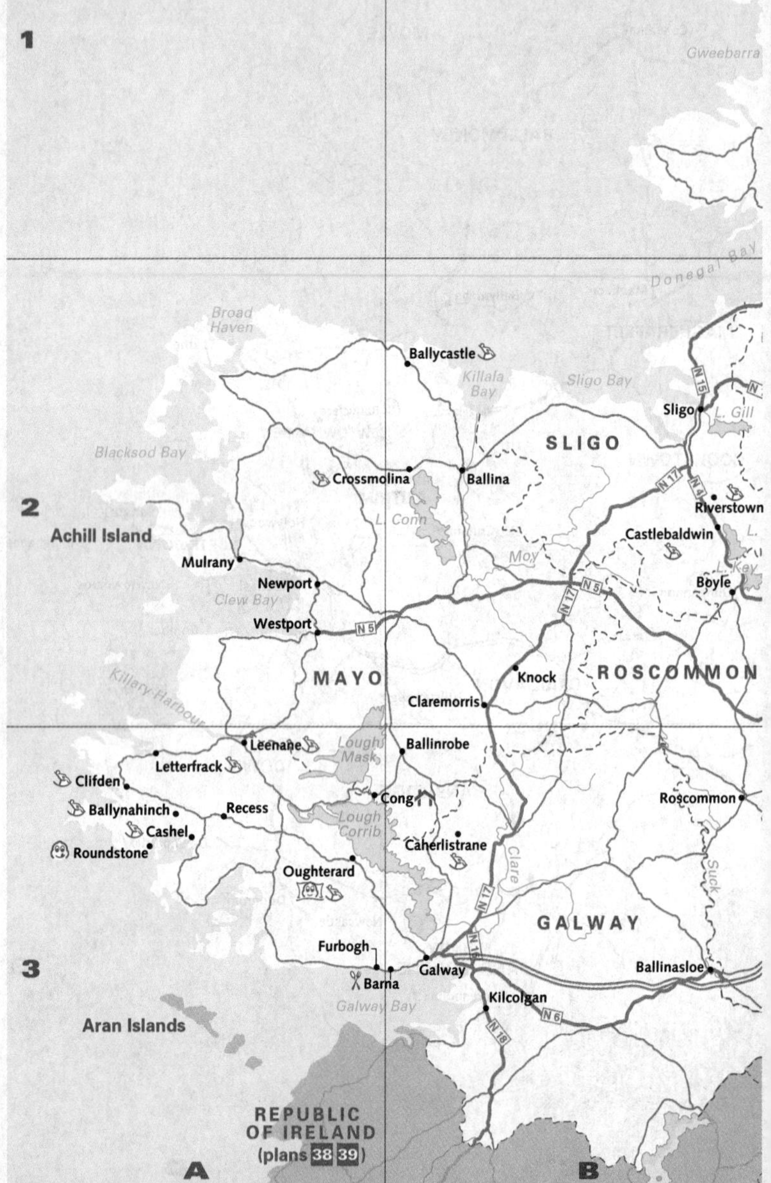

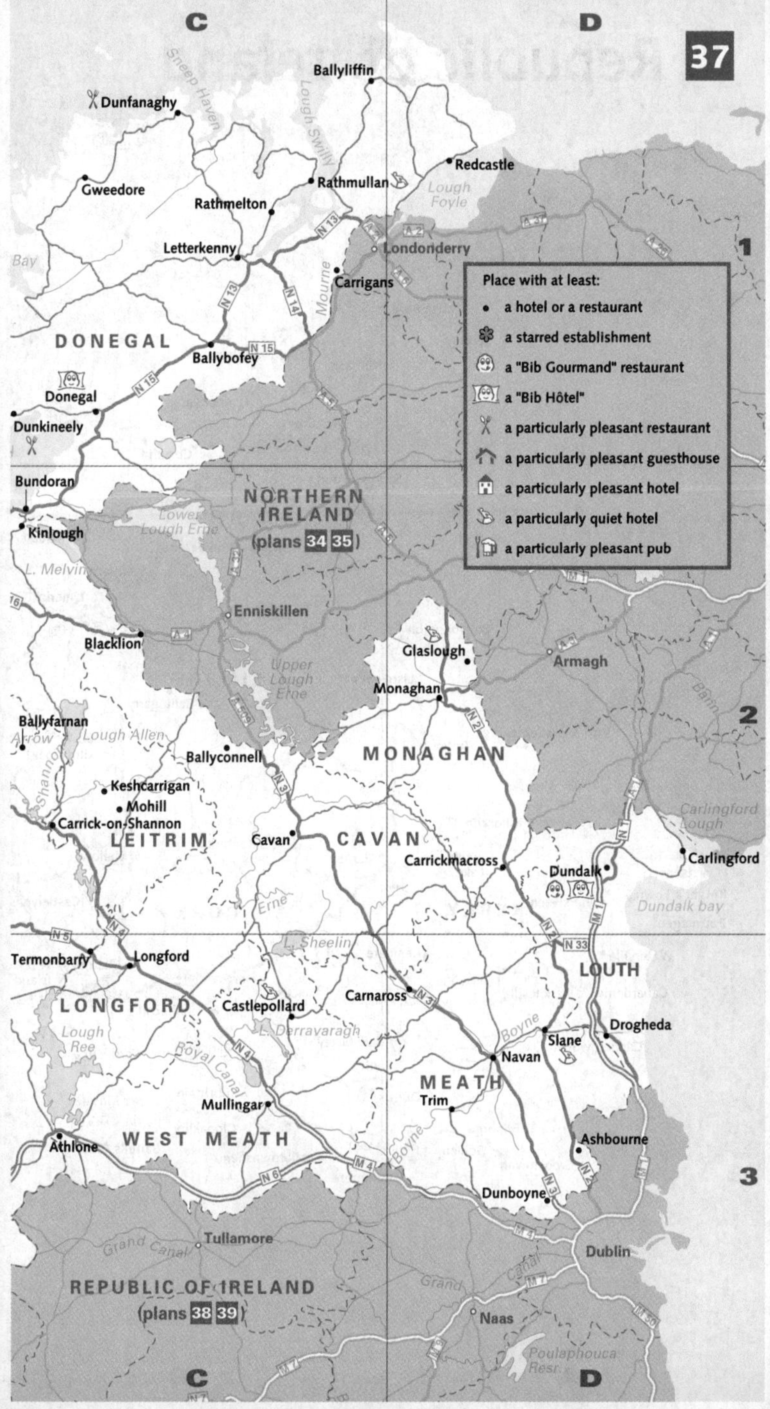
C
D
Ballyliffin
Dunfanaghy
Sheep Haven
Lough Swilly
Redcastle
Gweedore
Rathmullan
Lough Foyle
Rathmelton
Letterkenny
Londonderry
Bay
Carrigans
Mourne
DONEGAL
Ballybofey
Donegal
Dunkineely
Bundoran
Kinlough
L. Melvin
NORTHERN IRELAND
(plans 34 35)
Lower Lough Erne
Enniskillen
Blacklion
Upper Lough Erne
Glaslough
Monaghan
Armagh
Ballyfarnan
Arrow
Lough Allen
Shannon
Ballyconnell
MONAGHAN
Keshcarrigan
Mohill
Carrick-on-Shannon
LEITRIM
Cavan
CAVAN
Carrickmacross
Carlingford Lough
Carlingford
Dundalk
Dundalk bay
Erne
L. Sheelin
Termonbarry
Longford
LOUTH
LONGFORD
Castlepollard
Carnaross
Lough Ree
L. Derravaragh
Royal Canal
Boyne
Slane
Drogheda
Navan
MEATH
Trim
Mullingar
Athlone
WEST MEATH
Ashbourne
Dunboyne
Tullamore
Grand Canal
Dublin
REPUBLIC OF IRELAND
(plans 38 39)
Naas
Poulaphouca Resr.
1
2
3
Place with at least:
a hotel or a restaurant
a starred establishment
a "Bib Gourmand" restaurant
a "Bib Hôtel"
a particularly pleasant restaurant
a particularly pleasant guesthouse
a particularly pleasant hotel
a particularly quiet hotel
a particularly pleasant pub

38 Republic of Ireland

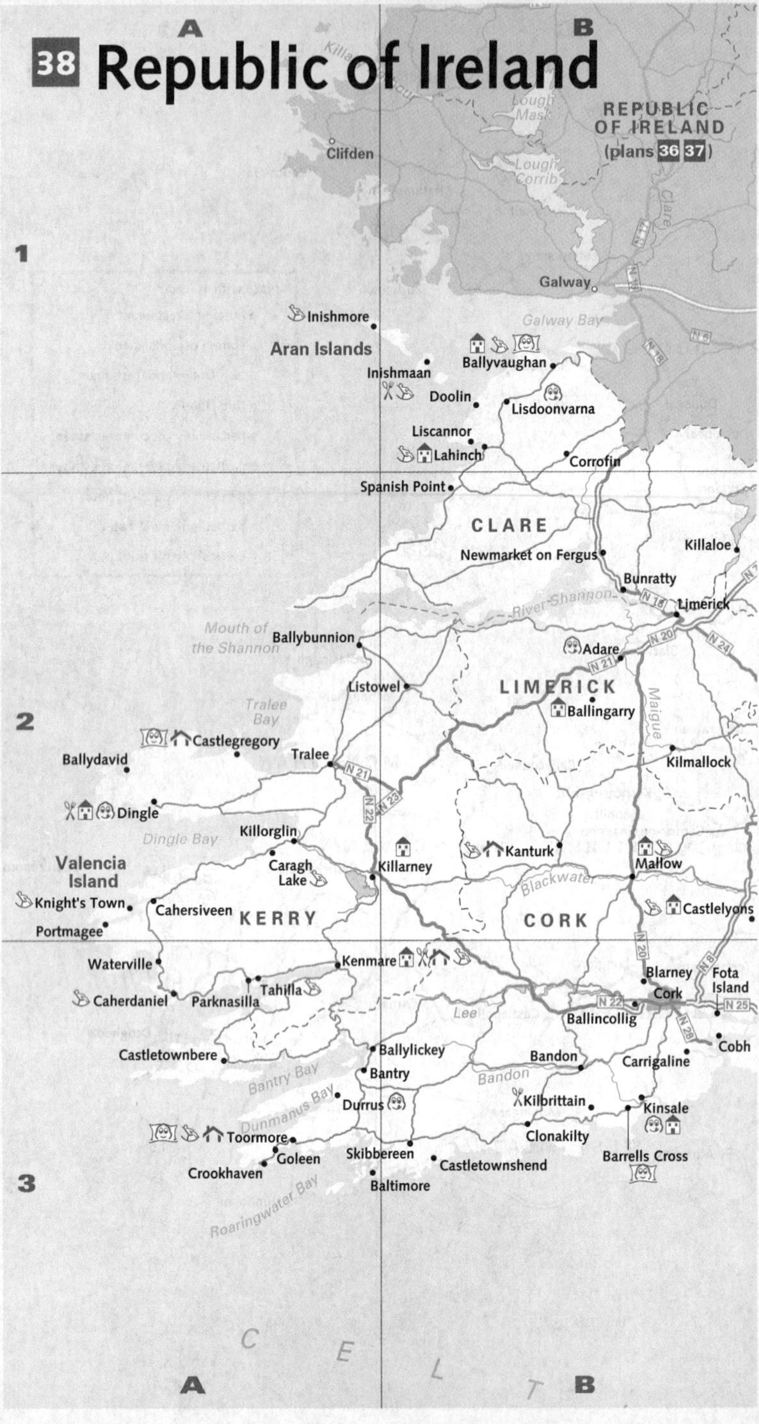
A
B
REPUBLIC OF IRELAND
(plans 36 37)
Lough Mask
Lough Corrib
Clifden
Clare
1
Galway
Galway Bay
Inishmore
Aran Islands
Inishmaan
Ballyvaughan
Doolin
Lisdoonvarna
Liscannor
Lahinch
Corrofin
Spanish Point
CLARE
Newmarket on Fergus
Killaloe
Bunratty
River Shannon
Limerick
Mouth of the Shannon
Ballybunnion
Adare
Listowel
LIMERICK
Ballingarry
Tralee Bay
Maigue
2
Castlegregory
Ballydavid
Tralee
Kilmallock
Dingle
Dingle Bay
Killorglin
Kanturk
Mallow
Valencia Island
Caragh Lake
Killarney
Blackwater
Knight's Town
Cahersiveen
KERRY
CORK
Castlelyons
Portmagee
Waterville
Kenmare
Blarney
Fota Island
Tahilla
Cork
Caherdaniel
Parknasilla
Lee
Ballincollig
Cobh
Castletownbere
Ballylickey
Bandon
Carrigaline
Bantry
Bantry Bay
Bandon
Dunmanus Bay
Durrus
Kilbrittain
Kinsale
Toormore
Clonakilty
Goleen
Skibbereen
Castletownshend
Barrells Cross
Crookhaven
Baltimore
3
Roaringwater Bay
C E L T
A
B
N 17
N 18
N 6
N 18
N 20
N 21
N 24
N 21
N 23
N 22
N 20
N 8
N 22
N 25
N 28

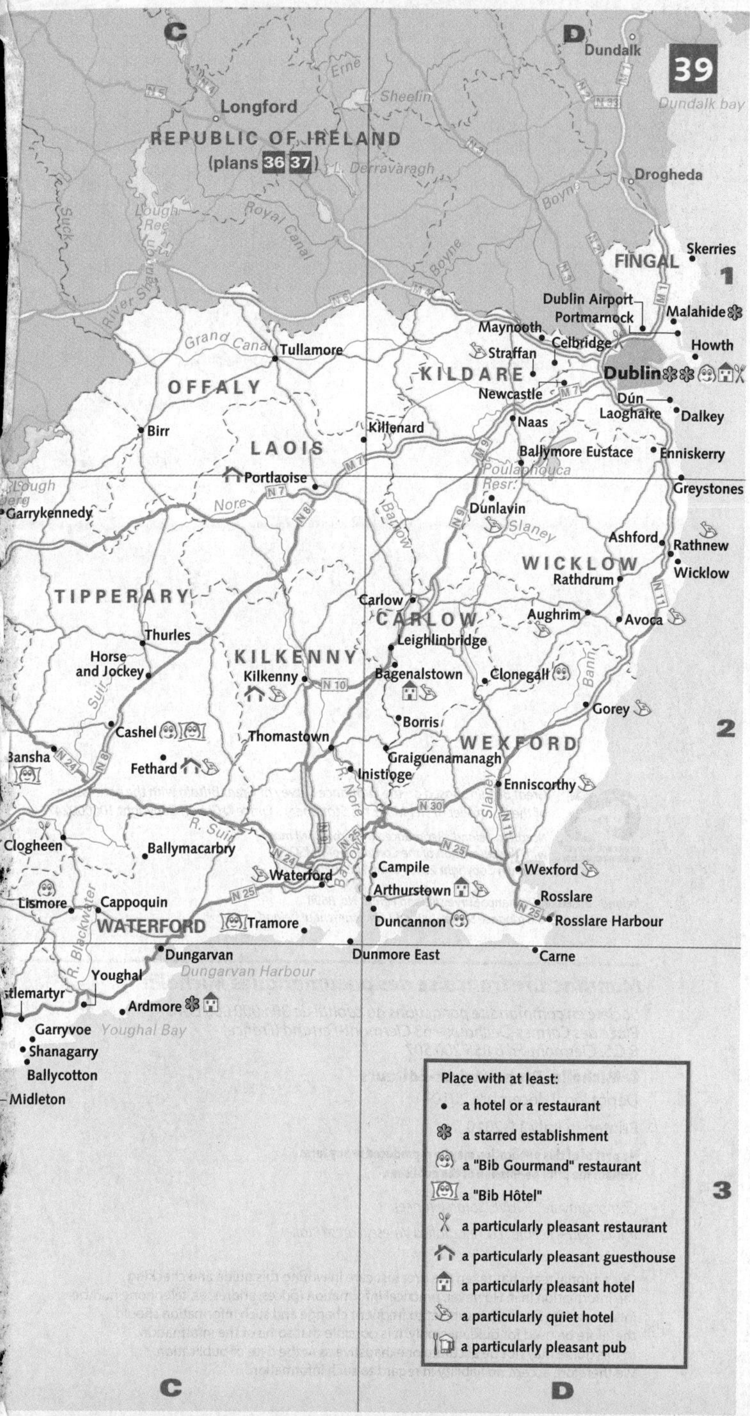
39
C
D
Dundalk
Dundalk bay
Longford
REPUBLIC OF IRELAND
(plans 36 37)
L. Sheelin
L. Derravaragh
Erne
Drogheda
Boyne
Royal Canal
Lough Ree
River Shannon
Suck
Skerries
FINGAL
1
Dublin Airport
Portmarnock
Malahide
Howth
Maynooth
Celbridge
Straffan
Grand Canal
Tullamore
KILDARE
Dublin
Newcastle
OFFALY
Dún Laoghaire
Dalkey
Naas
Birr
Killenard
LAOIS
Ballymore Eustace
Enniskerry
Poulaphouca Resr.
Portlaoise
Greystones
Garrykennedy
Nore
Dunlavin
Barrow
Slaney
Ashford
Rathnew
WICKLOW
Rathdrum
Wicklow
TIPPERARY
Carlow
CARLOW
Aughrim
Avoca
Thurles
Leighlinbridge
Horse and Jockey
KILKENNY
Kilkenny
Bagenalstown
Clonegall
Bann
Suir
Gorey
Borris
2
Cashel
Thomastown
WEXFORD
Graiguenamanagh
Bansha
Fethard
Inistioge
R. Nore
Enniscorthy
R. Suir
Clogheen
Ballymacarbry
Campile
Wexford
Waterford
Barrow
Arthurstown
Rosslare
Lismore
Cappoquin
WATERFORD
Tramore
Duncannon
Rosslare Harbour
Dungarvan
Dunmore East
Carne
Dungarvan Harbour
R. Blackwater
Youghal
stlemartyr
Ardmore
Garryvoe
Youghal Bay
Shanagarry
Ballycotton
Midleton
Place with at least:
a hotel or a restaurant
a starred establishment
a "Bib Gourmand" restaurant
a "Bib Hôtel"
a particularly pleasant restaurant
a particularly pleasant guesthouse
a particularly pleasant hotel
a particularly quiet hotel
a particularly pleasant pub
3
C
D

Manufacture française des pneumatiques Michelin

Société en commandite par actions au capital de 304 000 000 EUR.
Place des Carmes-Déchaux – 63 Clermont-Ferrand (France)
R.C.S. Clermont-Fd B 855 200 507

Dépôt légal décembre 2010

Printed in Italy 11-2010

Compogravure : JOUVE, Saran (France)
Impression – Reliure : La Tipografica Varese, Varese (Italie)